Lecture Notes in Computer Science   2350
Edited by G. Goos, J. Hartmanis, and J. van Leeuwen

Springer
Berlin
Heidelberg
New York
Barcelona
Hong Kong
London
Milan
Paris
Tokyo

Anders Heyden Gunnar Sparr
Mads Nielsen Peter Johansen (Eds.)

Computer Vision – ECCV 2002

7th European Conference on Computer Vision
Copenhagen, Denmark, May 28-31, 2002
Proceedings, Part I

 Springer

Series Editors

Gerhard Goos, Karlsruhe University, Germany
Juris Hartmanis, Cornell University, NY, USA
Jan van Leeuwen, Utrecht University, The Netherlands

Volume Editors

Anders Heyden
Gunnar Sparr
Lund University, Centre for Mathematical Sciences
Box 118, 22100 Lund, Sweden
E-mail: {Anders.Heyden,Gunnar.Sparr}@math.lth.se

Mads Nielsen
The IT University of Copenhagen
Glentevej 67-69, 2400 Copenhagen NW, Denmark
E-mail: malte@itu.dk

Peter Johansen
University of Copenhagen
Universitetsparken 1, 2100 Copenhagen, Denmark
E-mail: peterjo@diku.dk

Cataloging-in-Publication Data applied for

Die Deutsche Bibliothek - CIP-Einheitsaufnahme

Computer vision : proceedings / ECCV 2002, 7th European Conference on
Computer Vision, Copenhagen, Denmark, May 28 - 31, 2002. Anders Heyden ...
(ed.). - Berlin ; Heidelberg ; New York ; Barcelona ; Hong Kong ; London ;
Milan ; Paris ; Tokyo : Springer
Pt. 1 . - 2002
  (Lecture notes in computer science ; Vol. 2350)
  ISBN 3-540-43745-2

CR Subject Classification (1998): I.4, I.3.5, I.5, I.2.9-10

ISSN 0302-9743
ISBN 3-540-43745-2 Springer-Verlag Berlin Heidelberg New York

This work is subject to copyright. All rights are reserved, whether the whole or part of the material is
concerned, specifically the rights of translation, reprinting, re-use of illustrations, recitation, broadcasting,
reproduction on microfilms or in any other way, and storage in data banks. Duplication of this publication
or parts thereof is permitted only under the provisions of the German Copyright Law of September 9, 1965,
in its current version, and permission for use must always be obtained from Springer-Verlag. Violations are
liable for prosecution under the German Copyright Law.

Springer-Verlag Berlin Heidelberg New York
a member of BertelsmannSpringer Science+Business Media GmbH

http://www.springer.de

© Springer-Verlag Berlin Heidelberg 2002
Printed in Germany

Typesetting: Camera-ready by author, data conversion by PTP-Berlin, Stefan Sossna e.K.
Printed on acid-free paper   SPIN: 10870025   06/3142   5 4 3 2 1 0

Preface

Premiering in 1990 in Antibes, France, the European Conference on Computer Vision, ECCV, has been held biennially at venues all around Europe. These conferences have been very successful, making ECCV a major event to the computer vision community.

ECCV 2002 was the seventh in the series. The privilege of organizing it was shared by three universities: The IT University of Copenhagen, the University of Copenhagen, and Lund University, with the conference venue in Copenhagen. These universities lie geographically close in the vivid Öresund region, which lies partly in Denmark and partly in Sweden, with the newly built bridge (opened summer 2000) crossing the sound that formerly divided the countries.

We are very happy to report that this year's conference attracted more papers than ever before, with around 600 submissions. Still, together with the conference board, we decided to keep the tradition of holding ECCV as a single track conference. Each paper was anonymously refereed by three different reviewers. For the final selection, for the first time for ECCV, a system with area chairs was used. These met with the program chairs in Lund for two days in February 2002 to select what became 45 oral presentations and 181 posters. Also at this meeting the selection was made without knowledge of the authors' identity.

The high-quality of the scientific program of ECCV 2002 would not have been possible without the dedicated cooperation of the 15 area chairs, the 53 program committee members, and all the other scientists, who reviewed the papers. A truly impressive effort was made. The spirit of this process reflects the enthusiasm in the research field, and you will find several papers in these proceedings that define the state of the art in the field.

Bjarne Ersbøll as Industrial Relations Chair organized the exhibitions at the conference. Magnus Oskarsson, Sven Spanne, and Nicolas Guilbert helped to make the review process and the preparation of the proceedings function smoothly. Ole Fogh Olsen gave us valuable advice on editing the proceedings. Camilla Jørgensen competently headed the scientific secretariat. Erik Dam and Dan Witzner were responsible for the ECCV 2002 homepage. David Vernon, who chaired ECCV 2000 in Dublin, was extremely helpful during all stages of our preparation for the conference. We would like to thank all these people, as well as numerous others who helped in various respects. A special thanks goes to Søren Skovsgaard at the Congress Consultants, for professional help with all practical matters.

We would also like to thank Rachid Deriche and Theo Papadopoulo for making their web-based conference administration system available and adjusting it to ECCV. This was indispensable in handling the large number of submissions and the thorough review and selection procedure.

Finally, we wish to thank the IT University of Copenhagen and its president Mads Tofte for supporting the conference all the way from planning to realization.

March 2002

Anders Heyden
Gunnar Sparr
Mads Nielsen
Peter Johansen

Organization

Conference Chair

Peter Johansen — Copenhagen University, Denmark

Conference Board

Hans Burkhardt — University of Freiburg, Germany
Bernard Buxton — University College London, UK
Roberto Cipolla — University of Cambridge, UK
Jan-Olof Eklundh — Royal Institute of Technology, Sweden
Olivier Faugeras — INRIA, Sophia Antipolis, France
Bernd Neumann — University of Hamburg, Germany
Giulio Sandini — University of Genova, Italy
David Vernon — Trinity College, Dublin, Ireland

Program Chairs

Anders Heyden — Lund University, Sweden
Gunnar Sparr — Lund University, Sweden

Area Chairs

Ronen Basri — Weizmann Institute, Israel
Michael Black — Brown University, USA
Andrew Blake — Microsoft Research, UK
Rachid Deriche — INRIA, Sophia Antipolis, France
Jan-Olof Eklundh — Royal Institute of Technology, Sweden
Lars Kai Hansen — Denmark Technical University, Denmark
Steve Maybank — University of Reading, UK
Theodore Papadopoulo — INRIA, Sophia Antipolis, France
Cordelia Schmid — INRIA, Rhône-Alpes, France
Amnon Shashua — The Hebrew University of Jerusalem, Israel
Stefano Soatto — University of California, Los Angeles, USA
Bill Triggs — INRIA, Rhône-Alpes, France
Luc van Gool — K.U. Leuven, Belgium & ETH, Zürich, Switzerland
Joachim Weichert — Saarland University, Germany
Andrew Zisserman — University of Oxford, UK

Program Committee

Luis Alvarez	University of Las Palmas, Spain
Padmanabhan Anandan	Microsoft Research, USA
Helder Araujo	University of Coimbra, Portugal
Serge Belongie	University of California, San Diego, USA
Marie-Odile Berger	INRIA, Lorraine, France
Aaron Bobick	Georgia Tech, USA
Terry Boult	Leheigh University, USA
Francois Chaumette	INRIA, Rennes, France
Laurent Cohen	Université Paris IX Dauphine, France
Tim Cootes	University of Manchester, UK
Kostas Daniilidis	University of Pennsylvania, USA
Larry Davis	University of Maryland, USA
Frank Ferrie	McGill University, USA
Andrew Fitzgibbon	University of Oxford, UK
David J. Fleet	Xerox Palo Alto Research Center, USA
David Forsyth	University of California, Berkeley, USA
Pascal Fua	EPFL, Switzerland
Richard Hartley	Australian National University, Australia
Vaclav Hlavac	Czech Technical University, Czech Republic
Michal Irani	Weizmann Institute, Israel
Allan Jepson	University of Toronto, Canada
Peter Johansen	Copenhagen University, Denmark
Fredrik Kahl	Lund University, Sweden
Sing Bing Kang	Microsoft Research, USA
Ron Kimmel	Technion, Israel
Kyros Kutulakos	University of Rochester, USA
Tony Lindeberg	Royal Institute of Technology, Sweden
Jim Little	University of Brittish Columbia, Canada
Peter Meer	Rutgers University, USA
David Murray	University of Oxford, UK
Nassir Navab	Siemens, USA
Mads Nielsen	IT-University of Copenhagen, Denmark
Patrick Perez	Microsoft Research, UK
Pietro Perona	California Insititute of Technology, USA
Marc Pollefeys	K.U. Leuven, Belgium
Long Quan	Hong Kong University of Science and Technology, Hong Kong
Ian Reid	University of Oxford, UK
Nicolas Rougon	Institut National des Télécommunications, France
José Santos-Victor	Instituto Superior Técnico, Lisbon, Portugal
Guillermo Sapiro	University of Minnesota, USA
Yoichi Sato	IIS, University of Tokyo, Japan
Bernt Schiele	ETH, Zürich, Switzerland
Arnold Smeulders	University of Amsterdam, The Netherlands

Gerald Sommer — University of Kiel, Germany
Peter Sturm — INRIA, Rhône-Alpes, France
Tomas Svoboda — Swiss Federal Institute of Technology, Switzerland
Chris Taylor — University of Manchester, UK
Phil Torr — Microsoft Research, UK
Panos Trahanias — University of Crete, Greece
Laurent Younes — CMLA, ENS de Cachan, France
Alan Yuille — Smith-Kettlewell Eye Research Institute, USA
Josiane Zerubia — INRIA, Sophia Antipolis, France
Kalle Åström — Lund University, Sweden

Additional Referees

Henrik Aanaes
Manoj Aggarwal
Motilal Agrawal
Aya Aner
Adnan Ansar
Mirko Appel
Tal Arbel
Okan Arikan
Akira Asano
Shai Avidan
Simon Baker
David Bargeron
Christian Barillot
Kobus Barnard
Adrien Bartoli
Benedicte Bascle
Pierre-Louis Bazin
Isabelle Begin
Stephen Benoit
Alex Berg
James Bergen
Jim Bergen
Marcelo Bertamlmio
Rikard Berthilsson
Christophe Biernacki
Armin Biess
Alessandro Bissacco
Laure Blanc-Feraud
Ilya Blayvas
Eran Borenstein
Patrick Bouthemy
Richard Bowden

Jeffrey E. Boyd
Edmond Boyer
Yuri Boykov
Chen Brestel
Lars Bretzner
Alexander Brook
Michael Brown
Alfred Bruckstein
Thomas Buelow
Joachim Buhmann
Hans Burkhardt
Bernard Buxton
Nikos Canterakis
Yaron Caspi
Alessandro Chiuso
Roberto Cipolla
Dorin Comaniciu
Kurt Cornelis
Antonio Criminisi
Thomas E. Davis
Nando de Freitas
Fernando de la Torre
Daniel DeMenthon
Xavier Descombes
Hagio Djambazian
Gianfranco Doretto
Alessandro Duci
Gregory Dudek
Ramani Duraiswami
Pinar Duygulu
Michael Eckmann
Alyosha Efros

Michael Elad
Ahmed Elgammal
Ronan Fablet
Ayman Farahat
Olivier Faugeras
Paulo Favaro
Xiaolin Feng
Vittorio Ferrari
Frank Ferrie
Mario Figueireda
Margaret Fleck
Michel Gangnet
Xiang Gao
D. Geiger
Yakup Genc
Bogdan Georgescu
J.-M. Geusebroek
Christopher Geyer
Peter Giblin
Gerard Giraudon
Roman Goldenberg
Shaogang Gong
Hayit Greenspan
Lewis Griffin
Jens Guehring
Yanlin Guo
Daniela Hall
Tal Hassner
Horst Haussecker
Ralf Hebrich
Yacov Hel-Or
Lorna Herda

Shinsaku Hiura
Jesse Hoey
Stephen Hsu
Du Huynh
Naoyuki Ichimura
Slobodan Ilic
Sergey Ioffe
Michael Isard
Volkan Isler
David Jacobs
Bernd Jaehne
Ian Jermyn
Hailin Jin
Marie-Pierre Jolly
Stiliyan-N. Kalitzin
Behrooz Kamgar-Parsi
Kenichi Kanatani
Danny Keren
Erwan Kerrien
Charles Kervrann
Renato Keshet
Ali Khamene
Shamim Khan
Nahum Kiryati
Reinhard Koch
Ullrich Koethe
Esther B. Koller-Meier
John Krumm
Hannes Kruppa
Murat Kunt
Prasun Lala
Michael Langer
Ivan Laptev
Jean-Pierre Le Cadre
Bastian Leibe
Ricahrd Lengagne
Vincent Lepetit
Thomas Leung
Maxime Lhuillier
Weiliang Li
David Liebowitz
Georg Lindgren
David Lowe
John MacCormick
Henrik Malm

Roberto Manduchi
Petros Maragos
Eric Marchand
Jiri Matas
Bogdan Matei
Esther B. Meier
Jason Meltzer
Etienne Mémin
Rudolf Mester
Ross J. Micheals
Anurag Mittal
Hiroshi Mo
William Moran
Greg Mori
Yael Moses
Jane Mulligan
Don Murray
Masahide Naemura
Kenji Nagao
Mirko Navara
Shree Nayar
Oscar Nestares
Bernd Neumann
Jeffrey Ng
Tat Hieu Nguyen
Peter Nillius
David Nister
Alison Noble
Tom O'Donnell
Takayuki Okatani
Nuria Olivier
Ole Fogh Olsen
Magnus Oskarsson
Nikos Paragios
Ioannis Patras
Josef Pauli
Shmuel Peleg
Robert Pless
Swaminathan Rahul
Deva Ramanan
Lionel Reveret
Dario Ringach
Ruth Rosenholtz
Volker Roth
Payam Saisan

Garbis Salgian
Frank Sauer
Peter Savadjiev
Silvio Savarese
Harpreet Sawhney
Frederik Schaffalitzky
Yoav Schechner
Chrostoph Schnoerr
Stephan Scholze
Ali Shahrokri
Doron Shaked
Eitan Sharon
Eli Shechtman
Jamie Sherrah
Akinobu Shimizu
Ilan Shimshoni
Kaleem Siddiqi
Hedvig Sidenbladh
Robert Sim
Denis Simakov
Philippe Simard
Eero Simoncelli
Nir Sochen
Yang Song
Andreas Soupliotis
Sven Spanne
Martin Spengler
Alon Spira
Thomas Strömberg
Richard Szeliski
Hai Tao
Huseyin Tek
Seth Teller
Paul Thompson
Jan Tops
Benjamin J. Tordoff
Kentaro Toyama
Tinne Tuytelaars
Shimon Ullman
Richard Unger
Raquel Urtasun
Sven Utcke
Luca Vacchetti
Anton van den Hengel
Geert Van Meerbergen

Pierre Vandergheynst
Zhizhou Wang
Baba Vemuri
Frank Verbiest
Maarten Vergauwen
Jaco Vermaak
Mike Werman
David Vernon
Thomas Vetter

Rene Vidal
Michel Vidal-Naquet
Marta Wilczkowiak
Ramesh Visvanathan
Dan Witzner Hansen
Julia Vogel
Lior Wolf
Bob Woodham
Robert J. Woodham

Chenyang Xu
Yaser Yacoob
Anthony Yezzi
Ramin Zabih
Hugo Zaragoza
Lihi Zelnik-Manor
Ying Zhu
Assaf Zomet

Table of Contents, Part I

Active and Real-Time Vision

Tracking with the EM Contour Algorithm 3
  A.E.C. Pece, A.D. Worrall

M2Tracker: A Multi-view Approach to Segmenting and Tracking
People in a Cluttered Scene Using Region-Based Stereo 18
  A. Mittal, L.S. Davis

Image Features

Analytical Image Models and Their Applications 37
  A. Srivastava, X. Liu, U. Grenander

Time-Recursive Velocity-Adapted Spatio-Temporal Scale-Space Filters 52
  T. Lindeberg

Combining Appearance and Topology for Wide Baseline Matching 68
  D. Tell, S. Carlsson

Guided Sampling and Consensus for Motion Estimation 82
  B. Tordoff, D.W. Murray

Image Features / Visual Motion

Fast Anisotropic Gauss Filtering 99
  J.-M. Geusebroek, A.W.M. Smeulders, J. van de Weijer

Adaptive Rest Condition Potentials: Second Order Edge-Preserving
Regularization 113
  M. Rivera, J.L. Marroquin

An Affine Invariant Interest Point Detector 128
  K. Mikolajczyk, C. Schmid

Understanding and Modeling the Evolution of Critical Points under
Gaussian Blurring 143
  A. Kuijper, L. Florack

Image Processing Done Right 158
  J.J. Koenderink, A.J. van Doorn

Multimodal Data Representations with Parameterized Local Structures 173
  Y. Zhu, D. Comaniciu, S. Schwartz, V. Ramesh

The Relevance of Non-generic Events in Scale Space Models 190
    A. Kuijper, L. Florack

The Localized Consistency Principle for Image Matching under
Non-uniform Illumination Variation and Affine Distortion 205
    B. Wang, K.K. Sung, T.K. Ng

Resolution Selection Using Generalized Entropies of
Multiresolution Histograms 220
    E. Hadjidemetriou, M.D. Grossberg, S.K. Nayar

Robust Computer Vision through Kernel Density Estimation 236
    H. Chen, P. Meer

Constrained Flows of Matrix-Valued Functions: Application to
Diffusion Tensor Regularization 251
    C. Chefd'hotel, D. Tschumperlé, R. Deriche, O. Faugeras

A Hierarchical Framework for Spectral Correspondence 266
    M. Carcassoni, E.R. Hancock

Phase-Based Local Features 282
    G. Carneiro, A.D. Jepson

What Is the Role of Independence for Visual Recognition? 297
    N. Vasconcelos, G. Carneiro

A Probabilistic Multi-scale Model for Contour Completion Based on
Image Statistics 312
    X. Ren, J. Malik

Toward a Full Probability Model of Edges in Natural Images 328
    K.S. Pedersen, A.B. Lee

Fast Difference Schemes for Edge Enhancing Beltrami Flow 343
    R. Malladi, I. Ravve

A Fast Radial Symmetry Transform for Detecting Points of Interest 358
    G. Loy, A. Zelinsky

Image Features Based on a New Approach to 2D Rotation Invariant
Quadrature Filters 369
    M. Felsberg, G. Sommer

Representing Edge Models via Local Principal Component Analysis 384
    P.S. Huggins, S.W. Zucker

Regularized Shock Filters and Complex Diffusion 399
    G. Gilboa, N.A. Sochen, Y.Y. Zeevi

Multi-view Matching for Unordered Image Sets, or "How Do I
Organize My Holiday Snaps?" 414
   F. Schaffalitzky, A. Zisserman

Parameter Estimates for a Pencil of Lines: Bounds and Estimators 432
   G. Speyer, M. Werman

Multilinear Analysis of Image Ensembles: TensorFaces 447
   M.A.O. Vasilescu, D. Terzopoulos

'Dynamism of a Dog on a Leash' or Behavior Classification by
Eigen-Decomposition of Periodic Motions 461
   R. Goldenberg, R. Kimmel, E. Rivlin, M. Rudzsky

Automatic Detection and Tracking of Human Motion with
a View-Based Representation 476
   R. Fablet, M.J. Black

Using Robust Estimation Algorithms for Tracking Explicit Curves 492
   J.-P. Tarel, S.-S. Ieng, P. Charbonnier

On the Motion and Appearance of Specularities in Image Sequences 508
   R. Swaminathan, S.B. Kang, R. Szeliski, A. Criminisi, S.K. Nayar

Multiple Hypothesis Tracking for Automatic Optical Motion Capture 524
   M. Ringer, J. Lasenby

Single Axis Geometry by Fitting Conics 537
   G. Jiang, H.-t. Tsui, L. Quan, A. Zisserman

Computing the Physical Parameters of Rigid-Body Motion from Video 551
   K.S. Bhat, S.M. Seitz, J. Popović, P.K. Khosla

Building Roadmaps of Local Minima of Visual Models 566
   C. Sminchisescu, B. Triggs

A Generative Method for Textured Motion: Analysis and Synthesis 583
   Y. Wang, S.-C. Zhu

Is Super-Resolution with Optical Flow Feasible? 599
   W.Y. Zhao, H.S. Sawhney

New View Generation with a Bi-centric Camera 614
   D. Weinshall, M.-S. Lee, T. Brodsky, M. Trajkovic, D. Feldman

Recognizing and Tracking Human Action 629
   J. Sullivan, S. Carlsson

Towards Improved Observation Models for Visual
Tracking: Selective Adaptation 645
   J. Vermaak, P. Pérez, M. Gangnet, A. Blake

Color-Based Probabilistic Tracking 661
   P. Pérez, C. Hue, J. Vermaak, M. Gangnet

Dense Motion Analysis in Fluid Imagery 676
   T. Corpetti, É. Mémin, P. Pérez

A Layered Motion Representation with Occlusion and Compact
Spatial Support 692
   A.D. Jepson, D.J. Fleet, M.J. Black

Incremental Singular Value Decomposition of Uncertain Data with
Missing Values 707
   M. Brand

Symmetrical Dense Optical Flow Estimation with Occlusions Detection 721
   L. Alvarez, R. Deriche, T. Papadopoulo, J. Sánchez

Audio-Video Sensor Fusion with Probabilistic Graphical Models 736
   M.J. Beal, H. Attias, N. Jojic

Visual Motion

Increasing Space-Time Resolution in Video 753
   E. Shechtman, Y. Caspi, M. Irani

Hyperdynamics Importance Sampling 769
   C. Sminchisescu, B. Triggs

Implicit Probabilistic Models of Human Motion for Synthesis and
Tracking 784
   H. Sidenbladh, M.J. Black, L. Sigal

Space-Time Tracking 801
   L. Torresani, C. Bregler

Author Index 813

Table of Contents, Part II

Surface Geometry

A Variational Approach to Recovering a Manifold from Sample Points 3
J. Gomes, A. Mojsilovic

A Variational Approach to Shape from Defocus 18
H. Jin, P. Favaro

Shadow Graphs and Surface Reconstruction 31
Y. Yu, J.T. Chang

Specularities Reduce Ambiguity of Uncalibrated Photometric Stereo 46
O. Drbohlav, R. Šára

Grouping and Segmentation

Pairwise Clustering with Matrix Factorisation and the EM Algorithm 63
A. Robles-Kelly, E.R. Hancock

Shape Priors for Level Set Representations 78
M. Rousson, N. Paragios

Nonlinear Shape Statistics in Mumford–Shah Based Segmentation 93
D. Cremers, T. Kohlberger, C. Schnörr

Class-Specific, Top-Down Segmentation 109
E. Borenstein, S. Ullman

Structure from Motion / Stereoscopic Vision / Surface Geometry / Shape

Quasi-Dense Reconstruction from Image Sequence......................... 125
M. Lhuillier, L. Quan

Properties of the Catadioptric Fundamental Matrix 140
C. Geyer, K. Daniilidis

Building Architectural Models from Many Views Using Map Constraints 155
D.P. Robertson, R. Cipolla

Motion – Stereo Integration for Depth Estimation 170
C. Strecha, L. Van Gool

Lens Distortion Recovery for Accurate Sequential Structure and
Motion Recovery 186
    K. Cornelis, M. Pollefeys, L. Van Gool

Generalized Rank Conditions in Multiple View Geometry with
Applications to Dynamical Scenes 201
    K. Huang, R. Fossum, Y. Ma

Dense Structure-from-Motion: An Approach Based on Segment Matching 217
    F. Ernst, P. Wilinski, K. van Overveld

Maximizing Rigidity: Optimal Matching under Scaled-Orthography 232
    J. Maciel, J. Costeira

Dramatic Improvements to Feature Based Stereo 247
    *V.N. Smelyansky, R.D. Morris, F.O. Kuehnel, D.A. Maluf,
    P. Cheeseman*

Motion Curves for Parametric Shape and Motion Estimation 262
    P.-L. Bazin, J.-M. Vézien

Bayesian Self-Calibration of a Moving Camera 277
    G. Qian, R. Chellappa

Balanced Recovery of 3D Structure and Camera Motion from
Uncalibrated Image Sequences 294
    B. Georgescu, P. Meer

Linear Multi View Reconstruction with Missing Data 309
    C. Rother, S. Carlsson

Model-Based Silhouette Extraction for Accurate People Tracking 325
    R. Plaenkers, P. Fua

On the Non-linear Optimization of Projective Motion Using Minimal Parameters . 340
    A. Bartoli

Structure from Many Perspective Images with Occlusions 355
    D. Martinec, T. Pajdla

Sequence-to-Sequence Self Calibration 370
    L. Wolf, A. Zomet

Structure from Planar Motions with Small Baselines 383
    R. Vidal, J. Oliensis

Revisiting Single-View Shape Tensors: Theory and Applications 399
    A. Levin, A. Shashua

Tracking and Rendering Using Dynamic Textures on Geometric
Structure from Motion 415
  D. Cobzas, M. Jagersand

Sensitivity of Calibration to Principal Point Position 433
  R.I. Hartley, R. Kaucic

Critical Curves and Surfaces for Euclidean Reconstruction 447
  F. Kahl, R. Hartley

View Synthesis with Occlusion Reasoning Using
Quasi-Sparse Feature Correspondences 463
  D. Jelinek, C.J. Taylor

Eye Gaze Correction with Stereovision for Video-Teleconferencing 479
  R. Yang, Z. Zhang

Wavelet-Based Correlation for Stereopsis 495
  M. Clerc

Stereo Matching Using Belief Propagation 510
  J. Sun, H.-Y. Shum, N.-N. Zheng

Symmetric Sub-pixel Stereo Matching 525
  R. Szeliski, D. Scharstein

New Techniques for Automated Architectural Reconstruction from
Photographs 541
  T. Werner, A. Zisserman

Stereo Matching with Segmentation-Based Cooperation 556
  Y. Zhang, C. Kambhamettu

Coarse Registration of Surface Patches with Local Symmetries 572
  J. Vanden Wyngaerd, L. Van Gool

Multiview Registration of 3D Scenes by Minimizing Error between
Coordinate Frames 587
  G.C. Sharp, S.W. Lee, D.K. Wehe

Recovering Surfaces from the Restoring Force 598
  G. Kamberov, G. Kamberova

Interpolating Sporadic Data 613
  L. Noakes, R. Kozera

Highlight Removal Using Shape-from-Shading 626
  H. Ragheb, E.R. Hancock

A Reflective Symmetry Descriptor 642
    M. Kazhdan, B. Chazelle, D. Dobkin, A. Finkelstein, T. Funkhouser

Gait Sequence Analysis Using Frieze Patterns 657
    Y. Liu, R. Collins, Y. Tsin

Feature-Preserving Medial Axis Noise Removal 672
    R. Tam, W. Heidrich

Hierarchical Shape Modeling for Automatic Face Localization 687
    C. Liu, H.-Y. Shum, C. Zhang

Using Dirichlet Free Form Deformation to Fit Deformable Models to
Noisy 3-D Data 704
    S. Ilic, P. Fua

Transitions of the 3D Medial Axis under a One-Parameter Family of
Deformations 718
    P. Giblin, B.B. Kimia

Learning Shape from Defocus 735
    P. Favaro, S. Soatto

A Rectilinearity Measurement for Polygons 746
    J. Žunić, P.L. Rosin

Local Analysis for 3D Reconstruction of Specular Surfaces – Part II 759
    S. Savarese, P. Perona

Matching Distance Functions: A Shape-to-Area Variational Approach
for Global-to-Local Registration 775
    N. Paragios, M. Rousson, V. Ramesh

Shape from Shading and Viscosity Solutions 790
    E. Prados, O. Faugeras, E. Rouy

Model Acquisition by Registration of Multiple Acoustic Range Views 805
    A. Fusiello, U. Castellani, L. Ronchetti, V. Murino

Structure from Motion

General Trajectory Triangulation 823
    J.Y. Kaminski, M. Teicher

Surviving Dominant Planes in Uncalibrated Structure and Motion
Recovery 837
    M. Pollefeys, F. Verbiest, L. Van Gool

A Bayesian Estimation of Building Shape Using MCMC 852
    A.R. Dick, P.H.S. Torr, R. Cipolla

Structure and Motion for Dynamic Scenes – The Case of
Points Moving in Planes 867
   P. Sturm

What Does the Scene Look Like from a Scene Point? 883
   M. Irani, T. Hassner, P. Anandan

Author Index 899

Table of Contents, Part III

Shape

3D Statistical Shape Models Using Direct Optimisation of
Description Length 3
    R.H. Davies, C.J. Twining, T.F. Cootes,
    J.C. Waterton, C.J. Taylor

Approximate Thin Plate Spline Mappings 21
    G. Donato, S. Belongie

DEFORMOTION: Deforming Motion, Shape Average and the Joint
Registration and Segmentation of Images 32
    S. Soatto, A.J. Yezzi

Region Matching with Missing Parts 48
    A. Duci, A.J. Yezzi, S. Mitter, S. Soatto

Stereoscopic Vision I

What Energy Functions Can Be Minimized via Graph Cuts? 65
    V. Kolmogorov, R. Zabih

Multi-camera Scene Reconstruction via Graph Cuts 82
    V. Kolmogorov, R. Zabih

A Markov Chain Monte Carlo Approach to Stereovision 97
    J. Sénégas

A Probabilistic Theory of Occupancy and Emptiness 112
    R. Bhotika, D.J. Fleet, K.N. Kutulakos

Texture Shading and Colour / Grouping and Segmentation / Object Recognition

Texture Similarity Measure Using Kullback-Leibler Divergence
between Gamma Distributions 133
    J.R. Mathiassen, A. Skavhaug, K. Bø

All the Images of an Outdoor Scene 148
    S.G. Narasimhan, C. Wang, S.K. Nayar

Recovery of Reflectances and Varying Illuminants from Multiple Views 163
    Q.-T. Luong, P. Fua, Y. Leclerc

Composite Texture Descriptions 180
  A. Zalesny, V. Ferrari, G. Caenen, D. Auf der Maur, L. Van Gool

Constructing Illumination Image Basis from Object Motion 195
  A. Nakashima, A. Maki, K. Fukui

Diffuse-Specular Separation and Depth Recovery from Image Sequences 210
  S. Lin, Y. Li, S.B. Kang, X. Tong, H.-Y. Shum

Shape from Texture without Boundaries 225
  D.A. Forsyth

Statistical Modeling of Texture Sketch 240
  Y.N. Wu, S.C. Zhu, C.-e. Guo

Classifying Images of Materials: Achieving Viewpoint and
Illumination Independence 255
  M. Varma, A. Zisserman

Estimation of Multiple Illuminants from a Single Image of
Arbitrary Known Geometry 272
  Y. Wang, D. Samaras

The Effect of Illuminant Rotation on Texture Filters: Lissajous's
Ellipses 289
  M. Chantler, M. Schmidt, M. Petrou, G. McGunnigle

On Affine Invariant Clustering and Automatic Cast Listing in Movies 304
  A. Fitzgibbon, A. Zisserman

Factorial Markov Random Fields 321
  J. Kim, R. Zabih

Evaluation and Selection of Models for Motion Segmentation 335
  K. Kanatani

Surface Extraction from Volumetric Images Using Deformable Meshes:
A Comparative Study 350
  J. Tohka

DREAM^{2}S: Deformable Regions Driven by an Eulerian Accurate
Minimization Method for Image and Video Segmentation
(Application to Face Detection in Color Video Sequences) 365
  S. Jehan-Besson, M. Barlaud, G. Aubert

Neuro-Fuzzy Shadow Filter 381
  B.P.L. Lo, G.-Z. Yang

Parsing Images into Region and Curve Processes 393
  Z. Tu, S.-C. Zhu

Yet Another Survey on Image Segmentation: Region and Boundary
Information Integration 408
  J. Freixenet, X. Muñoz, D. Raba, J. Martí, X. Cufí

Perceptual Grouping from Motion Cues Using Tensor Voting in 4-D 423
  M. Nicolescu, G. Medioni

Deformable Model with Non-euclidean Metrics 438
  B. Taton, J.-O. Lachaud

Finding Deformable Shapes Using Loopy Belief Propagation 453
  J.M. Coughlan, S.J. Ferreira

Probabilistic and Voting Approaches to Cue Integration for
Figure-Ground Segmentation 469
  E. Hayman, J.-O. Eklundh

Bayesian Estimation of Layers from Multiple Images 487
  Y. Wexler, A. Fitzgibbon, A. Zisserman

A Stochastic Algorithm for 3D Scene Segmentation and Reconstruction 502
  F. Han, Z. Tu, S.-C. Zhu

Normalized Gradient Vector Diffusion and Image Segmentation 517
  Z. Yu, C. Bajaj

Spectral Partitioning with Indefinite Kernels Using the Nyström
Extension 531
  S. Belongie, C. Fowlkes, F. Chung, J. Malik

A Framework for High-Level Feedback to Adaptive,
Per-Pixel, Mixture-of-Gaussian Background Models 543
  M. Harville

Multivariate Saddle Point Detection for Statistical Clustering 561
  D. Comaniciu, V. Ramesh, A. Del Bue

Parametric Distributional Clustering for Image Segmentation 577
  L. Hermes, T. Zöller, J.M. Buhmann

Probabalistic Models and Informative Subspaces for Audiovisual
Correspondence 592
  J.W. Fisher, T. Darrell

Volterra Filtering of Noisy Images of Curves 604
  J. August

Image Segmentation by Flexible Models Based on Robust Regularized
Networks 621
  M. Rivera, J. Gee

Principal Component Analysis over Continuous Subspaces and
Intersection of Half-Spaces.................................... 635
    A. Levin, A. Shashua

On Pencils of Tangent Planes and the Recognition of Smooth 3D
Shapes from Silhouettes.. 651
    S. Lazebnik, A. Sethi, C. Schmid, D. Kriegman, J. Ponce, M. Hebert

Estimating Human Body Configurations Using Shape Context Matching 666
    G. Mori, J. Malik

Probabilistic Human Recognition from Video 681
    S. Zhou, R. Chellappa

SoftPOSIT: Simultaneous Pose and Correspondence Determination........... 698
    P. David, D. DeMenthon, R. Duraiswami, H. Samet

A Pseudo-Metric for Weighted Point Sets 715
    P. Giannopoulos, R.C. Veltkamp

Shock-Based Indexing into Large Shape Databases................. 731
    T.B. Sebastian, P.N. Klein, B.B. Kimia

EigenSegments: A Spatio-Temporal Decomposition of an Ensemble of Images .. 747
    S. Avidan

On the Representation and Matching of Qualitative Shape at
Multiple Scales.. 759
    A. Shokoufandeh, S. Dickinson, C. Jönsson, L. Bretzner, T. Lindeberg

Combining Simple Discriminators for Object Discrimination 776
    S. Mahamud, M. Hebert, J. Lafferty

Probabilistic Search for Object Segmentation and Recognition ... 791
    U. Hillenbrand, G. Hirzinger

Real-Time Interactive Path Extraction with On-the-Fly Adaptation
of the External Forces... 807
    O. Gérard, T. Deschamps, M. Greff, L.D. Cohen

Matching and Embedding through Edit-Union of Trees 822
    A. Torsello, E.R. Hancock

A Comparison of Search Strategies for Geometric Branch and Bound
Algorithms 837
    T. M. Breuel

Face Recognition from Long-Term Observations................... 851
    G. Shakhnarovich, J.W. Fisher, T. Darrell

Stereoscopic Vision II

Helmholtz Stereopsis: Exploiting Reciprocity for
Surface Reconstruction 869
  T. Zickler, P.N. Belhumeur, D.J. Kriegman

Minimal Surfaces for Stereo 885
  C. Buehler, S.J. Gortler, M.F. Cohen, L. McMillan

Finding the Largest Unambiguous Component of Stereo Matching 900
  R. Šára

Author Index 915

Table of Contents, Part IV

Object Recognition / Vision Systems Engineering and Evaluation

Face Identification by Fitting a 3D Morphable Model Using Linear
Shape and Texture Error Functions 3
    S. Romdhani, V. Blanz, T. Vetter

Hausdorff Kernel for 3D Object Acquisition and Detection 20
    A. Barla, F. Odone, A. Verri

Evaluating Image Segmentation Algorithms Using the Pareto Front 34
    M. Everingham, H. Muller, B. Thomas

On Performance Characterization and Optimization for Image Retrieval 49
    J. Vogel, B. Schiele

Statistical Learning

Statistical Learning of Multi-view Face Detection 67
    S.Z. Li, L. Zhu, Z. Zhang, A. Blake, H. Zhang, H. Shum

Dynamic Trees: Learning to Model Outdoor Scenes 82
    N.J. Adams, C.K.I. Williams

Object Recognition as Machine Translation: Learning a Lexicon for
a Fixed Image Vocabulary 97
    P. Duygulu, K. Barnard, J.F.G. de Freitas, D.A. Forsyth

Learning a Sparse Representation for Object Detection 113
    S. Agarwal, D. Roth

Calibration / Active and Real-Time and Robot Vision / Image and Video Indexing / Medical Image Understanding / Vision Systems / Engineering and Evaluations / Statistical Learning

Stratified Self Calibration from Screw-Transform Manifolds 131
    R. Manning, C. Dyer

Self-Organization of Randomly Placed Sensors 146
    R.B. Fisher

Camera Calibration with One-Dimensional Objects 161
    Z. Zhang

Automatic Camera Calibration from a Single Manhattan Image 175
    J. Deutscher, M. Isard, J. MacCormick

What Can Be Known about the Radiometric Response from Images? 189
   M.D. Grossberg, S.K. Nayar

Estimation of Illuminant Direction and Intensity of Multiple
Light Sources 206
   W. Zhou, C. Kambhamettu

3D Modelling Using Geometric Constraints: A Parallelepiped Based
Approach 221
   M. Wilczkowiak, E. Boyer, P. Sturm

Geometric Properties of Central Catadioptric Line Images 237
   J.P. Barreto, H. Araujo

Another Way of Looking at Plane-Based Calibration: The Centre
Circle Constraint 252
   P. Gurdjos, A. Crouzil, R. Payrissat

Active Surface Reconstruction Using the Gradient Strategy 267
   M. Mitran, F.P. Ferrie

Linear Pose Estimation from Points or Lines 282
   A. Ansar, K. Daniilidis

A Video-Based Drowning Detection System 297
   A.H. Kam, W. Lu, W.-Y. Yau

Visual Data Fusion for Objects Localization by Active Vision 312
   G. Flandin, F. Chaumette

Towards Real-Time Cue Integration by Using Partial Results 327
   D. DeCarlo

Tracking and Object Classification for Automated Surveillance 343
   O. Javed, M. Shah

Very Fast Template Matching 358
   H. Schweitzer, J.W. Bell, F. Wu

Fusion of Multiple Tracking Algorithms for Robust People Tracking 373
   N.T. Siebel, S. Maybank

Video Summaries through Mosaic-Based Shot and Scene Clustering 388
   A. Aner, J.R. Kender

Optimization Algorithms for the Selection of Key Frame Sequences
of Variable Length 403
   T. Liu, J.R. Kender

Multi-scale EM-ICP: A Fast and Robust Approach for Surface Registration 418
    S. Granger, X. Pennec

An Unified Approach to Model-Based and Model-Free Visual Servoing 433
    E. Malis

Comparing Intensity Transformations and Their Invariants in
the Context of Color Pattern Recognition 448
    F. Mindru, T. Moons, L. Van Gool

A Probabilistic Framework for Spatio-Temporal Video
Representation & Indexing 461
    H. Greenspan, J. Goldberger, A. Mayer

Video Compass 476
    J. Košecká and W. Zhang

Computing Content-Plots for Video 491
    H. Schweitzer

Classification and Localisation of Diabetic-Related Eye Disease 502
    A. Osareh, M. Mirmehdi, B. Thomas, R. Markham

Robust Active Shape Model Search 517
    M. Rogers, J. Graham

A New Image Registration Technique with Free Boundary
Constraints: Application to Mammography 531
    F. Richard, L. Cohen

Registration Assisted Image Smoothing and Segmentation 546
    B.C. Vemuri, Y. Chen, Z. Wang

An Accurate and Efficient Bayesian Method for Automatic
Segmentation of Brain MRI 560
    J.L. Marroquin, B.C. Vemuri, S. Botello, F. Calderon

A PDE Approach for Thickness, Correspondence, and Gridding of
Annular Tissues 575
    A. Yezzi, J.L. Prince

Statistical Characterization of Morphological Operator Sequences 590
    X. Gao, V. Ramesh, T. Boult

Image Registration for Foveated Omnidirectional Sensing 606
    F. Dornaika, J. Elder

Automatic Model Selection by Modelling the Distribution of Residuals 621
    T.F. Cootes, N. Thacker, C.J. Taylor

Assorted Pixels: Multi-sampled Imaging with Structural Models 636
   S.K. Nayar, S.G. Narasimhan

Robust Parameterized Component Analysis:
Theory and Applications to 2D Facial Modeling 653
   F. De la Torre, M.J. Black

Learning Intrinsic Video Content Using Levenshtein Distance in
Graph Partitioning 670
   J. Ng, S. Gong

A Tale of Two Classifiers: SNoW vs. SVM in Visual Recognition 685
   M.-H. Yang, D. Roth, N. Ahuja

Learning to Parse Pictures of People 700
   R. Ronfard, C. Schmid, B. Triggs

Learning Montages of Transformed Latent Images as Representations
of Objects That Change in Appearance 715
   C. Pal, B.J. Frey, N. Jojic

Exemplar-Based Face Recognition from Video 732
   V. Krüger, S. Zhou

Learning the Topology of Object Views 747
   J. Wieghardt, R.P. Würtz, C. von der Malsburg

A Robust PCA Algorithm for Building Representations from
Panoramic Images 761
   D. Skočaj, H. Bischof, A. Leonardis

Adjustment Learning and Relevant Component Analysis 776
   N. Shental, T. Hertz, D. Weinshall, M. Pavel

Texture, Shading, and Colour

What Are Textons? 793
   S.-C. Zhu, C.-e. Guo, Y. Wu, Y. Wang

Bidirectional Texture Contrast Function 808
   S.C. Pont, J.J. Koenderink

Removing Shadows from Images 823
   G.D. Finlayson, S.D. Hordley, M.S. Drew

Author Index 837

Active and Real-Time Vision

Tracking with the EM Contour Algorithm

Arthur E.C. Pece[1] and Anthony D. Worrall[2]

[1] Institute of Computer Science
University of Copenhagen
Universitetsparken 1
DK-2100 Copenhagen, Denmark
aecp@diku.dk
[2] Department of Computer Science
University of Reading
P.O. Box 225
Reading RG6 6AY, England
anthony.worrall@reading.ac.uk

Abstract. A novel active-contour method is presented and applied to pose refinement and tracking. The main innovation is that no "features" are detected at any stage: contours are simply assumed to remove statistical dependencies between pixels on opposite sides of the contour. This assumption, together with a simple model of shape variability of the geometric models, leads to the application of an EM method for maximizing the likelihood of pose parameters. In addition, a dynamical model of the system leads to the application of a Kalman filter. The method is demonstrated by tracking motor vehicles with 3-D models.

1 Introduction

Active contour methods can be divided into two main classes, depending on the principle used for evaluating the image evidence. One class (*e.g.* [3,2,7,11,21,20]) relies on the extraction of features from the image in the neighborhood of the contours and the assignment of one, and only one, correspondence between points on the contours and image features. Apart from the problem of finding correct correspondences, the thresholds necessary for feature detection inevitably make these methods sensitive to noise. Furthermore, a correct estimate of the model likelihood requires marginalization over possible correspondences *and* over possible features.

Other active-contour methods (*e.g.* [6,10,12,15,22]) avoid feature detection by maximizing feature *values* (without thresholding) underlying the contour, rather than minimizing the distance between locally-strongest feature and contour. Some form of smoothing (of the image or of the feature field) is necessary to ensure that the objective function is a smooth function of pose parameters. One disadvantage of these methods is that optimization of the contour positions is usually not gradient-based, and therefore slow to converge.

The EM contour algorithm introduced in this paper belongs to this latter class, with the important difference that smoothing is replaced by marginalization over possible deformations of the object shape. This model assumption, apart from being realistic, leads to an objective function which can be interpreted as a squared-distance measure, as in the case of contour methods of the first class.

The EM contour algorithm is a development of previous work [15,16,17]. The main development consists in the formulation of a generative model, leading to a sound theoretical basis and minor modifications of the mathematics.

The two basic model assumptions behind the method are simply stated:

1. Grey-level values of nearby pixels are correlated if both pixels belong to the object being tracked, or both belong to the background, but there are no correlations if the two pixels are on opposite sides of the contour. The form of correlations between nearby pixels is well known from research on the statistics of natural images (*e.g.* [8,9]); therefore, the log-likelihood of the pose and shape parameters of the object being tracked is easily obtained from the image.
2. The shape of the contour is subject to random local variability. Marginalizing over local shape variations (deformations) of the contours leads to the application of the EM method [4,13]. The covariance of the estimate of pose parameters is easily obtained and leads to proper weighting of the innovation in a Kalman filter.

The contour model introduced in this paper has a potentially wide range of applications in machine vision. This paper shows an application to tracking of rigid objects bound to the ground plane.

1.1 Organization of the Paper

Section 2 describes the generative model underlying the tracker and derives the log-likelihood for the state variables of the model. Section 3 introduces the EM contour algorithm used to optimize the log-likelihood in state space. Section 4 describes the dynamical model which underlies the Kalman filter, and lists the parameters of the tracker. Section 5 describes the method by which the state variables are initialized. Finally, Section 6 describes the results obtained on the PETS2000 test sequence and reviews the theoretical advantages of the method.

2 Generative Model

The tracker is based on finding the *MAP* (maximum *a posteriori*) estimate of the state parameters (*i.e.* pose, velocity, acceleration) of the object being tracked, given the image sequence up to the current frame. By Bayes' theorem, the posterior pdf (probability density function) is the product of the prior pdf and the likelihood (divided by a constant which can be neglected for optimization purposes).

In order to derive expressions for the prior pdf and likelihood of the state parameters, a generative model is introduced, consisting of two main components:

- a dynamical model, which defines the pdf over states of the object being tracked at a given point in time, given the state at an earlier time, *i.e.* the prior pdf;
- an observation model, which defines the pdf over images, given the current state of the object, *i.e.* the likelihood.

The dynamical model is fairly standard and is analyzed in section 4. At this stage, only 3 pose parameters of the object being tracked need to be considered: the X and Y coordinates on the ground plane and the orientation θ_Z. The vector of these pose parameters is defined as $\mathbf{y} = (X, Y, \theta_Z)$.

2.1 Observation Model

The observation model can itself be broken down into two components:

- a geometric component which defines a pdf over image locations of contours, given (a) the pose parameters of the object, (b) a 3-D geometric model of the object including an estimate of its shape variability, and (c) the camera geometry;
- a "coloring/shading" component which defines a pdf over grey-level differences between pixels, given the image locations of the contours.

The average geometric model is the shape of an "average" automobile. Given the current pose parameters of the object and the camera parameters, it is straightforward to project the 3-D boundaries between the facets of the geometric model onto the image plane (with hidden line removal), to obtain the expected image contours.

We begin by describing the case of no shape variability; this simplification will be removed in subsection 2.3.

2.2 Statistics of Grey-Level Differences

Grey levels at two close locations on the image plane are correlated, except for the case of two pixels which are known to lie on two different sides of an object boundary, in which case no correlation is expected. Research on the statistics of natural images shows that the pdf f_L of grey-level differences (gld's) between adjacent pixels is well approximated by a generalized laplacian [8]:

$$f_L(\Delta \mathcal{I}) = \frac{1}{Z_L} \exp\left(-\left|\frac{\Delta \mathcal{I}}{\lambda}\right|^\beta\right) \quad (1)$$

where $\Delta \mathcal{I}$ is the gld, λ is a parameter that depends on the distance between the two sampled image locations, β is a parameter approximately equal to 0.5, and Z_L is a normalization constant. For $\beta = 0.5$, it can be easily obtained that $Z_L = 4\lambda$.

Note that the generalized-laplacian pdf is obtained (reliably in all image ensembles which have been investigated) without manual intervention, *i.e.* without determining which gld's are measured across object boundaries and which gld's are measured within the same object. This means that the pdf includes the effect of *unpredicted* object boundaries, indeed it can be derived from a simple model of random occlusion [9]. This point is relevant in the following.

The pdf given by Eq.1 has been shown to fit the log-ratios of grey levels, rather than grey-level differences, but, for small values of the gld, the logarithmic transformation has only a small effect on the shape of the pdf. In addition, the gamma correction of most cameras already approximates a logarithmic transformation to some extent.

It will be clear at this point that the method is based on placing the contours in the image plane so as to minimize the sum of the log-prior pdf's of the gld's measured across the contours, under the constraints given by the shape model of the object being tracked. Similar principles were employed elsewhere [19,22].

We define the image coordinate system $\mathbf{u}$ and a binary indicator variable $\eta_{\Delta \mathbf{u}}(\mathbf{u})$, with value 1 if the boundary of the object being tracked is located between $\mathbf{u} - \Delta \mathbf{u}/2$ and $\mathbf{u} + \Delta \mathbf{u}/2$, and value 0 otherwise.

Given no boundary of the object of interest between two image locations, the pdf of gld's is given by Eq.1:

$$f[\Delta \mathcal{I}(\mathbf{u}) \,|\, \eta_{\Delta \mathbf{u}}(\mathbf{u}) = 0] = f_L[\Delta \mathcal{I}(\mathbf{u})] \tag{2}$$

where $\Delta \mathcal{I}(\mathbf{u}) = I(\mathbf{u} + \Delta \mathbf{u}/2) - I(\mathbf{u} - \Delta \mathbf{u}/2)$. Note that we are not assuming the total absence of boundaries between the two locations: only the absence of the boundary of the object of interest.

Grey levels observed on opposite sides of an object boundary are statistically independent, and therefore the conditional pdf of gld's, given an object boundary between the two image locations, can be assumed to be uniform[1]:

$$f[\Delta \mathcal{I}(\mathbf{u}) \,|\, \eta_{\Delta \mathbf{u}}(\mathbf{u}) = 1] \approx 1/m \tag{3}$$

where m is the number of grey levels.

Let us consider the normal to a point on a projected line segment, as illustrated in Fig. 1. The coordinate along this normal is denoted by ν, and the point of intersection of the line segment is denoted by μ, so that $\nu - \mu$ is the distance from the line segment along the normal. Given regularly-spaced samples of grey levels on the normal, with spacing $\Delta \nu$ and bilinear interpolation, we define the *observation* (at a given sample point on a contour) as $\Delta \mathcal{I} = \{\Delta \mathcal{I}(i \Delta \nu) \,|\, i \in \mathbb{Z}\}$. Assuming statistical independence between gld's, the pdf F_L of the observation in the absence of a contour is given by:

$$F_L(\Delta \mathcal{I}) \stackrel{\text{def}}{=} \prod_i f_L[\Delta \mathcal{I}(i \Delta \nu)] \tag{4}$$

while the pdf of the observation, given the contour location μ, is given by:

$$f(\Delta \mathcal{I} \,|\, \mu) = f[\Delta \mathcal{I} \,|\, \eta_{\Delta \nu}(\mu) = 1] \tag{5}$$
$$= \frac{1}{m} F_L(\Delta \mathcal{I}) \, f_L^{-1}[\Delta \mathcal{I}(\mu)]$$

---

[1] We ignore a possible dependency on the average grey level of the two image locations.

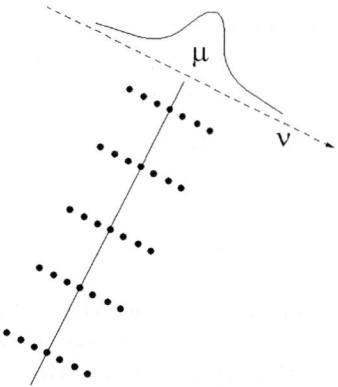

Fig. 1. Diagram illustrating the meaning of the symbols μ and ν and the spacing and sampling of the normals to a contour: one evaluation is performed on each normal, using the Gaussian window.

2.3 Marginalizing over Deformations

The geometric object model cannot be assumed to be perfect. In addition, it is desirable to make the log-likelihood smooth in parameter space. For these reasons, we postulate that the model is subject to random iid (independent, identically distributed) Gaussian deformations at each sample point on the contours: the actual image location of a point on a contour is assumed to have a Gaussian pdf with mean equal to the location predicted from the deterministic geometry, and constant variance. Random shape variability does not preclude additional parameterized shape variations, but shape recovery is not of interest in this paper.

For simplicity, the shape variability is defined in the image plane. For convenience, we define $\epsilon \stackrel{\text{def}}{=} \nu - \mu$, We also define the prior pdf of deformations $f_D(\epsilon)$:

$$f_D(\epsilon) = \frac{1}{Z_D} \exp \frac{-\epsilon^2}{2\sigma^2} \quad (6)$$

where $Z_D = \sqrt{2\pi}\sigma$ is a normalization factor.

The marginalized pdf of an observation is:

$$f_M(\boldsymbol{\Delta I} \mid \mu) = \int f(\boldsymbol{\Delta I} \mid \mu + \epsilon) \, f_D(\epsilon) \, d\epsilon$$

$$= \frac{1}{m} F_L(\boldsymbol{\Delta I}) \int f_L^{-1}[\Delta I(\mu + \epsilon)] \, f_D(\epsilon) \, d\epsilon \quad (7)$$

The integral can be approximated as a finite sum over the discrete set of possible deformations $\epsilon_j = j\Delta\nu - \mu$ (with $j \in \mathbb{Z}$):

$$f_M(\boldsymbol{\Delta I} \mid \mu) = \frac{1}{m} F_L(\boldsymbol{\Delta I}) \sum_j f_L^{-1}[\Delta I(j\Delta\nu)] \, f_D(\epsilon_j) \, \Delta\nu \quad (8)$$

The ratio between the marginalized pdf (Eq.8) and the pdf in the absence of a contour (Eq.4) is the likelihood ratio of the hypotheses that there is a contour at location μ and that there is no contour. The likelihood ratio is given by

$$R(\boldsymbol{\Delta I}\,|\,\mu) = \frac{f_M(\boldsymbol{\Delta I}\,|\,\mu)}{F_L(\boldsymbol{\Delta I})}$$
$$= \frac{1}{m}\sum_j f_L^{-1}[\Delta I(j\Delta\nu)]\, f_D(\epsilon_j)\,\Delta\nu \qquad (9)$$

Clearly, the same value of μ maximizes both the marginalized pdf and the likelihood ratio. However, the likelihood ratio is useful not only for parameter estimation, but also for testing the hypothesis that the contour is present.

Taking logarithms, we obtain the log-likelihood ratio:

$$h(\boldsymbol{\Delta I}\,|\,\mu) \stackrel{\mathrm{def}}{=} \log R(\boldsymbol{\Delta I}\,|\,\mu) \qquad (10)$$
$$= -\log m + \log\left\{\sum_j f_L^{-1}[\Delta I(j\Delta\nu)]\, f_D(\epsilon_j)\,\Delta\nu\right\}$$

which we define as the point-evaluation function. By inserting Eq.1 into Eq.10, and remembering that f_D is Gaussian with variance σ^2, we obtain

$$h(\boldsymbol{\Delta I}\,|\,\mu) = h_0 + \log\sum_j \exp\sqrt{\frac{|\Delta I(j\Delta\nu)|}{\lambda}}\,\exp\left(-\frac{\epsilon_j^2}{2\sigma^2}\right) \qquad (11)$$

where we define for simplicity:

$$h_0 \stackrel{\mathrm{def}}{=} \log\frac{Z_L}{m} - \log\frac{Z_D}{\Delta\nu} \qquad (12)$$

From Eq.11, it can be seen that, for a given observation $\boldsymbol{\Delta I}$, the point-evaluation becomes larger when the contour is placed at a location μ that maximizes a function of the absolute values $|\Delta I|$ under a Gaussian window centered on μ. The next section shows that maximization of the point-evaluation can be achieved by iterative minimization (and re-computation) of a squared distance which has greater intuitive appeal than the point-evaluation.

Before deriving the algorithm, however, statistical dependencies between point-evaluations must be considered.

2.4 Correction for Statistical Dependencies

Consider the set of sampled contour locations $\boldsymbol{\mu} \stackrel{\mathrm{def}}{=} \{\mu_k\,|\,1\leq k\leq n\}$, where the index k ranges over n observations on all observable line-segments. The number n of observations depends on the number and length of the visible line segments. The sum of all point-evaluations, collected over a finite set of sample points on the projected contours, needs to be corrected for statistical dependencies between different observations, to obtain the log-likelihood of $\boldsymbol{\mu}$.

Statistical parameters of natural images show considerable local variations within a single image (*e.g.* [18]). Therefore, the probability of a large point-evaluation is increased if other large point-evaluations have been observed nearby, independently of whether these large evaluations arise from the contours of interest or are due to the texture of the background.

To a first approximation, dependencies between measurements taken on different line segments can be ignored. Dependencies between measurements taken at different sampling points on the same line segment can be significantly reduced by scaling the corresponding point-evaluation functions by $1/\sqrt{L_k}$, where L_k is the length (in pixels) of the segment including sample point k. This scaling factor has been empirically found to give an approximately constant relationship between log-probabilities and sums of point-evaluations over a single line segment: more details are given in [16]. By this scaling, the objective function to be maximized becomes:

$$H = \sum_{k=1}^{n} \frac{1}{\sqrt{L_k}} h(\mu_k \mid \boldsymbol{\Delta \mathcal{I}_k}) \qquad (13)$$

3 The EM Contour Algorithm

When the log-likelihood is obtained by marginalization, it is often the case that optimization by the EM method leads to more robust convergence, as compared to Newton's method [4,13].

In introducing the algorithm, we begin by considering a single sample point on a contour. Optimization of the object pose under the constraint of rigid object motion on the ground plane is considered in the last subsection.

3.1 Simplified Description

This subsection gives an intuitive motivation for the EM contour algorithm.

Suppose that the true image location ν_b of the boundary between object and background were known. In this case, the image evidence could be ignored, since it would give no additional information: the likelihood of the contour location would be given simply by the likelihood of the deformation:

$$f(\nu_b|\mu) = f_D(\nu_b - \mu) \qquad (14)$$

Given that the true location of the boundary is not known, one possible solution is to estimate it from the observation. As an estimator, we choose the *center of mass* of the observation:

$$\widehat{\nu} \stackrel{\text{def}}{=} \sum_j p(j\Delta\nu)\, j\Delta\nu \qquad (15)$$

where $p(j\Delta\nu)$ is the probability that the contour is between locations $(j-1/2)\Delta\nu$ and $(j+1/2)\Delta\nu$ on the normal under consideration. This is obtained by normalization to unity of the sum (over all locations on the normal) of the pdf's of the observations:

$$p(j\Delta\nu) = \frac{f(\Delta\mathcal{I}|j\Delta\nu)\, f_D(j\Delta\nu - \mu)}{f(\Delta\mathcal{I}|i\Delta\nu)\, \sum_i f_D(i\Delta\nu - \mu)} \quad (16)$$

The center of mass is the *BLS* (Bayes-least-squares) estimate of the deformation. The use of the *BLS* estimator, rather than *e.g.* the *MAP* estimator, will be justified in the next subsection. For the moment, suffice it to say that it has the advantage of integrating over all the image evidence, rather than using only the image location with the strongest image derivative.

Assuming that the center of mass is a valid estimate, the log-likelihood becomes

$$\log f(\widehat{\nu}|\mu) = \log f_D(\widehat{\nu} - \mu) \quad (17)$$
$$= -\log Z_D - g(\widehat{\nu} - \mu) \quad (18)$$

where we define for convenience

$$g(\widehat{\nu} - \mu) = \frac{(\widehat{\nu} - \mu)^2}{2\sigma^2} \quad (19)$$

The definition of center of mass includes the current estimate of the contour location through Eq. 16. Therefore, an estimate of μ is needed to compute $\widehat{\nu}$, and an estimate of $\widehat{\nu}$ is needed to optimize μ. This fact suggests the following iterative algorithm:

- E step: estimate the deformation $\widehat{\epsilon} = \widehat{\nu} - \mu$ of the contour, using the image evidence $\Delta\mathcal{I}$ and the estimate $\mu^{(t-1)}$ of the contour location (where the superscript $(t-1)$ refers to iteration number);
- M step: re-estimate the contour locations $\mu^{(t)}$ so as to minimize the squared deformation, $g(\widehat{\nu} - \mu)$.

If the minimization is unconstrained, the second step is trivial: just set $\mu^{(t)} = \widehat{\nu}^{(t)}$. Constrained optimization will be considered in subsection 3.3.

3.2 Derivation of the Algorithm

The derivation is analogous to that of the EM clustering algorithm (*e.g.* [13], section 2.7). We begin by writing the expression for the complete-data log-likelihood, *i.e.* the log-pdf of the observation, given the current contour location and the vector of indicator variables $\boldsymbol{\eta}_{\Delta\nu} = \{\eta_{\Delta\nu}(j\Delta\nu)\}$:

$$h_C(\Delta\mathcal{I}|\mu, \boldsymbol{\eta}) = \sum_j \eta_{\Delta\nu}(j\Delta\nu) \log\left[f(\Delta\mathcal{I}|j\Delta\nu)\, f_D(\epsilon_j)\, \Delta\nu\right]$$

$$= h_0 + \sum_j \eta_{\Delta\nu}(j\Delta\nu) \left(\sqrt{\frac{|\Delta\mathcal{I}(j\Delta\nu)|}{\lambda}} - \frac{\epsilon_j^2}{2\sigma^2}\right) \quad (20)$$

Given that $\boldsymbol{\eta}_{\Delta\nu}$ is unknown, we substitute it by its expected value $\widehat{\boldsymbol{\eta}}_{\Delta\nu} = \{p(j\Delta\nu)\}$. By this substitution, we obtain the *expected complete-data log-likelihood*, or *negative free energy*:

$$\widehat{h}_C(\Delta\mathcal{I}|\mu, \widehat{\boldsymbol{\eta}}) = h_0 + \sum_j p(j\Delta\nu) \left(\sqrt{\frac{|\Delta\mathcal{I}(j\Delta\nu)|}{\lambda}} - \frac{\epsilon_j^2}{2\sigma^2}\right) \quad (21)$$

The negative free energy can be re-written to make explicit the dependency on μ:
$$\widehat{h}_C(\Delta \mathcal{I}|\mu, \widehat{\eta}) = h_0 + h_1 - g(\widehat{\nu} - \mu) \tag{22}$$

where $g(\widehat{\nu} - \mu)$ is defined by Eq.19 and

$$h_1 \stackrel{\text{def}}{=} \sum_j p(j\Delta\nu) \left[\sqrt{\frac{|\Delta \mathcal{I}(j\Delta\nu)|}{\lambda}} - \frac{(j\Delta\nu - \widehat{\nu})^2}{2\sigma^2} \right] \tag{23}$$

Once the probabilities $\{p(j\Delta\nu)\}$ are estimated in the E step of the EM algorithm, h_1 is a constant independent of μ.

From Eq.22, it can be seen that the negative free energy $\widehat{h}_C$ is equal to the negative squared distance $-g(\widehat{\nu} - \mu)$ between the contour and the center of mass, plus additive terms which do not depend on μ. We define $g(\widehat{\nu} - \mu)$ as the *differential free energy* that needs to be *minimized* with respect to μ.

A more general definition of the EM contour algorithm, which makes explicit its statistical basis, is as follows: initialize the contour locations by the prediction of a Kalman filter, or whatever initialization method is appropriate; thereafter, iterate to convergence the following steps:

- E step: estimate the posterior pdf over a discrete set of deformations, $p(j\Delta\nu)$, using Eq.16 with the image evidence $\mathcal{I}$ and the current estimate of μ:

$$p^{(t)}(j\Delta\nu) = \frac{f_D(j\Delta\nu - \mu^{(t-1)}) \, f(\mathcal{I}|j\Delta\nu)}{\sum_i f_D(i\Delta\nu - \mu^{(t-1)}) \, f(\mathcal{I}|i\Delta\nu)} \tag{24}$$

- M step: estimate the contour location

$$\mu^{(t)} = \underset{\mu}{\operatorname{argmax}} \, g^{(t)}(\mu)$$

that maximizes the current estimate of the negative free energy, or equivalently maximizes the current estimate of the free-energy term:

$$\widehat{h}_D^{(t)}(\mu) = \sum_j p^{(t)}(j\Delta\nu) \log f_D(j\Delta\nu - \mu) \tag{26}$$

In this general form, the EM contour algorithm does not involve any explicit estimation of the local shape deformation. Under the assumption of a Gaussian prior pdf for deformations, the EM contour algorithm reduces to the special case outlined in subsection 3.1, in which case the *BLS* estimates of deformations (*i.e.* the centers of mass) can be used for simplicity. In the rest of this paper, we restrict our attention to this special case.

The theory of the EM method ([13], chapter 3) proves that (a) the log-likelihood does not decrease from one iteration to the following and (b) the algorithm converges to an extremum of the log-likelihood.

3.3 Optimization of Pose Parameters

The differential free energy of the entire model can be obtained by substituting f with g in Eq.13:

$$\mathcal{G}(\mathbf{y}) = \sum_{k=1}^{n} \frac{1}{\sqrt{L_k}} g\left[\boldsymbol{\Delta\mathcal{I}}_k \mid \mu_k(\mathbf{y})\right] \quad (27)$$

where the dependencies on $\mathbf{y}$ have been made explicit for terms on both sides of the equation.

In order to minimize $\mathcal{G}$ in pose-parameter space (*i.e.* under the constraint of rigid translation and rotation of the object on the ground plane), the E and M steps of the EM algorithm must be appropriately modified:

- E step: use full perspective to obtain the current estimates of $\boldsymbol{\mu}$ from the pose parameters $\mathbf{y}^{(t-1)}$, and estimate the posterior pdf's over deformations, $p_k(j\Delta\nu)$, using Eq.16 with the image evidence $\boldsymbol{\Delta\mathcal{I}}_k$ and the current estimate of μ_k;
- M step: estimate the pose parameters $\mathbf{y}^{(t)}$ that minimize the differential free energy (Eq. 27), using the current estimates of the posterior pdf $p_k(j\Delta\nu)$ and linearized inverse perspective.

Since $g(\mu)$ is a quadratic function of μ, it follows that $\mathcal{G}(\mathbf{y})$ is a quadratic function of $\mathbf{y}$ within the range in which the linearized perspective is accurate.

Convergence of the EM contour algorithm depends only on linearized perspective being a valid approximation within the distance between $\mathbf{y}^{(t-1)}$ and $\mathbf{y}^{(t)}$: at the following iteration, full perspective is used to re-estimate the contour locations, the free energy and the linearized perspective.

4 Dynamical Model

In order to track an object over an image sequence, the complete state vector of the vehicle needs to be considered:

$$\mathbf{x} = \{X, Y, \theta_Z, v, \omega_Z, a\} \quad (28)$$

where v is the tangential velocity, ω_Z the angular velocity, and a the tangential acceleration of the object.

The observed pose[2] is equal to the first 3 terms of the state vector, plus an observation noise which includes the combined effect of the shape deformations and image noise:

$$\mathbf{y} = \mathbf{B} \cdot \mathbf{x} + \mathbf{n} \quad (29)$$

where $\mathbf{B}$ is a 3×6 matrix whose elements are all zero, except for $\mathbf{B}_{11} = \mathbf{B}_{22} = \mathbf{B}_{33} = 1$, and $\mathbf{n}$ is the observation noise.

---

[2] More precisely, the pose estimated by the EM contour algorithm.

In addition to Eq. 29, a dynamical model is needed to predict the state of the object at the next frame. The form of the model is as follows:

$$\mathbf{x}(t + \Delta t) = \mathbf{D}\left[\mathbf{x}(t)\right] + \mathbf{z}(t + \Delta t) \tag{30}$$

where Δt is the time interval between video frames (or, in the case of an iterated Kalman filter, between iteration steps), $\mathbf{D}$ describes the deterministic dynamics of the system and $\mathbf{z}$ is a random vector which includes unknown control inputs from the driver.

Simple physics leads to the following dynamical equations:

- position on the ground plane from orientation and tangential velocity:

$$X(t + \Delta t) = X(t) + v(t)\Delta t \cos \theta_Z(t)$$
$$Y(t + \Delta t) = Y(t) + v(t)\Delta t \sin \theta_Z(t) \tag{31}$$

- orientation and tangential velocity from angular velocity and tangential acceleration:

$$\theta_Z(t + \Delta t) = \theta_Z(t) + \omega_Z(t)\Delta t$$
$$v(t + \Delta t) = v(t) + a(t)\Delta t \tag{32}$$

- angular velocity and tangential acceleration from the driver's input:

$$\omega_Z(t + \Delta t) = \omega_Z(t)[1 - \exp(-\Delta t/\tau)] + \mathbf{z}_5(t + \Delta t)$$
$$a(t + \Delta t) = a(t)[1 - \exp(-\Delta t/\tau)] + \mathbf{z}_6(t + \Delta t) \tag{33}$$

The simplifying assumption is that changes of pressure on the gas pedal and of steering angle directly translate into tangential acceleration and angular velocity.

Assuming further that these inputs are uncorrelated, the (6 × 6) covariance matrix $\mathbf{Q}$ of the inputs should have only two non-zero elements: $\mathbf{Q}_{66} = \sigma_a^2$ for the tangential acceleration and $\mathbf{Q}_{55} = \sigma_\omega^2$ for the angular velocity.

In practice, better performance has been obtained by setting

$$\mathbf{Q}_{11} = \sigma_p^2 \sin^2 \theta_Z \tag{34}$$
$$\mathbf{Q}_{22} = \sigma_p^2 \cos^2 \theta_Z \tag{35}$$

where σ_p^2 is a spurious noise term in the vehicle position, in the direction normal to the vehicle orientation. This term helps to re-align the model with the object after an accidental misalignment.

A convenient measure of the covariance of the observation noise is the inverse of the *empirical observed information matrix* ([13], section 4.3, Eq. 4.41):

$$\mathbf{I}_e = \sum_k \frac{1}{\sqrt{L_k}} \nabla h(\Delta \mathcal{I}_k | \mu_k) \cdot \nabla^T h(\Delta \mathcal{I}_k | \mu_k) \tag{36}$$

where the sum is over all observations k and the gradient is in pose-parameter space.

Note that the nonlinearities in the system of Eq. 31 are due to the change from a Cartesian coordinate system (for the vehicle location, X and Y) to a polar coordinate system (for the vehicle orientation and velocity, θ_Z and v). Although the nonlinearities are inconvenient, this change of coordinates is a natural way of enforcing two constraints:

- the orientation of the vehicle θ_Z is directly observable by fitting the vehicle model to the image, as detailed in the previous section, while the vehicle velocity can only be inferred by observing the vehicle pose in two or more frames;
- the vehicle cannot move sideways.

It is also worth pointing out that the nonlinearity of the dynamical model is a lesser problem than the nonlinearity of the observation model.

Having specified the system, it is straightforward to implement an iterated extended Kalman filter [1] for the state variables.

4.1 Parameters of the Method

The observation model has 3 parameters: the scale parameter λ of the pdf of grey level differences; the standard deviation σ of the shape deformations; and the sampling interval $\Delta\nu$ on the normals to the contours.

The parameter λ is estimated from the average square root of gld's $\langle\sqrt{\Delta\mathcal{I}}\rangle$, measured over the entire image. For $\beta = 0.5$, the maximum-likelihood estimate of λ is given by $\lambda_{ML} = \langle\sqrt{\Delta\mathcal{I}}\rangle^2/4$. In the absence of large camera motion or lighting variations, it is only necessary to estimate λ in the first frame of the image sequence.

The scale parameter σ is varied in a range corresponding to a 3-D range of $0.3\ m$ to $0.1\ m$ at the viewing distance of the vehicle being tracked. The EM contour algorithm is applied to convergence at each scale. At each scale σ, the sampling interval is given by $\Delta\nu = \max(1, \sigma/4)$ (where both $\Delta\nu$ and σ are in pixels). At each scale, the termination criterion is that the root-mean-square displacement of sample points becomes less than $0.05\ \sigma$.

The parameters of the dynamical model are constrained to a realistic range by the physics of the objects under consideration. The values used in our application are as follows: $\tau = 0.1\ s$; $\sigma_a = 3\ m^2/s$; $\sigma_\omega = 16°/s$; $\sigma_p = 0.5\ m$. The standard deviations have been given relatively high values to compensate for the non-Gaussian nature of the inputs.

5 Initialization

The contour tracker is initialized when a new vehicle is detected and its pose and velocity are estimated. This is accomplished by cluster analysis of image differences. The method is fully described elsewhere [14]. Briefly, a reference image is subtracted from the current image. A new cluster/object is detected when the image difference has a significant amount of energy at a location distinct from the locations of all currently tracked clusters. The centroid and covariance of clusters are estimated by cluster analysis. When a new cluster is no longer in contact with the image boundaries, its centroid and covariance give initial estimates of the location and size of the corresponding object, under the assumption that the object is on the ground plane. If the estimated size is compatible with a car, then the orientation of the object and its velocity are determined by tracking its position for two frames.

6 Results and Conclusions

The method was tested on the PETS2000 test sequence [5]. The vehicles in the test sequence include a saloon car, a hatchback and a van. The proof of the robustness of the tracker is that the vehicles can be tracked (at 5 frames/second) using a grossly inappropriate geometric model (see Fig. 2), even when they move by almost their full length from one frame to the next. A video showing the tracking results is available at ftp://ftp.diku.dk/pub/diku/image/pece.eccv02.mpg.

Fig. 2. Tracking of the hatchback and van in the PETS2000 test sequence: the tracker is as effective with a generic vehicle model as with a specific model.

It is interesting that the equations for the log-likelihood are obtained by assuming a uniform pdf of grey-level differences under an object edge and a non-uniform pdf in the absence of an edge. At first sight, this would seem to imply that, paradoxically, the posterior pdf of the data is independent, and the prior pdf of the data dependent, on the state variables. In fact, a careful inspection of Eqs. 4 and 5 shows that this is not the case: the pdf of the image, given the pose variables (Eq.5) does depend on the pose, while the prior pdf of the image (Eq.4) depends on the image, but not on the model, and is not relevant to the optimization task.

One limitation of the method is that, if the object being tracked enters a highly textured region (*e.g.* bushes, cobblestones, other objects in the background), then large gld values will be measured on all normals, independently of the object pose. Whether the object can still be tracked under these conditions depends on how the average grey-level difference between object and background compares to the *local* gld statistics.

By contrast, the method should be relatively robust against occlusion and changes of illumination. In case of partial occlusion, if a few model lines can be reliably located in the image, then these can be sufficient to solve for the object pose, depending on the geometry of these visible lines. In case of changes of illumination, the initialization method can break down (since it is based on *temporal* image differences), but the contour tracker can still work as long as the λ parameter of the pdf of gld's is updated.

The main advantages of the EM contour tracker are its statistical basis in the EM method, its operation in 3-D and the two simple concepts on which the tracker is based: there are no correlations between image pixels on opposite sides of object edges, and it is necessary to marginalize over shape variations.

The fact that the generative model leads to a simple marginalization technique is an attractive feature. Methods that involve feature detection at any stage should marginalize over all possible correspondences of image features to model features, compatible with a hypothesis pose, in order to compute the correct likelihood of the pose. Similarly, 2-D contour methods should marginalize over all parameters of the 2-D contours, compatible with a state of a 3-D object, in order to compute the correct likelihood of the state. In practice, such marginalization is often difficult: avoiding feature detection makes marginalization easier to implement.

References

1. Y. Bar-Shalom, T. E. Fortmann, *Tracking And Data Association*. Academic Press, 1988.
2. A. Baumberg, D.C. Hogg, Learning Flexible Models from Image Sequences, Proc. of ECCV'94, Lecture Notes in Computer Science, vol. 800, *pp.*299-308, 1994.
3. A Blake, M Isard, *Active Contours*, Springer-Verlag, Berlin 1998.
4. A.P. Dempster, N.M. Laird, D.B. Rubin, Maximum likelihood from incomplete data via the EM algorithm (with discussion), *J. of the Royal Statistical Soc.* B 39: 1-38, 1977.

5. JM Ferryman, AD Worrall, Proc. of the 1st IEEE International Workshop on Performance Evaluation in Tracking and Surveillance: PETS 2000.
6. D Geman, B Jedynak, An active testing model for tracking roads in satellite images. IEEE Trans. PAMI 18(1): 1-14, 1996.
7. C Harris, Tracking with rigid models. In *Active Vision* (A Blake, A Yuille, eds) *pp.*59-73. MIT Press, 1992.
8. J. Huang, D. Mumford, Statistics of natural images and models. In *Proc. CVPR'99*, vol.1, *pp.*541-547, 1999.
9. A. Lee, D. Mumford, An Occlusion Model generating Scale-Invariant Images. In *Proc. Int. Workshop on Statistical and Computational Theories of Vision.* http://www.cis.ohio-state.edu/ szhu/SCTV2001.html, 1999.
10. M Kass, A Witkin, D Terzopoulos, Snakes: active contour models. In *Proc. ICCV'97, pp.*259-268, 1987.
11. D Koller, K Daniilidis, H-H Nagel, Model-based object tracking in monocular image sequences of road traffic scenes. *Int.J.Comp.Vis.* 10(3): 257-281, 1993.
12. H Kollnig, H-H Nagel, 3D pose estimation by fitting image gradients directly to polyhedral models. In *Proc. ICCV'95, pp.*569-574, 1995.
13. G.J. McLachlan, T. Krishnan, *The EM Algorithm and Extensions*, Wiley, New York, 1997.
14. A.E.C. Pece, Generative-model-based tracking by cluster analysis of image differences. Accepted for publication in *Robotics and Autonomous Systems.*
15. AEC Pece, AD Worrall, A statistically-based Newton method for pose refinement. *Image and Vision Computing* 16: 541-544, 1998.
16. AEC Pece, AD Worrall, A Newton method for pose refinement of 3D models. Proc 6th International Symposium on Intelligent Robotic Systems: SIRS'98, The University of Edinburgh.
17. A.E.C. Pece, A.D. Worrall, Tracking without feature detection. In [5], *pp.*29-37, 2000.
18. DL Ruderman, The statistics of natural images. *Network* 5: 517-548, 1994.
19. H. Sidenbladh, M.J. Black, Learning image statistics for Bayesian tracking, In *Proc. ICCV'01*, Vol. 2, *pp.*700 716, 2001.
20. P. Tissainayagam, D. Suter, Tracking multiple object contour with automatic motion model switching, In *Proc. ICPR'00, pp.*1146-1149, 2000.
21. AD Worrall, JM Ferryman, GD Sullivan, KD Baker, Pose and structure recovery using active models. Proc. BMVC'95, *pp.*137-146, 1995.
22. AL Yuille, JM Coughlan, Fundamental limits of Bayesian inference: order parameters and phase transitions for road tracking. *IEEE Trans. PAMI* 22(2): 160-173, 2000.

M2Tracker: A Multi-View Approach to Segmenting and Tracking People in a Cluttered Scene Using Region-Based Stereo

Anurag Mittal and Larry S. Davis

Department of Computer Science
University of Maryland
College Park, MD 20742
{anurag,lsd}@umiacs.umd.edu

Abstract. We present a system that is capable of segmenting, detecting and tracking multiple people in a cluttered scene using multiple synchronized cameras located far from each other. The system improves upon existing systems in many ways including: (1) We do not assume that a foreground connected component belongs to only one object; rather, we segment the views taking into account color models for the objects and the background. This helps us to not only separate foreground regions belonging to different objects, but to also obtain better background regions than traditional background subtraction methods (as it uses foreground color models in the algorithm). (2) It is fully automatic and does not require any manual input or initializations of any kind. (3) Instead of taking decisions about object detection and tracking from a single view or camera pair, we collect evidences from each pair and combine the evidence to obtain a decision in the end. This helps us to obtain much better detection and tracking as opposed to traditional systems.

Several innovations help us tackle the problem. The first is the introduction of a region-based stereo algorithm that is capable of finding 3D points inside an object if we know the regions belonging to the object in two views. No exact point matching is required. This is especially useful in wide baseline camera systems where exact point matching is very difficult due to self-occlusion and a substantial change in viewpoint. The second contribution is the development of a scheme for setting priors for use in segmentation of a view using bayesian classification. The scheme, which assumes knowledge of approximate shape and location of objects, dynamically assigns priors for different objects at each pixel so that occlusion information is encoded in the priors. The third contribution is a scheme for combining evidences gathered from different camera pairs using occlusion analysis so as to obtain a globally optimum detection and tracking of objects.

The system has been tested using different density of people in the scene which helps us to determine the number of cameras required for a particular density of people.

Keywords: Multi-camera Tracking, Region-Based Stereo, Grouping and Segmentation

A. Heyden et al. (Eds.): ECCV 2002, LNCS 2350, pp. 18–33, 2002.
© Springer-Verlag Berlin Heidelberg 2002

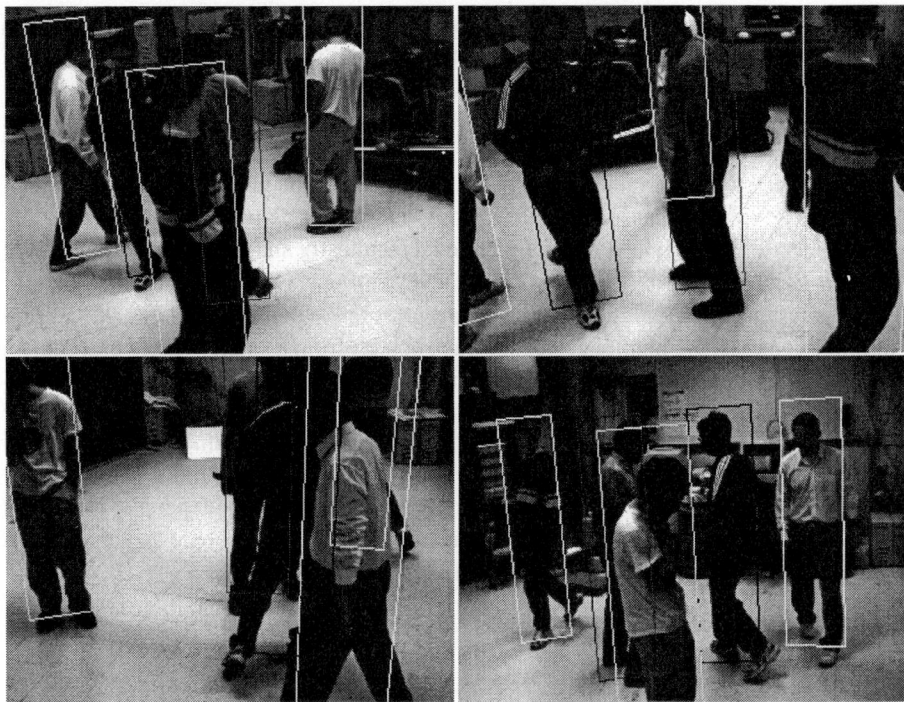

Fig. 1. Four images from a 6-perspective sequence at a particular time instant. The boxes show the positions found by the algorithm.

1 Introduction

In this paper we address the problem of segmenting, detecting and tracking multiple people using a multi-perspective video approach. In particular, we are concerned with the situation when the scene being viewed is sufficiently "crowded" that one cannot assume that any or all of the people in the scene would be visually isolated from any vantage point. This is normally the case in many surveillance applications. Figure 1 shows four images from a 6-perspective sequence that will be used to illustrate our algorithm. Notice that in all four images, there is substantial occlusion so that one cannot assume that we are seeing a person in isolation. We assume that our cameras are calibrated, and that people are moving on a calibrated ground plane. We also assume that the cameras are frame synchronized.

The paper develops several novel ideas in order to solve the problem. The first and most important is the introduction of a region-based stereo algorithm that is capable of finding 3D points inside an object if we know the regions belonging to the object in two views. No exact point matching is required. This is especially useful in wide baseline camera systems where exact matching is very difficult due to self-occlusion and a substantial change in viewpoint. The second contribution is the development of a scheme for setting priors for use in segmentation of a view using bayesian classification. The scheme, which assumes knowledge of approximate shape and location of objects, dynamically assigns priors for different objects at each pixel so that occlusion information is encoded in the priors. These priors are used to obtain good segmentation even in the case of partial occlusions. The third contribution is a scheme for combining evidences gathered from different camera pairs using occlusion analysis so as to obtain a globally optimum detection and tracking of objects. Higher weight is given to those pairs which have a clear view of that location than those whose view is potentially obstructed by some objects. The weight is also determined dynamically and uses approximate shape features to give a probabilistic answer for the level of occlusion.

Our system takes a unified approach to segmentation, detection and tracking using multiple cameras. We neither detect nor track objects from a single camera or a camera pair; rather evidence is gathered from multiple camera pairs and the decisions of detection and tracking are taken at the end by combining the evidences in a robust manner taking occlusion into consideration. Also, we do not simply assume that a connected component of foreground pixels corresponds to a single object. Rather, we employ a segmentation algorithm to separate out regions belonging to different people. This helps us to handle the case of partial occlusion and allows us to track people and objects in a cluttered scene where no single person is isolated in any view.

2 Related Work

There are numerous single-camera detection and tracking algorithms, all of which face the same difficulties of tracking 3D objects using only 2D information. These algorithms are challenged by occluding and partially-occluding objects, as well as appearance changes. Some researchers have developed multi-camera detection and tracking algorithms in order to overcome these limitations.

Haritaoglu et. al. [6] developed a single camera system which employs a combination of shape analysis and tracking to locate people and their parts (head, hands, feet, torso etc.) and tracks them using appearance models. In [7], they incorporate stereo information into their system. Kettnaker and Zabih [11] developed a system for counting the number of people in a multi-camera environment where the cameras have a non-overlapping field of view. Darrell et. al. [3] developed a tracking algorithm that uses a stereo pair of cameras and integrates stereo, color and face pattern detection. Dense stereo processing is used to isolate people from other objects and people in the background, and faces and bodies of people are tracked. All of these methods use a single viewpoint (using one or two cameras) for a particular part of the scene and would have problems in the case of objects occluded from that viewpoint.

Orwell et. al. [16] present a tracking algorithm to track multiple objects using multiple cameras using "color" tracking. They model the connected blobs obtained from background subtraction using color histogram techniques and use them to match and track objects. In [17], Orwell et. al. present a multi-agent framework for determining whether different agents are assigned to the same object seen from different cameras. This method would have problems in the case of partial occlusions where a connected foreground region does not correspond to one object, but has parts from several of them.

Cai and Aggarwal [1] extend a single-camera tracking system by starting with tracking in a single camera view and switching to another camera when the system predicts that the current camera will no longer have a good view of the subject. Since in our algorithm, we collect evidences from different pairs and only take the decision at the end, we expect our algorithm to perform better than this approach.

Intille et. al. ([9] and [10]) present a system which is capable of tracking multiple non-rigid objects. The system uses a top-view camera to identify individual blobs and a "closed-world" assumption to adaptively select and weight image features used for matching these blobs. Putting a camera(s) on the top is certainly a good idea since it reduces occlusion, but is not possible in many situations. Also, the advantage of a camera on top is reduced as we move away from the camera, which might require a large number of cameras. Such a camera system would also not be able to identify people or determine other important statistics (like height or color distributions) and hence may not be very useful for many applications.

Krumm et. al. [13] present an algorithm that has goals very similar to ours. They use stereo cameras and combine information from multiple stereo cameras (currently only 2) in 3D space. They perform background subtraction and then detect human-shaped blobs in 3D space. Color histograms are created for each person and are used to identify and track people over time. The method of using short-baseline stereo matching to back-project into 3D space and integrating information from different stereo pairs has also been used by Darrell et. al. [4]. In contrast to [13] and [4], our approach utilizes the wide-baseline camera arrangement that has the following advantages:

(1) It provides many more camera pairs that can be integrated (C_2^n as compared to $n/2$ for short baseline stereo, using n cameras),

(2) It has higher accuracy in back-projection and lower sensitivity to calibration errors, and

(3) It provides more viewing angles with the same number of cameras so that occlusion can be handled better.

On the other hand, the short-baseline stereo pair camera arrangement used, e.g., in [4] has the advantages of

(1) more accurate correspondences due to small change in viewpoint, and

(2) better understood matching algorithms.

It is not evident which method is better and it appears that a combination of the two methods might yield the best results.

Our region-based stereo algorithm can be considered to lie between wide-baseline stereo algorithms, which try to match exact 3D points across the views, and volume intersection algorithms which find the 3D shape of an object by intersection in 3D space without regard to the intensity values observed (except for background subtraction). Wide-baseline stereo algorithms have the challenge of incorrect matches due to a substantial change in viewpoint. Although some work has been done to improve upon these methods(e.g. [18] and [8]), they are still not very robust due to this fundamental difficulty.

On the other hand, volume intersection is very sensitive to background subtraction errors, so that errors in segmenting even one of the views can seriously degrade the recovered volume. Although there has been work recently (for e.g [20]) addressing some of these issues, these methods also have problems, especially in the case where the objects are occluded in some views by other objects. Back-projection in 3D space without regard to color also yields very poor results in cluttered scenes, where almost all of the camera view is occupied by the foreground.

In contrast, we do not match points exactly across views; neither do we perform volume intersection without regard to the objects seen. Rather, determination of regions belonging to different objects is sufficient to yield 3D points guaranteed to lie inside the objects.

3 General Overview of the Algorithm

Our system models different characteristics of people by observing them over time. These models include color models at different heights of the person and "presence" probabilities along the horizontal direction at different heights. These models are used to segment images in each camera view. The regions thus formed are matched across views using our region-matching stereo algorithm which yields 3D points potentially lying inside objects. These points are projected onto the ground plane and ground points are used to form an object location likelihood map using Gaussian kernels for a single image pair. The likelihood maps are combined using occlusion analysis to obtain a single map, which is then used to obtain ground plane positions of objects in the scene. The algorithm is then iterated using these new ground plane positions and this process is repeated until the ground plane positions are stable. The final ground plane positions are then used to update the person models, and the whole process is repeated for the next time step.

4 Modeling People

We model the appearance and locations of the people in the scene. These models, which are developed by observing people over time (method explained in section 9), help us segment people in the camera views. These models are developed from the sequences automatically; no manual input is required.

4.1 Color Models

One of the attributes useful to model is the color distribution at different heights of the person. A single color model for the whole person would not be able to capture the vertical variation of the color. On the other hand, modeling the horizontal distribution of color is very difficult without full 3D surface reconstruction, which would be too time-consuming and hence not too interesting for tracking and surveillance type of applications. In order to model the color distribution at different heights, we use the well-known method of non-parametric Gaussian kernel estimation technique which is well suited to our system. (see [5] for more details). Since the intensity levels change across cameras due to aperture effects, and due to shadow and orientation effects in the same view, we only use the ratios $r/(r+g+b)$ and $g/(r+g+b)$ in the color models.

4.2 "Presence" Probabilities

For our segmentation algorithm, we want to determine the probability that a particular person is "present" (i.e. occupies space) along a particular line of sight. Towards that end, we define "Presence" Probability (denoted by $L(h, w)$) as the probability that a person is present(i.e. occupies space) at height h and distance w from the vertical line passing through the person's center. This probability is a function of both the distance w and height h since, e.g., the width of a person near the head is less than the width near the center. This probability function also varies from person to person. The method for estimating this probability by observation is described in section 9.

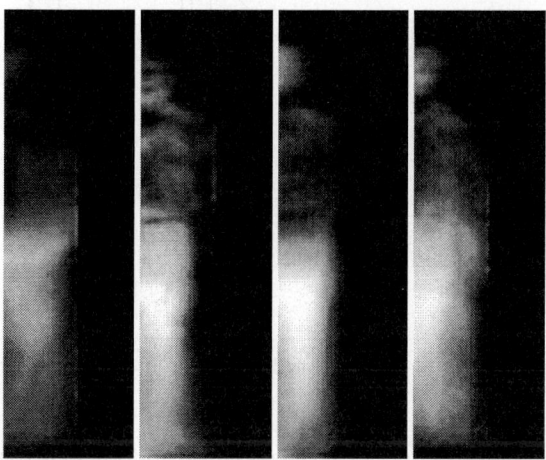

Fig. 2. Sample Presence Probabilities of people observed over time.

5 Pixel Classification in a Single View

We use Bayesian Classification to classify each pixel as belonging to a particular person, or the background. The *a posteriori* probability that an observed pixel $\mathbf{x}$ (containing both color and image position information) belongs to a person j (or the background) is

$$P_{posterior}(j/\mathbf{x}) \propto P_{prior}(j) P(\mathbf{x}/j) \tag{1}$$

The pixel is then classified as

$$\text{Most likely class} = \max_{j}(P_{posterior}(j/\mathbf{x})) \tag{2}$$

$P(\mathbf{x}/j)$ is given by the color model of the person at height h. For the background, we use a background model of the scene using the method described in [14].

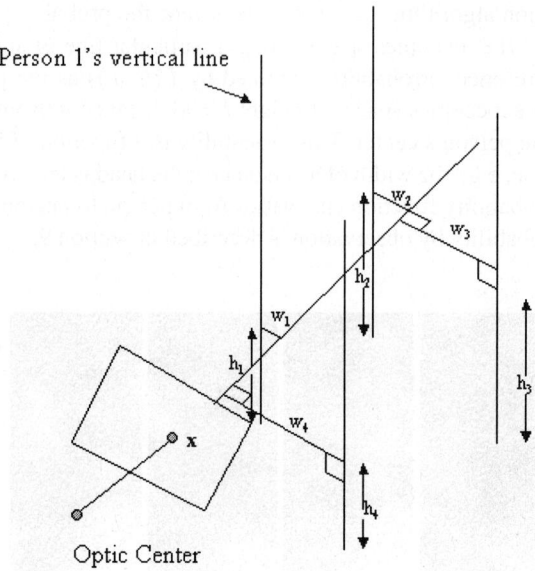

Fig. 3. Measuring distances (and heights) from the line of sight

We want the prior probabilities to include occlusion information so that the prior for a person in front is higher near his estimated position compared to the priors far away from him and compared to a person in rear. Doing this in a structured, consistent and logical manner is the challenge. We employ the following methodology. For each pixel **x**, we project a ray in space passing through the optical center of the camera (see Figure 3). We calculate the minimum distances w_j of this ray from the vertical lines passing through the currently estimated centers of the people. Also calculated are the heights h_j of the shortest line segments connecting these lines. Then, the prior probability that a pixel **x** is the image of person j is set as

$$P_{prior}(j) = L_j(h_j, w_j) \prod_{k \text{ occludes } j} (1 - L_k(h_k, w_k)) \quad (3)$$

$$P_{prior}(background) = \prod_{all\ j} (1 - L_j(h_j, w_j)) \quad (4)$$

where $L_j(h_j, w_j)$ is the "presence" probability described in section 4.2. A person "k occludes j" if the distance of k to the optical center of the camera is less than the distance of j to the center.

The motivation for the definition is that a particular pixel originates from a person if and only if (1) the person is present along that line of sight (Probability for this = L_j),

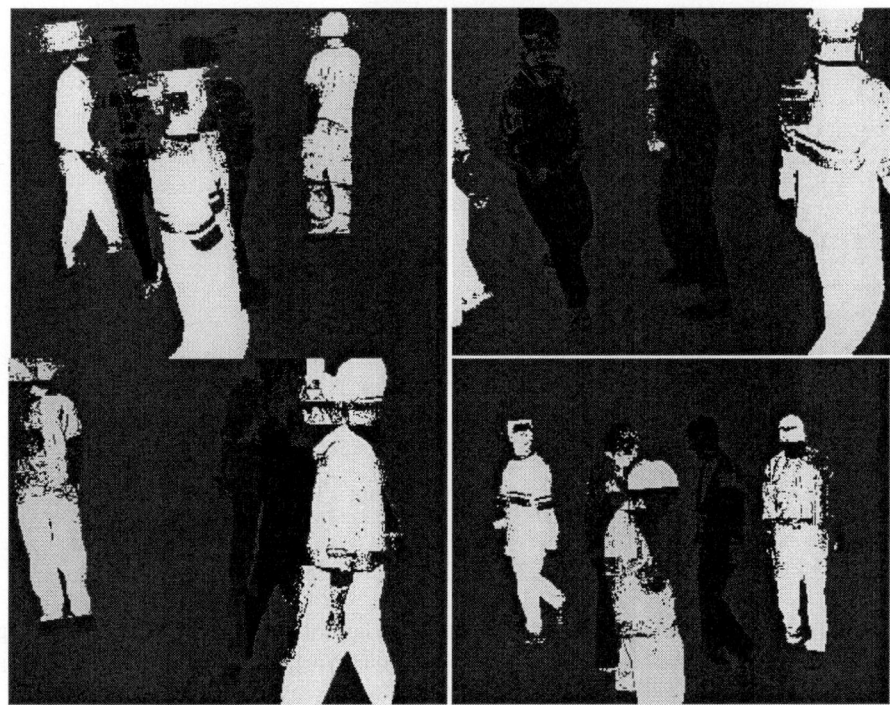

Fig. 4. The result of segmenting images shown in Figure 1

and (2) no other person in front of her is present along that line of sight (Probability = 1 - L_k). If no person is present along a particular line of sight, we see the background. The classification procedure enables us to incorporate both the color profile of the people, and the occlusion information available in a consistent and logical manner.

It is interesting to note that we expect to obtain better background subtraction using our segmentation procedure than using traditional background subtraction methods because we take into account models of the foreground objects in the scene in addition to information about the background that is the only input for traditional background subtraction methods. Indeed, this is what we observe during experiments.

We need a procedure to detect new people entering the scene and bootstraping the algorithm in order to make it fully automatic. Towards that end, we detect unclassified pixels as those for which $P_{prior} * P(c/j)$ is below a given threshold for all the person models and the background, i.e. none of the person models or the background can account for the pixel with a high enough probability. For these pixels, we use a simple color segmentation algorithm, which groups together pixels having similar color characteristics. This segmentation creates additional regions in the image and these regions are also matched across cameras as described in the next section.

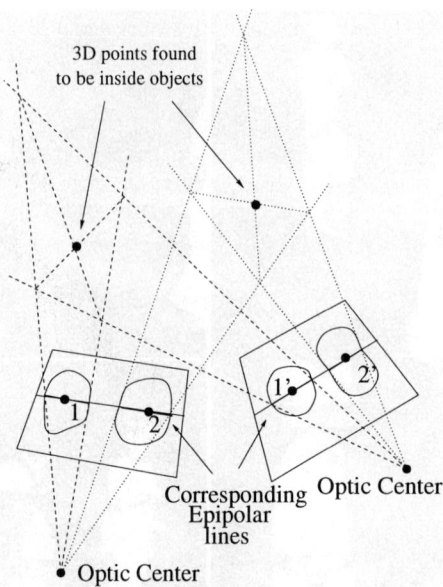

Fig. 5. The point of intersection of the diagonals of the quadrilateral formed by back-projecting the endpoints of the matched segments yields a 3D point lying inside an object. The matching segments are 1 and 1', and 2 and 2' respectively.

6 Region-Based Stereo

Along epipolar lines in pairs of views, we match regions from one camera view to the regions in the other. Segments belonging to the same person in different views (as determined by the classification algorithm) are matched to each other. Regions corresponding to unclassified pixels are matched to each other based on color characteristics. For each matched pair of segments, we project the end-points of the segments and form a quadrilateral in the plane of the corresponding epipolar lines. The point of intersection of the diagonals of this quadrilateral is taken to be belonging to the object (see Figure 5). This is because, for a convex object this is the only point that can be guaranteed to lie inside the object (see proof in Appendix). This is assuming that the complete object is visible and segmented completely as one region in each view. For any other 3D point in the plane of the epipolar lines, it is possible to construct a case in which this point will lie outside the object.

7 Producing Likelihood Estimates on the Ground Plane

Having obtained 3D points belonging to people, we want to detect and track people in a robust manner rejecting outliers. Assuming the people are standing upright or are otherwise extended primarily in the vertical direction, one natural way to do that would be to do the estimation on the ground plane after projecting the 3D points onto it. It is also possible to do clustering in 3D and this would be the method of choice for many applications. However, for our application, estimation on the ground plane is better since we are dealing with only walking people. We define a "likelihood" measure which estimates whether a particular location on the ground plane is occupied by an object. We develop likelihood maps for each camera pair used and then combine these maps in a robust manner using the occlusion information available.

7.1 Likelihood from a Single Camera Pair

A simple way to develop likelihood maps using ground points is to use Gaussian kernels. The weight and standard deviation of the kernels is based on the minimum width of the segments that matched to give rise to that point, and the camera instantaneous fields of view (IFOV). This gives higher weight to points originating from longer segments than from smaller ones. This is done for each pair of cameras for which the segmentation and matching is performed.

7.2 Combining Results from Many Camera Pairs Using Occlusion Analysis

Given the likelihood maps from matching across pairs of cameras, we describe a method for combining likelihood maps that makes use of occlusion information available from the approximate position of the people. For each of the cameras, we form a probability map that gives us the probability that a particular location $\mathbf{x}$ is visible from the camera. First of all, the camera center is projected onto the ground plane. Then, for each point $\mathbf{x}$ on the ground plane, we calculate the perpendicular distance w_j of each person j from the line joining the camera center and the point $\mathbf{x}$. Then, defining "presence" probabilities $L_j()$ in a way similar to section 4.2, but taking only the width as parameter (by averaging over the height parameter), we find the probability that the point $\mathbf{x}$ is visible from the camera c as

$$P_c(\mathbf{x}) = \prod_{j \text{ occludes } \mathbf{x}} (1 - L_j(w_j)) \tag{5}$$

where j occludes $\mathbf{x}$ if its distance from the camera is less than $\mathbf{x}$. Now, for a particular camera pair $(c1, c2)$, the weight for the ground point $\mathbf{x}$ is calculated as

$$w_{(c1,c2)}(\mathbf{x}) = P_{c1}(\mathbf{x})P_{c2}(\mathbf{x}) \tag{6}$$

The weight is essentially the probability that $\mathbf{x}$ is visible from both the cameras. The weighted likelihood value is then calculated as

$$Lk(\mathbf{x}) = \frac{\sum_{(c1,c2)} w_{(c1,c2)}(\mathbf{x}) Lk_{(c1,c2)}(\mathbf{x})}{\sum_{(c1,c2)} w_{(c1,c2)}(\mathbf{x})} \tag{7}$$

This definition helps us to dynamically weigh the different likelihood values such that the values with the highest confidence level (least occlusion) are weighted the most. Note that the normalization constant is different for each ground plane point and changes over time.

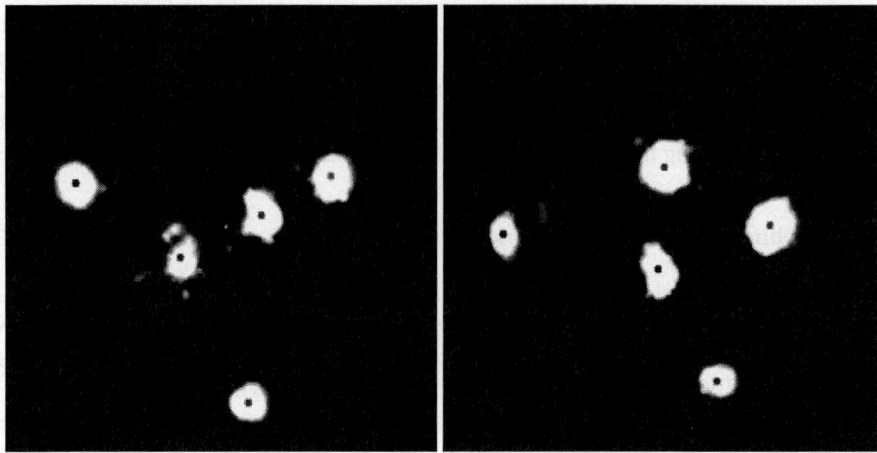

Fig. 6. (a) The likelihood map obtained for the image set shown in Figure 1 by applying the occlusion-analysis weighting scheme. The dots show the position state variable of the Kalman filter tracking the person. (b) The likelihood map for another time step from the same sequence.

8 Tracking on the Ground Plane

After obtaining the combined likelihood map, we identify objects by examining likelihood clusters and identifying regions where the sum of likelihoods exceeds a given threshold. The centroids of such likelihood "blobs" are obtained simply using

$$x_{centroid} = \frac{\sum_{\mathbf{x}, \mathbf{x} \in region} \mathbf{x} * Lk(\mathbf{x})}{\sum_{\mathbf{x}} Lk(\mathbf{x})} \tag{8}$$

where $Lk(\mathbf{x})$ is the likelihood at point **x**. These object blobs are then tracked over time using a *Kalman filter*.

9 Updating Models of People

Observed images and information about the current position of the people are used to update models of people and create ones for the "new" people detected. For each pixel, we calculate the "presence" probabilities L_j for each person as described earlier. We determine if L_j is above a certain threshold for a particular person and below another (lower) threshold for all others. This helps us in ensuring that the pixel is viewing the particular person only and nothing else (except the background). In order to determine if the pixel belongs to the background or not, we use the background model to determine the probability that the pixel color originates from the background. If this probability is below a certain threshold, then we determine that the pixel belongs to the person; else it belongs to the background. If it belongs to the person, it is added as a kernel to the color model of the person at that height. We update the "presence" probability L_j for the person by incrementing the count for the total number of observations at height h

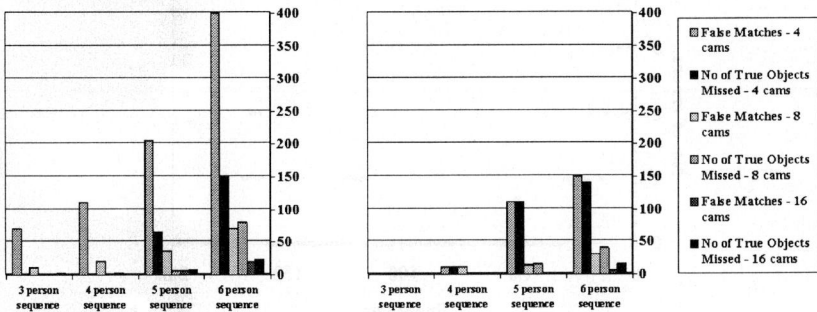

Fig. 7. Cumulative errors for four sequences of 200 time steps each by (a) averaging likelihoods and using no occlusion analysis, and (b) using occlusion analysis.

and width w for the person and incrementing the count for positive matches only if this pixel is determined to belong to the person (according to the above mentioned method). The "presence" probability at that height and width is then simply the second count divided by the first.

10 Implementation and Experiments

Image sequences are captured using up to 16 color CCD cameras. These cameras, which are attached to "Acquisition" PCs via frame grabbers, are capable of being externally triggered for synchronization purposes. Cameras are located at positions surrounding the lab so that they see the objects from different viewpoints. All of the cameras are calibrated using a global coordinate system and the ground plane is also determined. Frame synchronization across cameras is achieved using a TTL-level signal generated by a Data Translation DT340 card attached to a controller PC, and transmitted via coaxial cables to all the cameras. For video acquisition, the synchronization signal is used to simultaneously start all cameras. No timecode per frame is required.

In the distributed version of the algorithm where we use a Pentium II Xeon 450MHz PC for each of the cameras, the system currently takes about 2 seconds per iteration of the ground plane position finding loop. On the average, we need about 2 - 3 iterations per time step, so the running time of the algorithm is about 5 seconds per time step. We believe that by code optimizations and faster processors, we will be able to run the algorithm in real time.

In order to evaluate our algorithm, we conducted experiments on four sequences containing 3, 4, 5 and 6 people respectively. The attempt was to increase the density of people till the algorithm broke down and to study the breakdown thresholds and other characteristics. Each sequence consisted of 200 frames taken at the rate of 10 frames/second and people were constrained to move in a region approximately

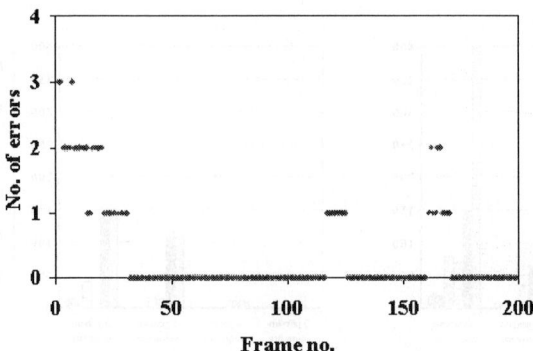

Fig. 8. Total errors as a function of time for the sequence with 5 people using 8 cameras. Note how the errors decrease with time as the models become more robust. Errors after the initial period occur mainly because of people coming too close to each other.

3.5mX3.5m in size. Matching was done for only adjacent pairs of cameras (n pairs) and not for all of the C_2^n pairs possible. This helps us control the time complexity of the algorithm, but reduces the quality of the results obtained.

For each of the sequences, we calculated the number of false objects found and the number of true objects missed by the algorithm. We calculated these metrics using 4, 8 and 16 cameras in order to study the effect of varying the number of cameras and to determine the breakdown characteristics, thus enabling us to determine the minimum number of cameras required to properly identify and track a certain number of objects. The cumulative errors over the 200 frames are shown in Figure 7(b). Also shown in Figure 7(a) are the error metrics obtained when the likelihood values obtained from different cameras are weighted equally and occlusion analysis is not used. This helps us observe the improvement obtained by using the occlusion analysis scheme. Most of the errors occur when the models for people are not very accurate, e.g., in the beginning and when a new person enters the scene. However, as models become better, it is able to correct itself after a few time steps only. The sequences containing 5 and 6 people have severe occlusion at many time steps such that a person is surrounded by the others in such a way that he is not visible from any of the cameras. This results in these people not being detected for those time steps.

11 Summary and Conclusions

In this paper, we have presented a system for segmenting, detecting and tracking multiple people using multiple synchronized cameras located far from each other. It is fully automatic and does not require any manual input or initialisations. It is able to handle occlusions and partial occlusions caused by the dense location of these objects and hence can be useful in many practical surveillance applications.

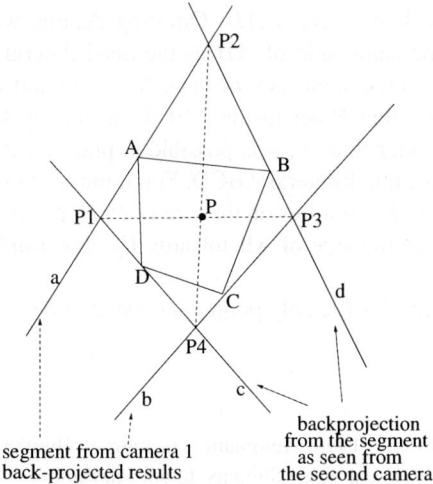

Fig. 9. Illustration for Appendix - shows that, for a convex object, the point of intersection of the diagonals of the quadrilateral formed by back-projecting the end-points of the matched segments is the only point guaranteed to lie inside the object

Acknowledgments

We would like to thank Ramani Duraiswami for reading the manuscript and suggesting improvements in it. This research has been funded by NSF grant no. EIA9901249.

Appendix

In this section, we prove that, in the case of a convex object O, the point of intersection of the diagonals of the quadrilateral formed by backprojecting the end-points of corresponding segments of that convex object is guaranteed to lie inside the object; and that no other point can be guaranteed thus.

We prove this with the help of an illustration showing the plane corresponding to the epipolar lines. (see Figure 9). Let a and b be the rays back-projected from the left and right ends of the segment as seen from the first camera. Let c and d be the corresponding rays from the second camera. Now, let P_1, P_2, P_3 and P_4 be the points of intersection of a, b, c and d as shown in the diagram. Let P be the point of intersection of the diagonals of $P_1 P_2 P_3 P_4$. Since camera 1 sees some point on line a that belongs to O, and O is guaranteed to lie between rays c and d, we can conclude that there exists a point on the line segment $P_1 P_2$ that lies on the boundary of O. Let this point be called A. Similarly, we can conclude the existence of points from O on line segments $P_2 P_3$, $P_3 P_4$ and $P_4 P_1$. Let these points be called B, C and D respectively. Since the object is convex, we can now conclude that all points lying inside the quadrilateral ABCD also lie within O.

Now, consider the line segment AB. Omitting details, we can easily prove that the point P lies on the same side of AB as the quadrilateral $ABCD$. Similarly, we can prove that P lies on the same side of lines BC, CD and DA as the quadrilateral $ABCD$. But this means that P lies inside $ABCD$, hence inside O.

For any point P' other than P, it is possible to place A, B, C and D such that the point P' lies outside the quadrilateral ABCD. For, it must lie on one side of at least one of the lines $P_1 P_3$ and $P_2 P_4$. If it lies on the side of $P_1 P_3$ towards P_2, then we can place AB such that P' lies on the side of AB towards P_2, thus implying that it lies outside ABCD.

Therefore, the point P is the only point guaranteed to lie inside O.

References

1. Cai Q. and Aggarwal J.K. 1998. Automatic Tracking of Human Motion in Indoor Scenes Across Multiple Synchronized video Streams. In *6th Internation Conference on Computer Vision,* Bombay, India, pp. 356-262.
2. Collins R.T., Lipton A.J., and Kanade T. 1999. A System for Video Surveillance and Monitoring. *American Nuclear Society Eighth International Topical Meeting on Robotics and Remote Systems,* Pittsburgh.
3. Darrell T., Gordon G., Harville M., and Woodfill J. 1998. Integrated Person Tracking Using Stereo, color, and Pattern Detection. *IEEE Computer Society Conference on Computer Vision and Pattern Recognition,* Santa Barbara, CA, pp. 601-608.
4. Darrell T., Demirdjian D., Checka N., and Felzenszwalb P. 2001. Plan-View Trajectory Estimation with Dense Stereo Background Models. In *IEEE International Conference on Computer Vision.,* Vancouver, Canada.
5. Elgammal A., Duraiswami R. and Davis L.S. 2001. Efficient Non-parametric Adaptive Color Modeling Using Fast Gauss Transform. *IEEE Conference on Computer Vision and Pattern Recognition,* Hawaii.
6. Haritaoglu I., Harwood D. and Davis, L.S. 1998. W4:Who, When, Where, What: A Real Time System for Detecting and Tracking People. *Third IEEE International Conference on Automatic Face and Gesture Recognition,* Nara, Japan, pp. 222-227.
7. Haritaoglu I., Harwood D., and Davis L.S. 1998. W4S: A real-time system for detecting and tracking people in 2 1/2D. *5th European Conference on Computer Vision,* Freiburg, Germany.
8. Horaud R. and Skordas T. 1989. Stereo Correspondence through Feature Grouping and Maximal Cliques. *IEEE Journal on Pattern Analysis and Computer Vision,* vol 11(11):1168-1180.
9. Intille S. S. and Bobick A. F. 1995. Closed-World Tracking. *5TH International Conference on Computer Vision,* Cambridge, MA, pp. 672-678.
10. Intille S.S., Davis, J.W. and Bobick A.F. 1997. Real-Time Closed-World Tracking. *IEEE Computer Society Conference on Computer Vision and Pattern Recognition,* pp. 697-703.
11. Kettnaker V. and Zabih R. 1999. Counting People from Multiple Cameras. In *IEEE International Conference on Multimedia Computing and Systems,* Florence, Italy, pp. 267-271.
12. Sander P.T., Vinet L, Cohen L. and Gagalowicz A. 1989. Hierarchical Region Based Stereo Matching. In *IEEE Conference on Computer Vision and Pattern Recognition,* San Diego.
13. Krumm J., Harris S., Meyers B., Brumitt B., Hale M. and Shafer S. 2000. Multi-camera Multi-person Tracking for EasyLiving. *3rd IEEE International Workshop on Visual Surveillance,* Dublin, Ireland.
14. Mittal A. and Huttenlocher D. 2000. Site Modeling for Wide Area Surveillance and Image Synthesis. In *IEEE Conference on Computer Vision and Pattern Recognition,* Hilton Head, South Carolina.

15. Mittal A. and Davis L.S. 2001. Unified Multi-Camera Detection and Tracking Using Region-Matching. In *IEEE Workshop on Multi-Object Tracking,* Vancouver, Canada.
16. Orwell J., Remagnino P. and Jones G.A. 1999. Multi-Camera Color Tracking. *Proceedings of the 2nd IEEE Workshop on Visual Surveillance,* Fort Collins, Colorado.
17. Orwell J., Massey S., Remagnino P., Greenhill D., and Jones G.A. 1999. A Multi-agent Framework for Visual Surveillance. *International Conference on Image Analysis and Processing,* Venice, Italy, pp 1104-1107.
18. Pritchett P., and Zisserman A. 1998. Wide Baseline Stereo Matching. In *Sixth International Conference on Computer Vision,* Bombay, India, pp. 754-760.
19. Rosales R. and Sclaroff S. 1999. 3D Trajectory Recovery for Tracking Multiple Objects and Trajectory Guided Recognition of Actions. *IEEE Computer Society Conference on Computer Vision and Pattern Recognition,* Fort Collins, Colorado, pp. 117-123.
20. Snow D., Viola P., and Zabih R. 2000. Exact Voxel Occupancy Using Graph Cuts. In *IEEE Conference on Computer Vision and Pattern Recognition*, Hilton Head, South Carolina.
21. Wren C.R., Azarbayejani A., Darrell T. and Pentland A.P. 1997. Pfinder: Real-time Tracking of the Human Body. *IEEE Transactions on Pattern Recognition and Machine Intelligence,* vol 19. 7.

Image Features

Image Features

Analytical Image Models and Their Applications

Anuj Srivastava[1], Xiuwen Liu[2], and Ulf Grenander[3]

[1] Department of Statistics, Florida State University, Tallahassee, 32306
[2] Department of Computer Science, Florida State University, Tallahassee, FL 32306
[3] Division of Applied Mathematics, Brown University, Providence, RI 021912

Abstract. In this paper, we study a family of analytical probability models for images within the spectral representation framework. First the input image is decomposed using a bank of filters, and probability models are imposed on the filter outputs (or spectral components). A two-parameter analytical form, called a **Bessel K form**, derived based on a generator model, is used to model the marginal probabilities of these spectral components. The Bessel K parameters can be estimated efficiently from the filtered images and extensive simulations using video, infrared, and range images have demonstrated Bessel K form's fit to the observed histograms. The effectiveness of Bessel K forms is also demonstrated through texture modeling and synthesis. In contrast to numeric-based dimension reduction representations, which are derived purely based on numerical methods, the Bessel K representations are derived based on object representations and this enables us to establish relationships between the Bessel parameters and certain characteristics of the imaged objects. We have derived a pseudo-metric on the image space to quantify image similarities/differences using an analytical expression for L^2-metric on the set of Bessel K forms. We have applied the Bessel K representation to texture modeling and synthesis, clutter classification, pruning of hypotheses for object recognition, and object classification. Results show that Bessel K representation captures important image features, suggesting its role in building efficient image understanding paradigms and systems.

Keywords: Image features, spectral analysis, Bessel K forms, clutter classification, object recognition.

1 Introduction

In the last few decades, statistical approach has become one of the dominating methods for computer vision and image understanding. Central to the promising success of statistical techniques in image understanding are efficient probability models for the observed images. To realize statistical inference algorithms efficiently, dimension reduction is required due to the high dimensionality of the image space. There are in general two approaches for dimension reduction: purely numerical, non-physical methods and physical-based methods. Purely numerical methods, which are closely related to the bottom-up approach for computer vision and image understanding, use one of the many techniques for dimension reduction by treating images as elements of a vector space and seeking a low-dimensional subspace that best represents those numbers under some chosen criteria. Principal components [12], independent components [4,3], sparse coding [16], Fisher's discriminant [2], local linear embedding [19], and many other statistical learning algorithms are all instances of this idea. The main advantage is the computational efficiency and the main drawback is knowledge deficiency. Lack of physical or contextual information leads to a limited performance, specially in challenging situations. In the second approach, which is closely related to the top-down approach for image understanding, images are characterized by the physical characteristics of the objects and the resulting physical variables are used to analyze images. An example of this idea is the *deformable template* theory [6] where images are studied through the transformations that match the templates to the observations. One drawback is that they are computationally expensive to implement, since they require synthesis of hypothesized images for image analysis.

In this paper, we study a framework that provides some interactions between the numeric-based and the template-based approaches. Consider a deformable template representation of the imaged objects, as laid out in [9,21]. The basic idea is that images are made up of objects, and their variability can be represented by physical variables. Using 3D models of objects, all occurrences of these objects can be generated using similarity transformations. 3D scenes containing these transformed objects lead to 2D images via occlusion and projection. To build probability models on I, we seek analytical forms that retain some physical considerations, although not as explicitly as the template approach. We replace 3D templates by their 2D profiles (called **generators**) and denote them as g's. Let $\mathcal{G}$ be the space of all possible generators associated with all objects, imaged from all angles. Random translation of 3D objects in a scene is modeled by random placements and scalings of g's in an image.

Each object contributes to the pixel value $I(z)$ according to $a_i g_i(\frac{1}{\rho_i}(z - z_i))$. Here $z \in W \equiv [0, L] \times [0, L]$ is a variable for pixel location, $g_i : W \mapsto \mathbb{R}_+$ is a generator of a randomly chosen object, $\rho_i \in [0, L]$ is a random scale, and $a_i \in \mathbb{R}$ is a random weight associated with g_i, which is drawn from the generator set $\mathcal{G}$ according to some measure dG. The image formation is now modeled by:

$$I(z) = \sum_{i}^{n} a_i g_i (\frac{1}{\rho_i}(z - z_i)), \quad z, z_i \in W, \ a_i \in \mathbb{R}, \ \rho_i \in [0, L] \ . \tag{1}$$

Since g_i's are assumed unknown, the related variables n, ρ_i's and z_i's are also indeterminable. We aim to derive probability models on I by implicitly incorporating their variability.

Motivated by a growing understanding of animal vision, a popular strategy has been to decompose images into their spectral components using a family of bandpass filters. Similarly, our probability model on I will be through its spectral representation. In the context of texture modeling, the marginal distributions are often chosen as sufficient statistics as the frequencies of values in the filtered images are relevant and the location information is discarded [11,10, 25]. Simoncelli et al. [18] have suggested using the lower order statistics (mean, variance, skewness, kurtosis) to specify the marginal densities of the wavelet coefficients of the images. Wainwright et al. [22] have studied a family of Gaussian mixtures, for different mixing densities, for modeling the observed histograms. Lee and Mumford [13] have presented a model for capturing the statistics in the images of leaves.

Using a physical model for image formation, we have extended a two-parameter probability model [8], to a full spectrum of bandpass filters and arbitrary images, called **Bessel K forms** [20]. We demonstrate the success of Bessel K forms in modeling the spectral components for video, infrared (IR), and range images of natural and artificial scenes and use the models for hypothesis pruning and object classification.

This paper is organized as follows. Section 2 applies Bessel K forms to model spectral components of images and associates the estimated Bessel K parameters with the observed shapes. Section 3 derives an L^2-metric on the Bessel K forms and on the image space, while Section 4 applies these metrics to texture modeling and synthesis, clutter classification, hypothesis pruning, and object classification. Section 5 concludes the paper.

2 Analytical Probability Models for Image Spectra

Given an image I and a bank of filters $\{F^{(j)}, j = 1, 2, \ldots, K\}$, we compute, for each filter $F^{(j)}$, a filtered image $I^{(j)} = I * F^{(j)}$, where $*$ denotes the 2D convolution operation. In this paper, we mainly use Gabor and Laplacian of Gaussian filters and do not address the issue of filter selection to best accomplish a specific task. Other filters can also be used as long as the resulting marginals are: (i) unimodal with the mode at zero, (ii) symmetric around zero, and (iii) are leptokurtic, i.e. their kurtosis is larger than that of a Gaussian random variable with the same variance.

2.1 Analytical Models

Applying 2D convolution to both sides of (1), we obtain a spectral component

$$I^{(j)}(z) \equiv (I * F^{(j)})(z) = \sum_i a_i g_i^{(j)}(\frac{1}{\rho_i}(z - z_i)) , \text{ where } g_i^{(j)} = F^{(j)} * g_i . \quad (2)$$

The *conditional* density of $I^{(j)}(z)$, given the Poisson points $\{z_i\}$, the scales $\{\rho_i\}$, and the profiles g_i's, is normal with mean zero and variance u, where $u \equiv \sum_i (g_i^{(j)}(\frac{1}{\rho_i}(z - z_i))^2$. Under this model and assuming u to be a scaled-Gamma random variable, the density function of $I^{(j)}(z)$ has been shown to be [8]: for $p > 0, c > 0$,

$$f(x; p, c) = \frac{1}{Z(p, c)} |x|^{p-0.5} K_{(p-0.5)}(\sqrt{\frac{2}{c}}|x|) , \quad (3)$$

where K is the modified Bessel function[1], Z is the normalizing constant given by $Z(p,c) = \sqrt{\pi}\Gamma(p)(2c)^{0.5p+0.25}$, and Γ is the gamma function. Let $\mathcal{D}$ be the space of all such densities: $\mathcal{D} = \{f(x;p,c)|p > 0, c > 0\}$. We refer to the elements of $\mathcal{D}$ as the **Bessel K forms** and the parameters (p,c) as the **Bessel parameters**. The elements of $\mathcal{D}$ are symmetric and unimodal for the mode at zero. For $p = 1$, $f(x;p,c)$ is the density of a double exponential. In general, it is the pth convolution power (for any $p > 0$) of a double exponential density. Therefore, it is unimodal with the mode at $x = 0$. For the same reason, it is symmetric around zero. One limitation of the Bessel K forms is that they are square-integrable only for $p > 0.25$. This property is due to the choice of Gamma density for u; as a result, the L^2-metric of the Bessel K forms is applicable when p-values are larger than 0.25.

As shown in [8], p and c can be estimated using moment estimator, which is given by

$$\hat{p} = \frac{3}{\text{SK}(I^{(j)}) - 3}, \quad \hat{c} = \frac{\text{SV}(I^{(j)})}{\hat{p}}, \qquad (4)$$

where SK is the sample kurtosis and SV is the sample variance of the pixel values in $I^{(j)}$. The computational task of estimating the marginal density is that of computing the second and the fourth moments of the filtered image. This moment estimator is sensitive to outliers and more robust estimators such as maximum likelihood estimator or robust estimation techniques can be used if needed.

We illustrate estimation results for a variety of images. Shown in the top panels of Fig. 1 are some images taken from the Groningen database. The middle panels display their specific filtered forms (or the spectral components) for Gabor filters chosen at arbitrary orientations and scales, and the bottom panels plot the marginal densities. On a log scale, the observed densities (histograms) are plotted in solid lines with dots and the estimated Bessel K forms ($f(x; \hat{p}, \hat{c})$) are plotted in solid lines.

Fig. 2(a) shows estimation results for two IR face images when filtered by Gabor filters. These results suggest the role of Bessel K forms in modeling images beyond the case of video images of natural scenes.

Shown in Fig. 2(b) are two examples of estimating marginal densities for the case of range images taken from the Brown range database. The images shown in top panels are filtered using Gabor filters and the resulting densities are plotted in the bottom panels.

A distinctive advantage of Bessel K representation, compared to numerical-based low-dimensional representations, is that Bessel K parameters can be related to physical characteristics of objects consisting of the observed image. Theoretically, the physical characteristics of the imaged objects, and the filter used in generating a spectral component, should dictate the resulting Bessel K

---

[1] Defined as
$$K_\nu(xy) = \frac{\Gamma(\nu+0.5)(2y)^\nu}{\Gamma(0.5)x^\nu} \int_0^\infty \frac{\cos(xz)}{(z^2+y^2)^{\nu+0.5}} dz,$$
for $\Re(\nu) > -0.5$, $x > 0$, and $|arg(y)| < \frac{\pi}{2}$.

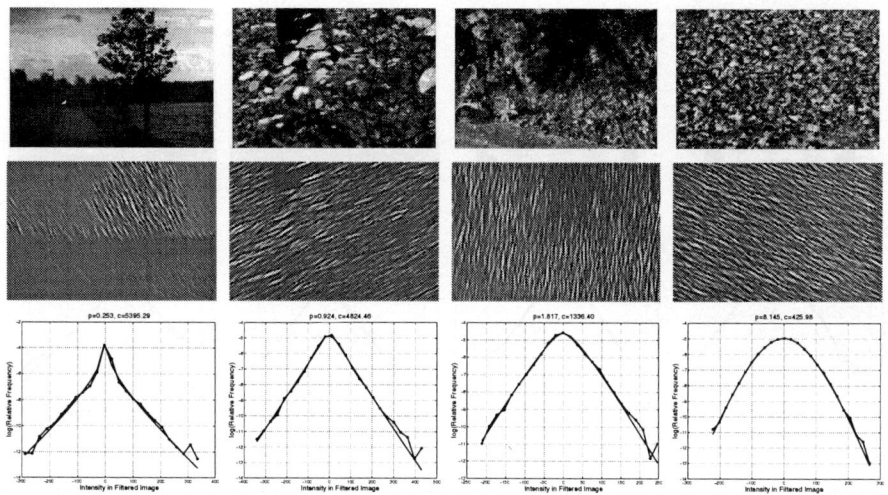

Fig. 1. Images (top panels), their Gabor components (middle panels), and the marginal densities (bottom panels). The observed densities are drawn in solid lines with dots and the estimated Bessel K forms are drawn in solid lines.

form. Since c is essentially a scale parameter relating to the range of pixels values in I, its role is not as important as p in image understanding.

Under certain assumptions of the generator model given in (2), specifically when $a_i \sim N(0,1)$, ρ_1 is fixed to be 1.0, and all the $g_i \equiv g$ (i.e. a fixed generator), then

$$p = \frac{1}{\frac{\kappa}{3\lambda} - 1}, \text{ where } \kappa = \frac{\left(\int_W g(z_1)^4 dz_1\right)}{\left(\int_W g(z_1)^2 dz_1\right)^2}. \tag{5}$$

This equation provides an important relationship between a generator g and the parameter p. According to (5), $p < 1$ occurs when $\lambda < \frac{\kappa}{6}$. If the generator g has sharp, distinct boundaries (i.e. κ is larger) then the p value is small unless the frequency of occurrence (λ) is large. Specifically, if a filter $F^{(j)}$ is used to extract a particular feature (e.g. oriented edges, junctions, bands, etc.) from the image I, then p is dictated by the **distinctness** (κ) and the **frequency of occurrence** (λ) of that feature in the image. For example, shown in Fig. 3 is a variation of p value when the images are filtered for extracting vertical edges ($\theta = 90$). The top row shows images with increasing frequency of vertical edges in going from left to right. Correspondingly, the estimated p value shows an increase (0.31, 0.77, 1.45, and 2.73). Summarizing the relation between p and κ, we have:

$$\text{If } \begin{cases} 0 < \lambda < \kappa/6 \text{ then } p < 1 \\ \kappa/6 < \lambda < \kappa/3 \text{ then } p > 1 \end{cases}.$$

2.2 Performance Analysis of Bessel K Forms

To quantify the performance in modeling observed histograms by estimated Bessel K forms, a number of quantities can be used and we choose the Kullback-

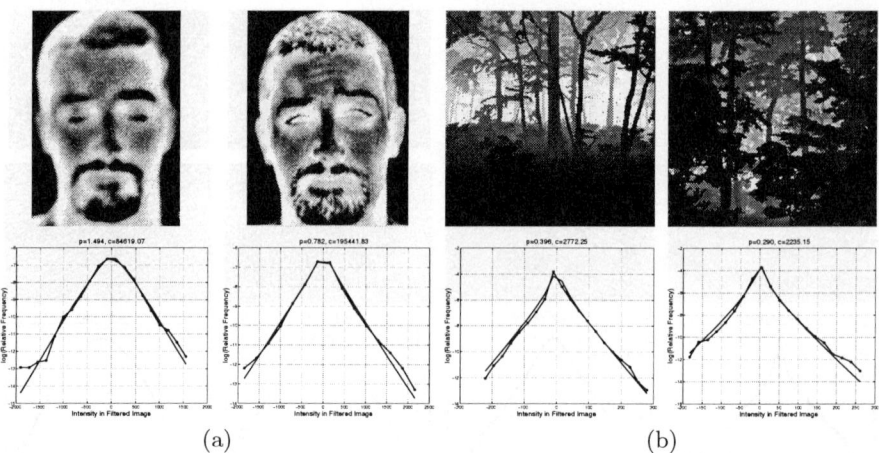

Fig. 2. Observed and estimated marginal densities (bottom panels) for (a) the IR face images (top panels) (b) range images of a forest of randomly chosen Gabor filters.

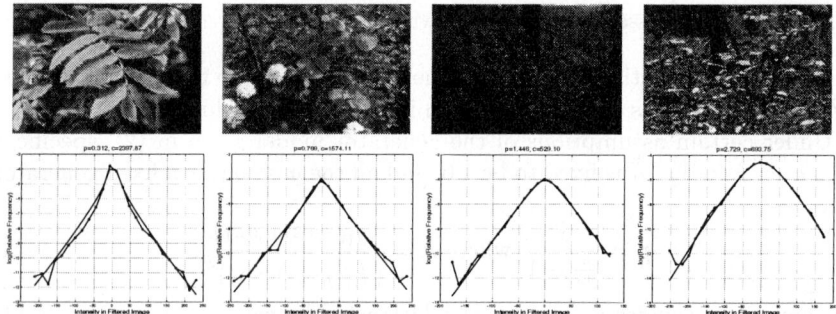

Fig. 3. Variation of p-values for extracting vertical edges ($\theta = 90$). Top panels are the original images, middle panels are the filtered images, and the bottom panels are the densities (log-scale). The estimated p-values are: 0.31, 0.77, 1.45, and 2.73, respectively.

Leibler (KL) divergence. For any two density functions f_1 and f_2, the divergence is defined as the quantity: $KL(f_1, f_2) = \int_{\mathbb{R}} f_1(x) \log(f_1(x)/f_2(x)) dx$. We have computed it by discretizing at the center points of the histogram bins. To evaluate match between the observed and the estimated densities, we have computed the KL divergence for two large databases. In each case, for a large combination of images and filters drawn randomly, we have averaged the KL divergence over thousands of resulting filtered marginals. The first database is made up of 300 natural video images downloaded from Groningen natural image database, and the second database is made up of 220 IR face pictures. Shown in Fig. 4 are the convergence plots of the average KL divergence, plotted against the sample size. The top plot is for the natural video images with a limiting value of 0.0657 while the bottom plot is for the infrared images with a limiting value of

0.0478. A comparison of these values underscores the degree of match between the observed histograms and the estimated Bessel K forms.

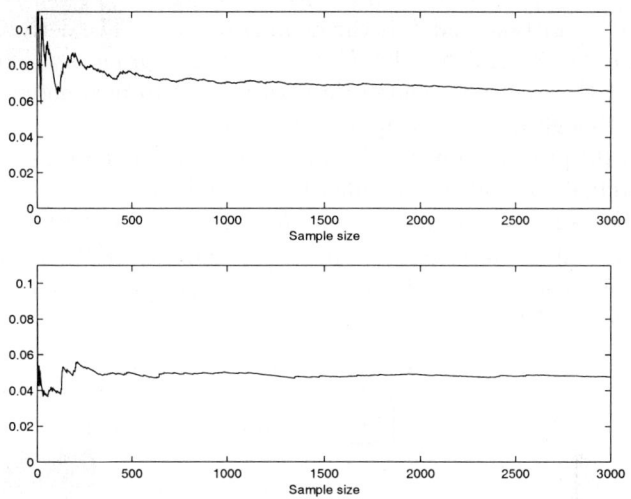

Fig. 4. Convergence of average KL-divergence between the observed and the estimated densities as the sample size increases. The top plot is for the Groningen database of natural images and the bottom plot is for the FSU IR face database.

3 Pseudo-Metrics for Comparing Images

We have chosen to represent images via the Bessel parameters of their spectral components. One distinct advantage, of having such analytical forms for the marginals of the spectral components, is the resulting theoretical framework for image analysis. To quantify the distance between two Bessel K forms, we have chosen the L^2-metric on $\mathcal{D}$. It is possible that other metrics, such as the Kullback-Leibler divergence or the L^1 metric, may prove more useful in certain situations. Since we are restricting ourselves to only $\mathcal{D}$, and not the full set of pdfs, we suggest that many of these choices will provide similar results, specially if the task is classification or hypothesis pruning. The main constraint of choosing L^2 is that Bessel K forms are not in L^2 for $p < 0.25$. In cases where the estimated $p < 0.25$, we can choose one of following: (i) drop that filter, (ii) approximate p (perhaps badly) by $0.25 + \epsilon$, and then compute the L^2-metric, or (iii) compute the L^2-metric numerically using the quadrature integration. For $f(x; p_1, c_1)$ and $f(x; p_2, c_2)$ in $\mathcal{D}$, the L^2-metric is $d(p_1, c_1, p_2, c_2) = \sqrt{\int_x (f(x; p_1, c_1) - f(x; p_2, c_2))^2 dx}$. Given $p_1, p_2 > 0.25$, $c_1, c_2 > 0$, this metric can be computed using the following closed form expression,

$$d(p_1,c_1,p_2,c_2) = \left(\frac{1}{2\sqrt{2\pi}}\Gamma(0.5)\left(\frac{\mathcal{G}(2p_1)}{\sqrt{c_1}} + \frac{\mathcal{G}(2p_2)}{\sqrt{c_2}} - \frac{2\mathcal{G}(p_1+p_2)}{\sqrt{c_1}}(\frac{c_1}{c_2})^{p_2}\mathcal{F}\right)\right)^{\frac{1}{2}} \tag{6}$$

where $\mathcal{G}(p) = \frac{\Gamma(p-0.5)}{\Gamma(p)}$, $\mathcal{F} = F((p_1+p_2-0.5), p_2; p_1+p_2; 1-\frac{c_1}{c_2})$, F is the hypergeometric function, and Γ is the gamma function. The derivation involves evaluation of the integral for the L^2-metric. For a proof, see [20]. It should be noted that the metric is symmetric with respect to parameters (p_1, c_1) and (p_2, c_2) even though it does not appear that way.

Equation (6) provides a metric between two Bessel K forms, or between two spectral marginals. It can be extended to a pseudo-metric on the image space as follows. For any two images, I_1 and I_2, and the filters $F^{(1)}, \ldots, F^{(K)}$, let the parameter values be given by: $(p_1^{(j)}, c_1^{(j)})$ and $(p_2^{(j)}, c_2^{(j)})$, respectively, for $j = 1, 2, \ldots, K$. Then, the L^2-distance, between the spectral representations of the two images, is defined as:

$$d_I(I_1, I_2) = \sqrt{\left(\sum_{j=1}^{K} d(p_1^{(j)}, c_1^{(j)}, p_2^{(j)}, c_2^{(j)})^2\right)}. \tag{7}$$

Note that d_I is not a proper metric on the image space because two different images can have $d_I = 0$ between them. Also, d_I is dependent upon the choice of filters. It has been established in the literature that different spectral components of the same images are often correlated, and therefore, this Euclidean form may not be appropriate. In such cases, another choice such as the *max* of all components may be pursued.

4 Applications of Bessel K Representations

Now we present some examples of applying these Bessel K formulations and the resulting metric to image understanding problems. We have selected examples from: (i) texture modeling and synthesis, (ii) clutter classification, (iii) hypothesis pruning, and (iv) object classification.

4.1 Texture Modeling and Synthesis

It has been shown [25,24] that homogeneous textures can be characterized sufficiently using their spectral responses. Because Bessel K forms provide a low-dimensional and analytical representation for spectral components, we use texture synthesis to further verify the effectiveness of Bessel K representation.

Given an observed image and K filters, we model the given texture by its marginals, represented by the estimated Bessel K densities. Besides using fewer numbers to represent a histogram, the density can be sampled to generate a histogram of any number of bins. An advantage of this model is that it can be verified systematically through generating images with matched histograms. As in [24], we impose a Gibbs-like distribution on the image space by:

$$P(I) = \frac{1}{Z} \exp(-\sum_{j=1}^{K} \sum_{i=1}^{L^{(j)}} \|H(I^{(j)})(i) - f(z_i; p^{(j)}, c^{(j)})\|^2 / T) ,$$

where $H(I^{(j)})$ denotes the histogram of the j-th filter response of I, $L^{(j)}$ is the number of bins, and z_i is the center value of i-th bin of the j-th histogram, T is a parameter corresponding to temperature, and Z is a normalizing constant. Here $p^{(j)}, c^{(j)}$ are estimated using an observed image. The texture synthesis is then to generate typical samples from $P(I)$. Here a Gibbs sampler [24] is used to generate the following examples while other sampling algorithms can also be used. Figure 5 shows three examples, where the histogram of the intensity filter is used directly as it does not satisfy the assumptions of Bessel K forms and for all other filters their estimated Bessel K densities are used. it is evident from these examples that Bessel K forms capture the perceptual important characteristics of textures. The basic elements are synthesized well as well as the global patterns.

4.2 Clutter Classification

An important application of this Bessel K representation is in the classification of clutter for ATR (automated target recognition) scenarios. In particular, given an observed image of a target, imaged in a cluttered environment, one would like to characterize the clutter to the extent that it improves the ATR performance. Some knowledge of clutter type, whether it is grass, buildings, trees, or roads, can help improve the task of target recognition. In this section, we utilize the Bessel K forms to represent the image spectra, and employ the metric defined in (7) to classify the clutter types from their images. We will demonstrate the strength of this model in the context of natural clutter classification. Consider the images of natural clutter shown in Fig. 6. For a simple illustration, let the images in the top row be training images that are already classified, and the bottom row be images that are to be classified. Using 27 small-scale Gabor filters ($K = 27$), for nine different orientations at three scales each, we have computed the pairwise distances d_I's.

Using the nearest neighbor approach, and the metric d_I one can perform clutter classification. To illustrate the classification of clutter types, we have plotted a clustering chart in the left panel of Fig. 7 using the dendrogram function in matlab. This function generates a clustering tree for points in image space when their pairwise distances are given. For comparison we run clustering program using an Euclidean metric on a principal subspace of the image space. We extracted non-overlapping patches of size 20×30 from the original images, performed principal component analysis (PCA) in $I\!R^{600}$, and retained only first 40 components. Images are then projected onto this linear subspace to compute coefficients and the resulting pairwise Euclidean distances.

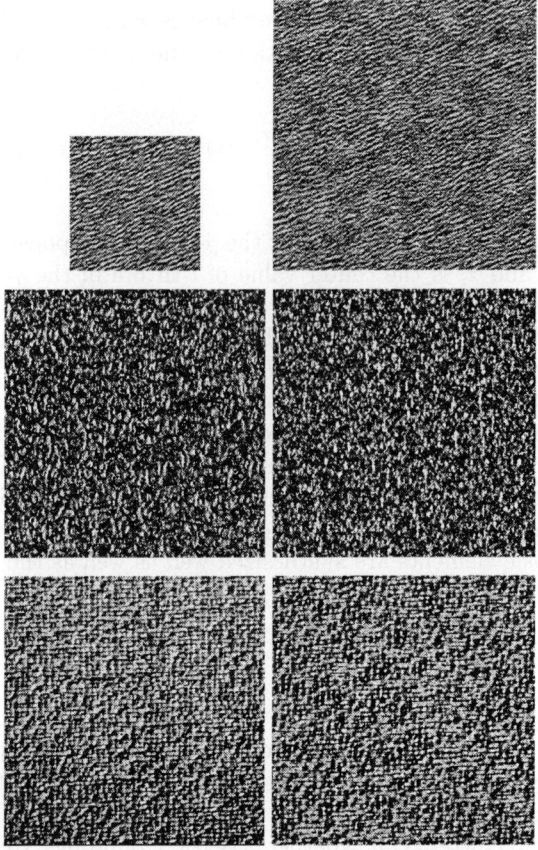

Fig. 5. Texture synthesis examples using Bessel K forms. In each row, the left shows the observed texture and the right a typical synthesized texture.

4.3 Hypothesis Pruning

The Bessel K forms also prove useful in pruning the hypothesis set in target recognition. Recognition of objects from their observed images corresponds to the selection of hypothesis in presence of the nuisance parameters [9]. As stated in Section 1, this hypothesis selection is often performed using detailed models involving physical shapes, texture, pose and motion [21,7,9]. Such methods are based on low- and high-dimensional deformations of targets' templates in order to match their synthesized images with the observed images. The deformations capture the variability in pose, motion, illumination, etc. and form the set of nuisance parameters, call it S, for hypothesis selection; they typically are computationally expensive to implement. Given an image, the task of searching over all possible templates is demanding and can benefit from a pruning that places significant probability only on a small subset.

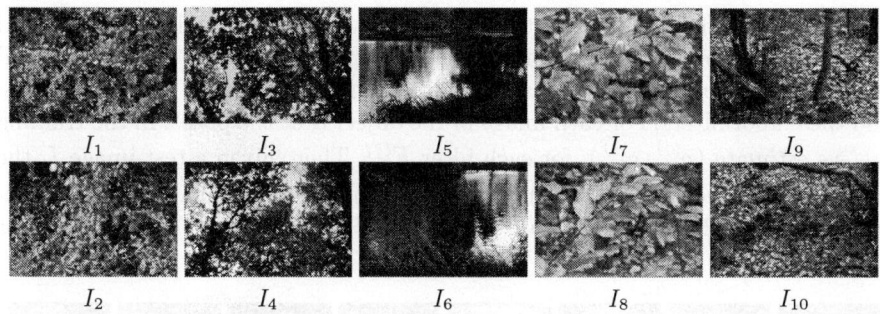

Fig. 6. Ten natural images from the Groningen database: top row are the training images and bottom row are the test images.

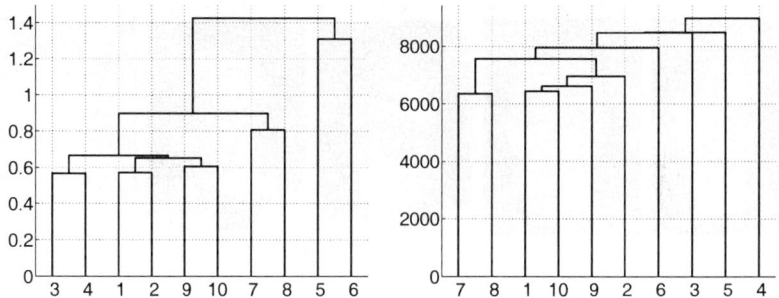

Fig. 7. Dendrogram clustering of images in Fig. 6 using d_I (left panel) and using an Euclidean metric on PCA (right panel). The labels on the horizontal axis correspond to the ones in Fig. 6 and the vertical axis shows the corresponding distance.

Let $\mathcal{A}$ be the set of all possible objects. Define a probability mass function on $\mathcal{A}$ according to:

$$P(\alpha|I) = \frac{\exp\left(-\min_{s \in S}(\sum_{j=1}^{K} d(p_{obs}^{(j)}, c_{obs}^{(j)}, p_{\alpha,s}^{(j)}, c_{\alpha,s}^{(j)})^2)/T\right)}{\sum_{\alpha'} \exp\left(-\min_{s \in S}(\sum_{j=1}^{K} d(p_{obs}^{(j)}, c_{obs}^{(j)}, p_{\alpha',s}^{(j)}, c_{\alpha',s}^{(j)})^2)/T\right)}, \quad (8)$$

where T controls our confidence (analogous to the temperature in Gibbs' energies) in this probability. Here $(p_{obs}^{(j)}, c_{obs}^{(j)})$ are the estimated parameters for the image I and filter $F^{(j)}$, and $(p_{\alpha,s}^{(j)}, c_{\alpha,s}^{(j)})$ are the estimated parameters for the filter $F^{(j)}$ and the target α rendered at the nuisance variable $s \in S$. Note that $(p_{\alpha,s}^{(j)}, c_{\alpha,s}^{(j)})$ can be pre-computed offline for all $\alpha \in \mathcal{A}$, $s \in S$, and $j \in \{1, 2, \ldots, K\}$.

To illustrate this idea, consider the following experiment. Shown in Fig. 8(a) are some sample images of objects from the Columbia object image library (COIL) [17]. This database consists of 72 images of each 100 objects, taken at five degree separation in azimuth, and has been widely used in testing object recognition algorithms. In this experiment, we have divide 7200 images into non-overlapping training and test sets. Some of the images are used as training and the remaining for testing, similar to the work presented in [17]. We have used $K = 39$ filters, including the gradient filters, the Laplacian of Gaussian filters, and the Gabor filters. For each image of the object α at the pose s in the training set, we estimate $(p_{\alpha,s}^{(j)}, c_{\alpha,s}^{(j)})$, for each filter $F^{(j)}$. Then, given a test image I, the estimated parameters $(p_{obs}^{(j)}, c_{obs}^{(j)})$ are used to compute the probability $P(\alpha|I)$ according to (8). Shown in Fig. 9 are the plots of $P(\alpha|I)$ versus α (for $T = 0.5$) for

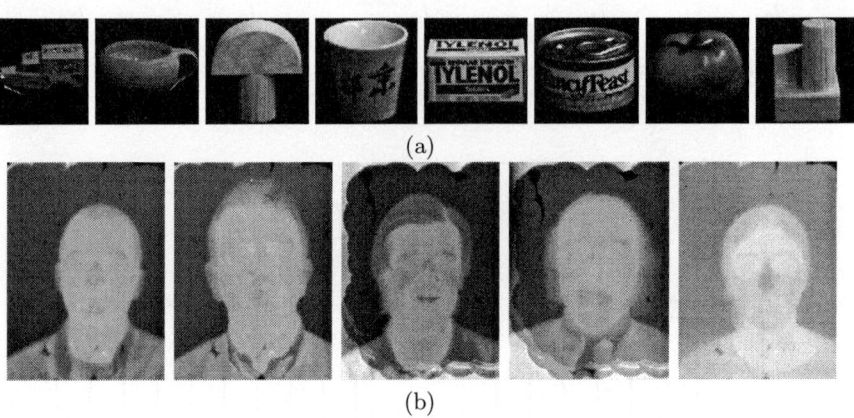

Fig. 8. Sample images from (a) COIL image dataset and (b) Equinox long wave infrared image dataset.

six different images I in the COIL database. All the objects with probabilities larger than some threshold, say 0.01, can be shortlisted for detailed hypothesis testing. As an example, the plot in left corresponds to an image of $\alpha = 1$. In the short-listing by thresholding, we are left with only 14 possible hypothesis, a significant reduction from 100. The middle plot displays the worst case of the whole experiment and still short-lists 35 objects. The right plot displays a best case, where the probability mass function on $\mathcal{A}$ is focused on one object and the hypothesis pruning gives a unique solution.

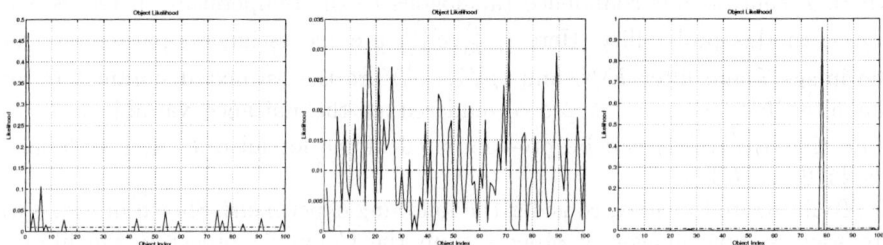

Fig. 9. Plots of $P(\alpha|I)$ versus α for six test images in the COIL database. The test images are of objects α_1, α_{15}, and α_{78}, respectively, for arbitrary orientations. Dotted lines suggest a threshold level for pruning.

4.4 Object Classification Using Bessel K Representation

Because Bessel K representation defines a distance measure between any images, it can also be used for object classification similar to purely numerical-based representations. One distinctive advantage of Bessel K representation is that it puts probability mass on images that may have large distance in the image-induced Euclidean space. In other words, the probability model on images has multiple modes in the image space, resulting in a more effective representation. Here we have used $P(\alpha|I)$ for object recognition and have compared our results with some other recently proposed procedures: principal component analysis (PCA), independent component analysis (ICA), support vector machines (SVM), and SNoW. Pontil and Verri [17] have applied SVM (Support Vector Machines) method to 3D object recognition and have tested it on a subset of the COIL-100 dataset with half for training and the other half for testing. As pointed out by Yang et al. [23], this dense sampling of training views simplifies the recognition problem. Hence, we have presented recognition results for different training to test ratios in splitting the COIL database. The number of components selected is such that complexity remains similar to that of Bessel representations. As Table 1 summarizes that Bessel representations, in addition to being analytic and parametric, mostly outperform these other methods. The significant performance decrease of the case with 4 training views per object is due to the nearest-neighbor classifier used, which does not generalize well; we expect significant improvement using more sophisticated classifiers, which will be investigated further.

Table 1. Correct recognition rate for the full COIL-100 dataset using PCA, ICA and Bessel forms

Training/test per object	PCA	ICA	SNoW [23]	SVM [23]	Bessel Forms
36 / 36	98.58%	98.47%	95.81%	96.03%	99.89%
18 / 54	96.67%	96.52%	92.31%	91.30%	99.00%
8 / 64	87.23%	87.91%	85.13%	84.80%	92.44%
4 / 68	75.82%	76.03%	81.46%	78.50%	78.65%

The Bessel K form has also been applied to a large infrared face dataset generated by Equinox company[2]. Because the dataset is still under development, here we use a subset consisting of 63 subjects with a total of 3,893 long-wave infrared images of faces. Fig. 8(b) shows some examples in the dataset. Tab. 2 shows the recognition results using the nearest neighbor classifier, which are almost perfect under all the conditions for this large dataset.

5 Conclusion

We have applied Bessel K forms to model the probability densities of the filtered marginals. The estimated parametric forms are shown to match well with the

---
[2] Available at http://www.equinoxsensors.com/products/HID.html

Table 2. Correct recognition rate with different training images of the Equinox dataset.

Total training/ test images	First correct	First two correct	First three correct
1948 / 1945	99.95%	100.0%	100.0%
993 / 2900	99.97%	100.0%	100.0%
527 / 3366	99.97%	100.0%	100.0%
343 / 3550	99.94%	99.97%	99.97%

observed histograms for a variety of images: video, IR, and range, for gradient, Gabor and Laplacian of Gaussian filters. Given the assumptions behind this construction, we expect this model to perform well in other imaging modalities such as MRI, PET, and radar imaging. We have used L^2 metric on the set of Bessel forms (restricted to $p > 0.25$) to derive a pseudo-metric on the image space. This metric can be used for, among other things, clutter classification and object recognition. Although the performance of Bessel representations in challenging object recognition situations remains to be tested, their ability to prune possible hypotheses, to feed to a more detailed model, seems promising.

Acknowledgments. This research was supported in part by the grants ARO DAAD19-99-1-0267, NMA 201-01-2010, and NSF DMS-0101429. The images used in the experiments are taken from the Groningen image database, the COIL database, Brown range database, Equinox IR face dataset, and FSU IR face database. We are grateful to the producers of these databases for making them public. We also thank Prof. J. Sethuraman for some useful discussions on this paper.

References

1. O. Barndorff-Nielsen, J. Kent, and M. Sorensen, "Normal variance-mean mixtures and z distributions," *International Statistical Review*, vol. 50, pp. 145–159, 1982.
2. P. N. Belhumeur, J. P. Hepanha, and D. J. Kriegman, "Eigenfaces vs. fisherfaces: Recognition using class specific linear projection," *IEEE Transactions on Pattern Analysis and Machine Intelligence*, vol. 19(7), pp. 711–720, 1997.
3. A. J. Bell and T. J. Sejnowski, "The "independent components" of natural scenes are edge filters," *Vision Research*, vol. 37(23), pp. 3327–3338, 1997.
4. P. Comon, "Independent component analysis, a new concept?" *Signal Processing, Special issue on higher-order statistics*, vo. 36(4), pp. 287-314, 1994.
5. I. S. Gradshteyn and I. M. Ryzhik, *Table of Integral Series and Products*, Academic Press, 2000.
6. U. Grenander, *General Pattern Theory*, Oxford University Press, 1993.
7. U. Grenander, M. I. Miller, and A. Srivastava, "Hilbert-schmidt lower bounds for estimators on matrix lie groups for atr," *IEEE Transactions on Pattern Analysis and Machine Intelligence*, vol. 20(8), pp. 790–802, 1998.
8. U. Grenander and A. Srivastava, "Probability models for clutter in natural images," *IEEE Transactions on Pattern Analysis and Machine Intelligence*, vol. 23(4), pp. 424-429, 2001.

9. U. Grenander, A. Srivastava, and M. I. Miller, "Asymptotic performance analysis of bayesian object recognition," *IEEE Transactions of Information Theory*, vol. 46(4), pp. 1658–1666, 2000.
10. D. J. Heeger and J. R. Bergen, "Pyramid-based texture analysis/synthesis," In *Proceedings of SIGGRAPHS*, pp. 229–238, 1995.
11. B. Julesz, "A theory of preattentive texture discrimination based on first-order statistics of textons," *Biological Cybernetics*, vol. 41, pp. 131–138, 1962.
12. M. Kirby and L. Sirovich, "Application of the karhunen-loeve procedure for the characterization of human faces," *IEEE Transactions on Pattern Analysis and Machine Intelligence*, vol. 12(1), pp. 103–108, 1990.
13. Ann B. Lee and David Mumford, "Occlusion models for natural images: A statistical study of scale-invariant dead leaves model," *International Journal of Computer Vision*, vol. 41, pp. 35–59, 2001.
14. M. I. Miller, A. Srivastava, and U. Grenander, "Conditional-expectation estimation via jump-diffusion processes in multiple target tracking/recognition," *IEEE Transactions on Signal Processing*, vol. 43(11), pp. 2678–2690, 1995.
15. D. Mumford, "Empirical investigations into the statistics of clutter and the mathematical models it leads to," *A lecture for the review of ARO Metric Pattern Theory Collaborative*, 2000.
16. B. A. Olshausen and D. J. Field, "Sparse coding with an overcomplete basis set: A strategy employed by V1?" *Vision Research*, vol. 37(23), pp. 3311–3325, 1997.
17. M. Pontil and A. Verri, "Support vector machines for 3d object recognition," *IEEE Transactions on Pattern Analysis and Machine Intelligence*, vol. 20(6), pp. 637–646, 1998.
18. J. Portilla and E. P. Simoncelli, "A parametric texture model based on joint statistics of complex wavelets," *International Journal of Computer Vision*, vol. 40(1), pp. 49–71, 2000.
19. S. T. Roweis and L. K. Saul, "Nonlinear dimensionality reduction by locally linear embedding," *Science*, vol. 290, pp. 2323–2326, 2000.
20. A. Srivastava, X. Liu, and U. Grenander, "Universal analytical forms for modeling image probabilities," *IEEE Transactions on Pattern Analysis and Machine Intelligence*, in press, 2002.
21. A. Srivastava, M. I. Miller, and U. Grenander, "Bayesian automated target recognition," *Handbook of Image and Video Processing, Academic Press*, pp. 869–881, 2000.
22. M. J. Wainwright, E. P. Simoncelli, and A. S. Willsky, "Random cascades on wavelet trees and their use in analyzing and modeling natural images," *Applied and Computational Harmonic Analysis*, vol. 11, pp. 89–123, 2001.
23. M. H. Yang, D. Roth, and N. Ahuja, "Learning to recognize 3d objects with SNoW," In *Proceedings of the Sixth European Conference on Computer Vision*, vol. 1, pp. 439–454, 2000.
24. S. C. Zhu, X. Liu, and Y. N. Wu, "Statistics matching and model pursuit by efficient MCMC," *IEEE Transactions on Pattern Recognition and Machine Intelligence*, vol. 22, pp. 554–569, 2000.
25. S. C. Zhu, Y. N. Wu, and D. Mumford, "Minimax entropy principles and its application to texture modeling," *Neural Computation*, vol. 9(8), pp. 1627–1660, 1997.

Time-Recursive Velocity-Adapted Spatio-Temporal Scale-Space Filters*

Tony Lindeberg

Computational Vision and Active Perception Laboratory (CVAP)
Department of Numerical Analysis and Computer Science
KTH, SE-100 44 Stockholm, Sweden
tony@nada.kth.se

Abstract. This paper presents a theory for constructing and computing velocity-adapted scale-space filters for spatio-temporal image data. Starting from basic criteria in terms of time-causality, time-recursivity, locality and adaptivity with respect to motion estimates, a family of spatio-temporal recursive filters is proposed and analysed. An important property of the proposed family of smoothing kernels is that the spatio-temporal covariance matrices of the discrete kernels obey similar transformation properties under Galilean transformations as for continuous smoothing kernels on continuous domains. Moreover, the proposed theory provides an efficient way to compute and generate non-separable scale-space representations without need for explicit external warping mechanisms or keeping extended temporal buffers of the past. The approach can thus be seen as a natural extension of recursive scale-space filters from pure temporal data to spatio-temporal domains.

1 Introduction

A basic property of real-world image data is that we may perceive and interpret them in different ways depending on the scale of observation. On spatial domains, the understanding of such multi-scale processes has grown substantially during the last decades, and lead to multi-scale representations such as pyramids (Burt 1981, Crowley 1981) and scale-space representation (Witkin 1983, Koenderink 1984, Lindeberg 1994, Florack 1997). In particular, the linear scale-space theory developed from these premises has close relations to biological vision (Young 1987), and has established itself as a canonical model for early visual processing. Output from linear multi-scale receptive fields can serve as input to a large set of visual modules, including feature detection, shape estimation, grouping, matching, optic flow and recognition.

The world around us, however, consists of spatio-temporal data, in which the temporal dimension plays a special role, and the future cannot be ac-

---

* The support from the Swedish Research Council for Engineering Sciences, TFR, and from the Royal Swedish Academy of Sciences as well as the Knut and Alice Wallenberg Foundation is gratefully acknowledged.

cessed (Koenderink 1988, Lindeberg & Fagerström 1996). Moreover, the spatio-temporal image data arising from a vision system that observes a coherent world will be special in the respect that spatial structures tend to be stable over time.

For analysing spatio-temporal image data with this preferred structure, mechanisms such as velocity adaptation are benefitial (Lindeberg 1997, Nagel & Gehrke 1998). For example, if we compute a separable spatio-temporal scale-space representation of a moving object, then the amount of motion blur will increase with the temporal scale. This issue can be partly dealt with by stabilizing the retinal image by tracking. In the case of imperfect stabilization, however, or for static cameras without tracking ability, alternatively a single camera that observes multiple independently moving objects, a complementary approach for reducing this effect is by adapting the shapes of the scale-space filters to the direction of motion. Moreover, as will be shown in section 2, velocity-adaptation is a necessary pre-requisite for defining spatio-temporal receptive field responses that are invariant under motion.

For image data defined on spatial domains, the related notion of shape adaption has proved to be highly useful for improving the accuracy in surface orientation estimates (Lindeberg & Gårding 1997), for handling image deformations in optic flow computations (Florack et al. 1998), for increasing the robustness when computing image features (Almansa & Lindeberg 2000) and for performing affine invariant segmentation (Ballester & Gonzalez 1998) and matching (Schaffalitzky & Zisserman 2001).

The purpose of this article is to develop a theory for formulating such velocity-adapted time-causal spatio-temporal filters. Specifically, it will be shown how temporal recursive filters can be extended into spatio-temporal recursive filters in such a way that we can control the orientation of the filter in space-time and allow for efficient implementation of non-separable scale-space filtering. It should be emphasized, however, that this paper is mainly concerned with the analysis of such recursive filters. In a companion paper (Laptev & Lindeberg 2002), it is shown how velocity-adapted spatio-temporal filters can be used for improving the performance of spatio-temporal recognition schemes.

2 Velocity-Adapted Spatio-Temporal Scale-Space

To model a spatio-temporal scale-space representation, there are several possible approaches. In his pioneering work, (Koenderink 1988) proposed to transform the time axis by a logarithmic transformation that maps the present moment to the unreachable future and applied Gaussian filtering on the transformed domain. Based on a classification of scale-space kernel that guarantee non-creation of local extrema on a one-dimensional domain (Lindeberg 1994), (Lindeberg & Fagerström 1996) formulated time-causal separable spatio-temporal scale-space representations, from which temporal derivatives could be computed without need for any other temporal buffering than the temporal multi-scale representation, with close relations to an earlier approach for estimating optical flow by (Fleet & Langley 1995) and the use of recursive filters on spatial domains (Deriche 1987). With regard to non-separable spatio-temporal scale-space, (Lindeberg 1997) formulated a scale-space theory for non-separable receptive fields, including velocity adaptation for discrete space-time. Other follow-up works based on Koenderinks separable scale-time model have been presented by (Florack 1997, ter Haar Romeny et al. 2001). Concerning non-linear scale-space concepts, (Guichard 1998) has proposed a morphological scale-space model model that commutes with Galilean transformations, and (Weickert 1998) has studied non-linear scale-spaces that comprise spatial shape adaptation.

2.1 Transformation Properties of Spatio-Temporal Scale-Space

For continuous data, a simplified spatio-temporal receptive field model in terms of Gaussian filtering can be used for illustrating the algebraic structure of a spatio-temporal scale-space, if we disregard temporal causality (Lindeberg 1994, Florack 1997). Consider the following shape- (or velocity-) adapted Gaussian kernels

$$g(x;\ \Sigma, m) = \frac{1}{(2\pi)^{D/2}\sqrt{\det \Sigma}}\, e^{-(x-m)^T \Sigma^{-1}(x-m)/2}, \qquad (1)$$

where the covariance matrix Σ describes the shape of the kernel and the mean vector m represents the position. This scale-space has the attractive property that it is *closed* under affine transformations. If two image patterns f_L and f_R are related by an affine transformation, $f_L(x_L) = f_R(x_R)$ where $x_R = Ax_L + b$, and if linear scale-space representations of these images are defined by

$$L(\cdot;\ \Sigma_L, v_L) = g(\cdot;\ \Sigma_L, v_L) * f_L(\cdot) \quad R(\cdot;\ \Sigma_R, v_R) = g(\cdot;\ \Sigma_R, v_R) * f_R(\cdot) \qquad (2)$$

then L and R are related according to $L(x;\ \Sigma_L, v_L) = R(y;\ \Sigma_R, v_R)$ where the covariance matrices Σ_L and Σ_R satisfy $\Sigma_R = A\Sigma_L A^T$ and the velocity terms v_L and v_R in the Gaussian kernels can be traded against coordinate shifts in x_L and x_R as long as the relation $x_R - v_R = A(x_L - v_L) + b$ is satisfied.

This closedness property is highly useful whenever we consider visual tasks involving affine image deformations (see figure 1), and has been explored in various respects by (Lindeberg 1994, Lindeberg & Gårding 1997, Florack 1997, Ballester & Gonzalez 1998, Nagel & Gehrke 1998, Schaffalitzky & Zisserman 2001). Specifically, with regard to Galilean motion in the image plane

$$\begin{cases} x' = x + v_x t \\ y' = y + v_y t \\ t' = t \end{cases} \quad \text{i.e.} \quad \begin{pmatrix} x' \\ y' \\ t' \end{pmatrix} = \begin{pmatrix} 1 & 0 & v_x \\ 0 & 1 & v_y \\ 0 & 0 & 1 \end{pmatrix} \begin{pmatrix} x \\ y \\ t \end{pmatrix} \qquad (3)$$

the spatio-temporal covariance matrix will transform as

$$\begin{pmatrix} C'_{xx} & C'_{xt} & C'_{xt} \\ C'_{xy} & C'_{yy} & C'_{yt} \\ C'_{xt} & C'_{yt} & C'_{tt} \end{pmatrix} = \begin{pmatrix} 1 & 0 & v_x \\ 0 & 1 & v_y \\ 0 & 0 & 1 \end{pmatrix} \begin{pmatrix} C_{xx} & C_{xt} & C_{xt} \\ C_{xy} & C_{yy} & C_{yt} \\ C_{xt} & C_{yt} & C_{tt} \end{pmatrix} \begin{pmatrix} 1 & 0 & 0 \\ 0 & 1 & 0 \\ v_x & v_y & 1 \end{pmatrix} \qquad (4)$$

while for the mean vector we have

$$\begin{pmatrix} C'_x \\ C'_y \\ C'_t \end{pmatrix} = \begin{pmatrix} 1 & 0 & v_x \\ 0 & 1 & v_y \\ 0 & 0 & 1 \end{pmatrix} \begin{pmatrix} C_x \\ C_y \\ C_t \end{pmatrix} = \begin{pmatrix} C_x + v_x C_t \\ C_y + v_y C_t \\ C_t \end{pmatrix} \quad (5)$$

It should be noted, however, that these transformation properties are not restricted to Gaussian smoothing kernels only. Rather, they hold for a rather wide family of rapidly decreasing non-negative smoothing functions. One idea we shall follow in this work is to define a family of discrete smoothing kernels such that a similar algebraic structure holds for their covariance matrices and mean vectors.

$$L(x;\ \Sigma_L, v_L) - \left\{ \begin{array}{c} x_R = Ax_L + b \\ \Sigma_R = A\Sigma_L A^T \\ x_R - v_R = A(x_L - v_L) + b \end{array} \right\} \to R(y;\ \Sigma_R, v_R)$$

$$\uparrow \qquad\qquad\qquad\qquad\qquad\qquad\qquad \uparrow$$
$$*g(\cdot;\ \Sigma_L, v_L) \qquad\qquad\qquad\qquad\qquad *g(\cdot;\ \Sigma_R, v_R)$$
$$| \qquad\qquad\qquad\qquad\qquad\qquad\qquad |$$
$$f_L(x_L) \qquad - \qquad x_R = Ax_L + b \qquad \to \qquad f_R(x_R)$$

Fig. 1. Commutative diagram of the Gaussian scale-space under linear transformations of the space-time coordinates, implying that the scale-space representations of two affinely deformed image patches can be aligned, either by adapting the shapes of the Gaussian kernels or equivalently by deforming the image data prior to smoothing.

2.2 Time-Recursive Temporal Scale-Space for Discrete Time in 0+1-D

In (Lindeberg 1994, Lindeberg & Fagerström 1996) it was shown that a natural and computationally efficient temporal scale-space concept for a one-dimensional temporal signal (without spatial extent) can be constructed by coupling first-order recursive filters in cascade

$$f_{out}(t) = \frac{\mu}{1+\mu} f_{out}(t-1) + \frac{1}{1+\mu} f_{in}(t) \quad (6)$$

The mean of such a filter is μ and the variance μ^2. Thus, by coupling k such filters in cascade, we obtain a filter with mean $M^{(k)} = \sum_{i=1}^{k} \mu_i$ and variance $V^{(k)} = \sum_{i=1}^{k} \mu_i^2 + \mu_i$.

It can be shown that if we for a given total variance τ^2 in the temporal domain let the time constants become successively smaller $\mu_i = \tau^2/K$ while increasing the number of filtering steps K, then with increasing K these kernels approach the Poisson kernel (Lindeberg 1997), which corresponds to the canonical temporal scale-space concept having a continuous scale parameter on a discrete temporal domain. In practice, however, we should of course rather choose the time constants μ_i such that the variances $V^{(k)}$ are distributed according to a geometric series, which means that the individual filter parameters should with $\gamma = (V^{(K)}/V^{(1)})^{1/K}$ in the minimal case be given by

$$\mu_k = \tfrac{1}{2}\left(\sqrt{1 + 4V^{(1)}(\gamma - 1)\gamma^{k-1}} - 1\right). \tag{7}$$

2.3 Time-Recursive Non-separable Scale-Space in 1+1-D

For spatial and spatio-temporal scale-space concepts in higher dimensions, it was shown in (Lindeberg 1997) that for a discrete scale-space representation with a continuous scale parameter, the requirement of non-enhancement of local extrema[1] implies that under variations of a scale parameter s the scale-space family must satisfy a semi-discrete differential equation of the form

$$(\partial_s L)(x;\ s) = (\mathcal{A}L)(x;\ s) = \sum_{\xi \in \mathbb{Z}^D} a_\xi L(x + \xi;\ s), \tag{8}$$

for some *infinitesimal scale-space generator* $\mathcal{A}$, characterized by

- the *locality* condition $a_\xi = 0$ if $|\xi|_\infty > 1$,
- the *positivity* constraint $a_\xi \geq 0$ if $\xi \neq 0$, and
- the *zero sum* condition $\sum_{\xi \in \mathbb{Z}^D} a_\xi = 0$.

When extending the temporal smoothing scheme (6) from a pure temporal domain to spatio-temporal image data, we propose to use the locality property obtained in this way to include nearest-neighbour computations in space. Thus, for a 1+1-D spatio-temporal signal with one spatial dimension and one temporal dimension, we propose to consider a smoothing scheme of the form

$$f_{out}(x,t) = \frac{1}{1+\mu_t}\begin{pmatrix}a\\b\\c\end{pmatrix}f_{out}(x,t-1) + \frac{1}{1+\mu_t}\begin{pmatrix}d\\e\\f\end{pmatrix}f_{in}(x,t) \tag{9}$$

where $a, b, c, d, e, f \geq 0$ and the vectors within parentheses denote computational symbols in the spatial domain, corresponding to the following explicit form of the smoothing scheme:

$$f_{out}(x,t) = \frac{1}{1+\mu_t}(a\,f_{out}(x+1,t-1) + b\,f_{out}(x,t-1) + c\,f_{out}(x-1,t-1)$$
$$+ d\,f_{in}(x+1,t) + e\,f_{in}(x,t) + f\,f_{in}(x-1,t)). \tag{10}$$

From the generating function $\varphi(w,z)$ of the corresponding filter $T(x,t;\ s)$

$$\varphi(w,z) = \sum_{x=-\infty}^{\infty}\sum_{t=-\infty}^{\infty} T(x,t;\ s)\,w^x z^t = \frac{dw^{-1} + e + fw}{1 + \mu_t - (aw^{-1} + b + cw)z} \tag{11}$$

---

[1] Non-enhancement of local extrema implies that the intensity value at a local maximum (minimum) must not increase (decrease) when the scale parameter s increases, i.e., $\partial_s L \leq 0\ (\geq 0)$ must hold at all local maxima (minima).

where w denotes the transformation variable in the spatial domain and z the corresponding transformation variable in the temporal domain, we get the mean vector M and the covariance matrix V of the smoothing kernel as

$$M = \begin{pmatrix} \varphi_w \\ \varphi_z \end{pmatrix}\bigg|_{(w,z)=(1,1)} = \begin{pmatrix} \mu_x \\ \mu_t \end{pmatrix}, \tag{12}$$

$$V = \begin{pmatrix} \varphi_{ww} + \varphi_w - \varphi_w^2 & \varphi_{wz} - \varphi_w\varphi_z \\ \varphi_{wz} - \varphi_w\varphi_z & \varphi_{zz} + \varphi_z - \varphi_z^2 \end{pmatrix}\bigg|_{(w,z)=(1,1)} = \begin{pmatrix} \mu_{xx} & \mu_{xt} \\ \mu_{xt} & \mu_t^2 + \mu_t \end{pmatrix}.$$

Our next aim is to solve for the parameters a, b, c, d, e and f in the recursive filter in terms of the parameters μ_x, μ_t, μ_{xx} and μ_{xt}. One additional constraint, $\varphi(1,1) = 1$, originates from the requirement that the filter should correspond to a normalized filter. While this problem formally has six degrees of freedom in $a \ldots f$ and six constraints in terms of the mass, mean and covariance of the filter, however, one complication originates from the fact that the mean and the variance of the kernel in the temporal domain are coupled. Thus, we expect the problem to have $6 - 1 - 2 - (3 - 1) = 1$ degree of freedom, and solve for a, b, c, d and f in terms of e and $\mu_x \ldots \mu_{xt}$. After some calculations it follows that

$$a = \frac{\mu_{xx} + \mu_x^2 + e - 1}{2} - \frac{\mu_{xt} + 2\mu_x \mu_{xt}}{2(1 + \mu_t)} \tag{13}$$

$$b = -\mu_{xx} - \mu_x^2 + 1 - e + \mu_t + \frac{2\mu_x \mu_{xt}}{(1 + \mu_t)}, \tag{14}$$

$$c = \frac{\mu_{xx} + \mu_x^2 + e - 1}{2} + \frac{\mu_{xt} - 2\mu_x \mu_{xt}}{2(1 + \mu_t)} \tag{15}$$

$$d = \frac{-\mu_x + 1 - e}{2} + \frac{\mu_{xt}}{2(1 + \mu_t)}, \tag{16}$$

$$f = \frac{+\mu_x + 1 - e}{2} - \frac{\mu_{xt}}{2(1 + \mu_t)}, \tag{17}$$

To interpret these relations, let us first parameterize the single degree of freedom in the solution in terms of $\nu = 1 - e$. Then, by rewriting the spatial computational molecules in terms of the spatial difference operators δ_x and δ_{xx} as

$$\begin{pmatrix} a \\ b \\ c \end{pmatrix} = \frac{1}{2}\left(\mu_{xx} + \mu_x^2 - \frac{2\mu_x\mu_{xt}}{1+\mu_t} - \frac{\nu}{2}\right)\begin{pmatrix} 1 \\ -2 \\ 1 \end{pmatrix} + \mu_t\begin{pmatrix} 0 \\ 1 \\ 0 \end{pmatrix} - \frac{\mu_{xt}}{1+\mu_t}\begin{pmatrix} 1/2 \\ 0 \\ -1/2 \end{pmatrix}$$

$$\begin{pmatrix} d \\ e \\ f \end{pmatrix} = -\mu_x\begin{pmatrix} 1/2 \\ 0 \\ -1/2 \end{pmatrix} + \begin{pmatrix} 0 \\ 1 \\ 0 \end{pmatrix} + \frac{\nu}{2}\begin{pmatrix} 1 \\ -2 \\ 1 \end{pmatrix} + \frac{\mu_{xt}}{(1+\mu_t)}\begin{pmatrix} 1/2 \\ 0 \\ -1/2 \end{pmatrix}$$

and by introducing mixed spatio-temporal derivatives according to

$$\delta_{xt}(f_{in}, f_{out})(x,t) = \begin{pmatrix} 1/2 \\ 0 \\ -1/2 \end{pmatrix} f_{in}(x,t) - \begin{pmatrix} 1/2 \\ 0 \\ -1/2 \end{pmatrix} f_{out}(x, t-1) \qquad (18)$$

$$\delta_{xxt}(f_{in}, f_{out})(x,t) = \begin{pmatrix} 1 \\ -2 \\ 1 \end{pmatrix} f_{in}(x,t) - \begin{pmatrix} 1 \\ -2 \\ 1 \end{pmatrix} f_{out}(x, t-1), \qquad (19)$$

we can with $\mu_{xxt} = \nu$ express the spatio-temporal smoothing scheme in (9) as

$$f_{out}(x,t) - f_{out}(x, t-1) = \frac{1}{1+\mu_t}(-\mu_x \delta_x f_{in}(x,t) + \delta_t(f_{in}, f_{out})(x,t)$$
$$+ \frac{1}{2}(\mu_{xx} + \mu_x^2 - \frac{2\mu_x \mu_{xt}}{1+\mu_t}) \delta_{xx} f_{out}(x, t-1)$$
$$+ \frac{2}{2} \frac{\mu_{xt}}{1+\mu_t} \delta_{xt}(f_{in}, f_{out})(x,t)$$
$$+ \frac{3}{6} \frac{\mu_{xxt}}{1+\mu_t} \delta_{xxt}(f_{in}, f_{out})(x,t)) \qquad (20)$$

Alternatively, after introducing the following notation for binomial smoothing with variance ν in the spatial domain

$$\text{Bin}(\nu) f_{in}(x,t) = \begin{pmatrix} \nu/2 \\ 1-\nu \\ \nu/2 \end{pmatrix} f_{in}(x,t) \qquad (21)$$

the recursive updating scheme can be expressed on the form

$$f_{out}(x,t) - f_{out}(x,t-1) = \frac{1}{1+\mu_t}(-\mu_x \delta_x f_{in}(x,t) + \text{Bin}(\nu) f_{in}(x,t) - f_{out}(x,t-1)$$
$$+ \frac{1}{2}(\mu_{xx} + \mu_x^2 - \frac{2\mu_x \mu_{xt}}{1+\mu_t} - \nu) \delta_{xx} f_{out}(x, t-1)$$
$$+ \frac{\mu_{xt}}{1+\mu_t} \delta_{xt}(f_{in}, f_{out})(x,t)) \qquad (22)$$

From this expression it is apparent how the mean and variance parameters μ_x, μ, μ_{xx} and μ_{xt} influence the recursive smoothing scheme. Moreover, we see how the free parameter $\nu = 1-e$ can be interpreted as a trade-off parameter between the amount of binomical pre-smoothing of the input signal and the amount of complementary spatial smoothing $\mu_{xx} - \nu$ in the recursive updating scheme. Regarding the existence of non-negative values of a, b, c, d, e and f, it can be shown that a necessary and sufficient condition is that

$$\max(\left|\mu_x - \frac{\mu_{xt}}{1+\mu_t}\right|, \mu_{xx} + \mu_x^2 - \mu_t - \frac{2\mu_x \mu_{xt}}{1+\mu_t}) \leq \nu \leq$$
$$\leq \min(1, \mu_{xx} + \mu_x^2 - \frac{2\mu_x \mu_{xt} + |\mu_{xt}|}{1+\mu_t}) \qquad (23)$$

Parametrization of filter shapes. Given that K such spatio-temporal smoothing filters with parameters $\mu_x^{(i)}$, $\mu_t^{(i)}$, $\mu_{xx}^{(i)}$ and $\mu_{xt}^{(i)}$ are coupled in cascade, the effective filter parameters of the composed kernel will be of the form

$$C_x^{(k)} = \sum_{i=1}^{k} \mu_x^{(i)}, \quad C_t^{(k)} = \sum_{i=1}^{k} \mu_t^{(i)}$$

$$C_{xx}^{(k)} = \sum_{i=1}^{k} \mu_{xx}^{(i)}, \quad C_{xt}^{(k)} = \sum_{i=1}^{k} \mu_{xt}^{(i)}, \quad C_{tt}^{(k)} = \sum_{i=1}^{k} (\mu_t^{(i)})^2 + \mu_t^{(i)}. \quad (24)$$

To parameterize these filter shapes, let us start from the transformation properties (4) and (5) of covariance matrices and mean vectors under Galilean motion. Then, with λ_{xx} and λ_t denoting the amount of spatial and temporal smoothing in a frame attached to the object (with separable smoothing), we have

$$\begin{pmatrix} C_{xx} & C_{xt} \\ C_{xt} & C_{tt} \end{pmatrix} = \begin{pmatrix} \lambda_{xx} + v^2 \lambda_t & v\lambda_t \\ v\lambda_t & \lambda_t \end{pmatrix} \quad \text{and} \quad \begin{pmatrix} C_x \\ C_t \end{pmatrix} = \begin{pmatrix} v\, C_t \\ C_t \end{pmatrix} \quad (25)$$

where C_t and C_{tt} are coupled according to (24).

Permissable combinations of filter parameters. To analyse for which combinations of λ_{xx}, λ_t and v non-negative discretization are possible, let us for simplicity consider one level of a recursive filter. From (24) and (25) it follows that

$$\mu_{xx} = \lambda_{xx} + v^2 \lambda_t \quad (26)$$

$$\mu_{xt} = v\lambda_t \quad (27)$$

$$\mu_t = \frac{1}{2}\left(\sqrt{1 + 4\lambda_t} - 1\right) \quad (28)$$

$$\mu_x = v\,\mu_t = \frac{v}{2}\left(\sqrt{1 + 4\lambda_t} - 1\right) \quad (29)$$

and for these specific values of the parameters, it holds that $\mu_x = \mu_{xt}/(1 + \mu_t)$. After some calculations it can be shown that a necessary prerequisite for the existence of a non-negative filter coefficients is that $|v| \leq 1$. In addition, the range of permissable spatial smoothing parameters λ_{xx} is delimited by

$$\frac{(|v| - v^2)}{2}\left(\sqrt{1 + 4\lambda_t} - 1\right) \leq \lambda_{xx} \leq \frac{1+v^2}{2} + \frac{1-v^2}{2}\sqrt{1 + 4\lambda_t} \quad (30)$$

If a larger amount of spatial smoothing is required than allowed by this inequality, a straightforward approach is to divide the smoothing step into several layers of the recursive filters coupled in cascade. Using k such filters with identical parameters, the filter parameters for one layer will be related to the filter parameters of the composed filter according to $\lambda'_{xx} = \lambda_{xx}/k$ and $\lambda'_t = \lambda_t/k$. To capture motions with $|v| > 1$, one possible approach is to complement this recursive filtering framework by an additional warping mechanism. Alternatively, we may carry out the computations at a coarser spatial resolution. Using the fact that the filter parameters transform as $\lambda''_{xx} = \lambda'_{xx}/h^2$, $\lambda''_t = \lambda'_t$ and $v'' = v'/h$ under a change of spatial resolution by a factor h, we finally obtain

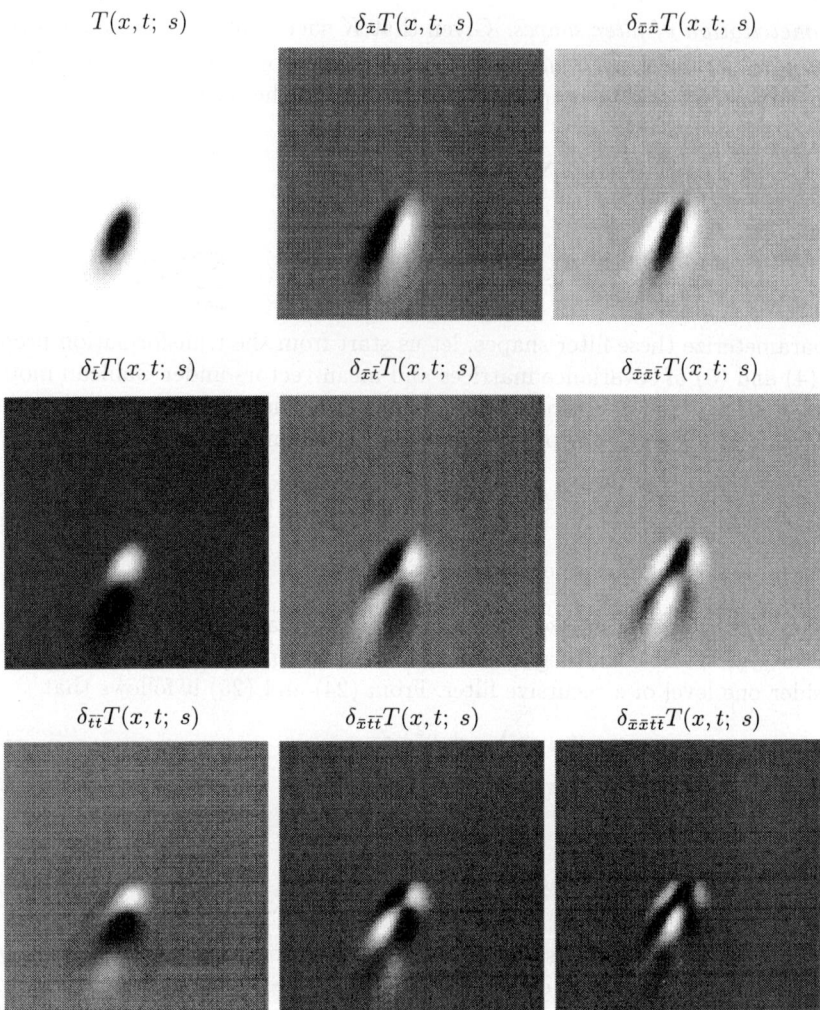

Fig. 2. Equivalent filter kernels corresponding to the result of using a discrete delta function as input and applying repeated non-separable recursive filtering according to (22) with a Galilean transformation parametrization of the filter shape (25) followed by subsequent Galilean based computation of velocity-adapted spatio-temporal derivatives according to (32) for different orders of spatial and temporal differentiation. (In all cases, the spatio-temporal smoothing parameters are the same ($\lambda_{xx} = 16, \lambda_t = 64, v = 1/3$) as well as the number of layers $k = 10$ and the image size 150×150 pixels. Horisontal axis: space x. Vertical axis: time t.)

$$\frac{k(h|v| - v^2)}{2}\left(\sqrt{1 + \frac{4\lambda_t}{k}} - 1\right) \leq \lambda_{xx} \leq k\left(\frac{h^2 + v^2}{2} + \frac{h^2 - v^2}{2}\sqrt{1 + \frac{4\lambda_t}{k}}\right)$$
(31)

where the upper bound on the image velocity is now given by $|v| \leq h$. Thus, we will be able to capture higher image velocites at coarser spatial scales using spatio-temporal recursive filtering only. However, if we want to capture rapid motions at fine spatial scales, then an additional warping mechanism is necessary.

Figure 2 shows a few examples of kernels computed in this way, followed by the computation of velocity-adapted spatio-temporal derivatives according to

$$\partial_{\bar{x}} = \partial_x \qquad \partial_{\bar{t}} = v\partial_x + \partial_t \qquad (32)$$

2.4 Recursive Non-separable Scale-Space in 2+1-D

To extend the previously developed recursive velocity adaptation scheme from one to two spatial dimensions, let us consider a smoothing scheme of the form

$$f_{out}(x,y,t) = \frac{1}{1+\mu_t}\begin{pmatrix} a & b & c \\ d & e & f \\ g & h & i \end{pmatrix}f_{out}(x,t-1) + \frac{1}{1+\mu_t}\begin{pmatrix} j & k & l \\ m & n & p \\ q & r & s \end{pmatrix}f_{in}(x,t) \quad (33)$$

where the matrices within parentheses denote computational symbols in the spatial domain (which relate the filter coefficients $a, b, \ldots, s$ to spatial positions). From the generating function of the corresponding filter

$$\varphi(u,v,z) =$$
$$= \frac{pu^{-1} + mu + kv^{-1} + rv + lu^{-1}v^{-1} + su^{-1}v + juv^{-1} + quv}{1 + \mu_t - (fu + du^{-1} + bv + hv^{-1} + cu^{-1}v^{-1} + iu^{-1}v + auv^{-1} + guv)z} \quad (34)$$

where u denotes the transformation variable in the spatial x-direction, v denotes the transformation variable in the spatial y-direction and z the corresponding transformation variable in the temporal domain, we obtain the mean vector M and the covariance matrix V as

$$M = \begin{pmatrix} \varphi_u \\ \varphi_v \\ \varphi_z \end{pmatrix}\bigg|_{(u,v,z)=(1,1,1)} = \begin{pmatrix} \mu_x \\ \mu_y \\ \mu_t \end{pmatrix}, \qquad (35)$$

$$V = \begin{pmatrix} \varphi_{uu} + \varphi_u - \varphi_u^2 & \varphi_{uv} - \varphi_u\varphi_v & \varphi_{uz} - \varphi_u\varphi_z \\ \varphi_{uv} - \varphi_u\varphi_v & \varphi_{vv} - \varphi_v - \varphi_v^2 & \varphi_{vz} - \varphi_v\varphi_z \\ \varphi_{uz} - \varphi_u\varphi_z & \varphi_{vz} - \varphi_v\varphi_z & \varphi_{zz} + \varphi_z - \varphi_z^2 \end{pmatrix}\bigg|_{(u,v,z)=(1,1,1)} \quad (36)$$

$$= \begin{pmatrix} \mu_{xx} & \mu_{xy} & \mu_{xt} \\ \mu_{xy} & \mu_{yy} & \mu_{yt} \\ \mu_{xt} & \mu_{yt} & \mu_t^2 + \mu_t \end{pmatrix}. \qquad (37)$$

Our next aim is to solve for the parameters $a, b, \ldots s$ in the recursive filter in terms of the parameters $\mu_x, \mu_y, \mu_t, \mu_{xx}, \mu_{xy}, \mu_{yy}, \mu_{xt}$ and μ_{yt}, with the additional constraint $\varphi(1,1,1) = 1$. Structurally, this problem has 18 degrees of freedom in the parameters $a, b, \ldots s$, one constraint due to normalization, three constraints in terms of the mean values and six constraints in terms of the covariance matrix, out of which one constraint is redundant due to the coupling between the mean and the variance in the temporal direction. Thus, we expect to problem to have $18 - 1 - 3 - (6 - 1) = 9$ degrees of freedom, After some calculations, it can be shown that in terms of the difference operators in figure 3, this non-separable recursive smoothing scheme can on incremental form be expressed as

$$f_{out}(x, y, t) - f_{out}(x, y, t - 1) =$$
$$= \frac{1}{1 + \mu_t}(D - \mu_x \, \delta_x \, f_{in}(x, y, t) - \mu_y \, \delta_y \, f_{in}(x, y, t)$$
$$+ \frac{1}{2}\left(\mu_{xx} + \mu_x^2 - \frac{2\mu_x\mu_{xt}}{1 + \mu_t}\right)\delta_{xx}f_{out}(x, y, t - 1)$$
$$+ \left(\mu_{xy} + \mu_x\mu_y - \frac{\mu_y\mu_{xt} + \mu_x\mu_{yt}}{1 + \mu_t}\right)\delta_{xy}f_{out}(x, y, t - 1)$$
$$+ \frac{1}{2}\left(\mu_{yy} + \mu_y^2 - \frac{2\mu_y\mu_{yt}}{1 + \mu_t}\right)\delta_{xy}f_{out}(x, y, t - 1)$$
$$+ \frac{\mu_{xt}}{1 + \mu_t}\delta_{xt}(f_{in}, f_{out})(x, y, t)$$
$$+ \frac{\mu_{yt}}{1 + \mu_t}\delta_{yt}(f_{in}, f_{out})(x, y, t)) \qquad (38)$$

where the nine degrees of freedom in the solution are contained in

$$D = f_{in}(x, y, t) - f_{out}(x, y, t - 1)$$
$$+ \tfrac{3}{6}\mu_{xxt}\,\delta_{xxt}(f_{in}, f_{out})(x, y, t) + \tfrac{6}{6}\mu_{xyt}\,\delta_{xyt}(f_{in}, f_{out})(x, y, t)$$
$$+ \tfrac{3}{6}\mu_{yyt}\,\delta_{yyt}(f_{in}, f_{out})(x, y, t)$$
$$+ \tfrac{3}{6}\mu_{xxy}\,\delta_{xxy}(f_{out})(x, y, t) + \tfrac{3}{6}\mu_{xyy}\,\delta_{xyy}(f_{out})(x, y, t)$$
$$+ \tfrac{12}{24}\mu_{xxyt}\,\delta_{xxyt}(f_{out}, f_{out})(x, y, t) + \tfrac{12}{24}\mu_{xyyt}\,\delta_{xyyt}(f_{out}, f_{out})(x, y, t)$$
$$+ \tfrac{6}{24}\mu_{xxyy}\,\delta_{xxyy}(f_{out})(x, y, t) + \tfrac{30}{120}\mu_{xxyyt}\,\delta_{xxyyt}(f_{out}, f_{out})(x, y, t). \qquad (39)$$

Parameterization of filter shapes based on Galilei transformations. To parameterize these filter shapes, let us first express the spatial part of the covariance matrix in terms of two eigenvalues (λ_1, λ_2) and one orientation α

$$\Sigma = \begin{pmatrix} C_{xx} & C_{xt} & C_{xt} \\ C_{xy} & C_{yy} & C_{yt} \\ C_{xt} & C_{yt} & C_t \end{pmatrix} = \begin{pmatrix} \lambda_1 \cos^2\alpha + \lambda_2 \sin^2\alpha & (\lambda_2 - \lambda_1)\cos\alpha\sin\alpha & 0 \\ (\lambda_2 - \lambda_1)\cos\alpha\sin\alpha & \lambda_1 \sin^2\alpha + \lambda_2 \cos^2\alpha & 0 \\ 0 & 0 & \lambda_t \end{pmatrix} \qquad (40)$$

Then, by subjecting this matrix to a Galilei transformation (4), we obtain

$$\Sigma' = \begin{pmatrix} \lambda_1 \cos^2\alpha + \lambda_2 \sin^2\alpha + v_x^2\lambda_t & (\lambda_2 - \lambda_1)\cos\alpha\sin\alpha + v_xv_y\lambda_t & v_x\lambda_t \\ (\lambda_2 - \lambda_1)\cos\alpha\sin\alpha + v_xv_y\lambda_t & \lambda_1 \sin^2\alpha + \lambda_2 \cos^2\alpha + v_y^2\lambda_t & v_y\lambda_t \\ v_x\lambda_t & v_y\lambda_t & \lambda_t \end{pmatrix} \qquad (41)$$

$$\delta_x f_{in}(x,y,t) = \begin{pmatrix} 0 & 0 & 0 \\ -1/2 & 0 & +1/2 \\ 0 & 0 & 0 \end{pmatrix} f_{in}(x,y,t)$$

$$\delta_{xx} f_{out}(x,y,t-1) = \begin{pmatrix} 0 & 0 & 0 \\ +1 & -2 & +1 \\ 0 & 0 & 0 \end{pmatrix} f_{out}(x,y,t-1)$$

$$\delta_{xy} f_{out}(x,y,t-1) = \begin{pmatrix} -1/4 & 0 & +1/4 \\ 0 & 0 & 0 \\ +1/4 & 0 & -1/4 \end{pmatrix} f_{out}(x,y,t-1)$$

$$\delta_{xt}(f_{in},f_{out})(x,y,t) = \begin{pmatrix} 0 & 0 & 0 \\ -1/2 & 0 & +1/2 \\ 0 & 0 & 0 \end{pmatrix} (f_{in}(x,y,t) - f_{out}(x,y,t-1))$$

$$\delta_{xxt}(f_{in},f_{out})(x,y,t) = \begin{pmatrix} 0 & 0 & 0 \\ +1 & -2 & +1 \\ 0 & 0 & 0 \end{pmatrix} (f_{in}(x,y,t) - f_{out}(x,y,t-1))$$

$$\delta_{xyt}(f_{in},f_{out})(x,y,t) = \begin{pmatrix} -1/4 & 0 & +1/4 \\ 0 & 0 & 0 \\ +1/4 & 0 & -1/4 \end{pmatrix} (f_{in}(x,y,t) - f_{out}(x,y,t-1))$$

$$\delta_{xyy}(f_{out})(x,y,t) = \begin{pmatrix} -1/2 & 0 & +1/2 \\ +1 & 0 & -1 \\ -1/2 & 0 & +1/2 \end{pmatrix} f_{out}(x,y,t)$$

$$\delta_{xyyt}(f_{in},f_{out})(x,y,t) = \begin{pmatrix} -1/2 & 0 & +1/2 \\ +1 & 0 & -1 \\ -1/2 & 0 & +1/2 \end{pmatrix} (f_{in}(x,y,t) - f_{out}(x,y,t-1))$$

$$\delta_{xxyy}(f_{out})(x,y,t) = \begin{pmatrix} 1 & -2 & 1 \\ -2 & +4 & -2 \\ 1 & -2 & 1 \end{pmatrix} f_{out}(x,y,t)$$

$$\delta_{xxyyt}(f_{in},f_{out})(x,y,t) = \begin{pmatrix} +1 & -2 & +1 \\ -2 & +4 & -2 \\ +1 & -2 & +1 \end{pmatrix} (f_{in}(x,y,t) - f_{out}(x,y,t-1))$$

Fig. 3. Difference operators used in the construction of the discrete recursive spatio-temporal scale-space representation in 2+1-D space-time (38). To reduce redundancy, operators that are mere rotations of corresponding operators in other directions are not shown. Thus, δ_y, δ_{yy}, δ_{yt}, δ_{yyt}, δ_{xxy} and δ_{xxyt} have been suppressed.

Velocity-adapted spatio-temporal derivatives are finally given by

$$\partial_{\bar{x}} = \partial_x \qquad \partial_{\bar{y}} = \partial_y \qquad \partial_{\bar{t}} = v_x \partial_x + v_y \partial_y + \partial_t \qquad (42)$$

Figures 4–5 show a few examples of spatio-temporal scale-space kernels generated in this way. Figure 4 shows filters corresponding to $v = 0$, while figure 5 shows corresponding velocity adapted (and non-separable) recursive filters for a non-

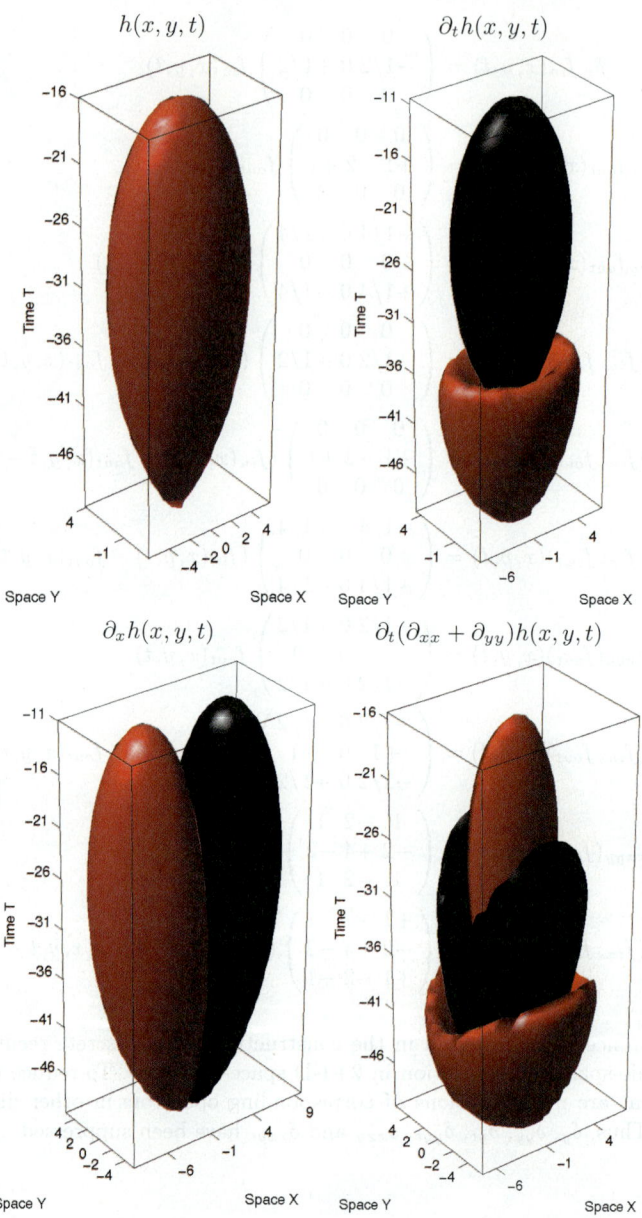

Fig. 4. Level surfaces of spatio-temporal receptive fields for the 2+1-D separable recursive spatio-temporal scale-space. (a) The raw smoothing kernel $h(x, y, t)$. (b) First-order temporal derivative $\partial_t h(x, y, t)$. (c) First-order spatial derivative $\partial_x h(x, y, t)$. (d) First-order temporal derivative of Laplacian response $\partial_t(\partial_{xx} + \partial_{yy})h(x, y, t)$. (In all cases, the smoothing parameters have been $\lambda_{xx} = 2$, $\lambda_{yy} = 1$, $\lambda_t = 4$, $v = 0$ and five identical recursive filters have been coupled in cascade.)

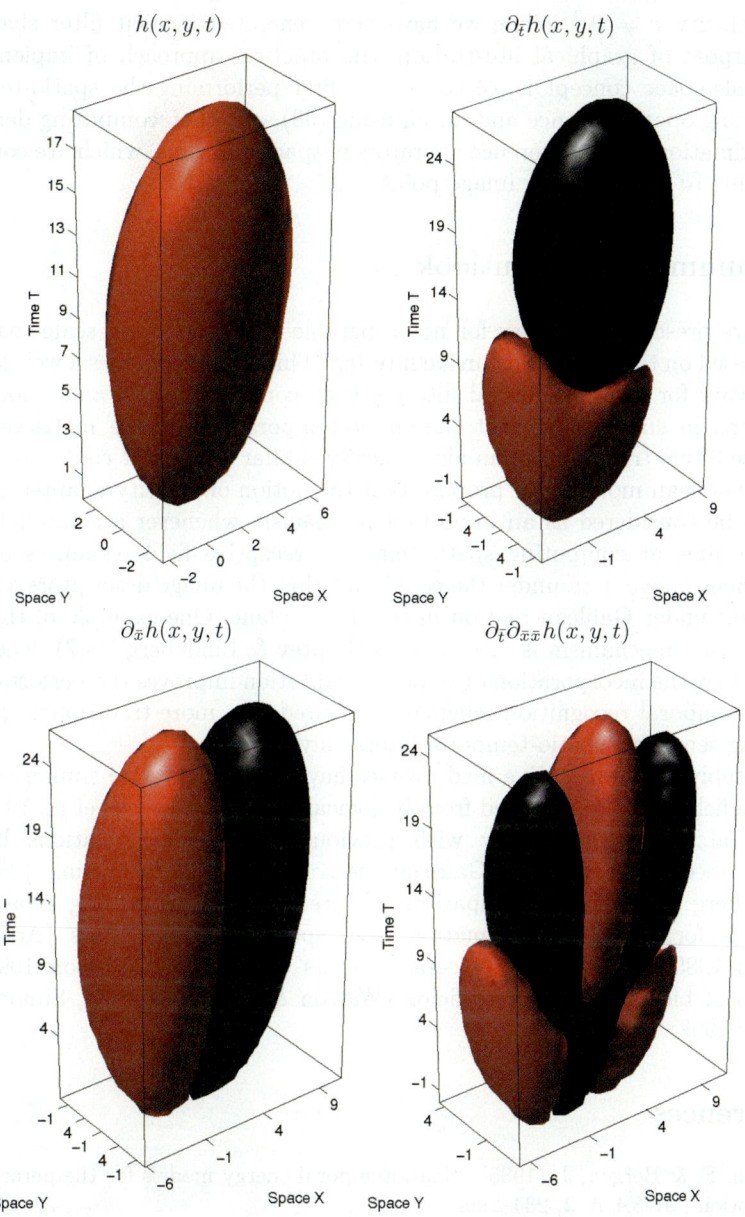

Fig. 5. Level surfaces of spatio-temporal receptive fields for the 2+1-D velocity-adapted spatio-temporal scale-space. (a) The raw smoothing kernel $h(x,y,t)$. (b) First-order temporal derivative $\partial_{\bar{t}} h(x,y,t)$. (c) First-order spatial derivative $\partial_{\bar{x}} h(x,y,t)$. (d) First-order temporal derivative of second-order derivative in the velocity direction $\partial_{\bar{t}} \partial_{\bar{x}\bar{x}} h(x,y,t)$. (In all cases, the smoothing parameters have been $\lambda_{xx} = 2$, $\lambda_{yy} = 1$, $\lambda_t = 4$, $(v_x, v_y) = (0.2, 0.0)$ and five identical filters have been coupled in cascade.)

zero velocity $v \neq 0$.[2] While we have here generated explicit filter shapes for the purpose of graphical illustration, the practical approach of implementing this scale-space concept is, of course, by first performing the spatio-temporal smoothing operation once and for all using (38), and then computing derivative approximations from difference operators in space and time, which are combined according to (42) at every image point.

3 Summary and Outlook

We have presented a theory for non-separable spatio-temporal scale-space kernels, based on time-causal recursive filtering. This theory provides a well-founded framework for spatio-temporal filtering with continuous scale and velocity parameters, in such a way that the spatio-temporal covariance matrices of the discrete filters transform in an algebraically similar way as for continuous filters under Galilean motion. We propose that the notion of velocity-adapted filtering should be considered as an important mechanism whenever a computer vision system aims at computing spatio-temporal receptive field responses of time-dependent image data under the constraint that the image descriptors are to be invariant under Galilean motion in the image plane. One example of the benefit of such a mechanism is presented in (Laptev & Lindeberg 2002), where it is shown how the incorporation of velocity adaptation improves the performance of spatio-temporal recognition schemes, compared to a more traditional approach of using separable spatio-temporal filters only.

Notably, these receptive field profiles have high qualitative similarity to receptive fields profiles recorded from biological vision (DeAngelis et al. 1995, Valois et al. 2000) in analogy with previously established relations between spatial receptive fields and Gaussian derivative operators (Young 1987); see (Lindeberg 2001) for a comparison. There are also interesting relations to methods for optic flow estimation from spatio-temporal filters (Adelson & Bergen 1985, Heeger 1988), steerable filters (Freeman & Adelson 1991) and models of biological receptive fields (Watson & Ahumada 1985, Simoncelli & Heeger 1998).

References

Adelson, E. & Bergen, J. (1985), 'Spatiotemporal energy models for the perception of motion', *JOSA* **A 2**, 284–299.
Almansa, A. & Lindeberg, T. (2000), 'Fingerprint enhancement by shape adaptation of scale-space operators with automatic scale-selection', *IEEE-TIP* **9**(12), 2027–2042.
Ballester, C. & Gonzalez, M. (1998), 'Affine invariant texture segmentation and shape from texture by variational methods', *J. Math. Im. Vis.* **9**, 141–171.
Burt, P. J. (1981), 'Fast filter transforms for image processing', *CVGIP* **16**, 20–51.

---

[2] For these filters, the choice of higher order filter parameters has been determined numerically. For graphical illustrations, the results are shown as level surfaces, where the colour of the level surface indicates the polarity.

Crowley, J. L. (1981), A Representation for Visual Information, PhD thesis, Carnegie-Mellon University, Pittsburgh, Pennsylvania.

DeAngelis, G. C., Ohzawa, I. & Freeman, R. D. (1995), 'Receptive field dynamics in the central visual pathways', *Trends in Neuroscience* **18**(10), 451–457.

Deriche, R. (1987), 'Using Canny's criteria to derive a recursively implemented optimal edge detector', *IJCV* **1**, 167–187.

Fleet, D. J. & Langley, K. (1995), 'Recursive filters for optical flow', *IEEE-PAMI* **17**(1), 61–67.

Florack, L. M. J. (1997), *Image Structure*, Kluwer, Netherlands.

Florack, L., Niessen, W. & Nielsen, M. (1998), 'The intrinsic structure of optic flow incorporating measurement duality', *IJCV* **27**(3), 263–286.

Freeman, W. T. & Adelson, E. H. (1991), 'The design and use of steerable filters', *IEEE-PAMI* **13**(9), 891–906.

Guichard, F. (1998), 'A morphological, affine, and galilean invariant scale-space for movies', *IEEE Trans. Image Processing* **7**(3), 444–456.

Heeger, D. (1988), 'Optical flow using spatiotemporal filters', *IJCV* **1**, 279–302.

Koenderink, J. J. (1984), 'The structure of images', *Biol. Cyb.* **50**, 363–370.

Koenderink, J. J. (1988), 'Scale-time', *Biol. Cyb.* **58**, 159–162.

Laptev, I. & Lindeberg, T. (2002), Velocity-adaption for direct recognition of activities using multi-scale spatio-temporal receptive field responses. Technical report ISRN KTH/NA/P-02/04-SE, KTH, Stockholm, Sweden.

Lindeberg, T. (1994), *Scale-Space Theory in Computer Vision*, Kluwer, Netherlands.

Lindeberg, T. (1997), Linear spatio-temporal scale-space, *in* 'Proc. Scale-Space'97', Utrecht, Netherlands, Vol. 1252 of Springer LNCS, pp. 113–127.

Lindeberg, T. (2001), Linear spatio-temporal scale-space, report, ISRN KTH/NA/P--01/22--SE, KTH, Stockholm, Sweden.

Lindeberg, T. & Fagerström, D. (1996), Scale-space with causal time direction, *in* 'ECCV'96', Vol. 1064, pp. 229–240.

Lindeberg, T. & Gårding, J. (1997), 'Shape-adapted smoothing in estimation of 3-D depth cues from affine distortions of local 2-D structure', *IVC* **15**, 415–434.

Nagel, H. & Gehrke, A. (1998), Spatiotemporal adaptive filtering for estimation and segmentation of optical flow fields, *in ECCV'98*, Freiburg, Germany, pp. 86–102.

Schaffalitzky, F. & Zisserman, A. (2001), Viewpoint invariant texture matching and wide baseline stereo, *in Proc. ICCV'01*, Vancouver, Canada.

Simoncelli, E. & Heeger, D. (1998), 'A model of neuronal responses in visual area MT', *Vis. Res.* **38**(5).

ter Haar Romeny, B., Florack, L. & Nielsen, M. (2001), Scale-time kernels and models, *in Scale-Space'01*, Vancouver, Canada.

Valois, R. L. D., Cottaris, N. P., Mahon, L. E., Elfer, S. D. & Wilson, J. A. (2000), 'Spatial and temporal receptive fields of geniculate and cortical cells and directional selectivity', *Vis. Res.* **40**(2), 3685–3702.

Watson, A. & Ahumada, A. (1985), 'Model of human visual-motion sensing', *JOSA* **2**(2), 322–341.

Weickert, J. (1998), *Anisotropic Diffusion in Image Processing*, Teubner-Verlag.

Witkin, A. P. (1983), Scale-space filtering, *in* '8th IJCAI', Karlsruhe, Germany, pp. 1019–1022.

Young, R. A. (1987), 'The Gaussian derivative model for spatial vision: I. Retinal mechanisms', *Spatial Vision* **2**, 273–293.

Combining Appearance and Topology for Wide Baseline Matching

Dennis Tell and *Stefan Carlsson*

Computational Vision and Active Perception Laboratory (CVAP)
Dept. of Numerical Analysis and Computer Science
KTH, SE-100 44 Stockholm, Sweden
Email: {dennis, stefanc}@nada.kth.se

Abstract. The problem of establishing image-to-image correspondences is fundamental in computer vision. Recently, several wide baseline matching algorithms capable of handling large changes of viewpoint have appeared. By computing feature values from image data, these algorithms mainly use appearance as a cue for matching. Topological information, i.e. spatial relations between features, has also been used, but not nearly to the same extent as appearance. In this paper, we incorporate topological constraints into an existing matching algorithm [1] which matches image intensity profiles between interest points. We show that the algorithm can be improved by exploiting the constraint that the intensity profiles around each interest point should be cyclically ordered. String matching techniques allows for an efficient implementation of the ordering constraint. Experiments with real data indicate that the modified algorithm indeed gives superior results to the original one. The method of enforcing the spatial constraints is not limited to the presented case, but can be used on any algorithm where interest point correspondences are sought.

1 Introduction

Recently, wide baseline image matching has received increased attention in computer vision. Unlike classical correlation based matching techniques, wide baseline matching algorithms can tolerate a large change in viewpoint between the images. The terms "wide baseline" and "large change" are quite vague, and available matching algorithms differ somewhat in the definition of these, but generally speaking, wide baseline algorithms are capable of handling more complicated transformations than image translations.

In applications such as 3D reconstruction or object recognition, better matching algorithms could potentially provide good results using only a few images to represent a scene or an object, as opposed to the 3D reconstruction algorithms of today [2] [3] which use image sequences, where the inter-frame difference between images is quite small. However, in cases where video sequences are not available, or difficult to record due to practical reasons, an algorithm capable of matching a few, quite disparate, images is needed. Another area where wide baseline matching could boost performance is content-based image retrieval. Fewer images to represent objects means smaller databases and shorter search times.

Existing matching algorithms can mainly tolerate two classes of transformations, similarity and affine. The work of Schmid and Mohr [4] as well as that of Gouet et al [5] and Baumberg [6], both using differential invariants, belong to the former class. These types of algorithms are adequate for image plane translations and rotations, but for general camera movement the image transformations will be more complex. Hence, methods capable of handling more general transformations have been developed. Torr and Davidson [7] used a coarse to fine approach in conjunction with cross correlation to handle larger baselines. Tuytelaars et al [8] developed an algorithm in which small image regions were found in an affine invariant way. Features were then computed from those regions. The first step of this method is quite complicated and there is no way to guarantee that the same regions are found in both images. The authors solve this problem by selecting several overlapping regions of different sizes and shapes.

All these algorithms use interest points, most often Harris corners, and the textured neighborhoods to discriminate among possible corner correspondences. However, the spatial relationships between corners is also a source of valuable information for matching. This was recognised by Zhang et al. [9] in a short baseline setting where matches were disambiguated using a relaxation technique where local consistency of matches was enforced. Schmid and Mohr [4] used what they called semi-local constraints to aid matching. Given a possible point correspondence, these constraints required that neighboring points be good correspondences as well. As Schmid and Mohrs algorithm dealt with similarity transformations, they also required that angles in the triangles formed by triplets of points be consistent across the images. Since we are dealing with affine or even projective transformations here, it is not necessarily true that angles are preserved in any way.

A more general, although heuristic apprach was taken by Belongie et al. in [10]. In their method, images were sampled sparsely along edges and for each sample point, a histogram was formed, in which each bin represented the density of sample points of the rest of the shape in a particular direction and at a particular distance from the point. Essentially, this histogram captured the appearance of the image as "seen" from every sampled point. By aligning the histogram with the direction of the image gradient, rotational invariance was achieved. Although the histogram was quite coarse, this method does not seem likely to be succesful if significant affine or projective transformations relate the images. Also, the method of Belongie et al. does not use texture in any way, which has proved to be a very good cue for matching considering the numerous references on texture based matching in the computer vision literature.

The property that each point of interest has an attached descriptor, which encodes a large portion of the image "as seen" from that point, is appealing, but a less heuristic method of enforcing topological constraints would be desirable.

So what we want is a method combining the idea of spatial relations between points of interest and local and global texture information.

2 Profile Matching

We will use the work introduced in [1] as a starting point for our algorithm. In [1], Tell and Carlsson introduce a matching method using affine invariants in which the complicated search for invariant image regions needed in [8] is avoided. The method is based on a comparison of the intensity profiles between pairs of Harris corners across the images (see fig. 1).

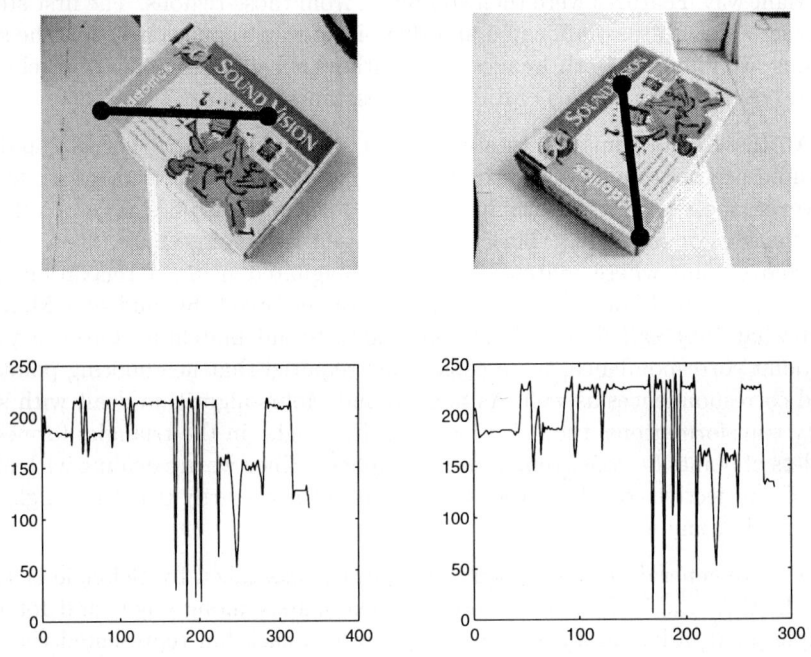

Fig. 1. The same intensity profile extracted from two different images. If the surface is planar along the profile, and if the images are related by an affine transformation, the texture of the profiles can be compared using any scale-invariant method.

The key idea is the observation that if an intensity profile lies along a planar surface, and if the viewing conditions are affine or if the images are related by an affine transformation, then corresponding intensity profiles are related by only one parameter - a scale change. This is because the profiles are related by a 1D affine transformation, which has 3 parameters. These parameters are completely specified by the known endpoints. Any scale-invariant way of comparing the texture along the profiles can be used for matching. In [1], fourier features are used, since they exhibit good information packing properties and are easy to compute. The distance between fourier feature vectors is then used to compare intensity profiles.

Since the goal of the algorithm is to find corner correspondences, and each corner can form many different intensity profiles with neighboring corners, Tell and Carlsson use a voting strategy. For each intensity profile in the first image, the second image is searched for profiles with similar feature vectors. One can either find all feature vectors within a given distance, or simply select the K closest ones. For each of these profiles, votes are cast for the correspondences of the endpoints of the profiles. The result of this process is a table $\mathbf{V}$ of votes, where the entry $\mathbf{V}(i,j)$ is the number of times corner i was associated with corner j. Fig. 2 shows a simple example where the profile in the left image matches the three profiles shown in the right image, which gives rise to a small voting table.

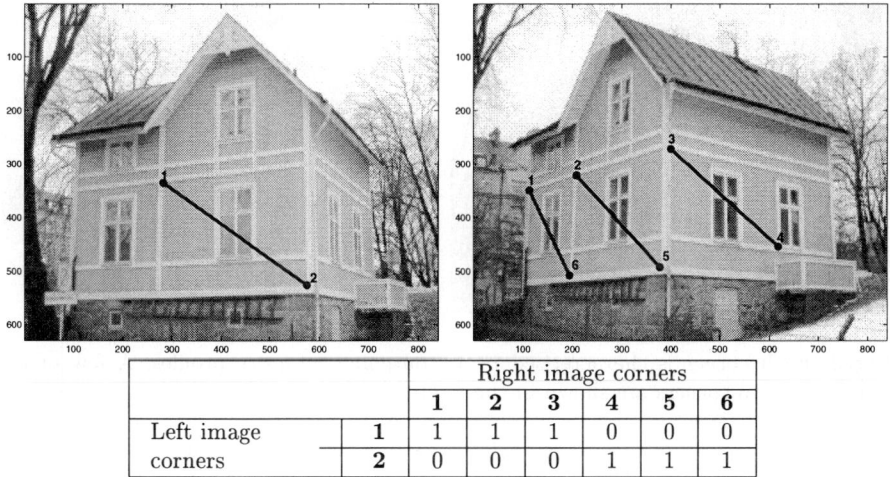

		Right image corners					
		1	2	3	4	5	6
Left image corners	1	1	1	1	0	0	0
	2	0	0	0	1	1	1

Fig. 2. Illustration of voting. The profile in the left image matches the three profiles in the right image. Hence votes are cast for the correspondences of the endpoints of the profiles. This table also illustrates the idea of voting; using only the displayed profiles, the voting table is highly ambiguous. However, if the voting procedure is performed for all profiles in the images, many ambiguities are resolved.

When the voting process is done, a set of candidate matches can be extracted from the voting table. Several methods are available for this step, for instance the greedy algorithm of iteratively selecting the largest entry and then eliminating that column and row. If one wishes to maximise the sum of the selected entries, graph matching algorithms such as maximum weight matching are applicable.

3 Drawback of the Original Method

To see why this method can be improved upon, consider one single corner in each image. These two corners are characterised by all their outgoing intensity profiles, as shown in fig. 3, where a few of the profiles around corner i in the left image and corner j in the right image are displayed. This collection of profiles serves as a signature which uniquely identifies the corner. This is basically the same idea as in the "shape contexts" of Belongie et al. [10], i.e. that every point of interest has an attached descriptor which represents the rest of the image as seen from that point.

Typically, every corner is allowed to form intensity profiles with its K closest neighboring corners. Formulated this way, it becomes clear that the voting matrix entry $V(i,j)$ for these two corners, is the number of times a profile from corner i in the left image matches a profile from corner j in the right image.

Fig. 3. Each corner is characterised by its outgoing intensity profiles. A few of the profiles for two corners are shown in the figure.

There are two problems with this measure of corner similarity. First, one of the profiles of the left image in fig. 3 may actually match several of the profiles in the right image, thereby voting for the same corner correspondence several times. This introduces a bias in the voting matrix. Second, the fact that intensity profiles should be cyclically ordered around the corners is not taken into account in any way. Again, considering fig. 3, given a subset of corresponding intensity profiles around the two corners, cyclic order should be preserved across the images. This is always true if the intensity profiles lie along planar surfaces, which is one of the basic assumptions of the method anyway.

To put this line of reasoning in a more formal context, first consider fig. 4, where the same profiles as in fig. 3 are shown with labels $\mathbf{p}_m$, $m \in (0, M)$, for the profiles around corner i in the left image, and $\mathbf{q}_n$, $n \in (0, N)$, for profiles around corner j in the right image.

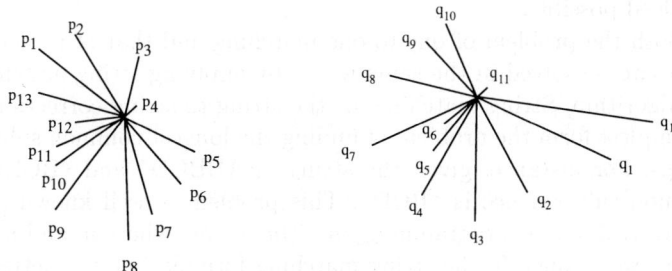

Fig. 4. The profiles extracted around corner i in the left image and corner j in the right image

Then, define a vote function v between two profiles, $\mathbf{p}_m$ and $\mathbf{q}_n$ as $v_{mn} = v(\mathbf{p}_m, \mathbf{q}_n)$. The form of the function v is defined by the voting strategy. For instance, by introducing the feature vectors of profiles as $\mathbf{p}_m^f$ and $\mathbf{q}_n^f$, and the covariance matrix $\mathbf{C}$, the following vote function could be used:

$$v(\mathbf{p}_m, \mathbf{q}_n) = \begin{cases} 1 & \text{if } \mathbf{p}_m^{f\,\top} \mathbf{C} \mathbf{q}_n^f < R^2 \\ 0 & \text{otherwise} \end{cases} \quad (1)$$

given some suitable distance threshold R. This method might give different numbers of matches depending on how "common" a particular profile is, so another possibility without this bias is the following:

$$v(\mathbf{p}_m, \mathbf{q}_n) = \begin{cases} 1 & \text{if } \mathbf{q}_n \in \{\text{the K profiles closest to } \mathbf{p}_m\} \\ 0 & \text{otherwise} \end{cases} \quad (2)$$

In this definition of the vote function, "closest to" means closest in the sense of Mahalanobis distance between feature vectors, as in eq. 1.

With these definitions, the vote matrix entry $\mathsf{V}(i,j)$ can be written as

$$\mathsf{V}(i,j) = \sum_{m=0}^{M} \sum_{n=0}^{N} v_{mn} \quad (3)$$

This equation makes it quite clear that one profile may vote several times in $\mathsf{V}(i,j)$, and that the angular order of profiles is not taken into account.

4 Suggested Solution - String Matching

It seems reasonable that the algorithm would be improved if cyclic order and one-to-one matching of intensity profiles were enforced somehow. However, since the method is already computationally quite expensive, it would be desirable to do this without increasing the time complexity too much. We believe that this is indeed possible.

Both the problem of one-to-one matching and that of preservation of cyclic order can be solved in the same way – by applying string matching methods to the algorithm. String matching, or the string to string correction problem, is in its simplest form the problem of finding the longest common subsequence of two strings. For instance, given the string "EABBCD" and "BCED", the longest common subsequence is "BCD". This problem is well known [11] and can be solved by dynamic programming in $O(mn)$ time where m and n are the lengths of the two strings. In the string matching formulation, two letters either match or don't match, but the dynamic programming algorithm can also handle the case of arbitrary similarities of letters. Each possible letter correspondence is simply assigned a weight which expresses the similarity of the letters. In this case, the algorithm still finds a one-to-one sequentially preserved solution, but now one of maximum sum weight instead of one of maximum length.

In our case, each corner is represented by a "string". These "strings" are the collection of outgoing intensity profiles from the corner. The "letters" are the individual profiles, sorted by their angle, and the weights can for instance be the normalized cross correlation between feature vectors.

A complicating property of our problem is that we don't know the starting points of the "strings". One image may well be rotated in relation to the other. The brute-force solution would be to try all possible starting points, resulting in a $O(mn^2)$ algorithm, but better solutions exist for this so-called "cyclic string-to-string correction problem". In [12], an $O(mn \log n)$ algorithm is proposed, and in [13] an $O(mn)$ algorithm is presented, but the latter one requires unit weights, which means that either letters match, or they don't. In the current implementation, the algorithm in [12] was used, since it allows arbitrary weights.

Using cyclic string matching, eq. 3 is changed to

$$\mathsf{V}(i,j) = \max_S \sum_{(m,n) \in S} v_{mn}. \tag{4}$$

The maximum in equation 4 is taken over all sequences S which are of the form $S = \{(m_1, n_1) \cdots (m_p, n_p)\}$, $p \leq \min(M, N)$, such that the following holds:

$$m_k > m_{k-1} \quad 0 \leq m_k \leq M$$
$$n_k > n_{k-1} \quad 0 \leq n_k \leq 2N$$
$$n_i \neq n_j \bmod N \quad \text{if } i \neq j.$$

The indexes n_k are used as $n_k \bmod N$ when accessing the intensity profiles. This complication is due to the fact that eq. 4 should be rotationally invariant.

This is a much more sensible measure of corner similarity than eq. 3. For instance, given the two strings "CDABBAA" and "ABCD", the original algorithm would find that the vote value is 7, whereas the one using cyclic string matching would find the correct value, which is 4. If ordinary string matching, and not cyclic string matching, was used, the result would be 2, which is not correct either, since rotational invariance is desired.

The next problem is how to apply the dynamic programming algorithm for string matching to the original matching algorithm. This is the topic of the next section. But before going into details about how the string matching methods were applied, an illustrative example might help to appreciate the results. Consider fig. 5, which shows the same row of a voting matrix both using the new approach and not using it. String matching clearly decreases the noise level in the vote matrix, and the correct match is more easily identified.

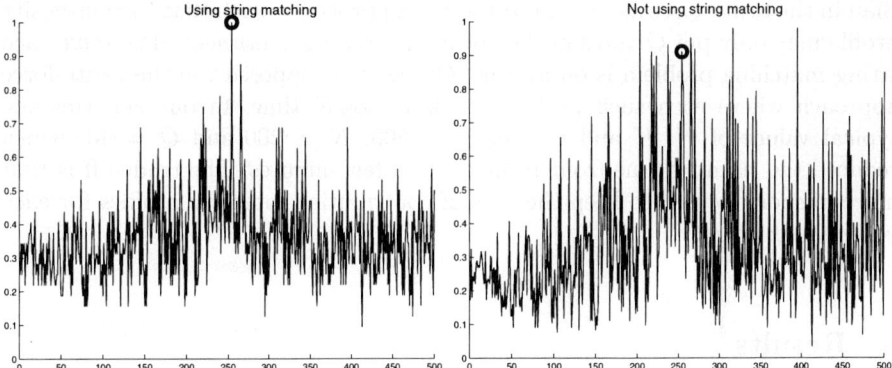

Fig. 5. Illustration of how the improved algorithm decreases noise in the votematrix. The graphs show an entire row of a voting matrix. The left image shows the results using the new approach, the right image shows the results using the original algorithm. The circles indicate the correctly matching column for the given row.

5 Applying the String Matching Algorithm

We see two possibilities of applying the string matching method. The first is the brute-force approach. Such an algorithm would consist of two steps. First, intensity profiles are extracted and features computed for each corner in order to find the "signature" (see fig. 4) of the corner. Second, the cyclic string matching problem is solved for every possible corner correspondence. Suppose that N corners are detected in each image, and that every corner will participate in K intensity profiles. Since there are N^2 possible corner correspondences, and each such candidate correspondence is evaluated using string matching with signatures of length K, the computational complexity of such an algorithm would be $O(N^2 K^2 \log K)$. If we allow a complete set of profiles to be formed, i.e. every corner may form profiles with every other corner, the time complexity becomes $O(N^4 \log N)$. Typical running times in our C++ implementation of the brute force algorithm with $N = 500$ is in the order of 10 hours on a Sun Blade 100 workstation.

Clearly, this is not practical with todays computers, so as an alternative, one might apply the string matching methods after the original algorithm. To do this, one must keep track of which intensity profiles that contributed to the voting matrix entry $V(i,j)$ (eq. 3). To do this, a list is kept for each entry in the voting matrix. Each time a vote is put in an entry, the list is appended with the identities of the two intensity profiles which gave rise to the vote.

Then for each voting matrix entry, the cyclic string matching problem is solved only for the contributing intensity profiles. With this approach, there are still N^2 string matching problems to solve, but each such problem is smaller than in the brute-force algorithm. If the voting process is such that each intensity profile may only put Q votes in the voting matrix, the time needed to solve each string matching problem is on average $Q^2 \log Q$, as opposed the the brute-force approach where each such problem took $K^2 \log K$ time. In our experiments, typical values of N, K and Q was $N = 500$, $K = 200$ and $Q = 40$, which reduced the running time from 10 hours to a few minutes. The trade-off is that more memory is used to keep the lists of contributing intensity profiles for each vote matrix entry.

6 Results

We have conducted a series of experiments designed to compare the performance of our extended algorithm using string matching to the original one. The first experiment compared the two algorithms by matching images of a piecwwise planar object using increasing differences in viewing angle. Both algorithms were run to find a candidate set of point correspondences, after which RANSAC was run to find a homography and a set of consistent matches. Fig. 6 shows the results and the number of consistent matches for the original algorithm, and fig. 7 shows the results using our string matching approach. Clearly, our method gives far more matches, and in the last image pair, where there is a very large difference in viewing angle, the original algorithm breaks down while the new approach still finds a reasonable solution.

The second experiment was made using a cylindrical object. Fig. 8(a) shows the results of the original algorithm and fig. 8(b) those of the new method. Here, the baseline can't be as wide as in the previous experiment for any of the algorithms, simply because the same part of the object can't be seen in both images if the difference in viewing angle is too large. Still, the method using string matching to enforce one-to-one matching and preservation of cyclic order of intensity profiles gives better results. It finds a solution in all three image pairs, while the original method only finds one in the first image pair.

The last experiment (fig. 6) shows a result on estimating a fundamental matrix instead of a homography. Again, the improved algorithm finds about 50% more matches. These may still contain outliers, since the epipolar constraint is quite weak, but that problem is present in both methods.

7 Conclusion

We have presented a general method of enforcing topological constraints such as one-to-one matching and cyclic order in matching algorithms. The method is based on applying cyclic string matching for every possible corner correspondence. Experiments have shown that the new method improved an existing wide baseline algorithm significantly, both by providing larger sets of correspondences, and by finding solutions in cases where the original algorithm failed completely.

However, the method is not limited to this matching algorithm. It can in principle be applied to other correspondence algorithms where interest points are used in the matching process, particularly those using the more traditional approach of computing features from small neighborhoods around corners [4] [5] [6]. Investigating this could be the topic of future work.

References

1. D. Tell and S. Carlsson. Wide baseline point matching using affine invariants computed from intensity profiles. In *ECCV*, volume 1, pages 814–828, 2000.
2. A. W. Fitzgibbon and A. Zisserman. Automatic camera recovery for closed or open image sequences. In *Proc. European Conference on Computer Vision*, pages 311–326. Springer-Verlag, June 1998.
3. D. Nistér. *Automatic dense reconstruction from uncalibrated video sequences*. KTH, 2001.
4. C. Schmid and R. Mohr. Local greyvalue invariants for image retrieval. *PAMI*, 19(5):872–877, 1997.
5. P. Montesinos, V. Gouet, and R. Deriche. Differential invariants for color images. In *ICPR*, 1998.
6. A. Baumberg. Reliable feature matching across widely separated views. In *CVPR*, pages 774–781, 2000.
7. P.H.S. Torr and C. Davidson. Impsac: Synthesis of importance sampling and random sample consensus. In *ECCV*, pages 819–833, 2000.
8. T. Tuytelaars and L. van Gool et. al. Matching of affinely invariant regions for visual servoing. In *ICRA*, pages 1601–1606, 1999.
9. Z. Zhang, R. Deriche, O. Faugeras, and Q.-T. Luong. A robust technique for matching two uncalibrated images through the recovery of the unknown epipolar geometry. *Artificial Intelligence Journal*, 78:87–119, oct 1995.
10. S. Belongie, J. Malik, and J. Puzicha. Matching shapes. In *Proc. ICCV01*, pages 454–461. IEEE, July 2001.
11. T. Cormen, C. Leiserson, and R. Rivest. *Introduction to algorithms*. MIT Press, 1992.
12. J. Gregor and M.G. Thomason. Dynamic programming alignment of sequences representing cyclic patterns. *IEEE Transactions on Pattern Analysis and Machine Intelligence (PAMI)*, 15:129–135, 1993.
13. G.M. Landau, E.W. Myers, and J.P.Schmidt. Incremental string comparison. *SIAM Journal of computing*, 27(2):557–582, 1998.

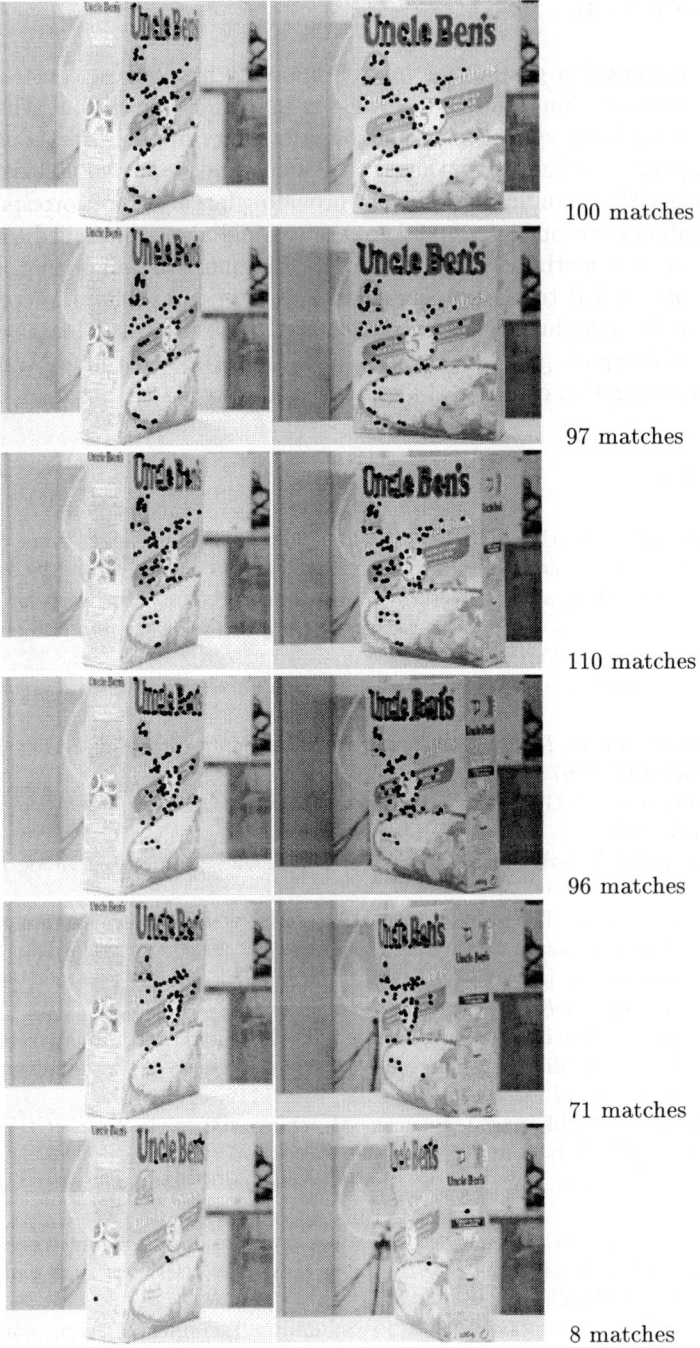

100 matches

97 matches

110 matches

96 matches

71 matches

8 matches

Fig. 6. Using the original matching method. Results on matching using increasing difference in viewing angle

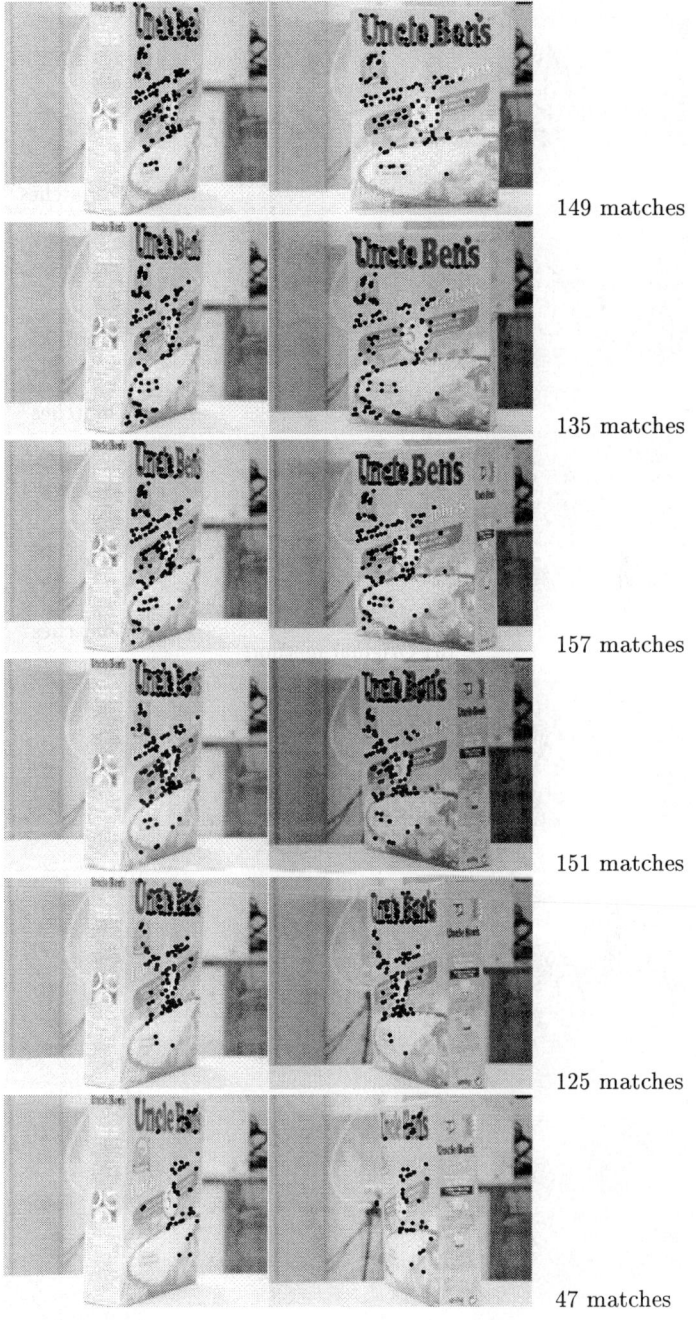

Fig. 7. Using string matching. Results on matching using increasing difference in viewing angle

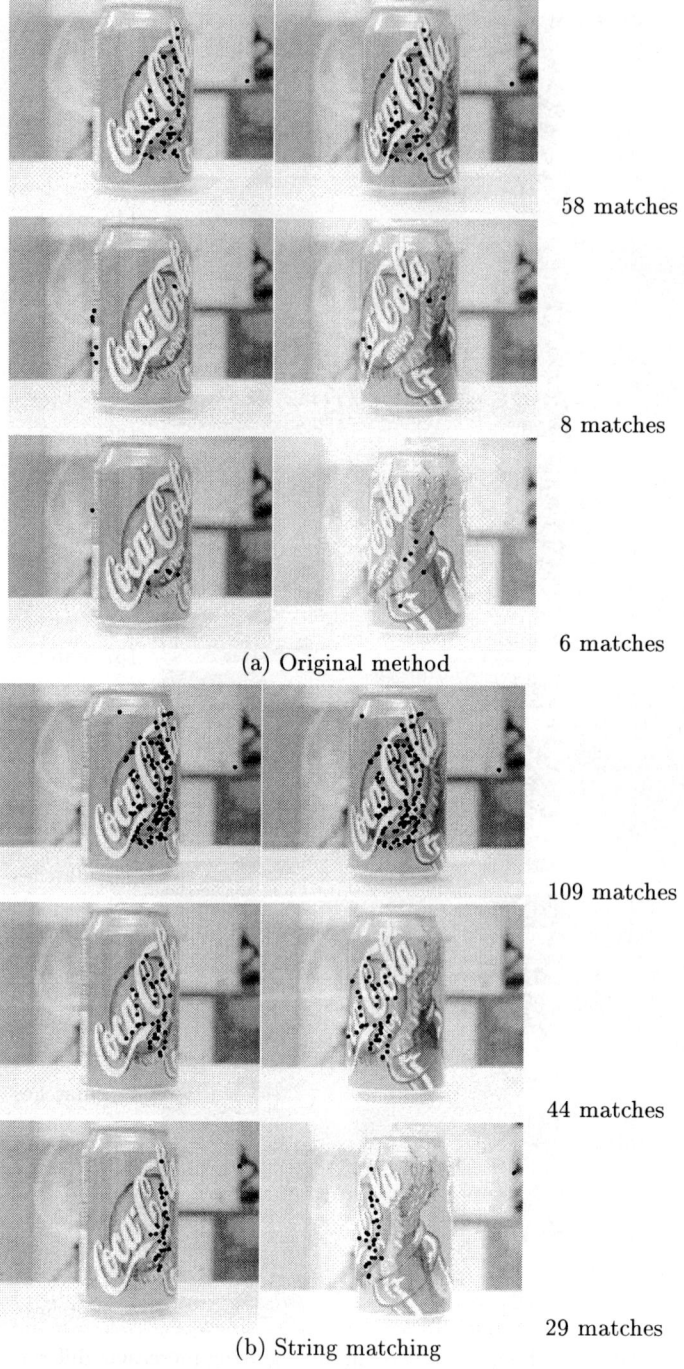

Fig. 8. Results on matching using increasing difference in viewing angle.

(a) Original method, 66 matches

(b) String matching, 105 matches

Fig. 9. Results on matching using fundamental matrix estimation in RANSAC.

Guided Sampling and Consensus for Motion Estimation

Ben Tordoff and David W Murray

Department of Engineering Science, University of Oxford
Parks Road, Oxford OX1 3PJ, UK
[bjt,dwm]@robots.ox.ac.uk

Abstract. We present techniques for improving the speed of robust motion estimation based on random sampling of image features. Starting from Torr and Zisserman's MLESAC algorithm, we address some of the problems posed from both practical and theoretical standpoints and in doing so allow the random search to be replaced by a guided search. Guidance of the search is based on readily-available information which is usually discarded, but can significantly reduce the search time. This guided-sampling algorithm is further specialised for tracking of multiple motions, for which results are presented.

1 Introduction

Since its introduction by Fischler and Bolles in 1981 [1] and later appearance in the statistical literature as Rousseeuw and Leroy's Least Median of Squares [4], random sampling and consensus (RANSAC) has been widely used in computer-vision — particularly in the areas of recovering epipolar geometry and 3D motion estimation [5, 7–10].

In [7], Torr and Zisserman describe a method of maximum likelihood estimation by sampling consensus (MLESAC). It follows the random sampling paradigm of its RANSAC ancestor, in that a minimal set of matches is used to estimate the scene motion and then support is sought in the remaining matches. However, whereas RANSAC just counts the number of matches which support the current hypothesis, MLESAC evaluates the likelihood of the hypothesis, representing the error distribution as a mixture model.

In this paper we seek ways to make iterative random sampling more suitable for use in applications where speed is of importance, by replacing random sampling with guided sampling based on other knowledge from the images.

We begin with a detailed review of the MLESAC algorithm, and in section 3 make observations on its performance. In section 4 we describe a scheme for resolving one issue in MLESAC's formulation and using this result guide the random sampling to reduce the search time. The possibility of incorporating multiple match-hypotheses is entertained in section 5, and section 6 shows that the search time is further reduced in the multiple motion case when information is propagated over time. Results and discussions appear in the sections to which they relate.

2 Maximum Likelihood Estimation by Sampling Consensus

As the basis for the remainder of this paper we will now describe Torr and Zisserman's MLESAC algorithm in detail. It is assumed that the feature detection and matching stages have given rise to a set of matches where each feature is only matched once, but some and possibly many, of the matches may be in error.

As mentioned earlier, MLESAC evaluates the likelihood of the hypothesis, representing the error distribution as a mixture model. Several assumptions are made, the veracity of which are discussed in section 3:

1. The probabilities of matches being valid are independent of one-another.
2. If a match is a mismatch, the error observed is uniformly distributed.
3. If a match is valid it will be predicted by the correct motion estimate up to Gaussian noise related to the noise in feature position estimates.
4. Every match has the same *prior* probability of being a mismatch.

A minimal set of matches h is chosen to estimate a motion hypothesis M_h, for which all matches $i = 1 \ldots n$ are either valid, v_i, or invalid, $\bar{v}_i$. The probability that M_h is a correct estimate of the true motion is denoted $\mathrm{p}(M_h)$. All n features are transferred between images using this motion and the differences between the estimated and actual match positions give rise to residual errors r_i, and hence to an overall error R_h. These errors may be calculated in just the second image, or more usually in both images (see [2], sec. 3.2). The aim is to sample randomly the space of possible motions and choose the hypothesised motion M_h that has maximum posterior probability given the data available, $\mathrm{p}(M_h|R_h)$. This cannot be measured directly and Bayes' rule is used:

$$M_{\mathrm{MAP}} = \max_h \left[\mathrm{p}(M_h|R_h)\right] = \max_h \left[\mathrm{p}(R_h|M_h)\frac{\mathrm{p}(M_h)}{\mathrm{p}(R_h)}\right]$$

where $\mathrm{p}(R_h|M_h)$ is the likelihood that it is correct and $\mathrm{p}(M_h)$, $\mathrm{p}(R_h)$ the prior probabilities of the motion and residuals respectively. If these terms can be measured then the maximum a posteriori (MAP) motion can be estimated.

The prior $\mathrm{p}(R_h)$ is constant irrespective of the choice of M_h, and nothing is known about the prior probability that the motion is correct, $\mathrm{p}(M_h)$. This means that the MAP estimate cannot be found and the new aim is to maximise the likelihood and hope that the motion with maximum likelihood (ML) estimate is similar to the maximum posterior (MAP) estimate. The new aim is to find

$$M_{\mathrm{MLESAC}} = \max_h \left[\mathrm{p}(R_h|M_h)\right]$$

2.1 Evaluating the Likelihood

To convert the likelihood into a usable form it is necessary to use assumption (1), that the probability of each residual is independent

$$\mathrm{p}(R_h|M_h) = \prod_i^n \mathrm{p}(r_i|M_h) \ .$$

Evaluation of the probability of each residual has two parts, according to whether it is a valid match or not. Assumption (2) states that if the feature is mismatched the probability of the residual is uniform, but will be related to the size of the search area w

$$\mathrm{p}(r_i|\bar{v}_i, M_h) = 1/w \ .$$

For a valid match the residual is due only to zero-mean Gaussian noise of deviation σ (related to the feature detector localisation error), and under assumption (3) the conditional probability is

$$p(r_i|v_i, M_h) = \frac{1}{\sigma\sqrt{2\pi}} e^{-\frac{r_i^2}{2\sigma^2}} .$$

The prior probabilities that match i is valid $p(v_i)$ or invalid $p(\bar{v}_i)$ are by definition mutually exclusive ($p(v_i, \bar{v}_i)=0$) and exhaustive ($p(v_i)+p(\bar{v}_i)=1$) so that the combined probability of observing the residuals given the hypothesised motion is given by the sum rule

$$p(r_i|M_h) = \left(\frac{1}{\sigma\sqrt{2\pi}} e^{-\frac{r_i^2}{2\sigma^2}}\right) p(v_i) + \left(\frac{1}{w}\right)(1 - p(v_i)) . \quad (1)$$

Assumption (4) states that $p(v_i)$ is constant across all matches and all hypothesised motions, that is $p(v_i) = p(v)$, the prior estimate of the proportion of valid matches. This controls the relative importance of the valid and invalid probability distributions, examples of which are shown in figure 1. Note the Gaussian curve when the residuals are small and the non-zero tails, giving a cost function which does not over-penalise extreme outliers. This shape is characteristic of the related robust method of M-estimation [3].

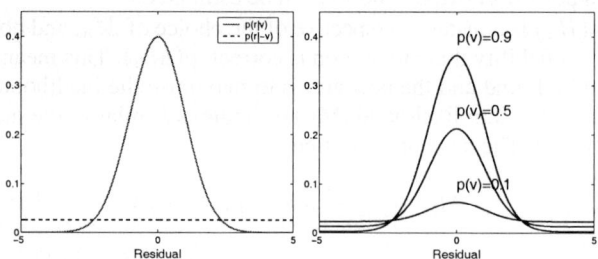

Fig. 1. (Left) the Gaussian and uniform distributions modelling valid and invalid residuals respectively. (Right) three examples of the combined distribution for different values of $p(v)$. Note the long tails which reduce the penalty for large residuals.

However, even assuming $p(v)$ to be the same for all features, it still must be estimated somehow. Torr and Zisserman approach this problem by using an iterative maximisation scheme to estimate $p(v)$ directly from each motion hypothesis and set of residuals. The goal is to find the $p(v)$ that maximises $p(R_h|M_h)$ for the current hypothesis M_h. As $p(R_h|M_h)$ varies smoothly with $p(v)$, any suitable ascent method can be used to find the maximum. However, in this approach each hypothesis M_h will generate its own estimate of $p(v)$, meaning that the comparison between likelihoods is based on different mixtures. We will return to this point in section 3.1.

We now have all the information required to calculate and compare the likelihood of each hypothesis. In practice for numerical stability the log likelihood is optimised:

$$M_{\text{MLESAC}} = \max_h \left[\sum_i^n \log \left\{ \left(\frac{1}{\sigma\sqrt{2\pi}} e^{-\frac{r_i^2}{2\sigma^2}} \right) p(v) + \left(\frac{1}{w} \right) (1 - p(v)) \right\} \right] \quad (2)$$

2.2 Knowing When to Stop Sampling

As in RANSAC [1] and Least Median of Squares [4], if the sampling and evaluation steps are repeated over a large number of samples it is hoped that at least one hypothesised motion will be close to the true motion. If the proportion of valid data is $p(v)$, and the minimum number of features required to form a hypothesis is m, then the probability, $p(M_c)$, that a correct hypothesis has been encountered after I iterations is approximately

$$p(M_c) \approx 1 - [1 - p(v)^m]^I \quad . \quad (3)$$

Although $p(v)$ is not generally known in advance, a lower bound can be estimated from the largest $p(v)$ observed in the mixture estimation step. A stopping condition is usually determined from a desired confidence level (eg. $p(M_c) > 95\%$).

2.3 Example Results

Figure 2 shows some results from running MLESAC on an image pair containing a moving object, a toy locomotive. The motion is pure-translation and, as the object exhibits little thickness, a planar homography can be used to model the transformation. Thus, four point matches between the two views are used for each MLESAC sample (shown in black) and the residual error for all other matches used to score the motion hypothesis. Matches which are inlying to the hypothesis are shown in white. Note that the better motion hypotheses give residual distributions which are highly peaked at low residual error but with a significant tail. The second peak observed in the final sample is due to the second motion present in the data-set — the stationary background.

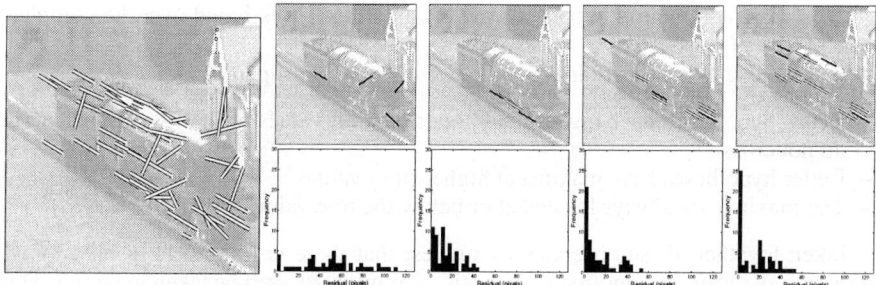

Fig. 2. The starting match-set for the train images (left) and several of the samples that MLE-SAC selects, along with the distribution of resulting residuals. The samples are arranged with increasing likelihood from left to right.

2.4 Summary of the Basic Algorithm

Robust computation of a single motion using MLESAC involves the following steps

1. For many trials do:
   (a) Choose a minimum number of matches and estimate a motion hypothesis M_h.
   (b) Calculate the residual error r_i for all matches when transformed by the hypothesised motion.
   (c) Estimate p(v) for a particular p(M_h) by maximising the sum-log-likelihood.
   (d) Retain the M_h which has the highest likelihood.
2. Use the estimated motion and list of valid matches as the starting point for a more accurate motion calculation, if required.

3 MLESAC Revisited

Having described the rationale underlying MLESAC and having demonstrated it in action, we now return to some specific points which merit closer examination.

3.1 Estimating the Mixture Parameter

In [7], Torr and Zisserman assume that the probability of a match being valid, p(v_i), is the same for all matches. Further, this constant value p(v) is re-estimated for each hypothesised motion. There are two deficiencies here:

1. All matches are not equal. Information which is usually freely available indicates that some matches are more likely to be valid than others (ie. we can refine the prior).
2. The prior probability that a match is valid does not depend on the hypothesised motion — it is a *prior* constant. Allowing it to vary makes the comparison of the likelihoods of the different motion hypotheses unfair.

However, as MLESAC works, and works well, these deficiencies appear to have little effect on the determination of which motion hypotheses are better. To reach an understanding of this, a large number of trials were conducted on a variety of imagery where the log-likelihood score (equation 2) was evaluated for a range of motion hypotheses. For each motion hypothesis the log-likelihood was found over the complete range of $0 \leq p(v) \leq 1$.

Typical results are shown in figure 3. The interesting properties are

- Better hypotheses have higher likelihoods over all values of p(v) — ie. the curves do not cross.
- Better hypotheses have maxima at higher p(v) values.
- The maxima are always located at or below the true value of p(v).

Taken together, these observations suggest that there is little to be gained by re-estimating p(v) for each motion hypothesis — it might as well be taken to be 0.5. This saves a small amount of computation time and overcomes the first of the objections that were raised above as the estimate is now constant across all hypotheses. Even if a more accurate estimate of p(v) is desired, the estimate from the best hypothesis seen so far should be used, rather than an estimate from the current hypothesis.

Note from figure 3 that poor motion hypotheses give curves with maximum p(v) at, or close to, zero, making all matches appear as outliers.

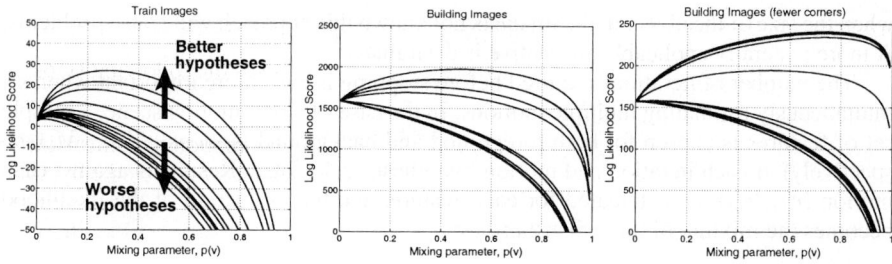

Fig. 3. The effect of varying the mixing parameter on the likelihood score of several motion hypotheses for three different sets of matching features.

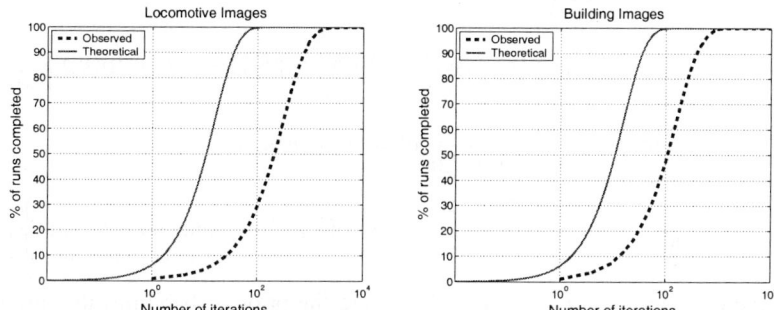

Fig. 4. MLESAC is run on the images 5000 times and the first iteration at which more than 75% of inliers is found recorded for each run. The proportion of runs that complete at or before a given iteration are shown.

3.2 Stopping Criterion

It is widely appreciated that the approximate stopping criterion (eqn. 3) specified for both RANSAC [6] and MLESAC [7] is often wildly optimistic. With about 50% valid data, equation (3) suggests that a confidence of 99% would require about 70 samples, but on the train images of the previous section the first reasonable solution was not seen until several hundred samples and the best solution at around 9500 samples.

To demonstrate, the MLESAC algorithm was repeatedly run on the locomotive images, stopping when a good solution was found, a "good" solution taken as one where at least 75% of the possible inliers are found. Figure 4 shows the number of iterations and the proportion of 5000 runs that had found a solution at or before this time for two sequences. In both cases the actual number of iterations required to observe a good motion hypothesis is significantly larger than predicted. The theoretical form of the stopping curve matches that observed from the data, but with around an order of magnitude shift.

The reason for this difference is that with noisy data it is not enough to have a sample composed only of inliers, they must be inliers that span the object so that the remaining matches are compared to an interpolated rather than an extrapolated motion. This significantly reduces the number of sample sets that will accurately hypothesise the motion. In cases where the motion is uniform over the image (eg. due to camera motion) a quick fix is to force the random sampling to pick points widely spaced, but when the size of the object in the image is not known this approach will cause problems. A more generally applicable alternative is desirable.

The number of iterations required before stopping is even more important when simultaneously estimating multiple motions. In the case of a two-motion scene, a sample set of features is chosen for both foreground and background motions (M_{fh}, M_{bh} respectively) at each iteration and motion hypotheses calculated. Residuals against each motion (r_{fi}, r_{bi}) are calculated for each feature, and the evaluation of the likelihood becomes the mixture of three distributions:

$$M_{\text{MLESAC}} = \max_h \left[p(R_h | M_{fh}, M_{bh}) \right]$$

$$= \max_h \prod_i^n \left\{ p(r_i | M_{fh}, f_i, v_i) p(f_i | v_i) p(v_i) \right.$$

$$\left. + p(r_i | M_{bh}, b_i, v_i) p(b_i | v_i) p(v_i) + p(r_i | \bar{v}_i) p(\bar{v}_i) \right\}$$

$$= \max_h \left[\sum_i^n \log \left\{ \frac{1}{\sigma\sqrt{2\pi}} e^{-\frac{r_{fi}^2}{2\sigma^2}} p(f_i | v_i) p(v_i) \right.\right.$$

$$\left.\left. + \frac{1}{\sigma\sqrt{2\pi}} e^{-\frac{r_{bi}^2}{2\sigma^2}} p(b_i | v_i) p(v_i) + \frac{1}{w}(1 - p(v_i)) \right\} \right] \quad (4)$$

where the extra terms $p(f_i|v_i)$ and $p(b_i|v_i)$ are the prior probabilities that the match belongs to the foreground or background respectively, given that it isn't a mismatch. Usually $p(f_i|v_i)$ and $p(b_i|v_i)$ are mutually exclusive and exhaustive so that $p(b_i|v_i) = 1 - p(f_i|v_i)$, and as $p(v_i)$, $p(\bar{v}_i)$ are also exclusive and exhaustive the parameters v_i, f_i and b_i are integrated out. As with the mixture parameter $p(v)$ in the single motion case, the background/foreground priors $p(b_i|v_i), p(f_i|v_i)$ could be assumed uniform over all features and estimated using expectation-maximisation at each MLESAC iteration. However this has the same deficiencies as in section 3.1 and it would be preferable to find a weighting for each feature that is constant across MLESAC trials. Such a weighting is discussed in section 6.

A conservative estimate of the number of iterations I that are required to find a good pair of hypothesised motions increases dramatically over the single motion case:

$$p(M_{fc}, M_{bc}) \approx 1 - \left[1 - p(f|v)^{m_f} p(b|v)^{m_b} p(v)^{(m_f + m_b)} \right]^I.$$

Consider an example with equal numbers of foreground and background features mapped by homographies between two images ($m_f = m_b = 4$), of which 25% are mismatched (ie. 37.5% are valid for each motion). The correct method of estimating both foreground and background simultaneously requires around 7660 iterations for 95% confidence and nearly 12000 for 99%.

An alternative is to estimate the motions individually. 37.5% of the data is valid for the first motion, requiring 150 iterations for 95% confidence or 230 for 99%. The second motion is estimated from the remaining matches (of which 60% is now valid) in 22 iterations for 95% confidence or 34 for 99%. These are clearly huge computational savings. However, evalutating the motions individually makes the assumption that the outliers to the first motion form a uniform distribution — visibly not the case in figure 2. In some cases it may be desirable to make this assumption and sacrifice accuracy for speed.

4 Guided Sampling

In the previous sections we have raised a couple of issues with the assumptions underlying MLESAC. We also noted that the number of iterations required for a good solution may be far higher than expected. To improve MLESAC we seek improved estimates of the following:

- $p(v_i)$, the prior probability that a feature is valid.
- $p(f_i|v_i)$, $p(b_i|v_i)$, the prior probabilities that a valid feature belongs to the foreground or background motions.

Although the discussion that follows is explicitly concerned with point features, similar arguments can be applied to estimation based on other feature types.

4.1 Using the Match Score

An obvious source of information on the validity of a feature-match is the match score. For point features, a common measure is the zero-normalised cross-correlation between image patches around the points in the two images being compared. The score is used to select the best consistent set of matches over all possible combinations.

Figures 5(a-c) show the distribution of correlation score; for both mismatches and valid matches determined over a range of image sequences whose pixel composition is quite different. The correct match distributions are always largely the same, and, provided there is little repeated texture within the search window, so too are the mismatch distributions. Normalising these histograms gives an approximation to the probability density of observing a particular match score s_{ik} given the validity of the putative match, $p(s_{ik}|v_{ik})$ and $p(s_{ik}|\bar{v}_{ik})$ (each feature i has several possible matches k).

Over the course of a tracking sequence, or when a camera repeatedly captures similar sequences (such as for a surveillance camera) then statistics for correct and incorrect matches can be built up online. However, where these distributions are unknown, we can approximate the distributions under the assumption of little repeated texture using simple functions. The mismatch distribution will be taken as quadratic

$$p(s_{ik}|\bar{v}_{ik}) \approx \frac{3}{4}(1 - s_{ik})^2 \qquad -1 \leq s_{ik} \leq 1$$

and for correct matches

$$p(s_{ik}|v_{ik}) \approx a\frac{(1 - s_{ik})}{\alpha^2} \exp -\left[\frac{1 - s_{ik}}{\alpha}\right]^2 \qquad -1 \leq s_{ik} \leq 1 \qquad (5)$$

where α is a "compactness" parameter and a is a normalisation constant such that the area under the curve is unity, as in figure 5(d). These expressions are chosen for their close fit to empirical data and their simplicity. Arguing from underlying image statistics might suggest more meaningful and accurate expressions. (For the image sequences used here, $\alpha = 0.15$ and $a = 1.0$ give a reasonable fit, although the final probabilities turn out not to be particularly sensitive to small variations in α.)

If a feature i has n_m potential matches with validity v_{ik} ($k = 1 \ldots n_m$), of which one is correct, then reasonable priors are $p(v_{ik}) = 1/n_m$ and $p(\bar{v}_{ik}) = (n_m - 1)/n_m$.

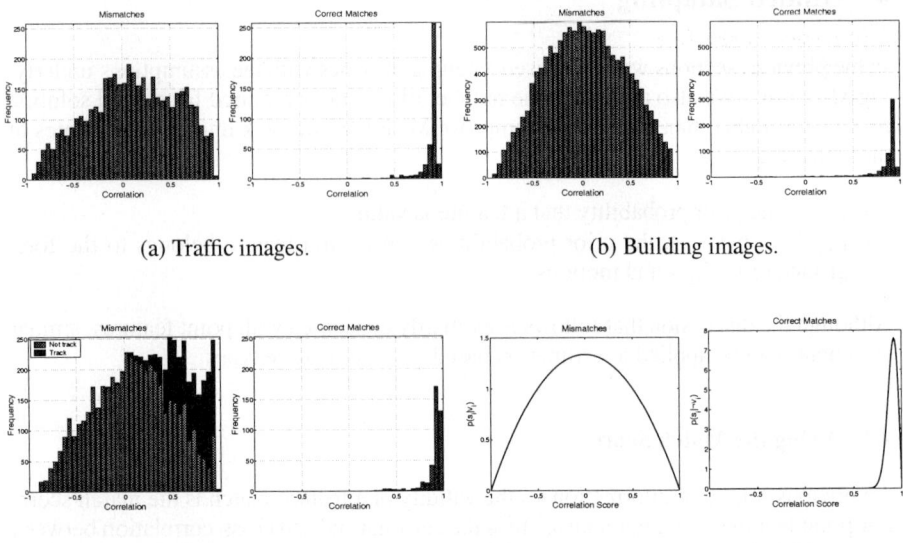

(a) Traffic images.

(b) Building images.

(c) Locomotive images (repeated structure mainly due to the track is shown in black).

(d) Approximations to the histogram shapes.

Fig. 5. Frequency of matches and mismatches against correlation score over all potential matches.

The probability of putative match k being correct when its match score is taken into account, but without considering the scores of the other matches is

$$p(v_{ik}|s_{ik}) = p(s_{ik}|v_{ik})\frac{p(v_{ik})}{p(s_{ik})} = p(s_{ik}|v_{ik})\frac{p(v_{ik})}{p(s_{ik}|v_{ik})p(v_{ik}) + p(s_{ik}|\bar{v}_{ik})p(\bar{v}_{ik})}$$

$$\approx p(s_{ik}|v_{ik})\frac{1}{p(s_{ik}|v_{ik}) + p(s_{ik}|\bar{v}_{ik})(n_m - 1)} . \quad (6)$$

It is also desirable to consider that all the putative matches might be wrong, in which case the feature matches an extra null feature. A simple way to represent this is to increase by one the number of putative matches in equation 6.

Furthermore we can also include the additional knowledge that only one putative match per feature is correct (if any are). We calculate the probability that a putative match k is valid given the scores of all the putative matches

$$p(v_{ik}|s_{i,1...n_m}) = \frac{p(v_{ik}|s_{ik})\prod_{j\neq k}^{n_m} p(\bar{v}_{ij}|s_{ij})}{\sum_l^{n_m}\left[p(v_{il}|s_{il})\prod_{j\neq l}^{n_m} p(\bar{v}_{ij}|s_{ij})\right] + \prod_j^{n_m} p(\bar{v}_{ij}|s_{ij})}$$

where the numerator gives the probability that this putative match is correct and all the others are wrong, and the denominator normalises by the sum of all possible match probabilities plus the possibility that none is correct. This makes the additional assumption that the probabilities $p(v_{ij}|s_{ij})$ are conditionally independent. Whichever of these putative matches is selected by the matching algorithm to be the single correct match, $p(v_{ik}|s_{i,1...n_m})$ can be used as $p(v_i)$ in equation 1 instead of using a constant $p(v)$.

Consider an example feature from the locomotive images. There are ten putative matches, and using $\alpha = 0.15$ and $a = 1$ in equation 5 the correlation scores map to probabilities as shown in figure 6.

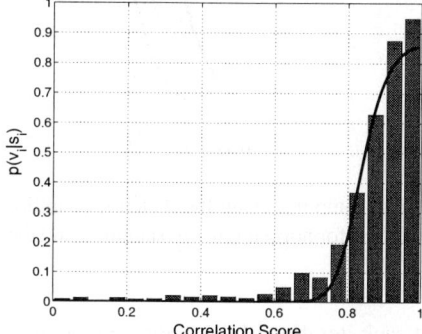

s_{ik}	$p(v_{ik}|s_{ik})$	$p(v_{ik}|s_{i,1\ldots n_m})$
-0.34	0.000	0.000
0.21	0.000	0.000
0.43	0.000	0.000
0.57	0.002	0.000
0.60	0.006	0.000
0.62	0.012	0.001
0.68	0.069	0.007
0.72	0.174	0.020
0.91	0.812	0.408
0.93	0.832	0.468

Fig. 6. Converting match scores into probabilities. Left: The observed histogram and approximation to it (from fig. 5) are transformed by equation 6 with $n_m = 10$. Right: The ten putative matches, their individual and combined probabilities of being valid.

4.2 Using $p(v_i)$ for Guided Sampling

We now have an estimate of the probability that a match is valid based on its match score and the scores of the other putative matches with which it competed. Whilst useful as a replacement for gradient descent estimation of an overall mixing parameter, we can also use it to guide the search — if we have evidence that one match is more likely to be valid than others, then it should be selected more often.

Each feature i has a single match selected using an optimal matcher which also delivers $p(v_i)$ for the selected match. The matches are sampled for use in the minimal motion computation set using a Monte-Carlo method according to $p(v_i)$. The increased cost of guiding the selection is marginal when compared to the other computations performed at each MLESAC iteration.

Figure 7 shows the "time to solution" test of section 3.2 repeated with guided sampling and the individual mixing parameters. This indicates that the computational cost of converting the correlation scores into validity likelihoods and performing weighted selection is easily offset by a dramatic reduction in the number of iterations required for a given confidence level. In real-time systems where the number of iterations may be fixed by time constraints, the confidence level is significantly increased — for instance in the building images 100 iterations gives 47% confidence for random sampling, but 99% when the sampling is guided by the match score.

5 Multiple Match-Hypotheses versus Rematching

Another possible change to the algorithm is that instead of choosing only the best putative match for use in the MLESAC algorithm, we include multiple matches for each feature, weighted in importance by their probabilities. This requires two small increases

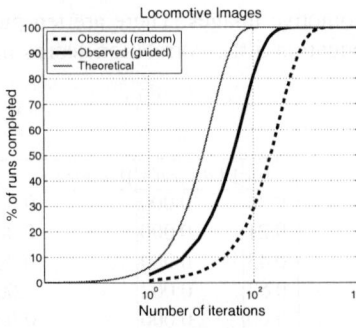 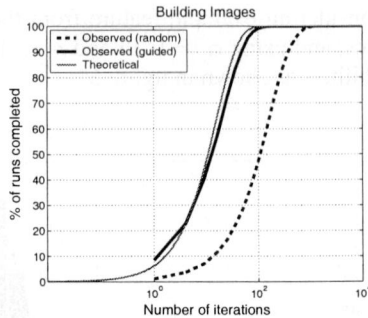

Fig. 7. The test of figure 4 is repeated with guided sampling using the match probability as in section 4.2. The dotted lines show the time-to-solution for normal random sampling and the thick solid line for guided.

in the amount of computation performed at each iteration of the algorithm, but makes a computational saving in that a global optimisation of the initial match set is not necessary.

At each MLESAC iteration when a match is selected to be part of the basis set all other putative matches for the matched features must then be removed from the list. The motions are calculated from minimal sets as before, but when evaluating the support for the motion hypothesis each putative match for each feature is tested, and the most likely one selected. In this way, even if the true match does not have the highest prior, it will still eventually be found in the MLESAC algorithm.

Using this technique, the total number of inliers that can be found by the algorithm increases by 25% for the locomotive images, and 7% for the building images. The increase depends on how well the prior $p(v_i)$ reflects the correctness of the matches — if $p(v_i)$ were a perfect indicator there would be no gain.

Whilst this method can significantly increase the number of matches that MLESAC finds, it also increases the sampling space from which seed matches are drawn — the average number of potential matches per feature was 1.4 for the locomotive images and 1.9 for the building, nearly doubling the sample space in the latter case. Furthermore, the extra matches that are included contain a large proportion of erroneous matches — we gain a little extra "signal" at the expense of a lot of extra "noise". Figure 8 shows the effect on the time-to-solution test for the locomotive and building images when all match hypotheses for ambiguous matches are included (ie. we have reduced the number of samples by only including multiple hypotheses when two or more matches score similarly).

We contrast this with the approach described in much of the sampling consensus literature, that of rematching. As before only one match-hypothesis is found per feature, but once MLESAC has been used and estimates of the motion(s) have been found, the likelihoods of all putative matches for all features are evaluated using these motions. For each feature, the putative match with highest likelihoods is kept in a manner similar to the initial match optimisation based on correlation score. Using this technique the time to solution remains as for the single hypothesis case, but again the total number of matches found increases. The totals observed are typically within one or two matches of the totals achieved by the multiple-hypothesis MLESAC, and there is little to choose between them on that basis.

The computational cost of rematching is one evaluation of the likelihood for every putative match. If there are an average of two putative matches per feature, then this is roughly equivalent to two iterations of MLESAC. The cost of the initial match optimisation is similarly between one and two iterations of MLESAC. When these costs are compared to the increased time-to-solution of the multiple-hypothesis approach, rematching is clearly faster in almost all cases. As each iteration of MLESAC is also slower in the multiple-hypothesis case, when speed is the goal rematching is preferable.

There are two cases where using the multiple-hypothesis approach proves advantageous. The first is in offline processing when computation time is irrelevant. The second is when the number of true matches that get mismatched is exceedingly high and if alternative matches are not included the correct motion may not be found. Although correlation matching is inadequate in many respects, enough correct matches were produced in all the sequences tested for multiple-hypothesis MLESAC to perform no better than rematching.

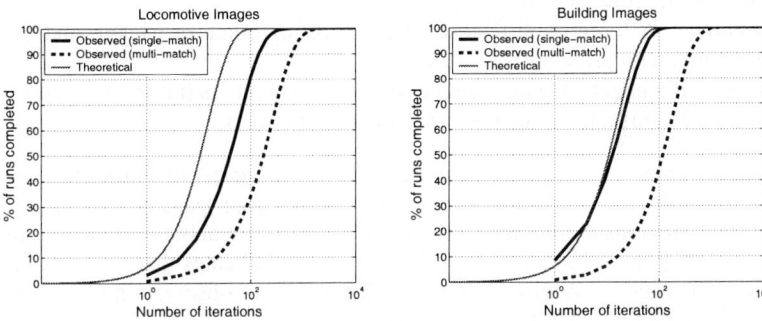

Fig. 8. Time-to-solution for guided sampling with and without multiple match-hypotheses. Including multiple match-hypotheses increases the number of inliers found, but at great computational cost.

6 Temporal Propagation of Information

Temporal consistency is a strong cue in the assignment of features to motion hypotheses — if a feature obeys the foreground motion in one frame it is likely to do so in the next. The output of MLESAC can be tailored to this purpose.

Following a successful run of guided MLESAC, we have maximum-likelihood estimates of the motions M_f, M_b, based on the overall residuals R and match scores S. As a by-product we have also evaluated the posterior probability that each match belongs to either motion, or is invalid. ie. although MLESAC is a maximum likelihood estimator of the motions, it is a maximum a posteriori estimator of the segmentation.

Without extra calculation we already have maximum likelihood estimates of the motion and the maximum a posteriori probability of each feature residual,

$$\max_h \{p(R_h|M_{hf}, S),\ p(R_h|M_{hb}, S),\ p(r_i|M_{hf}, M_{hb}, s_i)\}\ .$$

An extra rearrangement provides a posteriori estimates of the foreground-background-mismatch segmentation (see equation 4):

$$p(f_i, v_i | M_f, r_i, s_i) = p(r_i | M_f, f_i, v_i, s_i) \frac{p(f_i | v_i, s_i) p(v_i | s_i)}{p(r_i | M_f, M_b, s_i)}$$

$$p(b_i, v_i | M_b, r_i, s_i) = p(r_i | M_b, b_i, v_i, s_i) \frac{p(b_i | v_i, s_i) p(v_i | s_i)}{p(r_i | M_f, M_b, s_i)}$$

$$p(\bar{v}_i | M_f, M_b, r_i, s_i) = p(r_i | \bar{v}_i, s_i) \frac{p(\bar{v}_i | s_i)}{p(r_i | M_f, M_b, s_i)}$$

where all the probabilities shown are natural products of guided MLESAC and the score $s_{i,1...n_m}$ has been abbreviated s_i. To make use of this information in subsequent frames it is necessary to allow the following possibilities:

- **Propagation.** A foreground feature stays foreground, or background stays background, with probability β.
- **Cross-over.** A foreground feature becomes background, or background becomes foreground, with probability $1 - \beta$.
- **Absence.** If a matched feature did not exist in the previous frame, or was previously designated a mismatch it provides no prior information.

These relationships are summarised in the information graph of figure 9(a), where β measures the temporal efficacy of the information being propagated. Setting $\beta = 0.5$ indicates that previous assignments provide no information about current assignments, and $\beta = 1.0$ that the information is perfect. $\beta < 0.5$ indicates that previous information is in contradiction. Whilst β should be learned from observation of the extended sequence, here we fix it at 0.9 for experimentation.

At input to the first frame of a sequence we assume that features are equally likely to be background or foreground, from which point guided MLESAC increases or decreases these probabilities at each frame. (An alternative is that some heuristic initialisation might be used, such as weighting the foreground probability higher for features close to the centre of the view.) The evolution of the probabilities for a feature from the locomotive sequence is shown in figure 9(b).

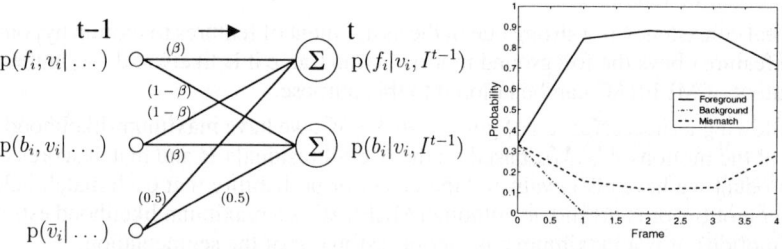

(a) β indicates the temporal efficacy of the data, and I^{t-1} the "previous frame's information".

(b) The evolution of the probabilities for one feature from the locomotive sequence.

Fig. 9. Propagating the assignment of a feature to a motion.

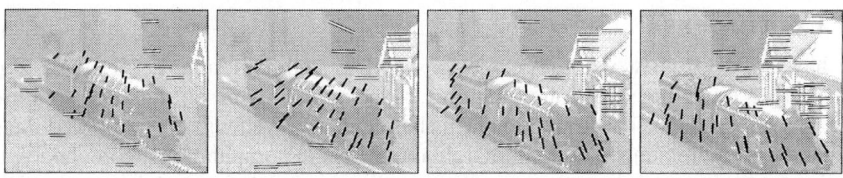

Fig. 10. Part of the locomotive sequence where both the locomotive and camera motions are approximated by planar homographies. Propagating the assignment of features to motions increases speed and ensures that the two motions are not exchanged.

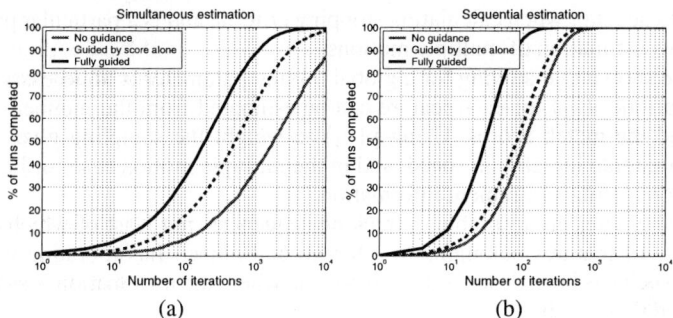

Fig. 11. An example of the improvement in speed when propagation is included. (a) simultaneous estimation of the multiple motions and (b) separate estimation of foreground then background. These tests were performed on the second frame from figure 10.

As with the improved prior on $p(v_i)$ (section 4.1), these improved estimates of $p(f_i|v_i)$ and $p(b_i|v_i)$ can be used to weight the selection of seed matches for the foreground and background motions. However, the speed advantage this brings is harder to quantify, depending entirely on the success of the segmentation in the previous frame.

6.1 Final Results: Multiple Motion Guided MLESAC

Figure 10 shows the first few frames from a sequence with motions tracked using guided MLESAC with assignment propagation. Both foreground and background motions are approximated by planar homographies, and feature matches are initialised with equal probability of belonging to either motion. Although simultaneous estimation of the two motions is the correct segmentation method, the results shown are for separately finding foreground then background motions using just 75 and 50 iterations respectively. Propagating the feature assignments helps to prevent the foreground and background motions interchanging during the sequence.

To get an idea of how much difference propagating the assignments makes to the speed, figure 11 shows the time-to-solution test performed on the second frame of the sequence. The test is repeated with no guidance, guided by match score, and guided by both the match score and previous assignment (as before, completion requires each of the two motions to find at least 75% of the maximum possible number of inliers). For simultaneous estimation of the motions (figure 11a), around 10000 iterations are needed for 90% confidence without guidance, compared to 1000 iterations when guided by score and previous data. When estimating the two motions sequentially (figure 11b), 90% confidence requires only 75 iterations when guided (this is the total for the two estimations, with around two-thirds of the iterations needed by the first estimation).

7 Conclusions

We have introduced two simple extensions to Torr and Zisserman's MLESAC algorithm which guide the selection of features, reducing the number of iterations required for a given confidence in the solution. This has been achieved without additional image or feature measurements, and with marginal increase in computational complexity. Including multiple match-hypotheses in the sampling is straightforward, but rarely yields benefits over a final re-evaluation of matches.

Through extensive experimentation it is clear that in sampling and consensus methods, the number of iterations required to find a "good" motion estimate is far higher than the number of iterations to find a sample which consists of only valid data. This *must* be taken into account when calculating stopping criteria, and is a particular problem for simultaneous estimation of multiple motions.

We have shown that solving for a global mixing parameter is unnecessary, and that individual priors $p(v_i)$ for each feature can be estimated from the number of possible matches and the match scores. Using $p(v_i)$ to weight the sampling gives around an order of magnitude increase in speed, and in the multiple motion case further gains are made by propagating assignment information.

Many other cues are available in tracking sequences, not least of which is the spatial grouping of features belonging to a foreground object. Incorporating these into a framework such has been described is simple and where the information is strong would further speed the search.

Acknowledgements

This work is supported by Grant GR/L58668 from the UK's Engineering and Physical Science Research Council, and BJT is supported by an EPSRC Research Studentship.

References

1. M.A. Fischler and R.C. Bolles. Random sample concensus: A paradigm for model fitting with applications to image analysis and automated cartography. *Comm. ACM*, 24(6):381–395, 1981.
2. R. Hartley and A. Zisserman. *Multiple View Geometry, 1st edition*. Cambridge University Press, 2000.
3. P.J. Huber. *Robust statistics*. John Wiley and Sons, 1985.
4. P.J. Rousseeuw and A.M. Leroy. *Robust regression and outlier detection*. Wiley, New York, 1987.
5. L. Shapiro. *Affine analysis of image sequences*. Cambridge University Press, Cambridge, UK, 1995.
6. P. H. S. Torr and A. Zisserman. Robust detection of degenerate configurations while estimating the fundamental matrix. *Computer Vision and Image Understanding*, 71(3):312–333, 1998.
7. P. H. S. Torr and A. Zisserman. MLESAC: A new robust estimator with application to estimating image geometry. *Computer Vision and Image Understanding*, 78:138–156, 2000.
8. P.H.S. Torr and D.W. Murray. Statistical detection of independent movement from a moving camera. *Image and Vision Computing*, 11(4):180–187, 1993.
9. P.H.S. Torr and D.W. Murray. The development and comparison of robust methods for estimating the fundamental matrix. *Int. Journal of Computer Vision*, 24(3):271–300, September 1997.
10. G. Xu and Z. Zhang. *Epipolar geometry in stereo, motion and object recognition*. Kluwer Academic Publishers, 1996.

Image Features / Visual Motion

Fast Anisotropic Gauss Filtering

Jan-Mark Geusebroek*, Arnold W. M. Smeulders, and Joost van de Weijer

Intelligent Sensory Information Systems, Department of Computer Science,
University of Amsterdam, Kruislaan 403, 1098 SJ Amsterdam, The Netherlands;
geusebroek@science.uva.nl

Abstract. We derive the decomposition of the anisotropic Gaussian in a one dimensional Gauss filter in the x-direction followed by a one dimensional filter in a non-orthogonal direction φ. So also the anisotropic Gaussian can be decomposed by dimension. This appears to be extremely efficient from a computing perspective. An implementation scheme for normal convolution and for recursive filtering is proposed. Also directed derivative filters are demonstrated.

For the recursive implementation, filtering an 512×512 image is performed within 65 msec, independent of the standard deviations and orientation of the filter. Accuracy of the filters is still reasonable when compared to truncation error or recursive approximation error.

The anisotropic Gaussian filtering method allows fast calculation of edge and ridge maps, with high spatial and angular accuracy. For tracking applications, the normal anisotropic convolution scheme is more advantageous, with applications in the detection of dashed lines in engineering drawings. The recursive implementation is more attractive in feature detection applications, for instance in affine invariant edge and ridge detection in computer vision. The proposed computational filtering method enables the practical applicability of orientation scale-space analysis.

1 Introduction

One of the most fundamental tasks in computer vision is the detection of edges and lines in images. The detection of these directional structures is often based on the local differential structure of the image. Canny's edge detector examines the magnitude of the first order image derivatives [3]. A well-founded approach for line detection is given by [16,20], where line structures are detected by examining the eigenvectors of the Hessian matrix, the Hessian being given by the local second order derivatives. Robust measurement of image derivatives is obtained by convolution with Gaussian derivative filters, a well known result from scale-space theory [6,13,15,21].

The difficulty of edge and line detection is emphasized when the structures run close together or cross each other, as is the case in engineering drawings or two-dimensional projections of complex (3D) scenes. In these cases, isotropic filtering strategies as used in e.g. [2,3,8,12,20] are not sufficient. Isotropic smoothing causes parallel lines to be blurred into one single line. Crossing lines are not

---

* This work was supported by the ICES Multimedia Information Analysis Project

well detected by isotropic filters [17], due to the marginal orientation selectivity of the Gaussian filter.

The task of edge and line detection is considered not trivial when disturbing influences have to be ignored, like shadows and shading, gaps in dashed lines, object borders locally blending together, partly occlusion of the object, or clutter in the background. In these cases, one would often like to have a detection method which ignores the distorting data aside the edge or line, while accumulating evidence of the edge or line data along its orientation. Hence, taking advantage of the anisotropic nature of lines and edges [1,10].

The use of isotropic Gaussians is for historical reasons, imposed by simplicity of derivation and efficiency in computation [13]. The assumption of isotropy for front-end vision [6,13,15,21] does not imply the scale-space operator to be isotropic, rather imposes the complete sampling of all possible orientations of the scene. The notion of orientation sampling suggest a combined scale and orientation space [12,14,22]. For a linear orientation scale-space, the anisotropic Gaussian is the best suited causal filter. We propose a method for fast filtering by anisotropic Gaussian's to construct an orientation scale-space.

Orientation analysis is often approached by steerable filters. Freeman and Adelson [7] put forward the conditions under which a filter can be tuned to a specific orientation by making a linear combination of basis filters. Their analysis included orientation tuning of the xy-separable first order isotropic Gaussian derivative filter. According to their framework, no exact basis exists for rotating an anisotropic Gaussian. Van Ginkel *et al.* proposed a deconvolution scheme for improving the angular resolution of the Gaussian isotropic filter. Under a linearity assumption on the input image, a steerable filter with good angular resolution is obtained. The method involves a Fourier based deconvolution technique, which is of high computational complexity. Perona [17] derived a scheme for generating a finite basis which approximates an anisotropic Gaussian. The scheme allowed both steering and scaling of the anisotropic Gaussian. However, the number of basis filters is large, and the basis filters are non-separable, requiring high computational performance.

We show the anisotropic Gaussian filter to be separable along two directions, not necessarily orthogonal. One of the axes is in a fixed, but in a freely selectable direction. The latter axis depends on the filter parameters $(\sigma_u, \sigma_v, \theta)$, the standard deviations and orientation, respectively. We show the resulting one-dimensional filters to be Gaussian filters. Hence, fast algorithms [4,5,23,24] can be used to calculate the orientation smoothed image and its derivatives. Van Vliet and Young propose [23,24] a recursive implementation of one-dimensional Gaussian filters. This is a great advantage over [5], as combining the one-dimensional filters into two-dimensional Gaussians will not introduce bias along the filter directions. The recursive filters need only 7 multiplications and 6 additions per pixel, independent of the standard deviation σ of the Gaussian filter. Moreover, the filter coefficients are simple to calculate.

In this paper, we show the decomposition of the anisotropic Gaussian in two Gaussian line filters in non orthogonal directions (Sect. 2). Choosing the

x-axis to decompose the filter along turns out to be extremely efficient from a computing perspective. We combine the decomposition with the recursive algorithms proposed in [23,24], yielding a constant calculation time with respect to the Gaussian scales and orientation (Sect. 3). We give timing results and compare accuracy with two-dimensional convolution in Sect. 4. Implementation of Gaussian derivative filters is given in Sect. 5.

2 Separation of Anisotropic Gaussian

A simple case of the isotropic Gaussian convolution filter in two dimensions is given by

$$g_\circ(x,y;\sigma) = \frac{1}{2\pi\sigma^2}\exp\left\{-\frac{1}{2}\left(\frac{x^2+y^2}{\sigma^2}\right)\right\} . \tag{1}$$

Anisotropy is obtained when scaling differently in the x- and y-direction. Then, an elliptic Gaussian with axes aligned along the coordinate system (see Fig. 1a) is given by

$$g_\perp(x,y;\sigma_x,\sigma_y) = \frac{1}{2\pi\sigma_x\sigma_y}\exp\left\{-\frac{1}{2}\left(\frac{x^2}{\sigma_x^2}+\frac{y^2}{\sigma_y^2}\right)\right\} . \tag{2}$$

Rotation of the coordinate system (x,y) over θ,

$$\begin{pmatrix} u \\ v \end{pmatrix} = \begin{bmatrix} \cos\theta & \sin\theta \\ -\sin\theta & \cos\theta \end{bmatrix}\begin{pmatrix} x \\ y \end{pmatrix} \tag{3}$$

results in the general case of oriented anisotropic Gaussian (Fig. 1b),

$$g_\theta(x,y;\sigma_u,\sigma_v,\theta) =$$
$$\frac{1}{2\pi\sigma_u\sigma_v}\exp\left\{-\frac{1}{2}\left(\frac{(x\cos\theta+y\sin\theta)^2}{\sigma_u^2}+\frac{(-x\sin\theta+y\cos\theta)^2}{\sigma_v^2}\right)\right\} \tag{4}$$

the u-axis being in the direction of θ, and the v-axis being orthogonal to θ.

From standard Fourier theory we have the convolution theorem,

$$f(x,y) * h(x,y) \;\overset{\mathcal{F}}{\Leftrightarrow}\; F(\omega_x,\omega_y)H(\omega_x,\omega_y) . \tag{5}$$

A linear filter is separable into two subsequent convolutions iff its Fourier transform can be written as a multiplication of two functions, one depending on ω_x, the other depending on ω_y,

$$h(x,y) = h_x(x) * h_y(y) \;\overset{\mathcal{F}}{\Leftrightarrow}\; H(\omega_x,\omega_y) = H_{\omega_x}(\omega_x)H_{\omega_y}(\omega_y) . \tag{6}$$

The Fourier transform of $g_\theta(.)$ (Eq. (4)) is given by

$$G_\theta(\omega_x,\omega_y;\sigma_u,\sigma_v,\theta) =$$
$$\exp\left\{-\frac{1}{2}\left((\omega_x\cos\theta+\omega_y\sin\theta)^2\sigma_u^2+(-\omega_x\sin\theta+\omega_y\cos\theta)^2\sigma_v^2\right)\right\} . \tag{7}$$

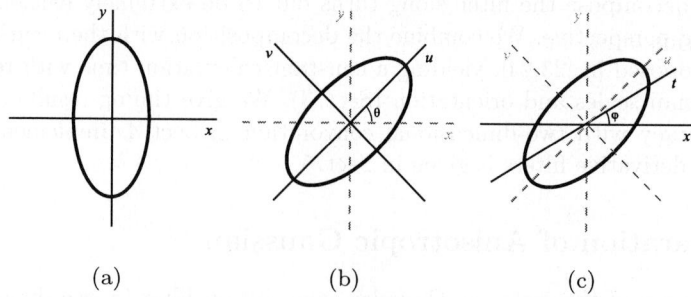

Fig. 1. Ellipse and its axes systems. An example of an anisotropic Gaussian with aspect ratio 1:2 and orientation $\theta = \frac{\pi}{4}$. **a.** Cartesian xy-aligned Gaussian. **b.** Principal axes uv-aligned Gaussian. **c.** uv-aligned Gaussian in a non-orthogonal xt-axes system. Axis t is rotated over $\varphi \approx \frac{\pi}{6}$ with respect to the x-axis.

The exponential is separable into two products if its argument is separable into sums ($e^{a+b} = e^a e^b$). From Eq. (7) it is easy to derive that the anisotropic Gaussian may be separated along the major axes u and v with (u, v) given by Eq. (3),

$$G_\theta(\omega_x, \omega_y; \sigma_u, \sigma_v, \theta) = \exp\left\{-\frac{1}{2}\left(\omega_u^2 \sigma_u^2 + \omega_v^2 \sigma_v^2\right)\right\} \ . \tag{8}$$

As we are interested in a convenient basis from a computational perspective, separation in u and v is uninteresting. What is needed is the decomposition into a filter in the x-direction and a filter along another direction. Therefore, we consider

$$(\omega_x \cos\theta + \omega_y \sin\theta)^2 \sigma_u^2 + (-\omega_x \sin\theta + \omega_y \cos\theta)^2 \sigma_v^2 \tag{9}$$

as the quadratic form in ω_x and ω_y,

$$a_{11}\omega_x^2 + 2a_{12}\omega_x\omega_y + a_{22}\omega_y^2 \tag{10}$$

where the coefficients are given by

$$\begin{aligned} a_{11} &= \sigma_u^2 \cos^2\theta + \sigma_v^2 \sin^2\theta \\ a_{12} &= \left(\sigma_u^2 - \sigma_v^2\right)\cos\theta\sin\theta \\ a_{22} &= \sigma_v^2 \cos^2\theta + \sigma_u^2 \sin^2\theta \ . \end{aligned} \tag{11}$$

We aim at separating the anisotropic Gaussian filter into a filter in the x-direction, followed by a filter along a line $t : y = x \tan\varphi$,

$$f(x,y) * h(x,y) = f(x,y) * h_x(x) * h_\varphi(t) \overset{\mathcal{F}}{\Leftrightarrow}$$
$$F(\omega_x, \omega_y) H(\omega_x, \omega_y) = F(\omega_x, \omega_y) H_x(\omega_x) H_\varphi(\omega_\varphi) \tag{12}$$

To achieve our goal, we collect in Eq. (10) all terms dependent on ω_y and separate out all terms independent of ω_y. Hence, Eq. (10) may be rewritten as

$$\left(a_{11} - \frac{a_{12}^2}{a_{22}}\right)\omega_x^2 + a_{22}\left(\omega_y + \frac{a_{12}}{a_{22}}\omega_x\right)^2. \tag{13}$$

Substitution in Eq. (7) yields

$$G_\theta(\omega_x, \omega_y; \sigma_u, \sigma_v, \theta) =$$

$$\exp\left\{-\frac{1}{2}\left(\left(a_{11} - \frac{a_{12}^2}{a_{22}}\right)\omega_x^2 + a_{22}\left(\omega_y + \frac{a_{12}}{a_{22}}\omega_x\right)^2\right)\right\}. \tag{14}$$

Separation of the exponential sum results in

$$G_\theta(\omega_x, \omega_y; \sigma_u, \sigma_v, \theta) =$$

$$\exp\left\{-\frac{1}{2}\left(a_{11} - \frac{a_{12}^2}{a_{22}}\right)\omega_x^2\right\}\exp\left\{-\frac{1}{2}a_{22}\left(\omega_y + \frac{a_{12}}{a_{22}}\omega_x\right)^2\right\}. \tag{15}$$

Back transformation to the spatial domain gives the separated anisotropic Gaussian filter,

$$g_\theta(x, y; \sigma_u, \sigma_v, \theta) = \frac{1}{2\pi\sigma_u\sigma_v} \tag{16}$$

$$\exp\left\{-\frac{1}{2}\frac{x^2}{a_{11} - \frac{a_{12}^2}{a_{22}}}\right\} * \exp\left\{-\frac{1}{2}\frac{\left(y + \frac{a_{12}}{a_{22}}x\right)^2}{a_{22}}\right\}. \tag{17}$$

The first factor represents a one-dimensional Gaussian in the x-direction at scale σ_x,

$$g_x(x; \sigma_x) = \frac{1}{\sqrt{2\pi}\sigma_x}\exp\left\{-\frac{1}{2}\frac{x^2}{\sigma_x^2}\right\} \tag{18}$$

where

$$\sigma_x = \sqrt{a_{11} - \frac{a_{12}^2}{a_{22}}}. \tag{19}$$

The second factor represents a one-dimensional Gaussian along the line $t: y = x\tan\varphi$,

$$g_\varphi(r; \sigma_\varphi) = \frac{1}{\sqrt{2\pi}\sigma_\varphi}\exp\left\{-\frac{1}{2}\frac{r^2}{\sigma_\varphi^2}\right\} \tag{20}$$

where $r = \sqrt{x^2 + y^2}$ is the distance from the origin, and with direction tangent

$$\tan \varphi = \frac{a_{12}}{a_{22}}$$

and standard deviation

$$\sigma_\varphi = \sqrt{a_{22}} \ . \tag{21}$$

Note that $\sqrt{2\pi\sigma_x}\sqrt{2\pi\sigma_\varphi} = 2\pi\sigma_u\sigma_v$, yielding the correct normalization (Eq. (16)). Rewriting Eq. (16) and substituting the quadratic coefficients Eq. (11) results in

$$g_\theta(x, y; \sigma_u, \sigma_v, \theta) = g_x(x; \sigma_x) * g_\varphi(\sqrt{x^2 + y^2}; \sigma_\varphi) \tag{22}$$

where

$$\tan \varphi = \frac{(\sigma_u^2 - \sigma_v^2) \cos \theta \sin \theta}{\sigma_v^2 \cos^2 \theta + \sigma_u^2 \sin^2 \theta} ,$$

$$\sigma_x = \frac{\sigma_u \sigma_v}{\sqrt{\sigma_v^2 \cos^2 \theta + \sigma_u^2 \sin^2 \theta}} ,$$

$$\sigma_\varphi = \sqrt{\sigma_v^2 \cos^2 \theta + \sigma_u^2 \sin^2 \theta} \ . \tag{23}$$

So we have achieved our goal namely that a Gauss filter at arbitrary orientation is decomposed into a one dimensional Gauss filter with standard deviation σ_x and another one dimensional Gauss filter at orientation φ and standard deviation σ_φ. For the anisotropic case $\sigma_u = \sigma_v = \sigma$, it is verified easily that $\sigma_x = \sigma$, $\sigma_\varphi = \sigma$, and $\tan \varphi = 0$. Further, for $\theta = 0$, trivially $\sigma_x = \sigma_u$, $\sigma_\varphi = \sigma_v$, and $\tan \varphi = 0$, and for $\theta = \frac{\pi}{2}$, $\sigma_x = \sigma_v$, $\sigma_\varphi = \sigma_u$, and $\tan \varphi = 0$.

An arbitrary example orientation of $\theta = \frac{\pi}{4}$ and $\sigma_v = \sigma, \sigma_u = 2\sigma$, results in $\sigma_x = \frac{4}{5}\sqrt{5}\sigma$, $\sigma_\varphi = \frac{1}{2}\sqrt{5}\sigma$, and $\tan \varphi = \frac{3}{5}$ ($\varphi \approx \frac{\pi}{6}$), see Fig. 1c.

3 Implementation

Implementation of Eq. (22) boils down to first applying a one dimensional Gaussian convolution in the x-direction. The resulting image is then convolved with a one-dimensional Gaussian in the φ-direction yielding the anisotropic smoothed image. The latter step implies interpolation, which can be achieved by linear interpolation between two neighboring x-pixels on the crossing between the image x-line of interest and the t-axis (see Fig. 1c). In this section, we consider two implementations of the anisotropic Gaussian, based on a common convolution operation, and based on a recursive filter [23], respectively.

Convolution Filter

Due to the filter symmetry, the x-filter Eq. (18) can be applied by adding pixel i left from the filter center with pixel i right from the filter center, and multiplying the summed pixels with filter weight i, or

$$g_x[x,y] = w_0 f[x,y] + \sum_{i=1}^{\lfloor N/2 \rfloor} w_i \left(f[x-i,y] + f[x+i,y] \right) . \quad (24)$$

Here, $f[x,y]$ is the input image, w_i is the filter kernel for half the sampled Gaussian from 0 to $\lfloor N/2 \rfloor$, and $g_x[x,y]$ is the filtered result image.

Filtering along the line $t : y = \mu x$, where $\mu = \tan \varphi$, is achieved by a sheared filter,

$$g_\theta[x,y] = w_0 g_x[x,y] + \sum_{i=1}^{\lfloor M/2 \rfloor} w_i \left(g_x[x-\mu i, y-i] + g_x[x+\mu i, y+i] \right) . \quad (25)$$

Notice that the $y \pm i$ coordinate falls exactly on a line, whereas the $x \pm \mu i$ coordinate may fall between two pixels. Hence, the value of the source pixel may be obtained by interpolating between the pixels at the line of interest. To achieve our goal of fast anisotropic filtering, we consider linear interpolation between the neighboring pixels at $x \pm \mu i$ with interpolation coefficient a. The filter equation then becomes

$$g_\theta[x,y] = w_0 g_x[x,y] + \sum_{i=1}^{\lfloor M/2 \rfloor} w_i \{ a \left(g_x[\lfloor x-\mu i \rfloor, y-i] + g_x[\lfloor x+\mu i \rfloor, y+i] \right)$$
$$+ (1-a) \left(g_x[\lfloor x-\mu i \rfloor - 1, y-i] + g_x[\lfloor x+\mu i \rfloor + 1, y+i] \right) \} . \quad (26)$$

The multiplication of $w_i a$ and $w_i (1-a)$ can be taken out of the loop to reduce the computational complexity of the filter.

Recursive Filter

Rather than applying convolution operators, Eq. (22) may be implemented by recursive filters. Van Vliet et al. [23,24] define a scheme for one-dimensional Gaussian filtering with infinite support. The recursive filter requires only 7 multiplications per pixel, an improvement over [5]. The complexity is independent of the Gaussian standard deviation σ. In [24] it is shown that the recursive filter is faster than its normal counterpart for $\sigma > 1$. When using the recursive filter, filtering along the x-line is given by the forward and backward filter pair,

$$g_x^f[x,y] = a_0 f[x,y] - a_1 g_x^f[x-1,y] - a_2 g_x^f[x-2,y] - a_3 g_x^f[x-3,y]$$
$$g_x^b[x,y] = a_0 y_x^f[x,y] - a_1 g_x^b[x+1,y] - a_2 g_x^b[x+2,y] - a_3 g_x^b[x+3,y] . \quad (27)$$

Here, a_i represent the filter coefficients as given by [23,24], and $g_x^b[x,y]$ is the x-filtered result image. The computational complexity of the recursive filter is 7 multiplications per pixel.

Filtering along the line $t : y = \mu x$, $\mu = \tan\varphi$, is achieved by a sheared recursive filter,

$$g_\theta^f[x,y] = g_\theta^f[t] = a_0 g_x^b[x+\mu y, y] - a_1 g_\theta^f[t-1] - a_2 g_\theta^f[t-2] - a_3 g_\theta^f[t-3]$$
$$g_\theta[x,y] = g_\theta^b[t] = a_0 g_\theta^f[x+\mu y, y] - a_1 g_\theta^b[t-1] - a_2 g_\theta^b[t-2] - a_3 g_\theta^b[t-3] \ . \tag{28}$$

Note that (x,y) are constraint to lie on the line t, hence may point to positions "between" pixels. Since interpolation of the recursive filter values is not possible, the filter history $g_\theta^f[t]$ and $g_\theta^b[t]$ has to be buffered, such that all t values are at the buffer "grid". The input values, $f[x,y]$ for the forward filter and $g_\theta^f[x,y]$ for the backward filter, are interpolated from the input data. The results $g_\theta^f[x,y]$ and $g_\theta[x,y]$ are interpolated to the output pixel grid by combining with the previous result. Since all pixels are at the exact line position, interpolation can be performed linearly between the current value and the previous value.

Computational complexity of the proposed implementations and a few common methods for Gaussian convolution is shown in Tab. 3. From the table it is expected that in the case of arbitrary θ, the xt-separated filter performs faster than the uv-separated filter with identical outcome.

Table 1. Complexity per pixel of various algorithms for Gaussian smoothing. Filter size is denoted by $N \times M$, depending on the Gaussian standard deviation σ.

Filter type	Separability	Complexity	
		Multiplications	Additions
convolution	xy^1	$\lfloor N/2 \rfloor + \lfloor M/2 \rfloor + 2$	$N + M - 2$
	uv^2	$2(N+M-1)$	$2(N+M-2)$
	xt^2	$\lfloor N/2 \rfloor + M + 1$	$N + 2M - 3$
recursive	xy^1	14	6
	uv^2	44	36
	xt^2	21	16
2D convolution	n.a.	NM	$NM - 1$
FFT convolution[3]	n.a.	$\log WH$	$\log WH$

[1] Restricted to Gaussian filters oriented along the x- and y-axis only, thus $\theta = 0°$ or $\theta = 90°$.
[2] Unrestricted θ.
[3] The complexity of a FFT based convolution depends on the image size $W \times H$. Note that the FFT based convolution was not fully optimized.

4 Results

Performance of the filter with respect to computation speed is shown in Tab. 4. The analysis was carried out on a normal PC (Intel Pentium III at 550 MHz) on a 512×512 image. The maximum calculation time for the proposed xt-separable recursive implementation was 65 msec. Small variations in the computation time for the xt-separable recursive implementation is due to the varying direction of the t-axis as function of σ_u, σ_v. The variation causes the processing of different pixels with respect to the filter origin, hence are influenced by the processor cache performance. The use of recursive filters is already beneficial for $\sigma_u > 1$ or $\sigma_v > 1$. The xt-separable recursive implementation is 1.5 times slower than isotropic recursive filtering (44 msec, xy-separable implementation), but takes only 0.5 times the computational load of an uv-separable anisotropic filter. The computation time for the xt-separable filter is only 1.5 times slower than xy-aligned recursive filtering (44 msec), in which case orientation selection is only horizontal or vertical. The results correspond to the predictions in Tab. 3. For the xt-separable convolution filter, calculation is approximately 1.6 times slower than xy-aligned filtering (data not shown), and 1.3 up to 2 times faster than uv-separable filtering. Normal convolution filtering is advantageous when considering locally steered filtering, as in tracking applications, for example Fig. 2. The recursive filtering is, given its computation speed, more attractive when smoothing or differentiating the whole image array, as in feature detection, see Fig. 3. Note that in this case 108 filters were applied to the image, each filter having different parameter values. The result shown represents the per pixel maximum response over all 108 filters. Calculation time was within 10 seconds.

Table 2. Performance of various anisotropic Gaussian filter implementations. All timings in [msec], averaged over 100 trials. Image size 512×512 pixels. Filter direction $\theta = 45°$.

σ_u	σ_v	2D convolution[1]	FFT convolution	1D convolution[1] uv[3]	xt	1D recursive[2] uv[3]	xt
1.0	1.0	515	1402	100	67	128	63
1.5	1.0	516	1402	114	81	128	63
2.0	1.0	828	1402	129	100	128	63
3.0	1.0	1610	1402	166	109	128	64
5.0	1.0	4282	1402	238	140	128	65
7.0	2.0	8047	1402	341	181	128	65
7.0	4.0	10203	1402	410	205	128	63
10.0	3.0	16594	1402	483	231	128	65
10.0	5.0	18000	1402	553	256	128	64
10.0	7.0	21125	1402	622	294	128	63

[1] Filter sizes truncated at 3σ.
[2] Approximation to Gauss, see Tab. 4.
[3] Implemented by scanning along the u and the v line, respectively, and by applying bilinear interpolation between pixels.

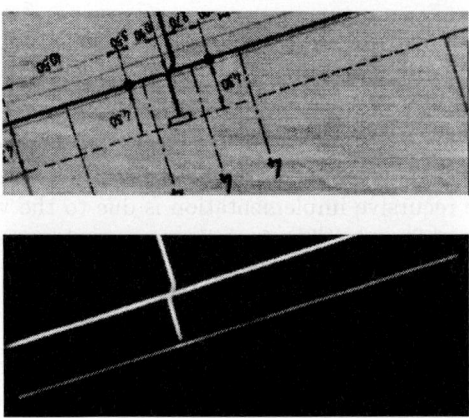

Fig. 2. Example of line detection by local anisotropic Gaussian filtering. Lines are tracked by steering the filter in the line direction. Hence, line evidence will be integrated by the large Gaussian standard deviation along the line, while maintaining spatial acuity perpendicular to the line. Original from an engineering drawing, courtesy of PNEM, The Netherlands.

The approximation of the two-dimensional Gaussian kernel of Eq. (4) by separable filters is not perfect due to interpolation of source values along the line $t = y + \tan\varphi \; x$. We evaluated the error for the xt-separable convolution filter in comparison to the full two-dimensional spatial convolution. The results are given in Tab. 4. Interpolation can be considered as a smoothing step with a small rectangular kernel. Hence, the effective filter is slightly larger than the theoretical size of the anisotropic Gaussian filter. As a result, the error is large for small σ_u, σ_v, as can be concluded from the table. For the convolution filters and $\sigma_u, \sigma_v \geq 3$, the interpolation error is of the same magnitude as the truncation error for a 3σ sized filter (last 4 rows in the table). The interpolation error is smaller for the xt-filter than for the uv-filter. For the latter, bilinear interpolation have to be performed, corresponding to a larger interpolation filter than the linear interpolation for the xt-separable filter. For the recursive filter, the interpolation error of the forward filter accumulates in the backward filter, causing a larger error. Especially the small filters are less accurate, as pointed out in [23,24]. Note that the error due to interpolation is neglectable compared to the error made by the recursive approximation of the Gaussian filter. For the uv-separated recursive filter, the bilinear interpolation caused the error accumulation to have such a drastic effect that the result was far from Gaussian (data not shown). In conclusion, accuracy for the xt-separated convolution filter is better than bilinear interpolation combined with uv-separated filtering. For recursive filtering, error is larger due to the recursive approximation of the Gauss

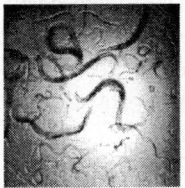
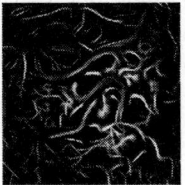

Fig. 3. Example of the detection of *C. Elegans* worms by applying recursive anisotropic Gauss filters. The original image is filtered at different orientations and scales, and the maximum response per pixel over all filters is accumulated. At each pixel, the local orientation and best fitting ellipse is available to be further processed for worm segmentation. Computation time was within 10 seconds for 5° angular resolution and 3 different aspect ratios (image size 512 × 512 pixels). Original courtesy of Janssen Pharmaceuticals, Beerse, Belgium.

filter. For numerous applications the computation speed is of more importance than the precision of the result.

Table 3. Accuracy of various anisotropic Gaussian filter implementations. The maximum error over all filter orientations is shown. Error measured as root of the sum squared differences with the true Gaussian kernel.

σ_u	σ_v	convolution uv	convolution xt	recursive xt
1.0	1.0	0	0	0.0196
1.5	1.0	0.0195	0.0132	0.0608
2.0	1.0	0.0160	0.0131	0.0536
3.0	1.0	0.0126	0.0114	0.0324
5.0	2.0	0.0018	0.0017	0.0062
7.0	2.0	0.0015	0.0014	0.0050
7.0	4.0	0.0003	0.0003	0.0012
10.0	3.0	0.0005	0.0004	0.0017
10.0	5.0	0.0001	0.0001	0.0008
10.0	7.0	0.0001	0.0001	0.0007

5 Derivative Filters

For the uv-separable filtering approach, as for the full two-dimensional convolution, Gaussian derivative filtering can be achieved by taking the derivatives of the kernel function. For the proposed xt-separable approach, kernel differentiation is not applicable due to the misalignment of the filter directions (x,t) with respect to the direction of derivation (u,v) (see Fig. 1c). Like in [23], sample differences may be used as approximations to the true image derivatives. Hence, filtering with a rotated version of the derivative kernel results in the image derivatives in the u, v direction, where the rotation kernel is given by Eq. (3).

The first order derivatives transform after rotation by

$$\begin{pmatrix} du \\ dv \end{pmatrix} = \begin{bmatrix} \cos\theta & \sin\theta \\ -\sin\theta & \cos\theta \end{bmatrix} \begin{pmatrix} dx \\ dy \end{pmatrix}. \qquad (29)$$

Hence, rotation of the sample differences $[1, 0, -1]$ yield

$$g_u^\theta = \frac{1}{2}\cos\theta \left(g_\theta[x+1, y] - g_\theta[x-1, y] \right) + \frac{1}{2}\sin\theta \left(g_\theta[x, y+1] - g_\theta[x, y-1] \right) \qquad (30)$$

$$g_v^\theta = -\frac{1}{2}\sin\theta \left(g_\theta[x+1, y] - g_\theta[x-1, y] \right) + \frac{1}{2}\cos\theta \left(g_\theta[x, y+1] - g_\theta[x, y-1] \right). \qquad (31)$$

The second order derivatives transform by

$$\begin{bmatrix} du^2 & dudv \\ dudv & dv^2 \end{bmatrix} = \begin{bmatrix} \cos\theta & \sin\theta \\ -\sin\theta & \cos\theta \end{bmatrix} \begin{bmatrix} dx^2 & dxdy \\ dxdy & dy^2 \end{bmatrix} \begin{bmatrix} \cos\theta & \sin\theta \\ -\sin\theta & \cos\theta \end{bmatrix}^T. \qquad (32)$$

Transforming the second order sample differences yields

$$g_{uu}^\theta = \cos^2\theta \left(g_\theta[x+1, y] - 2g_\theta[x, y] + g_\theta[x-1, y] \right) + 2\sin\theta \cos\theta$$
$$\left(g_\theta[x+1, y+1] + g_\theta[x-1, y-1] - g_\theta[x-1, y+1] - g_\theta[x+1, y-1] \right)$$
$$+ \sin^2\theta \left(g_\theta[x, y+1] - 2g_\theta[x, y] + g_\theta[x, y-1] \right) \qquad (33)$$

$$g_{uv}^\theta = \sin\theta \cos\theta \left\{ \left(g_\theta[x, y+1] - 2g_\theta[x, y] + g_\theta[x, y-1] \right) - \left(g_\theta[x+1, y] - 2g_\theta[x, y] + g_\theta[x-1, y] \right) \right\} + \left(\cos^2\theta - \sin^2\theta \right)$$
$$\left(g_\theta[x+1, y+1] + g_\theta[x-1, y-1] - g_\theta[x-1, y+1] - g_\theta[x+1, y-1] \right) \qquad (34)$$

$$g_{vv}^\theta = \sin^2\theta \left(g_\theta[x+1, y] - 2g_\theta[x, y] + g_\theta[x-1, y] \right) - 2\sin\theta \cos\theta$$
$$\left(g_\theta[x+1, y+1] + g_\theta[x-1, y-1] - g_\theta[x-1, y+1] - g_\theta[x+1, y-1] \right)$$
$$+ \cos^2\theta \left(g_\theta[x, y+1] - 2g_\theta[x, y] + g_\theta[x, y-1] \right). \qquad (35)$$

These filters can be included into the xt-separable filtering (Eq. (24), Eq. (26), Eq. (27), Eq. (28)).

6 Conclusion

We derived the decomposition of the anisotropic Gaussian in a one dimensional Gauss filter in the x-direction followed by a one dimensional filter in a non-orthogonal direction φ. The decomposition is shown to be extremely efficient from a computing perspective. An implementation scheme for normal convolution and for recursive filtering is proposed. Also directed derivative filters are demonstrated.

We proposed a scheme for both anisotropic convolution filtering and anisotropic recursive filtering. Convolution filtering is advantageous when considering locally steered filtering, as is the case in tracking applications [11,18,19]. Recursive filtering is more attractive when smoothing or differentiating the whole image array, for example in feature detection [3,15,20,21]. Error due to interpolation is neglectable compared to the error made by the recursive approximation of the Gaussian filter, and compared to the truncation error for convolution filters. The use of fast recursive filters [23,24] result in an calculation time of 65 msec. for a 512×512 input image on a normal PC.

Differentiation opposite to or along the filter direction is achieved by convolution with a rotated sample difference filters. For practical applicability of orientation scale-space analysis, we believe the exact approximation of Gaussian derivatives is of less importance than the ability to compute results in limited time.

Although the decomposition of Eq. (4) is possible in higher dimensions, the method is less beneficial for three dimensional filtering applications. Only one of the axes can be chosen to be aligned with the organization of the pixels in memory. For the other directions, traversing in arbitrary directions through the pixel data is required. Hence, computational gain is only marginal for higher dimensional smoothing.

The proposed anisotropic Gaussian filtering method allows fast calculation of edge and ridge maps, with high spatial and angular accuracy. The anisotropic filters can be applied in cases where edge and ridge data is distorted. Invariant feature extraction from a 2 dimensional affine projection of a 3D scene can be achieved by tuning the anisotropic Gaussian filter, an important achievement for computer vision. When structures are inherently interrupted, as is the case for dashed line detection, anisotropic Gaussian filter may accumulate evidence along the line while maintaining spatial acuity perpendicular to the line [9]. Orientation scale-space analysis can best be based on anisotropic Gaussian filters [22]. The proposed filtering method enables the practical applicability of orientation scale-space analysis.

References

1. A. Almansa and T. Lindeberg. Fingerprint enhancement by shape adaptation of scale-space operators with automatic scale selection. *IEEE Image Processing*, 9:2027–2042, 2000.
2. J. Bigün, G. H. Granlund, and J. Wiklund. Multidimensional orientation estimation with applications to texture analysis and optic flow. *IEEE Trans. Pattern Anal. Machine Intell.*, 13:775–790, 1991.
3. F. J. Canny. A computational approach to edge detection. *IEEE Trans. Pattern Anal. Machine Intell.*, 8(6):679–698, 1986.

4. R. Deriche. Separable recursive filtering for efficient multi-scale edge detection. In *Proceedings of the International Workshop on Machine Vision and Machine Intelligence*, pages 18–23, 1987.
5. R. Deriche. Fast algorithms for low-level vision. *IEEE Trans. Pattern Anal. Machine Intell.*, 12:78–87, 1990.
6. L. M. J. Florack, B. M. ter Haar Romeny, J. J. Koenderink, and M. A. Viergever. Scale and the differential structure of images. *Image and Vision Comput.*, 10(6):376–388, 1992.
7. W. T. Freeman and E. H. Adelson. The design and use of steerable filters. *IEEE Trans. Pattern Anal. Machine Intell.*, 13:891–906, 1991.
8. J. Gårding and T. Lindeberg. Direct computation of shape cues using scale-adapted spatial derivative operators. *Int. J. Comput. Vision*, 17(2):163–191, 1996.
9. J. M. Geusebroek, A. W. M. Smeulders, and H. Geerts. A minimum cost approach for segmenting networks of lines. *Int. J. Comput. Vision*, 43(2):99–111, 2001.
10. L. D. Griffin. Critical point events in affine scale space. In *Scale-Space Theories in Computer Vision*, pages 165–180. Springer-Verlag, 1997.
11. A. Jonk, R. van den Boomgaard, and A. W. M. Smeulders. A line tracker. *submitted to Comput. Vision Image Understanding*.
12. S. Kalitzin, B. ter Haar Romeny, and M. Viergever. Invertible orientation bundles on 2d scalar images. In *Scale-Space Theories in Computer Vision*, pages 77–88. Springer-Verlag, 1997.
13. J. J. Koenderink. The structure of images. *Biol. Cybern.*, 50:363–370, 1984.
14. J. J. Koenderink and A. J. van Doorn. Receptive field families. *Biol. Cybern.*, 63:291–297, 1990.
15. T. Lindeberg. *Scale-Space Theory in Computer Vision*. Kluwer Academic Publishers, Boston, 1994.
16. T. Lindeberg. Edge detection and ridge detection with automatic scale selection. In *Proceedings of the IEEE International Conference on Computer Vision and Pattern Recognition*, pages 465–470. IEEE Computer Society, 1996.
17. P. Perona. Steerable-scalable kernels for edge detection and junction analysis. *Image Vision Comput.*, 10:663–672, 1992.
18. E.P. Simoncelli. *Distributed Representation and Analysis of Visual Motion*. PhD thesis, Department of Electrical Engineering and Computer Science, MIT, Cambridge, MA, 1993.
19. E.P. Simoncelli, E.H. Adelson, and D.J. Heeger. Probability distributions of optical flow. In *Proceedings of the IEEE International Conference on Computer Vision and Pattern Recognition*, pages 310–315. IEEE Computer Society, 1991.
20. C. Steger. An unbiased detector of curvilinear structures. *IEEE Trans. Pattern Anal. Machine Intell.*, 20:113–125, 1998.
21. B. M. ter Haar Romeny, editor. *Geometry-Driven Diffusion in Computer Vision*. Kluwer Academic Publishers, Boston, 1994.
22. M. van Ginkel, P. W. Verbeek, and L. J. van Vliet. Improved orientation selectivity for orientation estimation. In M. Frydrych, J. Parkkinen, and A. Visa, editors, *Proceedings of the 10th Scandinavian Conference on Image Analysis*, pages 533–537, 1997.
23. L. J. van Vliet, I. T. Young, and P. W. Verbeek. Recursive Gaussian derivative filters. In *Proceedings ICPR '98*, pages 509–514. IEEE Computer Society Press, 1998.
24. I. T. Young and L. J. van Vliet. Recursive implementation of the Gaussian filter. *Signal Processing*, 44:139–151, 1995.

Adaptive Rest Condition Potentials: Second Order Edge-Preserving Regularization

Mariano Rivera and Jose L. Marroquin

Centro de Investigacion en Matematicas A.C.
Apdo. Postal 402, Guanajuato, Gto., 36000, Mexico
{mrivera,jlm}@cimat.mx
http://www.cimat.mx/~mrivera

Abstract. The propose of this paper is to introduce a new regularization formulation for inverse problems in computer vision and image processing that allows one to reconstruct second order piecewise smooth images, that is, images consisting of an assembly of regions with almost constant value, almost constant slope or almost constant curvature. This formulation is based on the idea of using potential functions that correspond to springs or thin plates with an adaptive rest condition. Efficient algorithms for computing the solution, and examples illustrating the performance of this scheme, compared with other known regularization schemes are presented as well.

Keywords. Edge-preserving regularization, image restoration, segmentation, anisotropic diffusion.

1 Introduction

In recent years, several methods for Edge-Preserving Regularization (EPR) for inverse problems in computer vision and image processing, have been published. These EPR methods are based on potentials that grow at a slower rate than quadratic ones. These methods have demonstrated their performance in detecting outliers in the data and reconstructing piecewise smooth images. The definition of piecewise smooth, however, has in most cases meant "almost piecewise constant", which means that the image can be represented as an assembly of regions such that inside them the gradient is close to zero. In the regularization framework, given the observed image g, the regularized solution f is computed as the minimizer of an energy functional U. Given a good initial guess for f, efficient algorithms for computing a local minimum have been reported in the literature. In spite of the success of robust regularization methods, there are still open important problems; in particular, the definition of piecewise smooth images has not been extended successfully to include regions with almost constant slope (second order smoothness). As a result, regions with constant slope are reconstructed with a "staircase" effect.

The purpose of this paper is to introduce a new formulation for energy potentials that allows one to reconstruct images with second order piecewise smoothness. In addition, efficient algorithms for computing the solution are presented.

The organization of the paper is as follows: section 2 presents a review of the EPR techniques based on robust potentials. In order to clarify the behavior of first order robust regularization an analogy with a Weak Spring System (WSS) is used. We show that this model has limitations for representing potentials for high order EPR.

In the third section, the new potentials for second order EPR are introduced. For first order potentials, the corresponding analogous model is a spring system with adaptive rest condition (ARC); we show that for this case, there is an equivalence between ARC and WSS potentials; however, ARC potentials can naturally be extended to high order EPR potentials, which do not have a direct representation in the WSS model.

Minimization algorithms are presented in section four and in section five, the performance of the proposed ARC potentials is demonstrated by experiments in both synthetic and real data. Finally, our conclusions are given in section six.

2 Robust Regularization

2.1 Statement of the Problem

The problem of reconstructing an image $\widehat{f}$ from noisy and degraded observations g given the following model of the observations:

$$g = F(\widehat{f}) + \eta, \qquad (1)$$

where η is additive noise and F is (in general) a non-linear operator that is assumed to be known, is an *ill posed* problem. Therefore, regularization of the problem is necessary. This means that, *prior* information or assumptions about the structure of $\widehat{f}$ need to be introduced in the reconstruction process. The regularized solution f^* is computed by minimizing an energy functional U:

$$f^* = \arg\min_f U(f)$$

where U is of the form:

$$U(f) = D(f,g) + \lambda R(f), \qquad (2)$$

The first term in (2) establishes that the reconstructed f should be consistent with the data g and the second term imposes a penalty for violating the prior assumptions of piecewise smoothness. The relative contribution of each term to the global energy is controlled by the positive parameter λ.

2.2 The Homogeneous Spring System

In the framework of Bayesian regularization, the data term in (2) is chosen as the negative log-likelihood and the prior constraints are incorporated in the form of a prior MRF model for f [1], so that the regularization term R in (2) takes the form of a sum, over the cliques of a given neighborhood system, of a set of "potential functions" supported on those cliques. One may take for instance as the neighborhood N of a pixel r its 8 closest neighbors:

$$N_r = \{s : |r - s| < 2\}$$

and cliques of size 2 $\langle r, s \rangle$ that correspond to horizontal, vertical and diagonal pixel pairs, where $r = (x, y)$ represents a site in the pixel lattice L. A quadratic regularized potential is obtained by assuming that η corresponds to Gaussian noise and choosing quadratic potentials over the first neighbor pairs:

$$U_H(f) = \sum_r \left\{ |F(f)_r - g_r|^2 + \frac{\lambda}{2} \sum_{s \in N_r} d_{rs} |f_r - f_s|^2 \right\} \quad (3)$$

with $d_{rs} = |r - s|^{-1}$. Functional (3) corresponds to the internal energy of the physical model of a Homogeneous Spring System (HSS). The HSS model is equivalent to a system of particles located at the sites of the pixel lattice, so that the vertical position of each particle is represented by the gray level of each pixel. Eq. (3) corresponds to the energy of the complete system where (when F is the identity) each particle f_r is connected by means of springs with the observation g_r and with its neighboring particles. The cost functional (3) does not preserve edges and will produce an over-smoothing of the real edges of the image.

2.3 The Weak Spring System: Robust Regularization

To alleviate that problem, there have been proposed potential functions for the regularization term that allow edge preservation, based on the idea of a breakable spring, that is, if the potential energy of a spring exceeds a given threshold θ, then the spring must be broken [2] or weakened [3][4][5][6]. To achieve this behavior, an auxiliary variable ω than acts as edge (outlier) detector is introduced; then the potential takes the form:

$$\rho(f_r - f_s, \omega_{rs}) = \omega_{rs}(f_r - f_s)^2 + \Psi(\omega_{rs}), \quad (4)$$

where ω_{rs} is associated to each pixel pair (r, s), and Ψ is a potential function that controls an over-detection of edges. In the case of the breakable spring model [2], ω_{rs} only takes the values $\{0, 1\}$; on other hand, in the case of the WSS model, $\omega_{rs} \in [0, 1]$, and is set close to 1 for $(f_r - f_s)^2 < \theta$ (where θ is a given threshold) and less that one otherwise. Black and Rangarajan [4] have shown that the potentials of the weak spring model correspond to the cost function for robust M-estimators. These potentials are, in general, non-convex and grow at a slower rate than the quadratic ones. This method is capable of finding the significant missing data of a noisy image and performing an edge-preserving restoration. Furthermore, the explicit outlier detection formulation allows one to incorporate additional constraints about the structure of the edge reject field ω [4]. For instance, one can penalize the "thickness" and the discontinuities on the edges, at the expense of an additional computational cost.

2.4 The Weak Thin Plate Model

The thin plate model [1,3] is obtained when one uses as potentials, squares of finite difference approximations to second derivatives:

$$\Delta^2 f_r = f_q - 2f_r + f_s. \qquad (5)$$

The computation of $\Delta^2 f_r$ involves cliques of size 3 $\langle q, r, s \rangle$ that correspond to horizontal, vertical and diagonals pixel triads (see figure 1).

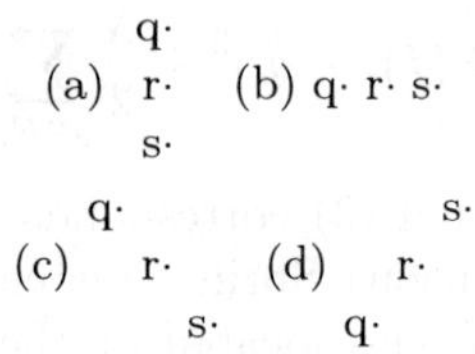

```
            q·
    (a)   r·      (b) q· r· s·
            s·

            q·                  s·
    (c)   r·        (d)   r·
            s·                  q·
```

Fig. 1. Cliques with triads of pixels

One could use the weak potential

$$\rho(\Delta^2 f_r, \omega_{qrs}) = \left[\Delta^2 f_r\right]^2 \omega_{qrs} + \mu \Psi(\omega_{qrs}),$$

as a second order edge-preserving potential; however, the results are not completely satisfactory, even for the reconstruction of piecewise constant images, where the first order model presents an excellent performance. The observed effect consists in the "ramping" or interpolation of first order discontinuities. In order to compute a second order solution, Geman and Reynolds [3] proposed to use the reconstruction computed with the first order model [using $\rho(f_r - f_s, \omega_{rs})$] as the starting point for the second order model. This improves the results, but still presents some problems, because the outliers for the first order model (jumps) do not correspond to the outliers for the second order one (large curvatures). Thus, the weak second order model does not work properly in the edges defined by jumps in the gray level (see section 5).

3 The Adaptive Rest Condition Potentials (ARC-Potentials)

In this section, we introduce potentials for EPR that are based on the paradigm of the Adaptive Rest Condition (ARC). The system we are proposing is based on the idea of using quadratic potentials with a non-zero (adaptive) rest condition:

$$\rho_{arc}(t, \phi_t) = |t - \phi_t|^2 + \Phi(\phi_t), \qquad (6)$$

where ϕ_t acts as the signed rest condition of the potential ρ_{arc}. In Refs. [9][10] a similar formulation is reported, in which ϕ are auxiliary variables introduced to minimize non-quadratic potentials by means of half-quadratic techniques—as in [3][4][5]. Here, however, we introduce the ARC potentials specifically to produce a novel generalization to the second order case. In the first order case, in fact, ARC potentials are equivalent to existing EPR potentials, as we show in the next subsection.

3.1 Spring System with Adaptive Rest Condition (SARC)

Consider $t = f_r - f_s$, thus,

$$\rho_{arc}(f_r - f_s, \phi_{rs}) = |f_r - f_s - \phi_{rs}|^2 + \Phi(\phi_{rs}), \tag{7}$$

Note that the desired behavior for the potential ρ_{arc} corresponds to choosing ϕ_{rs} close to zero for those values of $f_r - f_s$ that we want to smooth out, and close to the value of $f_r - f_s$ for those values that are considered edges. Φ is a given function that penalizes rest conditions different from zero. Figure 2-(a) shows the plot for a typical ϕ, and the corresponding ARC-potential is shown in panel 2-(b). As one can see the ρ_{arc} potential has a quadratic region (for $|t| < 0.5$) and outside this region an outlier rejection zone. In following we show how to choose the ARC and function Φ in order to have the desired effect.

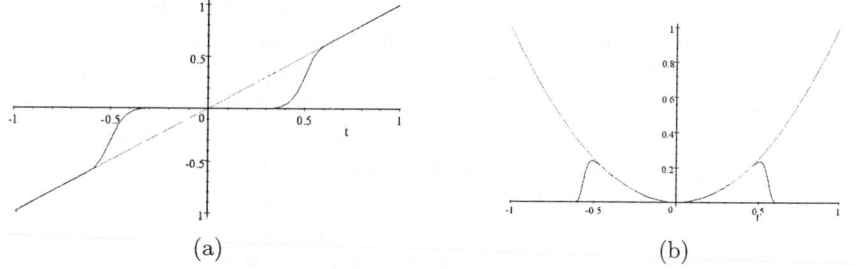

Fig. 2. (a) A typical rest condition ϕ (solid line) and the residual error $t = f_r - f_s$ (doted line). (b) ARC-Potential corresponding to $|t - \phi|^2$, with ϕ plotted in panel(a). Doted line: quadratic potential t^2

There are three possible strategies for choosing a spring system with ARC (SARC):

1. Explicit analogical line process (SARC-AL). In this case, one introduces auxiliary variables l, and chooses $\phi = lt$ and $\Phi(\phi) = \Psi(\phi/t)$ [see eq.(4)]. Where Ψ is a convex function. In this case, the SARC-AL potential corresponds to a half-quadratic potential. For instance, if we use $\Phi(\phi) = \mu(\phi/t)^2$, where μ is a positive parameter, one obtains the Ambrosio-Tortorelli[11] potential:

$$\rho_{arc}(t, l) = |t - lt|^2 + \mu(l)^2.$$

Note that in this case the optimal l is always in the interval $[0, 1]$.

2. Explicit binary line process (SARC-BL). In this case l is binary valued ($l \in \{0,1\}$) and $\Phi(t) = \mu V(t)$ where V is the Ising potential [1]:

$$V(t) = \begin{cases} -1 & if\ t=0 \\ 1 & otherwise. \end{cases} \qquad (8)$$

In this case, SARC-BL is equivalent to the breakable spring model [2].

3. Implicit line process (SARC-IL). In this case the ARC potential takes the form:

$$\rho_{arc}(t) = |t - \phi(t)|^2$$

where ϕ is a given function shaped as the one plotted in Figure 2. For instance, if one chooses $\phi(t) = t - \sqrt{\rho(t)}$, where ρ is a robust potential, we have $\rho_{arc}(t) = \rho(t)$, so that SARC-IL is equivalent to the robust potential formulation.

Although SARC models are equivalent to existing EPR techniques, we can obtain an extra benefit by using a combination of explicit and implicit line detection [12]:

$$\rho_{arc}(t, l) = |t - l\phi(t)|^2 + \frac{1}{\mu}(l)^2. \qquad (9)$$

where μ is positive parameter and the product $l\phi(t)$ is the ARC. The meaning of the extra variable l depends on the chosen function ϕ. In order to illustrate this combined formulation, one can assume that $\phi(t)$ corresponds to the function plotted in Fig. 2. In this case, for a small value of the parameter μ and if $|t| < 0.5$, one has that l is equal to zero (by effect of the penalization term). On the other hand, if $|t| > 0.5$, then l will be close to one. As a consequence, l represents an edge detector controlled by the function ϕ. This allows one to use ϕ to represent prior constraints about edge location; for example, in the edge-preserving regularization of optic flow, one may prevent edges from appearing in regions with small gray-level gradient by setting $\phi = 0$ in those regions [12].

3.2 Thin Plate System with Adaptive Rest Condition (PARC)

The greatest advantage of the ARC formulation is that it can be used to produce a novel extension to the second order case, by defining thin plate potentials with adaptive rest condition. These PARC regularization potentials have the property of not just adapting their stiffness, but also changing their behavior to SARC potentials at the edges of almost constant regions. This represents a significant advantage over the half-quadratic plate model based on robust potentials [3,4,5,7,8,9,10,13,14,15,16]

We have two cases for the PARC model: analogical line process (PARC-AL) and implicit line process (PARC-IL). In order to understand the PARC models, we first introduce the PARC-AL model.

We note that (5) can be written as:

$$\Delta^2 f_r = \Delta^+ f_r - \Delta^- f_r \qquad (10)$$

where

$$\Delta^+ f_r = f_q - f_r \quad \text{and} \quad \Delta^- f_r = f_r - f_s \tag{11}$$

(see figure 1).

Then, PARC potentials can be written in the general form:

$$\rho_{parc}(\Delta^2 f_r) = \left|\Delta^+ f_r - \Delta^- f_r - \phi_r\right|^2 + \Phi(\phi_r), \tag{12}$$

where the ARC ϕ should satisfy:

$$\phi_r \approx \begin{cases} 0 & if\ |\Delta^+ f_r| < \theta,\ |\Delta^- f_r| < \theta \\ \Delta^- f_r & if\ |\Delta^+ f_r| < \theta,\ |\Delta^- f_r| > \theta \\ \Delta^+ f_r & if\ |\Delta^+ f_r| > \theta,\ |\Delta^- f_r| < \theta \\ \Delta^2 f_r & if\ |\Delta^+ f_r| > \theta,\ |\Delta^- f_r| > \theta \end{cases}, \tag{13}$$

where θ is a given threshold. To obtain the desired behavior, one may represent ϕ_r as: $\phi_r \equiv \phi_r^+ + \phi_r^-$, where ϕ_r^+, ϕ_r^- depend on $\Delta^+ f_r$ and $\Delta^- f_r$, respectively, and penalize ϕ_r^+ and ϕ_r^- separately. Thus, (12) can be rewritten as:

$$\rho_{parc}(\Delta^2 f_r) = \left|\Delta^+ f_r - \Delta^- f_r - \phi_r^+ - \phi_r^-\right|^2 + \Phi(\phi_r^+) + \Phi(\phi_r^-)$$

One can now introduce "edge variables" $l_{qr} = \phi_r^+/\Delta^+ f_r$, $l_{rs} = \phi_r^-/\Delta^- f_r$, so that (12) can be written as:

$$\rho_{parc}(f, l)_{qrs} = \left|\Delta^+ f_r(1 - l_{qr}) - \Delta^- f_r(1 - l_{rs})\right|^2 + \mu\Psi(l_{qs}) + \mu\Psi(l_{rs}) \tag{14}$$

This potential is quadratic on f for a given l and satisfies the constraints (13) (see figure 3). $\Psi(\cdot)$ is a potential that penalizes an over-detection of edges, and must satisfy the constraints:

1. $\Psi(t) \geq 0\ \forall t$ with $\Psi(0) = 0$,
2. $\Psi(t) = \Psi(-t)$.
3. $\Psi'(t) = \partial\Psi(t(f))/\partial f$ and $\Psi''(t) \equiv \partial^2\Psi(t(f))/\partial f^2$ exist.

Note that there is no closed formula for l_{qr} and l_{rs}. Unlike the SARC-AL model, in PARC-AL there is no guarantee that $l \in [0, 1]$.

3.3 PARC-IL Models

The implicit line process PARC model (PARC-IL) is generated by using $\phi^+ = \phi(\Delta^+ f_r)$ and $\phi^- = \phi(\Delta^- f_r)$, where we use

$$\phi(t) = t(1 - \psi(t))$$

where ψ is chosen in a way such that $t\psi(t)$ is close to t for small values of t and close to zero for large values of t (we used $\psi(t) = \exp(-t^2)$ in our experiments of section IV). The edge penalization term takes in this case the form $\mu\left[|\Delta^+ f_r|^2 + |\Delta^- f_r|^2\right]$. Thus, the complete PARC-IL is given by

$$\rho_{parc}(f)_r = \left|\Delta^+ f_r \psi\left(\frac{\Delta^+ f_r}{k}\right) - \Delta^- f_r \psi\left(\frac{\Delta^- f_r}{k}\right)\right|^2 + \mu\left[|\Delta^+ f_r|^2 + |\Delta^- f_r|^2\right], \tag{15}$$

where k is a scale parameter and the parameter μ controls the granularity of the solution, since small regions surrounded by edges will be penalized by this term [13].

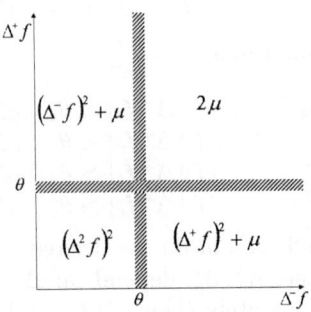

Fig. 3. Desired behavior of the PARC potential. For $\Delta^+ f > \theta$ and $\Delta^- f > \theta$ (θ is a given threshold) the potential is quadratic. $\rho_{arc} = \left|\Delta^- f\right|^2 + \mu$ if $\Delta^+ f > \theta$ and $\Delta^- f < \theta$. $\rho_{arc} = \left|\Delta^+ f\right|^2 + \mu$ if $\Delta^+ f < \theta$ and $\Delta^- f > \theta$. Finally, $\rho_{arc} = 2\mu$ if $\Delta^+ f > \theta$ and $\Delta^- f > \theta$, where μ is a fixed cost.

4 Minimization Algorithms

4.1 Half-Quadratic Coupled Minimization Algorithms for PARC-AL Models

In this case, the function to minimize is:

$$U(f,l) = \sum_r \Big\{ [F(f)_r - g_r]^2 \\
+ \lambda \sum_{q,s \in N_r} \Big([\Delta^+ f_r(1 - l_{qr}) - \Delta^- f_r(1 - l_{rs})]^2 \\
+ \mu \left[\Psi(l_{qr}) + \Psi(l_{rs})\right] \Big) \Big\} \tag{16}$$

where F is a linear operator. The solution may be computed by a two–step iterative minimization algorithm:

1. Quadratic minimization step: Update the restoration f^{t+1} (keeping l fixed), so that:

$$U(f^{t+1}, l^t) \leq U(f^t, l^t).$$

2. Update the second order edge detectors l (keeping f fixed), so that:

$$U(f^{t+1}, l^{t+1}) \leq U(f^{t+1}, l^t).$$

and set $t = t + 1$.

For the special case $\Psi(l_{qr}) = l_{qr}^2$, (16) is quadratic for f for a given l, and quadratic for l for a given f. Thus, the alternated minimization of (16) is performed by solving a coupled linear systems using any general algorithm as Gauss-Seidel or linear Conjugate Gradient. We have found a very good performance by alternating a single Gauss-Seidel iteration of each system. The experiments of the figures 3-(e) and 5-(b) correspond to this simple case.

4.2 Adaptive Non-linear Conjugate Gradient Algorithm (ANLCG) for PARC-IL Models

The cost functional with implicit edge detection is given by

$$U(f) = \sum_r \left\{ [F(f)_r - g_r]^2 \right.$$
$$+ \sum_{q,s \in N_r} \left(\left| \Delta^+ f_r \psi \left(\frac{\Delta^+ f_r}{k} \right) - \Delta^- f_r \psi \left(\frac{\Delta^- f_r}{k} \right) \right|^2 \right.$$
$$\left. \left. + \mu \left[|\Delta^+ f_r|^2 + |\Delta^- f_r|^2 \right] \right) \right\} \quad (17)$$

Note that U is differentiable, but non-quadratic in f, so a non-linear optimization algorithm needs to be used to find a local minimum of U. We propose here a modification to the Non-Linear Conjugate Gradient Algorithm (ANLCG), in which the step size is adaptively varied. Additionally, in order to accelerate the convergence rate, the algorithm introduces inertia in the descent. The algorithm is:

ANLCG
Set $n = 1, \beta_0 = 0, f_0$ equal to an initial guess, and $g_0 = G(f_0)$
Repeat until $|g_n| < \varepsilon$:

1. $s_n = -g_n + \beta_n s_{n-1}$
2. Compute the step α_n such that ensures energy reduction. i.e. $U(f_n + \alpha_n s_n) < U(f_n)$ (see below)
3. $f_{n+1} = f_n + \alpha_n s_n$,
   $n = n + 1$.
4. $g_n = \nabla U(f_n)$
5. $\beta_n = \max \left\{ 0, \frac{g_n^T (g_n - g_{n-1})}{g_{n-1}^T g_{n-1}} \right\}$,

where $\varepsilon \in (0,1)$ is a small positive constant. For computing the step α_n, we propose an algorithm that uses an adaptive local search. This algorithm is inspired in the one used in the Quasi-Gauss-Newton algorithm with an energy reduction constraint [17]. ANLCG algorithm (Step 2) requires that α_n is accepted only if it guarantees a sufficient reduction in the energy $U(f)$, that is , if

$$U(f_n + \alpha_n s_n) \leq (1-\varepsilon)U(f_n),$$

to achieve this we do the following:

Computation of α_n
Initially set $a = 0.01, m = 0$, and δ small enough (e.g. $\delta = 10^{-4}$).
2.1 $\alpha_n = a$
2.2   While $U(f_n + \alpha_n s_n) > (1 - \alpha_n \delta)U(f_n)$
          $\alpha_n = \alpha_n/c_1, m = 0$
2.3 $m = m + 1$
2.4   if $m > c_2$
          $a = c_3 \alpha_n, m = 0$
    else
          $a = \alpha_n$

Empirically, we have found that the values of parameters $c_1 = 2$, $c_2 = 5$ and $c_3 = 3$ and the initial step size a work properly. Note that since α_n ensures that the energy decreases at every iteration, the convergence of algorithm ANLCG is automatically guaranteed.

5 Experiments

In this section experiments (in both synthetic and real data) that demonstrate the performance of the PARC potentials are shown.

5.1 Comparison with the Half-Quadratic Second Order Model

The first experiment is a comparison of the performance of the PARC models with respect to other EPR model: the proposed by Geman and Reynolds [3]. The synthetic test image is shown in panel (a) in figure 4; the noise corrupted image is shown in panel (b). The test image was designed so that includes the following kind of regions: piecewise constant (delimited by first order discontinuities: edges), piecewise constant slope (second order discontinuities) and smooth (non-planar) regions. Panel (d) shows the reconstructed (filtered) image computed with a first order EPR model (the WSS). One can appreciate that WSS models promotes constant piecewise restorations. Panel (d) shows the reconstruction computed with (in our knowledge) the only second order model reported (see ref. [3]). This corresponds to the weak thin plate model (WTP). The used potential function corresponds to the one reported in [7]. This potential has been extensively used and has demonstrated its superior performance with respect to other first order EPR potentials (see [4] [5]). As one can see, in spite of the fact that the regions with constant and smooth changes in the slope are reconstructed with an acceptable quality, the gray level steps are over-smoothed. This

Fig. 4. (a) Synthetic real image. (b) Noisy data test image. Reconstructions computed with: (c) the weak membrane potential,(d) weak plate potential, (e) PARC-AL and (d) PARC-IL (see text).

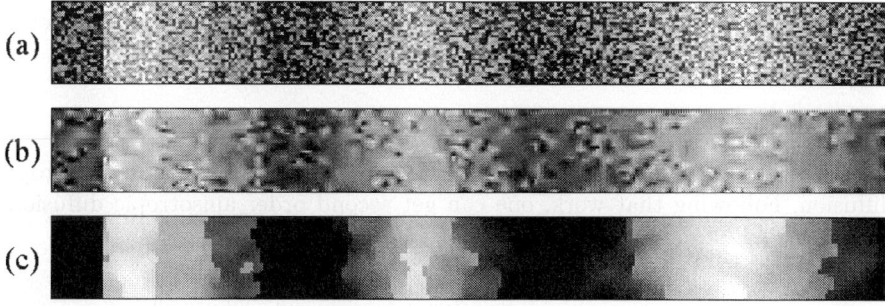

Fig. 5. (a) Noisy data test image. Reconstructions computed with: (b) weak plate potential and (c) PARC-AL

well-known effect is generated because the WTP changes the jumps by ramps. On the other hand, panels (e) and (f) show the reconstructions computed with the proposed PARC-AL and PARC-IL models, respectively. As one can note, the three different kinds of regions are reconstructed with high quality. The mean squared errors for the reconstructions are: 6.65e-4, 5.04e-4, and 4.09e-4; for the panels: (d), (e) and (f), respectively. The data were normalized to the interval [0,1] and corrupted with uniform noise with amplitude equal to 0.2, the MSE for the noisy data is 1.33e-2.

In our experiments, PARC models also have shown better performance for low signal to noise ratios. This is illustrated in figure 5. Panel (a) shows the corrupted image with uniform noise (with amplitude equal to 0.7, that corresponds to a MSE equal to 0.162). Panels (b) and (c) show the restorations computed with the WTP and PARC-AL models, respectively. The MSE for the computed restorations were 0.022 ans 0.004 for WTP and PARC-AL models, respectively. In fact, as was noted by Geman and Reynolds [3], WTP model is unstable for low SNR.

5.2 Comparison of PARC-AL vs. PARC-IL

In order to compare the relative performance of the two presented PARC models (PARC-AL and PARC-IL), we performed the following experiment with a real test image. In Figure 6, panel (a) is shown the cameraman picture corrupted with gaussian noise with σ^2 =0.05. Panel (b) and (c) the reconstructions computed with the AL and the IL model, respectively. The MSE were 1.5e-3 and 0.9e-3 Corresponding details are presented in panels (d), (e) and (f). As one can appreciate, the IL model performs a better restoration of the details. However, the computational time is larger for the IL model: 15 secs. while the restoration with the AL model took 3 secs. in a pentium III at 800 Mhz. based computer. The computational time for the WTP model (results not shown) was of 23 secs. We noted that for this case of high SNR, the restoration of the WTP model (with MSE equal to 1.6e-3) looks very similar to the one computed with the PARC-AL model. It should be noted that the convergence of the ANLCG minimization algorithm, used in the PARC-IL case, can always be guaranteed, which is not the case for PARC-AL; we have tested this last algorithm extensively, however, and it never has failed to converge.

5.3 Second Order Anisotropic Diffusion

Refs. [18][15] shown the relationship between robust potentials and anisotropic diffusion. Following that work, one can get second order anisotropic diffusions based on PARC potentials, for instance

$$f^{t+1} = f^t + h \frac{\partial}{\partial f_r^t} \sum_{q,s \in N_r} \rho_{parc}(f)_r, \tag{18}$$

where $\rho_{parc}(f)_r$ is given in (15), f^0 corresponds to the image in 6-(a) and the step size h is chosen small enough. Figure 7 shown images of a sequence computed with this method. We use the same PARC potential than in the experiment of figure 6.

6 Discussion and Conclusions

We have presented a new model for edge-preserving regularization, that allows one to reconstruct second order piecewise smooth images. This model is based

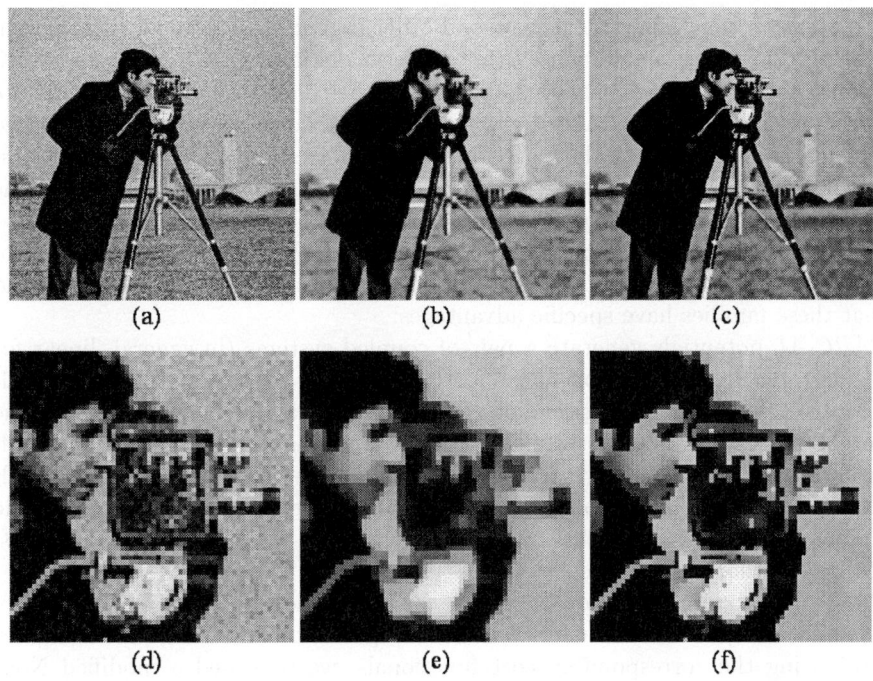

Fig. 6. (a) Cameraman picture corrupted with uniform noise. Reconstructions computed with: (b) PARC-AL and (c) PARC-IL. (d), (e), (f): corresponding details.

Fig. 7. Images of a sequence computed with an anisotropic diffusion algorithm based on PARC-IL potentials

on the physical analogy of adaptive rest condition potentials (ARC). In order to focus the paper on the characteristics of the ARC potentials, we dealt with the problem of restoring noisy images, but their use can be extended to other image processing and computer vision problems. We showed that the first order ARC model –which has been used before – is equivalent to the well known adaptive weak spring model, and hence, it has the problem of producing staircase–like solutions in regions of constant slope; to overcome this problem, we propose here an extension that generates new second order potentials; we called these potentials the thin plate model with adaptive rest condition (PARC). These PARC potentials have the property of changing their behavior to a first order EPR potential at the edges (steps in the gray level) of the image. As a result, regularized cost functionals based on the PARC model are more stable and perform a better restoration of edges and smooth regions, because PARC potentials extend the definition of smoothness to include regions with almost constant slope.

We introduced two kinds of PARC potentials: the PARC with analog line process (PARC-AL) and the PARC with implicit line process (PARC-IL). We found that these families have specific advantages:

PARC-AL potentials generate a pair of coupled systems (in general, linear for the restored image and non-linear for the auxiliary variables) that can be alternatively minimized. A special case results from selecting a coupled quadratic potential; in such case the resulting coupled systems are linear and can be efficiently minimized (in our case, we used the Gauss-Seidel algorithm in an alternated scheme). This model can incorporate potentials that penalize specific configurations of the auxiliary variable (for example the thickness of the edges; see [4,14,15] for more details).

PARC-IL potentials are non-linear; in this case, the line process is implicitly represented by a detection function that depends on the image gradient; for minimizing the corresponding cost functionals, we proposed a modified Nonlinear Conjugate Gradient Algorithm, for which one can guarantee convergence (at least to a local minimum). Experiments have shown that (in general) one obtains better reconstructions with the PARC-IL model although at a higher computational cost. An interesting open theoretical problem is to determine the precise relation between PARC-AL and PARC-IL potentials, as has been found in the case of WSS models.

Acknowledgments. This work was funded in part by CONACYT, Mexico under grant 34575-A.

References

1. Li, S.Z.: Markov Random Field Modeling in Image Analysis, Springer-Verlag, New York (2001)
2. Geman, S., Geman, D.: Stochastic relaxation, Gibbs distributions and Bayesian restoration of images, IEEE Trans. Pattern Anal. Machine Intell., 6 (1984) 721–741
3. Geman, D., Reynolds, G.: Constrained restoration and the recovery of discontinuities, IEEE Trans. Image Processing, 14 (1992) 367–383
4. Black, M.J., Rangarajan, A.: Unification of line process, outlier rejetion, and robust statistics with application in early vision, Int. Journal of Computer Vision, 19 (1996) 57–91
5. Charbonnier, P., Blanc-Féraud, L., Aubert, G., Barlaud, M.: Deterministic edge-preserving regularization in computer imagining, IEEE Trans. Image Processing, 6 (1997) 298–311

6. Kubota, T., Huntsberg, T.: Adaptive anisotropic parameter estimation in the weak membrane model, Proc. Int WS in EMMCVPR'97, Lecture Notes in Computer Vision 1223, Springer Verlag, Venice Italy, (1997) 179–194
7. Geman, S., McClure, D.E.: Bayesian image analysis methods: An application to single photon emission tomography, in Proc. Statistical Computation Section, Amer. Statistical Assoc., Washington, DC, (1985) 12–18
8. Blake A., Zisserman, A.: Visual reconstruction, The MIT Press, Cambridge, Massachusetts (1987)
9. Geman, D., Yang, C.: Nonlinear image recovery with half-quadratic regularization, IEEE Trans. Image Processing, 4 (1995) 932–946
10. Cohen, L.: Auxilar varibales and two-steps iterative algorithms in computer vision problems, Journal Mathematical Imaging and Vision, 6 (1996) 59–83
11. Ambrosio, L., Tortorelli, V.M.: Approximation of functionals depending on jumps by elliptic functionals via Γ-convergence, Commun. Pure Appl. Math, 43 (1990) 999–1036
12. Rivera, M., Marroquin, J.L.: The adaptive rest condition spring model: an edge preserving regularization techinque, in Proc. IEEE-ICIP 2000, Vol. II, Vancouver, BC, Canada (2000) 805–807
13. Rivera, M., Marroquin, J.L.: Efficient Half-Quadratic Regularization with Granularity Control, Techical Report: 05.06.2001, I-01-07 (CC), CIMAT, Mexico (2001)
14. Teboul, S., Blanc-Féraud, L., Aubert, G., Barlaud,M., Variational approach for edge-preserving regularization using coupled PDE's, IEEE Trans. Image Processing, 7 (1998) 387–397
15. Black, M.J., Sapiro, G., Marimont D.H., Heeger, D.: Robust anisotropic diffusion, IEEE Trans. Image Processing, 7 (1998) 421–432
16. Idier, J.: Convex half-quadratic criteria and interactig auxiliar variables for image restoration, IEEE Trans. Image Processing, 10 (2001) 1001–1009
17. Nocedal J., Wright, S.J.: Numerical Optimization (Springer Series in Operations Research), Springer-Verlag, New York (1999)
18. Perona, P., Malik, J.: Scale-space and edge detection using anisotropic diffusion, IEEE Trans. Pattern Anal. Machine Intell., 12 (1990) 629–639

An Affine Invariant Interest Point Detector

Krystian Mikolajczyk and Cordelia Schmid

INRIA Rhône-Alpes & GRAVIR-CNRS
655, av. de l'Europe, 38330 Montbonnot, France
{Name.Surname}@inrialpes.fr
http://www.inrialpes.fr/movi

Abstract. This paper presents a novel approach for detecting affine invariant interest points. Our method can deal with significant affine transformations including large scale changes. Such transformations introduce significant changes in the point location as well as in the scale and the shape of the neighbourhood of an interest point. Our approach allows to solve for these problems simultaneously. It is based on three key ideas : 1) The second moment matrix computed in a point can be used to normalize a region in an affine invariant way (skew and stretch). 2) The scale of the local structure is indicated by local extrema of normalized derivatives over scale. 3) An affine-adapted Harris detector determines the location of interest points. A multi-scale version of this detector is used for initialization. An iterative algorithm then modifies location, scale and neighbourhood of each point and converges to affine invariant points. For matching and recognition, the image is characterized by a set of affine invariant points; the affine transformation associated with each point allows the computation of an affine invariant descriptor which is also invariant to affine illumination changes. A quantitative comparison of our detector with existing ones shows a significant improvement in the presence of large affine deformations. Experimental results for wide baseline matching show an excellent performance in the presence of large perspective transformations including significant scale changes. Results for recognition are very good for a database with more than 5000 images.

Keywords : Image features, matching, recognition.

1 Introduction

Local characteristics have shown to be well adapted to matching and recognition, as they allow robustness to partial visibility and clutter. The difficulty is to obtain invariance under arbitrary viewing conditions. Different solutions to this problem have been developed over the past few years and are reviewed in section 1.1. These approaches first detect features and then compute a set of descriptors for these features. They either extract invariant features (and descriptors) or they compute invariant descriptors based on non-invariant features. In the case of significant transformations feature detection has to be adapted to the transformation, as at least a subset of the features must be present in both images in order to allow for correspondences. Features which have shown to be particularly appropriate are interest points. Scale invariant interest points detectors have been presented previously [10, 11]. However, none of the existing interest point detectors is invariant to affine transformations. In this paper we present an affine invariant interest point detector. For each interest point we simultaneously adapt location as well as scale and shape of the neighbourhood. We then obtain a truly affine invariant image description which gives excellent results in the presence of arbitrary viewpoint changes. Note that a perspective transformation of a smooth surface can be locally approximated by an affine transformation.

1.1 Related Work

Feature detection. Interest points are local features for which the signal changes two-dimensionally. They can be extracted reliably, are robust to partial visibility and the information content in these points is high. One of the first recognition techniques based on interest points has been proposed by Schmid and Mohr [14]. The points are extracted with the Harris detector [5] which is invariant to image rotation. To obtain invariance to scale changes interest points can be extracted in the scale space of an image [7]. Dufournaud et al. [3] use a multi-scale framework to match images at different scales. Interest points and descriptors are computed at several scales. A robust matching algorithm allows to select the correct scale. In the context of recognition, the complexity of a multi-scale approach is prohibitive. Lowe [10] proposes an efficient algorithm for recognition based on local extrema of difference-of-Gaussian filters in scale-space. Mikolajczyk and Schmid [11] use a multi-scale framework to detect points and then apply scale selection [8] to select characteristic points. These points are invariant to scale changes and allow matching and recognition in the presence of large scale factors. Tuytelaars and Van Gool [16] detect affine invariant regions based on image intensities. However, the number of such regions in an image is limited and depends on the content. They use colour descriptors computed for these regions for wide baseline matching.

Wide baseline matching and recognition. The methods presented in the following use standard feature detectors. They rely on the accuracy of these features which is a limitation in the presence of significant transformations.

Pritchett and Zisserman [12] estimate homographies of local planar surfaces in order to correct the cross-correlation and grow regions. The homographies are obtained by matching regions bound by four line segments. This approach has been applied to wide baseline matching and it is clearly difficult to extend to retrieval. Tell and Carlsson [15] also address the problem of wide baseline matching and use an affine invariant descriptors for point pairs. They compute an affine invariant Fourier description of the intensity profile along a line connecting two points. The description is not robust unless the two points lie on the same planar surface. Baumberg [2] extracts interest points at several scales and then adapts the shape of the region to the local image structure using an iterative procedure based on the second moment matrix [9]. Their descriptors are affine invariant for fixed scale and location, that is the scale and the location of the points are not extracted in an affine invariant way. The points as well as the associated regions are therefore not invariant in the presence of large affine transformations, see section 3.3 for a quantitative comparison to our approach. Furthermore, approximately four times more points are detected in comparison to our method. This increases the probability of false matches and in the case of retrieval the complexity is prohibitive. In our approach points that correspond to the same physical structure, but are detected at different locations in scale space, converge to the same point location. The number of points is therefore reduced. The properties of the second moment matrix were also explored by Schaffalitzky and Zisserman [13], but their goal was to obtain an affine invariant texture descriptor.

1.2 Our Approach

A uniform Gaussian scale-space is often used to deal with scale changes [3, 7, 10, 11]. However, an affine Gaussian scale-space is too complex to be practically useful, as three parameters have to be determined simultaneously. In this paper we propose a realistic solution which limits the search space to the neighbourhood of points and uses an iterative search procedure. Our approach is based on a method introduced by Lindeberg and Garding [9] which iteratively estimates an affine invariant neighbourhood. They explore the properties of the second moment descriptor to recover the surface orientation and compute the descriptors with non uniform Gaussian kernels.

Our affine invariant interest point detector is an affine-adapted version of the Harris detector. The affine adaptation is based on the second moment matrix [9] and local extrema over scale of normalized derivatives [8]. Locations of interest points are detected by the affine-adapted Harris detector. For initialization, approximate localizations and scales of interest points are extracted by the multi-scale Harris detector. For each point we apply an iterative procedure which modifies position as well as scale and shape of the point neighbourhood. This allows to converge toward a stable point that is invariant to affine transformations. This detector is the main contribution of the paper. Furthermore, we have developed a repeatability criterion which takes into account the point position as well as the shape of the neighbourhood. A quantitative comparison with existing detectors [2, 11] shows a significant improvement of our method in the presence of large affine transformations. Results for wide baseline matching and recognition based on our affine invariant points are excellent in the presence of significant changes in viewing angle and scale and clearly demonstrate their invariance.

Overview. This paper is organized as follows. Section 2 introduces the key ideas of our approach. In section 3 our affine invariant interest point detector is described in detail and compared to existing approaches. The matching and recognition algorithm is outlined in section 4. Experimental results are given in section 5.

2 Affine Gaussian Scale-Space

In this section we extend the idea of searching interest points in the scale space representation of an image and propose to search points in an affine Gaussian scale space. We extend the approach proposed in [11]; this approach explores the properties of the uniform Gaussian scale space and can handle significant scale changes. It is based on interest points which are local maxima of the Harris measure above a threshold. The Harris measure is the second moment matrix and describes the gradient distribution in a local neighbourhood of a point $\mathbf{x}$:

$$\mu(\mathbf{x}, \sigma_I, \sigma_D) = \sigma_D^2 g(\sigma_I) * \begin{bmatrix} L_x^2(\mathbf{x}, \sigma_D) & L_x L_y(\mathbf{x}, \sigma_D) \\ L_x L_y(\mathbf{x}, \sigma_D) & L_y^2(\mathbf{x}, \sigma_D) \end{bmatrix} \quad (1)$$

$$\det(\mu) - \alpha \operatorname{trace}^2(\mu) > threshold \quad (2)$$

where σ_I is the integration scale, σ_D the derivation scale, g the Gaussian and L the image smoothed by a Gaussian (cf. equation 3). To deal with significant scale changes, points are extracted at several scales and the characteristic scale is determined by automatic scale selection [8]. Scale selection is based on the maximum of the normalized Laplacian $|\sigma^2(L_{xx}(\mathbf{x}, \sigma) + L_{yy}(\mathbf{x}, \sigma))|$ where derivatives are computed with uniform Gaussian filters. A problem occurs in the case of affine transformations where the scale changes are not necessarily the same in all directions. In this case the selected scale does not reflect the real transformation of a point. It is well known that the local Harris maxima have different spatial locations when extracted at different detection scales (see figure 1). Thus, an additional error is introduced to the location of the point if the detection scales do not correspond to the scale factor between corresponding image patterns. In the case of affine transformations the detection scales in x and y directions have to vary independently to deal with possible affine scaling. Suppose both scales can be adapted to the local image structure. Hence, we face the problem of computing the second moment matrix in affine Gaussian scale space, where a circular window is replaced by an ellipse. An affine scale-space can be generated by convolution with non-uniform Gaussian kernels:

$$g(\Sigma) = \frac{1}{2\pi\sqrt{\det\Sigma}} \exp^{-\frac{\mathbf{x}^T \Sigma^{-1} \mathbf{x}}{2}},$$

where $\mathbf{x} \in \mathcal{R}^2$. If the matrix Σ is equal to an identity matrix multiplied by a scalar, this function corresponds to a uniform Gaussian kernel. Given any image function $I(\mathbf{x})$ the derivatives can be defined by

$$L_x(\mathbf{x}; \Sigma) = \frac{\partial}{\partial x} g(\Sigma) * I(\mathbf{x}) \quad (3)$$

This operation corresponds to the convolution with a rotated elliptical Gaussian kernel. If traditional uniform Gaussian filters are used, we deal with a three dimensional space (x, y, σ), and the Gaussian kernel is determined by one scale parameter σ. If Σ is a symmetric positive definite 2x2 matrix, the number of degrees of freedom of the kernel is three, which leads to a complex high dimensional search space. Thus, we have to apply additional constraints to reduce the search.

The selection of detection scales can be based on the second moment matrix. For a given point $\mathbf{x}$ the second moment matrix μ in non-uniform scale space is defined by

$$\mu(\mathbf{x}, \Sigma_I, \Sigma_D) = g(\Sigma_I) * ((\nabla L)(\mathbf{x}, \Sigma_D)(\nabla L)(\mathbf{x}, \Sigma_D)^T)$$

where Σ_I and Σ_D are the covariance matrices which determine the integration and the derivation Gaussian kernels. To reduce the search space we impose the

condition $\Sigma_I = a\Sigma_D$, where a is a scalar.
Consider an affine transformed point $\mathbf{x}_L = A\mathbf{x}_R$, the matrices μ are related by

$$\mu(\mathbf{x}_L, \Sigma_{I,L}, \Sigma_{D,L}) = A^T \mu(A\mathbf{x}_R, A\Sigma_{I,L}A^T, A\Sigma_{D,L}A^T) A \qquad (4)$$

Lindeberg [9] showed that if the second moment descriptor of the point $\mathbf{x}_L$ verifies

$$\mu(\mathbf{x}_L, \Sigma_{I,L}, \Sigma_{D,L}) = M_L \qquad \Sigma_{I,L} = tM_L^{-1} \qquad \Sigma_{D,L} = dM_L^{-1}$$

and the descriptor of the point $\mathbf{x}_R$ verifies corresponding conditions

$$\mu(\mathbf{x}_R, \Sigma_{I,R}, \Sigma_{D,R}) = M_R \qquad \Sigma_{I,R} = tM_R^{-1} \qquad \Sigma_{D,R} = dM_R^{-1}$$

then the matrices M_L and M_R are related by

$$M_L = A^T M_R A \qquad A = M_R^{-1/2} R M_L^{1/2} \qquad \Sigma_R = A\Sigma_L A^T \qquad (5)$$

where R is an arbitrary rotation. Note that the scalars t and d are the integration and derivation scales respectively. The relation 5 verifies equation 4. The proof and the outline of an iterative method for computing the matrices can be found in [9]. Matrices M_L and M_R, computed under these conditions, determine corresponding regions defined by $\mathbf{x}^T M \mathbf{x} = 1$. Baumberg [2] shows that if the neighbourhoods of points $\mathbf{x}_L$, $\mathbf{x}_R$ are normalized by transformations $\mathbf{x}'_L \mapsto M_L^{-1/2}\mathbf{x}_L$ and $\mathbf{x}'_R \mapsto M_R^{-1/2}\mathbf{x}_R$ respectively, then the normalized regions are related by a pure rotation $\mathbf{x}'_L \mapsto R\mathbf{x}'_R$. In the normalized frames M'_L and M'_R are equal up to a pure rotation matrix. In other words, the intensity patterns in the normalized frames are isotropic. We extend the approach proposed in [11]. We first transform the image locally to obtain an isotropic region and then search for a local Harris maximum and a characteristic scale. We then obtain a method for detecting points and regions invariant to affine transformations.

3 Affine Invariant Point Detector

In order to limit the search space we initialize the affine detector with interest points extracted by the multi-scale Harris detector [3]. Any detector can be used to determine the *spatial localization* of the initial points. However, the Harris detector is based on the second moment matrix, and therefore naturally fits into our framework. To obtain the *shape adaptation matrix* for each interest point we compute the second moment descriptor with automatically selected *integration* and *derivation* scale. The outline of our detection method is presented in the following:

- the *spatial localization* of an interest point for a given scale and shape is determined by the affine-adapted Harris detector,
- the *integration scale* is selected at the extremum over scale of normalized derivatives,
- the *derivation scale* is selected at the maximum of normalized isotropy,
- the *shape adaptation matrix* normalizes the point neighbourhood.

In the following we discuss in detail each step of the algorithm.

Shape adaptation matrix. Our iterative shape adaptation method works in the transformed image domain. Instead of applying an adapted Gaussian kernel we can transform the image and apply a uniform kernel. A recursive implementation of the uniform Gaussian filters can then be used for computing L_x and L_y. The second moment matrix is computed according to equation 1. A local window is transformed by $U^{(k-1)} = (\mu^{-\frac{1}{2}})^{(k-1)} \cdots (\mu^{-\frac{1}{2}})^{(1)} \cdot U^{(0)}$ in step (k) of the iterative algorithm. In the following we refer to this operation as U-transformation. Note that a new μ matrix is computed at each iteration and that the U matrix is the concatenation of square roots of the second moment matrices. By keeping the larger eigenvalue $\lambda_{max}(U) = 1$ we assure that the original image is not under-sampled. This implies that the image patch is enlarged in the direction of $\lambda_{min}(U)$. For a given point the integration and the derivation scale determine the second moment matrix μ. These scale parameters are automatically detected in each iteration step. Thus, the resulting μ matrix is independent of the initial scale.

Integration scale. For a given spatial point we can automatically select its characteristic scale. In order to preserve invariance to scale changes we select the integration scale σ_I for which the normalized Laplacian $|\sigma^2(L_{xx}(\sigma) + L_{yy}(\sigma))|$ attains a local maximum over scale [9]. Keeping this scale constant during iterations can be sufficient in the presence of weak affine distortions. In the case of large affine deformations the scale change is in general very different for the x and y directions. Thus, the characteristic scale detected in the image domain and in its U-transformed version can be significantly different. It is, therefore, essential to select the integration scale after each estimation of the U transformation. This allows to converge towards a solution where the scale and the second moment matrix do not change any more.

Derivation scale. The local derivation scale is less critical and can be set proportional to the integration scale $\sigma_D = s\sigma_I$. The factor s should not be too small, otherwise the smoothing is too large with respect to the derivation. On the other hand s should be small enough such that σ_I can average the covariance matrix $\mu(\mathbf{x}, \sigma_D, \sigma_I)$ by smoothing. Factor s is commonly chosen from the range $[0.5, \ldots, 0.75]$. Our solution is to select the derivation scale for which the local isotropy assumes a maximum over this range of scales. The local isotropy is measured by the local gradient distribution μ (equation 1). To obtain a normalized measure we use the eigenvalue ratio $(\lambda_{min}(\mu)/\lambda_{max}(\mu))$. Given the integration scale σ_I we select $s \in [0.5, \ldots, 0.75]$ for which the ratio assumes a maximum. The factor s has an important influence on the convergence of the second moment matrix. The iterative procedure converges toward a matrix with equal eigenvalues. The smaller the difference between the eigenvalues $(\lambda_{max}(\mu), \lambda_{min}(\mu))$ of the initial matrix, the closer is the final solution and the faster the procedure converges. Note that the Harris measure (equation 2) already selects the points with two large eigenvalues. A large difference between the eigenvalues leads to a large scaling in one direction by the U-transformation and the point does not converge to a stable solution due to noise. Thus, the selection of the local scale allows to obtain a reasonable eigenvalue ratio and allows convergence for points which would not converge if the ratio is too large. A similar approach for local scale selection was proposed in [1].

Spatial localization. It is well known that the local maxima of the Harris measure (equation 2) change their spatial location if the detection scale changes. This can also be observed if the scale change is different in each direction. The detection with different scales in x and in y direction is replaced by affine normalizing the image and then applying the same scale in both directions. The affine normalization of a point neighbourhood slightly changes the local spatial maxima of the Harris measure. Consequently, we re-detect the maximum in the affine normalized window W. We then obtain a vector of displacement to the nearest maximum in the U-normalized image domain. The location of the initial point is corrected with the displacement vector back-transformed to the original image domain $\mathbf{x}^{(k)} = \mathbf{x}^{(k-1)} + U^{(k-1)} \cdot (\mathbf{x}_w^{(k)} - \mathbf{x}_w^{(k-1)})$, where $\mathbf{x}_w$ are the coordinates in the transformed image domain.

Termination criterion. The important part of the iteration procedure is the termination criterion. The convergence measure can be based on either the μ or the U matrix. If the criterion is based on the μ matrix computed in each iteration step, we require that this matrix is sufficiently close to a pure rotation matrix. This implies that $\lambda_{max}(\mu)$ and $\lambda_{min}(\mu)$ are equal. In practice we allow for a small error $\lambda_{min}(\mu)/\lambda_{max}(\mu) > \epsilon_C$. Another possibility is to interpret the transformation $U = R^T \cdot D \cdot R$ as a rotation R and a scaling D and compare consecutive transformations. We stop the iteration if the consecutive R and D transformations are sufficiently similar. Both termination criteria give the same final results. Another important point is to stop the procedure in the case of divergence. We reject the point if $\lambda_{max}(D)/\lambda_{min}(D) > \epsilon_l$ (i.e. $\epsilon_l = 6$), otherwise it leads to unstable elongated structures.

3.1 Detection Algorithm

We propose an iterative procedure that allows initial points to converge to affine invariant points. To initialize our algorithm we use points extracted by the multi-scale Harris detector. These points are not affine invariant due to a non adapted Gaussian kernel, but provide an approximate localization and scale for initialization. For a given initial interest point $\mathbf{x}^{(0)}$ we apply the following procedure:

1. initialize $U^{(0)}$ to the identity matrix
2. normalize window $W(U^{(k-1)}\mathbf{x}_w) = I(\mathbf{x})$ centred in $U^{(k-1)}\mathbf{x}_w^{(k-1)} = \mathbf{x}^{(k-1)}$
3. select *integration scale* σ_I in $\mathbf{x}_w^{(k-1)}$
4. select *derivation scale* $\sigma_D = s\sigma_I$ which maximizes $\frac{\lambda_{min}(\mu)}{\lambda_{max}(\mu)}$
   with $s \in [0.5, \ldots, 0.75]$ and $\mu = \mu(\mathbf{x}_w^{(k-1)}, \sigma_D, \sigma_I)$
5. detect *spatial localization* $\mathbf{x}_w^{(k)}$ of the maximum of the Harris measure (equation 2) nearest to $\mathbf{x}_w^{(k-1)}$ and compute the location of interest point $\mathbf{x}^{(k)}$
6. compute $\mu_i^{(k)} = \mu^{-\frac{1}{2}}(\mathbf{x}_w^{(k)}, \sigma_D, \sigma_I)$
7. concatenate transformation $U^{(k)} = \mu_i^{(k)} \cdot U^{(k-1)}$ and normalize $U^{(k)}$ such that $\lambda_{max}(U^{(k)}) = 1$
8. go to step 2 if $\lambda_{min}(\mu_i^{(k)})/\lambda_{max}(\mu_i^{(k)}) < \epsilon_C$

Although the computation may seem to be very time consuming, note that most time is spent computing L_x and L_y, which is done only once in each step if the factor s is kept constant. The iteration loop begins with selecting the integration scale because we have noticed that this part of the algorithm is most robust to a small localization error of an interest point. However, scale σ_I changes if the shape of the patch is transformed. Given an initial approximate solution, the presented algorithm allows to iteratively modify the shape, the scale and the spatial location of a point and converges to a true affine invariant interest point.

The convergence properties of the shape adaptation algorithm are extensively studied in [9]. In general the procedure converges provided that the initial estimation of the affine deformation is sufficiently close to the true deformation and that the integration scale is well adapted to the local signal structure.

3.2 Affine Invariant Interest Point

Figure 1 presents two examples for interest point detection. Columns (a) display the points used for initialization which are detected by the multi-scale Harris detector. The circle around a point shows the scale of detection (the radius of the circle is $3\sigma_I$). Note that there is a significant change in location between points detected at different scales and that the circles in corresponding images (top and bottom row) do not cover the same image regions. The affine invariant points to which the initial points converge are presented in the columns (b). We can see that the method converges correctly even if the location and scale of the initial point is relatively far from the point of convergence. Convergence is in general obtained in less than 10 iterations. The minor differences between the

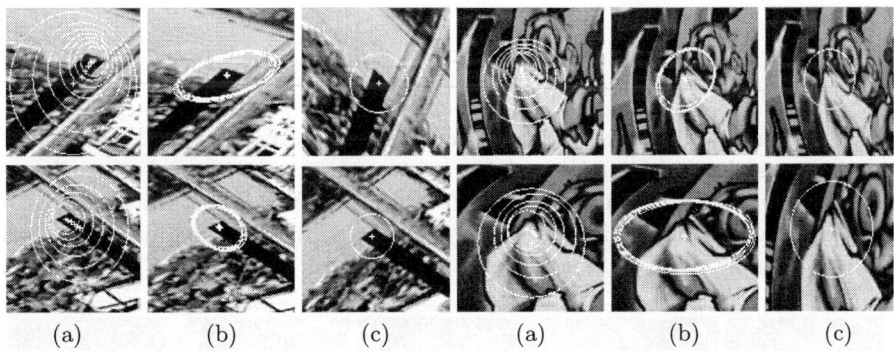

Fig. 1. Affine invariant interest point detection : (a) Initial interest points detected with the multi-scale Harris detector. (b) Points and corresponding affine regions obtained after applying the iterative algorithm. (c) Point neighbourhoods normalized with the estimated matrices to remove stretch and skew.

regions in columns (b) are caused by the imprecision of the scale estimation and the error ϵ_C. The relation between two consecutive scales is 1.2 and ϵ_C is set to 0.96. It is easy to identify these regions by comparing their locations, scales and second moment matrices and to keep only one of them. We then obtain a set of points where each one represents a different image location and structure.

Column (c) shows the points normalized with the estimated matrices to remove stretch and skew. We can clearly see that the regions correspond between the two images (top and bottom row).

3.3 Repeatability of Detectors

A comparative evaluation of different detectors is presented in the following. We compare our Harris-Affine method with two similar approaches [2, 11]. Mikolajczyk and Schmid [11] have developed a scale invariant interest point detector. Interest points are extracted at several scales with the Harris detector. Characteristic points are selected at the maxima over scale of the Laplacian function. We refer to this detector as Harris-Laplace. Baumberg [2] extracts Harris interest points at several scales and then adapts the shape of the region to the local image structure using an iterative procedure based on the second moment matrix. This method does not adapt location nor scale. It is referred to as Harris-AffineRegions.

An evaluation criterion for point detectors was described in [11]. It computes a repeatability score which takes into account the point location as well as the detection scale. We have extended this evaluation criterion to the affine case. The repeatability rate between two images is represented by the number of corresponding points with respect to the number of detected points. We consider two points $\mathbf{x}_a$ and $\mathbf{x}_b$ corresponding if :

1. the error in relative location of $\|\mathbf{x}_a, H \cdot \mathbf{x}_b\| < 1.5$ pixel, where H is the homography between images (planar scenes are used for our evaluation)
2. the error in image surface covered by point neighbourhoods is less than 20%

$$\epsilon_S = 1 - \frac{\mu_a \cap (A^T \mu_b A)}{\mu_a \cup (A^T \mu_b A)} < 0.2 \tag{6}$$

where μ_a and μ_b are the elliptical regions defined by $x^T \mu x = 1$. The union of the regions is $(\mu_a \cup (A^T \mu_b A))$ and $(\mu_a \cap (A^T \mu_b A))$ is their intersection. A is a local linearization of the homography H in point $\mathbf{x}_b$. We neglect the possible 1.5 pixel translation error while computing ϵ_S, because it has a small influence and the homography between real images is not perfect.

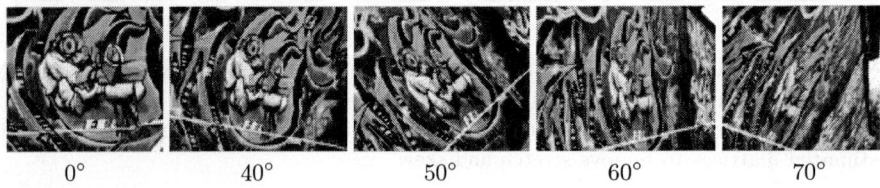

Fig. 2. Images of one test sequence. The corresponding viewpoint angles are indicated below the images.

Figures 3 and 4 display average results for three real sequences of planar scenes (see figure 2). The viewpoint varied in horizontal direction between 0 and

70 degree. There are also illumination and zoom changes between the images. The homography between images was estimated with manually selected point pairs. Figure 3 displays the repeatability rate and figure 4 shows the localization

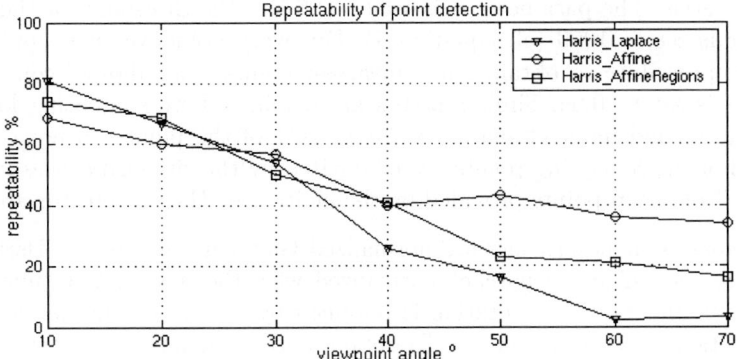

Fig. 3. Repeatability of detectors: a)$Harris\_Affine$ - approach proposed in this paper, b)$Harris\_AffineRegions$ - the multi-scale Harris detector with affine normalization of the point regions, c)$Harris\_Laplace$ - the multi-scale Harris detector with characteristic scale selection.

and intersection error for corresponding points. We can notice in figure 3 that our detector significantly improves the results for strong affine deformations, that is for changes in the viewpoint angle of more than 40 degrees. The improvement is with respect to localization as well as region intersection (see figure 4). In the presence of weak affine distortions the $Harris\_Laplace$ approach provides slightly better results. The affine adaptation does not improve the location and the point shape because the scaling is almost the same in every direction. In this case the uniform Gaussian kernel is sufficiently well adapted.

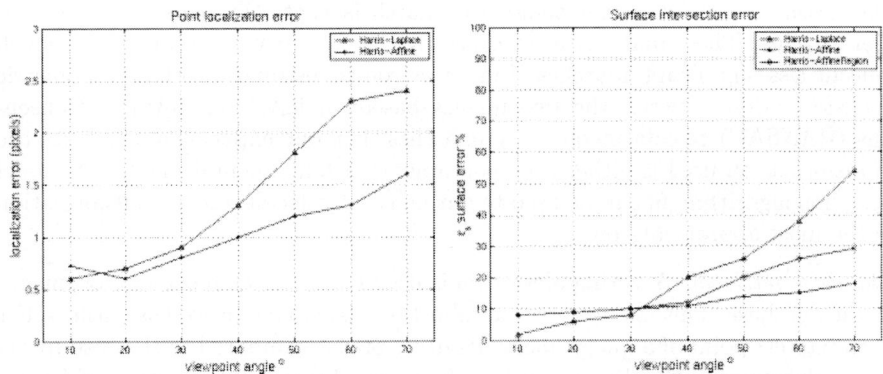

Fig. 4. Detection error of corresponding points : a) relative location b) surface intersection ϵ_S.

4 Matching and Recognition

Point detection. The initial set of interest points is obtained with the multi-scale Harris detector. The scale-space representation starts with a detection scale of 2.5 and the scale factor between two levels of resolution is 1.2. We have used 17 scale levels. The parameter α is set to 0.06 and the threshold for the Harris detector is set to 1000 (cf. equation 2). For every point we then applied the iterative procedure to obtain affine invariant points. The allowed convergence error ϵ_C is set to 0.96. Similar points are eliminated by comparing location, scale and second moment matrices. About 40% of the points do not converge and 2/3 of the remaining points are eliminated by the similarity measure, that is 20-30% of initial points provided by the multi-scale Harris detector are kept.

Descriptors. Our descriptors are normalized Gaussian derivatives. Derivatives are computed on image patches normalized with the matrix U estimated for each point. Invariance to rotation is obtained by "steering" the derivatives in the direction of the gradient [4]. To obtain a stable estimation of the gradient direction, we use an average gradient orientation in a point neighbourhood. Invariance to affine intensity changes is obtained by dividing the derivatives by the first derivative. We obtain descriptors of dimension 12 by using derivatives up to 4th order.

Similarity of descriptors. The similarity of descriptors is measured by the Mahalanobis distance. This distance requires the estimation of the covariance matrix Λ which encapsulates signal noise, variations in photometry as well as inaccuracy of the interest point location. Λ is estimated statistically over a large set of image samples. Given the scale, the gradient direction and the neighbourhood shape of points we can affine normalize the window and use cross-correlation as an additional distance measure.

Robust matching. To robustly match two images, we first determine point-to-point correspondences. We select for each descriptor in the first image the most similar descriptor in the second image based on the Mahalanobis distance. If the distance is below a threshold, the match is kept. We obtain a set of initial matches. These matches are verified by the cross-correlation measure which rejects less significant matches. Finally a robust estimation of the geometric transformation between the two images based on RANdom SAmple Consensus (RANSAC) rejects inconsistent matches. For our experimental results the transformation used is either a homography or a fundamental matrix. A model selection algorithm [6] can be used to automatically decide which transformation is the most appropriate one.

Database retrieval. A voting algorithm is used to select the most similar images in the database. This makes retrieval robust to mismatches as well as outliers. For each interest point of a query image, its descriptor is compared to the descriptors in the database. If the distance is less than a fixed threshold, a vote is added for the corresponding database image. Note that a point cannot vote several times for the same database image. The database image with the highest number of votes is the most similar one.

5 Experimental Results

In this section we present matching and recognition results based on the method described in section 4. All the tests were carried on real images [17].

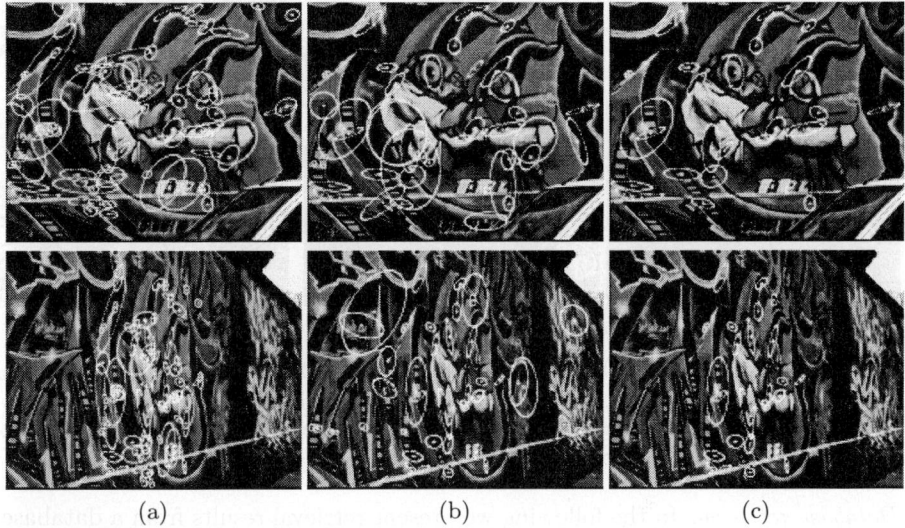

Fig. 5. Robust matching : (a) There are 78 couples of possible matches among the 287 and 325 detected points. (b) There are 43 point matches based on the descriptors and the cross-correlation score. 27 of these matches are correct. (c)There are 27 inliers to the robustly estimated homography. All of them are correct.

Matching. Figure 5 illustrates the results of the matching procedure. In order to separate the detection and matching results, we present all the possible correspondences determined with the homography in column (a). There are 78 corresponding point pairs among the 287 and 325 points detected in the first and second images respectively. We first match the detected points with the Mahalanobis distance and obtain 53 matches (29 correct and 24 incorrect). An additional verification based on the cross-correlation score rejects 10 matches (2 correct and 8 incorrect). These 43 matches (27 correct and 16 incorrect) are displayed in column (b). The images in column (c) show the 27 inliers to the robustly estimated homography. Note that there is a significant perspective transformation between the two images. A second example is presented in figure 6a. The images show a 3D scene taken from significantly different viewpoints. This image pair presents a more significant change in viewpoint than the images in figure 7c which were used in [13, 16] as an example for matching. In the figure 6b, we show a pair of images for which our matching procedure fails. The failure is not due to our detector, as the manually selected corresponding points show. It is caused by our descriptors which are not sufficiently distinctive. Note that the corners of sharp or wide angles, of light or dark intensity are almost the same once normalized to be affine invariant. If there is no distinctive texture in the region around the points, there are too many mismatches and additional constraints as for example semi-local constraints [3] should be used.

Fig. 6. (a) Example of a 3D scene observed from significantly different viewpoints. There are 14 inliers to a robustly estimated fundamental matrix, all of them correct. (b) An image pairs for which our method fails. There exist, however, corresponding points which we have selected manually.

Database retrieval. In the following we present retrieval results from a database with more than 5000 images. The images in the database are extracted from video sequences which include movies, sport events and news reports. Similar images are mostly excluded by taking one image per 300 frames. Furthermore, the database contains one image of each of our 4 test sequences. The second row of figure 7 shows these four images. The top row displays images for which the corresponding image in the database (second row) was correctly retrieved. Note the significant transformations between the query images and the images in the database. There is a scale change of a factor of 3 between images of pair (a). Image pairs (b) and (c) show large changes in viewing angle. Image pair (d) combines a scale change with a significant change in viewing angle. The displayed matches are the inliers to a robustly estimated transformation matrix between the query image and the most similar image in the database.

Conclusions and Discussion

In this paper we have described a novel approach for interest point detection which is invariant to affine transformations. Our algorithm simultaneously adapts location as well as scale and shape of the point neighbourhood. None of the existing methods for interest point detection simultaneously solves for all of these problems during feature extraction. Our affine invariant points and the associated corresponding regions allow matching and recognition in the presence of large scale and viewpoint changes. Experimental results for wide baseline matching and recognition are excellent. Future work includes the development of more discriminant descriptors as well as the use of neighbourhood constraints.

Fig. 7. For image pairs (a),(b) and (c) the top row shows the query images and the bottom row shows the most similar images in the database. For image pair (d) the left image is the query image and the right one the image in the database. The displayed matches are the inliers to a robustly estimated fundamental matrix or homography between the query image and the most similar image in the database. There are (a) 22 matches, (b) 34 matches, (c) 22 matches and (d) 33 matches. All of them are correct.

Acknowledgement

This work was supported by the European FET-open project VIBES. We are grateful to RobotVis INRIA Sophia-Antipolis for providing the Valbonne images and to the University of Oxford for the Dunster images. The authors would like to express special thanks to David Lowe and Matthew Brown for useful suggestions and constructive discussions during a preliminary part of this work.

References

1. A. Almansa and T. Lindeberg. Fingerprint enhancement by shape adaptation of scale-space operators with automatic scale selection. IEEE *Transactions on Image Processing*, 9(12):2027–2042, 2000.
2. A. Baumberg. Reliable feature matching across widely separated views. In *Proceedings of the Conference on Computer Vision and Pattern Recognition, Hilton Head Island, South Carolina, USA*, pages 774–781, 2000.
3. Y. Dufournaud, C. Schmid, and R. Horaud. Matching images with different resolutions. In *Proceedings of the Conference on Computer Vision and Pattern Recognition, Hilton Head Island, South Carolina, USA*, pages 612–618, 2000.
4. W. Freeman and E. Adelson. The design and use of steerable filters. IEEE *Transactions on Pattern Analysis and Machine Intelligence*, 13(9):891–906, 1991.
5. C. Harris and M. Stephens. A combined corner and edge detector. In *Alvey Vision Conference*, pages 147–151, 1988.
6. K. Kanatani. Geometric information criterion for model selection. *International Journal of Computer Vision*, 26(3):171–189, 1998.
7. T. Lindeberg. *Scale-Space Theory in Computer Vision*. Kluwer Publishers, 1994.
8. T. Lindeberg. Feature detection with automatic scale selection. *International Journal of Computer Vision*, 30(2):79–116, 1998.
9. T. Lindeberg and J. Garding. Shape-adapted smoothing in estimation of 3-D shape cues from affine deformations of local 2-D brightness structure. *Image and Vision Computing*, 15(6):415–434, 1997.
10. D. G. Lowe. Object recognition from local scale-invariant features. In *Proceedings of the 7th International Conference on Computer Vision, Kerkyra, Greece*, pages 1150–1157, 1999.
11. K. Mikolajczyk and C. Schmid. Indexing based on scale invariant interest points. In *Proceedings of the 8th International Conference on Computer Vision, Vancouver, Canada*, pages 525–531, 2001.
12. P. Pritchett and A. Zisserman. Wide baseline stereo matching. In *Proceedings of the 6th International Conference on Computer Vision, Bombay, India*, pages 754–760, 1998.
13. F. Schaffalitzky and A. Zisserman. Viewpoint invariant texture matching and wide baseline stereo. In *Proceedings of the 8th International Conference on Computer Vision, Vancouver, Canada*, pages 636–643, 2001.
14. C. Schmid and R. Mohr. Local grayvalue invariants for image retrieval. IEEE *Transactions on Pattern Analysis and Machine Intelligence*, 19(5):530–534, 1997.
15. D. Tell and S. Carlsson. Wide baseline point matching using affine invariants computed from intensity profiles. In *Proceedings of the 6th European Conference on Computer Vision, Dublin, Ireland*, pages 814–828, 2000.
16. T. Tuytelaars and L. Van Gool. Wide baseline stereo matching based on local, affinely invariant regions. In *The Eleventh British Machine Vision Conference, University of Bristol, UK*, pages 412–425, 2000.
17. Test sequences. http://www.inrialpes.fr/movi/people/Mikolajczyk/Database/

Understanding and Modeling the Evolution of Critical Points under Gaussian Blurring

Arjan Kuijper[1] and Luc Florack[2]

[1] Utrecht University, Department of Computer Science, Padualaan 14, NL-3584 CH Utrecht, The Netherlands
[2] Technical University Eindhoven, Department of Biomedical Engineering, Den Dolech 2, NL-5600 MB Eindhoven, The Netherlands

Abstract. In order to investigate the deep structure of Gaussian scale space images, one needs to understand the behaviour of critical points under the influence of parameter-driven blurring. During this evolution two different types of special points are encountered, the so-called scale space saddles and the catastrophe points, the latter describing the pairwise annihilation and creation of critical points. The mathematical framework of catastrophe theory is used to model non-generic events that might occur due to e.g. local symmetries in the image. It is shown how this knowledge can be exploited in conjunction with the scale space saddle points, yielding a scale space hierarchy tree that can be used for segmentation. Furthermore the relevance of creations of pairs of critical points with respect to the hierarchy is discussed. We clarify the theory with an artificial image and a simulated MR image.

1 Introduction

The presence of structures of various sizes in an image demands almost automatically a collection of image analysis tools that is capable of dealing with these structures. Essential is that this system is capable of handling the various, a priori unknown sizes or scales. To this end various types of multi-scale systems have been developed.

The concept of scale space has been introduced by Witkin [16] and Koenderink [8]. They showed that the natural way to represent an image at finite resolution is by convolving it with a Gaussian of various bandwidths, thus obtaining a smoothened image at a scale determined by the bandwidth. This approach has lead to the formulation of various invariant expressions – expressions that are independent of the coordinates – that capture certain features in an image at distinct levels of scale [4].

In this paper we focus on linear, or Gaussian, scale space. This has the advantage that each scale level only requires the choice of an appropriate scale; and that the image intensity at that level follows linearly from any previous level. It is therefore possible to trace the evolution of certain image entities over scale. The exploitation of various scales simultaneously has been referred to as *deep structure* by Koenderink [8]. It pertains to information of the change of the image from highly detailed –including noise – to highly smoothened. Furthermore, it may be expected that large structures "live" longer than small structures (a reason that Gaussian blur is used to suppress noise). The image together with its blurred version was called "primal sketch" by Lindeberg [12].

Since multi-scale information can be ordered, one obtains a hierarchy representing the subsequent simplification of the image with increasing scale. In one dimensional images this has been done by several authors [7,15], but higher dimensional images are more complicated as we will discuss below.

An essentially unsolved problem in the investigation of deep structure is how to establish meaningful links across scales. A well-defined and user-independent constraint is that points are linked if they are topological equal. Thus maxima are linked to maxima, etc. This approach has been used in 2-D images by various authors, *e.g.* [13], noticing that sometimes new extrema occurred, disrupting a good linking. This creation of new extrema in scale space has been studied in detail by Damon [2], proving that these creations are generic in images of dimension larger than one. That means that they are not some kind of artifact, introduced by noise or numerical errors, but that they are to be expected in any typical case.

Apart from the above mentioned catastrophe points (annihilations and creations) there is a second type of topologically interesting points in scale space, *viz.* scale space critical points. These are spatial critical points with vanishing scale derivative. This implies a zero Laplacean in linear scale space. Although Laplacean zero-crossings are widely investigated, the combination with zero gradient has only been mentioned occasionally, *e.g.* by [6,9,11].

Since linking of topologically identical points is an intensity based approach, also the shape of iso-intensity manifolds must be taken into account. Scale space critical points, together with annihilations and creations allow us to build a hierarchical structure that can be used to obtain a so-called pre-segmentation: a partitioning of the image in which the nesting of iso-intensity manifolds becomes visible.

It is sometimes desirable to use higher order (and thus non-generic) catastrophes to describe the change of structure. In this paper we describe several of these catastrophes in scale space and show the implications for both the hierarchical structure and the pre-segmentation.

2 Theory

Let $L(\mathbf{x})$ denote an arbitrary n dimensional image, the *initial image*. Then $L(\mathbf{x};t)$ denotes the $n+1$ dimensional *Gaussian scale space image* of $L(\mathbf{x})$. By definition, $L(\mathbf{x};t)$ satisfies the diffusion equation: $\Delta L = \partial_t L$, where ΔL denotes the Laplacean of L. *Spatial critical points*, i.e. saddles and extrema, at a certain scale t_0 are defined as the points at fixed scale t_0 where the spatial gradient vanishes: $\nabla L(\mathbf{x};t_0) = 0$. The type of a spatial critical point is given by the eigenvalues of the Hessian H, the matrix with the second order spatial derivatives, evaluated at its location. Note that the trace of the Hessian equals the Laplacean. For maxima (minima) all eigenvalues of the Hessian are negative (positive). At a spatial saddle point H has both negative and positive eigenvalues.

Since $L(\mathbf{x};t)$ is a continuous – even smooth – function in $(\mathbf{x};t)$-space, spatial critical points are part of a one dimensional manifold in scale space, the *critical curve*.

As a result of the maximum principle, critical points in scale space, i.e. points where both the spatial gradient and the scale derivative vanish: $\nabla L(\mathbf{x};t) = 0 \wedge \partial_t L(\mathbf{x};t) = 0$, are always saddle points and called *scale space saddles*

Consequently, the *extended Hessian* $\mathcal{H}$ of $L(\mathbf{x};t)$, the matrix of second order derivatives in scale space defined by

$$\mathcal{H} = \begin{pmatrix} \nabla \nabla^T L & \Delta \nabla L \\ (\Delta \nabla L)^T & \Delta \Delta L \end{pmatrix},$$

has both positive and negative eigenvalues at scale space saddles. Note that the elements of $\mathcal{H}$ are purely spatial derivatives. This is possible by virtue of the diffusion equation.

2.1 Catastrophe Theory

The spatial critical points of a function with non-zero eigenvalues of the Hessian are called *Morse critical points*. The *Morse Lemma* states that at these points the qualitative properties of the function are determined by the quadratic part of the Taylor expansion of this function. This part can be reduced to the *Morse canonical form* by a slick choice of coordinates. If at a spatial critical point the Hessian degenerates, so that at least one of the eigenvalues is zero (and consequently its determinant vanishes), the type of the spatial critical point cannot be determined. These points are called *catastrophe points*. The term catastrophe was introduced by Thom [14]. A thorough mathematical treatment can be found in the work of Arnol'd, e.g. [1]. More pragmatic introductions and applications are widely published, e.g. [5].

The catastrophe points are also called *non-Morse critical points*, since a higher order Taylor expansion is essentially needed to describe the qualitative properties. Although the dimension of the variables is arbitrary, the *Thom Splitting Lemma* states that one can split up the function in a Morse and a non-Morse part. The latter consists of variables representing the k "bad" eigenvalues of the Hessian that become zero. The Morse part contains the $n-k$ remaining variables. Consequently, the Hessian contains a $(n-k) \times (n-k)$ sub-matrix representing a Morse function. It therefore suffices to study the part of k variables. The canonical form of the function at the non-Morse critical point thus contains two parts: a Morse canonical form of $n-k$ variables, in terms of the quadratic part of the Taylor series, and a non-Morse part. The latter can by put into canonical form called the *catastrophe germ*, which is obviously a polynomial of degree 3 or higher.

Since the Morse part does not change qualitatively under small perturbations, it is not necessary to further investigate this part. The non-Morse part, however, does change. Generally the non-Morse critical point will split into a non-Morse critical point, described by a polynomial of lower degree, and Morse critical points, or even exclusively into Morse critical points. This event is called a *morsification*. So the non-Morse part contains the catastrophe germ and a perturbation that controls the morsifications.

Then the general form of a Taylor expansion $f(\mathbf{x})$ at a non-Morse critical point of an n dimensional function can be written as (*Thom's Theorem*): $f(\mathbf{x}; \lambda) = CG + PT + Q$, where $CG(x_1, \ldots, x_k)$ denotes the catastrophe germ, $PT(x_1, \ldots, x_k; \lambda_1, \ldots, \lambda_l)$ the perturbation germ with an l dimensional space of parameters, and the Morse part $Q = \sum_{i=k+1}^{n} \epsilon_i x_i^2$ with $\epsilon_i = \pm 1$.

The set of so-called simple real singularities have catastrophe germs given by the infinite series $A_k^\pm \stackrel{\text{def}}{=} \pm x^{k+1}, k \geq 1$ and $D_k^\pm \stackrel{\text{def}}{=} x^2 y \pm y^{k-1}, k \geq 4$. The germs A_k^+ and A_k^- are equivalent for $k=1$ and k even. Note that these catastrophes can be represented in a 2D coordinate system. In this paper we investigate the starting germs of both series, viz. the A_2, A_3, and D_4.

2.2 Catastrophes and Scale Space

The number of equations defining the catastrophe point equals $n + 1$ and therefore it is over-determined with respect to the n spatial variables. In scale space, however, the number of variables equals $n + 1$ and catastrophes occur as isolated points.

The transfer of the catastrophe germs to scale space has been made by may authors, [2,3,7,12], among whom Damon's account is probably the most rigorous. He showed that the only generic morsifications in scale space are the aforementioned A_2 (called Fold) catastrophes, describing *annihilations* and *creations* of pairs of critical points. These two points have opposite sign of the determinant of the Hessian before annihilation and after creation. All other events are compounds of such events.

Definition 1. *The scale space fold catastrophe germs are defined by*

$$f^A(x_1; t) \stackrel{def}{=} x_1^3 + 6x_1 t,$$
$$f^c(x_1, x_2; t) \stackrel{def}{=} x_1^3 - 6x_1(x_2^2 + t).$$

The Morse part is given by $\sum_{i=2}^n \epsilon_i(x_i^2 + 2t)$, *where* $\sum_{i=2}^n \epsilon_i \neq 0$ *and* $\epsilon_i \neq 0\ \forall i$.

Note that both the scale space catastrophe germs and the quadratic terms satisfy the diffusion equation. The germs f^A and f^c correspond to the two qualitatively different Fold catastrophes at the origin, an annihilation and a creation respectively. Non-generic scale space catastrophe events can be modelled by modifying the A_k and D_k series such, that they satisfy the diffusion equation. We will show that perturbation of the non-generic models resolves the generic Fold catastrophes. From Definition 1 it is obvious that annihilations occur in any dimension, but creations require at least 2 dimensions. Consequently, in 1D signals only annihilations occur. Furthermore, for images of arbitrary dimension it suffices to investigate the 2D case due to the Splitting Lemma.

2.3 Scale Space Hierarchy

From the previous section it follows that each critical curve in $(\mathbf{x}; t)$-space consists of separate branches, each of which is defined from a creation event to an annihilation event. We set $\#_C$ the number of creation events on a critical path and $\#_A$ the number of annihilation events. Since there exists a scale at which only one spatial critical point (an extremum) remains, there is one critical path with $\#_A = \#_C$, whereas all other critical paths have $\#_A = \#_C + 1$. That is, all but one critical paths are defined for a finite scale range.

One of the properties of scale space is non-enhancement of local extrema. Therefore, isophotes in the neighbourhood of an extremum at a certain scale t_0 move towards the spatial extremum at coarser scale, until at some scale t_1 the intensity of extremum equals the intensity of the isophote. The iso-intensity surface in scale formed by these isophotes form a dome, with its top at the extremum. Since the intensity of the extremum is monotonically in- or decreasing (depending on whether it is a minimum or a maximum, respectively), all such domes are nested. Retrospectively, each extremum branch carries a series of nested domes, defining increasing regions around the extremum in the input image.

These regions are uniquely related to one extremum as long as the intensity of the domes doesn't reach that of the so-called critical dome. The latter is formed by the iso-intensity manifold with its top at the extremum and containing a (nearby) scale space saddle, where both points are part of the same critical curve. That is, the scale space saddle is apparent at the saddle branch that is connected in an annihilation event with the extremum branch. The intensity at this point has a local extremum on the saddle branch.

In this way a hierarchy of regions of the input image is obtained in a straightforward manner, which can be regarded as a pre-segmentation. It also results in a partition of the scale space itself. See for more details Kuijper and Florack [10].

The crucial role is played by the scale space saddles and the catastrophe points. As long as only annihilation and creation events occur, the hierarchy is obtained straightforward. However, sometimes higher order catastrophes are needed to describe the local structure, viz. when two or more catastrophes happen to be almost incident and cannot be segregated due to numerical imprecision or (almost) symmetries in the image.

3 Catastrophes and Scale Space Saddles

In this section we discuss the appearance of catastrophe events in scale space and the effect on scale space saddles. Firstly, results on one dimensional images are given, because in this particular case scale space saddles coincide with catastrophe points. Secondly, multi-dimensional images are discussed. In higher dimensions the structure is more complicated, since generically scale space saddles do not coincide with catastrophe points. It suffices to investigate 2D images, since the A and D catastrophes are restricted to 2 bad variables.

3.1 A_2 Catastrophe in 1D

The A_2 catastrophe is called a Fold and is defined by $x^3 + \lambda x$. It scale space appearance is given by
$$L(x;t) = x^3 + 6xt.$$
The only perturbation parameter is given by t by the identification $\lambda = 6t$. It has a scale space saddle if both derivatives are zero. So it is located at the origin with intensity equal to zero. The determinant of the extended Hessian is negative, indicating a saddle. The parametrisation of the critical curve with respect to t is $(x(s); t(s)) = (\pm\sqrt{-2s}; s), s \leq 0$ and the parametrised intensity reads $P(s) = \pm 4s\sqrt{-2s}, s \leq 0$, see Figure 1a. The critical dome is given by the isophotes $L(x;t) = 0$ through the origin, so $(x;t) = (0;t)$ and $(x;t) = (x; -\frac{1}{6}x^2)$. Figure 1b shows isophotes $L = constant$ in the $(x;t, L(x;t))$-space, where the self-intersection of the isophote $L = 0$ gives the annihilation point. This isophote gives the separatrices of the different parts of the image. The separation curves in the $(x;t)$-plane are shown in Figure 1c: for $t < 0$ four segments are present, for $t > 0$ two remain.

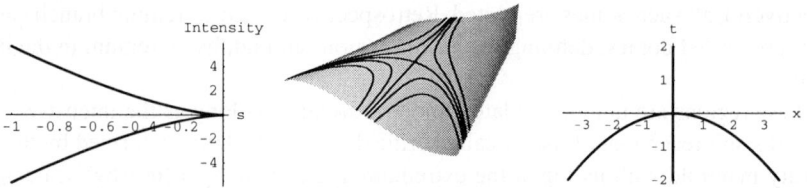

Fig. 1. Fold catastrophe in 1D: a) Parametrised intensity of the critical curve. b) 1+1D intensity scale space surface. c) Segments of b), defined by the scale space saddle.

3.2 A_3 Catastrophe in 1D

Although all catastrophes are generically described by fold catastrophes, one may encounter higher order catastrophes, e.g. due to numerical imprecision or symmetries in the signal when a set of two minima and one maximum change into one minimum, but one is not able to detect which minimum is annihilated. At such an event also the extended Hessian degenerates since one of the eigenvalues becomes zero.

The first higher order catastrophe describing such a situation is the A_3 (Cusp) catastrophe: $\pm x^4 + \lambda_1 x + \lambda_2 x^2$. The scale space representation of the catastrophe germ reads $\pm (x^4 + 12x^2 t + 12t^2)$. Obviously, scale fulfils the role of the perturbation by λ_2. Therefore the scale space form is given by

$$L(x;t) = x^4 + 12x^2 t + 12t^2 + \epsilon x,$$

where the two perturbation parameters are given by t for the second order term and ϵ for the first order term. If $\epsilon = 0$ the situation as sketched above occurs. The catastrophe takes place at the origin, where two minima and a maximum change into one minimum for increasing t. At the origin both L_{xx} and L_{xt} are zero, resulting in a zero eigenvalue of the extended Hessian. The parametrised intensity curves are shown in Figure 2a. Note that at the bottom left the two branches of the two minima with equal intensity coincide. The case $0 <|\epsilon| \ll 1$, where a morsification has taken place, is visualised in Figure 2b. This Figure shows the remaining Fold catastrophe of a minimum and a maximum (compare to Figure 1a), and the unaffected other minimum.

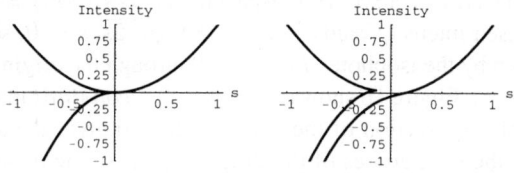

Fig. 2. Parametrised intensity of the Cusp catastrophe a) $\epsilon = 0$ b) $0 <|\epsilon| \ll 1$

Depending on the value and sign of ϵ one can find the three different types of catastrophe shown in Figure 3a-c. With an uncertainty in the measurement they may coincide, as shown in Figure 3d, where the oval represents the possible measure uncertainty.

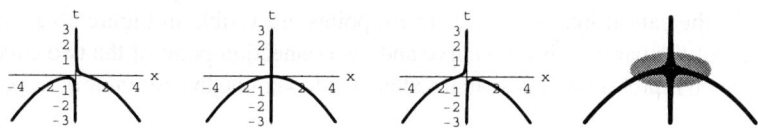

Fig. 3. Critical paths in the $(x; t)$-plane. a) $\epsilon < 0$ b) $\epsilon = 0$ c) $\epsilon > 0$ d) detection of the critical paths around the origin with uncertainty represented by the oval.

With the degeneration of the extended Hessian at the origin if $\epsilon = 0$, also the shape of the isophotes change, as shown in Figure 4. Since one eigenvalue is zero, the only remaining eigenvector is parallel to the t-axis. So there is no critical isophote in the t-direction, but both parts pass the origin horizontally. Furthermore the annihilating minimum cannot be distinguished from the remaining minimum.

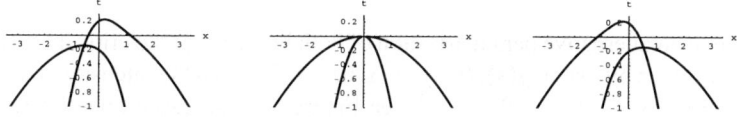

Fig. 4. Critical isophotes in the $(x; t)$-plane. a) $\epsilon < 0$ b) $\epsilon = 0$ c) $\epsilon > 0$

3.3 A_2 Catastrophe in 2D

The scale space Fold catastrophe in 2D is given by:

$$L(x, y; t) = x^3 + 6xt + \alpha(y^2 + 2t), \tag{1}$$

where $\alpha = \pm 1$. Positive sign describes a saddle – minimum annihilation, negative sign a saddle – maximum one. Without loss of generality we take $\alpha = 1$. The catastrophe takes place at the origin with intensity equal to zero and the scale space saddle is located at $(x, y; t) = (-\frac{1}{3}, 0; -\frac{1}{18})$ with intensity $-\frac{1}{27}$. The surface $L(x, y; t) = -\frac{1}{27}$ through the scale space saddle is shown in Figure 5a. It has a local maximum at $(x, y; t) = (\frac{1}{6}, 0; -\frac{1}{72})$: the top of the extremum dome. The iso-intensity surface through the scale space saddle can be visualised by two surfaces touching each other at the scale space saddle. One part of the surface is related to the corresponding extremum of the saddle. The other part encircles some other segment of the image. The surface belonging to the extremum forms an dome. The critical curve intersects this surface twice. The saddle branch has a intersection at the scale space saddle, the extremum branch at the top of the dome, as shown in Figure 5a.

The parametrisation of the two branches of the critical curve with respect to t is given by $(x(s), y(s); t(s)) = (\pm\sqrt{-2s}, 0; s)$, $s \leq 0$, see Figure 5b. The intensity of the critical curve reads $L(s) = 2s \pm 4s\sqrt{-2s}$, $s \leq 0$. The scale space saddle is located at $s = -\frac{1}{18}$, the catastrophe at $s = 0$. These points are visible in Figure 5b as the local minimum of the parametrisation curve and the connection point of the two curves (the upper branch representing the spatial saddle, the lower one the minimum), respectively.

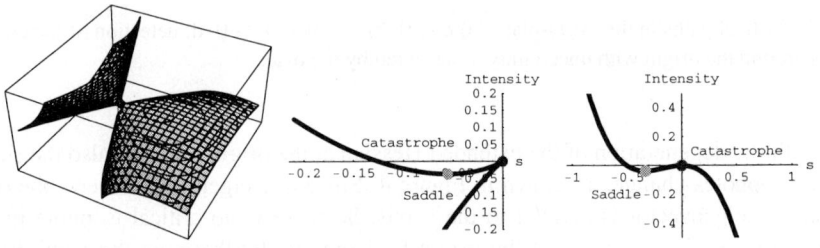

Fig. 5. a) 2D Surface trough the scale space saddle. b) Intensity of the critical curve, parametrised by the x-coordinate. c) Same for the t-coordinate.

Note that an alternative parametrisation of both branches of the critical curve simultaneously is given by $(x(s), y(s); t(s)) = (s, 0; -\frac{1}{2}s^2)$. Then the intensity of the critical curve is given by $L(s) = -2s^3 - s^2$, see Figure 5c. The catastrophe takes place at $s = 0$, the saddle at $s = -\frac{1}{3}$. These points are visible in Figure 5c as the extrema of the parametrisation curve. The branch $s < 0$ represents the saddle point, the branch $s > 0$ the minimum.

3.4 A_3 Catastrophe in 2D

With the similar argumentation as in the one dimensional case it is also interesting to investigate the behaviour around the next catastrophe event. The 2D scale space extension of the Cusp catastrophe is given by

$$L(x, y; t) = \frac{1}{12}x^4 + x^2 t + t^2 + \alpha(2t + y^2) + \epsilon x$$

where, again, $\alpha = \pm 1$. If $\epsilon \neq 0$ a fold catastrophe results. The critical curves in the $(x; t)$-plane at $\epsilon = 0, y = 0$ are shown in Figure 6a. They form a so-called pitchfork bifurcation at the origin, the catastrophe point.

One can verify that the critical points lay on the curves given by $(x(s), y(s); t(s)) = (0, 0; s)$ and $(x(s), y(s); t(s)) = (\pm\sqrt{-6s}, 0; s)$, $s \leq 0$.

The intensities are given by $L_1(s) = (0, 0; s) = s^2 + 2\alpha s$ with its extremum at $s = -\alpha$ and $L_2(s) = L(\pm\sqrt{-6s}, 0; s) = -2s^2 + 2\alpha s$, $s \leq 0$. The latter has an extremum at $s = \frac{1}{2}\alpha$. Since $s \leq 0$, these scale space saddles only occur if $\alpha < 0$. It is therefore essential to distinguish between the two signs of α.

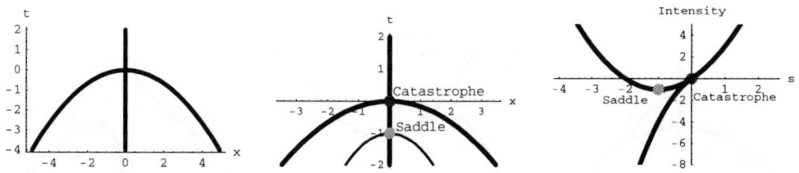

Fig. 6. a) Critical paths. b) Critical paths with zero-Laplacean, catastrophe point and scale space saddle if $\alpha > 0$. c) Intensity of the critical paths. The part bottom-left represents two branches ending at the catastrophe point.

Case $\alpha > 0$. For positive α, the curve $(x, y; t) = (0, 0; s)$ contains saddles if $t < 0$ and minima if $t > 0$. The other curve contains minima on both branches. At the origin a catastrophe occurs, at $(x, y; t) = (0, 0, -\alpha)$ a scale space saddle, see Figure 6b. The intensities of the critical curves are shown in Figure 6c; The two branches of the minima for $t < 0$ have equal intensity. The iso-intensity manifold in scale space forms a double dome since the two minima are indistinguishable, see Figure 7a.

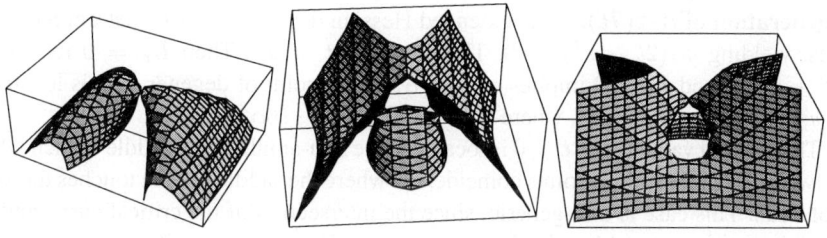

Fig. 7. 2D Surfaces trough the scale space saddles at a Cusp catastrophe, a) $\alpha > 0$, b) $\alpha < 0, t = \frac{1}{2}\alpha$ and c) $\alpha < 0, t = -\alpha$

A small perturbation $(0 <| \epsilon |\ll 1)$ leads to a generic image containing a Fold catastrophe and thus a single cone. However, as argued in section 3.2 this perturbation may be too small to identify the annihilating minimum. We will use this degeneration in Section 4 to identify multiple regions with one scale space saddle

Case $\alpha < 0$. If α is negative, the curve $(x, y; t) = (0, 0; s)$ contains a maximum if $t < 0$ and a saddle if $t > 0$, while the curve $(x, y; t) = (\pm\sqrt{-6s}, 0; s), s < 0$ contains saddles. Now 3 scale space saddles occur: at $(x, y; t) = (0, 0; -\alpha)$ and $(x, y; t) = (\pm\sqrt{-3\alpha}, 0; \frac{1}{2}\alpha)$, see Figure 8a. The corresponding intensities are shown in Figure 8b, where again the intensities of the two saddle branches for $t < 0$ coincide.

The iso-intensity surfaces through the scale space saddles are shown in Figure 7b-c. The scale space saddles at $t = \frac{1}{2}\alpha$ both encapsulate the maximum at the t-axis. The scale space saddle at $t = -\alpha$ is void: it is not related to an extremum. This is clear from the fact that there is only one extremum present.

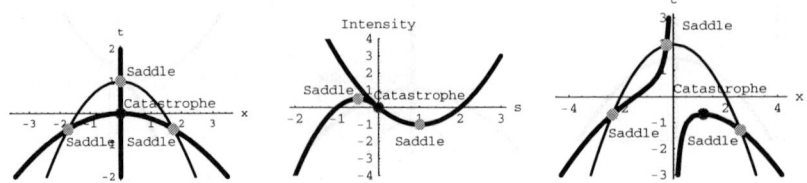

Fig. 8. a) Critical paths with zero-Laplacean, catastrophe point and scale space saddle if $\alpha = -1$. b) Intensity of the critical paths. The part bottom-left represents two branches ending at the catastrophe point. c) Critical paths with $\alpha < 0$, $4\epsilon^2 < -3\alpha^3$, zero-Laplacean, catastrophe point and scale space saddle.

If a small perturbation $(0 <|\epsilon| \ll 1)$ is added, the three scale space saddles remain present in the generic image. Their trajectories in the $(x;t)$-plane are shown in Figure 8c. Now a Fold catastrophe is apparent, but also a saddle branch containing two (void) scale space saddles, caused by the neighbourhood of the annihilating saddle-extremum pair.

Degeneration of det($\mathcal{H}$). The extended Hessian degenerates if its determinant vanishes, yielding $4\alpha(2t - x^2) = 0$. This implies $2t = x^2$. Then $L_x = 0$ reduces to $\frac{4}{3}x^3 + \epsilon = 0$ and $L_t = 0$ implies $x^2 = -\alpha$, so the point of degeneration is located at $(x, y; t) = (\sqrt{-\alpha}, 0, -\frac{1}{2}\alpha)$, where $\alpha < 0$ and $9\epsilon^2 = -16\alpha^3$.

This special value for α, $\epsilon \neq 0$ is located at the non-annihilating saddle branch where the two scale space saddle points coincide, i.e. where the saddle branch touches the zero-Laplacean. This case is non-generic, since the intersection of the critical curve and the hyperplane $\Delta L = 0$ at this value is not transverse. This value describes the transition of the case with two void scale space saddles to the case without scale space saddles: For $|\epsilon| < \frac{4}{3}\sqrt{-\alpha^3}$ two void scale space saddles occur on the non-annihilating saddle branch as shown in Figure 8c. For $|\epsilon| > \frac{4}{3}\sqrt{-\alpha^3}$ none occur since it does not intersect the zero-Laplacean. In other words: a Fold catastrophe *in scale space* occurs, regarding two scale space critical points (i.e. saddles) with different signs of det($\mathcal{H}$) and controlled by the perturbation parameter ϵ.

3.5 D_4^+ Catastrophe in 2D

The D_4^+ catastrophe, called hyperbolic umbilic, is given by $x^3 + xy^2$. The perturbation term contains three terms: $\lambda_1 x + \lambda_2 y + \lambda_3 y^2$. Its scale space addition is $8xt$. Obviously scale takes the role of λ_1. The scale space hyperbolic umbilic catastrophe germ with perturbation is thus defined by

$$L(x, y; t) = x^3 + xy^2 + 8xt + \alpha(y^2 + 2t) + \beta y$$

where the first part describes the scale space catastrophe germ. The set (α, β) form the extra perturbation parameters. One can verify that at the combination $(\alpha, \beta) = (0, 0)$ four critical points exist for each $t < 0$. At $t = 0$ the four critical curves annihilate simultaneously at the origin. This is non-generic, since this point is a scale space saddle with $\det(\mathcal{H}) = 0$.

Morsification takes place in the two parameters. Firstly, if $\alpha \neq 0$ and $\beta = 0$, the annihilations are separated. At the origin a Fold catastrophe occurs. On the saddle branch of the critical curve both a scale space saddle and a Cusp catastrophe are found. Secondly, if $\alpha = 0$ and $\beta \neq 0$, the double annihilation breaks up into two Fold annihilations with symmetric non-intersecting critical curves. A scale space saddle is not present.

Finally, if both α and β are non-zero, this second morsification results in two critical curves each of them containing an Fold annihilation. One the two critical curves contains a scale space saddle.

The extended Hessian degenerates for $x = -\alpha$. Then follows from $L_t = 0$ that $x = \alpha = 0$ and from L_y also $\beta = 0$, which is a non-generic situation.

3.6 D_4^- Catastrophe in 2D

The D_4^- catastrophe, called elliptic umbilic, is given by $x^3 - 6xy^2$. The perturbation term contains three terms: $\lambda_1 x + \lambda_2 y + \lambda_3 y^2$. Its scale space addition is $-6xt$. Obviously scale takes the role of λ_1. The scale space elliptic umbilic catastrophe germ with perturbation is thus defined by

$$L(x, y; t) = x^3 - 6xy^2 - 6xt + \alpha(y^2 + 2t) + \beta y \qquad (2)$$

where the first part describes the scale space catastrophe germ. The set (α, β) form the extra perturbation parameters. The combination $(\alpha, \beta) = (0, 0)$ gives two critical points for all $t \neq 0$. At the origin a so-called scatter event occurs: the critical curve changes from y-axis to x-axis with increasing t. Just as in the hyperbolic case, in fact two Fold catastrophes take place; in this case both an annihilation and a creation.

The morsification for $\alpha = 0$, $\beta \neq 0$ leads to the breaking into two critical curves without any catastrophe.

The morsification for $\alpha \neq 0$, $\beta = 0$ leads to only one catastrophe event at the origin: the Fold creation. The sign of α determines whether the critical curve contains a maximum – saddle pair or a minimum–saddle pair. Without loss of generality we may choose $\alpha = 1$. Then the generic creation germ (see Definition 1) is defined as

$$L(x, y; t) = x^3 - 6xt - 6xy^2 + y^2 + 2t \qquad (3)$$

The scale space saddle is located at $(x, y; t) = (\frac{1}{3}, 0; \frac{1}{18})$ and its intensity is $L(\frac{1}{3}, 0; \frac{1}{18}) = \frac{1}{27}$. The surface $L(x, y; t) = \frac{1}{27}$ has a local saddle at $(x, y; t) = (-\frac{1}{6}, 0; \frac{1}{72})$, see Figure 9. At creations newly created extremum domes can not be present, which is obvious from the maximum principle. Whereas annihilations of critical points leads to the annihilations of level-lines, creations of critical points are caused by the rearrangement of present level-lines. The intersection of the iso-surface through the scale space saddle and the critical curve therefore does not have a local extremum, but only local saddles.

This fact becomes clearer if we take a closer look at the structure of the critical curves. The creation containing critical curve is given by $(x, y; t) = (\pm\sqrt{2t}, 0; t)$. The

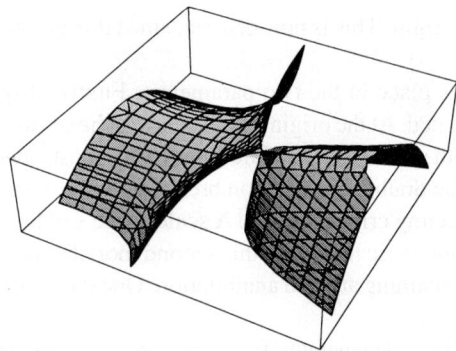

Fig. 9. Iso-intensity surface of the scale space saddle of the creation germ.

other critical curve, given by $(x, y; t) = (\frac{1}{6}, \pm\sqrt{\frac{1}{72} - t}; t)$, represents two branches connected at the second catastrophe. This point, located at $(x, y; t) = (\frac{1}{6}, 0; \frac{1}{72})$, is an element of both curves and obviously degenerates the extended Hessian. At this point two saddle points and the created extremum go through a Cusp catastrophe resulting in one saddle. Note that ignoring this catastrophe one would find the sudden change of extremum into saddle point while tracing the created critical points. Obviously this catastrophe is located between the creation catastrophe and the scale scale space saddle. The latter therefore does not invoke a critical dome around the created extremum.

A complete morsification by taking $\beta \neq 0$ resolves the scatter. It can be shown that the Hessian has two real roots if and only if $\|\beta\| < \frac{1}{32}\sqrt{6}$. At these root points subsequently a creation and an annihilation event take place on a critical curve. If $\|\beta\| > \frac{1}{32}\sqrt{6}$ the critical curve doesn't contain catastrophe points.

Due to this morsification the two critical curves do not intersect each other. Also in this perturbed system the minimum annihilates with one of the two saddles, while the other saddle remains unaffected. The scale space saddle remains on the non-catastrophe-involving curve. That is, the creation-annihilation couple and the corresponding saddle curve is not relevant for the scale space saddle and thus the scale space segmentation.

The iso-intensity surface of the scale space saddle due to the creation germ does not connect a dome-shaped surface to an arbitrary other surface, but shows only two parts of the surface touching each other at a void scale space saddle, see e.g. Figure 9.

4 Applications

In this section we give some examples to illustrate the theory presented in the previous sections. To show the effect of a cusp catastrophe in 2D, we firstly take a symmetric artificial image containing two Gaussian blobs and add noise to it. This image is shown in Figure 10a. Secondly, the effect is shown on the simulated MR image of Figure 10b. This image is taken from the web site http://www.bic.mni.mcgill.ca/brainweb.

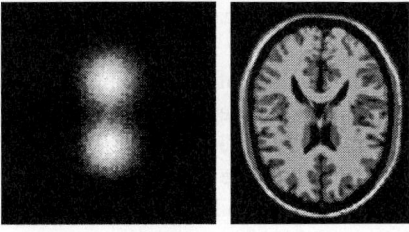

Fig. 10. 2D test images a: Artificial image built by combining two maxima and additive noise. b: 181 x 217 artificial MR image.

4.1 Artificial Image

Of the noisy image of Figure 10a, a scale space image was built containing 41 scales ranging exponentially from $e^{\frac{10}{8}}$ to $e^{\frac{20}{8}}$. The calculated critical paths are presented in Figure 11a. Ignoring the paths on the border, caused by the extrema in the noise, the paths in the middle of the image clearly shown the pitchfork-like behaviour. Note that since the symmetric image is perturbed, instead of a cusp catastrophe a fold catastrophe occurs. The scale space saddle on the saddle branch and its intensity define a closed region around the lower maximum, see Figure 11b. However, if the noise were slightly different, one could have found the region around the upper maximum. Knowing that the image should be symmetric and observing that the critical paths indeed are pitchfork-like, it is thus desirable to identify the catastrophe as a cusp-catastrophe. Then the scale space saddle defines the two regions shown in Figure 11c, which one may want to derive given Figure 10a.

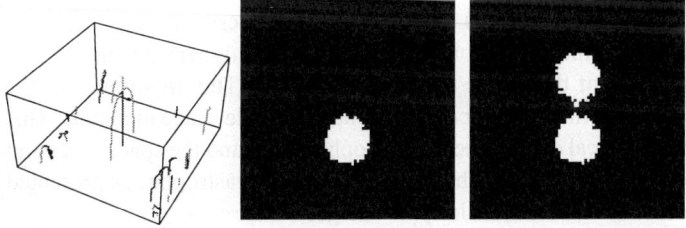

Fig. 11. Example of a cusp catastrophe: a: Critical paths in scale space. b: Segment according to a fold catastrophe. c: Segment according to a cusp catastrophe.

4.2 Simulated MR Image

Subsequently we took the 2D slice from an artificial MR image shown in Figure 10b. The scale space image at scale 8.37 with the large structures remaining is shown in Figure 12a. Now 7 extrema are found, defining a hierarchy of the regions around these extrema as shown in Figure 12b. In this case is it visually desirable to identify a region to segment S_1 with more or less similar size as region S_3. This is done by assigning a Cusp catastrophe to the annihilation of the extremum of segment S_3, in which the extremum of segment S_1 is also involved. Then the value of the scale space saddle defining segment S_3 also defines an extra region around the extremum in segment S_1. This is shown in Figure 12c, reflecting the symmetry present in Figure 12a. We mention that in this example several creation-annihilation events occurred, as described by the morsification of the D_4^- catastrophe.

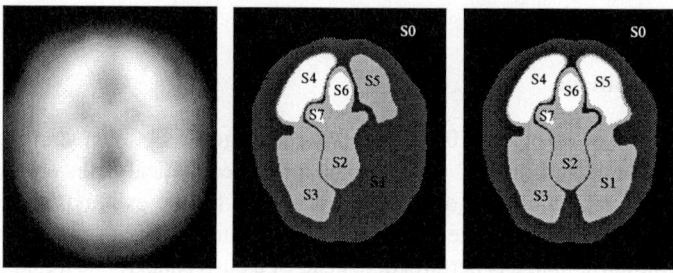

Fig. 12. a) Image on scale 8.4 b) Segments of the 7 extrema of a. c) Idem, with the iso-intensity manifold of S_1 chosen equally to S_3.

5 Summary and Discussion

In this paper we investigated the (deep) structure on various catastrophe events in Gaussian scale space. Although it is known that pairs of critical points are annihilated or created (the latter if the dimension of the image is 2 or higher), it is important to describe the local structure of the image around these events. The importance of this local description follows from its significance in building a scale space hierarchy. This algorithm depends on the critical curves, their catastrophe points and the space space saddle points. We therefore embedded the mathematically known catastrophes as presented in section 2 in the framework of linear scale space images.

Firstly, annihilations of extrema can occur in the presence of other extrema. In some cases it is not possible to identify the annihilating extremum due to numerical limitations, coarse sampling, or symmetries in the image. Then the event is described by a Cusp catastrophe instead of a Fold catastrophe. This description is sometimes desirable, e.g. if prior knowledge is present and one wishes to maintain the symmetry in the image. The scale space hierarchy can easily be adjusted to this extra information. We gave examples in section 4 on an artificial image and a simulated MR image. We discussed the A_3 and the D_4^+ for this purpose, but the higher order catastrophes in the sequences $A_k, k > 4$ and $D_k^+, k > 3$ can be dealt with in a similar fashion.

Secondly, the morsification of the D_4^- catastrophe was discussed, showing he successive appearance of a creation – annihilation event on a critical curve. This doesn't influence the hierarchical structure nor the pre-segmentation, but is only important with respect to the movement of the critical curve in scale space.

The theory described in this paper extends the knowledge of the deep structure of Gaussian scale space. It embeds higher order catastrophes within the framework of a scale space hierarchy. It explains how these events can in principle be used for segmentation, interpreted and implemented, *e.g.* if prior knowledge is available.

References

1. V. I. Arnold. *Catastrophe Theory*. Springer, Berlin, 1984.
2. J. Damon. Local Morse theory for solutions to the heat equation and Gaussian blurring. *Journal of Differential Equations*, 115(2):386–401, 1995.
3. L. M. J. Florack and A. Kuijper. The topological structure of scale-space images. *Journal of Mathematical Imaging and Vision*, 12(1):65–80, February 2000.
4. L. M. J. Florack, B. M. ter Haar Romeny, J. J. Koenderink, and M. A. Viergever. Cartesian differential invariants in scale-space. *Journal of Mathematical Imaging and Vision*, 3(4):327–348, 1993.
5. R. Gilmore. *Catastrophe Theory for Scientists and Engineers*. Dover, 1993. Originally published by John Wiley & Sons, New York, 1981.
6. L. D. Griffin and A. Colchester. Superficial and deep structure in linear diffusion scale space: Isophotes, critical points and separatrices. *Image and Vision Computing*, 13(7):543–557, September 1995.
7. P. Johansen, M. Nielsen, and O.F. Olsen. Branch points in one-dimensional Gaussian scale space. *Journal of Mathematical Imaging and Vision*, 13:193–203, 2000.
8. J. J. Koenderink. The structure of images. *Biological Cybernetics*, 50:363–370, 1984.
9. J. J. Koenderink. A hitherto unnoticed singularity of scale-space. *IEEE Transactions on Pattern Analysis and Machine Intelligence*, 11(11):1222–1224, 1989.
10. A. Kuijper and L. M. J. Florack. Hierarchical pre-segmentation without prior knowledge. In *Proceedings of the 8th International Conference on Computer Vision (Vancouver, Canada, July 9–12, 2001)*, pages 487–493, 2001.
11. L. M. Lifshitz and S. M. Pizer. A multiresolution hierarchical approach to image segmentation based on intensity extrema. *IEEE Transactions on Pattern Analysis and Machine Intelligence*, 12(6):529–540, 1990.
12. T. Lindeberg. *Scale-Space Theory in Computer Vision*. The Kluwer International Series in Engineering and Computer Science. Kluwer Academic Publishers, 1994.
13. A. Simmons, S.R. Arridge, P.S. Tofts, and G.J. Barker. Application of the extremum stack to neurological MRI. *IEEE Transactions on Medical Imaging*, 17(3):371–382, June 1998.
14. R. Thom. *Stabilité Structurelle et Morphogénèse*. Benjamin, New york, 1972.
15. T. Wada and M. Sato. Scale-space tree and its hierarchy. In *ICPR90*, pages Vol–II 103–108, 1990.
16. A.P. Witkin. Scale-space filtering. In *Proceedings of the Eighth International Joint Conference on Artificial Intelligence*, pages 1019–1022, 1983.

Image Processing Done Right

Jan J. Koenderink[1] and Andrea J. van Doorn[1]

Universiteit Utrecht, Buys Ballot Laboratory,
Princetonplein 5, Utrecht NL–3584CC, The Netherlands,
j.j.koenderink@phys.uu.nl,
http://www.phys.uu.nl/~wwwpm/HumPerc/koenderink.html

Abstract. A large part of "image processing" involves the computation of significant points, curves and areas ("features"). These can be defined as loci where absolute differential invariants of the image assume fiducial values, taking spatial scale and intensity (in a generic sense) scale into account. "Differential invariance" implies a group of "similarities" or "congruences". These "motions" define the geometrical structure of image space. Classical Euclidian invariants don't apply to images because image space is non–Euclidian. We analyze image structure from first principles and construct the fundamental group of image space motions. Image space is a Cayley–Klein geometry with one isotropic dimension. The analysis leads to a principled definition of "features" and the operators that define them.

Keywords. Image features, texture, image indexing, scale–space, image transformations, image space

1 Introduction

"Images" are often considered to be distributions of some "intensity" (a density of "stuff") over some spatial extent (the "picture plane" say). One thinks of a graph ("image surface") in the three dimensional product space defined by the picture plane and an intensity axis. Numerous conventional methods (often implicitly) involve the computation of differential invariants of this surface. One conventionally draws upon the large body of knowledge on the differential geometry of surfaces in $\mathbb{E}^3$.

There are grave problems with this approach though:
— the physical dimensions of the image plane are incommensurable with the dimension of the image intensity domain. The former are distances or angles, the latter radiances or irradiances;
— classical differential geometry deals with invariance under the Euclidian group of congruences. But to turn a region of "image space" about an axis parallel to the picture plane is impossible;
— the intensity domain is unlike the Euclidian line in that it is only a half–line and translations are undefined.
Thus the aforementioned methods lack a principled basis.

To accept that these methods are *ad hoc* doesn't necessarily mean that one should abandon them altogether. Rather, one should look for the proper group of congruences and adjust the differential geometry to be the study of invariants of that group[11]. One should investigate the proper geometry of the intensity domain. This is the quest undertaken in this paper: First we investigate the structure of the intensity domain, then we identify the proper group of congruences and similarities. We then proceed to develop the differential geometry of surfaces under the group actions in order to arrive at a principled discipline of "image processing".

2   Geometrical Structure of the "Intensity" Domain

"Intensity" is a generic name for a flux, the amount of stuff collected within a certain aperture centered at a certain location. In the case of a CCD array the aperture is set by the sensitive area and the flux is proportional with the number of absorbed photons collected in a given time window. One treats this as the continuous distribution of some "density", in the case of the CCD chip the number of absorbed photons per unit area per unit time, that is the irradiance. This goes beyond the observable and is often inadvisable because the "stuff" may be granular at the microscale. In the case of the CCD chip the grain is set by the photon shot noise. It is also inadvisable because natural images fail to be "nice" functions of time and place when one doesn't "tame" them via a finite collecting aperture or "inner scale". Only such tamed images are observable[4], this means that *any* image should come with an inner scale. This often is nilly willy the case. For instance, in the case of the CCD chip the inner scale is set by the size of its photosensitive elements. But no one stops you from changing the inner scale artificially. When possible this is a boon, because it rids one of the artificial pixelation. "Pixel fucking" is in a different ballpark from image processing proper, though it sometimes is a necessary evil due to real world constraints. Because of a number of technical reasons the preferred way to set the inner scale is to use Gaussian smoothing[4]. Here we assume that the "intensity" $z(x, y)$ is a smooth function of the Cartesian coordinates $\{x, y\}$ of the picture plane with a well defined inner scale. We assume that the intensity is positive definite throughout.

The photosensitive elements of the CCD chip can be used to illustrate another problem. Suppose we irradiate the chip with a constant, uniform beam. We count photons in a fixed time window. The photon counts are known to be Poisson distributed with parameter λ (say). Suppose a single measurement ("pixel value") yields n photons. What is the best estimate of the "intensity" λ on the basis of this sample? Let two observers A and B measure time in different units, *e.g.*, let $t_a = \mu t_B$, then their intensities must be related as $\lambda_A \, dt_A = \lambda_B \, dt_B$. Let A and B assign priors $f_A(\lambda_A) \, d\lambda_A$ and $f_B(\lambda_B) \, d\lambda_B$. We have to require that these be mutually consistent, that is to say, we require $f_A(\lambda_A) \, d\lambda_A = f_B(\lambda_B) \, d\lambda_B$. Both A and B are completely ignorant, and since their states of knowledge are equal, one arrives at the functional equation $f(\lambda) = \mu f(\mu \lambda)$, from which one concludes[9] that the prior that expresses complete ignorance and doesn't depend on the unit of time is $\lambda^{-1}\,d\lambda$, that is to say a *uniform prior on the log–intensity scale*.

This means that we only obtain some degree of symmetry between the Cartesian dimensions $\{x,y\}$ (where no particular place is singled out, and no particular scale has been established) and the intensity dimension if we use $Z(x,y) = \log(z(x,y)/z_0)$ instead of the intensity itself. Here the constant z_0 is an (arbitrary) unit of intensity. The choice of unit cannot influence the differential geometry of image space because it represents a mere shift of origin along the affine Z–dimension. Then the Z–axis becomes the affine line. Of course the global $\{x,y,Z\}$ space still fails to be Euclidian because the (log–)intensity dimension is incommensurable with the $\{x,y\}$ dimensions, whereas the $\{x,y\}$ dimensions are mutually compatible. The latter are measured as length or optical angle, the former in some unrelated physical unit (for instance photon number flux per area in the case of the CCD chip). But the approach to Euclidian space is much closer than with the use of intensity as such: As shown below we arrive at one of the 27 (three–dimensional) Cayley–Klein geometries[10,2] (of which Euclidian space is another instance).

3   The Geometry of Image Space

Consider "image space" $\mathbb{I}^3$ with coordinates $\{x,y,Z\}$. It is a (trivial) fiber bundle with the "picture plane" $\mathbb{P}^2$ as base space and the "log–intensity domain $\mathbb{L}$" as fibers. An image $Z(x,y)$ is a cross section of the bundle. We will use the term "pixels" for the fibers. A point $\{x,y,Z\}$ is said to have log–intensity Z and "trace" $\{x,y\}$. Image space is an infinite three dimensional space with the Euclidean metric in planes parallel to the xy–plane and a—quite independent— metric on the Z–axis. $\mathbb{I}^3$ can hardly be expected to be anything like a Euclidian space $\mathbb{E}^3$. For instance, it is hard to conceive of a rotation of an object by a quarter turn about the x–axis, because that would align the y-directions in the object with the Z–axis. What sense can anyone make of a "coincidence" of a distance in the picture plane with the intensity domain? $\mathbb{P}^2$ and $\mathbb{L}$ are absolutely incommensurable. This entails that *such operations should be forbidden by the geometry of* $\mathbb{I}^3$. To be precise, any geometrical operation should leave the pixels invariant[13].

We refer to these invariant lines (pixels) as "normal lines" (for reasons to be explained later) and planes that contain normal lines "normal planes". Such entities clearly cannot occur as tangent planes or lines in images because that would entail that the image gradient wouldn't exist. When we say "line" or "plane" we exclude the normal ones. This means that any plane can be represented as $Z(u,v) = Z_0 + (g_x u + g_y v)$. Here Z_0 is the intercept with the normal line through the origin and $\mathbf{g} = \nabla Z = \{g_x, g_y\}$ is the (log intensity) gradient of the plane. The normal planes cannot thus be represented, they are *special*. A similar reasoning applies to lines.

3.1 The Group of Congruences

Thus the space we are after is a three–dimensional space, such that the intensity domain (one–dimensional) and the picture plane (two–dimensional) "don't mix". The only transformations of any relevance thus leave a family of parallel lines (the "pixels") invariant. What other constraints does one *a priori* have? One obvious candidate is to require the space to be "homogeneous", *i.e.*, to require that a group of "congruences" exists, such that "free mobility" of configurations is guaranteed all over space. This assumption merely expresses the fact that one piece of picture is as good as the next, it expresses our total prior ignorance and simply extends the assumption needed to arrive at the structure of the intensity domain. *But then the case is settled:* The space has to be of constant curvature (or free mobility is jeopardized) and is one of the 27 Cayley–Klein geometries. The invariance of a family of parallel lines fixes it to the "simple isotropic geometry". This geometry is obtained from projective geometry when one singles out two intersecting lines in the plane at infinity as the "absolute conic". One may take the lines $x = \pm iy$ in the plane $Z = \infty$ with intersection $\{x, y, Z\} = \{0, 0, \infty\}$ as the absolute conic. Then all lines parallel to the Z–axis meet in the "vanishing point" $\{0, 0, \infty\}$. The group G_8 (8 parameters) of "direct isotropic similarities" that is the analog of the (7 parameter) group of Euclidian similarities[15] contains the projective transforms that leave the absolute conic invariant. (In this paper we stick to the notation introduced by Sachs[15] for this group and its subgroups.) We write it in a form such that the identity is obtained when all parameters are set to zero and such that the factors e^h and e^δ are positive definite.

$$\begin{aligned} x' &= e^h(x\cos\phi - y\sin\phi) + t_x \\ y' &= e^h(x\sin\phi + y\cos\phi) + t_y \\ Z' &= e^\delta Z(x,y) + \alpha_x x + \alpha_y y + \zeta \end{aligned} \quad (1)$$

G_8 is indeed the only group of transformations that conserves normal lines and generic planes as families (see figure 1).

The "movements" are thus very simple, namely (a special kind of) linear transformations combined with a shift. It is not likely to be a coincidence that the familiar transformations that apparently leave the picture "invariant" are members of G_8. Examples include the use of various "gradations" ("soft", "normal", "hard") in photography, the introduction of lightness gradients when enlarging negatives[1], *etc*. The latter equalize "uneven density" in the negative, often introduced when an off–axis piece of the image is being enlarged. Similar transformations are common in many image processing packages. The use of paper gradations is aptly caught by the "gamma transformations" of the form $z' = (z/z_0)^\gamma$, whereas gradients are approximated with $z'(x,y) = z(x,y)\exp(\sigma_x x + \sigma_y y)$. Here the exponential serves to ensure the definite positiveness of the intensity, necessary because a "linear gradient" is a nonentity. Such gradients commonly occur in unevenly lit scenes. Notice that all these "image preserving" operations are *linear* in the log–intensity domain. The transformations affect only the log–intensity

Fig. 1. Orbits of significant one–parameter subgroups. These groups appear either as identities, translations, or rotations in their traces on the picture plane. In image space the groups are far richer, for instance, the "rotations" may appear as screw motions with a normal line as axis, or as periodic motions that transform a paraboloid of rotation with normal axis in itself.

domain, not the traces. We suggest that the popularity of "gamma transformations" and "lightness gradients" derives from this fact. Image *structure* in the sense of curvatures of surfaces in $\mathbb{I}^3$ is indeed not in the least affected.

These transformations leave the "image" invariant (see figure 2) in the sense that photographers apply such transformations as they see fit, merely to "optimize" the image without in any way "changing" it[1]. Thus it is apt to say that *images are the invariants of* G_8. Hence we will consider G_8 as the *group of congruences and similitudes* of image space.

For any two points $\{x_{1,2}, y_{1,2}, Z_{1,2}\}$ we define the "reach" as the unsigned quantity $r_{12} = +\sqrt{(x_2 - x_1)^2 + (y_2 - y_1)^2}$. When the reach vanishes but the points are distinct we call them "parallel". In that case (and in that case only!) we define the "span" $s_{12} = Z_2 - Z_1$ (a signed quantity). Both reach and span are relative invariants of G_8. Consider the subgroups $\mathcal{B}_7$ of reach preserving and $\mathcal{S}_7$ of span preserving "isotropic similarities". Their intersection is the group $\mathcal{B}_6^{(1)}$ of "simple isotropic movements" (also known as "unimodular isotropic movements"). The group $\mathcal{B}_7$ is characterized by $h = 0$, $\mathcal{S}_7$ by $\delta = 0$, and $\mathcal{B}_6^{(1)}$ by $h = \delta = 0$. We define the "distance" between points as their reach when the reach is different from zero and their span if not. The distance is an absolute invariant of the simple isotropic movements.

Planes $Z(x, y) = Z_0 + (g_x x + g_y y)$ have "plane coordinates" $\{u, v, w\} = \{g_x, g_y, Z_0\}$. Two planes $\{u_{1,2}, v_{1,2}, w_{1,2}\}$ subtend a "skew", that is the unsigned quantity $s_{12} = +\sqrt{(u_2 - u_1)^2 + (v_2 - v_1)^2}$. When the skew vanishes but the planes are distinct we call them "parallel". In that case (and in that case only!) we define the "gap" $g_{12} = w_2 - w_1$ (a signed quantity). The "angle" subtended

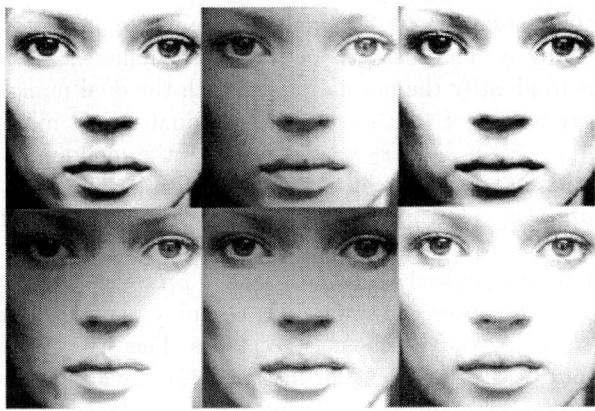

Fig. 2. An "image" is an invariant over variations such as these. Thus the figure suggests only a *single* image, not six! Infinitely other variations might be given of course.

by the planes is defined as the skew if the skew is not zero or the gap if it is. The skew is an absolute invariant of the subgroup $\mathcal{W}_7$ defined through $h = \delta$. The group of isotropic movements is the intersection of $\mathcal{W}_7$ and $\mathcal{B}_7$. Notice that there exist two types of similarities: Those of the "1st kind" ($\mathcal{W}_7$) scale distances and preserve angles, whereas those of the "2nd kind" ($\mathcal{B}_7$) scale angles and preserve distances (these are gamma transformations). There exists a full metric duality between points and planes, planes and points behave the same under the group G_8.

The metric $ds^2 = dx^2 + dy^2$ that is respected by $\mathcal{B}_6^{(1)}$ is of course degenerate. It is perhaps best understood as a degenerate Minkowski metric[7]. Then the pixels appear as degenerated "light cones" (of relativistic kinematics). All points on the normal line "above" a point (higher intensity) and "below" a point (lower intensity) are inside the light cone and thus *comparable* whereas a generic pair of points is outside the light cone ("elsewhere" in the relativistic kinematics) and *not comparable*. Such points only have a reach, namely their distance in the trace. Their log–intensities are not in a fixed relation but are typically changed by isometries of $\mathbb{I}^3$.

3.2 The Structure of Normal Planes

Much of the structure of image space can be understood from a study of the structure of normal planes[14]. In a way this is the study of one dimensional images and thus has frequent applications by itself. We use coordinates $\{x, y\}$, with the y–coordinate being interpreted as log–intensity, the x–coordinate as the distance in the image. This should yield no confusion since it will always be clear when we confine the discussion to normal planes.

It is often convenient to identify the Euclidian plane with the complex number plane ($z = x + iy$ with $i^2 = -1$). The reason is that linear transformations induce the similarities: $z' = pz + q$ implies a scaling by $|p|$, rotation over $\arg p$ and translation by q. The distance between two points is $|z_1 - z_2|$. It is no less convenient to identify the normal planes with the dual number plane. Dual numbers[3,8] are written $z = x + \varepsilon y$ where the dual unit is nilpotent ($\varepsilon^2 = 0$). The distance $|z_1 - z_2|$ is $x_1 - x_2$ when we define the modulus $|z|$ as x (signed quantity!). A linear transformation $z' = pz + q$ with $p = p_1 + \varepsilon p_2$, $q = q_1 + \varepsilon q_2$ implies $x' = p_1 x + q_1$, $y' = p_2 x + p_1 y + q_2$, which is in G_8. We have a scaling of distances by $|p| = p_1$, a "rotation" over $p_2/p_1 = \arg p$, and a translation over q. Notice that we can indeed write $p_1 + \varepsilon p_2 = p_1(1 + \varepsilon p_2/p_1) = |p|\exp \arg p$. Almost all of the structure of the familiar complex plane can immediately be put to good use in the study of the normal planes. This study is much simplified by the nilpotency of the dual unit, for instance, the Taylor expansion truncates after the first order. Thus $\sin \varepsilon \psi = \varepsilon \psi$, $\cos \varepsilon \psi = 1$, $\exp \varepsilon \psi = 1 + \varepsilon \psi$ and so forth.

The unit circle is given by $x^2 = 1$ and consists of the two normal lines $x = \pm 1$. The normal line $x = 0$ contains points that may equally be considered "centers" of the unit circle (thus all real lines are "diameters"!). The group of pure shears $x' = x$, $y' = y + \phi x$ moves the unit circle in itself, leaving the centers invariant. It is called a "rotation over ϕ", for apparently the group is to be understood as the group of *rotations* about the origin. If we define the orientation of a line through the origin as the (special) arc length of the arc cut from the unit circle, then the line from the origin to $\{x, y\}$ has an orientation $\phi = y/x$ and is transformed into the x–axis by the rotation over $-\phi$. It is perhaps disconcerting at first that this orientation is not periodic. Angles in the normal plane take on values on $(-\infty, +\infty)$, you cannot make a full turn in the normal plane. This is of course exactly what is called for given the incommensurability of the log–intensity and picture plane dimensions. Notice that the rotations correspond to the application of gradients in image processing.

The normal plane differs from the Euclidian plane in that the angle metric (like the distance metric) is parabolic (the Euclidian plane has an elliptic angle metric). This has the virtue that one enjoys full duality between points and lines. In the $\mathbb{E}^2$ one has parallel lines, but no parallel points (points that cannot be connected by a line), thus duality fails in this respect. Due to this fact the structure of the normal plane is much simpler than that of the Euclidian plane.

The bilinear expression $y + Y = xX$ defines a *line* (as a set of collinear points in point coordinates $\{x, y\}$) when we consider constant $\{X, Y\}$ and a *point* (as a set of concurrent lines in line coordinates $\{X, Y\}$) when we consider constant $\{x, y\}$. We define the distance of two points as $d_{12} = x_2 - x_1$, except when the points are "parallel", then we substitute the "special" distance $\delta_{12} = y_2 - y_1$. Similarly, we define the distance of two lines as the angle subtended by them, thus $\delta_{12} = X_2 - X_1$, except when the lines are parallel, then we substitute the "special" distance $d_{12} = Y_2 - Y_1$. These definitions make sense because either distance is invariant under general movements. Consider the polarity π which interchanges the point p with (point–)coordinates $\{x, y\}$ and the line P with (line–)coordinates $\{X, Y\}$, such that (numerically) $X = x$, $Y = y$. Suppose that p is on Q, thus $y_p + Y_Q = x_p X_Q$: then $q = \pi(Q)$ must be on $P = \pi(p)$ because

$y_q + Y_P = x_q X_P$. If $\pi(A) = a$ and $\pi(B) = b$ then $\delta_{AB} = d_{ab}$ in the generic case, whereas when a and b are parallel $\delta_{ab} = d_{AB}$. We also define the distance between a point u and a line V (say) as the distance between u and the point $\bar{u}$ on V such that u and $\bar{u}$ are parallel (the point on V nearest to u, or the "projection of u on V"). You have $|d_{uV}| = |x_u X_V - (y_u + Y_V)| = |d_{Uv}| = |X_U x_v - (Y_U + y_v)|$, which implies that when u is on V (thus $x_u X_V = y_u + Y_V$) then $d_{Uv} = d_{uV} = 0$. These properties indeed imply full metric duality of lines and points in the normal plane.

A circle like $x = \pm 1$ is more aptly called "circle of the 1st kind" to distinguish it from more general "cycles" defined as entities that can be moved into themselves (a circle of the 1st kind can also be rotated into itself and thus is a cycle too). In the normal plane the cycles include (apart from the circles of the 1st kind), the so called "circles of the 2nd kind" (which look like parabolas with normal axes), the generic lines and the normal lines. The circles are especially interesting. A circle $x + \varepsilon x^2/2\rho$ can be "rolled" over a line. One shows that distance traveled is ρ times the angle of rotation, which identifies ρ as "the radius" of the circle. The motion actually moves a whole family of "concentric" circles $x + \varepsilon(x^2/2\rho + \mu)$ in themselves. The "curvature" (reciprocal of the radius) equals y_{xx}. Notice that this expression is simpler than—and different from—the Euclidian $(y''/(1+y'^2)^{3/2})$. The circles of the 2nd kind hold many properties in common with the circles of the $\mathbb{E}^2$. Notice that the radius (or the curvature) may be negative though. The sign indicates whether the circle is a concave or convex one.

Since there exist two types of circles there exist two distinct notions of "inversion in a circle". Since we are only interested in transformations that conserve the normal rays (pixels!) individually, only the inversions in more general cycles are of interest though. Since lines are degenerated circles, inversions in lines are included. For instance the inversion induced by the x-axis turns an image into its negative and vice versa. Since inversions are conformal, they preserve local image structure.

Because of the full duality there exist two distinct types of similitudes in the normal plane. One type conserves distances and scales all angles by a common factor. The other type conserves angles and scales all distances by a common factor. Because of the constraint that normal lines should be conserved individually only the first mentioned type is of interest to us. Of course these transformations are nothing but the familiar gamma transformations.

Curves that run fully in the normal planes ("normal curves" say) are important in the study of surfaces via normal cuts. A curve $y(x)$ is parameterized by arc length x, thus the unit tangent is $\mathbf{T}(x) = \{1, y'(x)\}$. The curve's normal is simply $\mathbf{N} = \{0, 1\}$. The derivative of the tangent is $\dot{\mathbf{T}}(x) = y''(x)\mathbf{N}$, whereas $\dot{\mathbf{N}} = 0$. Thus the curvature of the curve is $\kappa_n(x) = y''(x)$. Here we distinguish the "normal curvature κ_n" from the curvature κ which vanishes identically since the projection of the curve in $\mathbb{P}^2$ is a straight line. The osculating circle at $x = x_0$ is $x + \varepsilon[y(x_0) + \kappa_n(x_0)(x - x_0)^2/2]$. When you specify the curvature as a function of arc length (its "natural equation") the curve is determined up to a motion.

3.3 The Geometry of Image Space Proper

In image space $\mathbb{I}^3$ the new (as compared with the normal planes) linear entities are planes. It is obvious how to define the distance between planes or of a plane and a line. One takes a point on one entity and drops a plumb line (normal line) on the other. The length of the gap divided by the distance to the common point(s) is the angle between the planes or the plane and the line. It is invariant under arbitrary motions and can thus serve as the distance measure. In case the entities are parallel one uses the gap.

It is convenient to introduce an orthonormal basis $\{\mathbf{e}_1, \mathbf{e}_2, \mathbf{e}_3\}$, $\mathbf{e}_1$ and $\mathbf{e}_2$ spanning the picture plane $\mathbb{P}^2$, and $\mathbf{e}_3$ the log-intensity dimension $\mathbb{L}$. One has $\mathbf{e}_i \cdot \mathbf{e}_j = 0$ for $i \neq j$, $\mathbf{e}_i \cdot \mathbf{e}_i = 1$ for $i = 1, 2$ and $\mathbf{e}_3 \cdot \mathbf{e}_3 = 0$. This introduces the degenerate metric

$$d_{12}^2 = (x_2 - x_1)^2 + (y_2 - y_1)^2. \tag{2}$$

For parallel points we again use the special distance.

The bivector $\pi = \mathbf{e}_1 \times \mathbf{e}_2$ represents the unit oriented area in the picture plane. The bivectors $\sigma_1 = \mathbf{e}_2 \times \mathbf{e}_3$ and $\sigma_2 = \mathbf{e}_3 \times \mathbf{e}_1$ represent oriented unit areas in normal planes and are of a different nature. The trivector $\tau = \mathbf{e}_1 \times \mathbf{e}_2 \times \mathbf{e}_3$ is the oriented unit volume of the space. Notice that you have $\pi^2 = -1$, a regular "pseudoscalar" in the picture plane, but $\sigma_i^2 = 0$ and also $\tau^2 = 0$. It is easy to set up the complete "geometric algebra" for image space. Many operations and geometrical relations can be handled elegantly in this framework. For instance, the bivector π generates the Euclidian rotations in the picture plane, whereas the bivectors σ_i generate shears in normal planes (also "rotations", but in the sense of image space).

Some properties of $\mathbb{I}^3$ may appear unfamiliar at first sight. For instance, two parallel lines in the picture plane are indeed parallel lines (in the sense of the metric) in $\mathbb{I}^3$, yet typically have different intensity gradients and thus are not necessarily coplanar. Any pair of points on a common perpendicular can be given equal intensities through a congruence, thus all such pairs of points are equivalent. This is similar to the phenomenon of "Clifford parallels" of elliptic space. There even exist surfaces ("Clifford planes") which are nonplanar, yet carry two mutually transverse families of parallel lines.

In the remainder of this paper we will be predominantly interested in differential properties of image space. Some of these are well known to photographers and universally used in the darkroom. An example is the practice of "burning" and "dodging" by which one introduces essentially arbitrary modulations of the type $z'(x, y) = z(x, y) \exp w(x, y)$, where $w(x, y)$ is quite arbitrary. Notice that $Z'(x, y) = Z(x, y) + w(x, y)$, thus locally (to first order) one has (at the point $\{x_0, y_0\}$ say) $Z'(x_0+dx, y_0+dy) = Z(x_0, y_0)+a+b\,dx+c\,dy$ (with $a = w(x_0, y_0)$, $\{b, c\} = \nabla(Z+w)(x_0, y_0)$), which is a *congruence* of image space. Thus dodging and burning represent *conformal transformations* of image space[16], which is most likely why they work as well as they do.

The topic of primary interest here is *differential geometry* of surfaces in image space[17,18,19,20,15]. We will only consider smooth surfaces (at least three times differentiable) with tangent planes that never contain a normal line. Notice that the degenerate metric allows us to point out the geodesics on arbitrary surfaces right away. They are the curves whose projections on the image plane are straight. The geodesic curvature of any curve on a surface is simply the Euclidian curvature of its projection on the picture plane.

We will write a generic point on a surface or a curve as $\mathbf{R} = \mathbf{r} + Z(\mathbf{r})\mathbf{e}_3$, where $\mathbf{r}$ is the component in the picture plane. Because the tangent of a curve or tangent plane of a surface never contains a normal line, we may globally parameterize a curve as $x(s)\mathbf{e}_1 + y(s)\mathbf{e}_2 + Z(s)\mathbf{e}_3$ and a surface as $x\mathbf{e}_1 + y\mathbf{e}_2 + Z(x,y)\mathbf{e}_3$, a "Monge parameterization". This is typically the most convenient way to represent curves and surfaces.

3.4 Surfaces

Again, the most natural way to parameterize a surface in image space is as a "Monge parameterization" $x\mathbf{e}_1 + y\mathbf{e}_2 + Z(x,y)\mathbf{e}_3$. Because the metric is degenerate it is immediately obvious that the "First Fundamental Form" $d\mathbf{R} \cdot d\mathbf{R}$ (or metric) is simply

$$\mathrm{I}(dx, dy) = dx^2 + dy^2 \qquad (3)$$

(thus $E = G = 1$, $F = 0$, that is what the Monge parameterization buys us). Thus all curves on the surface with straight traces are "geodesics".

A fruitful way to think of curvature is via the "spherical image". The tangent plane at $\{x_0, y_0\}$ is $\mathbf{R}(x_0 + dx, y_0 + dy) = \mathbf{R}(x_0, y_0) + [dx\mathbf{e}_1 + dy\mathbf{e}_2 + (Z_x\,dx + Z_y\,dy)\mathbf{e}_3]$. When we introduce the "Gaussian sphere" $\mathbf{G}(x,y) = x\mathbf{e}_1 + y\mathbf{e}_2 + (x^2 + y^2)/2\mathbf{e}_3$, we see that the tangent plane at $\mathbf{R}(x,y)$ is parallel to that at $\mathbf{G}(Z_x, Z_y)$. Thus the map that takes $\mathbf{R}(x,y)$ to $\mathbf{G}(Z_x, Z_y)$ is the analog of the "Gaussian image" of a surface[5]. When one applies a stereographical projection from the infinite focus of the Gaussian sphere, one obtains a mapping from a point $\mathbf{R}(x,y)$ of the surface to the point $\{Z_x, Z_y\}$ of what is generally known as "gradient space". Since the stereographic projection is isometric(!), gradient space is just as apt a representation as the Gaussian sphere itself. We hence refer to $\{Z_x, Z_y\} = \nabla Z(x,y)$ as the "attitude image" of the surface. It is indeed the analog of the spherical image, or Gauss map, of Euclidian geometry. Although the attitude image is in many respects simpler than the Gaussian image, it shares many of its properties. For instance, rotations of the surface in $\mathbb{I}^3$ lead to *translations* of the attitude image (of course translations of the surface don't affect the attitude image at all). Thus the shape of the attitude image is an invariant against arbitrary congruences of pictorial space. Similarities of $\mathbb{I}^3$ simply scale the attitude image (a possibility that cannot occur in Euclidian space which knows only similarities that conserve orientations.)

The area magnification of the attitude image is the intrinsic curvature $K(x,y)$. It is given by the determinant of the Hessian of the log–intensity

$$K(x,y) = Z_{xx}Z_{yy} - Z_{xy}^2. \qquad (4)$$

The trace of the Hessian of the log–intensity $Z_{xx} + Z_{yy}$ is another important invariant. It can be interpreted as twice the "mean curvature" H, for because it is invariant against Euclidian rotations of the picture plane the average of normal curvatures in any pair of orthogonal directions equals the mean curvature.

The magnification of the surface attitude map is typically anisotropic. This is just another way of saying that the "sectional" curvature of the surface differs for different orientations of the section. Notice that we need to study the sectional curvature, as the equivalent of the normal curvature of Euclidian differential geometry. This is because the only reasonable definition of "surface normal" in $\mathbb{I}^3$ is to let them be normal directions. But then these "normals" are essentially useless to measure shape properties since they don't depend on the nature of the surface to begin with! However, we certainly have a right to speak of "normal curvature" as synonymous with "sectional curvature", just like in classical differential geometry. (This is also the origin of our term "normal plane" introduced above.)

In order to measure the curvature of a section we may find the rate of change of the image in attitude space, or—and this is completely equivalent—we may find the best fitting (highest "order of contact") of sectional circles. This latter definition is obviously the geometer's choice. As we rotate the planar section the radius of the best fitting normal circle changes (periodically of course). The sectional planes are indeed normal planes and the circles "normal circles" (parabolas with normal axis).

Remember that the sectional curvature is simply the second derivative of the depth in the direction of the section. There will be two directions at which the radius of the normal circle reaches an extremum, we may call these the "directions of principal curvature". Exceptions are points where the radius of the best fitting circle doesn't depend on the orientation of the section. Such points are rare (generically isolated) and may be called "umbilical points" of the surface.

The orientation of the directions of principal curvature are given by

$$Z_{xy}dx^2 - (Z_{xx} - Z_{yy})dx\,dy - Z_{xy}dy^2 = 0. \tag{5}$$

These directions are invariant under arbitrary congruences.

The curvature of a normal section that subtends an angle Ψ with the first principal direction is

$$\kappa_n(\Psi) = \kappa_1 \cos^2 \Psi + \kappa_2 \sin^2 \Psi, \tag{6}$$

where κ_1, κ_2 are the principal curvatures. This is identical to Euler's formula from the classical differential geometry of surfaces.

At the umbilical points the curvilinear congruences of principal directions have a point singularity. Such points are key candidates for significant "features" of the surface.

The osculating paraboloid at a point is simply the Taylor expansion of log-intensity up to second order terms. For elliptic convex points these best fitting approximations are biaxial Gaussians in terms of intensity (not log-intensity).

Notice that the formalism is typically *much simpler* than that for Euclidian differential geometry, for instance, compare the simple expression for the mean curvature

$$2H = Z_{xx} + Z_{yy},$$

with the corresponding expression for Euclidian geometry:

$$\frac{(z_{xx}+z_{yy}) + z_{yy}z_x^2 + z_{xx}z_y^2 - 2z_{xy}z_xz_y}{(1+z_x^2+z_y^2)^{3/2}}.$$

Apart from being simpler the new expression has the additional advantage of being correct for a change and is thus to be recommended, despite the fact that it runs counter to conventional practice (or wisdom?).

4 Features and Significant Regions

A "feature" is the geometrical locus where some differential invariant vanishes. The value of the invariant is obtained by running an image operator at some scale. In most cases the required scale is obvious, in others a "best" scale has to be established[12]. One needs yet another scale in order to define the vanishing of the invariant, essentially the "bin width" at which one wishes to sample the values[6]. A "level set" such as $I(x,y) = I_0$ (in this example generically a *curve*) is really an (hopefully narrow) *area* $(I(x,y) - I_0)^2 < \epsilon^2$, where ϵ is the resolution in the I–domain, essentially the "bin–width". This can easily be captured in a neat formalism when the image scale space is augmented with a histogram scale space[6]. Level sets of differential invariants define "fuzzy features" $\exp(-(I(x,y) - I_0)^2/2\epsilon^2)$, that is to say, they assume the (maximum) value unity at the location of the feature and are near zero far from the location of the feature. This is the robust and principled way to find (or *define*) "features".

Examples of significant features (see figure 3) are the parabolic curves ($K = 0$), minimal curves ($H = 0$), ridges and ruts, and umbilical points. Special points of interest are the inflection points of the parabolic curves, and the points of crossing of ridges of unlike type. Notice that "points" are detected as fuzzy spots and "curves" as fuzzy ribbons or even areas. This makes perfect sense when you think of the nature of level "curves" on shallow slopes and in the presence of noise. Whether a pixel belongs to the level "curve" is a statistical issue and the fuzzy membership function expresses this.

Significant *regions* are obtained through thresholding of differential invariants, usually at zero value. Again, one needs to define "fuzzy" characteristic functions. One defines the characteristic region via $(1 + \mathrm{erf}((I(x,y) - I_0)/\epsilon))/2$. It equals near unity inside and near zero outside the region.

Here is a simple application: It is tempting to use thresholding as a coarse way of segmentation. The problem is that it cannot yield an invariant result. A local extremum is meaningless because I can shift it with a congruence of image space. In the place of a maximum (or hill area) you may substitute an area where $K > 0$ (elliptic) and $H < 0$ (convex). Any point in such elliptic convex areas can be turned into a maximum through the application of a suitable movement whereas no other points can. Likewise, in place of the minima (or valley areas)

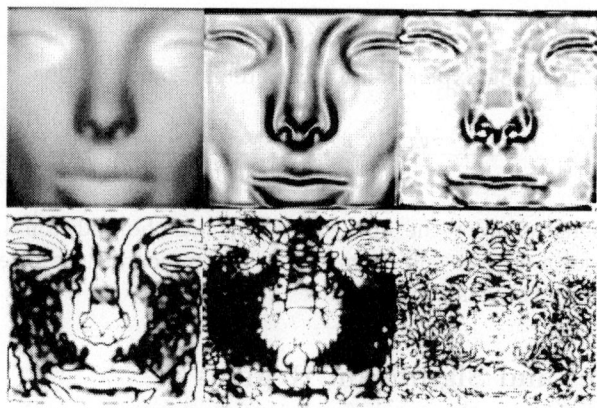

Fig. 3. Features for the case of a face image. Top from left to right: The image at the resolution of the operators (lighter is "more"), the gradient magnitude and the curvedness. These display scalar magnitudes. Bottom from left to right: Minimal ($H = 0$), parabolic ($K = 0$) loci and ridges (a 3rd-order invariant). These are (fuzzy!) curves. For all the invariants darker is "more".

you may put areas where $K > 0$ and $H > 0$. Notice that at the boundary of such areas one principal curvature vanishes and $H \neq 0$. Indeed, $K = 0$ and $H = 0$ only occurs at planar points which are not present in the generic case. Thus the areas are bounded by the parabolic curves and the sign of the mean curvature merely decides upon the type. One may denote such areas "domes" and "bowls" which is what they look like. Unlike the results of raw thresholding these are significant regions because invariant against arbitrary image space movements.

5 Conclusion

We have introduced a geometrical framework that allows one to handle image structures in a principled manner. The basic structure depends upon two major considerations. The first is a careful examination of the physical nature of the intensity domain. It turns out to be the case that only the log–intensity representation can be considered "natural" (in the geometrical sense) because it does not commit one to any particular choice of unit or fiducial intensity. The second is a careful examination of the group of transformations that leave image structure invariant (the "similitudes" and proper motions). We identify this group with the transformations that conserve the spatial structure ("pixels") and conserve lines and planes in image space as families. That this choice is particularly apt is evident from the fact that many of the common transformations used for more by a century by photographers and commonly available in image processing packages (of the Photoshop type) are easily identified as subgroups. Even nonlinear transformations as "dodging" and "burning" are easily identified as *conformal transformations* of the space[16].

Notice that all this derives from a single, very simple assumption, namely *Complete ignorance as to location in image space*. From this it follows that no intensity range is singled out and that the space is homogeneous (that "free mobility" is guaranteed). That the movements should conserve a family of parallel lines can hardly be counted as an "assumption": It is the only way to be consistent.

The geometry we obtain is one of the 27 Cayley–Klein geometries. It is the product of the Euclidian plane (with parabolic distance metric and elliptic angle metric) and the isotropic line[13] (with parabolic distance metric). This makes that the geometry of the isotropic planes (called "normal planes" in this paper) is governed by a degenerate, parabolic distance metric and a parabolic angle metric. This is exactly what makes this geometry a natural representation of image space. Since the slant of planes is not periodic but may take values on the full real axis, one cannot "turn around" in image space. This corrects the irritating oddity implicit in the conventional Euclidian choice where one may turn (in principle) the intensity domain so as to lie in the picture plane. Although we have seen no author explicitly admit this, it is implicit in the (very common) use of Euclidian expressions (for the curvature of image surfaces for instance) in image processing. Such Euclidian expressions are invariants under the group of *Euclidian* isometries, including rotations about *any* axis.

"Image processing done right" indeed implies that one uses the *isotropic* geometry. This may appear exotic at first blush, but some exposure soon leads to an intuitive understanding. The fact that the formalism becomes generally much simpler is perhaps an incentive to move over. The inadvertent use of differential invariants of G_8 is quite widespread in image processing applications. Such practices are justified through the fact that they work. The present theory puts such practices upon a principled foundation and—more importantly—allows a disciplined analysis and extension.

References

1. Adams, A.: *The Print: Contact Printing and Enlarging*. Basic Photo **3**. Morgan and Lester, New York, 1950
2. Cayley, A.: Sixth Memoir upon Quantics. Phil.Trans.Roy.Soc.Lond. **149** (1859) 61–70
3. Clifford, W. K.: Preliminary sketch of biquaternions. Proc.Lond.Math.Soc. (1873) 381–395
4. Florack, L.: *Image Structure*. Kluwer, Dordrecht, 1997
5. Gauss, C. F.: *Algemeine Flächentheorie*. (German translation of *Disquisitiones generales circa Superficies Curvas*), Hrsg. A. Wangerin, Ostwalds Klassiker der exakten Wissenschaften **5**. Engelmann, Leipzig, 1889 (orig. 1827)
6. Ginneken, B. van, Haar Romeny, B. M. ter: Applications of locally orderless Images. In: *Scale–Space Theories in Computer Vision*. Eds. M. Nielsen, P. Johansen, O. F. Olsen and J. Weickert. Second Int.Conf. Scale–Space'99, Lect.Notes in Computer Science **1682**. Springer, Berlin (1999) 10 21

7. Jaglom, I. M.: *A simple non–Euclidian geometry and its physical basis: an elementary account of Galilean geometry and the Galilean principle of relativity.* Transl. A. Shenitzer, ed.ass. B. Gordon. Springer, New York, 1979
8. Jaglom, I. M.: *Complex numbers in geometry.* Transl. E. J. F. Primrose. Academic Paperbacks, New York, 1968
9. Jaynes,E. T.: Prior Probabilities. IEEE Trans. on Systems Science and Cybernetics **4**(3) (1968) 227–241
10. Klein, F.: Über die sogenannte nichteuklidische Geometrie. Mathematische Annalen Bd.**6** (1871) 112–145
11. Klein, F.: *Vergleichende Betrachtungen über neue geometrische Forschungen* (the "Erlangen Program"). Programm zu Entritt in die philosophische Fakultät und den Senat der Universität zu Erlangen. Deichert, Erlangen, 1872
12. Lindeberg, T.: *Scale–Space Theory in Computer Vision.* Kluwer, Dordrecht, 1994
13. Pottmann, H., Opitz, K.: Curvature analysis and visualization for functions defined on Euclidian spaces or surfaces. Computer Aided Geometric Design **11** (1994) 655–674
14. Sachs, H.: *Ebene Isotrope Geometrie.* Vieweg, Braunschweig/Wiesbaden, 1987
15. Sachs, H.: *Isotrope Geometrie des Raumes.* Vieweg, Braunschweig/Wiesbaden, 1990
16. Scheffer, G.: Verallgemeinerung der Grundlagen der gewöhnlichen komplexen Funktionen. Sitz.ber.Sächs.Ges.Wiss., Math.–phys.Klasse, Bnd. **45** (1893) 828–842
17. Strubecker, K.: Differentialgeometrie des isotropen Raumes I. Sitzungsberichte der Akademie der Wissenschaften Wien **150** (1941) 1-43
18. Strubecker, K.: Differentialgeometrie des isotropen Raumes II. Math.Z. **47** (1942) 743–777
19. Strubecker, K.: Differentialgeometrie des isotropen Raumes III. Math.Z. **48** (1943) 369–427
20. Strubecker, K.: Differentialgeometrie des isotropen Raumes IV. Math.Z. **50** (1945) 1–92

Multimodal Data Representations with Parameterized Local Structures

Ying Zhu[1], Dorin Comaniciu[2], Stuart Schwartz[1], and Visvanathan Ramesh[2]

[1] Department of Electrical Engineering, Princeton University
Princeton, NJ 08544, USA
{yingzhu, stuart}@EE.princeton.edu
[2] Imaging & Visualization Department, Siemens Corporate Research
755 College Road East, Princeton, NJ 08540, USA
{Dorin.Comaniciu, Visvanathan.Ramesh}@scr.siemens.com

Abstract. In many vision problems, the observed data lies in a nonlinear manifold in a high-dimensional space. This paper presents a generic modelling scheme to characterize the nonlinear structure of the manifold and to learn its multimodal distribution. Our approach represents the data as a linear combination of parameterized local components, where the statistics of the component parameterization describe the nonlinear structure of the manifold. The components are adaptively selected from the training data through a progressive density approximation procedure, which leads to the maximum likelihood estimate of the underlying density. We show results on both synthetic and real training sets, and demonstrate that the proposed scheme has the ability to reveal important structures of the data.

1 Introduction

In this paper we address the problem of learning the statistical representation of multivariate visual data through parametric modelling. In many pattern recognition and vision applications, an interesting pattern is measured or visualized through multivariate data such as time signals and images. Its random occurrences are described as scattered data points in a high-dimensional space. To better understand and use the critical information, it is important to explore the intrinsic low dimensionality of the scattered data and to characterize the data distribution through statistical modelling. The general procedure in learning parametric distribution models involves representing the data with a family of parameterized density functions and subsequently estimating the model parameters that best fit the data.

Among the commonly used parametric models, principal component analysis (PCA) [1,2] and linear factor analysis [3] are linear modelling schemes that depict the data distribution either by a low-dimensional Gaussian or by a Gaussian with structured covariance. These approaches can properly characterize distributions in ellipsoidal shapes, but they are unable to handle situations where the data samples spread into a nonlinear manifold that is no longer Gaussian. The nonlinear structure of a multivariate data distribution is not unusual even when its intrinsic variables are distributed unimodally. For instance, the images of an object under varying poses form a nonlinear manifold in the high-dimensional space. Even with a fixed view, the variation in the facial expressions can still generate a face manifold with nonlinear structures. A similar situation occurs when we model the images of cars with a variety of outside designs. The nonlinearity can be characterized by multimodal distributions through mixtured density functions. Such methods include local PCA analysis [5], composite analysis [4], transformed component and its mixture analysis [24,25]. Alternative approaches have been proposed to describe the geometry of the principal manifold [6,22,23]. However, no probabilistic model is associated with the geometric representations.

This paper presents a new modelling scheme that characterizes nonlinear data distributions through probabilistic analysis. This scheme is built on parametric function representations and nonlinear factor analysis. Multivariate data is represented as a combination of parameterized basis functions with local supports. We statistically model the random parameterization of the local components to obtain a density estimate for the multivariate data. The probabilistic model derived here can provide likelihood measures, which are essential for many vision applications. We first introduced this idea in [26] to characterize the internally unimodal distributions with standard basis functions. Here we extend our discussion to cover multimodal distributions as well as the issue of basis selection. The paper is organized as follows. In section 2, we introduce the idea of parametric function representation. A family of multimodal distributions is formulated in section 3 to characterize an arbitrary data-generating process. In section 4, we solve the maximum likelihood (ML) density estimate through the procedure of progressive density approximation and the expectation-maximization (EM) algorithm. Related issues in basis selection and initial clustering are also addressed. In section 5, we show the experimental results of modelling both synthetic and real data. We finish with conclusions and discussions in section 6.

2 Data Representation with Parameterized Local Functions

Parameterized function representation [26] is built on function association and function parameterization (Fig. 1). In function association, an n-dimensional data $\mathbf{y} = [y_1, \cdots, y_n] \in R^n$ is associated with a function $y(\mathbf{t}) \in L^2 : R^d \to R^1 (\mathbf{t} \in R^d)$ such that

$$y_i = y(\mathbf{t}_i) \quad (i = 1, \cdots, n)$$

For images, $\mathbf{t}$ is a two dimensional vector and $y(\mathbf{t})$ is defined on R^2 ($\mathbf{t} \in R^2$). For time signals, $\mathbf{t}$ becomes a scalar and $y(\mathbf{t})$ is defined on R^1 ($\mathbf{t} \in R^1$). The function $y(\mathbf{t})$ is interpolated from the discrete components of $\mathbf{y}$, and the vector $\mathbf{y}$ is produced by sampling $y(\mathbf{t})$. The function association applies a smoothing process to the discrete data components. It is unique once the interpolation method is determined. Consequently, in the function space L^2, there exits a counterpart of the scattered multivariate data located in vector space R^n. The advantage of function association lies in its ease to handle the non-linearity by parametric effects embedded in the data. Its application to data analysis can be found in [6,8,9,10,19]. In function parameterization, we represent $y(\mathbf{t})$ with

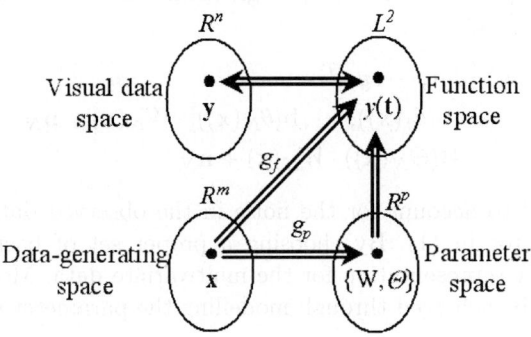

Fig. 1. Parametric function representation through space mappings. Multivariate data $\mathbf{y}$ is represented by function $y(\mathbf{t})$ parameterized by $\{W, \Theta\}$.

a basis of the function space L^2. Assume that the set of functions $\{b_\theta(\mathbf{t}) = b(\mathbf{t}; \theta) : R^d \to R(\mathbf{t} \in R^d)\}$, each parameterized and indexed by θ, construct a basis of L^2. With the proper choice of $b(\mathbf{t}; \theta)$, a function $y(\mathbf{t}) \in L^2$ can be closely approximated with a finite number (N) of basis functions,

$$y(\mathbf{t}) \cong [w_1, \cdots, w_N] \cdot \begin{bmatrix} b(\mathbf{t}; \theta_1) \\ \vdots \\ b(\mathbf{t}; \theta_N) \end{bmatrix} \quad (1)$$

In general, the basis function $b(\mathbf{t}; \theta)$ is nonlinear in θ. If locally supported functions such as wavelets are chosen to construct the basis $\{b(\mathbf{t}; \theta)\}$, then $y(\mathbf{t})$ is represented as a linear combination of nonlinearly parameterized local components. In the following discussion, we use W_N, Θ_N, and $\mathbf{\Theta}_N$ to denote the linear, nonlinear and overall parameter sets, where N is the number of basis functions involved.

$$W_N = \begin{bmatrix} w_1 \\ \vdots \\ w_N \end{bmatrix} ; \Theta_N = \begin{bmatrix} \theta_1 \\ \vdots \\ \theta_N \end{bmatrix} ; \mathbf{\Theta}_N = \begin{bmatrix} W_N \\ \Theta_N \end{bmatrix} \quad (2)$$

Assume $\mathbf{x} \in R^m$, in a vector form, to be the intrinsic quantities governing the data-generating process. With parametric function association, the observed data $\mathbf{y}$ is related to $\mathbf{x}$ through an unknown mapping $g_f : R^m \to L^2$, or equivalently, a mapping $g_p : R^m \to R^P$ from $\mathbf{x}$ to the parameter set,

$$g_p(\mathbf{x}) = [W_N(\mathbf{x}), \Theta_N(\mathbf{x})]^T \quad (3)$$

By defining the matrix

$$\mathbf{B}(\Theta_N) = [\mathbf{b}(\theta_1), \cdots, \mathbf{b}(\theta_N)]; \quad \mathbf{b}(\theta_i) = \begin{bmatrix} b(\mathbf{t}_1; \theta_i) \\ \vdots \\ b(\mathbf{t}_n; \theta_i) \end{bmatrix} \quad (i = 1, \cdots, N) \quad (4)$$

multivariate data $\mathbf{y}$ is related to $\mathbf{x}$ through the linear combination of local basis functions,

$$\begin{aligned} \mathbf{y} &= [y_1, \cdots, y_n]^T \\ &= [\mathbf{b}(\theta_1(\mathbf{x})), \cdots, \mathbf{b}(\theta_N(\mathbf{x}))] \cdot W_N(\mathbf{x}) + \mathbf{n}_N \\ &= \mathbf{B}(\Theta_N(\mathbf{x})) \cdot W_N(\mathbf{x}) + \mathbf{n}_N \end{aligned} \quad (5)$$

$\mathbf{n}_N$ is introduced to account for the noise in the observed data as well as the representation error in (1). By choosing a proper set of basis functions, (5) defines a compact representation for the multivariate data. Modelling the data distribution can be achieved through modelling the parameter set $\Theta_N(\mathbf{x})$.

3 Learning Data Distribution

In this section, we discuss the algorithms and the criteria for learning nonlinear data distributions with parametric data representation. Fig. 2 shows an example of how the parametric effect can cause the nonlinear structure of the data distribution. The observed multivariate data $\mathbf{y} = [y_1, \cdots, y_n]^T$ consists of n equally spaced samples from the random realizations of a truncated raised cosine function $y_0(t)$,

$$\begin{aligned} y_i &= y(t_i; w, \theta) \quad (t_i = i \cdot T) \\ y(t; w, \theta) &= w \cdot y_0(\tfrac{t-t_0}{s}) \quad (\theta = (s, t_0)) \\ y_0(t) &= \begin{cases} \tfrac{1}{2}(1 + \cos(t)) & (t \in [-\pi, \pi]) \\ 0 & (t \notin [-\pi, \pi]) \end{cases} \end{aligned} \quad (6)$$

where the generating parameters w, s and t_0 have a joint Gaussian distribution. Even though these intrinsic variables are distributed as a Gaussian, the conventional subspace Gaussian and Gaussian mixtures are either incapable or inefficient in describing the nonlinearly spread data. Such phenomena are familiar in many situations where the visual data is generated by a common pattern and bears similar features up to a degree of random deformation. Parameterized function representation decomposes the observed data into a group of local components with random parameters, which facilitates the characterization of locally deformed data.

3.1 Internally Unimodal Distribution

In most situations with a single pattern involved, the governing factor of the data-generating process is likely unimodal although the observed data $\mathbf{y}$ may

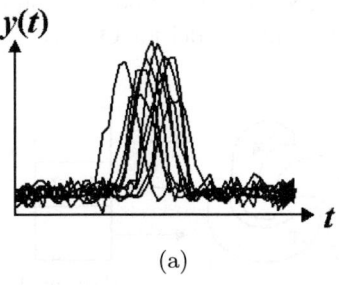 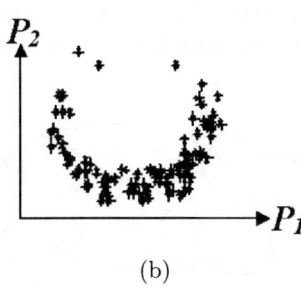

Fig. 2. Nonlinearly distributed manifold. (a) Curve samples. (b) 2D visualization of the data distribution. (P_1 and P_2 signify the sample projections on the top two principal components derived from the data.)

disperse into a nonlinear manifold. For such an internally unimodal distribution, we assume a normal distribution for the intrinsic vector $\mathbf{x}$, which, together with a proper mapping g_p, generates $\mathbf{y}$. When the mapping g_p is smooth, the linearization of $W_N(\mathbf{x})$ and $\Theta_N(\mathbf{x})$ is valid around the mean of $\mathbf{x}$,

$$W_N(\mathbf{x}) = W_{N,0} + A_{W,N} \cdot \mathbf{x}$$
$$\Theta_N(\mathbf{x}) = \Theta_{N,0} + A_{\Theta,N} \cdot \mathbf{x} \qquad (7)$$

hence $W_N(\mathbf{x})$ and $\Theta_N(\mathbf{x})$ can be modelled as a multivariate Gaussian. Assume $\mathbf{n}_N$ is white Gaussian noise with zero mean and variance σ_N^2. From the representation (5), the multivariate data $\mathbf{y}$ is effectively modelled as

$$p(\mathbf{y}) = \int_{\Theta_N} p(\Theta_N) \cdot p(\mathbf{y}|\Theta_N) d\Theta_N \qquad (8)$$

$$(\mathbf{y}|\Theta_N = \mathbf{b}(\Theta_N) \cdot W_N + \mathbf{n}_N)$$
$$\Theta_N \sim N(\mu_N, \Sigma_N); \qquad \mathbf{n}_N \sim N(0, \sigma_N^2 \cdot I_n) \qquad (9)$$

(8) defines a generative model of nonlinear factor analysis, where the parameter set $\Theta_N(\mathbf{x})$ has a unimodal Gaussian distribution.

3.2 Multimodal Distribution

The adoption of multimodal distribution for $\Theta_N(\mathbf{x})$ is necessary for two reasons. Firstly, if the process itself is internally multimodal, i.e. $\mathbf{x}$ can be modelled by mixtures of Gaussian, then the linearization of g_p around all the cluster means

$$W^q(\mathbf{x}) = W_0^q + A_W^q \cdot \mathbf{x}$$
$$\Theta^q(\mathbf{x}) = \Theta_0^q + A_\Theta^q \cdot \mathbf{x} \quad \mathbf{x} \in q\text{-th cluster} \qquad (q = 1, \cdots, C) \qquad (10)$$

leads to a mixture distribution for $\Theta_N(\mathbf{x})$. Secondly, even in the case of an internally unimodal distribution, if the smoothness and the valid linearization of g_p do not hold over all the effective regions of $\mathbf{x}$, piecewise linearization of g_p is necessary, which again leads to a Gaussian mixture model for $\Theta_N(\mathbf{x})$.

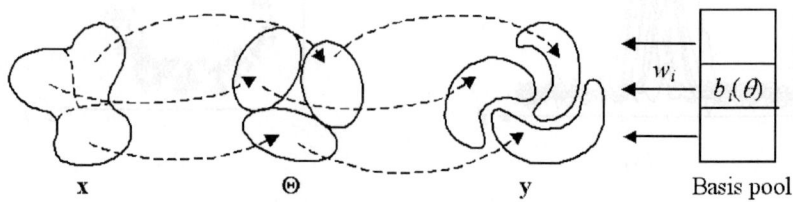

Fig. 3. Multimodal distribution and the basis pool for parameterized data representation.

Let c denote the cluster index, the generative distribution model for the observed data $\mathbf{y}$ is given by the multimodal factor analysis,

$$p(\mathbf{y}) = \sum_{q=1}^{C} P(c=q) \int_{\Theta_{N_q}} p(\Theta_{N_q}|c=q) \cdot p(\mathbf{y}|\Theta_{N_q}, c=q) d\Theta_{N_q} \quad (11)$$

$$P(c=q) = \pi_q \quad (q=1,\cdots,C) \quad (12)$$

$$p(\Theta_{N_q}|c=q) = N(\mu_{q,N_q}, \Sigma_{q,N_q}) \quad (13)$$

$$p(\mathbf{y}|\Theta_{N_q}, c=q) = N(\mathbf{B}(\Theta_{N_q}) \cdot W_{N_q}, \sigma_{q,N_q}^2 \cdot I_n) \quad (14)$$

$P(c=q)$ denotes the prior probability for the q-th cluster, $p(\Theta_{N_q}|c=q)$ denotes the density function of Θ_{N_q} in the q-th cluster, and $p(\mathbf{y}|\Theta_{N_q}, c=q)$ denotes the conditional density function of $\mathbf{y}$ given Θ_{N_q} in the q-th cluster. Define $\Phi_{q,N_q} = \{\mu_{q,N_q}, \Sigma_{q,N_q}, \sigma_{q,N_q}^2\}$, $\Phi = \{\pi_q, \Phi_{q,N_q}\}_{q=1}^{C}$. Equations (11)-(14) define a family of densities parameterized by Φ. The multivariate data $\mathbf{y}$ is statistically specified by the family of densities $p(\mathbf{y}|\Theta, c)$. The parameters $\{\Theta, c\}$, which characterize the cluster prior and the building components within each cluster, are specified by the family of densities $P(c)p(\Theta|c)$ that depend on another level of parameters Φ. Φ is therefore called the set of *hyper-parameters* [12]. The following discussion is devoted to finding the particular set of Φ such that the generative distribution $p(\mathbf{y}|\Phi)$ best fits the observed data.

3.3 Learning through Maximum Likelihood (ML) Fitting

Given M independently and identically distributed data samples $\{\mathbf{y}_1,\cdots,\mathbf{y}_M\}$, the density estimate $\hat{p}(\mathbf{y})$, in the maximum likelihood (ML) sense, is then defined by the ML estimate of Φ such that the likelihood

$$p(\mathbf{y}_1,\cdots,\mathbf{y}_M|\Phi) = \prod_{i=1}^{M} p(\mathbf{y}_i|\Phi) \quad (15)$$

is maximized over the parameterized family (11)-(14),

$$\hat{p}(\mathbf{y}) = p(\mathbf{y}|\hat{\mathbf{\Phi}})$$
$$\hat{\mathbf{\Phi}} = \text{argmax}_{\mathbf{\Phi} \in \Omega} \prod_{i=1}^{M} p(\mathbf{y}_i|\mathbf{\Phi}) \qquad (16)$$

Ω denotes the domain of $\mathbf{\Phi}$. Further analysis suggests that the ML criterion minimizes the Kullback-Leibler divergence between the density estimate and the true density. Denote the true density function for the observed data by $p_T(\mathbf{y})$. The Kullback-Leibler divergence $D(p_T||\hat{p})$ measures the discrepancy between p_T and $\hat{p}$,

$$\begin{aligned} D(p_T||\hat{p}) &= \int p_T(\mathbf{y}) \cdot \log \frac{p_T(\mathbf{y})}{\hat{p}(\mathbf{y})} d\mathbf{y} \\ &= E_{p_T}[\log p_T(\mathbf{y})] - E_{p_T}[\log \hat{p}(\mathbf{y})] \end{aligned} \qquad (17)$$

$D(p_T||\hat{p})$ is nonnegative and approaches zero only when the two densities coincide. Since the term $E_{p_T}[\log p_T(\mathbf{y})]$ is independent of the density estimate $\hat{p}(\mathbf{y})$, an equivalent similarity measurement is defined as

$$\begin{aligned} L(\hat{p}) &= E_{p_T}[\log \hat{p}(\mathbf{y})] \\ &= -D(p_T||\hat{p}) + E_{p_T}[\log p_T(\mathbf{y})] \\ &\leq E_{p_T}[\log p_T(\mathbf{y})] \end{aligned} \qquad (18)$$

$L(\hat{p})$ increases as the estimated density $\hat{p}$ approaches the true density p_T. It is upper bounded by $E_{p_T}[\log p_T(\mathbf{y})]$. Since p_T is unknown, $L(\hat{p})$, the expectation of $\log \hat{p}(\mathbf{y})$, can be estimated in practice by its sample mean.

$$\hat{L}(\hat{p}) = \frac{1}{M} \sum_{i=1}^{M} \log \hat{p}(\mathbf{y}_i) \qquad (19)$$

(19) defines the same target function as the ML estimate (16). Hence the ML fitting rule minimizes the Kullback-Leibler divergence between p_T and $\hat{p}$.

4 Hyper-Parameter Estimation and Basis Selection

Fig. 4 illustrates the process of density estimation. To solve the ML density estimate, we need to construct the local basis functions $\{b_i\}$ as well as their parameter set $\mathbf{\Theta}$. For each cluster, the local building components are gradually introduced through the *progressive density approximation* procedure. With a set of local components $\{b_1, \cdots, b_N\}$ parameterized by $\mathbf{\Theta}_N$, the multivariate data $\mathbf{y}$ is represented as a linear combination of nonlinearly parameterized local components. The *expectation-maximization* (EM) algorithm [12] is applied to estimate the hyper-parameter set $\mathbf{\Phi}$ that defines the distribution of $\mathbf{\Theta}_N$, $\mathbf{n}_N$, and the cluster prior $P(c)$. We first discuss the EM algorithm, and then address the issues of basis selection and parameterization as well as initial clustering.

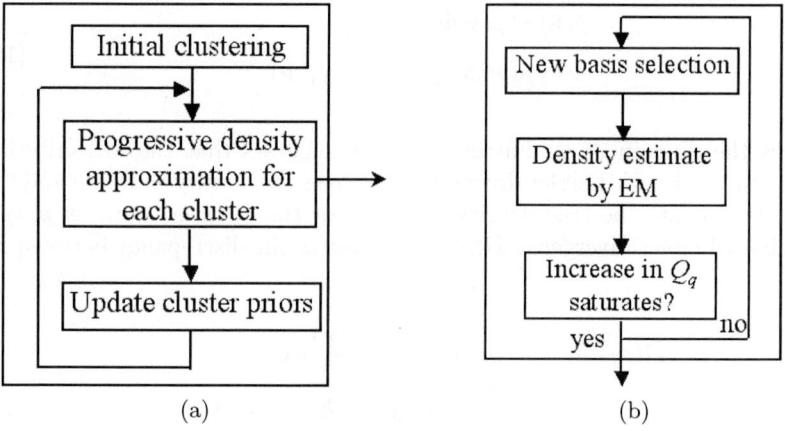

Fig. 4. Diagram of the EM-based modelling framework. (a) Iterative estimation of cluster prior and cluster density. (b) Progressive density approximation for each cluster.

4.1 EM Algorithm and Numerical Implementations

Assume that the set of local basis functions $\mathbf{B}_q(\Theta_{N_q}) = \{b_{q,1}(\theta_1), \cdots, b_{q,N_q}(\theta_{N_q})\}$ for the q-th cluster has already been established. Denote $\{\Theta_{N,j}, c_j\}$ as the hidden parameter set for the observed data $\mathbf{y}_j$, and $\mathbf{\Phi}^{(k)} = \{\pi_q^{(k)}, \mu_{q,N_q}^{(k)}, \Sigma_{q,N_q}^{(k)}, \sigma_{q,N_q}^{2(k)}\}_{q=1}^{C}$ as the estimate of $\mathbf{\Phi}$ from the k-th step. The EM algorithm maximizes the likelihood $p(\mathbf{y}_1, \cdots, \mathbf{y}_M | \Theta)$ through the iterative expectation and maximization operations.

E-Step: Compute the expectation of the log-likelihood of the complete data $\log p(\{\mathbf{y}_j, \Theta_{N,j}, c_j\}|\mathbf{\Phi})$ given the observed data $\{\mathbf{y}_j\}$ and the estimate $\mathbf{\Phi}^{(k)}$ from the last round,

$$Q(\mathbf{\Phi}|\mathbf{\Phi}^{(k)}) = \sum_{j=1}^{M} E[\log p(\mathbf{y}_j, \Theta_{N,j}, c_j | \mathbf{\Phi}) | \mathbf{y}_j, \mathbf{\Phi}^{(k)}] \qquad (20)$$

M-Step: Maximize the expectation

$$\mathbf{\Phi}^{(k+1)} = \operatorname{argmax}_{\mathbf{\Phi}} Q(\mathbf{\Phi}|\mathbf{\Phi}^{(k)}) \qquad (21)$$

Denote

$$p_q(\mathbf{y}_j|\Theta_{N_q,j}, \Phi_{q,N_q}) = p(\mathbf{y}_j|\Theta_{N_q,j}, c_j = q, \Phi_{q,N_q}) \qquad (22)$$

$$p_q(\Theta_{N_q,j}|\Phi_{q,N_q}) = p(\Theta_{N_q,j}|c_j = q, \Phi_{q,N_q}) \qquad (23)$$

$$p_q(\mathbf{y}_j|\Phi_{q,N_q}) = p(\mathbf{y}_j|c_j = q, \Phi_{q,N_q}) \qquad (24)$$

$$(q = 1, \cdots, C; \quad j = 1, \cdots, M)$$

$Q(\Phi|\Phi^{(k)})$ can be expressed as

$$Q(\Phi|\Phi^{(k)}) = \sum_{j=1}^{M}\sum_{q=1}^{C} P(c_j = q|\mathbf{y}_j, \Phi^{(k)}) \log \pi_q + \sum_{q=1}^{C} Q_q(\Phi_{q,N_q}|\Phi_{q,N_q}^{(k)}) \quad (25)$$

where

$$Q_q(\Phi_{q,N_q}|\Phi_{q,N_q}^{(k)}) = \sum_{j=1}^{M} \frac{P(c_j = q|\mathbf{y}_j, \Phi^{(k)})}{p_q(\mathbf{y}_j|\Phi_{q,N_q}^{(k)})} \int [\log p_q(\mathbf{y}_j|\Theta_{N_q,j}, \Phi_{q,N_q}) +$$
$$\log p_q(\Theta_{N_q,j}|\Phi_{q,N_q})] \cdot p_q(\mathbf{y}_j|\Theta_{N_q,j}, \Phi_{q,N_q}^{(k)}) p_q(\Theta_{N_q,j}|\Phi_{q,N_q}^{(k)}) d\Theta_{N_q,j} \quad (26)$$

(25) indicates that the cluster prior $\{\pi_q\}$ and the hyper-parameter set Φ_{q,N_q} for each cluster can be updated separately in the M-step. Generally, (26) has no closed form expression since the local component functions $\mathbf{B}_q(\Theta_{N_q})$ is nonlinear in Θ_{N_q}. The numerical approach can be adopted to assist the evaluation of the Q function. We detail the update rule for the hyper-parameters in the Appendix. The process of hyper-parameter estimation to maximize $p(\mathbf{y}_1, \cdots, \mathbf{y}_M|\Phi)$ is then summarized as follows:

1. Initially group $\{\mathbf{y}_1, \cdots, \mathbf{y}_M\}$ into C clusters. The initial clustering is addressed in later discussions. The number of clusters is preset. Set $\pi_q^{(0)} = \frac{M_q}{M}$, where M_q is the number of samples in the q-th cluster. Set $P(c_j = q|\mathbf{y}_j, \Phi^{(0)})$ to 1 if $\mathbf{y}_j$ is assigned to the q-th cluster, 0 otherwise.
2. Construct local basis functions $\{b_1, \cdots, b_{N_q}\}$. Estimate the hyper-parameters $\{\Phi_{q,N_q}\}$ separately for each cluster. In later discussions, the progressive density approximation algorithm is proposed to gradually introduce local components and the EM algorithm is carried out to find the ML estimate of $\{\Phi_{q,N_q}\}$.
3. Use the EM procedure to iteratively update the cluster prior $\{\pi_q\}$ and the hyper-parameters $\{\Phi_{q,N_q}\}$ through (38)-(41) in the appendix.

4.2 Progressive Density Approximation and Basis Selection

Unlike other modelling techniques with a fixed representation, the proposed generative model actively learns the component functions to build the data representation. The procedure is carried separately for each cluster. By introducing more basis components, the density estimate gradually approaches the true distribution. The progressive density approximation for the q-th cluster is stated as follows:

1. Start with $Nq = 1$.
2. Find the ML density estimate $\hat{p}_q(\mathbf{y}) = p_q(\mathbf{y}|\hat{\Phi}_{q,N_q})$ by iteratively maximizing $Q_q(\Phi_{q,N_q}|\Phi_{q,N_q}^{(k)})$ with (39)-(41) in the appendix.
3. Introduce a new basis function, increase N_q by 1, and repeat step 2 and 3 until the increase of Q_q saturates as N_q increases.

Since the domain of Φ_{q,N_q} is contained in the domain of Φ_{q,N_q+1}, the introduction of the new basis function increases Q_q, $Q_q(\hat{\Phi}_{q,N_q+1}|\hat{\Phi}_{q,N_q}) \geq Q_q(\hat{\Phi}_{q,N_q}|\hat{\Phi}_{q,N_q})$, which leads to the increase of the likelihood $p(\mathbf{y}_1,\cdots,\mathbf{y}_M|\hat{\Phi})$ and the decrease of the divergence $D(p_T||\hat{p})$.

Two issues are involved in basis selection. First, we need to choose the basis and its form of parameterization to construct an initial pool of basis functions (Fig. 3). Second, we need to select new basis functions from the pool for efficient data representation. Standard basis for the function space L^2, such as wavelets and splines with proper parameterization, is a natural choice to create the basis pool. In [26], we adopted wavelet basis (the Derivative-of-Gaussian and the Gabor wavelets) with its natural parameterization to represent the data:

Time signal $(y(t): R \to R)$:

$$b(t;\theta) = \psi_0(\tfrac{t-T}{s});$$
$$\psi_0(t) = t \cdot \exp(-\tfrac{1}{2}t^2); \quad \theta = \{T,s\} \in R \times R^+ \tag{27}$$

Image $(y(\mathbf{t}): R^2 \to R)$:

$$b(\mathbf{t};\theta) = \psi_0(SR_\alpha(\mathbf{t}-T))$$
$$\psi_0(\mathbf{t}) = t_x \cdot \exp(-\tfrac{1}{2}(t_x^2 + t_y^2)) \quad (\mathbf{t} = [t_x, t_y]^T)$$
$$S = \begin{bmatrix} s_x & 0 \\ 0 & s_y \end{bmatrix}, \quad R_\alpha = \begin{bmatrix} \cos(\alpha) & \sin(\alpha) \\ -\sin(\alpha) & \cos(\alpha) \end{bmatrix}, \quad T = \begin{bmatrix} T_x \\ T_y \end{bmatrix}$$
$$\theta = \{s_x, s_y, \alpha, T_x, T_y\} \in (R^+)^2 \times [0, 2\pi] \times R^2 \tag{28}$$

The parameters naturally give the location, scale and orientation of the local components. Details on selecting new basis functions from the pool are provided in [26], where the new basis function is selected to maximize the Q function used by the EM procedure. Its actual implementation minimizes a term of overall residual energy evaluated with the current density estimate $p(\mathbf{y}|\hat{\Phi}_{q,N_q})$.

The standard basis provides a universal and overcomplete basis pool for all L^2 functions [14]. However, it does not necessarily give an efficient representation, especially when the data contains structures substantially different from the base function ψ_0. In this case, the representation can have a low statistical dimension but high complexity in terms of large number of basis functions involved. Here we propose an *adaptive basis selection* scheme that keeps the parameterization of the standard basis and replaces the base function ψ_0 by the *base templates* extracted from the data. Denote the n-th base template by $\bar{b}_{q,n}$, and use (28) to define the parameters. The building components are constructed as transformed base templates,

$$b_{q,n}(\mathbf{t};\theta) = \bar{b}(Tr(\mathbf{t};\theta)) \tag{29}$$
$$Tr(\mathbf{t};\theta) = SR_\alpha(\mathbf{t}-T)$$

The hyper-parameter estimate $\hat{\Phi}_{q,N_q}$ with N_q components can be viewed as a special configuration of Φ_{q,N_q+1} where the (N_q+1)-th component is zero with probability 1. To select a new base template, $(w_{N_q+1}, \theta_{N_q+1})$ is initially assumed to be independent of Θ_{N_q} and uniformly distributed over its domain. From (37) and (22)-(24), we can approximate Q_q with the ML estimate of the sample parameters $(\hat{\Theta}_{N_q,j}, \hat{w}_{N_q+1,j}, \hat{\theta}_{N_q+1,j})$,

$$Q_q(\Phi_{q,N_q+1}|\hat{\Phi}_{q,N_q}) \cong \kappa - \frac{1}{2\hat{\sigma}_{q,N_q}^2} \sum_{j=1}^{M} a_{q,j} \| \hat{r}_{N_q,j} - \hat{w}_{N_q+1,j} b_{q,N_q+1}(\hat{\theta}_{N_q+1,j}) \|^2$$

$$\hat{\Theta}_{N_q,j} = \mathrm{argmax}_{\Theta_{N_q,j}} p_q(\mathbf{y}_j|\Theta_{N_q,j}, \hat{\Phi}_{q,N_q}) p_q(\Theta_{N_q,j}|\hat{\Phi}_{q,N_q})$$

$$\hat{r}_{N_q,j} = \mathbf{y}_j - \mathbf{B}(\hat{\Theta}_{N_q,j}) \cdot \hat{W}_{N_q,j}$$

$$a_{q,j} = \frac{P(c_j=q|\mathbf{y}_j, \Phi^{(k)})}{p_q(\mathbf{y}_j|\Phi_{q,N_q}^{(k)})} p_q(\mathbf{y}_j|\Theta_{N_q,j}, \hat{\Phi}_{q,N_q}) p_q(\Theta_{N_q,j}|\hat{\Phi}_{q,N_q})$$

The new basis is selected to maximize Q_q, or equivalently, to minimize the weighted residue energy

$$(\bar{b}_{q,N_q+1}, \{\hat{w}_{N_q+1,j}, \hat{\theta}_{N_q+1,j}\}_{j=1}^{M})$$
$$= \mathrm{argmin} \sum_{j=1}^{M} a_{q,j} \| \hat{r}_{N_q,j} - \hat{w}_{N_q+1,j} b_{q,N_q+1}(\hat{\theta}_{N_q+1,j}) \|^2 \qquad (30)$$

From (29), the right hand term in (30) is evaluated as

$$\sum_{j=1}^{M} a_{q,j} \| \hat{r}_{N_q,j}(\mathbf{t}) - \hat{w}_{N_q+1,j} \bar{b}_{q,N_q+1}(Tr(\mathbf{t};\hat{\theta}_{N_q+1,j})) \|^2$$
$$= \sum_{j=1}^{M} a_{q,j} \hat{\omega}_j \| \hat{r}_{N_q,j}(Tr^{-1}(\mathbf{t};\hat{\theta}_{N_q+1,j})) - \hat{w}_{N_q+1,j} \bar{b}_{q,N_q+1}(\mathbf{t}) \|^2$$
$$(Tr^{-1}(\mathbf{t};\theta) = R_{-\alpha}S^{-1}\mathbf{t} + T; \quad \hat{\omega}_j = \hat{s}_{x,q,N_q+1,j}^{-1} \hat{s}_{y,q,N_q+1,j}^{-1}) \qquad (31)$$

The new basis selection procedure is stated as follows:

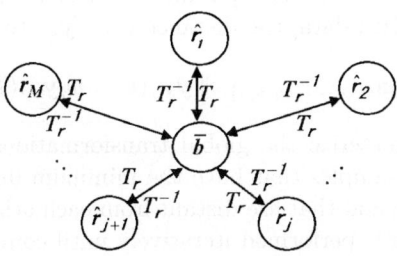

Fig. 5. Adaptive basis selection.

1. Locate the subregion where the residue $\sum_{j=1}^{M} a_{q,j} \| \hat{r}_{N_q,j}(\mathbf{t}) \|^2$ is most significant. Position the new base template to cover the subregion, and set $\bar{b}_{q,N_q+1}$ to be the subregion of $\hat{r}_{N_q,j_0}$ with $j_0 = \mathrm{argmax}_j a_{q,j} \| \hat{r}_{N_q,j}(\mathbf{t}) \|^2$.

2. Iteratively update $\bar{b}_{q,N_q+1}$ and $(\hat{w}_{N_q+1,j}, \hat{\theta}_{N_q+1,j})$ to minimize (31).

$$(\hat{w}_{N_q+1,j}, \hat{\theta}_{N_q+1,j}) = \mathrm{argmin}_{(w,\theta)} \parallel \hat{r}_{N_q,j}(\mathbf{t}) - w\bar{b}_{q,N_q+1}(Tr(\mathbf{t};\theta)) \parallel^2 \quad (32)$$

$$\bar{b}_{q,N_q+1}(\mathbf{t}) = \frac{1}{\sum_{j=1}^{M} a_{q,j}\hat{\omega}_j \hat{w}^2_{N_q+1,j}} \sum_{j=1}^{M}[a_{q,j}\hat{\omega}_j \hat{w}_{N_q+1,j}\hat{r}_{N_q,j}(Tr^{-1}(\mathbf{t};\hat{\theta}_{N_q+1,j}))] \quad (33)$$

3. Compute the hyper-parameters for Θ_{N_q+1} by (39)-(40), where $\Theta^{(k)}_{N_q,j,i,q}$ is replaced by the ML estimate $\hat{\Theta}_{N_q+1,j}$ and $K^{(k)}_{j,i,q}$ is replaced by the term derived from $\hat{\Theta}_{N_q+1,j}$.

The base template and the ML sample parameters are derived simultaneously through iterative procedures (Fig. 5). The base template is updated by the weighted average of the inversely transformed samples, where samples with higher likelihood are weighted more. The sample parameters are updated by the transformation that most closely maps the base template to the sample.

4.3 Initial Clustering

Initial clustering groups together the data samples that share dominating global structures up to a certain transformation. Through the expansion

$$\bar{b}_{q,n}(Tr(\mathbf{t};\theta_{q,n})) = \bar{b}_{q,n}(\mathbf{t}) + [\nabla_t \bar{b}_{q,n}(\mathbf{t})]^T \cdot (Tr(\mathbf{t};\theta_{q,n}) - \mathbf{t}) + \cdots \quad (34)$$

we notice that transformation effects are prominent in places where the local components have high-frequency (gradient) content. To emphasize the global structures for initial clustering, samples are smoothed by lowpass filters to reduce the effects of local deformations. Meanwhile, the sample intensity is normalized to reduce the variance of the linear parameters. Denote $\{\mathbf{y}_{s,1}, \cdots, \mathbf{y}_{s,M}\}$ as the smoothed and normalized data, the distance from $\mathbf{y}_{s,i}$ to $\mathbf{y}_{s,j}$ is defined as

$$d(\mathbf{y}_{s,i}, \mathbf{y}_{s,j}) = \min_{(w,\theta) \in \{(w_i,\theta_i)\}_i} \parallel \mathbf{y}_{s,j}(\mathbf{t}) - w_i \mathbf{y}_{s,i}(Tr(\mathbf{t};\theta_i)) \parallel^2 \quad (35)$$

where $\{(w_i, \theta_i)\}$ parameterize the global transformations. The cluster centers are first set to be the samples that have the minimum distance to a number of their nearest neighbors and that are distant from each other. Then the following procedure of clustering is performed iteratively until convergence.

1. Assign each sample to the cluster that has the minimal distance from its center to the sample.
2. For each cluster, find the new cluster center.

$$\mathbf{y}_{s,q} = \mathrm{argmin}_{\mathbf{y}_{s,j} \in C_q} \sum_{\mathbf{y}_{s,i} \in C_q} d(\mathbf{y}_{s,j}, \mathbf{y}_{s,i}) \quad (36)$$

5 Experiments

Examples of progressive density approximation with standard basis have been shown in [26] to learn unimodal distributions, where wavelet basis is used to model curves as well as pose manifolds for object identification. Here we show two examples of learning multimodal distribution with adaptive basis selection.

5.1 Multimodal Distribution of Synthetic Data

In this experiment, 200 images with 30x30 pixels have been synthesized as the training data, each containing a cross with its vertical bar shifted randomly. The shift is around one of two centers shown by the examples in Fig. 6(a). The data cannot be efficiently modelled by the transformed component analysis [24] with only global transformations. The proposed modelling scheme has been performed to estimate the multimodal distribution with 2 clusters. Adaptive basis selection is implemented by positioning rectangular base templates to cover the regions with significant residue. The parameterization of the base template is defined by the horizontal translation and scaling parameters (s_x, T_x) (28). As shown in Fig. 6(b), the two cluster centers have been successfully recovered. In each cluster, three local components have been selected to represent the data. Meanwhile, the intrinsic dimension 1 for both clusters has been identified. Fig. 6(c) shows the synthesized realizations along the nonlinear principal manifold of each cluster.

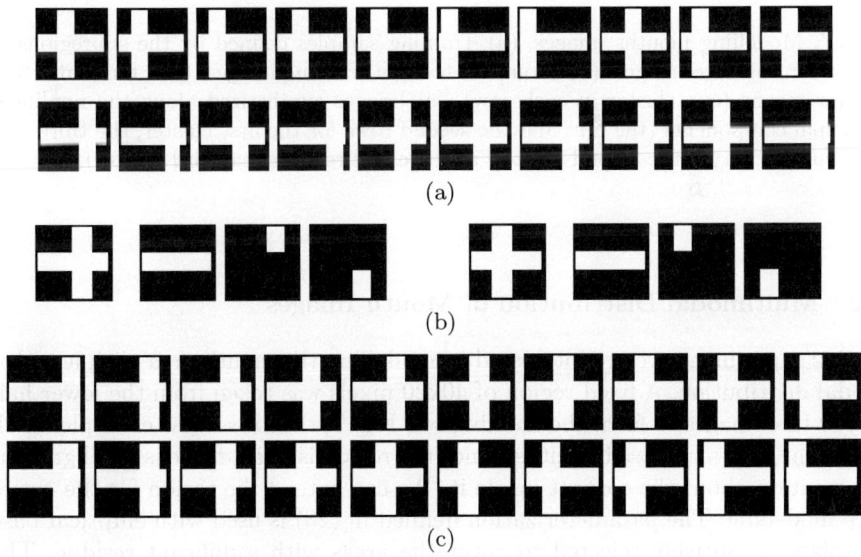

Fig. 6. Modelling synthetic data. (a) Training samples. (b) Cluster means and the three base templates selected for each cluster. (c) Synthesized samples on the principal manifolds learnt by the model. (one cluster in each row).

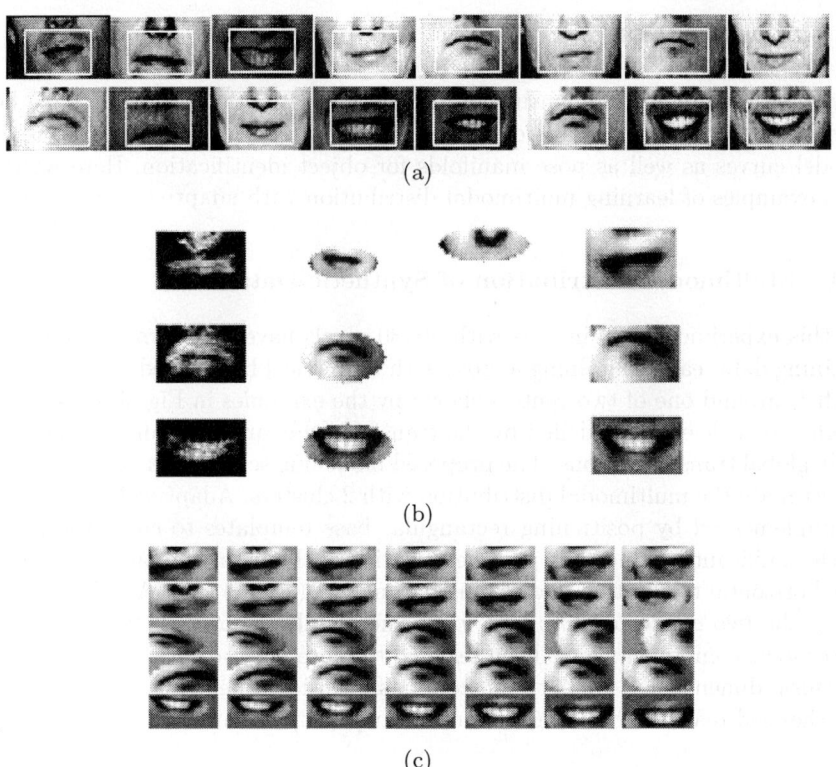

Fig. 7. Modelling mouths images. (a) Training samples defined by the subregions of the lower half face images. (b) From left to right: residue images, base templates and cluster means (one cluster in each row). (c) Images synthesized along the nonlinear principal components (the first and the second rows for the first cluster, the third and the fourth rows for the second cluster, and the last row for the third cluster).

5.2 Multimodal Distribution of Mouth Images

In this experiment, we are interested in modelling the mouth area with a multimodal distribution. A fixed region of 40x20 pixels was taken from the lower half of 100 face images to form the training set. Fig. 7(a) shows a few examples with open (smiling) and closed mouths. Since the region is fixed, there is no alignment information about the content inside it. We can extend the region for the entire face modelling. The parameterization defined in (28) is used with elliptical base templates adaptively selected to cover the areas with significant residue. The training images have been normalized before initial clustering. Three clusters and their nonlinear principal components identified by the model are shown in Fig. 7(b) and (c). The first cluster describes closed mouths from upright faces. Two local components have been selected to cover the mouth and the nose tip.

The second cluster describes closed mouths from slightly upward faces, and the third cluster describes the open mouths from smiling faces. Both the second and the third clusters use one component for the data representation. Fig. 7(c) indicates that horizontal and vertical translations are dominant deformations within the training set and they are represented by the nonlinear principal components.

6 Conclusions

In this paper, we have extended the idea of parameterized data representation to the statistical learning of multimodal data distributions. The building basis is adaptively selected from the training data to account for relevant local structures. The parameterized data representation by local components provides more flexibility than linear modelling techniques in describing the local deformations within the data. In addition, the EM-based generative model also provides a probabilistic description of the underlying data distribution. This allows various statistical approaches to be applied to vision problems. Both synthetic and real data are used to demonstrate the ability of the proposed modelling scheme to reveal the data structure and to obtain a good density estimate of the distribution manifold.

Through adaptive basis selection, the basis pool is adaptively defined by the data. It comprises the local patterns that are derived from the data. Compared with standard universal basis, the adaptive basis greatly reduces the complexity of the data representation. The algorithm finds, in a progressive and greedy fashion, the most efficient basis functions for the best modelling accuracy. Various applications of the proposed modelling scheme can be explored in further studies.

References

1. B. Moghaddam and A. Pentland, "Probabilistic Visual Learning for Object Representation", *IEEE Trans. Pattern Analysis and Machine Intelligence*, vol. 19, no. 7, Jul. 1997, pp. 696-710.
2. M. Tipping and C. Bishop. "Probabilistic Principal Component Analysis". Technical Report NCRG/97/010, Neural Computing Research Group, Aston University, September 1997.
3. R. A. Johnson and D. W. Wichern, *Applied Multivariate Statistical Analysis*, Prentice Hall, NJ, 1992.
4. J. Ng and S. Gong, "Multi-view Face Detection and Pose Estimation Using A Composite Support Vector Machine Across the View Sphere", *RATFG-RTS*, 1999, pp. 14-21.
5. N. Kambhatla and T. K. Leen, "Dimension Reduction by Local PCA", *Neural Computation*, vol. 9, no. 7, Oct. 1997, pp. 1493-1516.
6. B. Chalmond and S. C. Girard, "Nonlinear Modeling of Scattered Multivariate Data and Its Application to Shape Change", *IEEE Trans. Pattern Analysis and Machine Intelligence*, vol. 21, no. 5, May 1999, pp. 422-434.

7. B. Moghaddam, "Principal Manifolds and Bayesian Subspaces for Visual Recognition", *IEEE Int. Conf. on Computer Vision*, 1999, pp. 1131-1136.
8. J. O. Ramsay and X. Li, "Curve Registration", *J. R. Statist. Soc.*, Series B, vol. 60, 1998, pp. 351-363.
9. G. James and T. Hastie, "Principal Component Models for Sparse Functional Data", Technical Report, Department of Statistics, Stanford University, 1999.
10. M. Black, and Y. Yacoob, "Tracking and Recognizing Rigid and Non-Rigid Facial Motions Using Local Parametric Models of Image Motion", *IEEE Int. Conf. Computer Vision*, 1995, pp. 374-381.
11. Z. R. Yang and M. Zwolinski, "Mutual Information Theory for Adaptive Mixture Models", *IEEE Trans. Pattern Analysis and Machine Intelligence*, vol. 23, no. 4, Apr. 2001, pp. 396-403.
12. A. P. Dempster, N. M. Laird and D. B. Rubin, "Maximum Likelihood from Incomplete Data via EM Algorithm", *J. R. Statist. Soc.*, Series B, vol. 39, 1977, pp. 1-38.
13. H. Murase and S. K. Nayar, "Visual Learning and Recognition of 3D Objects from Appearance", *Int. J. Computer Vision*, vol. 14, 1995, pp. 5-24.
14. Q. Zhang and A. Benveniste, "Wavelet Networks", *IEEE Trans. Neural Networks*, vol. 3, no. 6, Nov 1992, pp. 889-898.
15. C. M. Bishop and J. M. Winn, "Non-linear Bayesian Image Modelling", *European Conf. on Computer Vision*, 2000, pp. 3-17.
16. B. Frey and N. Jojic, "Transformed Component Analysis: Joint Estimation of Spatial Transformations and image Components", *IEEE Int. Conf. Computer Vision*, 1999, pp. 1190-1196.
17. M. Weber, M. Welling and P. Perona, "Unsupervised Learning of Models for Recognition", *European Conf. on Computer Vision*, 2000, pp. 18-32.
18. T. S. Lee, "Image Representation Using 2D Gabor Wavelets", *IEEE Trans. Pattern Analysis and Machine Intelligence*, vol. 18, no. 10, 1996, pp. 959-971.
19. B.W. Silverman, "Incorporating Parametric Effects into Functional Principal Components Analysis, *J. R. Statist. Soc.*, Series B, vol. 57, no. 4, 1995, pp. 673-689.
20. M. Black, and A. Jepson, "Eigentracking: Robust Matching and Tracking of Articulated Objects Using A View-based Representation", *European Conf. on Computer Vision*, 1996, pp. 329-342.
21. A. R. Gallant, *Nonlinear Statistical Models*, John Wiley & Sons Inc., NY, 1987.
22. J. B. Tenenbaum, V. De Silva, and J. C. Langford, "A Global Geometric Framework for Nonlinear Dimensionality Reduction", *Science*, vol. 290, 2000, pp. 2319-2323.
23. S. Roweis and L. Saul, "Nonlinear Dimensionality Reduction by Locally Linear Embedding", *Science*, vol. 290, 2000, pp. 2323-2326.
24. B. J. Frey and N. Jojic, "Transformation-Invariant Clustering and Dimensionality Reduction Using EM", submitted to *IEEE Trans. Pattern Analysis and Machine Intelligence*, Nov. 2000.
25. C. Scott and R. Nowak, "Template Learning from Atomic Representations: A Wavelet-based Approach to Pattern Analysis", *IEEE workshop on Statistical and Computational Theories of Vision*, Vancouver, CA, July 2001.
26. Y. Zhu, D. Comaniciu, Visvanathan Ramesh and Stuart Schwartz, "Parametric Representations for Nonlinear Modeling of Visual Data", *IEEE Int. Conf. on Computer Vision and Pattern Recognition*, 2001, pp. 553-560.
27. K. Popat and R. W. Picard, "Cluster Based Probability Model and Its Application to Image and Texture Processing", *IEEE Trans. Image Processing*, Vol. 6, No. 2, 1997, pp. 268-284.

Appendix

Using the idea of importance sampling, for each cluster, a group of random realizations of $\Theta_{N_q,j}$, $\Theta_{N_q,j,i,q}^{(k)} = [W_{N_q,j,i,q}^{(k)}, \Theta_{N_q,j,i,q}^{(k)}]^T{}_i$, is chosen within the volume where the value of $p_q(\mathbf{y}_j|\Theta_{N_q,j}, \Phi_{q,N_q}^{(k)}) p_q(\Theta_{N_q,j}|\Phi_{q,N_q}^{(k)})$ is significant, and Q_q is evaluated as

$$Q_q(\Phi_{q,N_q}|\Phi_{q,N_q}^{(k)}) \cong \sum_{j=1}^{M} K_{j,i,q}^{(k)} [\log p_q(\mathbf{y}_j|\Theta_{N_q,j,i,q}^{(k)}, \Phi_{q,N_q}) + \log p_q(\Theta_{N_q,j,i,q}^{(k)}|\Phi_{q,N_q})]$$

$$K_{j,i,q}^{(k)} = \frac{P(c=q|\mathbf{y}_j, \Phi_{q,N_q}^{(k)})}{p_q(\mathbf{y}_j|\Phi_{q,N_q}^{(k)})} p_q(\mathbf{y}_j|\Theta_{N_q,j,i,q}^{(k)}, \Phi_{q,N_q}^{(k)}) p_q(\Theta_{N_q,j,i,q}^{(k)}|\Phi_{q,N_q}^{(k)}) \cdot \kappa_{q,j}^{(k)}$$

$$\kappa_{q,j}^{(k)} = \frac{p_q(\mathbf{y}_j|\Phi_{q,N_q}^{(k)})}{\sum_i p_q(\mathbf{y}_j|\Theta_{N_q,j,i,q}^{(k)}, \Phi_{q,N_q}^{(k)}) p_q(\Theta_{N_q,j,i,q}^{(k)}|\Phi_{q,N_q}^{(k)})} \quad (37)$$

Substitute the density function in (37) with (12)-(14), the cluster prior $\{\pi_q\}$ and the hyper-parameter set Φ_q for each cluster are updated separately in the M-step.

$$\pi^{(k+1)} = \frac{\sum_{j=1}^{M} P(c=q|\mathbf{y}_j, \Phi_{q,N_q}^{(k)})}{\sum_{q=1}^{C} \sum_{j=1}^{M} P(c=q|\mathbf{y}_j, \Phi_{q,N_q}^{(k)})} \quad (38)$$

$$\mu_{q,N_q}^{(k+1)} = \frac{1}{\sum_{j=1}^{M} \sum_i K_{j,i,q}^{(k)}} \sum_{j=1}^{M} \sum_i K_{j,i,q}^{(k)} \Theta_{N_q,j,i,q}^{(k)} \quad (39)$$

$$\Sigma_{q,N_q}^{(k+1)} = \frac{1}{\sum_{j=1}^{M} \sum_i K_{j,i,q}^{(k)}} \sum_{j=1}^{M} \sum_i K_{j,i,q}^{(k)} \cdot (\Theta_{N_q,j,i,q}^{(k)} - \mu_{q,N_q}^{(k+1)}) \cdot (\Theta_{N_q,j,i,q}^{(k)} - \mu_{q,N_q}^{(k+1)})^T$$

$$(40)$$

$$\sigma_{q,N_q}^{2(k+1)} = \frac{1}{Card(\mathbf{y}) \cdot \sum_{j=1}^{M} \sum_i K_{j,i,q}^{(k)}} \sum_{j=1}^{M} \sum_i K_{j,i,q}^{(k)} \| \mathbf{y}_j - \mathbf{B}_q(\Theta_{N_q,j,i,q}^{(k)}) \cdot W_{N_q,j,i,q}^{(k)} \|^2$$

$$(41)$$

$Card(\mathbf{y})$ denotes the cardinality of the multivariate data $\mathbf{y}$.

The Relevance of Non-generic Events in Scale Space Models

Arjan Kuijper[1] and Luc Florack[2]

[1] Utrecht University, Department of Computer Science, Padualaan 14, NL-3584 CH Utrecht, The Netherlands
[2] Technical University Eindhoven, Department of Biomedical Engineering, Den Dolech 2, NL-5600 MB Eindhoven, The Netherlands

Abstract. In order to investigate the deep structure of Gaussian scale space images, one needs to understand the behaviour of spatial critical points under the influence of blurring. We show how the mathematical framework of catastrophe theory can be used to describe the behaviour of critical point trajectories when various different types of generic events, *viz.* annihilations and creations of pairs of spatial critical points, (almost) coincide. Although such events are non-generic in mathematical sense, they are not unlikely to be encountered in practice. Furthermore the behaviour leads to the observation that fine-to-coarse tracking of critical points doesn't suffice. We apply the theory to an artificial image and a simulated MR image and show the occurrence of the described behaviour.

1 Introduction

The concept of scale space has been introduced in the English image literature by Witkin [16] and Koenderink [8]. They showed that the natural way to represent an image at finite resolution is by convolving it with a Gaussian , thus obtaining a smoothened image at a scale determined by the bandwidth. Consequently, each scale level only requires the choice of an appropriate scale and the image intensity at that level follows linearly from any previous level. It is therefore possible to trace the evolution of certain image entities, e.g. critical points, over scale. The exploitation of various scales simultaneously has been referred to as *deep structure* by Koenderink [8]. It pertains to the dynamic change of the image from highly detailed –including noise – to highly smoothened. Furthermore, it may be expected that large structures "live" longer than small structures (a reason that Gaussian blur is used to suppress noise). Since multi-scale information can be ordered, one obtains a hierarchy representing the subsequent simplification of the image with increasing scale [10].

In one dimensional images critical points can only vanish. Investigation of these locations has been done by several authors [7,15]. Higher dimensional images are more complicated since extrema can be created in scale space This phenomenon has been studied in detail by Damon, [2], proving that creations are generic in images of dimension larger than one. That means that they are not some kind of artifact, introduced by noise or numerical errors, but that they are to be expected in any typical case. This was somewhat counterintuitive, since blurring seemed to imply that structure could only disappear, thus suggesting that only annihilations could occur. Damon, however, showed that both annihilations and creations are generic catastrophes and gave a complete list of local perturbations of these generic events. Whereas Damons results were stated theoretically, application of these results were reported in *e.g.* [6,9,12]. The main outcome of the investigation of the generic results is that in order to be able to use the topological approach one necessarily needs to take into account both the annihilation and creation events.

In images the location of critical points can be found up to the numerical precision of the image. The same holds for the location of catastrophe points in scale space. So although the appearance of catastrophe events can be uniquely separated in annihilations or creations of pairs of critical points, due to *e.g.* numerical limitations, (almost) symmetries in the image, or coarse sampling also indistinguishable compounds of these annihilation and creation events can be found in practise. In this way a couple of nearby generic events may well look like a single, non-generic one. In this paper we describe these so-called non-generic catastrophes in scale space. The investigation is based on the description of the evolution of critical points in scale space, called (scale space) critical curves, in the neighbourhood of the catastrophe point(s). The compounds of generic events can be modelled using descriptions of "Catastrophe Theory". Obviously, the models obey the property that assuming infinite precision, in non-generic compounds the generic events can be distinguished.

Furthermore we investigate the appearance of creations as described by these models in more detail and explain why they are, albeit generic, rarely found, probably the reason for current applications to simply ignore them.

2 Theory

Gaussian Scale Space. Let $L(\mathbf{x})$ denote an arbitrary n-dimensional image, the initial image. Let $L(\mathbf{x};t)$ denotes the $(n+1)$-dimensional *Gaussian scale space image* of $L(\mathbf{x})$, obtained by convolution of an initial image with a normalised Gaussian kernel of zero mean and standard deviation $\sqrt{2t}$. Differentiation is now well-defined, since an arbitrary derivative of the image is obtained by the convolution of the initial image with the corresponding derivative of a Gaussian. Consequently, $L(\mathbf{x};t)$ satisfies the diffusion equation:

$$\partial_t L(\mathbf{x};t) = \Delta L(\mathbf{x};t)$$

Here $\Delta L(\mathbf{x};t)$ denotes the Laplacean. The type of a spatial critical point ($\nabla L(\mathbf{x};t) = 0$) is given by the eigenvalues of the Hessian H, the matrix with the second order spatial derivatives, evaluated at its location. The trace of the Hessian equals the Laplacean. For maxima (minima) all eigenvalues of the Hessian are negative (positive). At a spatial saddle point H has both negative and positive eigenvalues. Since $L(\mathbf{x};t)$ is a smooth function in $(\mathbf{x};t)$-space, spatial critical points are part of a one dimensional manifold in scale space, called the *critical curve*, by virtue of the implicit function theorem. Consequently, the intersection of all critical curves in scale space with a plane of certain fixed scale t_0 yields the spatial critical points of the image at that scale.

Catastrophe Theory. The spatial critical points of a function with non-zero eigenvalues of the Hessian are called *Morse critical points*. The *Morse Lemma* states that at these points the qualitative properties of the function are determined by the quadratic part of the Taylor expansion of this function. This part can be reduced to the *Morse canonical form* by a slick choice of coordinates. If at a spatial critical point the Hessian degenerates, so that at least one of the eigenvalues is zero (and consequently the determinant is zero), the type of the spatial critical point cannot be determined. Such a point is called a *catastrophe points*.

The term catastrophe was introduced by Thom [14]. It denotes a (sudden) qualitative change in an object as the parameters on which this object depends change smoothly. A thorough mathematical treatment on this topic can be found in the work of Arnol'd, see e.g. [1]. More pragmatic introductions and applications are widely published, e.g. [5]. The catastrophe points are also called *non-Morse critical points*, since a higher order Taylor expansion is essentially needed to describe the qualitative properties. Although the dimension of the variables is arbitrary, the *Thom Splitting Lemma* states that one can split up the function in a Morse and a non-Morse part. The latter consists of variables representing the k "bad" eigenvalues of the Hessian that become zero. The Morse part contains the $n - k$ remaining variables. Consequently, the Hessian contains a $(n - k) \times (n - k)$ sub-matrix representing a Morse function. It therefore suffices to study the part of k variables. The canonical form of the function at the non-Morse critical point thus contains two parts: a Morse canonical form of $n - k$ variables, in terms of the quadratic part of the Taylor series, and a non-Morse part. The latter can by put into canonical form called the *catastrophe germ*, which is obviously a polynomial of degree 3 or higher.

Since the Morse part does not change qualitatively under small perturbations, it is not necessary to further investigate this part. The non-Morse part, however, does change. Generally the non-Morse critical point will split into a non-Morse critical point, described by a polynomial of lower degree, and Morse critical points, or even exclusively into Morse critical points. This event is called a *morsification*. So the non-Morse part contains the catastrophe germ and a perturbation that controls the morsifications. Then the general form of a Taylor expansion $f(\mathbf{x})$ at a non-Morse critical point of an n dimensional function can be written as (*Thom's Theorem*) $f(\mathbf{x}; \lambda) = CG + PT + Q$, where $CG(x_1, \ldots, x_k)$ denotes the catastrophe germ, $PT(x_1, \ldots, x_k; \lambda_1, \ldots, \lambda_l)$ the perturbation germ with an l-dimensional space of parameters, and $Q = \sum_{i=k+1}^{n} \epsilon_i x_i^2$ with $\epsilon_i = \pm 1$, the Morse part. Of the so-called simple real singularities we will discuss the catastrophe germs given by the two infinite series $A_k^\pm \stackrel{\text{def}}{=} \pm x^{k+1}, k \geq 1$, and $D_k^\pm \stackrel{\text{def}}{=} x^2 y \pm y^{k-1}, k \geq 4$. For notational convenience we will rewrite the latter to $x^{k-1} \pm xy^2$.

Catastrophes and Scale Space. The number of equations defining the catastrophe point equals $n + 1$ and therefore it is over-determined with respect to the n spatial variables. Consequently, catastrophe points are generically not found in typical images. In scale space, however, the number of variables equals $n + 1$ and catastrophes occur as isolated points.

Although the list of catastrophes starts very simple, it is not trivial to apply it directly to scale space by assuming that scale is just one of the perturbation parameters. As Damon [2] points out: *"There are significant problems in trying to directly apply Morse theory to solutions of to the heat equation. First, it is not clear that generic solutions to the heat equation must be generic in the Morse sense. Second, standard models for Morse critical points and their annihilation and creation do not satisfy the heat equation. How must these models be modified? Third, there is the question of what constitutes generic behaviour. This depends on what notion of local equivalence one uses between solutions to the heat equation."* For example, in one-dimensional images the A_2 catastrophe reduces to $x^3 + \lambda x$. It describes the change from a situation with two critical points (a maximum and a minimum) for $\lambda < 0$ to a situation without critical points for $\lambda > 0$. This event can occur in two ways. The extrema are annihilated for increasing λ, but the opposite – creation of two extrema for decreasing λ – is also possible.

In scale space, however, there is an extra constraint: the germ has to satisfy the diffusion equation. Thus the catastrophe germ x^3 implies an extra term $6xt$. On the other hand, the perturbation term is given by λx, so by taking $\lambda = 6t$ scale plays the *role* of the perturbing parameter. This gives a directionality to the perturbation parameter, in the sense that the only remaining possibility for this A_2-catastrophe in one-dimensional images is an annihilation. So the Fold catastrophe is adjusted such that it satisfies the heat equation, but this adjustment only allows annihilations. However, it does not imply that only annihilations are generic in scale space. In higher dimensional images also the opposite – *i.e.* a A_2 catastrophe describing the creation of a pair of critical points – is possible. Then the perturbation $\lambda = -6t$ with increasing t requires an additional term of the form $-6xy^2$ in order to satisfy the diffusion equation as we will see.

The transfer of the catastrophe germs to scale space, taking into account the special role of scale, has been made by many authors, [2,3,7,9,12], among whom Damon's account – answering his questions – is probably the most rigorous. He showed that the only generic morsifications in scale space are the aforementioned A_2 catastrophes describing *annihilations* and *creations* of pairs of critical points. These two points have opposite sign of the determinant of the Hessian before annihilation and after creation.

Definition 1. *The generic scale space catastrophe germs are given [2] by*

$$f^A(\mathbf{x};t) \stackrel{\text{def}}{=} x_1^3 + 6x_1 t + Q(\mathbf{x};t),$$
$$f^c(\mathbf{x};t) \stackrel{\text{def}}{=} x_1^3 - 6x_1 t - 6x_1 x_2^2 + Q(\mathbf{x};t).$$

where $Q(\mathbf{x};t) \stackrel{\text{def}}{=} \sum_{i=2}^n \epsilon_i(x_i^2 + 2t)$, $\sum_{i=2}^n \epsilon_i \neq 0$, *and* $\epsilon_i \neq 0 \; \forall i$.

Note that the scale space catastrophe germs f^A and f^c, and the quadratic term Q satisfy the diffusion equation. The germs f^A and f^c correspond to the two qualitatively different A_2 catastrophes at the origin, an annihilation and a creation respectively. From Definition 1 it is obvious that annihilations occur in any dimension, but creations require at least 2 dimensions. Consequently, in 1D signals only annihilations occur. Furthermore, for images of arbitrary dimension and less than three vanishing eigenvalues of the Hessian at a degenerated point, it suffices to investigate the 2D case due to the Splitting Lemma. All other catastrophe events in scale space are compounds of Fold catastrophes. It is however possible that one may not be able to distinguish these generic events, *e.g.* due to numerical limitations, coarse sampling, or (almost) symmetries in the image. For instance, one may find at some scale three nearby critical points, e.g. two extrema and a saddle, and at the subsequent scale only one extremum. Obviously, one pair of critical points is annihilated, but one may not be able to identify the annihilating extremum at the former scale. This is illustrated in Figure 1.

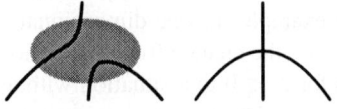

Fig. 1. Left: Annihilation of two critical points in the neighbourhood of a third critical point. The grey area represents the uncertainty in determining the catastrophe. Right: Non-generic representation and model of this event.

3 Scale Space Catastrophe Models

In this section we describe how catastrophes can be used to model events in $(2+1)$-dimensional scale space. The catastrophes describe in canonical coordinates how critical curves pass the origin yielding compounds of annihilations and / or creations of pairs of critical points. We will see that although most of these catastrophes are *non-generic*, they may still be relevant for modelling *compounds of generic events* that one is not capable of, or willing to, segregate as such. Recall, for example, Figure 1. The catastrophe germs are adjusted such that they satisfy the heat equation. Furthermore, by choosing the perturbation terms non-zero and adjusting them in the same way, descriptions of critical curves in scale space are obtained. These critical curves only contain the generic Fold annihilation(s) and/or creation(s).

A_2 **Fold catastrophe.** The Fold catastrophe in scale space is given by

$$L(x,y;t) = x^3 + 6xt + \delta(y^2 + 2t),$$

where $\delta = \pm 1$. One can verify that at the origin a saddle and an extremum (a minimum if $\delta = 1$, a maximum if $\delta = -1$) moving in the $y = 0$ plane meet and annihilate while increasing the scale parameter t.

A_3 **Cusp catastrophe.** The Cusp catastrophe germ is given by x^4. Its scale space addition is $12x^2 t + 12t^2$. The perturbation term contains two terms: $\lambda_1 x + \lambda_2 x^2$. Obviously, scale takes the role of λ_2. Taking the dual Cusp gives the same geometry by changing the sign of λ_1, or by setting $x = -x$. The scale space Cusp catastrophe germ with perturbation is thus defined by

$$L(x,y;t) = x^4 + 12x^2 t + 12t^2 + \lambda_1 x + \delta(y^2 + 2t),$$

with $\delta = \pm 1$. Morsification by the perturbation $\lambda_1 \neq 0$ yields one Fold catastrophe and one regular critical curve. One can verify that the $A_k, k > 3$ catastrophes describes the (non-generic) simultaneous annihilations of critical points in one dimension under the influence of blurring, albeit in more complicated appearances.

$D_4^\pm$ Umbilic catastrophes.

The $D_4^\pm$ Umbilic catastrophe germs are given by $x^3 + \delta xy^2$, where $\delta = \pm 1$. The scale space addition is $(6 + 2\delta)xt$, yielding $x^3 + xy^2 + 8xt$ for the Hyperbolic Umbilic catastrophe, and $x^3 - xy^2 + 4xt$ for the Elliptic Umbilic catastrophe. The perturbation contains three terms: $\lambda_1 x + \lambda_2 y + \lambda_3 y^2$. Obviously, scale takes the role of λ_1.

D_4^+ Hyperbolic Umbilic catastrophe.

The scale space D_4^+ Hyperbolic Umbilic catastrophe germ with perturbation is thus defined by

$$L(x, y; t) = x^3 + xy^2 + 8xt + \lambda_3(y^2 + 2t) + \lambda_2 y .$$

The critical curves and catastrophe points follow from

$$\begin{cases} L_x = 3x^2 + 8t + y^2 \\ L_y = 2xy + 2\lambda_3 y + \lambda_2 \\ \det(H) = 12x(x + \lambda_3) - 4y^2. \end{cases}$$

In the unperturbed situation four critical points exist for each $t < 0$ on the x- and y-axes. At $t = 0$ the four critical curves annihilate simultaneously at the origin, see Figure 2a. Taking perturbation into account, the curves are separated into two critical curves each

Fig. 2. Critical paths a) D_4^+-Unperturbed. b) D_4^+-Perturbed. c) D_4^--Unperturbed. d) D_4^--Small perturbation. e) D_4^--Large perturbation. Again, if the perturbation is small we may not be able to tell which configuration is the actual one.

containing a Fold catastrophe, see Figure 2b.

D_4^- Elliptic Umbilic catastrophes.

The scale space elliptic Umbilic catastrophe germ with perturbation is given by

$$L(x, y; t) = x^3 - xy^2 + 4xt + \lambda_3(y^2 + 2t) + \lambda_2 y . \tag{1}$$

Again, the critical curves and the catastrophe points follow from

$$\begin{cases} L_x = 6x^2 + 4t - y^2 \\ L_y = -2xy + 2\lambda_3 y + \lambda_2 \\ \det(H) = 12x(2\lambda_3 - 2x) - 4y^2. \end{cases}$$

The unperturbed equation gives two critical points for all $t \neq 0$. At the origin a so-called scatter event occurs: the critical curve changes from y-axis to x-axis with increasing t, see Figure 2c. Just as in the hyperbolic case, in fact two Fold catastrophes take place; in this case both an annihilation and a creation. The morsification is shown in Figure 2d. The critical curve on the right does not contain catastrophe points. The critical curve on the left, however, contains two Fold catastrophe points: a creation and an annihilation. So while increasing scale one will find two critical points, suddenly two extra critical points appear, of which one annihilates with one of the already existing ones. Finally, one end up with again two critical points. Clearly, if the samples in scale are taken too large, one could completely miss the subsequent catastrophes, see *e.g.* Figure 2e. The properties of the creations will be discussed in the next section.

Creations. As we showed, a creation event occurs in case of a morsified elliptic Umbilic catastrophe. In most applications, however, creations are rarely found, often giving rise to the (false) opinion that creations are caused by numerical errors and should be disregarded. The reason for their rare appearance lies in the specific requirements for the parameters in the (morsified) Umbilic catastrophe germ. Its general formulation is given by

$$L(x, y; t) = \frac{1}{6}L_{xxx}x^3 + \frac{1}{2}L_{xyy}xy^2 + L_{xt}xt + \frac{1}{2}L_{yy}(y^2 + 2t) + L_y y \quad (2)$$

In general, the spatial coefficients do *not* equal the derivatives evaluated in the coordinate system of the image. They follow from the alignment of the catastrophe in the plane defined by $y = 0$ and can have arbitrary value. Furthermore, the diffusion equation implies $L_{xt} \stackrel{\text{def}}{=} L_{xxx} + L_{xyy}$. Then the scale space evolution of the critical curves follow from

$$\begin{cases} \partial_x L = \frac{1}{2}L_{xxx}x^2 + L_{xt}t + \frac{1}{2}L_{xyy}y^2 \\ \partial_y L = L_{xyy}xy + L_{yy}y + L_y \\ \det(H) = L_{xxx}x(L_{xyy}x + L_{yy}) - L_{xyy}^2 y^2. \end{cases}$$

Firstly we consider the case $L_y = 0$. Then Eq. (2) describes a Fold catastrophe (either annihilation or creation) at the origin, where the critical curve is positioned in the (x, t)-plane. A creation necessarily requires the constraint $L_{xxx}L_{xt} < 0$ at the catastrophe point. This constraint is sufficient.

Theorem 1. *At a catastrophe point in two spatial dimensions, if the third order derivatives of the general local form as given by Eq. (2) with $L_y = 0$, are uncorrelated, the number of creations has an a priori likelihood of $1/4$ relative to the total number of catastrophes. In n dimensions it is $\frac{1}{\pi}\arccos\frac{1}{\sqrt{n}}$.*

Proof. The requirement $L_{xxx}L_{xt} < 0$ can be rewritten to $L_{xxx}(L_{xxx} + L_{xyy}) < 0$. In the (L_{xxx}, L_{xyy})-space this constraint is satisfied by all point sets in the area spanned by the lines through the origin with direction vectors $(1, 0)$ and $(1, -1)$, which is a quarter of the plane. For $n-D$ this extends to the area $L_{xxx}(L_{xxx} + L_{xy_1y_1} + \ldots + L_{xy_{n-1}y_{n-1}}) < 0$ in $(L_{xxx}, L_{xy_iy_i})$-space, with $\dim(\mathbf{y}) = n-1$. This representing two intersecting planes with normal vectors $(1, 0, \ldots, 0)$ and $(1, -1, \ldots, -1)$. They make an angle of ϕ radians, given by

$$\cos\phi = \frac{(1, 0, \ldots, 0) \cdot (1, -1, \ldots, -1)}{|(1, 0, \ldots, 0)| \cdot |(1, -1, \ldots, -1)|} = \frac{1}{\sqrt{n}}$$

Then the fraction of the space follows by taking twice this angle and dividing by the complete angle of 2π, i.e. $\frac{1}{\pi} \arccos \frac{1}{\sqrt{n}}$.

Note that if $n = 1$, the fraction of the space where creations can occur is zero, for $n = 2$ it is a quarter. The also interesting case $n = 3$ yields a fraction that is slightly more than a quarter, whereas for $n \to \infty$ the fraction converges to a half, see Figure 3a. That is: the higher the dimensions, the easier critical points can be created. The reason that in

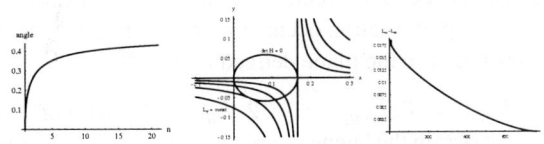

Fig. 3. a) The fraction of the space of the third order derivatives in which creations can occur as a function of the dimension according Theorem 1. b) Intersections of the curves $\det(H) = 0$ and $\partial_y L = 0$ with different values for L_y. For the value given by Theorem 2 the curves touch. c) Difference in intensity between the creation and the annihilation event for L_y increasing from 0 to its critical value.

practice in two dimensional images the number of creations observed is (much) smaller than a quarter, is caused by the role of the perturbation parameters. It is possible to give a tight bound to the perturbation of Equation (2) in terms of L_y:

Theorem 2. *A creation and subsequent annihilation event occur in Equation (2) if and only if*

$$| L_y | \le \frac{3}{16} L_{yy}^2 \sqrt{\frac{-3L_{xxx}}{L_{xyy}^3}} \tag{3}$$

Proof. The catastrophes satisfy $\partial_x L = \partial_y L = \det H = 0$. Since the solution of the system

$$\begin{aligned} \partial_y L = L_y + y(L_{yy} + L_{xyy}x) &= 0 \\ \det H = L_{xxx}x(L_{yy} + L_{xyy}x) - L_{xyy}^2 y^2 &= 0 \end{aligned} \tag{4}$$

only contains spatial coordinates, their intersections define the spatial coordinates of the catastrophes. The catastrophe points form the local extrema of the critical curve in $(x, y; t)$-space, i.e. at these points the tangent vector has no scale component. If the curves given by Eq. (4) touch, there is only a point of inflection in the critical curve, i.e. the critical curve in $(x, y; t)$-space has a (Fold) catastrophe point. At this point of inflection, the spatial tangent vectors of the curves defined by Eq. (4) are equal. Solving the system Eq. (4) with respect to y results in

$$y = -\frac{L_y}{L_{yy} + L_{xyy}x} = \pm \frac{1}{L_{xyy}} \sqrt{L_{xxx}x(L_{yy} + L_{xyy}x)}\,.$$

The equality of the tangent vectors at the point of inflection x_i, y_i yields

$$\frac{\partial}{\partial x} \left(-\frac{L_y}{L_{yy} + L_{xyy}x} \right) \Big|_{x_i, y_i} = \frac{\partial}{\partial x} \left(\pm \frac{1}{L_{xyy}} \sqrt{L_{xxx}x(L_{yy} + L_{xyy}x)} \right) \Big|_{x_i, y_i}$$

Solving both equalities results in

$$(x_i, y_i, L_y) = \left(-\frac{L_{yy}}{4L_{xyy}}, \pm\sqrt{\frac{-3L_{xxx}L_{yy}^2}{16L_{xyy}^3}}, \mp\frac{3L_{yy}^2}{16L_{xyy}}\sqrt{\frac{-3L_{xxx}}{L_{xyy}}}\right),$$

which gives the boundary values for L_y.

Note that Eq. (3) has only real solutions if $L_{xxx}L_{xyy} < 0$, i.e. at the D_4^- (morsified) catastrophe. As a consequence of Theorem 2, creations only occur if the perturbation is small enough. Again, this perturbation occurs in the coordinate system, obtained by the alignment of the catastrophe in the plane defined by $y = 0$.

Example 1. Taking $L_{xxx} = 6, L_{xyy} = -12, L_{yy} = 2$ yielding $L = x^3 - 6xy^2 - 6xt + y^2 + 2t + L_y$, we obtain the "generic creation example" as given in section 2 with perturbation. Then Theorem 2 gives $|L_y| \leq \frac{1}{32}\sqrt{6}$ as a –relatively small compared to the other derivative values– bound for the occurrence of a creation – annihilation couple. In Figure 3b the ellipse $\det(H) = 0$ is plotted, together with the curves $\partial_y L = 0$ for $L_y = 0$ (resulting in two straight lines at $y = 0$ and $x = \frac{1}{6}$, intersecting at $(x, y) = (\frac{1}{6}, 0)$), and $L_y = 2^{-i}\sqrt{6}, i = 4, \ldots, 7$. For $i > 5$, the perturbation is small enough and the intersection of $\partial_y L = 0$ and $\det H = 0$ contains two points. Thus a creation-annihilation is observed. If $i = 5$, L_y has its critical value and the curves touch. For larger values the curves do not intersect each other.

Obviously the perturbation L_y can be larger if L_{yy} increases. If so, the structure becomes more elongated. It is known by various examples of creations given in literature that elongated structures play an important role. In fact, the quintessential property is scale anisotropy. Another reason that creations are rarely found is that their lifetime is rather limited: with increasing t the created critical points annihilate. If the scale steps are taken too large, one simply misses the creation – annihilation couple. This may be regarded as a dual expression for the previous explanation. In the chosen coordinate system this can be calculated explicitly.

Theorem 3. *The maximum lifetime of a creation given by Equation (2) is*

$$t_{lifetime} = \frac{-L_{xxx}L_{yy}^2}{2L_{xyy}^2(L_{xxx} + L_{xyy})}.$$

The difference in intensity of the critical point that is created and subsequently annihilated is

$$\frac{L_{xxx}(2L_{xxx} - L_{xyy})L_{yy}^3}{6L_{xyy}^3(L_{xxx} + L_{xyy})}.$$

Proof. Observe that the lifetime is bounded by the two intersections of $\partial_y L = 0$ and $\det(H) = 0$, see Figure 3b. As $|L_y|$ increases from zero, the two points move towards each other over the arch $\det(H) = 0$ until they reach the value given by theorem 2 with lifetime equal to zero. The largest arch length is obtained for $L_y = 0$. Then the spatial coordinates are found by $\partial_y L(x, y; t) = y(L_{xyy}x + L_{yy}) = 0$ and $\det H = L_{xxx}x(L_{xyy}x + L_{yy}) - L_{xyy}^2 y^2 = 0$ i.e. $(x, y) = (0, 0)$ and $(x, y) = (-\frac{L_{yy}}{L_{xyy}}, 0)$ The location in scale space is given by $\partial_x L(x,y;t) = \frac{1}{2}L_{xxx}x^2 - \frac{1}{2}L_{xyy}y^2 + L_{xt}t = 0$. Consequently, the first catastrophe takes place at the origin - since also $t = 0$ - with zero intensity. The second one is located at

$$(x,y;t) = \left(-\frac{L_{yy}}{L_{xyy}}, 0; \frac{-L_{xxx}L_{yy}^2}{2L_{xyy}^2(L_{xxx} + L_{xyy})}\right)$$

with intensity

$$L_{cat} = \frac{L_{xxx}(2L_{xxx} - L_{xyy})L_{yy}^3}{6L_{xyy}^3(L_{xxx} + L_{xyy})}.$$

Then the latter is also the maximum difference in intensity.

Example 2. To show the effect of the movement along the arch $\det(H) = 0$, see Figure 3c. Without loss of generality we took again $L_{xxx} = 6, L_{xyy} = -12, L_{yy} = 2$. Firstly, the two solutions to $\nabla L = 0 \wedge \det(H) = 0$ were calculated as function of L_y. Secondly, the difference of the intensity of the solutions was calculated for 766 subsequent values of L_y, $L_y \in [0, \ldots, \frac{1}{32}\sqrt{6}]$. It is clearly visible that the intensity decreases monotonously with an increase of L_y. For this example we find that the lifetime is $\frac{1}{72}$, the difference in intensity $\frac{1}{18}$.

From the proof of Theorem 3 it is again apparent that L_{yy} plays an important role in enabling a (long)lasting creation. To observe this in more detail, note that the curve $\det H = 0$ is an ellipse (see also Figure 3b). Replacing x by $x - \frac{L_{yy}}{2L_{xyy}}$, it is centred at the origin. Setting $L_{xyy} = \frac{1}{b}$ and $L_{xxx}L_{xyy} = -\frac{1}{a^2}$, we find

$$\det H = 0 \Leftrightarrow x^2 + \frac{a^2}{b^2}y^2 - L_{yy}^2\frac{b^2}{4}$$

Assuming that we have a creation, $a^2 > 0$. The ellipse is enlarged with an increase of L_{yy}^2. Obviously, at the annihilations of the Hyperbolic Umbilic catastrophe $a^2 < 0$, so $\det H = 0$ then describes a hyperbola.

$D_5^\pm$ Parabolic Umbilic catastrophes. In the previous section we saw that the geometry significantly changed by taking either the term $-xy^2$, or the term $+xy^2$. Let us therefore, ignoring the perturbation terms λ_1, λ_2, and λ_3, define the scale space Parabolic Umbilic catastrophe germ by

$$L(x,y;t) = \frac{1}{4!}x^4 + \frac{1}{2!}x^2t + \frac{1}{2!}t^2 + \delta(\frac{1}{2}xy^2 + xt) \tag{5}$$

where $\delta = \pm 1$ and t takes the role of λ_4. Its critical curves and catastrophes follow from

$$\begin{cases} L_x = \frac{1}{6}x^3 + xt + \delta(t + \frac{1}{2}y^2) \\ L_y = \delta xy \\ \det(H) = \delta x(\frac{1}{2}x^2 + t) - y^2 \end{cases}$$

So the catastrophe points are located at the origin (a double point) and at $(x, y; t) = (-\frac{3}{2}\delta, 0; -\frac{9}{8}\delta^2)$. The latter is a simple annihilation (a fold catastrophe), the former is a cusp catastrophe (three critical point change into one) for both values of δ. Adding small perturbations by choosing the parameters λ_1, λ_2, and λ_3, the morsified Cusp catastrophe remains. The critical curves at the Cusp breaks up into two curves, one with a Fold catastrophe, one without a catastrophe.

$D_6^\pm$ Second Umbilic Catastrophes. Ignoring the perturbation terms $\lambda_1, \ldots, \lambda_4$ for the moment, the scale space expression of the $D_6^\pm$-catastrophes are given by

$$L(x, y; t) = \frac{1}{5!}x^5 + \frac{1}{3!}x^3 t + \frac{1}{2!}xt^2 + \delta(\frac{1}{2}xy^2 + xt), \quad (6)$$

where t takes the role of λ_5 and $\delta = \pm 1$. Its critical curves and catastrophes follow from

$$\begin{cases} L_x = \frac{1}{4!}x^4 + \frac{1}{2}x^2 t + \frac{1}{2}t^2 + \delta(t + \frac{1}{2}y^2) \\ L_y = \delta xy \\ \det(H) = \frac{1}{6}\delta x^2(x^2 + 6t) - y^2 \end{cases}$$

Setting $y = 0$, several catastrophes occur: At $(x, y; t) = (\pm\sqrt{-6\delta}, 0; \delta)$ two Fold annihilations if $\delta = -1$, at the origin a creation and at $(x, y; t) = (0, 0; -2\delta)$ again an annihilation, see Figure 4a for $\delta = 1$ and Figure 4b for $\delta = -1$. It is clear that

Fig. 4. Critical paths of the $D_6^\pm$-catastrophe. a) Unperturbed, $\delta = 1$. b) Unperturbed, $\delta = -1$. c) Perturbed, $\delta = 1$. d) Perturbed, $\delta = -1$.

the morsification by t of the D_6^+ yields a D_4^- scatter followed (while increasing scale) by a D_4^+ double annihilation at the origin. The D_6^- shows a D_4^- scatter at the origin, followed by again a D_4^- scatter at some higher scale. Both images show that a part of the critical curve forms a loop: The created critical points annihilate with each other. So if the perturbations are small (or if the measurement contains some uncertainty), one might not be able to distinguish between the involved Fold catastrophes. However, the scale space representation causes a separation into two non-generic catastrophes already mentioned. Further morsification gives more insight in the way *critical curves can behave*. By taking $\lambda_1, \ldots, \lambda_4 \neq 0$, the generic critical curves shown in Figure 4c-d are obtained. The morsification of the D_6^+ shows two critical curves behaving in an aesthetic way, combining the morsifications of the $D_4^\pm$ catastrophes, *i.e.* containing Fold annihilations and creations. Both created critical points on the right critical curve in Figure 4c annihilate at some larger scale. The morsification of the D_6^-, on the other hand, still shows the loop close to the origin. Consequently, in contrast to the elliptic Umbilic catastrophe, now *both created branches annihilate with each other*: the critical curve in the centre of Figure 4d is a closed loop in scale space.

Morsification summary. All non-Fold catastrophes morsify to Fold catastrophes and Morse critical points. The morsification gives insight in the structure around the catastrophe point regarding the critical curves. The morsification of the Umbilic catastrophes (the D_k) show that the trajectories in scale space of the created critical points fall into several classes. The morsified D_4^+-catastrophes describes two Fold annihilations. The morsified D_4^- catastrophe describes the creation of a pair of critical points and the annihilation of one of them with another critical point. So while tracing a critical branch of a critical curve both an annihilation and a creation event are traversed. The morsified D_6^+ catastrophe describes the creation of a pair of critical points and the annihilation of both of them with two other critical points. So while tracing a critical branch of a critical curve successively an annihilation, a creation and again an annihilation event are traversed. The morsified D_6^--catastrophe describes an *isolated* closed critical curve, appearing *ex nihilo* with two critical branches that disappear at some larger scale. So the morsified D_4^- (and its extension, the D_6^+) and D_6^--catastrophes describe essentially different creation events.

An important result lays on the area of tracing critical points. If one traces *only* critical points starting from the *initial* image, one will find the "D_4^-" creations, since they emerge as the starting point of a part of a critical curve that annihilates with one of the initial critical points. However, one will miss the "D_6^-" loops that occur somewhere in scale space, since they have no relation whatsoever to the critical points in the initial image. So fine-to-coarse tracing of critical points will not always yield the right result. Note that the full morsification of the non-generic catastrophes always yields the generic Fold annihilations and creations and Morse critical points.

4 Applications

In this section we give some examples to illustrate the theory presented in the previous sections. We will focus on the critical curves emerging from a creation event. Firstly, we will show the actual presence of a sequence of creation and annihilation events, modelled by the D_4^--catastrophe, on the (artificial) MR image of Figure 5a. This image is taken from the web site http://www.bic.mni.mcgill.ca/brainweb. Secondly, an example of creation *ex nihilo*, the D_6^--catastrophe, is shown by means of the classic "bridge"-image of Figure 6a and the MR image. The *practical* usefulness of critical curves (as they provide the ability for an uncommitted hierarchical structure and segmentation), as well as their non-generic modelling, is described by the authors in several papers, *e.g.* [10]. Results on an MR, a CT and a noise image with respect to the area where creations are possible have been presented elsewhere [9].

The artificial MR image of Figure 5a was used as initial image for the scale space image. For visualisation purposes, we restricted to the scale range $8.37 - 33.1$. The image at scale 8.37 (with only the large structures remaining) is shown in Figure 5b. This image contains 7 extrema.

Fig. 5. a: 181 x 217 artificial MR image. b) Image on scale 8.37 c) Critical paths of the MR image in scale range 8.37 − 33.1. d) Close-up of one of the critical paths of the MR image, showing a subsequent annihilation – creation event. e) Close-up, showing subsequent annihilation – creation events and loop events.

The scale space image in this scale range contains 161 logarithmically sampled scales. At all scales the spatial critical points were calculated and connected, forming the critical paths. Figure 5c shows these critical paths in the $(x, y; t)$-space. The bright curves represent the extrema, the dark ones the saddles. At the (approximate) catastrophe locations the curves are connected. Globally, the image shows annihilating pairs of critical points. Locally, however, the presence of extra branches of critical curves is visible. A close-up of one of the critical paths is shown in Figure 5d. It clearly shows a critical curve containing two subsequent Fold annihilation – creation events. The critical curve evidently shows the the appearance of an annihilation-creation-pair described by the D_3^- morsification. Note that the creation events would have been missed if the sampling was taking coarser, yielding one critical curve without protuberances in scale direction. Sampling without connecting critical paths yields the observation of temporarily created extrema (and saddles).

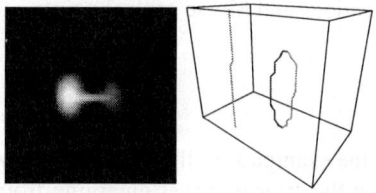

Fig. 6. a: Artificial bridge image. b) Critical paths of the bridge image.

Figure 6a shows the classical "bridge"-image: two mountains of different height (blobs with different intensity) connected by a small ramp and a deep valley between the mountains. This image was described by Lifshitz and Pizer [11] as possible initial image yielding a creation event in scale space. Firstly, there is only one maximum of the left blob. The right blob is not a maximum, since it is connected to the other blob by the ramp. Secondly, at some scale the ramp changes into a bridge with a deep dip in it due to the surrounding deep valleys: a maximum (right blob) – saddle (dip of the bridge) pair is created. Finally, at a large scale a saddle – extremum annihilation occurs. If the saddle annihilates with the left extremum, it can be modelled by the D_4^- catastrophe, as in the previous section. However, as shown by Figure 6b, it can also annihilate with the newly created extremum. This figure shows the critical paths of the scale space image of 6a. The left string represents the extremum of the brightest blob, the loop represents the created and annihilated maximum-saddle pair. The same behaviour is observed at the MR scale space image. Figure 5e shows a close-up of one of the critical curves. Besides several aforementioned subsequent Fold annihilation – creation events along the critical curve, here clearly also several "loop events" occur.

5 Discussion

In this paper we investigated the (deep) structure on various catastrophe events in Gaussian scale space. Although it is known that pairs of critical points are annihilated and created (the latter if the dimension of the image is 2 or higher), it is important to describe also the local structure of the image around the non-generic events. These events might be encountered in practical usage of scale spaces and the non-generic catastrophes can be used to model these occurrences. We therefore embedded catastrophes in scale space. Scale acts as one of the perturbation parameters. The morsification of the catastrophes yields generic Fold annihilations and creations of pairs of critical points.

The A_k series can be used to model (almost) simultaneous annihilations of pairs of critical points at a location (or indistinguishable region) in scale space. If k is even, it models the annihilation of k critical points, if k is odd, it models the collision of k critical points where $k-1$ annihilate and one remains.

For creations the D_k series can be used. Creations occur in different types. Critical paths in scale space can have protuberances, a subsequent occurrence of an annihilation and a creation. In scale space images this is visible by the creation of an extremum-saddle pair, of which one critical point annihilates at some higher scale with an already present critical point, while the other remains unaffected. It is also possible that critical paths form loops: the created pair annihilates at some higher scale. The possibility for both types to occur in practice was shown in the artificial MR image. This phenomena is known from physics, where it is used to describe the creation and successive annihilations of "virtual" elementary particles (and even the universe). Furthermore we showed that the protuberances in the critical paths, expressed in canonical coordinates, occur only in case of a small local perturbation. In addition, creations are less likely to happen due to a special constraint on the combination of third order derivatives and local perturbation. We gave a dimension dependent expectation of this event and an upper bound for the perturbation in canonical coordinates.

The lifetime of a created pair is enlarged if the local structure is elongated. This was derived from the canonical formulation and visualised by the example of the bridge image in section 4. Since the number of possible catastrophes is infinite, there is an infinite number of possible non-generic constellations in which ("infinite") critical points are annihilated and created. We restricted ourselves to the situations in which at most 6 critical points annihilate and in which critical points are created, the latter divided into models representing protuberances and loops.

Finally, the calculations were based on the canonical coordinates. In general, it is not trivial to transform the local coordinate system to these nice formulated catastrophe germs. In that sense, the numerical values have no direct meaning. They do describe, however, the qualitative behaviour of the critical curves close to the location of the catastrophes and can therefore be used to model the type of behaviour encountered in practical usage of a scale space. We gave examples of the appearances of this behaviour in section 4 based on an artificial MR image.

The theory described in this paper extends the knowledge of the deep structure of Gaussian scale space, especially with respect to the behaviour of critical curves in the vicinity of creation events and the scale space lifetime of the created critical points. It emphasises the relevance of investigating the complete scale space image, instead of a series of images at different scales.

References

1. V. I. Arnold. *Catastrophe Theory.* Springer, Berlin, 1984.
2. J. Damon. Local Morse theory for solutions to the heat equation and Gaussian blurring. *Journal of Differential Equations*, 115(2):386–401, 1995.
3. L. M. J. Florack and A. Kuijper. The topological structure of scale-space images. *Journal of Mathematical Imaging and Vision*, 12(1):65–80, February 2000.
4. L. M. J. Florack, B. M. ter Haar Romeny, J. J. Koenderink, and M. A. Viergever. Cartesian differential invariants in scale-space. *Journal of Mathematical Imaging and Vision*, 3(4):327–348, 1993.
5. R. Gilmore. *Catastrophe Theory for Scientists and Engineers.* Dover, 1993. Originally published by John Wiley & Sons, New York, 1981.
6. L. D. Griffin and A. Colchester. Superficial and deep structure in linear diffusion scale space: Isophotes, critical points and separatrices. *Image and Vision Computing*, 13(7):543–557, September 1995.
7. P. Johansen, M. Nielsen, and O.F. Olsen. Branch points in one-dimensional Gaussian scale space. *Journal of Mathematical Imaging and Vision*, 13:193–203, 2000.
8. J. J. Koenderink. The structure of images. *Biological Cybernetics*, 50:363–370, 1984.
9. A. Kuijper and L.M.J. Florack. Calculations on critical points under gaussian blurring. In *Nielsen et al. [13]*, pages 318–329, 1999.
10. A. Kuijper and L. M. J. Florack. Hierarchical pre-segmentation without prior knowledge. In *Proceedings of the 8th International Conference on Computer Vision (Vancouver, Canada, July 9–12, 2001)*, pages 487–493, 2001.
11. L. M. Lifshitz and S. M. Pizer. A multiresolution hierarchical approach to image segmentation based on intensity extrema. *IEEE Transactions on Pattern Analysis and Machine Intelligence*, 12(6):529–540, 1990.
12. T. Lindeberg. *Scale-Space Theory in Computer Vision.* The Kluwer International Series in Engineering and Computer Science. Kluwer Academic Publishers, 1994.
13. M. Nielsen, P. Johansen, O. Fogh Olsen, and J. Weickert, editors. *Scale-Space Theories in Computer Vision*, volume 1682 of *Lecture Notes in Computer Science*. Springer -Verlag, Berlin Heidelberg, 1999.
14. R. Thom. *Structural Stability and Morphogenesis.* Benjamin-Addison Wesley, 1975. translated by D. H. Fowler.
15. T. Wada and M. Sato. Scale-space tree and its hierarchy. In *ICPR90*, volume II, pages 103–108, 1990.
16. A. P. Witkin. Scale-space filtering. In *Proceedings of the Eighth International Joint Conference on Artificial Intelligence*, pages 1019–1022, 1983.

The Localized Consistency Principle for Image Matching under Non-uniform Illumination Variation and Affine Distortion

Bing Wang, Kah Kay Sung, Teck Khim Ng

School of Computing, National University of Singapore,
3 Science Drive 2, Singapore 117543
{wangb,ngtk}@comp.nus.edu.sg

Abstract. This paper proposes an image matching method that is robust to illumination variation and affine distortion. Our idea is to do image matching through establishing an imaging function that describes the functional relationship relating intensity values between two images. Similar methodology has been proposed by Viola [11] and Lai & Fang [6]. Viola proposed to do image matching through establishment of an imaging function based on a consistency principle. Lai & Fang proposed a parametric form of the imaging function. In cases where the illumination variation is not globally uniform and the parametric form of imaging function is not obvious, one needs to have a more robust method. Our method aims to take care of spatially non-uniform illumination variation and affine distortion. Central to our method is the proposal of a localized consistency principle, implemented through a non-parametric way of estimating the imaging function. The estimation is effected through optimizing a similarity measure that is robust under spatially non-uniform illumination variation and affine distortion. Experimental results are presented from both synthetic and real data. Encouraging results were obtained.

1. Introduction

Image matching is the process by which points of two images of essentially the same scene are geometrically transformed so that corresponding feature points of the two images have the same coordinates after transformation [8].

If two images are taken from different viewpoints, geometrical distortion arises. When the scene is far away from the camera, the geometric distortion can be approximated by affine distortion, which can account for translation, rotation, scale and shear. A geometric transformation needs to be performed to align the images.

Illumination variation between images further complicates the image matching problem. It is rarely the case that two images are taken under the same illumination condition. The position of light source such as the sun determines how shadows are formed. For the same scene the light source may also change. For example, the sun may be the main light source in daytime in which the illumination is essentially globally uniform and the localized floodlights may be the main light sources in the evening and night. When the illumination variation between the images is non-uniform across the scene, the problem becomes more complicated. For example, the sun illuminates the entire scene in daytime. At night, the floodlights may only illuminate part of the scene.

In this paper, we propose a method to solve the image matching problem for images taken under drastically different illumination condition, such as matching a day scene and a night scene. Our method is also robust to affine distortion so that the images need not be taken using the same camera pose.

We propose a localized consistency principle that takes into account spatially non-uniform illumination variation. We estimate the imaging function non-parametrically based on the localized consistency principle. We then develop a similarity measure based on the intuition that the imaging function is most accurately established when the images are matched. The experimental results show that the similarity measure is robust under spatially non-uniform illumination variation and affine transformation. The similarity measure also tolerates partial occlusion to a certain extent, as will be shown in our experiments.

Our proposed similarity measure is intensity based. It extends the consistency principle proposed by Viola to take into account spatially non-uniform illumination variation between images. It does not assume any particular parametric form for the complicated imaging function and uses non-parametric method for imaging function estimation, which makes it more robust to a general environment.

The paper is organized as follows. Section 2 describes related work. The localized consistency principle is presented in Section 3. The non-parametric estimation of the imaging function is formulated in Section 4 and the associated similarity measure is presented in Section 5. We present the experimental results in Section 6. Section 7 concludes the paper.

2. Related Work

The techniques for image matching under illumination variation can be classified into two categories:

2.1 Techniques Based on Image Representation Invariant to Illumination

This method is feature based. Image features free of illumination variation are extracted by filtering out the illumination variation. In this category, the feature constancy principle applies, i.e., the extracted feature remains unchanged between two images.

Stockham [9] proposed a homomorphic filtering technique to separate the slow varying low frequency illumination component from the high-frequency reflectance component that is intrinsic to the objects. Lange and Kyuma [7] introduced a wavelet representation and argued that the distance measure in the wavelet domain is psycho-visually more appropriate for judging facial similarity than in the spatial domain. Irani and Anandan [5] presented a high-pass energy representation to emphasize the common information between two multi-sensor images. Govindu and Shekhar [4] described a framework based on the statistical distribution of geometric properties of image contours.

The advantage of this category of work is that illumination invariant image representations greatly facilitate the development of similarity measure. The disadvantage is that the illumination variation may not be easily and cleanly separated from the intrinsic features. Therefore, useful and important intrinsic information may be lost together with the removal of illumination variation. Recent advances in deriving intrinsic images [12] may shed some light for future direction in this approach.

2.2 Techniques Based on the Modeling of Illumination Variation

Most methods in this category are intensity based. The relationship between corresponding points in two images is established by the modeling of illumination variation either implicitly or explicitly. Therefore, the similarity measure takes into account illumination variation.

Implicit illumination modeling includes the eigenspace and parametric space methods. Black and Jepson [1] propose that a set of basis images is constructed from multiple images on the same scene under varying illumination. Then the same scene under any illumination can be represented by the combination of the basis images. The basis images are computed based on principle component analysis (PCA). The matching is carried out in the eigenspace defined by these basis images. Tanaka, Sano, Ohara and Okudaira [10] presented a parametric template method. In this method, a parametric space is constructed from a given set of template images. Geometric transformation and illumination variation are accounted for in this space.

Explicit illumination modeling is to directly model the imaging function. Viola [11] proposed a method based on the consistency principle. The consistency principle is used to model the imaging function non-parametrically. Lai and Fang [6] used a low-order polynomial imaging function to account for spatially varying illumination. The imaging function is modeled by two illumination factors (multiplication and bias), which are functions of spatial location.

The advantage of modeling illumination is that the removal of illumination variation is not necessary and useful information is preserved. The disadvantage is that the modeling increases the complexity of the image matching algorithm, in particular, the formulation and computation of the similarity measure.

Our work belongs to the category based on explicit illumination modeling. Therefore, it is more closely related to the papers by Viola [11] and Lai & Fang [6]. The method by Viola assumes that consistency is established globally. The assumption is violated when the illumination variation between images is non-uniform across the scene. The method by Lai and Fang does take into account non-uniform illumination variation between images, but it requires a parametric form of imaging function which may not be readily available in a complicated environment.

In order to address the above-mentioned limitations, we propose the localized consistency principle to take into account spatially non-uniform illumination variation between images. Our formulation also takes care of affine distortion.

3. The Proposed Localized Consistency Principle

Before introducing our proposed localized consistency principle, we first review the consistency principle proposed by Viola [11].

3.1 Review of the Consistency Principle Proposed by Viola

Viola [11] proposed that the imaging function can be modeled non-parametrically using the consistency principle.

> **Definition 1.** The consistency principle states that if two points in one image have similar intensity values then the corresponding points in the other image will also have similar intensity values when the two images are taken on the same scene.

Based on the consistency principle, a consistent functional relationship can be established to relate intensity values in one image to intensity values in the other image. Hence, one can define an imaging function to project intensity values in one image $U(x, y)$ to intensity values in the other image $V(x', y')$, i.e.,

$$V(x', y') = V(T_x(x, y, \mathbf{t}), T_y(x, y, \mathbf{t})) = F(U(x, y)), \qquad (1)$$

where

$$\begin{cases} T_x(x, y, \mathbf{t}) = x' \\ T_y(x, y, \mathbf{t}) = y' \end{cases} \qquad (2)$$

are the transformation functions and **t** is the unknown parameter vector of the transformation functions.

3.2 The Shortcoming of the Consistency Principle

The consistency principle may not hold for images taken on a relatively large scene and at different time because the illumination variation may not be uniform across the scene. We will provide a simple illustration here.

Figure 1 shows two images of the same hypothetical scene but under different illumination conditions. The hypothetical illumination conditions are shown on top of the images. In image (a), the sun illuminates the entire scene. In image (b), the floodlight only illuminates the right part of the scene. Hence the illumination variation between images (a) and (b) is non-uniform.

In image (a), the intensity values of points A and C, which are far away from each other in the scene, are similar. According to the consistency principle, the relationship should also hold in image (b), i.e., the intensity values of A' and C' will also be similar. As the illumination variation is non-uniform between images, this relationship does not hold, as shown in image (b).

The consistency principle however holds in local neighborhood. In image (a), the intensity values of points A and B, which are in close proximity, are similar. In image (b), the intensity values of points A' and B' are also similar. Hence the consistency relationship holds in local neighborhood even when the illumination variation is spatially non-uniform between the images.

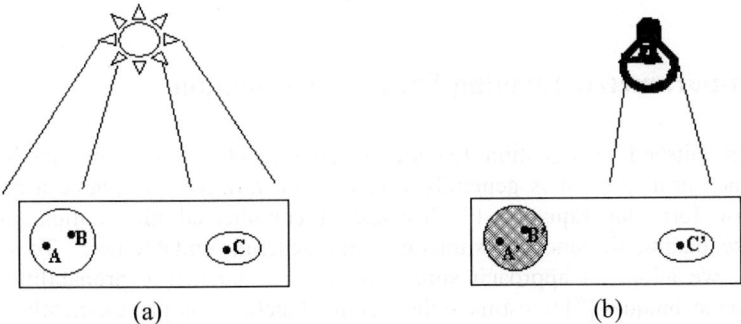

Fig. 1. Hypothetical scenes with spatially non-uniform illumination variation. (a) Scene under the sun. (b) Scene under a floodlight

3.3 The Proposed Localized Consistency Principle

To overcome the above-mentioned shortcoming, we propose to extend the consistency principle to include spatial similarity and name it the localized consistency principle.

Definition 2. The localized consistency principle states that if two points in one image have similar intensity values and are in proximate spatial location, then the corresponding points in the other image will also have similar intensity values when the two images are taken on the same scene.

The localized consistency principle takes into account spatially non-uniform illumination variation, which is expected when the images are taken on a large scene and at different time of the day. By this definition, we extend the definition of the consistency functional relationship between the images to be on both the intensity and spatial location domains, i.e.,

$$V(x', y') = V(T_x(x, y, t), T_y(x, y, t)) = F(x, y, U(x, y)). \tag{3}$$

3.4 The Localized Consistency Principle in Relation to Existing Work

It is interesting to review the parametric form of imaging function proposed by Lai & Fang [6]:

$$V(x', y') = \alpha(x, y)U(x, y) + \beta(x, y), \tag{4}$$

where $\alpha(x, y)$ is a multiplication factor and $\beta(x, y)$ is a bias factor. The two factors $\alpha(x, y)$ and $\beta(x, y)$ are approximated by low-order polynomials of (x, y) and their coefficients are derived by regression. We can regard Equation (4) as a special parametric form of Equation (3) that express our localized consistency principle. We shall present in the next section a non-parametric way of estimating the imaging function that is more robust to a wide range of real images.

4. Non-parametric Imaging Function Estimation

We established in Equation (3) the imaging function based on the localized consistency principle. It is generally very difficult however to assume a particular parametric form for Equation (3) because of complicated illumination variation. Therefore, parametric function estimation is not generally suitable here. To solve the problem, we adopt an approach similar to the non-parametric probability density estimation techniques [2] to estimate the imaging function non-parametrically.

4.1 General Non-parametric Function Estimation

The average value of $F(x)$ within a hypercube R is given by

$$\overline{F_R(\mathbf{x})} = \int_R F(\mathbf{x}) d\mathbf{x} / \int_R d\mathbf{x} . \tag{5}$$

Assuming $F(x)$ is continuous, region R is centered at $\mathbf{x}_0$ and region R is so small that $F(x)$ does not vary appreciably within it, we can write

$$\hat{F}(\mathbf{x}_0) = \overline{F_R(\mathbf{x})} = \int_R F(\mathbf{x}) d\mathbf{x} / \int_R d\mathbf{x} . \tag{6}$$

The equation can be rewritten in its discrete approximation form. Assuming there are k samples in region R, we have

$$\hat{F}(\mathbf{x}_0) = \sum_{\mathbf{x}_i \in R} F(\mathbf{x}_i) / k , \tag{7}$$

where $F(\mathbf{x}_i)$ is the i-th sample point in region R.

Defining a rectangular window function,

$$r(\mathbf{x}) = \begin{cases} 1 & |x_i| \le h/2 \quad i=1,...,d \\ 0 & \text{otherwise} \end{cases}, \tag{8}$$

where h is the length of the edge of the hypercube R and d is the dimension of the hypercube. Equation (7) can be rewritten as

$$\hat{F}(\mathbf{x}_0) = \sum_{\mathbf{x}_i \in U} r(\mathbf{x}_0 - \mathbf{x}_i) F(\mathbf{x}_i) / \sum_{\mathbf{x}_i \in U} r(\mathbf{x}_0 - \mathbf{x}_i) = \sum_{\mathbf{x}_i \in U} w(\mathbf{x}_0 - \mathbf{x}_i) F(\mathbf{x}_i) , \tag{9}$$

where U is the universal domain and

$$w(\mathbf{x}_0 - \mathbf{x}_i) = r(\mathbf{x}_0 - \mathbf{x}_i) / \sum_{\mathbf{x}_i \in U} r(\mathbf{x}_0 - \mathbf{x}_i), \tag{10}$$

$$\sum_{\mathbf{x}_i \in U} w(\mathbf{x}_0 - \mathbf{x}_i) = 1. \tag{11}$$

Equation (9) is an expression for the convolution of $w(x)$ and $F(x)$. In other words, the function estimate $\hat{F}(\mathbf{x})$ is a result of passing $F(x)$ through a filter with impulse response $w(x)$.

As in the case of digital filters, the window function $w(x)$ is not limited to the hypercube function. A more general class of window functions can be used instead, e.g., Gaussian window.

4.2 Non-parametric Imaging Function

Given two images $U(x, y)$ and $V(x', y')$, the relationship between the intensity values of corresponding pixels can be modeled by an imaging function $\hat{V}(x', y') = F(x, y, U(x, y))$ according to the localized consistency principle. Here $\hat{V}(x', y')$ represents the estimated value of $V(x', y')$ and the independent variable of $F()$ is a 3-tuple vector $(x, y, U(x, y))$. Since no parametric form of $F()$ is available, the function is estimated using a non-parametric method. Let A denote the sample space of pixels in U used to estimate the imaging function and B denote the corresponding sample space in V. Based on Equations (9) and (10), the imaging function can be written as

$$\begin{aligned} \hat{V}(x', y') &= F(x, y, U(x, y)) \\ &= \sum_{\substack{(x_a, y_a) \in A \\ (x_b, y_b) \in B}} w(x - x_a, y - y_a, U(x, y) - U(x_a, y_a)) V(x_b, y_b) \end{aligned} \tag{12}$$

where $\{x_a, y_a\} \in A$ and $\{x_b, y_b\} \in B$ are the corresponding sample points according to Equation (2) and

$$\begin{aligned} & w(x - x_a, y - y_a, U(x, y) - U(x_a, y_a)) \\ &= r(x - x_a, y - y_a, U(x, y) - U(x_a, y_a)) / \sum_{(x_a, y_a) \in A} r(x - x_a, y - y_a, U(x, y) - U(x_a, y_a)) \end{aligned} \tag{13}$$

where r is a window function centered at zero. A commonly used window function is Gaussian density function given by

$$r(x-x_a, y-y_a, U(x,y)-U(x_a,y_a)) \quad (14)$$
$$= g(x-x_a)g(y-y_a)g(U(x,y)-U(x_a,y_a))$$
$$= \frac{1}{(\sqrt{2\pi})^{3/2}\sigma_x\sigma_y\sigma_U} \exp\{-[\frac{(x-x_a)^2}{2\sigma_x^2} + \frac{(y-y_a)^2}{2\sigma_y^2} + \frac{(U(x,y)-U(x_a,y_a))^2}{2\sigma_U^2}]\}$$

The window function $r()$ is controlled by the standard deviation parameters σ_x, σ_y and σ_U, which represent the width of the window in each coordinate. It is clear from the above formula that the estimated function $\hat{V}(x',y') = F(x,y,U(x,y))$ is a weighted average of $V(x_b, y_b)$ with the weight given by Equation (13).

5. The Proposed Similarity Measure

The similarity measure can be formulated mathematically as an objective function that will achieve its minimum when two images are correctly aligned. The independent variables of the objective function are transformation parameters. Let C denote the sample space of pixels in $U(x, y)$ used to calculate the objective function and D denote the corresponding sample space in $V(x', y')$. We measure the similarity based on the following intuition:

- When the transformation parameters are correct, every pair of corresponding pixels $U(x, y)$ and $V(x', y')$ represents the same physical point of the scene. There is an intrinsic and consistent functional relationship between the images according to the localized consistency principle. In this case, the imaging function in Equation (12) is most accurately established. Hence for all $\{x_d, y_d\} \in D$, the estimated value $\hat{V}(x_d, y_d)$ given by Equation (12) will be close to the actual value $V(x_d, y_d)$.

- When the transformation parameters are not correct, the pair of corresponding pixels $U(x, y)$ and $V(x', y')$ represents different physical points in the scene. A consistent functional relationship can no longer be established between the images. Hence the estimated value $\hat{V}(x_d, y_d)$ will not be a good estimate of the actual value $V(x_d, y_d)$.

Based on the above analysis, we can formulate the similarity measure as the sum of squares (SSE) of the errors between the actual and estimated values

$$SSE = \sum_{(x_d,y_d) \in D} [V(x_d,y_d) - \hat{V}(x_d,y_d)]^2 . \quad (15)$$

The estimated value $\hat{V}(x_d, y_d)$ is given by

$$\hat{V}(x_d,y_d) = \sum_{\substack{(x_a,y_a) \in A \\ (x_b,y_b) \in B}} w(x_c-x_a, y_c-y_a, U(x_c,y_c)-U(x_a,y_a))V(x_b,y_b). \quad (16)$$

where $\{x_a, y_a\} \in A$ and $\{x_b, y_b\} \in B$ are the corresponding sample points used to estimate $\hat{V}(x_d, y_d)$, $\{x_c, y_c\} \in C$ and $\{x_d, y_d\} \in D$ are the corresponding sample points used to calculate the SSE. The correspondences are established in the transformation functions in Equation (2). Substituting Equation (16) into (15) and using the property in Equation (11), we have

$$SSE = \sum_{\substack{(x_c, y_c) \in C \\ (x_d, y_d) \in D}} [V(x_d, y_d) - \sum_{\substack{(x_a, y_a) \in A \\ (x_b, y_b) \in B}} w(x_c - x_a, y_c - y_a, U(x_c - x_a, y_c - y_a))V(x_b, y_b)]^2 \quad (17)$$

$$= \sum_{\substack{(x_c, y_c) \in C \\ (x_d, y_d) \in D}} [\sum_{\substack{(x_a, y_a) \in A \\ (x_b, y_b) \in B}} w(x_c - x_a, y_c - y_a, U(x_c - x_a, y_c - y_a))(V(x_d, y_d) - V(x_b, y_b))]^2$$

The image matching process is carried out using the simulated annealing algorithm. We downloaded the simulated annealing code provided by W. L. Goffe [3] from http://wuecon.wustl.edu/~goffe/. The simulated annealing algorithm refines the transformation parameter vector **t** in Equation (2) in such a way that the SSE, which is calculated according to Equation (17), is minimized. The resultant transformation parameter vector **t** is the best solution to align the two images.

It is important to note that when estimating the value $\hat{V}(x_d, y_d)$ in (17), we would like to exclude the sample point (x_c, y_c) in U and its corresponding point (x_d, y_d) in image V from the sample spaces A and B which are used to estimate the imaging function. In this way, the estimated value $\hat{V}(x_d, y_d)$ is calculated independent of the actual value $V(x_d, y_d)$.

6. Experimental Results

We conducted experiments to test our algorithm using synthetic and real data.

6.1 Synthetic Data

In this section, experiments using one-dimensional synthetic data are carried out to demonstrate the robustness of the proposed similarity measure based on the localized consistency principle.

As discussed in the previous sections, the consistency principle proposed by Viola only takes into account similarity in intensity values while the localized consistency principle takes into account similarity in both intensity values and spatial location. Let us assume that the spatial coordinate is denoted by x in 1-D. From Equations (13), (14) and (17), we can see that the similarity in spatial location is taken into account by the Gaussian window function in Equation (14). The width of the window in the spatial coordinate is controlled by the parameter σ_x. We will gradually decrease the value of σ_x (hence smaller spatial window) to study the effect on the SSE by the introduction of similarity in spatial location.

The signal, s_0, is a scan line from an image. A new signal, s_1, is constructed from s_0 by multiplying s_0 with a spatially varying factor, followed by adding with a spatially varying bias:

$$s_1[x] = (1 - 4xp + 3xp^2 + xp^3 + 2\sin(2\pi xp))s_0[x] + (2 - 3xp + xp^2) \tag{18}$$

where

$$x = 1, 2, ..., N \text{ and } xp = 2x/N - 1, \tag{19}$$

and both s_0 and s_1 are of size $N = 1280$.

We know that if we try to match s_1 with s_0, the correct value for the translation parameter is 0. We applied our similarity measure to this 1-D case. The SSE defined in Equation (17) is modified for 1-D and computed for various σ_x for the spatial window.

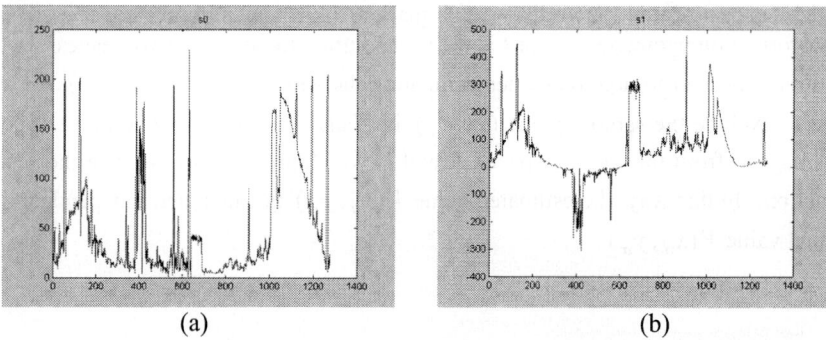

Fig. 2. One-dimensional signals. (a) A scan line s_0 from an image. (b) Constructed signal s_1

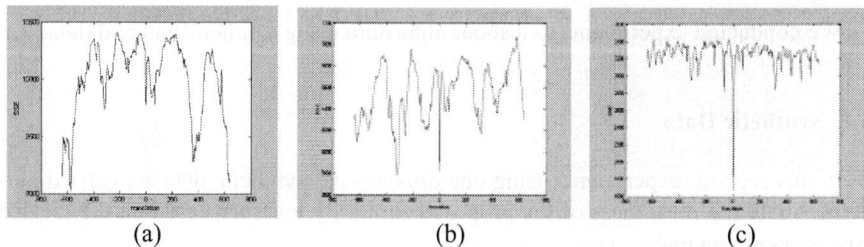

Fig. 3. SSE. (a) $\sigma_x = \infty$. (b) $\sigma_x = 185$. (c) $\sigma_x = 46$

When $\sigma_x = \infty$, no spatial similarity is measured and this is the case when the consistency principle applies. The true minimum at position 0 is overshadowed by other false minima.

When $\sigma_x = 185$, the two minima are more or less equal.

When $\sigma_x = 46$, the true minimum at zero is the only dominant one, as shown in Figure 3(c).

From the above results, we can see that as the value of σ_x decreases, the true minimum gradually becomes dominant. By introduction of spatial similarity in the similarity measure, the localized consistency principle is able to take into account the spatially non-uniform variation between two signals while the consistency principle fails in this aspect. Furthermore, the proposed similarity measure is able to handle high-order spatial variation (the sine component in the multiplication factor in Equation (18)).

6.2 Real Data

In this section, we will study the performance of the similarity measure on real images. Apart from the spatially varying illumination, the viewpoints from which the two images are taken will also be different in these experiments. Under the assumption that the scene is far away from the camera, the geometric distortion can be accounted for by affine transformation. The affine transformation can include translation, rotation, scaling and shear. The general form is

$$\begin{cases} x' = T_x(x, y, \mathbf{t}) = t_0 + t_1 x + t_2 y \\ y' = T_y(x, y, \mathbf{t}) = t_3 + t_4 x + t_5 y \end{cases} \quad (20)$$

where $\mathbf{t} = (t_0, t_1, t_2, t_3, t_4, t_5)$ is the parameter vector for the affine transformation.

6.2.1 University Buildings

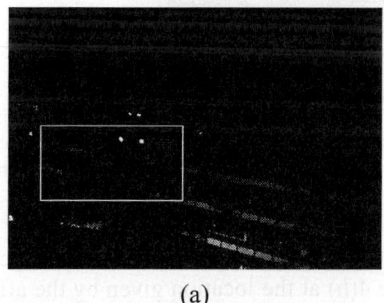
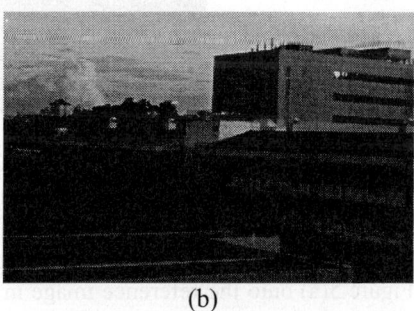

(a) (b)

Fig. 4. Image pair of university buildings. (a) Image taken in the evening (373x549[1]). (b) Image taken in daytime (reference image) (390x640).

The two images, as shown in Figure 4(a) and (b), are taken on buildings in a university campus in the evening and in daytime respectively. The ambient lighting

---

[1] Size (height x width) of the image is shown in the parenthesis.

in Figure 4(b) is bright. The ambient light in Figure 4(a) is very dark and the lighting is from floodlights inside and outside the buildings.

The subimage in Figure 5(a) is selected from Figure 4(a), as indicated by the white box. We will match this subimage against the reference image in Figure 4(b).

(a)   (b)

Fig. 5. Subimages. (a) Subimage of 4(a) (107x209). (b) Corresponding subimage of the reference image extracted using the transformation parameters given by the image matching algorithm (107x209).

After the affine transformation parameters are obtained by minimizing SSE in Equation (17), we observe the goodness of the match by extracting the corresponding subimage from the reference image in Figure 4(b) according to the affine transformation parameters. The corresponding subimage is shown in Figure 5(b). Comparing the two subimages in Figure 5(a) and (b), the spatial structures are the same although the illumination conditions are drastically different.

Fig. 6. Composed image by superimposing the subimage in Figure 5(a) onto the reference image in Figure 4(b) using the transformation parameters given by the image matching algorithm (390x640).

We can appreciate the accurate registration by superimposing the subimage in Figure 5(a) onto the reference image in Figure 4(b) at the location given by the affine transformation parameters. The superimposed image is shown in Figure 6. We can see that the spatial continuity is preserved in the superimposed image.

6.2.2 School Buildings

The two images, as shown in Figure 7(a) and (b), are taken on buildings in a school in the evening and in daytime respectively. The ambient lighting in Figure 7(b) is gray because of the cloudy weather. The ambient light in Figure 7(a) is extremely dark and the floodlights are extremely strong. The subimage in Figure 8(a) is selected from Figure 7(a), as indicated by the white box. The occlusion caused by different camera pose is indicated by ellipses in Figure 7(b) and 8(a).

The corresponding subimages in Figure 8(a) and (b) as well as the superimposed image, as shown in Figure 9, demonstrate good matches.

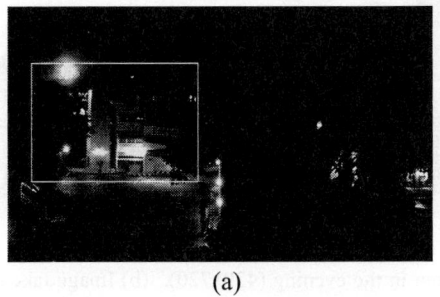 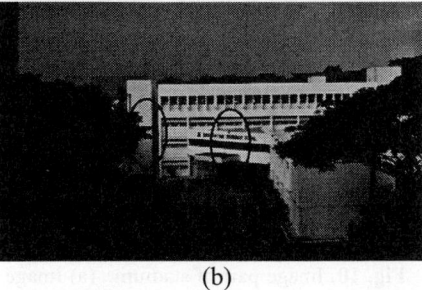

(a) (b)

Fig. 7. Image pair of school buildings. (a) Image taken in the evening (319x640). (b) Image taken in daytime (reference image) (322x640).

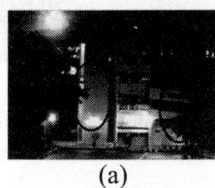 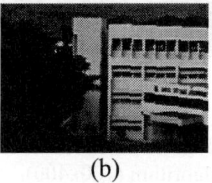

(a) (b)

Fig. 8. Subimages. (a) Subimage of Figure 7(a) (149x213). (b) Subimage of the reference image in Figure 7(b) extracted using the transformation parameters given by the image matching algorithm (149x213).

Fig. 9. Composed image by superimposing the subimage in Figure 8(a) onto the reference image in Figure 7(b) using the transformation parameters given by the image matching algorithm (322x640).

6.2.3 Stadium

The two images, as shown in Figure 10(a) and (b), are taken on a stadium in the evening and in daytime respectively. The ambient light in Figure 10(b) is bright. The ambient light in Figure 10(a) is dark and the floodlights are strong. The subimage in Figure 11(a) is selected from Figure 10(a), as indicated by the white box.

The corresponding subimages in Figure 11(a) and (b) as well as the superimposed image, as shown in Figure 12, demonstrate good matches.

Fig. 10. Image pair of stadium. (a) Image taken in the evening (429x720). (b) Image taken in daytime (reference image) (307x720).

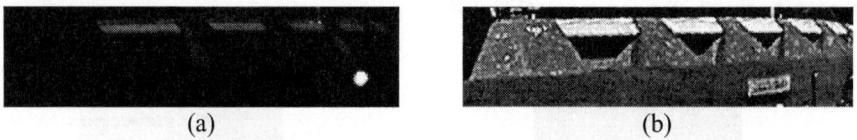

Fig. 11. Subimages. (a) Subimage of Figure 10(a) (100x400). (b) Subimage of the reference image in Figure 10(b) extracted using the transformation parameters given by the image matching algorithm (100x400).

Fig. 12. Composed image by superimposing the subimage in Figure 11(a) onto the reference image in Figure 10(b) using the transformation parameters given by the image matching algorithm (307x720).

7. Conclusion

In this paper, we proposed the localized consistency principle which states that if two points in one image have similar intensity values and are in proximate spatial location then the corresponding points in the other image will also have similar intensity values when the two images are taken on the same scene. The imaging function is estimated non-parametrically based on the localized consistency principle. The similarity measure is derived based on the intuition that the consistent functional relationship is most accurately established when the images are matched.

The similarity measure has been successfully tested in real and complicated environment as shown in Section 6. It is robust under spatially non-uniform illumination variation and affine distortion. It also tolerates partial occlusion.

Acknowledgment

In memory of Associate Professor Kah Kay Sung. The authors would also like to thank W. L. Goffe for providing the simulated annealing program code on the web.

References

1. Black, M.J., A.D. Jepson. 1998. EigenTracking: Robust Matching and Tracking of Articulated Objects Using a View-Based Representation. *International Journal of Computer Vision*, Vol. 26, No. 1, 63–84.
2. Duda, R.O., P.E. Hart. 1973. *Pattern Classification and Scene Analysis*. John Wiley & Sons, New York.
3. Goffe, W.L. 1997. SIMANN: A Global Optimization Algorithm Using Simulated Annealing. *Studies in Nonlinear Dynamics and Econometrics*, Vol. 1, No. 3, 169 – 176.
4. Govindu, V., C. Shekhar. 1999. Alignment using distributions of local geometric properties. *IEEE Trans. PAMI*, Vol. 21, No. 10, 1031 – 1043.
5. Irani, M., P. Anandan. 1998. Robust multi-sensor image alignment. *ICCV, 1998*, 959 – 966.
6. Lai, S.H., M. Fang. 1999. Robust and efficient image alignment with spatially varying illumination models. *CVPR*, 1999, Vol. 2, 167 – 172.
7. Lange, E., K. Kyuma. 1998. Wavelet-domain principal component analysis applied to facial similarity trees, caricaturing, and nonlinear illumination-invariant processing. *Third IEEE International Conference on Automatic Face and Gesture Recognition, 1998*, 171 – 176.
8. Shapiro, L.G., G.C. Stockman. 2001. *Computer Vision*. Prentice Hall, Upper Saddle River, New Jeysey.
9. Stockham, T.G., Jr. 1972. Image processing in the Context of a Visual Model. *Proc. IEEE*, Vol. 60, No. 7, 828 – 842.
10. Tanaka, K., M. Sano, S. Ohara, M. Okudaira. 2000. A parametric template method and its application to robust matching. *CVPR, 2000,* Vol. 1, 620 – 627.
11. Viola, P.A. 1995. *Alignment by maximization of mutual information*. Ph.D. Thesis, AI-Lab, M.I.T., Cambridge, AI Technical Report 1548.
12. Weiss, Y. 2001. Deriving intrinsic images from image sequences. *ICCV, 2001,* Vol. 2 , 68 –75.

Resolution Selection Using Generalized Entropies of Multiresolution Histograms

Efstathios Hadjidemetriou, Michael D. Grossberg, and Shree K. Nayar

Computer Science, Columbia University, New York, NY 10027, USA
{stathis, mdog, nayar}@cs.columbia.edu

Abstract. The performances of many image analysis tasks depend on the image resolution at which they are applied. Traditionally, resolution selection methods rely on spatial derivatives of image intensities. Differential measurements, however, are sensitive to noise and are local. They cannot characterize patterns, such as textures, which are defined over extensive image regions. In this work, we present a novel tool for resolution selection that considers sufficiently large image regions and is robust to noise. It is based on the generalized entropies of the histograms of an image at multiple resolutions. We first examine, in general, the variation of histogram entropies with image resolution. Then, we examine the sensitivity of this variation for shapes and textures in an image. Finally, we discuss the significance of resolutions of maximum histogram entropy. It is shown that computing features at these resolutions increases the discriminability between images. It is also shown that maximum histogram entropy values can be used to improve optical flow estimates for block based algorithms in image sequences with a changing zoom factor.

1 Introduction

The performances of many image analysis and interpretation algorithms depend on the image resolution at which they are applied. Therefore, the selection of the appropriate resolution is a critical preprocessing step. In this work we suggest the use of the generalized entropies of multiresolution histograms of an image for resolution selection. We first compute the multiresolution of an image, where resolution decreases with the standard deviation σ of a Gaussian filter [1,2]. Then, we transform the images of the various resolutions into their histograms. Finally, we compute the Tsallis generalized entropies of the histograms [3] for certain orders q. We call the plot of the Tsallis histogram entropy of order q as a function of image resolution σ the entropy–resolution plot of order q.

Histogram entropies have several properties which enable their use for resolution selection. One such property is that their values are directly related to the significance of a resolution. A high resolution busy image with many high count histogram bins has large histogram entropy. In the limit of low resolution, an image has uniform intensities, such as that shown in figure 1(g), and zero histogram entropy. Moreover, histogram entropies are inherently non–monotonic with resolution with one or more maxima. The local maxima correspond to significant resolutions.

Generalized histogram entropies are defined over the whole image. This is desirable when the detection of significant resolutions of an image requires the consideration of a certain image extend. This is obviously the case for textures which are commonly defined over extensive parts of images. Generalized histogram entropies can also detect multiple significant resolutions; for example, for textures with two levels of texel aggregation. Finally, they are robust to noise.

We first examine the entropy–resolution plots of images containing shapes and the sensitivity of these plots to the shape boundary. We then relate the entropy–resolution plots of shapes to those of textures. We also discuss the dependence of the entropy–resolution plots on their order q.

It is shown that computing image features at the resolution of maximum histogram entropy increases the discriminability between images. It is also shown that the maximum entropy values can be used to improve the performance of block based optical flow estimation for image sequences with a changing zoom factor.

2 Previous Work

The need for resolution selection was first realized, and exclusively used, in the context of edge detection. For example, Marr and Hildreth used multiple image resolutions to detect an arbitrary edge [4]. Later, several authors suggested the selection of image resolutions using the derivatives of pixels normalized by resolution [5,6]. To reduce noise, Lindeberg retained edges only if they fell along chains of connected pixels [6]. Elder and Zucker [7], as well as Marimont and Rubner [8], computed the edge magnitude at a number of resolutions and selected the lowest resolution that exceeded the sensor noise. Jeong and Kim [9] used pixel differential measurements to formulate a global regularizing function to select resolution.

Pixel differential measurements have more recently been used to select resolutions in problems other than edge detection. Lindeberg has used them to determine the characteristic length of objects [6], and to track features in an image sequence [10]. Another application has been to select resolutions that are appropriate to compute image features [11,12]. Finally, they have been used directly in image indexing systems [13,14].

It is not obvious, however, that differential measurements are the most appropriate technique for general resolution selection problems. Differential measurements have several limitations. In general, they are monotonically decreasing with image resolution. They can only be made non–monotonic by using normalized differential expressions. Both the expression and its normalization, however, are selected heuristically.

Pixel differential measurements are very sensitive to noise and are local. They cannot characterize textures, for example, which can cover extensive parts of an image. For large shapes, resolution selection requires two steps. First, the detection of the boundary pixels, and then the connection of the boundary pixels. Finally, differential measurements give only one significant resolution [6,7,8].

To alleviate these problems several researchers have suggested resolution selection using image entropy, which is a global image function. Further, image entropy is not dependent upon edge measurements, and is robust to noise [15, 16,17]. Sporring and Weickert [17] have considered resolutions as significant if they correspond to local maxima of the rate of entropy increase. Jagersand computed the characteristic length of objects based on resolutions which correspond to a local maximum of the rate of increase of mutual image entropy [15].

It has been shown, however, that image entropy is monotonic with resolution [18,19]. Similarly, image mutual entropy and generalized entropies are monotonic with resolution [18,20]. Moreover, the rates of change of both image entropy and mutual entropy with resolution have also been shown to be monotonic [21,22]. The monotonicity of image entropies limits their ability to select resolutions. Hence, in this work we use exclusively histogram entropies, which are inherently non–monotonic with resolution. They are also based on extensive image regions, they are robust to noise, and can detect multiple significant resolutions.

A similar application of entropies of histograms has been as an auto–focus criterion in the problem of depth from defocus [23], where it has been assumed that the histogram entropy is a monotonic function of focus. Another similar technique has been to compute the change of histogram entropy over an image, of a specific resolution, by varying the extend of the image region considered [24, 25,26]. This technique has been used for image segmentation.

In an early work Wong and Vogel [27] computed the Shannon entropy of histograms at multiple image resolutions for 2–3 images. Moreover, Roldan et al [28] derived some mathematical results about the Shannon histogram entropy of a critically subsampled pyramid constructed with a box filter. They showed that the histogram entropy normalized by the pyramid level is monotonically decreasing [28]. They also showed that an image in the form of a Gibbs distribution has maximum entropy at all pyramid levels [28].

3 Tsallis Entropies of Histograms

The Shannon entropy measures the average information of all the densities in the histogram. In some cases, however, it is desirable to use an information measure whose value is influenced selectively by some of the intensities. For example, ignore high bin count intensities of a uniform background, or increase sensitivity to high bin count significant intensities. To achieve this we use nonlinear generalized entropies. We choose the Tsallis generalized entropies because they simplify the analytical part of this work.

The Tsallis generalized entropy of order q over histogram $\mathbf{h}$ with unit L_1 norm is given by [3,29]:

$$S_q(\mathbf{h}) = \sum_{j=0}^{m-1} \frac{h_j - h_j^q}{q-1} \qquad (1)$$

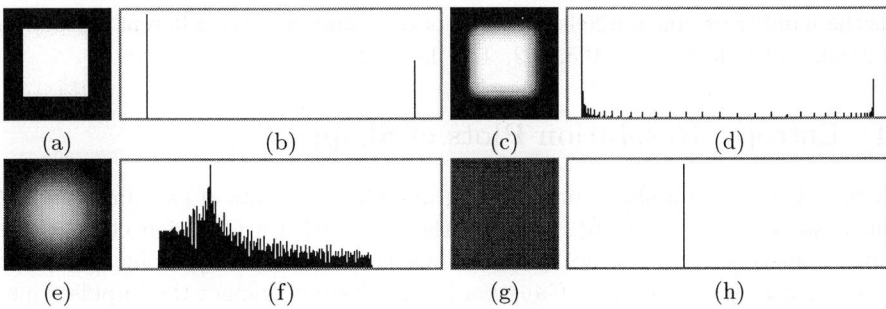

Fig. 1. The image in (a) is binary. Filtering the image in (a) moderately gives the image in (c). Filtering the image in (a) significantly gives the image in (e). Eventually filtering the image in (a) gives the image in (g) of uniform intensity equal to the average intensity of the image in (a). Next to each image is its histogram.

where m is the number of intensity levels, and h_j is the histogram density of intensity j. In the limit $q \to 1$ the Tsallis generalized entropies reduce to the Shannon entropy.

The minimum value of all Tsallis entropies is zero and occurs for histograms with non–zero count in a single intensity bin. That is, for uniform intensity images such as that shown in figure 1 (g). All Tsallis entropies obtain their maximum value for histograms where all intensities are equally frequent.

The sensitivity of the entropies for histograms which do not have minimum or maximum entropy values depend not only on the histogram, but also on the order q of the entropy. The order q appears as exponent in the numerator of the entropy expression given in equation (1). Hence, the entropies of $q < 1$ have a large value for histograms with many low bin count intensities and a low value for histograms with many high bin count intensities [3,20]. Conversely, entropies of $q \geq 1$ have a large value for histograms with many frequent intensities and a small value for histograms with many low bin count intensities [3,20].

An illustrative example are histograms which consist of a central main lobe together with sidelobes. In histograms with a narrow central main lobe and wide sidelobes the side lobes contribute many low bin count intensities. Thus, entropies with $q < 1$ have a large value. As the width of the main lobe increases, the number of frequent intensities increases with it. Consequently, the orders q of the entropies which attain large values also increase. For very large values of q large entropy values are attained only for extreme histograms with a very wide main lobe. All other histograms have a small entropy values. Similarly, for very small value of q large entropy values are attained only for extreme histograms with a very narrow main lobe. Again, all other histograms have a small entropy values. Therefore, in this work, we examine entropies in a range of q close to unity, $-0.5 \leq q \leq 2.5$.

The number of independent generalized entropies of the histogram of a discrete image is finite. It is shown in appendix A.1 that this number can be as large as the number of image pixels. In this work, we only use five different histogram entropies of orders $q = (-0.5, \ 0.2, \ 1.0, \ 1.3, \ 2.3)$.

4 Entropy–Resolution Plots of Shapes

A binary image of a shape has a histogram which consists of two impulses like those shown in figure 1 (b). Filtering the image with a Gaussian changes the binary image into grayscale by smoothing the intensity step along the shape boundary. In the histogram, Gaussian image filtering changes the impulses into wider distributions with long sidelobes like those shown in figure 1 (d). Each impulse in the histogram of the original binary image gives rise to a different distribution in the histogram. The low bin count intensities between the initial impulses correspond to the intensities of regions of steep intensity changes at the border between the shape and the background. This is particularly true for images whose initial histograms consist of distant impulses such as binary and halftone images.

When an image is filtered extensively the widths of the distributions in the histogram increase. Further, the peaks of the distributions move towards the mean image intensity. At some resolution the border between the shape and the background disappears and the two are joined. At that resolution, the individual distributions in the histogram meet to form a single distribution, like that shown in figure 1(f). Beyond that resolution the intensities of the image become uniform, the histogram has a count at a single bin such as that shown in figure 1 (h).

Limited image filtering simply increases the width of the main lobes of the histogram distributions. Therefore, it increases the order q of the histogram entropies which attain large values. Filtering, eventually, contracts the histogram towards the mean intensity and finally turns it into an impulse. Hence, the value of histogram entropy eventually decreases and finally becomes zero.

The images in figures 2 (a) and (g) have the same histogram. Some entropy–resolution plots of the two images are shown next to them in order of increasing q. The plots verify that the resolution of maximum entropy increases as a function of q. Note that the maxima of the entropy–resolution plots for which $q \geq 1$ occur at resolutions beyond those shown in the entropy–resolution plots of figure 2.

The resolutions at which the entropy–resolution plots attain large values also depend on the boundary of the shape in the original image. In appendix A.2 we examine the rates at which the Tsallis entropies of the histogram of image $\mathcal{L}$ change with Gaussian filtering. We show that they are linearly proportional to Fisher information measures of m different orders q. The generalized Fisher information measures $J_q(\mathcal{L})$ are given by [20,21,22]:

$$J_q(\mathcal{L}) = \int_D \left| \frac{\nabla \mathcal{L}(\mathbf{x})}{\mathcal{L}(\mathbf{x})} \right|^2 \mathcal{L}^q(\mathbf{x}) d^2 x. \tag{2}$$

where $\mathcal{L}(\mathbf{x})$ is the intensity value of image pixel $\mathbf{x}$. The Fisher information measures are nonlinearly weighted averages of pixel sharpness, which is defined as

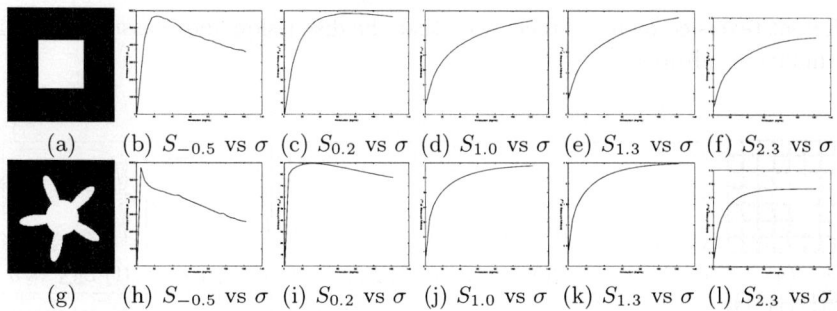

Fig. 2. The binary images of two shapes are shown in (a) and (g). Next to each image is a sequence of entropy–resolution plots of orders $q = (-0.5, 0.2, 1.0, 1.3, 2.3)$ left to right. The maxima in the entropy–resolution plots with $q < 1$ of the convoluted shape in (g) occur at finer resolutions than those of the entropy–resolution plots of the same orders of the image in (a).

$|\nabla \mathcal{L}(\mathbf{x})/\mathcal{L}(\mathbf{x})|^2$ [22]. The generalized Fisher information measures increase nonlinearly as the shapes become more eccentric or convoluted [30].

The maxima of the entropy–resolution plots in figures 2(h) and (i) occur at finer resolutions than the maxima of the plots in figures 2(b) and (c), respectively. This is because, compared to the shape in figure 2 (a), the boundary of the shape in figure 2 (g) is more convoluted with a higher rate of change of histogram entropy.

In summary, the entropy–resolution plots of binary shapes are initially increasing, they reach a maximum, and eventually decrease to zero. The resolution at which a plot reaches its maximum depends on its order q and on the boundary of the shape.

5 Entropy–Resolution Plots of Textures

In this section we consider a simple texture model where the texture is constructed by contracting shapes such as those discussed in the previous section to form texels. Subsequently the texels are tiled $r = p^2$ times to form a regular $p \times p$ texture. To preserve the size of the texture the texels are also contracted by a uniform transformation A whose determinant is given by $detA = 1/r$. Since, $(detA)r = 1$, textures for all p have the same histogram [31].

In appendix A.2 we show that the rate of change in the entropy–resolution plots of a shape multiplied by p^2 gives the rate of change in the entropy–resolution plots of of the corresponding regular texture. That is, in going from a shape to the corresponding regular texture the horizontal resolution coordinate of the entropy–resolution plot is scaled by $1/p$. Thus, the resolution of maximum entropy is scaled by the same factor. As discussed in section 4 the resolution of maximum entropy for shapes is attained at the resolution at which the border between the shape and the background disappears. For texture images, the resolution of maximum entropy corresponds to the resolution at which different texels come in contact. Note that the discussion above assumes circular boundary conditions.

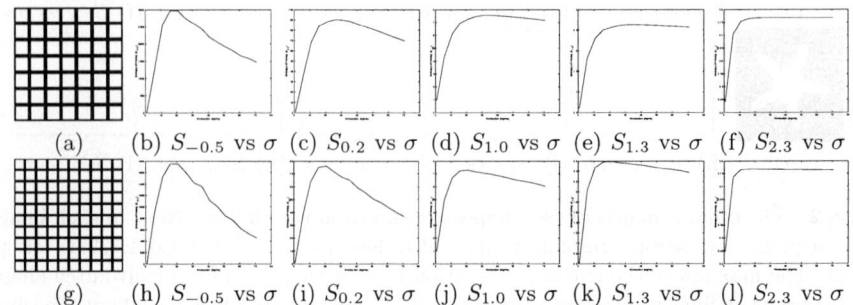

(a) (b) $S_{-0.5}$ vs σ (c) $S_{0.2}$ vs σ (d) $S_{1.0}$ vs σ (e) $S_{1.3}$ vs σ (f) $S_{2.3}$ vs σ

(g) (h) $S_{-0.5}$ vs σ (i) $S_{0.2}$ vs σ (j) $S_{1.0}$ vs σ (k) $S_{1.3}$ vs σ (l) $S_{2.3}$ vs σ

Fig. 3. The images in (a) and (g) are two synthetic textures. Next to each image is a sequence of some of its entropy–resolution plots of orders $q = (-0.5, 0.2, 1.0, 1.3, 2.3)$ left to right. The texture in (a) can be contracted to give part of the texture in (g). Similarly, the horizontal σ axis of each entropy–resolution plot of the image in (a) can be contracted to give part of the corresponding entropy–resolution plot of the image in (g).

The textures shown in figure 3(a) and figure 3(g) are obtained by minifying the same shape, shown in figure 2(a). The width of the texels in figure 3(g) is 70% of those in figure 3(a). Both textures have the same histogram entropies. The entropy–resolution plots are shown next to the textures. The horizontal coordinate σ of the entropy–resolution plots of the image in figure 3(a), shown in figure 3 (b–f), can indeed be contracted by 0.7 to give part of the entropy–resolution plots of the image in figure 3(g), shown in figures 3 (h–l). Moreover, the resolution of maximum entropy of the image in figure 3(a) can be multiplied by 0.7 to give the resolution of maximum entropy of the image in figure 3(g).

Above we examined texture models and entropy–resolution plots of regular textures. We now examine entropy–resolution plots of textures with random texel placement. Randomness monotonically increases image entropies and decreases the generalized Fisher informations [20], which are linearly related to the rate at which the histogram entropies change with resolution. Therefore, randomness in the placement of texels decreases the rate at which the histogram entropies change [20] and shifts their maxima to lower resolutions.

In figure 4(a) we show a regular texture and in figure 4(c) we show a random texture. Both textures are synthetic with identical texels and histograms. The maximum of the entropy–resolution plot of $q = 1.3$ of the regular texture shown in figure 4(b) occurs at a lower σ than the maximum of the entropy–resolution plot of the same order of the random texture in figure 4(d). The random textures consist of aggregates of texels. The distance between aggregate texels is larger than the distance between individual texels regularly placed. Thus, the maximum for randomly placed textures in figure 4 is shifted to a higher σ value.

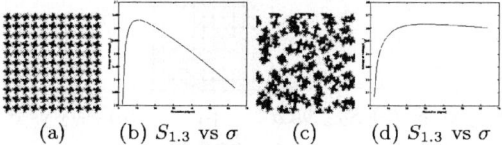

Fig. 4. The textures in (a) and (c) are synthetic with identical texels and histograms. The texel placement in the texture in (a) is regular, whereas the texel placement in the texture in (c) is random. Next to each image is its entropy–resolution plot of order $q = 1.3$. The maximum in the entropy–resolution plot of the regular texture occurs at a finer resolution than the maximum in the entropy–resolution plot of the random texture.

In summary, the resolution of maximum entropy depends on the entropy order, on the shape of the texels, on the size of the texels, and on the distance between them. Moreover, it depends on their placement pattern.

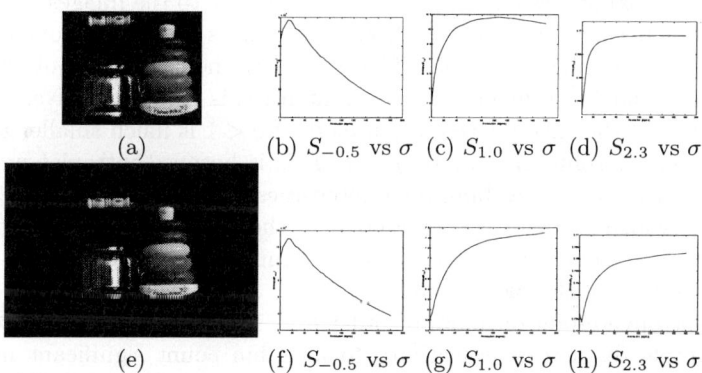

Fig. 5. The images, shown in (a) and (e), have identical foreground but differ in the area of the background. Next to each image are three of its entropy–resolution plots of orders $q = (-0.5, 1.0, 2.3)$ left to right. The entropy–resolution plot of order $q = -0.5$ is not sensitive to a change in the area of the background. The entropy–resolution plots of order $q \geq 1$, however, are significantly affected by the increase in the background area.

6 Significance of Entropy–Resolution Plots of $q \neq 1$

The entropy–resolution plots of order $q < 1$ are significant in cases where it is desirable to diminish the effect of the variation of the background. Figures 5 (a) and (e) show two images with identical foregrounds [32], but backgrounds of different size. In figure 5(a) the background is much smaller than in figure 5(e).

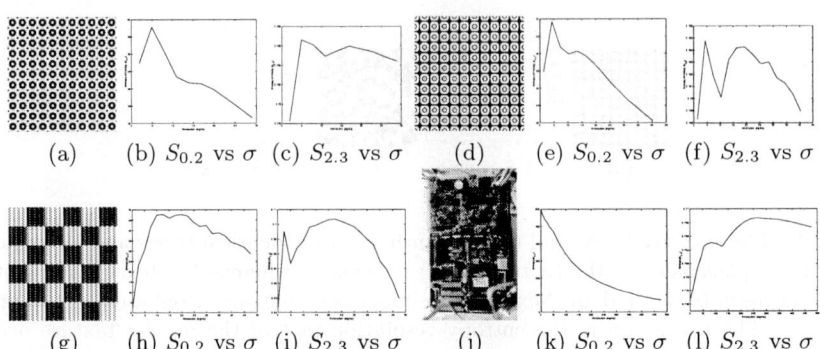

Fig. 6. In (a), (d), (g), and (j) are 4 images with fine structure. Next to each image are two of its entropy–resolution plots of orders $q = (0.2, 2.3)$ left to right. The images in (a) and (d) contain texels of more than one shape and size. The images in (g) and (j) contain two levels of structure. This is revealed by the two maxima in the entropy–resolution plots of order $q = 2.3$.

Some of the entropy–resolution plots are shown next to the images. These plots show that increasing the area of the background shifts the maxima of all entropy–resolution plots to higher σ values. This is because the filtering required to reach equilibrium, that is an image of uniform intensity, is more extensive.

The shift of the entropy–resolution plots of $q < 1$ is much smaller than that of the entropy–resolution plots of $q \geq 1$. This is because entropies with $q < 1$ are more sensitive to low bin count intensities and less sensitive to frequent intensities, which in this case correspond to the background [3]. On the other hand, entropy–resolution plots of $q > 1$ are significantly affected by the frequent image intensities of the background.

The entropy–resolution plots of order $q > 1$ are significant in cases where it is desirable to increase sensitivity to high bin count significant intensities of an image and decrease the sensitivity to low bin count ones. This can be used to decrease noise sensitivity. Also, in some histograms there are no low bin count intensities. Instead, all intensities are frequent. In such a case generalized entropies of $q \leq 1$ are not sensitive to histogram changes with image resolution, and it is necessary to use entropies of order $q > 1$.

A histogram with many high count bins can arise as a binary image containing multiple different shapes is filtered. The two impulses in the histogram of such a binary image meet more than once. In consecutive meetings after the first, however, the histogram has many high count bins. Therefore, only entropies of order $q > 1$ are sensitive to maxima corresponding to consecutive meetings.

In figures 6 (a), (d), (g), and (j) we can see textures that have texels of more than one shape and size. Next to each image we show 2 of its entropy–resolution plots of orders $q = (0.2, 2.3)$. Each of the images in figures 6 (a) and (d) has texels of 2 different sizes. This causes their entropy–resolution plots in figures 6 (c), and (e–f) to have 2 maxima. The image in figure 6 (g) shows a checkerboard pattern with stripes superimposed upon it. In the entropy–resolution plots in figures 6 (h–i) the first maximum corresponds to the size of the stripes. The second maximum corresponds to the size of the squares.

The image in figure 6 (j) shows a board with electronic components. The entropy–resolution plot in figure 6(l) has 2 maxima. The first maximum corresponds to the size of the components of the board. The second maximum corresponds to the size of the entire board. As we can see in figure 6, the multiple maxima in the entropy–resolution plots are more obvious for entropies of order $q > 1$. Also, entropy–resolution plots of orders $q > 1$ are less sensitive to noise.

In summary, entropy–resolution plots of order $q < 1$ are useful for shapes embedded in background, whereas plots of order $q > 1$ are useful for textures with multiple significant resolutions.

7 Applications

We demonstrate two different applications of the entropy–resolution plots. We first show that the resolutions at which the entropy–resolution plots are maximized can also maximize the discriminability between images in a database. We then use the entropy–resolution plot to adapt the block size in block based optical flow estimation for a zoom–in sequence. We show that motion estimation is improved.

7.1 Discrimination between Images

The discriminability of an image feature can be improved by appropriately selecting the image resolution at which it is computed. This is particularly true for image features which are non–monotonic with resolution. We demonstrate this for two features. The first is a vector which consists of the energy $E(C)$ and the Shannon entropy $S_1(C)$ of the cooccurrence matrix C [33]. The cooccurrence matrix is computed over a 3×3 neighborhood. The energy is given by $E(C) = \sum_{i,j=0}^{m-1} c_{ij}^2$, where c_{ij} is the element of the cooccurrence matrix at the ith row and j^{th} column. The Shannon entropy is given by $S_1(C) = \sum_{i,j=0}^{m-1} c_{ij}\, log\, c_{ij}$.

The second feature are the parameters of a Gauss Markov random field (GMRF) [34]. This model assumes that the intensity at each pixel is a linear combination of the intensities in the surrounding 5×5 window. Thus, each pixel gives an equation for 24 unknowns. Over the entire image this leads to an overconstraint system of linear equations that we solved with least squares.

The discriminability of the feature vectors can be measured using a database of images consisting of multiple disjoint classes [35]. Consider a database with k classes of p_j images in class j. The discriminability D can be modeled by the ratio of the between class scatter V_b to the within class scatter V_w, that is $D = \frac{V_b}{V_w}$ [35]. The within–class scatter is given by: $V_w = \sum_{j=1}^{k} \sum_{i=1}^{p_j} \|f_i - \mu_j\|_2^2$, where μ_j is the mean of class j. The between–class scatter is given by $V_b = \sum_{i=1}^{k} p_i \|\mu_i - \mu_{tot}\|_2^2$, where μ_{tot} is the mean of the entire database. We compute discriminability D as a function of image resolution σ for 2 databases of images.

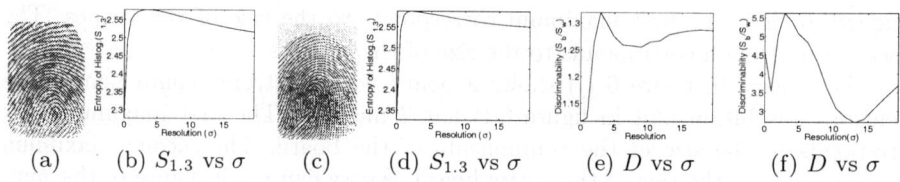

(a) (b) $S_{1.3}$ vs σ (c) (d) $S_{1.3}$ vs σ (e) D vs σ (f) D vs σ

Fig. 7. The images in (a) and (c) show fingerprints of two different persons. The images in (b) and (d) show the entropy–resolution plots of order $q = 1.3$ for the fingerprints in (a) and (c), respectively. The plot in (e) shows the discriminability–resolution plot of the cooccurrence matrix features for the fingerprint database. The plot in (f) shows the discriminability–resolution plot of the GMRF features for the fingerprint database. For both features the resolution of maximum discriminability coincides with that of the maxima of the entropy–resolution plots.

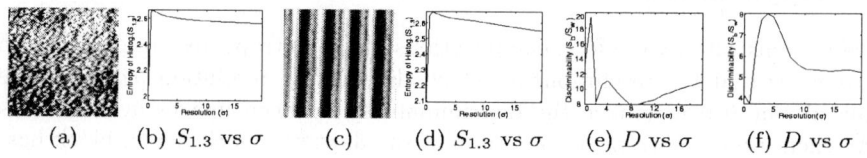

(a) (b) $S_{1.3}$ vs σ (c) (d) $S_{1.3}$ vs σ (e) D vs σ (f) D vs σ

Fig. 8. The images in (a) and (c) show two textures. The images in (b) and (d), respectively, show their entropy–resolution plots of order $q = 1.3$. The plot in (e) shows the discriminability–resolution plot of the cooccurrence matrix features for the texture database. The plot in (f) shows the discriminability–resolution plot of the GMRF features for the texture database. For both features the resolutions of maximum discriminability is approximately the same as the resolutions of the maxima of the entropy–resolution plots.

The first database consists of images of fingerprints of 4 different persons [36]. The fingerprints of each person form a different class. Thus, there are $k = 4$ different classes. Each class consists of 8 images of fingerprints from different fingers of the same person. The intensity resolution of all images is 8 bits and their size is 364×256 pixels. Figures 7(a) and (c) show two images from two different classes. Next to each image, in figures 7(b) and (d), respectively, is its entropy–resolution plot of order $q = 1.3$. The order of the entropy–resolution plots is chosen to be greater than one since the structure of the images is fine. Note that the resolution at which the entropy is maximum is the effective distance between the ridges of the fingerprints.

The plot in figure 7(e) shows the discriminability of the cooccurrence matrix features between the fingerprint classes as a function of resolution, namely, the discrimination–resolution plot. The plot in figure 7(f) shows the discrimination–resolution plot for the GMRF features. The range of the horizontal coordinate σ of all plots in figure 7 is the same. The discriminability in figures 7(e–f) is maximum at the resolution at which the entropy–resolution plots are maximized.

The second database consists of natural textures. It is a subset of the CUReT database [37]. It consists of images from $k = 61$ classes of textures. Each class consists of 5 instances of a physical texture. The 5 instances differ in the illumination and viewing directions. To account for these differences all images were histogram equalized. In total there are 305 images. The intensity resolution of all images is 8 bits and their size is 100×100 pixels.

In figure 8(a) and (c) we see images of two different textures from the database. Next to each image, in figures 8(b) and (d), respectively, is its entropy–resolution plot of order $q = 1.3$. The plot in figure 8(e) shows the discrimination–resolution plot of the cooccurrence matrix features. The plot in figure 8(f) shows the discrimination–resolution plot of the GMRF features. The range of the horizontal coordinate σ of all the plots in figure 8 is identical. The discriminability in figures 8(e–f) is maximized at approximately the resolution at which the entropy–resolution plots of the images achieve their maxima.

The plot in figure 8(e) has two maxima. This is because the images in the texture database have different resolutions of maximum histogram entropy. The peak at the finer resolution is higher because most textures are fine. Note that the discriminability in the plots in figures 7 (e–f) and figure 8(e) increases for large σ. This is because at those resolutions all images in a class have uniform intensity and are similar. Thus, the between–class scatter becomes very small.

7.2 Optical Flow Estimation

In optical flow estimation using block matching a very important parameter is the block size. Clearly, the appropriate block length b must be related to the size of the objects or the coarseness of the textures in an image sequence. Thus, for a zoom–in sequence the block size should vary.

We adapt the block size in a zoom–in sequence using the entropy–resolution plots of order $q = 0.2$. The order of the entropy–resolution plots used is less than one since the sequence zooms into the central part of the image which is surrounded by background. We use the maximum value of the entropy, $S_{0.2}^{max}$, which corresponds to the dominant image structure. The length of the block b_i used for the ith image is given by the block length used for image $(i-1)$ multiplied by the factor by which the maximum entropy changes. That is, $b_i = b_{i-1}(S_{0.2}^{i,max}/S_{0.2}^{i-1,max})$.

Figures 9(a) and (d) show 2 frames from two different synthetic zoom–in sequences where the optical axis coincides with the geometric center of the image. The size of the images is 281×224 pixels and 301×200 pixels, respectively. In each image in figures 9(b) and (e) we can see superimposed the vector field estimated from the zoom–in sequence. In figure 9(c) and (f) we plot the motion estimation error as a function of the block length. For the adaptive algorithm the horizontal axis is the block length used for the first image in the sequence. The error measure is proportional to the negative of the cosine of the angle by which the motion vectors deviate from the correct motion direction.

The dotted lines in the plots in figures 9(c) and (f) show the motion estimation error for constant block size. The solid lines show the motion estimation

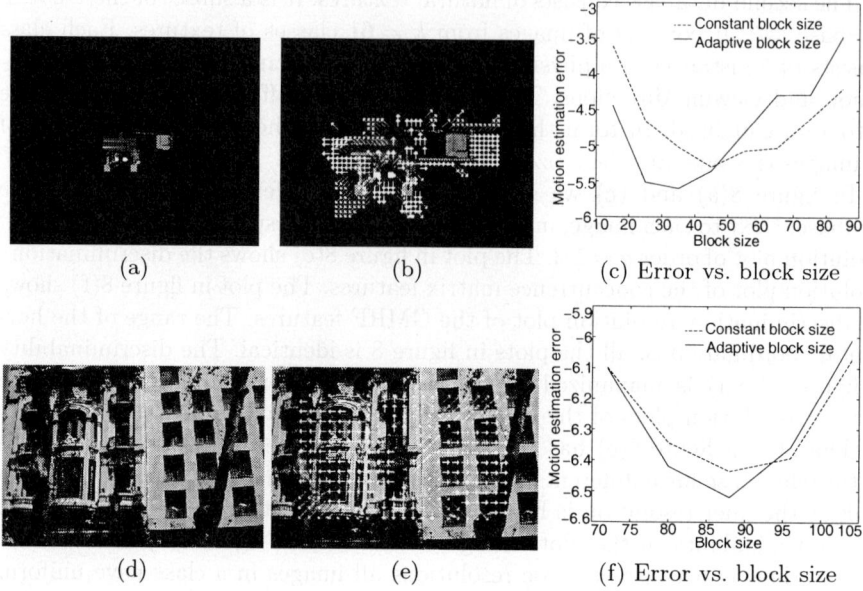

Fig. 9. The images in (a) and (d) are from 2 different zoom–in sequences. The images in (b) and (e) show images of the zoom–in sequences with motion vectors superimposed upon them. The plots in (c) and (f) are the motion estimation error as a function of the block size. The error of the constant block size algorithm is the dotted line and the error of the adaptive block size algorithm is the solid line. For both sequences the minimum error of the adaptively selected block size algorithm is smaller than the minimum error of the constant block size algorithm.

error for adaptively selected block size. In both plots the minimum error of the adaptively selected block size method is smaller than the minimum error of the fixed block size method.

8 Summary

We have suggested and examined the use of multiresolution histogram entropies for resolution selection. Multiresolution histogram entropies are appropriate for this objective because they are non–monotonic with resolution and robust to noise. Moreover, they represent sufficiently large image regions, and can detect multiple significant resolutions.

We examined the plot of the Tsallis entropy of order q of the histogram as a function of Gaussian image resolution, namely, the entropy–resolution plot of order q. We examined the entropy–resolution plots of images of shapes, regular textures, and random textures. Moreover, we discussed the fact that for $q < 1$ the entropy–resolution plots emphasize the foreground and for $q > 1$ the entropy–resolution plots are more sensitive to multiple significant resolutions.

We showed that the discriminability between images is larger at the resolution at which the histogram entropies are maximized. We also showed that the entropy–resolution plots can be used to adapt the block size in an optical flow algorithm and improve its performance.

A Appendix

A.1 Number of Independent Histogram Entropies

Property: The number of independent entropies of the histogram of an image can be at most equal to the number of the pixels in the image.

Proof: The histogram can be considered to be a distribution. It has been shown that the entropies of a distribution can be transformed into the histogram of the distribution [26]. Therefore, the entropies of the histogram can be transformed into the histogram of the histogram. The dimensionality of the histogram of the histogram can be as large as the number of image pixels. Therefore, the number of independent histogram entropies can be at most equal to the number of image pixels. □

A.2 Histograms Entropies and Fisher Information Measures

Lemma: The rate of change of the histogram with respect to Gaussian image filtering is linearly proportional to m different generalized Fisher information measures of the image.

Proof: The histogram $\mathbf{h}$ is equivalent to any complete set of Lyapunov exponents [17,26]. In particular, a histogram of m graylevels can be transformed linearly to a vector of m distinct Tsallis entropies. The transformation is given by $\mathbf{S}(\mathcal{L}) = R\,\mathbf{h}$, where R is an $m \times m$ matrix. Appropriate selection of the entropy orders makes R invertible [17]. Therefore, we have $\mathbf{h} = R^{-1}\mathbf{S}(\mathcal{L}) = T\,\mathbf{S}(\mathcal{L})$, where T is also an $m \times m$ matrix.

The rate at which the histogram changes with respect to image resolution is given by $\frac{d\mathbf{h}}{d\sigma} = T\,\frac{d\mathbf{S}(\mathcal{L})}{d\sigma}$. In turn, the rate at which the Tsallis entropies of the image change with respect to Gaussian filtering is proportional to the generalized Fisher information measures of the same order J_q given by equation (2) [20,21,22]. Therefore, we obtain $\frac{d\mathbf{h}}{d\sigma} = T\,\mathbf{J}(\mathcal{L})$, where $\mathbf{J}(\mathcal{L}) = (J_1(\mathcal{L})\ J_2(\mathcal{L}) \ldots J_m(\mathcal{L}))^{\mathrm{T}}$. In particular, for histogram density of intensity j we have $\frac{dh_j}{d\sigma} = \sum_{l=0}^{m-1} t_{jl} J_l(\mathcal{L})$, where t_{jl} are elements of matrix T. □

Property: The rate of change of Tsallis entropies of the histogram, $S_q(\mathbf{h})$, with respect to Gaussian filtering of the image is linearly proportional to generalized Fisher information measures of the image of m different orders q.

Proof: The rate of change of the Tsallis entropies of the histogram with respect to image resolution, σ, is obtained by differentiating equation (1) with respect to σ to obtain $\frac{dS_q(\mathbf{h})}{d\sigma} = \frac{1}{q-1}\sum_{j=0}^{m-1}\left((1-qh_j^{q-1})\frac{dh_j}{d\sigma}\right)$. By substituting the lemma above in this relation we obtain: $\frac{dS_q(\mathbf{h})}{d\sigma} = \frac{1}{q-1}\sum_{j,l=0}^{m-1}\left((1-qh_j^{q-1})t_{jl} J_l(\mathcal{L})\right)$. □

A.3 Effect of Texel Repetition on the Rate of Change of the Generalized Entropies of the Histogram

Lemma 1: Consider regular textures constructed from shapes as described in section 5. The relation between the generalized Fisher information of a shape, $J_q(\mathcal{L}_s)$, to that of the corresponding regular $p \times p$ texture, $J_q(\mathcal{L}_t)$, is: $J_q(\mathcal{L}_t) = p^2 J_q(\mathcal{L}_s)$.
The proof of Lemma 1 is given by Hadjidemetriou et al [30].
Property: The rate of change of the entropy of the histogram of the texture is p^2 times the rate of change of the entropy of the histogram of the shape.
Proof: The property derived in appendix A.2 for textures becomes $\frac{dS_q(\mathbf{h}_t)}{d\sigma} = \frac{1}{q-1}\sum_{j,l=0}^{m-1}\left((1-qh_j^{q-1})t_{jl}J_l(\mathcal{L}_t)\right)$. The corresponding relation holds for shapes $\frac{dS_q(\mathbf{h}_t)}{d\sigma}$. Substituting $J_q(\mathcal{L}_t) = p^2 J_q(\mathcal{L}_s)$ in the relation for textures we obtain $\frac{dS_q(\mathbf{h}_t)}{d\sigma} = p^2 \frac{dS_q(\mathbf{h}_s)}{d\sigma}$. □

References

1. Koenderink, J.: The structure of images. Biological Cybernetics **50** (1984) 363–370
2. Witkin, A.: Scale–space filtering. In: Proc. of IJCAI. (1983) 1019–1022
3. Tsallis, C.: Nonextensive statistics: Theoretical, experimental and computational evidences and connections. Brazilian Journal of Physics **29** (1999)
4. Marr, D., Hildreth, E.: Theory of edge detection. Proc. Royal society of London B **207** (1980) 187–217
5. Korn, A.: Toward a symbolic representation of intensity changes in images. IEEE Trans. on PAMI **10** (1988) 610–625
6. Lindeberg, T.: Edge detection and ridge detection with automatic scale selection. IJCV **30** (1998) 117–154
7. Elder, J., Zucker, S.: Local scale control for edge detection and blur estimation. IEEE Trans. on PAMI **20** (1998) 699–716
8. Marimont, D., Rubner, Y.: A probabilistic framework for edge detection and scale selection. In: Proc. of ICCV. Volume 1. (1998) 207–214
9. Jeong, H., Kim, C.: Adaptive discrimination of filter scales for edge detection. IEEE Trans. of PAMI **14** (1992) 579–585
10. Bretzner, L., Lindberg, T.: Feature tracking with automatic selection of spatial scales. CVIU **71** (1998) 385–392
11. Almansa, A., Lindberg, T.: Fingerprint enhancement by shape adaptation of scale–space operators with automatic scale selection. IEEE Trans. on IP **9** (2000) 2027–2042
12. Wiltschi, K., Lindberg, T., Pinz, A.: Classification of carbide distributions using scale selection and directional distributions. In: Proc. of ICIP. Volume 3. (1997) 122–125
13. Chomat, O., Verdiere, V., Hall, D., Crowley, J.: Local scale selection for Gaussian based description techniques. In: Proc. ECCV. Volume 1., Dublin (2000) 117–133
14. Crowley, J., A.C.Parker: A representation for shape based on peaks and ridges in the difference of low-pass transform. IEEE Trans. on PAMI **6** (1984) 156–170
15. Jagersand, M.: Saliency maps and attention selection in scale and spatial coordinates: An information theoretic approach. In: Proc. of ICCV. (1995) 195–202

16. Oomes, A., Snoeren, P.: Structural information in scale–space. In: Proc. of Workshop on Gaussian Scale–space Theory. Volume 96/19., Copenhagen, DIKU (1996) 48–57
17. Sporring, J., Weickert, J.: Information measures in scale–spaces. IEEE Trans. on IT **45** (1999) 1051–1058
18. Barron, A.: Entropy and the central limit theorem. The Annals of probability **14** (1986) 336–342
19. Carlen, E., Soffet, A.: Entropy production by block variable summation and central limit theorems. Communications in Mathematical Physics **140** (1991) 339–371
20. Plastino, A., Plastino, A., Miller, H.: Tsallis nonextensive thermostatistics and Fisher's information measure. Physica A **235** (1997) 577–588
21. Blackman, N.: The convolution inequality for entropy powers. IEEE Trans. on IT **11** (1965) 267–271
22. Stam, A.: Some inequalities satisfied by the quantities of information of Fisher and Shannon. Information and Control **2** (1959) 101–112
23. Thum, C.: Measurement of the entropy of an image with application to image focusing. Optica Acta **31** (1984) 203–211
24. Kadir, T., Brady, M.: Saliency, scale and image description. IJCV **45** (2001) 83–105
25. Koenderink, J., Doorn, A.: The structure of locally orderless images. IJCV **31** (1999) 159–168
26. Sporring, J., Colios, C., Trahanias, P.: Generalized scale–space. In: Proc. of ICIP. Volume 1. (2000) 920–923
27. Wong, A., Vogel, M.: Resolution-dependent information measures for image analysis. IEEE Trans. on Systems Man and Cybernetics **SMC-7** (1977) 49–61
28. Roldan, R., Molina, J., Aroza, J.: Multiresolution-information analysis for images. Signal Processing **24** (1991) 77–91
29. Tanaka, M., Watanabe, T., Mishima, T.: Tsallis entropy in scale–spaces. In: Proc. of the SPIE Conference on Vision Geometry VIII. Volume 3811. (1999) 273–281
30. Hadjidemetriou, E., Grossberg, M., Nayar, S.: Spatial information in multiresolution histograms. In: Proc. of CVPR. Volume 1. (2001) 702–709
31. Hadjidemetriou, E., Grossberg, M., Nayar, S.: Histogram preserving image transformations. In: Proc. of CVPR. (2000) I:410–416
32. Robotics Institute of CMU: (1998) CIL image database.
33. Haralick, R.: Statistical and structural approaches to texture. Proceedings of the IEEE **67** (1979) 786–804
34. Mao, J., Jain, A.: Texture classification and segmentation using multiresolution simultaneous autoregressive models. Pattern Recognition **25** (1992) 173–188
35. Fugunaka, K.: Introduction to Statistical Pattern Recognition. Academic Press, New York (1990)
36. Michigan State University: (2000) FVC database.
37. Dana, K., Nayar, S., van Ginneken, B., Koenderink, J.: Reflectance and texture of real-world surfaces. In: Proc. of CVPR. (1997) 151–157

Robust Computer Vision through Kernel Density Estimation

Haifeng Chen and Peter Meer

Electrical and Computer Engineering Department
Rutgers University, Piscataway, NJ, 08854-8058, USA
{haifeng, meer}@caip.rutgers.edu

Abstract. Two new techniques based on nonparametric estimation of probability densities are introduced which improve on the performance of equivalent robust methods currently employed in computer vision. The first technique draws from the projection pursuit paradigm in statistics, and carries out regression M-estimation with a weak dependence on the accuracy of the scale estimate. The second technique exploits the properties of the multivariate adaptive mean shift, and accomplishes the fusion of uncertain measurements arising from an unknown number of sources. As an example, the two techniques are extensively used in an algorithm for the recovery of multiple structures from heavily corrupted data.

1 Introduction

Visual data is complex and most often not all the measurements obey the same parametric model. For a satisfactory performance, robust estimators tolerating the presence of outliers in the data, must be used. These estimators are already popular in the vision community, see [17] for a representative sample of applications. Some of the robust techniques, like M-estimators and least median of squares (LMedS) were imported from statistics, while others, like Hough transform and RANSAC are innate, developed initially to solve specific vision problems.

It was shown in [2] that all the robust methods widely used in computer vision can be regarded as members of the same family of *M-estimators with auxiliary scale*, and that estimators with a smooth loss function (see Section 2) are to be preferred. In this paper we propose a novel approach toward computing M-estimators. The new approach combines several of the desirable characteristics of the different robust techniques already in use in computer vision and it is well suited for processing complex visual data.

A large class of computer vision problems can be modeled under the *linear errors-in-variables* (EIV) model. Under the EIV model *all* the measurements $\mathbf{y}_i \in \mathcal{R}^p$ are corrupted independently by zero mean noise, $\mathbf{y}_i = \mathbf{y}_{io} + \delta \mathbf{y}_i$, where the subscript 'o' denotes the unknown true value. In the sequel will consider the simplest case in which the noise covariance is $\sigma^2 \mathbf{I}_p$, however, our results can be easily extended to arbitrary covariance matrices. A linear constraint can be defined as

$$\mathbf{y}_{io}^\top \boldsymbol{\theta} - \alpha = 0 \qquad i = 1, \ldots, n \qquad \|\boldsymbol{\theta}\| = 1. \tag{1}$$

When the constraint is written under this form it can be shown that the Euclidean distance between a measurement $\mathbf{y}_i$ and $\hat{\mathbf{y}}_i$, its orthogonal projection on the hyperplane defined by the linear constraint is

$$\|\mathbf{y}_i - \hat{\mathbf{y}}_i\| = |\mathbf{y}_i^\top \boldsymbol{\theta} - \alpha| \qquad (2)$$

i.e., the geometric distance and the algebraic distance are the same.

The optimal estimator for the above model is the *total least squares* (TLS) technique. In the presence of outliers the corresponding robust M-estimator is defined as

$$[\hat{\alpha}, \hat{\boldsymbol{\theta}}] = \underset{\alpha, \boldsymbol{\theta}}{\operatorname{argmin}} \frac{1}{n} \sum_{i=1}^{n} \rho\left(\frac{1}{s}\|\mathbf{y}_i - \hat{\mathbf{y}}_i\|\right) \qquad \text{subject to} \quad \hat{\mathbf{y}}_i^\top \boldsymbol{\theta} - \hat{\alpha} = 0 \qquad (3)$$

where s is a scale parameter, and $\rho(u)$ is a nonnegative, even symmetric loss function, nondecreasing with $|u|$ and having the unique minimum $\rho(0) = 0$. Only the class of *redescending* M-estimators is considered here, and therefore we can always assume that $\rho(u) = 1$ for $|u| > 1$. A frequently used redescending M-estimator has the *biweight* loss function

$$\rho(u) = \begin{cases} 1 - (1-u^2)^3 & \text{if } |u| \leq 1 \\ 1 & \text{if } |u| > 1 \end{cases} \qquad (4)$$

and it will be the one employed throughout the paper.

The success of an M-estimation procedure, i.e., accurate estimation of the model parameters through rejection of the outliers, is contingent upon having a satisfactory scale parameter. (The issue of the breakdown point of the M-estimators is of lesser relevance in our context as will be seen later.) In [2] it was shown that the robust techniques imported from statistics differ from those developed by the vision community in the way the scale is obtained. For the former the scale is estimated from the data, while for the latter its value is set a priori.

It was implicitly assumed in (3) that a good scale estimate is already known. Statistical techniques for simultaneous estimation of the scale are available, e.g., [20], but they can not handle complex data of the type considered in this paper. Similarly, not in every vision application can a reliable scale estimate be obtained from the underlying physical properties. For example, in data containing multiple structures, i.e., several instances of the same model but with different sets of parameters, each structure may have been measured with a different uncertainty. A typical vision task generating such data is the recovery of the motion parameters for several moving objects in the presence of camera egomotion. In this case using a single global scale value for all the involved robust estimation procedures may not be satisfactory.

The performance of the robust M-type regression technique proposed in this paper has only a weak dependence on the accuracy of the scale estimate. Nevertheless, the technique provides a satisfactory inlier/outlier dichotomy for a wider range of contaminations than the traditional M-estimators. This performance improvement is achieved by recasting M-estimation as a kernel density estimation problem.

Kernel density estimation is a well known technique in statistics and pattern recognition. See the books [16] and [19] for a statistical treatment, and [7, Sec.4.3] for a pattern recognition description. Let x_i, $i = 1, \ldots, n$, be scalar measurements drawn from an arbitrary probability distribution $f(x)$. The kernel density estimate of this distribution $\hat{f}(x)$ (called the Parzen window estimate in pattern recognition), is obtained based on a *kernel function* $K(u)$ and a *bandwidth* h as

$$\hat{f}(x) = \frac{1}{nh} \sum_{i=1}^{n} K\left(\frac{x - x_i}{h}\right). \tag{5}$$

The kernel functions considered here satisfy the following properties

$$K(u) = K(-u) \geq 0 \qquad K(0) \geq K(u) \text{ for } u \neq 0$$

$$K(u) = 0 \text{ for } |u| > 1 \qquad \int_{-1}^{1} K(u) = 1. \tag{6}$$

Other conditions on the kernel function or on the density to be estimated [19, p.18], are always satisfied in practice. The even symmetry of the kernel function allows us to define its *profile*, $k(u)$ from

$$K(u) = c_k k(u^2) \tag{7}$$

where c_k is a normalization constant determined by (6). The importance of the profile is revealed in the case of multivariate kernel density estimation which will be be discussed in Section 3.

The quality of the density estimate $\hat{f}(x)$ is assessed using the *asymptotic mean integrated error* (AMISE), i.e., the integrated mean square error between the true density and its estimate for $n \to \infty$, while $h \to 0$ at a slower rate. The AMISE optimal bandwidth depends on the second derivative of $f(x)$, the unknown density [19, p.22]. While a good approximation of this bandwidth can be obtained employing a simple plug-in rule [19, p.72], for our purposes a bandwidth depending only on the kernel function and a raw scale estimate [19, Sec.3.2.2] suffices

$$\hat{h} = \left[\frac{243 R(K)}{35 \mu_2(K)^2 n}\right]^{1/5} \hat{\sigma} \qquad \hat{\sigma} = c \operatorname*{med}_{j} |x_j - \operatorname*{med}_{i} x_i| \tag{8}$$

$$R(K) = \int_{-1}^{1} K(u)^2 du \qquad \mu_2(K) = \int_{-1}^{1} u^2 K(u) du.$$

The data is taken into consideration through a median absolute deviations (MAD) scale estimate. The proportionality constant can be chosen as $c = 0.5$ or 1 to avoid oversmoothing of the estimated density [19, p.62]. In Section 2 the connection between the regression M-estimator (3) and the univariate density estimation (5) is established and then exploited to computational advantage.

In Section 3 kernel density estimation is reformulated under its most general multivariate form and will provide the tool to solve the following difficult problem. Let $\beta_j \in \mathcal{R}^p$, $j = 1, \ldots, m$, be a set of measurements whose uncertainty is also available through the covariance matrices $\mathbf{C}_j$. A large subset of these measurements is related to $M \ll m$ different data sources, while the rest are completely erroneous. The value of M is *not* known. Find the best (in statistical sense) estimates for the M vectors and covariances characterizing these sources. This is a fundamental feature space analysis problem and our approach, based on an extension of the variable bandwidth mean shift [4], provides a simple robust solution.

In Section 4 the two new techniques become the main building blocks of an algorithm for analyzing data containing multiple structures. The success of the algorithm is illustrated with 3D examples. Finally, in Section 5 the potential of the proposed techniques to solve difficult vision tasks, and the remaining open issues are discussed.

2 M-Estimators and Projection Pursuit

Projection pursuit is a nonparametric technique introduced in statistics in the 1970s for exploratory data analysis, and was soon applied also to nonlinear regression and density estimation problems. Projection pursuit seeks "interesting" low-dimensional (almost always one-dimensional) projections of multidimensional data. The informative value of a projection is measured with a *projection index*. Most often the projection index is a scalar functional of the univariate probability distribution estimated from the data projected on the chosen direction. The "best" direction is obtained through numerical optimization and corresponds to an extremum of the projection index. This is one step in an iterative procedure toward the solution. The current solution is then updated and a new search is initiated. For example, in projection pursuit regression at each iteration the shape of a smooth univariate nonlinear function which minimizes the sum of squared residuals is determined. At the subsequent iteration this function is incorporated into the current model. Convergence is declared when the squared error falls below a threshold. The papers [9], [11] offer not only excellent reviews on the projection pursuit paradigm, but also contain extensive discussions from researchers working on related topics.

There is a strong connection between robust linear regression estimators, such as least median of squares, and the projection pursuit procedure [6], [14, Sec.3.5]. This relationship, however, was investigated in statistics mostly for theoretical considerations and in the case of traditional regression, i.e., the case in which only one of the measured variables is corrupted by noise. In this paper will apply the projection pursuit paradigm to design a technique for the more general errors-in-variables (EIV) model which is better suited for vision tasks.

To prove the connection between EIV regression M-estimation and kernel density estimation, the definition (3) is rewritten as

$$[\hat{\alpha}, \hat{\boldsymbol{\theta}}] = \underset{\alpha, \boldsymbol{\theta}}{\operatorname{argmax}} \left[1 - \frac{1}{n} \sum_{i=1}^{n} \rho \left(\frac{\mathbf{y}_i^\top \boldsymbol{\theta} - \alpha}{s} \right) \right] = \underset{\alpha, \boldsymbol{\theta}}{\operatorname{argmax}} \frac{1}{n} \sum_{i=1}^{n} \kappa \left(\frac{\mathbf{y}_i^\top \boldsymbol{\theta} - \alpha}{s} \right) \quad (9)$$

where $\kappa(u) = c_\rho[1 - \rho(u)]$ will be called the *M-kernel function*, and c_ρ is the normalization constant making $\kappa(u)$ a proper kernel. Note that $\kappa(u) = 0$ for $|u| > 1$, and that the even symmetry of the loss function $\rho(u)$ allows the removal of the absolute values when (2) is plugged in. In Figs. 1a and 1b the biweight loss function and its corresponding M-kernel function is shown. Compare the M-kernel with the weight function

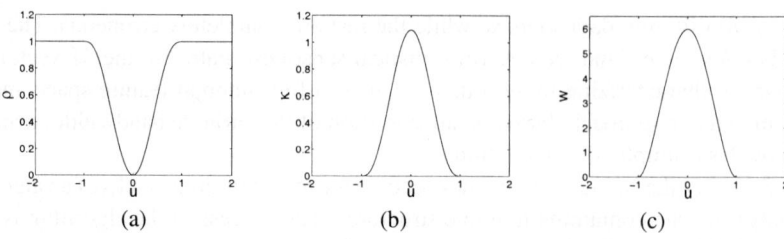

Fig. 1. The different functions associated with the *biweight* M-estimator. (a) The loss function $\rho(u)$. (b) The M-kernel function $\kappa(u)$. (c) The weight function $w(u)$.

$w(u) = u^{-1}\rho'(u)$ used in the well known iterative reweighted least squares implementation of M-estimators [13, p.306] (Fig. 1c). The two functions while look similar have different expressions.

Let $\boldsymbol{\theta}$ be a unit vector defining a line through the origin in $\mathcal{R}^p$. The projections of the data points $\mathbf{y}_i$ on this line have the intrinsic coordinates $x_i = \mathbf{y}_i^\top \boldsymbol{\theta}$. Given a kernel $K(u)$ and the bandwidth $\hat{h}$ (8), the estimated density of this sequence is

$$\hat{f}_{\boldsymbol{\theta}}(x) = \frac{1}{n\hat{h}_{\boldsymbol{\theta}}} \sum_{i=1}^{n} K\left(\frac{\mathbf{y}_i^\top \boldsymbol{\theta} - x}{\hat{h}_{\boldsymbol{\theta}}}\right) \tag{10}$$

where the dependence of the bandwidth on the direction of the projection (through the scale estimate of the projected points) was made explicit. The *mode* of the density estimate is defined as

$$\hat{x}_{\boldsymbol{\theta}} = \underset{x}{\operatorname{argmax}}\, \hat{f}_{\boldsymbol{\theta}}(x) \tag{11}$$

and can be easily computed. Comparing (9) and (10) we can remark that if $\kappa(u)$ is taken as the kernel function, $\boldsymbol{\theta}$ is chosen close to the true parameter of the linear model (1), and $\hat{h}_{\boldsymbol{\theta}}$ is a satisfactory substitute for the scale s, the mode (11) should provide a reasonable estimate for the intercept α.

Based on the above observation the EIV linear model M-estimation problem can be reformulated as

$$[\hat{\alpha}, \hat{\boldsymbol{\theta}}] = \underset{\boldsymbol{\theta}}{\operatorname{argmax}} \left[\hat{h}_{\boldsymbol{\theta}} \max_{x} \hat{f}_{\boldsymbol{\theta}}(x)\right] \tag{12}$$

which is the projection pursuit definition of the M-estimator, the projection index being the quantity inside the brackets. The equivalence between (3) and (12) is not perfectly rigorous since the scale was substituted with the bandwidth. However, this is an advantage since now the role of the scale is diminished and *any* bandwidth is satisfactory as long as it secures the reliable recovery of the mode. The bandwidth $\hat{h}_{\boldsymbol{\theta}}$ is proportional with the MAD scale estimate (8) which can be unreliable when the distribution is multimodal since the median is a biased estimator for nonsymmetric data. Similarly, for small measurement noise $\hat{h}_{\boldsymbol{\theta}}$ becomes small which can introduce artifacts if the bandwidth is not bounded downward.

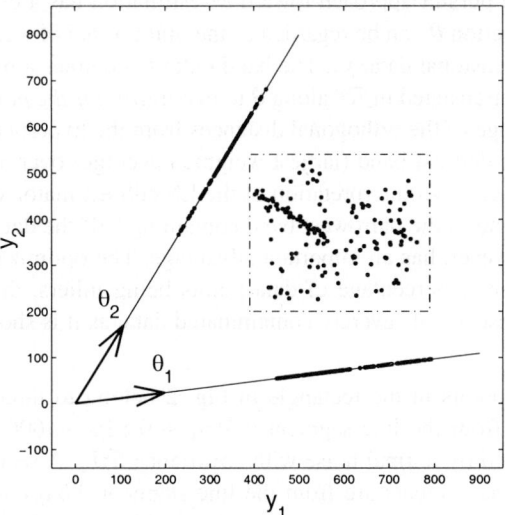

Fig. 2. Projection pursuit principle: the parameter estimates are sought by examining the projections of the data points on arbitrary directions.

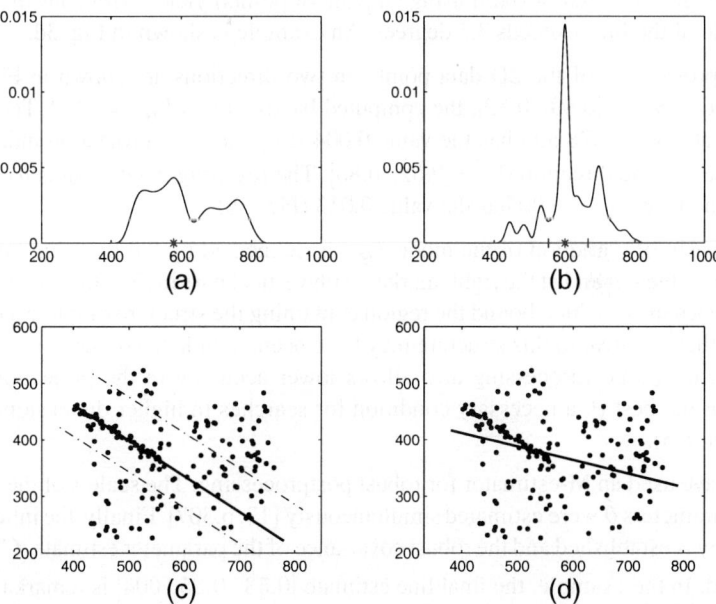

Fig. 3. Processing the data in Fig. 2. (a) Estimated density for the projection along direction $\hat{\theta}_1$. The detected mode is marked as ∗. (b) Estimated density for the projection along direction $\hat{\theta}_2$ which maximized the projection index. The points projecting inside the interval marked with the vertical bars are selected. (c) Projection pursuit based line estimate. The dashed lines bound the region delineated for robust postprocessing. (d) Hough transform based line estimate.

The projection pursuit approach toward M-estimation has a clear geometric interpretation. The direction θ can be regarded as the unit normal of a candidate hyperplane fitted to the p-dimensional data, $\mathbf{y}_i$. The bandwidth $\hat{h}_\theta$ defines a band centered on this plane. The band is translated in $\mathcal{R}^p$ along θ to maximize, *for the points within the band*, the weighted average of the orthogonal distances from the hyperplane. The M-estimate corresponds to the densest band (largest weighted average) over all θ. Note the similarity with the well known interpretation of the LMedS estimator where the parameter estimates correspond to the narrowest band containing half the data points [14, p.126]. Our approach, however, has an important advantage. The optimization criterion is not dependent on a *preset* percentage of data points being inliers, thus yielding a better behavior in the presence of severely contaminated data, as it is shown in the following example.

The 180 data points in the rectangle in Fig. 2 belong to three classes. There are 50 measurements from the line segment $0.54y_1 + 0.84y_2 - 606 = 0$ where $400 \leq y_1 \leq 560$, corrupted by normal noise with covariance $5^2 \mathbf{I}_2$. A second structure is also present. Its 30 measurements are from the line segment $0.54y_1 - 0.84y_2 - 60 = 0$ where $600 \leq y_1 \leq 750$, but were severly corrupted by normal noise with covariance $20^2 \mathbf{I}_2$ and became indistinguishable from the background. The background has 100 points uniformly distributed in the rectangle bounded by $(425, 225)$ and $(750, 525)$. By definition the LMedS estimator cannot handle such data. Similarly, the global maximum of the Hough accumulator (built using all pairs of points) yields erroneous fits once the angle side of the bins exceeds 3.6 degrees. An example is shown in Fig. 3d.

The projections of the 2D data points on two directions are shown in Fig. 2. For the direction $\theta_1 = [0.99, \ 0.12]$, the computed bandwidth is $h_{\theta_1} = 50.2$. The mode is detected at $\hat{x}_{\theta_1} = 578$ and has the value 0.004 (Fig. 3a). The projection index (12) is maximized by the direction $\theta_2 = [0.52, \ 0.85]$. The resulting bandwidth is $h_{\theta_2} = 23.8$ and the mode at $\hat{x}_{\theta_2} = 600$ has the value 0.013 (Fig. 3b).

The basin of attraction of the mode $\hat{x}_{\theta_2}$, is delineated by the first significant local minimum at the left and at the right, marked with vertical bars in Fig. 3b. They define two parallel lines in $\mathcal{R}^2$ which bound the region containing the structure of interest (Fig. 3c). Since outliers relative to this structure may have been included, a robust postprocessing is required. The postprocessing also allows lower accuracy in the projection pursuit search for the best θ, a necessary condition for searches in higher dimensional spaces (see Section 5).

We have used an M-estimator for robust postprocessing. The scale $\hat{s}$ of the structure and its parameters $\hat{\theta}$ were estimated simultaneously [13, p.307]. Finally, the inlier/outlier dichotomy is established and the robust covariance of the parameter estimate, $\mathbf{C}_{\hat{\theta}}$, is also computed. In the example, the final line estimate $[0.53, \ 0.85, \ 604]$ is remarkable close to the true values in spite of the severe contamination (Fig. 3c). Here the improvement due to the postprocessing was small, however, its role is increased when the projection pursuit based M-estimator is employed as a computational module in Section 4.

3 Robust Data Fusion

The following problem appears under many forms in computer vision tasks. The m measurements $\boldsymbol{\beta}_j \in \mathcal{R}^p$ are available together with their uncertainty described by the covariance matrices $\mathbf{C}_j$. Taking into account these uncertainties, classify the measurements into $M \ll m$ groups, where M is the number of clusters present in the data. The value of M is not known. The problem can also be regarded as a data fusion task in which the available evidence is to be reduced to the minimum number of plausible representations.

Will consider first the trivial case of $M = 1$, i.e., the case in which *all* the measurements belong to a single group. A satisfactory estimate for the center of the underlying cluster is obtained by minimizing the sum of Mahalanobis distances

$$\hat{\boldsymbol{\beta}} = \underset{\boldsymbol{\beta}}{\operatorname{argmin}} \sum_{j=1}^{m} (\boldsymbol{\beta} - \boldsymbol{\beta}_j)^\top \mathbf{C}_j^{-1} (\boldsymbol{\beta} - \boldsymbol{\beta}_j) \qquad (13)$$

where the covariances are assumed to have full rank. As expected, the solution

$$\hat{\boldsymbol{\beta}} = \left(\sum_{j=1}^{m} \mathbf{C}_j^{-1} \right)^{-1} \sum_{j=1}^{m} \mathbf{C}_j^{-1} \boldsymbol{\beta}_j \qquad (14)$$

is the covariance weighted average of the measurements. The more uncertain is a measurement (the inverse of its covariance has a smaller norm), the less it contributes to the result of the fusion.

To compute the covariance matrix $\mathbf{C}$ (uncertainty) associated with $\hat{\boldsymbol{\beta}}$, the covariances $\mathbf{C}_j$ are approximated as $\mathbf{C}_j \approx a_j \mathbf{C}$. The common covariance structure $\mathbf{C}$ and the positive proportionality factors a_j are determined from the minimization

$$[\hat{a}_j, \hat{\mathbf{C}}] = \arg \underset{a_j, \mathbf{C}}{\min} \sum_{j=1}^{m} \| \mathbf{C}_j - a_j \mathbf{C} \|_F^2 \qquad (15)$$

where $\|\mathbf{B}\|_F^2 = \operatorname{trace}[\mathbf{B}^\top \mathbf{B}]$ is the squared Frobenius norm of the matrix $\mathbf{B}$. Differentiating after a_j and taking the matrix gradient after $\mathbf{C}$, two relations connecting the unknown quantities are obtained

$$\hat{\mathbf{C}} = \frac{\sum_{j=1}^{m} \hat{a}_j \mathbf{C}_j}{\sum_{j=1}^{m} \hat{a}_j^2} \qquad \hat{a}_j = \frac{\operatorname{trace}[\mathbf{C}_j^\top \hat{\mathbf{C}}]}{\operatorname{trace}[\hat{\mathbf{C}}^\top \hat{\mathbf{C}}]}. \qquad (16)$$

The relations are evaluated iteratively starting from all $\hat{a}_j = 1$, which makes $\hat{\mathbf{C}}$ the average covariance. The $\hat{a}_j$-s are then refined, and the next value of $\hat{\mathbf{C}}$ is the one retained.

Will return now to kernel density estimation. A radially symmetric, p-dimensional multivariate kernel $K(\mathbf{u})$ is built from the profile $k(u)$ as

$$K(\mathbf{u}) = c_{k,p} k(\mathbf{u}^\top \mathbf{u}) \qquad (17)$$

where $c_{k,p}$ is the corresponding normalization constant and $\mathbf{u} \in \mathcal{R}^p$. The properties (6) can be easily extended to $\mathcal{R}^p$. In the most general case the bandwidth h is replaced by a symmetric positive definite *bandwidth matrix*, $\mathbf{H}$.

Given the data points $\mathbf{x}_i$, $i = 1, \ldots, n$, in $\mathcal{R}^p$, their multivariate density estimate computed with the kernel $K(\mathbf{u})$ and the bandwidth matrix $\mathbf{H}$ is [16, Sec.4.2.1]

$$\hat{f}(\mathbf{x}) = \frac{1}{n} \sum_{i=1}^{n} K_\mathbf{H}(\mathbf{x} - \mathbf{x}_i) \tag{18}$$

$$K_\mathbf{H}(\mathbf{x}) = [\det[\mathbf{H}]]^{-1/2} K(\mathbf{H}^{-1/2}\mathbf{x}) = c_{k,p}[\det[\mathbf{H}]]^{-1/2} k(\mathbf{x}^\top \mathbf{H}^{-1} \mathbf{x}). \tag{19}$$

Note that $\mathbf{H} = h^2 \mathbf{I}_p$ reduces (19) to the well known, traditional multivariate kernel density estimation expression.

In practice using a single bandwidth is often not satisfactory since the available data points are not spread uniformly over the region of existence of the unknown density. The *sample point* kernel density estimator is defined as

$$\hat{f}(\mathbf{x}) = \frac{1}{n} \sum_{i=1}^{n} K_{\mathbf{H}_i}(\mathbf{x} - \mathbf{x}_i) \tag{20}$$

where each data point $\mathbf{x}_i$ is considered in the computations through its own bandwidth matrix $\mathbf{H}_i$. The sample point estimator has superior performance relative to kernel density estimators in which the variable bandwidth is associated with the center of the kernel $\mathbf{x}$, [16, Sec.5.3]. From (20), taking into account (19) we obtain

$$\hat{f}(\mathbf{x}) = \frac{c_{k,p}}{n} \sum_{i=1}^{n} [\det[\mathbf{H}_i]]^{-1/2} k\left((\mathbf{x} - \mathbf{x}_i)^\top \mathbf{H}_i^{-1} (\mathbf{x} - \mathbf{x}_i)\right). \tag{21}$$

To solve the robust data fusion problem will compute the sample point density estimate of the m measurements $\boldsymbol{\beta}_j$. Multivariate Epanechnikov kernels built from the profile [19, p.30]

$$k(u) = \begin{cases} 1 - u & 0 \leq u \leq 1 \\ 0 & u > 1 \end{cases} \tag{22}$$

are used, and as bandwidth matrices the covariances $\mathbf{C}_j$ are employed. The covariance matrices are scaled to $\chi^2_{\gamma,p} \mathbf{C}_j$, where $\chi^2_{\gamma,p}$ is the chi-square value for p degrees of freedom and level of confidence γ (in our implementation $\gamma = 0.995$). Thus

$$K_{\mathbf{C}_j}(\mathbf{u}) = 0 \quad \text{for} \quad \mathbf{u}^\top \mathbf{C}_j^{-1} \mathbf{u} > \chi^2_{\gamma,p} \quad j = 1, \ldots, m \tag{23}$$

i.e., the kernel associated with a measurement is nonzero in the region of confidence of that measurement having coverage probability γ. The density estimate (21) becomes

$$\hat{f}(\boldsymbol{\beta}) = \frac{c_{k,p}}{m \left[\chi^2_{\gamma,p}\right]^{p/2}} \sum_{j=1}^{m} [\det[\mathbf{C}_j]]^{-1/2} k\left(\frac{1}{\chi^2_{\gamma,p}} (\boldsymbol{\beta} - \boldsymbol{\beta}_j)^\top \mathbf{C}_j^{-1} (\boldsymbol{\beta} - \boldsymbol{\beta}_j)\right). \tag{24}$$

Taking into account (22) we have obtained that solving the minimization problem (13) is equivalent to finding the maximum of the density estimate (24), i.e., its mode. (The apparent differences are only scalar normalization factors for the covariances.)

We are now ready to proceed to the proposed problem where the measurements come from an unknown number of sources M. To characterize these sources, first the M clusters are to be delineated, which as will be shown below is equivalent to finding *all* the significant modes of the density $\hat{f}(\beta)$

$$\hat{\beta}_l = \arg\max_{\beta} \hat{f}(\beta) \qquad l = 1,\ldots M. \tag{25}$$

Note that the value of M is determined automatically from the data. A mode of $\hat{f}(\beta)$ corresponds to a zero of its gradient

$$\nabla \hat{f}(\beta) = \frac{c_{k,p}}{m \left[\chi^2_{\gamma,p}\right]^{(p/2+1)}} \sum_{j=1}^{m} [\det[\mathbf{C}_j]]^{-1/2} \mathbf{C}_j^{-1}(\beta - \beta_j) \times \tag{26}$$
$$\times k'\left(\frac{1}{\chi^2_{\gamma,p}}(\beta-\beta_j)^\top \mathbf{C}_j^{-1}(\beta-\beta_j)\right).$$

The function $g(u) = -k'(u)$ defines a new profile which in our case is

$$I_\gamma(\mathbf{u}) = g\left(\frac{\mathbf{u}^\top \mathbf{C}_j^{-1} \mathbf{u}}{\chi^2_{\gamma,p}}\right) = \begin{cases} 1 & \mathbf{u}^\top \mathbf{C}_j^{-1} \mathbf{u} \leq \chi^2_{\gamma,p} \\ 0 & \mathbf{u}^\top \mathbf{C}_j^{-1} \mathbf{u} > \chi^2_{\gamma,p} \end{cases} \tag{27}$$

i.e., the indicator function selecting the data points inside the region of confidence of β_j. Defining the matrix $\mathbf{W}_j = [\det[\mathbf{C}_j]]^{1/2} \mathbf{C}_j$ the expression of the gradient (26) can be rewritten

$$\nabla \hat{f}(\beta) = \frac{c_{k,p}}{m \left[\chi^2_{\gamma,p}\right]^{(p/2+1)}} \left(\sum_{j=1}^{m} I_\gamma(\beta - \beta_j) \mathbf{W}_j^{-1}\right) \times \tag{28}$$
$$\times \left[\left(\sum_{j=1}^{m} I_\gamma(\beta-\beta_j)\mathbf{W}_j^{-1}\right)^{-1} \left(\sum_{j=1}^{m} I_\gamma(\beta-\beta_j)\mathbf{W}_j^{-1}\beta_j\right) - \beta\right]$$

where the presence of the indicator function assures the robustness computations. Indeed, the zeros of the gradient are given by an expression similar to (14), but with the computations restricted to local regions in $\mathcal{R}^p$. As long as the M clusters are reasonably separated, computing their centers is based only on the appropriate data points. By choosing a kernel other than Epanechnikov from the beta family [19, p.31], instead of a binary indicator function (27) additional weighting can be introduced in (28).

The modes of $\hat{f}(\beta)$ by definition are located in high density regions of $\mathcal{R}^p$. A versatile, robust mode detector is based on the *mean shift* property introduced first in pattern recognition [8], and which recently became popular in computer vision for a large variety of tasks [3]. The variable bandwidth version of the mean shift procedure was also developed [4].

The mean shift procedure recursively evaluates the second term of (28). The procedure starts by taking $\beta = \beta_j$, and a new value of β is computed using only the data

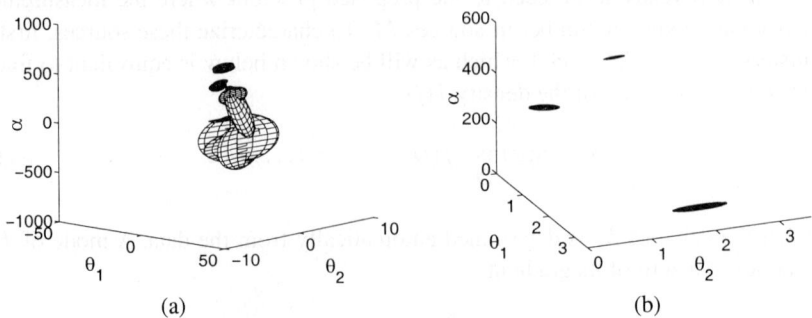

Fig. 4. An example of data fusion for $p = 3$, $m = 60$ and $M = 3$. (a) The measurements with regions of confidence. (b) The result of the multivariate variable bandwidth mean shift. Note the smaller scale.

points which yield nonzero values for the indicator function. The process is then repeated with the obtained β, i.e., the kernels are shifted according to the result of the previous step. Convergence is achieved when the shift becomes less than a threshold. See [3] and [4] for details about the mean shift procedure.

After the mean shift procedure was applied to all the m measurements, by associating these measurements with theirs point of convergence, arbitrarily shaped *basins of attraction* can be defined. Note that outliers, i.e., isolated erroneous measurements are not taken into account since they will fail to evolve. The points of convergence are characterized applying (14) and (16) to the data points in the basin of attraction. Pairs whose squared Mahalanobis distance is less than $\chi^2_{\gamma,p}$ (under both metrics) are merged. The resulting M modes are the output of the robust fusion procedure. An example is shown in Fig. 4. The large confidence regions in Fig. 4a correspond to erroneous measurements and hide the majority of the data. After robust fusion three modes are detected, each associated with a small uncertainty (Fig. 4b).

The fusion technique introduced here can provide a robust component for more traditional approaches toward combining classifiers, e.g., [18], or for machine learning algorithms which improve performance through resampling, e.g., bagging [1].

4 Robust Regression for Data with Multiple Structures

Data containing multiple structures is characterized by the presence of several instances of the same model, in our case (1), each defined with a different set of parameters. The need for reliable processing of such data distinguishes estimation problems in computer vision from those in applied statistics.

The assumption that the sought model is carried by the absolute majority of the data points, is embedded in all robust estimators in statistics. In vision tasks, such as, structure from motion, 3D scene representation, this assumption is violated once information about more than one object is to be acquired simultaneously. Among the four main classes of robust techniques employed in vision (see Section 1) only the Hough transform has the capability to handle complex multiple structured data. However, as our example in Section 2 has already shown, good performance of the Hough transform is contingent upon having access to the correct scale estimate (accumulator bin size), which in practice is often not possible. See [2] for a detailed discussion on the difficulties of traditional robust techniques in handling multiple structured data.

Four main processing steps can be distinguished in the implementation of the robust estimators based on a nondifferentiable optimization criterion: LMedS, RANSAC and Hough transform. First, several small random subsets of data points, i.e., samples, are selected. Next, from each sample a parameter estimate candidate is computed. In the third step, the quality of the candidates is assessed using all the data points and the candidate yielding the "best" quality measure is retained. Finally, the data is classified into inliers and outliers in relation to the model parameter estimates.

While some of these four steps can be intertwined and refined (or in the case of Hough transform disguised), they provide a general processing principle. This principle is still obeyed when the two techniques introduced in the paper are employed as computational modules in an algorithm for analyzing data with multiple structures.

1. *Definition of the random samples.*
   The data is quantized in $\mathcal{R}^p$ by defining a p-dimensional *bin* using the bandwidths (8) computed with a uniform kernel separately for each coordinate. The bins are ranked by the number of points inside, and at random one is chosen from the upper half of the ranking. Starting from this bin a *sample* is generated by probabilistic region growing. Any bin at the boundary of the current region selects a neighbor not yet in the region with probability equal to the normalized number of points of the neighbor. Normalization is by the total number of points of such neighbors. Region growing stops when the sample reaches the upper bound of allowed bins (in our 3D examples 6% of all nonempty bins), or no further growing is possible.
2. *Computation of the parameter estimate candidates.*
   For each of N samples (60 in our experiments) the projection pursuit based M-estimation procedure discussed in Section 2 is applied. For each sample the candidate vector $\hat{\theta}_l$ its covariance $\mathbf{C}_{\hat{\theta}_l}$, and a scale estimate $\hat{s}_l$ are obtained. For display purposes, the points declared inliers are delineated with a *bounding box*.
3. *Selection of the best candidates.*
   Using the N estimates and their covariances, the robust fusion procedure discussed in Section 3 is applied. The number of structures M present in the data is determined and their characteristics are computed.
4. *Classification of the data.*
   To refine the relation between the M structures and the data points declared inliers in the samples, each sample/structure association receives a vote. Only the points with more than 4 votes are retained for a structure. Finally, starting with the structure having the largest number of points, they are recursively removed from the data. Since the data classification starts from a reliable basis, other more sophisticated or application specific procedures can also be used.

Two experiments with 3D synthetic data containing $M = 3$ structures, are presented here. The first data set (Figures 5a and 5b) contains three planar regions in a chevron-type arrangement. Each region contains 100 points corrupted with normal noise having

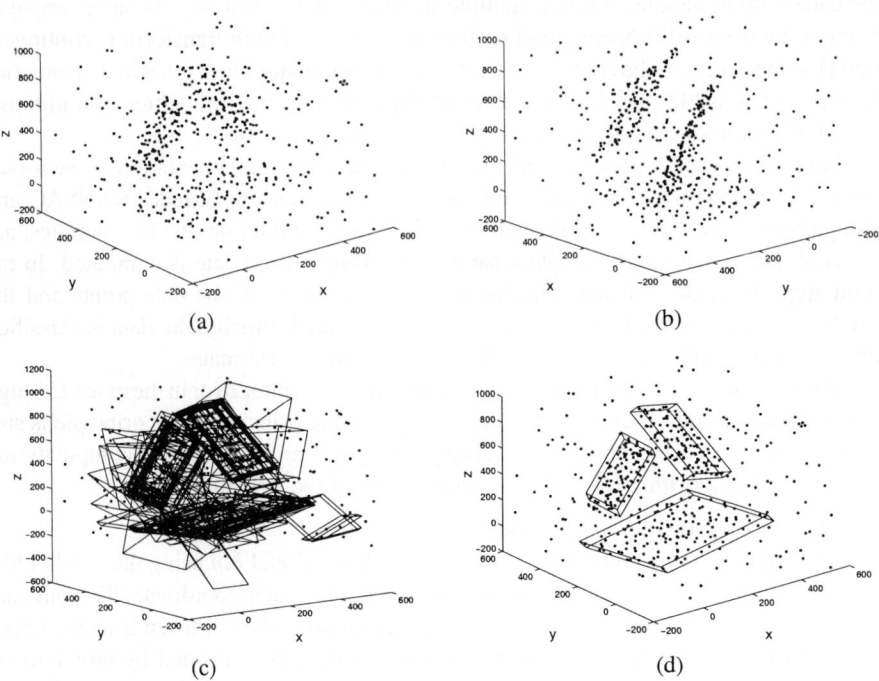

Fig. 5. Example of 3D data analysis containing multiple structures. (a), (b) Two views of the data. (c) Bounding boxes of the employed $N = 60$ samples. (d) Delineated structures.

covariance $10^2 I_3$. In the background 200 more data points are scattered uniformly in a cube incorporating all three structures. The 60 bounding boxes resulting at the end of the M-estimation procedures are shown in Figure 5c, while the feature space and the result of the robust fusion are in Figure 4. The output of the algorithm, the three structures delineated by their final bounding boxes, is shown in Figure 5d.

The second data set (Figures 6a and 6b) has the same characteristics, however, the three planar regions are now arranged in a Z-type configuration. In spite of the intersecting regions, the algorithm succeeded to distinguish the structures (Figure 5d). In both examples the estimated parameters were close to the true values for the planes.

5 Discussion

Many computer vision problems can be recast under the framework of robust analysis (regression) of data containing multiple structures. For example, the Costeira-Kanade algorithm for structure-from-motion factorization for multiple objects [5], was recently reformulated by Kanatani as finding for each tracked object a four-dimensional linear subspace in a space having the dimension twice the number of image frames [12]. Similarly, to build from an image sequence a scene-based representation of the visual environment, e.g. a mosaic, the multiple layer plane+parallax representation is the most

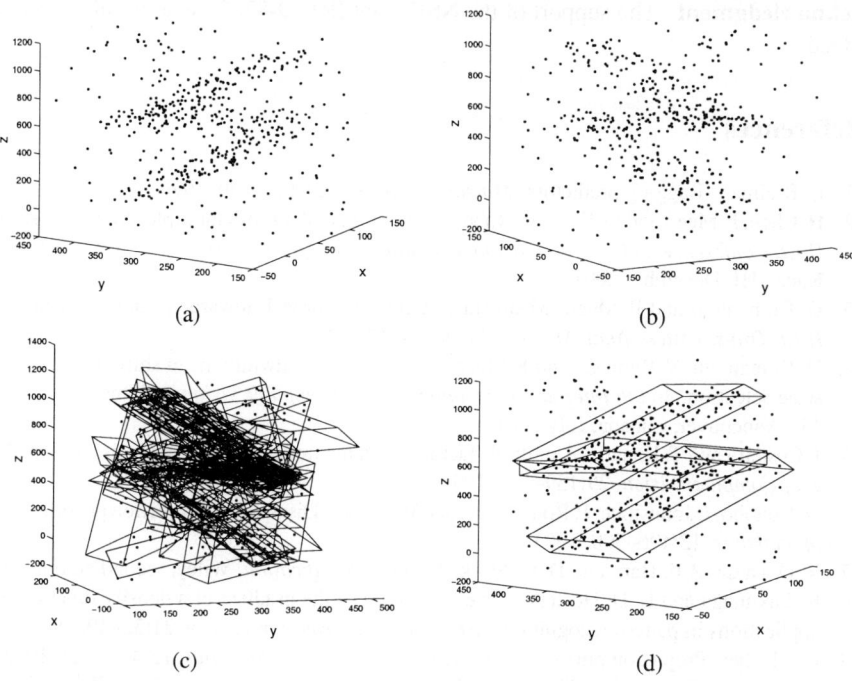

Fig. 6. Example of 3D data analysis containing multiple structures. (a), (b) Two views of the data. (c) Bounding boxes of the employed $N = 60$ samples. (d) Delineated structures.

general model [10], which can be also used for detecting independently moving objects [15]. The algorithm proposed in this paper offers a tool which can simultaneously extract all the significant model instances, instead of the usually employed recursive approach in which the "dominant" feature is detected first.

These vision tasks, however, require processing in high dimensional spaces. Thus, an efficient search strategy over θ has to be employed when the projection index is maximized (M-estimation). In the 3D examples described above, first 4^2 directions distributed uniformly over $\mathcal{R}^3$ were used, followed by a refinement of another 4^2 around the "best" direction from the previous step. The 3D examples were processed in MATLAB in less than a minute. Using a parametrization which takes into account that θ is a unit vector [20], we are currently developing a computationally feasible search strategy for higher dimensions. Ideally the search should also take into account a priori information specific to the vision task to be solved.

The two techniques presented in the paper make extensive use of nonparametric statistics tools which are more sensitive than the parametric methods, however, require more supporting data points to yield reliable results. See for example, [9, p.473] for a discussion of projection pursuit for small sample sizes. Nevertheless, the new data analysis algorithm tolerates "bad" data better than the robust techniques tradionally employed in computer vision.

Acknowledgment. The support of the NSF grant IRI 99-87695 is gratefully acknowledged.

References

1. L. Breiman. Bagging predictors. *Machine Learning*, 24:123–140, 1996.
2. H. Chen, P. Meer, and D. E. Tyler. Robust regression for data with multiple structures. In *2001 IEEE Conference on Computer Vision and Pattern Recognition*, volume I, pages 1069–1075, Kauai, HI, December 2001.
3. D. Comaniciu and P. Meer. Mean shift: A robust approach toward feature space analysis. *IEEE Trans. Pattern Anal. Machine Intell.*, 24, May 2002.
4. D. Comaniciu, V. Ramesh, and P. Meer. The variable bandwidth mean shift and data-driven scale selection. In *8th International Conference on Computer Vision*, volume I, pages 438–445, Vancouver, Canada, July 2001.
5. J. Costeira and T. Kanade. A multiple factorization method for motion analysis. *International J. of Computer Vision*, 29:159–179, 1998.
6. D. Donoho, I. Johnstone, P. Rousseeuw, and W. Stahel. Discussion: Projection pursuit. *Annals of Statistics*, 13:496–500, 1985.
7. R. O. Duda, P. E. Hart, and D. G. Stork. *Pattern Classification*. Wiley, second edition, 2000.
8. K. Fukunaga and L. D. Hostetler. The estimation of the gradient of a density function, with applications in pattern recognition. *IEEE Trans. Information Theory*, 21:32–40, 1975.
9. P. J. Huber. Projection pursuit (with discussion). *Annals of Statistics*, 13:435–525, 1985.
10. M. Irani and P. Anandan. Video indexing based on mosaic representations. *Proceedings of IEEE*, 86:905–921, 1998.
11. M. C. Jones and R. Sibson. What is projection pursuit? (with discussion). *J. of the Royal Stat. Soc. Series A*, 150:1–37, 1987.
12. K. Kanatani. Motion segmentation by subspace separation and model selection. In *8th International Conference on Computer Vision*, volume II, pages 301–306, Vancouver, Canada, July 2001.
13. G. Li. Robust regression. In D. C. Hoaglin, F. Mosteller, and J. W. Tukey, editors, *Exploring Data Tables, Trends, and Shapes*, pages 281–343. John Wiley & Sons, 1985.
14. P. J. Rousseeuw and A. M. Leroy. *Robust Regression and Outlier Detection*. Wiley, 1987.
15. H. S. Sawhney, Y. Guo, and R. Kumar. Independent motion detection in 3D scenes. *IEEE Trans. Pattern Anal. Machine Intell.*, 22:1191–1199, 2000.
16. B. W. Silverman. *Density Estimation for Statistics and Data Analysis*. Chapman & Hall, 1986.
17. Special Issue. Robust statistical techniques in image understanding. *Computer Vision and Image Understanding*, 78, April 2000.
18. D. M. J. Tax, M. van Breukelen, R. P. W. Duin, and J. Kittler. Combining multiple classifiers by averaging or by multiplying? *Pattern Recog.*, 33:1475–1486, 2000.
19. M. P. Wand and M. C. Jones. *Kernel Smoothing*. Chapman & Hall, 1995.
20. R. H. Zamar. Robust estimation in the errors-in-variables model. *Biometrika*, 76:149–160, 1989.

Constrained Flows of Matrix-Valued Functions: Application to Diffusion Tensor Regularization

C. Chefd'hotel, D. Tschumperlé, R. Deriche, and O. Faugeras

INRIA Sophia-Antipolis, France
{cchefd,dtschump,der,faugeras}@sophia.inria.fr

Abstract. Nonlinear partial differential equations (PDE) are now widely used to regularize images. They allow to eliminate noise and artifacts while preserving large global features, such as object contours. In this context, we propose a geometric framework to design PDE flows acting on constrained datasets. We focus our interest on flows of matrix-valued functions undergoing orthogonal and spectral constraints. The corresponding evolution PDE's are found by minimization of cost functionals, and depend on the natural metrics of the underlying constrained manifolds (viewed as Lie groups or homogeneous spaces). Suitable numerical schemes that fit the constraints are also presented. We illustrate this theoretical framework through a recent and challenging problem in medical imaging: the regularization of diffusion tensor volumes (DT-MRI).

Introduction

In the last decade, variational methods and nonlinear PDE's have been widely used to tackle computer vision problems, such as image restoration [19,24,26,35], segmentation [22], stereo-based 3D reconstruction [12], image inpainting [4,6], or image matching and optical flow estimation [1,2,11] (among other examples). Solutions to these problems, whether they are curves, surfaces, or images, are obtained by continuously deforming an initial estimation through a flow defined by a PDE. The corresponding evolution equations derive either from simple local heuristics or from cost functional minimizations. In the context of image and data restoration, which is considered in this paper, the idea is to achieve a selective smoothing that removes noise while preserving large global features, such as object contours (discontinuities of the signal). For this purpose, one generally uses anisotropic nonlinear diffusion PDE's, which often derive from variational principles (such as the ϕ-function formulation [7,19,24,25] which has proven its efficiency for gray-valued image restoration).

Generalizing these algorithms to multi-valued datasets is now attracting a growing interest. In effect, the increase of computer performances has made possible the implementation of PDE's acting on large fields of vectors or matrices. Recent works point toward this direction, with the definition of methods for color image restoration [26,28,31,35], or direction field regularization [5,17,23,29,33]. A flow on multi-valued data is generally not a straightforward generalization of its scalar counterpart, and new theoretical developments are involved. For instance, in the case of direction field restoration, vectors are constrained to have a unit norm. This yields a significant modification of the corresponding diffusion PDE's by introducing a coupling term between vector components.

The aim of this paper is to provide some formal and numerical tools to deal efficiently with this type of problems, with a particular emphasis on flows of matrix-valued functions undergoing orthogonal and spectral constraints. Our final objective concerns the restoration of diffusion tensor images of the human brain (DT-MRI) [21], modeled as fields of symmetric positive definite matrices (i.e. constrained to have positive eigenvalues). We start from the fact that most evolution PDE's can be viewed as ordinary differential equations (ODE) on a suitable function space. When nonlinear constraints are involved, the corresponding flows belong to an infinite dimensional submanifold[1] of the initial search space. Usually, this geometric viewpoint is hidden behind the use of Lagrange multipliers in constrained variational principles. It also appears implicitly in the nonlinear heat equation, borrowed from harmonic map theory, which has been recently proposed to regularize direction fields [5,29]. The interest of a fully geometric interpretation of the suitable function space is twofold. First, it provides a simple and unified framework to build constrained flows for matrix-valued functions, whether or not they derive from variational principles. Second, it naturally yields, through the use of exponential maps, suitable numerical schemes that are also constraint preserving.

This approach is presented as follows. Section 1 introduces a geometric setting to define constrained flows and their proper numerical implementations. Section 2 discusses the application of these methods to the definition of three different regularization techniques for DT-MRI datasets. Finally, section 3 presents results of numerical experiments on a real DT-MRI volume of the brain, leading to the construction of regular tissue fiber maps in the white matter.

1 Geometric Interpretation of Constraint Preserving Flows

1.1 Flows on Manifold

Let us consider the smooth trajectory $t \mapsto p(t)$ of a point moving on an arbitrary manifold $\mathcal{M}$. Any such trajectory can be defined, at least locally, as the integral curve of a smooth vector field V, and satisfies the evolution equation

$$\frac{\partial p(t)}{\partial t} = V(p(t)) \qquad \text{(where } p(0) \in \mathcal{M}\text{)}. \qquad (1)$$

Recall that since V is a vector field, we have $\forall\, p \in \mathcal{M}$, $V(p) \in T_p\mathcal{M}$, where $T_p\mathcal{M}$ denotes *the tangent space of $\mathcal{M}$ at p*. An example of such an integral curve, induced by a vector field on a sphere, is illustrated in Fig. 1a.

---
[1] Throughout this paper, we borrow some tools from differential geometry and Lie group theory. We refer to [18,20] for the corresponding background.

Despite its simplicity, eq. (1) contains the key elements to build all the constrained flows presented below. Let us assume that $\mathcal{M}$ is a submanifold corresponding to some nonlinear constraints on its embedding space $\mathcal{P}$. Then, we can say that a flow is *constraint preserving* if it is tangent to $\mathcal{M}$. Its form follows readily from the expression of the tangent space at any point p of the constrained set. This argument is valid for both finite and infinite dimensional manifolds. For our application, we will consider manifolds of the form $\mathcal{M} = \mathcal{F}(\Omega, \mathcal{N})$, where $\mathcal{F}(\Omega, \mathcal{N})$ is a set of functions $X : \Omega \to \mathcal{N}$, defined on an open subset Ω of the Euclidean space, and which take values in a constrained matrix manifold $\mathcal{N}$. This infinite dimensional manifold of mappings could be define on a suitable Banach or Hilbert space [16,18,20]. For a given point $X \in \mathcal{F}(\Omega, \mathcal{N})$, its tangent space is identified to the set of functions:

$$T_X \mathcal{F}(\Omega, \mathcal{N}) = \{x \mapsto V(x), \text{ such that } V(x) \in T_{X(x)} \mathcal{N}\},$$

where $T_{X(x)} \mathcal{N}$ is the tangent space to $\mathcal{N}$ at $X(x)$.

In the following, $\mathcal{M}$ is viewed as a submanifold of the linear space $\mathcal{P} = \mathcal{F}(\Omega, \mathbb{R}^{n \times n})$, where $\mathbb{R}^{n \times n}$ denotes the set of $n \times n$ real matrices[2]. Note that in the definition of the tangent space, we assumed that $\mathcal{F}(\Omega, \mathcal{N})$ inherits its constrained geometry directly from its codomain $\mathcal{N}$. We do not consider additional structural contraints, such as invertibility, which would yield more complex families of mappings (see for instance the groups of diffeomorphisms used in the image matching context [30]). In this setting, an evolution equation on $\mathcal{F}(\Omega, \mathcal{N})$ must satisfy:

$$\forall t > 0, \forall x \subset \Omega, \quad \begin{cases} \frac{\partial X(x)}{\partial t} = V(x), & \text{with } V(x) \in T_{X(x)} \mathcal{N}, \\ X_0 = X_{(t=0)} \in \mathcal{F}(\Omega, \mathcal{N}). \end{cases} \quad (2)$$

In order to specialize this equation to the practical cases studied in this paper, we can also notice that a wide range of orthogonal and spectral constraints on matrices define *Lie groups* and *homogeneous spaces*. They are submanifolds of $\mathbb{R}^{n \times n}$ which present some nice algebraic properties. In particular, the tangent space at any given point of a matrix Lie group is easily defined in terms of its tangent space at identity (its Lie algebra) [18]. This is particularly important since equation (2), together with the expression of the tangent space at any point on $\mathcal{N}$, will yield directly the constrained flows we are looking for. Regardless of the type of constraints discussed in the section 2, we will describe each point on $\mathcal{N}$ in terms of its extrinsic coordinates in $\mathbb{R}^{n \times n}$. The main reason is that a suitable parametrization of a constrained set is generally difficult, since several charts are often necessary to cover the underlying manifold. The constraint set may even have several connected components (the group of orthogonal matrices, for

---

[2] We naturally extend to $\mathcal{F}(\Omega, \mathbb{R}^{n \times n})$ all the operators existing on $\mathbb{R}^{n \times n}$. Let $X, Y, Z \in \mathcal{F}(\Omega, \mathbb{R}^{n \times n})$, the expression $Z = XY$ corresponds to the equality $Z(x) = X(x)Y(x), \forall x \in \Omega$ (product of matrices).

instance, has two connected components: the sets of rotations and anti-rotations (we call "anti-rotation" a reflection combined with a rotation)).

1.2 Gradient Flows and Cost Functionals

One way of building a constraint preserving flow (2) for a specific purpose is to minimize a cost functional f. The corresponding evolution equation is usually defined as a gradient flow that follows the direction of steepest descent toward the nearest critical point. To build such a flow, $\mathcal{M}$ is endowed with a *Riemannian metric* $\langle \cdot, \cdot \rangle_p$ which defines for all $p \in \mathcal{M}$ a scalar product between any two vectors of the tangent space $T_p\mathcal{M}$. Recall that the gradient is then defined as the unique vector field ∇f such that

$$\forall\, v \in T_p\mathcal{M}, \qquad df_p(v) = \langle \nabla f(p), v \rangle_p,$$

where $df_p(v)$ denotes the *first variation*[3] of f at p in the direction v. The corresponding minimizing flow is given by

$$\frac{\partial p(t)}{\partial t} = -\nabla f(p(t)) \qquad (p(0) \in \mathcal{M}).$$

When $\mathcal{M}$ is a linear function space equipped with the L^2-metric defined by $\langle v, w \rangle = \int_\Omega v(x) \cdot w(x)\, dx$, the equation $\nabla f(p) = 0$ corresponds to the usual Euler-Lagrange equation of variational calculus.

In our framework, we choose to endow $\mathcal{M} = \mathcal{F}(\Omega, \mathcal{N})$ with the metric $\langle U, V \rangle_X = \int_\Omega \langle U(x), V(x) \rangle_{X(x)}^{\mathcal{N}}\, dx$, where $\langle \cdot, \cdot \rangle_p^{\mathcal{N}}$ denotes a suitable Riemannian metric on $\mathcal{N}$, usually an *invariant* or a *normal metric* in the case of Lie groups and homogeneous spaces [15]. In practice, when the L^2-gradient is known for an arbitrary cost functional f on $\mathcal{F}(\Omega, \mathbb{R}^{n \times n})$, we will be able to reuse its expression to define the gradient of the restriction of f to $\mathcal{F}(\Omega, \mathcal{N})$. Up to a change of metric, the corresponding transformation is an orthogonal projection on the suitable tangent space.

1.3 Exponential Maps and Numerical Schemes

Standard numerical methods for differential equations are usually not suitable for constrained flows. Note that with a simple Euler method, the numerical integration of equation (1) yields the explicit scheme

$$p_{(t+dt)} = p_{(t)} + V(p_{(t)})\, dt \qquad \text{where} \qquad p_0 = p_{(t=0)} \in \mathcal{M}, \qquad (3)$$

where $dt > 0$ corresponds to the integration step. Since we are using extrinsic coordinates, there is a risk of stepping out from $\mathcal{M}$ for each (non infinitesimal) displacement. In fact, by writing (3) we implicitly assumed that the integral

---

[3] For an arbitrary curve p_ϵ on $\mathcal{M}$, such that $p_0 = p$ and $\left.\frac{\partial p_\epsilon}{\partial \epsilon}\right|_{\epsilon=0} = v$, one computes the first variation of f from the definition $df_p(v) = \left.\frac{\partial f(p_\epsilon)}{\partial \epsilon}\right|_{\epsilon=0}$.

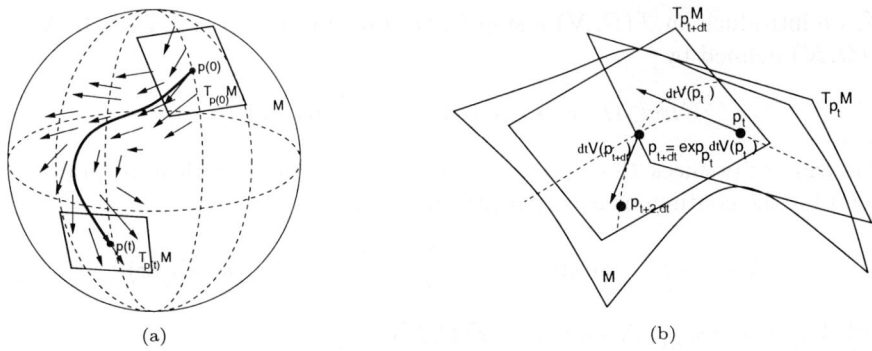

Fig. 1. (a) Integral curve of a vector field on a manifold $\mathcal{M}$, (b) Geodesic steps on a Riemannian manifold.

curve lies in a linear space. In our situation, we must adjust the integration method to accommodate the true constrained geometry of $\mathcal{M}$. The first idea is to project after each step the point $p_{(t+dt)}$ on the underlying manifold. We propose here to avoid this post-processing using a geometric integration step relying on *exponential maps*, following directly a geodesic path between each iteration. This technique is borrowed from existing numerical methods on Riemannian manifolds [15,27]. It consists of replacing (3) by

$$p_{(t+dt)} = \exp_{p_{(t)}}(dt\ V(p_{(t)})) \qquad p_0 \in \mathcal{M}, \qquad (4)$$

where $\exp_p$ denotes the exponential map at $p \in \mathcal{M}$. Recall that for a given point p on a (finite dimensional) manifold $\mathcal{M}$, and a vector $v \in T_p\mathcal{M}$, there exists a unique geodesic $t \mapsto \gamma_v(t)$ such that

$$\gamma_v(0) = p \quad \text{and} \quad \gamma_v'(0) = v.$$

The exponential map $\exp_p : T_p\mathcal{M} \longrightarrow \mathcal{M}$ is then defined by $\exp_p(v) = \gamma_v(1)$ ($\forall\ v$ such that $\gamma_v(1)$ exists). For dt sufficiently small, equation (4) corresponds to a geodesic step of length

$$\|dtV(p_{(t)})\|_{p_{(t)}} = \langle dtV(p_{(t)}), dtV(p_{(t)})\rangle_{p_{(t)}}^{1/2},$$

in the direction of $V(p_{(t)})$ (see Fig. 1b).

In general, the equation of a geodesic satisfies a second order differential equation. In this paper, we use the fact that for simple matrix manifolds, closed form solutions are often available (and thus the exponential map). Note that on linear manifolds endowed with the Euclidean metric, geodesics are straight lines. For instance, the tangent space at X in $\mathbb{R}^{n \times n}$ is defined by $T_X\mathbb{R}^{n \times n} \simeq \mathbb{R}^{n \times n}$ and we have $\forall X, V \in \mathbb{R}^{n \times n}$, $\exp_X V = X + V$. Then, equation (4) reduces to the original Euler integration method.

In our framework, these ideas extend naturally to the definition of a numerical integration scheme on $\mathcal{F}(\Omega, \mathcal{N})$. Given $\exp_p : T_p\mathcal{N} \mapsto \mathcal{N}$ the exponential map on

$\mathcal{N}$, we introduce on $\mathcal{F}(\Omega,\mathcal{N})$ a step-forward operator $\exp_X V : T_X \mathcal{F}(\Omega,\mathcal{N}) \mapsto \mathcal{F}(\Omega,\mathcal{N})$ defined by

$$\forall x \in \Omega, \ x \mapsto (\exp_X V)(x) = \exp_{X(x)} V(x).$$

One can easily check that $\exp_X V$ yields a consistent numerical integrator (in time) for the continuous equation (2), such that

$$X_{(t+dt)}(x) = \left(\exp_{X_{(t)}} dt\ V_{(t)}\right)(x) = \exp_{X_{(t)}(x)} dt\ V_{(t)}(x), \tag{5}$$

with $V_{(t)}(x) \in T_{X_{(t)}(x)}\mathcal{N}$ and $X_0 \in \mathcal{F}(\Omega,\mathcal{N})$.

Regarding the discretization in space of $V_{(t)}$ (on Ω), finite difference schemes developed for unconstrained equations still apply. Actually, constraints on the codomain $\mathcal{N}$ of $\mathcal{F}(\Omega, N)$ only change the time discretization scheme. If we had to deal with functions $\Omega \to \mathbb{R}^{n \times n}$ whose spatial domain Ω was an arbitrary manifold (for instance an implicit surface defined by a level set function), we could combine this technique with the framework introduced in [3].

2 Application of Constraint Preserving Flows to Diffusion Tensor Regularization

2.1 Context and Notations

We propose now to use the previous tools to address the problem of diffusion tensor regularization. Let $P(n)$ and $O(n)$ denote respectively the sets of symmetric positive definite, and orthogonal real matrices of size $n \times n$. Recall that

$$\forall\ X \in P(n), \quad X_{i,j} = X_{j,i} \quad \text{and} \quad \forall\ a \in \mathbb{R}^n \backslash \{0\}, \quad a^T X a > 0, \tag{6}$$
$$\forall\ X \in O(n), \quad XX^T = X^T X = I, \quad (I \text{ is the identity matrix}). \tag{7}$$

We are mainly interested in regularizing fields $X : \Omega \to P(3)$ of diffusion tensors coming from DT-MRI imaging. This recent and non-invasive 3D medical imaging modality consists in measuring the water molecule motion in the tissue fibers, using magnetic resonance techniques. Each voxel $X(x) \in P(3)$ of the acquired image X is defined by a symmetric and positive definite 3×3 matrix that defines the local water molecule motion (i.e. the fiber orientations) [9,10, 21,14,34]. These fiber structures are not explicitly given by the matrices $X(x)$, but can be retrieved by spectral decomposition $X(x) = U(x)D(x)U(x)^T$, where $U : \Omega \to O(3)$ is the field of 3×3 *orthogonal matrices* composed of the unit eigenvectors of X, and D is the field of the 3×3 matrices $D(x) = \text{diag}(\lambda_1, \lambda_2, \lambda_3)$ corresponding to its *positive eigenvalues*. Actually, the spectral decomposition splits the diffusion tensor field X into an *orientation feature* U (main directions of the water motion) and a *diffusivity feature* D (velocity of the water motion). A natural representation of X is then produced using ellipsoids whose axes and radii are respectively given by the eigenvectors in U and the corresponding

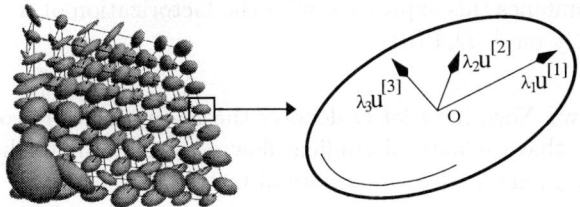

Fig. 2. View of a 3D diffusion tensor field $X : \Omega \to P(3)$.

positive eigenvalues $\lambda_1, \lambda_2, \lambda_3$ (see Fig. 2).
In the following, the mathematical reasoning developed in section 1 is applied through a progressive analysis of the diffusion tensor regularization problem. We refer to the research report version of this paper [8] for a detailed derivation of the results presented below. Note that this framework allows us to generalize previous regularization methods acting directly on the matrix representation of DT-MRI data [9,10,32].

2.2 Symmetric Positive Definite (SPD) Constraint

By analogy with scalar image regularization methods, the first idea to restore a DT-MRI field is to find a matrix-valued flow minimizing a regularization functional f,

$$\min_{X \in \mathcal{F}(\Omega, P(3))} f(X) = \int_\Omega \phi(\|\nabla_\Omega X\|) + \frac{\alpha}{2}(X - X_0)^2 \, d\Omega, \qquad (8)$$

(where $\|\nabla_\Omega X\| = \sqrt{\sum_{i,j} \|\nabla_\Omega X_{i,j}\|^2}$ and $\nabla_\Omega = (\frac{\partial}{\partial x}, \frac{\partial}{\partial y}, \frac{\partial}{\partial z})^T$ is the *spatial gradient* in Ω), while preserving the symmetric positive definite constraint (6). The fixed parameter $\alpha > 0$ prevents the expected solution from being too different from the given noisy field X_0, while $\phi : \mathbb{R} \to \mathbb{R}$ is *an increasing function* which controls the regularization behavior (this ϕ-function formulation was first introduced in the context of scalar image regularization with edge preservation [7,19,24]). Note that the functional (8) is invariant by matrix transposition and thus takes into account implicitly the symmetry property of the evolving matrices.

Constraint preserving flow: The simplest way to introduce flows on $\mathcal{F}(\Omega, P(n))$ is to consider the factorization of any symmetric positive definite matrix X into a product $R^T R$ where $R \in \mathrm{GL}(n, \mathbb{R})$, the Lie group of invertible $n \times n$ real matrices. Its Lie algebra $\mathfrak{gl}(n)$ is the set of real valued matrices, and we can identify any tangent vector W at point $R \in \mathrm{GL}(n, \mathbb{R})$ with a vector V of $\mathfrak{gl}(n)$ through $W = RV$. This leads to flows on $\mathcal{F}(\Omega, \mathrm{GL}(n))$ which are given by

$$\frac{\partial R}{\partial t} = R\,V \quad \text{where} \quad V \in \mathcal{F}(\Omega, \mathbb{R}^{n \times n}) \quad \text{and} \quad R_{(t=0)} = R_0 \in \mathcal{F}(\Omega, \mathrm{GL}(n)).$$

One simply combines this expression with the factorization of X to obtain flows that act directly on $\mathcal{F}(\Omega, \mathrm{P}(n))$.

Gradient flow: Now, if we let G denotes the L^2-gradient of f on $\mathcal{F}(\Omega, \mathbb{R}^{3 \times 3})$. We show in [8] that the natural gradient flow corresponding to the restriction of f to $\mathcal{F}(\Omega, \mathrm{P}(3))$ (endowed with its normal metric) satisfies

$$\frac{\partial X}{\partial t} = -\left((G+G^T) X^2 + X^2 (G+G^T)\right). \tag{9}$$

In our case, the matrix $G = (G_{i,j})$ is defined component by component with

$$G_{i,j} = \alpha(X_{i,j} - X_{0_{i,j}}) - \mathrm{div}\left(\frac{\phi'(\|\nabla_\Omega X\|)}{\|\nabla_\Omega X\|} \nabla_\Omega X_{i,j}\right). \tag{10}$$

Note that the PDE (9) allows to evolve directly the matrix coefficients while preserving the symmetric positive definiteness.

Numerical scheme: For equation (9), since the underlying manifold is an open region of a linear space, a simple Euler step could be used, provided the initial function X_0 is far enough from the constraint set boundaries. Using the exponential map theory presented before, we can introduce a more suitable scheme:

$$X_{(t+dt)} = \exp(-X_{(t)}(G+G^T)\, dt)^T\, X_{(t)} \exp(-X_{(t)}(G+G^T)\, dt), \tag{11}$$

where $\exp(A) = \sum_{i=0}^{\infty} \frac{A^i}{i!}$ denotes *the matrix exponential*, numerically implemented using a Padé approximation, as described in [13]. One can easily check by induction that this scheme satisfies the constraint. Let $K_{(t)} = \exp(-X_{(t)}(G_{(t)} + G_{(t)}^T)\, dt)$. If we assume $X_{(t)} \in \mathcal{F}(\Omega, \mathrm{P}(n))$, we have $\forall\, x \in \Omega, \forall\, v \in \mathbb{R}^n \setminus \{0\}, v^T X_{(t)}(x)v > 0$. Thus, $\forall\, x \in \Omega, \forall\, w \in \mathbb{R}^n \setminus \{0\}$,

$$w^T X_{(t+dt)}(x) w = w^T K_{(t)}^T(x) X_{(t)}(x) K_{(t)}(x) w$$
$$= (K_{(t)}(x)w)^T X_{(t)}(x) (K_{(t)}(x)w) > 0.$$

Experiments on synthetic data: An application of the symmetric positive definite regularizing flow (9) on a noisy, synthetic 3D tensor field is illustrated in Fig. 3. The tensor field is quite well restored, but suffers from *an eigenvalue swelling effect*, despite the anisotropic diffusion obtained with the ϕ-function formulation. Actually, when the noise does not affect the tensor orientations as much as the diffusivities (which is the case here), a global matrix regularization process quickly smoothes the diffusivities in regard of the orientations. Therefore, to avoid this eigenvalue smoothing, we have to split the regularization of the tensor orientations and diffusivities. Note that the same kind of behavior appears in color image restoration, where several methods propose to separate the chromaticity and the brightness information from a color vector, and restore them with different equations [5,17,29,31].

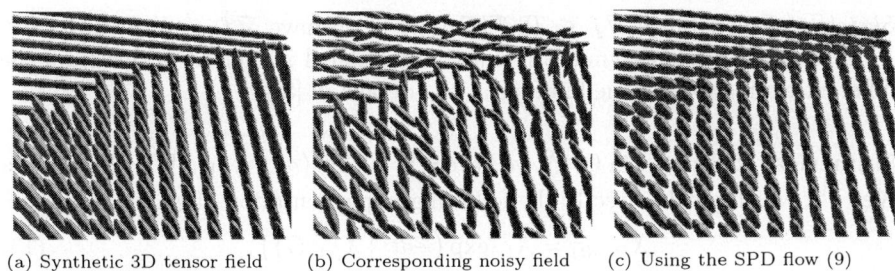

(a) Synthetic 3D tensor field   (b) Corresponding noisy field   (c) Using the SPD flow (9)

Fig. 3. Symmetric positive definite flow on a synthetic tensor field (with $\phi(s) = 2\sqrt{1+s^2} - 2$).

2.3 Orthogonal Flow

Eigenvalue over-smoothing can be avoided by regularizing the orientation part U and the diffusivity part D of a diffusion tensor field X, with different coupled equations. This problem has been already considered in [10,32]. Note that the regularization of the diffusivity field D can be handled with classic vector regularization PDE's [26,28,31,35], which must however satisfy the maximum principle in order to preserve the eigenvalue positiveness. We can then focus on the regularization of the orientation feature, i.e. the regularization flow that minimizes the following ϕ-functional:

$$\min_{U \in \mathcal{F}(\Omega, O(3))} f(U) = \int_\Omega \phi(\|\nabla_\Omega U\|) + \frac{\alpha}{2}(U - U_0)^2 \, d\Omega.$$

Constraint preserving flow: By definition, $O(n) = \{X \in GL(n, \mathbb{R}) \,/\, X^T X = I\}$. Its tangent space at X is $T_X O(n) = \{XA, \ A \in \mathfrak{so}(n)\}$, where $\mathfrak{so}(n)$ denotes its Lie algebra, the vector space of *skew-symmetric matrices*. Thus, any flow on $\mathcal{F}(\Omega, O(n))$ satisfies an equation of the form

$$\frac{\partial X}{\partial t} = X\,A, \quad \text{where} \quad \begin{cases} A \in \mathcal{F}(\Omega, \mathfrak{so}(n)) \\ X_0 = X_{(t=0)} \in \mathcal{F}(\Omega, O(n)). \end{cases} \quad (12)$$

Gradient flow: The gradient flow for the restriction of f to $\mathcal{F}(\Omega, O(n))$ with respect to its bi-invariant metric[4] is given by (see [8])

$$\frac{\partial X}{\partial t} = -\nabla f = -X\{X, G\} = X\,G^T\,X - G,$$

where $\{A, B\} = A^T B - B^T A$ denotes the generalized Lie brackets, and $G = (G_{i,j})$ is the usual gradient:

$$G_{i,j} = \alpha(U_{i,j} - U_{0_{i,j}}) - \operatorname{div}\left(\frac{\phi'(\|\nabla_\Omega U\|)}{\|\nabla_\Omega U\|}\nabla_\Omega U_{i,j}\right).$$

---
[4] $\langle XA, XB \rangle_X = -\int_\Omega \operatorname{Tr}(A(x)B(x))\, dx, \forall\ A, B \in \mathcal{F}(\Omega, \mathfrak{so}(n))$.

Sketch of Proof: Since $\nabla f \in T_X \mathcal{F}(\Omega, O(n))$, we have $\nabla f = XA$, with $A \in \mathcal{F}(\Omega, \mathfrak{so}(n))$. The skew-symmetric matrix function A is then identified from the different expressions of the first variation (details in [8]).

Numerical scheme: On $O(n)$, we have $\forall V \in T_X O(n)$, $\exp_X V = X e^{X^{-1} V} = X e^{X^T V}$, which yields directly the following implementation of eq. (12):

$$X_{(t+dt)} = X_{(t)} \exp\left(-dt \left\{X_{(t)}, G\right\}\right). \tag{13}$$

Remark: Note that in this case, for 3×3 skew-symmetric matrices, the matrix exponential can be expressed with *Rodrigues' formula*:

$$\exp(A) = I + \frac{\sin \|a\|}{\|a\|} A + \frac{1 - \cos \|a\|}{\|a\|^2} A^2 \quad \text{where} \quad A = \begin{bmatrix} 0 & -a_3 & a_2 \\ a_3 & 0 & -a_1 \\ -a_2 & a_1 & 0 \end{bmatrix} (\in \mathfrak{so}(3)),$$

and $a = [a_1 \; a_2 \; a_3]^T$. This equation can be used to improve the computational efficiency of the numerical implementation of eq. (13).

Experiments on synthetic data: The full regularization process of a diffusion tensor field X, using an orthogonal flow reads as follows:

1. Retrieve the orientation field U and the diffusivity field D of a tensor field X, i.e. $\forall x \in \Omega$, $X(x) = U(x) D(x) U(x)^T$.
2. Process the orientation field U with our orthogonal-constrained matrix flow (12). Note that one has to take care of the non-uniqueness of the orientation field U, as mentioned in [10,9,32]. Flipping one eigenvector $u^{[i]}$ (a column of U) does not change the tensor, but may affect the anisotropic regularization process. To overcome this problem, a local eigenvector alignment process is made before applying the PDE on each tensor of the field X. The neighboring eigenvector directions are aligned with the current one, by constraining the dot product between them to be positive:

$$\forall y \in \mathcal{V}(x), \quad u^{[i]}(y) := \text{sign}\left(u^{[i]}(x) . u^{[i]}(y)\right) u^{[i]}(y),$$

where $\mathcal{V}(x)$ is a neighborhood of x. This local operation allows to act only on the orientation feature of the tensors. The importance of this alignment step is shown on Fig. 4c.

3. Finally, process the diffusivity field D with a classic vector scheme, as in [35]:

$$\frac{\partial \lambda_i}{\partial t} = \alpha \left(\lambda_{0_i} - \lambda_i\right) + \text{div}\left(\Sigma \nabla_\Omega \lambda_i\right),$$

where Σ is a matrix that drive the diffusion process and may contain some *a-priori* physiological information.

As we can see in Fig. 4, the tensor field seems well restored. The final result is closer to the original image, and does not suffer from eigenvalue swelling. Note that the restoration of tensor orientations was initially proposed in [9,10, 32] using similar continuous flows but different numerical integration methods.

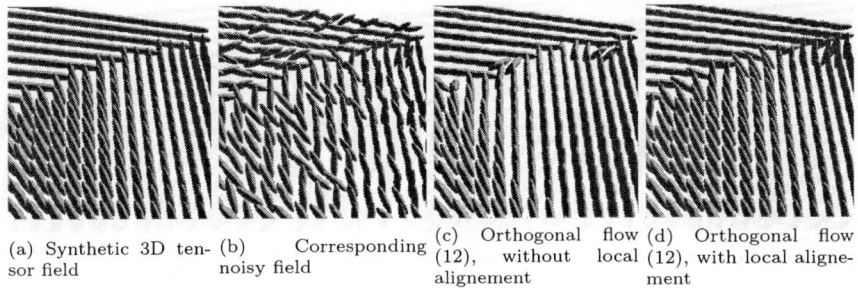

(a) Synthetic 3D tensor field.
(b) Corresponding noisy field.
(c) Orthogonal flow (12), without local alignement.
(d) Orthogonal flow (12), with local alignement.

Fig. 4. Orthogonal flow on a synthetic 3D tensor field.

2.4 Isospectral Flow

To avoid the eigenvector alignment step needed by the previous method (12), we propose here a simple way of regularizing directly tensor orientations. It consists in applying on the initial tensor field an *isospectral flow*, i.e. a regularizing flow that preserves the tensor diffusivities, while regularizing the tensor orientations.

Constraint preserving flow: We first consider the homogeneous space $M(Q) = \{H^T Q H, H \in O(n)\}$ of all the matrices orthogonally equivalent to a symmetric matrix Q. If all the values of X_0 had the same eigenvalues (the same as the matrix Q), we could model our configuration space as $\mathcal{F}(\Omega, M(Q))$. However, if we allow the eigenvalues of X_0 to vary spatially, we need to introduce a slightly more generic manifold $\mathcal{F}^{\text{iso}}_{X(0)}(\Omega) = \{H^T X(0) H, H \in \mathcal{F}(\Omega, O(n))\}$. From the expression of its tangent space $T_X \mathcal{F}^{\text{iso}}_{X(0)}(\Omega) = \{[X, A], A \in \mathcal{F}(\Omega, \mathfrak{so}(n))\}$ (the Lie brackets $[\cdot, \cdot]$ corresponds to the commutator $[A, B] = AB - BA$), the expected *isospectral* flows must satisfy

$$\frac{\partial X(t)}{\partial t} = [X, A(t)], \ A(t) \in \mathcal{F}(\Omega, \mathfrak{so}(n)).$$

Gradient flow: Given the L^2-gradient G on $\mathcal{F}(\Omega, \mathbb{R}^{n \times n})$ (defined by (10)), we show in [8] that a natural minimizing flow for f on $\mathcal{F}^{\text{iso}}_{X(0)}(\Omega)$ is defined by

$$\frac{\partial X}{\partial t} = [X, [X, -(G + G^T)]]. \qquad (14)$$

One can also obtain a suitable integration scheme for eq. (14), derived from the expression of the exponential map on the orthogonal group, and such that

$$\forall x \in \Omega, \ X_{(t+dt)}(x) = A_{(t)}(x)^T X_{(t)}(x) A_{(t)}(x), \text{ with}$$
$$A_{(t)}(x) = e^{-dt[G^T(x) + G(x), X_{(t)}(x)]}. \qquad (15)$$

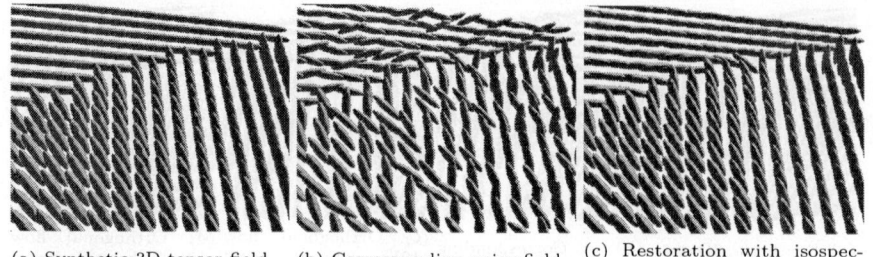

(a) Synthetic 3D tensor field. (b) Corresponding noisy field. (c) Restoration with isospectral flow (14).

Fig. 5. Isospectral flow on a synthetic 3×3 tensor field.

Experimental results: Equation (14) was applied to the usual noisy, synthetic tensor field. This experiment is illustrated in Fig. 5.

As expected, the results are similar to the ones obtained with the decomposition and the orthogonal constraints. However, the computation cost is significantly reduced (no local alignement steps are needed anymore for regularizing tensor orientations). The PDE (14) applies directly on the original matrix coefficients $X_{i,j}$.

3 Results on Real DT-MRI Datasets

We have tested the proposed diffusion tensor regularization PDE's (9), (12), (14), on a real $128 \times 128 \times 56$ DT-MRI dataset[5] of the brain (Fig. 6a,b). On the left side of each figure, we represent the tensors as ellipsoids, while the right side shows the corresponding fibers, tracked by following the main direction of each tensor. These fibers show the path followed by the water molecules. To make visualization easier, only one slice of the processed volume is represented. The computations have been carried out with a Pentium 1Ghz processor, 1Go RAM, and the corresponding computation times are given for the full volume restoration process. We noticed that the geodesic step approach allows time steps to be relatively high, and very few iterations are needed in practice. The ϕ-function used for these experiments is the "hypersurface" function, $\phi(s) = 2\sqrt{1 + s^2} - 2$ proposed in [7]. The results we obtained clearly illustrates the behavior of the different methods:

– The symmetric positive definite flow (9) tends to swell eigenvalues.
– The orthogonal constrained flow (12) works well with a local alignment step (Fig. 6e), but fails otherwise (Fig. 6d).
– The isospectral flow (14) has a quite similar behavior, but is more computationally efficient.

---

[5] The authors would like to thank J.-F. Mangin and J.-B. Poline (SHFJ-CEA) for providing us with the DT-MRI data (this work was partially supported by ARC MC2). We also thank R. Fournier for his visualization tool "TensView".

Even if the physiological validation of these results remains to be done, our methods seem to correct most artifacts (due to the image acquisition process) and retrieve the main global structures of the fiber network. It opens new perspectives to construct an accurate fiber map model of the brain.

Conclusion

In this paper, we proposed a geometric approach to construct general flows acting on constrained matrix-valued images. We also introduced numerical schemes that naturally fit into this framework thanks to the use of exponential maps. The efficiency and versatility of this setting has been illustrated with the problem of diffusion tensor regularization. Three different regularizing flows were introduced (symmetric positive definite, orthogonal, isospectral). Some of them generalize and extend previous works in this field. Numerical experiments show promising results even if, at this time, no physiological a-priori knowledge has been taken into account (for instance in the choice of a suitable ϕ-function). Future developments will include applications to other computer vision problems.

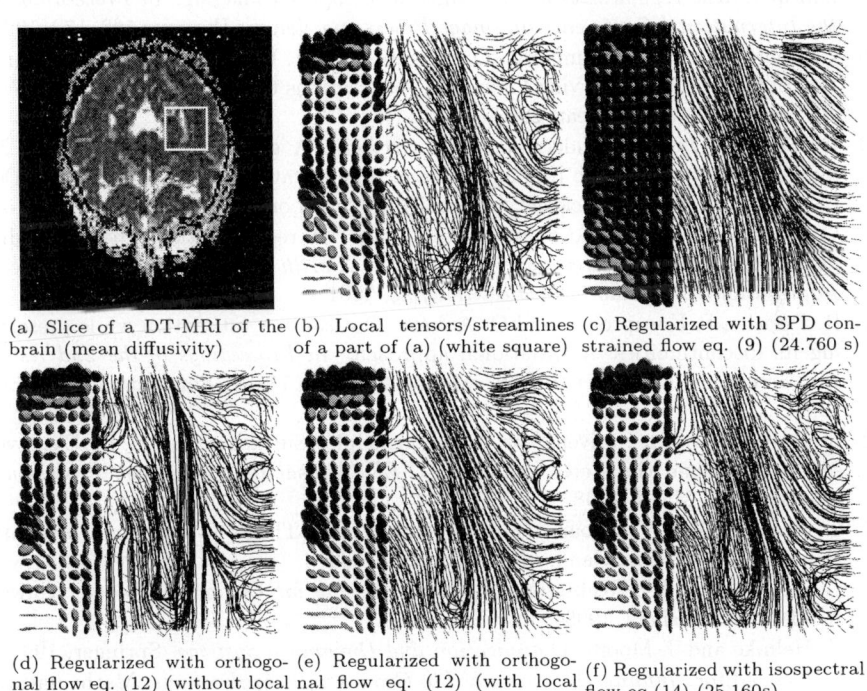

(a) Slice of a DT-MRI of the brain (mean diffusivity)
(b) Local tensors/streamlines of a part of (a) (white square)
(c) Regularized with SPD constrained flow eq. (9) (24.760 s)
(d) Regularized with orthogonal flow eq. (12) (without local alignment) (53.160s)
(e) Regularized with orthogonal flow eq. (12) (with local alignment) (1m21.360s)
(f) Regularized with isospectral flow eq.(14) (25.160s)

Fig. 6. Real diffusion tensor dataset (DT-MRI) regularization, using three different constrained methods (last numbers represent the computation time).

References

1. L. Alvarez, R. Deriche, J. Weickert, and J. Sánchez. Dense disparity map estimation respecting image discontinuities: A PDE and scale-space based approach. *International Journal of Visual Communication and Image Representation*, 2000.
2. Y. Amit. A nonlinear variational problem for image matching. *SIAM Journal on Scientific Computing*, 15(1), January 1994.
3. M. Bertalmio, L.T. Cheng, S. Osher, and G. Sapiro. Variational problems and partial differential equations on implicit surfaces: The framework and examples in image processing and pattern formation. *UCLA Research Report*, June 2000.
4. M. Bertalmio, G. Sapiro, V. Caselles, and C. Ballester. Image inpainting. In Kurt Akeley, editor, *Proceedings of the SIGGRAPH*, pages 417–424. ACM Press, ACM SIGGRAPH, Addison Wesley Longman, 2000.
5. T. Chan and J. Shen. Variational restoration of non-flat image features : Models and algorithms. *Research Report, Computational and applied mathematics, department of mathematics Los Angeles*, June 1999.
6. T. Chan and J. Shen. Mathematical models for local deterministic inpaintings. Technical Report 00-11, Department of Mathematics, UCLA, Los Angeles, March 2000.
7. P. Charbonnier, G. Aubert, M. Blanc-Féraud, and M. Barlaud. Two deterministic half-quadratic regularization algorithms for computed imaging. In *Proceedings of the International Conference on Image Processing*, volume II, pages 168–172, 1994.
8. C. Chefd'hotel, D. Tschumperlé, O. Faugeras and R. Deriche. Geometric Integration of Constraint Preserving Flows and Applications to Image Processing. *INRIA Research Report*, to appear, 2002.
9. O. Coulon, D.C. Alexander, and S.R. Arridge. A geometrical approach to 3d diffusion tensor magnetic resonance image regularisation. Technical Report, Department of Computer Science, University College London., 2001.
10. O. Coulon, D.C. Alexander, and S.R. Arridge. A regularization scheme for diffusion tensor magnetic resonance images. In *XVIIth International Conferenceon Information Processing in Medical Imaging*, 2001.
11. R. Deriche, P. Kornprobst, and G. Aubert. Optical flow estimation while preserving its discontinuities: A variational approach. In *Proceedings of the 2nd Asian Conference on Computer Vision*, volume 2, pages 71–80, Singapore, December 1995.
12. O. Faugeras and R. Keriven. Variational principles, surface evolution, PDE's, level set methods and the stereo problem. *IEEE Transactions on Image Processing*, 7(3):336–344, March 1998.
13. G. Golub and C. Van Loan. *Matrix computations*. The John Hopkins University Press, Baltimore, Maryland, second edition, 1989.
14. G. Granlund and H. Knutsson. *Signal Processing for Computer Vision*. Kluwer Academic Publishers, 1995.
15. U. Helmke and J. Moore. *Optimization and Dynamical Systems*. Springer, 1994.
16. V. Kac, editor. *Infinite Dimensional Lie Groups with Applications*. Mathematical Sciences Research Institute Publications 4. Springer, 1985.
17. R. Kimmel and N. Sochen. Orientation diffusion or how to comb a porcupine. Technical Report 2000-02, CIS, 2000. Accepted to special issue on PDEs in Image Processing, Computer Vision, and Computer Graphics, Journal of Visual Communication and Image Representation, 2000.

18. W. Klingenberg. *Riemannian Geometry.* de Gruyter Studies in Mathematics 1. Walter de Gruyter, 1982.
19. P. Kornprobst, R. Deriche, and G. Aubert. Nonlinear operators in image restoration. In *Proceedings of the International Conference on Computer Vision and Pattern Recognition,* pages 325–331, Puerto Rico, June 1997. IEEE Computer Society, IEEE.
20. S. Lang. *Differential Manifolds.* Springer, 1985.
21. D. Le Bihan. Methods and applications of diffusion MRI. In I.R. Young, editor, *Magnetic Resonance Imaging and Spectroscopy in Medicine and Biology.* John Wiley and Sons, 2000.
22. D. Mumford and J. Shah. Optimal approximations by piecewise smooth functions and associated variational problems. *Communications on Pure and Applied Mathematics,* 42:577–684, 1989.
23. P. Perona. Orientation diffusions. *IEEE Transactions on Image Processing,* 7(3):457–467, March 1998.
24. P. Perona and J. Malik. Scale-space and edge detection using anisotropic diffusion. *IEEE Transactions on Pattern Analysis and Machine Intelligence,* 12(7):629–639, July 1990.
25. L. Rudin, S. Osher, and E. Fatemi. Nonlinear total variation based noise removal algorithms. *Physica D,* 60:259–268, 1992.
26. G. Sapiro. *Geometric Partial Differential Equations and Image Analysis.* Cambridge University Press, 2001.
27. S. Smith. *Optimization Techniques on Riemannian Manifolds.* Hamiltonian and Gradient Flows, Algorithms and Control. American Mathematical Society, 1994, Fields Institute for Research in Mathematical Sciences, A. Bloch editor, 1994.
28. N. Sochen, R. Kimmel, and R. Malladi. A geometrical framework for low level vision. *IEEE Transaction on Image Processing, Special Issue on PDE based Image Processing,* 7(3):310–318, 1998.
29. B. Tang, G. Sapiro, and V. Caselles. Diffusion of general data on non-flat manifolds via harmonic maps theory : The direction diffusion case. *The International Journal of Computer Vision,* 36(2):149–161, February 2000.
30. A. Trouvé. Diffeomorphisms groups and pattern matching in image analysis. *International Journal of Computer Vision,* 28(3):213–21, 1998.
31. D. Tschumperlé and R. Deriche. Constrained and unconstrained PDE's for vector image restoration. In Ivar Austvoll, editor, *Proceedings of the 10th Scandinavian Conference on Image Analysis,* pages 153–160, Bergen, Norway, June 2001.
32. D. Tschumperlé and R. Deriche. Diffusion tensor regularization with constraints preservation. In *Proceedings of the IEEE Computer Society Conference on Computer Vision and Pattern Recognition,* Kauai Marriott, Hawaii, December 2001.
33. D. Tschumperlé and R. Deriche. Regularization of orthonormal vector sets using coupled PDE's. In *Proceedings of the 1st IEEE Workshop on Variational and Level Set Methods (VLSM'01),* July 2001.
34. B. Vemuri, Y. Chen, M. Rao, T. McGraw, T. Mareci, and Z. Wang. Fiber tract mapping from diffusion tensor MRI. In *Proceedings of the 1st IEEE Workshop on Variational and Level Set Methods in Computer Vision (VLSM'01),* July 2001.
35. J. Weickert. *Anisotropic Diffusion in Image Processing.* Teubner-Verlag, Stuttgart, 1998.
36. C.-F. Westin, S. Maier, B. Khidhir, P. Everett, F. Jolesz, and R. Kikinis. Image processing for diffusion tensor magnetic resonance imaging. In *Proceedings of the Second International Conference on Medical Image Computing and Computer-Assisted Intervention (MICCAI'99),* Springer-Verlag, 1999.

A Hierarchical Framework for Spectral Correspondence

Marco Carcassoni and Edwin R. Hancock

Department of Computer Science,
University of York, York YO1 5DD, UK.
{marco,erh}@cs.york.ac.uk

Abstract. The modal correspondence method of Shapiro and Brady aims to match point-sets by comparing the eigenvectors of a pairwise point proximity matrix. Although elegant by means of its matrix representation, the method is notoriously susceptible to differences in the relational structure of the point-sets under consideration. In this paper we demonstrate how the method can be rendered robust to structural differences by adopting a hierarchical approach. We place the modal matching problem in a probabilistic setting in which the correspondences between pairwise clusters can be used to constrain the individual point correspondences. To meet this goal we commence by describing an iterative method which can be applied to the point proximity matrix to identify the locations of pairwise modal clusters. Once we have assigned points to clusters, we compute within-cluster and between-cluster proximity matrices. The modal co-efficients for these two sets of proximity matrices are used to compute cluster correspondence and cluster-conditional point correspondence probabilities. A sensitivity study on synthetic point-sets reveals that the method is considerably more robust than the conventional method to clutter or point-set contamination.

1 Introduction

Eigendecomposition, or modal analysis, has proved to be an alluring yet elusive method for correspondence matching. Stated simply, the aim is to find the pattern of correspondence matches between two sets of objects using the eigenvectors of an adjacency matrix or an attribute proximity matrix. The problem has much in common with spectral graph theory [1] and has been extensively studied for both the abstract problem of graph-matching [17,16], and for point pattern matching [14,12,11]. In the case of graph-matching the adjacency matrix represents either the weighted or unweighted edges of the relational structure under study. For point pattern matching, the proximity matrix represents the pairwise distance relationships. The method may be implemented in a number of ways. The simplest of these is to minimize the distance between the modal co-efficients. A more sophisticated approach is to use a factorization method such as singular value decomposition to find the permutation matrix which minimizes the differences between the adjacency structures. Unfortunately, the method invariable fails when the sets of objects being matched are not of the same size due to structural differences. The reason for this is that the pattern of eigenvectors is unstable when structural differences are present.

There are several concrete examples in the pattern analysis literature. Turning our attention to graph-matching, Umeyama has an eigendecomposition method that recovers the permutation matrix that maximizes the correlation or overlap of the adjacency matrices for graphs of the same size [17]. This method uses a factorization method to find the permutation matrix that brings the two graphs into correspondence. Horaud and Sossa [5] have adopted a purely structural approach to the recognition of line-drawings. Their representation is based on the immanental polynomials for the Laplacian matrix of the line-connectivity graph. By comparing the coefficients of the polynomials, they are able to index into a large data-base of line-drawings. Of more direct relevance to this paper is the literature on point-pattern matching. Borrowing ideas from structural chemistry, Scott and Longuet-Higgins were among the first to use eigendecomposition methods for point correspondence analysis [12]. They showed how to recover correspondences via singular value decomposition on the point association matrix between different images. However, the method has a number of well documented problems relating to the small range of scale and angle differences for which it is effective. In an attempt to overcome these problems, Shapiro and Brady [14] have developed a method in which point sets are matched by comparing the eigenvectors of the point proximity matrix. Here the proximity matrix is constructed by computing the Gaussian weighted distance between points. Matching between different point-sets is effected by comparing the pattern of eigenvectors, or modal co-efficients, in different images. The method extends the range of angle and scale differences over which reliable correspondences can be recovered. However, the method fails for point sets of different sizes. In a recent paper [2] we have revisited the method of Shapiro and Brady. Our aim was to use the correspondence information delivered by the method to develop an EM algorithm for point-set alignment. For structurally intact point-sets subject to positional jitter, we showed that the performance of the Shapiro and Brady method could be improved using ideas from robust statistics to compute the proximity matrix and to compare the modal co-efficients. To overcome the difficulties encountered with point-sets of different size, an explicit alignment process was required.

The aim in this paper is to return to the Shapiro and Brady [14] method and to focus on how the method can be rendered robust to structural differences in the point-sets. We adopt a hierarchical approach. The method is based on the observation that the modes of the proximity matrix can be viewed as pairwise clusters. Moreover, the modal co-efficients represent the affinity of the raw points to the clusters. This idea has been exploited by several authors to develop powerful image segmentation [15] and grouping methods [13,8,6]. Sengupta and Boyer [13] have used property matrix spectra to characterise line-patterns. Various attribute representations are suggested and compared. Shokoufandeh, Dickinson and Siddiqi [16] have shown how graphs can be encoded using local topological spectra for shape recognition from large data-bases. Sarkar and Soundararajan [10] have shown how graph-spectral methods can be combined with cellular automata to learn grouping structure. Finally, a number of authors have used spectral methods to perform pairwise clustering on image data. Shi and Malik [15] use the second eigenvalue to segment images by performing an eigen-decomposition on a matrix of pairwise attribute differences using the iterative normalised cut method. Sarkar and Boyer [9] and Freeman and Perona [8] have developed matrix factorisation methods for line-grouping. In a recent paper, Weiss [18] has compared a number of matrix factorisation methods for matching and segmentation, and has commented on the way in which they compute the proximity matrix. His conclusion was that performance could be significantly improved if the matrix is correctly normalised. Inoue and Urahama [6] have shown how the sequential extraction of eigen-modes can be used to cluster pairwise pixel data as an alternative to computationally expensive methods, such as the mean-field annealing idea of Buhmann and Hoffman [4]. Rather than explicitly grouping the points prior to matching, here we aim to characterise the potential groupings in an implicit or probabilistic way and to exploit their arrangement to provide constraints on the pattern of correspondences.

Our approach is as follows. Each mode of the point-proximity matrix is taken to represent a potential grouping or cluster of points. For each group, we can compute a cluster centre point-position. While the pattern of modal co-efficients of the proximity matrix may be disturbed by structural differences in the pointsets, the centre-points of the groups or clusters may be more stable. Hence, we can use the cluster-centre proximity matrix to improve the correspondence process. Here we use an evidence combining method which is posed in a hierarchical framework. We compute the probability that pairs of points are in correspondence by developing a mixture model over the set of possible correspondences between the most significant groupings of points. In this way the cluster-centre correspondences, weight the point-correspondence probabilities. We discuss various alternative ways in which the correspondence process may be modelled using the modal co-efficients of the point and cluster centre proximity matrices. We compare these alternatives with both the Shapiro and Brady method and our previously reported method.

2   Point Correspondence

The modal approach to point correspondence introduced by Shapiro and Brady [14] commences by enumerating a point proximity matrix. This is a continuous or weighted counterpart of the graph adjacency matrix. Rather than setting the elements to unity or zero depending on whether or not there is a connecting edge between a pair of nodes, the elements of the proximity matrix are weights that reflect the strength of a pairwise adjacency relation. The weights of the proximity matrix are computed by taking a Gaussian function of the interpoint distances, Once the proximity matrix is to hand, then correspondences are located by computing its eigenvectors. The eigenvectors of the proximity matrix become the columns of a transformation matrix which operates on the original point identities. The rows of the transformation matrix represent the components of the original points in the directions of the eigenvectors. We can locate point correspondences by searching for rows of the transformation matrix which have maximal similarity.

Unfortunately there are two drawbacks with this modal method of correspondence. Firstly, there is no clear reason to use Gaussian weighting in favour of possible alternatives. Gaussian weighting may not be the most suitable choice to control the effects of pattern distortion due to point movement under measurement error or deformation under affine or perspective geometry. Secondly, the method proves fragile to structural differences introduced by the addition of clutter or point drop-out. In a recent paper we have addressed the first of these problems by using robust error kernels to compute the proximity matrix [2]. Here we focus on the second problem, and develop a hierarchical method matching point-sets.

In this section we review the existing work on the modal matching of point-sets, before detailing an improved method aimed at overcoming the problem of different point set size.

2.1 Shapiro and Brady

We are interested in finding the correspondences between two point-sets, a model point-set $\mathbf{z}$ and a data point-set $\mathbf{w}$. Each point in the image data set is represented by an position vector co-ordinates $\underline{w}_i = (x_i, y_i)^T$ where i is the point index. In the interests of brevity we will denote the entire set of image points by $\mathbf{w} = \{\underline{w}_i, \forall i \in \mathcal{D}\}$ where $\mathcal{D}$ is the point set. The corresponding fiducial points constituting the model are similarly represented by $\mathbf{z} = \{\underline{z}_j, \forall j \in \mathcal{M}\}$ where $\mathcal{M}$ denotes the index-set for the model feature-points $\underline{z}_j$.

The role of the weighting function used to compute the elements of the proximity matrix is to model the probability of adjacency relations between points. The standard way to represent the adjacency relations between points is to use the Gaussian proximity matrix. If i and i' are two data points, then the corresponding element of the proximity matrix is given by

$$H_D(i, i') = \exp\left[-\frac{1}{2s^2}||\underline{w}_i - \underline{w}_{i'}||^2\right] \quad (1)$$

The modal structure of the two point-sets is found by solving the eigenvalue equation $det[H - \lambda I] = 0$ together with the associated eigenvector equation $H\phi_l = \lambda_l \phi_l$, where λ_l is the lth eigenvalue of the matrix H and ϕ_l is the corresponding eigenvector. The vectors are ordered according to the magnitude of the associated eigenvalues. The ordered column-vectors are used to construct a modal matrix $\Phi = (\phi_1|\phi_2|\phi_3|.....)$. The column index of this matrix refers to the magnitude order of the eigenvalues while the row-index is the index of the original point-set. This modal decomposition is repeated for both the data and transformed model point-sets to give a data-point modal matrix $\Phi_D = (\phi_1^D|\phi_2^D|\phi_3^D|...|\phi_{|\mathcal{D}|}^D)$ and a model-point modal matrix $\Phi_M = (\phi_1^M|\phi_2^M|\phi_3^M|...|\phi_{|\mathcal{M}|}^M)$. Since the two point-sets are potentially of different size, the modes are truncated of the larger point-set. This corresponds to removing the last $||\mathcal{D}| - |\mathcal{M}||$ rows and columns of the larger matrix. The resulting matrix has $o = \min[\mathcal{D}, \mathcal{M}]$ rows and columns.

The modal matrices can be viewed as inducing a linear transformation on the original identities of the point-sets. Each row of the modal matrix represents one of the original points. The column entries in each row measure how the original point identities are distributed among the different eigen-modes.

Based on this eigendecomposition Shapiro and Brady [14] find correspondences by comparing the rows of the model matrices Φ_M and Φ_D. The decision concerning the correspondences is made on the basis of the similarity of different rows in the modal matrices for the data and the model. The measure of similarity is the Euclidean distance between the elements in the corresponding rows. According to Shapiro and Brady the correspondence probabilities are assigned according to the following binary decision

$$\zeta_{i,j}^{SB} = \begin{cases} 1 & \text{if } j = \arg\min_{j'} \sum_{l=1}^{o} ||\Phi_D(i,l) - \Phi_M(j',l)||^2 \\ 0 & \text{otherwise} \end{cases} \qquad (2)$$

The decision regarding the most likely correspondence can then be made on the basis of the maximum value of the probability.

2.2 Prior Work

In this section we briefly review our previous work aimed at improving the modal matching method. It must be stressed that the aim of this work was to compute correspondence probabilities for the purposes of point-set alignment using a variant of the EM algorithm. For point-sets of the same size which were not subject to contamination by clutter or dropout, we showed that the accuracy of correspondence matching could be improved by a) using a weighting function suggested by robust statistics to compute the point proximity matrix and b) comparing the modal co-efficients using a robust statistical procedure.

In Shapiro and Brady's original work the weighting function was the Gaussian [14]. Our first contribution has been to show that alternative weighting functions suggested by the robust statistics literature offer significant improvements [2].

According to robust statistics, there are some choices of possible weighting functions. In our previous work [2] we showed that the sigmoidal weighting function, generated by the hyperbolic tangent function

$$H_D(i,i') = \frac{2}{\pi ||\underline{w}_i - \underline{w}_{i'}||} \log \cosh \left[\frac{\pi}{s} ||\underline{w}_i - w_{i'}|| \right] \qquad (3)$$

gives improved performance under positional jitter.

The second contribution was to show that the method of assigning correspondences could be significantly improved if the elements of the modal matrix were compared using a robust statistical procedure. When there is a significant difference between one or more of the components of the eigenvectors, then these errors dominate the Euclidean distance measure used by Shapiro and Brady. One way to make the computation of correspondences robust to outlier measurement error is to accumulate probability on a component by component basis over the eigenvectors. To do this assume that the individual elements of the modal matrix are subject to Gaussian measurement errors and compute the correspondence probability using the formula

$$\zeta_{i,j}^{CH} = \frac{\sum_{l=1}^{o} \exp\left[-k||\Phi_D(i,l) - \Phi_M(j,l)||^2\right]}{\sum_{j' \in \mathcal{M}} \sum_{l=1}^{o} \exp\left[-k||\Phi_D(i,l) - \Phi_M(j',l)||^2\right]} \qquad (4)$$

where k is a constant. In this way large measurement errors contribute insignificantly through the individual exponentials appearing under the summation over the components of the eigenvectors.

These two refinements of Shapiro and Brady's method offer some improvements in terms of robustness to positional jitter and affine skew. However, when the point-sets under study are of different size, i.e. they are subject to structural corruption, then both methods fail. The reason for this is that the co-efficients of the modal matrices become unstable and can not be used for correspondence matching. Our aim in to this paper is to suggest a way of overcoming this problem.

3 Modal Clusters

Our aim if to pose the modal correspondence of point-sets in a hierarchical framework. We commence by locating the modal clusters of the point-sets under study. This is an iterative process which alternates between two steps. The first step involves computing the mean position vector for each mode of the proximity matrix. The second step involves computing a revised proximity matrix from the mean modal position vectors. Once this iterative process has converged, we select the mean position vectors associated with the most significant modes of the proximity matrix. These position-vectors are used to compute a modal-cluster proximity matrix. By using constraints provided by the modal correspondences of the cluster-centres, we aim to improve the correspondence matching of the raw point-sets. In this section, we describe how to perform the iterative modal clustering and how to compute the modal proximity matrix.

The coefficients of the modal matrix Φ can be viewed as providing information concerning pairwise clusters of points. Each mode, i.e. each column of the modal matrix Φ_D, is represented by an orthogonal vector in a $|\mathcal{D}|$ dimensional space. The columns associated with the eigenvalues of largest magnitude represent the most significant arrangements of points, while those associated with the eigenvalues of smallest magnitude represent insignificant structure. For a given point i the different modal co-efficients $\Phi(i,l), l = 1, ..., |\mathcal{D}|$ represent the affinity of the point to the different clusters. The larger the magnitude of the co-efficient, the greater the cluster affinity. In other words, the entries in the columns of the modal matrix represent the membership affinities for the different clusters. The row-entries, on the other hand represent the way in which the individual points are distributed among the different clusters. Here we aim to exploit this property of the modal matrix to develop a fast and robust matching method.

Our idea is based on the simple observation, that while the modal coefficients, i.e. the entries in the columns of the modal matrix, may not be stable under the addition of extra points, the physical centre of the associated cluster will be relatively robust to the addition of outliers.

3.1 Iterative Computation of the Modes

To locate the cluster-centres we adopt an iterative process. At each iteration, we use the modal co-efficients to compute a mean position vector for each eigen-mode. These modal-centres are then used to compute a revised proximity matrix. In their turn, the modal co-efficients for this revised proximity matrix are used to update the positions of the modal centres.

To this end we compute a mean position-vector for each eigen-mode. Let $\Phi_D^{(n)}$ be the modal matrix at iteration n. For the mode with eigenvalue λ_l, the position-vector for the cluster centre is

$$\underline{c}_l^{D\,(n)} = \frac{\sum_{i=1}^{|D|} |\Phi_D^{(n)}(i,l)| \underline{w}_i}{\sum_{i=1}^{|D|} \Phi_D^{(n)}(i,l)|} \tag{5}$$

Next, we compute the revised proximity matrix for the modal position vectors. The elements of the proximity matrix are again computed using the robust weighting kernel and are given by

$$H_D^{(n)}(l,l') = \frac{2}{\pi ||\underline{c}_l^{D\,(n)} - \underline{c}_{l'}^{D\,(n)}||} \log \cosh \left[\frac{\pi}{s} ||\underline{c}_l^{D\,(n)} - \underline{c}_{l'}^{D\,(n)}|| \right] \tag{6}$$

By solving the eigenvalue equation $det[H_D^{(n)} - \lambda^{(n)} I] = 0$ together with the associated eigenvector equation $H_D^{(n)} \phi_l^{(n)} = \lambda_l^{(n)} \phi_l^{(n)}$, we compute the updated a modal matrix $\Phi^{(n)} = (\phi_1^{(n)} | \phi_2^{(n)} | \phi_3^{(n)} | .....)$. This process is iterated until the modal position vectors stabilize. The final modal position vectors are noted by $\underline{c}_l^{D\,(\infty)}$ and the final modal co-efficient matrix by $\Phi_D^{(\infty)}$.

Once the pairwise clustering process has converged, then we can assign points to modal clusters. We represent the arrangement of points using both a set of within-cluster proximity matrices and a single between-cluster proximity matrixes. The modal structure of the between-cluster proximity matrix is used to compute the probabilities that individual cluster centres are in correspondence. The modal structure of the within-cluster proximity matrices are used to compute the probability that individual points within corresponding clusters match to one-another. Details of how the within-cluster and between-cluster modal structure is computed are outlined in the subsequent two subsections of the paper.

3.2 Within-Cluster Modal Matrices

When the iterative clustering process has converged, then the elements of the modal matrix can be used to assign points to clusters. We are interested in using the modal co-efficients and the cluster centre locations to compute the probability $P(i \in \omega_d)$ that the node i belongs to the cluster associated with mode ω_d of the original point-set. We use the co-efficients of the first S columns of the modal matrix $\Phi_D^{(\infty)}$ to compute the cluster membership probability. Here we assume that cluster membership probability is proportional to the magnitude of the entry in the row indexed i and column indexed ω_d of the modal matrix $\Phi_D^{(\infty)}$ and write

$$P(i \in \omega_d) = \Phi_D^*(i, \omega_d) = \frac{|\Phi_D^{(\infty)}(i, \omega_d)|}{\sum_{l=1}^{S} |\Phi_D^{(\infty)}(i, \omega_d)|} \quad (7)$$

For the points belonging to each cluster, we construct a within-cluster proximity matrix. To do this we first identify the points which belong to each modal cluster. This is done of the basis of the cluster-membership probabilities $P(i \in \omega_d)$. The set of points assigned to the cluster ω_D is $\mathcal{C}_{\omega_d}^D = \{i | P(i \in \omega_d) > T_c\}$ where T_c is a membership probability threshold. To construct this matrix we will need to relabel the points using a cluster point index which runs from 1 to $|\mathcal{C}_{\omega_d}|$. Accordingly we let δ_{i,ω_d}^D denote the point-index assigned to the node i in the cluster ω_d. The proximity matrix for the points belonging to this cluster is denoted by F_{ω_D} and the corresponding modal matrix is $\Theta_{\omega_d}^D$. The modal matrix for the cluster indexed ω_m in the model point-set is denoted by $\Theta_{\omega_m}^M$.

3.3 Between Cluster Modal Matrix

We also construct a between-cluster modal matrix to summarize the global structure or arrangement of the original point-set **w**. To do this we select the positions of the cluster-centres for the S largest eigenvalues, i.e. the first S columns of $\Phi_D^{(\infty)}$. There are a number of ways of choosing S. Here we set the value of S so that the co-efficients of the subsequent columns of $\Phi_D^{(\infty)}$ are insignificant. If T is a threshold, then the condition is that $|\Phi_D^{(\infty)}(i, l)| < T$ for $i = 1, ..., |\mathcal{D}|$ and $l > S$. Our idea is to use the modes of the $S \times S$ cluster-centre proximity matrix G_D for the purposes of matching. Accordingly, we solve the equation $det(G_D - \Lambda^D I) = 0$ to locate the eigenvalues of the modal cluster-centre proximity matrix. The eigenvectors ψ_L, $L = 1, .., S$ of the cluster-centre proximity matrix are found by solving the equation $G_D \psi_l^D = \Lambda_l^D \psi_l^D$ As before, these eigenvectors can be used to construct a modal-matrix for the cluster centre positions. The matrix has the eigenvectors of G as columns, i.e. $\Psi_D = \left(\psi_1^D | \psi_2^D | ..... \psi_S^D\right)$

This procedure is repeated to construct a second $S \times S$ cluster-centre modal matrix Ψ_M for the set of model points **z**. Since the principal modal-clusters are selected on the magnitude-order of the associated eigenvalues, there is no need to re-order them.

4 Matching

The aim in this paper is to explore whether the additional information provided by the modal clusters can be used to improve the robustness of the matching process to point addition and dropout. We would like to compute the probability $P(i \leftrightarrow j)$, that the data-point $i \in \mathcal{D}$ is in correspondence with the model data-point $j \in \mathcal{M}$. To do this we construct a mixture model over the set of possible correspondences between the set of S modal clusters extracted from the data point positions and the model point positions. Suppose that ω_d and ω_m respectively represent labels assigned to the modal clusters of the data and model point-sets. Applying the Bayes formula, we can write

$$P(i \leftrightarrow j) = \sum_{\omega_d=1}^{S} \sum_{\omega_m=1}^{S} P(i \leftrightarrow j | \omega_d \leftrightarrow \omega_m) P(\omega_d \leftrightarrow \omega_m) \qquad (8)$$

where $P(i \leftrightarrow j | \omega_d \leftrightarrow \omega_m)$ represents the cluster-conditional probability that the node i belonging to the data-graph cluster ω_d is in correspondence with the node j that belongs to the model-graph cluster ω_m. The quantity $P(\omega_d \leftrightarrow \omega_m)$ denotes the probability that the data point-set cluster indexed ω_d is in correspondence with the model point-set cluster indexed ω_m.

4.1 Cluster Conditional Correspondence Probabilities

To compute the cluster-conditional point correspondence probabilities we use the modal structure of the within-cluster proximity matrices. These correspondence probabilities are computed using the method outlined in Equation (4). As a result, we write

$$P(i \leftrightarrow j | \omega_d \leftrightarrow \omega_m) = \qquad (9)$$

$$= \frac{\sum_{l=1}^{O_{\omega_d,\omega_m}} \exp\left[-k_w \|\Theta_{\omega_d}^D(\delta_{i,\omega_d}^D, l) - \Theta_{\omega_m}^M(\delta_{j\omega_m}^D, l)\|^2\right]}{\sum_{j' \in \mathcal{M}} \sum_{l=1}^{O_{\omega_d,\omega_m}} \exp\left[-k_w \|\Theta_{\omega_d}^D(\delta_{i,\omega_d}^D, l) - \Theta_{\omega_m}^M(\delta_{j',\omega_m}^M, l)\|^2\right]}$$

where $O_{\omega_d,\omega_m} = \min[|\mathcal{C}_{\omega_m}|, |\mathcal{C}_{\omega_d}|]$ is the size of the smaller cluster.

4.2 Cluster Correspondence Probabilities

We have investigated two methods for computing the cluster correspondence probabilities $P(\omega_d \leftrightarrow \omega_m)$:

- **Modal eigenvalues:** The first method used to compute the cluster-centre correspondence probabilities relies on the similarity of the normalized eigenvalues of the cluster-centre modal matrix. The probabilities are computed in the following manner

$$P(\omega_d \leftrightarrow \omega_m) = \qquad (10)$$

$$\frac{\exp\left[-k_e \left\{\frac{|A_{\omega_d}^D|}{\sum_{\omega_d=1}^{S} |A_{\omega_d}^D|} - \frac{|A_{\omega_m}^M|}{\sum_{\omega_m=1}^{S} |A_{\omega_m}^M|}\right\}^2\right]}{\sum_{\omega_m=1}^{S} \exp\left[-k_e \left\{\frac{|A_{\omega_d}^D|}{\sum_{\omega_d=1}^{S} |A_{\omega_d}^D|} - \frac{|A_{\omega_m}^M|}{\sum_{\omega_m=1}^{S} |A_{\omega_m}^M|}\right\}^2\right]}$$

- **Modal co-efficients:** The mode correspondence probabilities have also been computed by performing a robust comparison of the co-efficients of the modal matrices of the cluster-centre proximity matrix. This is simply an application of the method outlined in Equation (4) to the modal co-efficients of the between-cluster proximity matrix. We therefore set

$$P(\omega_d \leftrightarrow \omega_m) = \frac{\sum_{L=1}^{S} \exp\left[-k_b ||\Psi_D(\omega_d, L)| - |\Psi_M(\omega_m, L)||^2\right]}{\sum_{\omega_m=1}^{S} \sum_{L=1}^{S} \exp\left[-k_b ||\Psi_D(\omega_d, L)| - |\Psi_M(\omega_m, L)||^2\right]} \quad (11)$$

Note that we no-longer have to truncate the number of modes of the larger point-set since we have chosen only the S principal clusters from both the model and data.

4.3 Correspondence Probabilities

Using these models for the within and between-cluster modal co-efficients we develop two models for the correspondence probabilities appearing in Equation (10):

- Modal co-efficients

$$P(i \leftrightarrow j) = \sum_{\omega_d=1}^{S} \sum_{\omega_m=1}^{S} \quad (12)$$

$$\frac{\sum_{l=1}^{O_{\omega_d,\omega_m}} \exp\left[-k_w ||\Theta_{\omega_d}^D(\delta_{i,\omega_d}^D, l) - \Theta_{\omega_m}^M(\delta_{j\omega_m}^D, l)||^2\right]}{\sum_{j' \in \mathcal{M}} \sum_{l=1}^{O_{\omega_d,\omega_m}} \exp\left[-k_w ||\Theta_{\omega_d}^D(\delta_{i,\omega_d}^D, l) - \Theta_{\omega_m}^M(\delta_{j',\omega_m}^M, l)||^2\right]}$$

$$\frac{\sum_{L=1}^{S} \exp\left[-k_b ||\Psi_D(\omega_d, L)| - |\Psi_M(\omega_m, L)||^2\right]}{\sum_{\omega_m=1}^{S} \sum_{L=1}^{S} \exp\left[-k_b ||\Psi_D(\omega_d, L)| - |\Psi_M(\omega_m, L)||^2\right]}$$

According to this formula, the correspondence match between the points i and j receives support if they belong to clusters which have a high probability of modal correspondence.

- Using eigenvectors and eigenvalues

$$P(i \leftrightarrow j) = \sum_{\omega_d=1}^{S} \sum_{\omega_m=1}^{S} \quad (13)$$

$$\frac{\sum_{l=1}^{O_{\omega_d,\omega_m}} \exp\left[-k_w ||\Theta_{\omega_d}^D(\delta_{i,\omega_d}^D, l) - \Theta_{\omega_m}^M(\delta_{j\omega_m}^D, l)||^2\right]}{\sum_{j' \in \mathcal{M}} \sum_{l=1}^{O_{\omega_d,\omega_m}} \exp\left[-k_w ||\Theta_{\omega_d}^D(\delta_{i,\omega_d}^D, l) - \Theta_{\omega_m}^M(\delta_{j',\omega_m}^M, l)||^2\right]}$$

$$\frac{\sum_{L=1}^{S} \exp\left[-k_b ||\Psi_D(\omega_d, L)| - |\Psi_M(\omega_m, L)||^2\right]}{\sum_{\omega_m=1}^{S} \sum_{L=1}^{S} \exp\left[-k_b ||\Psi_D(\omega_d, L)| - |\Psi_M(\omega_m, L)||^2\right]}$$

$$\frac{\exp\left[-k_e \left\{ \frac{|\Lambda_{\omega_d}^D|}{\sum_{\omega_d=1}^{S} |\Lambda_{\omega_d}^D|} - \frac{|\Lambda_{\omega_m}^M|}{\sum_{\omega_m=1}^{S} |\Lambda_{\omega_m}^M|} \right\}^2\right]}{\sum_{\omega_m=1}^{S} \exp\left[-k_e \left\{ \frac{|\Lambda_{\omega_d}^D|}{\sum_{\omega_d=1}^{S} |\Lambda_{\omega_d}^D|} - \frac{|\Lambda_{\omega_m}^M|}{\sum_{\omega_m=1}^{S} |\Lambda_{\omega_m}^M|} \right\}^2\right]}$$

4.4 Parameters

There are a number of parameters which need to be controlled in our correspondence matching method. The first of these are the widths s of the error kernels used to compute the proximity matrices for the original points, the individual clusters and the cluster-centres. In each case, we have found that the best method is to set s to be equal to the median interpoint distance. There are three exponential constants k_e, k_b and k_w which must be set for the correspondence probability computations. Here we set all three constants to 0.1.

5 Experiments

In this section we describe our experimental evaluation of the new modal correspondence method. This is divided into two parts. We commence with a sensitivity study on synthetic data. This is aimed at measuring the effectiveness of the method when the point sets under study are subject to clutter and positional jitter. The second part of the study focuses on real world data. Here we investigate the method when applied to finding point correspondences between curvature features in gesture sequences.

5.1 Sensitivity Study

In our sensitivity study, we have compared the new correspondence method with those of Shapiro and Brady [14] and our previous work [2]. The Shapiro and Brady method is based purely on modal correspondence analysis, while the our previous method uses modal correspondence probabilities to weight the estimation of affine alignment parameters in a dual-step EM algorithm.

Our sensitivity study uses randomly generated point-sets. We ensure that the point-sets have a clump structure by sampling the point positions from six partially overlapping Gaussian distributions with controlled variance. We have then added both new points at random positions, and, random point-jitter to the synthetic data. The randomly inserted points have been sampled from a uniform distribution. The positional jitter has been generated by displacing the points from their original positions by Gaussian measurement errors. The displacements have been randomly sampled from a circularly symmetric Gaussian distribution of zero mean and controlled standard deviation.

In Figure 1 we show the effect of increasing the number of randomly added points. In this experiment, we commence with a point-set of size 100. The plot shows the fraction of points correctly matched as a function of the number of randomly added points. The long-dashed curve, i.e. the one with gives the consistently lowest results, is the result of applying the Shapiro and Brady algorithm. Here the fraction of correct correspondences falls below 25% once the fraction of added clutter exceeds 2%. The dual-step EM used in our previous work which finds correspondences by explicitly aligning the points, is shown as a dot-dashed curve and performs best of all when the level of clutter is less than 20%. The remaining two curves show the results obtained with the two variants of our hierarchical correspondence algorithm detailed in Section 4.3. In the case of the dotted curve the cluster correspondences are computed using only the modal co-efficients of the between-cluster proximity matrix as described in Equation (12). The solid curve shows the results obtained if the eigenvalues are also used as described in Equation (13). There is little to distinguish the two methods. Both perform rather more poorly than the dual-step EM algorithm when the level of clutter is less than 20%. However, for larger clutter levels, they provide significantly better performance. The additional use of the eigenvlaues results in a slight improvement in performance.

Figure 2 investigates the effect of positional jitter. Here we plot the fraction of correct correspondence matches as a function of the standard deviation of the Gaussian position error added to the point-positions. We report the level of jitter using the ratio of the standard deviation of the Gaussian error distribution to the average closest inter-point distance. Here there is nothing to distinguish the behaviour of our hierarchical correspondence method from the dual-step alignment method. In each case the fraction of correct correspondences degrades slowly with increasing point-position jitter. However, even when the standard deviation of the position errors is 50% of the average minimum interpoint-distance then the fraction of correct correspondences is still greater than 50%. By contrast, the accuracy of the Shapiro and Brady method falls below 50% once the standard deviation of the positional error exceeds 10% of the minimum interpoint distance.

Our final set of experiments on synthetic data investigate the effect of diluting the cluster-structure of the point-sets. Here we have gradually moved the cluster-centres closer together and have investigated the effect on the fraction of correct correspondences when there is structural error present. The results are shown in figure 3. Here we represent the fraction of correct correspondences as a function of the overlap between the clusters. We have also included tests to show the performance of the algorithm when a 20% of clutter noise is added to the overlapping. The solid curve and the dashed curve respectively show the results obtained with the new method reported in this paper and the Shapiro and Brady method when the point-sets contain no clutter. The performance of the Shapiro and Brady method is poorer than the new method. Its sudden drop-off in performance is attributable to the effect of increased point-density as the clusters are overlapped. The dotted curve shows the result obtained with our new method when we match to the point-set with 20% clutter. Obviously the performance of the method is poorer than that obtained with the unclut-

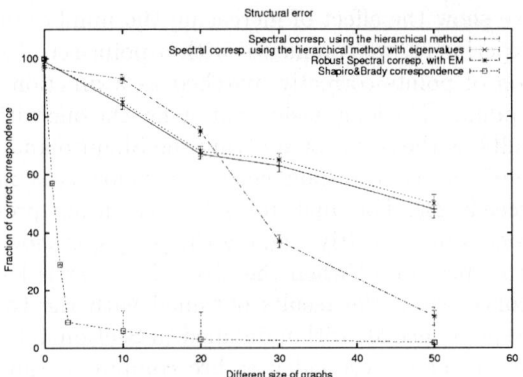

Fig. 1. Experimental results: structural error

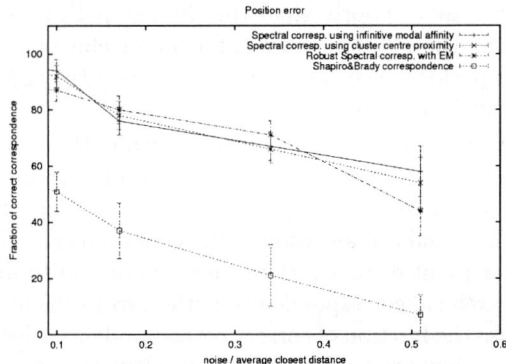

Fig. 2. Experimental results: position error

tered point-set. However, increased proximity of the clusters does not appear to significantly degrade performance.

5.2 Real World Data

In this section we provide some experiments with real world data. Our first experiment involves images from a gesture sequence of a hand. The images used in this study are shown in Figure 4. We commence by running the Canny edge detector over the images to locate the boundary of the hand. From this edge data, point features have been detected using the corner detector of Mokhtarian and Suomela [7]. The raw points returned by this method are distributed relatively uniformly along the outer edge of the hand and are hence not suitable for cluster analysis. We have therefore pruned the feature points using a curvature criterion. We have removed all points for which the curvature of the outline is smaller than a heuristically set threshold. Initially there are some 800 feature points, but after pruning this number is reduced to 271. The pruned feature-points are shown in

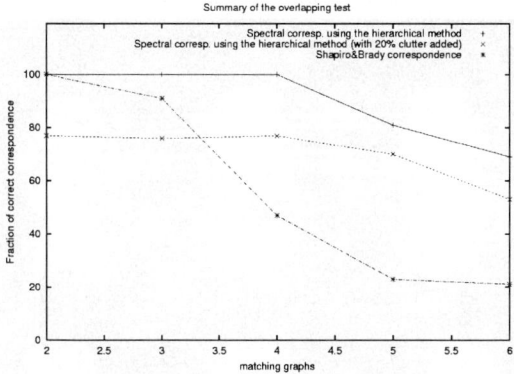

Fig. 3. Experimental results: final diagram for test on the cluster stability

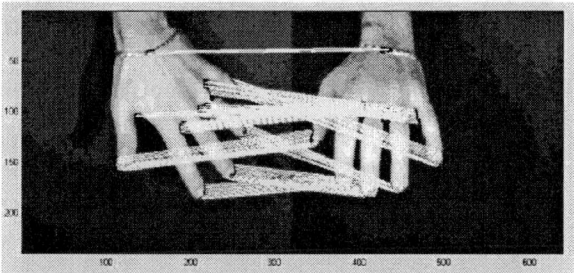

Fig. 4. Experimental results: real data experimentation

blue in the figure. They are clustered around the finger-tips and the points at which the fingers join the hand. After applying the clustering method, the set of centres shown in red is obtained. There are ten clusters in both images. The yellow lines between the two images show the detected correspondences. The fraction of correct correspondences is 81.2%.

Our second real world experiment involves a sequence of images obtained as a subject rotates and tilts their human head. The feature points here are highly non-planar. In Figure 5 we show the correspondences obtained. These are again good, and their appear to be no systematic problems.

A final example is shown in Figure 6 where we show the results obtained on an image pair from the roof-space of our lab. Here the correspondences are good despite the fact that there is no clear cluster-structure.

6 Conclusions

In this paper we have shown how constraints provided by the arrangement of modal groups of points can be used to improve the correspondence method of Shapiro and Brady [14]. The idea has been to use the modal co-efficients

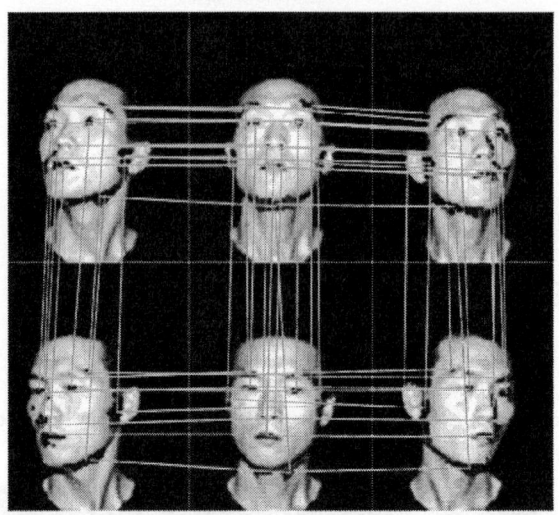

Fig. 5. Experimental results: real data experimentation

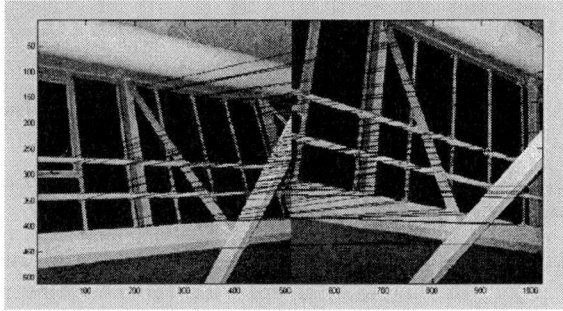

Fig. 6. Experimental results: real data experimentation

of the point-proximity matrix to establish the whereabouts of significant point groupings. We exploit these grouping to develop a hierarchical correspondence method. This is a two-step process. First, we use the spatial arrangements of the centre-points of the most significant groups to compute a between-cluster proximity matrix. The modal co-efficients of this between-cluster proximity matrix are used to establish correspondence probabilities between groups of points. Second, for each group of points we compute a within-cluster proximity matrix. The modal co-efficients of these within-cluster proxmity matrices are used to establish cluster-conditional point correspondence probabilities. Using the Bayes rule we combine these two sets of probabilities to compute individual point correspondence probabilities.

We have shown that while the Shapiro and Brady method fails once more than a few percent of clutter is added, the new method degrades more gracefully.

There are a number of ways in which the method described in this paper could be extended. One of the most important of these is to extend the method to line-pattern matching.

References

1. F.R.K. Chung, *Spectral Graph Theory*, CBMS series **92**, AMS Ed., 1997.
2. M.Carcassoni and E.R.Hancock , " Point Pattern Matching with Robust Spectral Correspondence ", *IEEE Computer Society Conference on Computer Vision and Pattern Recognition, IEEE Computer Society Press*, **I**, pp. 649-655 , 2000.
3. A.P. Dempster, Laird N.M. and Rubin D.B., "Maximum-likelihood from incomplete data via the EM algorithm", *J. Royal Statistical Soc. Ser. B (methodological)*, **39**, pp. 1-38, 1977.
4. T. Hofmann and J.M. Buhmann, "Pairwise Data Clustering by Deterministic Annealing", PAMI(19), No. 1, January 1997, pp. 1-14.
5. R. Horaud and H. Sossa, "Polyhedral Object Recognition by Indexing", *Pattern Recognition*, **28**, pp. 1855-1870, 1995.
6. K.Inoue and K. Urahama, "Sequential fuzzy cluster extraction by a graph spectral method", *Pattern Recognition Letters*, **20**, pp. 699-705, 1999.
7. F. Mokhtarian and R. Suomela, "Robust Image Corner Detection Through Curvature Scale Space", *IEEE PAMI*, **20**:12, pp. 1376–1381, December 1998.
8. P Perona and W Freeman, "A Factorisation Approach to Grouping", ECCV 98, Vol 1, pp 655-670, 1998.
9. S. Sarkar and K.L. Boyer, K.L., "Quantitative Measures of Change Based on Feature Organization: Eigenvalues and Eigenvectors", CVIU(71), No. 1, July 1998, pp. 110-136.
10. S. Sarkar and P. Soundararajan, "Supervised Learning of Large Perceptual Organization: Graph Spectral Partitioning and Learning Automata", PAMI(22), No. 5, May 2000, pp. 504-525.
11. S. Sclaroff and A. Pentland, "Modal Matching for Correspondence and Recognition", *IEEE PAMI*, **17**:6, pp. 545–561, 1995.
12. G.L. Scott and H.C. Longuet-Higgins, "An algorithm for associating the features of 2 images", *Proceedings of the Royal Society of London Series B (Biological)*, **244**, pp. 21–26, 1991.
13. K. Sengupta and K.L.Boyer, "Modelbase partitioning using property matrix spectra", *Computer Vision and Image Understanding*, **70**:2, pp. 177-196, 1998.
14. L.S. Shapiro and J.M. Brady, "Feature-based correspondence - an eigenvector approach", *Image and Vision Computing*, **10**, pp. 283–288, 1992.
15. J. Shi and J.Malik, "Normalized cuts and image segmentation", *Proc. of the IEEE Conf. on Computer Vision and Pattern Recognition*, 1997.
16. A. Shokoufandeh, S.J. Dickinson, K. Siddiqi and S.W. Zucker, "Indexing using a spectral encoding of topological structure", *Proc. of the IEEE Conf. on Computer Vision and Pattern Recognition*, pp.491-497, 1999.
17. S. Umeyama, "An eigen decomposition approach to weighted graph matching problems", *IEEE PAMI*, **10**, pp. 695–703, 1988.
18. Y. Weiss, "Segmentation using Eigenvectors: A Unifying View", International Conference on Computer Vision, pp. 975-982, 1999.

Phase-Based Local Features

Gustavo Carneiro and Allan D. Jepson

Department of Computer Science
University of Toronto
{carneiro,jepson}@cs.toronto.edu

Abstract. We introduce a new type of local feature based on the phase and amplitude responses of complex-valued steerable filters. The design of this local feature is motivated by a desire to obtain feature vectors which are semi-invariant under common image deformations, yet distinctive enough to provide useful identity information. A recent proposal for such local features involves combining differential invariants to particular image deformations, such as rotation. Our approach differs in that we consider a wider class of image deformations, including the addition of noise, along with both global and local brightness variations. We use steerable filters to make the feature robust to rotation. And we exploit the fact that phase data is often locally stable with respect to scale changes, noise, and common brightness changes. We provide empirical results comparing our local feature with one based on differential invariants. The results show that our phase-based local feature leads to better performance when dealing with common illumination changes and 2-D rotation, while giving comparable effects in terms of scale changes.

Keywords. Image features, Object recognition, Vision systems engineering and evaluation, Invariant local features, Local phase information.

1 Introduction

View-based object recognition has recently received a great deal of attention in the vision literature. In this paper we are particularly interested in approaches based on local features (e.g. differential invariants in [20], and local scale-invariant features in [13]). These approaches have demonstrated their unique robustness to clutter and partial occlusion, while keeping the flexibility and ease of training provided by classical view-based approaches (see [15,22]). However, to be successful for object recognition, local features must have the two properties: 1) be robust to typical image deformations; and 2) be highly distinctive to afford identity information.

We propose a novel local feature vector that is based on the phase and amplitude responses of complex-valued steerable filters. This builds on previous work [3] in which it was shown that the phase information provided by such filters is often locally stable with respect to scale changes, noise, and common brightness changes. Here we show it is also possible to achieve stability under rotation by selecting steerable filters.

The results of an empirical study described here show that the phase-based local feature performs better than local differential invariants for common illumination changes and 2-D rotation, while giving similar results for scale changes of up to 20%. We are currently investigating the use of brightness renormalization for the local differential invariants, as in [19], in order to reduce the brightness sensitivity of the differential invariant approach and provide a fairer comparison.

1.1 Previous Work

The use of local features is usually associated with the object recognition task. Currently, object recognition methods are of three types, namely: 1) systems that match geometric features, 2) systems that match luminance data, and 3) systems that match robustly detectable, informative, and relatively sparse local features. The first type of system, namely those that utilize geometric features (see [2,6,9,12]), are successful in some restricted areas, but the need of user-input models makes the representation of some objects, such as paintings or jackets, extremely hard. View-based methods (see [11,15,22]) have avoided this problem since they are capable of learning the object appearance without a user-input model. However they suffer from difficulties such as: 1) illumination changes are hard to be dealt with; 2) pose and position dependence; and 3) partial occlusion and clutter can damage the system performance (but see [1,11]).

The third type of object recognition method is based on local image descriptors extracted from robustly detectable image locations. Systems that are based on this method show promising results mainly because they solve most of the problems in the view-based methods, such as illumination changes, clutter, occlusion, and segmentation, while keeping most of their improvements in terms of flexibility and simplified model acquisition. Rao and Ballard [17] explore the use of local features for recognizing human faces. The authors use principal component analysis (PCA) to reduce the dimensionality of *localized natural image patches* at *multiple scales* rather than PCA of entire images at a single scale. In [16], Nelson presented a technique to automatically extract a geometric description of an object by detecting semi-invariants at localized points. A new concept was presented by Schmid and Mohr [20], where, instead of using geometric features, the authors use a set of differential invariants extracted from interest points. In [13,14] Lowe presents a novel method based on local scale-invariant features detected at interest points.

2 Image Deformations Studied

The image deformations considered here are: a) uniform brightness changes, b) non-uniform local brightness variations, c) noise addition, d) scale changes, and e) rotation changes. The uniform brightness change is simulated by adding a constant to the brightness value taking into account the non-linearity of the brightness visual perception, as follows:

$$I_h(\boldsymbol{x}) = 255 * \left[\max\left(0, \left(\frac{I(\boldsymbol{x})}{255}\right)^\lambda + k\right)\right]^{\frac{1}{\lambda}}, \qquad (1)$$

 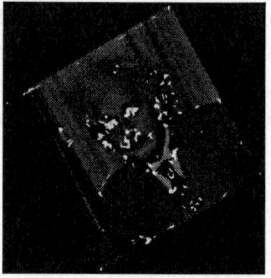

Fig. 1. Typical interest points detected on an image (brighter spots on the image). The right image shows the original points and the left one depicts the interest points detected after a 30°-degree rotation.

where $\lambda = 2.2$, and k is the constant the alters the final brightness value. The resulting image is linearly mapped to values between 0 and 255, and then quantized.

For the non-uniform local brightness variations, a highlight at a specific location of the image is simulated by adding a Gaussian blob in the following way:

$$I_h(\boldsymbol{x}) = I(\boldsymbol{x}) + 255 * G(\boldsymbol{x} - \boldsymbol{x}_0; \sigma), \qquad (2)$$

where $\sigma = 10$, $\boldsymbol{x}_0$ is a specific position in the image, and $G(\boldsymbol{x}; \sigma) = \exp\left(-x^2/(2\sigma^2)\right)$. Again, the resulting image is mapped to values between 0 and 255, and then quantized.

For noise deformations, we simply add Gaussian noise with varying standard deviation ($\sigma = 255 * [10^{-3}, 10^{-1}]$), followed by normalization and quantization, as above. The last two deformations involve spatial image warps. In particular, we consider 2D rotations (from $0°$ to $180°$ in intervals of $30°$) and uniform scale changes (with expansion factors in the range $[0.63, 1.58]$). Every image used in these deformation experiments is blurred, down-sampled and mapped to values between 0 and 255 in order to reduce high frequency artifacts caused by noise.

3 Interest Points

In the literature, view-based recognition from local information always relies on interest points, which represent specific places in an image that carry distinctive features of the object being studied. For example, in [13], interest points are represented by local extrema, with respect to both image location and scale, in the responses of difference of filters. Alternatively, a detector that uses the auto-correlation function in order to determine locations where the signal changes in two directions is used in [20]. A symmetry based operator is utilized in [10] to detect local interest points for the problem of scene and landmark recognition. In [16], a contour detection is run on the image, and points of high curvature around the shape are selected as interest points.

Fig. 2. The four images used for testing interest point detection. The right three images are also used for evaluating the local feature vectors.

Here we consider the Harris corner detector (see [7]) used in [20], where a matrix that averages the first derivatives of the signal in a window is built as follows:

$$\mathbf{C}(\boldsymbol{x}) = \exp{-\frac{x^2+y^2}{2\sigma^2}} \otimes \begin{bmatrix} I_x^2 & I_x I_y \\ I_x I_y & I_y^2 \end{bmatrix}, \quad (3)$$

where $\sigma = 2.0$, and $\otimes$ is the convolution operation. Here $I_x = G_x \otimes I$, where G_x is the x-derivative of a Gaussian with standard deviation 1, and similarly for I_y. The eigenvectors of this matrix encodes edge directions, while the eigenvalues, $\lambda_1(\boldsymbol{x})$ and $\lambda_2(\boldsymbol{x})$, represent edge strength. Corners, or interest points, can then be defined as locations at which $\lambda_1(\boldsymbol{x}) \geq \lambda_2(\boldsymbol{x}) \geq t$, where t is a threshold. Given the fact that the threshold function described in [7] does not produce a value between 0 and 1, we have found the following function to provide a more convenient threshold criterion:

$$R(\boldsymbol{x}) = \frac{\lambda_2(\boldsymbol{x})}{c + (1/2) * (\lambda_1(\boldsymbol{x}) + \lambda_2(\boldsymbol{x}))}, \quad (4)$$

where c is set based on the histogram of $R(\boldsymbol{x})$ of various types of images. Here, we select $c = 1$, and every point that has $R(\boldsymbol{x}) \geq 0.5$ is considered an interest point. Fig. 1 shows the corners detected for the Einstein image.

Two measures are computed to assess the performance of the interest point detector, namely the true positive rate and reliability. Given a point $\boldsymbol{x}_i$ in the original image space, and an image deformation specified by a matrix M and a translation vector $\boldsymbol{b}$, the transformed image location is

$$\boldsymbol{x}_j = M\boldsymbol{x}_i + \boldsymbol{b}. \quad (5)$$

Let us consider the set of interest points detected in an image I_i:

$$In(I_i) = \{\boldsymbol{x}_i | R(\boldsymbol{x}_i) \geq 0.5\}, \quad (6)$$

where $\boldsymbol{x}_i \in I_i$.

The true positive (TP_{rate}) rate of interest point detection, between the original image I_i and the transformed image I_j, is based on the following measure:

$$TP_{rate} = \frac{|\{\boldsymbol{x}_i | \exists \boldsymbol{x}_j \, s.t. ||M\boldsymbol{x}_i + \boldsymbol{b} - \boldsymbol{x}_j|| < \epsilon\}|}{|In(I_i)|}. \quad (7)$$

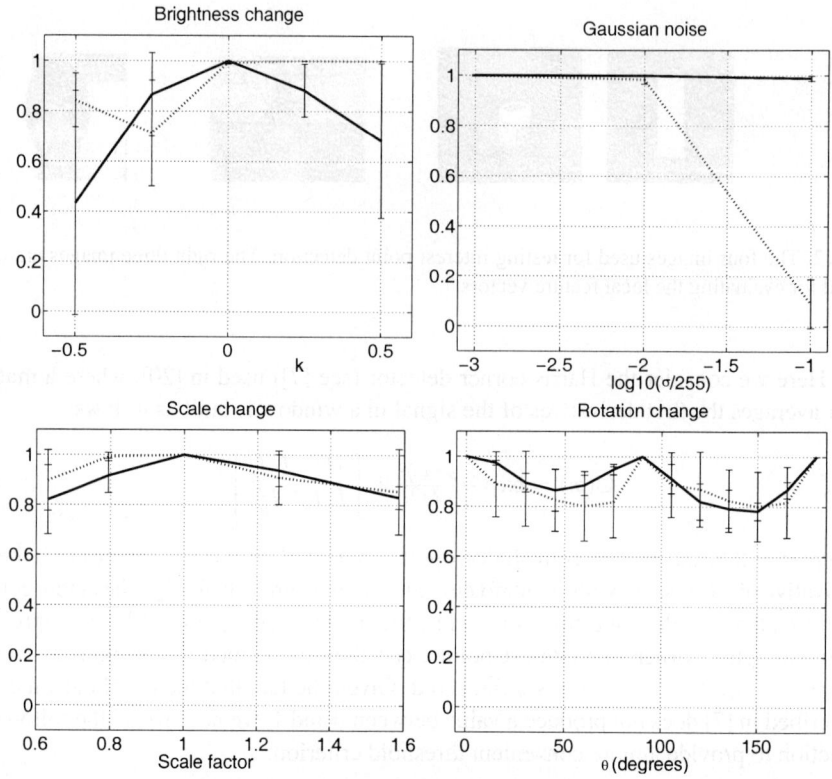

Fig. 3. Interest point repeatability. The graphs show the true positive (solid line) and reliability (dotted line) rates for the four types of image distortion.

where $x_i \in In(I_i)$, $x_j \in In(I_j)$, $||\cdot||$ denotes the *Euclidean* norm, and $\epsilon = 1.5$ pixels. However, this measure does not account for extraneous interest points in the transformed image. Therefore, we also measure the reliability of L_{rate} by calculating:

$$L_{rate} = \frac{|In(I_i)|}{|In(I_j)|}, \qquad (8)$$

where the maximum value for L_{rate} is constrained to be 1.

In Fig. 3, we can see common type of image deformations, the true positive rate and the reliability rate for the interest point detector (note: from left to right, image number 2 is extracted from the COIL database [18], and image number 4 is extracted from [21]).

4 Local Feature Vector

Ideally, the local features used to describe an object should have the following two properties: a) be complex enough to provide a strong information about a specific location of an image; and b) be relatively stable to changes in the object configuration, so that small transformations do not affect the efficiency of the correlation process. In this section we consider the problem of finding good candidates for such local features.

A recent proposal for local features described in [20] uses a set of derivatives, coined the "Local-Jet", that is invariant to rotation and is defined as follows:

$$\mathcal{V} = \begin{bmatrix} L \\ L_i L_i \\ L_i L_{ij} L_j \\ L_{ii} \\ L_{ij} L_{ji} \\ \epsilon_{ij}(L_{jkl} L_i L_k L_l - L_{jkk} L_i L_l L_l) \\ L_{iij} L_j L_k L_k - L_{ijk} L_i L_j L_k \\ -\epsilon_{ij} L_{jkl} L_i L_k L_l \\ L_{ijk} L_i L_j L_k \end{bmatrix} \in \Re^9, \tag{9}$$

where we use the tensor summation convention, ϵ_{ij} is the 2-D anti-symmetric epsilon tensor defined by $\epsilon_{12} = -\epsilon_{21} = 1$ and $\epsilon_{11} = \epsilon_{22} = 0$, and $L_i = \frac{\partial}{\partial x_i} G(x, \sigma) * I$ is the element of the local jet such that $G(x, \sigma)$ is a *Gaussian* function, and I is the image.

Alternatively, in [13], after detecting interest points, the image is locally characterized by a set of Scale Invariant Feature Transform (SIFT) features that represents a vector of local image measurements.

4.1 Phase and Amplitude Information

We use a local feature approach, similar to the ones described above, but with a new type of feature using phase information. The phase-based local feature is a complex representation of local image data that is obtained through the use of quadrature pair filters, tuned to a specific orientation θ and scale σ. More specifically, we use the steerable quadrature filter pairs described in [5] as follows: Let

$$\begin{aligned} g(x, \sigma, \theta) &= G_2(\sigma, \theta) * I(x), \\ h(x, \sigma, \theta) &= H_2(\sigma, \theta) * I(x), \end{aligned} \tag{10}$$

where $G_2(\sigma, \theta)$ is the second derivative of a Gaussian, $H_2(\sigma, \theta)$ is the approximation of Hilbert transform of G_2, and σ is the standard deviation of the Gaussian kernel used to derive G_2 and H_2. A complex polar representation can be written as:

$$g(x, \sigma, \theta) + i h(x, \sigma, \theta) = \rho(x, \sigma, \theta) e^{i\phi(x, \sigma, \theta)}, \tag{11}$$

where $\rho(x, \sigma, \theta)$ is the local amplitude information and $\phi(x, \sigma, \theta)$ is the local phase information.

4.2 Saturating the Amplitude Information

The amplitude saturation is similar to contrast normalization (see [8]) and to the constraint on a minimum absolute amplitude (see [4]). It is desirable to allow the amplitude to saturate in order to reduce the system's sensitivity to brightness change. Therefore, whenever the local amplitude is high enough the saturated amplitude should be roughly constant. Here we use

$$\tilde{\rho}(x, \sigma, \theta) = 1 - e^{\frac{-\rho^2(x,\sigma,\theta)}{2*\sigma_\rho^2}}, \qquad (12)$$

where $\sigma_\rho = 2.5$. As a result, $\tilde{\rho}$ is roughly 1 for ρ over $2\sigma_\rho$, and near 0 for small amplitudes.

4.3 Local Image Description

Since a single pixel does not provide a distinctive response we consider several sample points, say $\{x_{i,m}\}_{m=1}^{M}$, taken from a region around each interest point, x_i. We use the sampling pattern depicted in Fig. 4, with the center point $x_{i,1}$ denoting the specific interest point x_i (the reasons for selecting this particular sampling pattern are discussed further below). At each spatial sample point $x_{i,m}$ the filters are steered to N equally spaced orientations, namely

$$\theta_n(x_i) = \theta_M(x_i) + (n-1)\frac{180°}{N}, \quad \text{for } n = 1, \ldots, N. \qquad (13)$$

Here $\theta_M(x_i)$ is the main orientation of the pixel computed as described in [5], except we use the sign of the imaginary response of the filter steered to this orientation to resolve a particular direction (i.e. mod $360°$) from this orientation. Notice that this main orientation $\theta_M(x_i)$ therefore determines both the orientations that the filters are steered to and the positions of the sample points along circle centered on the interest point x_i (see Fig. 4).

The feature vector $F(x_i)$ has individual components specified by the saturated complex filter responses. We use $\tilde{\rho}_i(n,m)e^{\phi_i(n,m)}$ to denote the filter response evaluated at $x_{i,m}$ and steered to orientation $\theta_n(x_i)$, for $n = 1, \ldots, N$, and $m = 1, \ldots, M$. Together these responses form the NM-dimensional complex feature vector $F(x_i)$.

4.4 Phase Correlation

The similarity between local features is computed using phase correlation since this is known to provide some stability to typical image deformations such as brightness changes and near identity image warps. The similarity measure for our feature vector is the normalized phase correlation

$$S(F(x_i), F(x_j)) = \left| \frac{\sum_{m=1}^{M}\sum_{n=1}^{N} \tilde{\rho}_i(n,m)\tilde{\rho}_j(n,m)e^{i(\phi_i(n,m)-\phi_j(n,m))}}{1 + \sum_{m=1}^{M}\sum_{n=1}^{N} \tilde{\rho}_i(n,m)\tilde{\rho}_j(n,m)} \right|. \qquad (14)$$

The reason for adding the 1 in the denominator above is to provide a low-amplitude cutoff for the normalization. This results in similarity values $S(F(x_i), F(x_j)) \in [0, 1]$.

4.5 Feature Vector Configuration

An empirical study was conducted to select the remaining parameters of the local feature vector. These are: a) the number of steering directions, N; b) the number of sample points $P = M - 1$ on the circle surrounding the interest point x_i; and c) the radius, l, of the circle. Each of these parameters represents a compromise between stability (better for small values of the parameters), and expressiveness (better at larger values). By evaluating the detection rates and false target rates (in the manner described for the experiments below) we selected $M = 9$, $N = 4$, and $l = 3$ as providing a reasonable trade-off between expressiveness and stability.

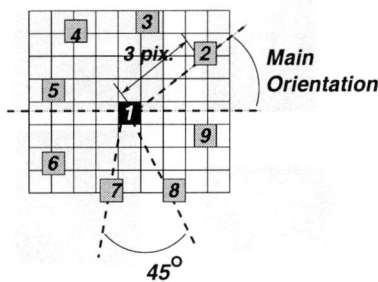

Fig. 4. Configuration of local descriptor.

5 Experiment Setup

In order to compare our feature with the differential invariant feature in (9), 3 test images were selected (see Fig. 2), and 5 image databases (see Fig. 5) were selected consisting of 12 images each. None of the test images were included in these databases. Some of the images inserted into the databases were selected due to appearance similarities with the test images, and other images were just natural scenes.

Given the 5 types of image deformations studied (see Section 2), the comparison is based on the Receiver Operating Characteristics (ROC) curves where the detection rate vs false positive rate is computed for each of the local feature types. In order to define these rates, let x_i be an interest point in a test image. Suppose $x_i{}^0 = Mx_i + b$ denotes the correct position of this interest point in the transformed test image, according to the spatial deformation used. The detection rate (DT) is then defined to be the proportion of interest points x_i such that there exists some interest point, x_j in the transformed image which is both sufficiently close to the mapped point (i.e. $||x_j - x_i{}^0|| < \epsilon$) and which has a similar local feature vector (i.e. $S(F(x_i), F(x_j)) > \tau$). Here ϵ was fixed at 1.5 pixels, while τ was varied to generate the ROC curves. Similarly, given this same interest point x_i in the test image, a false positive is defined by the presence of a similar interest point x_j in the database (i.e. $S(F(x_i), F(x_j)) > \tau$). The false positive rate

(FP) is defined to be the number of these false positives divided by the total number of test image interest points evaluated.

The threshold for both similarity functions is varied as follows: for the phase correlation, that has values in $[0, 1]$, the variation step is 0.1; the differential invariant feature uses the Mahalanobis distance, as described in [20], which can have practically any value above 0, so the variation step is 1 until $DT_{rate} \geq 0.99$. The actual curves are computed using intervals of 0.03 for the false positive rate, and these are plotted using linear interpolation.

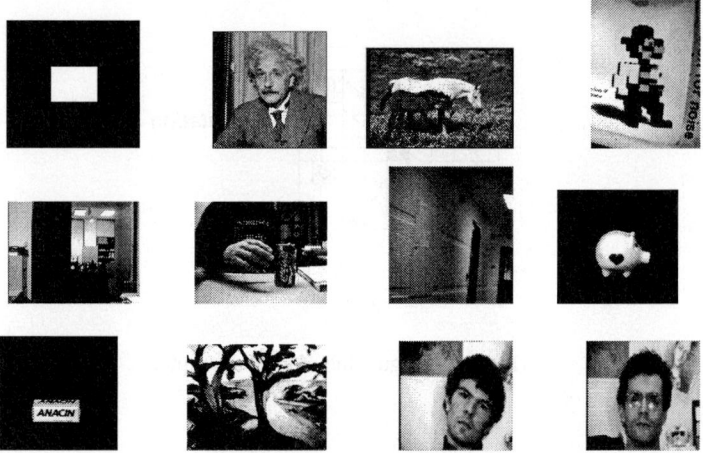

Fig. 5. Database of images.

6 Results

Fig. 6 shows the ROC curve for uniform brightness changes. It is clear that the phase-based feature displays consistently better results, and, due to amplitude saturation, the feature is almost unaffected by an increase in brightness. However, it is more sensitive to decreases in brightness, which is presumably due to the appearance of unsaturated low amplitude responses. The differential invariant feature, on the other hand, is seen to be quite sensitive to these changes. This is also clear from Fig. 7, where we show the detection rate for thresholds τ at which the false positive rate is fixed at 0.1. It is clear from this plot that the phase-based approach is much less sensitive to brightness changes. The same is true for non-uniform brightness changes, as shown in Fig. 8.

The phase-based feature also gives good results for other types of image deformations. As shown in Fig. 9, the performance of both types of features is seen to be similar for additive Gaussian noise. For scale changes, the differential invariant feature is seen to have a somewhat larger detection rate, for the same level of false positives(see Figure 10). This is true primarily for the larger scale changes. For scale changes between ±20%, the phase-based local feature provides comparable performance (see Fig. 11). Finally, the ROC curves show the phase-based feature is somewhat better under image rotation (see Fig. 12). In order to control for small brightness changes which may have occurred during the rotation and scale deformations, we computed the ROC curves with and without rescaling the transformed image to values between 0 and 255. Both cases gave similar results to the ones reported here.

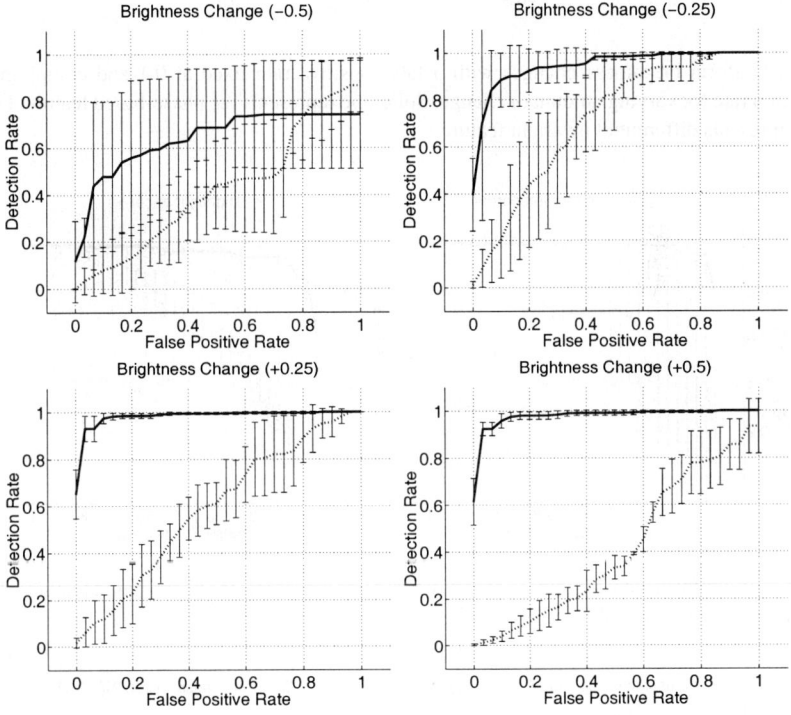

Fig. 6. Uniform brightness changes. Solid line represents the phase-based feature. Dotted line represents differential invariant feature.

7 Conclusions and Future Work

A new type of local feature based on the phase and amplitude of steerable bandpass filters is proposed here. An empirical study is conducted in order to demonstrate that it has the basic characteristics necessary for useful local features, that is, they are robust to common image deformations and distinctive. Moreover, an empirical comparison with

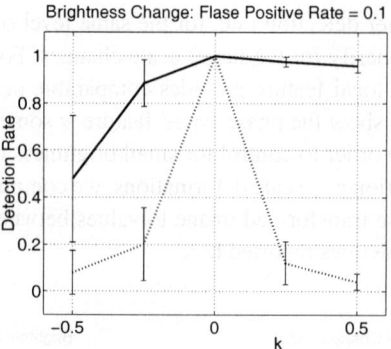

Fig. 7. Uniform brightness changes with a false positive rate fixed at 0.1 and computing the detection rate for varying amount of change. Solid line represents the phase-based feature. Dotted line represents differential invariant feature.

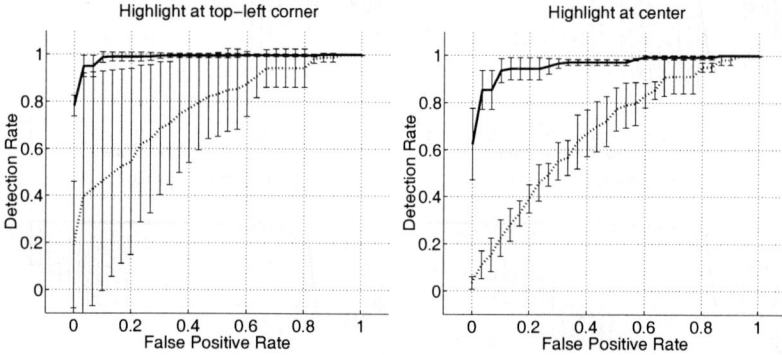

Fig. 8. Non-uniform local brightness changes. Solid line represents the phase-based feature. Dotted line represents differential invariant feature.

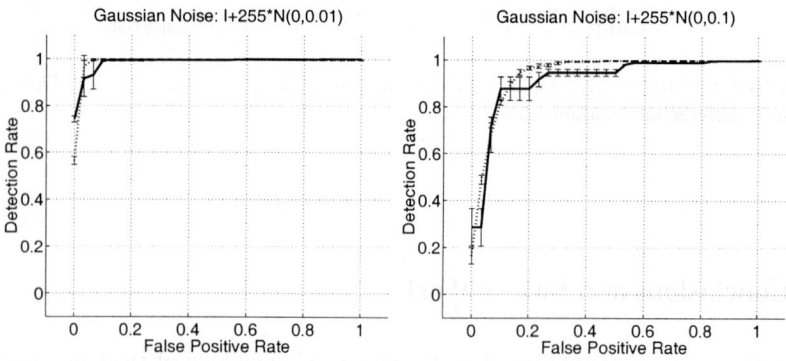

Fig. 9. Gaussian noise changes. Solid line represents the phase-based feature. Dotted line represents differential invariant feature.

Phase-Based Local Features   293

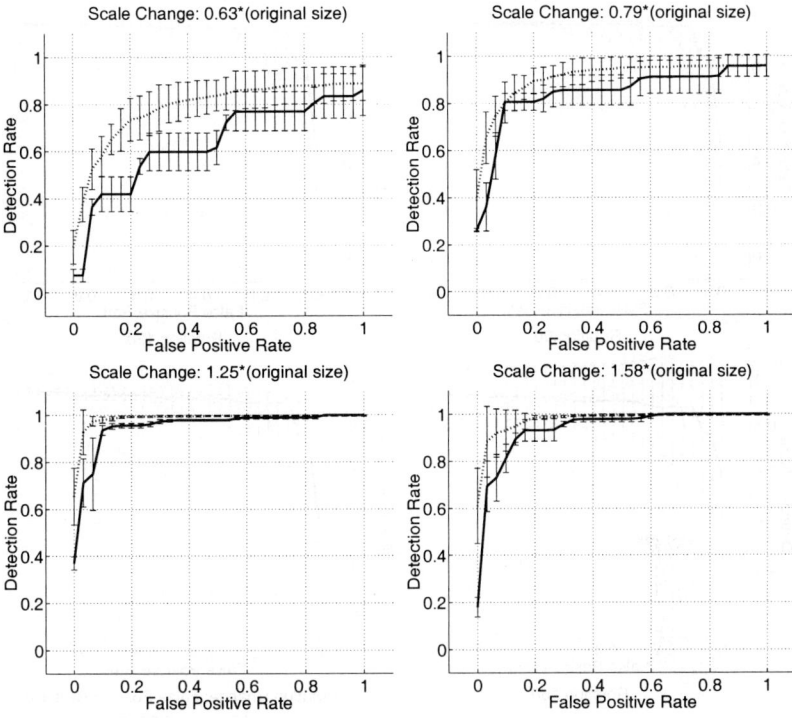

Fig. 10. Scale changes. Solid line represents the phase-based feature. Dotted line represents differential invariant feature.

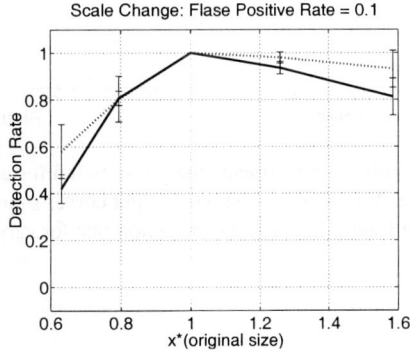

Fig. 11. Scale changes with a false positive rate fixed at 0.1 and computing the detection rate for varying amount of change. Solid line represents the phase-based feature. Dotted line represents differential invariant feature.

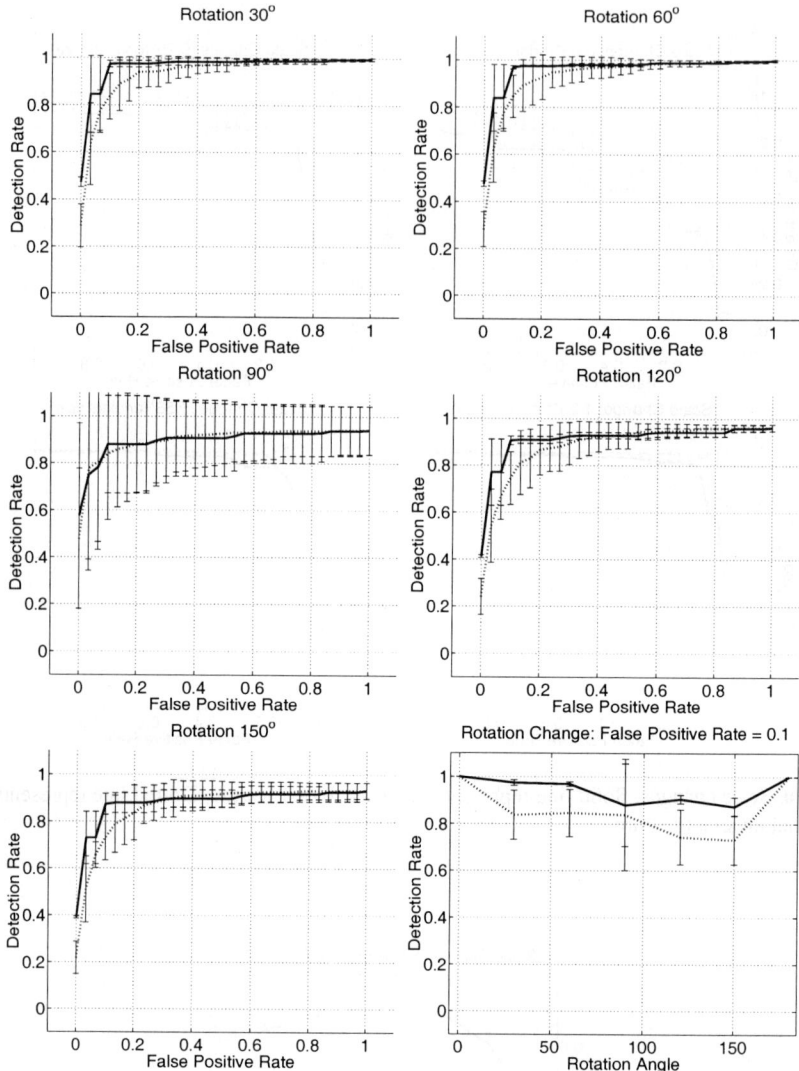

Fig. 12. Rotation changes. Solid line represents the phase-based feature. Dotted line represents differential invariant feature. The graph at the bottom-right corner shows rotation changes with a false positive rate fixed at 0.1 and computing the detection rate for varying amount of change.

differential invariant features shows that the phase-based local feature performs better in terms of common illumination changes and 2-D rotation, while giving comparable or slightly worse results when dealing with scale changes. An important area for further study is the use of brightness normalization in the differential invariant features, and the comparison of the result with our phase-based approach.

The phase-based local feature has obvious applications in object recognition, but a few issues must be dealt with before exploring its capabilities. The interest point detector used here can be replaced by another one that provides a better response in terms of the information being studied here, (i.e., phase and amplitude), and presents a better response to scale changes. The high dimensionality of the vector can represent a burden, so methods for reducing it, or search methods that perform well in high dimensions must be sought. Finally, grouping features before searching the database of models is an important component that should be added.

References

1. M. J. Black and A. D. Jepson. Eigentracking: Robust matching and tracking of articulated objects using a view-based representation. In *4th European Conf. on Computer Vision*, pages 329–342, Cambridge, April 1996.
2. R. Brooks. Model-based 3-d interpretations of 2-d images. *IEEE Transactions on Pattern Analysis and Machine Intelligence*, 5(2):140–150, 1983.
3. D. Fleet. *Measurement of Image Velocity*. Kluwer Academic Publishers, 1992.
4. D. Fleet, A. D. Jepson, and M. Jenkin. Phase-based disparity measure. In *CVGIP: Image Understanding*, pages 198–210, 1991.
5. W. T. Freeman and E. H. Adelson. The design and use of steerable filters. *IEEE Transactions on Pattern Analysis and Machine Intelligence*, 13(9):891–906, 1991.
6. W. E. L. Grimson and T. Lozano-Pérez. Localizing overlapping parts by searching the interpretation tree. *IEEE Transactions on Pattern Analysis and Machine Intelligence*, 9(4):469–482, 1987.
7. C. Harris and M. Stephens. A combined corner and edge detector. In *Alvey Vision Conference*, 1988.
8. D. J. Heeger. Computational model of cat striate physiology. Technical report, Massachusetts Institute of Technology, October 1989.
9. D. Huttenlocher and S. Ullman. Object recognition using alignment. In *International Conference on Computer Vision*, pages 102–111, London, UK, 1987.
10. D. Jugessur and G. Dudek. Local appearance for robust object recognition. In *IEEE Computer Vision and Pattern Recognition*, pages 834–839, Hilton Head, USA, June 2000.
11. A. Leonardis and H. Bischoff. Dealing with occlusions in the eigenspace approach. In *IEEE Conference on Computer Vision and Pattern Recognition*, pages 453–458, San Francisco, USA, June 1996.
12. D. G. Lowe. Three-dimensional object recognition from single two-dimensional images. *Artificial Intelligence*, 31(3):355–395, 1987.
13. D. G. Lowe. Object recognition from local scale-invariant features. In *International Conference on Computer Vision*, pages 1150–1157, Corfu, Greece, September 1999.
14. D. G. Lowe. Towards a computational model for object recognition in it cortex. In *First IEEE International Workshop on Biologically Motivated Computer Vision*, pages 20–31, Seoul, Korea, May 2000.
15. H. Murase and S. Nayar. Visual learning and recognition of 3-d objects from appearance. *International Journal of Computer Vision*, 14(1):5–24, 1995.
16. R. C. Nelson. Memory-based recognition for 3-d objects. In *ARPA Image Understanding Workshop*, pages 1305–1310, Palm Springs, USA, February 1996.
17. R.P.N. Rao and D.H. Ballard. Natural basis functions and topographic memory for face recognition. In *International Joint Conference on Artificial Intelligence*, pages 10–17, 1995.

18. S. K. Nayar S. A. Nene and H. Murase. Columbia object image library (coil-20). Technical report, Department of Computer Science, Columbia University, February 1996.
19. B. Schiele and J.L. Crowley. Object recognition using multidimensional receptive field histograms. In *4th European Conference on Computer Vision*, volume 1, pages 610–619, April 1996.
20. C. Schmid and R. Mohr. Local grayvalue invariants for image retrieval. *IEEE Transactions on Pattern Analysis and Machine Intelligence*, 19(5):530–535, 1997.
21. M. Turk and A. Pentland. Eigenfaces for recognition. *Journal of Cognitive Neuroscience*, 3(1), 1991.
22. M. Turk and A. P. Pentland. Face recognition using eigenfaces. In *IEEE Computer Vision and Pattern Recognition*, pages 586–591, 1991.

What Is the Role of Independence for Visual Recognition?

Nuno Vasconcelos[1]* and Gustavo Carneiro[2]

[1] Compaq Computer Corporation,
Cambridge Research Laboratory,
nuno.vasconcelos@compaq.com
[2] Department of Computer Science,
University of Toronto,
carneiro@cs.toronto.edu

Abstract. Independent representations have recently attracted significant attention from the biological vision and cognitive science communities. It has been 1) argued that properties such as sparseness and independence play a major role in visual perception, and 2) shown that imposing such properties on visual representations originates receptive fields similar to those found in human vision. We present a study of the impact of feature independence in the performance of visual recognition architectures. The contributions of this study are of both theoretical and empirical natures, and support two main conclusions. The first is that the intrinsic complexity of the recognition problem (Bayes error) is higher for independent representations. The increase can be significant, close to 10% in the databases we considered. The second is that criteria commonly used in independent component analysis are not sufficient to eliminate all the dependencies that impact recognition. In fact, "independent components" can be less independent than previous representations, such as principal components or wavelet bases.

1 Introduction

After decades of work in the area of visual recognition (in the multiple guises of object recognition, texture classification, and image retrieval, among others) there are still several fundamental questions on the subject which, by large, remain unanswered. One of the core components of any recognition architecture is the feature transformation, a mapping from the space of image pixels to a feature space with better properties for recognition. While numerous features have been proposed over the years for various recognition tasks, there has been small progress towards either 1) a universally good feature set, or 2) a universal and computationally efficient algorithm for the design of optimal features for any particular task.

In the absence of indisputable universal guidelines for feature design, one good source of inspiration has always been the human visual system. Ever since

---

* A longer version of the paper containing all proofs is available from the author.

the work of Hubel and Wiesel [9], it has been established that 1) visual processing is local, and 2) different groups in primary visual cortex (i.e. area V1) are tuned for detecting different types of stimulus (e.g. bars, edges, and so on). This indicates that, at the lowest level, the architecture of the human visual system can be well approximated by a multi-resolution representation localized in space and frequency, and several "biologically plausible" models of early vision are based on this principle [2,3,8,13,18,19]. All these models share a basic common structure consisting of three layers: a *space/space-frequency* decomposition at the bottom, a middle stage introducing a non-linearity, and a final stage pooling the responses from several non-linear units. They therefore suggest the adoption of a mapping from pixel-based to space/space-frequency representations as a suitable universal feature transformation for recognition.

A space/space-frequency representation is obtained by convolving the image with a collection of elementary filters of reduced spatial support and tuned to different spatial frequencies and orientations. Traditionally, the exact shape of the filters was not considered very important, as long as they were localized in both space and frequency, and several elementary filters have been proposed in the literature, including *differences of Gaussians* [13], *Gabor functions* [16,8], and *differences of offset Gaussians* [13], among others. More recently, this presumption has been challenged by various authors on the basis that the shape of the filters determines fundamentally important properties of the representation, such as sparseness [7,15] and independence [1].

These claims have been supported by (quite successful) showings that the enforcement of sparseness or independence constraints on the design of the feature transformation leads to representations which exhibit remarkable similarity to the receptive fields of cells found in V1 [1,15]. However, while the arguments are appealing and the pictures compelling, there is, to the best of our knowledge, no proof that sparseness or independence are, indeed, fundamental requirements for visual recognition. On the contrary, not all evidence supports this conjecture. For example, detailed statistical analysis of the coefficients of wavelet transforms (an alternative class of sparse features which exhibit similar receptive fields) has revealed the existence of clear inter-dependencies [17].

In what concerns the design of practical recognition systems, properties such as sparseness or independence are important only insofar as they enable higher-level goals such as computational efficiency or small probability of error. Under a Bayesian view of perception [12], these two goals are, in fact, closely inter-related: implementation of minimum probability of error (MPE) decisions requires accurate density estimates, which are very difficult to obtain in high-dimensional feature spaces. The advantage of an independent representation is to decouple the various dimensions of the space, allowing high dimensional estimates to be computed by the simple multiplication of scalars. In this sense, independence can be a crucial enabler for accurate recognition with reduced complexity. On the other hand, it is known that any feature transformation has the potential to increase Bayes error, the ultimate lower-bound on the probability of error that any recognition architecture can achieve, for a given feature space. It is not clear that independent feature spaces are guaranteed to exhibit lower Bayes error than non-independent ones. In fact, since the independence constraint restricts the set of admissible transforms, it is natural to expect the opposite.

Due to all of this, while there seem to be good reasons for the use of independent or sparse representations, it is not clear that they will lead to optimal recognition. Furthermore, it is usually very difficult to determine, in practice, if goals such as independence are actually achieved. In fact, because guaranteeing independence is a terribly difficult endeavor in high-dimensions, independent component analysis techniques typically resort to weaker goals, such as minimizing certain cumulants, or searching for non-Gaussian solutions. While an independent representation will meet these weaker goals, the reverse does not usually hold. In practice, it is in general quite difficult to evaluate by how much the true goal of independence has been missed.

In this work we address two questions regarding the role of independence. The first is fundamental in nature: "how important is independence for visual recognition?". The second is relevant for the design of recognition systems: "how realistic is the expectation of actually enforcing independence constraints in real recognition scenarios?". To study these questions we built a complete recognition system and compared the performance of various feature transforms which claim different degrees of independence: from generic features that make no independence claims (but were known to have good recognition performance), to features (resulting from independent component analysis) which are supposed to be independent, passing through transforms that only impose very weak forms of independence, such as decorrelation.

It turns out that, with the help of some simple theoretical results, the analysis of the recognition accuracy achieved by the different transforms already provides significant support for the following qualitative answers to the questions above. First, it seems to be the case that imposing independence constraints increases the intrinsic complexity (Bayes error) of the recognition problem. In fact, our data supports the conjecture that this intrinsic complexity is monotonically increasing on the degree of independence. Second, it seems clear that great care needs to be exercised in the selection of the independence measures used to guide the design of independent component transformations. In particular, our results show that approaches such as minimizing cumulants or searching for non-Gaussian solutions are not guaranteed to achieve this goal. In fact, they can lead to "independent components" that are less independent than those achieved with "decorrelating" representations such as principal component analysis or wavelets.

2 Bounds on Recognition Accuracy

A significant challenge for empirical evaluation is to provide some sort of guarantees that the observed results are generalizable. This challenge is particularly relevant in the context of visual recognition, since it is impossible to implement all the recognition architectures that could ever be conceived. For example, the fact that we rely on a Bayesian classification paradigm should not compromise the applicability of the conclusions to recognition scenarios based on alternative classification frameworks (e.g. discriminant techniques such as neural networks or support vector machines). This goal can only be met with recourse to theoretical insights on the performance of recognition systems, which are typically available in the form of bounds on the probability of classification error.

The most relevant of these bounds is that provided by the Bayes error, which is the minimum error that any architecture can achieve in a given classification problem.

Theorem 1 *Given a feature space $\mathcal{X}$ and a query $\mathbf{x} \in \mathcal{X}$, the decision function which minimizes the probability of classification error is the Bayes or maximum a posteriori (MAP) classifier*

$$g^*(\mathbf{x}) = \arg\max_i P_{Y|\mathbf{X}}(i|\mathbf{x}), \tag{1}$$

where Y is a random variable that assigns $\mathbf{x}$ to one of M classes, and $i \in \{1,\ldots,M\}$. Furthermore, the probability of error is lower bounded by the Bayes error

$$L^* = 1 - E_{\mathbf{x}}[\max_i P_{Y|\mathbf{X}}(i|\mathbf{x})], \tag{2}$$

where $E_{\mathbf{x}}$ means expectation with respect to $P_{\mathbf{X}}(\mathbf{x})$.

The significance of this theorem is that any insights on the Bayes error that may be derived from observations obtained with a particular recognition architecture are valid for all architectures, as long as the feature space $\mathcal{X}$ is the same. The following theorem shows that a feature transformation can never lead to smaller error in the transformed space than that achievable in the domain space.

Theorem 2 *Given a classification problem with observation space $\mathcal{Z}$ and a feature transformation*

$$T : \mathcal{Z} \to \mathcal{X},$$

then

$$L_{\mathcal{X}}^* \geq L_{\mathcal{Z}}^* \tag{3}$$

where $L_{\mathcal{Z}}^*$ and $L_{\mathcal{X}}^*$ are, respectively, the Bayes errors on $\mathcal{Z}$ and $\mathcal{X}$. Furthermore, equality is achieved if and only if T is an invertible transformation.

The last statement of the theorem is a worst-case result. In fact, for a specific classification problem, it may be possible to find non-invertible feature transformations that do not increase Bayes error. What is not possible is to find 1) a feature transformation that will reduce the Bayes error, or 2) a universal non-invertible feature transformation guaranteed not to increase the Bayes error on all classification problems.

Since Bayes error is an intrinsic measure of the complexity of a classification problem, the theorems above are applicable to any classification architecture. The following upper bounds are specific to a family of architectures that we will consider throughout this work, and are usually referred to as plug-in decision rules [6]. The basic idea is to rely on Bayes rule to invert (1)

$$g^*(\mathbf{x}) = \arg\max_i P_{\mathbf{X}|Y}(\mathbf{x}|i)P_Y(i), \qquad (4)$$

and then estimate the quantities $P_{\mathbf{X}|Y}(\mathbf{x}|i)$ and $P_Y(i)$ from training images. This leads to the following upper bound on the probability of error.

Theorem 3 *Given a classification problem with a feature space $\mathcal{X}$, unknown class probabilities $P_Y(i)$ and class conditional likelihood functions $P_{\mathbf{X}|Y}(\mathbf{x}|i)$, and a decision function*

$$g(\mathbf{x}) = \arg\max_i \hat{p}_{\mathbf{X}|Y}(\mathbf{x}|i)\hat{p}_Y(i), \qquad (5)$$

the difference between the actual and Bayes error, is upper bounded by

$$P(g(\mathbf{X}) \neq Y) - L^*_{\mathcal{X}} \leq \sum_i \int |P_{\mathbf{X}|Y}(\mathbf{x}|i)P_Y(i) - \hat{p}_{\mathbf{X}|Y}(\mathbf{x}|i)\hat{p}_Y(i)|d\mathbf{x}. \qquad (6)$$

In the remainder of this work we assume that the classes are a-priori equiprobable, i.e. $P_Y(i) = 1/M, \forall i$. This leads to the following corollary.

Corollary 1 *Given a classification problem with equiprobable classes, a feature space $\mathcal{X}$, unknown class conditional likelihood functions $P_{\mathbf{X}|Y}(\mathbf{x}|i)$, and a decision function*

$$g(\mathbf{x}) = \arg\max_i \hat{p}_{\mathbf{X}|Y}(\mathbf{x}|i), \qquad (7)$$

the difference between the actual and Bayes error is upper bounded by

$$P(g(\mathbf{X}) \neq Y) - L^*_{\mathcal{X}} \leq \Delta_{g,\mathcal{X}} \qquad (8)$$

where

$$\Delta_{g,\mathcal{X}} = \sum_i KL[P_{\mathbf{X}|Y}(\mathbf{x}|i)||\hat{p}_{\mathbf{X}|Y}(\mathbf{x}|i)], \qquad (9)$$

is the estimation error and

$$KL[P_{\mathbf{X}}(\mathbf{x})||Q_{\mathbf{X}}(\mathbf{x})] = \int P_{\mathbf{X}}(\mathbf{x}) \log \frac{P_{\mathbf{X}}(\mathbf{x})}{Q_{\mathbf{X}}(\mathbf{x})} d\mathbf{x} \qquad (10)$$

is the relative entropy, or Kullback-Leibler divergence, between $P_{\mathbf{X}}(\mathbf{x})$ and $Q_{\mathbf{X}}(\mathbf{x})$.

Bounds (3) and (8) reflect the impact of both feature selection and density estimation on recognition accuracy. While the feature transformation determines the best possible achievable performance, the quality of the density estimates determines how close the actual error is to this lower bound. Hence, for problems where density estimation is accurate one expects the actual error to be close to the Bayes error. On the other hand, when density estimates are poor, there are no guarantees that this will be the case.

The latter tends to be the case for visual recognition, where high-dimensional feature spaces usually make density estimation a difficult problem. It is, therefore, difficult to determine if the error is mostly due to the intrinsic complexity of the problem (Bayes error) or to poor quality of density estimates. One of the contributions of this work is a strategy to circumvent this problem, based on the notion of embedded feature spaces [21].

Definition 1 *Given two vector spaces $\mathcal{X}_m$ and $\mathcal{X}_n$, $m < n$, such that $dim(\mathcal{X}_m) = m$ and $dim(\mathcal{X}_n) = n$ an embedding is a mapping*

$$\epsilon : \mathcal{X}_m \to \mathcal{X}_n \tag{11}$$

which is one-to-one.

A canonical example of embedding is the zero padding operator for Euclidean spaces

$$\iota_m^n : \mathbb{R}^m \to \mathbb{R}^n \tag{12}$$

where $\iota_m^n(\mathbf{x}) = (\mathbf{x}, \mathbf{0})$, $\mathbf{x} \in \mathbb{R}^m$, and $\mathbf{0} \in \mathbb{R}^{n-m}$.

Definition 2 *A sequence of vector spaces $\{\mathcal{X}_1, \ldots, \mathcal{X}_d\}$, such that $dim(\mathcal{X}_i) < dim(\mathcal{X}_{i+1})$, is called embedded if there exists a sequence of embeddings*

$$\epsilon_i : \mathcal{X}_i \to \mathcal{X}'_{i+1}, \ i = 1, \ldots, d-1, \tag{13}$$

such that $\mathcal{X}'_{i+1} \subset \mathcal{X}_{i+1}$.

The inverse operation of an embedding is a submersion.

Definition 3 *Given two vector spaces $\mathcal{X}_m$ and $\mathcal{X}_n$, $m < n$, such that $dim(\mathcal{X}_m) = m$ and $dim(\mathcal{X}_n) = n$ a submersion is a mapping*

$$\gamma : \mathcal{X}_n \to \mathcal{X}_m \tag{14}$$

which is surjective.

A canonical example of submersion is the projection of Euclidean spaces along the coordinate axes

$$\pi_m^n : \mathbb{R}^n \to \mathbb{R}^m \tag{15}$$

where $\pi_m^n(x_1, \ldots, x_m, x_{m+1}, \ldots, x_n) = (x_1, \ldots, x_m)$. The following theorem shows that any linear feature transformation originates a sequence of embedded vector spaces with monotonically decreasing Bayes error, and monotonically increasing estimation error.

Theorem 4 *Let*

$$T : \mathbb{R}^d \to \mathcal{X} \subset \mathbb{R}^d,$$

be a linear feature transformation. Then,

$$\mathcal{X}_i = \pi_i^d(\mathcal{X}), i = 1, \ldots, d-1 \tag{16}$$

is a sequence of embedded feature spaces such that

$$L^*_{\mathcal{X}_{i+1}} \leq L^*_{\mathcal{X}_i}. \tag{17}$$

Furthermore, if $\mathbf{X}_1^d = \{\mathbf{X}_1, \ldots, \mathbf{X}_d\}$ is a sequence or random variables such that $\mathbf{X}_i \in \mathcal{X}_i$,

$$\mathbf{X}_i = \pi_i^d(\mathbf{X}), i = 1, \ldots, d \tag{18}$$

and $\{g(\mathbf{x})\}_1^d$ a sequence of decision functions

$$g_i(\mathbf{x}) = \arg\max_k \hat{p}_{\mathbf{X}_i|Y}(\mathbf{x}|k) \tag{19}$$

then

$$\Delta_{g_{i+1}, \mathcal{X}_{i+1}} \geq \Delta_{g_i, \mathcal{X}_i}. \tag{20}$$

Figure 1 illustrates the evolution of the upper and lower bounds on the probability of error as one considers successively higher-dimensional subspaces of $\mathcal{X}$. Since accurate density estimates can usually be obtained in low-dimensions, the two bounds tend to be close when the subspace dimension is small. In this case, the actual probability of error is dominated by the Bayes error. For higher-dimensional subspaces two distinct scenarios are possible, depending on the independence of the individual random variables X_i. Whenever these variables are dependent, the decrease in Bayes error tends to be cancelled by an increase in estimation error and the actual probability of error increases. In this case, the actual probability of error exhibits the concave shape depicted in the left plot, where an inflection point marks the subspace dimension for which Bayes error ceases to be dominant.

The right plot depicts the situation where the variables X_i are independent. In this case, it can be shown that

$$\Delta_{g_{i+1}, \mathcal{X}_{i+1}} - \Delta_{g_i, \mathcal{X}_i} = \sum_k KL[P_{X_{i+1}|Y}(x|k) \| \hat{p}_{X_{i+1}|Y}(x|k)], \tag{21}$$

i.e. the increase in overall estimation error is simply the sum of the errors of the individual scalar estimates. Since these errors tend to be small, one expects the overall probability of error to remain approximately flat.

Hence, the shape of the curve of probability of error as a function of the subspace dimension carries significant information about 1) the Bayes error in the full space $\mathcal{X}$ and 2) the independence of the component random variables X_i. We will see in section 5 that this information is sufficient to draw, with reasonable certainty, conclusions such as "the Bayes error of transform T is greater than that of transform U". With regards to independence, the ultimate test is, of course, to implement a recognition system based on estimates of the joint density $P_\mathbf{X}(\mathbf{x})$ and compare with a recognition system based on the independence assumption, i.e. $P_\mathbf{X}(\mathbf{x}) = \prod_i P_{X_i}(x_i)$. When independence holds, the two systems will achieve the same recognition rates. From now on, we will refer to the former system as based on *joint modeling* and to the latter as based on *independent modeling* or on the *product of marginals*.

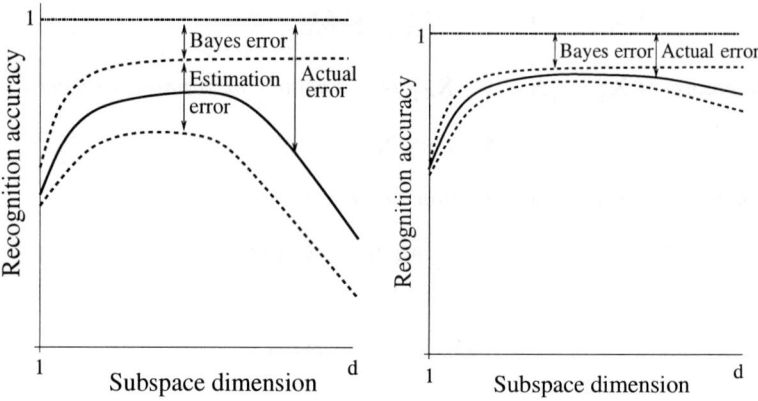

Fig. 1. Upper bound, lower bound, and actual probability of error as a function of subspace dimension. Left: dependent features. Right: independent features.

3 Feature Transforms

Since the goal is to evaluate the impact of independence on visual recognition, it is natural to study transformations that lead to features with different degrees of independence. We restrict our attention to the set of transformations that perform some sort of space/space-frequency decomposition. In this context, the feature transformation is a mapping

$$T : \mathbb{R}^k \to \mathbb{R}^d$$
$$\mathbf{z} \to \mathbf{x} = \mathbf{Wz}$$

where $\mathbf{z} \in \mathbb{R}^k$ is a $n \times n$ image patch with columns stacked into a k-dimensional vector ($k = n^2$) and $\mathbf{W}$ the transformation matrix. In general, $k \geq d$, and one can also define a reconstruction mapping

$$R : \mathbb{R}^d \to \mathbb{R}^k$$
$$\mathbf{x} \to \mathbf{z} = \mathbf{Ax}$$

from features $\mathbf{x}$ to pixels $\mathbf{z}$. The columns of $\mathbf{A}$ are called basis functions of the transformation. When $d = k$ and $\mathbf{A} = \mathbf{W}^T$ the transformation is orthogonal. Various popular space/space-frequency representations are derived from orthogonal feature transforms.

Definition 4 *The Discrete Cosine Transform (DCT) [11] of size n is the orthogonal transform whose basis functions are defined by:*

$$A(i,j) = \alpha(i)\alpha(j) \cos \frac{(2x+1)i\pi}{2n} \cos \frac{(2y+1)j\pi}{2n}, \ 0 \leq i,j,x,y < n \qquad (22)$$

where $\alpha = \sqrt{1/n}$ for $i = 0$, and $\alpha = \sqrt{2/n}$ otherwise.

The DCT has empirically been shown to have good decorrelation properties [11] and, in this sense, DCT features are at the bottom of the independence spectrum. Previous recognition results had shown, however, that it can lead to recognition rates comparable to or better than those of many features proposed in the recognition literature [20]. It is possible to show that, for certain classes of stochastic processes, the DCT converges asymptotically to the following transform [11].

Definition 5 *Principal Components Analysis (PCA) is the orthogonal transform defined by*

$$\mathbf{W} = \mathbf{D}^{-1/2}\mathbf{E}^T, \qquad (23)$$

where $\mathbf{EDE}^T$ is the eigenvector decomposition of the covariance matrix $E[\mathbf{zz}^T]$.

It is well known (and straightforward to show) that PCA generates uncorrelated features, i.e. $E[\mathbf{xx}^T] = \mathbf{I}$. While they originate spatial/spatial-frequency representations, the major limitation of the above transforms as models for visual perception is the arbitrary nature of their spatial localization (enforced by arbitrarily segmenting images into blocks). This can result in severe scaling mismatches if the block size does not match that of the image detail. Such scaling problems are alleviated by the wavelet representation.

Definition 6 *A wavelet transform (WT) [14] is the orthogonal transform whose basis functions are defined by*

$$A(i,j) = \sqrt{2^{k+l}}\Psi\left(2^k x - i\right)\Psi\left(2^l y - j\right) \begin{matrix} 0 \leq k,l < \log_2 n \\ (0,0) \leq (i,j) < (2^k, 2^l) \end{matrix} \qquad (24)$$

where $\Psi(x)$ is a function (wavelet) that integrates to zero.

Like the DCT, wavelets have been shown empirically to achieve good decorrelation. While this is an important part of independence (all of it when the inputs are Gaussian) there is in general a significant amount of higher-order dependencies that cannot be captured by orthogonal components [15]. Eliminating such dependencies is the goal of independent component analysis.

Definition 7 *Independent Component Analysis (ICA) [4] is a feature transform such that*

$$P_\mathbf{X}(\mathbf{x}) = \prod_i P_{\mathbf{X}_i}(\mathbf{x}_i) \qquad (25)$$

where $\mathbf{X} = \{X_1, \ldots, X_d\}$ is the random process from which feature vectors are drawn.

An equivalent definition is to require that the mutual information between features is zero (see [1] for details). The exact details of ICA depend on the particular algorithm used to learn the basis from a training sample. Since independence is usually difficult to measure and enforce if d is large, ICA techniques tend to settle for less ambitious goals. The most popular solution is to minimize a contrast function which is guaranteed to be zero if the inputs are independent. Examples of such contrast functions are higher order correlations and information-theoretic objective functions[4]. In this work, we consider representatives from the two types: the method developed by Comon [5], which uses a contrast function based on high-order cumulants, and the FastICA algorithm [10], that relies on the negative entropy of the features.

4 Experimental Set-Up

In order to evaluate the recognition accuracy achievable with the various feature transformations, we conducted experiments on two image databases: the Brodatz texture database, and the Corel database of stock photography. Brodatz is a standard benchmark for texture classification under controlled imaging conditions, and no distractors. Corel is a good testing ground for recognition in the context of natural scenes (e.g. no control over lighting or object pose, cluttered backgrounds).

Brodatz contains 112 gray-scale textures that were broken down into 9 128×128 patches, leading to a total of 1008 images. This set was split into two subgroups, a *query* database containing the first patch of each texture and a *retrieval* database containing the remaining 8. In the case of Corel, we selected 15 image classes[1] each containing 100 color images. We then created a query and retrieval database by assigning each image to the query set with a probability 0.2.

All color images were converted to the YBR color space. Where applicable, the feature transformations were applied to each channel separately and the resulting feature vectors combined by interleaving the color components according to the pattern $YBRYBR\ldots$. For each channel, the feature space was 64-dimensional (three layers of wavelet decomposition and 8×8 image blocks in the remaining cases) and consecutive observations were extracted with a step of 2 (Brodatz) or 4 (Corel) pixels in each of the x and y directions. Public domain software by the authors of the techniques was used for learning the feature transformations. All learning was based in two $100,000$-point samples extracted randomly from the retrieval databases. Figure 2 presents the basis functions learned from Brodatz for PCA, ICA with the method by P. Comon, and ICA with the FastICA algorithm, as well as the DCT basis (wavelet basis do not have block-based support and are not shown).

Once the different bases were computed, all image patches were projected into each of them leading to a sample of feature vectors per image. Maximum likelihood (ML) parameters of a Gaussian mixture model were then estimated using the EM algorithm. The number of Gaussian components was held constant (several values were tried with qualitatively similar results, here we report results

---
[1] Arabian horses, Auto racing, Owls, Roses, Ski scenes, religious stained glass, sunsets and sunrises, coasts, Divers and diving, Land of the pyramids (pictures of Egypt), English country gardens, fireworks, Glaciers and mountains, Mayan and Aztec ruins, and Oil Paintings.

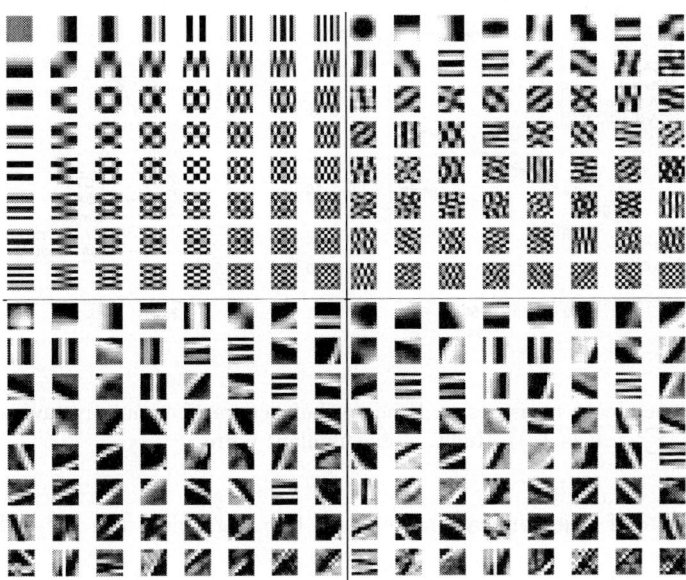

Fig. 2. Basis functions for DCT (top left), PCA (top right) ICA learned with Comon's method (bottom left) and ICA learned with the fastICA method (bottom right).

with 8 components), and a joint density for each of the embedded subspaces $\mathcal{X}_i$ was obtained by downward-projection of the joint density in $\mathcal{X}$ [21]. A Gaussian mixture with the same number of components was also fit to each of the scalar variables X_i to obtain the independent model.

To double-check the independence results we computed various statistical measures of independence. The first was the KL divergence between the joint and independent models $KL\left[P_\mathbf{X}(\mathbf{x}) \| \prod_i P_{X_i}(x_i)\right]$. Since we wanted an alternative measure of independence not affected by the quality of the mixture parameter estimates, we used histograms to compute this statistic. However, in order to avoid well known problems of histogram-based estimates in high dimensions, we only considered average pairwise divergences

$$\hat{KL}(X_i) = \frac{1}{d-1} \sum_{j \neq i} KL\left[P_{X_i, X_j}(x_i, x_j) \| P_{X_i}(x_i) P_{X_j}(x_j)\right]. \tag{26}$$

These divergence are measures of pairwise independence and should be zero whenever independence holds.

One popular way to measure dependencies of order larger than two is through high-order statistics, such as cross-cumulants. While the 2nd order cross-cumulant

$$Cum[X_i, X_j] = E[X_i X_j], \forall i \neq j \tag{27}$$

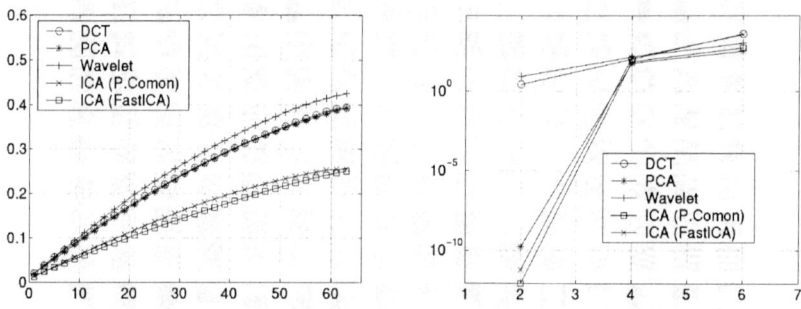

Fig. 3. Independence measures on Brodatz. Left: curve of cumulative average KL divergence $(i, \sum_{j=1}^{i} \hat{KL}(X_j))$. Right: cross-cumulant norm.

is a measure of the correlation between two variables, the 4th-order cross-cumulant

$$Cum[X_i, X_j, X_k, X_l] = E[X_i X_j X_k X_l] - E[X_i X_j]E[X_k X_l]$$
$$- E[X_i X_k]E[X_j X_l] - E[X_i X_l]E[X_j X_k], \forall i \neq (j, k, l),$$

can serve both as a measure of 1) linear fourth-order dependence and 2) distance from Gaussianity [10], and higher-order cumulants capture dependencies of higher order. Unfortunately, the number of terms in a cumulant grows exponentially with its order and the computations involved rapidly become infeasible. We computed cumulants up to 6th-order, but omit the formulas. All cumulant information was summarized by the norm of the off-diagonal terms (cross-cumulants), e.g.

$$||Cum_4|| = \sum_{i,j,k,l \neq (c,c,c,c)} Cum^2[X_i, X_j, X_k, X_l] \qquad (28)$$

for the fourth-order cumulant. These statistics are zero when independence holds.

5 Results

Figure 3 presents the independence measures obtained on Brodatz. The curves on the left plot represent the cumulative average KL divergence (26) after reordering the X_j such that $\hat{KL}(X_{j+1}) < \hat{KL}(X_j)$. These curves suggest the existence of two groups: the first, consisting of the ICA techniques, achieves significantly better pairwise independence than the second, consisting of the decorrelating transforms. A somewhat different picture starts to emerge from the right plot which shows the evolution of the cumulant norm as a function of its order. While the ICA techniques (together with PCA) achieve the lowest 2nd and 4th order cumulant norms, the slope of the curve (between 4th and 6th order) is larger

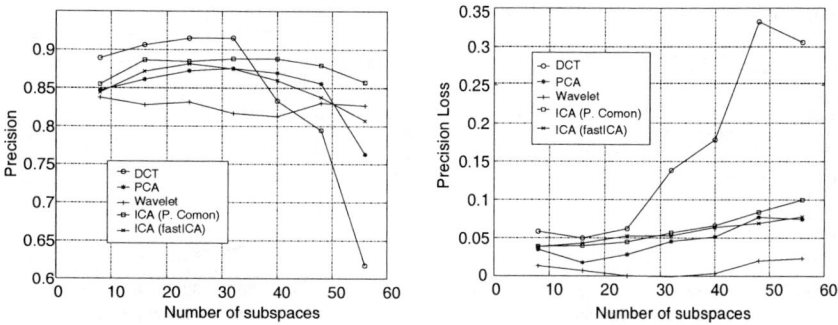

Fig. 4. Recognition results on Brodatz. Left: Precision, at 30% recall, achieved with joint modeling. Right: Precision loss inherent to the independence assumption.

than that of the wavelet features. This indicates that, for higher orders, the curves are likely to cross, in which case the wavelet representation would be the most independent. This observation is supported by the results that follow and suggests that minimizing cumulants up to a certain order does not really provide any independence guarantees, since the dependencies can simply become of higher-order.

In order to evaluate recognition accuracy we measured precision at various levels of recall[2]. Since the results were qualitatively similar for all levels, we only present curves of precision, as a function of subspace dimension, at 30% recall on Brodatz and 10% recall on Corel. The left plot of Figure 4 shows the precision achieved on Brodatz with joint modeling. The right plot presents the associated precision loss[3] when the joint model is replaced by the product of the marginals. This precision loss is a measure of the dependence between the features, since both models should lead to the same result when independence holds.

Two major conclusions can be taken from the figure. First, the ordering of transformations by degree of independence is quite surprising, with wavelets at the top, followed by PCA, the two ICA methods, and the DCT (as a distant last). While we want to avoid conclusions such as "feature transform X leads to weaker dependencies" that may not generalize to other databases, it is clear that this ordering is very different from that of Figure 3 (ICA techniques on top, then DCT and PCA, and finally wavelets). This can only mean that quantities such as pairwise KL divergence or a limited set of cross-cumulants do not really capture what is going on in terms of independence, at least the aspects that are important for recognition. While this is not completely surprising, since these measures only capture *pairwise* or *linear* dependencies, it clearly indicates that

---

[2] When the n most similar images to a query are retrieved, recall is the percentage of all relevant images that are contained in that set, and precision the percentage of the n which are relevant.

[3] By precision loss we mean the difference between the precision achieved with the joint and independent models.

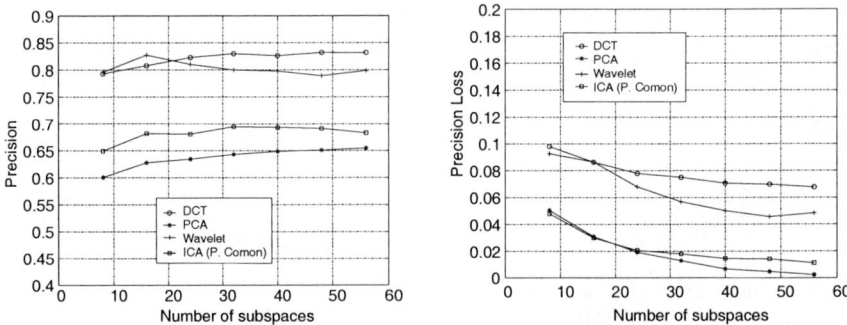

Fig. 5. Recognition results on Corel. Left: Precision, at 10% recall, achieved with joint modeling. Right: Precision loss inherent to the independence assumption.

recognition is affected by much more sophisticated patterns of dependence. The logical conclusion is that ICA techniques designed to minimize measures such as those of Figure 3 may not always be of great use for recognition.

Second, the precision curves seem to comply very well with the theoretical arguments of section 2. In particular, they are concave (there is a large increase in precision from 1 to 8 dimensions that we do not show for clarity of the graph), and tend to be flatter when the features are more independent. Remember that compliance with the theory implies that the curves are dominated by the Bayes error for all dimensions when the features are independent, and up to the inflection point when they are not. This is an important observation, since the more independent features (flatter curves) have smaller precision than that achieved at the inflection point of the less independent ones. In fact, a comparison of the two plots reveals significant evidence in support of the conjecture that precision at the inflection point is a monotonic function of the degree of dependence of the features! The natural conclusion is then that independence has a non-negligible cost in terms of Bayes error. In particular, the precision achieved with the most independent features (wavelet coefficients) is almost 10% bellow the peak precision achieved with the less independent ones (DCT).

This conclusion is also supported by Figure 5, which presents recognition results on Corel. Since this is a larger database and contains colored images, 192-dimensional feature space, the queries take significantly longer to compute. For this reason, we restricted the analysis to the first 64 dimensions (and only considered one of the ICA techniques) which are probably not enough to reach the inflection point in all cases. Nevertheless, one can still confidently say that the precision of the more independent feature transforms is roughly 10% lower than the peak precision of the less independent transforms. The only significant difference with respect to the results obtained on Brodatz is that ICA does appear to produce features which are very close to independent, while the wavelet coefficients are not independent.

References

1. A. Bell and T. Sejnowski. The independent components of natural scenes are edge filters. *Vision Research*, 37(23):3327–3328, December 1997.
2. J. Bergen and E. Adelson. Early Vision and Texture Perception. *Nature*, 333(6171):363–364, 1988.
3. J. Bergen and M. Landy. Computational Modeling of Visual Texture Segregation. In M. Landy and J. Movshon, editors, *Computational Models of Visual Processing*. MIT Press, 1991.
4. J. Cardoso. Blind Signal Separation: Statistical Principles. *Proceedings of the IEEE*, 90(8):2009–20026, October 1998.
5. P. Comon. Independent Component Analysis, A New concept? *Signal Processing*, 36:287–314, 1994.
6. L. Devroye, L. Gyorfi, and G. Lugosi. *A Probabilistic Theory of Pattern Recognition*. Springer-Verlag, 1996.
7. D. Field. What is the goal of sensory coding? *Neural Computation*, 6(4):559–601, January 1989.
8. I. Fogel and D. Sagi. Gabor Filters as Texture Discriminators. *Biol. Cybern.*, 61:103–113, 1989.
9. D. Hubel and T. Wiesel. Brain Mechanisms of Vision. *Scientific American*, September 1979.
10. A. Hyvarinen and E. Oja. Independent Component Analysis: Algorithms and Applications. *Neural Networks*, 13:411–430, 2000.
11. N. Jayant and P. Noll. *Digital Coding of Waveforms: Principles and Applications to Speech and Video*. Prentice Hall, 1984.
12. D. Knill and W. Richards. *Perception as Bayesian Inference*. Cambridge Univ. Press, 1996.
13. J. Malik and P. Perona. Preattentive Texture Discrimination with Early Vision Mechanisms. *Journal of the Optical Society of America*, 7(5):923–932, May 1990.
14. S. Mallat. A Theory for Multiresolution Signal Decomposition: the Wavelet Representation. *IEEE Trans. on Pattern Analysis and Machine Intelligence*, Vol. 11:674 693, July 1989.
15. B. Olshausen and D. Field. Emergence of simple-cell receptive field properties by learning a sparse code for natural images. *Nature*, 381:607–609, 1996.
16. M. Porat and Y. Zeevi. Localized Texture Processing in Vision: Analysis and Synthesis in the Gaborian Space. *IEEE Trans. on Biomedical Engineering*, 36(1):115–129, January 1989.
17. J. Portilla and E. Simoncelli. Texture Modeling and Synthesis using Joint Statistics of Complex Wavelet Coefficients. In *IEEE Workshop on Statistical and Computational Theories of Vision, Fort Collins, Colorado*, 1999.
18. D. Sagi. The Psychophysics of Texture Segmentation. In T. Papathomas, editor, *Early Vision and Beyond*, chapter 7. MIT Press, 1996.
19. A. Sutter, J. Beck, and N. Graham. Contrast and Spatial Variables in Texture Segregation: testing a simple spatial-frequency channels model. *Perceptual Psychophysics*, 46:312–332, 1989.
20. N. Vasconcelos. *Bayesian Models for Visual Information Retrieval*. PhD thesis, Massachusetts Institute of Technology, 2000.
21. N. Vasconcelos and A. Lippman. A Probabilistic Architecture for Content-based Image Retrieval. In *Proc. IEEE Computer Vision and Pattern Recognition Conf., Hilton Head, North Carolina*, 2000.

A Probabilistic Multi-scale Model for Contour Completion Based on Image Statistics

Xiaofeng Ren and Jitendra Malik

Computer Science Division
University of California at Berkeley, Berkeley, CA 94720
{xren,malik}@cs.berkeley.edu

Abstract. We derive a probabilistic multi-scale model for contour completion based on image statistics. The boundaries of human segmented images are used as "ground truth". A probabilistic formulation of contours demands a prior model and a measurement model. From the image statistics of boundary contours, we derive both the prior model of contour shape and the local likelihood model of image measurements. We observe multi-scale phenomena in the data, and accordingly propose a higher-order Markov model over scales for the contour continuity prior. Various image cues derived from orientation energy are evaluated and incorporated into the measurement model. Based on these models, we have designed a multi-scale algorithm for contour completion, which exploits both contour continuity and texture. Experimental results are shown on a wide range of images.

1 Introduction

Traditionally there are two approaches to grouping: region-based methods and contour-based methods. Region-based approaches, such as the Normalized Cut framework [19], have been popular recently. Region-based methods seem to be a natural way to approach the grouping problem, because (1) regions arise from objects, which are natural entities in grouping; (2) many important cues, such as texture and color, are region-based; (3) region properties are more robust to noise and clutter.

Nevertheless, contours, even viewed as boundaries between regions, are themselves very important. In many cases boundary contour is the most informative cue in grouping as well as in shape analysis. The intervening contour approach [9] has provided a framework to incorporate contour cues into a region-based framework. However, how to reliably extract contour information, despite years of research, is largely an open problem. Contour extraction is hard, mainly for the following reasons:

1. texture: natural scenes are often highly textured. Contour-based approaches often have difficulty dealing with textured regions and find a lot of false positives, largely because they do not have an inherent concept of texture.
2. low contrast: contrast varies a lot in natural scenes. For example, camouflage of animals. In many cases, contours are perceptually salient only because they form a consistent group.

The problem of contour completion has been studied extensively [4,14,17,13,20,5,18,2]. Most of these approaches are two-stage: an early stage of detection, where hard decisions are made locally and prematurely; and a later stage of linking or grouping. This two-stage paradigm ignores the crucial fact that contour elements are not independent. A pixel is an edge if and only if there is a contour passing through it. The probability of a pixel being an edge is the posterior probability that there exists a contour passing through this pixel given the image.

Based on this observation, we propose a multi-scale Bayesian approach to contour completion and the classical problem of contour extraction. Two questions we need to answer in a Bayesian framework: a prior model of contour shape; and a local model of contour measurements, how the image arises from contours. These two questions we answer by empirical measurements of contours in natural images. There have been many recent studies on the statistics of natural images [22,8,7,11,3] . In our work we use the database of human segmented images reported in [11]. The contours in these segmentations are explored to understand natural scenes and to motivate our contour completion algorithm. Driven by this empirical analysis in Section 3, *higher order Markov models* are proposed as the prior model for contour shape. This is a significant distinction in our work from the related approaches such as Mumford [13], Williams and Jacobs [21], who used a first-order Markov model for contour shape. We also make use of the database of human segmented images to arrive at a measurement model, incorporating various local cues such as orientation energy and textureness. Based on the Markov assumption, we use dynamic programming to efficiently compute the posterior probability. The multi-scale contour completion algorithm is presented in Section 5. Experimental results are shown in Section 6.

2 Bayesian Contour Completion

In this section we give a formal analysis of our intuition in the introduction and motivate our work on images statistics. The key is that how likely a pixel is an edge is quantified by the posterior probability that there exists a contour passing through it:

Consider a pixel p in a given image I. Let M_p denote the measurement, or a feature vector, at the pixel p, and M the collection $\{M_p\}$ for all p. Let $\mathbf{b}_p \in \{0, 1\}$ be the binary random variable which denotes the existence of a boundary contour at pixel p. What we want to compute is the posterior distribution:

$$P(\mathbf{b}_p|M) = \frac{P(M, \mathbf{b}_p)}{P(M)} \propto P(M, \mathbf{b}_p) \qquad (1)$$

The posterior probability of the non-contour case is determined by our background model. If we make the simplifying assumption that $\mathbf{b}_p = 0$ does not constrain the existence of contours at other pixels, we have

$$\begin{aligned}P(\mathbf{b}_p = 0|M) &\propto P(M|\mathbf{b}_p = 0)P(\mathbf{b}_p = 0)\\ &= P(\mathbf{b}_p = 0)P(M_p|\mathbf{b}_p = 0)P(M_{I\setminus\{p\}})\end{aligned} \qquad (2)$$

By the law of large numbers, the marginal probability M_Λ can be well approximated by an exponential function $P(M_\Lambda) \approx r^{|\Lambda|}$, where $|\Lambda|$ is the number of pixels in the subset Λ, and r is the expected likelihood.

In the contour case $P(\mathbf{b}_p = 1)$, we can not make the independence assumption. Indeed, $\mathbf{b}_p = 1$ if and only if there is a boundary contour passing through the pixel p. Let $\mathcal{C} = \{\gamma |\ \gamma$ is a curve passing through $p\ \}$ be the collection of all such contours. Since one and only one such contour passes through p in the image I, we have

$$P(M, \mathbf{b}_p = 1) = \sum_{\gamma \in \mathcal{C}} P(M, \gamma)$$

For each such curve γ,

$$P(M, \gamma) = P(M|\gamma) P(\gamma)$$

What we need in this probabilistic formulation is:

1. $P(\gamma)$, the prior model on contour shape;
2. $P(M|\gamma)$, the model of local image measurements conditioned on the presence or the absence of a contour.

3 Modeling Contour Shape

The key fact we need to keep in mind when studying contours, or any object in natural images, is that these objects are multi-scale. This multi-scale phenomenon mainly arises from two sources:

1. Objects in the natural world are themselves multi-scale. For example, a object has parts: the parts in the figure of a person include nose, head, torso, arm, hand, finger, etc., all of which are different in scale.
2. Despite the possible bias introduced by the observer, objects are usually viewed from an arbitrary distance and angle.

3.1 Scale Invariance

Scale invariance in natural images has been reported by various authors. An in-depth study of scale invariance in boundary contours is beyond the scope of this paper. We study one phenomenon here: contours consist of segments, which roughly correspond to the parts of objects or the scale of local details. We consider the decomposition of contours at extremal points, i.e., the points whose curvatures are locally maximal. Figure 1(a) shows some examples of this decomposition. The distribution of the length of the resulted contour segments reveals to us properties of the underlying mechanism which generates the contours. For example, if a first-order Markov model were accurate, then this distribution of segment length, or the time to wait until a high curvature event occurs, is exponential.

Figure 1 (b) shows the distribution of contour segment length. Ignoring the range where the length is small, in which the decompositions are not reliably, we observe from this distribution the following power law:

$$\text{frequency} \propto \frac{1}{(\text{contour length})^{1.994}}$$

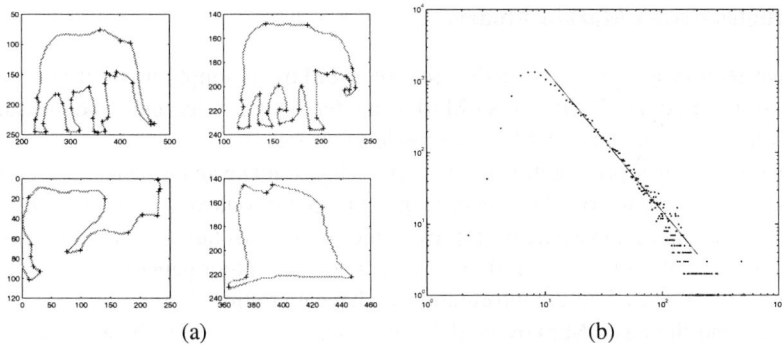

Fig. 1. Examples of the contour decomposition. High curvature points, where the contours are segmented, are shown in the plots. The decompositions are consistent with human perception.

This power law is consistent with the distribution of region area [11], and with the intuition that natural objects are self-similar. We can formalize this intuition and give a simple explanation: suppose we have a contour of fixed length l_0 at a base scale. When viewed at scale s (say $s = d$ where d is the distance to the observer), its apparent length is l_0/s. At the same time, because the field of view is s^2 times larger, the probability of observing this contour increases by s^2. Hence the frequency of observing this contour of an apparent length l is proportional to $s^2 = (l_0^2)/(l^2)$. I.e., this contour induces a whole distribution:

$$f(l) \propto \int_s s^2 \delta_{l_0}(ls) ds = \frac{l_0^2}{l^2}$$

We take the expectation w.r.t. l_0 to obtain the overall distribution. This does not change the structure of the power law:

$$\bar{f}(l) = E[f(l)] \propto \frac{E[l_0^2]}{l^2}$$

it still decreases quadratically with contour length l.

We can compare this inverse square law with the predictive first-order Markov model as used by Mumford [13], Williams and Jacobs [21]. In their work, curvature is assumed to be white noise; hence the tangent direction is a Brownian motion. That would imply that the frequency a contour appears decreases exponentially with its length. Exponential models are common; they have the memoryless property and are easy to work with. We would like to assume that. However, *This is not true empirically.*

The next question we want to explore is *self-similarity*. We use region area as an indication for the scale of the object. We study whether the distribution of the contour segment length is the same for different ranges of region area. Our results, which we omit here, show that the distributions are almost identical for groups of different region sizes. This result justifies the intuition that objects themselves are multi-scale and self-similar in nature. *It suggests that any algorithm for contour completion should be intrinsically multi-scale.*

3.2 Higher-Order Markov Models

We have seen in the previous section that the Markov assumption is not accurate. In this section we extend the first-order Markov model to high-order ones, and measure the information these higher-order Markov models convey.

Let $C(\cdot)$ be the representation of the curve. This could be an intrinsic representation, e.g., curvature parameterized by curve length. Or, in the context of contour completion, to make the computation easier we represent the curve by its tangent directions parameterized by time. We adopt the random process view of contour generation, in which we predict $C(t+1)$ based on the information we have up to time t.

We extend the basic Markov model over scale. Let $C^{(0)} = C$ be a curve γ at the base scale. $C^{(1)}, \cdots, C^{(k-1)}$ are the scaled versions of the original curve γ. Define the k-th Markov model over scales to be:

$$P(C^{(0)}(t+1)|\gamma) = P(C^{(0)}(t+1)|C^{(0)}(t), C^{(1)}(t), \cdots, C^{(k-1)}(t)) \quad (3)$$

Figure 2 shows the information gain when we extend the Markov model over scales. We observe that there is a substantial gain from combining orientation information at coarser scales. The use of higher-order Markov models is empirically justified by cross-validation (Figure 2 (b)). The intuition is that scaled curves, at coarser scales, combine information in a neighborhood. For example, if $C^{(1)}(t)$ is to the left of $C^{(0)}(t)$, it makes a left turn at t and therefore $C^{(0)}(t+1)$ is more likely to turn to the left. This intuition has been confirmed empirically from samples of conditional distributions, which we omit here. Since long-range dependencies in contours is likely caused by interactions at coarser scales, these models over scales are a natural choice for local contour modeling. This is not intended to be a global model of contours, since in these models there is no notion of topological constraints, such as closure and no self-intersection; nevertheless, it is sufficient for our purpose of contour completion.

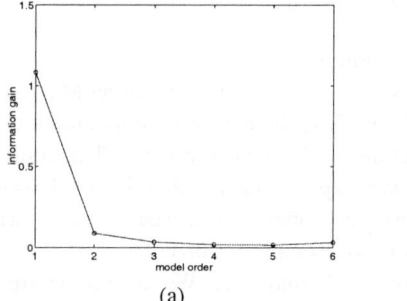
(a)

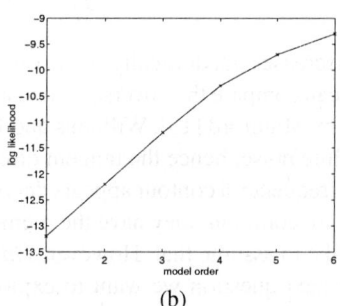
(b)

Fig. 2. (a) Information gain as the order of our Markov models increase. The model of order 1 corresponds to the traditional Markov model. (b) 10-fold cross validation of higher-order Markov models. The log-likelihood is normalized by the length of contours.

4 Local Measurement Model

We have seen the use of higher order Markov models to represent the prior distribution of contour shape. In this section we turn to the images themselves. We study how the contours locally give rise to image measurements. We formalize the problem as computing the local posterior distribution of contour elements. In Section 4.1 we derive the posterior model of local contour detection from image statistics of both the orientation energy and textureness. In Section 4.2 we derive a probabilistic model of positional uncertainty to go beyond the assumption of conditional independence. And in Section 4.3 we derive in a similar fashion a model of local orientation uncertainty.

4.1 Detection Uncertainty

The use of orientation energy (e.g., [12,16]) has been an essential part of computer vision. The orientation energy at an angle θ is defined as:

$$OE_\theta^2 = (I * f_{1,\theta})^2 + (I * f_{2,\theta})^2 \qquad (4)$$

where $f_{1,\theta}$ and $f_{2,\theta}$ are the second Gaussian derivative and its Hilbert pair oriented at the angle θ. It has roots in biological vision, and it has proven to be extremely successful in both contour and texture analysis. However, people have also realized the difficulties which come with the success. One major problem is the wide existence of textured regions, which typically have high responses to traditional contour-based techniques. Recently people have started to look into the interaction of texture cues with contour cues (e.g., Malik et. al. [10]). They introduced the notion of $p_{texture}$, based on the χ^2 distance of texton histograms (see detailed explanations in their paper):

$$p_{texture} = 1 - \frac{1}{exp[-(\chi_{LR}^2 - \tau)/\beta]} \qquad (5)$$

They target at suppressing OE responses in homogeneous texture regions, by multiplying p_{con}, a non-linear transform of OE, by $p_{texture}$. In this paper we extend the notion of $p_{texture}$ to be orientation dependent; i.e., χ_{LR}^2 is computed for each angle θ. Let $p_{con,\theta} = 1 - exp(-OE_\theta/\sigma_{IC})$ as in [10]. We gate $p_{con,\theta}$ with $p_{texture,\theta}$ separately in each angle θ

$$p_{b,\theta} = p_{con,\theta} * (1 - p_{texture,\theta}) \qquad (6)$$

After the gating, we take the maximum $p_b^* = \max p_{b,\theta}$. Let θ^* denote the angle where $p_{b,\theta}$ achieves the maximum, i.e., $p_{b,\theta^*} = p_b^*$.

In Figure 3, we show the power of this cue combination. At the back of the zebra, the orientation energy is strong in the vertical direction. This is not the true direction of the boundary contour (in the scale where the human segmentations are done). However, $p_{texture}$ is low only at the horizontal direction. This enables us to locally detect the maximum p_b^* in the correct direction.

Figure 4 shows the statistics of $p_{con,\theta}$ and $p_{texture,\theta}$. The likelihood ratio in Part (a) is used in our contour completion algorithm. Part (c) and (d) justifies the multiplicative

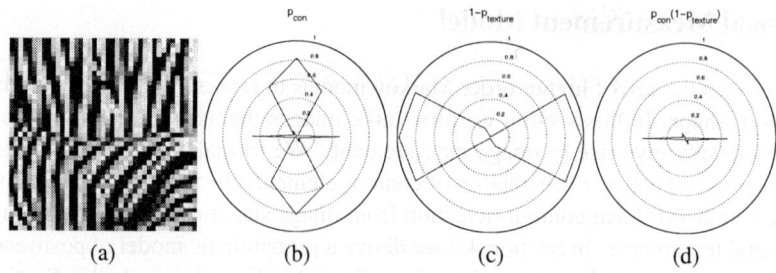

Fig. 3. Illustration of $p_{texture,\theta}$. (a) a patch from a zebra image; we consider the pixel at the center. (b) the distribution of raw $p_{con,\theta}$ (not gated with $p_{texture}$), maximal in the vertical direction. (c) $1 - p_{texture,\theta}$, maximal in the horizontal direction. (d) the product $p_{b,\theta} = p_{con,\theta}(1 - p_{texture,\theta})$, sharply peaked in the horizontal direction.

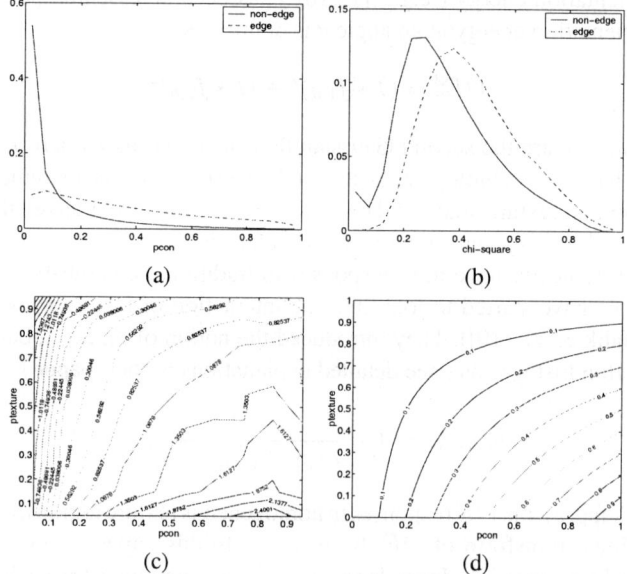

Fig. 4. Image statistics of orientation energy ($p_{con,\theta}$) and textureness ($p_{texture,\theta}$). (a) the marginal distributions of $p_{con,\theta}$, both the edge case and non-edge case. (b) the marginal distributions of the χ^2 distance used in Equation eqrefeq:ptexture to produce of $p_{texture,\theta}$. (c) the contour plot of the likelihood ratio $\frac{P(\cdot|edge)}{P(\cdot|non-edge)}$. (d) the contour plot of the multiplicative cue combination (Equation (6)).

form of our definition of $p_{b,\theta}$. We also empirically measure the information gain of the cues from histograms of the joint distribution. In our experiments, the marginal entropy of $\mathbf{b}_p$, *edge* vs. *non-edge*, is 0.2492 (in bits); the information gain of $p_{con,\theta}$ is 0.0425; and the information gain of $p_{texture,\theta}$ over $p_{con,\theta}$ is 0.0091. These information-theoretic measures illustrate the relative importance of these local cues.

4.2 Positional Uncertainty

So far in our local model, the posterior probability p_b^* is estimated independently at each pixel. We have ignored the important relationship: the correlation between neighboring pixels. Traditionally this is done by non-maximum suppression. However, due to image noise we can never be certain about the contour localization. There is always a positional uncertainty. To be consistent with our philosophy of avoiding local hard decisions, we again make use of image statistics to derive a probabilistic model of positional uncertainty, which serves as a soft non-maximum suppression.

We base our analysis on the quadratic model originally proposed in [15]. Empirically we have found it to perform well on real images. Their approach is to fit a parabola in a local neighborhood, and use the information from the parabola fitting, such as d, the distance to the center of the parabola, and c, the curvature of the parabola. Details are omitted here. In Figure 5 (a)-(c) we show the statistics of the various outputs from this parabola fitting. In this study of non-maximum suppression, we compare the statistics of edge pixels to near-edge pixels (i.e., pixels that are within a distance of 4 from a human marked contour). The results are qualitatively different from what we have seen in the previous section, where we compare edge pixels to non-edge pixels. p_b^* alone is not a good cue for non-maximum suppression. Instead, both the distance d and the curvature c are informative. For edge pixels, the curvature tends to be negative, and the distance to the center of the parabola tends to be small. In this work we choose d, the distance , for our model of positional uncertainty. We observe the following relationship

$$P(\mathbf{b}_p|M_p, d_p) = P(\mathbf{b}_p|M_p)\frac{P(d_p|M_p, \mathbf{b}_p)}{P(d_p|M_p)}$$

Accordingly we collect the statistics for the ratio $P(d_p|p_b^*, \mathbf{b}_p = 1)/P(d_p|p_b^*, \mathbf{b}_p = 0)$, as shown in Figure 5 (d). Motivated by this statistics, we choose the following model to update p_b^*:

$$p_b^* \leftarrow p_b^* \left[(\alpha_1 + \alpha_2 d)^{-\beta_1 - \beta_2 p_b^*}\right] \quad (7)$$

In this parametric model, when d is large the multiplicative factor is small, and p_b^* is suppressed. This suppression is more significant when p_b^* is large.

4.3 Orientation Uncertainty

In the previous sections we have studied the posterior probability of $\mathbf{b}_p$, i.e., the existence of a boundary contour at a pixel, as a function of $p_{con,\theta}$, $p_{texture,\theta}$, and d (the distance to the center of a local parabolic fit). However, due to image noise and further complications such as junctions, the true contour might not be oriented at θ^*, the maximum $p_{b,\theta}$ orientation. We represent the orientation uncertainty with a distribution $\{p_\theta\}$ over θ at each pixel. We further assume that this distribution is Gaussian, and θ^* is an unbiased estimate of the peak. We use two features to estimate the variance σ_θ^2: p_b^* and $p_b^\perp$. $p_b^\perp$ is defined as follows: if θ^* is the angle of the maximum $p_{b,\theta}$, we choose the angle $\theta^\perp$ perpendicular to θ^* and define $p_b^\perp = p_{b,\theta^\perp}$. Figure 6 (a) shows the statistics of the

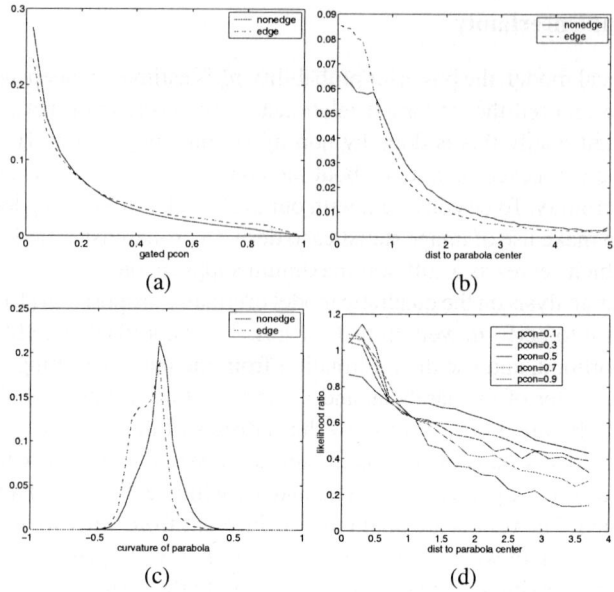

Fig. 5. Image statistics for probabilistic non-maximum suppression. (a) the marginal distributions of $Pcon$, edge vs. non-edge. Note here we are comparing edge pixels with near-edge pixels, hence the orientation energy alone gives us little information. (b) the marginal distributions of the distance d in parabola fitting. c) the marginal distributions of the curvature c in parabola fitting. (d) the distributions of the likelihood ratio, as a function of the distance d, conditioned on p_b^*.

variance of local orientation for each $(p_b^*, p_b^\perp)$ pair. Motivated by this statistics, we use a simple parametric model as shown in Figure 6 (b):

$$\sigma_\theta^2 = \exp(-\beta \frac{p_b^*}{p_b^\perp + \alpha}) \tag{8}$$

When p_b^* is large, the uncertainty is low; similarly when $p_b^\perp$ is large, the uncertainty is high. This simple parametric model has the desired properties; clearly other models could be used as well. Once we obtain an estimate of σ_θ^2, we distribute the probability mass p_b^* over θ according to the uncertainty.

There are three important cases here: (1) when the contrast is high, we have a reliable estimate of local orientation; (2) when the contrast is low, local orientation can be arbitrary; (3) at a junction, the $p_{b,\theta}$ profile is complicated. Building a local junction detector is extremely difficult. Our approach is to make a soft decision locally, and let contour completion to find the most probable orientation. This frees us from searching for a precise solution for the distribution of orientation $\{p_\theta\}$.

5 Multi-scale Contour Completion

To motivate the multi-scale model from a practical viewpoint, Figure 7 shows the output of a single-scale contour completion algorithm on the same image scaled to different

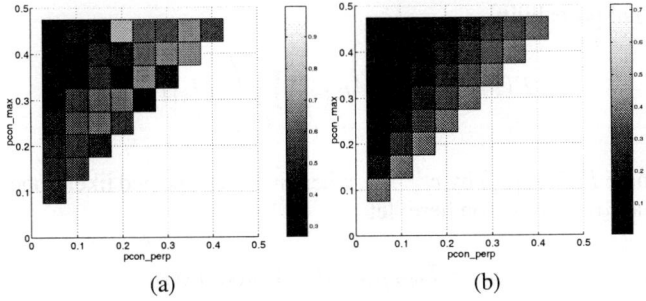

Fig. 6. The uncertainty of local orientation σ_θ^2 as a function of p_b^* and $p_b^\perp$. (a) the statistics from real images. (b) fitting the parametric model (Equation (8)).

sizes. The results are dramatically different. At finer scales, the algorithm is unable to complete contours over a long distance in the image. At coarser scales, the algorithm is unable to properly detect and enhance curved contours. For any model based on the Markov assumption and the underlying preference for straight lines, no matter how the parameters are tuned, it only works at a certain scale, therefore unable to handle the wide range of scales existing in natural images.

Fig. 7. A synthetic image and the outputs of a single-scale contour completion algorithm on this image at different sizes. The figures correspond to completion over increasingly coarse scales.

We will start with a single-scale version of our probabilistic contour completion algorithm and then extend it to multi-scale. The multi-scale property comes in two ways: (a) contour propagation is done at each scale and the results are combined to produce the final estimate; (b) prior models at finer scales are conditioned on the results from coarser scales.

5.1 Single-Scale Version

We represent a curve γ by $\{q(t), T(t)\}$, where $q(t)$ denote the locations and $T(t)$ the tangent directions of γ at $q(t)$. Let $P_{\text{length}}(n)$ be the distribution of contour lengths and $|\gamma|$ the length of the curve γ. The prior probability of γ can be written as

$$P(\gamma) = P_{\text{length}}(|\gamma|) P(T(\cdot)) P(\gamma(\cdot)|T(\cdot)) \tag{9}$$

The conditional probability

$$P(M|\gamma) \approx P(M_{I\setminus\{\gamma\}}) \prod_t P(M_\gamma | T(t)) \qquad (10)$$

We approximate $P(M_{I\setminus\{\gamma\}})$ by $r^{|I|-|\gamma|}$, where r is the expected likelihood in Section 2. Apply the Markov assumption here; let

$$g_t^+ = P_{location}(q(t+1)|q(t), T(t))$$
$$g_t^- = P_{location}(q(t-1)|q(t), T(t))$$
$$h_t^+ = P_{tangent}(T(t+1)|T(t))$$
$$h_t^- = P_{tangent}(T(t-1)|T(t))$$
$$m_t = P_{measurement}(M_{q(t)}|T(t))/r$$

Then we have the likelihood ratio:

$$\begin{aligned}L(M,\gamma) &= \frac{P(M,\gamma)}{P(M,\mathbf{b}_p=0)} \propto P(\gamma)\frac{P(M_\gamma|\gamma)}{P(M_\gamma|\mathbf{b}_{\gamma(\cdot)}=0)} \\ &\approx P_{length}(|\gamma|)P(T(0))\frac{P(M_p|T(0))}{P(M_p|\mathbf{b}_p=0)} \\ &\quad \times \prod_{t<0} g_{t+1}^- h_{t+1}^- m_t \prod_{t>0} g_{t-1}^+ h_{t-1}^+ m_t\end{aligned} \qquad (11)$$

This is a Hidden Markov Model with $q(t)$ and $T(t)$ as hidden variables. Because of the one-dimensional nature of contours, we can apply dynamical programming to solve this computational problem, which is essentially the same as the alpha-beta algorithm or the stochastic completion approach in [21]. The details are omitted here. Let γ^+ denote the partial contour $\{\gamma(t); t > 0\}$, and γ^- for $\{\gamma(t); t < 0\}$. Let $\phi(p,\theta,k)$ be the sum of the messages arriving at (p,θ) at step k. We maintain:

$$\phi(p,-\theta,k) \propto P(M, \exists \gamma \text{ through } (p,\theta) \text{ s.t. } |\gamma^+| = k)$$
$$\phi(p,\theta,k) \propto P(M, \exists \gamma \text{ through } (p,\theta) \text{ s.t. } |\gamma^-| = k)$$

$\phi(p,\theta,k)$ are recursively computed using propagation and diffusion as in [21,20]. Given ϕ, we can calculate the likelihood ratio $L_p = \frac{P(M,\mathbf{b}_p=1)}{P(M,\mathbf{b}_p=0)}$ as:

$$\begin{aligned}L_p &\propto \sum_\theta P(T(0)=\theta)P(M_p|T(0)=\theta) \\ &\quad \times \sum_{n>1}\left(P_{length}(n)\sum_{k=1}^{n-2}\phi(p,\theta,k)\phi(p,-\theta,n-k-1)\right)\end{aligned} \qquad (12)$$

With this probabilistic interpretation, we can incorporate contour cues, avoid making premature hard decisions, and readily extend the model to multi-scale.

Fig. 8. Results on a few classical synthetic images.

5.2 Multi-scale Version

At the coarsest scale, the single-scale version of the contour completion algorithm is applied. Suppose we have obtained the posterior distributions $P(b_p^{(s)} = 0|M^{(s)})$ and $P(T_p^{(s)}|M^{(s)})$ for scales $s = 1, \cdots, k-1$. (note $\sum_\theta P(T_p^{(s)} = \theta|M^{(s)}) = P(b_p^{(s)} = 1|M^{(s)})$.)

The prior distributions in Equation (9) is now all conditioned on the coarser scales. We see that the message passing algorithm remains the same, except that the prior of tangent directions $P_{\text{tangent}}(\theta'|\theta)$ now becomes

$$P_{\text{tangent}}^{(k)}(\theta'|\theta) = E_{\{T_q^{(s)}, s<k\}} \left[P_{\text{tangent}}(\theta'|\theta, \{T_q^{(s)}, s < k\}) \right] \quad (13)$$

We refer to this multi-scale processing as *multi-scale conditioning*. In practice, we simplify the computation by conditioning $P_{\text{tangent}}^{(k)}$ at scale k only on $T_q^{(k-1)}$ at scale $k-1$, and use the maximum-probability direction $T_q^{*(s)}$ to replace the expectation over all the possible directions $\{T_q^{(s)}\}$. Some results obtained by the multi-scale algorithm are shown in the next section. Finally, to combine the results from individual scales, we have

$$P(M, T_p = \theta) = \sum_s P_{\text{scale}}(s) P^{(s)}(M, T_p = \theta)$$

where we use the self-similar $1/s^2$ distribution in Section 3.1 for P_{scale}.

(a)   (b)   (c)   (d)

Fig. 9. A synthetic example of the use of multi-scale conditioning. (a) the original input. (b) the completion at the coarse scale. (c) the completion at the fine scale without using the conditioning in Equation (13). (d) the completion with the conditioning.

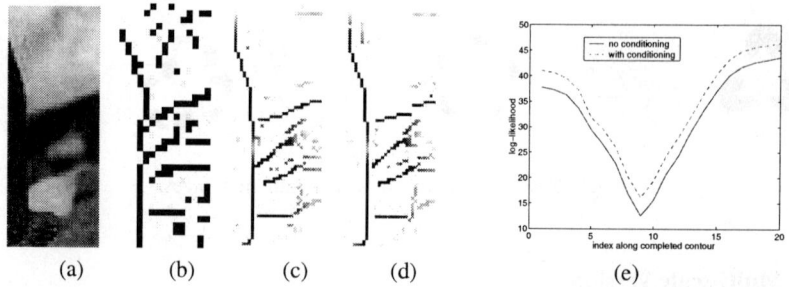

Fig. 10. A further example of the use of multi-scale conditioning. It is a patch extracted from the penguin image in Figure 11. (a) the original image. (b) the completion at the coarse scale. (c) the completion at the fine scale without conditioning. (d) the completion with conditioning. (e) the posterior log-likelihood at the pixels along the central low-contrast contour. Both algorithms successfully complete the low-contrast contour in the middle of the patch. The signal is significantly enhanced by the use of multi-scale conditioning at low-contrast locations.

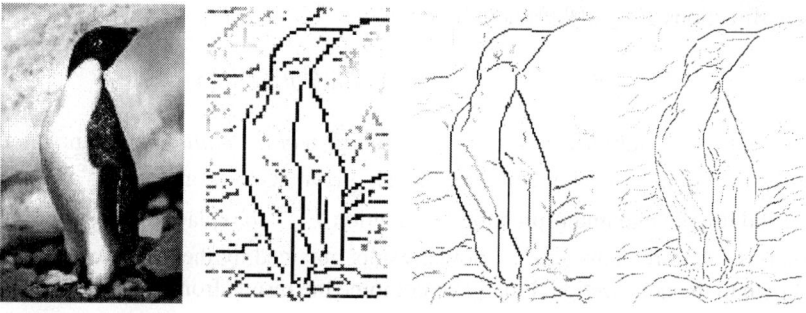

Fig. 11. A complete example of multi-scale contour completion. The completion is done at three distinct scales, from coarse to fine. We notice that the results are qualitatively different. At the coarse scale, large gaps of low contrast contours are easily completed, and noise are generally suppressed. But there are some details which we can only see at fine scales.

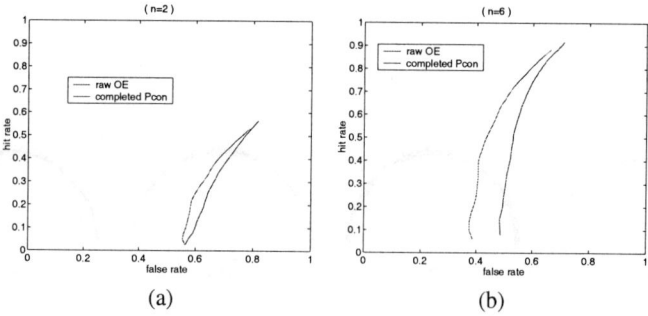

Fig. 12. ROC-like curves for performance evaluation. (a) with $n = 2$ (see text). (b) with $n = 6$.

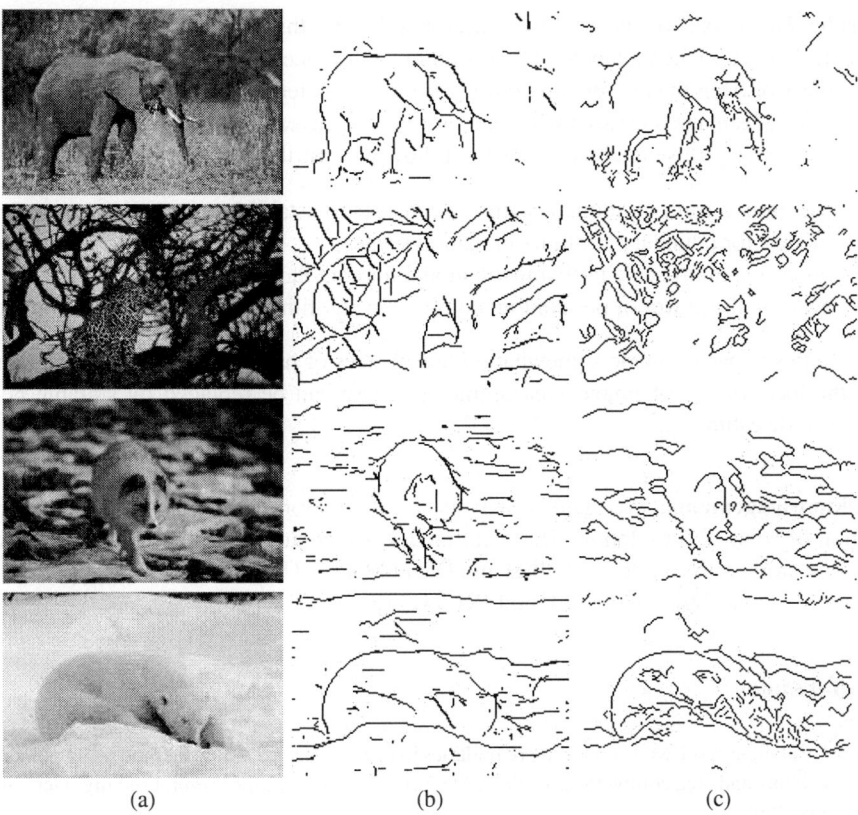

Fig. 13. More results on real images with low contrast contours and stochastic textures. (a) the original images, at the resolution of 179 × 115. (b) the thresholded results of our algorithm. (c) the Canny edges with approximately the same number of pixels. Notice how the algorithm recovers low-contrast contours and suppresses noise, for example, in the first row the back and the left leg of the elephant; in the second row the branches on the right and the cheetah in the middle; and in the third row the outline of the wolf.

6 Experiments and Evaluation

Figure 8 shows our results on a few simple synthetic images with subjective contours. Figure 9 shows the use of multi-scale completion on a synthetic image. Figure 10 shows the use of multi-scale conditioning for real images. Figure 11 shows the completion results at various scales. And Figure 13 contains more completion results. Please see the interpretations therein.

We have quantitatively evaluated the performance of our algorithm on a large set of images. We again turn to the ground truth from our segmentation database. The problem of edge detection by itself is a classification problem. We define the following two performance measures: *hit rate*, the number of correctly labeled edge pixels divided by the total number of edge pixels; and *false rate*, the number of labeled pixels which are not true edges divided by the total number of labeled pixels. Figure 12 shows our results. The plots correspond to two different tolerance thresholds on localization error. We declare a hit when a labeled pixel is within a distance of n from a true contour. We can observe from the curves, that our algorithm consistently outperforms the raw OE cue. This advantage increases when the threshold n increases.

In summary, this paper has made the following contributions:

1. use ground truth on human segmented images to establish prior and measurement models for boundary contours in natural scenes;
2. propose a multi-scale probabilistic model for contour completion;
3. evaluate the power of our contour completion algorithm on a wide range of images.

In this paper we made somewhat *ad hoc* choices of parametric forms for the terms in the local model of image measurements. These can be replaced by suitable non-parametric estimates.

Acknowledgements. We thank Yair Weiss for discussions on the probabilistic formulation of contour completion. The local models for contour measurements are related to joint work with Charless Fowlkes and David Martin. This research was supported by NSF through a Digital Library Grant IRI-9411334.

References

1. S. Belongie and J. Malik. Finding boundaries in natural images: A new method using point descriptors and area completion. In *Proc. 5th Euro. Conf. Computer Vision*, Freiburg, Germany, June 1998.
2. J.H. Elder and S.W. Zucker. Computing contour closures. In *Proc. Euro. Conf. Computer Vision*, volume I, pages 399–412, Cambridge, England, Apr 1996.
3. W. S. Geisler, J. S. Perry, B. J. Super, and D. P. Gallogly. Edge co-occurrence in natural images predicts contour grouping performance. *Vision Research*, 41:711–724, 2001.
4. S. Geman and D. Geman. Stochastic relaxation, gibbs distribution, and the bayesian retoration of images. *IEEE Trans. Pattern Analysis and Machine Intelligence*, 6:721–41, Nov. 1984.
5. G. Guy and G. Medioni. Inferring global perceptual contours from local features. *Int'l. Journal of Computer Vision*, 20(1-2):113–33, Oct. 1996.
6. F. Heitger and R. von der Heydt. A computational model of neural contour processing. In *Proc. Int. Conf. Computer Vision*, pages 32–40, Berlin, Germany, May 1993.
7. J. Huang and D. Mumford. Statistics of natural images and models. In *Proc. IEEE Conf. Comput. Vision and Pattern Recognition*, pages I:541–547, 1999.
8. S. Konishi, A.L. Yuille, J.M. Coughlan, and S.C. Zhu. Fundamental bounds on edge detection: An information theoretic evaluation of different edge cues. pages I:573–579, 1999.
9. T. Leung and J. Malik. Contour continuity in region-based image segmentation. In H. Burkhardt and B. Neumann, editors, *Proc. Euro. Conf. Computer Vision*, volume 1, pages 544–59, Freiburg, Germany, June 1998. Springer-Verlag.
10. J. Malik, S. Belongie, T. Leung, and J. Shi. Contour and texture analysis for image segmentation. *Int'l. Journal of Computer Vision*, 43(1):7–27, June 2001.
11. D. Martin, C. Fowlkes, D. Tal, and J. Malik. A database of human segmented natural images and its application to evaluating segmentation algorithms and measuring ecological statistics. In *Proc. 8th Int'l. Conf. Computer Vision*, volume 2, pages 416–423, July 2001.

12. M.C. Morrone and R.A. Owens. Feature detection from local energy. *Pattern Recognition Letters*, 6:303–13, 1987.
13. D. Mumford. Elastica and computer vision. In Chandrajit Bajaj, editor, *Algebraic Geometry and Its Applications*, pages 491–506. Springer Verlag, 1994.
14. P. Parent and S.W. Zucker. Trace inference, curvature consistency, and curve detection. *IEEE Trans. Pattern Analysis and Machine Intelligence*, 11(8):823–39, Aug. 1989.
15. P. Perona and J. Malik. Boundary detection using quadratic filters: Performance criteria and experimental assessment. In *SPIE*, 1708.
16. P. Perona and J. Malik. Detecting and localizing edges composed of steps, peaks and roofs. In *Proc. Int. Conf. Computer Vision*, pages 52–7, Osaka, Japan, Dec 1990.
17. L. Rosenthaler, F. Heitger, O. Kubler, and R. von der Heydt. Detection of general edges and key-points. In *Proc. 2nd Europ. Conf. Comput. Vision, G. Sandini (Ed.), LNCS-Series Vol. 588, Springer-Verlag*, pages 78–86, 1992.
18. E. Sharon, A. Brandt, and R. Basri. Completion energies and scale. *IEEE Trans. Pattern Analysis and Machine Intelligence*, 22(10):1117–1131, October 2000.
19. J. Shi and J. Malik. Normalized cuts and image segmentation. In *Proc. IEEE Conf. Computer Vision and Pattern Recognition*, pages 731–7, San Juan, Puerto Rico, June 1997.
20. L. Williams, J. Zweck, T. Wang, and K. Thornber. Computing stochastic completion fields in linear-time using a resolution pyramid. *CVIU*, 76(3):289–297, December 1999.
21. L.R. Williams and D.W. Jacobs. Stochastic completion fields: a neural model of illusory contour shape and salience. In *Proc. 5th Int. Conf. Computer Vision*, pages 408–15, Cambridge, MA, June 1995.
22. S.C. Zhu. Embedding gestalt laws in markov random fields. *IEEE Trans. Pattern Analysis and Machine Intelligence*, 21(11):1170–1187, November 1999.

Toward a Full Probability Model of Edges in Natural Images

Kim S. Pedersen[1] and Ann B. Lee[2]

[1] DIKU, University of Copenhagen
Universitetsparken 1,
DK-2100 Copenhagen Ø, Denmark
[2] Division of Applied Mathematics,
Box F, Brown University,
Providence, RI 02912, USA

Abstract. We investigate the statistics of local geometric structures in natural images. Previous studies [13,14] of high-contrast 3×3 natural image patches have shown that, in the state space of these patches, we have a concentration of data points along a low-dimensional non-linear manifold that corresponds to edge structures. In this paper we extend our analysis to a filter-based multiscale image representation, namely the local 3-jet of Gaussian scale-space representations. A new picture of natural image statistics seems to emerge, where primitives (such as edges, blobs, and bars) generate low-dimensional *non-linear* structures in the state space of image data.

Keywords: Natural image statistics, probability model of local geometry, scale-space, image features, biologically-inspired computational models

1 Introduction

The study of natural image statistics is an active research area and different approaches have been taken in this field [4,7,8,13,14,22,24,26,27]. It has previously been shown that natural image statistics — such as the marginal distributions of image intensity L and the gradient magnitude $\|\nabla L\|$ — are highly non-Gaussian, and approximately invariant to changes in scale [4,17,22]. Roughly speaking, the research in natural image statistics can be divided into two related directions: Researchers such as Zetzsche et al. [27], Simoncelli [24], and Huang et al.[7,8] have looked at the 1D marginal and 2D joint statistics of filter responses for a fixed wavelet basis. They have, for example, explored complex dependencies between pairs of wavelet coefficients at nearby spatial positions, orientations and scales. Others have looked at the state space of image data and tried to find a set of directions (or projections of the data) that lead to an optimal image representation in some sense; see e.g. sparse coding [21] and ICA [2,9].

In this paper, we take a different approach to natural image statistics. We believe that in order to fully understand the statistics of natural images one needs to explore the *full probability distribution* of the salient structures of local image patches. The analysis is free from such restrictive assumptions as independent components, or even linear decompositions of an image into basis images.

Our work is inspired by David Marr's ideas [18] that the structure of images can be described by primitives such as edges, bars, blobs and terminations — the so-called "primal sketch". The basic questions we ask are: *What are the probability distributions of Marr's primitives and how are these primitives represented geometrically in the state space of image data?* Can we develop models that will tell us how likely we are to observe a local geometric structure (such as an edge, ridge, blob, corner etc.) of a certain size in an image? Not much work has been done in this direction to our knowledge. Such probability models would, however, be useful as a priori knowledge in image processing and computer vision applications as diverse as feature detection [3], segmentation [16] and enhancement [23,28]. In particular, probability models on features could be used as prior distributions on features in image coding and reconstruction. Nielsen and Lillholm [20] have, for example, suggested that one can reconstruct an image by solving a variational optimization problem constrained by a feature prior and localized feature measurements.

To study the distribution of local geometric image structures, one first has to choose a representation that captures the image geometry in a neighborhood of some fiducial point. We will use a representation based on a set of local measurements of the luminance captured through a set of sensors — a sensorium. The concept of a sensorium makes sense both from a biological vision point of view (the receptive fields in the early visual system have been compared to feature detectors [11]) and from a mathematical point of view: Florack and Mumford [5,19] have both argued that an image I is not a function or a pointwise estimate $I(x,y)$ but a Schwartz distribution that can only be probed by averaging (or measuring) $\int\int I(\xi,\eta)\phi_j(x-\xi,y-\eta)d\xi d\eta$ through smooth "test" functions or sensors ϕ_j.

In our previous study [13,14] of natural image statistics, the sensorium is defined by the sensors in the CCD camera used to collect the images. More specifically, we study the joint statistics of the *pixel* intensity values in high-contrast 3×3 natural image patches. We found (for optical images) that the state space of the patch data is extremely sparse, with most of the data concentrated around a continuous non-linear manifold in state space. This manifold corresponds to edges of different orientations α and positions l.

In this work, we investigate whether our previous results (such as the existence of an ideal edge manifold in state space and the concentration of natural image data around this manifold) generalize to different scales and more general image representations.

In the context of linear Gaussian scale-space theory [10], Koenderink and van Doorn [11] proposed the so-called *local jet* of an image as a biologically plausible representation of local image geometry. In this setting, the sensorium consists of partial derivatives of the Gaussian kernel function. Convolving an image with these kernels is equivalent to measuring the partial derivatives of a coarse-grained representation of the image — the so-called scale-space image. The jet space captures the local geometry in a neighborhood of a point in the image, where the size of the neighborhood is determined by the standard deviation or *scale* of the Gaussian kernel.

In this work, we choose an image representation defined by Gaussian scale-space image derivatives up to third order — the 3-jet. This sensorium can distinguish between image structures such as edges, ridges, blobs and corners [11], but is blind to structures that require the descriptive power of image derivatives of order higher than 3.

We believe that such a representation of image data has certain advantages compared to many other types of multiscale representations. First of all, the Gaussian scale-space representation gives us a sensible way of defining image derivatives — the scale-space image derivatives. With these derivatives, we can use the language of differential geometry to define and interpret local features in images. The Gaussian kernel and its derivatives are furthermore similar to the receptive fields found in the mammalian visual system [10,11]. Both the mammalian receptive fields and the Gaussian scale-space derivatives are tuned to structures at different scales, orientations and spatial frequencies.

As in [13,14], we focus our analysis on edge structures. We first define a model of an ideal edge in Gaussian scale-space, and show that the 3-jet representations of edges define a 2-dimensional differentiable manifold in jet space. We then study how empirical data, extracted from a large database of natural images, are distributed in 3-jet space with respect to this manifold. We find, in accordance with previous results in [13,14], that the natural image data are densely distributed around the edge manifold with a probability density function of the form $\theta^{-\gamma}$, where θ is the distance to the edge manifold and γ is close to 0.7. Furthermore, we show that the results are approximately invariant to a change of scale.

This work is an attempt to develop a *full probability model of edges* in natural images that is universal, i.e. independent of scale and image representation. In the future, we plan to extend the analysis to representations of other image primitives (such as bars, blobs, and T-junctions).

The organization of the paper is as follows: In Sec. 2 we provide the necessary background on jet space and linear Gaussian scale-space theory. We introduce the Gaussian edge model in Sec. 3. In Sec. 4, we describe our image data set, the whitening and contrast normalization of this data, and the results of our analysis. Finally, we finish with concluding remarks (Sec. 5).

2   Multi-scale Local Jet

Linear Gaussian scale-space was proposed among others by Koenderink [10] as a sound theoretical framework for doing multi-scale image analysis. The Gaussian scale-space $L : \Omega \mapsto \mathbb{R}$ of an image $f : \Omega \mapsto \mathbb{R}$ (where $\Omega \subseteq \mathbb{R}^2$) can be defined as the solution to the heat diffusion equation

$$\frac{\partial L}{\partial t} = \frac{1}{2}\nabla^2 L \qquad (1)$$

under the constraint $L(x,y; s=0) = f(x,y)$. The *scale* $s \geq 0$ is related to t by $t = s^2$. The Gaussian scale-space representation of an image is thus a convolution

$$L(x,y;s) = \iint_\Omega f(\xi,\eta)\phi(x-\xi, y-\eta; s)\, d\xi\, d\eta \qquad (2)$$

with a Gaussian kernel function $\phi : \mathbb{R}^2 \mapsto \mathbb{R}$ where

$$\phi(x,y;s) = \frac{1}{2\pi s^2} e^{-\frac{(x^2+y^2)}{2s^2}} . \qquad (3)$$

We interpret the parameter s as the measurement scale of the scale-space image $L(x,y;s)$ as it corresponds to the width (or standard deviation) of the "smoothing filter" $\phi(\cdot)$.

An image is in general not a differentiable function, but in scale-space we obtain a family of smoothed versions of the image which are C^∞-differentiable. We can compute partial derivatives $\partial_{x^n}\partial_{y^m} (\equiv \frac{\partial^{n+m}}{\partial x^n \partial y^m})$ of the scale-space representation by convolving the image $f(\cdot)$ with partial derivatives of the Gaussian kernel function $\phi(\cdot; s)$, as

$$L_{x^n y^m}(\cdot; s) \equiv \partial_{x^n}\partial_{y^m}(f * \phi) = f * (\partial_{x^n}\partial_{y^m}\phi) . \qquad (4)$$

Note that the scale-space derivatives $L_{x^n y^m}$ constitute a scale-space as they also satisfy the previous heat diffusion equation.

Various approaches exist for discretization of scale-space representations (see e.g. [15]). Here we evaluate the convolution in Eq. (2) by multiplying the discrete Fourier transform of the discrete image with discretized Fourier transformed Gaussian derivatives $\partial_{x^n}\partial_{y^m}\phi$.

To be able to compare scale-space derivatives at different scales, it is convenient to use dimensionless coordinates (the so-called natural coordinates) and scale-normalized differential operators [15]. In the (x,y)-coordinate system the dimensionless coordinates are given by

$$(x', y') = \left(\frac{x}{s}, \frac{y}{s}\right) \qquad (5)$$

and the scale-normalized partial derivatives are

$$L_{x'^n y'^m}(x,y;s) = \partial_{x'^n}\partial_{y'^m} L(x,y;s) = s^{n+m}\partial_{x^n}\partial_{y^m} L(x,y;s) . \qquad (6)$$

In the rest of this paper we will assume that *all* scale-space derivatives $L_{x^n y^m}$ are scale normalized.

We can describe the local geometry of an image by the so-called local jet [6, 11]. Since the scale-space image $L(x,y;s)$ is a smoothed, differentiable version of an image, we can use a Taylor series to describe its behavior around a point

(x_0, y_0). For $(x_0, y_0) = (0, 0)$, for example, we have

$$L(x, y; s) = L + L_x x + L_y y + \frac{1}{2}(L_{xx}x^2 + 2L_{xy}xy + L_{yy}y^2)$$
$$+ \frac{1}{6}(L_{xxx}x^3 + 3L_{xxy}x^2y + 3L_{xyy}xy^2 + L_{yyy}y^3) + \ldots \quad (7)$$

where the scale-space derivatives $L, L_x, L_y, \ldots$ are evaluated at $(x_0, y_0) = (0, 0)$. Consider now the truncated Taylor expansion of degree k. The so-called *local k-jet* (of $L(x, y; s)$ at (x_0, y_0)) is an equivalence class of smooth functions with respect to the map $j^k L : \mathbb{R}^2 \mapsto \mathcal{J}^k(\mathbb{R}^2 \mapsto \mathbb{R}) \subset \mathbb{R}^N$, $N = (2+k)!/(2k!)$, where

$$j^k L(x, y; s) = (L(x, y; s), L_x(x, y; s), L_y(x, y; s), \ldots, L_{x^n y^m}(x, y; s))^T \quad (8)$$

and $n + m = k$. The space $\mathcal{J}^k(\mathbb{R}^2 \mapsto \mathbb{R})$ of all k-jets of functions $\mathbb{R}^2 \mapsto \mathbb{R}$ is sometimes called a *k-jet space*. Images that belong to the same k-jet (i.e. the same point in $\mathcal{J}^k(\mathbb{R}^2 \mapsto \mathbb{R})$) "look" the same up to order k, in the sense that we can not distinguish between them by only looking at scale-space derivatives up to order k. Koenderink and van Doorn [12] named this class a metamer inspired by the terminology of Schrödinger's theory of colorimetry.

We limit our analysis to the partial derivatives parameterizing the 3-jet, as the 3-jet captures the characteristics of common geometric structures such as edges, ridges, blobs, and corners [11,12]. In the following, we will study the statistics of images mapped into 3-jet space by $\tilde{j}^3 L : \mathbb{R}^2 \mapsto \tilde{\mathcal{J}}^3$, where

$$\tilde{j}^3 L(x, y; s) = (L_x, L_y, L_{xx}, L_{xy}, L_{yy}, L_{xxx}, L_{xxy}, L_{xyy}, L_{yyy})^T \quad (9)$$

and the measurement scale $s > 0$. The scale-space derivatives $L_x, L_y, L_{xx}, \ldots$ are evaluated at $(x, y; s)$, and are *scale normalized* according to Eq. (6), i.e. $L_{x^n y^m}(x, y; s) = s^{n+m} \partial_{x^n} \partial_{y^m} L(x, y; s)$. In the above 3-jet representation, we have excluded the intensity $L(x, y; s)$ of the blurred image, as we are only interested in variations in the local image geometry. The tilde notation is to indicate that $\tilde{\mathcal{J}}^3 \subset \mathcal{J}^3(\mathbb{R}^2 \mapsto \mathbb{R})$.

3 The Edge Manifold

We will investigate a simple model of edges mapped into jet space. We model edges by the scale-space of an ideal step edge (step edges blurred with a Gaussian — a Gaussian edge). In this section, we show that the contrast-normalized 3-jet representations of blurred step edges of different orientations, positions and scales trace out a differentiable 2D submanifold in the jet space $\tilde{\mathcal{J}}^3$.

For convenience, we define the edge model in the local orthonormal (u, v)-coordinate system where the v-axis has the direction of the local gradient at any point P_0 and the u-axis is perpendicular, i.e. we define unit vectors

$$e_v = (\cos \alpha, \sin \alpha)^T = \frac{1}{\sqrt{L_x^2 + L_y^2}} (L_x, L_y)^T \bigg|_{P_0} \quad (10)$$

and

$$e_u = (\sin \alpha, -\cos \alpha)^T. \tag{11}$$

In this coordinate system, an ideal step edge (defined on $\mathbb{R}^2$) has the form

$$f(u, v; l) = \begin{cases} 1 & \text{if } v \geq l \\ 0 & \text{if } v < l \end{cases} \tag{12}$$

where $l \in \mathbb{R}$ is the displacement of the edge from the origin in the v-direction. The scale-space representation of the ideal step edge is (according to Eq. (2)) given by

$$G(u, v; l, s) = f(u, v; l) * \phi(u, v; s) = \int_{v'=-\infty}^{v} \psi(v'; l, s) \, dv' \tag{13}$$

where $\psi(v; l, s) = \frac{1}{\sqrt{2\pi s^2}} e^{-\frac{(v-l)^2}{2s^2}}$ is a one-dimensional Gaussian kernel centered at l. For the scale-normalized partial derivatives of the edge model $G(u, v; l, s)$ along the u and v-axes, we have

$$\begin{aligned} G_{u^n}(u, v; l, s) &= 0 \\ G_{v^n}(u, v; l, s) &= s^n \partial_{v^{n-1}} \psi(v; l, s) \end{aligned} \tag{14}$$

for $n \geq 1$.

We now map the edge model $G(u, v; \alpha, l, s)$ into the jet space $\tilde{\jmath}^3$ by computing the nine components of the map $\tilde{\jmath}^3 G(0, 0; \alpha, l, s)$ defined by Eq. (9). Since

$$\begin{aligned} \partial_x &= \cos \alpha \, \partial_v + \sin \alpha \, \partial_u \\ \partial_y &= \sin \alpha \, \partial_v - \cos \alpha \, \partial_u, \end{aligned} \tag{15}$$

we get that

$$\begin{aligned} G_{x^m, y^n}(0, 0; \alpha, l, s) &= \cos^m \alpha \, \sin^n \alpha \, G_{v^{m+n}}(u, v; l, s) \Big|_{(u,v)=(0,0)} \\ &= s^{m+n} \cos^m \alpha \, \sin^n \alpha \, \partial_{v^{m+n-1}} \psi(v; l, s) \Big|_{v=0}. \end{aligned} \tag{16}$$

Denote the map that takes the edge model to the 3-jet space $\tilde{\jmath}^3$ by $\mathcal{E}$: $[0, 2\pi) \times \mathbb{R} \times \mathbb{R}_+ \backslash \{0\} \mapsto \tilde{\jmath}^3$, where

$$\begin{aligned} \mathcal{E}(\alpha, l, s) = (&G_x(0, 0; \alpha, l, s), G_y(0, 0; \alpha, l, s), G_{xx}(0, 0; \alpha, l, s), \\ &G_{xy}(0, 0; \alpha, l, s), G_{yy}(0, 0; \alpha, l, s), G_{xxx}(0, 0; \alpha, l, s), \\ &G_{xxy}(0, 0; \alpha, l, s), G_{xyy}(0, 0; \alpha, l, s), G_{yyy}(0, 0; \alpha, l, s))^T. \end{aligned} \tag{17}$$

Although the edge map $\mathcal{E}$ is a function of three variables (the angle α, the displacement l and the scale s), the loci of all points $\mathcal{E}(\alpha, l, s)$ trace out a 2-dimensional C^∞ differentiable manifold in $\mathbb{R}^9$ that only depends on α and the ratio l/s (see Appendix A). Note that the edge manifold is periodic in α for fixed l/s ratio.

Fig. 1. Sample images from the van Hateren still image collection. We show the log-transformed intensity values, $\log(f(x,y)+1)$.

4 Statistics of Edge Structures

4.1 The Empirical Data Set

In our experiments, we use the van Hateren still image collection consisting of 4167 1020×1532 pixels gray-scale images[1] [25] (see Fig. 1 for samples from the database). Before doing any processing of the images $f(x,y)$ in the database, we compress the intensity range by taking the logarithm $\log(f(x,y)+1)$ of the intensity.

For each scale-space image $L^{(i)}(x,y;s)$ at a fixed scale s, where $s = 1, 2, 4, 8, 16, 32$ pixels and $i = 1, \ldots, 4167$, we extract a random set of 1000 spatial coordinates $X^{(i,s)} \subseteq \Omega$ ($\Omega \subseteq \mathbb{R}^2$ denotes the image domain). At these spatial coordinates, we compute the 3-jet representations defined according to Eq. (9). This gives us data sets

$$J_s = \left\{ \tilde{j}^3 L^{(i)}(x,y;s) \subseteq \tilde{\mathfrak{j}}^3 \,\middle|\, (x,y) \in X^{(i,s)}; i = 1, \ldots, 4167 \right\} \quad (18)$$

where $s = 1, 2, 4, 8, 16, 32$ pixels. Elements in each set J_s are points in $\tilde{\mathfrak{j}}^3$ that have been sampled from different spatial positions and different images at a fixed scale s. The total number of data points[2] in each set J_s is $|J_s| \approx 4.1 \cdot 10^6$.

4.2 Whitening and Contrast Normalization

The lighting conditions may vary across and between images. We are interested in variations in the local *geometry* of the image and would like to disregard variations caused by changing lighting.

---

[1] We use the raw image set (.iml) where the intensity values have been linearized by the camera's lookup table.

[2] To prevent numerical problems during contrast normalization (see Sec. 4.2 and Eq. (20)), we discard data points y with a norm $\|y\|$ that is close to zero after whitening. This corresponds to 1% of all data points.

Before contrast-normalizing we first whiten the data. This will lead to a vector representation of the 3-jets where the elements are uncorrelated and of the same order of magnitude.

Assume that $\boldsymbol{x} \in J_s$ where J_s is our data set (Eq. (18)). The covariance or correlation matrix $C = <\boldsymbol{xx}^T>$ is scale invariant, so we can get a robust estimate of C from the joined data set $\boldsymbol{x} \in \bigcup_s J_s$ where s denotes the scale. The mean $<\boldsymbol{x}> = \boldsymbol{0}$ due to the convolution with mean-zero scale-space filters.

The first step in the data preprocessing is to define transformed input variables

$$\boldsymbol{y} = \Lambda^{-1/2} U^T \boldsymbol{x} , \qquad (19)$$

where U is a 9×9-matrix with the normalized eigenvectors of C as columns, and Λ is a diagonal 9×9-matrix with the corresponding eigenvalues of C as diagonal elements. The transformed data $\boldsymbol{y}$ is "white" in the sense that the covariance matrix $<\boldsymbol{yy}^T> = \boldsymbol{1}$.

The second step is to contrast-normalize the data according to

$$\hat{\boldsymbol{p}} = \frac{\boldsymbol{y}}{\|\boldsymbol{y}\|} \qquad (20)$$

so that scale-space images of similar geometric structure have the same representation. The whitened and contrast-normalized data points $\hat{\boldsymbol{p}}$ all lie on a 8-dimensional unit sphere

$$S^8 \equiv \{\hat{\boldsymbol{p}} | \; \|\hat{\boldsymbol{p}}\| = 1\} \in \mathbb{R}^9 . \qquad (21)$$

The 8-sphere S^8 is the *state space of whitened and contrast-normalized* 3-jet representations. The whitened and contrast-normalized data set J_s at a fixed scale s is denoted by $\hat{J}_s \in S^8$.

Similarly, we define the map $\hat{\mathcal{E}} : [0, 2\pi) \times \mathbb{R} \mapsto S^8$ that takes the edge map $\mathcal{E}(\alpha, l, s)$ (Eq. (17)) to the state space of whitened and contrast normalized 3-jet representations by

$$\hat{\mathcal{E}}(\alpha, l/s) = \frac{\Lambda^{-1/2} U^T \mathcal{E}(\alpha, l/s, 1)}{\|\Lambda^{-1/2} U^T \mathcal{E}(\alpha, l/s, 1)\|} . \qquad (22)$$

We measure the *distance* between two data points $\hat{\boldsymbol{p}}_0, \hat{\boldsymbol{p}}_1 \in S^8$ on the 8-sphere by their angular separation, i.e.

$$\text{dist}(\hat{\boldsymbol{p}}_0, \hat{\boldsymbol{p}}_1) \equiv \arccos(\hat{\boldsymbol{p}}_0^T \hat{\boldsymbol{p}}_1) . \qquad (23)$$

4.3 Density Results for the Empirical Data Set

In Sec. 3, we described the theoretical manifold of edges in 3-jet space. In this section, we verify that the *empirical* data from natural images (i.e. the whitened and contrast-normalized data in sets $\hat{J}_s$ from Sec. 4.1 and Sec. 4.2) are really densely distributed around the manifold of edges. By putting parallel bins around

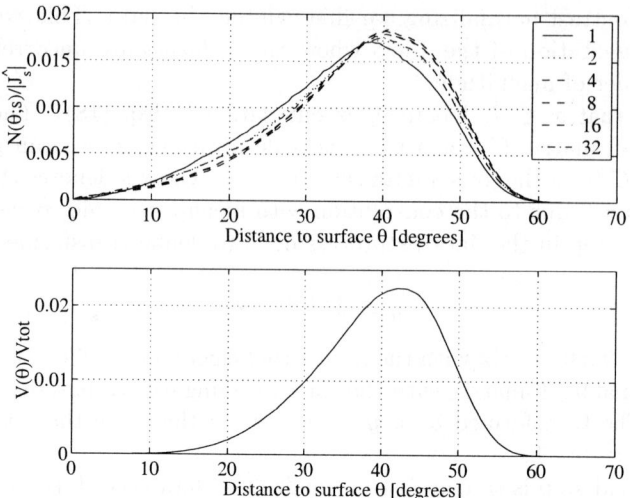

Fig. 2. (Top) The normalized histograms $N(\theta;s)/|\hat{J}_s|$ of the data sets $\hat{J}_s$ ($|\hat{J}_s| \approx 4.1 \cdot 10^6$ points), where $s = 1, 2, 4, 8, 16, 32$ (see legend) and θ is the distance to the edge manifold $\hat{\mathcal{E}}(\alpha, l/s) \subset S^8$. (Bottom) Normalized histogram $V(\theta)/V_{\text{tot}}$, which corresponds to the Monte Carlo estimated volume on S^8 of the histogram bins of $N(\theta;s)$ ($V_{\text{tot}} = 10^7$ points).

the manifold and computing histograms of the data, we can get an estimate of the functional form of the probability density around the surface.

First we divide the whitened and constrast-normalized edge manifold $\hat{\mathcal{E}}(\alpha, l/s)$ of Eq. (22) into a mesh of spherical triangles in the same fashion as in [13]. We sample the edge manifold with parameters $l \in [-4s, 4s]$ and $\alpha \in [0, 2\pi)$. We refine the mesh of triangles until no vertices in a triangle are more than 11 degrees apart. This gives us a triangulated mesh with a total of 22944 triangles. We use the triangulated mesh of the manifold to estimate the distances between the data points of $\hat{J}_s$ and the manifold of edges $\hat{\mathcal{E}}(\alpha, l/s)$ on the 8-sphere S^8. The distance $\text{dist}(\boldsymbol{x}, \hat{\mathcal{E}}(\alpha, l/s))$ between a data point $\boldsymbol{x} \in \hat{J}_s$ and the edge manifold $\hat{\mathcal{E}}(\alpha, l/s)$ is approximated by the distance to the center point of the closest triangle in the mesh.

Fig. 2 (top) shows a normalized histogram of the number of whitened and contrast-normalized data points $\hat{\boldsymbol{p}}_n^s \in \hat{J}_s$ ($n = 1, \ldots, |\hat{J}_s|$) versus the distance θ to the edge manifold $\hat{\mathcal{E}}(\alpha, l/s) \subset S^8$. Let

$$N(\theta; s) = \#\left\{n \left| \theta - \frac{\Delta\theta}{2} \leq \text{dist}(\hat{\boldsymbol{p}}_n^s, \hat{\mathcal{E}}(\alpha, l/s)) < \theta + \frac{\Delta\theta}{2}\right.\right\} \quad (24)$$

where $\Delta\theta$ is the histogram bin width and $\text{dist}(\hat{\boldsymbol{p}}_n^s, \hat{\mathcal{E}}(\alpha, l/s))$ is the angular distance (Eq. (23)) from the data point $\hat{\boldsymbol{p}}_n^s$ to the closest point on the triangulated mesh of the edge manifold $\hat{\mathcal{E}}(\alpha, l/s)$.

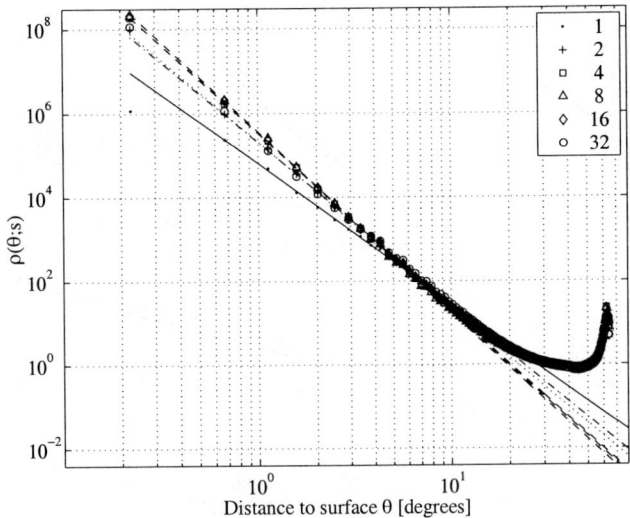

Fig. 3. Density $\rho(\theta;s)$ versus the distance θ to the edge manifold $\hat{\mathcal{E}}(\alpha,l/s) \subset S^8$ for data points in $\hat{J}_s$. Each graph represents the density at a fixed scale s, where $s = 1, 2, 4, 8, 16, 32$ pixels (see legend). By linear regression for $\theta < 9$ degrees we get that $\rho_{\mathrm{fit}}(\theta;s) \sim \theta^{-\gamma_s}$, where $\gamma_s = 1.7, 1.0, 0.7, 0.7, 0.7, 1.1$ ($s = 1, 2, 4, 8, 16, 32$).

To get an estimate of the probability density of points around the edge manifold, we also need to calculate the volume of the bins $[\theta - \frac{\Delta\theta}{2}, \theta + \frac{\Delta\theta}{2})$ in the state space S^8. We here estimate the bin volume by sampling $V_{\mathrm{tot}} = 10^7$ uniformly randomly distributed points $\boldsymbol{v}_n$ ($n = 1, \ldots, V_{\mathrm{tot}}$) on the 8-sphere. The histogram

$$V(\theta) = \#\left\{ n \middle| \theta - \frac{\Delta\theta}{2} \leq \mathrm{dist}(\boldsymbol{v}_n, \hat{\mathcal{E}}(\alpha,l/s)) < \theta + \frac{\Delta\theta}{2} \right\} \quad (25)$$

of the number of samples versus the distance θ to the surface of edges is a Monte Carlo estimate of the volume of the histogram bins. Fig. 2 (bottom) shows the normalized histogram $V(\theta)/V_{\mathrm{tot}}$.

We define the empirical *density* of data points around the edge manifold as

$$\rho(\theta;s) = \frac{N(\theta;s)/|\hat{J}_s|}{V(\theta)/V_{\mathrm{tot}}}. \quad (26)$$

Fig. 3 shows the calculated density for the data sets $\hat{J}_s$, where $s = 1, 2, 4, 8, 16, 32$ pixels. These results seem to indicate that the probability distribution of data points in the jet space has an *infinite* density at the manifold of blurred step edges (where $\theta = 0$). This is consistent with the results on high-contrast 3×3 pixel image patches in [13]. Furthermore, the density function $\rho(\theta;s)$ is approximately *scale invariant* and seems to converge towards the functional form $\rho(\theta;s) \sim \theta^{-0.7}$ as we increase the scale s. The latter results are consistent with many of the

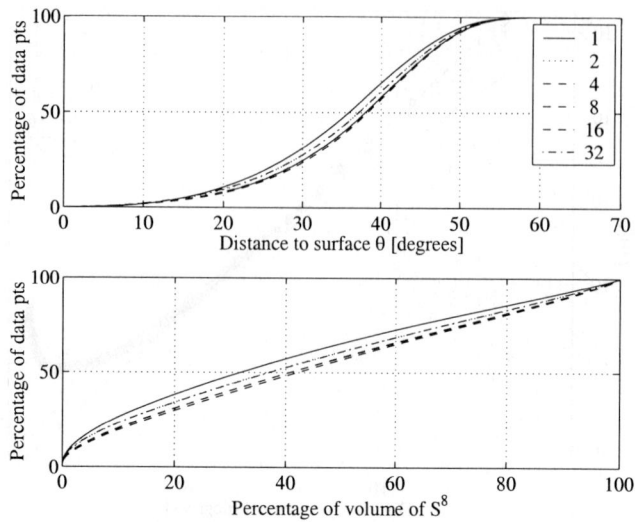

Fig. 4. (Top) Cumulative sum $\sum_{\beta \leq \theta} N(\beta; s)/|\hat{J}_s|$ (in percent) of the number of data points in $\hat{J}_s$ as a function of the distance to the manifold of edges. (Bottom) Cumulative volume versus cumulative number of data points for data sets $\hat{J}_s$.

previous empirical findings on scale invariance of natural image statistics; see e.g. [4,22].

In Fig. 4 (top), we calculate the cumulative sum $\sum_{\beta \leq \theta} N(\beta; s)/|\hat{J}_s|$ (in percent) of the number of data points as a function of the distance θ to the manifold of edges. For all scales s, we get that 20% of all data points are within 29 degrees of the manifold of edges, which corresponds to less than 12% of the total surface area of the 8-sphere S^8 (see Fig. 4 (bottom)). In other words, points in these subsets of $\hat{J}_s$ are densely clustered around the low-dimensional manifold of edges.

To better illustrate the connection between the density function $\rho(\theta; s)$ and the image space, we end this section by computing $\rho(\theta; s)$ for pixels in the classical "Lena" image. Fig. 5 shows both scale-space images of Lena and the corresponding densities $\rho(\theta; s)$ for different scales s. In the density calculation, we first map the pixels in the scale-space of Lena into the jet space $\tilde{j}^3$ in Eq. (9) and then whiten and contrast normalize according to Sec. 4.2. We subsequently compute the distance θ of these points to the edge manifold $\hat{\mathcal{E}}(\alpha, l/s) \subset S^8$ and, finally, we look up the fitted density values $\rho_{\text{fit}}(\theta; s) \sim \theta^{-\gamma_s}$ (see Fig. 3) corresponding to the computed θ-values. The gray values in the second and fourth columns of Fig. 5 code for the magnitude of $\rho_{\text{fit}}(\theta; s) \sim \theta^{-\gamma_s}$ for different scales $s = 1, 2, 4, 8, 16, 32$. The first and third columns show the corresponding scale-space images.

Fig. 5. The first and third columns show scale-space images of "Lena" (226 × 226 pixels) for scales $s = 1, 2, 4, 8, 16, 32$ pixels. The second and fourth columns show the corresponding log-densities $\log(\rho(\theta; s))$ in jet space (a bright pixel corresponds to a high density at that position in the image). The densities $\rho(\theta; s)$ are estimated at each pixel by first computing the distance θ to the manifold of blurred step edges and then looking up the density values $\rho_{\text{fit}}(\theta; s)$ (see Fig. 3) that correspond to these θ-values.

5 Conclusions

We have extended the results of [13,14] from a pixel-based image representation to the jet space representation of linear Gaussian scale-space. The goal of this work is to investigate whether our previous findings on small image patches generalize to larger scales and general filter-based image representations.

In this work, we analyze Gaussian scale-space derivatives computed at randomly chosen points in (a large database of) natural images. At each chosen location, we compute the 3-jet representation (a 9-dimensional vector of up to 3rd order scale-space image derivatives) at different fixed scales. After whitening and a contrast-normalization, the data is on the surface of a unit 8-sphere in $\mathbb{R}^9$ centered at the origin.

Analysis shows that the probability distribution of empirical data has an infinite density at a 2-dimensional C^∞-differentiable manifold in the 8-sphere (the state space of whitened and contrast-normalized 3-jet representations). This nonlinear surface corresponds to the loci in jet space of Gaussian blurred step edges of different orientations α, positions l and scales s. Our results are approximately invariant to a change of scale. In fact, for increasing scales s, the density around the surface seems to converge towards the functional form $\rho(\theta) \sim \theta^{-0.7}$, where

θ is the distance to the edge manifold. For all scales, we find that 20% of the randomly chosen image points have a 3-jet representation that are within 29 degrees of the edge manifold. This region around the manifold corresponds to less than 12% of the total surface volume of the 8-sphere.

The results above are consistent with our earlier findings in [13,14] for 3×3 natural image patches. In this work, we have studied the manifold of Gaussian blurred step edges parametrized by the orientation α and the scale-normalized position $l' = l/s$ of an edge. More generally, we believe that one can define a dictionary of probability models on representations of *general* primitives (edges, bars, blobs, T-junctions) parametrized by $\Phi = \{\phi_1, \phi_2, \ldots\}$ for *any* set of filters $f_1, \ldots, f_N$ in a sensorium. In the N-dimensional state space of the filter-based image representations, the image primitives will define manifolds of the general form

$$M(\Phi) = [f_1(\cdot) * I(\cdot; \Phi), \ldots, f_N(\cdot) * I(\cdot; \Phi)]^T . \tag{27}$$

The picture that seems to emerge is that natural images are extremely sparse with most of the data in state space concentrated along these low-dimensional structures that correspond to edges, blobs, bars etc. One has to realize that these manifolds are in general highly *non-linear* — this makes our approach fundamentally different from, for example, ICA and sparse coding where one studies linear projections in state space. It should also be noted that the dimension of the state space of the image data is determined by the number of filters in the analysis (which is usually very large), while the dimension of the manifolds of image primitives is fixed and determined by the complexity of the primitives only. Because of the *low dimensionality* of the primitive manifolds (2 for edges, 3 for bars, etc), a "probabilistic primal sketch" of natural images may have important implications on the information-theoretic bounds one can put on compression of these images.

Acknowledgments. We would like to thank Associate Professor Mads Nielsen, Professor Peter Johansen and Professor David Mumford for their valuable comments.

A Appendix: The Edge Manifold

Theorem 1. *The loci of all points $\mathcal{E}(\alpha, l, s)$ (Eq. (17)) trace out a 2-dimensional C^∞-differentiable manifold in the jet space $\tilde{j}^3 \subset \mathbb{R}^9$. This manifold of edge representations is parametrized by the angle α and the ratio l/s between the displacement l and the scale s.*

Proof. The edge map $\mathcal{E}$ (Eq. (17)) is *infinitely differentiable*, as

$$G_{x^m, y^n}(x, y; \alpha, l, s) = s^{m+n} \cos^m \alpha \, \sin^n \alpha \, \partial_{v^{m+n-1}} \psi(v; l, s) \tag{28}$$

and the functions $\cos \alpha$, $\sin \alpha$ and $\psi(v; l, s)$ are C^∞-differentiable with respect to α, l and s (for $s > 0$).

Furthermore, if we introduce the dimensionless variables

$$u' = \frac{u}{s}, \quad v' = \frac{v}{s}, \quad l' = \frac{l}{s}, \quad s' = 1 \tag{29}$$

and assume scale-normalized derivatives as in Eq. (14), we get that

$$G_{v^n}(u,v;l,s) = G_{v'^n}(u',v';l',s') \tag{30}$$

for $n \geq 1$. Eq. (30) follows from the scaling properties of the Gaussian function $\psi(v;l,s)$: We have that

$$\psi(v';l',s') = s\psi(v;l,s) \tag{31}$$

and [1]

$$\partial_{v^k}\psi(v;l,s) = \left(\frac{-1}{s\sqrt{2}}\right)^k H_k\left(\frac{v-l}{s\sqrt{2}}\right)\psi(v;l,s) \tag{32}$$

for $k \geq 0$. Hence,

$$\begin{aligned}\partial_{v^k}\psi(v;l,s) &= \frac{1}{s^k}\left(\frac{-1}{s'\sqrt{2}}\right)^k H_k\left(\frac{v'-l'}{s'\sqrt{2}}\right)\frac{1}{s}\psi(v';l',s') \\ &= \frac{1}{s^{k+1}}\partial_{v'^k}\psi(v';l',s'),\end{aligned} \tag{33}$$

which is equivalent to (Eq. (30))

$$\underbrace{s^{k+1}\partial_{v^k}\psi(v;l,s)}_{G_{v^n}(u,v;l,s)} = \underbrace{s'^{k+1}\partial_{v'^k}\psi(v';l',s')}_{G_{v'^n}(u',v';l',s')} \tag{34}$$

where $n = k+1 \geq 1$.

Although the edge map $\mathcal{E}$ in Eq. (17) is a function of three variables (the angle α, the displacement l and the scale s), the loci of all points $\mathcal{E}(\alpha, l, s)$ trace out a *2-dimensional* manifold (in the jet space) which only depends on α and the dimensionless ratio l/s.

References

1. G. Arfken. *Mathematical Methods for Physicists*. Computational Imaging and Vision. Academic Press, London, 1985.
2. A. J. Bell and T. J. Sejnowski. The "independent components" of natural scenes are edge filters. *Vision Research*, 37:3327–3338, 1997.
3. A. Desolneux, L. Moisan, and J. Morel. Partial gestalts. Technical Report CMLA 2001-22, CMLA, Cachan, France, 2001.
4. D. J. Field. Relations between the statistics of natural images and the response proporties of cortical cells. *J. Optic. Soc. of Am.*, 4(12):2379–2394, 1987.
5. L. Florack. *Image Structure*. Computational Imaging and Vision. Kluwer Academic Publishers, Dordrecht, 1997.
6. L. Florack, B. ter Haar Romeny, M. Viergever, and J. Koenderink. The gaussian scale-space paradigm and the multiscale local jet. *IJCV*, 18:61–75, 1996.

7. J. Huang, A. Lee, and D. Mumford. Statistics of range images. In *Proc. of CVPR'00*, 2000.
8. J. Huang and D. Mumford. Statistics of natural images and models. In *Proc. of CVPR'99*, 2000.
9. A. Hyvärinen. Survey on independent component analysis. *Neural Computing Surveys*, 2:94–128, 1999.
10. J. J. Koenderink. The structure of images. *Biol. Cybern.*, 50:363–370, 1984.
11. J. J. Koenderink and A. J. van Doorn. Representation of local geometry in the visual system. *Biol. Cybern.*, 55:367–375, 1987.
12. J. J. Koenderink and A. J. van Doorn. Metamerism in complete sets of image operators. In K. Bowyer and N. Ahuja, editors, *Advances in Image Understanding*, pages 113–129. IEEE Comp. Soc. Press, 1996.
13. A. B. Lee, K. S. Pedersen, and D. Mumford. The complex statistics of high-contrast patches in natural images. In *WWW Proc. of 2nd Int. IEEE Workshop on Statistical and Computational Theories of Vision*, Vancouver, Canada, 2001. http://www.cis.ohio-state.edu/~szhu/SCTV2001.html.
14. A. B. Lee, K. S. Pedersen, and D. Mumford. The nonlinear statistics of high-contrast patches in natural images. Technical Report APPTS Report #01-3, Brown University, USA, 2001.
15. T. Lindeberg. *Scale-Space Theory in Computer Vision*. Kluwer, 1994.
16. J. Malik, S. Belongie, T. Leung, and J. Shi. Contour and texture analysis for image segmentation. *IJCV*, 43(1):7–27, 2001.
17. S. Mallat. A theory for multiresolution signal decomposition: The wavelet representation. *IEEE Transaction on PAMI*, 11:674–693, 1989.
18. D. Marr. *Vision*. W. H. Freeman, New York, 1982.
19. D. Mumford and B. Gidas. Stochastic models for generic images. *Quarterly of Applied Mathematics*, 59(11):85–111, March 2001.
20. M. Nielsen and M. Lillholm. What do features tell about images? In Michael Kerckhove, editor, *Scale-Space and Morphology in Computer Vision*, LNCS 2106, pages 39–50, 2001.
21. B. A. Olshausen and D. J. Field. Natural image statistics and efficient coding. *Network: Computation in Neural Systems*, 7(2):333–339, May 1996.
22. D. Ruderman and W. Bialek. Statistics of natural images: Scaling in the woods. *Physical Review Letters*, 73(6):814–817, August 1994.
23. E. P. Simoncelli. Bayesian denoising of visual images in the wavelet domain. In P. Müller and B Vidakovic, editors, *Bayesian Inference in Wavelet Based Models*, pages 291–308. Springer-Verlag, New York, 1999.
24. E. P. Simoncelli. Modelling the joint statistics of images in the wavelet domain. In *Proc. of SPIE, 44th Annual Meating*, volume 3813, pages 188–195, Denver, 1999.
25. J. H. van Hateren and A. van der Schaaf. Independent component filters of natural images compared with simple cells in primary visual cortex. *Proc. R. Soc. Lond. Series B*, 265:359 – 366, 1998.
26. M. J. Wainwright and E. P. Simoncelli. Scale mixtures of gaussians and the statistics of natural images. In S. A. Solla et al., editor, *Advances in Neural Information Processing Systems 12*, pages 855–861. MIT Press, 2000.
27. C. Zetzsche, B. Wegmann, and E. Barth. Nonlinear aspects of primary vision: Entropy reduction beyond decorrelation. In *Int'l Symposium, Society for Information Display*, volume 24, pages 933–936, 1993.
28. S. C. Zhu and D. Mumford. Grade: Gibbs reaction and diffusion equations. — a framework for pattern synthesis, image denoising, and removing clutter. In *Proc. of ICCV'98*, 1998.

Fast Difference Schemes for Edge Enhancing Beltrami Flow*

R. Malladi and I. Ravve

Mail Stop: 50A-1148, 1 Cyclotron Road
Lawrence Berkeley National Laboratory
Computing Science Department
University of California, Berkeley, CA 94720
{malladi,ravve}@math.lbl.gov

Abstract. The Beltrami flow [13,14] is one of the most effective denoising algorithms in image processing. For gray-level images, we show that the Beltrami flow equation can be arranged in a reaction-diffusion form. This reveals the edge-enhancing properties of the equation and suggests the application of additive operator split (AOS) methods [4,5] for faster convergence. As we show with numerical simulations, the AOS method results in an unconditionally stable semi-implicit linearized difference scheme in $2D$ and $3D$. The values of the edge indicator function are used from the previous step in scale, while the pixel values of the next step are used to approximate the flow. The optimum ratio between the reaction and diffusion counterparts of the governing PDE is studied, in order to achieve a better quality of segmentation. The computational time decreases by a factor of ten, as compared to the explicit scheme. For 2D color images, the Beltrami flow equations are coupled, and do not yield readily to the AOS technique. However, in the proximity of an edge, the cross-products of color gradients nearly vanish, and the coupling becomes weak. The principal directions of the edge indicator matrix are normal and tangent to the edge. Replacing the action of the matrix on the gradient vector by an action of its eigenvalue, we reduce the color problem to the gray level case with a reasonable accuracy. The scalar edge indicator function for the color case becomes essentially the same as that for the gray level image, and the fast implicit technique is implemented.

Keywords: Beltrami Flow, Unconditionally Stable Schemes, Color Images, Segmentation.

1 Introduction

The main objective in early computer vision is to smooth images without destroying the semantic content, i.e. edges, features, corners, etc. In other words,

---

* This work was supported by the Director, Office of Science, Office of Advanced Scientific Research, Mathematical, Information, and Computational Sciences Division, U.S. Department of Energy under Contract No. DE-AC03-76SF00098, and LBNL Directed Research and Development Program

the boundaries between objects in the image should survive as long as possible along the scale, while homogeneous regions should be simplified and flattened in a rapid way. This is particularly important since the denoising an image is usually a precursor to segmentation and representation which often rely on edge fidelity.

The use of diffusion equations for image processing in computer vision originated with the work of [1] where the authors pre-select a diffusion coefficient function in the image that preserves the edge information. A more rigorous view was achieved with the realization that the iso-intensity contours of an image can be moved under their curvature following the work of Osher and Sethian [6]. This lead to a series of papers starting with the one by Alvarez, Lions and Morel [2], of viewing the images as a set of level contours and moving then under their curvature. Image smoothing by way of level set curvature motion [3,7] thwarts the diffusion in the edge direction, thereby preserving the edge information. The work by Malladi and Sethian [7,8] showed that in addition to this basic approach, a natural stopping criterion can also be chosen to prevent over smoothing a given image. For a comprehensive look at various approaches that rely on geometric diffusion, the reader is referred to [10]. Another crucial idea in [8] was also to diffuse an image by viewing it as a graph of a function and moving it under the mean curvature.

An important question still remained, what is the natural way to treat vector-valued images and images in higher dimensions? An answer to this and other questions was attempted in [13,14] by Sochen, Kimmel, and Malladi. The result is a general mathematical framework for feature-preserving image smoothing that applies seamlessly to gray level, vector-value (color) images, volumetric images, and movies. The main idea is to view images as embedded maps between two Riemannian manifolds and to define an action potential that provides a measure on the space of these maps. The authors in [14] showed that many classical geometric flows emerge as special cases in this view as well as a new flow, the so called Beltrami flow that moves a gray level image under a scaled mean curvature, and also succeeds in finding a natural coupling between otherwise decoupled component-wise diffusion that was often used in the past in vector-valued image diffusion. In the case of gray value images, and by following a different approach, Yezzi in [21] arrived at a similar equation.

Smoothing of noisy images and edge enhancement usually presents a numerical integration of a parabolic PDE with one dimension in scale and two dimensions in space. This is often the most time consuming component of nonlinear image processing algorithms. Smoothing technique governed by the Beltrami flow equation is one of the most effective since it incorporates the edge indicator function, that minimizes diffusion at and across the edges and extensive diffusion elsewhere. On the other hand, solving the equations using explicit methods can be very time consuming due to the scaling and small time step requirement. We aim to build faster methods to solve the Beltrami flow equation in $2D$ gray level and color, and volumetric imagery. we use the method of Additive Operator Split (AOS). This technique was introduced by Weickert [4] for the nonlinear diffusion flow and later applied by Goldenberg et al. [5] to implement a fast version of the geodesic contour model.

On a different note, the Beltrami flow equation results from minimizing a (natural) generalization of $L2$ Euclidean norm to non-Euclidean manifolds, see [13] for details. This suggests that the governing equation is an "edge-preserving" in contrast to being an "edge-enhancing" flow. In other words, on grey level images, the equation simulates a mean curvature flow scaled by an edge-indicator function, thereby preserving the edge features in scale. In a recent note on the study of intermediate asymptotics of certain commonly used anisotropic diffusion equations, Barenblatt [9] reports that Beltrami flow equation forms a sharp step in the viscinity of edges. In this work, an asymptotic self-similar solution was obtained for a particular case of the Beltrami equation, suggesting an "edge-sharpening" behavior. In the present context, while performing operator splitting, we confirm that Beltrami flow has both edge-preserving and edge-sharpening components.

Our goal is to build a fast and reliable method to solve the Beltrami flow equations and it is based on AOS technique. This paper is organized as follows. In Section 2, we rearrange the governing equation for the Beltrami flow. This approach leads to a semi-implicit linearized difference scheme. In Section 3, we present numerical simulations for $2D$ and $3D$ gray level images. We run the flow to different scales and different relative magnitudes of reaction term vs. diffusion components are considered. In Section 4 we consider the color images where the edge indicator function is expressed by a matrix [11,14]. Equations for two-dimensional images become coupled, and this does not allow us to apply the AOS splitting immediately. However, in the proximity of the edge, the cross-products of color gradients all vanish or almost vanish. The Beltrami operator then becomes weakly coupled, and the principal directions of the edge indicator matrix are normal and tangent to the edge. The action of this matrix on the gradient vector of a specific color component may be replaced by the action of the eigenvalue on this vector. Thus, the problem is reduced to a scalar gray level case with a reasonable degree of accuracy, and the fast implicit smoothing scheme is implemented. Section 5 presents the results of numerical simulation for color images. We summarize this work in Section 6.

2 Implicit Scheme for Gray Level Images

Let us denote by (Σ, g) the image manifold and its metric and by (M, h) the space-feature manifold and its metric, then the map $X : \Sigma \to M$ has the following measure, [16]:

$$S[X^i, g_{\mu\nu}, h_{ij}] = \int d^n \sigma \sqrt{g} g^{\mu\nu} \partial_\mu X^i \partial_\nu X^j h_{ij}(X), \qquad (1)$$

where m is the dimension of Σ, g is the determinant of the image metric, $g^{\mu\nu}$ is the inverse of the image metric, the range of indices is $\mu, \nu = 1, \ldots, \dim \Sigma$, and $i, j = 1, \ldots, \dim M$, and h_{ij} is the metric of the embedding space. This is a natural generalization of the $L2$ norm to manifolds. As an example, a grey level image can be treated as a $2D$ manifold embedded in R^3, i.e. a mapping $X : (x, y) \to (X^1 = x, X^2 = y, X^3 = U(x, y))$.

Many scale-space methods, linear and non-linear can be shown to be a gradient descent flows of this functional with appropriately chosen metric of the image manifold. The gradient descent equation is $X_t^i = -\frac{1}{\sqrt{g}} \frac{\delta S}{\delta X^i}$. As shown in [13], minimizing the area action in Eqn. 1, with respect to the feature coordinate U, we obtain the following Beltrami flow equation,

$$\dot{U} = \frac{U_{xx}(U_y^2 + 1) - 2U_x U_y U_{xy} + U_{yy}(U_x^2 + 1)}{(1 + U_x^2 + U_y^2)^2}. \tag{2}$$

The nonlinear diffusion equation is the following reaction-diffusion partial differential equation [4,5]

$$\dot{U} = \nabla \cdot \left(\frac{\nabla U}{g}\right) = \frac{\partial}{\partial x}\left(\frac{U_x}{g}\right) + \frac{\partial}{\partial y}\left(\frac{U_y}{g}\right) \tag{3}$$

where $g = (1 + U_x^2 + U_y^2)$ is the gradient magnitude.

The Beltrami equation may be reduced to a similar reaction-diffusion form, namely

$$\dot{U} = \nabla \cdot \left(\frac{\nabla U}{2g}\right) + \frac{\nabla^2 U}{2g} = h \nabla^2 U + 1/2 \nabla h \cdot \nabla U \tag{4}$$

where $h = 1/g$, is the edge indicator function. In this form, the Beltrami flow equation is not a "pure" diffusion equation. It has both an (parabolic) edge-preserving and an (hyperbolic) edge-sharpening terms. In addition, the reaction-diffusion form of Eq. (4) hides the mixed derivative U_{xy}, thereby making it conducive to the AOS approach. In other words, the equation can be rearranged into the form $\dot{U} = (A_x + A_y)U$, where A_x and A_y are the following differential operators:

$$A_x = \frac{\partial}{\partial x}\left(\frac{h}{2}\frac{\partial}{\partial x}\right) + \frac{h}{2}\frac{\partial^2}{\partial x^2} \qquad A_y = \frac{\partial}{\partial y}\left(\frac{h}{2}\frac{\partial}{\partial y}\right) + \frac{h}{2}\frac{\partial^2}{\partial y^2}. \tag{5}$$

Applying the backward difference formula to the above form we get,

$$\frac{\boldsymbol{U}^{n+1} - \boldsymbol{U}^n}{\Delta t} = (\boldsymbol{A}_x + \boldsymbol{A}_y)\,\boldsymbol{U}^{n+1} \tag{6}$$

The superscript n is related to the present and $n+1$ to the next time step. The subscripts i, j index the discrete pixel location; $\boldsymbol{U}_{i,j}^n$ are known values, and $\boldsymbol{U}_{i,j}^{n+1}$ are to be found. Using $\boldsymbol{U}^{n+1}$ on the right side of Eq. (6) makes the integration scheme implicit and unconditionally stable, namely

$$[\boldsymbol{I} - \Delta t\,(\boldsymbol{A}_x + \boldsymbol{A}_y)]\,\boldsymbol{U}^{n+1} = \boldsymbol{U}^n \tag{7}$$

where $\boldsymbol{I}$ is the identity matrix. Before proceeding in time, we calculate the values of the edge indicator function g, using the known values of $\boldsymbol{U}^n$. Thus, the scheme is only semi-implicit. Although g depends on the gradient of U, we treat it like a given function of (x, y), making the governing PDE "quasi-linear".

Note that Eq. (7) includes a large bandwidth matrix, because all equations, related to new pixel values U^{n+1} are coupled. Our aim is to decouple the set (7) so that each row and each column of pixels can be handled separately. For this, we re-arrange the equations into the following form:

$$U^{n+1} = [I - \Delta t (A_x + A_y)]^{-1} U^n \tag{8}$$

Of course, we do not intend to invert the matrix to solve the linear set. This is only a symbolic form used for further derivation. For a small value of Δt, the matrix in the brackets on the right side of Eq. (8) is close to the identity I. Thus, its inverse can be expanded into the Taylor series in the proximity of I: $[I - \Delta t (A_x + A_y)]^{-1} \approx I + \Delta t (A_x + A_y)$, where the linear term is retained and the high order terms are neglected. Introducing this form into (8), we get,

$$2U^{n+1} = (I + 2\Delta t A_x) U_n + (I + 2\Delta t A_y) U^n \tag{9}$$

Introducing the notations $V = (I + 2\Delta t A_x)U^n$ and $W = (I + 2\Delta t A_y)U^n$ the solution is simply

$$U^{n+1} = \frac{V + W}{2} \tag{10}$$

In order to get an implicit scheme, we apply the differential matrix operators A_x and A_y to U^{n+1} (and not to U^n), namely

$$(I + 2\Delta t A_x)^{-1} V = U^n \qquad (I + 2\Delta t A_y)^{-1} W = U^n \tag{11}$$

Following the procedure of expanding the matrix inverses into Taylor series and applying the linearization for small Δt, we finally obtain the equation sets for V and W as follows:

$$(I - 2\Delta t A_x) V = U^n \qquad (I - 2\Delta t A_y) W = U^n \tag{12}$$

These equations can be solved with either the Dirichlet or Neumann boundary conditions; these and other details are described in [17].

3 Simulation Results for Gray Level Images

We ran a series of numerical simulations to demonstrate the performance of the implicit scheme for the Beltrami flow. We introduced an acceleration factor f that is defined as the ratio of the step size used in the implicit scheme to the maximum allowed step size for the explicit scheme. For a square grid, and assuming the pixels are a unit length apart, the maximun time step size for the explicit scheme is 0.25. We ran the scheme with values of f ranging between 1 and 200. The results are shown in Fig. 1. As we see, the implicit scheme is always stable, but for $f \gg 50$, the resulting accuracy may be insufficient for certain applications.

The next series of numerical simulations are carried out to study the edge enhancemeent effect on gray level images. We fix the acceleration factor to 10 and solve the following normalized reaction-diffusion equation in this series:

$$\frac{\partial U}{\partial t} = \cos\beta \; \nabla h \cdot \nabla U \; + \; \sin\beta \; h \; \nabla^2 U \qquad (13)$$

The first term on the right side of Eq. (13) is a reaction term, while the second is a diffusion term and β is a parameter controlling the relative contribution of these opposing effects. The reaction term is responsible for edge enhancement, while the diffusion term smooths the noise away from the edges. Results of varying β between 0 to 90° is shown in Fig. 2. The first row in Fig. 2, presents the initial image and the results for $\beta = 0$ (pure reaction) and $\beta = 30°$. The second row presents the results for $\beta = 45°$ (a nonlinear diffusion flow equation), $\beta = \arctan 2 \approx 63.4°$ (the Beltrami flow), and $\beta = 90°$ (scaled "linear" diffusion). According to Eq. (13), the edge enhancement effect should decay with increasing β. Indeed, we see that the edge enhancement is stronger for the nonlinear diffusion flow ($\beta = 45°$) than for the Beltrami flow ($\beta = 63.4°$).

Fig. 1. Results of implicit difference scheme for Beltrami flow till scale = 250; the first row shows the initial image and results with $f = 1, 2$; second row corresponds to $f = 5, 10, 20$; third row corresponds to values of $f = 50, 100, 200$.

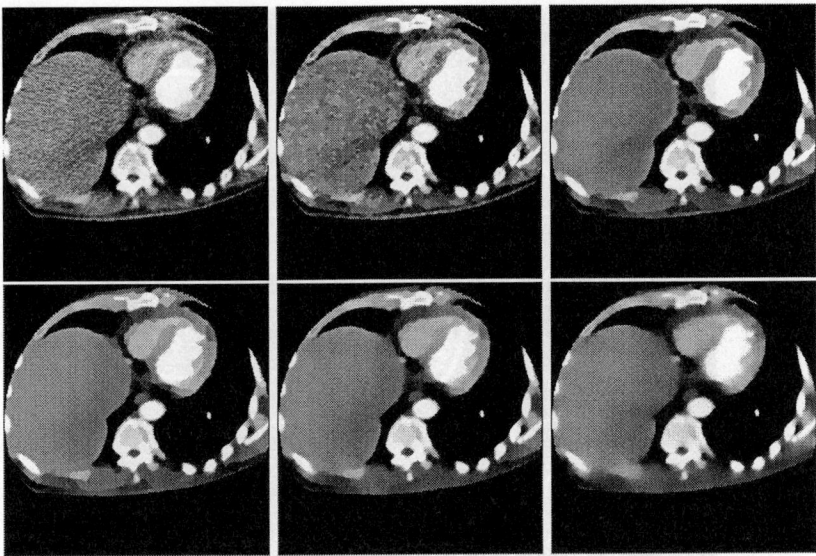

Fig. 2. Results of solving Eq. 13 until scale = 250 with different values of β.

In Fig. 3, the implicit difference scheme in $3D$ for the Beltrami flow is applied to a volumetric image of the brain. The image consists of 124 slices of 256×256 images. In the first column of Fig. 3, we show the original slice # 20, and results of running the flow until scale = 50 and 100. The other two columns show exactly the same results for slice #50 and #100. An acceleration factor of 12 was applied in all the simulations. We note that the $3D$ Beltrami flow can also be arranged as follows:

$$\dot{U} = \nabla \cdot \left(\frac{h\nabla U}{2}\right) + \frac{h\nabla^2 U}{2} \qquad (14)$$

where $h = 1/(1 + U_x^2 + U_y^2 + U_z^2)$ is the edge indicator function.

Note that due to the additional component U_z^2 in the denominator, the $3D$ Beltrami flow is slower than the corresponding $2D$ flow. This means that to achieve the same degree of noise reduction and edge enhancement, larger scale values should be employed in $3D$.

4 Beltrami Smoothing for Color Images

The Beltrami flow for color images is governed by the following set of partial differential equations [11,14]:

$$\frac{\partial I_i}{\partial t} = \frac{\frac{\partial P_i}{\partial x} + \frac{\partial Q_i}{\partial y}}{g} - \frac{\frac{\partial g}{\partial x} P_i + \frac{\partial g}{\partial y} Q_i}{2\,g^2} \qquad (15)$$

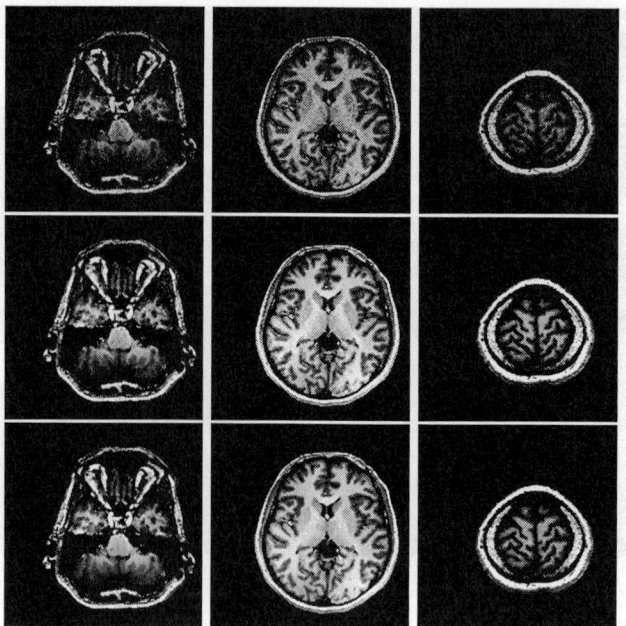

Fig. 3. Results of 3D Beltrami edge enhancing flow

where $i = 1, 2, 3$ corresponds to the color channel (red, green, blue), I_i is the corresponding pixel value, and P_i, Q_i are defined by:

$$P_i = g_{22} \frac{\partial I_i}{\partial x} - g_{12} \frac{\partial I_i}{\partial y} \qquad Q_i = -g_{12} \frac{\partial I_i}{\partial x} + g_{11} \frac{\partial I_i}{\partial y}. \qquad (16)$$

g_{11}, g_{12} and g_{22} are components of a symmetric matrix (tensor) $\boldsymbol{G}$ of dimension 2×2, and g is its discriminant, i.e.

$$\boldsymbol{G} = \begin{bmatrix} g_{11} & g_{12} \\ g_{12} & g_{22} \end{bmatrix} \qquad (17)$$

$$g_{11} = 1 + \sum_{j=1}^{3} \left(\frac{\partial I_j}{\partial x}\right)^2 \qquad g_{22} = 1 + \sum_{j=1}^{3} \left(\frac{\partial I_j}{\partial y}\right)^2$$

$$g_{12} = \sum_{j=1}^{3} \frac{\partial I_j}{\partial x} \frac{\partial I_j}{\partial y} \qquad g = \det \boldsymbol{G} = g_{11} g_{22} - g_{12}^2. \qquad (18)$$

For the time being, instead of Beltrami flow (15), let us consider a simplified smoothing flow, which is an analog of the nonlinear diffusion for gray level image:

$$\frac{\partial I_i}{\partial t} = \frac{\frac{\partial P_i}{\partial x} + \frac{\partial Q_i}{\partial y}}{g} - \frac{\frac{\partial g}{\partial x} P_i + \frac{\partial g}{\partial y} Q_i}{g^2} \qquad (19)$$

Note that the factor 2 is missing in the denominator of Eq. (19). This form is easier to handle in the following analysis. The above equation can be rearranged into a vector equation, namely

$$\frac{\partial I}{\partial t} = \frac{\partial}{\partial x}\left(\frac{P}{g}\right) + \frac{\partial}{\partial y}\left(\frac{Q}{g}\right) \qquad (20)$$

Let us define vector $\boldsymbol{S}_i$ of length 2, whose components are P_i/g and Q_i/g. We can then show that

$$\boldsymbol{S}_i = \boldsymbol{G}^{-1} \nabla I_i = \boldsymbol{R} \nabla I_i \qquad (21)$$

where $\boldsymbol{R}$ is the inverse of matrix $\boldsymbol{G}$, and the component wise flow becomes

$$\frac{\partial I_i}{\partial t} = \nabla \cdot \boldsymbol{S}_i = \nabla \cdot (\boldsymbol{R}\, \nabla I_i) \qquad (22)$$

Note that there are three pixel value gradient vectors ∇I_i (for each color component), three vector components $\boldsymbol{S}_i$, but only one matrix $\boldsymbol{R}$. This is 2×2 edge indicator matrix, similar to a scalar edge indicator function for a gray level case. Expanding the last equation, we obtain a reaction term with the first derivatives of pixel values, and a diffusion term with containing the second derivatives

$$\frac{\partial I_i}{\partial t} = (\nabla \cdot \boldsymbol{R}) \cdot \nabla I_i + \boldsymbol{R} \cdot \nabla\nabla I_i. \qquad (23)$$

The first term is a scalar product of two vectors (divergence of tensor $\nabla \cdot \boldsymbol{R}$ yields a vector), and $\boldsymbol{R} \cdot \nabla\nabla I_i$ is a full scalar product of two tensors; $\nabla\nabla I_i$ is the following matrix of second derivatives:

$$\nabla\nabla I_i = \begin{bmatrix} I^i_{xx} & I^i_{xy} \\ I^i_{xy} & I^i_{yy} \end{bmatrix} \qquad (24)$$

Note that while this nonlinear diffusion flow includes the reaction term and the diffusion term, the Beltrami color flow includes an additional reaction term not considered here.

Now, consider the nonlinear diffusion flow, Eq. (22), and replace the action of matrix $\boldsymbol{R}$ on vector ∇I_i by the action of the eigenvalue on that vector, see [18,15,12]. For this, we de-compose the gradient vector ∇I_i into the basis of principal directions $\boldsymbol{V}_1$ and $\boldsymbol{V}_2$, as follows:

$$\nabla I_i = k_1 \boldsymbol{V}_1 + k_2 \boldsymbol{V}_2, \qquad (25)$$

where $\boldsymbol{V}_1$ and $\boldsymbol{V}_2$ are normalized eigenvectors of the edge indicator tensor $\boldsymbol{R}$. Assume λ_1 and λ_2 are eigenvalues, corresponding to these eigenvectors, i.e.,

$$\boldsymbol{R}\boldsymbol{V}_k = \lambda_k \boldsymbol{V}_k \qquad k = 1, 2 \qquad (26)$$

Consider the expression inside the brackets on the right side of Eq. (22),

$$\boldsymbol{R}\nabla I_i = \boldsymbol{R}(k_1\boldsymbol{V}_1 + k_2\boldsymbol{V}_2) = k_1\boldsymbol{R}\boldsymbol{V}_1 + k_2\boldsymbol{R}\boldsymbol{V}_2 = k_1\lambda_1\boldsymbol{V}_1 + k_2\lambda_2\boldsymbol{V}_2 \qquad (27)$$

Note that λ_k are real positive numbers since matrix $\boldsymbol{R}$ is symmetric and positive definite. Recall that

$$g = 1 + \sum_{j=1}^{3}\left(\frac{\partial I_j}{\partial x}\right)^2 + \sum_{j=1}^{3}\left(\frac{\partial I_j}{\partial y}\right)^2 + \sum_{j=1}^{3}\left(\frac{\partial I_j}{\partial x}\right)^2 \cdot \sum_{j=1}^{3}\left(\frac{\partial I_j}{\partial y}\right)^2 - \sum_{j=1}^{3}\left(\frac{\partial I_j}{\partial x}\frac{\partial I_j}{\partial y}\right)^2 \tag{28}$$

and the eigenvalues λ_k of matrix $\boldsymbol{R}$ are roots of a quadratic equation:

$$\lambda \cdot g = 1 + \frac{\sum_{j=1}^{3}\left(\frac{\partial I_j}{\partial x}\right)^2 + \sum_{j=1}^{3}\left(\frac{\partial I_j}{\partial y}\right)^2}{2} \pm \sqrt{\frac{\left[\sum_{j=1}^{3}\left(\frac{\partial I_j}{\partial x}\right)^2 + \sum_{j=1}^{3}\left(\frac{\partial I_j}{\partial y}\right)^2\right]^2}{4} - A} \tag{29}$$

where

$$A = \sum_{j=1}^{3}\left(\frac{\partial I_j}{\partial x}\right)^2 \cdot \sum_{j=1}^{3}\left(\frac{\partial I_j}{\partial y}\right)^2 - \left(\sum_{j=1}^{3}\frac{\partial I_j}{\partial x}\frac{\partial I_j}{\partial y}\right)^2 \tag{30}$$

Expanding powers and products in Eq. (30) we can express A to be the sum of squares of lengths for cross-products of pairs of gradients $\nabla I_m \times \nabla I_{m+1}$;

$$A = \sum_{j=1}^{3}\left(\nabla I_j \times \nabla I_{(j+1)\ div\ 3}\right)^2 \tag{31}$$

For the gray level image, the edge is a line which divides region into segments with different pixel values. In other words, when passing across the edge, the pixel value changes in a discontinuous manner. The magnitude of the gradient vector is large and its direction is normal to the edge.

For the color image, the gradients of red-green-blue components may have different directions. However, we assume that in the proximity of the edge at least one of them has a large magnitude. The direction of this gradient is normal to the edge. The directions of other color gradients are collinear to this direction provided the magnitudes of gradients of these other components are also large. For the component(s) of small gradient magnitude, the direction of gradient does not matter. Thus, in the close proximity of the "true" edge, the value A in Eq. (31) will be small because all cross-products of gradients vanish or almost vanish; this is because either the components of the cross-product are collinear, or due to the fact that one of them or both have small magnitude.

Since the cross-products are small in the proximity of the edge, the value A in Eq. (29) may be neglected and the eigenvalues become:

$$\lambda_1 \approx \frac{1}{g} \qquad \lambda_2 \approx 1 \qquad g \approx 1 + \sum_{j=0}^{3}\left(\frac{\partial I_j}{\partial x}\right)^2 + \sum_{j=0}^{3}\left(\frac{\partial I_j}{\partial y}\right)^2 \tag{32}$$

In the proximity of the edge, the principal direction V_1 of the edge indicator matrix R, corresponds to the smaller eigenvalue $1/g$:

$$\frac{V_1^y}{V_1^x} = \sqrt{\sum_{j=1}^{3}\left(\frac{\partial I_j}{\partial y}\right)^2 \Big/ \sum_{j=1}^{3}\left(\frac{\partial I_j}{\partial x}\right)^2} \tag{33}$$

Since we assumed that all gradients have approximately collinear directions in the proximity of the edge, it follows from Eq. (33) that the principal direction V_1 coincides with these gradients and is normal to the edge. The second principal direction, corresponds to a larger eigenvalue 1:

$$\frac{V_2^x}{V_2^y} = -\sqrt{\sum_{j=1}^{3}\left(\frac{\partial I_j}{\partial x}\right)^2 \Big/ \sum_{j=1}^{3}\left(\frac{\partial I_j}{\partial y}\right)^2} \tag{34}$$

The second eigenvector is tangent to the edge. Note that even when the cross products of color components' gradients do not vanish exactly, it is reasonable to define the direction of the edge as a principal direction of the edge indicator matrix corresponding to the larger eigenvalue $\lambda_2 \approx 1$.

Now consider Eq. (27). Since the edge is normal to the gradient,

$$k_1 \approx |\nabla I_i| \qquad k_2 \approx 0 \tag{35}$$

$$R\nabla I_i = k_1\lambda_1 V_1 + k_2\lambda_2 V_2 \approx \frac{\nabla I_i}{g} \tag{36}$$

where g is given by Eq. (32). In the proximity of the edge, the governing equation for the color image flow becomes:

$$\frac{\partial I_i}{\partial t} = \nabla \cdot (R\nabla I_i) = \nabla \cdot \left(\frac{\nabla I_i}{g}\right) = \nabla\left(\frac{1}{g}\right) \cdot \nabla I_i + \frac{\nabla^2 I_i}{g} \tag{37}$$

Now, recall that Eq. (37) describes the nonlinear diffusion flow which differs from the Beltrami flow. It follows from Eqs. (15, 19 and 37) that the Beltrami flow has an additional reaction term, namely

$$\frac{\partial I_i}{\partial t} = \nabla\left(\frac{1}{g}\right) \cdot \nabla I_i + \frac{\nabla^2 I_i}{g} + \frac{\frac{\partial g}{\partial x} P_i + \frac{\partial g}{\partial y} Q_i}{2 g^2}. \tag{38}$$

Rearranging the last term in Eq. (38) to a tensor form:

$$\frac{\frac{\partial g}{\partial x} P_i + \frac{\partial g}{\partial y} Q_i}{2 g^2} = -P_i \frac{\partial}{\partial x}\frac{1}{2 g} - Q_i \frac{\partial}{\partial y}\frac{1}{2 g} = -\nabla\left(\frac{1}{2 g}\right) \cdot g \, R \, \nabla I_i \tag{39}$$

and applying Eq. (36) in the proximity of the edge, i.e., $g\,\boldsymbol{R}\,\nabla I_i \approx \nabla I_i$, the governing equation (38) for Beltrami flow can be expressed as:

$$\frac{\partial I_i}{\partial t} \approx \nabla\left(\frac{1}{2\,g}\right)\cdot \nabla I_i + \frac{\nabla^2 I_i}{g} = \nabla\cdot\left(\frac{\nabla I_i}{2\,g}\right) + \frac{\nabla^2 I_i}{2\,g} \qquad (40)$$

This corresponds exactly with the governing partial differential equation for the Beltrami flow equation fro a gray level image. This means that the mechanism of the edge enhancement is exactly the same. In the proximity of the edge, $1/g$ reaches minimum values. The gradient of $1/g$ is directed outside the thin pass of the edge. The gradient of the pixel value is also normal to the edge, but its direction coincides with the gradient of $1/g$ for larger pixel values, and is opposite to that direction for smaller pixel values. The reactive component of the equation becomes positive for larger pixel values and negative for smaller pixel in the proximity of the edge. So, the large values become even larger, and the small values become even smaller. thereby enhancing and sharpening the edge.

Note that the simplified decoupled form of the Beltrami smoothing may be used for numerical computations. Close to the edge this form is justified because the coupling between x and y components of gradient becomes weak. Away from the edge, the decoupled form brings a definite inaccuracy, and the flow is no longer exactly Beltrami. However, we consider that the accuracy is crucial at the proximity of the edge and less important elsewhere. In this case, the decoupled form of the governing equation (40) leads to a considerable saving of the computational time. Furthermore, the decoupled form makes it possible to apply the additive splitting algorithm leading to a semi-implicit linearized difference scheme, and this yields much faster and unconditionally stable computation. For a specific raw or column of pixels, the left-side matrix of the difference equation set is the same for all three color components, and only the right-side vectors differ. Thus, we solve the three sets of equations simultaneously.

5 Simulation Results for Color Images

The goal of this numerical experiment is to show that the weakly coupled Beltrami smoothing operator may be replaced by its decoupled approximation without essential loss of accuracy and with a great saving of the computational time.

Fig. 4 presents the simulation results for implicit scheme with different values of acceleration factor $f = 2\ldots 50$. The first row includes the initial image (left picture) and the smoothing simulation results for the Beltrami filtering, using the coupled explicit difference scheme with a full edge indicator matrix (central picture) and explicit difference scheme with decoupled governing equation with the eigenvalue instead of the mathix (right picture). In the second row the results are plotted for implicit difference scheme with decoupled governing equation and acceleration factor $f = 1, 2, 5$. The third row corresponds to $f = 10, 20, 50$. As we see, for acceleration factors of up to 20, the flow is simulated with a reasonable accuracy.

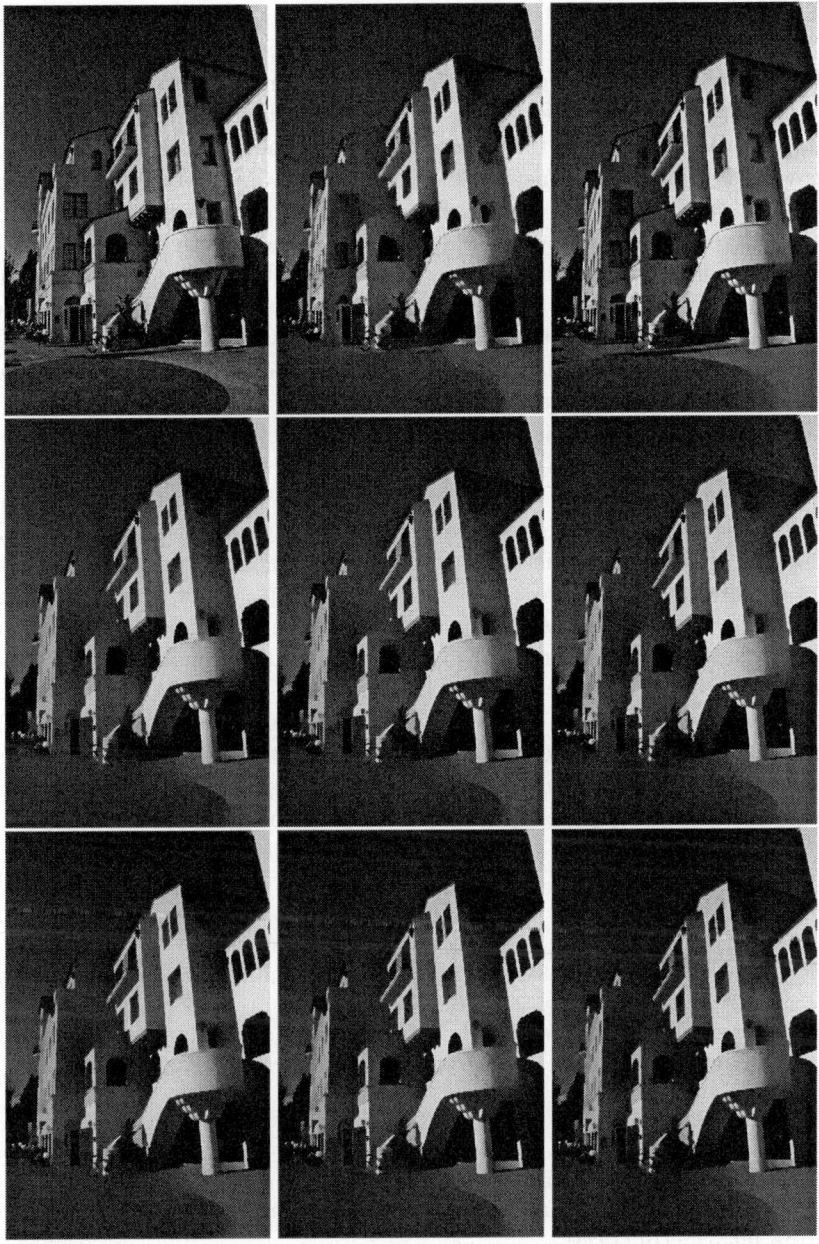

Fig. 4. Semi-implicit AOS implementation of Beltrami flow for Color Images; scale 1000

6 Closing Remarks

The anisotropic Beltrami operator for gray level images is reduced to reaction-diffusion form and this makes it possible to apply the Additive Operator Split (AOS) approach. Based on this approach, the uncondiotionally stable difference scheme is developed. The method uses the known values of the edge indicator function from the previous scale step, and incorporates the unknown pixel values from the next step, thus making the difference scheme semi-implicit and linearized. The implicit scheme leads to considerable saving of the computational time as compared to the explicit scheme: up to ten times and even more, depending on the value of the scale step, with no visible loss of accuracy. The approach may be applied also to the mean curvature flow in a similar way, with a different edge indicator function.

The eigenvalue analysis is applied to study the Beltrami smoothing technique for color images. It is shown that in the proximity of the edge the coupling of the Beltrami operator becomes weak. The principal directions of the edge indicator matrix are normal to the edge and tangent to the edge. This allows us to replace the action of the edge indicator matrix on the gradient vector by the action of its eigenvalue on that vector. The main assumption for fast processing of color images is that the cross-products of the gradients of color components are negligibly small in the proximity of edge, since their directions are all parallel and normal to the edge. When these cross-products are small, the coupling becomes weak. Weak coupling of the Beltrami operator for color images makes it possible to apply the AOS technique and unconditionably stable fast implicit difference scheme. The difference scheme is similar to that for gray-level images. Numerical simulations confirm the validity of the assumption about the weak coupling.

References

1. P. Perona, J. Malik, "Scale-space and edge-detection using anisotropic diffusion," IEEE Trans. of PAMI, Vol. 12, pp. 629–639, 1990.
2. L. Alvarez, P.L. Lions, J.M. Morel, "Image selective smoothing and edge detection by non-linear diffusion II," SIAM Journal on Numerical Analysis, Vol. 29(3), pp. 845–866, 1992.
3. L. Rudin, S. Osher, and E. Fatemi, "Nonlinear total variation based noise removal algorithms," Physica D, Vol. 60, pp. 259–268, 1992.
4. J. Weickert, B.M. ter Haar Romeny, and M.A. Viergever. "Efficient and reliable scheme for nonlinear diffusion filtering". *IEEE Trans on Image Processing.*, Vol. 7(3), pp. 398-410 (1998).
5. R. Goldenberg, R. Kimmel, E. Rivlin, and M. Rudzsky. "Fast Geodesic Active Contours". M. Nielsen, P. Johansen, O.F. Olsen, J. Weickert (Editors), Scale-space theories in computer vision, Lecture Notes in Computer Science, Vol. 1682, Springer, Berlin, 1999.
6. S. Osher and J. A. Sethian, "Fronts propagating with curvature dependent speed: Algorithms based on Hamilton-Jacobi formulation," Journal of Computational Physics, Vol. 79, pp. 12-49, 1988.

7. R. Malladi and J. A. Sethian, "Image processing via level set curvature flow," Proc. of Natl. Acad. of Scie., Vol. 92, pp. 7046–7050, July 1995.
8. R. Malladi and J. A. Sethian, "Image Processing: Flows under Min/Max curvature and Mean curvature," Graphical Models and Image Processing, Vol. 58(2), pp. 127–141, 1996.
9. G.I. Barenblatt. "Self-Similar Intermediate Asymptotics for Nonlinear Degenerate Parabolic Free-Boundary Problems which Occur in Image Processing". to appear in Proceedings of the National Academy of Science, 2001.
10. B. M. ter Harr Romeny, editor, Geometry-driven diffusion in computer vision, Kluwer Academic publishers, The Netherlands, 1994.
11. R. Kimmel, R. Malladi, and N. Sochen. "Images as embedded maps and minimal surfaces: movies, color, texture, and volumetric medical images". International Joornal of Computer Vision, 1999.
12. R. Kimmel, "A natural norm for color processing," in Proceedings of 3-rd ACCV, Springer-Verlag LNCS 1352, pp. 88–95, Hong-Kong, January 1998.
13. N. Sochen, R. Kimmel and R. Malladi, "From high energy physics to low level vision," LBNL Report # 39243, Lawrence Berkeley National Laboratory, University of California, Berkeley, Aug. 1996.
14. N. Sochen, R. Kimmel and R. Malladi, "A genearal framework for low level vision". IEEE Transactions, Vol. 7, No. 3, 1998.
15. G. Sapiro, "Vector-valued active contours," in Proceedings of CVPR '96, pp. 650–655, 1996.
16. A. M. Polyakov, "Quantum geometry of bosonic strings," in Physics Letters B, 103B(3), pp. 207–210, 1981.
17. R. Malladi and I. Ravve, "Fast difference scheme for anisotropic Beltrami smoothing and edge contrast enhancement of gray level and color images," LBNL report # 48796, Lawrence Berkeley National Laboratory, University of California, Berkeley, August, 2001.
18. J. Weickert. Anisotropic Diffusion in Image Processing. Ph. D. Thesis, Kaiserslautern University, 1996.
19. Curtis E. Gerald and Patric O. Wheatley. Applied Numerical Analysis, Addison Wesley, NY, 1999.
20. William H. Press, Saul A. Tekolsky, William T. Vetterling and Brian F. Flannery. Numerical Recipes in C, Cambridge University Press, 1992
21. A. Yezzi, "Modified curvature motion for image smoothing and enhancement," IEEE Tran. of Image Processing, Vol. 7, No. 3, 1998.

A Fast Radial Symmetry Transform for Detecting Points of Interest

Gareth Loy and Alexander Zelinsky

Australian National University, Canberra 0200, Australia.
{gareth, alex}@syseng.anu.edu.au
http://www.syseng.anu.edu.au/~gareth

Abstract. A new feature detection technique is presented that utilises local radial symmetry to identify regions of interest within a scene. This transform is significantly faster than existing techniques using radial symmetry and offers the possibility of real-time implementation on a standard processor. The new transform is shown to perform well on a wide variety of images and its performance is tested against leading techniques from the literature. Both as a facial feature detector and as a generic region of interest detector the new transform is seen to offer equal or superior performance to contemporary techniques whilst requiring drastically less computational effort.

1 Introduction

Automatic detection of points of interest in images is an important topic in computer vision. Point of interest detectors can be used to selectively process images by concentrating effort at key locations in the image, they can identify salient features and compare the prominence of such features, and real-time interest detectors can provide attentional mechanisms for active vision systems [11].

In this paper a new point of interest operator is presented. It is a simple and fast gradient-based interest operator which detects points of high radial symmetry. The approach was inspired by the results of the generalised symmetry transform [8,4,9], although the method bares more similarity to the work of Sela and Levine [10] and the circular Hough transform [5,7]. The approach presented herein determines the contribution each pixel makes to the symmetry of pixels around it, rather than considering the contribution of a local neighbourhood to a central pixel. Unlike previous techniques that have used this approach [5,7,10] it does not require the gradient to be quantised into angular bins, the contribution of *every* orientation is computed in a single pass over the image. The new method works well with a general fixed parameter set, however, it can also be tuned to exclusively detect particular kinds of features. Computationally the algorithm is very efficient, being of order $O(KN)$ when considering local radial symmetry in $N \times N$ neighbourhoods across an image of K pixels.

Section 2 of this paper defines the new radial symmetry transform. Section 3 discusses the application of the transform, including selection of parameters and some additional refinements. Section 4 shows the performance of the new transform on a variety of images, and compares it to existing techniques, and Section 5 presents the conclusions.

2 Definition of the Transform

The new transform is calculated over a set of one or more ranges N depending on the scale of the features one is trying to detect. The value of the transform at range $n \in N$ indicates the contribution to radial symmetry of the gradients a distance n away from each point. Whilst the transform can be calculated for a continuous set of ranges this is generally unnecessary as a small subset of ranges is normally sufficient to obtain a representative result.

At each range n an *orientation projection image* O_n and a *magnitude projection image* M_n are formed. These images are generated by examining the gradient **g** at each point **p** from which a corresponding *positively-affected pixel* $\mathbf{p}_{+ve}(\mathbf{p})$ and *negatively-affected pixel* $\mathbf{p}_{-ve}(\mathbf{p})$ are determined, as shown in Figure 1. The *positively-affected pixel* is defined as the pixel that the gradient vector $\mathbf{g}(\mathbf{p})$ is pointing to, a distance n away from **p**, and the *negatively-affected pixel* is the pixel a distance n away that the gradient is pointing directly away from.

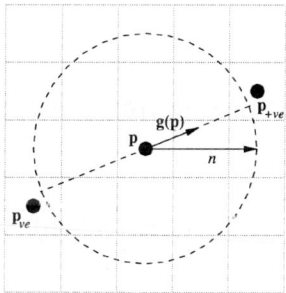

Fig. 1. The locations of pixels $\mathbf{p}_{+ve}(\mathbf{p})$ and $\mathbf{p}_{-ve}(\mathbf{p})$ affected by the gradient element $\mathbf{g}(\mathbf{p})$ for a range of $n = 2$. The dotted circle shows all the pixels which can be affected by the gradient at **p** for a range n.

The coordinates of the positively-affected pixel are given by

$$\mathbf{p}_{+ve}(\mathbf{p}) = \mathbf{p} + \text{round}\left(\frac{\mathbf{g}(\mathbf{p})}{\|\mathbf{g}(\mathbf{p})\|}n\right)$$

while those of the negatively-affected pixel are

$$\mathbf{p}_{-ve}(\mathbf{p}) = \mathbf{p} - \text{round}\left(\frac{\mathbf{g}(\mathbf{p})}{\|\mathbf{g}(\mathbf{p})\|}n\right)$$

where 'round' rounds each vector element to the nearest integer.

The orientation and projection images are initially zero. For each pair of affected pixels the corresponding point $\mathbf{p}_{+ve}$ in the orientation projection image O_n and magnitude projection image M_n is incremented by 1 and $\|\mathbf{g}(\mathbf{p})\|$ respectively, while the point corresponding to $\mathbf{p}_{-ve}$ is decremented by these same quantities in each image. That is

$$O_n(\mathbf{p}_{+ve}(\mathbf{p})) = O_n(\mathbf{p}_{+ve}(\mathbf{p})) + 1$$

$$O_n(\mathbf{p}_{-ve}(\mathbf{p})) = O_n(\mathbf{p}_{-ve}(\mathbf{p})) - 1$$

$$M_n(\mathbf{p}_{+ve}(\mathbf{p})) = M_n(\mathbf{p}_{+ve}(\mathbf{p})) + \|\mathbf{g}(\mathbf{p})\|$$

$$M_n(\mathbf{p}_{-ve}(\mathbf{p})) = M_n(\mathbf{p}_{-ve}(\mathbf{p})) - \|\mathbf{g}(\mathbf{p})\|$$

The radial symmetry contribution at a range n is defined as the convolution

$$S_n = F_n * A_n \qquad (1)$$

where

$$F_n(\mathbf{p}) = \|\tilde{O}_n(\mathbf{p})\|^{(\alpha)} \tilde{M}_n(\mathbf{p}), \qquad (2)$$

$$\tilde{O}_n(\mathbf{p}) = \frac{O_n}{\max_{\mathbf{p}}\{\|O_n(\mathbf{p})\|\}},$$

$$\tilde{M}_n(\mathbf{p}) = \frac{M_n}{\max_{\mathbf{p}}\{\|M_n(\mathbf{p})\|\}},$$

α is the radial strictness parameter, and A_n is a two-dimensional Gaussian. These parameters are discussed in more detail in Section 3.

The full transform is defined as the sum of the symmetry contributions over all the ranges considered,

$$S = \sum_{n \in N} S_n \qquad (3)$$

If the gradient is calculated so it points from dark to light then the output image S will have positive values corresponding to bright radially symmetric regions and negative values indicating dark symmetric regions (see Figure 2 for example).

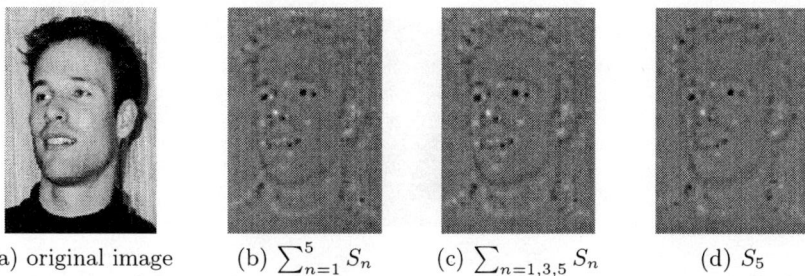

(a) original image (b) $\sum_{n=1}^{5} S_n$ (c) $\sum_{n=1,3,5} S_n$ (d) S_5

Fig. 2. Varying the set of ranges N.

3 Applying the Transform

In order to apply the transform there are a number of parameters that must first be defined, namely, the a set of ranges $N = \{n_1, n_2, ...\}$ at which to calculate S_n, the Gaussian kernels A_n, and the radial strictness parameter α. Some additional refinements are also considered, including ignoring small gradient elements, and only searching for dark or light radially symmetric regions.

The traditional approach to local symmetry detection [3,8,10] is to calculate the symmetry apparent in a local neighbourhood about each point. This can be achieved by calculating S_n for a continuous set of ranges $N = \{1, 2, ..., n_{max}\}$ and combining using equation 3. However, since the symmetry contribution is calculated independently for each range n it is simple to determine the result at a single range, or an arbitrary selection of ranges that need not be continuous. Furthermore, the results obtained by examining a representative subset of ranges give a good approximation of the output obtained by examining a continuous selection of ranges, while saving on computation.

Figure 2 shows the combined output S calculated for a continuous range of n from 1 to 5 (b) is closely approximated by combining only $n = 1$, 3 and 5 (c). Also, if the scale of a radially symmetric feature is know *a priori* then the feature can be efficiently detected by only determining the transform at the appropriate range, this is demonstrated by the effective highlighting of the eyes (that have radius 5 pixels) by S_5 in Figure 2 (d).

The purpose of the Gaussian kernel A_n is to spread the influence of the positively- and negatively-affected pixels as a function of the range n. A two-dimensional Gaussian is chosen because it is radially symmetric so it will have a consistent effect over all gradient orientations, and it is separable so its convolution can be efficiently determined. Figure 3 shows the contribution for a single gradient element $\mathbf{g}(\mathbf{p})$. By scaling the standard deviation linearly with the range n, we define an arc of influence that applies to all affected pixels. The width of the arc is defined by scaling the standard deviation of A_n with respect to n.

The parameter α determines how strictly radial the radial symmetry must be for the transform to return a high interest value. Figure 4 shows the effect of choosing α to be 1, 2 and 3 on S_1 for an image exhibiting strong radial values

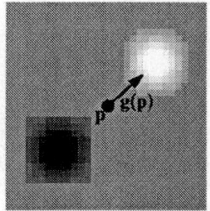

Fig. 3. The contribution of a single gradient element, with A_n chosen to be a 2D Gaussian of size $n \times n$ and standard deviation $\sigma = 0.25n$, and $n = 10$.

around the eyes. Note how a higher α eliminates non-radially symmetric features such as lines. A choice of $\alpha = 2$ is suitable for most applications. Choosing a higher α starts attenuating points of interest, whilst a lower α gives too much emphasis to non-radially symmetric features, however, choosing α as 1 minimises the computation when determining F_n in Equation 2.

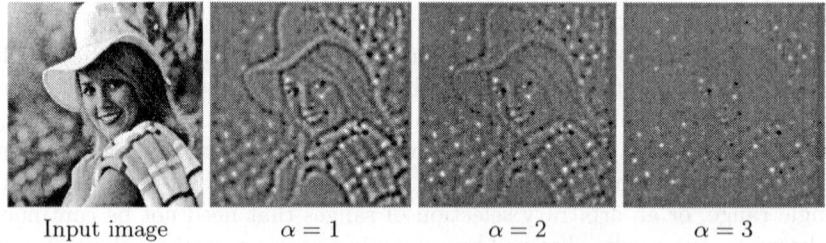

Input image $\alpha = 1$ $\alpha = 2$ $\alpha = 3$

Fig. 4. Effect of varying α. Original image from USC-SIPI Image Database [1]

Gradient elements with small magnitudes have less reliable orientations, are more easily corrupted by noise, and tend to correspond to features that are not immediately apparent to the human eye. Since the purpose of the transform is to pick out points of interest in the image it is logical to ignore such elements in our calculation. A gradient threshold parameter β is introduced for this purpose, and when calculating images O_n and M_n all gradient elements whose magnitudes are below β are ignored. The effect of a non-zero β is shown in Figure 5. The main advantage of a non-zero β is an increase in the speed of the algorithm, since there are less gradient elements considered, and hence less affected pixels to be calculated.

The transform can be tuned to look only for dark or bright regions of symmetry. To look exclusively for dark regions, only the negatively-affected pixels need be considered when determining M_n and O_n (see Section 2). Likewise, to detect bright symmetry only positive affected pixels need be considered. Examples of dark symmetry are shown in Section 4.

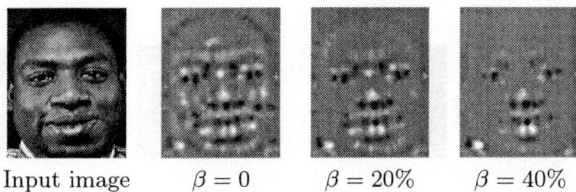

Input image $\beta = 0$ $\beta = 20\%$ $\beta = 40\%$

Fig. 5. The effect of different values of β on S. Here β is measured as a percentage of the maximum possible gradient magnitude. Original image from Database of Faces, AT&T Laboratories Cambridge [2]

4 Performance of the Transform

The performance of the new transform was demonstrated on a range of images and compared with several prominent transforms from the literature.

Figure 6 demonstrates the performance of the new transform on faces and other images. These figures were generated using the parameter settings presented in Table 1, and show how the transform can provide a useful cue for the location of facial features – especially eyes – in face images, as well as highlighting generic points of interest that are characterised by high contrast and radial symmetry.

Table 1. Parameter Settings used for Experimentation

Parameter	Setting		
	Full	Fast	Fast Dark
Set of ranges N	$\{n : n = 1, 2, ..., 6\}$	$\{n : n = 1, 3, 5\}$	$\{n : n = 1, 3, 5\}$
Gaussian kernel			
Volume under kernel	n^2	n^2	n^2
Size	n	n	n
Standard deviation	$0.5n$	$0.5n$	$0.5n$
Radial strictness α	2	2	2
Small gradients ignored	0	20% ignored	20% ignored
Dark symmetry	Yes	Yes	Yes
Bright symmetry	Yes	Yes	No

Figure 7 compares the performance of the transform against existing techniques from the literature. Each transform is applied to the image in the centre of the figure (the standard 256 × 256 lena image) for which the intuitive points of interest are the eyes.

All methods were implemented with a local neighbourhood radius of 6 pixels, and where necessary the gradient orientation was quantised into 8 bins.

Each of the transforms was implemented in Matlab. For the majority of the transforms an estimate of the approximate number of floating point operations

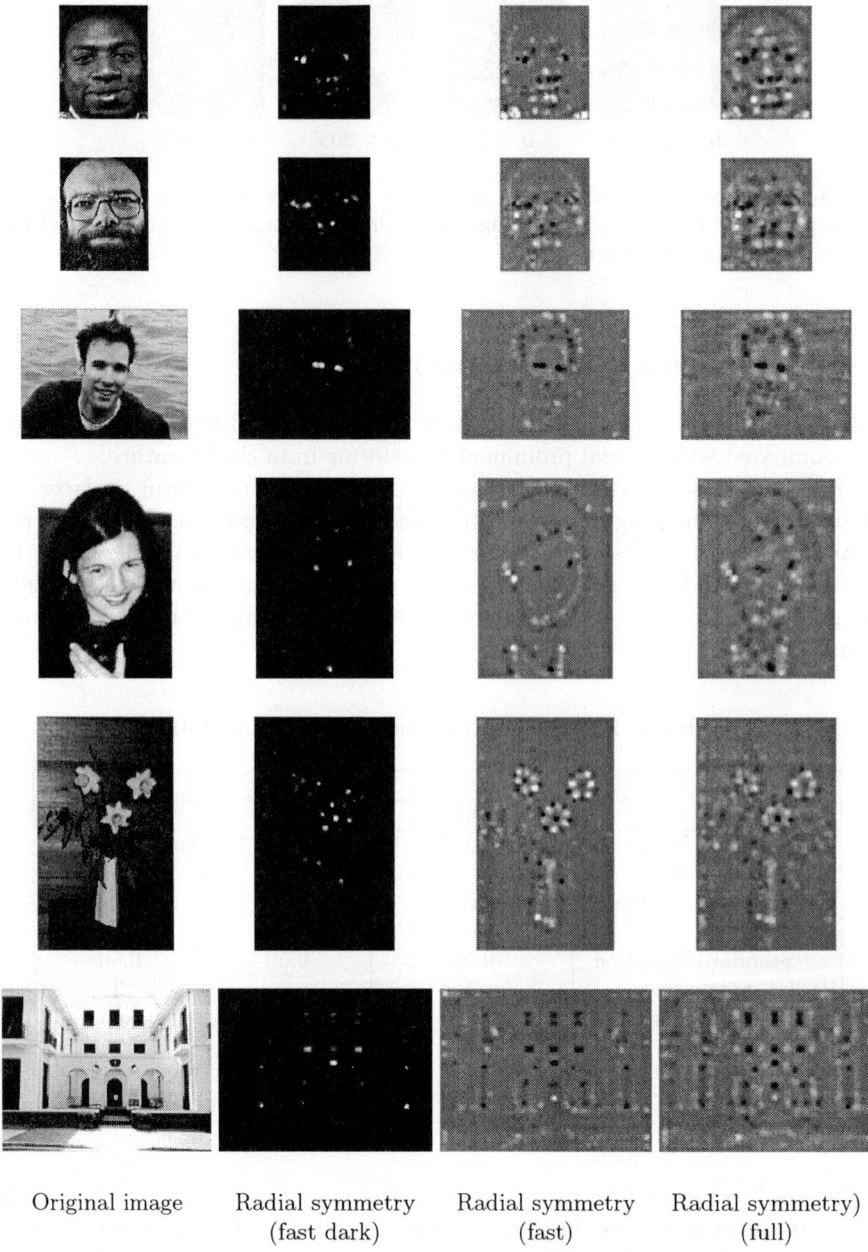

Original image   Radial symmetry   Radial symmetry   Radial symmetry)
                             (fast dark)   (fast)   (full)

Fig. 6. The new transform applied to a variety of images. The parameter settings are indicated beneath each column and refer to the values detailed in Table 1. The two top most images are from the Database of Faces [2].

involved was obtained from Matlab, however, for Di Gesù et al.'s discrete symmetry transform and Sela and Levine's real-time attention mechanism this was not feasible. These transforms involve optimised low-level processes that were not practical to implement in Matlab, so the number of operations required is not reported here. It suffices to say that the *non-optimised* implementations used to generate the visual results shown required computation well in excess of the other methods. The estimated computations obtained are presented in Table 2.

The new transform effectively highlights the points of interest (eyes) in Figure 7. Of the existing transforms Reisfeld's generalised (dark and radial) symmetry provide the next best result, and while the other transforms do highlight the eye regions they tend to highlight many other points as well reducing their overall effectiveness.

Table 2. Estimated Computation Required for Different Transforms to compute the results in Figure 7

Transform	Computations (Mflop)
New Transform	
Full	19.7
Fast	7.93
Fast Dark	7.02
Existing Transforms	
Generalised Symmetry	
Radial [8]	259
Dark [9]	179
Circular Hough [7]	33.9

Table 3 lists the theoretical order of computation required to compute the transforms on an image of K pixels, where local symmetry is considered in an $N \times N$ neighbourhood, and for those methods that require gradient quantisation the gradient is quantized into B bins. The complexity $O(KN)$ of the new transform is lower than all other transforms considered, with the possible exception of Di Gesu et al.'s Discrete Symmetry Transform that has complexity $O(KB)$. However, as was discussed in Section 3, it is not necessary to calculate the new transform at all ranges $1..N$, so the computational order can be further reduced, whereas it is essential to calculate Di Gesu et al.'s Discrete Symmetry Transform across four or more angular bins. Furthermore the results from the Discrete Symmetry Transform do not appear as effective for locating points of interest (see Figure 7).

Figure 7 and Tables 2 and 3 demonstrate that the new transform can provide comparable or superior results to existing techniques whilst requiring significantly less computation and complexity.

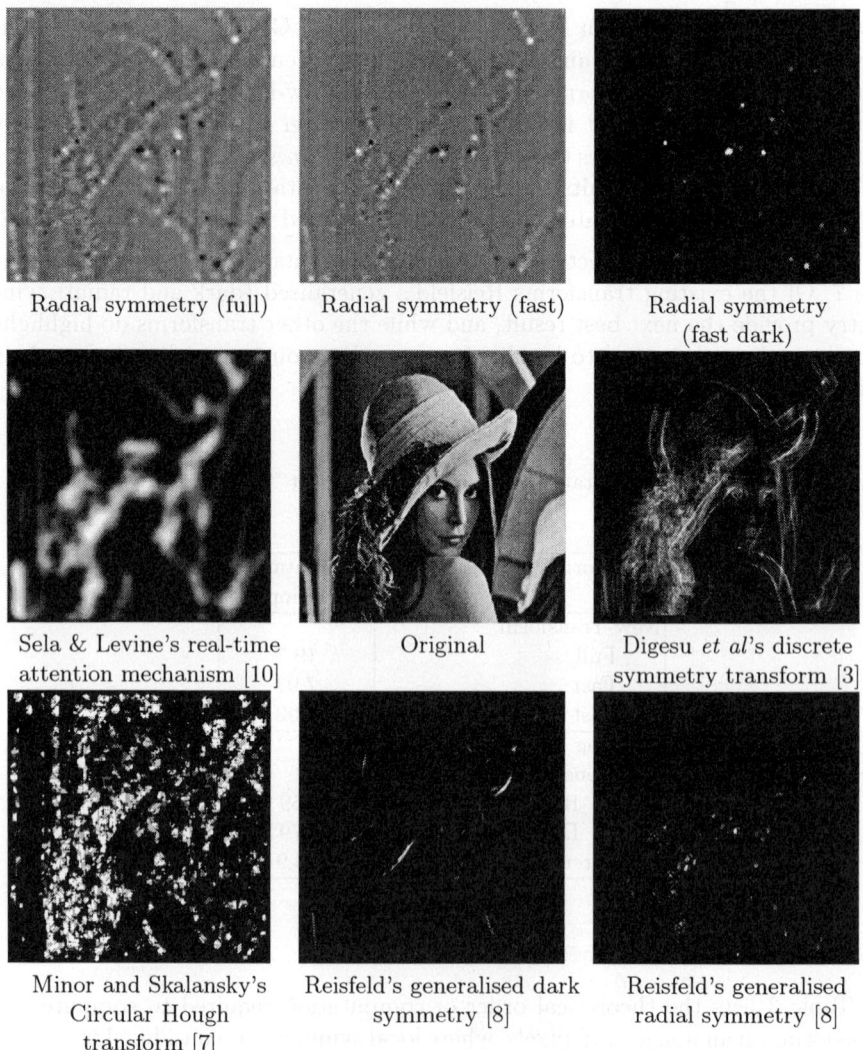

Fig. 7. Comparison of new transform (top row) with other available transforms. In order to compare the output of Sela & Levine's real-time attention mechanism with the other transforms, the final step, which involved identifying local maximums in the output as points of interest, has been omitted.

The key to the speed of the new transform lies in the use of *affected pixels* to project the effect of gradient elements. This allows an approximation of the effect of each gradient element on the radial symmetry of the pixels around it, without specifically considering neighbourhoods about each point, as did [6,8], or requiring multiple calculations for different gradient orientations, as did [3,7,10].

Table 3. Computational Order of Different Transforms

Transform	Order
New Radial Symmetry Transform	KN
Reisfeld's Generalised Symmetry Transform [8]	KN^2
Lin and Lin's Gradient-based Inhibitory Mechanism [6]	KN^2
Di Gesu et al.'s Discrete Symmetry Transform [3]	KB
Sela and Levine's Real-Time Attentional Mechanism [10]	KBN
Circular Hough Transform [7]	KBN

Unlike other transforms the fast symmetry transform differentiates between dark and bright regions of radial symmetry, while allowing both to be computed simultaneously. Alternatively just dark (or bright) points of symmetry can be considered exclusively with an associated reduction in computation.

5 Conclusion

A novel point of interest detector has been presented that uses the gradient of an image to locate points of high radial symmetry. The method has been demonstrated on a series of face images and other scenes, and compared against a number of contemporary techniques from the literature. As a point of interest operator the new transform provides equal or superior performance on the images tested while offering significant savings in both the computation required and the complexity of the implementation. The efficiency of this transform makes it well suited to real-time vision applications.

References

1. The USC-SIPI Image Database, University of Southern California Signal & Image Processing Institute. *http:// sipi.usc.edu/ services/ database/ Database.html*.
2. Database of Faces. AT&T Laboratories Cambridge, *http:// www.cam-orl.co.uk/ facedatabase.html*.
3. V. Di Gesù and C. Valenti. The discrete symmetry transform in computer vision. Technical Report DMA 011 95, Palermo University, 1995.
4. N. Intrator, D. Reisfeld, and Y. Yeshurun. Extraction of facial features for recognition using neural networks, 1995.
5. C. Kimme, D. Ballard, and J. Sklansky. Finding circles by an array of accumulators. *Communications of the Association for Computing Machinery*, 18(2):120–122, February 1975.
6. Cheng-Chung Lin and Wei-Chung Lin. Extracting facial features by an inhibitory mechanism based on gradient distributions. *Pattern Recognition*, 29(12):2079–2101, 1996.
7. L. G. Minor and J. Sklansky. Detection and segmetaion of blobs in infrared images. *IEEE Tranactions on Systems Man and Cyberneteics*, SMC-11(3):194–201, March 1981.

8. D. Reisfeld, H. Wolfson, and Y. Yeshurun. Context free attentional operators: the generalized symmetry transform. *International Journal of Computer Vision, Special Issue on Qualitative Vision*, 14:119–130, 1995.
9. D. Reisfeld and Y. Yeshurun. Preprocessing of face images: Detection of features and pose normalisation. *Computer Vision and Image Understanding*, 71(3):413–430, September 1998.
10. Gal Sela and Martin D. Levine. Real-time attention for robotic vision. *Real-Time Imaging*, 3:173–194, 1997.
11. Orson Sutherland, Harley Truong, Sebastien Rougeaux, and Alexander Zelinsky. Advancing active vision systems by improved design and control. In *Proceedings of International Symposium on Experimental Robotics (ISER2000)*, December 2000.

Image Features Based on a New Approach to 2D Rotation Invariant Quadrature Filters[*]

Michael Felsberg[1] and Gerald Sommer[2]

[1] Linköping University, Linköping S-58183, Sweden,
mfe@isy.liu.se, www.isy.liu.se/~mfe
[2] Christian-Albrechts-University of Kiel, Kiel D-24105, Germany,
gs@ks.informatik.uni-kiel.de, www.ks.informatik.uni-kiel.de/~gs

Abstract. Quadrature filters are a well known method of low-level computer vision for estimating certain properties of the signal, as there are local amplitude and local phase. However, 2D quadrature filters suffer from being not rotation invariant. Furthermore, they do not allow to detect truly 2D features as corners and junctions unless they are combined to form the structure tensor. The present paper deals with a new 2D generalization of quadrature filters which is rotation invariant and allows to analyze intrinsically 2D signals. Hence, the new approach can be considered as the union of properties of quadrature filters and of the structure tensor. The proposed method first estimates the local orientation of the signal which is then used for steering some basis filter responses. Certain linear combination of these filter responses are derived which allow to estimate the local isotropy and two perpendicular phases of the signal. The phase model is based on the assumption of an angular band-limitation in the signal. As an application, a simple and efficient point-of-interest operator is presented and it is compared to the Plessey detector.

Keywords: image features, quadrature filters, analytic signal, structure tensor, point-of-interest operator, orientation estimation

1 Introduction

This section deals with some basic ideas about quadrature filters and describes related approaches which occur in the literature.

1.1 Quadrature Filters and Feature Detection

Quadrature filters are a well known issue in signal processing and low-level computer vision. They are suited for estimating the local amplitude and the local

---

[*] This work has been developed during M. Felsberg's PhD studies in Kiel, and it has been supported by German National Merit Foundation and by DFG Graduiertenkolleg No. 357 (M. Felsberg) and by DFG Grant So-320-2-2 (G. Sommer).

phase of signals. Whereas the local amplitude is a measure for the local intensity of a structure, the local phase describes the structure or shape of the signal [1]. For 1D signals, quadrature filters are obtained by a bandpass filter and its Hilbert transform which form a pair of an even and an odd filter. This Hilbert pair of filters can be used to detect certain shapes of signals, e.g., peaks and jumps. Furthermore, the local phase allows to distinguish or to classify detected structures. The amplitude response of a quadrature filter is chosen as a bandpass filter in order to isolate certain frequency components, i.e., to reduce the original signal to a signal with small bandwidth, which is necessary to obtain a reasonable interpretation of the local phase [2], page 171. The local amplitude and the local phase can be considered as features of the signal. They are obtained by applying some postprocessing (a change to polar coordinates) to the quadrature filter responses and they locally characterize the signal, at least if they are considered for several scales (for a more detailed discussion on features, see e.g. [3]).

For image processing, it is also desirable to have such an approach which simultaneously allows to detect and to classify image features. Even without going into mathematical details it is obvious that the 2D generalization of quadrature filters is far from being trivial. Consider for example the classes of 2D structures which correspond to 1D peaks and jumps. Lines and edges are projections of the former signals but they are themselves intrinsically 1D, i.e., they differ with respect to one direction only [4]. This is different for corners, line-crossings, and general junctions which are all i2D structures. This qualitative extension of structures should be reflected in the applied 2D feature set, such that it should not just contain 2D projections of 1D features but it should also include a new quality of features which are intrinsically 2D.

Besides this new quality of features, a further degree of freedom for the features is introduced: the orientation of the feature. For the detection and classification of features it is reasonable to have a rotation invariant approach since the orientation information neither affects the intensity nor the classification of a feature. Nevertheless, the orientation information is worth to be reflected in an additional distinct component. Using such an approach instead of a set of orientation dependent operators extends the invariance – equivariance idea [2] to three parts of information about a feature: classification, intensity, and orientation. An appropriate generalization of quadrature filters to 2D should take into account the previous considerations, at least if the 2D quadrature filters are designed with respect to the application of feature detection and classification.

1.2   2D Quadrature Filters

Unfortunately, all approaches for 2D quadrature filters ignore one or several of the formerly proposed properties. Except for the quaternionic analytic signal [5], no 2D extension of the quadrature principle exists which explicitly deals with the intrinsic dimension of the considered signal. However, according to the previous discussion, it is not sufficient just to project 1D quadrature filters onto 2D space.

A projection of 1D quadrature filters to 2D is performed if the partial Hilbert transform is used to create the odd filter. The partial Hilbert transform is obtained by projecting the frequency vector onto a preference direction and applying the frequency response of the 1D Hilbert transform to this scalar product [2]. Special cases of the partial Hilbert transform are the Hilbert transforms with respect to the coordinate axes. The symmetry of the partial Hilbert transform is illustrated in Fig. 1, left. Quadrature filters obtained from the partial Hilbert transform are obviously not rotation invariant and are not adequate for detecting intrinsically 2D features. It should be mentioned that the steerable quadrature filters proposed in [6] do not have the drawback of being rotation variant since they are orientation adaptive. However, they are not capable to deal with intrinsically 2D signals either.

A second 2D extension of quadrature filters is obtained by means of the total Hilbert transform which is just the successive application of the Hilbert transforms with respect to both coordinate axes [7]. The resulting symmetry of the total Hilbert transform is even with respect to point symmetry and odd with respect to line-symmetry (see Fig. 1, second from the left). Quadrature filters obtained from the total Hilbert transform are obviously not rotation invariant and are not capable of detecting intrinsically 1D features.

A further quadrature approach is obtained by combining the previous two methods. The resulting quadrature filter is only non-zero in the first quadrant of the frequency domain [7]. Unfortunately, the reduction to one quadrant yields a loss of information and therefore, Hahn suggests to consider a second operator output which is non-zero either in the second or in the fourth quadrant. However, the representation in two complex signals is not totally satisfactory and therefore, Bülow and Sommer proposed to use the quaternionic Fourier transform [8,9] instead of the complex one. The resulting quaternionic analytic signal consists of four parts instead of two [5]. Two parts correspond to the partial Hilbert transforms with respect to the coordinate axes and one corresponds to the total Hilbert transform (see Fig. 1, third, fourth, and fifth from the left). The phase approach of the quaternionic analytic signal also reflects the intrinsic dimension to some extent. However, the quaternionic analytic signal is not rotation invariant.

The only non-steered, rotation invariant approach to quadrature filters which occurred in the literature so far, is obtained from the monogenic signal [10]. It is adequate for treating intrinsically 1D signals but delivers no information about the 2D part of a signal. The monogenic signal is based on the Riesz transform which is a 2D generalization of the Hilbert transform. The Riesz transform is antisymmetric with respect to the origin since its frequency response is basically given by the normalized frequency vectors [11] (see also Fig. 1, right). Note that the monogenic signal contains no steering by the orientation but the latter is obtained as an additional feature.

Hence, it is desirable to combine the rotation invariance of the monogenic signal with the symmetry decomposition of the quaternionic analytic signal. This combination directly leads to the new approach which is the main topic of this paper. In order to visualize the drawbacks of the previously mentioned methods, the local amplitudes of the filter responses to the signal $f(x,y) = \cos(x)\cos(y)$ are illustrated in Fig. 2.

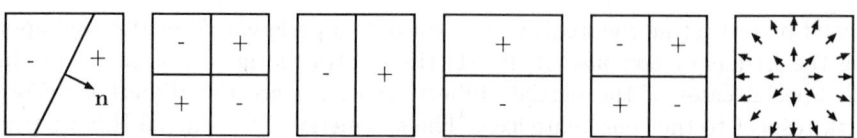

Fig. 1. Symmetries of the odd filters obtained from the considered quadrature approaches. From left to right: the partial Hilbert transform with preference direction **n**, the total Hilbert transform, the three imaginary components of the quaternionic analytic signal, and the Riesz transform (vector valued)

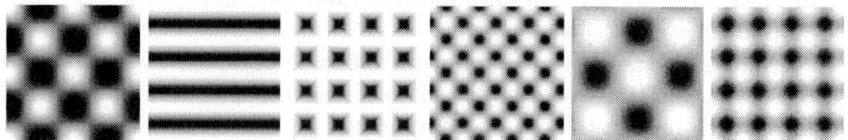

Fig. 2. Amplitudes of the various known approaches to the 2D analytic signal for a simple 2D signal. From left to right: original signal (black indicates -1 and white indicates 1), the local amplitudes obtained from the partial Hilbert transform with respect to x, the orientation adaptive Hilbert transform, the total Hilbert transform, the quaternionic analytic signal, and the monogenic signal. All amplitude images are in a range from zero (black) to one (white). For the quaternionic analytic signal the signal has been rotated by $\pi/4$

1.3 Other Related Approaches

Talking about the analysis of intrinsically 1D and 2D signals, it is natural to consider also the structure tensor [12,13]. The structure tensor can either be computed by a set of classical quadrature filters (see e.g. [2]) or by partial derivatives (see e.g. [14]). In the latter case, the structure tensor can be considered in the context of an approximation of the autocorrelation of the signal [15]. Hence, the two eigenvalues of the structure tensor are related to the principal curvatures of the autocorrelation function, whereas the eigenvectors indicate the corresponding coordinate system. Therefore, the structure tensor can be used to estimate the main orientation of a structure by means of the eigenvector which corresponds to the larger eigenvalue.

The eigenvalues themselves and their relation also provide a measure for the intrinsic dimension of the signal. In [14], the coherence is used for this purpose and it is defined by the square ratio of the difference and the sum of the eigenvalues. However, there exist other definitions for coherence measures in the literature (see e.g. [16]).

According to [2], the structure tensor fulfills the invariance – equivariance requirement with respect to rotations and changes of the signal structure. The estimation of the local orientation is independent of the underlying shape of the signal (e.g. line-like or edge-like) and its energy, whereas the coherence and the norm of the tensor are rotation invariant. Hence, the design principle of the structure tensor is to some extent related to the properties of quadrature filters, i.e., local features are mutually independent. The new approach which is presented below extends the invariance – equivariance property to the full superset of features obtained from quadrature filters (i.e., local phase and local amplitude) and from the structure tensor (i.e., local orientation, local coherence, and a local intensity measure).

2 The New Approach

As pointed out in the introduction, it is desirable to have an approach which combines the properties of quadrature filters and of the structure tensor in order to obtain a sophisticated 2D analytic signal. The theory which is developed in the sequel is based on a signal model which is similar to that of the structure tensor.

2.1 The 2D Signal Model

Intrinsically 2D signals have a much greater variety than 1D signals. Actually, the number of possible 2D signals is infinite times larger than the (already infinite) number of 1D signals. This increase of possible signal realizations can be considered more formally by means of symmetries. Whereas 1D signals can be distinguished into locally even and locally odd functions, a 2D signal can contain infinite many even or odd 1D functions with different orientations.

In order to analyze arbitrary 2D signals with respect to all components, infinite many basis filters are necessary. The local signal analysis could be thought of as a spherical Fourier series which is known to have infinite many basis function. This is true unless the signals under consideration are sampled. In the latter case it is not reasonable to apply basis filters with arbitrary high angular frequencies. If the main coefficients of the basis filters are obtained from the samples adjacent to the origin, it is even necessary to restrict the spherical Fourier basis functions to be of order less or equal to three in order to avoid aliasing. Hence, the signal model introduced below is not a heuristic choice but it is the most complete local model which does not suffer from angular aliasing.

As we will show in the subsequent section, the restriction of the basis functions directly correspond to a decomposition of 2D signals into two perpendicular[1] intrinsically 1D signals. The Fourier basis functions of order zero to three establish a 4D space of angular functions. Since each of the two involved 1D functions consist of an odd and an even part, two perpendicular 1D functions can be expressed as a 4D vector. Accordingly, we define the following local 2D signal model which will be used in the sequel to approximate arbitrary 2D functions. Let f_1 and f_2 be two arbitrary 1D signals and let $\mathbf{n}(\mathbf{x}) = (\cos\theta(\mathbf{x}), \sin\theta(\mathbf{x}))^T$ be a unit vector with direction $\theta(\mathbf{x})$ where $\mathbf{x} = (x,y)^T$ indicates the spatial vector. Then, the 2D signal $\tilde{f}(\mathbf{x})$ is obtained as

$$\tilde{f}(\mathbf{x}) = f_1(\mathbf{x} \cdot \mathbf{n}(\mathbf{x})) + f_2(\mathbf{x} \cdot \mathbf{n}^\perp(\mathbf{x})) ,\tag{1}$$

where $\mathbf{n}^\perp(\mathbf{x})$ is the vector obtained by rotating $\mathbf{n}(\mathbf{x})$ by $\pi/2$ anticlockwise.

---
[1] We use the term perpendicular for two 1D signals with orthogonal orientation vectors. Opposed to that, orthogonality of signals refers to their linear independence in the vector space of functions.

Any 2D signal can be approximated by an appropriate choice of such a 2D signal $\tilde{f}$. Considering the original signal and its approximation in the Fourier domain, the approximation corresponds to a suppression of all frequency components which are not lying either on the main orientation line or on the line perpendicular to the main orientation. However, Fourier theory and a correct estimate of the main orientation ensure that this approximation is L^2 optimal.

2.2 The Basis Functions

For the sake of a more formal investigation, consider the following signal representation. Apart from the ordinary 2D Fourier basis, an arbitrary 2D function can be represented by means of the following set of basis functions:

$$b_1(\mathbf{x}, \mathbf{u}) = \cos(2\pi xu)\cos(2\pi yv) \qquad (2)$$
$$b_2(\mathbf{x}, \mathbf{u}) = \cos(2\pi xu)\sin(2\pi yv) \qquad (3)$$
$$b_3(\mathbf{x}, \mathbf{u}) = \sin(2\pi xu)\cos(2\pi yv) \qquad (4)$$
$$b_4(\mathbf{x}, \mathbf{u}) = \sin(2\pi xu)\sin(2\pi yv) \;, \qquad (5)$$

see e.g. [8]. Each of these basis functions can be rewritten by means of the trigonometric addition theorems as sums of trigonometric functions:

$$b_1(\mathbf{x}, \mathbf{u}) = (\cos(2\pi(xu - yv)) + \cos(2\pi(xu + yv)))/2 \qquad (6)$$
$$b_2(\mathbf{x}, \mathbf{u}) = (-\sin(2\pi(xu - yv)) + \sin(2\pi(xu + yv)))/2 \qquad (7)$$
$$b_3(\mathbf{x}, \mathbf{u}) = (\sin(2\pi(xu - yv)) + \sin(2\pi(xu + yv)))/2 \qquad (8)$$
$$b_4(\mathbf{x}, \mathbf{u}) = (\cos(2\pi(xu - yv)) - \cos(2\pi(xu + yv)))/2 \;. \qquad (9)$$

The basis functions $b_1, \ldots, b_4$ also establish a basis if the coordinate system is rotated. Moreover, the representation of the rotated basis functions as sums of trigonometric functions is nothing else but a signal representation according to the 2D model which has been introduced in the previous section since each basis function consists of two perpendicular harmonic oscillations.

The signal which has been used in Fig. 2 is the basis function $b_1(\mathbf{x}, (1, 1)^T)$. Obviously, all known approaches to the 2D analytic signal fail to decompose the latter function into its amplitude and phase information, except for the quaternionic analytic signal. The latter yields a constant (and therefore correct) amplitude for b_1 but it fails if the latter is rotated by $\pi/4$ (see also Fig. 2).

In order to understand what happens if the amplitude is estimated correctly, consider Fig. 3.

These illustrations show the basis functions $b_1, \ldots, b_4$ in the frequency domain with respect to the coordinate system spanned by $\mathbf{n}$ and $\mathbf{n}^\perp$. The sum of all four functions yields just one impulse in the quadrant between $\mathbf{n}$ and $\mathbf{n}^\perp$. Setting the other three quadrants to zero is similar to the idea of the quaternionic analytic signal with the important difference that the quadrants are not fixed to the coordinate system but they are attached to the vector $\mathbf{n}$.

The principle of quadrature in 1D is to replace pairs of impulses in the frequency domain (i.e., the Fourier transform of an arbitrary harmonic oscillation)

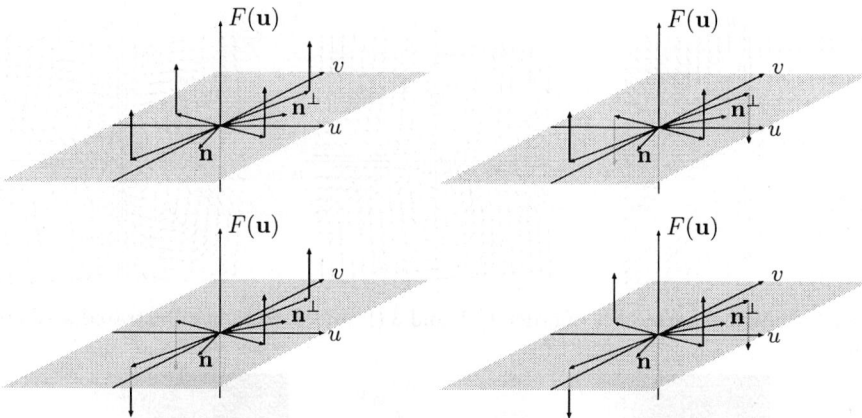

Fig. 3. The basis functions $B_1, \ldots, B_4$ for $\mathbf{u} = (1,1)^T$ with respect to the coordinate system spanned by $\mathbf{n}$ and $\mathbf{n}^\perp$. Upper left: B_1, bottom left: iB_2, upper right: iB_3, bottom right: $-B_4$

with a single impulse. In 2D however, this principle can be extended in several ways. If intrinsically 1D signals are to be considered, it is sufficient to replace pairs of impulses with a single impulse. However, if intrinsically 2D signals are to be considered, quadruples or $2n$-tuples have to be replaced with one single impulse. The number of applied basis functions must be identical to the number of impulses which are to be replaced. Hence, intrinsically 2D approaches require at least four basis functions but can potentially be infinitely dimensional. According to the previous discussion about the signal model we retain with quadruples of impulses and hence, with four basis functions.

2.3 General Formulation

Up to now it is unclear how to obtain rotation invariant basis functions although the method to be applied has already been mentioned: spherical harmonics. Spherical harmonics allow to design steerable filters [6] which are orientation adaptive and therefore, rotation invariant.

The spherical harmonics of order 1, 2, and 3 are illustrated as vector fields in Fig. 4.

The vector fields are obtained according to the frequency response

$$H_n(\mathbf{u}) = \left(\frac{u+iv}{|\mathbf{u}|}\right)^n, \qquad (10)$$

where $H_1(\mathbf{u})$ is basically identical to the Riesz transform. By appropriate steering operations and linear combinations, the vector fields can be used to create the desired symmetry properties sketched in Fig. 3.

The symmetry of B_1 is trivial and is obtained by a simple allpass frequency response. The symmetry of B_4 is obtained by projecting the second spherical harmonic onto the double-angle orientation vector (see Fig. 5, left).

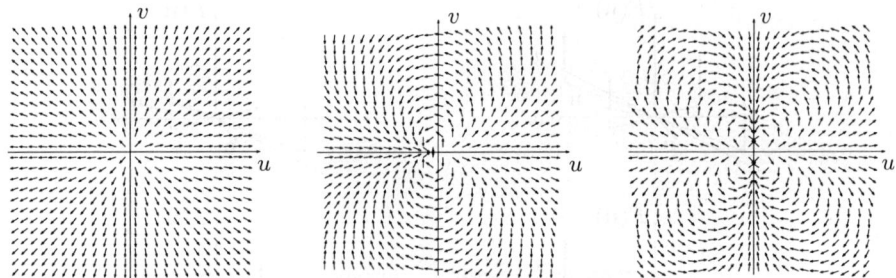

Fig. 4. Spherical harmonics of order 1, 2, and 3 (from left to right) illustrated as vector fields

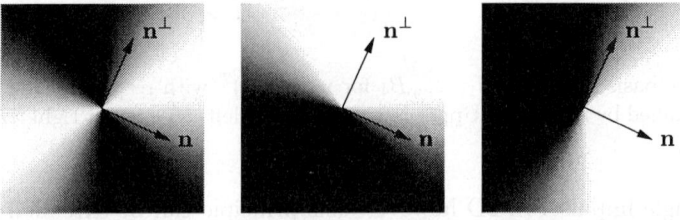

Fig. 5. From left to right: projection of the second order harmonic, linear combination and projection of odd order spherical harmonics to achieve B_2 symmetry, and linear combination and projection of odd order spherical harmonics to achieve B_3 symmetry

If θ_0 indicates the main orientation (for the estimation of the main orientation see next section), the B_4-symmetry is obtained according to

$$B_4(\mathbf{u}) = \text{real}\{\exp(-i2\theta_0)H_2(\mathbf{u})\} = \cos(2(\theta - \theta_0)) \ . \quad (11)$$

Note that the main orientation of the signal is not identical to the argument of $\mathbf{n}$ but lies on the diagonal of the quadrant between $\mathbf{n}$ and $\mathbf{n}^\perp$ (see also Fig. 3).

The two basis functions $B_1 \equiv 1$ and B_4 can be combined in order to obtain the angular windowing functions

$$W_1(\mathbf{u}) = 1 + B_4(\mathbf{u}) = 2\cos^2(\theta - \theta_0) \quad (12)$$
$$W_2(\mathbf{u}) = 1 - B_4(\mathbf{u}) = 2\sin^2(\theta - \theta_0) \ . \quad (13)$$

The angular shape of these window functions is the same as for the filters which are involved in the calculation of the structure tensor [2,14].

The remaining two symmetries can be obtained by applying $H_1(\mathbf{u})$ (i.e., the Riesz transform) to the two windowing functions and steering them. Since $H_1(\mathbf{u})$ is complex valued, the resulting functions are also complex valued:

$$\begin{aligned}W_3'(\mathbf{u}) &= \exp(-i\theta_0)H_1(\mathbf{u})W_1(\mathbf{u}) \\ &= \cos(\theta - \theta_0) + \frac{1}{2}(\exp(i3(\theta - \theta_0)) + \exp(i(\theta - \theta_0)))\end{aligned} \quad (14)$$

$$\begin{aligned}W_4'(\mathbf{u}) &= \exp(-i\theta_0)H_1(\mathbf{u})W_2(\mathbf{u}) \\ &= i\sin(\theta - \theta_0) - \frac{1}{2}(\exp(i3(\theta - \theta_0)) - \exp(i(\theta - \theta_0))) \ .\end{aligned} \quad (15)$$

Since we need scalar valued functions rather than complex valued ones, the frequency responses W_3' and W_4' must be projected without changing the amplitude or losing the antisymmetry. This would be done by considering the (signed) absolute value of the frequency response. However, taking the absolute value is not linear and therefore, this operation cannot be transferred to the spatial domain, which is necessary in order to steer the responses. Fortunately, the signed absolute value can be replaced by taking the real part and the imaginary part without introducing large errors. The relative mean square error is less than 2.3% and it is concentrated on the diagonals between the main orientation and the line perpendicular to it, which means that it only affects those signals which violate the assumed signal model[2]. Hence, the necessary scalar valued functions are obtained as

$$W_3(\mathbf{u}) = \text{real}\{W_3'\} = \frac{3}{2}\cos(\theta - \theta_0) + \frac{1}{2}\cos(3(\theta - \theta_0)) \qquad (16)$$

$$W_4(\mathbf{u}) = \text{imag}\{W_4'\} = \frac{3}{2}\sin(\theta - \theta_0) - \frac{1}{2}\sin(3(\theta - \theta_0)) \ . \qquad (17)$$

Adding and subtracting these two functions yields the remaining two basis functions $B_2 = W_3 + W_4$ and $B_3 = W_3 - W_4$. The resulting frequency responses can be found in Fig. 5 (center and right) and realize the symmetries according to Fig. 3.

Although the previous results have been developed and illustrated in the frequency domain, the filters, the steering operations, and the various linear combinations are actually applied in the spatial domain, see Fig. 6.

Finally, all of the previously described filters have an allpass amplitude response. In order to decompose the signal into its distinct frequency components, the filters are combined with radial bandpass filters. The choice of the specific bandpass design is not crucial. However, for the subsequent experiments, we have used the difference of Poisson filters bandpass (see [17]) which is similar to the lognormal bandpass (see e.g. [2]).

3 Feature Detection

From the filter responses produced by $b_1, \ldots, b_4$ several local properties and features of the signal can be extracted. Although we started the discussion with the basis functions $b_1, \ldots, b_4$, we will now rather focus upon the responses of $w_1, \ldots, w_4$. However, since both sets of filters can easily be exchanged there is no fundamental difference.

---

[2] The linear factors $\frac{3}{2}$ and $\frac{1}{2}$ can be numerically optimized which gives a further improvement of the approximation. Note that for 2D signals according to the assumed model, taking the real part and imaginary part yields exact solutions. The approximation however improves the robustness of the approach.

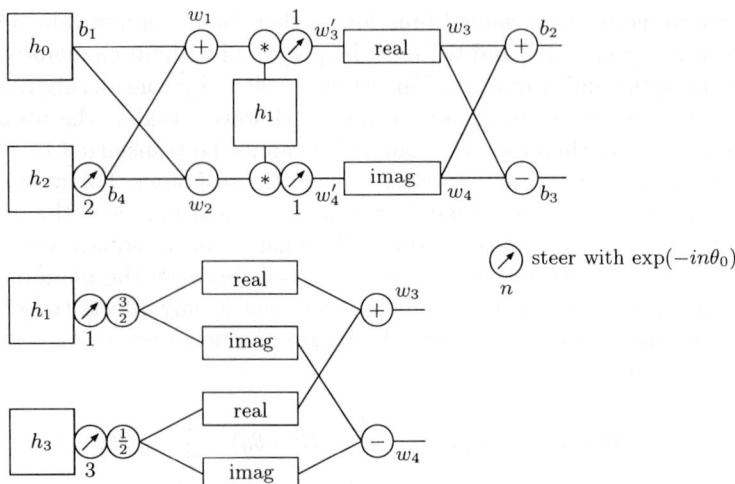

Fig. 6. Overview of the filter design process. In the upper part of the figure, the filter responses of b_2 and b_3 are obtained from those of b_1 and b_4 whereas in the bottom part they are directly computed from the spherical harmonics of order one and three

3.1 Local Orientation Estimation

In the previous section, several steering operations have been performed which depend on the local orientation. Although there are several methods for estimating the local orientation which could be applied beforehand, it is more efficient to use the responses of the spherical harmonics to estimate the orientation. However, the spherical harmonics yield phase-dependent estimates of the orientation. Consider e.g. the first order harmonic. For phases close to zero and close to π the orientation estimate becomes unreliable (see [18] and Fig. 7). In order to obtain a stable and efficient method for orientation estimation, the impact of the phase to the mean estimation error has to be investigated. In turns out, that the spherical harmonics of odd order and of even order show an opposite behavior (see Fig. 7), which implies that a combination of odd order and even order terms improves the estimate.

It is sufficient to estimate the orientation within $[0, \pi/2)$ since orientation information is normally within $[0, \pi)$ and due to the supposed signal model, the remaining interval $[\pi/2, \pi)$ is covered by the perpendicular component. Hence, any product of spherical harmonics which has a maximal order of four can be used to estimate the orientation in the reduced interval. Since the energy of the filter responses is proportional to the square of the sine and of the cosine of the local phase for odd and even order harmonics respectively, a reasonable choice to combine the filter responses for estimating the orientation independent of the phase[3] is given by

$$\theta_e = \arg((h_2 * f)^2 + (h_1 * f)(h_3 * f))/4 \ . \tag{18}$$

---

[3] Actually, the proposed estimate is phase independent for i1D signals. For i2D signals, orientation information can be totally undetermined (e.g. at local extrema) which is

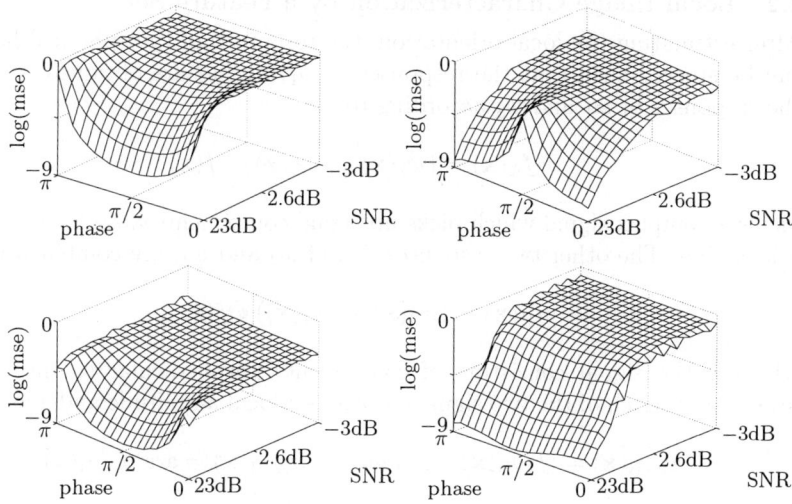

Fig. 7. Phase dependence of the mean square error of some orientation estimate methods. Top left: first order harmonic, top right: second order harmonic, bottom left: third order harmonic, and bottom right: method according to (18). The figures show the logarithm of the mean square error drawn against the local phase and the signal to noise ratio. A value of 0 means an error of $\pi/2$, which is the maximal possible orientation error. Actually, the orientation errors have been evaluated by taking the second, fourth, and sixth power of a complex exponential, yielding a maximal error of $\pi/2$, $\pi/4$, and $\pi/6$, respectively. Therefore, the error for low SNR seems to decrease with the order of the harmonic which is basically not true. The test signal which has been used for this investigation is a radial modulation, i.e., $\cos(\sqrt{x^2+y^2})$

The resulting mean square error of this orientation estimation can also be found in Fig. 7. For all subsequent experiments the orientation has been estimated by the previous formula.

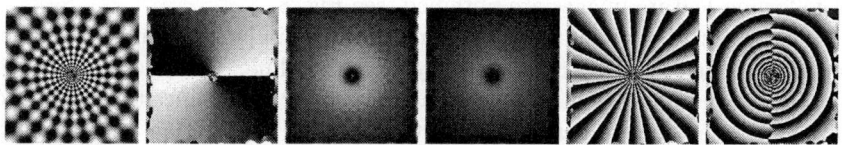

Fig. 8. From left to right: test image consisting of a superposition of an angular and a radial modulation, estimated main orientation, amplitude of the dominant part, amplitude of the non-dominant part, phase of the dominant part, and phase of the non-dominant part. Note the correspondence between orientation wrapping and phase inversion

---

also reflected be the proposed method since the magnitude of the complex number in (18) is zero in that case.

3.2 Local Image Characterization by a Feature Set

After estimating the local orientation, the responses of the spherical harmonics can be steered such that the responses of $w_1, \ldots, w_4$ are obtained. Combining the responses of w_1 and w_3 according to

$$f_A(\mathbf{x}) = (w_1(\mathbf{x}) + iw_3(\mathbf{x})) * f(\mathbf{x}) \qquad (19)$$

yields a complex signal which picks up signal components close to the estimated orientation. The other two responses, i.e. of w_2 and w_4, are combined as

$$f_B(\mathbf{x}) = (w_2(\mathbf{x}) + iw_4(\mathbf{x})) * f(\mathbf{x}) \; , \qquad (20)$$

which is the signal consisting of components perpendicular to the estimated orientation. Each of the two signals provides a local amplitude and a local phase:

$$A_{A/B}(\mathbf{x}) = |f_{A/B}(\mathbf{x})| \quad \text{and} \quad \varphi_{A/B}(\mathbf{x}) = \arg(f_{A/B}(\mathbf{x})) \; . \qquad (21)$$

Comparing A_A and A_B yields the dominant partial signal and allows to change the orientation estimate θ_e into the main orientation: If $A_A(\mathbf{x}) \geq A_B(\mathbf{x})$ the estimated orientation is the main orientation θ_m and otherwise $\theta_m = \theta_e + \pi/2$. Furthermore, a measure for the local isotropy is provided by the ratio of the two amplitudes:

$$c(\mathbf{x}) = \min\{A_B(\mathbf{x})/A_A(\mathbf{x}), A_A(\mathbf{x})/A_B(\mathbf{x})\} \; , \qquad (22)$$

so that $c(\mathbf{x})$ is zero if the signal is intrinsically 1D and it is one if the signal is either intrinsically 2D or constant, i.e., if the energy is distributed isotropically.

The two local amplitudes can be combined to form a total local amplitude measure according to

$$A_T(\mathbf{x}) = A_A(\mathbf{x}) + A_B(\mathbf{x}) \; . \qquad (23)$$

For a synthetic image which is much harder to separate than that in Fig. 2, the following feature images are obtained, see Fig. 8.

According to the orientation wrapping of the main orientation at π and zero, the phase image shows a phase inversion on that line. The phase of the non-dominant part of the signal is inverted along a vertical line since the orientation-shift of $\pi/2$ for the perpendicular part moves the orientation wrapping to a vertical line.

3.3 Detection of Points of Interest

The energy of the non-dominant structure provides a mean for detecting intrinsically 2D points, e.g., corners, line crossing, or general junctions. This can directly be compared to the Plessey (or Harris-Stephens) detector [19] which is itself closely related to the structure tensor and to coherence measures. In Fig. 9 the results of the new point-of-interest detector are compared to those of the Plessey detector.

Fig. 9. Upper two rows from left to right: Output of the proposed point-of-interest detector without noise, with noise (white, Gaussian distribution, variance 25), and of the Plessey detector. The original images and the output of the Plessey detector are taken from [20]. Bottom row: detection in rotated images (left and center), the right image shows the reference image (left half) and a test image (right half) for the illumination experiment

The new method just detects local maxima of the non-dominant local amplitude in a neighborhood with a radius of seven pixels. Only those maxima are kept which are above a certain threshold, where the latter is given by two times the mean amplitude. The results of the proposed method are better than those of the Plessey detector, with respect to false-positives, false-negatives, and noise-sensitivity. The outputs of other corner detectors like the SUSAN detector, the Kitchen/Rosenfeld detector, and the CSS approach can be found at [20]. The new approach performs nearly as good as the CSS approach and in contrast to the mentioned methods, the new approach also provides information about the

Table 1. Repeatability rates for illumination changes. A detection is repeated if the detected point in the reference image is adjacent to the one in the test image

mean (10^2)	1.56	1.20	0.92	0.71	1.75	1.44	1.09	0.79	1.28	1.02	0.81	0.60
var (10^3)	4.80	4.06	2.91	2.08	5.71	4.69	3.19	2.03	4.74	4.19	3.08	2.05
rep. rate	1.00	0.80	0.73	0.62	0.72	0.73	0.68	0.62	0.74	0.64	0.58	0.54
mean (10^2)	1.50	1.15	0.85	0.65	1.28	1.02	0.75	0.58	1.69	1.33	1.02	0.78
var (10^3)	4.72	4.15	2.83	1.97	4.80	4.32	2.91	2.06	5.30	4.19	2.96	2.06
rep. rate	0.75	0.71	0.56	0.52	0.68	0.62	0.55	0.52	0.77	0.74	0.70	0.65

kind of the point-of-interest. Hence, it allows to distinguish between corners, endstoppings, line-crossings, etc..

In two further experiments, the detector has been applied to images with added noise and to rotated images. The detector output is fairly the same as in the original experiment. In order to assess the performance of the new detector in further detail, we made a similar investigation as proposed in [21]. We evaluated the repeatability rate for various kinds of different illuminations of the scene in Fig. 9, bottom right. The images are taken from [22]. The results can be found in Tab. 1 where the change of illumination is represented by the mean and the variance of the test images. The results are close to those in [21].

4 Conclusion

We have presented a new approach to 2D quadrature filters which generalizes the idea of invariance – equivariance. Combining the features which are obtained from the classical quadrature filters and the structure tensor, our method allows to estimate five features at a time: local orientation, local isotropy, local amplitude, and two local phases. Due to the invariance – equivariance property, all features are mutually independent of each other.

As an application we have presented a corner detector and compared it to other approaches. Although the local phases at the detected point of interest allow to classify that point, further investigations have to be done in order to obtain a stable algorithm. However, the results from the synthetic image in Fig. 8 show that the presented method yields reliable estimates of the local phases. Furthermore, the proposed algorithm is quite efficient, since it consists of only one real valued and three complex valued convolutions and of three complex multiplications for the steering operations.

References

1. Oppenheim, A., Lim, J.: The importance of phase in signals. Proc. of the IEEE **69** (1981) 529–541
2. Granlund, G.H., Knutsson, H.: Signal Processing for Computer Vision. Kluwer Academic Publishers, Dordrecht (1995)
3. Koenderink, J.J.: What is a "feature"? Journal of Intelligent Systems **3** (1993) 49–82

4. Krieger, G., Zetzsche, C.: Nonlinear image operators for the evaluation of local intrinsic dimensionality. IEEE Trans. on Image Processing **5** (1996) 1026–1041
5. Bülow, T., Sommer, G.: The hypercomplex signal – a novel approach to the multidimensional analytic signal. IEEE Trans. on Signal Processing **49** (2001) 2844–2852
6. Freeman, W.T., Adelson, E.H.: The design and use of steerable filters. IEEE Trans. on Pattern Analysis and Machine Intelligence **13** (1991) 891–906
7. Hahn, S.L.: Hilbert Transforms in Signal Processing. Artech House, Boston, London (1996)
8. Bülow, T., Sommer, G.: Algebraically extended representation of multi-dimensional signals. In: Proc. of the 10th Scand. Conf. on Image Analysis. (1997) 559–566
9. Sangwine, S.J.: Fourier-transforms of color images using quaternion or hypercomplex numbers. Electronic Letters **32** (1996) 1979–1980
10. Felsberg, M., Sommer, G.: The monogenic signal. IEEE Trans. on Signal Processing **49** (2001) 3136–3144
11. Stein, E., Weiss, G.: Introduction to Fourier Analysis on Euclidean Spaces. Princeton University Press, New Jersey (1971)
12. Bigün, J., Granlund, G.H.: Optimal orientation detection of linear symmetry. In: Proc. of the IEEE First Intern. Conference on Computer Vision. (1987) 433–438
13. Förstner, W., Gülch, E.: A fast operator for detection and precise location of distinct points, corners and centres of circular features. In: ISPRS Intercommission Workshop, Interlaken. (1987) 149–155
14. Jähne, B.: Digitale Bildverarbeitung. Springer-Verlag, Berlin (1997)
15. Förstner, W.: Statistische Verfahren für die automatische Bildanalyse und ihre Bewertung bei der Objekterkennung und -vermessung. Number 370 in C. Verlag der Bayerischen Akademie der Wissenschaften (1991)
16. Weickert, J.: A review of nonlinear diffusion filtering. In ter Haar Romeny, B., Florack, L., Koenderink, J., Viergever, M., eds.: Scale-Space Theory in Computer Vision. Volume 1252 of LNCS., Springer, Berlin (1997) 260–271
17. Felsberg, M., Sommer, G.: Scale adaptive filtering derived from the Laplace equation. In: 23. DAGM Symposium Mustererkennung, München. Volume 2191 of LNCS., Springer-Verlag, Heidelberg (2001) 124–131
18. Felsberg, M., Sommer, G.: A new extension of linear signal processing for estimating local properties and detecting features. In: 22. DAGM Symposium Mustererkennung, Kiel. Springer-Verlag, Heidelberg (2000) 195–202
19. Harris, C.G., Stephens, M.: A combined corner and edge detector. In: 4th Alvey Vision Conference. (1988) 147–151
20. Mokhtarian, F.: Image corner detection through curvature scale space. http://www.ee.surrey.ac.uk/Research/VSSP/demos/corners/ (2001) (Accessed 16 Nov 2001).
21. Schmid, C., Mohr, R., C., B.: Evaluation of interest point detectors. International Journal of Computer Vision **37** (2000) 151–172
22. Pauli, J.: Kiel appearance image library. http://www.ks.informatik.uni-kiel.de/~jpa/images.html (1998) (Accessed 22 Feb 2002).

Representing Edge Models via Local Principal Component Analysis

Patrick S. Huggins and Steven W. Zucker*

Department of Computer Science
Yale University, New Haven CT 06520, USA
{huggins,zucker}@cs.yale.edu

Abstract. Edge detection depends not only upon the assumed model of what an edge is, but also on how this model is represented. The problem of how to represent the edge model is typically neglected, despite the fact that the representation is a bottleneck for both computational cost and accuracy. We propose to represent edge models by a partition of the edge manifold corresponding to the edge model, where each local element of the partition is described by its principal components. We describe the construction of this representation and demonstrate its benefits for various edge models.

1 Introduction

Underlying any given edge detection scheme is a model of what an edge actually is. These models typically possess several parameters, e.g., position, contrast, orientation, and 'scale' (or 'blur'), and while edge detection *per se* is concerned only with determining the presence or absence of an edge at some location, to ignore these parameters is to invite error [46][68][71]. Furthermore, the parameters that characterize the edge are of interest themselves: they can be used to determine the physical nature of the edge [26][72][57][30] and scene geometry [36], or to support subsequent processing such as perceptual organization and recognition [44]. These considerations have led researchers to develop progressively complex models of edges. See Table 1.

Table 1. Some edge parameters and a sampling of edge models incorporating them. A complete edge model would include all of these and more. How do we represent this complexity?

Parameter	Detector
Orientation	[27][49][19][12]
Blur (or 'scale')	[8][60][42][18]
Subpixel location	[32][67][28][47]
Intensity variations	[55][53][59][69]
Curvature	[17][35][37][73]

Solving edge detection in light of the effects of these parameters is equivalent to parameter estimation [70][33][63]: given a neighborhood of an image $\mathcal{I}$ and an

---
* Supported by AFOSR and DARPA

A. Heyden et al. (Eds.): ECCV 2002, LNCS 2350, pp. 384–398, 2002.
© Springer-Verlag Berlin Heidelberg 2002

edge model $\mathcal{E}$ with parameter space Θ, we seek the 'best' explanation of $\mathcal{I}$, e.g., finding $\hat{\boldsymbol{\theta}} \in \Theta$ that maximizes $p(\mathcal{E}(\boldsymbol{\theta})|\mathcal{I})$.

The parameter estimation problem can be viewed geometrically [27][3]: the edge model $\mathcal{E}$ is a low-dimensional manifold embedded in a high-dimensional space, where the dimensionality is given by the number of pixels in the image neighborhood. Our contribution here is to develop a representation of this manifold that reflects its intrinsic geometry. We construct our representation using the method of local principal component analysis [34].

The advantages of our representation lie in its relationship to the geometry of the edge manifold. This leads to an accurate representation, and it can be applied to a wide variety of models, even nonparametric ones.

2 Edge Manifolds

Edge detection is generally treated as a local process. An image point is identified as an edge if the neighborhood of the image centered on that point, as defined by the edge detector window, is determined to be 'edge-like', as defined by the assumed edge model. These neighborhoods are images themselves, and so edge detection is then the classification of these images into *edge* and *non-edge*. We can view each image (i.e., windowed neighborhood of an image) as a point in a high-dimensional space, with the dimension of the space equal to the number of pixels in the image and the coordinates of the image as the intensity values at the corresponding pixels. The class of edge images is some subset of this space. If the class of edge images is defined by a model where the image of an edge varies smoothly as the parameters vary, then the trace of the model in the high-dimensional space is a manifold (note that some regularization is required for discrete images).

Consider a simple edge model $\mathcal{E} : [0, 2\pi) \to (X \times Y \to \mathbb{R}^n)$ where the only parameter $\theta \in [0, 2\pi)$ is orientation, $x \in X$ and $y \in Y$ are image coordinates, n is the number of pixels in an image ($n = |X \times Y|$), and intensity takes on real values. The image intensity function is given by $\mathcal{E}(x, y; \theta) = \mathcal{G} * f(x, y; \theta)$, where $\mathcal{G}$ is a regularization operator, e.g., a Gaussian, $*$ denotes convolution, and

$$f(x, y; \theta) = \begin{cases} 1 & \text{if } -\sin(\theta)x + \cos(\theta)y > 0 \\ 0 & \text{otherwise} \end{cases}.$$

As θ varies, $\mathcal{E}(\theta)$ traces out a curve in $\mathbb{R}^n$. See Figure 1(a). Given an observed image $\mathcal{I}$, we would like to determine whether or not it is an edge according to our model. The parameter estimation computations to achieve this can be described in terms of the geometry of this manifold (Section 2.1). To support this we develop a representation of the manifold based on local principal component analysis (Section 2.2), which is particularly well suited to the problem.

2.1 Parameter Estimation

Let $\mathcal{E}(\boldsymbol{\theta}) \subset \mathbb{R}^n$ be the edge manifold where $\boldsymbol{\theta} \in \Theta$ is a vector of edge parameters and let $\mathcal{I} \in \mathbb{R}^n$ be an image. The parameter estimation problem is then to find

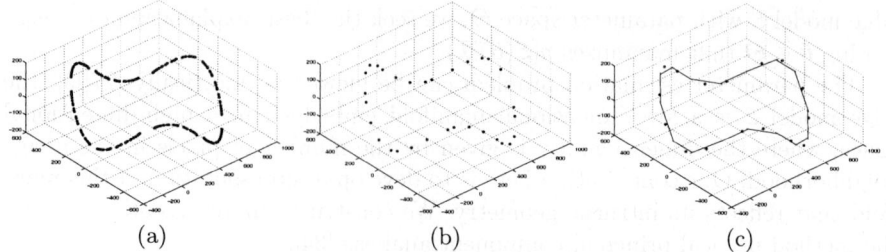

Fig. 1. (a) The edge manifold for an edge model where the only parameter is orientation. The manifold is embedded in a 197-dimensional space; here we display the manifold projected to the first 3 principal components of the entire manifold data set (see also [3]). Since orientation is periodic, the manifold is a closed loop. (b) The manifold sampled at 32 points. (c) Local PCA: The manifold sampled at 16 points with the first principal component of the neighborhood of the samples. The principal components approximate the local tangent space to the manifold, enabling better reconstruction than in (b).

the 'best' element of $\mathcal{E}$ that 'explains' $\mathcal{I}$ and the corresponding parameters $\hat{\theta}$. These parameters can subsequently be used for the edge decision procedure. This can be interpreted geometrically, as we show, highlighting the importance of the representation $\mathcal{E}$.

Parameter estimation is well studied [70], and the maximum likelihood estimator (MLE) is often used. It is defined as the parameter which maximizes the likelihood function for a given observation. Previous work in edge parameter estimation [33][63] show that, for certain restricted edge models, the MLE is a minimum variance unbiased estimator, i.e., it achieves or approaches the Cramér-Rao lower bound. Under simple assumptions, i.e., additive Gaussian noise and a uniform probability distribution over Θ, the MLE for the general edge model is,

$$\hat{\theta}_{ML} = \underset{\theta}{\operatorname{argmax}}\ L(\mathcal{E}(\theta)|\mathcal{I}) = \underset{\theta}{\operatorname{argmax}}\ \frac{1}{(2\pi)^{n/2}} e^{-\frac{1}{2}\|\mathcal{I}-\mathcal{E}(\theta)\|^2},$$

where L is the likelihood function. This shows that the best estimate, in the maximum likelihood sense, is the closest point on the manifold to $\mathcal{I}$. This result also shows the importance of the manifold's geometry: one source of bias for the MLE is curvature asymmetry in the manifold; see [1]. Other sources of estimator error include variations in noise [52] and preprocessing [2]. In what follows we assume that the MLE is adequate, however the representation we suggest is certainly not limited to this case. In all cases, the representation of $\mathcal{E}$ that we choose determines the nature of the computations used to find $\hat{\theta}$, and ultimately dictates the accuracy of parameter estimation.

2.2 Representing Edge Manifolds

The most straightforward approach to representation, where computational cost is not an issue, is to simply sample the manifold finely enough so that the distance between samples is less than the amount of error we are willing to accept. See Figure 1(b). The problem of finding the closest point on the manifold to a given image is then a search problem [3]. Such an approach is not optimal in that it does not take advantage of the smoothness of the manifold.

Another approach is to construct a linear approximation to the manifold, e.g., via the Karhunen-Loève transform [16]. Unfortunately, in most cases the manifold is highly nonlinear, and as a result the approximation is poor.

Our approach is to take advantage of the merits of the Karhunen-Loève transform by applying it to a subset of the manifold where it is appropriate. The intuition is that since the manifold is smooth, it can *locally* be well approximated by a linear subspace. The resulting representation is a piecewise linear one, where the parameter space Θ is partitioned into subsets $\Theta_1, \Theta_2, \ldots, \Theta_N$ and each corresponding subset of the manifold $\mathcal{E}(\Theta_1), \mathcal{E}(\Theta_2), \ldots, \mathcal{E}(\Theta_N)$ is represented by a linear approximation $\hat{\mathcal{E}}_1, \hat{\mathcal{E}}_2, \ldots, \hat{\mathcal{E}}_N$, i.e., $\mathcal{E} \approx \hat{\mathcal{E}} = \bigcup_i \hat{\mathcal{E}}_i$. The estimation problem is now one of finding the closest point to a given image $\mathcal{I}$ on $\hat{\mathcal{E}}$, which is computed using a combination of search and linear projection. See Figure 1(c). The procedure to construct this representation is called *local principal component analysis*, developed by Kambhatla and Leen [34].

Local Principal Component Analysis (Local PCA). The procedure consists of two main ingredients: a partitioning the manifold, and the principal components of the elements of the partition.

Various procedures exist for solving the optimal partitioning of a set, depending on what measure of optimality is chosen, e.g., [41]. Given that we are interested in partitions where linear approximations work, an optimal partition, in the sense of minimizing reconstruction error, can be formally described as minimizing the expected distance between points in the elements of a partition and their reconstructions. We compute the partition via the generalized Lloyd algorithm [22] with reconstruction error as the distortion metric [34].

Computing the linear approximation of a given partition element is a matter of computing its principal components. If $\mathcal{E}(\Theta_i)$ is the partition element under consideration, then the principal components are the eigenvectors of the covariance matrix of $\mathcal{E}(\Theta_i)$, i.e., the eigenvectors ψ_i and corresponding eigenvalues λ_i are solutions to

$$C\psi = \lambda\psi$$

where C is the covariance matrix

$$C = \mathbb{E}[(\mathcal{E}(\boldsymbol{\theta}) - \mathbb{E}[\mathcal{E}(\boldsymbol{\theta})])(\mathcal{E}(\boldsymbol{\theta}) - \mathbb{E}[\mathcal{E}(\boldsymbol{\theta})])^T]$$

for $\boldsymbol{\theta} \in \Theta_i$. These can be computed using standard techniques [62]. The components are orthogonal vectors aligning with the directions along which $\mathcal{E}(\Theta_i)$

varies maximally, the first component accounting for most of the variance, the second for the the second-most, and so on.

The number of components we store to define the representation should be commensurate with the dimension of the manifold. The measured dimension may of course depend upon the extent over which the samples are taken; thus ideally the dimension selection should be coupled with the partitioning algorithm, with a maximum acceptable reconstruction error determining the stopping. In our examples we simply fix the dimension based on the number of parameters in the model.

Determining the closest point on the manifold to a given point in the ambient space is done by searching for the closest element of the partition to the point in space followed by a projection onto the corresponding principal components. Given an image $\mathcal{I}$, the algorithm searches for the closest subset of the edge manifold $\mathcal{E}(\Theta_\mathcal{I})$, where

$$\Theta_\mathcal{I} = \arg \min_{\Theta_i} \|\mathcal{I} - \mathbb{E}[\mathcal{E}(\Theta_i)]\|.$$

The approximate closest manifold point is given by

$$\hat{\mathcal{I}} = \mathbb{E}[\mathcal{E}(\Theta_\mathcal{I})] + \sum_i c_i \psi_{\Theta_\mathcal{I},i}$$

where $\psi_{\Theta_\mathcal{I},i}$ are the principal components associated with $\Theta_\mathcal{I}$ and

$$c_i = (\mathcal{I} - \mathbb{E}[\mathcal{E}(\Theta_\mathcal{I})]) \cdot \psi_{\Theta_\mathcal{I},i}.$$

See Figures 2 and 3. The distance to the manifold is $\|\mathcal{I} - \hat{\mathcal{I}}\|$. The estimated 'parameters' are the local coordinates of $\hat{\mathcal{I}}$, i.e., the c_i. To relate these to the model parameters requires a labeling of the partition element centers and the associated diffeomorphism from the subspace to the global coordinates.

2.3 Elaborating the Edge Manifold

So far we have only considered the orientation dimension of an edge model to illustrate our approach. Here we consider some additional dimensions to illustrate the generality of the approach and some geometric issues of significance.

Orientation × Curvature. An example of a two-dimensional manifold is an edge model with parameters for orientation (θ_1)[1] and curvature (θ_2). We can describe an image generated by this model as $\mathcal{E}(x, y; \boldsymbol{\theta}) = \mathcal{G} * f(x', y'; \theta_2)$ where

$$f(x', y'; \theta_2) = \begin{cases} 1 & \text{if } y' > \theta_2 x'^2 \\ 0 & \text{otherwise} \end{cases},$$

and $x' = \cos(\theta_1)x + \sin(\theta_1)y$ and $y' = -\sin(\theta_1)x + \cos(\theta_1)y$. We show a set of the corresponding filters in Figure 4.

---
[1] Note that θ_i takes on a different meaning with each different model.

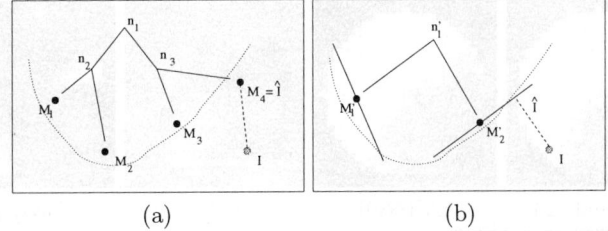

(a) (b)

Fig. 2. Determining the closest point on a manifold $\mathcal{E}$ (dotted line) to a given image $\mathcal{I}$ (grey circle). (a) For the manifold representation given in Figure 1(b) the reconstruction $\hat{\mathcal{I}}$ is the closest subset center M_4, where $M_i = \mathbb{E}[\mathcal{E}(\Theta_i)]$, the Θ_i being the elements of the partition in the parameter space. The reconstruction is found by simply searching through the M_i. (b) For the manifold representation of Figure 1(c) the closest subset center is found by search, followed by a projection onto the linear approximation of the subset.

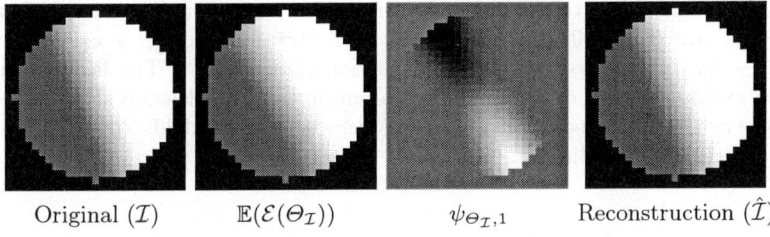

Original ($\mathcal{I}$) $\mathbb{E}(\mathcal{E}(\Theta_\mathcal{I}))$ $\psi_{\Theta_\mathcal{I},1}$ Reconstruction ($\hat{\mathcal{I}}$)

Fig. 3. Approximating an edge manifold. An edge image, $\mathcal{I}$, is generated by a model, $\mathcal{E}$ parameterized by orientation; $\mathcal{I} = \mathcal{E}(1.98\text{rad})$. The algorithm finds the nearest subspace center to $\mathcal{I}$, $\mathbb{E}[\mathcal{E}(\Theta_\mathcal{I})]$, and projects the image onto the first principal component of the subspace, $\psi_{\Theta_\mathcal{I},1}$; here we use only one component as the manifold is one-dimensional. The reconstruction is given by $\hat{\mathcal{I}} = \mathbb{E}[\mathcal{E}(\Theta_\mathcal{I})] + c_1 \psi_{\Theta_\mathcal{I},1}$, where $c_1 = (\mathcal{I} - \mathbb{E}[\mathcal{E}(\Theta_\mathcal{I})]) \cdot \psi_{\Theta_\mathcal{I},1}$. In this case, $\|\mathcal{I} - \mathbb{E}[\mathcal{E}(\Theta_\mathcal{I})]\|/\|\mathcal{I}\| = 6.86\%$, $\|\mathcal{I} - \mathbb{E}[\mathcal{E}'(\Theta_\mathcal{I})]\|/\|\mathcal{I}\| = 3.55\%$, where $\mathcal{E}'$ is the same edge manifold represented by twice as many subsets but no principal components, and $\|\hat{\mathcal{I}} - \mathcal{I}\|/\|\mathcal{I}\| = 0.48\%$.

Intensity Variation. One well known shortcoming of step-edge models is that edges observed in the natural world are typically not steps [26][4]. Local energy based detectors [53][59] improve the situation but fail to capture the full variety of intensity variation on either side of the discontinuity. Local PCA is an attractive approach to model higher order intensity variations because the added cost of representation is simply additional principal components for each partition, but no additional partition elements. Intensity variation in the neighborhood of an edge can be captured up to its Taylor approximation, with the order dictated by the number of filters. The model is given by $\mathcal{E}(x, y; \boldsymbol{\theta}) = \mathcal{G} * f(x, y; \boldsymbol{\theta})$, where

$$f(x,y;\boldsymbol{\theta}) = \begin{cases} \theta_1 + \theta_2 x + \theta_3 y + \theta_4 x^2 + \theta_5 xy + \theta_6 y^2 & \text{if } y > 0 \\ \theta_7 + \theta_8 x + \theta_9 y + \theta_{10} x^2 + \theta_{11} xy + \theta_{12} y^2 & \text{otherwise} \end{cases}.$$

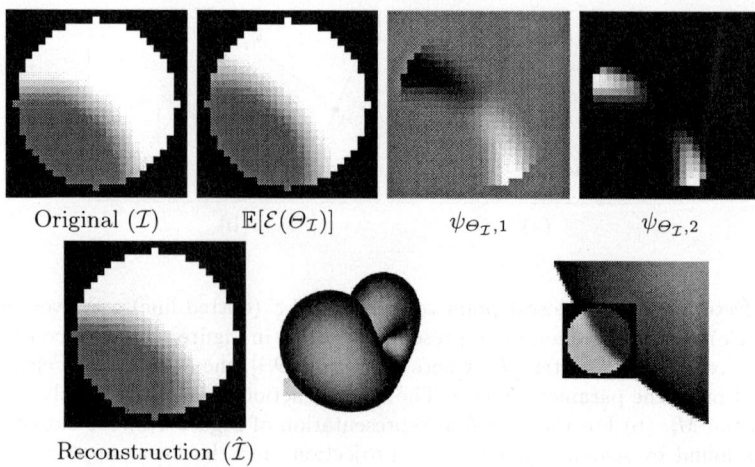

Fig. 4. Manifold $\mathcal{E}$ has two parameters, orientation and curvature. $\mathcal{I}$ has orientation 2.5rad and curvature -0.48. As before, $\hat{\mathcal{I}} = \mathbb{E}[\mathcal{E}(\Theta_{\mathcal{I}})] + c_1 \psi_{\Theta_{\mathcal{I}},1} + c_2 \psi_{\Theta_{\mathcal{I}},2}$, where $c_i = (\mathcal{I} - \mathbb{E}[\mathcal{E}(\Theta_{\mathcal{I}})]) \cdot \psi_{\Theta_{\mathcal{I}},i}$. The reconstruction error is 2.2%. The last two images show an example of this operator applied to an image. The close up shows a piece of the image as reconstructed by the local PCA represented manifold. Note the curvature bias induced by the shading.

We show a set of second order filters in Figure 5. Note that identifying quadratic intensity variation may be fundamental to edge classification [4], e.g., similar filters have proven useful in occluding contour identification [29].

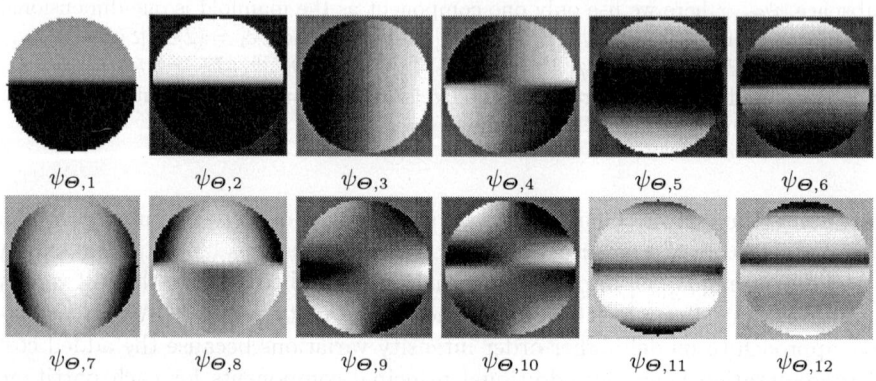

Fig. 5. The principal components specifying a 12 parameter edge manifold where the edge orientation is fixed horizontally and all variation is up to quadratic in intensity. Filters $\psi_{\Theta,1}$ and $\psi_{\Theta,2}$ account for contrast, filters $\psi_{\Theta,3}$ and $\psi_{\Theta,4}$ account for linear variation along the edge, filters $\psi_{\Theta,5}$ and $\psi_{\Theta,6}$ account for linear variation in the direction normal to the edge, while the remainder account for quadratic variations.

Orientation × Position × Blur. A three-dimensional manifold we consider is given by the parameters for edge position (θ_1), blur (θ_2), and orientation (θ_3). The model is given by $\mathcal{E}(x,y;\boldsymbol{\theta}) = \mathcal{G}(\theta_2) * f(x,y;\theta_1,\theta_3)$

$$f(x,y;\theta_1,\theta_3) = \begin{cases} 1 & \text{if } -\sin(\theta_3)x + \cos(\theta_3)y > \theta_1 \\ 0 & \text{otherwise} \end{cases}.$$

See Figure 7 for the associated filters.

2.4 Geometry of the Edge Manifold

Considering progressively more complex edge manifolds raises the question: how do these parameters interact? The local PCA representation, by construction, creates a local orthogonal coordinate frame describing each subset of the manifold. In the one-dimensional case we saw (Figure 1(c)) that the first principal component (Figure 3 $\psi_{\Theta_\mathcal{I},1}$) was approximately tangent to the manifold (indeed, in the limit that the subset shrinks to zero, it becomes exact), which corresponds to the derivative of the manifold with respect to θ. In the multi-parameter case, the principal components span the (approximate) tangent space to the manifold and point in the so-called principal directions [14]. In Figure 6 in $\mathcal{E}(\Theta_1)$ the components ψ_1 and ψ_2 are roughly parallel to the parameter curves; this also occurs on the orientation × position × blur manifold, see Figure 7. In general, the edge manifolds are twisted, and there is no guarantee that a simple relationship exists between the principal components and the parameter curves or between the parameter curves themselves. See Figure 6, $\mathcal{E}(\Theta_2)$. In contrast, the coordinates of the the local PCA representation are naturally coupled to the geometry of the manifold, the eigenvalues of each axis depending on curvature; furthermore this coordinate system is automatic - a nonparametric manifold where the data points are observed as opposed to constructed would be equally well represented by local PCA.

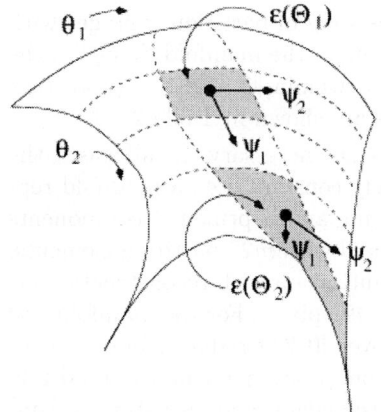

Fig. 6. An edge manifold $\mathcal{E}$ defined by two parameters, θ_1 and θ_2. The canonical coordinate curves (dashed lines) have an arbitrary relationship with the local principal components, ψ_1 and ψ_2, which are dependent on the intrinsic geometry of the manifold. They may align, as in $\mathcal{E}(\Theta_1)$. In general the coordinate curves are neither orthogonal nor aligned with the principal components, as in $\mathcal{E}(\Theta_2)$.

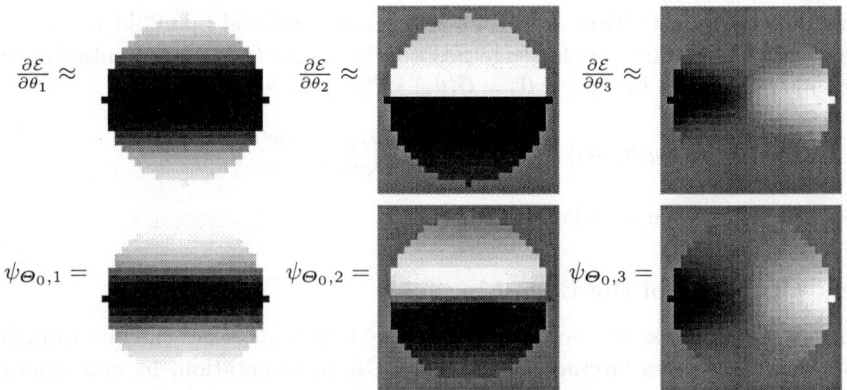

Fig. 7. *Top row*: The 'partial derivatives' of an edge manifold $\mathcal{E}$ with parameters corresponding to location (θ_1), blur (θ_2), and orientation (θ_3), where location is measured normal to the edge. These are obtained by computing the first principal component of the subset of the submanifold defined by considering variation in only a single parameter, centered on $\mathcal{E}([0,0,0])$, where each subset is approximately of the same length in the ambient space. *Bottom row*: The first three principal components of the cell centered on $\mathcal{E}([0,0,0])$. The correspondence with the partial derivatives suggests that the coordinate curves are near orthogonal at $\mathcal{E}([0,0,0])$.

3 Results

We tested the reconstruction performance of the local PCA representation on edge manifolds of increasing complexity. As a measure of performance, we calculate the percent error in the reconstruction of manifold points, averaged over the whole manifold: Error $= \mathbb{E}\left[\frac{\|\hat{\mathcal{I}}-\mathcal{E}(\theta)\|}{\|\mathcal{E}(\theta)\|}\right]$, for $\theta \in \Theta$. For comparison, we measure the performance of the representation consisting of partition averages with no principal components, i.e., given a partitioning of the manifold $\mathcal{E}_1, \mathcal{E}_2, ...,$ the reconstruction is given by $\hat{\mathcal{I}} = \mathbb{E}[\mathcal{E}_j]$ where $j = \mathrm{argmin}_i \|\mathcal{I} - \mathbb{E}[\mathcal{E}_i]\|$ (note that this is simply vector quantization). The results are shown in Table 2.

Before discussing the results, some details are necessary. In all cases the number of computations was kept approximately constant, i.e., a manifold represented by local PCA with m partition elements and n principal components per element would be compared against a manifold with $m2^n$ partition elements. The partitions were computed using vector quantization with reconstruction error as the distortion metric. The window size is 491 pixels. For the manifolds we considered, orientation is sampled uniformly over $[0, 2\pi)$ radians, blur is sampled uniformly over $[0, 8]$ pixels standard deviation, position is sampled uniformly over $[-8, 8]$ pixels (in the direction normal to the edge), and curvature is sampled uniformly over $[-0.083, 0.083]$. Note that the uniform sampling may bias the representation computed by local PCA.

Table 2. Comparison of local PCA and vector quantization (0 components) representations of three manifolds. Error values given are the expected reconstruction percent errors. In each case we indicate the size of the partition and the number of principal components used. See text for a discussion.

Model Parameters	Partition Size × Components	Error
Orientation	36 × 0	2.31%
	18 × 1	0.69%
	12 × 2	0.45%
Orientation, curvature	512 × 0	3.29%
	128 × 2	2.21%
Orientation, blur, position	512 × 0	11.1%
	64 × 3	8.9%

Our first test considers the one-dimensional edge manifold parameterized by orientation. The comparison is essentially between the representations shown in Figure 1(b) and (c). For the local PCA representation with a single principal component, the necessary filters are depicted in Figure 3. The errors show the benefit of the local PCA representation, suggesting that the manifold is well approximated by the linear subspaces at the scale chosen.

Despite the fact that the edge manifold is one-dimensional, we see that adding a second principal component further reduces the error. From this it is clear that the tangent space to the manifold varies within the partition elements: the second component is capturing the curvature of the manifold. The representation in some sense 'dilates' the manifold, as a point that lies on the plane determined by the two components is interpreted as being on the manifold.

We represent the orientation × curvature manifold in the second case. The manifold is two dimensional and the filters used by the local PCA representation are depicted in Figure 4. Here we see that again the local PCA is more efficient, though not as dramatically as in the previous case. This suggests that the manifold is highly curved in the curvature dimension.

The last manifold we consider is three-dimensional, with parameters varying edge location, orientation, and blur. Local PCA filters for this manifold appear in Figure 7. Here we have chosen a coarse partition, typical of many edge detectors (see, e.g., the discussion in [58]). Even at this resolution, the structure of the manifold is still captured significantly by the local PCA representation, as evidenced in the errors.

We have illustrated that for a variety of edge models, the local PCA representation yields better reconstructions than the vector quantization method. The amount of computation is marginally less for the local PCA, while the storage cost for the local PCA is significantly less ($O(m \log m + mn)$ vs. $O(m2^n \log(m2^n))$). Optimization of the method is the subject of ongoing work.

4 Related Work

The treatment of edge detection as a model matching problem is classical (Hueckel [27]). The statistical formulation and analysis of the problem as one of parameter estimation [64][33][52][9][63] is still ongoing, in part because as the edge model is elaborated, the analysis becomes less tractable, hence our acceptance of the maximum-likelihood estimator. The geometric nature of the problem on which our analysis depends is nicely highlighted by Baker et al. [3]. Perhaps the earliest effort to explicitly represent an edge manifold is due to Meer et al. [50], using self-organizing maps [38].

Following Hueckel [27], Hummel [31] applied the Karhunen-Loève transform to edge space to obtain an optimal basis in which to represent the edge manifold. Note that this is different from the representation itself, which is nonlinear (see Figure 1(a)), and that we would still need to represent the manifold, only now embedded in a reduced dimensional space. The same approach has been used to determine optimal bases in which to represent arbitrary image patches [23][43] and by Perona [58] to represent steerable filters [20][65].

Our approach is to use the Karhunen-Loève transform for the representation itself, applying it to a neighborhood of the manifold as opposed to the whole manifold (as in the optimal bases case [31][58]) or some superset containing the manifold (as in the natural image statistics literature [23][43][7][56]). The advantage is that the resulting representation reflects the intrinsic dimensionality of the manifold rather than the dimensionality of the space it lies in. While here we use knowledge of the parameters of the edge model to determine the dimensionality of the manifold, methods to estimate the dimensionality, e.g., [21], may be used in conjunction with local PCA (see [11]) when such information is not available.

An alternative formulation of steerable filters uses Lie group theory to derive the basis [40][51][25]. While again the result is only a basis and not a representation, it is interesting to note that the construction of the basis depends upon derivative operators that act on the edge manifold.

Researchers in learning have developed various representations for nonlinear manifolds, e.g., nonlinear principal component analysis (NLPCA) [39], principal curves [24], and local PCA [34]. Local PCA is approximately a first order representation of principal curves, and has the attraction that it is easily computed; this is not the case for some of the nonlinear methods [48]. Alternative nonlinear methods include population coding [66][45] and radial basis functions [61]. We also note that related local linear methods have been successfully applied in computer vision [10][5][13].

5 Conclusions

Motivated by the need to represent complex models of edge appearance, we considered the geometry of the corresponding edge manifold. The global structure of the edge manifold reveals the limitation of standard linear dimension reduction techniques. The smoothness of the manifold suggests its tangent space as a means of local approximation. We achieve just such a representation using local principal component analysis.

We construct local PCA representations of edge manifolds of varying complexity. These constructions give rise to image filters which correspond to points on and tangents to the edge manifold. Using these filters we compute the distance of an image patch to the edge manifold, which is equivalent to estimating the edge model parameters. Furthermore, these filters are not designed: they are direct consequences of the intrinsic geometry of the manifold.

Appearance-based approaches to object recognition, e.g., [54], bypass edge detection to model intensity distributions directly. These approaches are ultimately limited by complexity at the object level [6][15]. However, the variation that is captured by such models can also be captured locally by sufficiently complex features, e.g., occlusion edges [29]. Here we achieve a representation of edges that balances their local nature with the complexity of their appearance.

References

[1] S. Amari, O.E. Barndorff-Nielsen, R.E. Kass, S.L. Lauritzen, and C.R. Rao. *Differential Geometry in Statistical Inference*. IMS, 1987.
[2] S. Baker. On the parameter estimation accuracy of model-matching feature detectors. Technical Report CUCS-011-97, Columbia, 1997.
[3] S. Baker, S.K. Nayar, and H. Murase. Parametric feature detection. *International Journal of Computer Vision*, 27(1):27–50, 1998.
[4] H.G. Barrow and J.M. Tenenbaum. Recovering intrinsic scene characteristics from images. In A.R. Hanson and E.M. Riseman, editors, *Computer Vision Systems*. Academic Press, New York, 1978.
[5] R. Basri, D. Roth, and D.W. Jacobs. Clustering appearances of 3d objects. In *CVPR'98*, pages 414–420, 1998.
[6] P.N. Belhumeur and D.J. Kriegman. What is the set of images of an object under all possible lighting conditions? In *CVPR'96*, 1996.
[7] A.J. Bell and T.J. Sejnowski. The "independent components" of natural scenes are edge filters. *Vision Research*, 37(23):3327–3338, 1997.
[8] F. Bergholm. Edge focusing. *IEEE Trans. Pattern Analysis and Machine Intelligence*, 9(6), 1987.
[9] T. Blaszka and R. Deriche. Recovering and characterizing image features using an efficient model based approach. Technical Report 2422, INRIA, November 1994.
[10] C. Bregler and S. Omohundro. Nonlinear manifold learning for visual speech recognition. In *ICCV'95*, pages 494–499, 1995.
[11] J. Bruske and G. Sommer. Intrinsic dimensionality estimation with optimally topology preserving maps. *IEEE Trans. Pattern Analysis and Machine Intelligence*, 20(5), 1998.
[12] J. Canny. A computational approach to edge detection. *IEEE Trans. Pattern Analysis and Machine Intelligence*, 8(6):679–698, November 1986.
[13] R. Cappelli, D. Maio, and D. Maltoni. Multispace kl for pattern representation and classification. *IEEE Trans. Pattern Analysis and Machine Intelligence*, 23(9), September 2001.
[14] M.P. Do Carmo. *Differential geometry of curves and surfaces*. Prentice-Hall, Englewood Cliffs, NJ, 1976.

[15] J.L. Crowley and F. Pourraz. Continuity properties of the appearance manifold for mobile robot position estimation. *Image and Vision Computing*, 19:741–752, 2001.
[16] P.A. Devijver and J. Kittler. *Pattern Recognition: a statistical approach*. Prentice-Hall, Englewood Cliffs, NJ, 1982.
[17] A. Dobbins, S.W. Zucker, and M.S. Cynader. Endstopped neurons in the visual cortex as a substrate for calculating curvature. *Nature*, 329(6138):438–441, October 1987.
[18] J.H. Elder and S.W. Zucker. Local scale control for edge detection and blur estimation. *IEEE Trans. Pattern Analysis and Machine Intelligence*, 20(7):699–716, July 1998.
[19] M. Fahle and T. Poggio. Visual hyperacuity: spatiotemporal interpolation in human vision. In *IU84*, pages 49–77, 1984.
[20] W.T. Freeman and E.H. Adelson. The design and use of steerable filters. *IEEE Trans. Pattern Analysis and Machine Intelligence*, 13(9), 1991.
[21] K. Fukunaga and D.R. Olsen. An algorithm for finding intrinsic dimensionality of data. *IEEE Trans. on Computers*, 20(2), 1971.
[22] A. Gersho and R.M. Gray. *Vector Quantization and Signal Compression*. Kluwer, 1992.
[23] P.J.B. Hancock, R.J. Baddeley, and L.S. Smith. Principal components of natural images. *Network*, 3(1):61–70, 1992.
[24] T. Hastie and W. Stuetzle. Principal curves. *J. Am. Stat. Assoc.*, 84(406), June 1989.
[25] P.C. Hel-Or, Y. Teo. Canonical decomposition of steerable functions. *Journal of Mathematical Imaging and Vision*, 9:83–95, 1998.
[26] B.K.P. Horn. Understanding image intensities. *AI*, 8:201–231, 1977.
[27] M.H. Huekel. An operator which locates edges in digitized pictures. *JACM*, 18(1):113–125, January 1971.
[28] A. Huertas and G.G. Medioni. Detection of intensity changes with subpixel accuracy using laplacian-gaussian masks. *IEEE Trans. Pattern Analysis and Machine Intelligence*, 8(5):651–664, September 1986.
[29] P.S. Huggins, H.F. Chen, P.N. Belhumeur, and S.W. Zucker. Finding folds: on the appearance and identification of occlusion. In *CVPR*, 2001.
[30] P.S. Huggins and S.W. Zucker. Folds and cuts: how shading flows into edges. In *ICCV*, 2001.
[31] R.A. Hummel. Edge detetcion using basis functions. *Computer Vision, Graphics, and Image Processing*, 9(1):40–55, 1979.
[32] P.D. Hyde and L.S. Davis. Subpixel edge estimation. *Pattern Recognition*, 16(4):413–420, 1983.
[33] R. Kakarala and A.O. Hero. On acheivable accuracy in edge localization. *IEEE Trans. Pattern Analysis and Machine Intelligence*, 14(7):777–781, July 1992.
[34] N. Kambhatla and T.K. Leen. Dimension reduction by local principal component analysis. *Neural Computation*, 9:1493–1516, 1997.
[35] M. Kass, A.P. Witkin, and D. Terzopoulos. Snakes: active contour models. *International Journal of Computer Vision*, 1(4):321–331, January 1988.
[36] J.J. Koenderink. What does the occluding contour tell us about solid shape? *Perception*, 13:321–330, 1984.
[37] J.J. Koenderink and W. Richards. Two-dimensional curvature operators. *J. Opt. Soc. Am. A*, 5(7), July 1988.
[38] T. Kohonen. *Self-Organizing Maps*. Springer, 1997.

[39] M.A. Kramer. Nonlinear principal component analysis using autoassociative neural networks. *AIChE Journal*, 37(2), February 1991.
[40] R. Lenz. *Group Theoretical Methods in Image Processing*. Number 413 in Lecture Notes in Computer Science. Springer-Verlag, Berlin, 1990.
[41] Y. Linde, A. Buzo, and R. Gray. An algorithm for vector quantization design. *IEEE Trans. Communications*, 28(1):84–95, January 1980.
[42] T. Lindeberg. Edge detection and ridge detection with automatic scale selection. *International Journal of Computer Vision*, 30(2):117–154, 1998.
[43] Y. Liu and H. Shouval. Localized principal components of natural images - an analytic solution. *Network*, 5(2), 1994.
[44] D.G. Lowe. *Perceptual Organization and Visual Recognition*. Kluwer, 1985.
[45] N. Ludtke, R.C. Wilson, and E.R. Hancock. Population codes for orientation estimation. In *ICPR'00*, 2000.
[46] W.H.H.J. Lunscher and M.P. Beddoes. Optimal edge detector design i: parameter selection and noise effects. *IEEE Trans. Pattern Analysis and Machine Intelligence*, 8(2), March 1986.
[47] E.P. Lyvers, O.R. Mitchell, M.L. Akey, and A.P. Reeves. Subpixel measurements using a moment-based edge operator. *IEEE Trans. Pattern Analysis and Machine Intelligence*, 11(12):1293–1309, December 1989.
[48] E.C. Malthouse. Some theoretical results on nonlinear principal components analysis. Technical report, Northwestern University, 1996.
[49] D. Marr and E. Hildreth. Theory of edge detection. *Proc. R. Soc. Lond. B*, 207:187–217, 1980.
[50] P. Meer, S. Wang, and H. Wechsler. Edge detection by associative mapping. *Pattern Recognition*, 22(5):491–503, 1989.
[51] M. Michaelis and G. Sommer. A lie group approach to steerable filters. *Pattern Recognition Letters*, 16:1165–1174, 1995.
[52] D. Mintz. Robust consensus based edge-detection. In *CVPR92*, pages 651–653, 1992.
[53] M. Morrone and D. Burr. Feature detection from local energy. *Pattern Recognition Letters*, 6:303–313, 1987.
[54] H. Murase and S.K. Nayar. Visual learning and recognition of 3-d objects from appearance. *International Journal of Computer Vision*, 14:5–24, 1995.
[55] V.S. Nalwa and T.O. Binford. On detecting edges. *IEEE Trans. Pattern Analysis and Machine Intelligence*, 8(6):699–714, November 1986.
[56] B.A. Olshausen and D.J. Field. Sparse coding with an overcomplete basis set: a strategy employed by v1? *Vision Research*, 37(23):3311–3325, 1997.
[57] A.P. Pentland. A new sense for depth of field. *IEEE Trans. Pattern Analysis and Machine Intelligence*, 9(4):523–531, July 1987.
[58] P. Perona. Deformable kernels for early vision. *IEEE Trans. Pattern Analysis and Machine Intelligence*, 17(5), May 1995.
[59] P. Perona and J. Malik. Detecting and localizing edges composed of steps, peaks and roofs. In *ICCV'90*, pages 52–57, 1990.
[60] M. Petrou and J. Kittler. Optimal edge detectors for ramp edges. *IEEE Trans. Pattern Analysis and Machine Intelligence*, 13(5):483–491, May 1991.
[61] T. Poggio and F. Girosi. A theory of networks for approximation and learning. Technical Report A.I. Memo 1140, MIT, July 1989.
[62] W.H. Press, S.A. Teukolsky, W.T. Vetterling, and B.P. Flannery. *Numerical Recipes in C, 2nd Ed.* Cambridge, 1992.
[63] Karl Rohr. On the precision in estimating the location of edges and corners. *Journal of Mathematical Imaging and Vision*, 7(1):7–22, 1997.

[64] A. Rosenfeld and S. Banerjee. Maximum-likelihood edge detection in digital signals. *Computer Vision, Graphics, and Image Processing*, 55(1):1–13, January 1992.

[65] E.P. Simoncelli, W.T. Freeman, E.H. Adelson, and D.J. Heeger. Shiftable multiscale transforms. *IEEE Trans. Information Theory*, 38(2):587–607, March 1992.

[66] H.P. Snippe. Parameter extraction from population codes: a critical assessment. *Neural Computation*, 8(3), April 1996.

[67] A.J. Tabatabai and O.R. Mitchell. Edge location to subpixel values in digital imagery. *IEEE Trans. Pattern Analysis and Machine Intelligence*, 6(2):188–200, March 1984.

[68] V. Torre and T.A. Poggio. On edge detection. *IEEE Trans. Pattern Analysis and Machine Intelligence*, 8(2), March 1986.

[69] F. Ulupinar and Medioni G. Refining edges detected by a log operator. *Computer Vision, Graphics, and Image Processing*, 51:275–298, 1990.

[70] H.L. van Trees. *Detection, Estimation, and Modulation Theory, Part I*. John Wiley & Sons, 1968.

[71] P.W. Verbeek and van Vliet L.J. On the location error of curved edges in low-pass filtered 2-d and 3-d images. *IEEE Trans. Pattern Analysis and Machine Intelligence*, 16(7), July 1994.

[72] A. Witkin. Intensity-based edge classification. In *Proc. 2nd Nat. Conf. A.I.*, pages 36–41, 1982.

[73] M. Worring and A.W.M. Smeulders. Digital curvature estimation. *Computer Vision, Graphics, and Image Processing*, 58(3):366–382, November 1993.

Regularized Shock Filters and Complex Diffusion

Guy Gilboa[1], Nir A. Sochen[2], and Yehoshua Y. Zeevi[1]

[1] Department of Electrical Engineering, Technion – Israel Institute of Technology
Technion City, Haifa 32000, Israel
gilboa@tx.technion.ac.il, www.ee.technion.ac.il/∼gilboa
zeevi@ee.technion.ac.il, www.ee.technion.ac.il/∼zeevi
[2] Department of Applied Mathematics, University of Tel-Aviv, Tel-Aviv 69978, Israel
sochen@math.tau.ac.il, www.math.tau.ac.il/∼sochen

Abstract. We address the issue of regularizing Osher and Rudin's shock filter, used for image deblurring, in order to allow processes that are more robust against noise. Previous solutions to the problem suggested adding some sort of diffusion term to the shock equation. We analyze and prove some properties of coupled shock and diffusion processes. Finally we propose an original solution of adding a complex diffusion term to the shock equation. This new term is used to smooth out noise and indicate inflection points simultaneously. The imaginary value, which is an approximated smoothed second derivative scaled by time, is used to control the process. This results in a robust deblurring process that performs well also on noisy signals.

Keywords: Shock filters, deblurring, denoising, image enhancement, complex diffusion, image features.

1 Introduction

1.1 Background

In the past decade there has been a growing amount of research concerning partial differential equations in the fields of computer vision and image processing. Applications, supported by rigorous theory, were developed for purposes such as image denoising and enhancement, segmentation, object tracking and many more. A review of topics in the subject can be seen in [14]; see [9] for more recent studies. The research is focused mostly on linear and nonlinear parabolic schemes of diffusion-type processes. In [11] Osher and Rudin proposed a hyperbolic equation called shock filter that can serve as a stable deblurring algorithm approximating deconvolution.

1.2 Problem Statement

The formulation of the shock filter equation is:

$$I_t = -|I_x|F(I_{xx}), \tag{1}$$

where F should satisfy $F(0) = 0$, $F(s)\mathrm{sign}(s) \geq 0$. Note: the above equation and all other evolutionary equations in this paper have initial conditions $I(x,0) = I_0(x)$ and Neumann boundary conditions ($\frac{\partial I}{\partial n} = 0$ where n is the direction perpendicular to the boundary).

Choosing $F(s) = \mathrm{sign}(s)$ gives the classical shock filter equation:

$$I_t = -\mathrm{sign}(I_{xx})|I_x|. \tag{2}$$

In the 2D case the shock filter equation is commonly generalized to:

$$I_t = -\mathrm{sign}(I_{\eta\eta})|\nabla I|, \tag{3}$$

where η is the direction of the gradient.

The 1D process (Eq. 2) is approximated by the following discrete scheme:

$$I_i^{n+1} = I_i^n - \Delta t |DI_i^n| \mathrm{sign}(D^2 I_i^n), \tag{4}$$

where

$$\begin{aligned} DI_i^n &\doteq m(\Delta_+ I_i^n, \Delta_- I_i^n)/h, \\ D^2 I_i^n &\doteq (\Delta_+ \Delta_- I_i^n)/h^2, \end{aligned} \tag{5}$$

$m(x,y)$ is the minmod function:

$$m(x,y) \doteq \begin{cases} (\mathrm{sign}\, x) \min(|x|,|y|) & \text{if } xy > 0, \\ 0 & \text{otherwise,} \end{cases}$$

and $\Delta_\pm \doteq \pm(u_{i\pm 1} - u_i)$. The CFL condition in the 1D case is $\Delta t \leq 0.5 h$.

The shock filter main properties are:

- Shocks develop at inflection points (second derivative zero-crossings).
- Local extrema remain unchanged in time. No new local extrema are created. The scheme is total variation preserving (TVP).
- The steady state (weak) solution is piece-wise constant (with discontinuities at the inflection points of I_0).
- The process approximates deconvolution.

Most rigorous analysis and proofs of these properties were based on the discrete scheme (Eq. 4).

As already noted in the original paper, any noise in the blurred signal will also be enhanced. As a matter of fact this process is extremely sensitive to noise. Theoretically, in the continuous domain, any white noise added to the signal may add an infinite number of inflection points, disrupting the process completely. Discretization may help somewhat, but in general the same sensitivity to noise occurs. In Fig. (1) we compare the process acting on a sine wave without noise and with very low additive white Gaussian noise (SNR=40dB). Clearly the signal in the noisy case is not enhanced and the process results mainly in noise amplification.

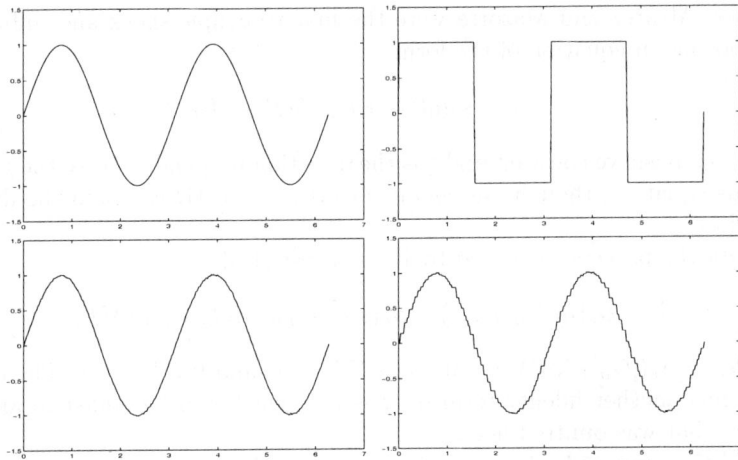

Fig. 1. Signal (sine wave) and its steady state shock filter solution without noise (top) and with very low additive white Gaussian noise, SNR=40dB (bottom).

2 Previous Works

The noise sensitivity problem is critical and unless properly solved - might prevent most practical uses of shock filters. Previous studies addressed the issue suggesting several solutions. The common way seen in literature to increase robustness ([1,3,10,12]) is to convolve the signal's second derivative with a lowpass filter, such as a Gaussian:

$$I_t = -\text{sign}(G_\sigma * I_{xx})|I_x|, \qquad (6)$$

where G_σ is a Gaussian of standard deviation σ.

This is generally not sufficient to overcome the noise problem: convolving the signal with a Gaussian of moderate width will in many cases not cancel the inflection points produced by the noise. Their magnitude will be considerably lower, but there will still be a change of sign at these points, which will lead the flow to go in opposite direction at each side. For very wide (large scale) Gaussians - most inflection points produced by the noise are diminished, but at a cost: the location of the signal's inflection points are less accurate. Moreover, the effective Gaussian's width σ is in many cases larger than the length of the signal, thus causing the boundary conditions imposed on the process to strongly affect the solution. Lastly, from a computational point of view, the convolution process in each iteration is costly.

A more complex approach, that we will also follow later, is to address the issue as an enhancing-denoising problem: smoother parts are denoised, whereas edges are enhanced and sharpened. The main idea is to add some sort of anisotropic diffusion term with an adaptive weight between the shock and the diffusion processes. Alvarez and Mazorra were the first to couple shock and diffusion in [1] proposing an equation of the form:

$$I_t = -\text{sign}(G_\sigma * I_{\eta\eta})|\nabla I| + c I_{\xi\xi} \qquad (7)$$

where c is a positive constant and ξ is the direction perpendicular to the gradient ∇I. This equation, though, degenerates to (6) in the 1D case and the diffusion part is lost.

In [10] the process suggested by Kornprobst et al. is:

$$I_t = \alpha_r(h_\tau I_{\eta\eta} + I_{\xi\xi}) - \alpha_e(1 - h_\tau)\text{sign}(G_\sigma * I_{\eta\eta})|\nabla I|, \qquad (8)$$

where $h_\tau = h_\tau(|G_{\tilde\sigma} * \nabla I|) = 1$ if $|G_{\tilde\sigma} * \nabla I| < \tau$, and 0 otherwise. The original scheme has another fidelity term $\alpha_f(I - I_0)$, which can be added to any such schemes, that was omitted here.

In [3] the proposed scheme of Coulon and Arridge is:

$$I_t = \text{div}(c\nabla I) - (1-c)^\alpha \text{sign}(G_\sigma * I_{\eta\eta})|\nabla I|, \qquad (9)$$

where $c = \exp(-\frac{|G_{\tilde\sigma} * \nabla I|^2}{k})$. Originally, the process was used for classification, based on a probabilistic framework. Eq. (9) is the adaptation for direct processing on images.

Later we will show examples of these schemes and compare the results to ours.

3 Coupling Shock and Diffusion

In the following section we analyze two discrete schemes involving shock filter and diffusion. We provide a few theorems regarding the behavior of these schemes. The proofs are in Appendix I. For simplicity, our analysis is done in one dimension.

3.1 Shock and Linear Diffusion

We start by adding a linear diffusion term to the shock filter equation:

$$I_t = -\text{sign}(I_{xx})|I_x| + \lambda I_{xx}, \qquad (10)$$

where $\lambda > 0$ is a constant weight parameter. The discrete scheme of (10) is:

$$I_i^{n+1} = I_i^n + \Delta t(-\text{sign}(D^2 I_i^n)|DI_i^n| + \lambda D^2 I_i^n), \qquad (11)$$

with CFL condition $\lambda \Delta t \leq 0.5 h^2$, $(h \leq 1)$.

Theorem 1. *The scheme of (11) obeys the strong minimum-maximum principal (no new local extrema are created and the global maximum and minimum at any time are bounded by those of the initial condition) and reaches a trivial constant steady state solution* $\lim_{n\to\infty} I^n(x) = \text{const}$ *for any* $\lambda > 0$.

This process is a mix between denoising and enhancement processes, where for low λ it behaves more like an enhancing shock filter and for large λ denoising is more dominant (with some edge preservation). Some characteristics of the shock filter are lost: Real shocks are actually not created; the scheme is not total-variation preserving; the signal diminishes with time - the steady state solution is a constant function.

3.2 A TVP Shock and Diffusion Process

An interesting modification of equation (10) is:

$$I_t = -\text{sign}(I_{xx})|I_x| + \lambda I_{xx}|\text{sign}(I_x)|, \tag{12}$$

and its discrete equivalent:

$$I_i^{n+1} = I_i^n + \Delta t(-\text{sign}(D^2 I_i^n)|DI_i^n| + \lambda D^2 I_i^n |\text{sign}(DI_i^n)|). \tag{13}$$

The diffusion term is multiplied by $|\text{sign}(I_x)|$. The value of this expression is always 1 except for the case $I_x = 0$, in which the value is 0. This relatively small change makes an important difference in the behavior of the equation. We should comment that (12) has the most simple shock-diffusion coupling for the sake of straitforward analysis, it is not intended for use on noisy signals.

Theorem 2. *The scheme of (13) is total variation preserving (TVP), local extrema remain unchanged in time and no new local extrema are created.*

Let us define $I_{i+\frac{1}{2}}^n$ as a discrete inflection point if $(D^2 I_i^n)(D^2 I_{i+1}^n) < 0$.

Theorem 3. *If there is a single discrete inflection point between two points of extrema, then its location is preserved through the evolution of (13).*

Theorem 2 implies Eq. (13) can have a nontrivial steady state. Assuming these properties are valid in the continuous domain of Eq. (12) we can simplify the equation locally and calculate in some cases the steady state solution analytically. Here we give an example of how to do it. We consider the case where there is a finite set E of local extrema points of the initial condition $I_0(x) \in C^2$, $x \in [0, 1]$. Between every two extrema points there is one inflection point. The calculation of the solution is as follows:

- Let us define by S the set of location of extrema points of $I_0(x)$ and by S_V their value: $S \doteq \{s_1, s_2, .., s_L\} : I_{0x}(s_i) = 0,\quad s_1 < s_2.. < s_L$, $S_V \doteq \{v_1, v_1, .., v_L\} : v_i = I_0(s_i),\quad 1 < i < L$.
- Let us define by T the set of location of inflection points of $I_0(x)$, $T \doteq \{t_1, t_1, .., t_{L-1}\} : I_{0xx}(t_i) = 0,\quad t_1 < t_2.. < t_{L-1}$. In this example we assume $0 < s_1 < t_1 < s_2 < .. < t_{L-1} < s_L < 1$.
- Let us define the value at the 2 boundary points $v_0 = I_0(0)$, $v_{L+1} = I_0(1)$ and denote $s_0 = 0$, $s_{L+1} = 1$.

- Following Theorems 2,3 - the location of extrema and inflection points do not change in time. Therefore we can separate the original equation on $x \in [0,1]$ to $2L$ equations with appropriate boundary conditions. Each equation is between an extrema point and an inflection point, except at the boundaries. The $2L$ equations are defined on $[0, s_1], [s_1, t_1], [t_1, s_2], ..[t_{L-1}, s_L], [s_L, 1]$.
- For each equation the first and second derivatives do not change their sign in the entire region. Therefore Eq. (12) can be rewritten at each region as: $I_t = \pm I_x \pm \lambda I_{xx}$ depending on the signs of I_x and I_{xx} at that region. At steady state $(I_t(x) \equiv 0)$ at each region the equation reduces to two possible options: $I_x = \pm \lambda I_{xx}$ and the solution is: $I(x) = c_1 \exp(\pm x/\lambda) + c_2$, where c_1, c_2 are arbitrary constants.
- Imposing the following boundary conditions:

$$\begin{aligned} I(s_i) &= v_i & 0 < i < L+1, \\ I(s_i^-) &= I(s_i^+) & 1 < i < L, \\ I(t_i^-) &= I(t_i^+) & 1 < i < L-1, \\ I_x(t_i^-) &= I_x(t_i^+) & 1 < i < L-1, \end{aligned}$$

We get $4L$ linear equations from the boundary conditions which allow us to calculate the $4L$ constants appearing in the $2L$ equations. Actually there is almost no coupling and we can solve separately every two equations between extrema points, that is on neighboring regions $[s_i, t_i], [t_i, s_{i+1}]$. The two equations on the boundary regions $[0, s_1], [s_L, 1]$ are independent. The weak solution is piece-wise differentiable (for the entire domain $x \in [0,1]$ we get $I(x, t \to \infty) \in C^0$).

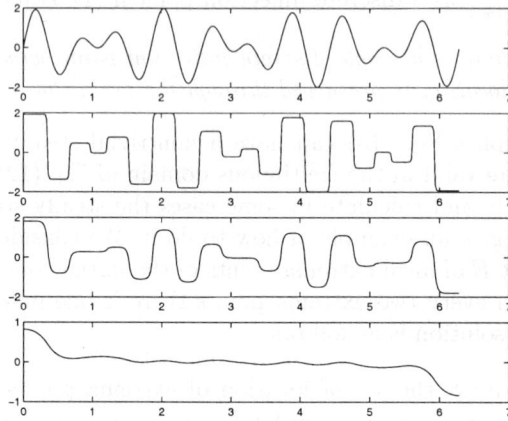

Fig. 2. Three examples of numerical solutions to equation (10) for different values of λ. From top: Initial condition ($I_0 = \sin 7x + \sin 10x$), I(x,t) after 1000 iterations for $\lambda = 0.1, 1, 10$, respectively.

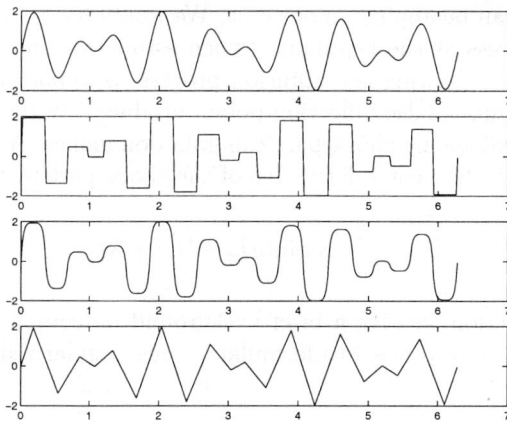

Fig. 3. Three examples of numerical solutions to equation (12) for different values of λ. From top: Initial condition ($I_0 = \sin 7x + \sin 10x$), I(x,t) at steady state for $\lambda = 10^{-4}, 1, 10^4$, respectively.

In Fig. 3 we show the behavior of equation (12) for different values of λ.

3.3 Considering the Second Derivative's Magnitude

in order to account for the magnitude of the second derivative controlling the flow - we return to the original shock filter formulation of (1) and choose $F(s) = \frac{2}{\pi} \arctan(as)$. This function is a "soft" sign, where a is a parameter that controls the sharpness of the slope near zero. The equation is therefore:

$$I_t = -\frac{2}{\pi} \arctan(aI_{xx})|I_x| + \lambda I_{xx}. \tag{14}$$

In this way the inflection points are not of equal weight anymore; regions near edges, with large magnitude of the second derivative near the zero crossing, will be sharpened much faster than relatively smooth regions.

3.4 Incorporating Time Dependency to the Process

Another desirable goal is the ability to change the process behavior with time in a controlled manner. In [5] we elaborate the idea of explicitly incorporating the time t to Perona-Malik type schemes ([13]). The basic idea is that processes controlled by the gradient magnitude have large errors in estimating gradients at the initial stages, where the signal is still very noisy. Therefore a preliminary phase of mainly noise removal can be advantageous. We suggested two processes with continuous transition in time, beginning with linear diffusion at time zero (strong denoising), advancing towards high nonlinearity (strong edge-preserving properties).

Similar ideas can be applied in our case. We would like to decrease the shock affects of the process at the beginning (when estimating the signal's inflection points is difficult) - allowing the diffusion process to smooth out the noise. As the evolution advances, false inflection points produced by the noise are greatly reduced and the enhancing shock part can gain dominance. A simple way to do that is to multiply the second derivative of the shock part by the time t:

$$I_t = -\frac{2}{\pi} \arctan(aI_{xx}t)|I_x| + \lambda I_{xx}. \tag{15}$$

In the next section we give a brief background on complex diffusion. Later we will use this type of process to formulate a new regularized shock filter.

4 Complex Diffusion

4.1 Introduction

Complex diffusion-type processes are encountered i.e. in quantum physics and in electro-optics. In [4] we analyzed a diffusion equation with a complex diffusion coefficient and showed some applications for image filtering. This process is a generalization of the *diffusion equation* and the *time dependent Schrödinger equation* with zero potential. There are little related studies in that field in the vision community. A recent paper by Barbaresco ([2]) presented the closely related issues of calculus of variations in the complex domain and its applications to spectral analysis. In this section we summarize the relevant results of [4].

4.2 Linear Complex Diffusion

Problem Definition. Let us consider the following initial value problem:

$$I_t = cI_{xx}, \quad t > 0, \quad x \in \mathbb{R} \tag{16}$$
$$I(x;0) = I_0 \in \mathbb{R}, \quad c, I \in \mathbb{C}.$$

We rewrite the complex diffusion coefficient as $c \doteq re^{i\theta}$, and, since there does not exist a stable fundamental solution of the inverse diffusion process, restrict ourselves to a positive real value of c, that is $\theta \in (-\frac{\pi}{2}, \frac{\pi}{2})$.

The fundamental solution is:

$$h(x;t) = G_\sigma(x;t)e^{i\alpha(x)}, \tag{17}$$

where

$$\alpha(x) = \frac{x^2 \sin\theta}{4tr}, \quad \sigma(t) = \sqrt{\frac{2tr}{\cos\theta}}. \tag{18}$$

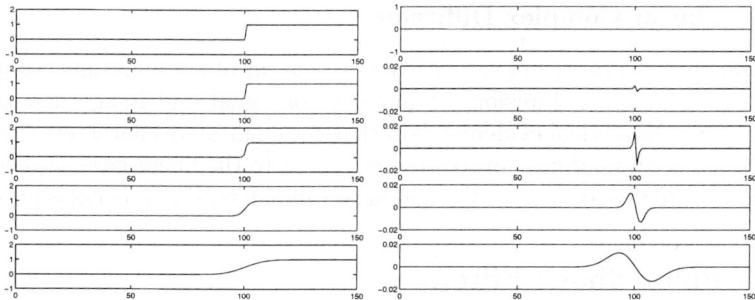

Fig. 4. Complex diffusion of a small theta applied to a step signal ($\theta = \pi/30$). Left - real values, right - imaginary values. Each frame depicts from top to bottom: original step, diffused signal after times: 0.025, 0.25, 2.5, 25.

Fig. 5. Complex diffusion of the cameraman image for small theta ($\theta = \pi/30$) after 10 iterations. Left - real values, right - imaginary values (factored by 20).

Approximate Solution for Small Theta. We showed in our previous study that as $\theta \to 0$ the imaginary part can be regarded as a smoothed second derivative of the initial signal, factored by θ and the time t. Generalizing the solution to any dimension with Cartesian coordinates $\mathbf{x} \doteq (x_1, x_2, ..x_N) \in \mathbb{R}^N$, $I(\mathbf{x};t) \in \mathbb{C}^N$ and denoting that in this coordinate system $\mathbf{G}_\sigma(\mathbf{x};t) \doteq \prod_i^N G_\sigma(x_i;t)$, we get:

$$\lim_{\theta \to 0} \frac{Im(I)}{\theta} = t\Delta \mathbf{G}_{\hat{\sigma}} * I_0, \qquad (19)$$

where $Im(\cdot)$ denotes the imaginary value and $\hat{\sigma} = \sqrt{2t}$.

In Figs. (4), (5) 1D and 2D examples are shown of the complex diffusion evolution process for small θ. The edge detection (smoothed second derivative) properties are clearly apparent in the imaginary part, whereas the real value depicts the properties of ordinary Gaussian scale-space.

4.3 Nonlinear Complex Diffusion

Nonlinear complex processes can be derived from the above mentioned properties of the linear complex diffusion for purposes of signal and image denoising or enhancement. Numerical evidence show that the qualitative characteristics of the imaginary part in nonlinear processes are similar to the linear case, especially at the zero-crossing locations. In [4] a nonlinear ramp denoising process is presented.

5 Complex Shock Filters

From (15) and (19) we derive the complex shock filter formulation:

$$I_t = -\frac{2}{\pi}\arctan(a\mathrm{Im}(\frac{I}{\theta}))|I_x| + \lambda I_{xx}, \qquad (20)$$

where $\lambda = re^{i\theta}$ is a complex scalar. Implementation of equation (20) is done by the same discrete approximations (except that all computations are complex); the CFL condition in 1D is $\Delta t \leq 0.5h^2 \frac{\cos\theta}{r}$.

The complex shock filter generalization to 2D is:

$$I_t = -\frac{2}{\pi}\arctan(a\mathrm{Im}(\frac{I}{\theta}))|\nabla I| + \lambda I_{\eta\eta} + \tilde{\lambda}I_{\xi\xi}, \qquad (21)$$

where $\tilde{\lambda}$ is a real scalar.

The complex filter is an elegant way to avoid the need of convolving the signal in each iteration and still get smoothed estimations. The time dependency of the process is inherent, without the need to explicitly use the evolution time t. Moreover, the imaginary value receives feedback - it is smoothed by the diffusion and enhanced at sharp transitions by the shock, thus can serve better for controlling the process then a simple second derivative.

In Fig. 6 a noisy sine wave is processed by several shock-filter based processes described earlier. The original shock filter (Eq. (2)) and the one with Gaussian convolved second derivative (Eq. (6)) are clearly not suitable for this task. The process of Kornprobst et al. (Eq. (8)) performs relatively well but the minimum and maximum of the signal decay quite fast and the deblurring is not so strong. Moreover there are 5 parameters that need to be adjusted and from our experience the performance of the process is quite sensitive to a few of them (esp. to τ). The process of Coulon and Arridge (Eq. (9)) behaves somewhat better in this 1D example, it produces shock structures but is strongly affected by to the boundary conditions and tends to move the shocks towards the center. Our complex shock filter scheme (Eq. (20)) seems to produce the best result, compared to the ideal result shown at the top right. The scheme is stable in time, decays slowly and preserves well the location of the shocks. Another advantage of our scheme is that we basically have only two parameters: $|\lambda|$ and a (in the 1D case, three in 2D). Note: as the process is normalized - it is not affected by the exact value of θ as long as it is small. In all our experiments we took $\theta = 0.01$. At the bottom right we can see the imaginary value of the complex process (the scale

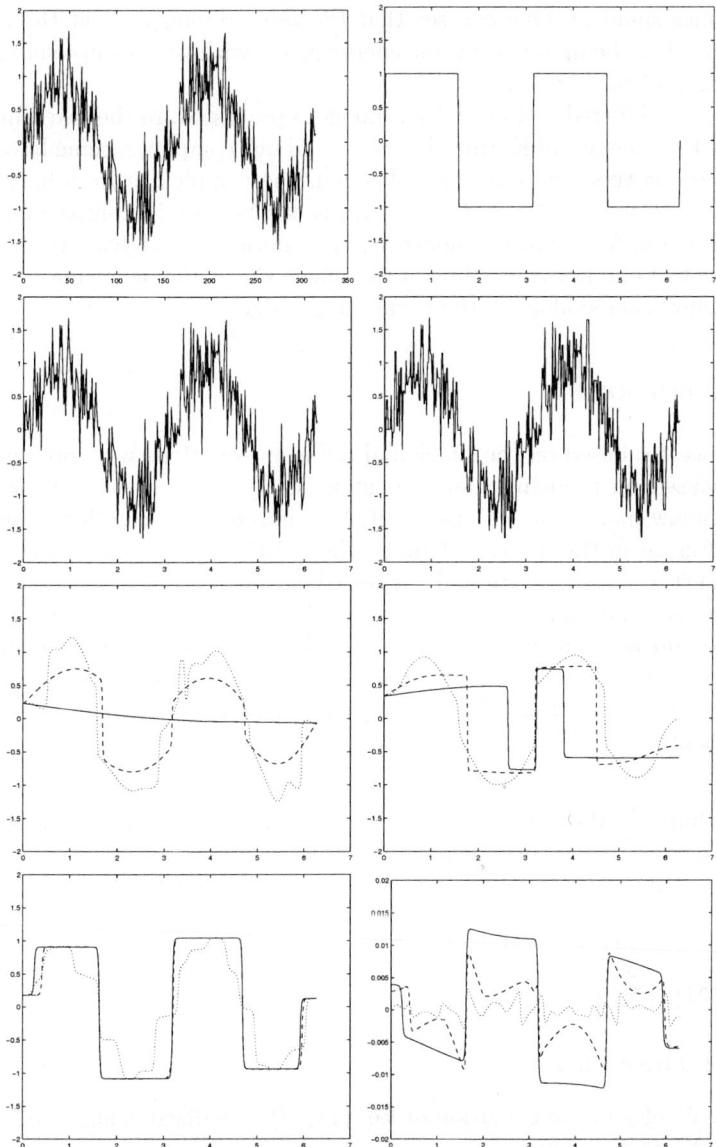

Fig. 6. Noisy signal (sine wave) processed by several algorithms. From top, left: signal with additive white Gaussian noise (SNR=5dB), right: ideal steady state shock result; left: steady state of original shock filter Eq. (2), right: steady state of Eq. (6) - Gaussian convolved derivative, $\sigma = 100$; left: evolution of Eq. (8) - Kornprobst et al. ($\alpha_r = 1, \alpha_e = 0.5, \tau = 0.04, \sigma = 30, \tilde{\sigma} = 5$), right: evolution of Eq. (9) - Coulon-Arridge ($k = 0.01, \alpha = 1, \sigma = 30, \tilde{\sigma} = 5$); bottom: evolution of Eq. (20) - complex shock filter (our proposed scheme), left: real values, right: imaginary values, ($|\lambda| = 0.5, a = 5$). All evolution graphs depict 3 time points along the evolution: 300 (dotted), 3,000 (dashed) and 30,000 (solid) iteration.

is 100 times smaller). One can see that the zero crossings are at the inflection points and that the imaginary value energy grows with time - thus enabling good preservation of the shocks.

In Fig. 7 a blurred and noisy tools image is processed. In the two dimensional case only the schemes of Kornprobst et at. and our complex scheme have acceptable results at this levels of noise. Though, the complex process have sharper edges and is closer to the shock process (as can be seen in comparison to ideal shock response, for a blurred image without noise - top right). At the bottom right a plot of one horizontal line of the image shows the denoising achieved by the complex scheme along with sharper large edges.

6 Conclusion

Some processes based on the shock and diffusion equations were presented. The paper focused on reducing the inherent noise sensitivity of the shock filter in order to allow more practical uses of it. We analyzed the coupling of shock and linear diffusion in the discrete domain, showed that the process converges to a trivial constant steady state and suggested a modification for a total variation preserving scheme. For the purpose of regularizing the shock filter our suggestion is to add a complex diffusion term and to use the imaginary value as the controller for the direction of the flow instead of the second derivative. This results in a robust and stable deblurring process that can still be effective in noisy environments.

Acknowledgments. This research has been supported in part by the Ollendorf Minerva Center, by the Fund for the Promotion of Research at the Technion, by the Israeli Ministry of Science, Israeli Academy of Science and by the Technion V.P.R. Fund.

APPENDIX I

Proof of Theorem 1

All lemmas refer to the evolution of Eq. (11). I_i^n is a discrete signal of N points ($1 \leq i \leq N$) at iteration n.

Lemma 1. *If ($I_i^n \geq I_{i+1}^n$ and $I_i^n > I_{i-1}^n$) or ($I_i^n > I_{i+1}^n$ and $I_i^n \geq I_{i-1}^n$) then $I_i^{n+1} < I_i^n$.*

Proof. From the definition of the minmod function it follows that $DI_i^n = 0$. From (5) $D^2 I_i^n < 0$ and therefore $I_i^{n+1} = I_i^n + \Delta t(\lambda D^2 I_i^n) < I_i^n$.

Lemma 2. *If $I_i^n = I_{i-1}^n = I_{i+1}^n$ then $I_i^{n+1} = I_i^n$.*

Proof. $DI_i^n = 0$, $D^2 I_i^n = 0$.

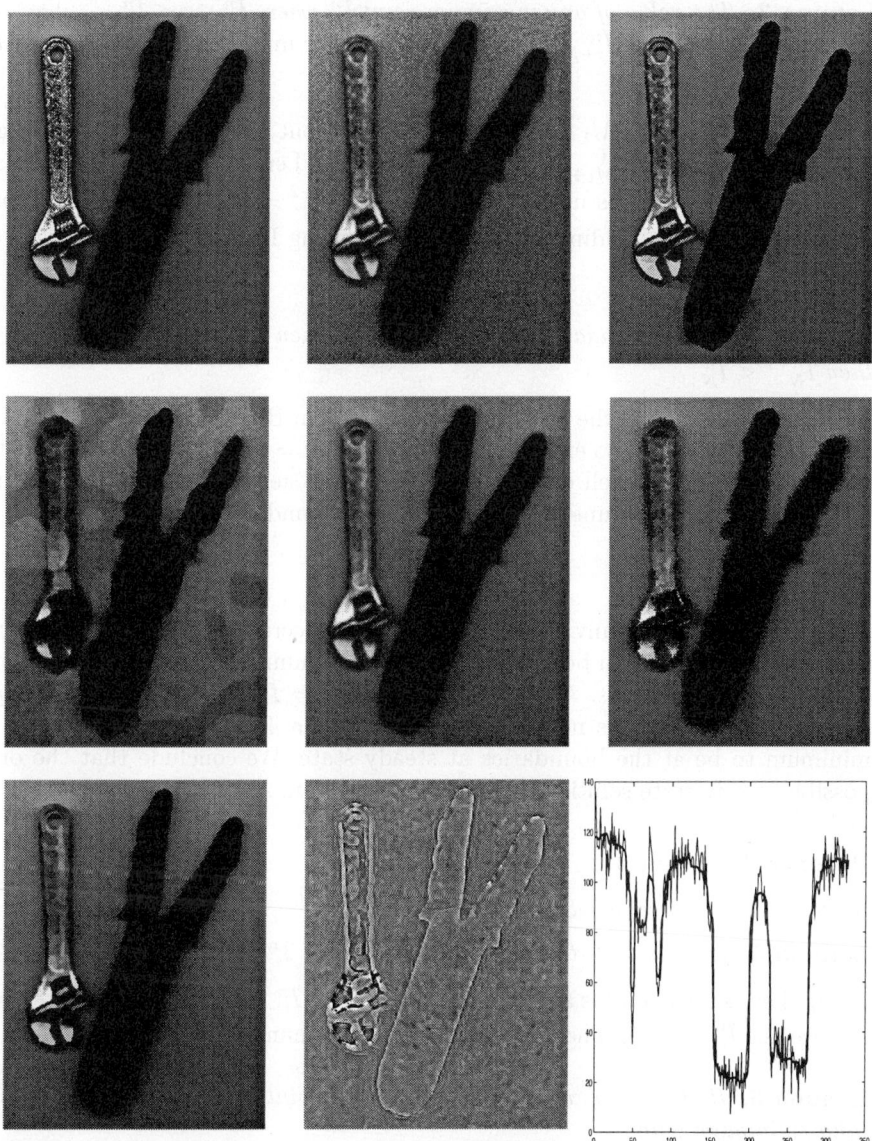

Fig. 7. Top row (from left): Original tools image, Gaussian blurred ($\sigma = 2$) with added white Gaussian noise (SNR=15dB), ideal shock response (of blurred image without the noise); middle row: evolutions of Eq. (7) - Alvarez-Mazorra ($\sigma = 10$), Eq. (8) - Kornprobst et al. ($\alpha_r = 0.2, \alpha_e = 0.1, \tau = 0.2, \sigma = 10, \tilde{\sigma} = 1$), Eq. (9) - Coulon-Arridge ($k = 5, \alpha = 1, \sigma = 10, \tilde{\sigma} = 1$); bottom: evolution of Eq. (20) - complex process, left: real values, middle: imaginary values ($|\lambda| = 0.1, \tilde{\lambda} = 0.5, a = 0.5$), right: one horizontal line showing the gray level values of the complex evolution (thin line - iteration 1, bold line - iteration 100). All evolution results are for 100 iterations, dt=0.1.

Lemma 3. *The value of any maximum point I_i^n where $I_{i-M_1}^n < I_{i-M_1+1}^n = .. = I_i^n = .. = I_{i+M_2-1}^n > I_{i+M_2}^n$ will be reduced after $\min(M_1, M_2)$ steps, that is: $I_i^{n+\min(M_1,M_2)} < I_i^n$.*

Proof. Let us assume $M_1 = \min(M_1, M_2)$, without loss of generality (wlog). Following Lemma 1 $I_{i-M_1+1}^{n+1} < I_{i-M_1+1}^n$. Following Lemma 2 $I_i^{n+1} = I_i^n$. We can repeat this $M_1 - 1$ steps until $I_{i-1}^{n+M_1-1} < I_{i-1}^{n+M_1-2} = I_i^n$. Then the conditions of Lemma 2 are not holding anymore and following Lemma 1 we get $I_i^{n+M_1} < I_i^{n+M_1-1} = I_i^n$.

Lemma 4. *At the boundary points: If $I_1^n > I_2^n$ then $I_1^{n+1} < I_1^n$; if $I_N^n > I_{N-1}^n$ then $I_N^{n+1} < I_N^n$.*

Proof. Let us examine the point I_1^n. The Neumann BC dictates $DI_1^n = 0$. This condition is equivalent to extending the signal (to $i = 0$) and setting $I_0^n \equiv I_1^n$ for any n. Thus $D^2 I_1^n$ is well defined. As $I_1^n > I_2^n$ we get $D^2 I_1^n < 0$ and therefore $I_1^{n+1} < I_1^n$. Similar arguments are valid for the boundary point I_N^n.

Theorem 1

Proof. From Lemma 3 any local maximum point decreases after a finite number of steps. Similarly, it can be shown that any local minimum point increases after a finite number of steps. At steady state $I_i^{n+M} = I_i^n$ for any positive integer M, therefore it contains no local extrema. Lemma 4 forbids the maximum or minimum to be at the boundaries at steady state. We conclude that the only possible steady state solution is a constant function.

Proof of Theorem 2

All lemmas refer to the evolution of Eq. (13).

Lemma 5. *If I_i^n is an extrema point then $I_i^{n+1} = I_i^n$.*

Proof. Let us assume I_i^n is a maximum point: $I_i^n \geq I_{i-1}^n, I_{i+1}^n$. Therefore $DI_i^n = 0$ and we get $I_i^{n+1} = I_i^n$. The same applies for minimum points.

Lemma 6. *If I_i^n is a maximum/minimum point then I_i^{n+1} is a maximum/minimum point.*

Proof. Let us assume I_i^n is a maximum point: $I_i^n \geq I_{i-1}^n, I_{i+1}^n$. We should prove the relations at the next step are: $I_i^{n+1} \geq I_{i-1}^{n+1}, I_{i+1}^{n+1}$. We examine the point I_{i-1}^n. There are two possible cases: if I_{i-1}^n is an extrema point itself, then by Lemma 5 it is not changed and we have $I_i^{n+1} = I_i^n \geq I_{i-1}^n = I_{i-1}^{n+1}$. If I_{i-1}^n is not an extrema point then $I_i^n > I_{i-1}^n > I_{i-2}^n$, $DI_{i-1}^n \neq 0 \Rightarrow |\text{sign}(DI_{i-1}^n)| = 1$ and we get: $I_{i-1}^{n+1} = I_{i-1}^n + \Delta t[|I_{i-1}^n - I_i^n|/h + (I_i^n - 2I_{i-1}^n + I_{i-2}^n)/h^2]$. The last term $((..)/h^2)$ is negative. using the CFL relation: $\Delta t \leq 0.5 h^2 \leq 0.5 h$ for any $h \leq 1$ we get $I_{i-1}^{n+1} < I_{i-1}^n + 0.5(I_i^n - I_{i-1}^n) = 0.5(I_i^n + I_{i-1}^n) < I_i^n = I_i^{n+1}$. The same can be proven for I_{i+1}^{n+1} and similar arguments hold for minimum points.

From Lemmas 5,6 it follows that extrema points are stable and their value does not change through the evolution process. As extrema points are unchanged and no new local extrema are created - the scheme is TVP.

Theorem 3

The proof of this theorem is somewhat more lengthy and will appear in our technical report ([7]). The intuition behind it is that near inflection points the diffusion is weaker than the shock. Therefore in the evolution process there will be a point where $|D^2 I| < |DI|$ and the shock will prevent the inflection point from being vanished or moved.

References

1. L. Alvarez, L. Mazorra, "Signal and image restoration using shock filters and anisotropic diffusion", SIAM J. Numer. Anal. Vol. 31, No. 2, pp. 590-605, 1994.
2. F. Barbaresco, "Calcul des variations et analyse spectrale: equations de Fourier et de Burgers pour modeles autoregressifs regularises", Traitement du Signal, vol. 17, No. 5/6, 2000.
3. O. Coulon, S.R. Arridge, "Dual echo MR image processing using multi-spectral probabilistic diffusion coupled with shock filters", MIUA'2000, British Conference on Medical Image Understanding and Analysis, London, United-Kingdom, 2000.
4. G. Gilboa, Y.Y. Zeevi, N. Sochen, "Complex diffusion processes for image filtering", Michael Kerckhove (Ed.): Scale-Space 2001, LNCS 2106, pp. 299-307, Springer-Verlag 2001.
5. G. Gilboa, N. Sochen, Y.Y. Zeevi, "Image enhancement segmentation and denoising by time dependent nonlinear diffusion processes", ICIP-'01, Thessaloniki, Greece, October 2001.
6. G. Gilboa, N. Sochen, Y.Y. Zeevi, "Anisotropic selective inverse diffusion for signal enhancement in the presence of noise", Proc. IEEE ICASSP-2000, Istanbul, Turkey, vol. I, pp. 211-224, June 2000.
7. G. Gilboa, N. Sochen, Y.Y. Zeevi, "Complex diffusion for image filtering", CCIT Technical Report, Technion-IIT, Haifa, Israel - to appear.
8. F. Guichard, J-M. Morel, "A note on two classical shock filters and their asymptotics", M. Kerckhove (Ed.): Scale-Space 2001, LNCS 2106, pp. 75-84, Springer-Verlag 2001.
9. M. Kerckhove (Ed.), "Scale-Space and morphology in computer-vision", Scale-Space 2001, LNCS 2106, Springer-Verlag 2001.
10. P. Kornprobst, R. Deriche, G. Aubert, "Image coupling, restoration and enhancement via PDE's", Proc. Int. Conf. on Image Processing 1997, pp. 458–461, Santa-Barbara (USA), 1997.
11. S.J. Osher and L. I. Rudin, "Feature-oriented image enhancement using shock filters", SIAM J. Numer. Anal. 27, pp. 919-940, 1990.
12. N.Rougon, F.Preteux, "Controlled anisotropic diffusion", Proc. SPIE Conf. on Nonlinear Image Processing VI - IS&T / SPIE Symp. on Electronic Imaging, Science and Technology '95, San Jose, CA, Vol. 2424, 1995, pp. 329-340.
13. P. Perona and J. Malik, "Scale-space and edge detection using anisotropic diffusion", IEEE Trans. PAMI, vol. PAMI-12,no. 7, pp. 629-639, 1990.
14. B M ter Haar Romeny Ed., "Geometry driven diffusion in computer vision", Kluwer Academic Publishers, 1994.

Multi-view Matching for Unordered Image Sets, or "How Do I Organize My Holiday Snaps?"

F. Schaffalitzky and A. Zisserman

Robotics Research Group
University of Oxford
{fsm,az}@robots.ox.ac.uk

Abstract. There has been considerable success in automated reconstruction for image sequences where small baseline algorithms can be used to establish matches across a number of images. In contrast in the case of widely separated views, methods have generally been restricted to two or three views.

In this paper we investigate the problem of establishing relative viewpoints given a large number of images where no ordering information is provided. A typical application would be where images are obtained from different sources or at different times: both the viewpoint (position, orientation, scale) and lighting conditions may vary significantly over the data set.

Such a problem is not fundamentally amenable to exhaustive pair wise and triplet wide baseline matching because this would be prohibitively expensive as the number of views increases. Instead, we investiate how a combination of image invariants, covariants, and multiple view relations can be used in concord to enable efficient multiple view matching. The result is a matching algorithm which is linear in the number of views.

The methods are illustrated on several real image data sets. The output enables an image based technique for navigating in a 3D scene, moving from one image to whichever image is the next most appropriate.

1 Introduction

Our objective in this work is the following: given an unordered set of images, divide the data into clusters of related (i.e. from the same scene) image and determine the viewpoints of each image, thereby spatially organizing the image set. The need for solving this problem arises quite commonly. For example, the image set may have been acquired by a person photographing a scene (e.g. a castle or mountain) at various angles while walking back and forth around the area. Or the set may be the response from a query to an image database (e.g. a web search engine). Typical examples of such image sets are given in figures 1 and 2.

Much of the research on structure and motion recovery has concentrated on image sequences, and there are two consequences of this: first, there is an *ordering* on the image set, and it is natural to use this ordering, at least initially, in the processing; second, it has allowed small baseline algorithms to be used

Fig. 1. Fifteen images of the church in Valbonne, France.

Fig. 2. Fifteen images (from a set of 46) of Raglan Castle, Wales.

between consecutive frames of the sequence. Many successful systems strongly use this ordering [1,3,4] as a means of sewing together long feature tracks through the sequence and generating initial structure and camera estimates. Given these estimates further matches may then be sought between non-contiguous frames based on approximate spatial overlap of the views [7,17].

In our case we do not have an ordering, so there is no natural sequence in which to process the images, and also we cannot know *a priori* that between-view motions are small. Consequently we will require wide baseline matching methods [2,10,12,11,15,16,18,21,23,24] to compute multiview relations. In practice, computing view clusters will be difficult because wide baseline matching is difficult but in this paper we will see how far we can go by applying imperfect wide baseline stereo techniques to multi-view data sets.

How to proceed? We could attempt to mimic the image sequence (ordered set) processing paradigm and compute a fundamental matrix between all N-choose-2 views (using a suitable wide baseline algorithm), then follow this by computing trifocal geometry over all N-choose-3 views, and finally sew together the resulting matches into tracks throughout our view set. Clearly we would rather not do this as it will become prohibitively expensive as N increases – a complexity of at least $O(N^3)$ for trifocal geometry and to this must be added the cost of sewing together all three-view matches.

Instead we divide the problem into three stages: first (section 2) we develop an efficient indexing scheme based on invariant image patches. The output is a table of features vs views, so that for each feature point its putative matches over multiple views are known. The table at this stage will contain many ambiguous (i.e. not one-to-one matches) and many erroneous matches. The overall complexity of this stage is data dependent but the main parameter is the total number of features in the data set, which is linear in the number of images.

In the second stage (section 3) the quality of the matches is improved by a number of global "clean-up" operations such as selective use of two-view and three-view matching constraints. The output is a feature vs view table with considerably more correct matches, and fewer incorrect matches. The complexity of this stage, which is opportunistic, is linear in the number of views.

In the third stage (section 4) a 3D reconstruction of cameras and points is computed for connected sub-sets of views using the multiple view tracks. The difficulty is that between some views there will be no matches because the viewpoint footprints do not overlap or the images might even have been taken from two different scenes. In either case, the set of input images should be expected to split into clusters and the objective is to find those clusters, the larger the better.

Once the cameras are computed the images can be viewed coherently by embedding them in a VRML model, or by driving an image based renderer directly from the estimated scene geometry.

2 From Images to Multiview Matches

In this section our objective is to efficiently determine putative multiple view matches, i.e. a point correspondence over multiple images.

To achieve this we follow the, now standard, approach in the wide baseline literature, and start from features with viewpoint invariant descriptors. The viewpoint transformations which must be considered are an affine geometric transformation and an affine photometric transformation.

Features are determined in two stages: first, regions which transform covariantly with viewpoint are detected in each image, second, a vector of invariant descriptors is then computed for each region. The invariant vector is a label for that region, and will be used as an index into an indexing structure for matching between views — the corresponding region in other images will (ideally) have an identical vector.

These features are determined in all images independently. The descriptors for all images are then stored in the indexing structure. Features with 'close' descriptors establish a putative multiple view match. These steps are described in more detail in the following subsections.

Fig. 3. Invariant neighbourhood process. Left: close-up of original image. Middle: three detected interested points, their associated scale indicated by the size of the circles. Right: the corresponding affine-adapted neighbourhoods.

2.1 Covariant Regions

We use two types of features: one based on interest point neighbourhoods, the other based on the "Maximally Stable Extremal" (MSE) regions of Matas and Paleček [11]. Both features are described in more detail below. Each feature defines an elliptical region which is used to construct an invariant descriptor.

Invariant neighbourhoods: In each image independently we compute interest points, to each of which is associated a characteristic scale. The scale is computed using the method of [13] and is necessary in order to handle scale changes between the views. For each point we then attempt to compute an affine invariant neighbourhood using the method proposed by Baumberg [2]. The method is an adaptive procedure based on isotropy of the second moment gradient matrix [8]. If successful, the output is an image point with an elliptical neighbourhood which transforms co-variantly with viewpoint Similar neighbourhoods have been developed by Mikolajczyk and Schmid [14].

For a 768 × 512 image the number of neighbourhoods computed is typically 2000 but the number depends of course on the image. See figure 3 for an example. The computation of the neighbourhood generally succeeds at points where there is signal variation in more than one direction (e.g. near "blobs" or "corners").

To illustrate "what the computer sees", figure 4 shows just those parts of an image which are in a support region of some invariant neighbourhood.

Fig. 4. The support regions used to compute invariants are shown here using original image intensities. The representation is clearly dense and captures most of the salient image parts while discarding smooth regions, such as the sky. The large "sea" in the right-most image is a featureless lawn.

MSE regions: The regions are obtained by thresholding the intensity image and tracking the connected components as the threshold value changes. A MSE region is declared when the area of a component being tracked is approximately stationary. The idea (and implementation used here) is due to Matas and Paleček [11] (see figure 5 for an example). Typically the regions correspond to blobs of high contrast with respect to their surroundings. For example a dark window on a grey wall. Once the regions have been detected we construct ellipses by replacing each region by an ellipse with the same 2nd moments.

2.2 Choice of Invariant Descriptor

Given an elliptical image region which is co-variant with 2D affine transformations of the image, we wish to compute a description which is *invariant* to such geometric transformations *and* to 1D affine intensity transformations. The choice of descriptors we use is novel, and we now discuss this.

Invariance to affine lighting changes is achieved simply by shifting the signal's mean (taken over the invariant neighbourhood) to zero and then normalizing its power to unity.

The first step in obtaining invariance to image transformation is to affinely transform each neighbourhood by mapping it onto the unit disk. The process

Fig. 5. MSE regions (shown in white) detected in views 3 and 7 of the Valbonne data set.

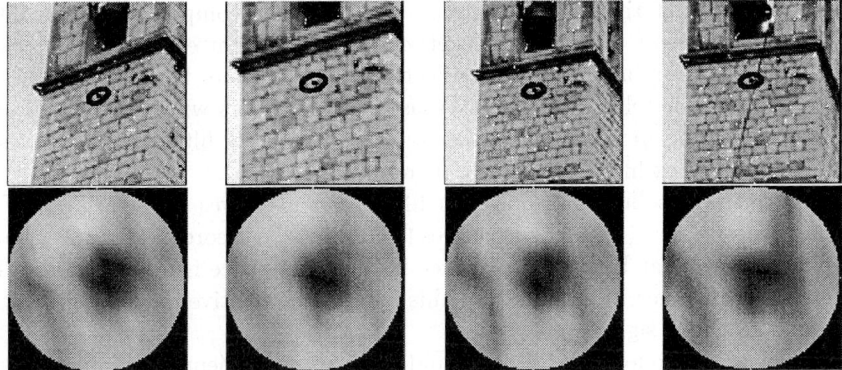

Fig. 6. Illustration of the invariant indexing stage. The query point is taken from the second image (from the left) and the hits found in the index structure are shown in the other images. Below each image is the corresponding affine normalized image patch. Note that the patches are approximately rotated versions of each other. This shows only four of the eight "hits" correctly found for this particular point.

is canonical except for a choice of rotation of the unit disk, so this device has reduced the problem from one of affine invariance to computing rotational invariants of a scalar function (the image intensity) defined on the unit disk. This idea was introduced by Baumberg in [2].

The objective of invariant indexing is to reduce the cost of search by discarding match candidates whose invariants are different. While two very different features can have similar invariants, similar features cannot have very different invariants. Conceptually, the "distance" in invariant space predicts a lower bound on the "distance" in feature space. Our invariant scheme is designed so that Euclidean distance between invariant vectors actually (and not just conceptually) provide a lower bound on the SSD difference between image patches. By contrast Schmid [20] and Baumberg [2] both learn a distance metric in invariant space from training data, which has the disadvantage of tuning the metric to the domain of training data.

We apply a bank of linear filters, similar to derivatives of a Gaussian, and compute rotational invariants from the filter responses. The filters used are derived from the family

$$K_{mn}(x,y) = (x+iy)^m (x-iy)^n G(x,y)$$

where $G(x,y)$ is a Gaussian. Under a rotation by an angle θ, the two complex quantities $z = x+iy$ and $\bar{z} = x-iy$ transform as $z \mapsto e^{i\theta}z$ and $\bar{z} \mapsto e^{-i\theta}\bar{z}$, so the effect on K_{mn} is simply multiplication by $e^{i(m-n)\theta}$. Along the "diagonal" given by $m-n = $ const the group action is the same and filters from different "diagonals" are orthogonal so if we orthonormalize each "diagonal" separately we arrive at a new filter bank with similar group action properties but which is also orthonormal. This filter bank differs from a bank of Gaussian derivatives by a linear coordinates change in filter response space. The advantage of our formulation is that the group acts separately on each component of the filter response and doesn't "mix" them together, which makes it easier to work with. Note that the group action doesn't affect the magnitude of filter responses but only changes their relative phases. We used all the filters with $m+n \leq 6$ and $m \geq n$ (swapping m nd n just gives complex conjugate filters) which gives a total of 16 complex filter responses per image patch.

Taking the absolute value of each filter response gives 16 invariants. The inequality $||z|-|w|| \leq |z-w|$ guarantees (by Parseval's theorem – the filter bank is orthonormal) that Euclidean distance in invariant space is a lower bound on image SSD difference. Unfortunately, this ignores the relative phase between the components of the signal.

Alternatively, following [13] one could estimate a gradient direction over the image patch and artifically "rotate" each coefficient vector to have the same gradient direction. This would give twice as many (32) invariants, but doesn't work well when the gradient is close to zero.

Instead, we find, among the coefficients for with $p = m - n \neq 0$ the one with the largest absolute value and artificially "rotate" the patch so as to make the phase 0 (i.e. the complex filter response is real and positive). When $p > 1$ there are p ways to do this (p roots of unity) and we just put all the p candidate invariant vectors into the index table. The property of distance in invariant space being a lower bound on image SSD error is also approximately true for this invariant scheme, the source of possible extra error coming from feature localization errors.

Summary: We have constructed, for each invariant neighbourhood, a feature vector which is invariant to affine intensity and image transformations. Morever, the Euclidean distance between feature vectors directly predicts a lower bound on the SSD distance between image patches, obviating the need to learn this connection empirically.

2.3 Invariant Indexing

By comparing the invariant vectors for each point over all views, potential matches may be hypothesized: i.e. a match is hypothesized if the invariant vectors of two points are within a threshold distance. See figure 6 for illustration. These are the "hits" in the indexing structure, and since each must be attended to, the overall complexity depends at the very least on the total number of hits.

Indexing structure: The query that we wish to support is "find all points within distance ε of this given point". We take ε to be one tenth of the image dynamic range (recall this is an image intensity SSD threshold).

For the experiments in this paper we used a binary space partition tree, found to be more time efficient than a k-d tree, despite the extra overhead. The high dimensionality of the invariant space (and it is generally the case that performance increases with dimension) rules out many indexing structures, such as R-trees, whose performances do not scale well with dimension.

2.4 Verification

Since two different patches may have similar invariant vectors, a "hit" match does not mean that the image regions are affine related. For our purposes two points are deemed matched if there exists an affine geometric and photometric transformation which registers the intensities of the elliptical neighbourhood within some tolerance. However, it is too expensive, and unecessary, to search exhaustively over affine transformations in order to verify every match. Instead we compute an approximate estimate of the local affine transformation between the neighbourhoods from the characteristic scale and invariants. If after this approximate registration the intensity at corresponding points in the neighbourhood differ by more than a threshold, or if the implied affine intensity change between the patches is outside a certain range, then the match can be rejected. Table 1 shows the time taken by, and the number of matches involved in, this process.

Table 1. Typical timings for the initial stages on a 2.0GHz Xeon processor. Most of the time is taking up by querying the index table, although it is an empirical observation that the majority of multi-tracks are small. Verification by correlation typically removes 30% of the putatives matches.

	Valbonne	Raglan
Total number of features	39544	402622
Intra-image hashing (ms)	8130	159400
Distintive features	37628	384068
Inter-image hashing (ms)	30760	2513520
Number of matches	14349	717721
Correlation (ms)	6930	313530
Number of matches	9168	332063

The outcome of the indexing and verification stages is a large collection of putative "multi-tracks"; a multi-track is simply the set of matches resulting from a query to the index table. A multi-track thus gives rise to a number of feature track hypotheses by selecting a subsets with at most one feature taken from each image. The index table matches two features if they merely "look" similar up to an affine transformation, so the possible putative tracks contain many false matches (e.g. one corner of a window in one image will match all the corner of the window in another image). To reduce the confusion, we only consider features which are "distinctive" in the sense that they have at most 5 intra-image matches. Thus, we use within-image matching (a process that is linear in the number of views) to reduces the cost inter-matching.

For the 15-image Valbonne sequence, the result of hashing and verification is summarized in table 7. Each entry counts the number of putative two-view matches implied by the list of multi-tracks. Note, this is only a *picture* of the feature vs view data structure; one could also generate from it an $N \times N \times N$ table of 3-view match counts, or 4-view match counts etc.

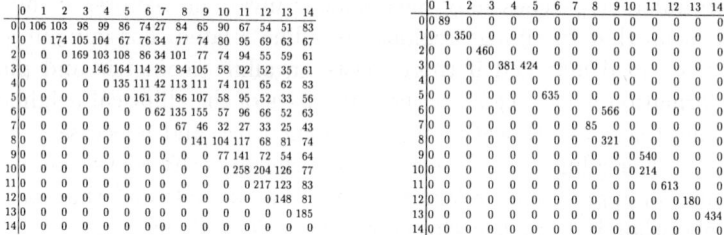

Fig. 7. Left: Number of initial two-view connections found between the view of the Valbonne image set. Right: Number of new two-view connections found (see section 3.3).

The problem now is that there are still many false matches. These can be resolved by robustly fitting multi-view constraints to the putative correspondences but to do so naively is prohibitively expensive since the number, say, of fundamental matrices is quadratic in the number of views. Instead, we will use the table to guide a heuristic for singling out pairs of views which it will be worth spending computational effort on.

For each pair of views that we do single out, we want out algorithm to have the best chance of working. This is the subject of the next section.

3 Improving the Multiview Matches

Given the putative multiple matches of section 2 our objective in this section is to build up a sufficient number of *correct* point matches between the views in order to support camera computation over a significant sub-set of the views. The computation of cameras from these matches is then the subject of section 4.

Our task here then is to "clean-up" the multiple view matches: remove erroneous and ambigous matches and add in new correct matches.

The matching constraint tools at our disposal range from semi-local to global across the image. Semi-local constraints are on how sets of neighbouring points transform (for example a similar photometric or geometric transformation), and global are the multi-view relations which apply to point matches globally across the image (such as epipolar and trifocal geometry). These constraints can be applied at various points and order in a matching strategy, and can be used both to generate new matches and to verify or refute existing matches.

The strategy we employ here is to improve the matches between selected view *pairs*. There are three steps (1) select view pair, (2) grow additional matches, (3) compute the epipolar geometry to reject incorrect matches. These three steps are described below.

However, it is important to note that in improving matches between a particular view pair has consequences for the matches between other pairs of images (by tracking a feature from view to view) in the view set. This is a key point because it means that a linear number of operations results in improvements that naively would require quadratic, or cubic etc time.

3.1 Growing Matches

Given a verified match between two views, the estimated affine transformation between the patches can be refined using direct photometric registration (similar to the Lucas-Kanade [9] algorithm) with correction for affine intensity changes. This verification is expensive as it involves a six-parameter (four geometric and two photometric) numerical optimization which is carried out using the Levenberg-Marquardt algorithm. Even a special-purpose implementation of this is quite slow and it is unwise to apply it indiscriminantly.

Once computed, the fitted local intensity registration provides information about the local orientation of the scene near the match; for example, if the camera is rotated about its optical axis, this will be reflected directly by cyclo-rotation in the local affine transformation. The local affine transformation can thus be used to guide the search for further matches. This idea of growing matches [16] enables matches which have been missed as hits, perhaps due to feature localization errors, to be recovered and is crucial in increasing the number of correspondences found to a sufficient level.

Growing is the opposite of the approach taken by several previous researchers [20,25], where the aim was to measure the consistency of matches of neighbouring points as a means of verifying or refuting a particular match. In our case we have a verified match and use this as a "seed" for growing. The objective is to obtain other verified matches in the neighbourhood, and then use these to grow still further matches etc.

We use the estimated affine transformation provided by the initial verified match to guide the search for further matches (see figure 8) which are then verified in the standard manner. Figure 9 demonstrates that many new matches can be generated from a single seed.

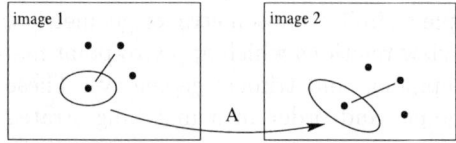

Fig. 8. Illustration of the use of local registration to guide the search for further matches.

Fig. 9. A seed match (left) and the 25 new matches grown from it (right).

3.2 Robust Global Verification

Having grown matches the next step is to use fundamental matrix estimation between pairs of views with a sufficient number of matches. This is a global method to reject outlying two-view matches between each pair of views. A novelty here is to use the affine transformations between the patches in the computation, by imposing the constraint that points transferred under the affine transformation agree with the fundamental matrix in an infinitesimal neighbourhood. The consequence is that only 3 points are needed for each RANSAC sample, as opposed to 7 if only the position of the point is used [6].

3.3 Greedy Algorithm

The next objective is to efficiently select pairs of views to process using two-view matching constraints in order to "clean up" the putative matches in the feature vs view table. Our approach will be to construct a spanning tree on the set of images in the data set. How do we select the edges of the tree? Starting from the pair of images with the most putative two-view matches, we robustly impose the epipolar constraint and then join up those images in the graph. Then we do the same for the pair of images with the highest number of two-view matches, subject to the constraint that joining those images will not create a cycle in the graph. If there are N images, the spanning tree will have $N - 1$ edges so this process is linear in the number of views.

Figure 10 shows the spanning tree obtained in this way and table 7 shows the difference between the number of two-view matches before and after this process has been applied to the Valbonne data set. It can be seen that in all cases considered, the number of matches increased, sometimes significantly. Once the spanning tree has been constructed, we delete any edges corresponding to fewer than 100 matches. In the Valbonne example, this has no effect but in

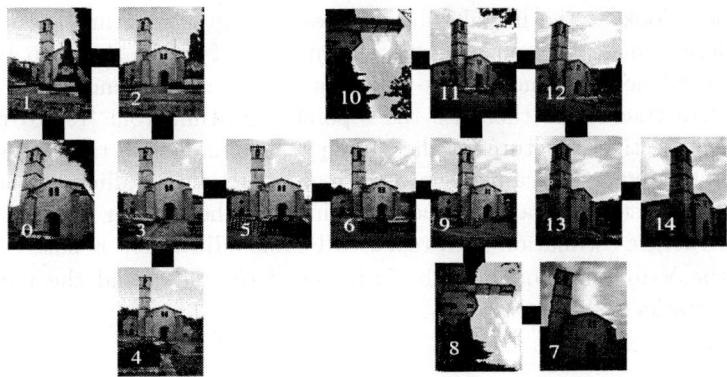

Fig. 10. Two-view connections found between the views of the Valbonne image set.

the Raglan data set it causes the graph to break into 11 connected components corresponding to distinct scenes, or views of the same scene that were difficult to match. In the next stage, each such component is treated separately.

In summary, we have described a method for singling out particular views for processing which allows us to split the data set into subsets that are likely to be related. The complexity of all stages is linear in the number of views. This process is of course sub-optimal compared to enforcing epipolar constraints between all pairs of images but on the data sets tried, it gives almost comparable performance.

4 From Matches to Cameras

The objective now is to compute cameras and scene structure for each of the components from the previous section separately. Our sub-goal is to find many long tracks (i.e. correspondences across many views) as this is likely to correlate with large a baseline, and a large baseline increases the chance of a successful reconstruction. To achieve this we use a greedy algorithm.

Since we wish to use the reconstruction as a means of spatially organizing the views we require a metric (or at least quasi-affine [5]) reconstruction, and we use the standard approach of first computing a projective reconstruction, followed by auto-calibration [6] using the constraint that the camera has square pixels.

Estimating cluster geometry: In general the cluster of views we are faced with will not have many complete tracks across them, which makes it necessary to compute structure for a sub-set of views first and then enlarge to more views using common scene points. The question is how to select the initial sub-set of views.

Our approach is to order the views in each component, again greedily, by starting with the pair with the most matches and sequentially adding in the next view with the largest number of matches, subject to it being adjacent to a view already included. Now we have an ordering on our image set.

We next look at the initial subsequences of length two, three, four, ... in each ordered image set and compute the number of tracks that can be made across the whole subsequence. We take the longest subsequence with at least 25 complete tracks and then use the 6-point algorithm from [19] to robustly compute projective structure for the subsequence, bundle and then sequentially re-section the remaining cameras into the reconstruction, bundling [22] as we go. The process of selecting a subsequence is linear in the number of views but, of course, structure estimation with repeated bundle adjustment is not.

For the Valbonne sequence, the ordering of the views and the number of complete tracks is shown in table 2.

Table 2. As the number k of views used increases, the number of complete tracks (those seen in all views) decreases. The number of reconstructed points tends to increase initially, then plateau and eventually decrease. A compromise must be reached.

k	views	tracks	points
2	11,12	377	377
3	9,11,12	94	423
4	6,9,11,12	52	666
5	5,6,9,11,12	33	869
6	3,5,6,9,11,12	18	1072
7	2,3,5,6,9,11,12	11	1208
8	2,3,4,5,6,9,11,12	8	1200
9	1,2,3,4,5,6,9,11,12	6	1319

For the resectioning it is important to have Euclidean reconstruction because when image overlap is small the scene is often nearly flat so one needs to make calibration assumptions in order to be able to re-section the cameras. We assume square pixels.

Overall we have moved from a sparse "backbone" of good two-view matches (end of section 3) to a "weaving" together of the views [7,17] via the computed structure. Instead of sparse connections between pairs of views we now have a global view of our data set, facilitated by being able to quickly look up relationships in the feature vs view table.

4.1 Results

In the case of the Valbonne image set the views have sufficient overlap to form a single cluster, but the Raglan image set splits into three clusters of size eight, five and two.

Valbonne: This is a 15 image set, and cameras are computed in a single reconstruction over all the views, shown in figure 11.

Raglan: This is a set of 46 images which breaks into several clusters, the largest consisting of 8 views. Some such clusters are shown if figures 12 and 13

5 Algorithm Summary

The strategy involves hypothesizing matches (the hash table) with hypotheses being refuted, verified or grown based on progressively more global image neighbourhood and multiple view constraints.

1. Detect two types of feature independently in each image, and compute their invariant descriptors.
2. Use hashing (followed by correlation, but no registration) to find initial putative matches and make a table counting two-view matches.
3. Greedy spanning tree growing stage:
    a) Choose the pair i, j of images with the largest number of matches, subject to i, j not already being in the same component.
    b) Apply full two-view matching to images i and j, that is:
        i. Increase correlation neighbourhood sizes if this improves the score.
        ii. Intensity based affine registration.
        iii. Growing using affine registrations.
        iv. Robustly fit epipolar geometry.
    c) Join images i and j in the graph.
    d) Repeat till only one component is left.
4. Form connected components of views as follows:
    a) Erase from the spanning tree all edges corresponding to fewer than 100 matches.
    b) Greedily grow connected components as before; this induces an ordering on the images in each component.
    c) From each ordered component, choose the largest initial subsequence of images with at least 25 complete tracks.
    d) Compute (Euclidean) structure for that subsequence.
    e) Re-section the remaining views into the reconstruction in order, bundling the structure and cameras at each stage.

5.1 Discussion, Conclusion, and Future Work

We have achieved our aim of constructing an $O(N)$ method of organizing an unordered image set. The algorithm is greedy but performs reasonably well. There are still plenty of issues to be addressed, though:

Three-view constraints: Applying two-view matching constraints exhaustively is expensive because there are $O(N^2)$ pairs of images and each computation is independent of the other. For three-view matching constraints there is a qualitative difference, which is that while there are $O(N^3)$ triples of images, the outcome of outlier rejection for one triplet *can* affect the outcome for another triplet (if the triplets share two views). Essentially, the RANSAC robust fitting is able to terminate more quickly as the number of mismatches is reduced. Empirically, it has been observed that the robust fits speed up towards the end of the set of triplets.

This is an example of how structure constraints reduce complexity of matching; quantifying when estimated structure is reliable enough to be used for guiding the matching is an important problem.

Once a spanning tree has been formed (e.g. by our greedy method) it might be beneficial to run a multi-view structure constraint filter "along" the tree to clear up bad matches. For example, at each vertex of the tree one could apply a filter to the vertex and its neighbours. The complexity of this would still be linear in the number of views.

Fig. 11. VRML model of the scene computed for the Valbonne image set. Note that the distribution of images in the computed scene reflects the impression of proximity, adjacency etc that one gets by looking at the original images. There number of 3D scene points is 1034.

Cleaning up the matches: The initial match candidates produced by the indexing structure are based on appearance alone so when trying to form tracks across a few images one is easy prey for mismatched features. The larger the set of images, the greater the risk of false matches. Applying two- or three-view matching constraints can help illuminate the global picture, though. For example, if we believe in the results of two-view matching between image A and B and between image B and C then we can infer matches between image A and C and also reject matches between these images that were previously putative. The practical difficulty with this sort of approach is knowing when estimated two- or three-view can be trusted for inference with and when it can't.

Image based viewer: Although our aim is to compute the cameras, and results are given for this below, if our only requirement is an approximate spatial organization (in terms of relations such as "to-the-left-of", or "a-close-up-of"),

Fig. 12. The largest cluster (8 views), for the Raglan image set, showing the interior of the hexagonal keep.

Fig. 13. Two smaller clustesr (5 views and 2 views) from the Raglan image set, the left one showing the exterior of the keep and the right one showing the top of the keep. Ideally the latter should have been connected to the 8-view cluster of views.

then simply computing homographies between the views and organizing the results with a spherical topology, will suffice. This is a sufficient basis for an image based navigator.

Variations and extensions: Our framework could be specialized (in transformation) by reducing the degree of invariance of the interest point neighbourhood descriptors (e.g. from affine to similarity only) or generalized (in scene type) by including other types of invariant descriptor, e.g. those developed by [12,21,23, 24].

Other heuristics: Section 2 outlined one strategy for obtaining sufficient multiview matches, and are now looking at other methods to quickly find subsets of hits that are likely to yield good structure estimates which can then be brought in earlier to guide matching, such as the voting techniques used by Schmid [20].

To conclude, we have achieved our objective of spatially organizing an unordered image set, and have set up a framework which is applicable to large data sets. We are currently investigating if the scheme can be extended as far as, say, video shot-matching where there can be thousands of shots in a single movie.

Acknowledgements. This paper is dedicated to Richard Szeliski. We are very grateful to Jiri Matas for supplying the MSE region code and to Andrew Fitzgibbon for his assistance with the structure-from-motion engine used for the experiments. The Valbonne images were provided by INRIA Sophia, and the Raglan images by Julian Morris. Funding was provided by Balliol College, Oxford, and EC project Vibes.

References

1. S. Avidan and A. Shashua. Threading fundamental matrices. In *Proc. ECCV*, pages 124–140. Springer-Verlag, 1998.
2. A. Baumberg. Reliable feature matching across widely separated views. In *Proc. CVPR*, pages 774–781, 2000.
3. P. Beardsley, P. Torr, and A. Zisserman. 3D model acquisition from extended image sequences. In *Proc. ECCV*, LNCS 1064/1065, pages 683–695. Springer-Verlag, 1996.
4. A. W. Fitzgibbon and A. Zisserman. Automatic camera recovery for closed or open image sequences. In *Proc. ECCV*, pages 311–326. Springer-Verlag, Jun 1998.
5. R. Hartley, L. de Agapito, E. Hayman, and I. Reid. Camera calibration and the search for infinity. In *Proc. ICCV*, pages 510–517, September 1999.
6. R. I. Hartley and A. Zisserman. *Multiple View Geometry in Computer Vision*. Cambridge University Press, ISBN: 0521623049, 2000.
7. R. Koch, M. Pollefeys, B. Heigl, L. Van Gool, and H. Niemann. Calibration of hand-held camera sequences for plenoptic modeling. In *Proc. ICCV*, pages 585–591, 1999.
8. T. Lindeberg and J. Gårding. Shape-adapted smoothing in estimation of 3-d depth cues from affine distortions of local 2-d brightness structure. In *Proc. ECCV*, pages 389–400, May 1994.
9. B. D. Lucas and T. Kanade. An iterative image registration technique with an application to stereo vision. In *Proc. of the 7th International Joint Conference on Artificial Intelligence*, pages 674–679, 1981.
10. J. Matas, J. Burianek, and J. Kittler. Object recognition using the invariant pixel-set signature. In *Proc. BMVC.*, pages 606–615, 2000.

11. J. Matas, O. Chum, and T. Urban, M. an Pajdla. Distinguished regions for widebaseline stereo. Research Report CTU–CMP–2001–33, Center for Machine Perception, K333 FEE Czech Technical University, Prague, Czech Republic, November 2001.
12. J Matas, M Urban, and T Pajdla. Unifying view for wide-baseline stereo. In B Likar, editor, *Proc. Computer Vision Winter Workshop*, pages 214–222, Ljubljana, Sloveni, February 2001. Slovenian Pattern Recorgnition Society.
13. K. Mikolajczyk and C. Schmid. Indexing based on scale invariant interest points. In *Proc. ICCV*, 2001.
14. K. Mikolajczyk and C. Schmid. An affine invariant interest point detector. In *Proc. ECCV*. Springer-Verlag, 2002.
15. P. Pritchett and A. Zisserman. Matching and reconstruction from widely separated views. In R. Koch and L. Van Gool, editors, *3D Structure from Multiple Images of Large-Scale Environments, LNCS 1506*, pages 78–92. Springer-Verlag, Jun 1998.
16. P. Pritchett and A. Zisserman. Wide baseline stereo matching. In *Proc. ICCV*, pages 754–760, Jan 1998.
17. H. S. Sawhney, S. Hsu, and R. Kumar. Robust video mosaicing through topology inference and local to global alignment. In *Proc. ECCV*, pages 103–119. Springer-Verlag, 1998.
18. F. Schaffalitzky and A. Zisserman. Viewpoint invariant texture matching and wide baseline stereo. In *Proc. ICCV*, Jul 2001.
19. F. Schaffalitzky, A. Zisserman, Hartley, R. I., and P. H. S. Torr. A six point solution for structure and motion. In *Proc. ECCV*, pages 632–648. Springer-Verlag, Jun 2000.
20. C. Schmid and R. Mohr. Local greyvalue invariants for image retrieval. *IEEE PAMI*, 19(5):530–534, May 1997.
21. D. Tell and S. Carlsson. Wide baseline point matching using affine invariants computed from intensity profiles. In *Proc. ECCV*. Springer-Verlag, Jun 2000.
22. W. Triggs, P. McLauchlan, R. Hartley, and A. Fitzgibbon. Bundle adjustment: A modern synthesis. In W. Triggs, A. Zisserman, and R. Szeliski, editors, *Vision Algorithms. Theory and Practice*, LNCS. Springer Verlag, 2000.
23. T. Tuytelaars and L. Van Gool. Content-based image retrieval based on local affinely invariant regions. In *Int. Conf. on Visual Information Systems*, pages 493–500, 1999.
24. T. Tuytelaars and L. Van Gool. Wide baseline stereo matching based on local, affinely invariant regions. In *Proc. BMVC.*, pages 412–425, 2000.
25. Z. Zhang, R. Deriche, O. D. Faugeras, and Q.-T. Luong. A robust technique for matching two uncalibrated images through the recovery of the unknown epipolar geometry. *Artificial Intelligence*, 78:87–119, 1995.

Parameter Estimates for a Pencil of Lines: Bounds and Estimators

Gavriel Speyer and Michael Werman

Computer Science, The Hebrew University, Jerusalem.
Gavriel_Speyer@amat.com, werman@cs.huji.ac.il

Abstract. Estimating the parameters of a pencil of lines is addressed. A statistical model for the measurements is developed, from which the Cramer Rao lower bound is determined. An estimator is derived, and its performance is simulated and compared to the bound. The estimator is shown to be asymptotically efficient, and superior to the classical least squares algorithm.

1 Introduction

Identifying straight lines and estimating their common point of intersection is a frequent task in image processing applications. The particular problem of estimating the parameters of a single line from two dimensional measurements has been studied in [1], [4], [8]. When multiple lines are known to intersect at a common point, however, parameter estimates for a given line can be improved owing to the common information available from the other lines. Moreover, the structure of the estimator changes from that presented in [1] and [8]. It is the purpose of this paper to present the line parameter estimation problem by providing a parameterized statistical model of the measurements, analyzing the limitations imposed by this model on the line parameter estimates, and finally by proposing an estimator for the line parameters.

The analysis begins in Section 2, where the measurements of points on a line are statistically modelled by the parameters of interest. In Section 3, parameter estimation is addressed by using the parameterized statistical model of Section 2 to determine the Fisher information matrix for the line parameters. From the Fisher information matrix, the Cramer-Rao lower bounds for line parameter estimates are determined explicitly in terms of the line parameters and the statistical parameters influencing the measurements. Section 4 addresses the problem of estimating line parameters from a pencil of lines when each of these lines is modelled according to Section 2. The methods of Section 3 are used to find the Fisher information matrix for the totality of line parameters and their point of intersection. The performance benefit attained by using a mutual point of intersection is reflected in the Cramer Rao lower bound, which is compared with the results of Section 3. An estimator for the point of intersection and the respective line parameters is then developed in Section 5. In Section 6 the performance of this estimator is simulated and compared with the Cramer Rao lower bounds from Sections 3 and 4. In addition, the proposed estimator is compared with the least squares estimator for the point of intersection when the lines are parameterized independently of each other.

2   The Line Data Model

One method for fitting two dimensional point measurements to a line is proposed by Ponce and Forsyth in [1]. The N line measurements (x_n, y_n), $n = 1, \ldots, N$ in the coordinate system (x, y) are modelled as a rotation by ϕ of points (χ_n, γ_n), $n = 1, \ldots, N$ in an initial coordinate system (χ, γ). In (χ, γ) coordinates, a line is assumed to be described by $\gamma = A$, although the measurements γ_n are perturbed from A by zero mean noise ν_n. Thus, line modelling begins with the transformation by coordinate rotation

$$\begin{bmatrix} x_n \\ y_n \end{bmatrix} = \begin{bmatrix} \cos\phi & \sin\phi \\ -\sin\phi & \cos\phi \end{bmatrix} \begin{bmatrix} \chi_n \\ \gamma_n \end{bmatrix}$$
$$= \begin{bmatrix} b & a \\ -a & b \end{bmatrix} \begin{bmatrix} \chi_n \\ A + \nu_n \end{bmatrix}$$
$$= -\mathbf{S} \begin{bmatrix} \chi_n \\ c - \nu_n \end{bmatrix} \quad (1)$$

where the rotation matrix $\mathbf{S}$ is given by

$$\mathbf{S} = \begin{bmatrix} -b & a \\ a & b \end{bmatrix} \quad (2)$$

and

$$\begin{bmatrix} a \\ b \\ c \end{bmatrix} = \begin{bmatrix} \sin\phi \\ \cos\phi \\ -A \end{bmatrix} \quad (3)$$

In this notation, a line is described in (x, y) coordinates by $ax + by + c = 0$.

In order to model the points (x_n, y_n) statistically, it is sufficient to characterize χ_n and ν_n, as (x_n, y_n) are related to these by the linear transformation (1). For simplicity of analysis, assume the noise samples ν_n to be zero mean, independent, and identically distributed Gaussian random variables with variance σ_ν^2, and denote this distribution by $\nu_n \sim N(0, \sigma_\nu^2)$, $n = 1, \ldots, N$. Similarly, the coordinates χ_n are assumed to be independent and identically distributed samples from a Gaussian distribution having mean μ_χ and variance σ_χ^2, such that $\chi_n \sim N(\mu_\chi, \sigma_\chi^2)$, $n = 1, \ldots, N$. As σ_ν^2 is the measurement noise and σ_χ^2 the spread of the points on the line, it must be that $\sigma_\chi^2 \gg \sigma_\nu^2$.

As the two random variables ν_n and χ_n are Gaussian and independent, they are jointly Gaussian [3]. Thus, the vector $\mathbf{z}_n = \begin{bmatrix} x_n & y_n \end{bmatrix}^T$ has Gaussian distribution $\mathbf{z}_n \sim N(\boldsymbol{\mu}_z, \mathbf{C}_z)$ with mean vector $\boldsymbol{\mu}_z = E\{\mathbf{z}_n\}$ found from (1) as

$$\boldsymbol{\mu}_z = -\mathbf{S} \begin{bmatrix} \mu_\chi \\ c \end{bmatrix} \quad (4)$$

The correlation matrix $\mathbf{C_z}$ is found from equations (1) and (4), and by noting that by the independence of χ_n and ν_n, $E\{(\chi_n - \mu_\chi)\nu_n\} = E\{\chi_n - \mu_\chi\}E\{\nu_n\} = 0$.

$$\begin{aligned}\mathbf{C_z} &= E\left\{\mathbf{S}\begin{bmatrix}\chi_n - \mu_\chi \\ -\nu_n\end{bmatrix}\begin{bmatrix}\chi_n - \mu_\chi \\ -\nu_n\end{bmatrix}^T \mathbf{S}^T\right\} \\ &= \mathbf{S}\begin{bmatrix}\sigma_\chi^2 & 0 \\ 0 & \sigma_\nu^2\end{bmatrix}\mathbf{S}^T \\ &= \mathbf{S}\Lambda\mathbf{S}^T\end{aligned} \quad (5)$$

Since the matrix $\mathbf{S}$ is unitary and diagonalizes $\mathbf{C_z}$, it holds the eigenvectors of $\mathbf{C_z}$. From (2) and (5), the eigenvector $[a\ b]^T$ of $\mathbf{S}$ is associated with the eigenvalue σ_ν^2, the variance of the measurement noise.

The joint statistics of z_n can be expressed succinctly in terms of the concatenation vector Z given by

$$Z = \begin{bmatrix}z_1^T & z_2^T & \cdots & z_N^T\end{bmatrix}^T \quad (6)$$

The measurements z_n are jointly Gaussian, so the vector Z has Gaussian distribution $Z \sim N(\boldsymbol{\mu_Z}, \mathbf{C_Z})$. The mean $\boldsymbol{\mu_Z} = E\{Z\}$ is given by the $2N \times 1$ vector

$$\boldsymbol{\mu_Z} = \begin{bmatrix}\boldsymbol{\mu_z}^T & \cdots & \boldsymbol{\mu_z}^T\end{bmatrix}^T \quad (7)$$

By virtue of the independent and identically distributed nature of the random variables ν_n and χ_n, $E\{\nu_n\nu_m\} = \sigma_\nu^2 \delta_{n-m}$ and $E\{(\chi_n - \mu_\chi)(\chi_m - \mu_\chi)\} = \sigma_\nu^2 \delta_{n-m}$, where δ_n is the Dirac function. The $2N \times 2N$ covariance matrix $\mathbf{C_Z}$ is then given by

$$\mathbf{C_Z} = \begin{bmatrix}\mathbf{C_z} & 0 & \cdots & 0 \\ 0 & \mathbf{C_z} & & 0 \\ \vdots & & \ddots & \vdots \\ 0 & 0 & \cdots & \mathbf{C_z}\end{bmatrix} \quad (8)$$

3 Cramer Rao Bounds for Line Parameter Estimates Given a Single Line

Having statistically characterized the joint distribution of the samples (x_n, y_n), $n = 1, \ldots, N$, the influence of this statistical model on parameter estimates can be determined. First, note from equations (2), (4) and (5) that the mean vector $\boldsymbol{\mu_z}$ and covariance matrix $\mathbf{C_z}$ are seen to be functions of the parameters ϕ, c, μ_χ, σ_χ^2, and σ_ν^2, denoted by the vector $\boldsymbol{\theta}$ as

$$\boldsymbol{\theta} = \begin{bmatrix}\phi & c & \mu_\chi & \sigma_\chi^2 & \sigma_\nu^2\end{bmatrix}^T \quad (9)$$

Since the random vectors z_n have the Gaussian distribution $z_n \sim N(\boldsymbol{\mu}_z(\boldsymbol{\theta}), \mathbf{C}_z(\boldsymbol{\theta}))$ for any choice of $\boldsymbol{\theta}$, the random vector $\mathbf{Z}$, by (7) and (8), is also statistically parameterized as $\mathbf{Z} \sim N(\boldsymbol{\mu}_Z(\boldsymbol{\theta}), \mathbf{C}_Z(\boldsymbol{\theta}))$. The random vectors z_n, $n = 1, \ldots, N$ and $\mathbf{Z}$ are therefore called Generalized Gaussian random vectors [2]. The significance of this characterization lies in the fact that the parameters $\boldsymbol{\theta}$ are assumed deterministic and unknown, like the line parameters in (3), for example, which are being estimated. Estimates of fixed parameters, like the components of $\boldsymbol{\theta}$, have their minimum variance bounded by the Cramer Rao Lower Bound (CRLB), which is determined by relating the $K \times K$ covariance matrix $\mathbf{C}_{\hat{\boldsymbol{\theta}}}$ of the K unbiased parameter estimates $\hat{\boldsymbol{\theta}}$ to the inverse Fisher information matrix $\mathbf{I}^{-1}(\boldsymbol{\theta})$ as [2]

$$\mathbf{C}_{\hat{\boldsymbol{\theta}}} \geq \mathbf{I}^{-1}(\boldsymbol{\theta}) \tag{10}$$

So that for each estimate $\hat{\theta}_i$ of the true parameter θ_i, the variance $\sigma_{\hat{\theta}_i}^2$ is given by $\mathbf{C}_{\hat{\boldsymbol{\theta}}}(i,i)$, and the CRLB by $\mathbf{I}^{-1}(\boldsymbol{\theta})(i,i)$. For the case of a Generalized Gaussian random vector $\mathbf{X} \sim N(\boldsymbol{\mu}_X(\boldsymbol{\theta}), \mathbf{C}_X(\boldsymbol{\theta}))$, the elements of $\mathbf{I}(\boldsymbol{\theta})$ are given by [2], equation (3.31)

$$[\mathbf{I}(\boldsymbol{\theta})]_{ij} = \left[\frac{\partial \boldsymbol{\mu}_X(\boldsymbol{\theta})}{\partial \theta_i}\right]^T \mathbf{C}_X^{-1}(\boldsymbol{\theta}) \left[\frac{\partial \boldsymbol{\mu}_X(\boldsymbol{\theta})}{\partial \theta_j}\right] \\ + \frac{1}{2}\mathrm{tr}\left[\mathbf{C}_X^{-1}(\boldsymbol{\theta}) \frac{\partial \mathbf{C}_X(\boldsymbol{\theta})}{\partial \theta_i} \mathbf{C}_X^{-1}(\boldsymbol{\theta}) \frac{\partial \mathbf{C}_X(\boldsymbol{\theta})}{\partial \theta_j}\right] \tag{11}$$

where $\mathrm{tr}[\mathbf{D}]$ denotes the trace of the matrix $\mathbf{D}$, and $\partial \boldsymbol{\mu}_X(\boldsymbol{\theta})/\partial \theta_j$ is the partial derivative of every element in the mean vector $\boldsymbol{\mu}_X(\boldsymbol{\theta})$ with respect to the jth element of the parameter vector $\boldsymbol{\theta}$, just as $\partial \mathbf{C}_X(\boldsymbol{\theta})/\partial \theta_i$ is the partial derivative of every component of the covariance matrix $\mathbf{C}_X(\boldsymbol{\theta})$ with respect to the ith element of $\boldsymbol{\theta}$.

Applying (11) to the measurements $\mathbf{Z} \sim N(\boldsymbol{\mu}_Z(\boldsymbol{\theta}), \mathbf{C}_Z(\boldsymbol{\theta}))$ with (7) and (8), then the elements $[\mathbf{I}(\boldsymbol{\theta})]_{ij}$ are found as

$$[\mathbf{I}(\boldsymbol{\theta})]_{ij} = N \left[\frac{\partial \boldsymbol{\mu}_z(\boldsymbol{\theta})}{\partial \theta_i}\right]^T \mathbf{C}_z^{-1}(\boldsymbol{\theta}) \left[\frac{\partial \boldsymbol{\mu}_z(\boldsymbol{\theta})}{\partial \theta_j}\right] \\ + \frac{N}{2}\mathrm{tr}\left[\mathbf{C}_z^{-1}(\boldsymbol{\theta}) \frac{\partial \mathbf{C}_z(\boldsymbol{\theta})}{\partial \theta_i} \mathbf{C}_z^{-1}(\boldsymbol{\theta}) \frac{\partial \mathbf{C}_z(\boldsymbol{\theta})}{\partial \theta_j}\right] \tag{12}$$

Equation (12) states that the Fisher information matrix for N measurements z_n is that for a single measurement scaled by N.

Noting from (2) that $\mathbf{S}^T = \mathbf{S}$, the following identities from (5) make determining the components of (11) straightforward

$$\frac{\partial \mathbf{C}_z}{\partial \phi} = \frac{\partial \mathbf{S}}{\partial \phi} \boldsymbol{\Lambda} \mathbf{S} + \mathbf{S} \boldsymbol{\Lambda} \frac{\partial \mathbf{S}}{\partial \phi} \tag{13}$$

$$\mathbf{S}\mathbf{S}^T = \mathbf{S}^T\mathbf{S} = \begin{bmatrix} 1 & 0 \\ 0 & 1 \end{bmatrix} \tag{14}$$

$$S\frac{\partial S}{\partial \phi} = \begin{bmatrix} 0 & -1 \\ 1 & 0 \end{bmatrix} \quad (15)$$

$$\frac{\partial S}{\partial \phi}S = \begin{bmatrix} 0 & 1 \\ -1 & 0 \end{bmatrix} \quad (16)$$

$$C_z^{-1} = S\Lambda^{-1}S \quad (17)$$

By applying the identities (13) through (17) in (12) for all combinations of the parameter elements in (9), it can be shown that the Fisher information matrix takes the form

$$\mathbf{I}(\boldsymbol{\theta}) = \begin{bmatrix} \mathbf{I}(\phi, c, \mu_\chi) & 0 \\ 0 & \mathbf{I}(\sigma_\chi^2, \sigma_\nu^2) \end{bmatrix} \quad (18)$$

The block diagonal structure of (18) implies that the inverse of (18) is similarly block diagonal, so that to find the bounds on estimating the line parameters ϕ, c, and μ_χ, one need only consider the Fisher information matrix $\mathbf{I}(\phi, c, \mu_\chi)$. This matrix is found as

$$\mathbf{I}(\phi, \mathbf{c}, \mu_\chi) = \frac{N}{\sigma_\nu^2 \sigma_\chi^2} \begin{bmatrix} \sigma_\chi^2 \mu_\chi^2 + c^2 \sigma_\nu^2 + \left(\sigma_\nu^2 - \sigma_\chi^2\right)^2 & \mu_\chi \sigma_\chi^2 & -c\sigma_\nu^2 \\ \mu_\chi \sigma_\chi^2 & \sigma_\chi^2 & 0 \\ -c\sigma_\nu^2 & 0 & \sigma_\nu^2 \end{bmatrix} \quad (19)$$

and the inverse is given by

$$\mathbf{I}(\phi, \mathbf{c}, \mu_\chi)^{-1} = \frac{1}{N\left(\sigma_\nu^2 - \sigma_\chi^2\right)^2} \begin{bmatrix} \sigma_\chi^2 \sigma_\nu^2 & -\mu_\chi \sigma_\chi^2 \sigma_\nu^2 & c\sigma_\chi^2 \sigma_\nu^2 \\ -\mu_\chi \sigma_\chi^2 \sigma_\nu^2 & \kappa_1 & -c\mu_\chi \sigma_\chi^2 \sigma_\nu^2 \\ c\sigma_\chi^2 \sigma_\nu^2 & -c\mu_\chi \sigma_\chi^2 \sigma_\nu^2 & \kappa_2 \end{bmatrix} \quad (20)$$

where $\kappa_1 = \sigma_\nu^2 \left[\sigma_\chi^2 \mu_\chi^2 + \left(\sigma_\nu^2 - \sigma_\chi^2\right)^2\right]$ and $\kappa_2 = \sigma_\chi^2 \left[c^2 \sigma_\nu^2 + \left(\sigma_\nu^2 - \sigma_\chi^2\right)^2\right]$. From (20), the CRLB for any estimate $\hat{\phi}$ of the rotation angle ϕ is given by the first diagonal entry

$$\text{CRLB}\left(\hat{\phi}\right) = \frac{\sigma_\nu^2 \sigma_\chi^2}{N\left(\sigma_\chi^2 - \sigma_\nu^2\right)^2} \quad (21)$$

To find the CRLB for the parameter estimates of $a = \sin\phi$, $b = \cos\phi$, and $c = c$ from (3), we use [2] p45 (3.30)

$$\mathbf{I}^{-1}(\mathbf{g}(\boldsymbol{\theta})) = \frac{\partial \mathbf{g}(\boldsymbol{\theta})}{\partial \boldsymbol{\theta}} \mathbf{I}^{-1}(\boldsymbol{\theta}) \frac{\partial \mathbf{g}(\boldsymbol{\theta})}{\partial \boldsymbol{\theta}}^T \quad (22)$$

which determines the inverse of the Fisher information matrix for estimating the functions $\mathbf{g}(\boldsymbol{\theta}) = \begin{bmatrix} g_1(\boldsymbol{\theta}) & g_2(\boldsymbol{\theta}) & \cdots & g_r(\boldsymbol{\theta}) \end{bmatrix}$ of the parameter vector $\boldsymbol{\theta}$ from the inverse of the Fisher information matrix for $\boldsymbol{\theta}$ itself. The matrix $\partial \mathbf{g}(\boldsymbol{\theta})/\partial \boldsymbol{\theta}$ in (22) is the $r \times p$ Jacobian matrix

$$\frac{\partial \mathbf{g}(\boldsymbol{\theta})}{\partial \boldsymbol{\theta}} = \begin{bmatrix} \frac{\partial g_1(\boldsymbol{\theta})}{\partial \theta_1} & \frac{\partial g_1(\boldsymbol{\theta})}{\partial \theta_2} & \cdots & \frac{\partial g_1(\boldsymbol{\theta})}{\partial \theta_p} \\ \frac{\partial g_2(\boldsymbol{\theta})}{\partial \theta_1} & \frac{\partial g_2(\boldsymbol{\theta})}{\partial \theta_2} & \cdots & \frac{\partial g_2(\boldsymbol{\theta})}{\partial \theta_p} \\ \vdots & \vdots & \ddots & \vdots \\ \frac{\partial g_r(\boldsymbol{\theta})}{\partial \theta_1} & \frac{\partial g_r(\boldsymbol{\theta})}{\partial \theta_2} & \cdots & \frac{\partial g_r(\boldsymbol{\theta})}{\partial \theta_p} \end{bmatrix} \quad (23)$$

Letting $\mathbf{g}(\boldsymbol{\theta}) = \begin{bmatrix} a & b & c \end{bmatrix}$ as in (3), then substitution into (23) yields

$$\frac{\partial [a\,b\,c]}{\partial \boldsymbol{\theta}} = \begin{bmatrix} \cos\phi & 0 & 0 \\ -\sin\phi & 0 & 0 \\ 0 & 1 & 0 \end{bmatrix} \tag{24}$$

Applying (22) with (20) and (24) and noting (21) yields

$$\mathbf{I}^{-1}(a,b,c) = \mathrm{CRLB}\left(\hat{\phi}\right) \begin{bmatrix} \cos^2\phi & -\sin\phi\cos\phi & -\mu_x\cos\phi \\ -\sin\phi\cos\phi & \sin^2\phi & \mu_x\sin\phi \\ -\mu_x\cos\phi & \mu_x\sin\phi & \mu_x^2 + \frac{\sigma_\nu^2}{N\mathrm{CRLB}(\hat{\phi})} \end{bmatrix} \tag{25}$$

The terms along the main diagonal in (25) are the Cramer Rao lower bounds on the variance of the line parameter estimates $\hat{a}$, $\hat{b}$, and $\hat{c}$, respectively.

$$\begin{bmatrix} \sigma_{\hat{a}}^2 \\ \sigma_{\hat{b}}^2 \\ \sigma_{\hat{c}}^2 \end{bmatrix} \geq \begin{bmatrix} b^2 \mathrm{CRLB}\left(\hat{\phi}\right) \\ a^2 \mathrm{CRLB}\left(\hat{\phi}\right) \\ \mu_x^2 \mathrm{CRLB}\left(\hat{\phi}\right) + \frac{\sigma_\nu^2}{N} \end{bmatrix} \tag{26}$$

4 Cramer Rao Bounds for Line Parameter Estimates Given a Pencil of Lines

The results of the previous section can be extended to find the influence of a common point of intersection (x_0, y_0) on line parameter estimates for a pencil of L lines. In this case, each line ℓ, $\ell = 1, \ldots, L$ has associated with it a distinct group of data $\mathbf{Z}_\ell$ of the form (6), each having N_ℓ two dimensional data points z_{n_ℓ}. The fact that the data families $\mathbf{Z}_\ell$, $\ell = 1, \ldots, L$ are all distinct means that the noise models that generate them, as in (1), are all independent. The vectors $\mathbf{Z}_\ell$, $\ell = 1, \ldots, L$ are jointly Gaussian with

$$E\left\{(\mathbf{Z}_\ell - \boldsymbol{\mu}_{\mathbf{Z}_\ell})(\mathbf{Z}_k - \boldsymbol{\mu}_{\mathbf{Z}_k})^T\right\} = \delta_{\ell-k}\mathbf{C}_{\mathbf{Z}_\ell} \tag{27}$$

where $\mathbf{C}_{\mathbf{Z}_\ell}$, $\ell = 1, \ldots, L$ are of the form (8). A vector $\mathbf{Q}$ defined as the concatenation of the measurements $\mathbf{Z}_\ell$, $\ell = 1, \ldots, L$ such that

$$\mathbf{Q} = \begin{bmatrix} \mathbf{Z}_1^T & \cdots & \mathbf{Z}_L^T \end{bmatrix}^T \tag{28}$$

is therefore distributed as $\mathbf{Q} \sim N(\boldsymbol{\mu}_\mathbf{Q}, \mathbf{C}_\mathbf{Q})$ with mean vector $\boldsymbol{\mu}_\mathbf{Q} = E\{\mathbf{Q}\}$

$$\boldsymbol{\mu}_\mathbf{Q} = \begin{bmatrix} \boldsymbol{\mu}_{\mathbf{Z}_1}^T & \cdots & \boldsymbol{\mu}_{\mathbf{Z}_L}^T \end{bmatrix}^T \tag{29}$$

and, using (27), the covariance matrix $\mathbf{C}_\mathbf{Q}$ is

$$\mathbf{C}_\mathbf{Q} = \begin{bmatrix} \mathbf{C}_{\mathbf{Z}_1} & 0 & \cdots & 0 \\ 0 & \mathbf{C}_{\mathbf{Z}_2} & & 0 \\ \vdots & & \ddots & \vdots \\ 0 & 0 & \cdots & \mathbf{C}_{\mathbf{Z}_L} \end{bmatrix} \tag{30}$$

By substitution of $\boldsymbol{Q}$ in (11), and using (29) and (30), its not hard to show that the elements of the Fisher Information matrix are given by

$$[\mathbf{I}(\boldsymbol{\vartheta})]_{ij} = \sum_{\ell=0}^{L} N_\ell \left[\frac{\partial \boldsymbol{\mu}_{z_\ell}(\boldsymbol{\vartheta})}{\partial \vartheta_i}\right]^T \mathbf{C}_{z_\ell}^{-1}(\boldsymbol{\vartheta}) \left[\frac{\partial \boldsymbol{\mu}_{z_\ell}(\boldsymbol{\vartheta})}{\partial \vartheta_j}\right]$$
$$+ \frac{N_\ell}{2} \text{tr}\left[\mathbf{C}_{z_\ell}^{-1}(\boldsymbol{\vartheta}) \frac{\partial \mathbf{C}_{z_\ell}(\boldsymbol{\vartheta})}{\partial \vartheta_i} \mathbf{C}_{z_\ell}^{-1}(\boldsymbol{\vartheta}) \frac{\partial \mathbf{C}_{z_\ell}(\boldsymbol{\vartheta})}{\partial \vartheta_j}\right] \quad (31)$$

where $\boldsymbol{\mu}_{z_\ell}$ and $\mathbf{C}_{z_\ell}$ are from (4) and (5). The parameter vector $\boldsymbol{\vartheta}$ holds the parameter vectors $\boldsymbol{\theta}_\ell$ defined in (9) for each family of line data $\ell = 1, \ldots, L$. This parameter space is reduced for the pencil of lines by noting that the common point of intersection (x_0, y_0) lies on each of the L lines, and thus satisfies $a_\ell x_0 + b_\ell y_0 + c_\ell = 0$, $\ell = 1, \ldots, L$. Thus, $c_\ell = -a_\ell x_0 - b_\ell y_0$ and the parameter vector $\boldsymbol{\vartheta}$ is given by

$$\boldsymbol{\vartheta} = \begin{bmatrix} \phi_1 \; \mu_{\chi_1} \; \sigma_{\nu_1}^2 \; \sigma_{\chi_1}^2 \; \cdots \; \phi_L \; \mu_{\chi_L} \; \sigma_{\nu_L}^2 \; \sigma_{\chi_L}^2 \; x_0 \; y_0 \end{bmatrix} \quad (32)$$

It should be clear from (31) and the definitions (4) and (5) that $\partial \boldsymbol{\mu}_{z_i}/\partial \vartheta_j = 0$ and $\partial \mathbf{C}_{z_i}/\partial \vartheta_j = 0$ for $i \neq j$ where ϑ_j are the line parameters of the jth line, excluding x_0 and y_0. By applying the identities (13) through (17) in (31), it's straightforward to show that parameter estimates of ϕ_ℓ, μ_{χ_ℓ}, x_0 and y_0 are independent of those for $\sigma_{\nu_\ell}^2$ and $\sigma_{\chi_\ell}^2$, $\ell = 1, \ldots, L$, exactly as for (18). The Fisher information matrix for the reduced parameter vector $\boldsymbol{\vartheta}'$

$$\boldsymbol{\vartheta}' = \begin{bmatrix} \phi_1 \; \mu_{\chi_1} \; \cdots \; \phi_L \; \mu_{\chi_L} \; x_0 \; y_0 \end{bmatrix} \quad (33)$$

is then given by

$$\mathbf{I}(\boldsymbol{\vartheta}') = \begin{bmatrix} I_{\phi_1,\phi_1} & I_{\phi_1,\mu_{\chi_1}} & 0 & \cdots & 0 & 0 & I_{\phi_1,x_0} & I_{\phi_1,y_0} \\ I_{\mu_{\chi_1},\phi_1} & I_{\mu_{\chi_1},\mu_{\chi_1}} & 0 & \cdots & 0 & 0 & I_{\mu_{\chi_1},x_0} & I_{\mu_{\chi_1},y_0} \\ 0 & 0 & \ddots & & \vdots & \vdots & \vdots & \vdots \\ \vdots & \vdots & & & I_{\phi_L,\phi_L} & I_{\phi_L,\mu_{\chi_L}} & I_{\phi_L,x_0} & I_{\phi_L,y_0} \\ 0 & 0 & 0 & \cdots & I_{\mu_{\chi_L},\phi_L} & I_{\mu_{\chi_L},\mu_{\chi_L}} & I_{\mu_L,x_0} & I_{\mu_{\chi_L},y_0} \\ I_{x_0,\phi_1} & I_{x_0,\mu_{\chi_1}} & I_{x_0,\phi_2} & \cdots & I_{x_0,\phi_L} & I_{x_0,\mu_{\chi_L}} & I_{x_0,x_0} & I_{x_0,y_0} \\ I_{y_0,\phi_1} & I_{y_0,\mu_{\chi_1}} & I_{y_0,\phi_2} & \cdots & I_{y_0,\phi_L} & I_{y_0,\mu_{\chi_L}} & I_{y_0,x_0} & I_{y_0,y_0} \end{bmatrix} \quad (34)$$

where the elements of (34) are given by $I_{\phi_\ell,\phi_\ell} = N_\ell \left(\frac{(\mu_{\chi_\ell} - b_\ell x_0 + a_\ell y_0)^2}{\sigma_{\nu_\ell}^2} + \frac{(a_\ell x_0 + b_\ell y_0)^2}{\sigma_{\chi_\ell}^2} + \frac{(\sigma_{\nu_\ell}^2 - \sigma_{\chi_\ell}^2)^2}{\sigma_{\nu_\ell}^2 \sigma_{\chi_\ell}^2}\right)$, $I_{\phi_\ell,\mu_{\chi_\ell}} = I_{\mu_{\chi_\ell},\phi_\ell} = N_\ell \frac{a_\ell x_0 + b_\ell y_0}{\sigma_{\chi_\ell}^2}$, $I_{\phi_\ell,x_0} = I_{x_0,\phi_\ell} = N_\ell \frac{a_\ell(b_\ell x_0 - a_\ell y_0 - \mu_{\chi_\ell})}{\sigma_{\nu_\ell}^2}$, $I_{\phi_\ell,y_0} = I_{y_0,\phi_\ell} = N_\ell \frac{b_\ell(b_\ell x_0 - a_\ell y_0 - \mu_{\chi_\ell})}{\sigma_{\nu_\ell}^2}$, $I_{\mu_{\chi_\ell},\mu_{\chi_\ell}} = \frac{1}{\sigma_{\chi_\ell}^2}$, $I_{\mu_{\chi_\ell},x_0} = I_{x_0,\mu_{\chi_\ell}} = I_{\mu_{\chi_\ell},y_0} = I_{y_0,\mu_{\chi_\ell}} = 0$, $I_{x_0,x_0} = \sum_{\ell=1}^{L} \frac{a_\ell^2}{\sigma_{\nu_\ell}^2}$, $I_{x_0,y_0} = I_{y_0,x_0} = \sum_{\ell=1}^{L} \frac{a_\ell b_\ell}{\sigma_{\nu_\ell}^2}$, and $I_{y_0,y_0} = \sum_{\ell=1}^{L} \frac{b_\ell^2}{\sigma_{\nu_\ell}^2}$.

The Fisher information matrix for line parameter estimates of a_ℓ, b_ℓ, $\ell = 1, \ldots, L$ and (x_0, y_0) is found from (22) using the transformation $g(\vartheta')$ of the parameter vector ϑ' given by

$$g(\vartheta') = \begin{bmatrix} \sin\phi_1 & \cos\phi_1 & \sin\phi_2 & \cos\phi_2 & \cdots & \sin\phi_L & \cos\phi_L & x_0 & y_0 \end{bmatrix} \quad (35)$$

Then

$$\mathbf{I}^{-1}(g(\vartheta')) = \frac{\partial g(\vartheta')}{\partial \vartheta'} \mathbf{I}^{-1}(\vartheta') \frac{\partial g(\vartheta')}{\partial \vartheta'}^T \quad (36)$$

where $\mathbf{I}^{-1}(\vartheta')$ is from (34), and the matrix $\partial g(\vartheta')/\partial \vartheta'$ is determined by applying (23) to (35) in the same manner as was done for (24). The bounds afforded by (36) can be compared to the bounds of (26) for unassisted line parameter estimation. Figure 1 illustrates the improved performance of joint estimation by plotting the minimum variance $\sigma_{\hat{a}_1}^2$ as a function of the number of lines L using (36) and (26). The simulation parameters are $x_0 = 1000.0$, $y_0 = 0$, $N = 64$, $\mu_\chi = 0$, $\sigma_\nu^2 = 1$, $\sigma_\chi^2 = 16$, and $\Delta_\phi = \pi/6$.

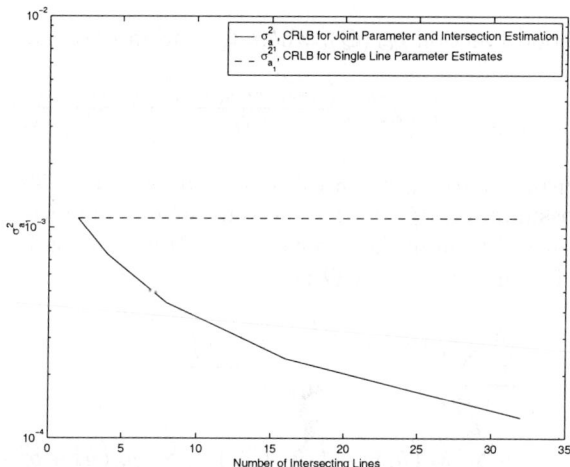

Fig. 1. Comparison of CRLBs from (36) and (26) for estimating parameter a_1 from a pencil of L lines.

5 A Point of Intersection Estimator

To motivate an estimator for the point of intersection $(\hat{x}_0, \hat{y}_0)$ of L lines, consider a particular line ℓ, whose measurements are of the form (1), such that

$$\begin{bmatrix} x_{n,\ell} \\ y_{n,\ell} \end{bmatrix} = \begin{bmatrix} \cos\phi_\ell & \sin\phi_\ell \\ -\sin\phi_\ell & \cos\phi_\ell \end{bmatrix} \begin{bmatrix} \chi_{n,\ell} \\ \gamma_{n,\ell} \end{bmatrix} \quad (37)$$

Multiplying both sides of (37) by a test vector $[\sin\hat{\phi}_\ell \ \cos\hat{\phi}_\ell]$ yields

$$\sin\hat{\phi}_\ell x_{n,\ell} + \cos\hat{\phi}_\ell y_{n,\ell} = \sin\left(\hat{\phi}_\ell - \phi_\ell\right)\chi_{n,\ell} + \cos\left(\hat{\phi}_\ell - \phi_\ell\right)\gamma_{n,\ell} \quad (38)$$

The variance of the left hand side of (38) is the same as the variance of the right hand side of (38), which is given by

$$\sin^2\left(\hat{\phi}_\ell - \phi_\ell\right)\sigma_{\chi,\ell}^2 + \cos^2\left(\hat{\phi}_\ell - \phi_\ell\right)\sigma_{\nu,\ell}^2 \quad (39)$$

As $\sigma_{\nu,\ell}^2 < \sigma_{\chi,\ell}^2$ by assumption, (39) is minimized when $\hat{\phi}_\ell = \phi_\ell$. Thus, defining $[\hat{a}_\ell \ \hat{b}_\ell] = [\sin\hat{\phi}_\ell \ \cos\hat{\phi}_\ell]$ and a constant $\hat{c}_\ell$ for $\ell = 1,\ldots,L$, then these are line parameters as in (3), with the constraint

$$\hat{a}_\ell^2 + \hat{b}_\ell^2 = [\hat{a}_\ell \ \hat{b}_\ell]\begin{bmatrix}\hat{a}_\ell\\\hat{b}_\ell\end{bmatrix} = 1 \quad (40)$$

In addition, these lines are constrained to intersect at $(\hat{x}_0, \hat{y}_0)$

$$\hat{a}_\ell \hat{x}_0 + \hat{b}_\ell \hat{y}_0 + \hat{c}_\ell = 0 \quad (41)$$

Now, the likelihood function $p_\Theta(Q)$, where Q is from (28), can be expressed

$$p_\Theta(Q) = C_0 e^{-\sum_{\ell=1}^{L}\sum_{n=1}^{N_\ell}\frac{(a_\ell x_{n_\ell} + b_\ell y_{n_\ell} + c_\ell)^2}{2\sigma_{\nu_\ell}^2} + \frac{(-b_\ell x_{n_\ell} + a_\ell y_{n_\ell} - \mu_{\chi_\ell})^2}{2\sigma_{\chi_\ell}^2}} \quad (42)$$

with $\Theta = [a_1 \ b_1 \ c_1 \ \ldots \ a_L \ b_L \ c_L \ x_0 \ y_0]$. Given the variance (39), the constraint (40), and the assumption $\sigma_{\nu_\ell}^2 < \sigma_{\chi_\ell}^2$, choosing Θ to minimize the double sum over the first squared term in the exponent of (42) will maximize $p_\Theta(Q)$. Thus, a suitable cost for an estimator of Θ is

$$C(Q) = \sum_{\ell=1}^{L}\sum_{n=1}^{N_\ell}\frac{\left(\hat{a}_\ell x_{n,\ell} + \hat{b}_\ell y_{n,\ell} + \hat{c}_\ell\right)^2}{2\sigma_\ell^2}$$
$$+ \sum_{\ell=1}^{L}\lambda_\ell\left(\hat{a}_\ell \hat{x}_0 + \hat{b}_\ell \hat{y}_0 + \hat{c}_\ell\right) + \sum_{\ell=1}^{L}\rho_\ell\left(\hat{a}_\ell^2 + \hat{b}_\ell^2 - 1\right) \quad (43)$$

To decouple the parameter estimates for the separate lines in the minimization of (43), the point of intersection $(\hat{x}_0, \hat{y}_0)$ is viewed as a known parameter. The minimization of (43) with respect to the parameters $\hat{a}_\ell$, $\hat{b}_\ell$, and $\hat{c}_\ell$ of line ℓ is then

$$\mathbf{A}_\ell\begin{bmatrix}\hat{a}_\ell\\\hat{b}_\ell\end{bmatrix} = -\frac{2\sigma_\ell^2\rho_\ell}{N_\ell}\begin{bmatrix}\hat{a}_\ell\\\hat{b}_\ell\end{bmatrix} - \frac{\lambda_\ell\sigma_\ell^2}{N_\ell}\begin{bmatrix}(\hat{x}_0 - \overline{x_\ell})\\(\hat{y}_0 - \overline{y_\ell})\end{bmatrix} \quad (44)$$

As in [1], $\mathbf{A}_\ell$ is the modal matrix of the data associated with the ℓth line.

$$\mathbf{A}_\ell \equiv \begin{bmatrix}\left(\overline{x_\ell^2} - \overline{x_\ell}^2\right) & \left(\overline{y_\ell x_\ell} - \overline{x_\ell}\,\overline{y_\ell}\right)\\\left(\overline{y_\ell x_\ell} - \overline{x_\ell}\,\overline{y_\ell}\right) & \left(\overline{y_\ell^2} - \overline{y_\ell}^2\right)\end{bmatrix} \quad (45)$$

where the notation $\overline{z}$ means
$$\overline{z} = \frac{\sum_{k=1}^{K} z_k}{K} \tag{46}$$
Clearly, $\mathbf{A}_\ell$ tends asymptotically to $\mathbf{C}_{z_\ell}$ from (8). In addition, note the identity
$$\hat{c}_\ell = -\hat{a}_\ell \overline{x_\ell} - \hat{b}_\ell \overline{y_\ell} - \frac{\sigma_\ell^2 \lambda_\ell}{N_\ell} \tag{47}$$
which is the result of minimizing (43) with respect to $\hat{c}_\ell$, and helps to realize the form (44).

To complete the solution for $\hat{a}_\ell, \hat{b}_\ell$, denote the (column) eigenvectors of $\mathbf{A}_\ell$ by ψ_{0_ℓ} and ψ_{1_ℓ}, and the matrix $\mathbf{\Psi}_\ell = [\psi_{0_\ell}\ \psi_{1_\ell}]$ such that
$$\mathbf{A}_\ell = \mathbf{\Psi}_\ell \mathbf{\Lambda}_\ell \mathbf{\Psi}_\ell^T \tag{48}$$
where $\mathbf{\Lambda}_\ell$ is the associated diagonal matrix whose entries are the eigenvalues β_{0_ℓ} and β_{1_ℓ} of $\mathbf{A}_\ell$. The relevant parameters can all be defined then as
$$\left[(\hat{x}_0 - \overline{x_\ell})\ (\hat{y}_0 - \overline{y_\ell})\right]^T = \mathbf{\Psi}_\ell \mathbf{d}_\ell \tag{49}$$
$$[\hat{a}_\ell\ \hat{b}_\ell]^T = \mathbf{\Psi}_\ell \mathbf{f}_\ell \tag{50}$$
Using (50) and (49), equation (44) may be written
$$\mathbf{\Psi}_\ell \mathbf{\Lambda}_\ell \mathbf{f}_\ell = \alpha_\ell \mathbf{\Psi}_\ell \mathbf{f}_\ell - \frac{\lambda_\ell \sigma_\ell^2}{N_\ell} \mathbf{\Psi}_\ell \mathbf{d}_\ell \tag{51}$$
where $\alpha_\ell = -2\sigma_\ell^2 \rho_\ell / N_\ell$. By multiplying both sides of (51) by $\mathbf{\Psi}_\ell^T$, noting that $\mathbf{\Psi}_\ell^T \mathbf{\Psi}_\ell = \mathbf{I}_{2 \times 2}$ and then rearranging, its not hard to show that the solution for $(\hat{a}_\ell, \hat{b}_\ell)$ is given by
$$\begin{bmatrix} \hat{a}_\ell \\ \hat{b}_\ell \end{bmatrix} = -\frac{\lambda_\ell \sigma_\ell^2}{N_\ell} \mathbf{\Psi}_\ell \begin{bmatrix} \frac{1}{\beta_{0,\ell} - \alpha_\ell} & 0 \\ 0 & \frac{1}{\beta_{1,\ell} - \alpha_\ell} \end{bmatrix} \mathbf{d}_\ell \tag{52}$$
The Lagrangian multipliers α_ℓ and λ_ℓ in (52) must now be determined. α_ℓ is found from backwards substitution of (52) into (41). Using (47) and after some manipulation, it can be shown that
$$\frac{d_{0,\ell}^2}{(\beta_{0,\ell} - \alpha_\ell)} + \frac{d_{1,\ell}^2}{(\beta_{1,\ell} - \alpha_\ell)} = -1 \tag{53}$$
Equation (53) yields the Lagrangian multiplier α_ℓ
$$\alpha_\ell = \frac{1}{2}\left(\beta_{0,\ell} + \beta_{1,\ell} + d_{0,\ell}^2 + d_{1,\ell}^2\right)$$
$$\pm \frac{1}{2}\sqrt{\left(\beta_{0,\ell} + \beta_{1,\ell} + d_{0,\ell}^2 + d_{1,\ell}^2\right)^2 - 4\left(d_{0,\ell}^2 \beta_{1,\ell} + d_{1,\ell}^2 \beta_{0,\ell} + \beta_{0,\ell}\beta_{1,\ell}\right)} \tag{54}$$
$$= \frac{\left(\beta_{0,\ell} + \beta_{1,\ell} + d_{0,\ell}^2 + d_{1,\ell}^2\right)}{2} \pm \frac{\sqrt{\left(\beta_{0,\ell} - \beta_{1,\ell} + d_{0,\ell}^2 - d_{1,\ell}^2\right)^2 + 4 d_{0,\ell}^2 d_{1,\ell}^2}}{2} \tag{55}$$
$$= \frac{1}{2}\varsigma_\ell \pm \frac{1}{2}\xi_\ell \tag{56}$$

where (55) shows that the discriminant is always positive, so that α_ℓ is always real and positive.

The second Lagrangian multiplier λ_ℓ is found from the constraint (40) which can be rewritten using (52) as

$$\lambda_\ell^2 \left[\left(\frac{d_{0,\ell}}{(\beta_{0,\ell} - \alpha_\ell)} \right)^2 + \left(\frac{d_{1,\ell}}{(\beta_{1,\ell} - \alpha_\ell)} \right)^2 \right] = \frac{N_\ell^2}{(\sigma_\ell^2)^2} \tag{57}$$

This yields λ_ℓ as

$$\lambda_\ell = \pm \frac{N_\ell}{\sigma_\ell^2} \frac{(\beta_{0,\ell} - \alpha_\ell)(\beta_{1,\ell} - \alpha_\ell)}{\sqrt{d_{0,\ell}^2 (\beta_{1,\ell} - \alpha_\ell)^2 + d_{1,\ell}^2 (\beta_{0,\ell} - \alpha_\ell)^2}} \tag{58}$$

The denominator of (58) can be put in a more useful form substituting (53) into (57) for each of the ratios in d_0 and d_1. After some algebra, and substituting (58) for λ_ℓ, it can be shown that

$$d_{0,\ell}^2 (\beta_{1,\ell} - \alpha_\ell)^2 + d_{1,\ell}^2 (\beta_{0,\ell} - \alpha_\ell)^2 = \pm (\beta_{0,\ell} - \alpha_\ell)(\beta_{1,\ell} - \alpha_\ell) \xi_\ell \tag{59}$$

with ξ_ℓ from (56). The parameters $(\hat{a}_\ell, \hat{b}_\ell)$ in (52) can then be rewritten with (58) and (59) as

$$\begin{bmatrix} \hat{a}_\ell \\ \hat{b}_\ell \end{bmatrix} = \frac{\Psi_\ell \begin{bmatrix} d_{0,\ell} (\beta_{1,\ell} - \alpha_\ell) \\ d_{1,\ell} (\beta_{0,\ell} - \alpha_\ell) \end{bmatrix}}{\sqrt{(\beta_{0,\ell} - \alpha_\ell)(\beta_{1,\ell} - \alpha_\ell) \xi_\ell}} \tag{60}$$

Returning to the cost (43) and observing that $(\hat{a}_\ell, \hat{b}_\ell)$ implicitly satisfy the constraints, its not hard to show that

$$C(\mathbf{Q}) = \sum_{\ell=1}^{L} N_\ell \frac{\begin{bmatrix} \hat{a}_\ell \\ \hat{b}_\ell \end{bmatrix}^T \left(\mathbf{A}_\ell + \begin{bmatrix} (\bar{x}_\ell - \hat{x}_0) \\ (\bar{y}_\ell - \hat{y}_0) \end{bmatrix} \begin{bmatrix} (\bar{x}_\ell - \hat{x}_0) \\ (\bar{y}_\ell - \hat{y}_0) \end{bmatrix}^T \right) \begin{bmatrix} \hat{a}_\ell \\ \hat{b}_\ell \end{bmatrix}}{2\sigma_m^2} \tag{61}$$

Substituting (60) into (61), noting (48) and (49) and making prudent use of equation (53), it can be shown that this cost reduces to

$$C(\mathbf{Q}) = \sum_{\ell=1}^{L} \frac{N_\ell}{2\sigma_\ell^2} \alpha_\ell \tag{62}$$

The α_ℓ which minimize (62) are found from (54) by subtracting the radical. To find the point of intersection $(\hat{x}_0, \hat{y}_0)$, (62) can be minimized using Newton Raphson, but an initial guess for $(\hat{x}_0, \hat{y}_0)$ is required. Noting from (55) that for any $\mathbf{d}_\ell$ given by (49), $\min(\beta_{0,\ell}, \beta_{1,\ell}) \leq \alpha_\ell \leq \max(\beta_{0,\ell}, \beta_{1,\ell})$, the choice of $\mathbf{d}_\ell$ such that $\alpha_\ell = \min(\beta_{0,\ell}, \beta_{1,\ell})$ occurs when the vector $[(\hat{x}_0 - \bar{x}_\ell)(\hat{y}_0 - \bar{y}_\ell)]$ from (49) projects entirely onto the eigenvector $\psi_{\max}$ corresponding to the maximum eigenvalue $\beta_{\max}$. To minimize $C(\boldsymbol{Q})$, this condition should be satisfied for as many lines as possible, so that if $[\tilde{a}_\ell\ \tilde{b}_\ell]$ are the components of the eigenvector $\psi_{\min}$ corresponding to the minimum eigenvalue $\beta_{\min}$, then $\tilde{a}_\ell(\hat{x}_0 - \bar{x}_\ell) + \tilde{b}_\ell(\hat{y}_0 - \bar{y}_\ell) = 0$. A point $(\hat{x}_0, \hat{y}_0)$ that seeks to minimize every α_ℓ is thus found from

$$\begin{bmatrix} \tilde{a}_1 & \tilde{b}_1 \\ \tilde{a}_2 & \tilde{b}_2 \\ \vdots & \vdots \\ \tilde{a}_N & \tilde{b}_N \end{bmatrix} \begin{bmatrix} \hat{x}_0 \\ \hat{y}_0 \end{bmatrix} = - \begin{bmatrix} \tilde{c}_1 \\ \tilde{c}_2 \\ \vdots \\ \tilde{c}_N \end{bmatrix} \quad (63)$$

where $\tilde{c}_\ell = -\tilde{a}_\ell \bar{x}_\ell - \tilde{b}_\ell \bar{y}_\ell$. Since $\tilde{a}_\ell$, $\tilde{b}_\ell$, and $\tilde{c}_\ell$ minimize α_ℓ and (62) for $L = 1$, the parameter estimators of a single line from [1] are in fact a special case of the current approach.

With the initial guess $(\hat{x}_0, \hat{y}_0)$, the Newton-Raphson method computes [2]

$$\begin{bmatrix} \hat{x}_0[n+1] \\ \hat{y}_0[n+1] \end{bmatrix} = \begin{bmatrix} \hat{x}_0[n] \\ \hat{y}_0[n] \end{bmatrix} - \left\{ \begin{bmatrix} \frac{\partial^2 C(\boldsymbol{Q})}{\partial \hat{x}_0^2} & \frac{\partial^2 C(\boldsymbol{Q})}{\partial \hat{x}_0 \partial \hat{y}_0} \\ \frac{\partial^2 C(\boldsymbol{Q})}{\partial \hat{y}_0 \partial \hat{x}_0} & \frac{\partial^2 C(\boldsymbol{Q})}{\partial \hat{y}_0^2} \end{bmatrix}^{-1} \begin{bmatrix} \frac{\partial C(\boldsymbol{Q})}{\partial \hat{x}_0} \\ \frac{\partial C(\boldsymbol{Q})}{\partial \hat{y}_0} \end{bmatrix} \right\}_{\hat{x}_0 = \hat{x}_0[n], \hat{y}_0 = \hat{y}_0[n]} \quad (64)$$

An algorithm for the point of intersection estimator is given by

1. Estimate the initial point of intersection $(\hat{x}_0[0], \hat{y}_0[0])$ from (63)
2. Compute the modal matrices $\mathbf{A}_\ell$ from (45) and the resulting eigenvectors $\boldsymbol{\Psi}_\ell$ and eigenvalues $\beta_{0,\ell}$, $\beta_{1,\ell}$ for each family of line data $\ell = 1, \ldots, L$.
3. Determine $\boldsymbol{d}_\ell$ from (49) using $(\hat{x}_0[n], \hat{y}_0[n])$
4. Compute $C(\boldsymbol{Q})$ from (62) and its partial derivatives in terms of α_ℓ from (54) to construct (64).
5. Repeat from 3. until (62) is minimum

6 Simulation and Discussion

In keeping with the figures of Section 4, simulations are performed with the same parameters: $\sigma_\nu^2 = 1$, $\sigma_\chi^2 = 16$, $\mu_\chi = 0$, $\hat{x}_0 = 1000$, $\hat{y}_0 = 0$, and $10{,}000$ iterations. When multiple lines intersect at $(\hat{x}_0, \hat{y}_0)$, they do so by equally dividing an angle of $\pi/6$. Figure 2 illustrates the error variance of the proposed intersection estimator (64) for the estimate of coordinate $\hat{x}_0$ when only two lines intersect, one coincident with the x axis and the second with angle of intersection $\pi/6$. As seen from the figure, for N as low as 16, the simulated variance is within an order of magnitude of the CRLB from (36). Moreover, the estimator (64) is seen to asymptotically attain the CRLB, consistent with the expected behavior of maximum likelihood estimators [2].

The line parameter estimate $\hat{a}_1$ from the pencil is found by substituting the point of intersection estimate $(\hat{x}_0, \hat{y}_0)$ from (64) into (60) using (54) for α_ℓ. The

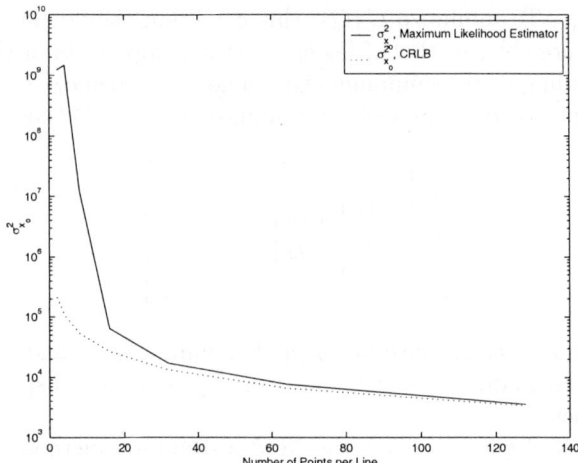

Fig. 2. Simulated $\sigma^2_{\hat{x}_0}$, as estimated from (64) and CRLB from (36) versus number of points N.

curves of figure 3 depict simulations of the estimator variance $\sigma^2_{\hat{a}_1}$, $\sigma^2_{\tilde{a}_1}$ and the CRLB from (36) as a function of the number of intersecting lines L. As can be seen from the figure, $\hat{a}_1$ provides a clear improvement over the alternative of estimating the line parameter $\tilde{a}_1$ from its line data alone, confirming the predictions of figure 1. The number of points per line in the simulation is $N = 64$.

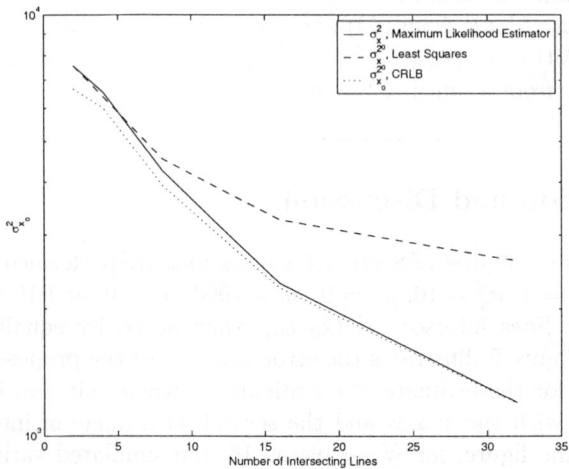

Fig. 3. Simulated $\sigma^2_{\hat{x}_0}$, as estimated from (64), Least Squares, and the CRLB from (36), versus the number of lines L.

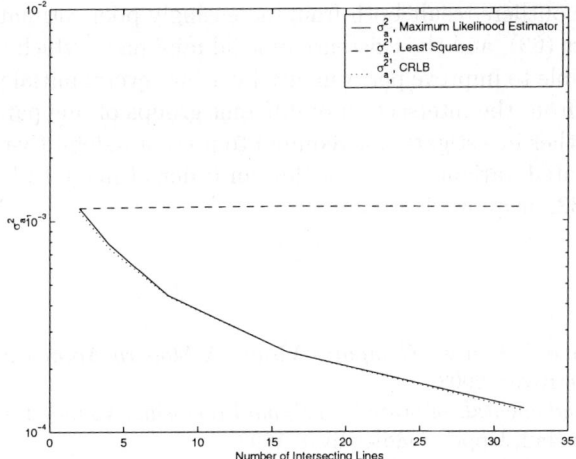

Fig. 4. Simulated $\sigma_{\hat{a}_1}^2$, by applying (60) to estimates $(\hat{x}_0, \hat{y}_0)$ from (64), the Single Line parameter estimator from [1], and the CRLB from (36), versus the number of lines L.

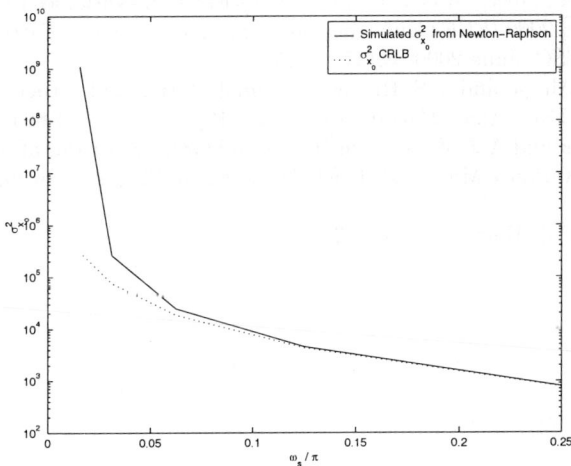

Fig. 5. Simulated $\sigma_{\hat{x}_0}^2$ from (64) and the CRLB from (36) versus ω_s from (65).

The performance of (64) using the least squares estimate of $(\hat{x}_0, \hat{y}_0)$ from (63) is simulated in figure 5 as a function of the subtending angle ω_s

$$\omega_s = \max \left\{ \omega_{\ell,k} = \cos^{-1}\left(a_\ell a_k + b_\ell b_k\right), \ \ell, k = 1, \ldots, L \right\} \qquad (65)$$

The simulation parameters are $L = 16$, $N_\ell = 64$, $\sigma_{\nu_\ell}^2 = 1$, $\sigma_{\chi_\ell}^2 = 16$ and ω_s is equally divided by the L intersecting lines. It is apparent from the figure that as ω_s becomes increasingly small, the performance of the method degrades. The large variance $\sigma_{\hat{x}_0}^2$ of the estimator results from a small number of very large outliers. These outliers result both from increasingly poor estimates afforded by the initial guess (63), and the existence of local minima to which (64) converges. It may be possible to improve performance by using several initial points $(\hat{x}_0, \hat{y}_0)$, each obtained from the intersection of different groups of line parameters $\tilde{a}_\ell$, $\tilde{b}_\ell$, and $\tilde{c}_\ell$, but further investigation is required to present a definitive solution. Note that the simulated variance $\sigma^2_{\hat{x}_0}$ is within an order of magnitude of the CRLB for $\omega_s/\pi = 1/32$, or about 1.4 degrees.

References

1. D. Forsyth and J. Ponce , *Computer Vision: A Modern Approach*. Prentice Hall, Upper Saddle River, 2003.
2. SM Kay , *Fundamentals of Statistical Signal Processing, Volume I, Estimation Theory*. Prentice Hall, Upper Saddle River, 1993.
3. A. Papoulis, *Probability and Random Variables, Third Edition*. McGraw-Hill, 1991.
4. K. Kanatani, "Introduction to Statistical Optimization for Geometric Computation". A.I. Laboratory, Department of Computer Science, Gunma University, Japan. http://www.suri.it.okayama-u.ac.jp/~kanatani/e/
5. B. Matei and P. Meer, "A General Method for Errors-in-Variables Problems in Computer Vision". *2000 IEEE Conference on Computer Vision and Pattern Recognition*, Hilton Head, SC, June 2000, vol.II, 18-25
6. J. Weng, N. Ahuja, and T.S. Huang, "Optimal Motion and Structure Estimation". *IEEE Trans. Patt. Anal. Machine Intell.*, Vol 15, no. 9, pp.864-884, 1993
7. B. Friedlander and A.J. Weiss, "On the Second Order Statistics of the Eigenvectors of Sample Covariance Matrices". *IEEE Trans. Signal Process.*, Vol 46, no. 11, pp.864-884, 1998
8. R.O. Duda, P.E. Hart , *Pattern Classification and Scene Analysis*. John Wiley & Sons, 1973.

Multilinear Analysis of Image Ensembles: TensorFaces

M. Alex O. Vasilescu and Demetri Terzopoulos

Courant Institute, New York University, USA
Department of Computer Science, University of Toronto, Canada

Abstract. Natural images are the composite consequence of multiple factors related to scene structure, illumination, and imaging. Multilinear algebra, the algebra of higher-order tensors, offers a potent mathematical framework for analyzing the multifactor structure of image ensembles and for addressing the difficult problem of disentangling the constituent factors or modes. Our multilinear modeling technique employs a tensor extension of the conventional matrix singular value decomposition (SVD), known as the N-mode SVD. As a concrete example, we consider the multilinear analysis of ensembles of facial images that combine several modes, including different facial geometries (people), expressions, head poses, and lighting conditions. Our resulting "TensorFaces" representation has several advantages over conventional eigenfaces. More generally, multilinear analysis shows promise as a unifying framework for a variety of computer vision problems.

1 Introduction

Natural images are formed by the interaction of multiple factors related to scene structure, illumination, and imaging. Human perception remains robust despite significant variation of these factors. For example, people possess a remarkable ability to recognize faces when confronted by a broad variety of facial geometries, expressions, head poses, and lighting conditions, and this ability is vital to human social interaction. Developing a similarly robust computational model of face recognition remains a difficult open problem whose solution would have substantial impact on biometrics for identification, surveillance, human-computer interaction, and other applications.

Linear algebra, i.e., the algebra of matrices, has traditionally been of great value in the context of image analysis and representation. The Fourier transform, the Karhonen-Loeve transform, and other linear techniques have been veritable workhorses. In particular, principal component analysis (PCA) has been a popular technique in facial image recognition, as has its refinement, independent component analysis (ICA) [2]. By their very nature, however, these offspring of linear algebra address single-factor variations in image formation. Thus, the conventional "eigenfaces" facial image recognition technique [13,17] works best when person identity is the only factor that is permitted to vary. If other factors, such as lighting, viewpoint, and expression, are also permitted to modify facial images, eigenfaces face difficulty.

In this paper, we employ a more sophisticated mathematical approach in the analysis and representation of images that can account explicitly for each of the multiple factors inherent to image formation. Our approach is that of multilinear algebra—the algebra of higher-order tensors. The natural generalization of matrices (i.e., linear operators defined over a vector space), tensors define multilinear operators over a *set* of vector spaces. Subsuming conventional linear analysis as a special case, tensor analysis offers a unifying mathematical framework suitable for addressing a variety of computer vision problems. Tensor analysis makes the assumption that images formed as a result of some multifactor confluence are amenable to linear analysis as each factor or mode is allowed to vary in turn, while the remaining factors or modes are held constant.[1]

We focus in this paper on the higher-order generalization of PCA and the singular value decomposition (SVD) of matrices for computing principal components. Unlike the matrix case for which the existence and uniqueness of the SVD is assured, the situation for higher-order tensors is not as simple. Unfortunately, there does not exist a true "tensor SVD" that offers all the nice properties of the matrix SVD [6]. There are multiple ways to decompose tensors orthogonally. However, one multilinear extension of the matrix SVD to tensors is most natural. We demonstrate the application of this N-*mode SVD* to the representation of collections of facial images, where multiple modes are permitted to vary. The resulting representation separates the different modes underlying the formation of facial images, hence it is promising for use in a robust facial recognition algorithm.

The remainder of this paper is organized as follows: Section 2 reviews related work. Section 3 covers the foundations of tensor algebra that are relevant to our approach. Section 4 formulates the tensor decomposition algorithm which is central to our multilinear analysis. Section 5 applies our multilinear analysis algorithm to the analysis of facial images. Section 6 concludes the paper and proposes future research topics.

2 Related Work

Prior research has approached the problem of facial representation for recognition by taking advantage of the functionality and simplicity of matrix algebra. The well-known family of PCA-based algorithms, such as eigenfaces [13,17] and Fisherfaces [1] compute the PCA by performing an SVD on a $P \times XY$ *data matrix* of "vectorized" $X \times Y$ pixel images of P people. These linear models are suitable in the case where the identity of the subject is the only variable accounted for in image formation. Various researchers have attempted to deal with the shortcomings of PCA-based facial image representation in less constrained (multi-factor) situations, for example, by employing better classifiers [11].

Bilinear models have attracted attention because of their richer representational power. The *2-mode analysis* technique for analyzing (statistical) data matrices of scalar entries is described by Magnus and Neudecker [8]. 2-mode analysis was extended to vector entries by Marimont and Wandel [9] in the context of characterizing color surface and illuminant spectra. Freeman and Tenenbaum [4,14] applied this extension in three different perceptual domains, including face recognition.

As was pointed out by Shashua and Levin [12], the natural representation of a collection of images is a three-dimensional array, or 3rd-order tensor, rather than a simple matrix of vectorized images. They develop compression algorithms for collections of images, such as video images, that take advantage of spatial (horizontal/vertical) and

---
[1] Also of interest is the fact that, from a probabilistic point of view, multilinear algebra is to higher-order statistics what linear algebra is to second-order statistics [3].

temporal redundancies, leading to higher compression rates compared to applying conventional PCA on vectorized image data matrices.

In addressing the motion analysis/synthesis problem, Vasilescu [19,18] structured motion capture data in tensor form and developed an algorithm for extracting "human motion signatures" from the movements of multiple subjects each performing several different actions. The algorithm she described performed 3-mode analysis (with a dyadic decomposition) and she identified the more general motion analysis problem involving more than two factors (people, actions, cadences, ...) as one of N-mode analysis on higher-order tensors. N-mode analysis of observational data was first proposed by Tucker [16], who pioneered 3-mode analysis, and subsequently developed by Kapteyn et al. [5, 8] and others, notably [3].

The N-mode SVD facial image representation technique that we develop in this paper subsumes the previous methods reviewed above. In particular, when presented with matrices of vectorized images that are amenable to simple, linear analysis, our method reduces to SVD, hence PCA; i.e., the eigenfaces of Sirovich and Kirby or Turk and Pentland. When the collection of images is more appropriately amenable to bilinear analysis, our technique reduces to the "style/content" analysis of Freeman and Tenenbaum. More importantly, however, our technique is capable of handling images that are the consequence of any number of multilinear factors of the sort described in the introduction.

3 Relevant Tensor Algebra

We now introduce the notation and basic definitions of multilinear algebra. Scalars are denoted by lower case letters $(a, b, \ldots)$, vectors by bold lower case letters $(\mathbf{a}, \mathbf{b} \ldots)$, matrices by bold upper-case letters $(\mathbf{A}, \mathbf{B} \ldots)$, and higher-order tensors by calligraphic upper-case letters $(\mathcal{A}, \mathcal{B} \ldots)$.

A *tensor*, also known as n-way array or multidimensional matrix or n-mode matrix, is a higher order generalization of a vector (first order tensor) and a matrix (second order tensor). Tensors are multilinear mappings over a set of vector spaces. The *order* of tensor $\mathcal{A} \in \mathbb{R}^{I_1 \times I_2 \times \ldots \times I_N}$ is N. An element of $\mathcal{A}$ is denoted as $\mathcal{A}_{i_1 \ldots i_n \ldots i_N}$ or $a_{i_1 \ldots i_n \ldots i_N}$ or where $1 \leq i_n \leq I_n$.

An Nth–order tensor $\mathcal{A} \in \mathbb{R}^{I_1 \times I_2 \times \ldots \times I_N}$ has *rank-1* when it is expressible as the outer product of N vectors: $\mathcal{A} = \mathbf{u}_1 \circ \mathbf{u}_2 \circ \ldots \circ \mathbf{u}_N$. The tensor element is expressed as $a_{ij\ldots m} = u_{1i}u_{2j}\ldots u_{Nm}$, where u_{1i} is the ith component of $\mathbf{u}_1$, etc. The *rank* of a Nth order tensor $\mathcal{A}$, denoted R=rank($\mathcal{A}$), is the minimal number of rank-1 tensors that yield $\mathcal{A}$ in a linear combination:

$$\mathcal{A} = \sum_{r=1}^{R} \sigma_r \mathbf{u}_1^{(r)} \circ \mathbf{u}_2^{(r)} \circ \ldots \circ \mathbf{u}_N^{(r)}. \qquad (1)$$

A singular value decomposition (SVD) can be expressed as a *rank decomposition* as is shown in the following simple example:

$$\mathbf{M} = \begin{bmatrix} a & b \\ c & d \end{bmatrix} \begin{bmatrix} \sigma_{11} & 0 \\ 0 & \sigma_{22} \end{bmatrix} \begin{bmatrix} f & g \\ h & i \end{bmatrix} = \sigma_{11} \begin{bmatrix} a \\ c \end{bmatrix} \circ \begin{bmatrix} f \\ g \end{bmatrix} + \sigma_{22} \begin{bmatrix} b \\ d \end{bmatrix} \circ \begin{bmatrix} h \\ i \end{bmatrix} \qquad (2)$$

$$= \mathbf{U}_1 \Sigma \mathbf{U}_2^T \tag{3}$$

$$= \begin{bmatrix} \mathbf{u}_1^{(1)} & \mathbf{u}_1^{(2)} \end{bmatrix} \begin{bmatrix} \sigma_{11} & 0 \\ 0 & \sigma_{22} \end{bmatrix} \begin{bmatrix} \mathbf{u}_2^{(1)} & \mathbf{u}_2^{(2)} \end{bmatrix}^T \tag{4}$$

$$= \sum_{i=1}^{R=2} \sum_{j=1}^{R=2} \sigma_{ij} \mathbf{u}_1^{(i)} \circ \mathbf{u}_2^{(j)} \tag{5}$$

Note that a singular value decomposition is a *combinatorial orthogonal rank decomposition* (5), but that the reverse is not true; in general, rank decomposition is not necessarily singular value decomposition. For further discussion on the differences between matrix SVD, rank decomposition and orthogonal rank decomposition for higher order tensors see [6].

Next, we generalize the definition of column and row rank of matrices. In tensor terminology, column vectors are referred to as mode-1 vectors and row vectors as mode-2 vectors. The mode-n vectors of an Nth order tensor $\mathcal{A} \in \mathbb{R}^{I_1 \times I_2 \times \ldots \times I_N}$ are the I_n-dimensional vectors obtained from $\mathcal{A}$ by varying index i_n while keeping the other indices fixed. The mode-n vectors are the column vectors of matrix $\mathbf{A}_{(n)} \in \mathbb{R}^{I_n \times (I_1 I_2 \ldots I_{n-1} I_{n+1} \ldots I_N)}$ that results from *flattening* the tensor $\mathcal{A}$, as shown in Fig. 1. The n-*rank* of $\mathcal{A} \in \mathbb{R}^{I_1 \times I_2 \times \ldots \times I_N}$, denoted R_n, is defined as the dimension of the vector space generated by the mode-n vectors:

$$R_n = rank_n(\mathcal{A}) = rank(\mathbf{A}_{(n)}). \tag{6}$$

A generalization of the product of two matrices is the product of a tensor and a matrix. The *mode-n product* of a tensor $\mathcal{A} \in \mathbb{R}^{I_1 \times I_2 \times \ldots \times I_n \times \ldots \times I_N}$ by a matrix $\mathbf{M} \in \mathbb{R}^{J_n \times I_n}$, denoted by $\mathcal{A} \times_n \mathbf{M}$, is a tensor $\mathcal{B} \in \mathbb{R}^{I_1 \times \ldots \times I_{n-1} \times J_n \times I_{n+1} \times \ldots \times I_N}$ whose entries are computed by

$$(\mathcal{A} \times_n \mathbf{M})_{i_1 \ldots i_{n-1} j_n i_{n+1} \ldots i_N} = \sum_{i_n} a_{i_1 \ldots i_{n-1} i_n i_{n+1} \ldots i_N} m_{j_n i_n}. \tag{7}$$

The mode-n product can be expressed in tensor notation as follows:

$$\mathcal{B} = \mathcal{A} \times_n \mathbf{M}, \tag{8}$$

or, in terms of flattened matrices,

$$\mathbf{B}_{(n)} = \mathbf{M} \mathbf{A}_{(n)}. \tag{9}$$

The mode-n product of a tensor and a matrix is a special case of the inner product in multilinear algebra and tensor analysis. In the literature, it is often denoted using Einstein summation notation. For our purposes, however, the mode-n product symbol is more suggestive of multiplication and expresses better the analogy between matrix and tensor SVD [16] (see Section 4). The mode-n product has the following properties:

1. Given a tensor $\mathcal{A} \in \mathbb{R}^{I_1 \times \ldots I_n \times \ldots I_m \ldots}$ and two matrices, $\mathbf{U} \in \mathbb{R}^{J_m \times I_m}$ and $\mathbf{V} \in \mathbb{R}^{J_n \times I_n}$ the following property holds true:

$$\mathcal{A} \times_m \mathbf{U} \times_n \mathbf{V} = (\mathcal{A} \times_m \mathbf{U}) \times_n \mathbf{V} \tag{10}$$
$$= (\mathcal{A} \times_n \mathbf{V}) \times_m \mathbf{U} \tag{11}$$
$$= \mathcal{A} \times_n \mathbf{V} \times_m \mathbf{U} \tag{12}$$

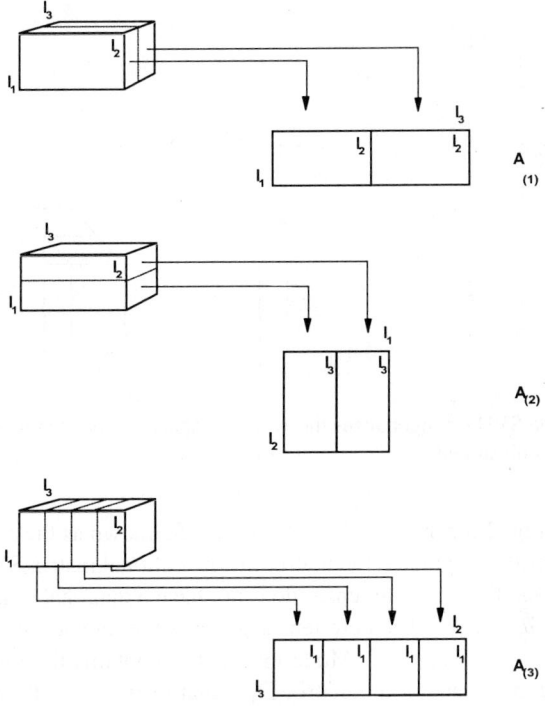

Fig. 1. Flattening a (3rd-order) tensor. The tensor can be flattened in 3 ways to obtain matrices comprising its mode-1, mode-2, and mode-3 vectors.

2. Given a tensor $\mathcal{A} \in \mathbb{R}^{I_1 \times \ldots \times I_n \times \ldots \times I_N}$ and two matrices, $\mathbf{U} \in \mathbb{R}^{J_n \times I_n}$ and $\mathbf{V} \in \mathbb{R}^{K_n \times J_n}$ the following property holds true:

$$(\mathcal{A} \times_n \mathbf{U}) \times_n \mathbf{V} = \mathcal{A} \times_n (\mathbf{VU}) \tag{13}$$

4 Tensor Decomposition

A matrix $\mathbf{D} \in \mathbb{R}^{I_1 \times I_2}$ is a two-mode mathematical object that has two associated vector spaces, a row space and a column space. SVD orthogonalizes these two spaces and decomposes the matrix as $\mathbf{D} = \mathbf{U}_1 \mathbf{\Sigma} \mathbf{U}_2^T$, the product of an orthogonal column-space represented by the left matrix $\mathbf{U}_1 \in \mathbb{R}^{I_1 \times J_1}$, a diagonal singular value matrix $\mathbf{\Sigma} \in \mathbb{R}^{J_1 \times J_2}$, and an orthogonal row space represented by the right matrix $\mathbf{U}_2 \in \mathbb{R}^{I_2 \times J_2}$. In terms of the mode-$n$ products defined in the previous section, this matrix product can be rewritten as $\mathbf{D} = \mathbf{\Sigma} \times_1 \mathbf{U}_1 \times_2 \mathbf{U}_2$.

By extension, an order $N > 2$ tensor or n-way array $\mathcal{D}$ is an N-dimensional matrix comprising N spaces. "N-mode SVD" is a an extension of SVD that orthogonalizes these N spaces and expresses the tensor as the mode-n product (7) of N-orthogonal spaces

$$\mathcal{D} = \mathcal{Z} \times_1 \mathbf{U}_1 \times_2 \mathbf{U}_2 \ldots \times_n \mathbf{U}_n \ldots \times_N \mathbf{U}_N, \tag{14}$$

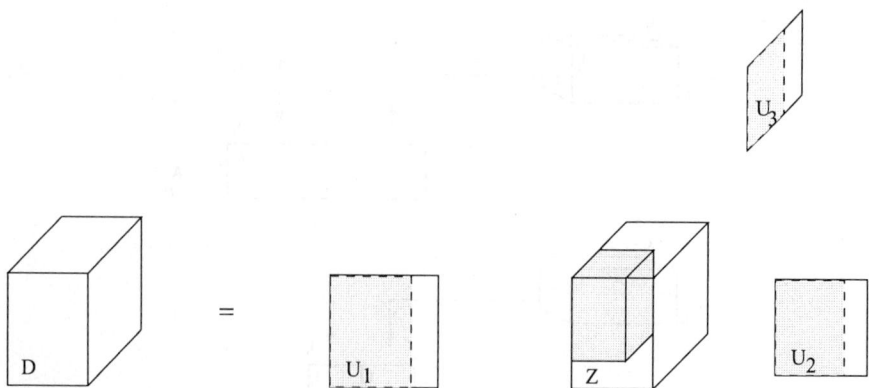

Fig. 2. An N-mode SVD orthogonalizes the N vector spaces associated with an order-N tensor (the case $N = 3$ is illustrated).

as illustrated in Fig. 2 for the case $N = 3$. Tensor $\mathcal{Z}$, known as the *core tensor*, is analogous to the diagonal singular value matrix in conventional matrix SVD. It is important to realize, however, that the core tensor does not have a diagonal structure; rather, $\mathcal{Z}$ is in general a full tensor [6]. The core tensor governs the interaction between the *mode matrices* $\mathbf{U}_n$, for $n = 1, \ldots, N$. Mode matrix $\mathbf{U}_n$ contains the orthonormal vectors spanning the column space of the matrix $\mathbf{D}_{(n)}$ that results from the mode-n flattening of $\mathcal{D}$, as was illustrated in Fig. 1. [2]

4.1 The N-Mode SVD Algorithm

In accordance with the above theory, our N-mode SVD algorithm for decomposing $\mathcal{D}$ is as follows:

1. For $n = 1, \ldots, N$, compute matrix $\mathbf{U}_n$ in (14) by computing the SVD of the flattened matrix $\mathbf{D}_{(n)}$ and setting $\mathbf{U}_n$ to be the left matrix of the SVD.[3]

---

[2] Note that the N-mode SVD can be expressed as an expansion of mutually orthogonal rank-1 tensors (analogous to equation (5)), as follows:

$$\mathcal{D} = \sum_{i_1=1}^{R_1} \cdots \sum_{i_n=1}^{R_n} \cdots \sum_{i_N=1}^{R_N} z_{i_1 \ldots i_N} \mathbf{U}_1^{(i_1)} \circ \ldots \circ \mathbf{U}_n^{(i_n)} \circ \ldots \mathbf{U}_N^{(i_N)},$$

where $\mathbf{U}_n^{(i_n)}$ is the i_n column vector of the matrix $\mathbf{U}_n$. In future work, we shall address the problem of finding the best rank-$(R_1, R_2, \ldots, R_N)$ tensor. This is not to be confused with the classical "rank-R problem" [7].

[3] When $\mathbf{D}_{(n)}$ is a non-square matrix, the computation of $\mathbf{U}_n$ in the singular value decomposition $\mathbf{D}_{(n)} = \mathbf{U}_n \mathbf{\Sigma} \mathbf{V}_n^T$ can be performed efficiently, depending on which dimension of $\mathbf{D}_{(n)}$ is smaller, by decomposing either $\mathbf{D}_{(n)} \mathbf{D}_{(n)}^T = \mathbf{U}_n \mathbf{\Sigma}^2 \mathbf{U}_n^T$ and then computing $\mathbf{V}_n^T = \mathbf{\Sigma}^+ \mathbf{U}_n^T \mathbf{D}_{(n)}$ or by decomposing $\mathbf{D}_{(n)}^T \mathbf{D}_{(n)} = \mathbf{V}_n \mathbf{\Sigma}^2 \mathbf{V}_n^T$ and then computing $\mathbf{U}_n = \mathbf{D}_{(n)} \mathbf{V}_n \mathbf{\Sigma}^+$.

2. Solve for the core tensor as follows

$$\mathcal{Z} = \mathcal{D} \times_1 \mathbf{U}_1^T \times_2 \mathbf{U}_2^T \ldots \times_n \mathbf{U}_n^T \ldots \times_N \mathbf{U}_N^T. \qquad (15)$$

5 TensorFaces: Multilinear Analysis of Facial Images

As we stated earlier, image formation depends on scene geometry, viewpoint, and illumination conditions. Multilinear algebra offers a natural approach to the analysis of the multifactor structure of image ensembles and to addressing the difficult problem of disentangling the constituent factors or modes.

Fig. 3. The facial image database (28 subjects × 45 images per subject). (a) The 28 subjects shown in expression 2 (smile), viewpoint 3 (frontal), and illumination 2 (frontal). (b) The full image set for subject 1. Left to right, the three panels show images captured in illuminations 1, 2, and 3. Within each panel, images of expressions 1, 2, and 3 are shown horizontally while images from viewpoints 1, 2, 3, 4, and 5 are shown vertically. The image of subject 1 in (a) is the image situated at the center of (b).

In a concrete application of our multilinear image analysis technique, we employ the Weizmann face database of 28 male subjects photographed in 15 different poses under 4 illuminations performing 3 different expressions. We used a portion of this database, employing images in 5 poses, 3 illuminations, and 3 expressions.[4] Using a global rigid optical flow algorithm, we roughly aligned the original 512×352 pixel images relative to one reference image. The images were then decimated by a factor of 3 and cropped as shown in Fig. 3, yielding a total of 7943 pixels per image within the elliptical cropping window. Our facial image data tensor $\mathcal{D}$ is a $28 \times 5 \times 3 \times 3 \times 7943$ tensor. The number of modes is $N = 5$.

We apply multilinear analysis to the facial image data using the N-mode decomposition algorithm described in Section 4. The 5-mode decomposition of $\mathcal{D}$ is

$$\mathcal{D} = \mathcal{Z} \times_1 \mathbf{U}_{\text{people}} \times_2 \mathbf{U}_{\text{views}} \times_3 \mathbf{U}_{\text{illums}} \times_4 \mathbf{U}_{\text{expres}} \times_5 \mathbf{U}_{\text{pixels}}, \qquad (16)$$

where the $28 \times 5 \times 3 \times 3 \times 7943$ core tensor $\mathcal{Z}$ governs the interaction between the factors represented in the 5 mode matrices: The 28×28 mode matrix $\mathbf{U}_{\text{people}}$ spans the space of people parameters, the 5×5 mode matrix $\mathbf{U}_{\text{views}}$ spans the space of viewpoint parameters, the 3×3 mode matrix $\mathbf{U}_{\text{illums}}$ spans the space of illumination parameters and the 3×3 mode matrix $\mathbf{U}_{\text{expres}}$ spans the space of expression parameters. The 7943×7943 mode matrix $\mathbf{U}_{\text{pixels}}$ orthonormally spans the space of images.

Our multilinear analysis, which we call *TensorFaces*, subsumes linear, PCA analysis or conventional eigenfaces. Each column of $\mathbf{U}_{\text{pixels}}$ is an "eigenimage". These eigenimages are identical to conventional eigenfaces [13,17], since the former were computed by performing an SVD on the mode-5 flattened data tensor $\mathcal{D}$ which yields the matrix $\mathbf{D}_{\text{(pixels)}}$ whose columns are the vectorized images. To further show mathematically that PCA is a special case of our multilinear analysis, we write the latter in terms of matrix notation. A matrix representation of the N-mode SVD can be obtained by unfolding $\mathcal{D}$ and $\mathcal{Z}$ as follows:

$$\mathbf{D}_{(n)} = \mathbf{U}_n \mathbf{Z}_{(n)} (\mathbf{U}_{n+1} \otimes \mathbf{U}_{n+2} \otimes \ldots \otimes \mathbf{U}_N \otimes \mathbf{U}_1 \otimes \ldots \otimes \mathbf{U}_{n-1})^T, \qquad (17)$$

where $\otimes$ denotes the matrix Kronecker product. Using (17) we can express the decomposition of $\mathcal{D}$ as

$$\underbrace{\mathbf{D}_{\text{(pixels)}}}_{\text{image data}} = \underbrace{\mathbf{U}_{\text{pixels}}}_{\text{basis vectors}} \underbrace{\mathbf{Z}_{\text{(pixels)}} (\mathbf{U}_{\text{people}} \otimes \mathbf{U}_{\text{views}} \otimes \mathbf{U}_{\text{illums}} \otimes \mathbf{U}_{\text{expres}})^T}_{\text{coefficients}}. \qquad (18)$$

The above matrix product can be interpreted as a standard linear decomposition of the image ensemble, where the mode matrix $\mathbf{U}_{\text{pixels}}$ is the PCA matrix of basis vectors and the associated matrix of coefficients is obtained as the product of the flattened core tensor times the Kronecker product of the people, viewpoints, illuminations, and expressions mode matrices. Thus, as we stated above, our multilinear analysis subsumes linear, PCA analysis.

---

[4] A computer-controlled robot arm positioned the camera to $\pm 34°$, $\pm 17°$, and $0°$, the frontal view in the horizontal plane. The face was illuminated by turning on and off three light sources fixed at the same height as the face and positioned to the left, center, and right of the face. For additional details, see [10].

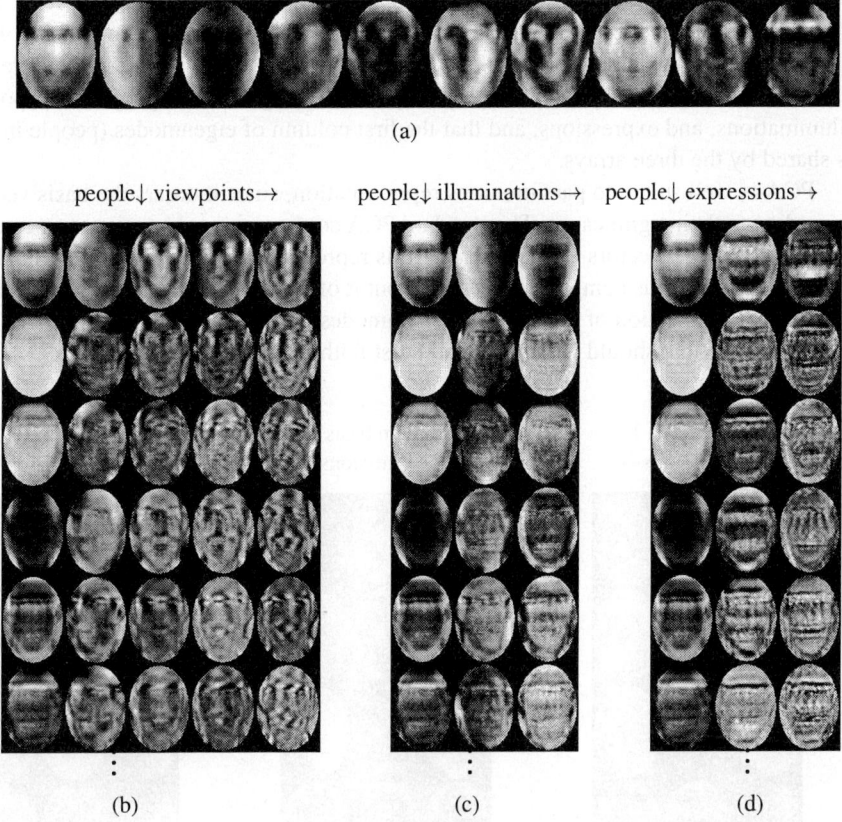

Fig. 4. Some of the basis vectors resulting from the multilinear analysis of the facial image data tensor $\mathcal{D}$. (a) The first 10 PCA eigenvectors (eigenfaces), which are contained in the mode matrix $\mathbf{U}_{\text{pixels}}$, and are the principal axes of variation across all images. (b,c,d) A partial visualization of the product $\mathcal{Z} \times_5 \mathbf{U}_{\text{pixels}}$, in which the core tensor $\mathcal{Z}$ transforms the eigenvectors $\mathbf{U}_{\text{pixels}}$ to yield a 5-mode, $28 \times 5 \times 3 \times 3 \times 7943$ tensor of eigenmodes which capture the variability across modes (rather than images). Some of the first few eigenmodes are shown in the three arrays. The labels at the top of each array indicate the names of the horizontal and vertical modes depicted in that array. Note that the basis vector at the top left of each panel is the average over all people, viewpoints, illuminations, and expressions (the first column of eigenmodes (people mode) is shared by the three arrays).

The advantage of multilinear analysis is that the core tensor $\mathcal{Z}$ can transform the eigenimages present in the matrix $\mathbf{U}_{\text{pixels}}$ into *eigenmodes*, which represent the principal axes of variation across the various modes (people, viewpoints, illuminations, expressions) and represents how the various factors interact with each other to create an image. This is accomplished by simply forming the product $\mathcal{Z} \times_5 \mathbf{U}_{\text{pixels}}$. By contrast, PCA basis vectors or eigenimages represent only the principal axes of variation across images. To demonstrate, Fig. 4 illustrates in part the results of the multilinear analysis of the facial image tensor $\mathcal{D}$. Fig. 4(a) shows the first 10 PCA eigenimages contained in $\mathbf{U}_{\text{pixels}}$.

Fig. 4(b) illustrates some of the eigenmodes in the product $\mathcal{Z} \times_5 \mathbf{U}_{\text{pixels}}$. A few of the lower-order eigenmodes are shown in the three arrays. The labels at the top of each array indicate the names of the horizontal and vertical modes depicted by the array. Note that the basis vector at the top left of each panel is the average over all people, viewpoints, illuminations, and expressions, and that the first column of eigenmodes (people mode) is shared by the three arrays.

PCA is well suited to parsimonious representation, since it orders the basis vectors according to their significance. The standard PCA compression scheme is to truncate the higher order eigenvectors associated with this representation. Our multilinear analysis enables an analogous compression scheme, but it offers much greater control. It allows the strategic truncation of higher-order eigenmodes depending on the task at hand and the modalities that should be represented most faithfully.

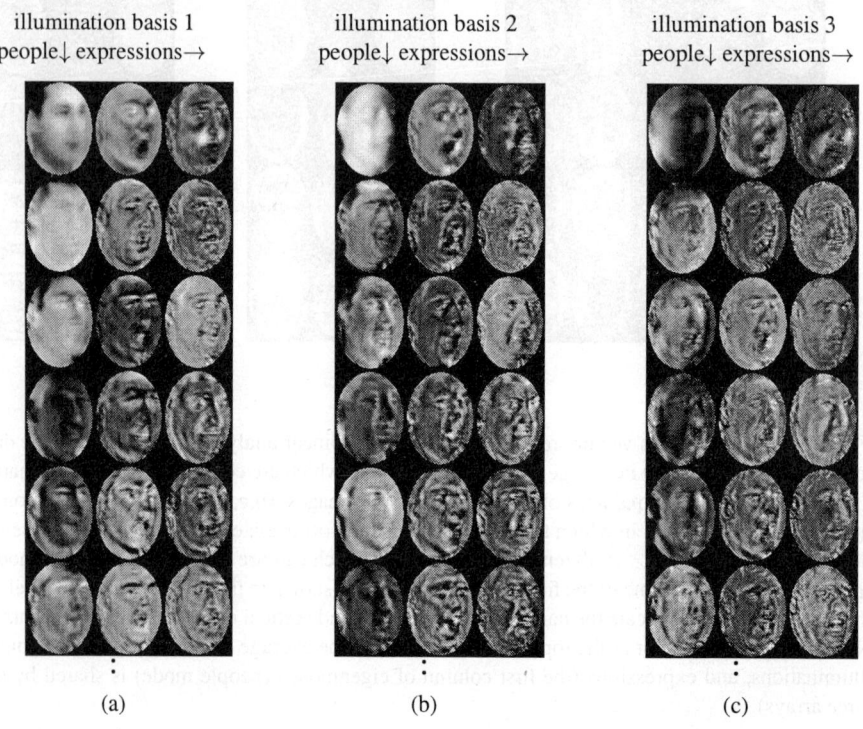

(a) (b) (c)

Fig. 5. Some of the eigenvectors in the $28 \times 3 \times 3 \times 7943$ tensor $\mathcal{Z} \times_2 \mathbf{U}_{\text{views}} \times_5 \mathbf{U}_{\text{pixels}}$ for viewpoint 1. These eigenmodes are viewpoint specific.

Multilinear analysis subsumes mixtures of probabilistic PCA or view-based models [15,11] when one uses a different choice of basis functions. Starting with the eigenmodes $\mathcal{Z} \times_5 \mathbf{U}_{\text{pixels}}$, we multiply the viewpoint parameter matrix $\mathbf{U}_{\text{views}}$ to form the product $\mathcal{Z} \times_2 \mathbf{U}_{\text{views}} \times_5 \mathbf{U}_{\text{pixels}}$, which yields the principal axes of variation of the image ensemble across the people mode, illumination mode, and expression mode for each of the 5 viewpoints. Fig. 5 shows the eigenvectors that span all the images in viewpoint 1.

In essence, the multilinear analysis provides for each viewpoint the principal axes of a multidimensional Gaussian.

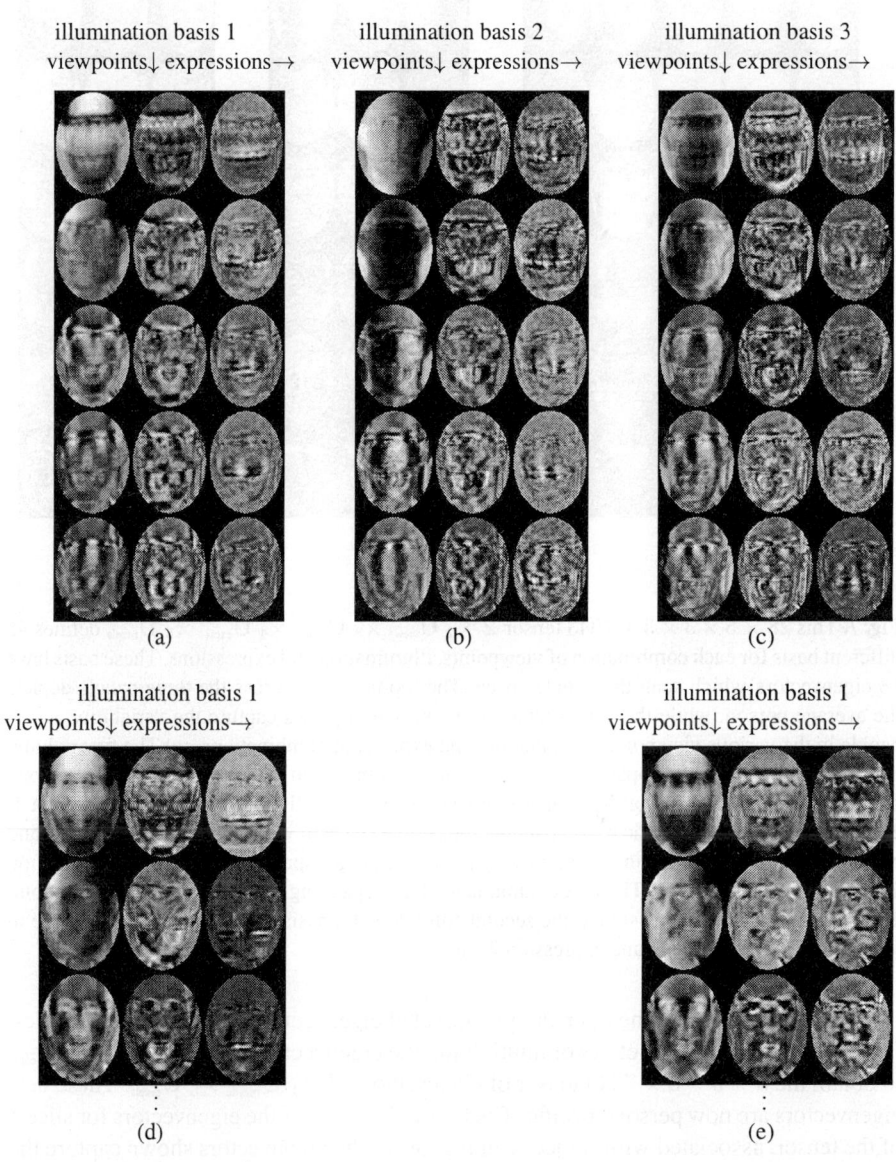

Fig. 6. (a,b,c) All the eigenvectors in the $5 \times 3 \times 3 \times 7943$ tensor $\mathcal{Z} \times_1 \mathbf{U}_{people} \times_5 \mathbf{U}_{pixels}$ for subject 1. This is the top slice (subject 1 in Fig. 3(a)) of the tensor depicted in Fig. 4(b–d) but multiplied by $\mathbf{U}_{people}$, which makes the eigenvectors person-specific. (d) Person specific eigenvectors for subject 2 and (e) for subject 3; the upper 3×3 portions of arrays analogous to that in (a) are shown.

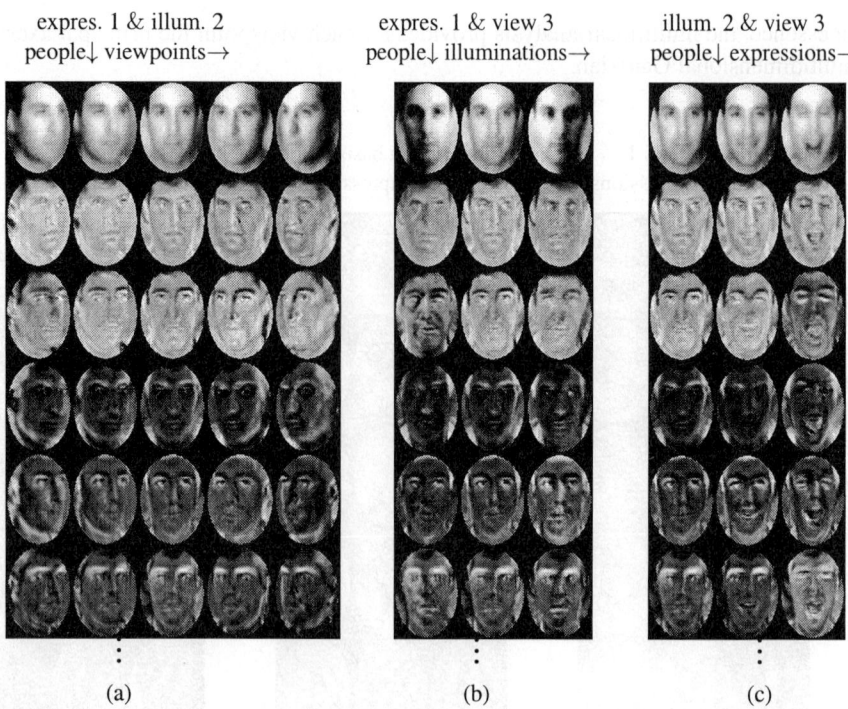

Fig. 7. This $28 \times 5 \times 3 \times 3 \times 7943$ tensor $\mathcal{Z} \times_2 \mathbf{U}_{\text{views}} \times_3 \mathbf{U}_{\text{illums}} \times_4 \mathbf{U}_{\text{expres}} \times_5 \mathbf{U}_{\text{pixels}}$ defines 45 different basis for each combination of viewpoints, illumination and expressions. These basis have 28 eigenvectors which span the people space. The topmost row across the three panels depicts the average person, while the eigenvectors in the remaining rows capture the variability across people in the various viewpoint, illumination, and expression combinations. (a) The first column is the basis spanning the people space in viewpoint 1, illumination 2 and expression 1, the second column is the basis spanning the people space in viewpoint 2, illumination 2 and expression 1, etc. (b) The first column is the basis spanning the people space in viewpoint 1, illumination 1 and expression 1, the second column is the basis spanning the people space in viewpoint 1, illumination 2 and expression 1, etc. (c) The first column is the basis spanning the people space in viewpoint 3, illumination 2 and expression 1, the second column is the basis spanning the people space in viewpoint 3, illumination 2 and expression 2, etc.

Similarly, we can define a person specific set of eigenvectors that span all the images. Fig. 6(a–c) illustrates the effect of multiplying the eigenvectors of Fig. 4(b–d) by $\mathbf{U}_{\text{people}}$ to obtain the $5 \times 3 \times 3 \times 7943$ tensor of eigenvectors $\mathcal{Z} \times_1 \mathbf{U}_{\text{people}} \times_5 \mathbf{U}_{\text{pixels}}$. These new eigenvectors are now person-specific. The figure shows all of the eigenvectors for slice 1 of the tensor, associated with subject 1 in Fig. 3(a). The eigenvectors shown capture the variations across the distribution of images of this particular subject over all viewpoints, expressions, and illuminations. Fig. 6(d–e) shows portions of slices 2 and 3 through the tensor (the upper 3×3 portions of arrays analogous to that in (a) of the figure are shown), showing some of the eigenvectors specific to subject 2 and to subject 3, respectively.

An important advantage of multilinear analysis is that it maps all images of a person, regardless of viewpoint, illumination and expression, to the same coefficient vector, given the appropriate choice of basis, thereby achieving zero intra-class scatter. Thus, multilinear analysis creates well separated people classes by maximizing the ratio of inter-class scatter to intra-class scatter [1]. By comparison, PCA will represent each different image of a person with a different vector of coefficients.

In our facial image database there are 45 images per person that vary with viewpoint, illumination, and expression. PCA represents each person as a set of 45 vector-valued coefficients, one for each image in which the person appears. The length of each PCA coefficient vector is $28 \times 5 \times 3 \times 3 = 1215$. By contrast, multilinear analysis enables us to represent each person with a single vector coefficient of dimension 28 relative to the bases comprising the tensor $\mathcal{Z} \times_2 \mathbf{U}_{views} \times_3 \mathbf{U}_{illums} \times_4 \mathbf{U}_{expres} \times_5 \mathbf{U}_{pixels}$, some of which are shown in Fig. 7. Each column in the figure is a basis and it is composed of 28 eigenvectors. In any column, the first eigenvector depicts the average person and the remaining eigenvectors capture the variability across people, for the particular combination of viewpoint, illumination, and expression associated with that column. The eigenvectors in any particular row play the same role in each column. This is the reason why images of the same person taken under different viewpoint, illumination, and expression conditions are projected to the same coefficient vector by the bases associated with these conditions.

6 Conclusion

We have identified the analysis of an ensemble of images resulting from the confluence of multiple factors related to scene structure, illumination, and viewpoint as a problem in multilinear algebra. Within this mathematical framework, the image ensemble is represented as a higher-dimensional tensor. This image data tensor must be decomposed in order to separate and parsimoniously represent the constituent factors. To this end, we prescribe the "N-mode SVD" algorithm, a multilinear extension of the conventional matrix singular value decomposition (SVD).

Although we have demonstrated the power of N-mode SVD using ensembles of facial images, which yielded TensorFaces, our tensor decomposition approach shows promise as a unifying mathematical framework for a variety of computer vision problems. In particular, it subsumes as special cases the simple linear (1-factor) analysis associated with conventional SVD and principal components analysis (PCA), as well as the incrementally more general bilinear (2-factor) analysis that has recently been investigated in the context of computer vision [4,14]. Our completely general multilinear approach accommodates any number of factors by taking advantage of the mathematical machinery of tensors.

Not only do tensor decompositions play an important role in the factor analysis of multidimensional datasets, as described in this paper, but they also appear in conjunction with higher order statistics (higher order moments and cumulants) that are employed in independent component analysis (ICA). Hence, we can potentially apply tensor decomposition to ICA.

In future work, we will develop algorithms that exploit our multilinear analysis framework in a range of applications, including image compression, resynthesis, and recognition.

References

1. P.N. Belhumeur, J. Hespanha, and D.J. Kriegman. Eigenfaces vs. fisherfaces: Recognition using class specific linear projection. In *Proceedings of the European Conference on Computer Vision*, pages 45–58, 1996.
2. R. Chellappa, C.L. Wilson, and S. Sirohey. Human and machine recognition of faces: A survey. *Proceedings of the IEEE*, 83(5):705–740, May 1995.
3. L. de Lathauwer. *Signal Processing Based on Multilinear Algebra*. PhD thesis, Katholieke Univ. Leuven, Belgium, 1997.
4. W. Freeman and J. Tenenbaum. Learing bilinear models for two-factor problems in vision. In *Proceedings of the IEEE Conference on Computer Vision and Pattern Recognition*, pages 554–560, 1997.
5. A. Kapteyn, H. Neudecker, and T. Wansbeek. An approach to n-mode component analysis. *Psychometrika*, 51(2):269–275, June 1986.
6. T. G. Kolda. Orthogonal tensor decompositions. *SIAM Journal on Matrix Analysis and Applications*, 23(1):243–255, 2001.
7. J. B. Kruskal. Rank, decomposition, and uniqueness for 3-way and n-way array. In R. Coppi and S. Bolasco, editors, *Multiway Data Analysis*, pages 7–18, Amsterdam, 1989. North Holland.
8. J. R. Magnus and H. Neudecker. *Matrix Differential Calculus with Applications in Statistics and Econometrics*. John Wiley & Sons, New York, New York, 1988.
9. D.H. Marimont and B.A. Wandell. Linear models of surface and illuminance spectra. *J. Optical Society of America, A.*, 9:1905–1913, 1992.
10. Y. Moses, S. Edelman, and S. Ullman. Generalization to novel images in upright and inverted faces. *Perception*, 25:443–461, 1996.
11. A. Pentland and B. Moghaddam. View-based and modular eigenspaces for face recognition. In *Proc. IEEE Conf. on Computer Vision and Pattern Recognition*, 1994.
12. A. Shashua and A. Levin. Linear image coding for regression and classification using the tensor-rank principle. In *Proceedings of the IEEE Conference on Computer Vision and Pattern Recognition*, page in press, Hawai, 2001.
13. L. Sirovich and M. Kirby. Low dimensional procedure for the characterization of human faces. *Journal of the Optical Society of America A.*, 4:519–524, 1987.
14. J.B. Tenenbaum and W.T. Freeman. Separating style and content. In M. Moser, M. Jordan, and T. Petsche, editors, *Advances in Neural Information Processing Systems*, pages 662–668. MIT Press, 1997.
15. M. E. Tipping and C. M. Bishop. Mixtures of probabilistic principal component analysers. *Neural Computation*, 11(2):443–482, 1999.
16. L. R. Tucker. Some mathematical notes on three-mode factor analysis. *Psychometrika*, 31:279–311, 1966.
17. M. A. Turk and A. P. Pentland. Eigenfaces for recognition. *Journal of Cognitive Neuroscience*, 3(1):71–86, 1991.
18. M. A. O. Vasilescu. An algorithm for extracting human motion signatures. In *IEEE Conference on Computer Vision and Pattern Recognition*, Hawai, 2001. in press.
19. M. A. O. Vasilescu. Human motion signatures for character animation. In *ACM SIGGRAPH 2001 Conf. Abstracts and Applications*, page 200, Los Angeles, August 2001.

'Dynamism of a Dog on a Leash'
or
Behavior Classification by Eigen-Decomposition of Periodic Motions

Roman Goldenberg, Ron Kimmel, Ehud Rivlin, and Michael Rudzsky

Computer Science Department,
Technion—Israel Institute of Technology
Technion City, Haifa 32000, ISRAEL

Abstract. Following Futurism, we show how periodic motions can be represented by a small number of eigen-shapes that capture the whole dynamic mechanism of periodic motions. Spectral decomposition of a silhouette of an object in motion serves as a basis for behavior classification by principle component analysis. The boundary contour of the walking dog, for example, is first computed efficiently and accurately. After normalization, the implicit representation of a sequence of silhouette contours given by their corresponding binary images, is used for generating eigen-shapes for the given motion. Singular value decomposition produces these eigen-shapes that are then used to analyze the sequence. We show examples of object as well as behavior classification based on the eigen-decomposition of the binary silhouette sequence.

1 Introduction

Futurism is a movement in art, music, and literature that began in Italy at about 1909 and marked especially by an effort to give formal expression to the dynamic energy and movement of mechanical processes. A typical example is the 'Dynamism of a Dog on a Leash' by Giacomo Balla, who lived during the years 1871-1958 in Italy, see Figure 1 [2]. In this painting one could see how the artist captures in one still image the periodic walking motion of a dog on a leash. Following Futurism, we show how periodic motions can be represented by a small number of eigen-shapes that capture the whole dynamic mechanism of periodic motions. Singular value decomposition of a silhouette of an object serves as a basis for behavior classification by principle component analysis. Figure 2 present a running horse video sequence and its eigen-shape decomposition. One can see the similarity between the first eigen-shapes - Figure 2(c,d), and another futurism style painting "The Red Horseman" by Carlo Carra [2] - Figure 2(e). The boundary contour of the moving non-rigid object is computed efficiently and accurately by the fast geodesic active contours [15]. After normalization, the implicit representation of a sequence of silhouette contours given by their corresponding binary images, is used for generating eigen-shapes for the given motion. Singular value decomposition produces the eigen-shapes that are used to analyze the sequence. We show examples of object as well as behavior classification based on the eigen-decomposition of the sequence.

Fig. 1. 'Dynamism of a Dog on a Leash' 1912, by Giacomo Balla. Albright-Knox Art Gallery, Buffalo.

2 Related Work

Motion based recognition received a lot of attention in the last several years. This is due to the general recognition of the fact that the direct use of temporal data may significantly improve our ability to solve a number of basic computer vision problems such as image segmentation, tracking, object classification, etc., as well as the availability of a low cost computer systems powerful enough to process large amounts of data.

In general, when analyzing a moving object, one can use two main sources of information to rely upon: changes of the moving object position (and orientation) in space, and object deformations.

Object position is an easy-to-get characteristic, applicable both for rigid and non-rigid bodies that is provided by most of the target detection and tracking systems, usually as a center of the target bounding box. A number of techniques [17], [16], [11], [26] were proposed for the detection of motion events and for the recognition of various types of motions based on the analysis of the moving object trajectory and its derivatives. Detecting object orientation is a more challenging problem which is usually solved by fitting a model that may vary from a simple ellipsoid [26] to a complex 3D vehicle model [18] or a specific aircraft-class model adapted for noisy radar images as in [9].

While object orientation characteristic is more applicable for rigid objects, it is object deformation that contains the most essential information about the nature of the non-rigid body motion. This is especially true for natural non-rigid objects in locomotion that exhibit substantial changes in their apparent view,

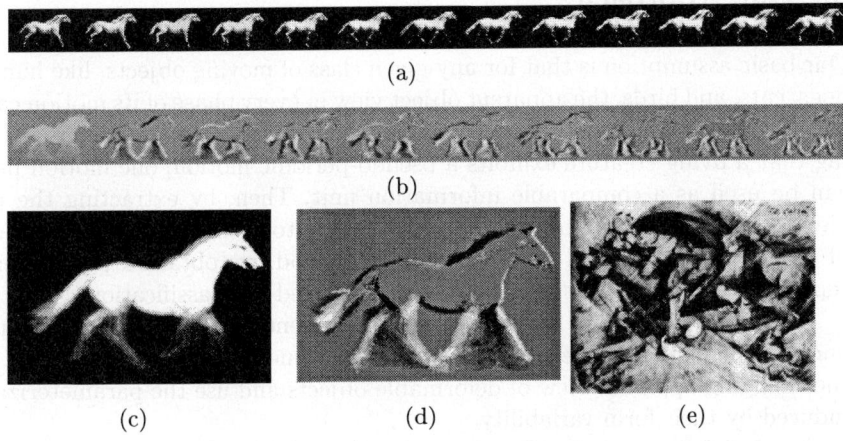

Fig. 2. (a) running horse video sequence, (b) first 10 eigen-shapes, (c,d) first and second eigen-shapes enlarged, (e) 'The Red Horseman', 1914, by Carlo Carra, Civico Museo d'Arte Contemporanea, Milan.

as in this case the motion itself is caused by these deformations, e.g. walking, running, hoping, crawling, flying, etc.

There exists a large number of papers dealing with the classification of moving non-rigid objects and their motions, based on their appearance. Lipton et al. describe a method for moving target classification based on their static appearance [19] and using the skeletonization [13]. Polana and Nelson [24] used local motion statistics computed for image grid cells to classify various types of activities. An original approach using the temporal templates and motion history images (MHI) for action representation and classification was suggested by Davis and Bobick in [3]. Cutler and Davis [10] describe a system for real-time moving object classification based on periodicity analysis. It would be impossible to describe here the whole spectrum of papers published in this field and we refer the reader to the following surveys [5], [14] and [21].

The most related to our approach is a work by Yacoob and Black [29], where different types of human activities were recognized using a parameterized representation of measurements collected during one motion period. The measurements were eight motion parameters tracked for five body parts (arm, torso, thigh, calf and foot).

In this paper we concentrate on the analysis of the deformations of moving non-rigid bodies in an attempt to extract characteristics that allow us to distinguish between different types of motions and different classes of objects.

3 Our Approach

Our basic assumption is that for any given class of moving objects, like humans, dogs, cats, and birds, the apparent object view in every phase of its motion can be encoded as a combination of several basic body views or configurations. Assuming that a living creature exhibits a pseudo-periodic motion, one motion period can be used as a comparable information unit. Then, by extracting the basic views from a large training set and projecting onto them the observed sequence of object views collected from one motion period, we obtain a parameterized representation of object's motion that can be used for classification.

Unlike [29] we do not assume an initial segmentation of the body into parts and do not explicitly measure the motion parameters. Instead, we work with the changing apparent view of deformable objects and use the parameterization induced by their form variability.

In what follows we describe the main steps of the process that include,

- Segmentation and tracking of the moving object that yield an accurate external object boundary in every frame.
- Periodicity analysis, in which we estimate the frequency of the pseudo-periodic motion and split the video sequence into single-period intervals.
- Frame sequence alignment that brings the single-period sequences above to a standardized form by compensating for temporal shift, speed variations, different object sizes and imaging conditions.
- Parameterization by building an eigen-shape basis from a training set of possible object views and projecting the apparent view of a moving body onto this basis.

3.1 Segmentation and Tracking

As our approach is based on the analysis of deformations of the moving body, the accuracy of the segmentation and tracking algorithm in finding the target outline is crucial for the quality of the final result. This rules out a number of available or easy-to-build tracking systems that provide only a center of mass or a bounding box around the target and calls for more precise and usually more sophisticated solutions.

Therefore we decided to use the geodesic active contour approach [4] and specifically the 'fast geodesic active contour' method described in [15], where the segmentation problem is expressed as a geometric energy minimization. We search for a curve C that minimizes the functional

$$S[\mathcal{C}] = \int_0^{L(\mathcal{C})} g(\mathcal{C}) ds,$$

where ds is the Euclidean arclength, $L(\mathcal{C})$ is the total Euclidean length of the curve, and g is a positive edge indicator function in a 3D hybrid spacial-temporal space that depends on the pair of consecutive frames $I^{t-1}(x,y)$ and $I^t(x,y)$. It gets small values along the spacial-temporal edges, i.e. moving object boundaries, and higher values elsewhere.

In addition to the scheme described in [15], we also use the background information whenever a static background assumption is valid and a background image $B(x,y)$ is available. In the active contours framework this can be achieved either by modifying the g function to reflect the edges in the difference image $D(x,y) = |B(x,y) - I^t(x,y)|$, or by introducing additional area integration terms to the functional $S(\mathcal{C})$:

$$S[\mathcal{C}] = \int_0^{L(\mathcal{C})} g(\mathcal{C}) ds + \lambda_1 \int_{in(\mathcal{C})} |D(x,y) - c_1|^2 da + \lambda_2 \int_{out(\mathcal{C})} |D(x,y) - c_2|^2 da,$$

where λ_1 and λ_2 are fixed parameters and $c1$, $c2$ are given by:

$$c_1 = average_{inside(\mathcal{C})}[D(x,y)]$$
$$c_2 = average_{outside(\mathcal{C})}[D(x,y)]$$

The latter approach is inspired by the 'active contours without edges' model proposed by Chan and Vese [6] and forces the curve $\mathcal{C}$ to close on a region whose interior and exterior have approximately uniform values in $D(x,y)$. A different approach to utilize the region information by coupling between the motion estimation and the tracking problem was suggested by Paragios and Deriche in [22].

Figure 3 shows some results of moving object segmentation and tracking using the proposed method.

Contours can be represented in various ways. Here, in order to have a unified coordinate system and be able to apply a simple algebraic tool, we use the implicit representation of a simple closed curve as its binary image. That is, the contour is given by an image for which the exterior of the contour is black while the interior of the contour is white.

3.2 Periodicity Analysis

Here we assume that the majority of non-rigid moving objects are self-propelled alive creatures whose motion is almost periodic. Thus, one motion period, like a step of a walking man or a rabbit hop, can be used as a natural unit of motion and extracted motion characteristics can by normalized by the period size.

The problem of detection and characterization of periodic activities was addressed by several research groups and the prevailing technique for periodicity detection and measurements is the analysis of the changing 1-D intensity signals along spatio-temporal curves associated with a moving object or the curvature analysis of feature point trajectories [23], [20], [25], [27]. Here we address the problem using global characteristics of motion such as moving object contour deformations and the trajectory of the center of mass.

By running frequency analysis on such 1-D contour metrics as the contour area, velocity of the center of mass, principal axes orientation, etc. we can detect

Fig. 3. Non-rigid moving object segmentation and tracking.

the basic period of the motion. Figures 4 and 5 present global motion characteristics derived from segmented moving objects in two sequences. One can clearly observe the common dominant frequency in all three graphs.

The period can also be estimated in a straightforward manner by looking for the frame where the external object contour best matches the object contour in the current frame. Figure 6 shows the deformations of a walking man contour during one motion period (step). Samples from two different steps are presented and each vertical pair of frames is phase synchronized. One can clearly see the similarity between the corresponding contours. An automated contour matching can be performed in a number of ways, e.g. by comparing contour signatures or by looking at the correlation between the object silhouettes in different frames. Figure 7 shows four graphs of inter-frame silhouette correlation values measured for four different starting frames taken within one motion period. It is clearly visible that all four graphs nearly coincide and the local maxima peaks are approximately evenly spaced. The period, therefore, can be estimated as the average distance between the neighboring peaks.

3.3 Frame Sequence Alignment

One of the most desirable features of any classification system is the invariance to a set of possible input transformations. As the input in our case is not a static image, but a sequence of images, the system should be robust to both spacial and temporal variations.

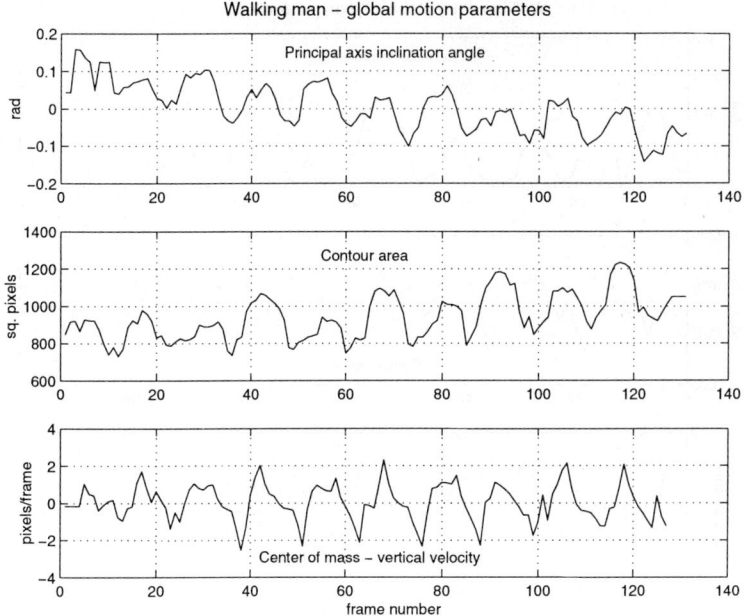

Fig. 4. Global motion characteristics measured for walking man sequence.

Spatial Alignment: Scale invariance is achieved by cropping a square bounding box around the center of mass of the tracked target silhouette and re-scaling it to a predefined size (see Figure 8).

One way to have orientation invariance is to keep a collection of motion samples for a wide range of possible motion directions and then look for the best match. This approach was used by Yacoob and Black in [29] to distinguish between different walking directions. Although here we experiment only with motions nearly parallel to the image plane, the system proved to be robust to small variations in orientation. Since we do not want to keep models for both left-to-right and right-to-left motion directions, the right-to-left moving sequences are converted to left-to-right by horizontal mirror flip.

Temporal Alignment: A good estimate of the motion period allows us to compensate for motion speed variations by re-sampling each period subsequence to a predefined duration. This can be done by interpolation between the binary silhouette images themselves or between their parameterized representation as explained below. Figure 9 presents an original and re-sampled one-period subsequence after scaling from 11 to 10 frames.

Temporal shift is another issue that has to be addressed in order to align the phase of the observed one-cycle sample and the models stored in the training base. In [29] it was done by solving a minimization problem of finding the

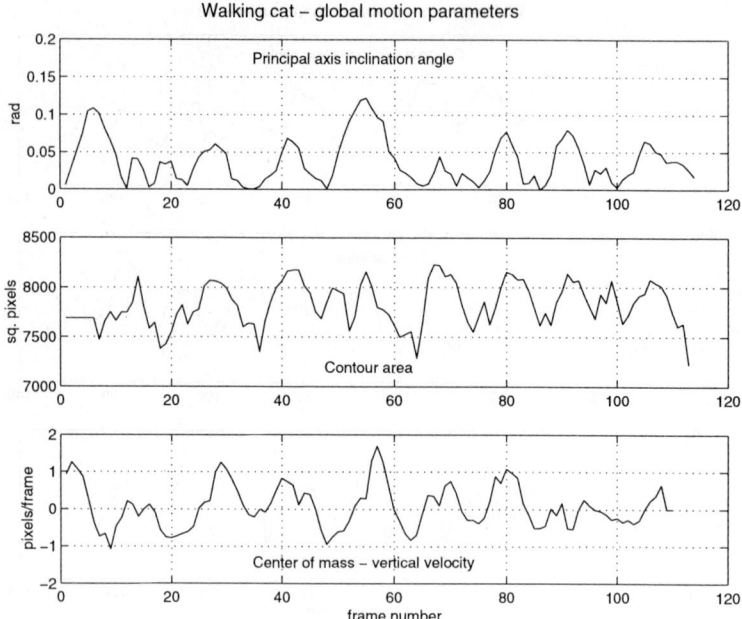

Fig. 5. Global motion characteristics measured for walking cat sequence.

optimal parameters of temporal scaling and time shift transformations so that the observed sequence is best matched to the training samples. Polana and Nelson [24] handled this problem by matching the test one-period subsequence to reference template at all possible temporal translations.

Assuming that in the training set all the sequences are accurately aligned, we find the temporal shift of a test sequence by looking for the starting frame that best matches the generalized (averaged) starting frame of the training samples, as they all look alike. Figure 10 shows (a) - the reference starting frame taken as an average over the temporally aligned training set, (b) - a re-sampled single-period test sequence and, (c) the correlation between the reference starting frame and the test sequence frames. The maximal correlation is achieved at the seventh frame, therefore the test sequence is aligned by cyclically shifting it 7 frames to the left.

3.4 Parameterization

In order to reduce the dimensionality of the problem we first project the object image in every frame onto a low dimensional base that represents all possible appearances of objects that belong to a certain class, like humans, four-leg animals, etc.

Let n be number of frames in the training base of a certain class of objects and M be a training samples matrix, where each column corresponds to

Fig. 6. Deformations of a walking man contour during one motion period (step). Two steps synchronized in phase are shown. One can see the similarity between contours in corresponding phases.

a spatially aligned image of a moving object written as a binary vector. In our experiments we use 50×50 normalized images, therefore, M is a $2500 \times n$ matrix. The correlation matrix MM^T is decomposed using Singular Value Decomposition as $MM^T = U\Sigma V^T$, where U is an orthogonal matrix of principal directions and the Σ is a diagonal matrix of singular values. In practice, the decomposition is performed on $M^T M$, which is computationally more efficient [28]. The principal basis $\{U_i, i = 1..k\}$ for the training set is then taken as k columns of U corresponding to the largest singular values in Σ. Figure 11 presents a principal basis for the training set formed of 800 sample images collected from more than 60 sequences showing dogs and cats in motion. The basis is built by taking the $k = 20$ first principal component vectors.

We assume that by building such representative bases for every class of objects and then finding the basis that best represents a given object image in a minimal distance to the feature space (DTFS) sense, we can distinguish between various object classes. Figure 12 shows the distances from more than 1000 various images of people, dogs and cats to the feature space of people and to that of dogs and cats. In all cases, images of people were closer to the people feature space than to the animals' feature space and vise a versa. This allows us to distinguish between these two classes. A similar approach was used in [12] for the detection of pedestrians in traffic scenes.

If the object class is known (e.g. we know that the object is a dog), we can parameterize the moving object silhouette image I in every frame by projecting it onto the class basis. Let B be the basis matrix formed from the basis vectors $\{U_i, i = 1..k\}$. Then, the parameterized representation of the object image I is given by the vector $\overline{p}$ of length k as $\overline{p} = B^T \overline{v_I}$, where $\overline{v_I}$ is the image I written as a vector.

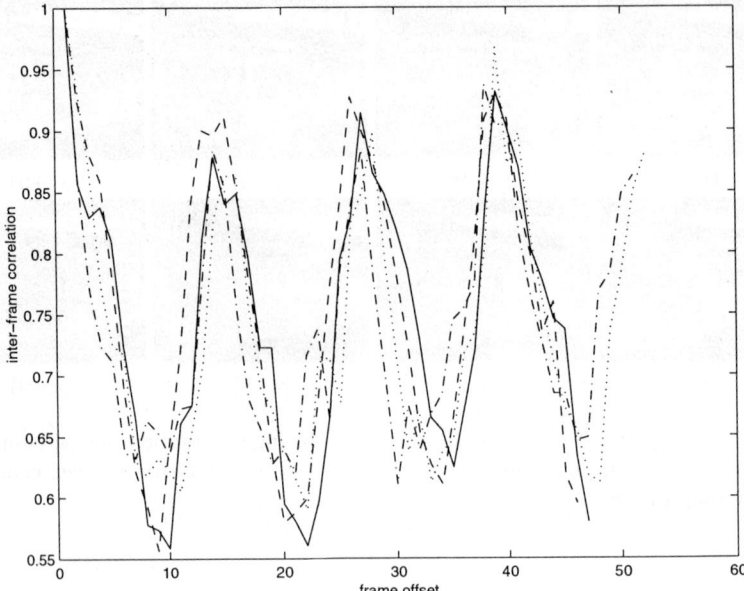

Fig. 7. Inter-frame correlation between object silhouettes. Four graphs show the correlation measured for four initial frames.

The idea of using a parameterized representation in motion-based recognition context is certainly not a new one. To name a few examples we mention again the work of Yacoob and Black [29]. Cootes et al. [8] used similar technique for describing feature point locations by a reduced parameter set. Baumberg and Hogg [1] used PCA to describe a set of admissible B-spline models for deformable object tracking. Chomat and Crowley [7] used PCA-based spatio-temporal filter for human motion recognition.

Figure 13 shows several normalized moving object images from the original sequence and their reconstruction from a parameterized representation by back-projection to the image space. The numbers below are the norms of differences between the original and the back-projected images. These norms can be used as the DTFS estimation.

Now, we can use these parameterized representations to distinguish between different types of motion. The reference base for the activity recognition consists of temporally aligned one-period subsequences, whereas the moving object silhouette in every frame of these subsequences is represented by its projection to the principal basis. More formally, let $\{I_f : f = 1..T\}$ be a one-period, temporally aligned set of normalized object images, and $\overline{p_f}, f = 1..T$ a projection of the image I_f onto the principal basis B of size k. Then, the vector P of length kT formed by concatenation of all the vectors $\overline{p_f}, f = 1..T$, represent a one-period subsequence. By choosing a basis of size $k = 20$ and the normalized duration of

Fig. 8. Scale alignment. A minimal square bounding box around the center of the segmented object silhouette (a) is cropped and re-scaled to form a 50 × 50 binary image (b).

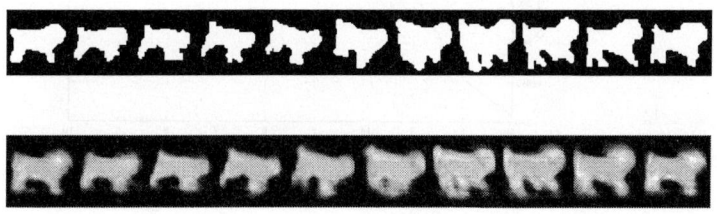

Fig. 9. Temporal alignment. Top: original 11 frames of one period subsequence. Bottom: re-sampled 10 frames sequence.

one-period subsequence to be $T = 10$ frames, every single-period subsequence is represented by a feature point in a 200-dimensional feature space.

In the following experiment we processed a number of sequences of dogs and cats in various types of locomotion. From these sequences we extracted 33 samples of walking dogs, 9 samples of running dogs, 9 samples with galloping dogs and 14 samples of walking cats. Let $S_{200 \times m}$ be the matrix of projected single-period subsequences, where m is the number of samples and the SVD of the correlation matrix is given by $SS^T = U^S \Sigma^S V^S$. In Figure 14(a) we depict the resulting feature points projected for visualization to the 3-D space using the three first principal directions $\{U_i^S : i = 1..3\}$, taken as the column vectors of U^S corresponding to the three largest eigen values in Σ^S. One can easily observe four separable clusters corresponding to the four groups.

Another experiment was done over the 'people' class of images. Figure 14(b) presents feature points corresponding to several sequences showing people walking and running parallel to the image plane and running at oblique angle to the camera. Again, all three groups lie in separable clusters.

The classification can be performed, for example, using the k-nearest-neighbor algorithm. We conducted the 'leave one out' test for the dogs set above, classifying every sample by taking them out from the training set one at a time, and the three-nearest-neighbors strategy resulted in 100% success rate.

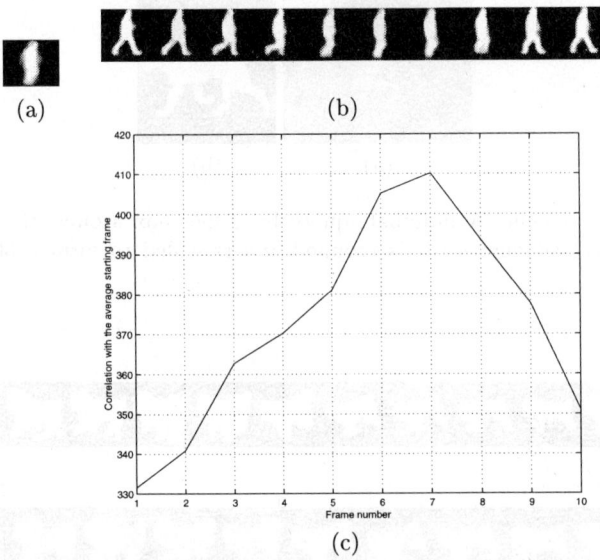

Fig. 10. Temporal shift alignment: (a) - average starting frame of all the training set sequences, (b) - temporally shifted single-cycle test sequence, (c) - the correlation between the reference starting frame and the test sequence frames

4 Concluding Remarks

We presented a new framework for motion-based classification of moving non-rigid objects. The technique is based on the analysis of changing appearance of moving objects and is heavily relying on high accuracy results of segmentation and tracking by using the fast geodesic contour approach. The periodicity analysis is then performed based on the global properties of the extracted moving object contours, followed by video sequence spatial and temporal normalization. Normalized one-period subsequences are parameterized by projection onto a principal basis extracted from a training set of images for a given class of objects. A number of experiments show the ability of the system to analyze motions of humans and animals, to distinguish between these two classes based on object appearance, and to classify various type of activities within a class, such as walking, running, galloping. The 'dogs and cats' experiment demonstrate the ability of the system to discriminate between these two very similar by appearance classes by analyzing their locomotion.

5 Acknowledgments

We thank Alfred M. Bruckshtein for sharing with us his observation of the connection between the Futurism art movement and the periodic motion presentation using eigen shapes.

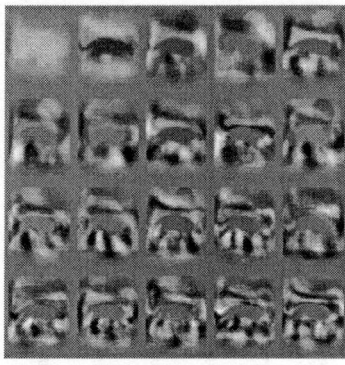

Fig. 11. The principal basis for the 'dogs and cats' training set formed of 20 first principal component vectors.

References

1. A Baumberg and D Hogg. An efficient method for contour tracking using active shape models. In *In Proc. IEEE Workshop on Motion of Non-Rigid and Articulated Objects*, pages 194–199, Austin, 1994.
2. J R Beniger. The Arts and New Media site. In *www.usc.edu/schools/annenberg/asc/projects/ comm544/*, University of South California, Annenberg School for Communication.
3. A Bobick and J Davis. The representation and recognition of action using temporal templates. *IEEE Trans. on PAMI*, 23(3):257–267, 2001.
4. V. Caselles, R. Kimmel, and G. Sapiro. Geodesic active contours. *IJCV*, 22(1):61–79, 1997.
5. C Cedras and M Shah. Motion-based recognition: A survey. *IVC*, 13(2):129–155, March 1995.
6. T F Chan and L A Vese. Active contours without edges. *IEEE trans. on Image Processing*, 10(2):266–277, February 2001.
7. O Chomat and J Crowley. Recognizing motion using local appearance, 1998.
8. T F Cootes, C J Taylor, D H Cooper, and J Graham. Active shape models: Their training and application. *CVIU*, 61(1):38–59, January 1995.
9. N J Cutaia and J A O'Sullivan. Automatic target recognition using kinematic priors. In *Proceedings of the 33rd Conference on Decision and Control*, pages 3303–3307, Lake Buena Vista, FL, December 1994.
10. R Cutler and L Davis. Robust real-time periodic motion detection, analysis, and applications. *PAMI*, 22(8):781–796, August 2000.
11. S A Engel and J M Rubin. Detecting visual motion boundaries. In *Proc. Workshop on Motion: Representation and Analysis*, pages 107–111, Charleston, S.C., May 1986.
12. U Franke, D Gavrila, S Gorzig, F Lindner, F Paetzold, and C Wohler. Autonomous driving goes downtown. *IEEE Intelligent System*, 13(6):40–48, 1998.
13. H Fujiyoshi and A Lipton. Real-time human motion analysis by image skeletonization. In *Proc. of the Workshop on Application of Computer Vision*, October 1998.

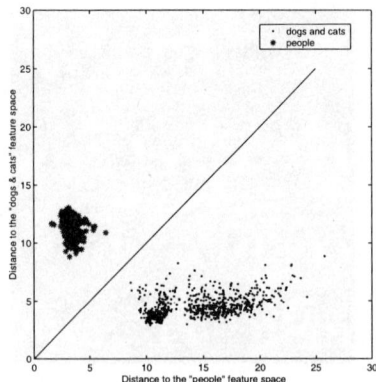

Fig. 12. Distances to the 'people' and 'dogs and cats' feature spaces from more than 1000 various images of people, dogs and cats.

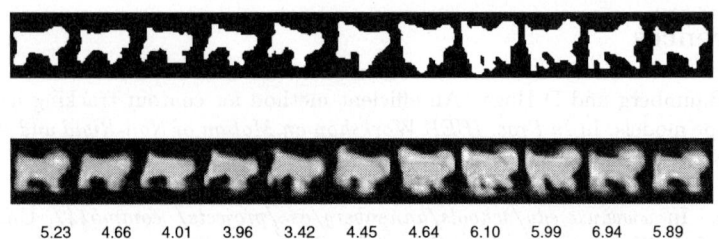

Fig. 13. Image sequence parameterization. Top: 11 normalized target images of the original sequence. Bottom: the same images after the parameterization using the principal basis and back-projecting to the image basis. The numbers are the norms of the differences between the original and the back-projected images.

14. D M Gavrila. The visual analysis of human movement: A survey. *CVIU*, 73(1):82–98, January 1999.
15. R Goldenberg, R Kimmel, E Rivlin, and M Rudzsky. Fast geodesic active contours. *IEEE Trans. on Image Processing*, 10(10):1467–75, October 2001.
16. K Gould, K Rangarajan, and M Shah. Detection and representation of events in motion trajectories. In *Advances in Image Processing and Analysis, chapter 14*. SPIE Optical Engineering Press, June 1992. Gonzalez and Mahdavieh (Eds.).
17. K Gould and M Shah. The trajectory primal sketch: a multi-scale scheme for representing motion characteristics. In *Proc. Conf. on Computer Vision and Pattern Recognition, San Diego, CA*, pages 79–85, 1989.
18. D Koller, K Daniilidis, and H-H Nagel. Model-based object tracking in monocular image sequences of road traffic scenes. *International Journal of Computer Vision*, 10:257–281, 1993.
19. A Lipton, H Fujiyoshi, and R Patil. Moving target classification and tracking from real-time video. In *In Proc. IEEE Image Understanding Workshop*, pages 129–136,

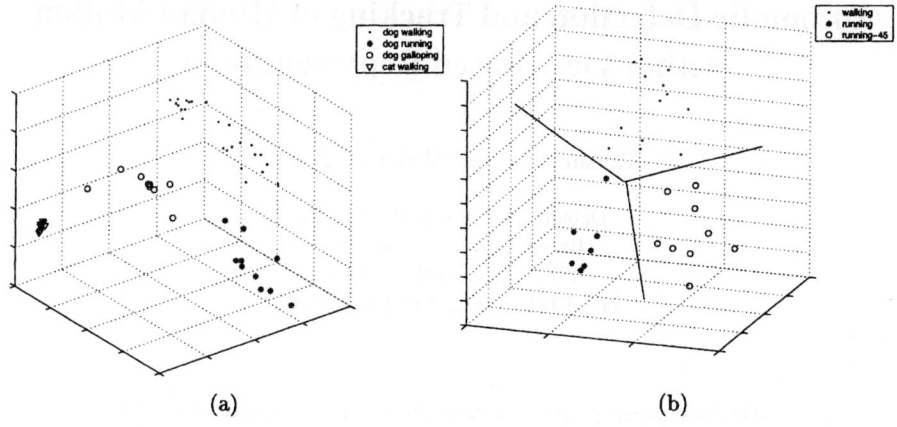

(a) (b)

Fig. 14. Feature points extracted from the sequences with (a) walking, running and galloping dogs and walking cats, and (b) people walking and running parallel to the image plane and at 45 degrees angle to the camera. Feature points are projected to the 3-D space for visualization.

1998.
20. F Liu and R W Picard. Finding periodicity in space and time. In *Proc. of the 6th Int. Conf. on Computer Vision*, pages 376–383, Bombay, India, 1998.
21. D M Moeslund and E Granum. A survey of computer vision-based human motion capture. *CVIU*, 81(3):231–268, March 2001.
22. N Paragios and R Deriche. Geodesic active regions for motion estimation and tracking. In *Proc. of the 7th Int. Conf. on Computer Vision*, pages 688–694, Kerkyra, Greece, 1999.
23. R Polana and R C Nelson. Detecting activities. *Journal of Visual Communication and Image Representation*, 5:172–180, 1994.
24. R. Polana and R.C. Nelson. Detection and recognition of periodic, nonrigid motion. *IJCV*, 23(3):261–282, June 1997.
25. S M Seitz and C R Dyer. View invariant analysis of cyclic motion. *Int. Journal of Computer Vision*, 25(3):231–251, December 1997.
26. J M Siskind and Q Morris. A maximum-likelihood approach to visual event classification. In *Proceedings of the Fourth European Conference on Computer Vision*, pages 347–360, Cambridge, UK, April 1996.
27. P S Tsai, M Shah, K Keiter, and T Kasparis. Cyclic motion detection for motion based recognition. *Pattern Recognition*, 27(12):1591–1603, December 1994.
28. M. Turk and A. Pentland. Eigenfaces for recognition. *Journal of Cognitive Neuro Science*, 3(1):71–86, 1991.
29. Y Yacoob and M J Black. Parameterized modeling and recognition of activities. *CVIU*, 73(2):232–247, February 1999.

Automatic Detection and Tracking of Human Motion with a View-Based Representation

Ronan Fablet and Michael J. Black

Department of Computer Science
Brown University, Box 1910
Providence, RI02912, USA
{rfablet,black}@cs.brown.edu

Abstract. This paper proposes a solution for the automatic detection and tracking of human motion in image sequences. Due to the complexity of the human body and its motion, automatic detection of 3D human motion remains an open, and important, problem. Existing approaches for automatic detection and tracking focus on 2D cues and typically exploit object appearance (color distribution, shape) or knowledge of a static background. In contrast, we exploit 2D optical flow information which provides rich descriptive cues, while being independent of object and background appearance. To represent the optical flow patterns of people from arbitrary viewpoints, we develop a novel representation of human motion using low-dimensional spatio-temporal models that are learned using motion capture data of human subjects. In addition to human motion (the foreground) we probabilistically model the motion of generic scenes (the background); these statistical models are defined as Gibbsian fields specified from the first-order derivatives of motion observations. Detection and tracking are posed in a principled Bayesian framework which involves the computation of a posterior probability distribution over the model parameters (i.e., the location and the type of the human motion) given a sequence of optical flow observations. Particle filtering is used to represent and predict this non-Gaussian posterior distribution over time. The model parameters of samples from this distribution are related to the pose parameters of a 3D articulated model (e.g. the approximate joint angles and movement direction). Thus the approach proves suitable for initializing more complex probabilistic models of human motion. As shown by experiments on real image sequences, our method is able to detect and track people under different viewpoints with complex backgrounds.

Keywords: Visual motion, motion detection and tracking, human motion analysis, probabilistic models, particle filtering, optical flow.

1 Introduction

The extraction and the tracking of humans in image sequences is a key issue for a variety of application fields, such as, video-surveillance, animation, human-computer interface, and video indexing. The focus of a great deal of research has been the detection and tracking of simple models of humans by exploiting knowledge of skin color or static backgrounds [10,15,22]. Progress has also been made on the problem of accurate 3D tracking of high-dimensional articulated body models given a known initial starting pose [9,11,25]. A significant open issue that limits the applicability of these 3D models is the problem of automatic initialization. Simpler, lower-dimensional, models are needed that can be automatically initialized and provide information about the 3D body parameters. Towards that end, we propose a novel 2D view-based model of human motion based on optical flow that has a number of benefits. First, optical flow provides some insensitivity to variations in illumination, clothing, and background structure. Second, the dimensionality of the model is sufficiently low to permit automatic detection and tracking of people in video sequences. Third, the parameters of the model can be related to the pose of a 3D articulated model and are hence suitable for initializing more complex models. Finally, we develop a probabilistic formulation that permits our motion estimates to be exploited by higher level tracking methods.

The key idea behind our view-based representation is summarized in Figure 1. Motion capture data of actors performing various motions is used to generate many idealized training flow fields from various viewpoints. For each viewpoint, singular value decomposition (SVD) is used to reduce the dimensionality of the training flow fields to give a low-dimensional linear model. Training motions are projected onto this linear basis and temporal models of the linear coefficients for different activities are learned. It is worth noting that there is some psychophysical evidence for the existence of view-based representations of biological motions such as human walking [6,27].

Given this model, the automatic detection and tracking of human motion in image sequences is formulated using a principled Bayesian framework. In addition to the view-based human motion model, we learn a model for the optical flow of general scenes which is used to distinguish human motions from general background motions. Both foreground (person) and background statistical models are defined as Gibbsian fields [12,32] specified from the first-order statistics of motion measurements. Hence, we can exactly evaluate the likelihood of given motion observations w.r.t. learned probabilistic motion models. Therefore, the detection and tracking of human motion can be stated as Bayesian estimation, which involves the evaluation of the posterior distribution of model parameters w.r.t. a sequence of motion observations. For tracking, the prediction

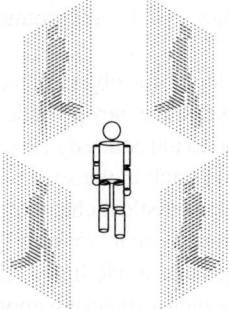

Fig. 1. The motion of a 3D articulated model is projected to derive the 2D image motion (optical flow) of a person from a variety of views. Natural 3D human motions are acquired with a commercial motion-capture system.

in time of this posterior distribution is derived from a prior distribution on the temporal dynamics of model parameters. Since we exploit general non-parametric probabilistic models, the posterior distribution is non-Gaussian and has no straightforward analytic form. Thus, we represent it explicitly using a discrete set of samples in a particle filtering framework [13,16].

2 Problem Statement and Related Work

In this paper, we focus, on the automatic detection and tracking of human motion in image sequences, without the complete recovery of the 3D body motion. While recent advances have been obtained for the tracking of 3D human motion using 2D image cues from monocular image sequences [14,25,30] or multi-view image sequences [4,9,11], these techniques require manual initialization (see [20] for a more complete review). Despite these successes, the complete recovery of 3D body motion is not always necessary and the detection and tracking of 2D human motion is sufficient for numerous applications. Furthermore, this 2D stage can also be regarded as a primary step towards the automatic initialization of more complex 3D schemes.

View-based models for object recognition are not new but here we apply these ideas to biological motion recognition [6,27]. We see these models as existing within a hierarchy from low-level image measurements to 3D motion models. Bregler [5] proposed a similar probabilistic hierarchy of models but the approach lacked powerful mid-level representations of human motion such as those proposed here and hence attempted to interpret at a high level, very low-level motion measurements. There have been other proposed intermediate representations such as the "cardboard" person model [19] and the scaled prismatic model [7] but these proved too high dimensional for automatic initialization.

Current approaches for the detection and the tracking of people in images and videos mainly rely on human appearance analysis and modeling. For instance, pedestrian detection has been achieved using low-resolution wavelet images of people [22] or body shape [10]. In [18], a Bayesian framework is also developed for object localization based on probabilistic modeling of object shape. The most successful of recent tracking methods exploit statistical models of object appearance (color or grey-level histograms [8], mixture models of color distributions [17], background subtraction [15], or edge-based models of object shape [16,29]).

Among all the methods developed for object detection and tracking, Bayesian approaches appear the most attractive, since they provide a principled probabilistic framework to combine multiple cues and to introduce *a priori* knowledge or constraints related to the class of objects to detect and track in the scene. For these statistical schemes, the key point is to provide appropriate statistical characterization of the entities of interest (foreground) and of the background. Recent work on Bayesian tracking has focused on this problem of foreground/background modeling [17,24,26,28].

In this paper, we also consider such a Bayesian approach. Unlike previous work, our main focus is on the definition of appropriate probabilistic models of dynamic information for human motion. As previously mentioned, whereas motion cues provide generic and rich information independent of object appearance, they are rarely exploited for the detection and tracking of predefined types of objects. Motion information is indeed mainly exploited in motion detection schemes [21,23], when no *a priori* information is available about the class of entities to extract. This is due to the lack of generic probabilistic models of object motion, which could be used as alternatives or complements to statistical modeling of object appearance. However, in the context of human motion analysis, recent studies [2,31] targeted at motion estimation and activity recognition have stressed that human motion examples share specific characteristics, which make the definition and the identification of generic models of human motion feasible.

We further exploit and extend these previous approaches to handle the automatic detection and tracking of human motion in image sequences. Similarly to [2,31], we rely on learned bases of human motion. However, instead of considering only one motion basis set as in [2,31], we use a set of these motion bases. Consequently, our probabilistic modeling can be viewed as a mixture of human motion models. Moreover, unlike these previous approaches, our main concern is to design well-founded probabilistic models of human motion. Instead of assuming particular noise distributions such as Gaussian or some more robust distribution [2], our models are defined as Gibbsian fields [12,32] specified from the first-order statistics of motion measurements, and are directly learned from training examples. These probabilistic models are then used as the foreground motion models in our approach. In the same fashion we construct a statistical background model that accounts for generic motion situations (cf. [17,24,26]). Both models are exploited in the Bayesian framework for detection and tracking. These motion models could be combined with more traditional probabilistic models of appearance in this Bayesian framework. It would be straightforward to extend this work to detect and track other kinds of objects for other applications.

3 Human Motion Modeling

To detect and track human motion in image sequences, we rely on generative models, which are computed from training examples for different view angles using PCA (Principal Component Analysis). What is critical is that these models be sufficiently low-dimensional so as to permit efficient search and sufficiently expressive so as to be useful for initializing more complex models. Given these linear human motion bases, we build probabilistic likelihood models from the statistical analysis of the reconstruction error and of the distribution of the projection onto basis vectors.

In this section, we first present the training stage used to learn human motion bases. Then, the different features of the probabilistic human motion models are introduced.

3.1 Learning Human Motion Bases

The learning of motion bases from training examples has already been successfully exploited for parameterized motion estimation and activity recognition [2,31]. Similarly, we learn bases for full-body human motion from synthetic training examples generated from motion capture data. Here we focus on walking motions but the approach can be extended to more general human motion.

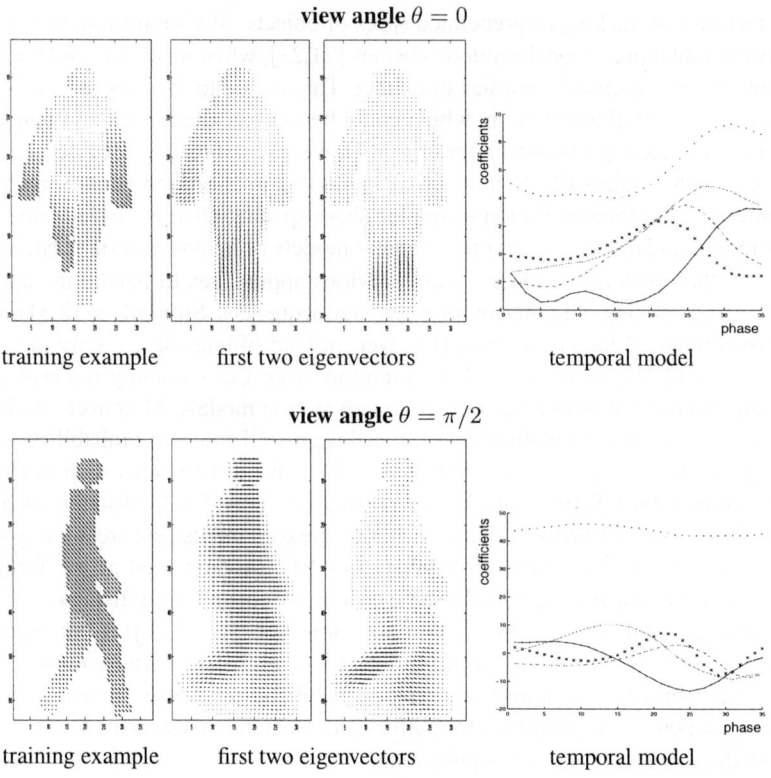

Fig. 2. Learning human motion models

Our training set consists of multiple walking sequences from four professional dancers (two men and two women). Given the 3D position of the body and its motion at any time instant we can predict the actual 2D flow field that this motion would generate from any viewing direction. To our knowledge, complex motion models such as those described here have never been used before because of the lack of reasonable training data. Here however, with 3D "ground truth" we can generate high-quality training flow fields from any desired viewpoint. Fig. 2 displays two example flow fields from the training set. To cope with the changes in optical flow as a function of viewing angle, we adopt a view-based model and separately learn motion bases for different viewing directions. Specifically, we generate a training set of 480 flow fields for each of twelve view angles $\{0, \pi/6, ..., 11\pi/6\}$. For each view, we perform PCA and keep as motion bases the first fifteen eigenvectors accounting on average for 0.95 of the total variance. Fig.2 shows the two first basis vectors for the view angles 0 and $\pi/2$. For a given human motion model $\mathcal{M}$, $\theta(\mathcal{M})$ denotes the associated view angle, $N_B(\mathcal{M})$ the number of basis vectors and $B(\mathcal{M}) = \{B_k(\mathcal{M}), k \in \{1, ..., N_B(\mathcal{M})\}\}$ the eigenvectors for the human motion basis.

These learned motion bases constrain the spatial configuration of the detected and tracked human motion. Additionally we model the temporal characteristics of human motion. In this work, we use the method described in [1]. However, other kinds of temporal models could be employed (e.g. Hidden Markov Models (HMM), auto-regressive models or other time series models). The exploited temporal model is specified by a sequence $\tau(\mathcal{M}) = [a_1(\mathcal{M}), ..., a_{\phi_{max}}(\mathcal{M})]$, where $a_\phi(\mathcal{M})$ is a vector of linear coefficients at phase ϕ of the cyclic walking gait [2]. Given the motion basis $B(\mathcal{M})$, we learn the temporal model $\tau(\mathcal{M})$ using the method described in [1]. For each model $\mathcal{M}$, we compute the associate trajectories of the motion coefficients of the projection of the associated training examples onto basis $B(\mathcal{M})$ and the mean trajectories form the temporal models. In Fig. 2, the temporal models for $\theta = 0$ and $\theta = \pi/2$ are displayed.[1]

Hence, given a model $\mathcal{M}$, a phase ϕ and a magnitude γ, we can generate an optical flow field $w(\mathcal{M}, \phi, \gamma)$ corresponding to the human motion:

$$w(\mathcal{M}, \phi, \gamma) = \gamma \sum_{k=1}^{N_B(\mathcal{M})} a_{\phi,k}(\mathcal{M}) B_k(\mathcal{M}). \tag{1}$$

3.2 Statistical Modeling of Human Motion

Now, let $w(\mathcal{W})$ be an observed flow field in a window $\mathcal{W}$. Our generative model states that $w(\mathcal{W})$ equals $w(\mathcal{M}, \phi, \gamma)$ plus noise for some setting of the model parameters $\mathcal{M}$, $\mathcal{W}$, the phase ϕ and magnitude γ. Rather than assume an arbitrary noise model (e.g. Gaussian), here we learn it from training data.

We note that we can reduce the dimensionality of the model further by computing the optimal magnitude term γ' that minimizes the reconstruction error

$$E(w(\mathcal{W}), \phi, \mathcal{M}\}) = w(\mathcal{W}) - \gamma' \sum_{k=1}^{N_B(\mathcal{M})} a_{\phi,k}(\mathcal{M}) B_k(\mathcal{M}) \tag{2}$$

where γ' is given by

$$\gamma' = \left[\sum_{k=1}^{N_B(\mathcal{M})} \alpha_k a_{\phi,k}(\mathcal{M}) \right] / \left[\sum_{k=1}^{N_B(\mathcal{M})} \alpha_k^2 \right] \tag{3}$$

where $\{\alpha_k\}$ are the coefficients of the projection of $w(\mathcal{W})$ onto the bases $B(\mathcal{M})$.

The likelihood $P_{HM}(w(\mathcal{W})|\phi, \gamma, \mathcal{M})$ of the flow field $w(\mathcal{W})$ given the model parameters $(\phi, \gamma, \mathcal{M})$ is then specified from the reconstruction error $E(w(\mathcal{W}), \phi, \mathcal{M})$ and magnitude γ' as follows:

$$P_{HM}(w(\mathcal{W})|\phi, \gamma, \mathcal{M}) = P\left(E(w(\mathcal{W}), \phi, \mathcal{M}), \gamma'|\phi, \gamma, \mathcal{M}\right). \tag{4}$$

We can rewrite this as:

$$P_{HM}(w(\mathcal{W})|\phi, \gamma, \mathcal{M}) = P\left(E(w(\mathcal{W}), \phi, \mathcal{M})|\gamma', \phi, \gamma, \mathcal{M}\right) P\left(\gamma'|\phi, \gamma, \mathcal{M}\right). \tag{5}$$

---

[1] Observe that we have chosen to separately compute the spatial and temporal models for each view. This simplifies the learning and estimation problems compared to building a single spatio-temporal model for each view.

Since the magnitude of the reconstruction error obviously depends on the magnitude of the human motion, the likelihood $P(E(w(\mathcal{W}), \phi, \mathcal{M})|\gamma', \phi, \gamma, \mathcal{M})$ is evaluated from the normalized reconstruction error $\widetilde{E}(w(\mathcal{W}), \phi, \mathcal{M})$ defined by:

$$\widetilde{E}(w(\mathcal{W}), \phi, \mathcal{M}) = E(w(\mathcal{W}), \phi, \mathcal{M})/[\gamma' \|a_\phi(\mathcal{M})\|], \qquad (6)$$

as $\gamma' \|a_\phi(\mathcal{M})\|$ is the magnitude of the human motion. Thus, further simplifying conditional dependencies, the likelihood $P_{HM}(w(\mathcal{W})|\phi, \gamma, \mathcal{M})$ is defined as the product of two terms as follows:

$$P_{HM}(w(\mathcal{W})|\phi, \gamma, \mathcal{M}) = P\left(\widetilde{E}(w(\mathcal{W}), \phi, \mathcal{M})|\mathcal{M}\right) P(\gamma'|\phi, \gamma, \mathcal{M}). \qquad (7)$$

The first term, $P(\widetilde{E}(w(\mathcal{W}), \phi, \mathcal{M})|\mathcal{M})$, represents the likelihood distribution and will be learned from training examples. The second term, $P(\gamma'|\phi, \gamma, \mathcal{M})$, is exploited to specify the minimum motion magnitude of the motion to be detected and tracked and to smooth the temporal evolution of the magnitude γ of the tracked area.

3.3 Likelihood Distribution of the Reconstruction Error

The definition of the likelihood distribution $P\left(\widetilde{E}(w(\mathcal{W}), \phi, \mathcal{M})|\mathcal{M}\right)$ is based on the first-order statistics of $\widetilde{E}(w(\mathcal{W}), \phi, \mathcal{M})$. Let Λ denote the quantization space of these flow field differences and $\Gamma(\widetilde{E}(w(\mathcal{W}), \phi, \mathcal{M})) = \{\Gamma(\lambda, \widetilde{E}(w(\mathcal{W}), \phi, \mathcal{M}))\}_{\lambda \in \Lambda}$ the histogram of $\widetilde{E}(w(\mathcal{W}), \phi, \mathcal{M})$ quantized over Λ. The computation of the likelihood $P(\widetilde{E}(w(\mathcal{W}), \phi, \mathcal{M})|\mathcal{M})$ must be independent of the size of the window $\mathcal{W}$ in order to compare the likelihoods of the projection error over a set of windows with different sizes. This leads us to consider the normalized histogram $\overline{\Gamma}(\widetilde{E}(w(\mathcal{W}), \phi, \mathcal{M}))$ as the characteristic statistics of $\widetilde{E}(w(\mathcal{W}), \phi, \mathcal{M})$.

Based on the Maximum Entropy criterion (ME) [32], $P(\widetilde{E}(w(\mathcal{W}), \phi, \mathcal{M})|\mathcal{M})$ is expressed using the following Gibbsian formulation:

$$P\left(\widetilde{E}(w(\mathcal{W}), \phi, \mathcal{M})|\mathcal{M}\right) \propto \exp\left[\Psi_\mathcal{M} \bullet \overline{\Gamma}(\widetilde{E}(w(\mathcal{W}), \phi, \mathcal{M}))\right], \qquad (8)$$

where $\Psi_\mathcal{M} = \{\Psi_\mathcal{M}(\lambda)\}_{\lambda \in \Lambda}$ are the Gibbsian potentials which explicitly specify the distribution $P(\widetilde{E}(w(\mathcal{W}), \phi, \mathcal{M})|\mathcal{M})$. $\Psi_\mathcal{M} \bullet \overline{\Gamma}(\widetilde{E}(w(\mathcal{W}), \phi, \mathcal{M}))$ is the dot product between model potentials $\Psi_\mathcal{M}$ and normalized histogram $\overline{\Gamma}(\widetilde{E}(w(\mathcal{W}), \phi, \mathcal{M})$ defined by:

$$\Psi_\mathcal{M} \bullet \overline{\Gamma}(\widetilde{E}(w(\mathcal{W}), \phi, \mathcal{M})) = \sum_{\lambda \in \Lambda} \Psi_\mathcal{M}(\lambda) \overline{\Gamma}(\lambda, \widetilde{E}(w(\mathcal{W}), \phi, \mathcal{M})). \qquad (9)$$

Since we will compare values of the likelihood $P(\widetilde{E}(w(\mathcal{W}), \phi, \mathcal{M})|\mathcal{M})$ for different windows $\mathcal{W}$ and models $\mathcal{M}$, the normalization constant $Z_\mathcal{M}$ defined by:

$$Z_\mathcal{M} = \sum_{(w(\mathcal{W}),\phi)} \exp\left[\Psi_\mathcal{M} \bullet \overline{\Gamma}(\widetilde{E}(w(\mathcal{W}), \phi, \mathcal{M}))\right], \qquad (10)$$

has to be explicitly known and computable. Let us stress that this issue was not handled in [2,31] since only one motion basis was considered. It can be rewritten as:

$$Z_\mathcal{M} = \left(\sum_{\lambda \in \Lambda} exp\left[\frac{\Psi_\mathcal{M}(\lambda)}{|\mathcal{W}|}\right]\right)^{|\mathcal{W}|}. \qquad (11)$$

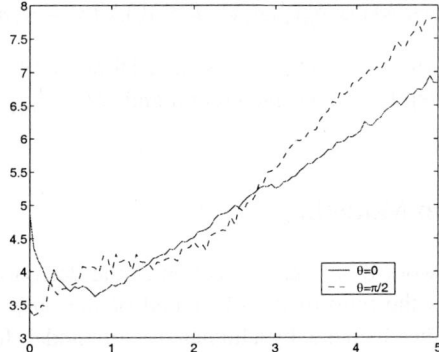

Fig. 3. Potentials $\Psi_\mathcal{M}$ specifying the likelihood of the reconstruction error $P(\widetilde{E}(w(\mathcal{W}), \phi, \mathcal{M}) | \mathcal{M})$. We give the plots of $\{-\Psi_\mathcal{M}(\lambda)\}_{\lambda \in \Lambda}$ for the view angles $\theta = 0$ and $\theta = \pi/2$.

Thus, the exact expression of the likelihood $P(\widetilde{E}(w(\mathcal{W}), \phi, \mathcal{M}) | \mathcal{M})$ is

$$P\left(\widetilde{E}(w(\mathcal{W}), \phi, \mathcal{M}) | \mathcal{M}\right) = \left(\sum_{\lambda \in \Lambda} \exp\left[\frac{\Psi_\mathcal{M}(\lambda)}{|\mathcal{W}|}\right]\right)^{-|\mathcal{W}|} \exp\left[\Psi_\mathcal{M} \bullet \overline{\Gamma}(\widetilde{E}(w, \phi, \mathcal{M}))\right]. \tag{12}$$

In this expression, only the first term depends on $|\mathcal{W}|$ whereas it is by definition independent of the observed motion error $\widetilde{E}(w(\mathcal{W}), \phi, \mathcal{M})$. Therefore, to make the comparison of the likelihoods according to different window sizes feasible, we will compute the expression (12) for a reference window size $|\mathcal{W}|_{ref}$. In practice, we use the window size of the training examples.

We learn the potentials $\Psi_\mathcal{M}$ for a model $\mathcal{M}$ from the training examples used to compute the motion basis $B(\mathcal{M})$. More precisely, given the normalized histogram $\overline{\Gamma}(\mathcal{M})$ of the reconstruction error for this training set, the potentials $\Psi_\mathcal{M}$ estimated w.r.t. the Maximum Likelihood (ML) criterion are given by:

$$\Psi_\mathcal{M}(\lambda) = \log\left(\overline{\Gamma}(\lambda, \mathcal{M}) / \sum_{\lambda' \in \Lambda} \overline{\Gamma}(\lambda', \mathcal{M})\right). \tag{13}$$

Fig. 3 displays the plot of the potentials $\Psi_\mathcal{M}$ for the view angles $\theta = 0$ and $\theta = \pi/2$. These two distributions are non-Gaussian. Besides, it is also worth mentioning that the main peak does not necessarily occur in 0. Thus, there can be a weak bias in the reconstruction from the learned motion basis.

3.4 Prior Distribution of Magnitude

To further constrain the detection and tracking of human motion, we exploit the fact that we aim at identifying moving entities with a motion magnitude greater than a given motion detection level μ. In addition, the magnitude γ' is more likely to evolve smoothly over time. Therefore, $P(\gamma' | \phi, \gamma, \mathcal{M})$ is written as:

$$P(\gamma'|\phi,\gamma,\mathcal{M}) \propto \delta_\mu(\|w(\mathcal{M},\phi,\gamma')\|)\mathcal{N}(\gamma'-\gamma,\sigma^2_{mag}), \qquad (14)$$

where $\|w(\mathcal{M},\phi,\gamma')\|$ is the norm of the reconstructed flow $w(\mathcal{M},\phi,\gamma')$ given by relation (1). $\delta_\mu(.)$ is a smooth step function centered in μ and $\mathcal{N}(.,\sigma^2_{mag})$ a normal distribution with variance σ^2_{mag}.

4 Generic Motion Modeling

In the Bayesian framework described in Section 5, the detection and the tracking of human motion exploits the ratio of the likelihood of the observation within a given window explained, on the one hand, by a human motion model (foreground model) and on the other hand by a generic motion model (background model). Since no ground truth exists for the flow fields of general scenes, we cannot directly derive this model using observed statistics of the flow field w. As an alternative, it is defined from the statistics of temporal image differences. Thus, it allows us to handle noise on a static background but also dynamic situations which do not correspond to human motion.

The probabilistic distribution attached to this model is specified using the first-order statistics of the difference of pairs of successive images. Given a window $\mathcal{W}$ and an image difference ΔI, we evaluate its normalized histogram $\overline{\Gamma}(\Delta I(\mathcal{W})) = \{\overline{\Gamma}(n, \Delta I(\mathcal{W}))\}_{n\in\{-N,...,N\}}$ where N is the number of grey-levels in the images. Similarly to the statistical modeling of the reconstruction error in ubsection 3.3, the likelihood $P_{GM}(\Delta I(\mathcal{W}))$, that the image difference $\Delta I(\mathcal{W})$ within window $\mathcal{W}$ is a sample of the generic motion model, is expressed as:

$$P_{GM}(\Delta I(\mathcal{W})) \propto \exp\left[\Psi_{GM} \bullet \overline{\Gamma}(\Delta I \mathcal{W})\right], \qquad (15)$$

$$\text{with } \Psi_{GM} \bullet \overline{\Gamma}(\Delta I(\mathcal{W})) = \sum_{n=-N}^{N} \Psi_{GM}(n)\overline{\Gamma}(n,\Delta I(\mathcal{W})). \qquad (16)$$

We cope with the normalization issue in a similar way as in Subsection 3.3. To estimate the potentials Ψ_{GM}, we consider a set of image sequences acquired with a static camera, involving different kinds of moving objects (pedestrians, cars, trees) and backgrounds. The normalized histogram $\overline{\Gamma}_{GM}$ of the image differences is evaluated from this set of sequences and the estimation of the potentials Ψ_{GM} w.r.t. the ML criterion leads to:

$$\Psi_{GM}(n) = \log\left(\overline{\Gamma}_{GM}(n) / \sum_{n'=-N}^{N} \overline{\Gamma}_{GM}(n')\right). \qquad (17)$$

Fig. 4 displays the plot of the estimated potentials Ψ_{GM} of the generic motion model. While this distribution is obviously non-Gaussian, it is similar in spirit to the robust function as used for robust motion estimation [3].

5 Bayesian Formulation

The detection and the tracking of human motion is stated as a Bayesian inference problem. More precisely, given a sequence of observations, i.e. a sequence of observed flow

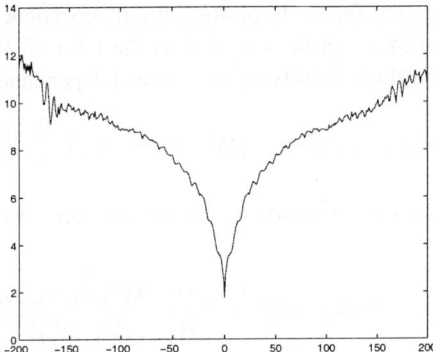

Fig. 4. Plot of the potentials Ψ_{GM} of the generic motion model.

fields and image differences, we aim at evaluating the posterior distribution of the model parameters which are in our case the location (i.e., the window $\mathcal{W}$) and type of human motion (i.e., model $\mathcal{M}$, phase ϕ and magnitude γ of the sought human motion sample).

In this Section, we detail this Bayesian formulation which exploits the statistical motion models, that we have previously defined, in a data-driven likelihood. We will define prior distribution over model parameters appropriate for detection and tracking. Then, we will briefly outline how we evaluate in practice the posterior distribution using particle filtering.

5.1 General Overview

Let us denote by $\overline{w}_t = \{w_0, w_1, \ldots, w_t\}$ and $\overline{\Delta I}_t = \{\Delta I_0, \Delta I_1, \ldots, \Delta I_t\}$ the sequences of flow fields and image differences up to time t. The flow fields $\{w_t\}$ are estimated using the robust technique described in [3].

The goal of detecting and tracking human motion at time t is regarded as the evaluation of the posterior distribution $P(\phi_t, \gamma_t, \mathcal{W}_t, \mathcal{M}_t | \overline{w}_t, \overline{\Delta I}_t)$. Below, we will denote by Θ_t the model parameters $[\phi_t, \gamma_t, \mathcal{W}_t, \mathcal{M}_t]$. Using Bayes rule and assuming that observations at time t are independent from observations at previous instants given model parameters Θ_t, we obtain:

$$P(\Theta_t | \overline{w}_t, \overline{\Delta I}_t) = k \underbrace{P(w_t, \Delta I_t | \Theta_t)}_{\text{data-driven likelihood}} \underbrace{P(\Theta_t | \overline{w}_{t-1}, \overline{\Delta I}_{t-1})}_{\text{prior at time } t-1}, \quad (18)$$

where k is a constant independent of Θ_t.

5.2 Data-Driven Likelihood

The data-driven distribution $P(w_t, \Delta I_t | \Theta_t)$ evaluates the likelihood that the observations at time t account for human motion model $\mathcal{M}_t$ within the window $\mathcal{W}_t$. Assuming the motion characteristics within the window $\mathcal{W}_t$ are independent on those of the background $\mathcal{R} \setminus \mathcal{W}_t$, where $\mathcal{R}$ is the image support, $P(w_t, \Delta I_t | \Theta_t)$ is explicitly given by:

$$P(w_t, \Delta I_t | \Theta_t) = k' P_{HM}(w_t(\mathcal{W}_t) | \phi_t, \gamma_t, \mathcal{M}_t) P_{GM}(\Delta I_t(\mathcal{R} \setminus \mathcal{W}_t) | \mathcal{W}_t), \quad (19)$$

where k' is a normalization factor. Exploiting the independence between $\mathcal{R}\backslash \mathcal{W}_t$ and $\mathcal{W}_t$, $P_{GM}(\Delta I_t(\mathcal{R}\backslash \mathcal{W}_t)|\mathcal{W}_t)$ can be rewritten as the ratio of $P_{GM}(\Delta I_t(\mathcal{R})|\mathcal{W}_t)$ and $P_{GM}(\Delta I_t(\mathcal{W}_t)|\mathcal{W}_t)$. Further simplifying conditional dependencies, we obtain:

$$P(w_t, \Delta I_t | \Theta_t) = k' P_{HM}(w_t(\mathcal{W}_t)|\phi_t, \gamma_t, \mathcal{M}_t) \frac{P_{GM}(\Delta I_t(\mathcal{R}))}{P_{GM}(\Delta I_t(\mathcal{W}_t))}, \qquad (20)$$

Since $P_{GM}(\Delta I_t(\mathcal{R}))$ does not depend on model parameters Θ_t, this simplifies into the following expression:

$$P(w_t, \Delta I_t | \Theta_t) = k'' \frac{P_{HM}(w_t(\mathcal{W}_t)|\phi_t, \gamma_t, \mathcal{M}_t)}{P_{GM}(\Delta I_t(\mathcal{W}_t))}, \qquad (21)$$

where k'' is a normalization factor.

Thus, the data-driven term $P(w_t, \Delta I_t | \phi_t, \gamma_t, \mathcal{W}_t, \mathcal{M}_t)$ is completely determined from the expression of the likelihoods $P_{HM}(w_t(\mathcal{W}_t)|\phi_t, \gamma_t, \mathcal{M}_t)$ and $P_{GM}(\Delta I_t(\mathcal{W}_t))$ given by relations (12), (14) and (15).

5.3 Prior Distribution on Model Parameters

The prior distribution $P(\Theta_t | \overline{w}_{t-1}, \overline{\Delta I}_{t-1})$ describes the temporal dynamics of the model parameters Θ_t. For the detection task at time $t = 0$, this prior reduces to $P(\Theta_0)$. Since we have neither *a priori* knowledge about the location of the human motion in the image nor the human motion type, the initial prior distribution is chosen to be uniform.

For tracking purpose, the prior distribution $P(\Theta_t | \overline{w}_{t-1}, \overline{\Delta I}_{t-1})$ is expressed as the marginalization of the joint distribution over all model parameters up to time t over all observations up to time t. Adopting a first-order Markov assumption on model parameters, this leads to the following integral formulation:

$$P(\Theta_t | \overline{w}_{t-1}, \overline{\Delta I}_{t-1}) = \int P(\Theta_t | \Theta_{t-1}, \overline{w}_{t-1}, \overline{\Delta I}_{t-1}) \underbrace{P(\Theta_{t-1} | \overline{w}_{t-1}, \overline{\Delta I}_{t-1})}_{\text{posterior at time } t-1} d\Theta_{t-1}. \quad (22)$$

This integral involves the product of two terms: $P(\Theta_{t-1} | \overline{w}_{t-1}, \overline{\Delta I}_{t-1})$ the posterior distribution at time $t-1$ and $P(\Theta_t | \Theta_{t-1}, \overline{w}_{t-1}, \overline{\Delta I}_{t-1})$ the prior distribution over model parameters describing their temporal dynamics. Assuming conditional independence of model parameters ϕ_t, γ_t and $\mathcal{M}_t$ w.r.t. to $[\Theta_{t-1}, \overline{w}_{t-1}, \overline{\Delta I}_{t-1}]$, the latter term is rewritten as:

$$\begin{aligned} P(\Theta_t | \Theta_{t-1}, \overline{w}_{t-1}, \overline{\Delta I}_{t-1}) &= P(\mathcal{M}_t | \Theta_{t-1}, \overline{w}_{t-1}, \overline{\Delta I}_{t-1}) \\ &\times P(\phi_t | \Theta_{t-1}, \overline{w}_{t-1}, \overline{\Delta I}_{t-1}) \\ &\times P(\gamma_t | \Theta_{t-1}, \overline{w}_{t-1}, \overline{\Delta I}_{t-1}) \\ &\times P(\mathcal{W}_t | \gamma_t, \phi_t, \mathcal{M}_t, \Theta_{t-1}, \overline{w}_{t-1}, \overline{\Delta I}_{t-1}). \end{aligned} \qquad (23)$$

$P(\mathcal{M}_t | \Theta_{t-1}, \overline{w}_{t-1}, \overline{\Delta I}_{t-1})$ defines the evolution of the human motion model assigned to the tracked window. It is directly related to the temporal evolution of the view angles between the tracked entity and the camera. We can assume that $\mathcal{M}_t$ depends only on $\mathcal{M}_{t-1}$. We thus resort to the specification of the first-order Markov chain $P(\mathcal{M}_t|\mathcal{M}_{t-1})$. Assuming the view angle evolves smoothly over time, these transitions are defined by:

$$P(\mathcal{M}_t|\mathcal{M}_{t-1}) = \begin{cases} \alpha, & \text{if } \mathcal{M}_t = \mathcal{M}_{t-1} \\ \dfrac{1-\alpha}{2}, & \text{if } \theta(\mathcal{M}_t) = \theta(\mathcal{M}_{t-1}) \pm \pi/6[2\pi] \end{cases}. \qquad (24)$$

Typically, we set in practice $\alpha = 0.7$.

Concerning phase ϕ_t, it can be assumed that it evolves smoothly along time and $P(\phi_t|\Theta_{t-1}, \overline{w}_{t-1}, \overline{\Delta I}_{t-1})$ is taken to be a wrapped Gaussian distribution centered in ϕ_{t-1} modulo the length of the walk cycle. For the magnitude γ_t, we exploit that we have estimated at time $t-1$ the magnitude which leads to the lowest reconstruction error. We then assign this value to γ_t.

The prior distribution $P(\mathcal{W}_t|\Theta_{t-1}, \overline{w}_{t-1}, \overline{\Delta I}_{t-1})$ over the window position $\mathcal{W}_t$ is assumed to be Gaussian around the predicted window $\mathcal{W}_t^{pred}$.

$$P(\mathcal{W}_t|\phi_t, \gamma_t, \mathcal{M}_t, \Theta_{t-1}, \overline{w}_{t-1}, \overline{\Delta I}_{t-1}) = \mathcal{N}(\mathcal{W}_t - \mathcal{W}_t^{pred}, \sigma_{pos}), \qquad (25)$$

where $\mathcal{N}(., \sigma_{pos})$ is a Gaussian distribution with diagonal covariance σ_{pos}. The location of the predicted window $\mathcal{W}_t^{pred}$ is computed from the displacement of the center of the previous window $\mathcal{W}_{t'1}$ according to the reconstructed flow $w(\mathcal{M}_{t-1}, \gamma_t, \phi_{t-1})$.

5.4 Computation of the Posterior Distribution

The direct computation of the posterior distribution $P(\Theta_t|\overline{w}_t, \overline{\Delta I}_t)$ is not feasible, since no analytic form of this likelihood function over the whole model parameter space can be derived. However, for any values of the model parameters Θ_t, we can evaluate the likelihood of the observations formed by the flow field and the image difference at time t given these model parameter values. Therefore, we can approximate the posterior distribution $P(\Theta_t|\overline{w}_t, \overline{\Delta I}_t)$ by a set of samples using a particle filtering framework [13, 16].

At time t, we first draw N_{part} particles $\{s_n\}$, each one being assigned model parameter values $\Theta_{t-1}^{s_n}$. We propagate this set of particles at time t using the temporal dynamics specified by the prior distributions $P(\Theta_t|\Theta_{t-1}, \overline{w}_{t-1}, \overline{\Delta I}_{t-1})$. This supplies us with a new set of particles $\{s'_n\}$, for which we compute the likelihoods $P(w_t, \Delta I_t|\Theta_t^{s'_n})$ using (21). When normalized to sum to one, these likelihoods (or weights) associated with each particle s'_n approximate the posterior distribution at time t.

At time $t = 0$, for detection purposes, we need to perform a global search over model parameters (i.e., position, motion type, phase and scale). We exploit an hierarchical strategy to approximate the posterior distribution by subsampling at different resolutions the space of the model parameters. This scheme provides a coarse location of the detected human motion, which will be refined by tracking.

Fig. 5. Tracking a human walking in a straight line. We display the location of the expected window at frames 0, 10, 20, 30, 40 and 50.

6 Experiments

Parameter setting. We present preliminary results of detection and tracking of human motion in different real image sequences acquired with a static camera. In order to visualize the posterior distribution in the frame at time t, we display the expected location $<\mathcal{W}_t|\overline{w_t}, \overline{\Delta I_t}>$ of the detected and tracked window including human motion, which is approximated by the following sum over the set of particles $\{s_n\}_{n \in \{1,...,N_{part}\}}$ at time t: $<\mathcal{W}_t|\overline{w_t}, \overline{\Delta I_t}> = \sum_{n=1}^{N_{part}} \pi^{s_n} \mathcal{W}_t^{s_n}$ where π_{s_n} is the normalized version of the likelihood $P(w_t, \Delta I_t | \Theta_t^{s_n})$.

In the subsequent experiments, we used the following parameter settings. As far as the data-driven likelihood is concerned, the main parameter to set is the motion detection level μ. Since this parameter has a physical meaning in terms of average displacement within the expected window comprising the human motion, it is easy to set. We will use $\mu = 1.0$. Besides, the variance of the prediction for the magnitude γ is taken to be $\sigma_{mag}^2 = 1.0$. These parameters could be learned from training data.

For the prior distribution specifying the temporal dynamics, we set $\alpha = 0.7$ for the Markov chain characterizing the transitions between human motion models, and the covariance σ_{pos} has diagonal terms equaling 5.0 for the square root of the variance on the position of the center of the tracked window, and 1.0 for the variance in terms of window scaling.

Human walking in a straight line. The first processed example is an sequence of 60 frames involving a human walking in a straight line. We display in Fig. 5 the results for frames 0, 10, 20, 30, 40 and 50. Our method accurately recovers the window size and the location of the walking pedestrian with no manual initialization. As previously mentioned, the initialization provides a coarse estimate of the location of the human

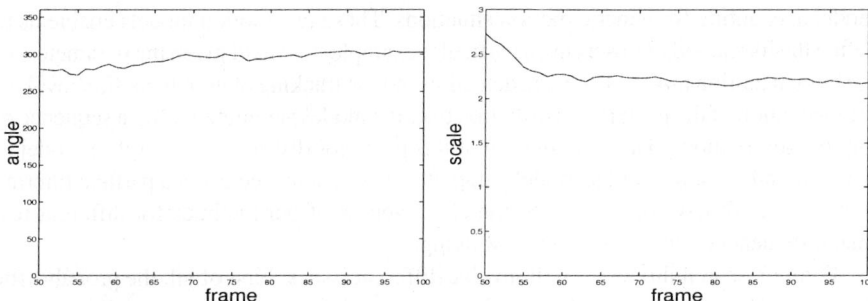

Fig. 6. Tracking a human walking in a straight line. Plot of the estimated values of scale and view angle parameters.

Fig. 7. Tracking a human walking in a straight line. We display the location of the expected window at frames 0, 10, 20, 30, 40 and 50.

motion, since the coarse-to-fine strategy is not iterated until the finest resolution. Also, as shown in Fig. 6, the expected value of the viewing angle stabilizes around $10\pi/6$, whereas one could expect to obtain $3\pi/2$. Even though there is a bias (corresponding to the quantization step of the view angles), it provides us with correct direction of the human motion. This bias might be due to differences in magnitude between the observed human motion and the training examples.

Walking pedestrian in presence of background motion. The second processed example is a video of a street acquired from the top a building. Therefore, it does not exactly refer to the kind of motion situation learned from the training examples. In this sequence, the tree in the upper right corner is slightly moving in the wind. In spite of these difficulties, our approach recovers the location of the walking pedestrian and the expected view angle is estimated to be approximately $8\pi/6$, which gives a correct guess of the direction of the human motion.

Note further, that with the position, scale, viewing direction, and phase of the gate, that we could now predict the 3D configuration of the body (since we knew this during training). Thus our posterior distribution provides the basis for a probabilistic proposal distribution for more detailed tracking. In future work, we will use our 2D models for initialisation of 3D human motion tracking.

7 Conclusion

We have presented a Bayesian framework for the automatic detection and tracking of human motion in image sequences. It relies on the design of probabilistic generative models of human motion learned for training examples. We also define a statistical model accounting for generic motion situations. These two motion models enable us to define the likelihood of observing a particular example flow field given the parameters of the human motion model. Then, the detection and the tracking of human motion involves the evaluation of the posterior distribution over the model parameters w.r.t. a sequence of motion observations. The computation of this posterior distribution exploits a model of the temporal dynamics of the model parameters and is achieved using a particle filtering framework. We have demonstrated the effectiveness of our methods for different real image sequences comprising human walking.

Future research directions will involve different issues. First of all, the probabilistic human motion models provide complementary tools to appearance modeling usually considered for the detection and tracking of people. The Bayesian framework exploited in our work could be easily extended to combine both appearance and motion models. Additionally, we could enrich the characterization of human motion by learning more complex temporal models of human motion using time series analysis tools such as HMMs or linear and non-linear auto-regressive models. With a more varied training set, we could learn more general models of 2D image motion. Finally, the proposed probabilistic human motion models could also be used to characterize and analyze other categories of dynamic events, not necessarily human related, such as dynamic phenomena occurring in meteorological image sequences.

Acknowledgments. This work was support in part by an INRIA postdoctoral grant, by the DARPA HumanID Project (ONR contract N000140110886) and by a gift from the Xerox Foundation.

We thank Michael Gleicher for providing the 3D motion capture database, Manolis Kamvysselis and Hedvig Sidenbladh for help processing the mocap data and Robert Altschuler for providing video data used to train the generic motion model. Michael J. Black thanks Allen Jepson for discussions on foreground and background models.

References

1. M. Black, Y. Yacoob, A. Jepson, and D. Fleet. Learning parametrized models of image motion. *CVPR*, pp. 561–567, 1997.
2. M.J. Black. Explaining optical flow events with parametrized spatio-temporal tracking. *CVPR*, pp. 326–332, 1999.
3. M.J. Black and P. Anandan. The robust estimation of multiple motions: Parametric and piecewise-smooth flow fields. *CVIU*, 63(1):74–104, 1996.
4. C. Bregler and J. Malik. Tracking people with twists and exponential maps. *CVPR*, pp. 8–15, 1998.
5. C. Bregler. Learning and recognizing human dynamics in video sequences. *CVPR*, pp. 568–574, 1997.
6. I. Bülthoff, H.H. Bülthoff, and P. Sinha. A survey on the automatic indexing of video data. *Nature Neuroscience*, 1(3):254–257, 1998.
7. T-J. Cham and J. M. Rehg. A multiple hypothesis approach to figure tracking. *CVPR*, 1:239–245, 1999.
8. D. Comaniciu, V. Ramesh, and P. Meer. Real-time tracking of non-rigid objects using mean shift. , *CVPR*, pp. 142–149, 2000.

9. J. Deutscher, A. Blake, and I. Reid. Articulated motion capture by annealing particle filtering. *CVPR*, pp. 126–133, 2000.
10. D. Gavrila. Pedestrian detection from a moving vehicle. *ECCV*, II, pp.37–49, 2000.
11. D. Gavrila and L. Davis. 3-D model-based tracking of human in action: a multi-view approach. *CVPR*, pp. 73–80, 1996.
12. S. Geman and D. Geman. Stochastic relaxation, Gibbs distribution and the Bayesian restoration of images. *PAMI*, 6(6):721–741, 1984.
13. N. Gordon, D.J. Salmond, and A.F. Smith. A novel approach to nonlinear/non-Gaussian bayesian estimation. *IEEE Trans. on Radar, Sonar and Navigation*, 140(2):107–113, 1996.
14. Nicholas R. Howe, Michael E. Leventon, and William T. Freeman. Bayesian reconstruction of 3D human motion from single-camera video. *NIPS*, 12, pp. 820–826, 2000.
15. I. Haritaoglu, D. Harwood and L. Davis. A real time system for detecting and tracking people *IVC*, 1999
16. M. Isard and A. Blake. Condensation: conditional density propagation for visual tracking. *IJCV*, 29(1):5–28, 1998.
17. M. Isard and J. MacCormick. BraMBLE: a Bayesian multiple-blob tracker. *ICCV*, II, pp. 34–41, 2001.
18. M. Isard J. Sullivan, A. Blake and J. MacCormick. Object localization by bayesian correlation. *ICCV*, pp. 1068–1075, 1999.
19. S. X. Ju, M. J. Black, and Y. Yacoob. Cardboard people: A parameterized model of articulated motion. *Int. Conf. on Automatic Face and Gesture Recog.*, pp. 38–44, 1996.
20. T. Moeslund and E. Granum. A survey of computer vision-based human motion capture. *CVIU*, to appear.
21. J.M. Odobez and P. Bouthemy. Separation of moving regions from background in an image sequence acquired with a mobile camera. *Video Data Compression for Multimedia Computing*, chapter 8, pp. 295–311. H. H. Li, S. Sun, and H. Derin, eds, Kluwer, 1997.
22. C. Papageorgiou and T. Poggio. Trainable pedestrian detection. *ICCV*, pp. 1223–1228, 1999.
23. N. Paragios and R. Deriche. Geodesic active contours and level sets for the detection and tracking of moving objects. *PAMI*, 22(3):266–280, 2000.
24. J. Rittscher, J. Kato, S. Joga, A. Blake. A probabilistic background model for tracking. *ECCV*, 2:336-350, 2000.
25. H. Sidenbladh, M. Black, and D. Fleet. Stochastic tracking of 3d human figures using 2d image motion. *ECCV*, pp. 702–718, 2000.
26. H. Sidenbladh and M. J. Black. Learning image statistics for Bayesian tracking. *ICCV*, II, pp. 709–716, 2001.
27. P. Sinha, H.H. Bülthoff, and I. Bülthoff. View-based recognition of biological motion sequences. *Invest. Ophth. and Vis. Science*, 36(4):1920, 1995.
28. J. Sullivan, A. Blake, and J. Rittscher. Statistical foreground modelling for object localisation. *ECCV*, II pp. 307–323, 2000.
29. K. Toyama and A. Blake. Probabilistic tracking in a metric space. *ICCV*, 2:50–57, 2001.
30. S. Wachter and H. Nagel. Tracking of persons in monocular image sequences. *CVIU*, 74(3):174–192, 1999.
31. Y. Yacoob and M.J. Black. Parametrized modeling and recognition of activities. *CVIU*, 73(2):232–247, 1999.
32. S.C. Zhu, T. Wu, and D. Mumford. Filters, random fields and maximum entropy (FRAME) : towards a unified theory for texture modeling. *IJCV*, 27(2):107–126, 1998.

Using Robust Estimation Algorithms for Tracking Explicit Curves

Jean-Philippe Tarel[1], Sio-Song Ieng[1], and Pierre Charbonnier[2]

[1] LIVIC (INRETS-LCPC), 13, Route de la Minière, 78000 Versailles, France.
tarel@lcpc.fr, ieng@inrets.fr
[2] LRPC, 11, Rue Jean Mentelin, BP 9, 67200 Strasbourg, France.
Pierre.Charbonnier@equipement.gouv.fr

Abstract. The context of this work is lateral vehicle control using a camera as a sensor. A natural tool for controlling a vehicle is recursive filtering. The well-known Kalman filtering theory relies on Gaussian assumptions on both the state and measure random variables. However, image processing algorithms yield measurements that, most of the time, are far from Gaussian, as experimentally shown on real data in our application. It is therefore necessary to make the approach more robust, leading to the so-called robust Kalman filtering. In this paper, we review this approach from a very global point of view, adopting a constrained least squares approach, which is very similar to the half-quadratic theory, and justifies the use of iterative reweighted least squares algorithms. A key issue in robust Kalman filtering is the choice of the prediction error covariance matrix. Unlike in the Gaussian case, its computation is not straightforward in the robust case, due to the nonlinearity of the involved expectation. We review the classical alternatives and propose new ones. A theoretical study of these approximations is out of the scope of this paper, however we do provide an experimental comparison on synthetic data perturbed with Cauchy-distributed noise.

1 Introduction

Automatic driving and assistance systems development for vehicle drivers has been subject of investigations from many years [1]. Usually, this kind of problem is decomposed into two different tasks: perception and control. We focus on the particular problem of the lateral control of a vehicle on its lane, or lane-keeping.

The perception task must provide an accurate and real-time estimation of the orientation and lateral position of the vehicle within its lane. Since the road is defined by white lane-markings, a camera is used as a perception tool. The control task requires computing, in real time, the wheel angle in such a way that the vehicle stays at the center of the lane.

A key problem is to decide about the choice of the parameters transmitted between the control and perception modules. This raises the question of designing an approach which integrates both control and perception aspects. A popular technique in control theory is the well-known Kalman filtering. Kalman theory is very powerful and convenient, but it is based on the assumption that the state and the measures are Gaussian random variables. Most of the time, outputs of vision processes are far from the Gaussian assumption. This has been shown in several vision problems, for instance [2][3][4]. This leads us to consider robust Kalman theory when measures are not Gaussian, but corrupted by *outliers*. Various algorithms [5][6][7] were proposed to tackle the problem of robust Kalman filtering. The first algorithm proposed in [6] is difficult to apply in practice. Alternatives described in [5] and [7] outline an approach leading to weighted least squares algorithms. However, these approaches are restricted to a small number of convex functions, while the one we propose here is valid for a large class of not necessarily convex functions. Also, contrary to our approach, the estimation step of the algorithm in [5][7] is not iterative.

We propose here an overview of the problem based on Lagrange multipliers for deriving the equations of the robust Kalman filtering leading to a iterative reweighted least squares algorithm. To our knowledge, in the existing derivations, the explanation of why the robust Kalman filtering is not exact is rarely discussed. The main advantage of this derivation, which is equivalent to the half-quadratic approach [2][3], is to allow us to see two levels of approximations. One consists in assuming a Gaussian summary of the past and the other concerns the covariance matrix of the estimated state at every time step. Different possible approximate covariance matrices are proposed and experimentally compared.

The paper is organized as follows. First, we describe the system inboard the vehicle, and show that the features we are extracting from every image are not Gaussian. Second, for the sake of clarity, we gradually review least squares, recursive least squares, and Kalman filtering theory, and finally derive the robust Kalman filtering. Finally, we show the advantages of the designed robust Kalman filtering for the estimation of lane-markings position on perturbed road images and provide a comparison between the different approximate covariance matrices.

Fig. 1. Side camera system.

2 Image Feature Extraction

We have developed a system for measuring the lateral position and orientation of a vehicle using a vertical camera on its side. Due to the camera specifications and position, the accuracy of this system should be about 2 cm in position. Fig. 1 shows a first version of the system. A second version, where the camera is inside the left side mirror, is in progress. The image plane is parallel to the road surface, and the camera is mechanically aligned with the vehicle axis. This geometry reduces the calibration of the system to very simple manipulations.

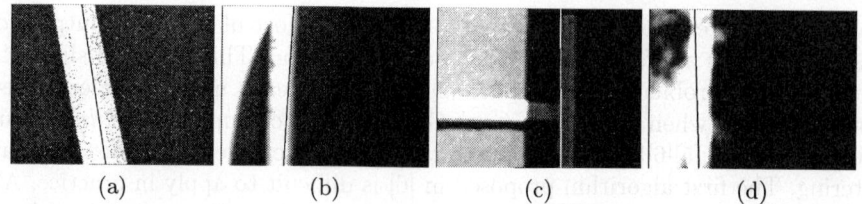

Fig. 2. Typical image without perturbation (a), and perturbations due to another markings, shadows, lighting conditions (b) (c) (d). Solid lines are the fitted lane-markings centers assuming Gaussian noise.

Fig. 2(a) displays a typical example of images observed by the camera. The seen lane-marking is very close to a straight line, even in curves. Images (b), (c) and (d) are examples of perturbations due to other markings and lighting conditions. The image processing consists in first, extracting features in each newly grabbed image and second, in robustly fitting a line (or another kind of curve, as described in the next section). The first step is required for real time processing. The set of extracted features must provide a summary of the image content relevant to the application. On every line of an image, a lane-marking is approximatively seen as a white hat function on the intensity profile. Lane-marking centers, on every image line, are chosen as the extracted features.

Following the approach in [8], we want to reduce as much as possible the effect of low image contrast on the extracted features. Consequently, we have to design a detector which is relatively invariant to contrast changes. When the threshold on the intensity is reduced, features in images are numerous, and a criterion for selecting these becomes mandatory. We believe that selection based on geometrical considerations is a better alternative than selection based on intensity contrast. Since the system is calibrated, the feature extraction is performed on the width of lane-markings which is assumed to range between 8 and 23 cm.

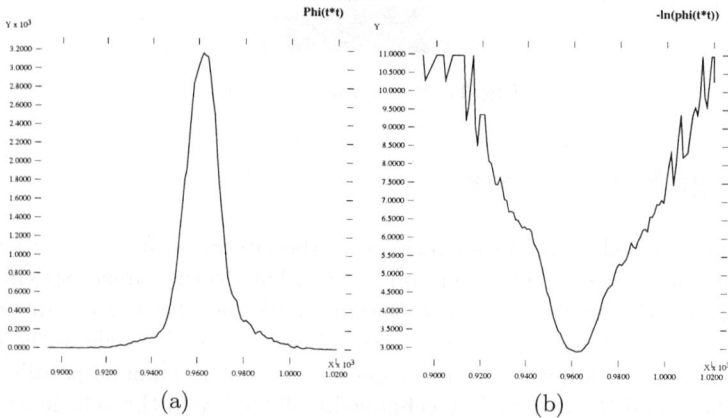

Fig. 3. (a) Distribution of errors, (b) negative of its logarithm as a function of noise b.

The obtained set of points is used by the line fitting. The question arises about the probability distribution function (pdf) of the extracted points around the true line. Most of the time, this pdf is assumed to be Gaussian. In Fig. 3(a), the measured pdf from a sequence of more than 100 real images is displayed. The pdf is not Gaussian, since Fig. 3(b) does not look like a parabola. Indeed, deeper investigations have shown that the curve in Fig. 3(b) can be very well approximated by $\phi(b^2) = \sqrt{1 + \frac{b^2}{\sigma^2}} - c$ with $\sigma = 5$, in a range of $[-20, 20]$ pixels around the minimum. For a good approximation on a larger range, a linear combination of the same kinds of functions with different values of σ seem to be needed.

3 Robust Estimation Framework

We consider that the lane-marking centers, extracted as described in the previous section, are noisy measurements of an underlying curve explicitly described as a function of one of its image coordinates:

$$y = \sum_{i=0}^{d} f_i(x) a_i = X(x)^t A \tag{1}$$

where (x, y) are the image coordinates of a point on the curve, $A = (a_i)_{0 \leq i \leq d}$ is the coefficient vector of the curve parameters, and $X(x) = (f_i(x))_{0 \leq i \leq d}$ is a vector of basis functions of the image coordinate x. In the context of our application, the basis functions are chosen as $f_i(x) = x^i$. The underlying curve is therefore a polynomial of degree d (i.e, a line when $d = 1$, a parabola when $d = 2$). Other bases may be used with their corresponding advantages or disadvantages.

In our model, the vertical coordinate is chosen as the x and assumed non-random. Thus only the other coordinate of the extracted point, y, is considered as a noisy measurement, i.e. $y = F(x)^t A + b$. In all that follows, the measurement noise b is assumed independent and identically distributed (iid), and centered.

For an intuitive understanding, we make a gradual presentation of the robust Kalman framework. Non-recursive least squares fitting is first recalled. Then, robust estimators are presented based on Lagrange multipliers approach and approximate inverse covariance matrices are proposed. In the fourth subsection, we introduce recursive and robust least squares (recursive least squares is a simple case of Kalman filter, using a constant state model). Finally, the robust Kalman filter is described.

3.1 Least Squares Fitting

First, we remember the very simple situation where only one image is observed and where the noise b is Gaussian. The goal is to estimate the curve parameters A_{LS} on the whole n extracted points (x_i, y_i), $i = 1, ..., n$. This issue is also known as a regression problem. Let $\mathcal{A}$ denote the underlying curve parameters we want to approximate with A_{LS}. Let σ be the standard deviation of the Gaussian noise

b. The probability of a measurement point (x_i, y_i), given the curve parameters A, is:
$$p_i((x_i, y_i)/A) = \frac{1}{\sqrt{2\pi}\sigma} e^{-\frac{1}{2}(\frac{F(x_i)^t A - y_i}{\sigma})^2}$$

For simpler equations, from now, we denote $X_i = X(x_i)$. We can write the probability of the whole set of points as the product of the individual probabilities:
$$p \propto \prod_{i=1}^{i=n} e^{-\frac{1}{2}(\frac{X_i^t A - y_i}{\sigma})^2} \qquad (2)$$

where p is the so-called likelihood of the point data set, given curve parameter A. $\propto$ denotes the equality up to a factor. Maximizing likelihood p with respect to A is equivalent to minimizing the negative of its logarithm, namely:
$$e_{LS}(A) = \frac{1}{2\sigma^2} \sum_{i=1}^{i=n} (X_i^t A - y_i)^2$$

It is the so-called least squares error. Since the fitting error is quadratic and positive, the minimization of e_{LS} is equivalent to canceling the vector of its first derivative with respect to A. It gives the well-known normal equations:
$$XX^t A = XY \qquad (3)$$

where $Y = (y_i)_{1 \le i \le n}$ is the vector of y coordinates, the matrix $X = (X_i)_{1 \le i \le n}$ is the *design matrix*, and $S = XX^t$ is the *scatter matrix* which is always symmetric and positive. If S is definite, (3) has the unique solution $A_{LS} = S^{-1}XY$. Computing the best fit A_{LS} simply requires solving the linear system (3). As seen before, it is also the Maximum Likelihood Estimate (MLE).

Since only Y is random, the expectation of A_{LS} is $\overline{A_{LS}} = S^{-1}X\overline{Y}$. The point coordinates in $\overline{Y}$ correspond to points exactly on the underlying curve, thus $\mathcal{A} = S^{-1}X\overline{Y}$. Therefore, $\overline{A_{LS}}$ equals $\mathcal{A}$, i.e. the estimator A_{LS} of $\mathcal{A}$ is unbiased. The covariance matrix C_{LS} of A_{LS} is $\overline{(A_{LS} - \overline{A_{LS}})(A_{LS} - \overline{A_{LS}})^t} = S^{-1}X\overline{(Y-\overline{Y})(Y-\overline{Y})^t}X^t S^{-t}$. We have $\overline{(Y-\overline{Y})(Y-\overline{Y})^t} = \sigma^2 I_d$, since the noise b is iid with variance σ^2. I_d denotes the identity matrix of size $n \times n$. Finally, the inverse covariance matrix of A_{LS} is deduced:
$$C_{LS}^{-1} = \frac{1}{\sigma^2} S = Q_{LS} \qquad (4)$$

Q_{LS} is also known as Fisher's information matrix for the set of n data points. Q_{LS} is defined as the expectation of the second derivative of e_{LS} with respect to A.

Finally, since e_{LS} is minimum in A_{LS} with second derivative matrix Q_{LS}, (2) can be rewritten as:
$$p \propto e^{-\frac{1}{2}(A - A_{LS})^t Q_{LS}(A - A_{LS})} \qquad (5)$$

As clearly shown on Fig. 2, least squares fitting does not provide correctly fit curves in the presence of image perturbations.

3.2 Robust Fitting

We still assume that only one image is observed, and that measurement noises are iid and centered. But now, the noise is not assumed Gaussian, but having heavier tails. The heaviest observed noise is specified by a function $\phi(t)$ in such a way that the probability of measurement point (x_i, y_i), given curve parameter A, is:

$$p_i((x_i,y_i)/A) \propto e^{-\frac{1}{2}\phi((\frac{X_i^t A - y_i}{\sigma})^2)}$$

Similarly to the half-quadratic approach [2][3], $\phi(t)$ is assumed:

- **H0**: defined and continuous on $[0, +\infty[$ as its first and second derivatives,
- **H1**: $\phi'(t) > 0$ (thus ϕ is increasing),
- **H2**: $\phi''(t) < 0$ (thus ϕ is concave).

These three assumptions are very different from the ones used in M-estimator approach for the convergence proof. Indeed in [9], the convergence proof requires that $\rho(b) = \phi(b^2)$ is convex. In our case, the concavity and monotony of $\phi(t)$ implies that $\phi'(t)$ is bounded, but $\phi(b^2)$ is not *necessarily convex* with respect to b. Note that, the pdf of Sec. 2, observed in practice on real data, verifies these three assumptions.

Following [9], the role of this ϕ function is to saturate the error in case of an important measurement noise $|b_i| = |X_i^t A - y_i|$, and thus to lower the importance of outliers. The scale parameter, σ, sets the distance from which a measurement noise has a good chance to be considered as outliers. Notice that with certain ϕ, the associated pdf cannot be integrated on its support. Without difficulties, a bounded support with fixed bounds can be introduced to maintain the statistical interpretation of the fitting.

Following the same MLE approach than for least squares, the problem is set as the minimization with respect to A of the robust error:

$$e_R(A) = \frac{1}{2} \sum_{i=1}^{i=n} \phi((\frac{X_i^t A - y_i}{\sigma})^2)$$

Notice that the Gaussian case corresponds to the particular case in which $\phi(t) = t$, but this last function does not strictly agree with assumption (H2). $e_{LS}(A)$ is indeed a limit case of $e_R(A)$. Contrary to the Gaussian case, the previous minimization is in general not quadratic. This last minimization can be done iteratively using the Gradient or Steepest Descent algorithms. But, since $\phi(b^2)$ and thus $e_R(A)$ are not necessarily convex, these algorithms can be relatively slow when the gradient slope is near zero. Indeed, the speed of convergence is only linear, when quasi-Newton algorithms achieve a quadratic speed of convergence. But generally, with quasi-Newton algorithms, the convergence to a local minimum is not sure. Therefore, we prove next that the used quasi-Newton algorithm always converges towards a local minimum. A global minimum can be obtained using simulated annealing, despite an expensive computational cost [2].

We now explain how this e_R can be solved iteratively, using the well known quasi-Newton algorithm named iterative reweighted least squares. The same algorithm is also a particular case obtained with the half-quadratic approach [3]. First, we rewrite $e_R(A)$ as the search for a saddle point of the associated Lagrange function. Then, the algorithm is obtained as a alternated minimization of the dual function.

First, we rewrite the minimization of $e_R(A)$ as the maximization of $-e_R$. This will allow us to later write $-e_R(A)$ as the extremum of a convex function rather than a concave one, since the negative of a concave function is convex. Second, we introduce the auxiliary variables $w_i = (\frac{X_i^t A - y_i}{\sigma})^2$. These variables are needed to rewrite $-e_R(A)$ as the value achieved at the minimum of a constrained problem. This apparent complication is in fact precious since it allows us to introduce the Lagrange multipliers. Indeed using (H1), $-e_R(A)$ can be seen as the minimization with respect to $W = (w_i)_{1 \leq i \leq n}$ of:

$$E(A, W) = \frac{1}{2} \sum_{i=1}^{i=n} -\phi(w_i)$$

subject to n constraints $h_i(A, W) = w_i - (\frac{X_i^t A - y_i}{\sigma})^2 \leq 0$.

For any A, we now focus on the minimization of $E(A, W)$ with respect to W only subject to the n constraints $h_i(A, W) \leq 0$, with respect to W only. This problem is well-posed because it is a minimization of a convex function subject to convex constraints. Therefore using the classical Kuhn and Tucker's theorem [10], if a solution exists, the minimization of $E(A, W)$ with respect to W is equivalent to the search of the unique saddle point of the Lagrange function of the problem:

$$L_R(A, W, \lambda_i) = \frac{1}{2} \sum_{i=1}^{i=n} -\phi(w_i) + \lambda_i (w_i - (\frac{X_i^t A - y_i}{\sigma})^2)$$

where λ_i are Kuhn and Tucker multipliers ($\lambda_i \geq 0$). More formally, we have proved for any A:

$$-e_R(A) = \min_{w_i} \max_{\lambda_i} L_R(A, W, \lambda_i) \quad (6)$$

Notice that the Lagrange function L_R is now quadratic with respect to A, contrary to the original error e_R. Using the saddle point property, we can change the order of the variables w_i and λ_i in (6). $L_R(A, W, \lambda_i)$ being convex with respect to W, it is equivalent to search for a minimum of $L_R(A, W, \lambda_i)$ with respect to W and to have its first derivative zero. Thus, we deduce:

$$\lambda_i = \phi'(w_i) \quad (7)$$

This last equation can be used with (H2) to substitute w_i in L_R and then to deduce that the original problem is equivalent to the following minimization:

$$\min_A e_R(A) = \min_{A, \lambda_i} -L_R(A, {\phi'}^{-1}(\lambda_i), \lambda_i)$$

$\mathcal{E}(A, \lambda_i) = -L_R(A, {\phi'}^{-1}(\lambda_i), \lambda_i)$ is the dual function. The dual function is convex with respect to A. $\mathcal{E}$ is also convex with respect to λ_i (Indeed, $\frac{\partial^2 \mathcal{E}}{\partial \lambda_i^2} =$

$-\frac{1}{\phi''(\phi'^{-1}(\lambda_i))}$). Since $e_R(b^2)$ is not convex, it is not necessary that $\mathcal{E}$ is convex with respect to A and λ_i. Therefore, $\mathcal{E}(A, \lambda_i)$ does not have a unique minimum.

An alternate minimization of the dual function leads to the classical robust algorithm, used in the half-quadratic and M-estimator approaches:

1. Initialize A_0, and set $j = 1$,
2. For all indexes i ($1 \leq i \leq n$), compute the auxiliary variable $w_{i,j} = (\frac{X_i^t A_{j-1} - y_i}{\sigma})^2$,
3. Solve the linear system $\sum_{i=1}^{i=n} \phi'(w_{i,j}) X_i X_i^t A_j = \sum_{i=1}^{i=n} \phi'(w_{i,j}) X_i y_i$,
4. If $\|A_j - A_{j-1}\| > \epsilon$, increment j, and go to 2, else $A_{RLS} = A_j$.

The convergence test can be also performed on the error variation. A test on a maximum number of iterations can be added too. It can be shown that the previous algorithm always strictly decreases the dual function if the current point is not a stationary point (i.e a point where the first derivatives are all zero) of the dual function [11]. Using the previous Lagrange function, this proves that the previous algorithm is globally convergent, i.e, it converges towards a local minimum of $e_R(A)$ for all initial A_0s which are not a maximum of $e_R(A)$. As a quasi-Newton algorithm, it can be also proved that the speed of convergence of the algorithm around a local minimum is quadratic, when S is definite.

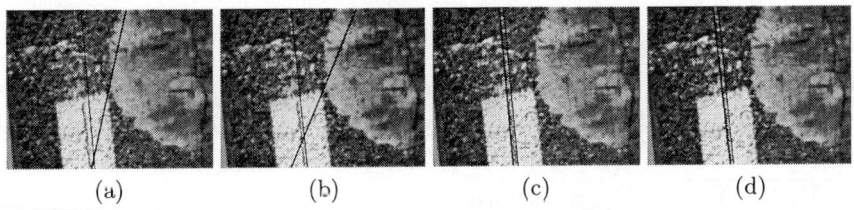

Fig. 4. Fitting on a real image assuming (a) Gauss, (b) quasi-Laplace, (c) Cauchy, and (d) Geman & McClure distributed noise. Thin black lines are the initial A_0's. Thick ones are the fitting results. See Sec. 4 for a definition of the pdfs.

Finally, Fig. 4 illustrates the importance of robust fitting in images with many outliers. The thin black lines depict the initial A_0's. The thicker ones are the fitting results A_R, assuming (a) Gauss, (b) quasi-Laplace, (c) Cauchy, and (d) Geman & McClure distributed noise. A correct fitting is achieved only with the last two pdfs which are not convex.

3.3 Covariance Matrix in Robust Fitting

The covariance matrix C_R of the estimate A_R is required for a correct management of uncertainties in a recursive process. Contrary to the least squares case, where the covariance matrix was easy to compute using its definition, the estimation of C_R as the expectation of $(A_R - \overline{A_R})(A_R - \overline{A_R})^t$ is difficult in the robust framework, due to the non-linearities. An alternative is to use an approximation.

Similar to [9], p. 173-175, an approximation based on extending (4) is proposed. The inverse covariance matrix is approximated by the second derivative of e_R at the achieved minimum:

$$C_{R,Huber}^{-1} = \sum_{i=1}^{i=n}(2w_i\phi''(w_i) + \phi'(w_i))X_iX_i^t \tag{8}$$

where w_i is computed once the minimum of e_R is achieved. The value $\frac{d^2\phi((\frac{b}{\sigma})^2)}{db^2} = 2w\phi''(w) + \phi'(w)$ is not always positive, since $\phi((\frac{b}{\sigma})^2)$ is not necessarily convex with respect to b. Nevertheless, the second derivative of e_R with respect to A at A_R is a positive matrix since A_R achieves a minimum. This property is a necessary condition for the matrix being interpreted as a covariance matrix.

In [5][7], another approximation is implicitly used in the context of approximate robust Kalman filtering. The proposed approximate inverse covariance matrix can be seen as the second derivative of $-L_R$ with respect to A, at the achieved saddle point:

$$C_{R,Cipra}^{-1} = \sum_{i=1}^{i=n}\lambda_i X_i X_i^t \tag{9}$$

where λ_i is computed when the minimum of e_R is achieved. However, p. 175 of [9], Huber warns us against the use of this matrix (9).

Another approximation can be obtained if we forget that λ_i is a random variable. Let us rewrite the last equation of the robust algorithm as:

$$XRX^tA = XRY \tag{10}$$

where R is a $n \times n$ matrix with diagonal values λ_i, $1 \leq i \leq n$. Using these notations, the covariance matrix $C_{R,new1}$ is $\overline{(A_R - \overline{A_R})(A_R - \overline{A_R})^t}$ and equals $(XRX^t)^{-1}XR\overline{(Y-\overline{Y})(Y-\overline{Y})^t}R^tX^t(XRX^t)^{-t}$. Recalling from Sec. 3.1, that $\overline{(Y-\overline{Y})(Y-\overline{Y})^t} = \sigma^2 I_d$, we deduce:

$$C_{R,new1}^{-1} = \frac{1}{\sigma^2}(XRX^t)^t(XR^2X^t)^{-1}(XRX^t) \tag{11}$$

We also propose, without justification, another approximation:

$$C_{R,new2}^{-1} = \frac{1}{\sigma^2}\sum_{i=1}^{i=n}\lambda_i^2 X_i X_i^t \tag{12}$$

Now, the question is "what is the best choice for an approximate inverse covariance matrix?" A theoretical study is out of the scope of this paper, but we provide an experimental comparison in Sec. 4.

3.4 Recursive Fitting

We now consider the problem of sequentially processing images. The steady-state situation consists in supposing that we observe, at every time step t, the same underlying curve. Suppose that images are indexed by t and that for each image t, we have to fit its n_t data points $(x_{i,t}, y_{i,t})$, $i = 1, ..., n_t$. Of course, assuming that every point in every image is iid and centered, it is clear that we could directly apply what is explained in the two previous sections, on the whole data set. However, it is better to take advantage of the sequential arrival of images and deploy a recursive algorithm, in particular for saving memory space and number of computations, especially in the context of real time processing.

Recursive Least Square Fitting: When least squares error is used, recursive algorithms are based on an exhaustive summary of the data points, observed before t. Indeed, the error of the data points from time 1 to t is:

$$e_{rLS,t}(A) = \frac{1}{2\sigma^2} \sum_{k=1}^{k=t} \sum_{i=1}^{i=n} (F(x_{i,k})^t A - y_{i,k})^2$$

This sum can be rewritten as the sum of the error at time t alone and of the error from time 1 to $t-1$:

$$e_{rLS,t}(A) = \frac{1}{2}(A - A_{rLS,t-1})^t Q_{rLS,t-1}(A - A_{rLS,t-1}) + \frac{1}{2\sigma^2} \sum_{i=1}^{i=n_t} (X_{i,t}^t A - y_{i,t})^2 \tag{13}$$

Using (5), the summary of the past error consists in the previously fitted solution $A_{rLS,t-1}$ and its Fisher's matrix $Q_{rLS,t-1}$. By comparing $e_{rLS,t}$ with e_{LS}, the exhaustive summary by $A_{rLS,t-1}$ and $Q_{rLS,t-1}$ can be interpreted as a Gaussian prior on A at time t.

The error $e_{rLS,t}$ is quadratic and using (5) its second order matrix is $Q_{rLS,t}$. Taking second derivative of (13), we deduce:

$$Q_{rLS,t} = Q_{rLS,t-1} + \frac{1}{\sigma^2} S_t \tag{14}$$

where $S_t = \sum_{i=1}^{i=n_t} X_{i,t} X_{i,t}^t$. The recursive update of the fit is obtained by solving the following linear system obtained by canceling the first derivative of $e_{rT,t}$ with respect to A:

$$Q_{rLS,t} A_{rLS,t} = Q_{rLS,t-1} A_{rLS,t-1} + \frac{1}{\sigma^2} T_t \tag{15}$$

with $T_t = \sum_{i=1}^{i=n_t} y_{i,t} X_{i,t}$. As a consequence, the recursive fitting algorithm consists of the following steps:

1. Initialize the recursive fitting by setting $Q_{rLS,0}$ and $A_{rLS,0}$ to zero, and set t=1.
2. For the data set associated to step t, compute the matrix $S_t = \sum_{i=1}^{i=n_t} X_{i,t} X_{i,t}^t$ and the vector $T_t = \sum_{i=1}^{i=n_t} y_{i,t} X_{i,t}$ only related to the current data set.
3. Update the Fisher's matrix $Q_{rLS,t}$ using (14).
4. Compute the current fit $A_{rLS,t}$ by solving the linear system (15).
5. If a new dataset is available, increment t and go to 2.

The solution, obtained by this recursive algorithm at step t, is the same that the one obtained by standard least squares using all points of time steps from 1 to t. It is the so-called recursive (or sequential) least squares algorithm (subscript rLS). Note that no matrix inverse is explicitly needed. Only one linear system is solved at every time step t. This can be crucial in real time applications, since the complexity for solving the linear system is $O(d^2)$, when it is $O(d^3)$ for a matrix inverse.

Note that (14) gives the recursive update of the Fisher's matrix $Q_{rLS,t}$ as a function of the previous Fisher's matrix $Q_{rLS,t-1}$ and of the current scatter matrix S_t. A better initialization of $Q_{rLS,0}$ than 0 consists in β times the identity matrix, where β has a positive value close to zero. This initialization insures that the solution of (15) is unique. Indeed, $Q_{rLS,t}$ is definite for any t, even if S_t in (14) is not. This is equivalent to the *Ridge Regression* regularization [12]. More generally, $Q_{rLS,0}$ is the inverse covariance matrix on the Gaussian prior on the curve parameters A, leading to a Maximum A Posteriori (MAP) estimate.

Recursive Robust Fitting: Is it possible to generalize this recursive scheme in the robust case? In general, an exact answer is negative : it is not possible to rewrite (13) excepted for a very narrow class of function ϕ, that do not satisfy our assumptions (see sufficient statistics in [13]). Moreover, to obtain a solution without approximation, the computation of the weights λ_i would require storing all past observed points in memory up to the current time step. For real time application, this is a problem, since it means that the number of computations will increase with time t. Clearly, a second level of approximation is needed - remember that the first one consists in the approximate computation of the inverse covariance matrix as described in Sec. 3.3. It is usual to consider $A_{rR,t-1}$ as Gaussian with a covariance matrix $C_{rR,t-1} = Q_{rR,t-1}^{-1}$, while it is a seldom pointed out that it is an approximation. The summary by $A_{rR,t-1}$ and $Q_{rR,t-1}$ is not exhaustive, but can still be included as a prior during the robust fitting at every time step:

$$e_{rR,t}(A) = \frac{1}{2}\sum_{i=1}^{i=n_t} \phi((\frac{X_{i,t}^t A - y_{i,t}}{\sigma})^2) + \frac{1}{2}(A - A_{rR,t-1})^t Q_{rR,t-1}(A - A_{rR,t-1})$$

Thus, $e_{rR,t}$ can be minimize by following the same approach than in Sec. 3.2. If Huber's (8) approximate is used, the new approximate inverse covariance matrix at time step t is:

$$Q_{rR,t,Huber} = \sum_{i=1}^{i=n_t}(2w_{i,t}\phi''(w_{i,t}) + \phi'(w_{i,t}))X_{i,t}X_{i,t}^t + Q_{rR,t-1,Huber} \quad (16)$$

where $w_{i,t} = w_{i,j,t}$ with j the last iteration when the minimum of e_{rR} is reached. Similarly, other approximations can be derived using Cipra's (9) and our approximations (11) and (12).

Finally, the recursive and robust algorithm consists of the following steps:

1. Initialize $Q_{rR,0}$ and $A_{rR,0}$ to zero or to a prior, and set t=1,
2. Initialize $A_{0,t} = A_{rR,t-1}$, and set $j = 1$,

3. For all indexes i ($1 \leq i \leq n_t$), compute the auxiliary variable $w_{i,j,t} = (\frac{X_{i,t}^t A_{j-1,t} - y_{i,t}}{\sigma})^2$,
4. Solve the linear system

$$(\sum_{i=1}^{i=n_t} \phi'(w_{i,j,t}) X_{i,t} X_{i,t}^t + Q_{rR,t-1}) A_{j,t} = \sum_{i=1}^{i=n_t} \phi'(w_i) X_i y_i + Q_{rR,t-1} A_{rR,t-1}$$

5. If $\|A_{j,t} - A_{j-1,t}\| > \epsilon$, increment j, and go to 3, else continue,
6. $A_{rR,t} = A_{j,t}$ and its approximate inverse covariance matrix $Q_{rR,t}$ is given by (16) or similar. If a new dataset is available, increment t, and go to 2

In the recursive context, it is clear that, a better estimate of the covariance matrix leads to better recursive estimators. In particular, if the covariance matrix is under-estimated with respect to the true covariance matrix, information about the past will be gradually lost. On the contrary, if the covariance matrix is over-estimated, the impact of the most recent data is always diminished.

3.5 Robust Kalman

Kalman filtering is a stochastic, recursive estimator, which estimates the state of a system based on the knowledge of the system input, the measurement of the system output, and a model of the link between input and output.

We can identify state A_t at time t with $A_{rLS,t}$ or $A_{rR,t}$, depending of the measurement noise pdf. As in Sec. 3.1, we introduce $Y_t = (y_{i,t})_{1 \leq i \leq n_t}$, which is the so-called measurement vector, and $X_t = (X_{i,t})_{1 \leq i \leq n}$, the measurement matrix. The link between measurements and state can thus be written as $Y_t = X_t A_t + B$ where B is a vector of iid, centered measurement noises. This equation is the so-called measurement equation.

Compared to the recursive least squares, discrete Kalman filtering consists in assuming linear dynamics for the state model. More precisely, we assume $A_t = U_t A_{t-1} + V_t + u$ where u is a centered iid Gaussian model noise. This last equation is the so-called model, or state-transition, equation. As a summary, the Kalman model is:

$$\begin{cases} A_t = U_t A_{t-1} + V_t + u \\ Y_t = X_t A_t + v \end{cases} \quad (17)$$

When v is Gaussian, (17) models the classical Kalman (subscript K). When v is non Gaussian, (17) models the robust to non-Gaussian measurement Kalman, or robust Kalman for short (subscript RK). The steady-state case we dealt with in the previous section, is a particular case of (17), where the first equation is deterministic and reduced to $A_{t+1} = A_t$.

In the dynamic case with v Gaussian, the prior on A is not A_{t-1} but the prediction $\hat{A}_{K,t} = U_t A_{K,t-1} + V_t$, given by the model equation. Using the model equation, the covariance matrix of the prediction $\hat{A}_{K,t}$ is derived as $\hat{C}_{K,t} = U_t C_{K,t-1} U_t^t + \Sigma$, where Σ is the covariance matrix of the Gaussian model noise u. Thus the inverse covariance matrix of the prediction $\hat{Q}_{K,t} = \hat{C}_{K,t}^{-1}$ using the matrix lemma, is:

$$\hat{Q}_{K,t} = \Sigma^{-1} - \Sigma^{-1} U_t (U_t^t \Sigma^{-1} U_t + Q_{K,t-1})^{-1} U_t^t \Sigma^{-1} \quad (18)$$

This last equation is interesting in the context of real time applications, since it involves only one matrix inverse at every time t. As in (13), the prediction is used as a Gaussian prior on A. The associated error, to be compared with (13), is now:

$$e_{K,t}(A) = \frac{1}{2}\sum_{i=1}^{i=n_t}\frac{1}{\sigma^2}(X_{i,t}^t A - y_{i,t})^2 + \frac{1}{2}(A - \hat{A}_{K,t})^t \hat{Q}_{K,t}(A - \hat{A}_{K,t})$$

The recursive equations of the Kalman filtering are obtained by derivations from $e_{K,t}$. When $\hat{Q}_{K,t}$ is computed, only one linear system has to be solved at every t.

How does this method extend to the robust case? As before with recursive least squares, generally, an exact solution of the robust Kalman is not achievable. The two levels of approximations must be performed. Like in Sec. 3.4, we assume that $A_{RK,t-1}$ is approximatively Gaussian, and its inverse covariance matrix is given by one of the approximations of Sec. 3.3. As a consequence, the associated error is:

$$e_{RK,t}(A) = \frac{1}{2}\sum_{i=1}^{i=n_t}\phi((\frac{X_{i,t}^t A - y_{i,t}}{\sigma})^2) + \frac{1}{2}(A - \hat{A}_{RK,t})^t \hat{Q}_{RK,t}(A - \hat{A}_{RK,t})$$

In the robust Kalman, the Huber's approximation (16), translates as:

$$Q_{RK,t,Huber} = \sum_{i=1}^{i=n_t}(2w_{i,t}\phi''(w_{i,t}) + \phi'(w_{i,t}))X_{i,t}X_{i,t}^t + \hat{Q}_{RK,t} \quad (19)$$

Other approximate inverse covariance matrix can be derived using Cipra's (9) and our approximations (11) and (12).

Finally, the robust Kalman algorithm consists of the following steps:

1. Initialize $Q_{RK,0}$ and $A_{RK,0}$ to zero or to a prior, and set t=1,
2. Compute the predicted solution $\hat{A}_{RK,t} = U_t A_{RK,t-1} + V_t$, and its covariance matrix $\hat{Q}_{RK,t}$ using (18),
3. Initialize $A_{0,t} = \hat{A}_{RK,t}$, and set $j = 1$,
4. For all indexes i ($1 \leq i \leq n_t$), compute the auxiliary variable $w_{i,j,t} = (\frac{X_{i,t}^t A_{j-1,t} - y_{i,t}}{\sigma})^2$,
5. solve the linear system

$$(\sum_{i=1}^{i=n_t}\phi'(w_{i,j,t})X_{i,t}X_{i,t}^t + \hat{Q}_{RK,t})A_{j,t} = \sum_{i=1}^{i=n_t}\phi'(w_i)X_i y_i + \hat{Q}_{RK,t}\hat{A}_{RK,t}$$

6. If $\|A_{j,t} - A_{j-1,t}\| > \epsilon$, increment j, and go to 4, else continue,
7. $A_{RK,t} = A_{j,t}$ and its approximate inverse covariance matrix $Q_{RK,t}$ is given by (19) or similar. If a new dataset is available, increment t, and go to 2.

Note that in [5][7], one single weighted least squares iteration is performed at each time step. We believe for each iteration one should achieve convergence in the approximation done in steps 4-6. Moreover the weights in [7] are binary. This corresponds to a truncated Gaussian pdf, violating (H0). In such a case, the choice of the scale parameter becomes critical: a small variation of the scale parameter can produce a very different solution.

As a conclusion, the Lagrange multipliers approach (and half-quadratic approach) of robust fitting allows us to have new insight in why robust Kalman filtering provides approximate estimates. Robust Kalman is not exact because: the amount of past data cannot be reduced without loss of information, and the covariance matrix of the predicted state is an approximation. Contrary to [5][7], this formulation also suggests that it is important to iteratively search for the best solution A_t at every time steps.

Table 1. Correspondence between particular values of α and classical ϕs and pdfs proposed in the literature.

α	Name	pdf $\propto e^{-\frac{1}{2}\phi(b^2)}$	error=$\phi(b^2)$	weight=$\phi'(t)$
1	Gauss	$\propto e^{-\frac{1}{2}b^2}$	b^2	1
0.5	quasi-Laplace	$\propto e^{-\frac{1}{2}\sqrt{1+b^2}}$	$2(\sqrt{1+b^2}-1)$	$\frac{1}{\sqrt{1+t}}$
0	Cauchy	$\propto \frac{1}{1+b^2}$	$ln(1+b^2)$	$\frac{1}{1+t}$
-1	Geman & McClure [2]	$\propto e^{\frac{1}{2}\frac{1}{1+b^2}}$	$\frac{b^2}{1+b^2}$	$\frac{1}{(1+t)^2}$

4 Experiments

We have restrict ourselves in the choice of ϕ to the following one parameter family of functions:

$$\phi_\alpha(t) = \frac{1}{\alpha}((1+t)^\alpha - 1)$$

These functions verify the three assumptions (H0), (H1), and (H2), when $\alpha < 1$.

This family is very convenient, since it allows us to catch many of the classical ϕs and pdfs proposed in the literature. Tab. 1 illustrates this fact. Notice that the pdf obtained in the experiments of Sec. 2 corresponds to $\alpha = 0.5$. The pdf obtained for $\alpha = 0.5$, also known as the hypersurface function, is a good differentiable approximation of Laplace's pdf. Thus we have preferred to name it the quasi-Laplace function.

Table 2. Comparison between the covariance matrices obtained with various approximations. The relative standard deviations are also shown.

Name	$\sqrt{C_{00}}$	$\sqrt{C_{11}}$	$\sqrt{C_{00}}$ rel. Std.	$\sqrt{C_{11}}$ rel. Std.
C_{new1}	0.138	0.00474	7.8%	10.6%
C_{Cipra}	0.162	0.00555	9.8%	13.2%
C_{Huber}	0.189	0.00647	10.5%	14.1%
C_{new2}	0.190	0.00653	13.1%	17.6%
reference	0.195	0.00688		

A simulation was performed using 50000 fits on simulated 101 noisy points along a line with true parameters $a_0 = 100$ and $a_1 = 1$. a_0 is the pose of the line and a_1 is its slope. The noise pdf for each sample is Cauchy $\propto \frac{1}{1+(\frac{b}{\sigma})^2}$ with $\sigma = 1$. The Cauchy noise was simulated by applying the function $tan(\frac{\pi}{2}v)$ on v, a uniform noise on $[-1, 1]$. The variance of the Cauchy pdf is not defined, thus the simulated noise can have very large values (outliers). Robust fits were obtained using the Cauchy-distributed pdf of Sec. 3.2. For every fit, the Huber's, Cipra's, and ours approximate covariance matrices were computed and averaged. These are denoted C_{Huber}, C_{Cipra}, C_{new1} and C_{new2}, respectively. The square roots of the averaged diagonal matrix components are shown in Tab. 2. The covariance matrix of the 50000 fits is also estimated and is the reference displayed in the last line of Tab. 2 (Monte-Carlo estimates).

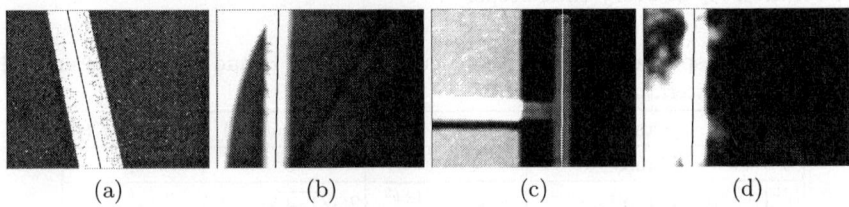

Fig. 5. Typical image without perturbation (a), and perturbations due to another markings, shadows, lighting conditions (b) (c) (d). Solid lines are the fitted lane-markings centers assuming Geman & McClure noise.

Tab. 2 shows that the closest approximation is C_{new2}. All these approximations can be ordered in terms of proximity, with respect to the reference one, in the following order: C_{new2}, C_{Huber}, C_{Cipra} and C_{new1}. Notice that the closer to the reference one the matrix is, the larger its relative variation from one fit to another is. For instance, this variation is 7.8% for C_{new1} when it is 13.1% for C_{new2}. Clearly, the choice of the approximation is a trade-off between accuracy and stability. We also notice that all the approximations under-estimate the true matrix. A different weighting of the two right terms in (16) and (19) can be introduced for correcting this.

Finally, we show in Fig. 5, the same images than in Fig. 2 using Geman & McClure noise assumption. Unlike the Gaussian assumption, the obtained fits are correct even in presence of important perturbations due to other lane-markings and difficult lighting conditions.

5 Conclusion

In this paper, we have reviewed the problem of making Kalman filtering robust to outliers, in a unified framework. The link with Lagrange multipliers yields a revised half-quadratic theory and justifies the use of iterative reweighted least squares algorithms in M-estimator theory even for non-convex $\rho(b) = \phi(b^2)$. Moreover, in contrast to previous works, we do not restrict ourselves to a single potential function but the half-quadratic framework is valid for a large class of functions, involving non-convex *and hence more robust* ones. We have shown that, as soon as non-Gaussian likelihoods are involved, two levels of approximation are needed. First, in contrast with the non-robust case, there is no obvious closed-form expressions for the covariance matrix. After reviewing classical solutions, we proposed new approximations and experimentally studied their behavior in terms of accuracy and stability. An accurate covariance matrix is very important to tackle the problem of missing data on a long sequence of images, an important subject for future investigations. Second, to design a recursive filter in the robust case, the pdf of previous estimates must be considered as Gaussian. In existing algorithms, only one iteration is performed at each time step to obtain the robust estimate. We believe it is better to let the iterative least squares algorithm to converge. Further exploration than presented in [5] is needed to treat the case where the noise involved in the state-transition equation is non-Gaussian. Here the challenge is to derive an integrated and consistent framework.

References

1. E.D. Dickmanns and A. Zapp. A curvature-based scheme for improving road vehicle guidance by computer vision. In *Proceedings of SPIE Conference on Mobile Robots S.161-16*, volume 727, 1986.
2. D. Geman and G. Reynolds. Constrained restoration and the recovery of discontinuities. *IEEE Trans. on Pattern Analysis and Intelligence*, 14(3):367–383, 1992.
3. P. Charbonnier, L. Blanc-Féraud, G. Aubert, and M. Barlaud. Deterministic edge-preserving regularization in computed imaging. *Trans. on Image Processing*, 6(2):298–311, 1997.
4. P.H.S. Torr and A. Zisserman. Mlesac: A new robust estimator with application to estimating image geometry. *Computer Vision and Image Understanding*, 78(1):138–156, 2000.
5. T. Cipra and R. Romera. Robust kalman filtering and its application in time series analysis. *Kybernetika*, 27(6):481–494, 1991.
6. C. Masreliez. Approximate non-gaussian filtering with linear state and observation relations. *IEEE Transactions on Automatic Control*, 18:107–110, February 1975.
7. R. Rao. Robust kalman filters for prediction, recognition, and learning. Technical Report TR645, University of Rochester, 1996.
8. F. Guichard and J.-P. Tarel. Curve extraction combining perceptual grouping and a kalman like fitting. In *IEEE International Conference on Computer Vision*, Kerkyra, Greece, 1999.
9. P. J. Huber. *Robust Statistics*. John Wiley and Sons, New York, New York, 1981.
10. M. Minoux. *Mathematical Programming: Theory and Algorithms*. Chichester: John Wiley and Sons, 1986.
11. D. G. Luenberger. *Introduction to linear and nonlinear programming*. Addison Wesley, 1973.
12. T. Tasdizen, J.-P. Tarel, and D.B. Cooper. Improving the stability of algebraic curves for applications. *IEEE Transactions on Image Processing*, 9(3):405–416, March 2000.
13. H. W. Sorenson. *Parameter Estimation*. Marcel Dekker, Inc., New York, New York, 1980.

On the Motion and Appearance of Specularities in Image Sequences

Rahul Swaminathan[1], Sing Bing Kang[2], Richard Szeliski[2],
Antonio Criminisi[2], and Shree K. Nayar[1]

[1] Columbia University, New York NY 10027, USA,
srahul@cs.columbia.edu
[2] Microsoft Research,
One Microsoft Way, Redmond 98052, WA, USA

Abstract. Real scenes are full of specularities (highlights and reflections), and yet most vision algorithms ignore them. In order to capture the appearance of realistic scenes, we need to model specularities as separate layers. In this paper, we study the behavior of specularities in static scenes as the camera moves, and describe their dependence on varying surface geometry, orientation, and scene point and camera locations. For a rectilinear camera motion with constant velocity, we study how the specular motion deviates from a straight trajectory (*disparity deviation*) and how much it violates the epipolar constraint (*epipolar deviation*). Surprisingly, for surfaces that are convex or not highly undulating, these deviations are usually quite small. We also study the appearance of specularities, i.e., how they interact with the body reflection, and with the usual occlusion ordering constraints applicable to diffuse opaque layers. We present a taxonomy of specularities based on their photometric properties as a guide for designing separation techniques. Finally, we propose a technique to extract specularities as a separate layer, and demonstrate it using an image sequence of a complex scene.

1 Introduction

Specularities are all around us. There are reflections in windows, monitors, and picture frames, glossy sheen on books and furniture, and bright highlights on coffee mugs and fruits. The presence of specular reflections[1] in an environment is what gives it a true sense of realism. Understanding the behavior of specularities has been one of the long-standing research areas in optics (see Euclid's Optica). In the 18th century, the results obtained in optics became the basis of new and powerful descriptive geometry tools (page 60 of [Kem01]). Descriptive geometry and its novel ways of representing 3D objects and specular reflections, combined

---
[1] In this paper, the term *specularity* or specular reflection is used to describe any non-Lambertian component. *Highlights* are isolated bright spots due to reflections of point or small area light sources, and *reflections* are virtual images with discernible structures.

with the well-established rules of linear perspective, allowed artists and architects to greatly enhance the sense of realism of the environments they depicted.

From an *image-based rendering* perspective, realistic scene synthesis requires extensive appearance capture. However, the number of images required can be reduced using geometry. Also, one must deal with specularities and reflections in real scenes. One approach is that of modeling specularities and reflections as separate layers [LS97]. Thus, the diffuse component of the image sequence contains the structure information while the specular component contains higher order appearance information. We propose a simple technique to recover scene structure as layers while at the same time detecting specularities and estimating the underlying diffuse component.

Many approaches have been suggested to separate the specular and diffuse layers. These can be broadly categorized into physics-based approaches and image-based approaches. Physics-based methods either use the Dichromatic Reflectance Model to recover specularities [KSK88,SHW92] or use the polarizing effect on specularities [Wol90,NFB97,SSK98,FA99]. Image-based approaches include dominant motion based techniques such as [IRP94,SAA00]. However, current techniques (except [KSK88,SHW92]) can only handle planar objects reflected off planar surfaces or require the use of added imaging components such as polarizer filters. Lee and Bajcsy [LB92] proposed a spectral differencing technique to detect specularities from multiple views. However, the diffuse component could not be estimated nor could it deal with dis-occlusion events.

Many vision algorithms that compute scene structure typically ignore specularities. For example, it has been common practice in stereo to ignore specular scenes or to treat specular pixels as outliers. This is because specularities alter the appearance of a scene point from multiple views, which can lead to errors during the matching process. However, attempts to make use of specularities to recover the shape of objects have also been demonstrated in the past [BN98, BB88,Ike81,HB88,Sch94,ON97]. In [ON97], the estimated 3D caustic surface is used to recover shape and classify image features as being either specular or diffuse.

The problem of recovering structure while at the same time separating the diffuse and specular layers is very hard under general camera motions. We simplify our analysis by assuming linear camera motion with constant velocity. This enables us to illustrate our ideas using the concept of Epipolar Plane Image (EPI) [BB89] in a spatial-temporal volume (a stacked image sequence). An EPI is a cross-section of the spatial-temporal volume corresponding to a particular scan-line.

Using the EPI framework, we study the motion of specularities not only in the scene but also within each EPI. Unlike in [ON97], we perform the analysis within the EPI framework. We define metrics to distinguish between traces of specular and diffuse features in the EPI and study the factors on which they depend (§ 2 and § 3). These metrics are also experimentally validated for real specular objects.

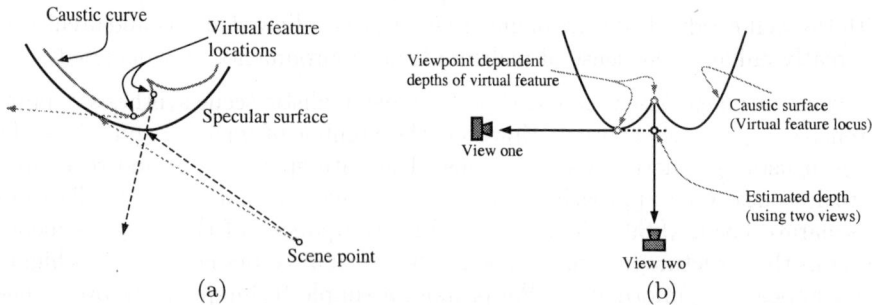

Fig. 1. Reflections on curved surfaces: (a) The geometry of reflection on curved specular surfaces. The position of the virtual feature at two viewpoints lies on the caustic curve at two distinct points. Any point on the caustic is visible only along the tangent to the caustic at the point. (b) Simple two view stereo algorithms estimate an erroneous depth for the virtual feature.

We also show the limits to which geometry alone can be used to separate the two layers and propose the use of photometry as well. We build a taxonomy of specular reflections in § 4, which aids in the design of hybrid algorithms to separate the diffuse and specular layers of a scene. Finally, we demonstrate the effectiveness of our approach on a real scene with specularities (§ 5).

2 Specular Motion in 2D

In general, for flat surfaces, we know that the reflected scene point (virtual feature) lies at a single point behind the surface. However, for curved surfaces, the position of the virtual feature is viewpoint dependent (Fig. 1)[ON97]. The locus of the virtual feature is a *catacaustic* [Ham28], referred to in this paper as just a caustic.

2.1 A Circular Reflector

For purposes of demonstration we assume the specular curve (in 2D) to be circular. The caustic is defined by the geometry of the specular curve and the scene point being reflected. Thus, we can compute the caustic curve in closed form [BS73,BG84].

Given a camera position, we derive the point on the caustic where the virtual feature is seen. It's image location is simply a projection of the caustic point onto the image plane. We derive the image location of a virtual feature as a function of camera pose, specular surface geometry and the scene point.

To compute the EPI trace of the specularities, we assume that the camera motion is linear in the plane parallel to the imaging plane. The linear camera motion implies that the EPI trace of any scene point must lie along straight lines within the EPI-slice. However, reflected points move along their caustic. Thus, their EPI traces would be expected to be curved.

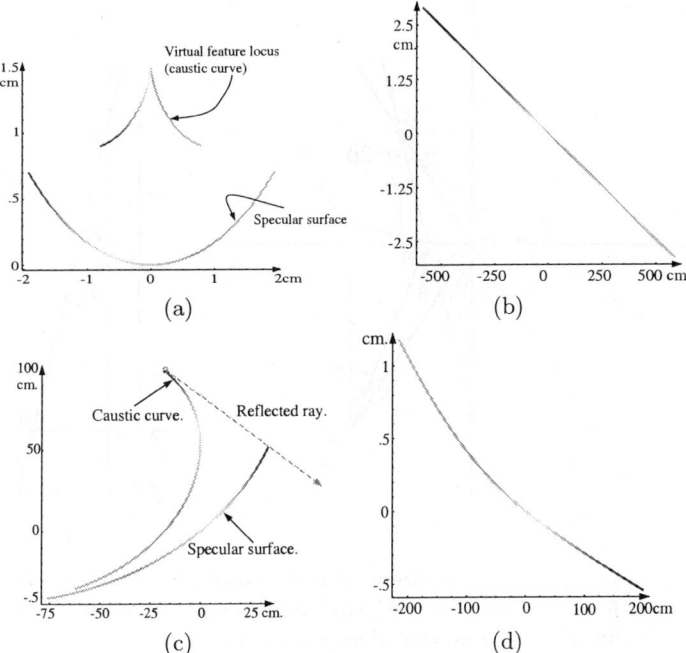

Fig. 2. Plots of actual surfaces, associated caustic curves, and EPI traces. Please note that correspondence between points on the actual surface, caustic curve, and EPI trace, is color-coded. (a) A high curvature surface, such as a soda can, for which the caustic curve is also small and has high curvature. (b) The corresponding EPI trace is almost linear since the virtual feature undergoes minimal motion. (c) An extreme case: In the vicinity of the drawn reflected ray, the camera observes reflection on an almost flat surface (e.g., a monitor screen) at an oblique angle. The corresponding part of the caustic has the least curvature. Thus for small viewpoint changes, the virtual feature moves significantly. (d) The corresponding EPI trace is noticeably bent and therefore appears non-rigid.

We define the deviation of an EPI-trace from a straight line as *disparity deviation* (DD). Disparity deviation depends entirely on the movement of the virtual feature and distance of the viewer from the scene. Motion along the caustic in turn depends on the curvature of the surface, surface orientation and the distance of the reflected point from the surface. The greater this distance, the greater the motion along the caustic surface.

Fig. 2 shows sample EPI curves for two specular curves. Surprisingly, the curve with higher curvature shows little disparity deviation. Although high curvatures lead to faster angular motion along the caustic, this motion is contained within a very small area. Lower curvatures, on the other hand, can produce noticeable disparity deviation in the EPI. For a given curvature, disparity deviation is accentuated at grazing angles of reflections (as we show below).

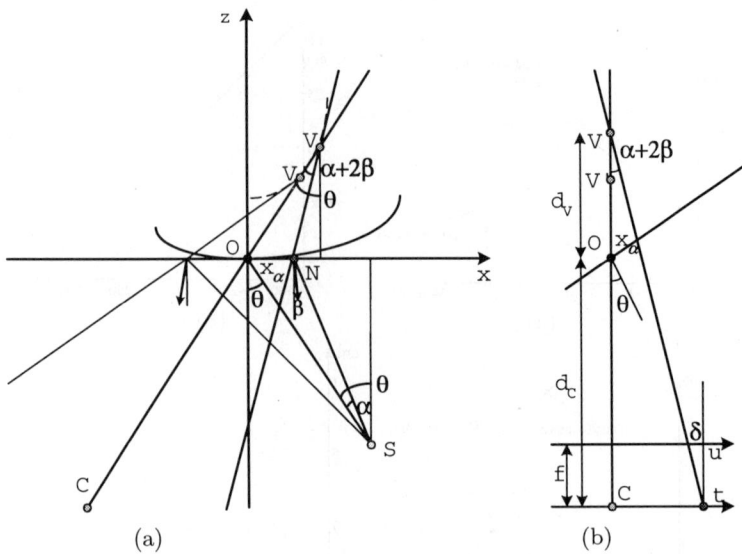

Fig. 3. 2D analysis of specular reflection: (a) Reflection of surface point S by the curved surface at point O as seen by camera C; (b) Projection of the reflected image into the camera C with image plane u moving along the t axis.

2.2 Infinitesimal Motion

We now characterize the local behavior of a specularity, starting with the 2D case (Fig. 3). The scene point being reflected is at S, the camera is at C, and the reflected surface point O is at the origin, with the surface normal along the Z-axis. The incident angle to the surface is θ, while the surface itself has a curvature $\kappa = 1/\rho$.

Consider an infinitesimal change of angle $\alpha = \angle OSN$ in the direction of the light ray leaving S. This corresponds to a motion along the surface from O to N of length x_α,

$$x_\alpha = d_S[\sin\theta - \sin(\theta - \alpha)], \tag{1}$$

where, d_S is the distance from S to O. At the new reflection point N, the surface normal has changed by an angle $\beta = \kappa x_\alpha + \frac{1}{2}\dot\kappa x_\alpha^2 + O(x_\alpha^3)$. Thus, while the incidence angle is $\theta - \alpha$, the emittance angle is $\theta - \alpha - 2\beta$.

This emittance angle determines the angle $\angle OVN = \alpha + 2\beta$, where V is the virtual image point, formed by the intersection of the reflected ray at the origin and the reflected ray at the new point N. We obtain

$$x_\alpha = d_V[\sin\theta - \sin(\theta - \alpha - 2\beta)], \tag{2}$$

where, d_V is the distance from V to O.

Equating (1) and (2) and taking the limit of d_V as $\alpha \to 0$ gives us

$$\lim_{\alpha \to 0} d_V = \frac{d_S}{1 + 2d_S\kappa\cos\theta}. \tag{3}$$

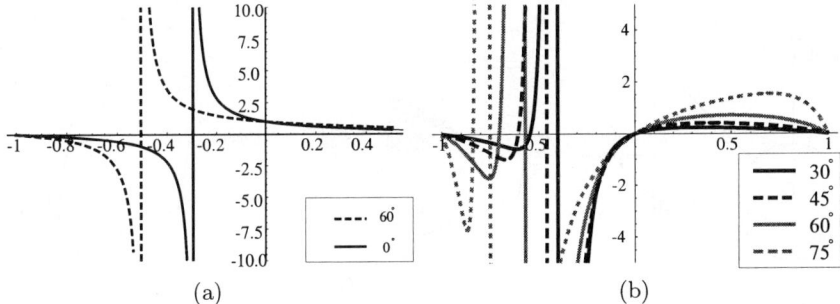

Fig. 4. (a) Plot of virtual depth d_V as a function of curvature κ for $d_S = 1$ and $\theta = 0°$ and $60°$. (b) Disparity deviation for $f = 100$ as a function of κ for $d_S = 1$, $d_C = 4$, and $\theta = 30°, 45°, 60°, 75°$. The horizontal axis in both cases is actually $2/\pi \tan^{-1} \kappa$, so that the full range $\kappa = (-\infty, 0, \infty)$ can be visualized.

In the limiting case as $d_S \to \infty$ or $\kappa \to \infty$ ($\rho \to 0$), i.e., as the scene point distance becomes large relative to the radius of curvature, we get $d_V = \frac{\rho}{2} \sec \theta$. This result is quite intuitive: the virtual image sits at the focal point behind (or in front of) the reflector for head-on viewing condition, and further away for tilted surfaces.

The behavior in the general case when the source is closer to the surface is plotted in Fig. 4(a). The virtual depth slowly decreases for a convex reflector as the curvature increases. For a concave reflector, the virtual depth decreases, moving rapidly towards negative infinity as the radius of curvature approaches the object distance (as the object approaches the focal point), and then jumps back to positive virtual depths. The actual distance seen by the camera is $d_V + d_C$, so that impossible apparent depths only occur when $d_V < -d_C$.

These results are consistent with the shapes of the caustics presented previously for the circular reflector. Now, how does the disparity (curvature in the EPI) change as we vary the camera position? In other words, what is the disparity deviation of a specular feature? From Fig. 3(b), we see that the disparity D is given by $D = \delta/t = f/(d_V + d_C)$. To see how D varies with t, we apply the chain rule to obtain

$$\dot{D} = \frac{\partial D}{\partial t} = \frac{f d_V^3}{(d_V + d_C)^3} \left(\dot{\kappa}(1 + \cos 2\theta) + 4 \frac{\kappa}{d_S} \sin \theta + 2\kappa^2 \sin 2\theta \right). \quad (4)$$

(The full derivation is given in our technical report [CKSS02].) Notice that there is no disparity deviation for planar reflection, i.e., $\dot{D} = 0$ when $\kappa = \dot{\kappa} = 0$, as expected.

We can now examine each component in (4). The first ratio $(d_V/(d_C + d_V))$ becomes large when $d_C \approx -d_V$, i.e., when the virtual image appears very close to the camera, which is also when the disparity itself becomes very large. The term that depends on the curvature variation $\dot{\kappa}$ decreases for slanted surfaces. It is most significant for undulating surfaces. At their inflection points, the apparent location of the virtual image can move very rapidly.

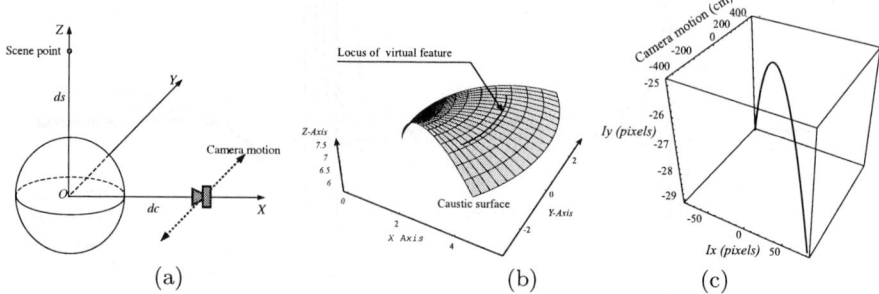

Fig. 5. (a) Analytic setup showing the location of the scene point in relation to the specular surface and camera path. (b) Section of the 3D caustic surface associated with (a). The thin curve on this surface is the locus of virtual features and is neither stationary nor planar. (c) The corresponding EPI-curve clearly exhibits significant epipolar deviations.

The term κ/d_S might at first appear to blow up for $d_S \to 0$, but since d_V is proportional to d_S, this behavior is annihilated. However, for moderate values of d_S, we can get a strong disparity deviation for slanted surfaces. The last term is strongest at a 45° surface slant. It would appear that this term would blow up for large κ, but since d_V is inversely proportionally to κ in these cases, it does not.

To summarize, the two factors that influence the disparity deviation the most are (1) when $d_C + d_V \approx 0$, which is when disparities are very large to start with (because the camera is near the reflector's focal point), and (2) fast undulations in the surface. Ignoring undulations, Fig. 4(b) shows how $\dot{D}$ varies as a function of κ for a variety of slants, with $d_S = 1$ and $d_C = 4$. Therefore, under many real-world conditions, we expect the disparity deviation to be small enough that treating virtual features as if they were real features should work in practice.

3 Specular Motion in 3D

We now discuss the effect of specularities in 3D, again using the caustic surface to perform our analysis. We present our results for a spherical reflector although the results can be extended to arbitrary surface geometries.

Consider a spherical specular surface whose center lies at the origin. The scene point being reflected is located along the positive Z-axis at a distance d_S from the origin. We again derive the caustic surface using the Jacobian technique [BS73,SGN01]. To study the motion of specularities, we assume the camera to move in the X, Y-plane, parallel to the Y-axis at a distance d_C from the origin (Fig. 5(a)). Note, this camera path is not critical to the results we derive.

We need to derive the image location of a virtual feature as a function of camera pose. From the setup in Fig. 5(a), the Z-axis forms the axis of symmetry for the caustic surface (see [SGN01]). Thus, all rays that reflect on the spherical surface, must pass through the axis at some point. Hence, for any camera position, the Z-axis and the camera location determine a plane on which the virtual feature must also lie. Given the camera pose and caustic surface, determining the position of the virtual feature is now reduced to a 2D problem for which an analytic solution exists (details are in [CKSS02]). The image location of the virtual feature is simply a projection of the derived virtual feature onto the image plane.

3.1 Epipolar Deviations for a Spherical Reflector

Under linear camera motion, the images of a rigid scene point must all lie on the same epipolar line (or plane). However, the motion of a virtual feature on the caustic surface (Fig. 5(b)) violates this constraint. As seen in Fig. 5(c), the image of the virtual feature does not lie on a single scan-line. We refer to this phenomenon as *epipolar deviation (ED)*.

In general, epipolar deviations depend on three primary factors: surface curvature, orientation of surface, and distance of the camera from the reflecting surface. We only consider scene points distant from the surface as they usually produce the largest caustic surfaces [CKSS02]. We now analyze each factor for its contribution to ED. This study helps determine situations when ED effects can be neglected and when they provide significant cues to the presence of highlights and specularities.

Surface Curvature: We know that for planar mirrors, the virtual feature is stationary at a single point behind the surface. Similarly, high curvature surfaces such as sharp corners have very localized tiny caustic surfaces. Between these two extreme curvatures, surfaces exhibit higher epipolar deviations as seen in Fig. 6(a).

Surface Orientation: The angle of incidence of an observed reflection is also critical to epipolar deviation. The more oblique the incidence, the greater the motion of the virtual feature along the caustic surface, causing larger ED. From Fig. 6(b) we can see how ED drops to zero at an angle which corresponds to the plane in which the caustic curve is planar. Beyond this point, the virtual feature locus is again non-planar and causes epipolar deviations. As one moves to near-normal reflections, we see that the feature locus is restricted to the cusp region of the caustic. This implies very small feature motion, in turn reducing ED.

Camera Distance: As camera distance from the scene increases, disparity between scene points decreases. Thus, decreasing disparities imply lower virtual feature motions, in turn decreasing epipolar deviation (Fig. 6(c)).

To empirically validate these analytical results, we took a series of pictures of a mirrored ball at different distances and orientations, and manually plotted the specularity trajectories (measured to the nearest pixel). As seen in Fig. 6(d–f), the results of our experiments are in agreement with our theoretical prediction.

In general, specular reflections or virtual features do not adhere to epipolar geometry. In our geometric analysis, we assume large camera field of view and range of motion, and on occasion, large scene distances. However, in typical real situations, both the camera's range of motion and field of view are limited; as

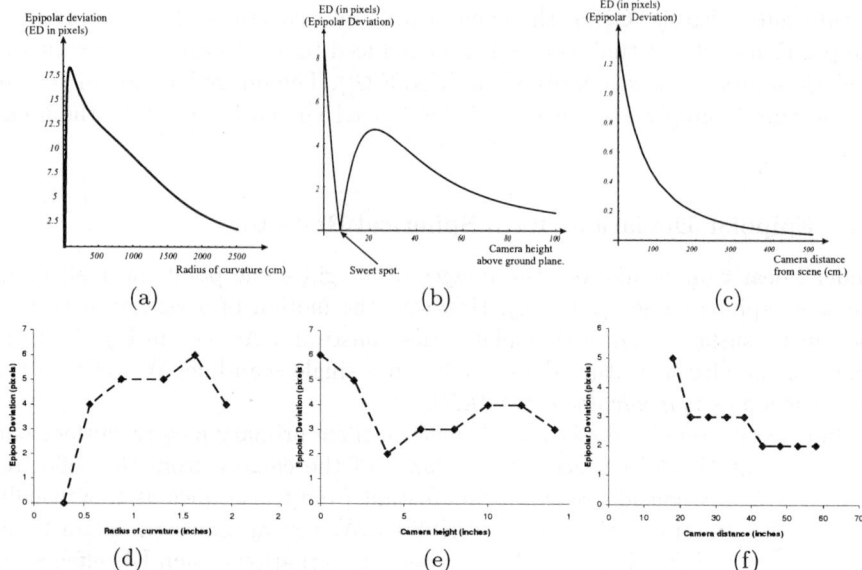

Fig. 6. Epipolar Deviations as a function of the three most significant factors: (a) surface curvature (b) surface orientation (c) camera distance from scene. (d-f) are the corresponding results of experiments using real objects. (d) We used reflective balls with radii ranging from 1.95 to 0.3 inches; each was placed about 3 feet away from the camera. (e) The ball of radius 1.95 inches was placed 3 feet away from the camera. The height of the ball was changed up to 14 inches. (f) The same ball was used, with the distance of the camera to the ball varied from 1.5 to 5 feet. Notice the similar trends between the theoretical and experimental plots.

a result, the specular features appear to adhere closely to epipolar constraints. This makes it hard to disambiguate between specular and diffuse streaks in the EPI. Thus, for any diffuse-specular separation technique to be effective, pure geometric analysis may be insufficient. Of course, other effects such as changing shape of the reflection is a geometric cue towards the reflector's geometry. However, such area based approaches are beyond the scope of this paper. We propose the use of photometric constraints to dis-ambiguate the problem.

4 Photometry of Specularities

We now present a photometric analysis of specularities under linear camera motion. Within the framework of EPIs, we develop a taxonomy of specularities and motivate the need for hybrid algorithms that use geometric and photometric constraints to separate the diffuse and specular layers. In the following discussion, we define an *EPI-strip* to be a strip within an EPI where all the associated physical points are contiguous and share a *common fate* (e.g., similar color or true depth).

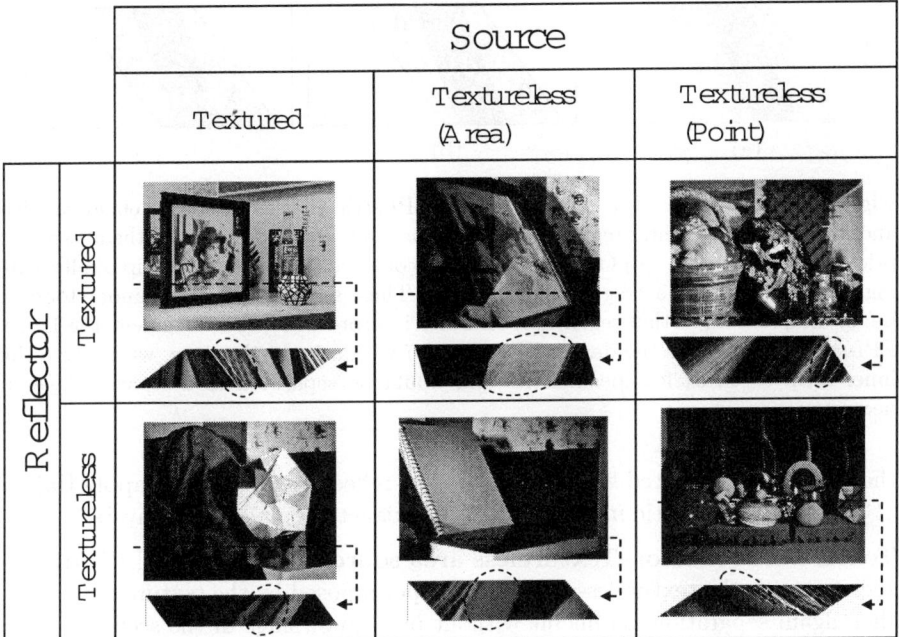

Fig. 7. Taxonomy of specularities with example snapshots of sequences. Below each image is the EPI associated with the marked scan-line. Note that all of the EPIs were sheared for visual clarity.

4.1 Taxonomy of Specularities

We categorize the type of observed specularities based on whether the reflecting and reflected surfaces (which we term *reflector* and *source* respectively) are textured (Fig. 7). Furthermore, we differentiate between area and point sources, since this has an impact on how separation can be accomplished.

Textured reflector–Textured source: The EPI-strip associated with this type of specularity is characterized by a blending between the reflector and source textures leading to a criss-cross pattern. Effective techniques for separation tend to analyze the entire area (e.g., [SAA00,Wei01]).

Textured reflector–Textureless area source: In this case, most of the EPI strip is brightened by a uniform color associated with the source. This causes ambiguity in separation, as the modified part of the strip may be misclassified as a separate strip.

Textured reflector–Textureless point source: In principle, this is similar with the previous case, except that the source is highly localized (Fig. 7). As a result, separation can be accomplished by analyzing constant color sub-strips of the EPI-strip, e.g., using the Dichromatic Reflectance Model [KSK88].

Textureless reflector–Textured source: This presents a similar problem as the textured reflector-textureless source case. If, however, we are able to extract

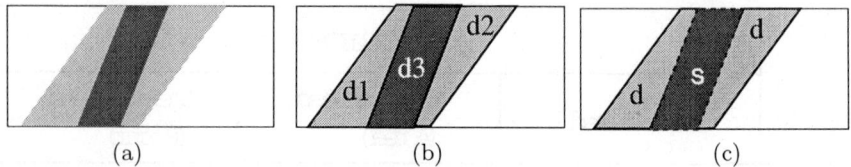

Fig. 8. (a) A typical EPI in which a smaller EPI-strip (darker region) is enclosed with another EPI-strip (lighter region). This EPI has many interpretations in the absence of prior scene knowledge. (b) One interpretation could be that each thin strip of alternating colors, represents a "region" in the scene. Thus, each (d_1, d_2, d_3) is understood to be an unique Lambertian region. (c) Another interpretation could segment the larger EPI-strip (d) includes the darker EPI-strip (s) within it. In this case, we analyze the inner strip to check for specularities and would be separated as a separate layer if necessary.

the EPI-strip associated with the textureless reflector, we can then apply Bajcsy et al.'s multi-chromatic model [BLL96] to extract the underlying layers.

Textureless reflector–Textureless area source: If most of the EPI-strip associated with the textureless reflector is superimposed by the textureless source, then again separation is difficult without prior knowledge of the scene. A more detailed explanation of this case is given in the following section (§4.2).

Textureless reflector–Textureless point source: As with the textured reflector – textureless point source case, there exist separation techniques, including the Dichromatic Reflectance Model [KSK88].

4.2 EPI-Strips and Their Inherent Ambiguity

There exists an inherent ambiguity in EPI analysis for specularities and diffuse regions when considering individual EPI. Fig. 8(a) illustrates such an EPI. One EPI-strip (darker) is completely enclosed by another EPI-strip (lighter). Individual layers can now be extracted in one of many ways leading to valid and unique interpretations.

Fig. 8(b) is one interpretation where each EPI-strip was extracted separately representing three unique diffuse layers $(d_1 \ldots d_3)$. The varying tilts of their bordering edges in the EPI lead to slanted segments in the scene of varying depths. In contrast, another equally valid extraction includes the inner EPI-strip (Fig. 8(c)). If this inner strip conforms to the photometric constraints discussed earlier, we interpret it as a specularity s over the otherwise diffuse region d.

Such ambiguities arise in purely Lambertian scenes as well as those containing occlusions. In principle, one can reduce the ambiguities by analyzing multiple EPIs all at once. However, this still does not guarantee an ambiguity-free scenario.

4.3 Surface Curvature and Specularities

Within an EPI, closer scene surfaces have a more horizontal orientation than those farther away. Also, for opaque surfaces, these more horizontal EPI-strips run across (occlude) more vertical EPI-strips.

In the presence of specularities, these depth ordering constraints are often violated. The manner in which these violations occur are cues to the local surface curvature in the scene.

For convex surfaces, the locus of virtual features resides behind the surface. The corresponding EPI-strip of specular reflection has a more vertical orientation than that of the underlying diffuse component (Fig. 9(a,b)). In contrast, concave surfaces typically form the virtual feature in front of the surface. The EPI-strip of the specular component is therefore more horizontal.

On separating the diffuse and specular component within an EPI-strip, one can estimate the local curvature of the surface. If the specular EPI-strip component is more horizontal, the underlying surface must be concave. However, if the specular EPI-strip is more vertical, the surface is most likely to be convex.

5 A Technique for Removing Specularities

We now describe a technique to remove the specular components from an image sequence and estimate the underlying diffuse colors associated with the specular regions.

The technique first extracts EPI-strips from each EPI. Each EPI-strip is then rectified so that trails within it are vertical. The rectified EPI-strip is then analyzed for specularities using a variant of [SAA00]. Our technique is more general in that it is designed to work with textured reflectors and all the three types of sources shown in the first row of Fig. 7 and is not constrained to planar surfaces. Once separation is achieved, the corresponding region within the EPI is marked and excluded from future computations. This process is repeated for all other EPI-strips within the EPI.

5.1 Extracting Good EPI-Strips

A critical stage of the technique is the extraction of EPI-strips within each EPI. Since the camera is assumed to move linearly, the EPI-strips of scene points should be straight lines. As a result, edge detection with straight line fitting is sufficient to detect the bounding sides of EPI-strips.

The slope of an edge in the EPI is directly related to the distance of the associated point from the viewer. We order the edges based on their distance from the viewer, beginning with the closest strip and ending with the farthest. Pairs of depth-ordered edges define candidate EPI-strips. Each EPI-strip is rectified (sheared) such that the slanted bounding edges are vertical (Fig. 9(b)). Every column of the rectified EPI-strip now corresponds to a stabilized scene point viewed over time.

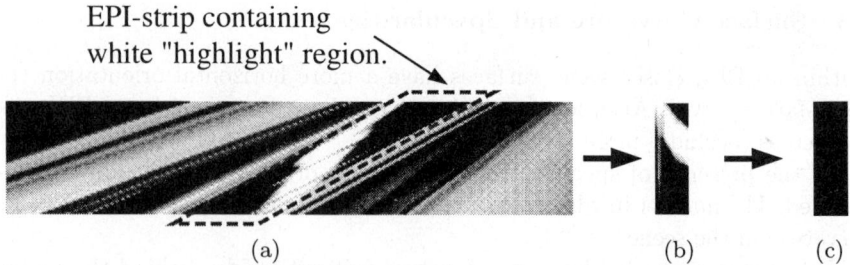

Fig. 9. An EPI of the sequence in Fig. 10. (a) Typical highlight pattern seen on convex specular surfaces. Chromatically, the highlight region seems to occlude the underlying texture of the surface. However, the orientation of the highlight is more vertical implying a farther depth. This confirms the bright pattern to be caused by a specularity. (b) Rectified section of the marked EPI-strip. The diffuse component is now made vertical, while the specular component is oriented beyond 90°. (c) Using photometric analysis along with geometric reasoning, the highlight is extracted to reveal the underlying diffuse component.

An EPI-strip candidate is deemed to be good if most of the edges within the rectified strip are vertical. However, specularities and occluding regions would produce slanted edges within the rectified EPI-strip. Since we order the edges from nearest to farthest, the closer EPI-strips would have already been extracted, leaving behind specular strips. Rather than defining goodness of an EPI-strip candidate using photometric constraints, a metric based on predominant orientation is far more robust in practice (details are in [CKSS02]).

5.2 Specularity Extraction

An EPI-strip that is selected is then analyzed for the presence of highlights. The scenario assumed here is that of a textured reflector with an arbitrary source. Many highlight regions tend to be saturated in parts. To simplify our process, we look for specularities in EPI-strips containing pixel intensities above a predefined minimum value.

In any column of the rectified EPI-strip, the pixel with lowest intensity gives us an upper bound on the diffuse component of that scene point. For every column, we estimate this upper bound and assume the scene point to have the associated color. The residual is then the specularity. To validate this step, we group all pixels that are strongly specular and observe their relative orientation within the EPI-strip. If they have a more vertical orientation, then they must be specularities. Note that this is only true for convex surfaces. In our current implementation, we do not consider the effect of concave reflectors.

5.3 Results Using an Image Sequence of a Real Scene

To validate our technique, we took an image sequence of a real scene that contains both specular and Lambertian objects. The camera was mounted on a linear

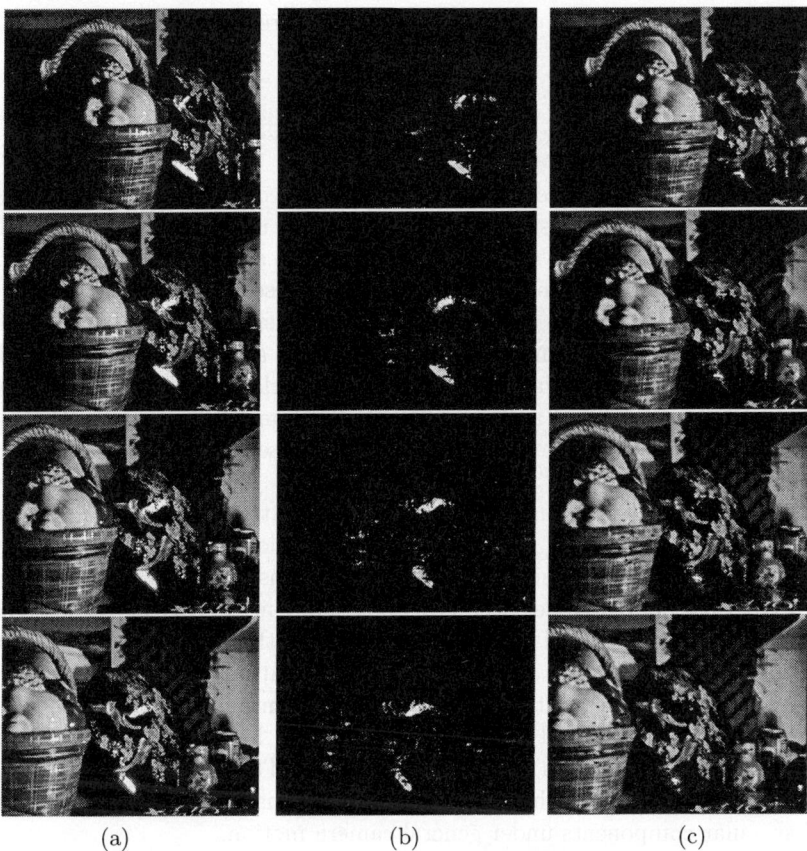

(a) (b) (c)

Fig. 10. (a) A subset of our images of a real scene. (b) On performing EPI analysis using a combination of geometric as well as photometric constraints, the specular components were removed from the image sequence. The two strong highlights regions in sequence (a) are robustly detected. (c) The diffuse component video stream is almost void of specular effects. Some artifacts show up in this sequence due to incorrect EPI-strip selection as well as re-sampling issues while computing the rectified EPI-strip (Fig. 9(b)).

translation stage about 3 feet away from the scene. A set of 50 images were captured at uniform intervals as the camera was translated from left to right. A subset of the acquired images can be seen in Fig. 10(a).

This sequence of images were then stacked together to form a spatio-temporal volume on which the above EPI analysis was performed. As seen from Fig. 10 (b), the specular regions were effectively segmented out from the image sequence. Also, the underlying diffuse component of the scene was recovered successfully (Fig. 10(c)).

However, inaccurate EPI-strip extraction and interpolation issues while creating the rectified EPI-strip result in some visible artifacts (black spots and residual specularities in Fig. 10(c)). Since we use a relatively simple technique to detect and separate specular layers, the results are quite sensitive to the EPI-strip selection process.

6 Conclusions

In this paper, we first present a geometric analysis of the behavior of specularities in typical scenes. We study their image traces under linear camera motion and introduced the metrics *disparity deviation* (DD) and *epipolar deviation* (ED) to characterize specular motion. We show that these deviations depend on the surface curvature as well as the orientation of the specular surface. One might expect that reflections from curved surfaces would always produce curved EPI traces. Surprisingly, both flat and highly curved surfaces do not produce significant deviations. Instead, it is the mildly curved (especially convex) surfaces that produce the largest deviations. In addition, the closer the object, the larger the deviations tend to be.

Our findings suggest that it might be difficult to differentiate diffuse from specular components using geometric constraints alone. As a result, we supplement our geometric analysis with photometric considerations, which make up the second part of our paper. We develop a taxonomy of specular reflections to aid in the design of hybrid algorithms that use both geometric and photometric constraints. Finally, we present results on a real image sequence, using our hybrid algorithm to separate the two components into different layers.

In the future, we would like to move from the "local" edge-based approach for selecting EPI-strips to a more global approach. This should significantly help the photometric analysis phase. Our ultimate goal is to able to separate diffuse and specular components under general camera motion.

References

[BB88]   A. Blake and G. Brelstaff. Geometry from specularity. *Proc. International Conference on Computer Vision*, pages 394–403, 1988.

[BB89]   H. H. Baker and R. C. Bolles. Generalizing epipolar-plane image analysis on the spatiotemporal surface. *International Journal of Computer Vision*, 3(1):33–49, 1989.

[BG84]   J. W. Bruce and P. J. Giblin. *Curves and Singularities*. Cambridge University Press, Cambridge, 1984.

[BLL96] R.K. Bajcsy, S.W. Lee, and A. Leonardis. Detection of diffuse and specular interface reflections and inter-reflections by color image segmentation. *International Journal of Computer Vision*, 17(3):241–272, March 1996.

[BN98]   D. N. Bhat and S. K. Nayar. Stereo and specular reflection. *International Journal of Computer Vision*, 26(2):91–106, February 1998.

[BS73]   D. G. Burkhard and D. L. Shealy. Flux Density for Ray Propagation in Geometrical Optics. *Journal of the Optical Society of America*, 63(3):299–304, March 1973.

[CKSS02] A. Criminisi, S.B. Kang, R. Swaminathan, and R. Szeliski. Separating Diffuse and Specular Layers using EPI Analysis, MSR-TR(in preparation). Technical report, Microsoft Research, 2002.

[FA99]   H. Farid and E.H. Adelson. Separating reflections and lighting using independent components analysis. In *Proc. Computer Vision and Pattern Recognition*, pages I:262–267, 1999.

[Ham28]   W. R. Hamilton. Theory of Systems of Rays. *Transactions of the Royal Irish Academy*, 15:69–174, 1828.

[HB88]   G. Healey and T. O. Binford. Local shape from specularity. *CVGIP*, pages 62–86, 1988.

[Ike81]   K. Ikeuchi. Determining surface orientation of specular surfaces by using the photometric stereo method. *IEEE Transactions on Pattern Analysis and Machine Intelligence*, 3(6):661–669, 1981.

[IRP94]   M. Irani, B. Rousso, and S. Peleg. Computing occluding and transparent motions. *International Journal of Computer Vision*, 12(1):5–16, January 1994.

[Kem01]   M. Kemp. *Visualizations: The Nature Book of Art and Science*. University of California Press, 2001.

[KSK88]   G. J. Klinker, S. A. Shafer, and T. Kanade. The measurement of highlights in color images. *International Journal of Computer Vision*, 2(1):7–32, June 1988.

[LB92]   S.W. Lee and R. Bajcsy. Detection of specularity using colour and multiple views. In *Proc. European Conference on Computer Vision*, pages 99–114, 1992.

[LS97]   J. Lengyel and J. Snyder. Rendering with coherent layers. In *Computer Graphics Proceedings, Annual Conference Series*, pages 233–242, Proc. SIGGRAPH'97 (Los Angeles), August 1997. ACM SIGGRAPH.

[NFB97]   S.K. Nayar, X. S. Fang, and T. Boult. Separation of reflectance components using color and polarization. *International Journal of Computer Vision*, 21(3):163–186, February 1997.

[ON97]   M. Oren and S. Nayar. A theory of specular surface geometry. *International Journal of Computer Vision*, 24(2):105–124, September 1997.

[SAA00]   R. Szeliski, S. Avidan, and P. Anandan. Layer extraction from multiple images containing reflections and transparency. In *Proc. Conference on Computer Vision and Pattern Recognition*, volume 1, pages 246–253, June 2000.

[Sch94]   H. Schultz. Retrieving shape information from multiple images of a specular surface. *IEEE Transactions on Pattern Analysis and Machine Intelligence*, 16(2):195–201, February 1994.

[SGN01]   R. Swaminathan, M. D. Grossberg, and S. K. Nayar. Caustics of Catadioptric Cameras. In *Proc. International Conference on Computer Vision*, pages II:2–9, July 2001.

[SHW92]   S. A. Shafer, G. Healey, and L. Wolff. *Physics-Based Vision: Principles and Practice*. Jones & Bartlett, Cambridge, MA, 1992.

[SSK98]   Y. Schechner, J. Shamir, and N. Kiryati. Polarization-based decorrelation of transparent layers: The inclination angle of an invisible surface. In *Proc. International Conference on Computer Vision*, pages 814–819, 1998.

[Wei01]   Y. Weiss. Deriving intrinsic images from image sequences. In *Proc. International Conference on Computer Vision*, pages II: 68–75, 2001.

[Wol90]   L.B. Wolff. Polarization-based material classification from specular reflection. *IEEE Transactions on Pattern Analysis and Machine Intelligence*, 12(11):1059–1071, November 1990.

Multiple Hypothesis Tracking for Automatic Optical Motion Capture

Maurice Ringer and Joan Lasenby

Cambridge University, Engineering Dept
Cambridge CB2 1PZ, UK
{mar39,jl}@eng.cam.ac.uk

Abstract. We present a technique for performing the tracking stage of optical motion capture which retains, at each time frame, multiple marker association hypotheses and estimates of the subject's position. Central to this technique are the equations for calculating the likelihood of a sequence of association hypotheses, which we develop using a Bayesian approach. The system is able to perform motion capture using fewer cameras and a lower frame rate than has been used previously, and does not require the assistance of a human operator. We conclude by demonstrating the tracker on real data and provide an example in which our technique is able to correctly determine all marker associations and standard tracking techniques fail.

Keywords. Visual motion, correspondence problem, tracking, optical motion capture

1 Introduction

A significant problem in optical motion capture is determining which of the markers worn by the actor, if any, generated a particular detection on a particular camera's image plane at a particular time. This problem is most apparent when two markers appear close together in the view of one camera or when markers become occluded. In such cases, most motion capture systems will often attribute a detection to the wrong marker, or lose track of the given marker for the remainder of the sequence [9,10]. For this reason, nearly all motion capture systems require a human operator to guide the tracking process.

In this paper, we present a technique which retains, at each time frame of video input, more than one marker association hypothesis. We show how to calculate the likelihood of each of these hypotheses and the most likely path through these hypotheses over the video sequence for the specific case of tracking human motion.

The multiple hypothesis technique which we propose was first used by the engineers of radar systems and has since been used extensively in this field [13,1]. It is similar to the Viterbi algorithm [6], which is widely used in communications and other pattern recognition systems, however its use in computer vision has been limited. Cox and Hingorani [4] describe a multiple hypothesis technique for tracking corners in a video sequence, although each detected feature is tracked independently in the 2D camera plane. In constrast, we make use of a skeletal model of a human figure and thus incorporate the inter–dependence of marker positions to better associate detections to markers and to track markers occluded by another part of the figure [9,16,15,12].

Cham and Rehg [3], who claim to be first to use a multiple hypothesis approach to visually track human figures, also use a kinematic model, however detection is done by template matching so that feature corrspondence is a continuous variable. For this reason, they resort to Monte Carlo techniques to estimate the most likely figure positions.

Rasmussen and Hager [11] use point measurements and thus discrete correspondences, similar to us, and develop an expression for the likelihood of a correspondence similar to that developed in this paper. They do not, however, propogate multiple hypotheses nor use a 3D kinematic model.

Song et al [17,18] also provide good work on tracking markers detected on people. Their focus is on developing a highly constrained model in order to assist in marker association, however their work is specific to single camera views and they also do not propagate multiple association hypotheses.

To the knowledge of the authors, this paper presents the first adaptation of multiple hypothesis tracking to optical motion capture in which a 3D kinematic model of the figure is used and in which point measurements are detected in multiple cameras. We believe that our technique is capable of performing motion capture using fewer cameras and a lower frame rate than has been used previously. More significantly, the tracker is able to output the complete orientation and position of the figure throughout the sequence without requiring the assistance of a human operator.

The computational requirements of the proposed tracker mean that it is unlikely to execute in real-time. However, due to being fully automatic, only a few minutes are required to track most motion capture sequences. Thus, the tracker could be run during the motion capture session. The director could assess the actor's performance almost immediately and decide whether to keep the sequence or shoot it again.

The following section describes the multiple hypothesis tracker for optical motion capture. It provides the equations for calculating the most likely path through the trellis of hypotheses, which is the primary contribution of this paper.

The third section of this paper details the results when the tracker is used to capture the motions of a dancer, which include both high accelerations and significant marker occlusions. For this analysis, only two digital cameras operating at 25 frames/second and a single Pentium PC were used. We present real motion capture data for which the multiple hypothesis tracker is able to determine the correct marker association for each frame of the sequence and standard tracking techniques are not.

2 Method

It is well known that skeleton-based models significantly assist motion capture systems [9,16,15,12]. In these systems, the desired system state, x_k, at time k, is a vector containing the global position of the actor, the relative orientations of each limb and possibly the lengths of the limbs (or the deviation of the limb lengths from some base skeleton).

The measurement, z_k, is a vector containing the 2D coordinates of the bright points detected by the motion capture cameras at time k. The length of this vector will vary over time as markers become hidden and revealed due to the movement of the actor.

Let Ω_k be a possible association at time k. This discrete-valued variable specifies which markers generated each detected point, which markers were not detected and which detections were erroneous (not due to a marker). The state, measurement and association are related via the non-linear measurement function,

$$z_k = h(x_k, \Omega_k) + w_k \tag{1}$$

where w_k is noise present in the detection process.

Posing the problem in a Bayesian framework, we desire to estimate, at each time frame k, the state that maximises the posterior density function,

$$P(x_k|z_1,..,z_k) = \sum_{\Omega_k} P(x_k|\Omega_k, z_1,..,z_k) P(\Omega_k). \tag{2}$$

Most motion capture systems do this by first estimating the most likely assocation, $\Omega_k^{(1)}$, using a predicted value of the state, $\hat{x}_k$, which is calculated using previous values of the state (x_{k-1}, etc) and some model of how the state is expected to evolve over time. The new state, x_k, is then a function only of this association, thus assuming only one non-zero term in the above summation and forcing the state posterior density function to be uni-modal.

In Multiple Hypothesis Tracking, up to I estimates of the state, $x_k^{(i)}$, where $i \in \{1,..,I\}$, are retained at each time frame, k. At a new time frame, $k+1$, the J most likely marker associations, $\Omega_{k+1}^{(i,j)}$, where $j \in \{1,..,J\}$, are calculated, and from each of these, the state at time $k+1$ is estimated. Thus, the term $P(x_k|\Omega_k, z_1,..,z_k)$ in equation (2) contains I modes and the summation contains J terms. Combining these probability densities provides a new state posterior of up to IJ modes, of which only the most likely I are propagated forward so as to stop the trellis of possible hypotheses and states growing exponentially.

The following sections discuss these stages of the multiple hypothesis tracker for optical motion capture in further detail.

2.1 Determining the Likely Association Hypotheses

The probability of a given marker association hypothesis, Ω_k, at time k, is

$$P(\Omega_k|z_k, x_k) = \frac{1}{c} p(z_k|\Omega_k, x_k) P(\Omega_k|x_k) \tag{3}$$

where c is a constant. In order to maximise this function, we require x_k, the unknown state. Typically, x_k is replaced with a prediction, $\hat{x}_k$, calculated using previous values of the state and a model of how a human body is expected to move. It is assumed that the true and predicted values of the state are close enough that, independent of which is used in equation (3), the same value of Ω_k provides its maximum.

The multiple hypothesis tracker, however, does not make this assumption. Instead, the J most likely association hypotheses are calculated using equation (3) and each of the I predicted states. It is assumed that one of these J hypotheses, not necessarily the first, maximises this equation had the true state been used. The probability of these hypotheses constitute the weighting, $P(\Omega_k)$, of the J terms of equation (2).

Let M be the number of cameras and N be the number of markers worn by the subject under observation. Let Ω_k be the set $\{\Omega_k^m\}$, where Ω_k^m is the marker association for camera m and $m \in \{1,..,M\}$. Let Ω_k^m be the set $\{Q_k^m, R_k^m, \phi_k^m, \zeta_k^m, \xi_k^m\}$, where

- Q_k^m is the number of detected bright points in camera m at time k,
- R_k^m is the number of markers detected in camera m at time k,
- $\phi_k^m(r)$ is the detection generated by marker r in camera m at time k ($r \in \{1,..,R_k^m\}$),
- $\xi_k^m(q)$ is the qth detection in camera m which was not generated from a marker (false detections) ($q \in \{1,..,Q_k^m - R_k^m\}$), and
- $\zeta_k^m(n)$ is the nth marker not detected in camera m ($n \in \{1,..,N - R_k^m\}$).

The first term of equation (3), $p(z_k|x_k, \Omega_k)$, is the likelihood that the measurement at time k resulted from the state x_k and the particular association Ω_k. It is,

$$p(z_k|x_k, \Omega_k) = \prod_{m=1}^{M} \left(\prod_{q=1}^{Q_k^m - R_k^m} p_{FA}(\xi_k^m(q)) \prod_{r=1}^{R_k^m} p_D(\phi_k^m(r), r) \right) \quad (4)$$

where $p_{FA}(q)$ is the likelihood that detection q is a false detection and $p_D(q,r)$ is the likelihood that detection q is due to marker r.

We assume that false detections are uniformly distributed over the image plane of the camera and that a single detection is corrupted by Gaussian noise (the measurement noise, w_k). Thus,

$$p_{FA}(q) = \frac{1}{A} \quad (5)$$

$$p_D(q,r) = \frac{1}{c} \exp\left(([z_k]_q - [h(\hat{x}_k)]_r)^T \Sigma^{-1} ([z_k]_q - [h(\hat{x}_k)]_r) \right) \quad (6)$$

where A is the area of the image plane of the camera on which the detection occurred and Σ is the covariance of the detection error, w_k. The notation $[v]_i$ extracts the ith point from the stacked vector of 2D coordinates in v.

The final term in equation (3), $P(\Omega_k|x_k)$, is the probability that a certain marker association is correct given a particular position of the subject. It is not conditioned on the measurement but instead weights $p(z_k|x_k, \Omega_k)$ by how likely it is that each marker is visible in each camera. For example, if the predicted state suggests a particular marker is occluded in a given camera's view, we should be less inclined to associate a detection in that camera to the marker. Most motion capture systems do not utilise this information when estimating the association hypothesis and the advantage of doing so is discussed in [15,9].

Let the associations assigned to the detections in each camera be independent. Thus,

$$P(\Omega_k|x_k) = \prod_{m=1}^{M} P(\Omega_k^m|x_k) \qquad (7)$$

where

$$P(\Omega_k^m|x_k) = P_{FA}(Q_k^m - R_k^m) \prod_{r=1}^{R_k^m} P_D(\phi_k^m(r)) \prod_{n=1}^{N-R_k^m} (1 - P_D(\zeta_k^m(n))). \qquad (8)$$

$P_{FA}(q)$ is the probability of detecting q erroneous bright points and is assumed to be a Poisson distribution of mean λ_{FA}. λ_{FA} is the number of false detections expected in a single camera/frame and is assumed constant.

$P_D(r)$ is the probability of detecting marker r and is calculated by ray–tracing the predicted position of the marker onto the camera's image plane. $P_D(r)$ is zero if the ray from the marker passes through any part of the actor's body, which is modelled using cylinders and spheres, and λ_D, the probability that a visible marker is detected, if the ray does not. We model $P_D(r)$ as changing gradually, so that when the ray from the marker to the camera plane passes close to the edge of a limb, $P_D(r)$ is between 0 and λ_D. That is, the limb edges are considered "blurry".

We observe that equation (3) can be written as

$$P(\Omega_k|z_k, x_k) = \prod_{m=1}^{M} f(\Omega_k^m, z_k^m, x_k) \qquad (9)$$

Thus, in order to find the J most likely association hypotheses, we find the values of Ω_k^m which produce the J largest values of $f(\Omega_k^m, z_k^m, x_k)$ for each camera, m. Only combinations of these J values are substituted into the above equation, reducing the number of association hypotheses to test to J^M.

We note that it is possible to calculate $f(\cdot, z_k^m, x_k)$ by constructing a square matrix F of size $(N + Q^m)$ whose first N rows correspond to the markers and whose first Q^m columns correspond to the detections. Different values of the association, Ω_k^m, correspond to selecting different elements of F so that no row or column is selected twice, and the value of $-\log[f(\Omega_k^m, z_k^m, x_k)]$ is the sum of the selected elements. Selecting element (i, j), where $i \leq N$ and $j \leq Q^m$, corresponds to assigning marker i to detection j. Selecting elements in columns $(Q^m + 1)$ to $(Q^m + N)$ correspond to assigning a marker as being not detected and selecting elements in rows $(N + 1)$ to $(N + Q^m)$ correspond to assigning a detection as being not due to a marker (a false detection).

From equations (4) and (7), it straightforward to show that the elements of F are

$$F(q,r) = \begin{cases} -\log\left[p_D(q,r) P_D(r)\right] & \text{if } r \leq N,\ q \leq Q^m \\ -\log\left[p_{FA}(r-N) P_{FA}(r-N)\right] & \text{if } r > N,\ q \leq Q^m \\ -\log\left[1 - P_D(r)\right] & \text{if } r \leq N,\ q = n + Q^m \\ \infty & \text{if } r \leq N,\ q \neq n + Q^m \\ 0 & \text{if } r > N,\ q > Q^m \end{cases} \quad (10)$$

The problem of maximising $f(\cdot, z_k^m, x_k)$ is thus reduced to determining a sequence, $\Omega'(q)$, of $N + Q^m$ unique column indices ($q \in [1, N + Q^m]$) which minimises

$$E = \sum_{q=1}^{N+Q^m} F(q, \Omega'(q)). \quad (11)$$

This task is often refered to as the Linear Assignment Problem (LAP) and fast and efficient algorithms exist for solving it [2,19].

The most likely association hypothesis, $\Omega^{(1)}$, is the unconstrained LAP solution, Ω'. Further hypotheses are found by fixing elements of F which occur in Ω' to ∞ and re-calculating the LAP solution. This technique for determining the best J solutions to the LAP is detailed in [5].

2.2 Updating the State Estimate

For each of the I estimates of the state, $x_{k-1}^{(i)}$, at time $k-1$, a prediction for time k is made and the J most likely association hypotheses, $\Omega_k^{(i,j)}$, are calculated using the procedure described in the previous section. That is, each of the I modes of the state posterior density function are considered independently when estimating the association hypotheses.

Given an association hypothesis at time k, the next step of the tracking process is to use this to estimate the the state, x_k.

We define $\Psi_k^{(i)}$ as a sequence of association hypotheses, $\{\Omega_1^{(i_1,j_1)}, .., \Omega_k^{(i_k,j_k)}\}$. That is, $\Psi_k^{(i)}$ defines a single path through the trellis of possible hypotheses. The best estimate of x_k is then one which maximises

$$P(x_k | z_1, .., z_k, \Psi_k) = \frac{1}{c} p(z_k | x_k, \Omega_k) P(\Omega_k | x_k) P(x_k | z_1, .., z_{k-1}, \Psi_{k-1}) \quad (12)$$

where Ω_k is the final element of Ψ_k. The first two terms of this expression have been defined in the previous section, while the third is the distribution of the predicted state, $\hat{x}_k$.

Equation (12) is similar to equation (3) although the unknown variable is now the state so the manipulations of the previous section do not help. A number of techniques have been proposed to solve this problem, such as the particle filter [7,

8] and the extended Kalman filter [1], although these techniques usually consider only the first and third terms of this expression. One method of incorporating the effect of the term $P(\Omega_k|x_k)$ into the state estimation is discussed in [14].

We have found that a good estimate of x_k is given by maximising the likelihood function, $p(z_k|x_k, \Omega_k)$, using a gradient ascent algorithm, initialised using the predicted value of the state, $\hat{x}_k$.

Upon determining the new state, $x_k^{(i,j)}$, from each marker association hypothesis, $\Omega_k^{(i,j)}$, we are able to calculate the probability of the path of hypotheses $\Psi_k^{(i,j)} = \{\Psi_{k-1}^{(i)}, \Omega_k^{(i,j)}\}$, which is given by

$$\begin{aligned}
P_k^\Psi &\equiv P(\Psi_k|z_1, .., z_k, x_1, .., x_k) \\
&= \frac{1}{c} p(z_1, .., z_k|\Psi_k, x_1, .., x_k) P(\Psi_k|x_1, .., x_k) \\
&= \frac{1}{c} p(z_k|\Omega_k, x_k) P(\Omega_k|x_k) \, P(\Psi_{k-1}|z_1, .., z_{k-1}, x_1, .., x_{k-1}) \\
&= \frac{1}{c} p(z_k|\Omega_k, x_k) P(\Omega_k|x_k) P_{k-1}^\Psi.
\end{aligned} \quad (13)$$

Thus, the procedure for calculating the probability of a path of hypotheses is recursive: at each new time frame, we need only calculate $p(z_k|\Omega_k, x_k) P(\Omega_k|x_k)$ and multiply this with the probably of the path at time $k-1$. Note that at first glance, it may appear that $p(z_k|\Omega_k, x_k) P(\Omega_k|x_k)$ was calculated when determining the probability of the association hypothesis (the sum of the elements of the LAP solution, from equation 3), however this calculation was performing using $\hat{x}_k$, not the MAP estimate of the state, x_k.

Upon calculating the probabilities of $\Psi_k^{(i,j)}$, only the I most likely are retained, so as to stop the trellis of possible hypotheses growing exponentially. The state estimates which correspond to these I hypotheses are then used to predict the state at time $k+1$ and repeat the algorithm for the next time frame.

It is possible that two different state estimates produce the same association hypothesis when estimating likely hypotheses. That is, $\Omega_k^{(i_1,j_1)} = \Omega_k^{(i_2,j_2)}$ for $i_1 \neq i_2$. In this case, two hypothesis paths have merged and it is not necessary to retain both, even if the probability of both fall within the best I, because it is likely that both hypothesis paths will generate the same state estimate and likely association hypotheses in future time frames. When paths merge, the most likely path is retained. That is, the I most likely values of $\Psi_k^{(i,j)}$ are chosen so that their final elements, $\Omega_k^{(i,j)}$, are unique.

Note that as k increases and association hypotheses are added to each of the retained paths, the most likely path may change and the most likely state at any time $j < k$, may change also. This occurs when the tracking system determines a particular association hypothesis at one time is most likely, but when future frames and detections reveal that this was not the case. It is in these situations that typical single hypothesis trackers fail.

The final output of the tracking system is the sequence of state estimates, $\{x_1^{(i_1)}, .., x_K^{(i_2)}\}$, corresponding to the most likely hypothesis path.

3 Results

The multiple hypothesis tracker was implemented and tested using two cameras operating at 25 frames/sec. The actor wore 15 markers.

Figure 1 shows the actor at some time k during a sequence in which she was dancing. Figure 2 shows the detections made by each camera at this time (indicated by the circles). Also shown in this figure is the predicted position of the actor (indicated by the shadow) and the markers (the crosses), calculated from the most likely state estimate, $\hat{x}_k^{(1)}$.

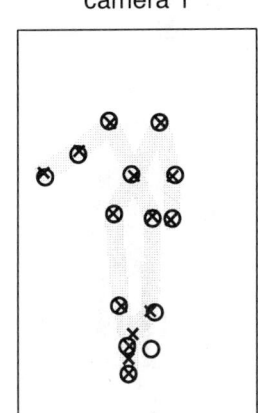
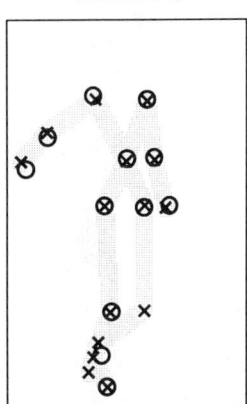

Fig. 1. View of the actor at frame k.

Fig. 2. Detections made at each camera plane (circles) and the predicted position of each marker (crosses) at time k.

In the previous time frame, the dancer's left foot was behind her right leg and the markers on her left toe and left ankle were occluded from both cameras. At time k, however, the marker on her left toe was detected in camera 1, as can be seen in these two figures.

The three most likely association hypotheses, given $\hat{x}_k^{(1)}$, are shown in figure 3. The most likely association, as given by equation (3), is shown on the left of this figure and suggests the new detection resulted from the dancer's left ankle. It is the association hypothesis $\Omega_k^{(1,2)}$, shown in the centre of figure 3, which is correct. The third association hypothesis suggested switches the assignment between the markers on the left and right ankles.

At this point, typical motion capture trackers would fail. The state they would generate, $x_k^{(1,1)}$, is incorrect.

Figure 4 shows the likely association hypotheses at time $k+1$ for each of the 3 state estimates retained at time k. In this frame, the marker on the dancer's

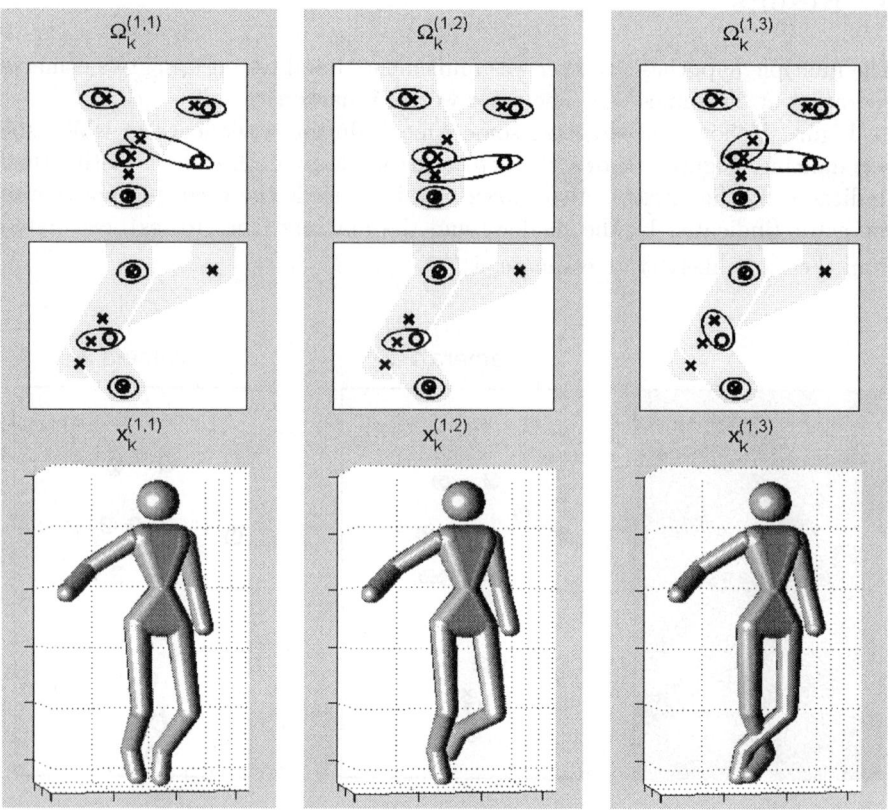

Fig. 3. The likely association hypotheses at time k and the resulting state estimate using each (each of the three columns represent a different hypothesis). The upper two rows show the associations for the two cameras, marked by the ellipses. Circles in these figures represent the detections made by the camera while the shadow and markers show the predicted state and marker locations projected onto that camera's image plane, as given by $\hat{x}_k$. The bottom row shows the state estimates given these three association hypotheses.

left toe is detected in both cameras while the marker on her left ankle continues to remain occluded to both.

It can be seen from figure 4, that the most likely association hypothesis at time $k+1$, given the most likely state estimate, $x_k^{(1,1)}$, at time k, is to assign the new detection to the dancer's left ankle, propagating the error made in the previous frame. The multiple hypothesis tracker realises this mistake when it evaluates the likelihoods of each of the six possible paths (equation 13). The additional detection in the second camera is enough to make $\Omega_{k+1}^{(2,1)}$ more likely than $\Omega_{k+1}^{(1,1)}$.

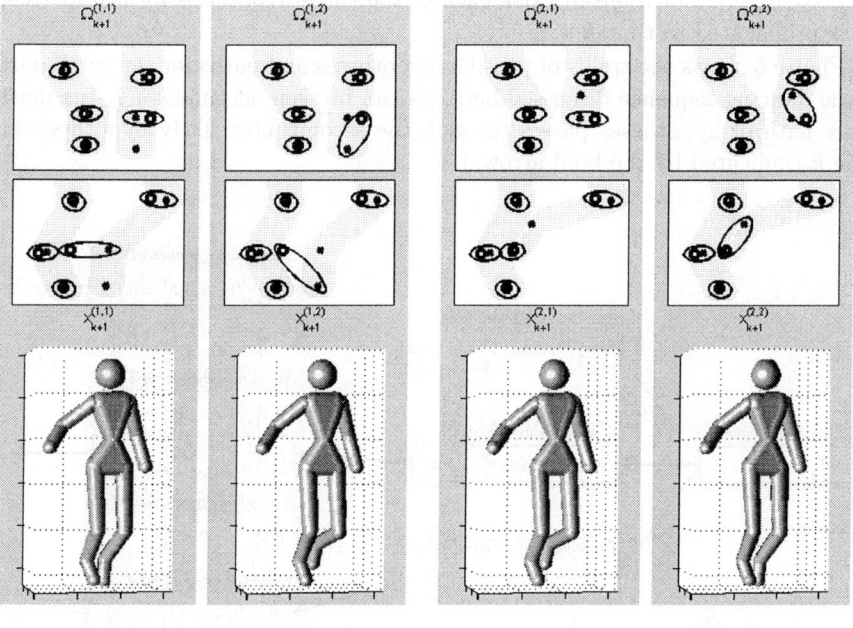

Fig. 4. The likely association hypotheses at time $k+1$, and the resulting state estimate using each, for the three state estimates retained at time k. At this time frame, the two most likely hypotheses were calculated.

Note that $\Omega_{k+1}^{(1,1)} = \Omega_{k+1}^{(2,2)}$. In this case, two hypothesis paths have merge and only one path containing this association hypothesis is retained. Similarly,

$\Omega_{k+1}^{(1,2)} = \Omega_{k+1}^{(2,1)}$, which ensures one each of the three hypothesis formed at time k are propagated to time $k+2$.

Figure 5 shows the trellis of possible hypotheses and paths for the small part of the dancing sequence discussed here. As can be seen, at time $k+1$, the most likely path of hypotheses passes through the second most likely hypothesis at time k (indicated by the bold arrows).

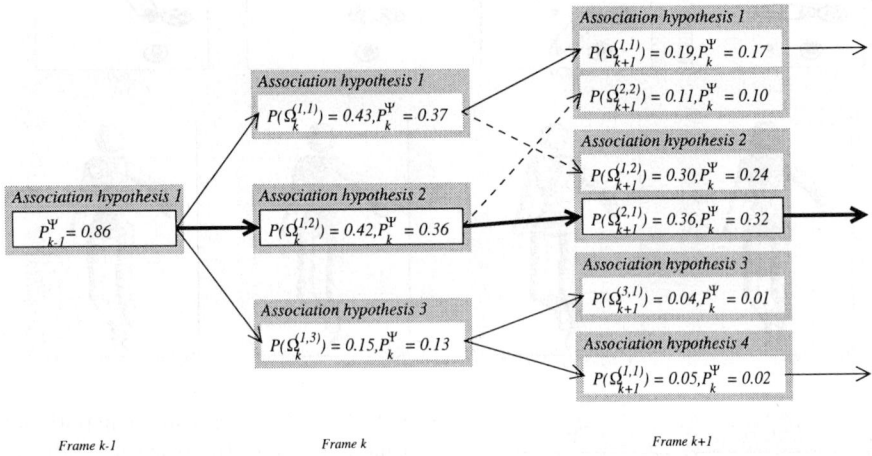

Fig. 5. Section of the trellis of possible hypothesis paths for the dancer sequence. The bold arrows mark the most likely path at time $k+1$ and the dashed arrows mark the paths that were disregarded because they merged with ones more likely.

4 Conclusions

We have presented a technique for performing the tracking stage of optical motion capture which retains, at each time frame, multiple marker association hypotheses and estimates of the subject's position. We have derived, using a Bayesian approach, the equations for calculating the likelihood of a particular association hypothesis and for a path of possible hypotheses through the video sequence.

As the multiple hypothesis tracker considers the most likely marker association when evaluating hypothesis paths, it performs at least as well as a typical single hypothesis system. It has been found, however, that situations occur in which typical systems fail to determine the correct association and in which our tracker succeeds. An example of such a case from real data has been shown. The system appears able to perform successfully using fewer cameras and a lower frame rate than has been used previously, but most significantly, it does not require the assistance of a human operator.

The number of state estimates to retain, I, and the number of hypotheses to calculate, J, at each time frame is a function of the complexity of the system: the number of cameras, markers and the type of motion being captured. Although the processing power required at each time frame increases exponentially with IJ, the multiple hypothesis process is ideally suited to adaptation for parallel processing, in which real time performance becomes a possibility.

References

1. S. Blackman and R. Popoli. *Design and analysis of modern tracking systems.* Artech House, 1999.
2. G. Carpaneto and P. Toth. Algorithm 548: Solution of the assignment problem [H]. *ACM Transactions on Mathematical Software*, 6(1):104–111, March 1980.
3. T.-J. Cham and J. Rehg. A multiple hypothesis approach to figure tracking. In *Proc. 1999 Comp Vision and Pattern Recognition (CVPR 99)*, volume 2, pages 239–245, Fort Collins, USA, 1999.
4. I. J. Cox and S. L. Hingorani. An efficient implementation and evaluation of Reid's multiple hypothesis tracking algorithm for visual tracking. *IEEE Trans. on PAMI*, 18(2):138–150, February 1996.
5. R. Danchick and G. Newnam. A fast method for finding the exact N-best hypothesis for multitarget tracking. In *IEEE trans on Aerospace and Elec Sys*, volume 29, pages 555–560, Apr 1993.
6. D. G. Forney Jr. The Viterbi algorithm. *Proceedings of the IEEE*, 61(3):268–268, March 1973.
7. S. J. Godsill, A. Doucet, and M. West. Maximum a posteriori sequence estimation using Monte Carlo particle filters. *Ann. Inst. Statist. Math*, 52(1), March 2001.
8. N. Gordon, D. Salmond, and A. Smith. Novel approach to nonlinear/non-gaussian bayesian state estimation. In *IEEE Proc F, No 140*, pages 107–113, 1993.
9. L. Herda, P. Fua, R. Plänkers, R. Boulic, and D. Thalmann. Skeleton–based motion capture for robust reconstruction of human motion. In *Proc. Computer Animation*, IEEE CS Press, 2000.
10. A. Menache. *Understanding Motion Capture for Computer Animation and Video Games.* Korgan Kaufmann Publishers, Academic Press, 2000.
11. C. Rasmussen and G. D. Hager. Joint porbabilistic techniques for tracking multipart objects. In *Proc. Computer Vision and Pattern Recognition (CVPR)*, pages 16–21, 1998.
12. J. Rehg and T. Kanade. Visual tracking of self-occluding articulated objects. In *Proc of the International Conf on Computer Vision (ICCV)*, Boston, USA, June 1995.
13. D. Reid. An algorithm for tracking multiple targets. In *IEEE Trans on Automatic Control*, volume AC-24, pages 843–854, Dec 1979.
14. M. Ringer, T. Drummond, and J. Lasenby. Using occlusions to aid pose estimation for visual motion capture. In *Proc. Computer Vision and Pattern Recognition (CVPR)*, Kauai, USA, 2001.
15. M. Ringer and J. Lasenby. Modelling and tracking articulated motion from multiple camera views. In *Proc. 11th British Machine Vision Conference (BMVC2000)*, volume 1, pages 172–181, Bristol, UK, September 2000.
16. L. Schiff. The future of motion-capture animation: Building the perfect digital human. *Animation World Magazine*, Issue 4.11, February 2000.

17. Y. Song, L. Goncalves, E. Di Bernardo, and P. Perona. Monocular perception of biological motion – detection and labeling. In *Proc. 7th Int. Conf. on Computer Vision (ICCV99)*, pages 805–812, Corfu, Greece, 1999.
18. Y. Song, L. Goncalves, and P. Perona. Monocular perception of biological motion – clutter and partial occlusion. In *Proc. 6th European Conf. on Computer Vision (ECCV00)*, volume 2, pages 719–733, Dublin, Ireland, 2000.
19. H. A. Taha. *Operations Research, An Introduction.* Prentice-Hall, 6th edition, 1997.

Single Axis Geometry by Fitting Conics

Guang Jiang[1,4], Hung-tat Tsui[1], Long Quan[2], and Andrew Zisserman[3]

[1] Dept. of Electronic Engineering, The Chinese University of Hong Kong,
New Territory, Hong Kong
{gjiang,httsui}@ee.cuhk.edu.hk
[2] Dept. of Computer Science, Hong Kong University of Science and Technology,
Kowloon, Hong Kong
quan@cs.ust.hk
[3] Department of Engineering Science, University of Oxford,
Parks Road, Oxford OX1 3PJ, UK
az@robots.ox.ac.uk
[4] School of Technical Physics, Xidian University, Xi'an 710071, P.R. China

Abstract. In this paper, we describe a new approach for recovering 3D geometry from an uncalibrated image sequence of a single axis (turntable) motion. Unlike previous methods, the computation of multiple views encoded by the fundamental matrix or trifocal tensor is not required. Instead, the new approach is based on fitting a conic locus to corresponding image points over multiple views. It is then shown that the geometry of single axis motion can be recovered given at least two such conics. In the case of two conics the reconstruction may have a two fold ambiguity, but this ambiguity is removed if three conics are used. The approach enables the geometry of the single axis motion (the 3D rotation axis and Euclidean geometry in planes perpendicular to this axis) to be estimated using the minimal number of parameters. It is demonstrated that a Maximum Likelihood Estimation results in measurements that are as good as or superior to those obtained by previous methods, and with a far simpler algorithm. Examples are given on various real sequences, which show the accuracy and robustness of the new algorithm.

1 Introduction

Acquiring 3D models from single axis motion sequences, particularly turntables, has been widely used by computer vision and graphics researchers. The key component of the 3D reconstruction is the recovery of the rotation angles. Traditionally, rotation angles are obtained by careful calibration [4,17,22,23]. Fitzgibbon et al. [8] extended the single axis approach to recover unknown rotation angles using a projective geometry model of the motion. In their method, corresponding points are carefully tracked over each pair of images for the fundamental matrices and each triplet of images for the trifocal tensors. Mendonça et al. [15] recover the rotation angles from profiles of surfaces. The search for corresponding points is transformed into a search for epipolar tangencies. All of the above papers have some discussion on the invariants in this special single axis motion. However the ideal points **i** and **j**, which play a very important role in rotation angle recovery, are not discussed explicitly.

Recently a new method has been proposed [11] which does not incur the expense of computing trifocal tensors or of the nonlinear optimization involved in computing epipolar tangencies. Instead, corresponding points in different images are fitted to a conic. It is then shown that rotation angles can be directly computed from only one conic and one fundamental matrix. The remaining geometric quantities can be obtained using more conics.

In this paper, we show further that even one fundamental matrix is unnecessary. All single axis geometry can be computed from at least two conics by directly calculating the image of the circular points. Thence all invariant quantities of the single axis motion can be computed. The advantage of the new method over the existing ones is straightforward. First, it is intrinsically a multiple view approach as all geometric information from the whole sequence is nicely summarized in the conics! This contrasts with the computation of fundamental matrices and trifocal tensors which use only a subsequence of 2 and 3 views respectively. Second, as will be shown in section 4, the essential geometry of the image single axis geometry may be specified by six parameters and this may be minimally estimated from two conics (a total of 10 parameters). Previous methods have involved estimating more than this minimum number of parameters, e.g. 18 tensor parameters from 3 views.

The paper is organized as follows. A review of the geometry of single axis motion is given in Section 2. Section 3 describes the invariants under the single axis motion case and the rotation angle recovery based on these invariants. A Maximum Likelihood Estimation method for these invariants and conics fitting is given in Section 4. Section 5 demonstrates two experiments. One is on the reconstruction of the Hannover dinosaur from a turntable image sequence. The other is on a reconstruction of a girl who is seated in a rotating chair. The latter is a short video sequence and we want to show that 3D photography can be easily done. Finally, a short conclusion is given in Section 6.

2 Review of the Geometry of Single Axis Motion

Throughout the paper, scalars are denoted in plain letters or lower case Greek. Assuming a pin-hole camera model, the object space may be considered as embedded in $\mathcal{P}^3$ and the image space embedded in $\mathcal{P}^2$. Vectors in $\mathcal{P}^2$ are denoted in lower case boldface and vectors in $\mathcal{P}^3$ and matrices in upper case boldface. The camera performs the projection from $\mathcal{P}^3$ to $\mathcal{P}^2$, and can be represented by a 3×4 matrix $\mathbf{P}_{3\times 4}$ of rank 3 whose kernel is the projection center. The relationship between a point $\mathbf{X}$ in $\mathcal{P}^3$ and a point $\mathbf{x}$ in $\mathcal{P}^2$ can be written as

$$\lambda \mathbf{x} = \mathbf{P}_{3\times 4}\mathbf{X}, \tag{1}$$

where $\mathbf{x}$ and $\mathbf{X}$ are in homogeneous coordinates and λ is a non-zero scalar.

A typical set up for single axis motion consists of a stationary CCD camera in front of a turntable on which the object to be reconstructed is placed [17,18]. The internal parameters of the camera are assumed fixed.

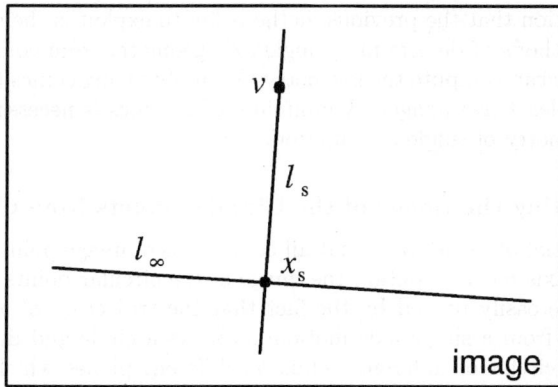

Fig. 1. Fixed image entities

For a single axis motion, without loss of generality, the rotation axis of the turntable is chosen to be the z-axis the world coordinate. Then each point on the object is moving in its plane that is perpendicular to the z-axis. Indeed, there is a pencil of horizontal planes. The invariants related to the geometry of single axis motion have been established in [8]. These invariants on the image plane are:

1. The line $\mathbf{l}_s$ which is the image of the rotation axis.
2. The line $\mathbf{l}_\infty$ which is the image of the intersection line for all horizontal planes. Actually, it is the vanishing line of all the horizontal planes.
3. The point $\mathbf{x}_s$ which is the image of the intersection of the rotation axis with the horizontal plane through the camera center.
4. The point $\mathbf{v}$ which is the vanishing point of the rotation axis.

These fixed image entities are illustrated schematically in Figure 1.

3 Single Axis Geometry and Conic Loci

Our first remark is that the trajectory of the corresponding points in different images of any given space point, displayed in any particular image plane, is a conic by the very definition of single axis motion (Figure 2) [19]. This extremely

Fig. 2. Dinosaur sequence and Conics

trivial observation that the previous methods fail to exploit is the starting point of our new methods of determining single axis geometry from conic loci. It will be seen that we can compute the geometry by simply fitting conics to the tracked points over at least five images. A minimum of 2 conics is necessary to recover the entire geometry of single axis motion.

3.1 Computing the Image of the Circular Points from Conics

The first essential observation is that all conic locus of image points of an object from a single axis motion contain the image of the circular points.

This can be easily proved by the fact that the trajectory of a given object point in space from a single axis motion is always a circle and different points therefore give circles of different radius on different planes which are all parallel and perpendicular to the single rotation axis. All circles go through their respective circular points of the plane they are lying on by the very definition of the circular points [20]. As all these supporting planes are parallel, i.e. they share a common line at infinity on which the circular points lie. We may thus conclude that all circles of different radius on different parallel planes from the single axis motion share the common pair of circular points $\mathbf{i}$ and $\mathbf{j}$. Because this is a projective property it remains true for the projection onto any image plane. In any particular image plane, this means that all conic loci of corresponding points intersect in the pair of common circular points $\mathbf{i}$ and $\mathbf{j}$. Thus, by just computing intersection points of at least two conic loci, we obtain the image of the circular points, and also the vanishing line of the parallel planes.

Consider the intersection of a pair of conics, there are always 4 intersection points including complex and infinite points according to Bezout's theorem. In terms of real intersection points, they may be 0, 1, 2, 3, or 4 according to the configurations.

- For the case of 1 or 2 real intersection points, it is straightforward that the only pair of complex conjugate points is the image of the circular points.
- It is generally impossible to have 3 or 4 real intersection points if the conics are real perspective image of the circles from the single axis motion by its definition.

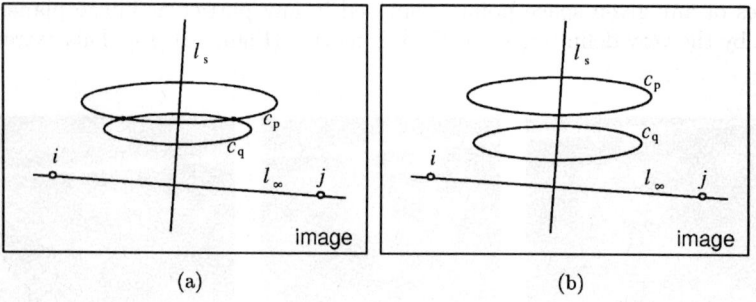

Fig. 3. The intersections of two conics

– The most difficult case is when there is no real intersection points. This is in fact very common if we just look at the illustrative conic loci in Figure 3. In this case, we obtain two pairs of complex conjugate points. There is a reconstruction ambiguity coming from the ambiguity of the two pairs of complex conjugate points. Of course, this ambiguity can be immediately removed as soon as we have more than 2 conics.

3.2 The Complete Computation Method

After having described the key components of computing the image of the circular points from at least two conics, we can summarize the complete method of computing rotational angles and the underlying single axis geometry.

1. Fit two conics $\mathbf{C}_p$ and $\mathbf{C}_q$ to all tracked points over the sequence for two given points respectively. At this stage, two points tracked over at least 5 images are needed.
2. Compute the intersection points of the two conics $\mathbf{C}_p$ and $\mathbf{C}_q$. We may have either one pair of complex conjugates or two pairs of complex conjugates. If there is a unique pair of complex conjugates, the image of circular points $\mathbf{i}$ and $\mathbf{j}$ are exactly this pair of complex conjugates. However if there are two possible pairs of complex conjugate points, we obtain two possible solutions. This double solution ambiguity can be removed by using any additional conic.
3. Compute the vanishing line
$$\mathbf{l}_\infty = \mathbf{i} \times \mathbf{j}.$$
4. Obtain the projection of the two circle centers as the pole of the line $\mathbf{l}_\infty$
$$\mathbf{o}_p = \mathbf{C}_p^{-1} \mathbf{l}_\infty,$$
$$\mathbf{o}_q = \mathbf{C}_q^{-1} \mathbf{l}_\infty.$$
5. Compute the rotation axis as
$$\mathbf{l}_s = \mathbf{o}_p \times \mathbf{o}_q.$$
6. Compute the angular motion between two views from the tracked points. i.e. points $\mathbf{a}$ and $\mathbf{b}$ on two views are tracked points on conic $\mathbf{C}_p$, the rotation angle of the two views can be calculated by using Laguerre's formula [20]
$$\theta_{ab} = \frac{1}{2i} \log(\{\mathbf{l}_{o_p a}, \mathbf{l}_{o_p b}; \mathbf{l}_{o_p i}, \mathbf{l}_{o_p j}\}).$$

The fixed image entities for the single axis motion deduced from two conics are shown in Figure 4.a and the rotation angle with respected to the image entities is shown in Figure 4.b.

Compare with Figure 1, the vanishing point $\mathbf{v}$ of the rotation axis cannot be obtained from the conics. This means that although metric structure in all planes perpendicular to the rotation axis can be accurately determined, the reconstruction along the rotation axis has a 1D projective ambiguity. This same result is also shown by Fitzgibbon et al. [8] and other researchers [1,16,24] which have two parameters not determined. The ambiguity can be removed by specifying camera aspect ratio and parallel vertical scene lines.

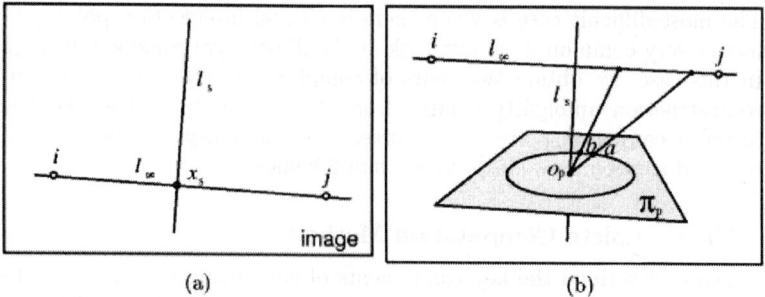

Fig. 4. (a) Fixed image entities deduced from conics. (b) The rotation angle with respect to the image entities.

3.3 Recovering Lost Angles

In practice, some points are missing in some views along the tracking path. The rotation angles for these views in which the tracked points are missing cannot be recovered. We show in this section how to find the 'missing' corresponding points and then how to recover the angles of these views.

Figure 5 illustrates this configuration to help the following development. The conic $\mathbf{C}$ on the plane π_1 has been obtained from at least a point tracked over five images. The point $\mathbf{a}$ is visible in views m_1 and m_2 as $\mathbf{a}_1$ and $\mathbf{a}_2$, but missing in view m_3, so the point $\mathbf{a}_3$ is not available. However, a point $\mathbf{b}$ is available in the three views m_1, m_2, and m_3 as $\mathbf{b}_1$, $\mathbf{b}_2$ and $\mathbf{b}_3$. Let us assume its unknown conic trajectory is the conic $\mathbf{C}_i$ on the plane π_i. As we know the two planes π_1 and π_i are parallel in space, they therefore share the same vanishing line $\mathbf{l}_\infty$ and the circular points $\mathbf{i}$ and $\mathbf{j}$. Since the rotation angle between the view m_1 and m_2 is known from the conic $\mathbf{C}$. We may use Laguerre's formula for the point $\mathbf{b}$ on the plane π_i:

$$\theta_{12} = \frac{1}{2i} \log(\{\mathbf{l}_{o_1 b_1}, \mathbf{l}_{o_1 b_2}; \mathbf{l}_{o_1 i}, \mathbf{l}_{o_1 j}\}),$$

where the point $\mathbf{o}_1$ is the only unknown vector of the image of the circle center. Since $\mathbf{o}_1$ lies on $\mathbf{l}_s$, the one unknown component of this point can be calculated from the known cross ratio $\{\mathbf{l}_{o_1 b_1}, \mathbf{l}_{o_1 b_2}; \mathbf{l}_{o_1 i}, \mathbf{l}_{o_1 j}\}$.

From the reconstructed point $\mathbf{o}_1$, the rotation angle θ_{23} between the view m_2 and m_3 can be obtained.

$$\theta_{23} = \frac{1}{2i} \log(\{\mathbf{l}_{o_1 b_2}, \mathbf{l}_{o_1 b_3}; \mathbf{l}_{o_1 i}, \mathbf{l}_{o_1 j}\}).$$

Once the angle θ_{23} has been determined, Laguerre's formula can be applied again to the computation of the line $\mathbf{l}_{o a_3}$. By intersecting the line $\mathbf{l}_{o a_3}$ with the conic $\mathbf{C}$, the missing point $\mathbf{a}_3$ is recovered.

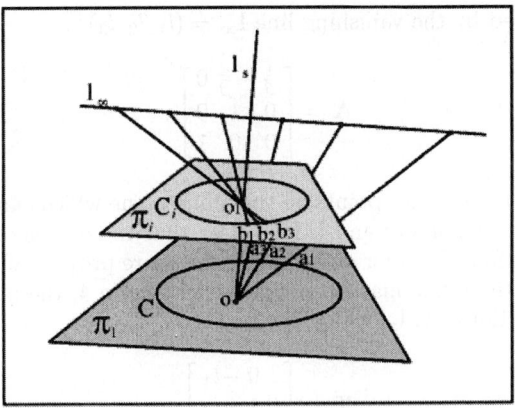

Fig. 5. Finding missing points and recovering missing angles.

4 Invariants Estimation and Conic Fitting Based on Maximum Likelihood Estimation

It has been shown that the geometry of single axis motion can be recovered given at least two conics. With the minimum of two conics the reconstruction may have a two fold ambiguity, but one or more additional conics makes the solution unique. In this section, a Maximum Likelihood Estimation (MLE) method is given for simultaneous estimation of the fixed geometric entities and conics.

As mentioned earlier, each point on the object is moving on its plane which is perpendicular to the z-axis and different points therefore form a pencil of horizontal planes. For each such plane, there is a plane homography $\mathbf{H}$ which maps the conic in the image plane to the circle lying on the horizontal plane,

$$\mathbf{C}_{cirle} = \mathbf{H}^{-\top} \mathbf{C}_{conic} \mathbf{H}^{-1}. \qquad (2)$$

And we assume the center of the circle is the origin of the plane and its radius is one. We will derive a formula for this homography which will be used to parametrize the MLE.

The homography can be decomposed into a concatenation of five matrices $\mathbf{R}$, $\mathbf{S}$, $\mathbf{T}$, $\mathbf{A}$ and $\mathbf{P}_u$, representing rotation, isotropic scaling, translation, affine and 'pure projective' transformations respectively [12,6,13]:

$$\mathbf{H} = \mathbf{RSTAP}_u. \qquad (3)$$

where

$$\mathbf{P}_u = \begin{bmatrix} 1 & 0 & 0 \\ 0 & 1 & 0 \\ l_1 & l_2 & l_3 \end{bmatrix},$$

can be determined by the vanishing line $\mathbf{l}_\infty = (l_1, l_2, l_3)^\top$.

$$\mathbf{A} = \begin{bmatrix} \frac{1}{\beta} & -\frac{\alpha}{\beta} & 0 \\ 0 & 1 & 0 \\ 0 & 0 & 1 \end{bmatrix},$$

$(\alpha \mp i\beta, 1, 0)^T$ is the circular points on the affine plane which can be obtained by $\mathbf{P}_u$ through circular points $\mathbf{i}$ and $\mathbf{j}$. It is clear that the degree of freedom of the circular points is four. Two for determining the 'pure projective' matrix and two for determining the affine matrix. As shown in Figure 4, the other fixed image entity is the rotation axis $\mathbf{l}_s$, which has two d.o.f.

$$\mathbf{T} = \begin{bmatrix} 1 & 0 & -t_1 \\ 0 & 1 & -t_2 \\ 0 & 0 & 1 \end{bmatrix},$$

$(t_1, t_2, 1)^\top$ is the pole of vanishing line $\mathbf{l}_\infty$ with respect to conic $\mathbf{C}_n$ on the metric plane. Since the pole is constrained by the rotation axis $\mathbf{l}_s$, only one degree of freedom exists in the translation matrix.

$$\mathbf{S} = \begin{bmatrix} s & 0 & 0 \\ 0 & s & 0 \\ 0 & 0 & 1 \end{bmatrix},$$

After processing by the matrices of $\mathbf{P}_u$, $\mathbf{A}$ and $\mathbf{T}$, the conic is transformed into a circle with center at the original point. The isotropic scaling matrix scales the circle to a circle with radius unity. There is one d.o.f. for each conic. Since the rotation matrix does not affect the circle with center at the original point, no degree of freedom lies in the matrix $\mathbf{R}$ for the circle.

In summary, there are in total 6 d.o.f. for the fixed entities (2 for each of the two circular point, 2 for $\mathbf{l}_s$) and 2 for each conic (which correspond to where the center is along the rotation axis (1) and its radius (1)). The cost function for the MLE involves minimizing the sum of squared geometric distances (one for each of the m measured points) over all $6 + 2n$ parameters for the fixed entities and n conics.

$$\mathcal{C} = \sum_n \sum_m d_\perp(\mathbf{x}, \mathbf{C})^2. \qquad (4)$$

However, as is shown in [10] this nonlinear cost function $\mathcal{C}$ can be approximated as

$$d_\perp(\mathbf{x}, \mathbf{C})^2 = \frac{(\mathbf{x}^T \mathbf{C} \mathbf{x})^2}{4((\mathbf{C}\mathbf{x})_1^2 + (\mathbf{C}\mathbf{x})_2^2)},$$

where $(\mathbf{C}\mathbf{x})_i$ denotes the i-th component of the 3-vector $\mathbf{C}\mathbf{x}$. This function is optimized using the standard Levenberg-Marquart algorithm.

The $6 + 2n$ parameters are initialized by the method in Section 3 as follows. First, each conic is fitted to corresponding points from more than 4 views [3,7]. Then the pole of each conic with respect to the vanishing line is calculated, and the point on the rotation axis which is nearest to the pole is used to estimate the initial value of t_1 (1 dof). Now, each conic can be transformed into a circle. The radius of this circle determines the initial value of s (1 dof). Finally, each conic is mapped to a unit circle with center at the origin and the points on the conic is mapped to the points near the unit circle for the optimum procedure.

5 Experiments

The new algorithm of computing single axis geometry from only conics has been implemented. The whole computational procedure is simple and robust. We just give two examples to demonstrate the method. The first example is from the popular dinosaur image sequence from the University of Hannover. In this experiment, we have introduced a robust method for computing the rotation angles. We also show directly the projective meaning of rotation angles in an image plane. Another example is a video sequence of a girl in a rotating chair. This example also shows the practicality of this algorithm and the ease of computation.

The dinosaur sequence contains 36 views from a turntable with a constant 10 degrees angular motion. The angular accuracy is about 0.05 degrees[17]. Figure 6.a shows the tracking of some interest points of the sequence. Results of conic fitting of the same sequence using MLE is shown in Figure 6.b. Figure 7 shows the results of recovered rotation angles.

Actually, the rotation angles can be labeled on the vanishing line after randomly selecting a reference point. For instance, we may select the cross point of lines $\mathbf{l}_\infty$ and $\mathbf{l}_s$ in Figure 8 as the reference point for zero rotation angle. Any rotation angle can then be computed directly by applying Laguerre's formula and labeled on the vanishing line.

For any fitted conic, the intersections on the vanishing line with the lines joining the conic pole and known corresponding points represent the angles of

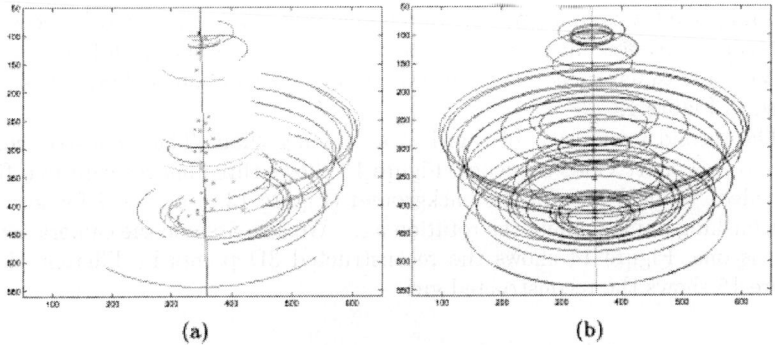

Fig. 6. (a) Some tracked points from the dinosaur sequence. The marks of '×' indicate the initial poles of the direct fitted conics with respected to the vanishing line. (b) Fitted conics with the MLE. The marks of '+' indicate the poles of the MLE fitted conics with respected to the vanishing line. The marks '+' are neatly located on the rotation axis.

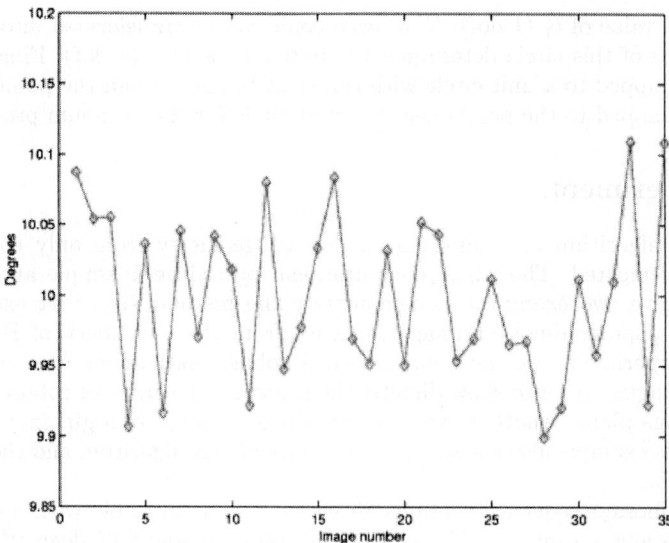

Fig. 7. Recovered rotation angles for the whole sequence of 36 views.

views with respect to the reference point. Thus, the angles (with respect to the reference point) of unknown corresponding points can be marked out on the vanishing line with the recovered rotation angles. Then, an unknown corresponding point on the conic is given by the intersection between the conic and the line joining its angle mark on the vanishing line and the conic pole. The corresponding points in all views (Figure 9) can be determined.

Using the Shape-from-Silhouettes approach described in [5,17], the horizontal slices of the dinosaur model can be obtained as illustrated in Figure 10. As the vanishing point **v** is unknown, there remains unknown ratios among slices and the reconstruction is up to two projective parameters as shown in Figure 11.

With a reasonable choice of the ratio, full reconstruction is obtained as illustrated in Figure 12.

The second example is of a girl in a rotating chair. The reconstruction is done from a short video sequence. Figure 13 shows three images captured from the video. Vertical lines in the background (Figure 13.c) are used for locating the vanishing point **v** along the rotation axis. We also assume the camera aspect ratio is one. Figure 14 shows the reconstructed 3D points in different views. Figure 15 shows the reconstructed girl.

6 Conclusion

We have presented a novel intuitive method of computing single axis geometry by fitting conic loci only to the corresponding points. The novelty of this algorithm is that it does not need to calculate any multiple view geometry such as

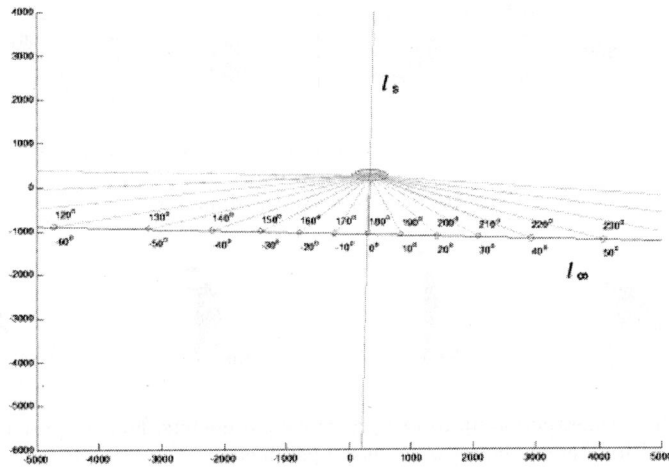

Fig. 8. Labeled rotation angles on the vanishing line (Dinosaur sequence). By selecting one reference point on the vanishing line, any rotation angle can be labeled on the vanishing line according to the Laguerre's formula.

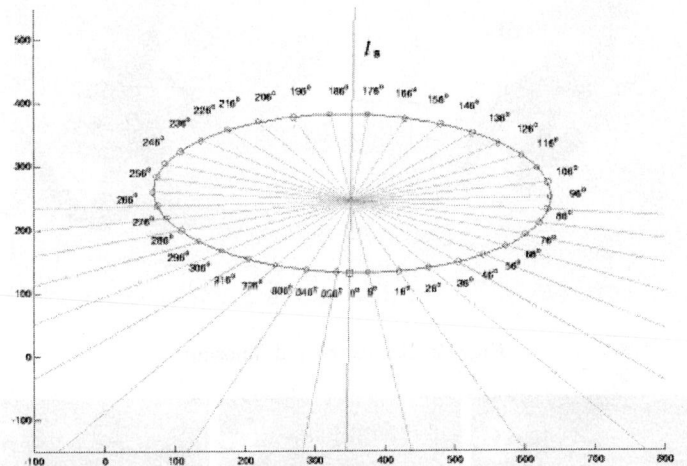

Fig. 9. Recovered corresponding points on one conic (Dinosaur sequence). After knowing the rotation angles in 36 views, with the fitted conic and a point on the conic, the corresponding points in 36 views can be recovered.

fundamental matrices and trifocal tensors. We need only to compute two, or at most three conics without any other geometric quantities in our new approach. Using MLE and more than three conics can improve the estimation and reconstruction. The algorithm is simple and robust and the number of parameters to be estimated is substantially reduced compared to previous approaches. This fact is verified by experiments on real data showing very good results.

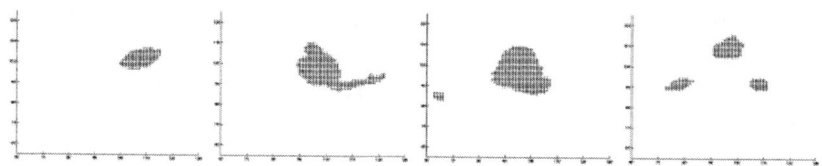

Fig. 10. Four Slices of the dinosaur.

Fig. 11. 3D reconstruction up to two projective parameters. Four reconstructions are displayed with different choices of unknown parameters.

Fig. 12. Reconstructed dinosaur.

Fig. 13. Three images captured from the video. The video is a girl in a rotating chair. A vertical line in the background is marked out for searching the vanishing point along the rotation axis.

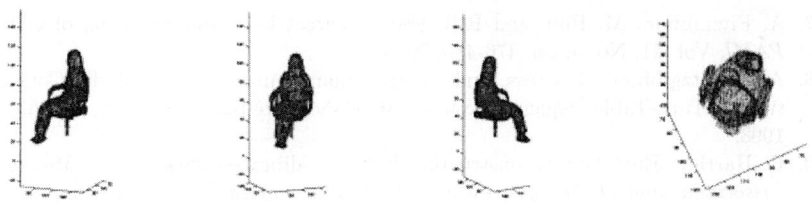

Fig. 14. 3D points of reconstructed girl from four different views.

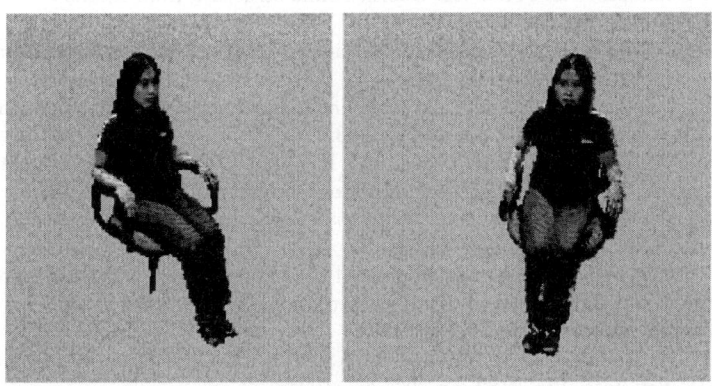

Fig. 15. Reconstructed girl.

Acknowledgments. This research is partially supported by RGC grant CUHK 4310/98E.

References

1. L. de Agapito, R. Hartley, and E. Hayman: Linear self-calibration of a rotating and zooming camera, *CVPR*, Vol. 1, pp. 15-21, 1999.
2. M. Armstrong, A. Zisserman, and R. Hartley: Self-Calibration from Image Triplets, *ECCV*, pp. 3-16, 1996.
3. F. Bookstein: Fitting conic sections to scattered data, *CVGIP*, vol. 9, pp. 56-71, 1979.
4. E. Boyer: Object models from contour sequences, *ECCV*, pp. 109-118, 1996.
5. C.H. Chien and J.K. Aggarwal: Identification of 3D objects from multiple silhouettes using quadtrees/octrees. *Comp. Vision, Graphics, and Image Processing* 36, 1986, pp.256-273.
6. O. Faugeras: Stratification of three-dimensional vision: projective, affine, and metric representation. *J. Opt. Soc. Am., A*, Vol. 12, pp. 465-484, 1995.

7. A. Fitzgibbon, M. Pilu, and R.B. Fisher: Direct least square fitting of ellipses. *PAMI*, Vol. 21, No. 5, pp. 476-480, 1999.
8. A.W. Fitzgibbon, G. Cross, and A. Zisserman: Automatic 3D Model Construction for Turn-Table Sequences, *SMILE Workshop*, Freiburg, Germany, pp. 155-170, 1998.
9. R. Hartley: Euclidean reconstruction from uncalibrated views, In J. Mundy, A. Zisserman, and D. Forsyth, editors, *Applications of Invariance in Computer Vision*, LNCS 825, SpringerVerlag, pp. 237-256, 1994.
10. R. Hartley and A. Zisserman: Multiple View Geometry in Computer Vision, *Cambridge University Press*, 2000.
11. G. Jiang, H.T. Tsui, L. Quan and S.Q. Liu: Recovering the Geometry of Single Axis Motions by Conic Fitting, *CVPR*, pp. 293-298, 2001.
12. J.J. Koenderink and A.J. van Doorn: Affine structure from motion. *J. Opt. Soc. Am., A*, 8(2), pp. 377-385, 1991.
13. D. Liebowitz and A. Zisserman: Metric rectification for perspective images of planes. *CVPR*, pp. 482-488, 1998.
14. Q.-T. Luong and O.D. Faugeras: The Fundamental matrix: theory, algorithms, and stability analysis, *IJCV*, pp. 43-76, 1996.
15. P.R.S. Mendonça, K.-Y.K. Wong, and R. Cipolla: Camera pose estimation and reconstruction from image profiles under circular motion. In D. Vernon, editor, *Proc. 6th European Conf. on Computer Vision*, volume II, pp. 864-877, Dublin, Ireland, Jun 2000. Springer-Verlag.
16. J. Mundy, and A. Zisserman: Repeated Structures: Image Correspondence Constraints and Ambiguity of 3D Reconstruction, *In Applications of invariance in computer vision*, SpringerVerlag, 1994.
17. W.Niem: Robust and Fast Modelling of 3D Natural Objects from Multiple Views, *SPIE*, San Jose, Vol. 2182, pp. 388-397, 1994.
18. W. Niem, and R. Buschmann: Automatic Modelling of 3D Natural Objects from Multiple Views, *Yakup Paker and Sylvia Wilbur: Image Processing for Broadcast and Video Production. Workshops in computing series*, Springer, Hamburg, 1994.
19. H.S. Sawhney, J. Oliensis, and A.R. Hanson: Image Description and 3-D Reconstruction from Image Trajectories of Rotational Motion. *PAMI*, Vol. 15, No. 9, pp. 885-898, 1993.
20. J. Semple, and G. Kneebone: Algebraic Projective Geometry. *Oxford University Press*, 1952.
21. P.F. Sturm, and S.J. Maybank: On plane-based camera calibration: A general algorithm, singularities, applications, *CVPR*, pp. 432-437, 1999.
22. S. Sullivan, and J. Ponce: Automatic model construction, pose estimation, and object recognition from photographs using triangular splines, *PAMI*, Vol. 20, No. 10, pp. 1091-1097, 1998.
23. R. Szeliski: Shape from rotation, *CVPR*, pp. 625-630, 1991.
24. A. Zisserman, D. Liebowitz, and M. Armstrong: Resolving Ambiguities in Auto-Calibration, *In Philosophical Transactions of the Royal Society of London*, SERIES A, vol. 356, no. 1740, pp. 1193-1211, 1998.

Computing the Physical Parameters of Rigid-Body Motion from Video

Kiran S. Bhat[1], Steven M. Seitz[2], Jovan Popović[3], and Pradeep K. Khosla[1]

[1] Carnegie Mellon University, Pittsburgh, PA, USA
{kiranb,pkk}@cs.cmu.edu
[2] University of Washington, Seattle, WA, USA
seitz@cs.washington.edu
[3] Massachusetts Institute of Technology, Cambridge, MA, USA
jovan@lcs.mit.edu

Abstract. This paper presents an optimization framework for estimating the motion and underlying physical parameters of a rigid body in free flight from video. The algorithm takes a video clip of a tumbling rigid body of known shape and generates a physical simulation of the object observed in the video clip. This solution is found by optimizing the simulation parameters to best match the motion observed in the video sequence. These simulation parameters include initial positions and velocities, environment parameters like gravity direction and parameters of the camera. A global objective function computes the sum squared difference between the silhouette of the object in simulation and the silhouette obtained from video at each frame. Applications include creating interesting rigid body animations, tracking complex rigid body motions in video and estimating camera parameters from video.

1 Introduction

The motion of real objects is governed by their underlying physical properties and their interactions with the environment. For example, a coin tossed in the air undergoes a complex motion that depends on its initial position, orientation, and velocity at the time at which it is thrown. Replacing the coin with a bowling pin produces a distinctly different motion, indicating that motion is also influenced by shape, mass distribution, and other intrinsic properties of the object. Finally, the environment also affects the motion of an object, through the effects of gravity, air drag, and collisions.

In this paper we present a framework for recovering physical parameters of objects and environments from video data. We focus specifically on the case of computing the parameters underlying the motion of a tumbling rigid object in free flight assuming the object shape and mass distribution are known. Our algorithm models tumbling dynamics using ordinary differential equations, whose parameters include gravity, inertia and initial velocities. We present an optimization framework to identify these physical parameters from video.

Our dynamic model captures the true rotational physics of a tumbling rigid body. This aspect distinguishes our work from prior work in motion tracking and analysis [4,7,11,5], where the focus is on identifying object kinematics, i.e., motion trajectories. Moreover,

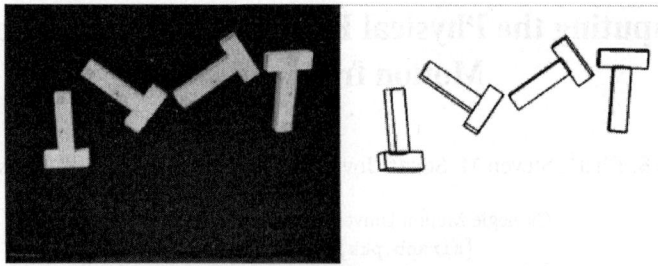

Fig. 1. Four frames of a tumbling object superimposed (left) and a physical simulation generated from the estimated motion parameters. The object is thrown from right to left. Our optimization framework computes the object, camera and environment parameters to match the simulated wireframe object with the video at every frame.

our algorithm uses information from all frames in the video sequence simultaneously, unlike feedforward filter based methods. Figure 2 compares the results of our offline batch algorithm with an online Kalman filter applied to a synthetic example of 2D ballistic motion with gaussian noise. Our algorithm tries to find the best fit parabola to the data, whereas a Kalman filter fits a higher order curve to the data. Although the Kalman filter approach *tracks* the data better, our algorithm finds the true parameters describing the physics of the ballistic motion. These parameters can now be used to *animate* a particle in simulation, that *moves like* the given data. However, most tracking tasks require only kinematic properties and therefore, our approach of accurately modeling the underlying physics might seem to be unnecessary or prohibitively difficult.

We argue that estimating physical parameters has important benefits for the analysis of rigid-body motion. First, the use of an accurate physical model actually *simplifies* the task of recovering kinematics, since the complete motion is determined by the initial state and a small number of other parameters. Second, the recovered model enables the behavior of the object to be *predicted* in new or unseen conditions. For instance, from a short video clip of a object at any point in its trajectory, we can reason from where it was launched and where and in what attitude it will land. This same ability allows the path to be followed *through occlusions*. In addition, we can predict how the object would behave in different conditions, i.e., with more angular velocity. In the same manner, by recovering parameters of the environment, we can predict how different objects would move in that environment. As one application of measuring the environment, we show how estimating the direction of gravity in an image sequence can be used to rectify a video to correct for camera roll.

We estimate parameters of a rigid-body motion with an optimization that seeks to match the resulting motion with the frames of the video sequence. Rather than operating in a feed-forward manner, as is typical of object tracking techniques [16,17, 7,4], we cast the problem in a global optimization framework that optimizes over all frames at once. Using this framework, we show how it is possible to simultaneously compute the object, camera, and environment parameters from video data. Unlike previous analytical methods [15,14], our method does not require any velocity, acceleration, or torque measurements to compute the body state as a function of time. Furthermore, an important element of our estimation approach is that it relies only on easily computable metrics such as image silhouettes and 2D bounding boxes, avoiding the need to compute optical flow or track features on the object over time. Our optimizer employs general-purpose rigid-body simulators [1] that model a wide range of behaviors, such as collisions and articulated structures.

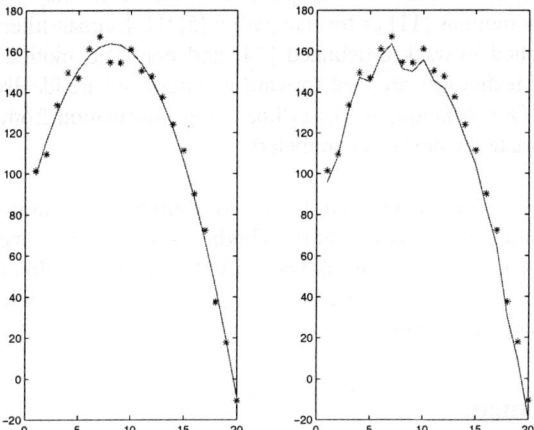

Fig. 2. Illustrating the differences between parameter estimation using optimization (left) and a Kalman filter (right) on a simplistic 2D example. The input data is the trajectory of a point mass in free flight, corrupted with gaussian noise. Our optimization algorithm uses all the data points simultaneously to fit a path that globally satisfies physical laws; in this simple case, a parabolic path. The Kalman filter processes the data sequentially and fits a higher order curve to the data.

2 Related Work

Several researchers in the computer vision community have focussed on the problem of extracting body shape and camera motion from video [23,12,8]. There is very little work on extracting the underlying physical properties of the object or the environment. Several groups [20,3] have modeled the dynamics of point masses (free flight and collisions) from video to design controllers for robots performing juggling or playing air hockey. Ghosh et al. [9] use estimation theory to recover the riccati dynamics and shape of planar objects using optical flow. Masutani et al. [15] describes an algorithm to extract the inertial parameters of a tumbling rigid body from video. Their system tracks feature points in the images to get instantaneous velocity measurements and uses the Poinsot's solution [22] to compute the inertial parameters. The problem of simultaneously recovering the physical parameters of the object, camera, and environment from a single camera has not been previously addressed.

Our work is closely related to prior work on model based tracking in computer vision [11,5,21,4,7,24,17,16]. However, the notion of a dynamic model in the tracking literature is different from the one presented here. We use ordinary differential equations to model the non-linear rotational dynamics of tumbling rigid bodies, and extract its parameters from video. These parameters include initial velocities, gravity and inertias. In contrast, most of the prior tracking algorithms use a Kalman filter to update the state variables of the moving object. In many instances, the dynamic model that relates the current and previous states is extremely simple [11,5]. However, they are sufficient for tracking rigid-body motions [11] or for navigation [5,21]. Kalman filters have also been successfully applied to track articulated [24] and non-rigid motion [16,17] in video. The filter based techniques are feed-forward in nature and are ideally suited for tracking applications. Our technique works offline using information from all frames simultaneously to estimate the physical parameters.

Several techniques have been developed [19,6] to estimate the parameters of a simulation to design computer animations of rigid bodies. Although these methods have been used for synthesis, to date, they have not been used to analyze motion from video. Our technique is similar to recent parameter estimation techniques for designing rigid body animations in computer graphics [19,18].

3 Problem Statement

Our goal is to infer the physical parameters underlying the motion of a rigid body in free flight from a pre-recorded video sequence of its motion. Free flight motion of the rigid body in video is determined by a relatively small set of parameters. They can be categorized into three groups:

- **Object Parameters**: We distinguish two types of object parameters: intrinsic parameters (object shape, mass distribution and location of center of mass), extrinsic parameters (initial position, orientation, velocity, angular velocity).
- **Environment Parameters**: Parameters such as gravity direction and air drag.
- **Camera**: We distinguish two types of camera parameters: intrinsic (focal length, principle point, etc.), extrinsic parameters (position and orientation).

In this paper, we extract the extrinsic parameters of the object and the direction of the gravity vector. We assume that the shape and inertial properties of the object are known and the effect of air drag is negligible. Without loss of generality, we place the origin of the world coordinate system at the camera center, with the principle axes aligned with the camera coordinate system. Due to the choice of this coordinate system, the direction of gravity depends on the orientation of the camera, and is not necessarily vertical.

We employ the standard mathematical model from classical mechanics to represent the motion of a rigid body in free flight. A set of nonlinear ordinary differential equations (ODE) model the motion of a rigid body by computing the evolution of its state, which includes the body's position and velocities, over time. As a result, the motion of a rigid body is succinctly described by the parameters that affect the solution of the ODE. We use the term *simulation* to refer to the process of computing the body's motion by integrating the ODE.

4 Estimation from Video

In this section, we describe the equations of motion of a rigid body in free flight, and identify the parameters that affect the motion. We present an optimization framework to identify these parameters from a video sequence.

4.1 Equations of Motion

The tumbling motion of a rigid body in free flight is characterised by its position, orientation, linear and angular velocity. Let us define the state $q(t) = [X(t), \theta(t), V(t), \omega(t)]$ to be the values of these parameters at time t. $X(t) \in \mathbf{R}^3$ and $\theta(t) \in SO(3)$ specify the position and orientation in a world coordinate system. We use a quaternion representation to represent the orientation with four parameters. $V(t) \in \mathbf{R}^3$ and $\omega(t) \in \mathbf{R}^3$ specify the linear and angular velocity coordinates. The time derivative of the state $q(t)$, called the simulation function $F(t, q(t))$, is governed by the ODE

$$F(t, q(t)) = \frac{d}{dt}(q(t)) = \frac{d}{dt}\begin{pmatrix} X(t) \\ \theta(t) \\ V(t) \\ \omega(t) \end{pmatrix} = \begin{bmatrix} V(t) \\ \frac{1}{2}(\theta(t) * \omega(t)) \\ g \\ -I(t)^{-1}\left(\frac{dI(t)}{dt}\omega(t)\right) \end{bmatrix} \quad (4.1)$$

Here, $I(t)$ is the inertia matrix in world coordinates, and $g \approx (0, -9.81, 0)$ is the acceleration due to gravity. The product $*$ refers to the quaternion multiplication. The state $q(t)$ at any time instant $t = t_f$ is determined by integrating Eq (4.1):

$$q(t_f) = q(t_0) + \int_{t_0}^{t_f} F(t, q(t)) dt \quad (4.2)$$

The state at any time $q(t)$ depends on the initial state $q(t_0)$ and inertial matrix. In this paper, we assume that the inertia matrix is known. Consequently, it is sufficient to solve for the initial state, which we denote by $\mathbf{p_{obj}}$.

4.2 Estimating Parameters from 3D Data

The state of the body $q(t)$ describes the configuration of the body at any time. From the state $q(t_i)$ at any time t_i, we can compute the state $q(t_j)$ at any other time t_j by running the simulation forwards or backwards. However, obtaining the full state information from the real world requires linear and angular velocity measurements, which are hard to measure accurately.

4.3 Estimating Parameters from Video

This section describes techniques to extract the simulation parameters $\mathbf{p} = (\mathbf{p_{obj}}, \mathbf{p_{env}})$ from video. In this paper, we recover the object parameters $\mathbf{p_{obj}}$ and gravity direction $\mathbf{p_{env}}$. The gravity direction in our framework is encoded by two angles (tilt and roll). Video provides strong cues about the instantaneous pose and velocities of an object. However, the complex motion of a tumbling rigid body limits the information that can be reliably extracted from video. In particular, it is difficult to track a point on a tumbling object over many frames because of self occlusion. The high speeds of typical tumbling motions induces significant motion blur making measurements like optical flow very noisy. In contrast, it is easier to measure the bounding box or silhouettes of a tumbling body.

We solve for simulation parameters $\mathbf{p}$ by minimizing the least square error between the silhouettes from video and silhouettes from the simulation at each frame. The details of this optimization are given in Section 5. The object parameters in our formulation include both initial position and velocities. Alternatively, we can reduce the search space by first recovering the 3D pose (position and orientation) from the sequence using prior vision techniques, and then optimizing for the velocities that generate the set of 3D poses. Several researchers in the recognition community describe algorithms to recover the 3D pose of an object from silhouettes [13,10]. Let $(\boldsymbol{X}(t_0), \boldsymbol{\theta}(t_0)), ..., (\boldsymbol{X}(t_k), \boldsymbol{\theta}(t_k))$ be the sequence of poses computed from a sequence of k frames. The optimization algorithm finds *a feasible* solution for the initial linear and angular velocity by minimizing the following objective function:

$$\min_{\boldsymbol{\omega}(t_0), \boldsymbol{v}(t_0)} \sum_{i=t_0, t_1 ... t_k} (\boldsymbol{X}(i) - \boldsymbol{X}^s(i))^2 + (\boldsymbol{\theta}(i) - \boldsymbol{\theta}^s(i))^2 \qquad (4.3)$$

where $\boldsymbol{X}^s(t_j)$ is the position and $\boldsymbol{\theta}^s(t_j)$ is the orientation of the object (in simulation) at time $t = t_j$ for the current estimate of inital velocities $\boldsymbol{v}(t_0)$ and $\boldsymbol{\omega}(t_0)$. Section 5 provides details on computing the analytical derivatives required for this minimization.

Although this method reduces the number of variables to be optimized, its performance depends on the accuracy of the pose estimates obtained from silhouettes. Since recognition-based methods do not enforce dynamics (they operate on a per frame basis), they might introduce discontinuities in pose measurements, leading to incorrect solutions for initial velocities. Hence, we decided to optimize for the pose and velocity and gravity parameters simultaneously in our framework. However, the error space with our formulation has several local minima, and hence our technique is sensitive to initialization. Moreover, fast tumbling motion could result in aliasing problems, especially with slow cameras. Hence, the solution obtained from optimization is not *unique*. The details of this optimization are given in Section 5.

5 Optimization

This section describes the details of the unconstrained optimization employed to estimate physical parameters from video. The algorithm solves for the object, camera, and environment parameters simultaneously which generate a simulation that *best matches* the video clip. We use shape-based metrics to compare the real and simulated motions. The resulting objective function computes the sum squared differences of the metric over all the frames in the sequence. Our algorithm works offline and analyzes all frames in the video sequence to compute the parameters. We first preprocess the video to obtain a background model of the scene. Then, we segment the moving object and compute its bounding box and silhouette at each frame. The bounding box **B** is stored a vector of four numbers, which are the positions of its extreme corners. The silhouette **S** is represented by a binary image enclosed within the bounding box.

Recall that the motion of a rigid body is fully determined by the parameters **p**. For a given set of parameters, the optimizer simulates the motion to compute the bounding boxe and silhouette at each frame. It also computes the gradients of the metrics, which is used to update the parameters in the next optimization step. The goal of the optimization algorithm is to minimize the deviation between the silhouettes of the simulated motion and the silhouettes detected in the video sequence. We provide an initial estimate for the parameters **p** and use a gradient descent to update it at each step of the optimization. Gradient based methods are fast, and with reasonable initialization, converge quickly to the correct local minima.

5.1 Objective Function

The objective function measures the difference between the motion observed in video and the motion computed in the simulation. For example, at every frame, our implementation performs a pixel by pixel comparison between the silhouette from simulation and silhouette from video and computes a sum squared difference. This amounts to counting the non-overlapping pixels between the two silhouettes at each frame. This difference is accumulated over all the frames in the sequence. Alternatively, we could compare the second moments of the silhouette at each frame, and compute a SSD of the moments over all frames. The objective function for the silhouette metric has the form:

$$E = \min_{\mathbf{p}} \sum_{i=t_1, t_2 \ldots t_f} (\mathbf{S}^v(i) - \mathbf{S}^s(i, \mathbf{p}))^2 \qquad (5.1)$$

where $\mathbf{S}^v(i)$ and $\mathbf{S}^s(i)$ is the silhouette obtained at time i from the video and simulation respectively. Gradient descent is used to minimize this error function. The update rule for parameters is:

$$\mathbf{p} = \mathbf{p} + \lambda \frac{\partial E}{\partial \mathbf{p}} \qquad (5.2)$$

where λ is the magnitude of the step in the gradient direction. The following subsections describe the gradient computation in detail.

5.2 Gradient Computation

The optimization algorithm requires computing the gradients of the objective function. This in turn, requires computing the gradients of the silhouette at each frame. Although the state $\mathbf{q}(t)$ is a continuous function of the parameters $\mathbf{p}$ (Eq. 4.1), quantities like bounding boxes and silhouettes are not continuously differentiable functions of parameters $\mathbf{p}$. One straightforward approach is to compute the gradients of the metrics (e.g. $\partial \mathbf{S}(\mathbf{q})/\partial \mathbf{p}$) numerically, using finite differences. This, however, has two major drawbacks. First, computing the gradients of the metric with respect to $\mathbf{p_{obj}}$ (initial conditions) using finite differences is extremely slow, since the simulation function has to be evaluated several times during the gradient computation. Secondly, determining robust step sizes that yield an accurate finite difference approximation is difficult. We resort to a hybrid approach for computing the gradients. First, we analytically compute the gradients of the state with respect to parameters $\partial \mathbf{q}(t)/\partial \mathbf{p}$. We then compute the derivative of the metric with respect to the state using finite differences, e.g. $\partial \mathbf{S}(\mathbf{q})/\partial \mathbf{q}$. We use the chain rule to combine the two gradients:

$$\frac{\partial \mathbf{S}}{\partial \mathbf{p}} = \frac{\partial \mathbf{S}}{\partial \mathbf{q}} \frac{\partial \mathbf{q}}{\partial \mathbf{p}} \qquad (5.3)$$

Since the metric (e.g. silhouette $\mathbf{S}$) depends only on the position and orientation terms of the state $\mathbf{q}$, the gradient $\partial \mathbf{S}(\mathbf{q})/\partial \mathbf{q}$ can be computed quickly and accurately using finite differences. Finally, we note that the camera parameters do not depend on the 3D state of the object. Therefore, we use finite differences to compute the gradients with respect to gravity vector $\mathbf{p_{env}}$.

Jacobian for Free Flight. The motion of a rigid body in free flight (in 3D) is fully determined by the control vector $\mathbf{p_{obj}}$. Rewriting Eq. (4.1) to show this dependence explicitly yields:

$$\frac{d\mathbf{q}(t)}{dt} = \mathbf{F}(t, \mathbf{p_{obj}}) \qquad (5.4)$$

We evaluate the jacobian $\partial \mathbf{q}(t_f)/\partial \mathbf{p_{obj}}$ at time t_f by numerically integrating the equation

$$\frac{d}{dt}\left(\frac{\partial \mathbf{q}(t)}{\partial \mathbf{p_{obj}}}\right) = \frac{\partial \mathbf{F}(t, \mathbf{p_{obj}})}{\partial \mathbf{p_{obj}}} \qquad (5.5)$$

until time t_f with the initial condition $\partial \mathbf{q}(t_0)/\partial \mathbf{p_{obj}}$. We use a fourth order Runge-Kutta method with fixed step size to perform this numerical integration.

Derivatives of Silhouettes. We use finite differences to compute the derivative of silhouette with respect to the current state $\mathbf{q}(t)$. We compute the silhouette at the given state by rendering the simulated object. The derivative of the silhouette with respect to a scalar component q_i of the state $\mathbf{q}$ has the form:

$$\frac{\partial \mathbf{S}}{\partial q_i} = \lim_{\Delta q_i \to 0} \left(\frac{\mathbf{S}(\mathbf{q}+\Delta q_i) - \mathbf{S}(\mathbf{q})}{\Delta q_i}\right) \qquad (5.6)$$

The jacobian of the silhouette is obtained by applying chain rule

$$\frac{\partial \mathbf{S}}{\partial \mathbf{p_{obj}}} = \frac{\partial \mathbf{S}}{\partial \mathbf{q}} \frac{\partial \mathbf{q}}{\partial \mathbf{p_{obj}}} \qquad (5.7)$$

Derivatives with Respect to Gravity direction. We compute the jacobian of the silhouette with respect to a scalar component p^i_{env} of the gravity direction $\mathbf{p_{env}}$ using finite differences, as shown:

$$\frac{\partial \mathbf{S}}{\partial p^i_{env}} = \lim_{\Delta p^i_{env} \to 0} \left(\frac{\mathbf{S}(\mathbf{p_{env}} + \Delta p^i_{env}) - \mathbf{S}(\mathbf{p_{env}})}{\Delta p^i_{env}} \right) \quad (5.8)$$

The overall jacobian matrix is given by:

$$\frac{\partial \mathbf{S}}{\partial \mathbf{p}} = \begin{pmatrix} \frac{\partial \mathbf{S}}{\partial \mathbf{p_{obj}}} \\ \frac{\partial \mathbf{S}}{\partial \mathbf{p_{env}}} \end{pmatrix} \quad (5.9)$$

6 Results

Our system has three main modules: *Preprocessor*, *Rigid body simulator* and *Optimizer*. We first preprocess the video sequence to compute the silhouettes and bounding boxes of the rigid object. We build a background model for the scene and use autoregressive filters [2] to segment the moving object from the background. We then compute the bounding box and silhouette metrics from the segmented image at each frame. Our tumbling video sequences are typically 35-40 frames long when captured with a digital camera operating at 30 Hz. The optimizer typically takes a couple of minutes to compute the parameters from the sequence on a SGI R12000 processor.

Experiment 1: The goal of this example is to match the motion of a simulation with a complex tumbling motion of a T shaped object (Figure 3). Our user interface lets the user specify an approximate value for the initial positions and velocities of the body. The algorithm robustly estimates the initial position and linear velocity, even with a poor initial guess. However, it is very sensitive to the initial estimate of the orientation and angular velocities. From numerous experiments, we have found the error space of the silhouette metric to be very noisy, containing many local minima. However, with a reasonable initialization for the orientation and angular velocity parameters, we find that our algorithm converges to a reasonable local minima. This convergence is seen in Figure 3(a), where the overall motion of the simulation closely matches the motion in video. We superimpose the bounding boxes obtained from simulation onto the frames from video (the white boxes in the first row) to show the match. We also show the match between the trajectory of a corner point in video with the corresponding trajectory in simulation. The small square boxes show the trajectory of a corner point, identified by hand, from the video sequence. These trajectories are shown for visualization purposes only and are not used in the optimization. As the algorithm proceeds, the trajectory of the 3D corner point in simulation (black line) overlaps with these boxes. This sequence also highlights some limitations with our optimization framework and metrics. Row (c) shows an example where the simulated and the real object have totally different orientations but have silhouettes that look very similar. Finally, we note that our algorithm generates a 3D reconstruction of the object's trajectory that matches the given video sequence.

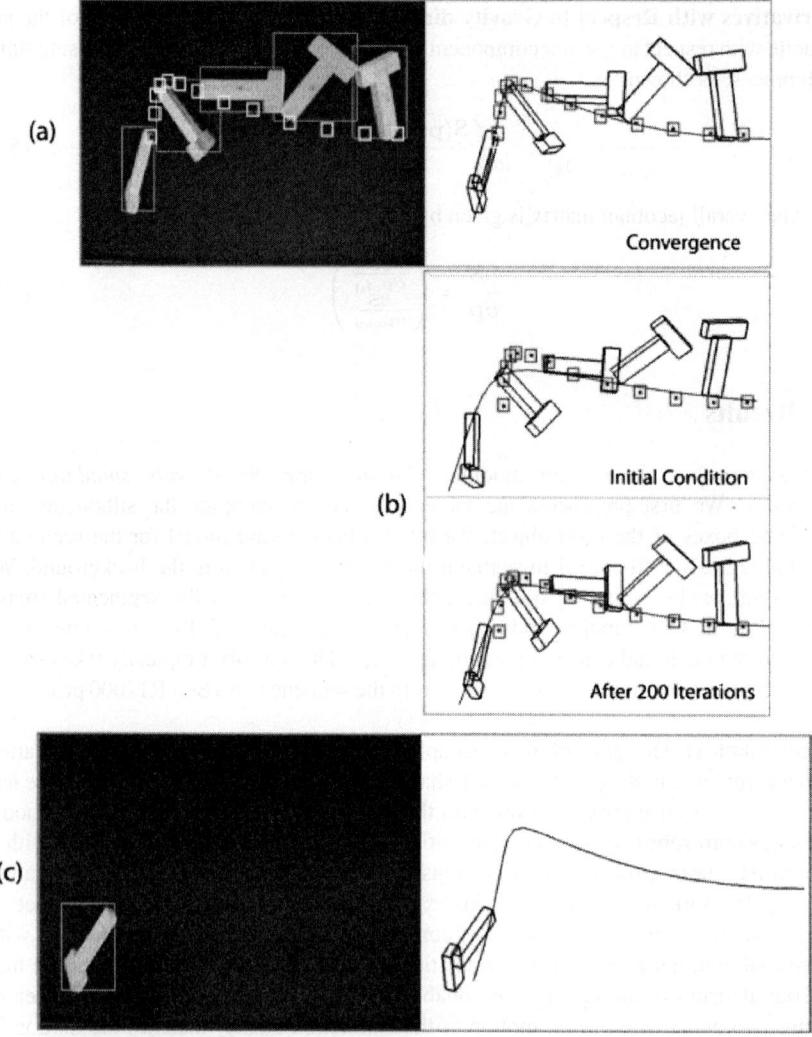

Fig. 3. Computing the parameters of a T-shaped object thrown in the air. The first row (a) shows a few frames from the video (right to left) and the corresponding physical simulation generated by our algorithm. The bounding boxes from simulation are superimposed over the video to show the match. The small square boxes indicate the trajectory of a corner point in video. The thin line indicates the motion of the corresponding corner in simulation. Row (b) shows the results of the algorithm at different stages of optimization. Notice that the match improves as the number of iterations increases. Row (c) highlights a limitation of the silhouette based metric. Note that although the orientation of the simulated object is flipped relative to the real object, they both have similar silhouettes

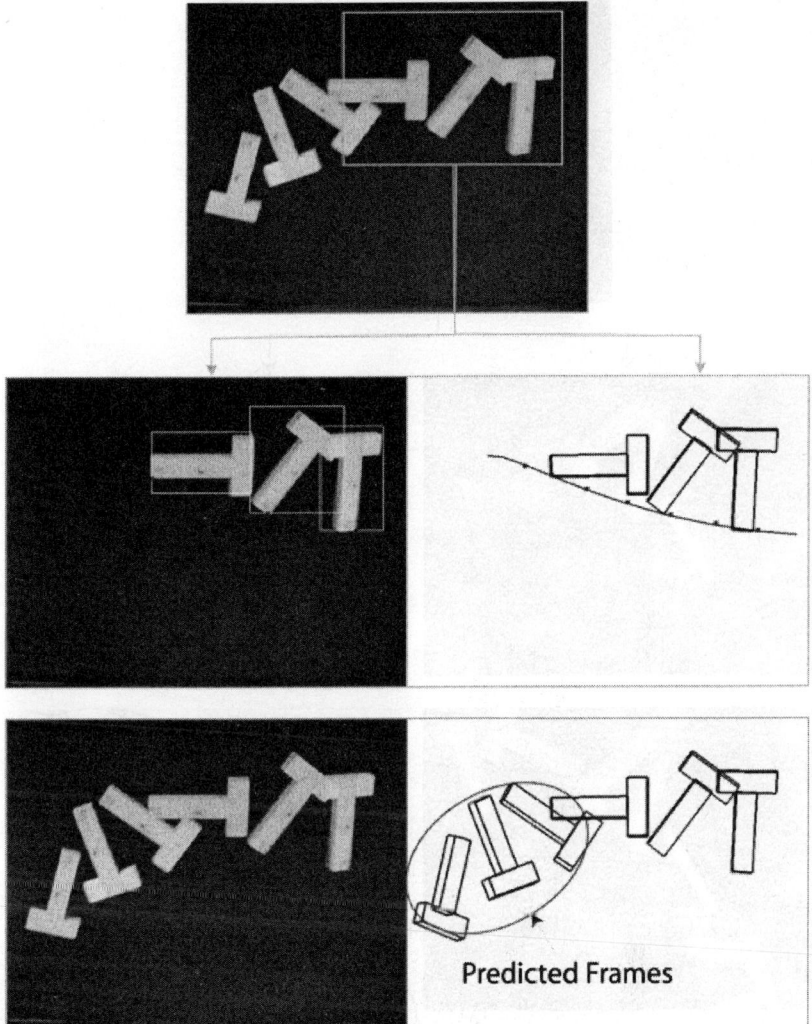

Fig. 4. Predicting the motion of tumbling bodies in video. The first row shows a long sequence of a tumbling object thrown from right to left. We select a portion of this sequence and match its motion in simulation. The second row shows a portion of the original clip contained inside the yellow box, and the corresponding frames of a simulation. We use these parameters to predict the motion of the tumbling object across the whole sequence.

Experiment 2: The objective of this experiment is to predict the motion of a rigid-body in a long video sequence of free flight from a subset of frames of the same sequence. Figures 4 and 5 show two different video clips of a rigid body in free flight, with different

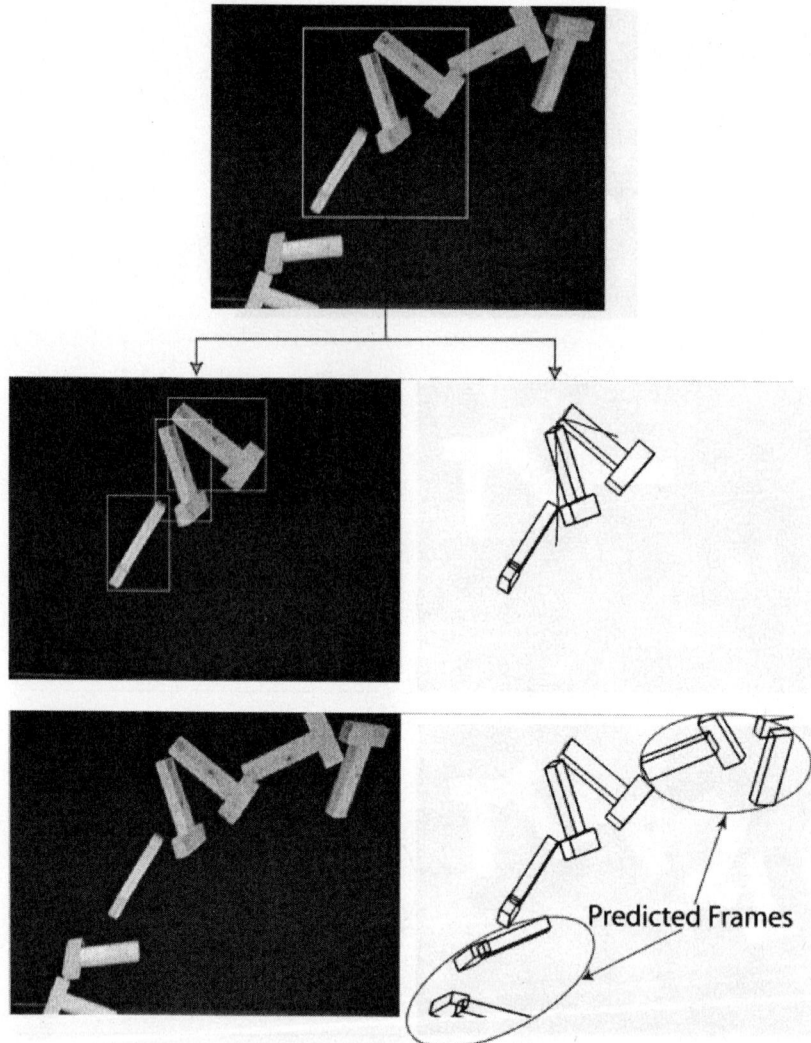

Fig. 5. Predicting the motion of a complicated tumbling object. The second row shows the match between a small portion of the video clip and a simulation. The simulation matches the video quite well for the frames on which it optimized, but the small errors propogates to larger error in the predicted frames.

motion trajectories. We match the motion of the shorter clip to a simulation and use the simulation parameters to predict the motion of the longer clip.

In Figure 4, the object tumbles about its major axis, and the essence of this motion is captured in the shorter sequence. Hence the simulation parameters computed by matching this small sequence correctly predicts the motion in the overall clip. However, the motion of the object in Figure 5 is about the body's intermediate axis, and is much more complicated. Small errors in the estimated values of simulation parameters results in large orientation error in the predicted frames, as time increases. We see this effect in the results obtained in Figure 5.

Experiment 3: Our algorithm optimizes the direction of the gravity vector along with the motion parameters from a video sequence. Figure 6 shows results of roll correction performed using the parameters obtained from our optimization algorithm. The first row shows four frames of a video sequence captured from a camera with significant roll distortion. We compute the camera pitch and roll parameters which minimize the silhouette error. These parameters are used to warp the original sequence such that the camera vertical axis aligns with the gravity vector. The last row shows the result of this rectification. Notice that the people in the first row are in a slanted pose, whereas they are upright in the last row.

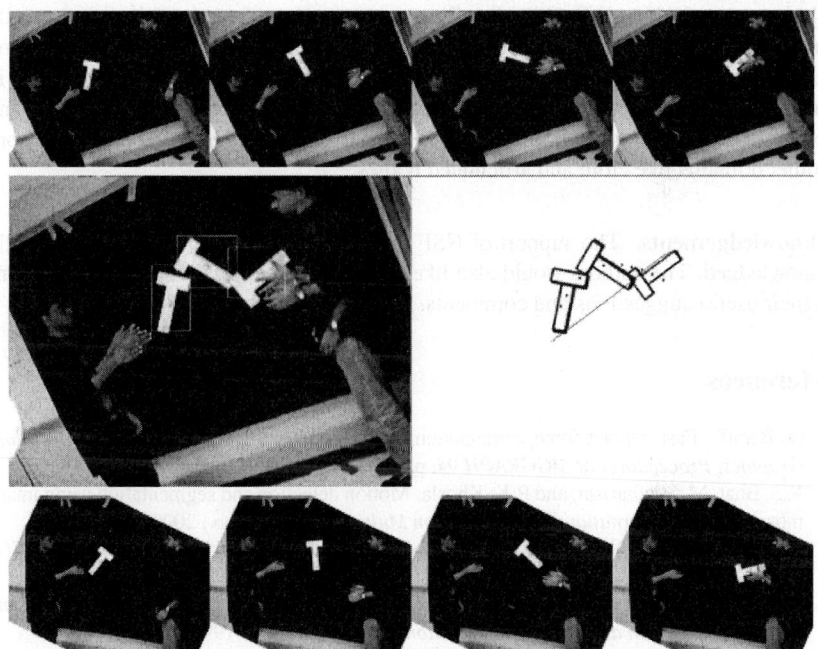

Fig. 6. Using rigid-body motion estimation to correct for camera roll. An object is thrown in the air from left to right (top row) and captured from a video camera with significant roll. The video is difficult to watch on account of the image rotation. The motion of the object is estimated (middle row), as well as the camera roll (defined by the orientation with respect to the gravity direction). The video frames are automatically rectified to correct for the camera roll.

7 Conclusion

This paper describes an optimization framework to extract the motion and underlying physical parameters of a rigid body from video. The algorithm minimizes the least square error between the silhouettes obtained in simulation and silhouettes from video at each frame. The paper presents a gradient based approach to perform this minimization.

The error space of the silhouettes is very noisy with many local minima. From our experiments, we have noticed several different combinations of initial orientations and angular velocities which result in silhouette sequences that look *similar*. This is especially true for shorter sequences, where there is not enough information (from video) to uniquely identify the true control parameters. Moreover, the performance of our simple gradient descent algorithm is sensitive to the initial guess for the control parameters. We are working on implementing better gradient based optimization algorithms and using a mixture of discrete-continuous techniques for multiple initializations. Silhouette metric has difficulties handling motions of symmetric objects, especially when multiple poses of the object project to similar silhouettes. We are investigating the use of simple color based techniques to alleviate this problem. We are interested in optimizing for the object intrinsic parameters like the location of the center of mass and the inertia matrix using our framework. We are also looking at applying our framework to other domains like cloth and articulated bodies.

Acknowledgements. The support of NSF under ITR grant IIS-0113007 is gratefully acknowledged. The authors would also like to thank Alfred Rizzi and Jessica Hodgins for their useful suggestions and comments.

References

1. D. Baraff. Fast contact force computation for nonpenetrating rigid bodies. *In Computer Graphics, Proceedings of SIGGRAPH 94*, pages 23–34, 1994.
2. K.S. Bhat, M. Saptharishi, and P. K. Khosla. Motion detection and segmentation using image mosaics. *IEEE International Conference on Multimedia and Expo.*, 2000.
3. B.E. Bishop and M.W. Spong. Vision-based control of an air hockey playing robot. *IEEE Control Systems*, pages 23–32, June 1999.
4. C. Bregler. Learning and recognizing human dynamics in video sequences. *Proc. IEEE Conf. on Computer Vision and Pattern Recognition*, pages 8–15, June 1997.
5. S. Chandrashekhar and R. Chellappa. Passive navigation in a partially known environment. *Proc. IEEE Workshop on Visual Motion*, pages 2–7, 1991.
6. S. Chenney and D.A. Forsyth. Sampling plausible solutions to multi-body constraint problems. *In Computer Graphics, Proceedings of SIGGRAPH 00*, pages 219–228, 2000.
7. Q. Delamarre and O. Faugeras. 3d articulated models and multi-view tracking with silhouettes. *In Proc. of the Seventh International Conference on Computer Vision, IEEE*, pages 716–721, 1999.
8. O. Faugeras, Q.T Luong, and T. Papadopoulo. *The Geometry of Multiple Images*. MIT Press, 2001.
9. B.K. Ghosh and E.P. Loucks. A perspective theory for motion and shape estimation in machine vision. *SIAM Journal of Control and Optimization*, 33(5):1530–1559, 1995.

10. W.E. Grimson. *Object recognition by computer: the role of geometric constraints.* MIT Press, 1990.
11. C. Harris. Tracking with rigid models. In A. Blake and A. Yuille, editors, *Active Vision*, chapter 4, pages 59–73. The MIT Press, 1992.
12. R. Hartley and A. Zisserman. *Multiple View Geometry in Computer Vision.* Cambridge University Press, 2000.
13. D. Jacobs and R. Basri. 3-d to 2-d pose determination with regions. *International Journal of Computer Vision*, 34(2/3):123–145, 1999.
14. P. K. Khosla. Estimation of robot dynamics parameters: Theory and application. *International Journal of Robotics and Automation*, 3(1):35–41, 1988.
15. Y. Masutani, T. Iwatsu, and F. Miyazaki. Motion estimation of unknown rigid body under no external forces and moments. *IEEE International Conference on Robotics and Automation*, 2:1066–1072, 1994.
16. D. Metaxas and D. Terzopoulos. Shape and nonrigid motion estimation through physics-based synthesis. *IEEE Trans. Pattern Analysis and Machine Intelligence*, 15(6):580–591, 1993.
17. A. Pentland and B. Horowitz. Recovery of nonrigid motion and structure. *IEEE Trans. Pattern Analysis and Machine Intelligence*, 13(7):730–742, July 1991.
18. J. Popovic. *Interactive Design of Rigid-Body Simulation for Computer Animation.* Ph.D Thesis, CMU-CS-01-140, Carnegie Mellon University, July 2001.
19. J. Popovic, S.M. Seitz, M. Erdmann, Z. Popovic, and A. Witkin. Interactive manipulation of rigid body simulations. *In Computer Graphics, Proceedings of SIGGRAPH 00*, pages 209–218, 2000.
20. A.A. Rizzi and D.E. Koditschek. An active visual estimator for dexterous manipulation. *IEEE Transactions on Robotics and Automation*, 12(5):697–713, 1996.
21. J. Schick and E.D. Dickmanns. Simultaneous estimation of 3d shape and motion of objects by computer vision. *Proc. IEEE Workshop on Visual Motion*, pages 256–261, 1991.
22. K. Symon. *Mechanics, Third Edition.* Addison-Wesley Publishing Company, Reading, Massachussetts, 1971.
23. C. Tomasi and T. Kanade. Shape and motion from image streams under orthography: a factorization method. *International Journal of Computer Vision*, 9(2):137–154, November 1992.
24. C. Wren. *Understanding Expressive Action.* Ph.D Thesis, Massachusetts Institute of Technology, March 2000.

Building Roadmaps of Local Minima of Visual Models

Cristian Sminchisescu and Bill Triggs

INRIA Rhône-Alpes, 655 avenue de l'Europe, 38330 Montbonnot, France.
{Cristian.Sminchisescu,Bill.Triggs}@inrialpes.fr
http://www.inrialpes.fr/movi/people/{Sminchisescu,Triggs}

Abstract. Getting trapped in suboptimal local minima is a perennial problem in model based vision, especially in applications like monocular human body tracking where complex nonlinear parametric models are repeatedly fitted to ambiguous image data. We show that the trapping problem can be attacked by building 'roadmaps' of nearby minima linked by *transition pathways* — paths leading over low 'cols' or 'passes' in the cost surface, found by locating the *transition state* (codimension-1 saddle point) at the top of the pass and then sliding downhill to the next minimum. We know of no previous vision or optimization work on numerical methods for locating transition states, but such methods do exist in computational chemistry, where transitions are critical for predicting reaction parameters. We present two families of methods, originally derived in chemistry, but here generalized, clarified and adapted to the needs of model based vision: *eigenvector tracking* is a modified form of damped Newton minimization, while *hypersurface sweeping* sweeps a moving hypersurface through the space, tracking minima within it. Experiments on the challenging problem of estimating 3D human pose from monocular images show that our algorithms find nearby transition states and minima very efficiently, but also underline the disturbingly large number of minima that exist in this and similar model based vision problems.

Keywords: Model based vision, global optimization, saddle points, 3D human tracking.

1 Introduction

Many visual modelling problems can be reduced to cost minimization in a high dimensional parameter space. Local minimization is usually feasible, but practical cost functions often have large numbers of local minima and it can be very difficult to ensure that the desired one is found. Exhaustive search rapidly becomes impracticable in more than 2–3 dimensions, so most global optimization methods focus on heuristics for finding 'good places to look next'. This includes both deterministic techniques like branch-and-bound and pattern search, and stochastic importance samplers like simulated annealing, genetic algorithms and tabu search.

Unfortunately, global optimization remains expensive with any of these methods. In this paper we develop an alternative strategy based on building 1-D 'roadmaps' of the salient minima, linked by paths passing over **saddle points**: stationary (zero gradient) points that have one or more negative curvature directions, so that they represent 'cols' rather than 'hollows' in the cost surface. We will restrict attention to **transition states** (saddles with just one negative curvature direction), as these give the minimum-peak-cost pathways between local minima. Our focus is on methods for finding the salient transitions surrounding an initial minimum. Given these, adjacent minima can be found simply by sliding downhill using local minimization.

Despite the omnipresence of local minima, we know of no previous vision or optimization work on systematic numerical algorithms for locating transition states. As far as we can judge, this was generally considered to be intractable. However such methods *do* exist in the computational chemistry / solid state physics community, where transitions are central to the theory of chemical reactions[1]. We will describe two families of transition-finding algorithms that have roots in computational chemistry: **eigenvector tracking** is a modified form of damped Newton minimization, while **hypersurface sweeping** sweeps a moving hypersurface through the space, tracking minima within it. These methods are potentially useful in almost any visual modelling problem where local minima cause difficulties. Examples include model based tracking, reconstruction under correspondence ambiguities, and various classes of camera pose and calibration problems. We present experimental results on monocular model based human pose estimation.

1.1 Literature Review

We start with a brief overview of the computational chemistry / solid state physics literature on locating transition states. This literature should be accessible to vision workers with high-school chemistry and a working knowledge of optimization. However the underlying ideas can be difficult to disentangle from chemistry-specific heuristics, and some papers are rather naive about numerical optimization issues. We therefore give a self-contained treatment of two of the most promising approaches below, in numerical analysts language.

A transition state is a local minimum along its $n-1$ positive curvature directions in parameter space, but a local maximum along its remaining negative curvature one. So transition state search methods often reduce to a series of $(n-1)$-D minimizations, while moving or maximizing along the remaining direction. The main differences lie in the methods of choosing the directions to use.

Eigenvector tracking methods [10, 17, 6, 39, 40, 23, 16, 31, 24, 15, 11, 5] are modified Newton minimizers designed to increase the cost along one of the curvature eigendirections, rather than reducing it along all eigendirections. If the lowest curvature direction is chosen they attempt to find the lowest gradient path to a transition state by walking along the 'floor' of the local cost 'valley'. However this behaviour can not be guaranteed [19, 36, 18] and valleys need not even lead to saddle points: they might be 'blind', with the transition states located off to one side. An early method [17] used explicit Newton

---

[1] Atomic assemblies can be modelled in terms of the potential energy induced by interactions among their atoms, *i.e.* by an energy function defined over the high-dimensional configuration space of the atoms' relative positions. A typical assembly spends most of its time near an energy minimum (a stable or quasi-stable state), but thermal perturbations may sometimes cause it to cross a transition state to an adjacent minimum (a chemical reaction). The energy of the lowest transition joining two minima determines the likelihood of such a perturbation, and hence the reaction pathway and rate.

minimization in the $(n-1)$-D space obtained by eliminating the coordinate with the largest overlap with the desired up-hill direction. Later quasi-Newton methods use Lagrange multipliers [6, 39, 40] or shifted Hessian eigenvalues [31, 24, 15, 11, 5] to ensure that the cost function is increased along the chosen 'uphill eigenvector' direction while being minimized in all orthogonal ones. Maintaining a consistent direction to follow can be delicate and several competing methods exist, including using a fixed eigenvector index [17, 6, 39, 40, 23, 16] and attempting to track corresponding eigenvectors from step to step [31, 24, 15, 11, 5]. Eigenvector tracking can be motivated as a 'virtual cost minimization' obtained by inverting the sign of the negative Hessian eigenvalue and the corresponding gradient component [22, 15]. This gives an intuitive algebraic analogy with minimization, but none of its convergence guarantees as the virtual cost function changes at each step.

Constraint based methods [10, 1, 2, 3, 22, 16] aim to use some form of constrained optimization to guarantee more systematic global progress towards a transition state. Crippen & Sheraga's early method [10] builds an uphill path by minimizing in the orthogonal hyperplane of a ray emanating from the initial minimum and passing through the current configuration. Mousseau [22] uses a similar but less rigorous technique based on changing the gradient sign in one direction followed by conjugate root-finding in the other directions. Barkema [3] uses a biased repulsive spherical potential and optimizes subject to this soft constraint. New minima are found but the method does not attempt to pass exactly through a saddle point. Abashkin & Russo [1, 2] minimize on successively larger radius hyperspheres centred at a minimum, and also include a method for refining approximately located saddle points. The use of hyperspheres forces the search to move initially along the valley floor of the cost surface [18], so usually at most two distinct saddles can be found. Below we show how to steer the initial search along any desired direction using ellipsoidal surfaces.

There are also stochastic search methods designed to find transition states. See our companion paper [35] for references.

2 Algorithms for Finding Transition States

Many efficient methods exist for finding local minima of smooth high dimensional cost surfaces. Minimization allows strong theoretical guarantees as the reduction in the function value provides a clear criterion for monitoring progress. For example, for a bounded-below function in a bounded search region, any method that ensures 'sufficient decrease' in the function at each step is 'globally convergent' to some local minimum [13]. Finding saddle points is much harder as there is no universal progress criterion and no obvious analogue of a 'downhill' direction. Newton-style iterations provide rapid *local* convergence near the saddle, but it is not so obvious how to find sufficiently nearby starting points. We will consider several methods that extend the convergence zone. We are mainly interested in saddles as starting points for finding adjacent minima, so we will focus on methods that can be started from a minimum and tuned to find nearby transition states. (Efficient 'rubber band relaxation' methods also exist for finding the transition state(s) linking two given minima [29]).

2.1 Newton Methods

Let $f(\mathbf{x})$ be the cost function being optimized over its n-D parameter vector $\mathbf{x}$, $\mathbf{g} \equiv \frac{\partial f}{\partial \mathbf{x}}$ be the function's **gradient** and $\mathbf{H} \equiv \frac{\partial^2 f}{\partial \mathbf{x}^2}$ be its **Hessian**. We seek **transition states**, stationary points $\mathbf{g}(\mathbf{x}) = \mathbf{0}$ at which the Hessian has one negative and $n{-}1$ positive eigenvalues. If there is a stationary point at $\mathbf{x}{+}\boldsymbol{\delta x}$, a first order Taylor approximation at $\mathbf{x}$ gives $\mathbf{0} = \mathbf{g}(\mathbf{x}{+}\boldsymbol{\delta x}) \approx \mathbf{g}(\mathbf{x}) + \mathbf{H}\,\boldsymbol{\delta x}$. Solving this linear system for $\boldsymbol{\delta x}$ and iterating to refine the approximation gives the **Newton iteration**: $\mathbf{x} \leftarrow \mathbf{x}{+}\boldsymbol{\delta x}$ with update $\boldsymbol{\delta x} = -\mathbf{H}^{-1}\mathbf{g}$. When started sufficiently close to any regular[2] stationary point, Newton's method converges to it, but how close you need to be is a delicate point in practice.

For Newton-based minimization, convergence can be globalized by adding suitable damping to shorten the step and stabilize the iteration. The standard methods use the **damped Newton** update $\boldsymbol{\delta x} = -(\mathbf{H}{+}\lambda\mathbf{D})^{-1}\mathbf{g}$, where $\mathbf{D}$ is a positive diagonal matrix (often the identity). The damping factor $\lambda > 0$ is manipulated by the algorithm to ensure stable and reliable progress downhill towards the minimum. Damping can be viewed as Newton's method applied to a modified local model for f, whose gradient at $\mathbf{x}$ is unchanged but whose curvature is steepened to $\mathbf{H}{+}\lambda\mathbf{D}$.

Similarly, to reduce the step and stabilize the iteration near a saddle point, negative curvatures must be made more negative, and positive ones more positive. In a Hessian eigenbasis $\mathbf{H} = \mathbf{V}\mathbf{E}\mathbf{V}^\top$, where $\mathbf{E} = \mathrm{diag}(\lambda_1,...,\lambda_n)$ are the eigenvalues of $\mathbf{H}$ and the columns of $\mathbf{V}$ are its eigenvectors, the undamped Newton update becomes $\boldsymbol{\delta x} = -\mathbf{V}\,(\bar{g}_1/\lambda_1,\ldots,\bar{g}_n/\lambda_n)^\top$ where $\bar{g}_i \equiv (\mathbf{V}^\top\mathbf{g})_i$ are the eigen-components of the gradient. Damping can be introduced by replacing this with[3]:

$$\boldsymbol{\delta x} = -\mathbf{V}\,\mathbf{u}(\lambda), \quad \mathbf{u}(\lambda) \equiv \left(\frac{\bar{g}_1}{\lambda_1+\sigma_1\lambda},\ldots,\frac{\bar{g}_n}{\lambda_n+\sigma_n\lambda}\right)^\top = \left(\frac{\sigma_1\bar{g}_1}{\sigma_i\lambda_1+\lambda},\ldots,\frac{\sigma_n\bar{g}_n}{\sigma_n\lambda_n+\lambda}\right)^\top \quad (1)$$

where $\sigma_i = \pm 1$ is a desired sign pattern for the λ_i. Damping $\lambda > \max_i(-\sigma_i\lambda_i, 0)$ ensures that the denominators are positive, so that the iteration moves uphill to a maximum along the eigendirections with $\sigma_i = -1$ and downhill to a minimum along the others. At each step this can be viewed as the minimization of a virtual local function with curvatures $\sigma_i\lambda_i$ and sign-flipped gradients $\sigma_i\bar{g}_i$. But the model changes at each step so none of the usual convergence guarantees of well-damped minimization apply: f itself is *not* minimized.

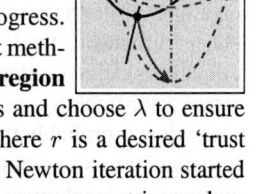

As in minimization, λ must be varied to ensure smooth progress. There are two main strategies for this: **Levenberg-Marquardt** methods manipulate λ directly, while the more sophisticated **trust region** ones maintain a local region of supposed-'trustworthy' points and choose λ to ensure that the step stays within it, e.g. $\|\boldsymbol{\delta x}(\lambda)\| = \|\mathbf{u}(\lambda)\| \lesssim r$ where r is a desired 'trust radius'. (Such a λ can be found efficiently with a simple 1-D Newton iteration started at large λ [13]). In both cases, convergence criteria and model accuracy metrics such as the relative f-prediction error:

---

[2] 'Regular' means that $\mathbf{H}$ is nonsingular and 2nd order Taylor expansion converges.

[3] There is nothing absolute about eigenvalues! Affine changes of coordinates leave the original Newton method unchanged but produce essentially inequivalent eigen-decompositions and dampings.

$$\beta = \left| \frac{f(\mathbf{x}+\delta\mathbf{x}) - f(\mathbf{x})}{\mathbf{g}^\top \delta\mathbf{x} + \delta\mathbf{x}^\top \mathbf{H}\delta\mathbf{x}/2} - 1 \right| \qquad (2)$$

are monitored, and the damping is increased (larger λ or shorter r) if the accuracy is low, decreased if it is high, and left unchanged if it is intermediate (*e.g.*, by scaling λ or r up or down by fixed constants).

As in minimization, if the exact Hessian is unavailable, quasi-Newton approximations based on previously computed gradients can be used. Positive definiteness is not required so update rules such as Powell's are preferred [5]: $\mathbf{H} \leftarrow \mathbf{H} - \frac{\delta\mathbf{x}^\top \boldsymbol{\xi}}{\|\delta\mathbf{x}\|^4} \delta\mathbf{x}\, \delta\mathbf{x}^\top + \frac{\boldsymbol{\xi}\, \delta\mathbf{x}^\top + \delta\mathbf{x}\, \boldsymbol{\xi}^\top}{\|\delta\mathbf{x}\|^2}$, where $\boldsymbol{\xi} = \mathbf{g}(\mathbf{x}+\delta\mathbf{x}) - \mathbf{g}(\mathbf{x}) - \mathbf{H}(\mathbf{x})\delta\mathbf{x}$.

2.2 Eigenvector Tracking

Now consider the choice of the signs σ_i. Roughly speaking, the damped iteration moves uphill to a maximum along directions with $\sigma_i = -1$ and downhill to a minimum along directions with $\sigma_i = +1$, *i.e.* it tries to find a stationary point whose principal curvatures λ_i have signs σ_i. To find minima we need $\sigma_i = +1$, and for transition states exactly one σ_i should be made negative[4]. The question is, which one.

This question is thornier than it may seem. To ensure continued progress we need to track and modify "the same" eigenvector(s) at each step. Unfortunately, there is no globally well defined correspondence rule linking eigenvectors at different points, especially given that the trajectory followed depends strongly on the eigenvector(s) chosen. So in practice we must resort to one of several imperfect correspondence heuristics. For transition state searches we need only track one eigenvector (the one that is given $\sigma_i = -1$), so we will concentrate on this case. A simple approach would be to choose a fixed direction in space (perhaps the initial eigendirection) and take the eigenvector with maximal projection along this direction. But many such directions are possible and the most interesting saddles may happen not to have negative curvature along the particular direction chosen. Alternatively, we can try to track a given eigenvector as it changes. The problem is that globally, eigendirections are by no means stable. Eigenvalues change as we move about the space, but generically (in codimension 1) they never cross. When they approach one another, the eigenbasis of their 2D subspace becomes ill-conditioned and slews around through roughly $90°$ to avoid the collision. Seen from a large enough scale, the eigenvalues do seem to cross with more or less constant eigenvectors, but on a finer scale there is no crossing, only a smooth but rapid change of eigendirection that is difficult to track accurately. Whichever of the two behaviours is desired, it is difficult to choose a step length that reliably ensures it, so the numerical behaviour of eigenvector-tracking methods is often somewhat erratic. In fact, the imprecise coarse scale view is probably the desired one: if we are tracking a large eigenvalue and hoping to reduce it to something negative, it will have to "pass through" each of the smaller eigenvalues. Tracking at too fine a scale is fatal as it (correctly) prevents such crossings, instead making the method veer off at right angles to the desired trajectory.

Even without these problems there would be no guarantee that a saddle point of the desired signature was found (*e.g.* the trajectory could diverge to infinity). Also, as with

---

[4] This holds irrespective of the λ_i and $\bar{g}_i$ at the *current* state, which affect only the damping required for stability.

other damped Newton methods, the whole process is strongly dependent on the affine coordinate system used. Nevertheless, eigenvector tracking is relatively lightweight, simple to implement, and it often works well in practice.

2.3 Hypersurface Sweeping

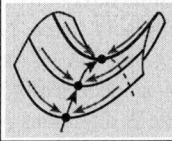

Eigenvector trackers do not enforce any notion of global progress, so they can sometimes behave erratically, *e.g.* cycling or stalling. To prevent this we can take a more global approach to the '$(n-1)$-D minimization and 1D maximization' required for transition state search. 'Hypersurface sweeping' approaches sweep an $(n-1)$-D hypersurface across the parameter space — typically a moving hyperplane or an expanding hyper-ellipsoid centred at the initial minimum — tracking local minima within the hypersurface and looking for temporal maxima in their function values. The intuition is that as the hypersurface expands towards a transition state, and assuming that it approaches along its negative curvature direction, the $(n-1)$-D minimization forces the hypersurface-minimum to move along the lowest path leading up to the saddle's 'col', and the 1-D maximization detects the moment at which the col is crossed. The method can not stall or cycle as the hypersurface sweeps through each point in the space exactly once.

The moving hypersurface can be defined either implicitly as the level sets $c(\mathbf{x}) = t$ of some function $c(\mathbf{x})$ on the parameter space (a linear form for hyperplanes, a quadratic one for hyper-ellipsoids...), or explicitly in terms of a local parametrization $\mathbf{x} = \mathbf{x}(\mathbf{y}, t)$ for some hypersurface-t-parametrizing $(n-1)$-D vector $\mathbf{y}$. The minimum-tracking problem becomes:

$$\text{local\_max}_t \ f_c(t) \quad \text{where} \quad f_c(t) \equiv \begin{cases} \text{local\_min}_{c(\mathbf{x})=t} \ f(\mathbf{x}) \\ \text{local\_min}_{\mathbf{y}} \ f(\mathbf{x}(\mathbf{y}, t)) \end{cases} \quad (3)$$

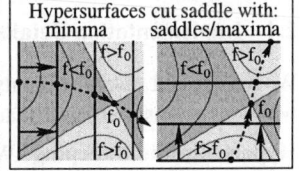

Different local minima on the hypersurface typically lead to different transition states. To find the lowest cost transition we would in principle have to track every minimum. More seriously, transitions that are cut by the hypersurfaces in negative curvature directions are missed: they appear as saddle points or local maxima within the hypersurface, and so can not be found by tracking only minima. Nor do local maxima of $f_c(t)$ always indicate true transition states. At any hypersurface-stationary point, f's isosurface is necessarily tangent to the local hypersurface: $\mathbf{g} \propto \frac{\partial c}{\partial \mathbf{x}}$ or $\mathbf{g}^\top \frac{\partial \mathbf{x}}{\partial \mathbf{y}} = \mathbf{0}$. The point is a hypersurface-minimum, -saddle, or -maximum respectively as the cost isosurface has higher/mixed/lower signed curvature than the local hypersurface (*i.e.* as the isosurface is locally inside/mixed/outside the hypersurface). At points where the moving hypersurface transitions from being outside to being mixed w.r.t. the local isosurface, the minimum being tracked abruptly disappears and the solution drops away to some other local minimum on the hypersurface, causing an abrupt 'sawtooth' maximum in $f_c(t)$ (generically, the hypersurface-minimum collides with a hypersurface-saddle and is annihilated). The search

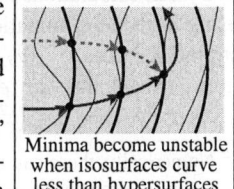

can continue from there, but it is important to verify that the maxima found really are saddle points.

As any given family of hypersurfaces is necessarily blind to some saddle orientations, it is wise to try a range of different families. Hyperplanes search preferentially along a fixed direction whereas hyper-ellipsoids can find saddles lying in any direction. The initial direction of the minimum trajectory is determined by the hyperplane normal or the ellipsoid shape. Near a minimum $\mathbf{x}_0$ with Hessian $\mathbf{H}_0$, consider the ellipsoids $c(\mathbf{x}) = (\mathbf{x}-\mathbf{x}_0)^\top \mathbf{A} (\mathbf{x}-\mathbf{x}_0) = t$, where $\mathbf{A}$ is some positive definite matrix. To second order, $f(\mathbf{x})$ generically has exactly two local minima on an infinitesimal ellipsoid $c(\mathbf{x}) = t$: the $\pm$ directions of the smallest eigenvector of the matrix pencil[5] $\mathbf{A}+\lambda\mathbf{H}$. For most $\mathbf{A}$ there are thus only two possible initial trajectories for the moving minimum, and so at most two first saddles will be found. To find additional saddles we need to modify $\mathbf{A}$. We can enforce any desired initial direction $\mathbf{u}$ by taking the 'neutral' search ellipsoids $\mathbf{A} = \mathbf{H}$ (on which f is constant to second order, so that all initial directions are equally good) and flattening them slightly relative to the cost isosurfaces in the $\mathbf{u}$ direction. E.g., to satisfy the Lagrange multiplier condition for a constrained minimum, $\frac{\partial c}{\partial \mathbf{x}} \propto \frac{\partial f}{\partial \mathbf{x}}$, we can take $\mathbf{A} = \mathbf{H} + \mu \frac{\mathbf{g}\mathbf{g}^\top}{\mathbf{u}^\top \mathbf{g}}$ where $\mathbf{g} = \mathbf{H}\mathbf{u}$ is the cost gradient (and hence isosurface normal) at displacements along $\mathbf{u}$ and μ is a positive constant, say $\mu \sim 0.1$ for mild flattening. Similarly, for hyperplanes $c(\mathbf{x}) = \mathbf{n}^\top (\mathbf{x}-\mathbf{x}_0) = t$ with normal $\mathbf{n}$, the initial minimum direction is $\mathbf{u} = \pm\mathbf{H}^{-1}\mathbf{n}$, so to search in direction $\mathbf{u}$ we need to take $\mathbf{n} = \mathbf{H}\mathbf{u}$.

The minimum tracking process is a fairly straightforward application of constrained optimization, but for completeness we summarize the equations needed in the appendix.

Summary: None of the current methods are foolproof. Damped Newton iteration is useful for refining estimated saddles but its convergence domain is too limited for general use. Eigenvector tracking extends the convergence domain but it is theoretically less sound (or at least, highly dependent on the step size and 'same eigenvector' heuristics). Hypersurface sweeping is better founded and provides at least weak guarantees of global progress, but it is more complex to implement and no single sweep finds all saddle points.

2.4 Implementation Details

We have tested several variants of each of the above methods. In the experiments below we focus on just two, which are summarized in fig. 1:

Hyper-ellipsoid sweeping: We start at a local minimum and use centred, curvature-eigenbasis-aligned ellipsoidal hypersurfaces flattened along one eigendirection, say the eth. This restricts the initial search to an eigendirection (the eth). This limitation could easily be removed, but gives a convenient, not-too-large set of directions to try. All calculations are performed in eigen-coordinates and the minimum is tracked using variable elimination (6) on x_e. In eigen-coordinates, the on-hypersurface constraint becomes $\sum_i (x_i/\sigma_i')^2 = t^2$, where the σ_i' are the principal standard deviations, except that the eth (eliminated) one is shrunk by say 20%. Solving for x_e gives $x_e(\mathbf{y},t) = \pm\sigma_e'(t^2 - \sum_{i \neq e}(x_i/\sigma_i')^2)^{1/2}$ where $\mathbf{y} = (x_1, ..., x_{e-1}, x_{e+1}, ..., x_n)$.

---

[5] Numerically, these can be found by generalized eigen-decomposition of $(\mathbf{A}, \mathbf{H})$, or standard eigen-decomposition of $\mathbf{L}^{-\top}\mathbf{H}\mathbf{L}^{-1}$ where $\mathbf{L}\mathbf{L}^\top$ is the Cholesky decomposition of $\mathbf{A}$.

Hyper-ellipsoid Sweeping Transition State Search
1. Initialization Given initial minimum $\mathbf{x}_0$ with Hessian $\mathbf{H}$, eigen-decompose $\mathbf{H}$ to $(\lambda_i, \mathbf{v}_i)$ with principal radii $\sigma_i = 1/\sqrt{\lambda_i}$. Choose an initial search eigen-direction e. Shrink σ_e by say 20% and prepare to eliminate x_e. Set initial step $\mathbf{x}_1 = \mathbf{x}_0 + t_1 \sigma_e \mathbf{v}_e$ where t_1 is say 3. Go to step 2.B.
2. Loop, Updating Hypersurface and Minimizing A. $k=k+1$. Estimate an initial $\mathbf{x}_k$ by linear extrapolation to the trust radius. Compute the resulting t_k. B. Minimize f on the t_k ellipsoid to get $f_c(t_k)$: $\mathbf{y}_k = \arg\min_\mathbf{y} f(\mathbf{x}_k(\mathbf{y}, t_k))$. C. Compute $f'_c = \frac{\partial}{\partial t} f_c(t_k)$. If $f'_c < \epsilon$ we are near or past saddle: go to step 3.A. Otherwise go to step 2.A.
3. Line Search for Transition State Refinement A. If $|f'_c| < \epsilon$, exit. B. $k=k+1$. Estimate t_{saddle} by linear interpolation of last two f'_c values. B. Optimize $\mathbf{y}_k$ as in step 2.B and go to step 3.A.
Eigenvector Tracking Transition State Search
Initialization Set starting point $\mathbf{x}_0$, initial tracking direction $\mathbf{t}$ and initial trust radius r.
Eigenvector Tracking Loop A. At $\mathbf{x}_k$, find $f_k, \mathbf{g}_k, \mathbf{H}_k$, the Hessian eigen-decomposition $(\lambda_i, \mathbf{v}_i)$ and eigen-basis gradient $\bar{g}_k$. Set n_- to the number of negative eigenvalues. If the problem has active internal constraints, project $\mathbf{t}$ onto the constraint surface. B. If $k > 0$ choose $e = \max_i |\mathbf{v}_i^T \mathbf{t}|$. Set $\alpha = |\mathbf{v}_e^T \mathbf{t}|$ and $\mathbf{t} = \mathbf{v}_e$. C. If $\lambda_e > 0$ set $\bar{g}_e = -\bar{g}_e$. Take an undamped Newton step if $n_- = 1$ and $\|\delta \mathbf{x}\| \leq r$. Otherwise take a damped one with λ chosen so that $\|\delta \mathbf{x}\| \leq r$. D. Find the new f and the modelling error β (2). If $\beta > 0.3$ (say) or $\alpha < 0.7$ (say), shrink the trust radius r by say 50%. Otherwise, if $\beta < 0.2$ (say) and we took a damped step, grow r by say 40%. E. If $\beta \geq 1$ go to step C. If $\|\mathbf{g}_k\| < \epsilon$ return success if $n_- = 1$, failure otherwise. Otherwise, go to step A.

Fig. 1. Our ellipsoid sweeping and eigenvector tracking algorithms for transition state search.

Derivatives are easily found. At each time step we predict the new minimum by linear extrapolation from the previous two, $\mathbf{x} = \mathbf{x}_k + r \frac{\mathbf{x}_k - \mathbf{x}_{k-1}}{\|\mathbf{x}_k - \mathbf{x}_{k-1}\|}$ where r is a trust region radius for $\delta \mathbf{x}$, then solve for the corresponding t_{k+1} using the ellipsoid constraint.

Eigenvector tracker: We use the damped Newton saddle step (1), moving away from the minimum by reversing the sign of the gradient in the tracked eigendirection if this has positive curvature. The damping $\lambda > 0$ is controlled to keep the step within a trust radius r and to dominate any undesired negative eigenvalues. The trust radius is set by monitoring the accuracy (2) of the local model for f.

In some of our target applications, the underlying problem has bound constraints that must be maintained. For hypersurface sweeping this just adds additional constraints to the within-hypersurface minimizations. For eigenvector following, our trust region step routine uses a projection strategy to handle constraints on x, and also projects the eigenvector-tracking direction t along the constraints to ensure stability.

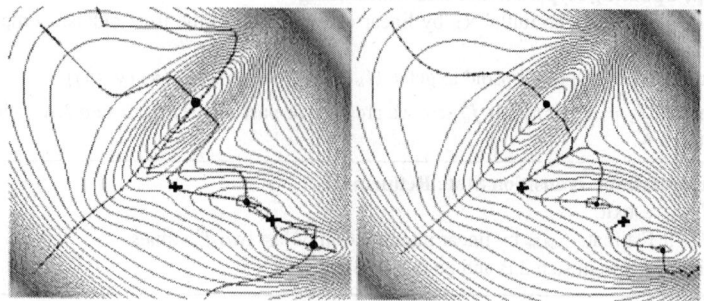

Fig. 2. Trajectories for the hyper-ellipsoid sweeping (left) and eigenvector following (right) algorithms on the Müller cost surface, initialized along the ± eigendirections of the 3 minima.

3 Human Domain Modelling

Representation: The 3D body model used in our human tracking experiments consists of a kinematic 'skeleton' of articulated joints controlled by angular joint parameters, covered by a 'flesh' built from superquadric ellipsoids with additional global deformations [4]. A typical model has 30–35 joint parameters; 8 internal proportions encoding the positions of the hip, clavicle and skull tip joints; and 9 deformable shape parameters for each body part. The complete model is encoded in a single large parameter vector x. During tracking and static pose estimation we usually estimate only joint parameters, but during initialization some length ratios are also estimated. In use, the superquadric surfaces are discretized into 2D meshes and the mesh nodes are mapped to 3D points using the kinematic body chain then projected to predicted image points $r_i(x)$ using perspective image projection.

Observation Likelihood: Robust model-to-image matching cost metrics are evaluated for each predicted image feature r_i, and the results are summed over all observations to produce the image contribution to the parameter space cost function. Cost gradient and Hessian contributions g_i, H_i are also computed and assembled. We use a robust combination of extracted-feature-based metrics and intensity-based ones such as optical flow, robustified normalized edge energy and potentials derived from silhouette distance transforms [32]. The feature-based terms associate the predictions r_i with nearby image features $\bar{r}_i$, the cost being a robust function of the prediction errors $\Delta r_i(x) = \bar{r}_i - r_i(x)$. We also give results for a simpler likelihood designed for model initialization, based on squared distances between reprojected model joints and their specified image positions.

Priors and Constraints: Our model [33, 34] incorporates both hard constraints (for joint angle limits) and soft priors (penalties for anthropometric model proportions, collision avoidance between body parts, and stabilization of useful but hard-to-estimate model parameters such as internal d.o.f. of the clavicle complex). In the experiments below we use mainly joint angle limits and body part non-interpenetration constraints. The priors provide additional cost, gradient and Hessian contributions for the optimization.

Estimation: We apply Bayes rule and maximize the total posterior probability to give locally MAP parameter estimates:

$$\log p(\mathbf{x}|\bar{\mathbf{r}}) \propto \log p(\mathbf{x}) + \log p(\bar{\mathbf{r}}|\mathbf{x}) = \log p(\mathbf{x}) - \int e(\bar{\mathbf{r}}_i|\mathbf{x}) \, di \quad (4)$$

Here, $p(\mathbf{x})$ is the prior on the model parameters, $e(\bar{\mathbf{r}}_i|\mathbf{x})$ is the cost density associated with observation i, and the integral is over all observations (assumed independent). Equation (4) gives the model likelihood in a single image, under the model priors but without initial state or temporal priors. During tracking, the temporal prior at time t is determined by the previous posterior $p(\mathbf{x}_{t-1}|\mathbf{R}_{t-1})$ and the system dynamics $p(\mathbf{x}_t|\mathbf{x}_{t-1})$, where we have collected the observations at time t into vector $\mathbf{r}_t$ and defined $\mathbf{R}_t = \{\mathbf{r}_1, \ldots, \mathbf{r}_t\}$. The posterior at t becomes:

$$p(\mathbf{x}_t|\mathbf{R}_t) \propto p(\bar{\mathbf{r}}_t|\mathbf{x}_t) \, p(\mathbf{x}_t) \int_{\mathbf{x}_{t-1}} p(\mathbf{x}_t|\mathbf{x}_{t-1}) \, p(\mathbf{x}_{t-1}|\mathbf{R}_{t-1})$$

Together $p(\mathbf{x}_t|\mathbf{x}_{t-1})$ and $p(\mathbf{x}_{t-1}|\mathbf{R}_{t-1})$ form the time t prior $p(\mathbf{x}_t|\mathbf{R}_{t-1})$ for the image correspondence search (4).

4 Experiments

We illustrate our transition state search algorithms on a 2 d.o.f. toy problem, and on 3D human pose and motion estimation from monocular images.

The Müller Potential: This simple analytical 2D cost function[6] is often used to illustrate transition state methods in chemistry. Fig. 2 shows its 3 minima and 2 saddles (the black dots and crosses) and plots the trajectories of the two methods starting from each minimum. The hypersurface sweeping algorithm is run for extended trajectories through several saddles and minima (left plot). In this simple example, a single sweep started at the top left minimum successfully finds all of the other minima and transition states.

Articulated 3D Human Motion Estimation: There is a large literature on human motion tracking but relatively little work on the thorny issue of local minima in the difficult 3D-from-monocular case. Cham & Rehg [7] combine local optimization and condensation sampling for 2D tracking. Deutscher et al [12] use an annealed sampling method and multiple cameras. Sidenbladh et al [30] use particle filtering with importance sampling based on a learned walking model. Sminchisescu & Triggs [34] combine robust constraint-consistent local continuous optimization with a covariance-scaled sampling

---

[6] It has the form: $V(x,y) = \sum_{i=1}^{4} A_i \, e^{a_i(x-x_i)^2 + b_i(x-x_i)(y-y_i) + c_i(y-y_i)^2}$, where: $\mathbf{A} = (-200, -100, -170, 15)$, $\mathbf{a} = (-1, -1, -6.5, 0.7)$, $\mathbf{b} = (0, 0, 11, 0.6)$, $\mathbf{c} = (-10, -10, -6.5, 0.7)$, $\mathbf{x} = (1, 0, -0.5, -1)$, $\mathbf{y} = (0, 0.5, 1.5, 1)$.

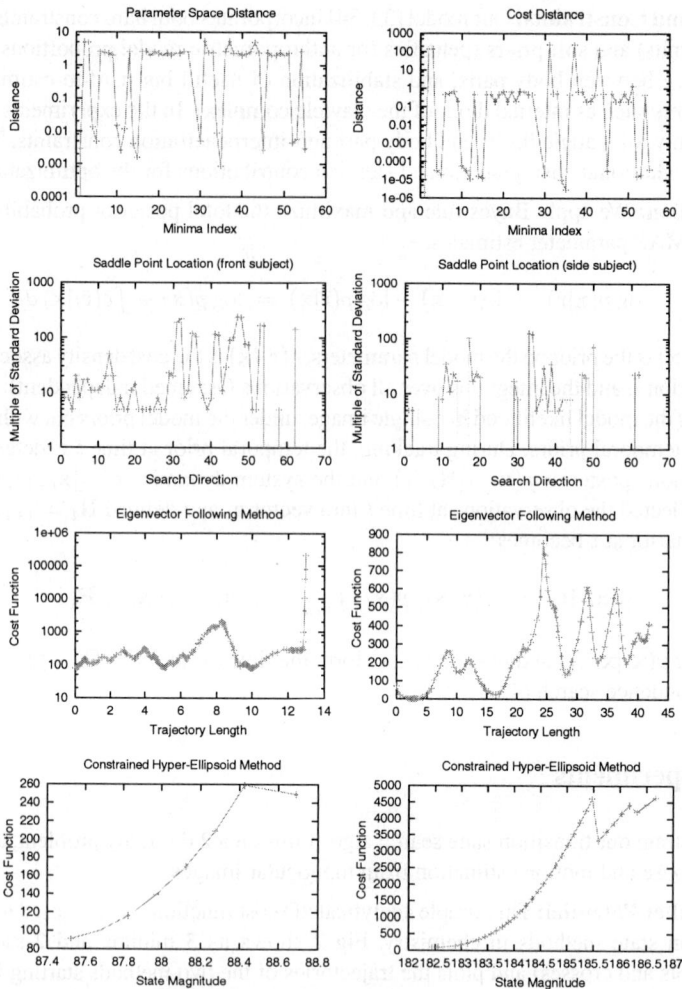

Fig. 3. Transition state and minimum location algorithms for ±32-eigendirection search trials. Top row: parameter space distance and cost difference between initial and current minimum. Second row: saddle point distances in standard deviations for a frontal and a partly side-on 3D pose. Third and fourth rows: cost profiles for different trajectories and constraints (see text).

method that focuses samples in regions likely to have low cost. All of these works note the difficulty of the multiple-minimum problem and attempt to develop techniques or constraints (on the scene, motion, number of cameras or background) to tackle it.

Here we show a few examples from a larger set of experiments with a 32 d.o.f. articulated full-body model, including pose estimation and tracking in monocular images using cost surfaces based on different combinations of image cues. The figures show

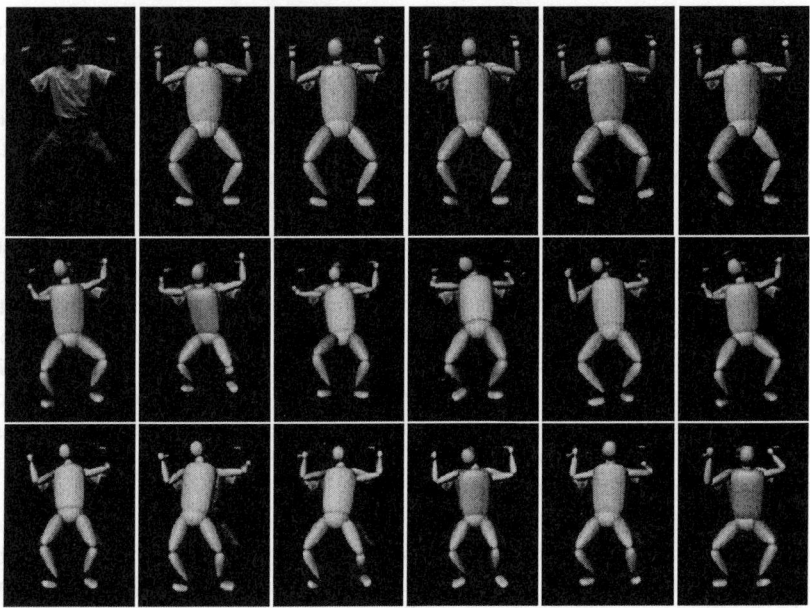

Fig. 4. Minima of image-based cost functions. Top row: contour and optical flow likelihood. Middle and bottom rows: silhouette and edge likelihood.

examples of minima found in likelihood models based on image contours and optical flow (fig. 4, top row), contours and silhouette-image data (fig. 4, middle and bottom rows), and model-to-image joint correspondences (fig. 5).

Fig. 3 attempts to capture some more quantitative information about the methods, here for the joint correspondence cost function. The first row displays the parameter space and cost distances of the 56 minima found during a set of 64 constrained searches (the ± directions of the 32 eigenvectors of an initial minimum, distances being measured w.r.t. this minimum, in radians and metres for the parameter space). The second row again shows parameter space distances, but now measured in standard deviations and for saddles rather than minima, for the same frontal view and for a slightly more side-on one (fig. 5, respectively top and bottom). The plots reveal the structure of the cost surface, with nearby saddles at 4–8 standard deviations and progressively more remote ones at 20–50, 80–100 and 150–200 standard deviations. It follows that no multiple-minimum exploration algorithm can afford to search only within the 'natural' covariance scale of its current minima: significantly deeper sampling is needed to capture even nearby minima (as previously noted, *e.g.* by [33, 34]).

The last two rows of fig. 3 show some sample cost profiles for typical runs of the eigenvector following (row 3) and constrained hyper-surface (row 4) saddle search methods. In the eigenvector method, it is preferable to represent the joint limits using a 'hard' active set strategy (row 3 right) rather than soft constraints (row 3 left): the stiff 'cost walls' induced by the soft constraints tend to force the eigenvector follower into head-on collision with the wall, with the cost climbing rapidly to infinity. The active set strategy avoids this problem at the price of more frequent direction changes as the joint limits switch on and off. The hyper-ellipsoid method (row 4) produces more stable trajectories that do not require special joint limit processing, but its cost profiles have characteristic sawtooth edges (row 4 right) associated with sudden state readjustments on the hypersphere at points where the tracked minimum becomes locally unstable.

Fig. 4 shows minima for costs based on various combinations of image cues. In the first row the minima correspond to a small interframe motion, using contour and robust optical flow information. This case has relatively few, but closely spaced local minima owing to the smoothing/quadratic effect of the flow. (Remoter minima do still exist at points where the robust contributions of sets of flow measurements turn off, particularly when these coincide with incorrect edge assignments). The second and third rows show minima arising from a silhouette and edge based cost function. The minima shown include 'reflective' (depth-related) ambiguities, incorrect edge assignments and singular 'inside-silhouette' configurations (which can be alleviated to some extent by augmenting the likelihood term as in [32]).

Finally, fig. 5 shows depth ambiguities for articulated 3D frontal and side poses, under model to image joint correspondences. The arm-shoulder complex is very flexible and therefore tends to induce more minima than the legs. We also find that side views tend to generate fewer minima than frontal ones, perhaps due to presence of body-part non-self-intersection and joint constraints that render many 'purely reflective' minima infeasible.

5 Conclusions and Future Work

We have described two families of deterministic-optimization-based algorithms for finding 'transition states' (saddle points with 1 negative eigenvalue) in high-dimensional multi-modal cost surfaces. These allow us to build topological 'roadmaps' of the nearby local minima and the transition states that lead to them. The methods are based on ones developed in computational chemistry, but here generalized, clarified and adapted for use in computational vision. Experiments on the difficult problem of articulated 3D human pose from monocular images show that our algorithms can stably and efficiently recover large numbers of transition states and minima, but also serve to underline the very large numbers of minima that exist in this problem.

We are currently applying our methods to other multimodal problems in vision, including structure from motion. We are also trying to use them to quantify the degrees of ambiguity of different cost functions, with the longer term goal of designing better cost functions based on higher-level features and groupings.

Acknowledgements. This work was supported by an EIFFEL doctoral grant and European Union FET-Open project VIBES. We would like to thank Alexandru Telea for discussions on implementation.

Fig. 5. 'Reflective' kinematic ambiguities under the model/image joint correspondence cost function. Each pair of rows displays the original image overlayed with the projected model, and the 3D model position seen from a fixed synthetic overhead camera. Note the pronounced forwards-backwards character of these reflective minima, and the large parameter space distances that often separate of them.

Appendix: Implementation of Hypersurface Sweeping

Here we summarize the equations needed to implement hypersurface sweeping for both implicit and parametric hypersurfaces. For the implicit approach, let $\mathbf{g}_c \equiv \frac{\partial c}{\partial \mathbf{x}}$ and also $\mathbf{H}_c \equiv \frac{\partial^2 c}{\partial \mathbf{x}^2}$. The hypersurface constraint is enforced with a Lagrange multiplier λ, solving $\frac{\partial}{\partial \mathbf{x}}(f + \lambda c) = \mathbf{g} + \lambda \mathbf{g}_c = 0$ subject to $c = t$. If we are currently at $(\mathbf{x}, \lambda)$, second order Taylor expansion of these equations for a constrained minimum at $(\mathbf{x}+\delta\mathbf{x}, \lambda+\delta\lambda)$ gives the standard **sequential quadratic programming** update rule for $(\delta\mathbf{x}, \delta\lambda)$:

$$\begin{pmatrix} \mathbf{H}_\lambda & \mathbf{g}_c \\ \mathbf{g}_c^\top & 0 \end{pmatrix} \begin{pmatrix} \delta\mathbf{x} \\ \delta\lambda \end{pmatrix} = - \begin{pmatrix} \mathbf{g} + \lambda \mathbf{g}_c \\ c - t \end{pmatrix} \quad \text{where} \quad \mathbf{H}_\lambda \equiv \mathbf{H} + \lambda \mathbf{H}_c \quad (5)$$

(The $\lambda \mathbf{H}_c$ term in the Hessian is often dropped for simplicity. This slows the convergence but still gives correct results). Similarly, in the parametric approach let $\mathbf{J} \equiv \frac{\partial}{\partial \mathbf{y}} \mathbf{x}(\mathbf{y}, t)$. The chain rule gives the reduced gradient $\mathbf{g}_\mathbf{y} = \mathbf{J} \mathbf{g}$ and Hessian $\mathbf{H}_\mathbf{y} = \mathbf{J} \mathbf{H} \mathbf{J}^\top + (\frac{\partial}{\partial \mathbf{y}} \mathbf{J}) \mathbf{g}$. These can be used directly in the Newton update rule $\delta\mathbf{y} = -\mathbf{H}_\mathbf{y}^{-1} \mathbf{g}_\mathbf{y}$. In particular, if we eliminate one x-variable — say x_n so that $\mathbf{y} = (x_1, ..., x_{n-1})$ and $x_n = x_n(\mathbf{y}, t)$ — we have:

$$\mathbf{J} = \left(\mathbf{I} \mid \frac{\partial x_n}{\partial \mathbf{y}} \right), \qquad \mathbf{g}_\mathbf{y} = \frac{\partial f}{\partial \mathbf{y}} + g_n \frac{\partial x_n}{\partial \mathbf{y}}, \qquad \mathbf{H}_\mathbf{y} = \mathbf{J} \mathbf{H} \mathbf{J}^\top + g_n \frac{\partial x_n}{\partial \mathbf{y}} \quad (6)$$

To save optimization work and for convergence testing and step length control, it is useful to be able to extrapolate the position and value of the next minimum from existing values. This can be done, e.g., by linear extrapolation from two previous positions, or analytically by solving the constrained minimum state update equations $(\mathbf{g} + (\lambda + \delta\lambda)\mathbf{g}_c)(\mathbf{x} + \delta\mathbf{x}) = 0$ or $\mathbf{g}_\mathbf{y}(\mathbf{y} + \delta\mathbf{y}, t + \delta t) = 0$ to first order, assuming that $\mathbf{x}, t$ is already a minimum and $t \to t + \delta t$:

$$(\delta\mathbf{x}, \delta\lambda) = \frac{\delta t}{\mathbf{g}_c^\top \mathbf{H}_\lambda^{-1} \mathbf{g}_c} (\mathbf{H}_\lambda^{-1} \mathbf{g}_c, -1) \quad (7)$$

$$\delta\mathbf{x} = \mathbf{J}\, \delta\mathbf{y} + \frac{\partial \mathbf{x}}{\partial t} \delta t, \qquad \delta\mathbf{y} = -\mathbf{H}_\mathbf{y}^{-1} \left(\frac{\partial \mathbf{J}}{\partial t} \mathbf{g} + \mathbf{J} \mathbf{H} \frac{\partial \mathbf{x}}{\partial t} \right) \delta t \quad (8)$$

Taylor expansion of $f(\mathbf{x}+\delta\mathbf{x})$ then gives $f_c(t+\delta t) \approx f_c(t) + f'_c \delta t + \frac{1}{2} f''_c \delta t^2$ with $f'_c = \mathbf{g} \frac{\delta \mathbf{x}}{\delta t}$ and $f''_c = \frac{\delta \mathbf{x}}{\delta t}^\top \mathbf{H} \frac{\delta \mathbf{x}}{\delta t}$. For step length control, we can either fix δt and solve for $\delta\mathbf{x}$ or $\delta\mathbf{y}$ (and hence $\mathbf{x} + \delta\mathbf{x} \equiv \mathbf{x}(\mathbf{y} + \delta\mathbf{y}, t + \delta t)$), or fix a desired trust region for $\delta\mathbf{x}$ or $\delta\mathbf{y}$ and work backwards to find a δt giving a step within it.

References

[1] Y. Abashkin and N. Russo. Transition State Structures and Reaction Profiles from Constrained Optimization Procedure. Implementation in the Framework of Density Functional Theory. *J. Chem. Phys.*, 1994.

[2] Y. Abashkin, N. Russo, and M. Toscano. Transition States and Energy Barriers from Density Functional Studies: Representative Isomerization Reactions. *International Journal of Quantum Chemistry*, 1994.

[3] G. T. Barkema. Event-Based Relaxation of Continuous Disordered Systems. *Physical Review Letters*, 77(21), 1996.
[4] A. Barr. Global and Local Deformations of Solid Primitives. *Computer Graphics*, 18:21–30, 1984.
[5] J. M. Bofill. Updated Hessian Matrix and the Restricted Step Method for Locating Transition Structures. *Journal of Computational Chemistry*, 15(1):1–11, 1994.
[6] C. J. Cerjan and W. H. Miller. On Finding Transition States. *J. Chem. Phys.*, 75(6), 1981.
[7] T. Cham and J. Rehg. A Multiple Hypothesis Approach to Figure Tracking. In *CVPR*, volume 2, pages 239–245, 1999.
[8] A. Chiusso, R. Brockett, and S. Soatto. Optimal structure from motion: Local ambiguities and global estimates. *IJCV*, 39(3):195–228, 2000.
[9] K. Choo and D. Fleet. People Tracking Using Hybrid Monte Carlo Filtering. In *ICCV*, 2001.
[10] G. M. Crippen and H. A. Scheraga. Minimization of Polypeptide Energy. XI. The Method of Gentlest Ascent. *Archives of Biochemistry and Biophysics*, 144:462–466, 1971.
[11] P. Culot, G. Dive, V. H. Nguyen, and J. M. Ghuysen. A Quasi-Newton Algorithm for First-Order Saddle Point Location. *Theoretica Chimica Acta*, 82:189–205, 1992.
[12] J. Deutscher, A. Blake, and I. Reid. Articulated Body Motion Capture by Annealed Particle Filtering. In *CVPR*, 2000.
[13] R. Fletcher. Practical Methods of Optimization. In *John Wiley*, 1987.
[14] D. Gavrila and L. Davis. 3-D Model Based Tracking of Humans in Action:A Multiview Approach. In *CVPR*, pages 73–80, 1996.
[15] T. Helgaker. Transition-State Optimizations by Trust-Region Image Minimization. *Chemical Physics Letters*, 182(5), 1991.
[16] G. Henkelman and H. Jonsson. A Dimer Method for Finding Saddle Points on High Dimensional Potential Surfaces Using Only First Derivatives. *J. Chem. Phys.*, 111(15):7011–7022, 1999.
[17] R. L. Hilderbrandt. Application of Newton-Raphson Optimization Techniques in Molecular Mechanics Calculations. *Computers & Chemistry*, 1:179–186, 1977.
[18] F. Jensen. Locating Transition Structures by Mode Following: A Comparison of Six Methods on the Ar_8 Lennard-Jones potential. *J. Chem. Phys.*, 102(17):6706–6718, 1995.
[19] P. Jorgensen, H. J. A. Jensen, and T. Helgaker. A Gradient Extremal Walking Algorithm. *Theoretica Chimica Acta*, 73:55–65, 1988.
[20] J. MacCormick and M. Isard. Partitioned Sampling, Articulated Objects, and Interface-Quality Hand Tracker. In *ECCV*, volume 2, pages 3–19, 2000.
[21] D. Morris and J. Rehg. Singularity Analysis for Articulated Object Tracking. In *CVPR*, pages 289–296, 1998.
[22] N. Mousseau and G. T. Berkema. Traveling Through Potential Energy Lanscapes of Desordered Materials: The Activation-Relaxation Technique. *Physical Review E*, 57(2), 1998.
[23] L. J. Munro and D. J. Wales. Defect Migration in Crystalline Silicon. *Physical Review B*, 59(6):3969–3980, 1999.
[24] J. Nichols, H. Taylor, P. Schmidt, and J. Simons. Walking on Potential Energy Surfaces. *J. Chem. Phys.*, 92(1), 1990.
[25] J. Oliensis. The Error Surface for Structure from Motion. Technical report, NECI, 2001.
[26] R. Plankers and P. Fua. Articulated Soft Objects for Video-Based Body Modeling. In *ICCV*, pages 394–401, 2001.
[27] J. Rehg and T. Kanade. Model-Based Tracking of Self Occluding Articulated Objects. In *ICCV*, pages 612–617, 1995.
[28] R. Rosales and S. Sclaroff. Inferring Body Pose without Tracking Body Parts. In *CVPR*, pages 721–727, 2000.

[29] E. M. Sevick, A. T. Bell, and D. N. Theodorou. A Chain of States Method for Investigating Infrequent Event Processes Occuring in Multistate, Multidimensional Systems. *J. Chem. Phys.*, 98(4), 1993.
[30] H. Sidenbladh, M. Black, and D. Fleet. Stochastic Tracking of 3D Human Figures Using 2D Image Motion. In *ECCV*, 2000.
[31] J. Simons, P. Jorgensen, H. Taylor, and J. Ozmen. Walking on Potential Energy Surfaces. *J. Phys. Chem.*, 87:2745–2753, 1983.
[32] C. Sminchisescu. Consistency and Coupling in Human Model Likelihoods. In *CFGR*, 2002.
[33] C. Sminchisescu and B. Triggs. A Robust Multiple Hypothesis Approach to Monocular Human Motion Tracking. Technical Report RR-4208, INRIA, 2001.
[34] C. Sminchisescu and B. Triggs. Covariance-Scaled Sampling for Monocular 3D Body Tracking. In *CVPR*, 2001.
[35] C. Sminchisescu and B. Triggs. Hyperdynamics Importance Sampling. In *ECCV*, 2002.
[36] J. Q. Sun and K. Ruedenberg. Gradient Extremals and Stepest Descend Lines on Potential Energy Surfaces. *J. Chem. Phys.*, 98(12), 1993.
[37] B. Triggs, P. McLauchlan, R. Hartley, and A. Fitzgibbon. Bundle Adjustment - A Modern Synthesis. In Springer-Verlag, editor, *Vision Algorithms: Theory and Practice*, 2000.
[38] S. Wachter and H. Nagel. Tracking Persons in Monocular Image Sequences. *CVIU*, 74(3):174–192, 1999.
[39] D. J. Wales. Finding Sadle Points for Clusters. *J. Chem. Phys.*, 91(11), 1989.
[40] D. J. Wales and T. R. Walsh. Theoretical Study of the Water Pentamer. *J. Chem. Phys.*, 105(16), 1996.

A Generative Method for Textured Motion: Analysis and Synthesis

Yizhou Wang and Song-Chun Zhu

Dept. of Comp. and Info. Sci., Ohio State Univ., Columbus, OH 43210, USA
{wangyiz, szhu}@cis.ohio-state.edu

Abstract. Natural scenes contain rich stochastic motion patterns which are characterized by the movement of a large number of small elements, such as falling snow, raining, flying birds, firework and waterfall. In this paper, we call these motion patterns *textured motion* and present a generative method that combines statistical models and algorithms from both texture and motion analysis. The generative method includes the following three aspects. 1). Photometrically, an image is represented as a superposition of linear bases in atomic decomposition using an overcomplete dictionary, such as Gabor or Laplacian. Such base representation is known to be generic for natural images, and it is low dimensional as the number of bases is often 100 times smaller than the number of pixels. 2). Geometrically, each moving element (called moveton), such as the individual snowflake and bird, is represented by a deformable template which is a group of several spatially adjacent bases. Such templates are learned through clustering. 3). Dynamically, the movetons are tracked through the image sequence by a stochastic algorithm maximizing a posterior probability. A classic second order Markov chain model is adopted for the motion dynamics. The sources and sinks of the movetons are modeled by birth and death maps. We adopt an EM-like stochastic gradient algorithm for inference of the hidden variables: bases, movetons, birth/death maps, parameters of the dynamics. The learned models are also verified through synthesizing random textured motion sequences which bear similar visual appearance with the observed sequences.

1 Introduction: Objectives and Previous Work

Natural scenes contain rich stochastic motion patterns which are characterized by the movement of a large number of small deformable elements (or particles). For example, raining, snowing, bird flock, moving crowd, firework, waterfalls, and so on. The analysis and synthesis of such motion patterns, called *textured motion* in this paper, are important for a variety of applications in both vision and graphics, and stimulate growing interest of the two communities.

Graphics methods. In graphics, the objective is to render textured motion in video or cartoon animation, and the quality of the rendered motion is usually measured by three basic criteria.

1. It should be *realistic*. This motivates work for modeling and learning the photometric and dynamic properties from real video due to the complexity of textured motion. Usually, data driven statistical modeling is often more appropriate than physically-based modeling.
2. It should be *stylish*. This is required for applications in non-photo realistic rendering (NPR), for example, rendering a waterfall in a cartoon movie. It is desirable to separate the dynamics of motion from its photometric appearances, so that the video appears symbolic but with realistic motion.
3. It should be *controllable*. For a better blending of the motion with other 3D objects in a scene, one should increase the degree of freedoms in maneuvering the motion. For example, it is desirable to control the sources and sinks where the motion elements appear and disappear, to control the individual moving elements, to change its motion direction etc.

In the graphics literature, both physically-based and data driven models are reported. The former includes the work which create animations of fire and gaseous phenomena with particles [12, 5]. The latter includes the 1). video texture[14] which finds smooth transition points in a video sequence from which the video could be replayed with minimum artifacts; 2). 3D volume texture[18] which generates motion through non-parametric sampling from an observed video motivated by recent work on texture synthesis. Though the statistical models of the video texture or 3D volume texture can render some realistic animations, such models do not model the dynamic and geometric properties of the moving elements.

Vision methods. In computer vision, the analysis of textured motion has applications for video analysis, such as motion segmentation, annotation, recognition and retrieval, detecting abnormal motion in a crowd, and so on. Needless to say that a good vision model of textured motion is useful for animation in graphics as mentioned above. For such applications, a vision model should satisfy the following properties.

1. It should be *sufficient* and *general*. It is not enough to just render a synthesized sequence that looks like the original as the video texture do, the model should also be able to capture the variability and therefore can be generalized to new data.
2. It should be *parsimonious* and *low dimensional* for computation. This requests the model capture the semantics of the motion. This also requests the modeling of photometric, geometric, and dynamic aspects of the motion — consistent with the graphics criteria.

In the vision literature, as these motion patterns lie in the domains of both motion analysis and texture modeling, statistical models are proposed from both directions with a trend of merging the two. In the following, we briefly review these work to set the background of our method.

Early vision work on textured motion was done by (Szummer and Picard, 1996)[17] who adopt a spatial-temporal auto-regression (STAR) model from

(Cliff and Ord, 1976)[4]. Let $\mathbf{I}(x, y, t)$ be the intensity of a pixel (x, y) at time t, a STAR model assumes that $\mathbf{I}(x, y, t)$ is a regression of its neighboring pixels

$$\mathbf{I}(x, y, t) = \sum_{i=1}^{p} a_i \mathbf{I}(x + \delta x_i, y + \delta y_i, t + \delta t_i) + N(0, \sigma^2), \tag{1}$$

where $(\delta x_i, \delta y_i, \delta t_i)$ is the displacement of a neighboring pixel in space and time, and $a_i, i = 1, ..., p$ are parameters to be fit. A linear (or partial) order is imposed so that $\mathbf{I}(x, y, t)$ only depends on pixels at previous frames $\delta t_i < 0, \forall i$ for fast synthesis. Such model can be considered as an extension from a causal Gaussian Markov random field model (GMRF) used in texture modeling by adding the time dimension. Along the line of texture modeling, Bar-Joseph et.al.[1] extended the work by Heeger and Bergen (1995) and others[19] to multi-resolution analysis in a tree structured representation, in a similar spirit to (Wei and Lovoy, 2000).

Although these algorithms can show synthesis of good motion, we argue that the concept of treating a motion pattern as a solid texture is perhaps not appropriate. Because textures are physically the status of systems with massive elements at thermodynamic equilibrium characterized by maximum entropy distributions[19]. However, this assumption is not observed in textured motions, for example, fire or gaseous turbulence, which are clearly not at equilibrium.

The recent work (Soatto, Doretto, and Wu, 2001)[15] engages the motion dynamics explicitly. By a SVD analysis, Soatto et al. represent an image $\mathbf{I}(t)$ by a small number of principal components. The projections of $\mathbf{I}(t)$ on these components, denoted by $x(t)$, is modeled by a Markov model,

$$x(t + 1) = Ax(t) + Bv(t), \quad \mathbf{I}(t) = Cx(t) + n(t), \tag{2}$$

where $v(t)$ is the noise driving the motion and $n(t)$ is the image noise for the reconstruction residues. The parameters A, B, C are learned by maximum likelihood estimation (MLE). This model can generate impressive synthesis for a variety of motion patterns and can also be used for recognition[13].

Being considered as an extension the work [15], Fitzgibbon considered not only the stochastic part for textured motion, but also the parametric component introduced by the camera motion [16]. In [16], the images are also represented by the principal components with peroidc coefficients, and the Auto-Regression (AR) model is used to handel stochastic textured motion. The parametric component for camera motion is governed by projective geometry model. The objective of the method is to both efficiently fit the AR model and correctly register the image sequence.

Our method. In this paper, we present a generative method for the analysis and synthesis of textured motion, motivated by the vision and graphics criteria discussed above. Our model includes the following three aspects.

1. *Photometrically*, an image is represented as a superposition of linear bases in atomic decomposition using an over-complete dictionary, such as Gabor or Laplacian. Such base representation is known to be generic for natural

images, and it is low dimensional as the number of bases is often 100 times smaller than the number of pixels.
2. *Geometrically*, each moving element (called moveton), such as the individual snowflake, bird, is represented by a template which is a group of several spatially adjacent bases. Such templates are deformable to account for the variabilities of the elements and are learned through clustering.
3. *Dynamically*, the movetons are tracked through the image sequence by a stochastic algorithm maximizing a posterior probability. A classic Markov chain model is adopted for the motion dynamics, as in[15]. The sources and sinks of the movetons are modeled by birth and death maps.

We adopt an EM-like stochastic gradient algorithm for inference of the hidden variables: bases, movetons, birth/death maps, parameters of the dynamics.

2 A Generative Model for Images and Video

To fix notation, let $\mathbf{I}[0, \tau]$ denote an image sequence on a 2D lattice $\Lambda = \{(x,y) : 0 \leq x, y \leq L\}$ in a discretized time interval $[0, \tau] = \{0, 1, 2, ..., \tau\}$. For $(x, y) \in \Lambda$ and $t \in [0, \tau]$, $\mathbf{I}(x, y, t)$ denotes the pixel intensity, and $\mathbf{I}(t) \in \mathbf{I}[0, \tau]$ is a single image frame.

2.1 Image Representation: From Pixels to Bases

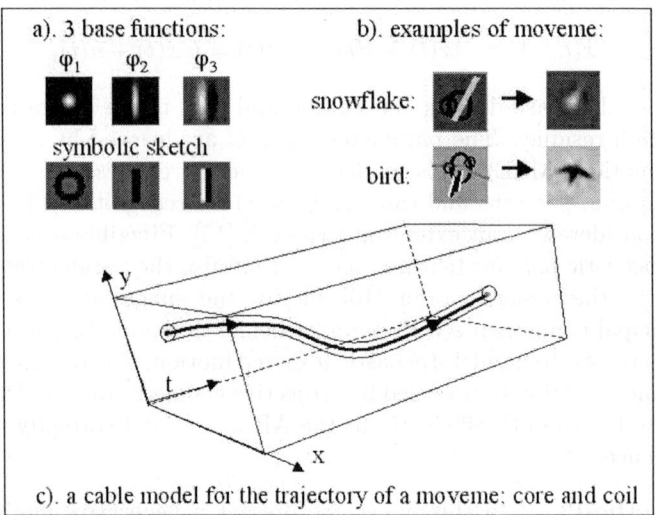

Fig. 1. A "cable model" for movetons.

In this section, we study the representation of a single image frame $\mathbf{I} \in \mathbf{I}[0, \tau]$. For clarity, we remove the time index. We represent an image as a superposition of a small number of image bases, in a scheme which is often called *atomic decomposition* in wavelets and image coding[9, 10, 3].

$$I = \sum_{j=1}^{N} \alpha_j \mathbf{b}_j + \mathbf{n}, \quad \mathbf{b} \in \Delta. \qquad (3)$$

In equation (3), $\mathbf{b}_j$ is an image base from a dictionary Δ, α_j is its coefficient, and $\mathbf{n}$ is a noise process for the residues. The dictionary includes all bases which are transformed versions of three base functions (mother wavelets) $\psi_\ell, \ell = 1, 2, 3$,

$$\Delta = \{T_{x,y,\theta,\sigma} \circ \psi_\ell \; : \; (x,y) \in \Lambda, \theta \in [0, 2\pi), \sigma \in [\sigma_{\min}, \sigma_{\max}], \ell = 1, 2, 3\}$$

$T_{x,y,\theta,\sigma}$ denotes a transform with (x, y, θ, σ) for translation, rotation, and scaling respectively.

We denote the set of base functions by $\Psi = \{\psi_\ell, \ell = 1, 2, 3\}$. We choose the Laplacian of Gaussian (LoG), Gabor cosine (Gcos), and Gabor sine (Gsin) shown in Figure 1.a. These base functions represent blobs, bars and step edges respectively (see the symbolic sketches in Figure 1.a). We choose 8 scales, and 12 orientations.

Thus we transform an image $\mathbf{I}$ into a base representation, called a *base map*.

$$\mathbf{B} = (\mathbf{b}_j = (\alpha_j, \ell_j, x_j, y_j, \theta_j, \sigma_j) \; : \; j = 1, 2, ..., N).$$

As Δ is over-complete, we should discuss how $\mathbf{B}$ is inferred from $\mathbf{I}$ later. We choose the base representation for two reasons.

1. *Low dimensionality*. The number of bases is usually 100-fold smaller than the number of pixels. Figure 2 shows a snowing sequence, each frame can be approximated by $N \approx 100$ bases (see Figure 2.b). When N increases to 800 bases, the reconstructed images in Figure 2.c) are of very high precision. This also introduces a *coarse-to-fine* strategy for computation.
2. *Generality*. It is well known that the LoG and Gabor bases are generic representations for the ensemble of natural images[11], and are also fundamental to human visual perception.

2.2 Image Representation: From Bases to Movetons

In natural image sequences, the image bases often form spatially coherent groups. This is most evident in sequences where the moving elements (or "movetons") are identifiable, such as the individual snow flakes, and flying birds. Figure 1.b shows two examples. A snow flake is a sum of three bases: 2 ψ_1's and 1 ψ_2 at various scales and space displacements. A bird consists of 7 bases: 3 ψ_1's, 2 ψ_2's 2 ψ_3's. The number of bases, and their relative positions and coefficients may vary between the movetons. By defining a distance between the movetons, one can cluster the movetons into a small number of deformable templates.

$$\Phi = \{\phi_\ell(\beta) : \ell = 1, 2, ..., n\}$$

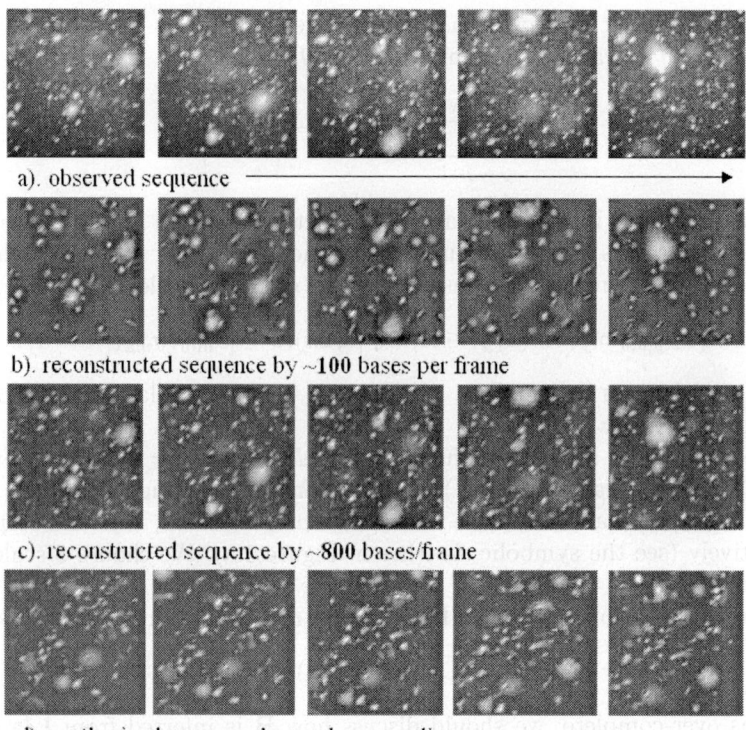

Fig. 2. Example of a snowing sequence. (see snow_obs.avi and snow_syn.avi for movies)

with ℓ indexing the moveton types and β being the parameters for relative deformations of the bases within a moveton. Thus we obtain a dictionary of movetons with some transformations,

$$\Pi = \{\, T_{x,y,\theta,\sigma} \circ \phi_\ell \ : \ (x,y) \in \Lambda, \theta \in [0, 2\pi), \sigma \in [\sigma_{\min}, \sigma_{\max}], \ell \,\}. \tag{4}$$

In practice, not all bases are necessarily grouped into movetons. We call the ungrouped ones *free bases*, which are treated as degenerated movetons, i.e. each moveton has one base, for clarity of notation. For the N bases in the base map **B**, suppose we group them into J movetons, then we arrive at a more meaningful representation of the image, with dimensions further reduced than **B**.

$$\mathbf{M} = (\pi_j = (\ell_j, x_j, y_j, \theta_j, \sigma_j, \beta_j), j = 1, 2, ..., J), \qquad J \ll N.$$

Each moveton π_j is represented by $1 \leq \ell_j \leq n$ for the type of the deformable template, $x_j, y_j, \theta_j, \sigma_j$ for the position, orientation, and scale of the overall moveton, and β for the deformable within the moveton.

During the computation, we should learn the deformable templates Φ_ℓ and compute the movetons and free bases **M** from images. For example, Figure 3.a displays the symbolic sketches for a set of typical deformable templates of the

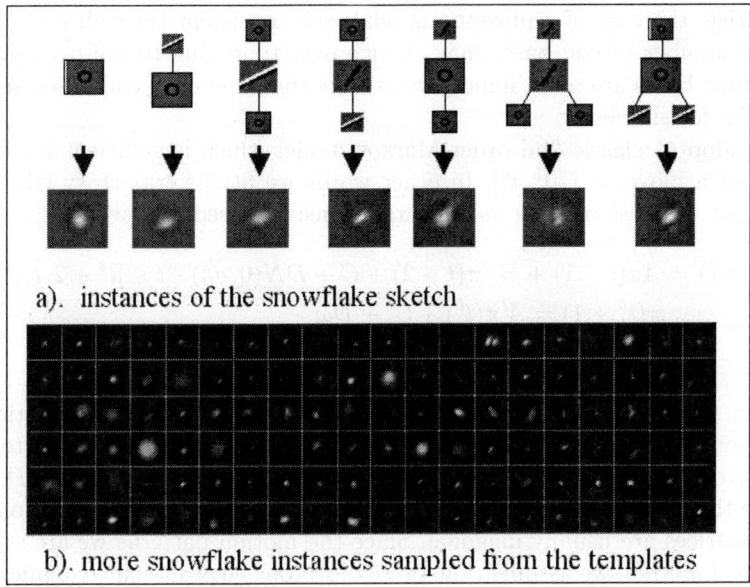

Fig. 3. The computed motion elements: snow flakes and random examples.

snowing sequence shown in Figure 2. Figure 3.b shows 120 random movetons sampled from the moveton dictionary Π. Each moveton is a snow flake. This sample shows the variety and generality of the deformable models learned with bases.

To summarize, we have a following generative model for an image **I**, with dimensions reduced sequentially,

$$\mathbf{M} \xrightarrow{\Phi} \mathbf{B} \xrightarrow{\Psi} \mathbf{I}$$

2.3 Motion Representation: Dynamics, Sources, Sinks, and State Transition

Now we turn to the image sequence $\mathbf{I}[0, \tau]$. As shown in Figure 1.c, a moveton π can be traced over a certain time interval $[t_b, t_e]$ and thus its trajectory is what we call a "cable". Typically in a moveton template, one base has relatively large coefficient and scale, such as the main body of the bird or snow flake, and its trajectory forms the *core* of the cable. The core base is surrounded by a number of minor bases which account for the deformations. Due to self-rotation, the trajectories of these minor bases form the *coil* surrounding the cable core. In a coarse-to-fine computation, we can compute the trajectories of the cores first, and then add the coils sequentially. Thus we denote a cable by

$$C[t^b, t^e] = (\pi(t^b), \pi(t^b + 1), ..., \pi(t^e)). \tag{5}$$

In practice, the core of a moveton is relatively consistent through its life span, and the number of coil bases may change over time, due to self-occlusion etc. Since these bases are often minor, we assume the number of coil bases are fixed in a cable for simplicity.

We adopt a classic 2nd order Markov model which is sufficient for the dynamics of a moveton $C[t^b, t^e]$. In other words we fit the trajectory (the cable) $C[t^b, t^e]$ by regression. Such models are extensively used in tracking[8].

$$\pi(t) = A\pi(t-1) + B \cdot \pi(t-2) + C + DN(0, \sigma_0^2) \quad t \in [t^b + 2, t^e]$$
$$\pi(t^b + 1) = A'\pi(t^b) + C' + D\omega$$
$$(\pi(t^b), t^b) \sim P_B(\pi, \lambda), \quad (\pi(t^e), t^e - t^b) \sim P_D(\pi, \lambda).$$

One can simplify the equation in a canonical form expressed in equation (2). $\pi(t)$ is a vector representing a number of bases including both the photometric (by base coefficients) and geometric information. The matrices A, B, C, D, A', C' capture the change of image appearances and the motion of the movetons, and these matrices are usually diagonal. Since the motion patterns we are studying is *textured motion*, we assume that those movetons have similar dynamics. That means those trajectories share the same A, B, C, D, A', C'.

The first moveton $\pi(t^b)$ and its timing t^b follows a probability $P_B(\pi, \lambda)$ which we call the *birth map* for movetons. P_B specifies the "sources" of the movetons where the movetons are often originated. Similarly, the end of the trajectory $\pi(t^e)$ and its life span $t^e - t^b$ are governed by a *death map* $P_D(\pi, \lambda)$. P_D reveals the "sinks" in a lattice. π is a long vector, P_B and P_D are high dimensional. Although other attributes in π can be modeled if necessary, we are most interested in the location (x, y).

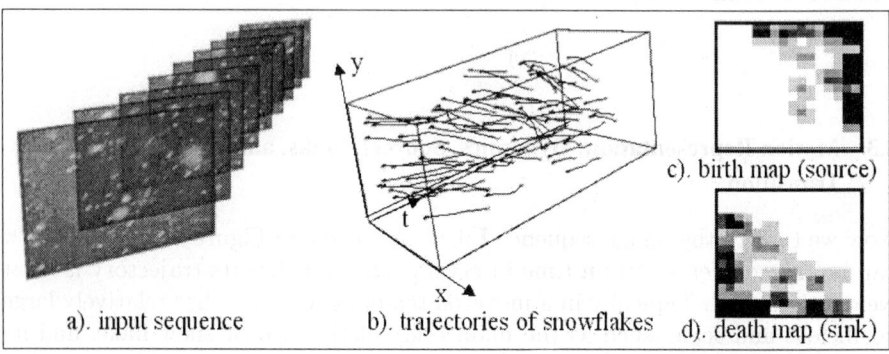

a). input sequence   b). trajectories of snowflakes   c). birth map (source)   d). death map (sink)

Fig. 4. The computed trajectories of snow flakes and the source and sink maps.

For example, Figure 4 displays the computed trajectories (4.b), birth (source) map (4.c), and death (sink) map (4.d) of the snowing sequence shown in Figure 2. The dark locations at the death/birth maps indicate high probabilities. Thus the algorithm "understands" that the snow flakes enter mostly from the upper-right corner and disappear around the lower-left corner. We sum over the other variables at each (x, y).

During the learning process, suppose we have computed K cables from a sequence $\mathbf{I}[0, \tau]$, $C_i[t_i^b, t_i^e], i = 1, 2, ..., K$, we represent P_B and P_D in a non-parametric form,

$$P_B(\pi, \lambda) = \frac{1}{K} \sum_{i=1}^{K} \delta(\pi - \pi_i(t_i^b), \lambda - t_i^b), \quad P_D(\pi, \lambda) = \frac{1}{K} \sum_{i=1}^{K} \delta(\pi - \pi_i(t_i^b), \lambda - (t_i^e - t_i^b))$$

where $\delta()$ is a Parzen window centered at 0. Then we can project P_B and P_D to the (x, y) dimensions as marginal probabilities.

In practice, the death and birth of movetons may be synchronized. For example, in the firework scene shown in Figure 10, a large number of movetons can come and go together. This requests the P_B and P_D be joint probabilities for a large number of movetons.

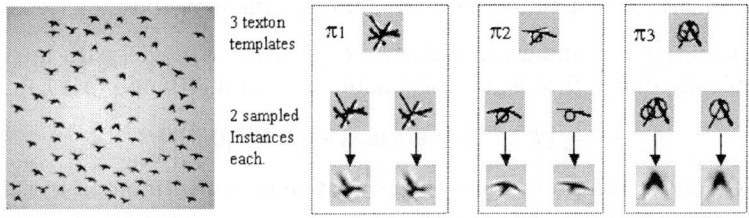

Fig. 5. Three transition states while birds flying.

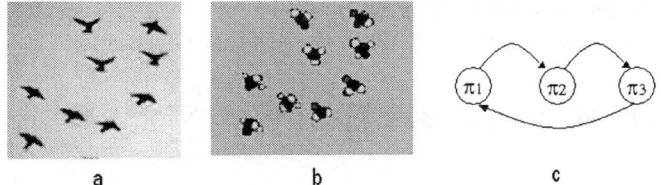

Fig. 6. 3D graphic model of flying birds and their flying states transition.

Furthermore, sometimes when the movetons are non-rigid objects or articulated objects, we may observe certain repeating states in their movements, for example, the birds flapping their wings while flying. Thus we also need to model the state transition of those movetons. As the result, we extend the motion dynamics model with more states. Figure 5 shows the clustered three states ($\pi 1$, $\pi 2$, $\pi 3$) of the poses when birds flying. And Figure 6 displays the 3D graphic model for the birds and their flying states transition. During the synthesis of birds fly, once we determine the birds' flying pathes, we can make those birds flapping their wings by sampling the transition states from the model.

To summarize, we denote all parameters in the motion equation above by,

$$\Gamma = (A, B, C, D, B, A', C', P_B, P_D, T(\pi_j))$$

3 Problem Formulation

Given an observed image sequence $\mathbf{I}^{obs}[0, \tau]$ as training data, we want to achieve two objectives.

1. Make inference about all the hidden (latent) variable which are represented by an unknown of K cables,

$$W[0, \tau] = (K, \{(t_i^b, t_i^e, C_i) : [t_i^b, t_i^e] \subset [0, \tau], i = 1, 2, ..., K\}).$$

2. Compute the optimal fit for all parameters in the generative model $\Theta = (\Phi, \Gamma)$, with Φ being the set of deformable templates for the movements, and Γ governing the birth, death, and motion of the movetons.

The formulation is standard in statistics for learning a model with latent variables (missing data), that is, the maximum likelihood estimate (MLE),

$$\Theta^* = (\Phi^*, \Gamma^*) = \arg\max \log p(\mathbf{I}^{obs}[0, \tau]; \Theta). \tag{6}$$

The likelihood is computed from the generative model with latent variables integrated (summed) out, For clarity of notation, we assume W are continuous variables.

$$p(\mathbf{I}^{obs}[0, \tau]; \Theta) = \int p(\mathbf{I}^{obs}[0, \tau] | W[0, \tau]; \Phi) p(W[0, \tau]; \Gamma) dW.$$

Let $\mathbf{B}(t) = \{\mathbf{b}_{t,j}, j = 1, 2, ..., N(t)\}$ be the collection of all bases in the K movetons (cables) at time t, then we can re-express $W[0, \tau]$ as $(\mathbf{B}(0), ..., \mathbf{B}(\tau))$, by equation (3), $p(\mathbf{I}[0, \tau] | W[0, \tau]; \Phi)$ is the product Gaussians,

$$p(\mathbf{I}^{obs}[0, \tau] | W[0, \tau]; \Phi) = \prod_{t=0}^{\tau} G(\mathbf{I}^{obs}(t) - \sum_{j=1}^{N(t)} \alpha_{t,j} \mathbf{b}_{t,j}; \sigma_o^2),$$

as we assume iid Gaussian noise $G(0, \sigma_o^2)$ for $\mathbf{n}$.

Following the motion representation, $p(W[0, \tau]; \Gamma)$ is also a product of Gaussians,

$$p(W[0, \tau]; \Gamma) = \prod_{i=1}^{K} P_B(\pi(t_i^b), t^b) P_D(\pi(t_i^e), t_i^e) p(\pi(t_i^b + 1) | \pi(t_i^b); A', C', D)$$

$$\times \prod_{t=t_i^b+2}^{t_i^e} p(\pi(t) | \pi(t-1), \pi(t-2); A, B, C, D).$$

4 Computation: Learning and Inference

To solve the MLE in eqn. (6), we set $\frac{\partial \log p(\mathbf{I}^{\text{obs}};\Theta)}{\partial \Theta} = 0$. This leads to

$$\int [\frac{\partial \log p(\mathbf{I}^{\text{obs}}|W;\Phi)}{\partial \Phi} + \frac{\partial \log p(W;\Gamma)}{\partial \Gamma}] p(W|\mathbf{I};\Theta) dW = 0. \qquad (7)$$

Instead of using the classic EM algorithm, we adopt the stochastic gradient algorithm[6] which is capable of being global optimal Θ. It iterates three steps with s indexing steps.

Step 1. Sampling $W^{\text{syn}}[0,\tau] \sim p(W|\mathbf{I}^{\text{obs}};\beta)$. This includes computing the bases, grouping bases into movetons, and tracking the movetons. The computation is realized by a data driven Markov chain Monte Carlo techniques, including the following reversible dynamics.

1). The death or birth of a motion trajectory Γ of length one.
2). Extending or shrinking a trajectory.
3). Mutating two nearby trajectories at a certain base.
4). Diffusing the coefficient, location, orientation, scale of a base in a trajectory (Inferring **B**).

Step 2. Updating the motion dynamics parameters Γ by regression,

$$\Gamma(s+1) = (1-\rho)\Gamma(s) + \rho \frac{\partial \log p(W^{\text{syn}}[0,\tau];\Gamma)}{\partial \Gamma}.$$

Step 3. Updating the moveton parameters Γ by clustering and grouping,

$$\Phi(s+1) = (1-\rho)\Phi(s) + \rho \frac{\partial \log p(\mathbf{I}^{\text{obs}}|W^{\text{syn}};\Phi)}{\partial \Phi}.$$

Finally, the birth, death maps, P_B and P_D, are updated by counting the the head and tail of each cable at their locations in the frames.

The algorithm is initialized by a stochastic version of match pursuit[9] for the base maps which is often very effective. We adopt a coarse-to-fine scheme and track the core bases whose coefficients and scales are higher than a threshold, and learn the motion dynamics Γ. Then we lower the threshold to add the coil bases quickly following the learned trajectory.

Our method for tracking movetons is similar to the condensation algorithm[8], while is distinguished from it in two main aspects. Firstly, we have a full generative model of image rather than the tracking model whose likelihood can only be evaluated relatively. Secondly, we are optimizing the whole trajectories and thus will trace back in time during the computation, which means we don't have to remember a huge samples for each movetons. This, in combination with the generative model, saves large amount of time and memory.

For a typical sequence of 30 frames, the learning takes about 10-20 minutes in a Pentium IV PC, and the synthesis of sequence can be done in nearly real-time.

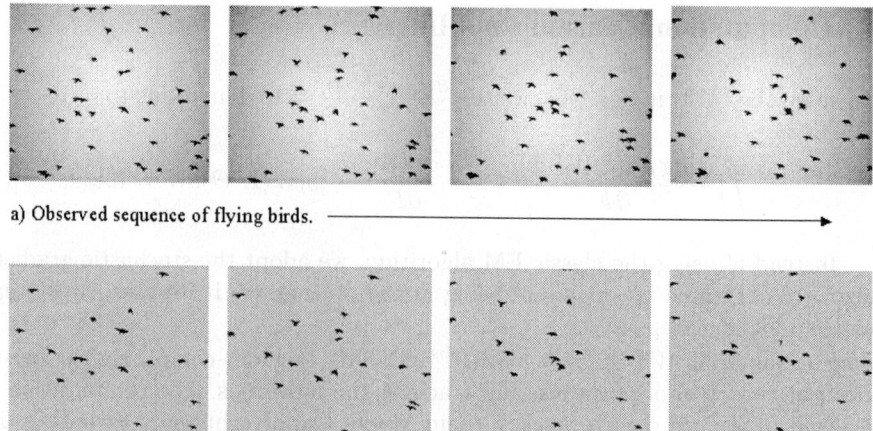

a) Observed sequence of flying birds.

b) Synthesized sequence of flying birds by random sampling (reduced number of birds for photo editing).

Fig. 7. Example of the bird sequence (see bird_obs.avi, bird_syn.avi).

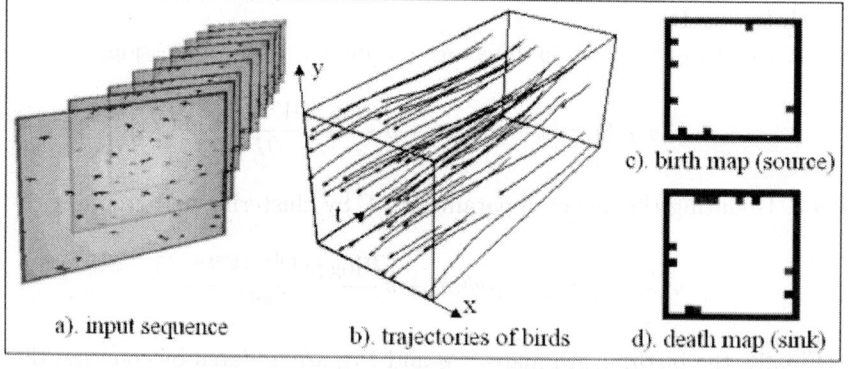

a). input sequence   b). trajectories of birds   c). birth map (source)   d). death map (sink)

Fig. 8. The computed trajectories of flying birds and the source and sink maps.

5 Experiments

We report the results on four textured motion sequences.

   1. The snowing sequence. Fig. 2 shows the reconstruction of the snowing images by bases, and a synthesized sequence. For movie, see the observed and synthesized sequence at the attached avi files snow_obs.avi and snow_syn.avi respectively. The algorithm also computes the movetons (snow flake) templates, and random samples are shown in Fig. 3 The trajectories and source/sink maps are shown in Fig 4.

   2. The flying bird sequence. Fig. 7.a and b show the observed and synthesize sequences. The animation can be seen at the attached avi files bird_obs.avi and bird_syn.avi. The trajectories and source/sink maps are shown in Fig.8. The

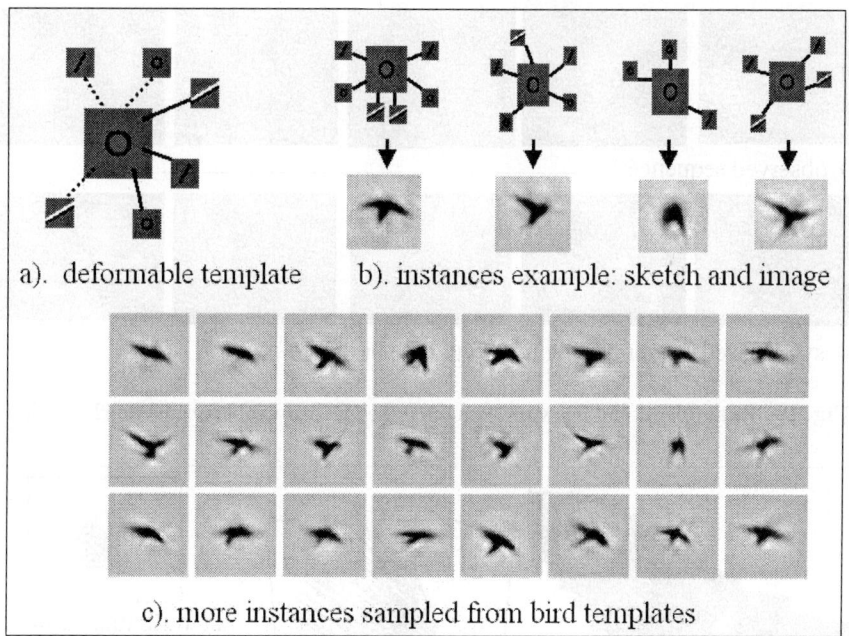

Fig. 9. The computed motion elements: flying birds and random examples

birds enter and exit the picture from the image boundary. The maps are rather sparse because we reduced the number of cables (birds) for photo editing effect. Fig.9 shows the deformable templates (a) where a core base is surrounded by a number of small coil bases. The dashed connection means the coil base may or may not appear all the time. A variety of templates and image instances of birds (movetons) are shown in (b) and (c).

3. *The firework sequence.* Fig. 10.a and b show the observed and synthesized sequences. See attached firework_obs.avi and firework_syn.avi for the movies. The trajectories and source/sink maps are shown in Fig.11. In the synthesis, we edit the birth map $P_B(\pi, \lambda)$ by changing its birth rate, assume a uniform distribution for the sources over then lattice. Thus the synthesis has more fireworks.

4. *The waterfall sequence.* Fig.12 shows the observed and synthesized sequences. See attached waterfall_obs.avi and waterfall_syn.avi for the movies. The trajectories and source sinks are shown in Fig.13. Fig.14 shows 10 typical water drops in the waterfall which are a cluster of bases.

6 Discussion and Future Work

The generative model in this paper is motivated by the graphics and vision criteria discussed in Section (1). It learns realistic motion patterns from real data, separates the motion dynamics with photometric and geometric styles, and thus achieves good controllability. For example, we can change the source/sink,

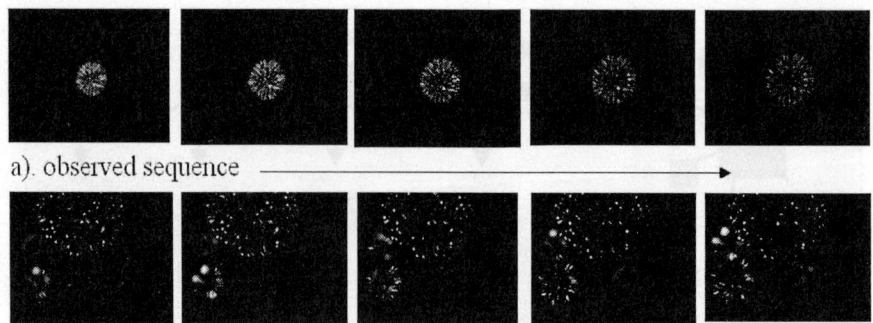

Fig. 10. Example of the firework sequence (see firework_obs.avi, firework_syn.avi)

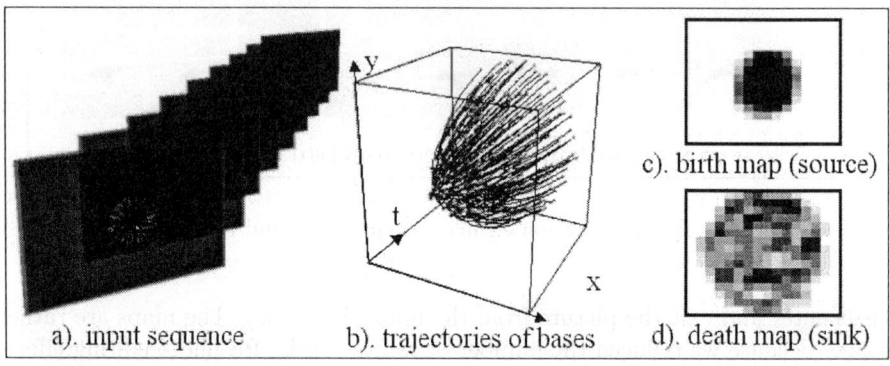

Fig. 11. The computed trajectories of fireworks and the source and sink maps.

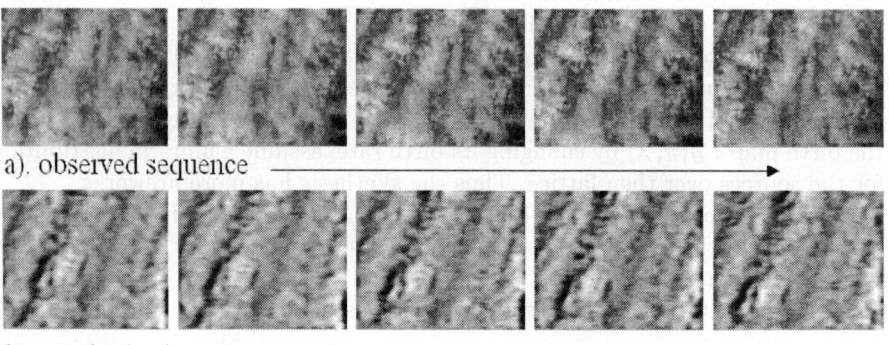

Fig. 12. Example of the waterfall sequence (see waterfall_obs.avi, waterfall_syn.avi)

alter the dynamics or geometry of movetons by group or by individuals. The representation is semantically meaningful for vision applications as well because

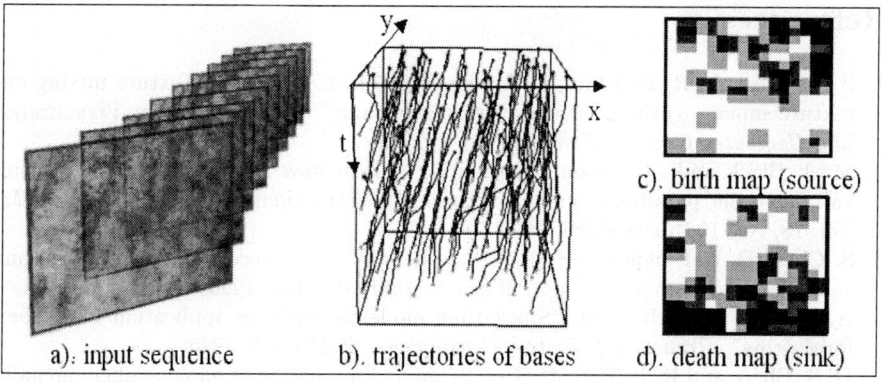

Fig. 13. The computed trajectories of waterfalls and the source and sink maps.

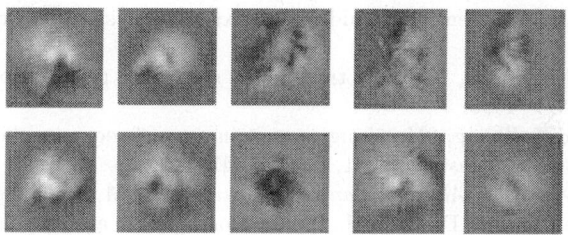

Fig. 14. The random examples of water drops.

the recovered trajectories etc. Needless to say that the generative description $W[0,\tau]$ achieves tremendous compression (usually 10^2-fold) compared to image $\mathbf{I}[0,\tau]$.

In future work we should extend the model in the following aspects.

1. We shall study the spatial interactions of the moving elements, bifurcation and merging of trajectories, and thus integrate good properties of the STAR model to account for lighting variation in motions such as water.
2. We shall study the 3D positions of the moving elements (structure from motion).

Acknowledgments

We'd like to thank for the support of three research grants, NSF IIS-98-77-127, NSF IIS-00-92-664 and an ONR grant N000140-110-535. Cheng-en Guo and Adrian Barbu are very helpful in programming and creating some of the figures. We also thank the MIT motion texture database.

References

1. Z. Bar-Joseph, R. El-Yaniv, D. Lischinski, and M. Werman. "Texture mixing and texture movie synthesis using statistical learning", *IEEE Trans on Visualization and Computer Graphics*, (to appear).
2. M. J. Black and A. Jepson, "Estimating optical flow in segmented images using variable-order parametric models with local deformations", *IEEE Trans on PAMI*, Vol. 18, No. 10, pp. 972-986, 1996.
3. S. Chen, D. L. Donoho, and M. A. Saunders, "Atomic decompostion by basis pursuit", *Technical preprint*, Dept. of Stat., Stanford Univ., 1996.
4. A. D. Cliff and J.K. Ord, "Space-time modeling with an application to regional forecasting", *Trans. Inst. British Geographers*, 66:119-128, 1975.
5. D. S. Ebert and R. E. Parent, "Rendering and animation of gaseous phenomena by combining fast volume and scaleline A-buffer techniques", *SIGGRAPH*, 1990.
6. M. G. Gu, "A stochastic approximation algorithm with MCMC method for incomplete data estimation problems", *Preprint*, Dept. of Stat., McGill Univ. 1998.
7. D. Heeger and J. Bergen, "Pyramid-based texture analysis and synthesis", *Proc. of SIGGRAPH*, 1995.
8. M. Isard and A. Blake, "Contour tracking by stochastic propagation of conditional density", *ECCV*, 1996.
9. S. Mallat and Z. Zhang, "Matching pursuit in a timef-requency dictionary", *IEEE trans. on Signal Processing*, vol.41, pp3397-3415, 1993.
10. Y. Meyer, *Wavelets: Algorithm and Applications*, SIAM, Philadelphia, 1993.
11. B. A. Olshausen and D. J. Field, "Sparse coding with an overcomplete basis set: A strategy employed by V1?", *Vision Research*, Vo.37, No. 23, pp3311-3325, 1997.
12. W. T. Reeves and R. Blau, "Approximate and probabilistic algorithms for shading and rendering structured particle systems", *Proc. of SIGGRAPH*, 1985.
13. P. Saisan, G. Doretto, Y.N. Wu, S. Soatto, "Dynamic Texture Recognition," *CVPR*, 2001.
14. A. Schodl, R. Szeliski, D. Salesin, and I. Essa, "Video texture", *Proc. of SIGGRAPH*, 2000.
15. S. Soatto, G. Doretto, and Y.N. Wu, "Dynamic texture", *ICCV*, 2001.
16. A. W. Fitzgibbon, "Stochastic rigidity: image registration for nowhere-static scenes.", *Proc. ICCV*, pages 662–669, July 2001.
17. M. O. Szummer and R. W. Picard, "Temporal texture modeling", *Proc. of Int'l Conf. on Image Processing*, Lausanne, Switzerland, 1996.
18. L.Y. Wei and M. Levoy, "Fast texture synthesis using tree structured vector quantization", *Proc. of SIGGRAPH*, 2000.
19. S. C. Zhu, Y.N. Wu, and D. B. Mumford, "Minimax entropy principle and Its Applications to Texture Modeling", *Neural Computation*, Vol. 9, Nov. 1997

Is Super-Resolution with Optical Flow Feasible?

WenYi Zhao and Harpreet S. Sawhney

Sarnoff Corporation
201 Washington Road, Princeton, NJ 08540
{wzhao, hsawhney}@sarnoff.com

Abstract. Reconstruction-based super-resolution from motion video has been an active area of study in computer vision and video analysis. Image alignment is a key component of super-resolution algorithms. Almost all previous super-resolution algorithms have *assumed* that standard methods of image alignment can provide accurate enough alignment for creating super-resolution images. However, a systematic study of the demands on accuracy of multi-image alignment and its effects on super-resolution has been lacking. Furthermore, implicitly or explicitly most algorithms have assumed that the multiple video frames or specific regions of interest are related through global parametric transformations. From previous works, it is not at all clear how super-resolution performs under alignment with piecewise parametric or local optical flow based methods. This paper is an attempt at understanding the influence of image alignment and warping errors on super-resolution. Requirements on the *consistency* of optical flow across multiple images are studied and it is shown that errors resulting from traditional flow algorithms may render super-resolution infeasible.

1 Introduction

Enhancement of image resolution, called *super-resolution*, by processing multiple video images has been studied by many researchers over the past decade. The majority of super-resolution algorithms formulate the problem as a signal reconstruction problem from multiple samples. These algorithms are based on sampling theorems which state that given enough uniform or non-uniform samples, signals can be reconstructed. In single images captured over discrete grids, super-resolution may not be possible since all parts of the scene may not be adequately sampled by a single image. Multiple images captured using motions of the sensor or objects potentially provide adequate samples for super-resolution of any given image frame. However, ensuring the accuracy of sample locations from multiple images demands adequate alignment between multiple images that may be related through arbitrarily complex motion models. Almost all previous super-resolution algorithms have *assumed* that standard methods of image alignment can provide accurate enough alignment for creating super-resolution images. Implicitly or explicitly most algorithms have assumed that the multiple video frames or specific regions of interest are related through global parametric transformations. However, a systematic study of the demands on accuracy of multi-image alignment and its effects on super-resolution has been lacking. Moreover, when multiple video frames cannot be aligned by global parametric models, local models like optical flow need to be used for alignment. From previous works, it is not at all clear how super-resolution performs under alignment with piecewise parametric or local optical flow based methods.

This paper is an attempt at understanding the influence of image alignment and warping errors on super-resolution. We first present an analysis on how optical flow affects super-resolution algorithms. In particular, we adopt a general motion model composed of a global parametric model plus local flow [15]. To understand what is the impact of flow error on super-resolution, we introduce an image degradation model that explicitly incorporates the motion/flow error. We then convert such a geometric error into image noise. Focusing on the gradient-based flow computation leads us to discover an interesting phenomenon: large/small motion errors are associated with small/large image gradients. This suggests that image warping error is not as catastrophic as the flow error, and implies that image warping process may be well-behaved and hence flow-based super-resolution is feasible.

In order to address the core alignment issue itself, we experiment with novel flow algorithms. Though we show that it is image warping not flow that is directly linked to the super-resolution process, flow is especially critical for reconstruction of high-frequency components in the signal. The flow algorithms we employ address two issues: *flow consistency* and *flow accuracy*. Flow consistency implies that the flow computed from frame A to frame B should be consistent with that computed from B to A. Flow accuracy measures the absolute error in flow. The new algorithms take advantage of multi-image alignment in contrast with traditional flow algorithms devoted to pairwise image alignment. By computing all flows simultaneously, we propose a method that is similar to "bundle adjustment" used in parametric registration. Consistent and bundled flow estimation addresses the issues of flow consistency and accuracy.

2 Related Work

Work on super-resolution can be divided into two main categories: reconstruction-based methods [1-9] and learning-based methods [11-13]. The theoretical foundations for reconstruction methods are (non-)uniform sampling theorems while learning-based methods employ generative models that are learned from samples. The goal of the former is to *reconstruct* the original (super-sampled) signal while that of the latter is to *create* the signal based on learned generative models. In contrast with reconstruction methods, learning-based super-resolution methods assume that corresponding low-resolution and high-resolution training image pairs are available [11-13]. In [12], a general-purpose learning is applied and has demonstrated some good results for super-resolution.

The majority of super-resolution algorithms belong to the signal reconstruction paradigm. Among this category are frequency-based methods [9], Bayesian methods [4-6], BP (back-projection) methods [1], POCS (projection onto convex set) methods [3], non-uniform sampling based methods [7-8] and hybrid methods [2]. These methods are deeply root in sampling theorems. According to these theorems, perfect reconstruction can be achieved as long as adequate sub-samples are available. Image alignment is typically used to ensure the availability of samples. Knowing if the samples are enough is important since in general the condition could vary from point to point in the images. There exist techniques that can be used to handle this issue automatically, e.g., regularization techniques. As for alignment, it is the key for the success of all reconstruction-based super-resolution algorithms. With accurate alignment, the reconstruction task is relatively easy. This is clearly demonstrated in [7].

The emphasis of this work is on the feasibility of super-resolution under general non-parametric motion models. Consistent estimation of *global* motion models (e.g. homographies) are therefore not reviewed here. Accurate alignment demanded by super-resolution may be difficult under general motion models since the system is not heavily over-determined as in the case of global parametric models. Another factor that contributes to the difficulty is that motion is typically estimated from noisy low-resolution images and interpolated to the higher resolution. Ideally, accurate motion estimation should be estimated from high-resolution images that are not available. Restricting the motion models to global parametric limits the application of super-resolution greatly. To work with general image sequences, we have to loosen such requirements. Otherwise, we would have to resort to solving a difficult segmentation problem: segment out moving objects and compute the parametric motion models for the objects. For non-rigid objects, it is even more difficult. In [17], a method for reliable block motion estimation is suggested for super-resolution in which multiple motion vectors are created for each block. However, our work shows that for reconstruction based methods, cross-frame consistency of motion estimates is important for super-resolution.

3 Flow-Based Super-Resolution

We first address the issue of feasibility of flow-based super-resolution.

3.1 Analysis of Flow Error for Super-Resolution

Classical Signal Reconstruction. Without loss of generality, we use 1D signals for analysis. We assume that the original high-resolution digital signal $f(n)$ has bandwidth $(-\omega_0, \omega_0)$ with $\omega_0 > \pi/2$ and two sub-sampled versions of the signal, $f1(n)$ and $f2(n)$, are available. There are two sub-sampling modes considered here: (i) decimation only, and (ii) blurring and decimation. In the decimation-only case: $f_1(n) = f(2n)$ and $f_2(n) = f(2n-1)$. Assume that the two sub-sampled signals are aliased, that is their spectra are created by wrapping the high-frequency part of the original signal into its low-frequency band. Mathematically, their Fourier transforms [18] are related to the Fourier transform of the original high-resolution signal as:

$$F_1(\omega) = \begin{cases} F(\omega/2), & |\omega| \leq 2\pi - 2\omega_0 \\ F(\omega/2) + A_1(\omega/2), & otherwise \end{cases}$$

and

$$F_2(\omega) = \begin{cases} F(\omega/2)\exp(-j\omega/2), & |\omega| \leq 2\pi - 2\omega_0 \\ F(\omega/2)\exp(-j\omega/2) - A_1(\omega/2)\exp(-j\omega/2), & otherwise \end{cases}$$

where $A_1(\omega/2) = F((\omega - 2\pi)/2) + F((\omega + 2\pi)/2)$ is the aliased component composed of the original mid-frequency and wrapped high-frequency. To recover the original signal using an estimated signal shift $\tilde{n}_0$, we perform the following operation: $F(\omega) = (F_1(2\omega) + F_2(2\omega)\exp(j\omega\tilde{n}_0))/2$.

In the case of perfect alignment $\tilde{n}_0 = 1$, the original signal can be perfectly recovered since the aliasing items are cancelled. In the case of imperfect alignment, $\delta\tilde{n}_0 \neq 0$, the reconstructed signal is as follows:

$$\tilde{F}(\omega) = \begin{cases} F(\omega)(1+\exp[j\omega\delta\tilde{n}_0])/2, & |\omega| \leq 2\pi - 2\omega_0 \\ F(\omega)(1+\exp[j\omega\delta\tilde{n}_0])/2 + (A_1(\omega) + A_2(\omega)\exp[j\omega\delta\tilde{n}_0])/2, & otherwise \end{cases}$$

Thus, while the reconstructed signal is affected across the whole spectrum by mis-alignment, the effect on the high-frequency components is more severe. In the case of blurring and decimation, we first recover the blurred signal and then perform de-blurring. The same analysis applies as long as the cut-off frequency of the blurring filter is equal to or larger than ω_0. In summary, alignment is critical for perfect reconstruction.

The above analysis does not take into account that alignment is computed from the sub-sampled signals. In the following we study the relationship between signal alignment and signal warping for a 2D signal.

Reconstruction based on Alignment and Warping. In order to model the high-to-low resolution image formation process, we adopt the matrix notations used in [2]. Specifically,

$$Y_k = D_k C_k F_k X + N_k \tag{1}$$

where X is the original high-resolution image, Y_k is the kth low-resolution frame, D_k, C_k, F_k are decimation, blurring and motion-warping matrices, respectively, that embody the corresponding transformations, N_k is the noise model at low-resolution. Note that given a motion representation (including optical flow), F_k can be used to represent the corresponding warping transformation. Based on this model and the assumption of zero-mean Gaussian noise, the ML-estimator of X from Y_k is

$$\tilde{X} = \arg_X \min\{(Y - HX)^T W(Y - HX)\} \tag{2}$$

where W is the weight matrix determined by noise N_k, matrix H is defined as $[H]_k = D_k C_k F_k$. However, this model does not allow for alignment error. In order to account for the uncertainty of estimated alignment, we augment the above model as:

$$Y_k = D_k C_k (F_k + \delta F_k) X + N_k = D_k C_k F_k X + (N_k + N_X^{F_k}) \tag{3}$$

where $N_X^{F_k} \stackrel{\text{def}}{=} \delta F_k X$. Comparing Eqs. (1) and (3), we notice an additional noise term. Now the ML-estimator needs to be modified as:

$$\tilde{X} = \arg_X \min\{(Y - HX)^T W^F (Y - HX)\} \tag{4}$$

where the new weight matrix is computed from both the noise terms $N_X^{F_k}$ and N_k.

Image warping. Before we study the misalignment induced noise term, it is important to review the basic warping technique. Given a source image I^s and the alignment transformation from this image to the warped image I^w, image warping can be formulated as:

$$I^w(\mathbf{p}) = \sum_i \alpha_i I^s(\mathbf{q}_i) \tag{5}$$

where α_i's are the interpolation coefficients, $I^s(\mathbf{q}_i)$ are pixels that surround the center pixel $I(\mathbf{q}_0)$ (very often $\mathbf{q}_0$ is not on the integer grid) in the source image and $I^w(\mathbf{p})$ is the corresponding pixel in the warped image. The given alignment parameter $\mathbf{u}$ defines the relation between $\mathbf{q}_0$ and $\mathbf{p}$: $\mathbf{p} = \mathbf{q}_0 + \mathbf{u}[\mathbf{p}]$.

Model for $N_X^{F_k}$ without N_k. We convert the geometric motion error into additional image noise via image warping. To simplify the analysis, we first assume that the original image noise can be ignored.

Using Eq. 5, the warped image $I^{F_k}(\mathbf{p})$ (matrix notation of $F_k X$) is obtained from I (matrix notation of X). Assuming an error in the estimated motion, the warped image changes to $\tilde{I}^{F_k}(\mathbf{p})$. For *small* motion error $d\mathbf{u}$, we can use a linear approximation:

$$\tilde{I}^{F_k}(\mathbf{p}) \approx I^{F_k}(\mathbf{p}) + I_x^{F_k}(\mathbf{p}) d\mathbf{u}_x + I_y^{F_k}(\mathbf{p}) d\mathbf{u}_y. \tag{6}$$

In the iterative process of estimating motion from the reference image I to a image I_k, at each iteration I is warped to match I_k [15]:

$$I_k(\mathbf{p}) \approx \sum_i \alpha_i I(\mathbf{q}_0 + \mathbf{u}[\mathbf{p}]). \tag{7}$$

Note that the alignment parameters are in the same coordinates $\mathbf{p}$ in Eqs. 6 and 7. Hence the components of $N_X^{F_k}$ can be obtained as:

$$\delta I^{F_k}(\mathbf{p}) \approx I_x^{F_k}(\mathbf{p}) d\mathbf{u}[\mathbf{p}]_x + I_y^{F_k}(\mathbf{p}) d\mathbf{u}[\mathbf{p}]_y. \tag{8}$$

This image noise (warping error) is dependent on pixel location. Now let us model the motion error and image noise across the whole image region. We further assume that the motion error is zero-mean (this might not be true in general but appears to be a valid assumption from our experiments), then the image noise has zero-mean. Its covariance can be computed as:

$$\text{var}(\delta I^{F_k}) = I_x^2 (\sum I_y^2) + I_y^2 (\sum I_x^2) - 2I_x I_y (\sum I_x I_y),$$

using the covariance matrix for the estimated motion:

$$\text{cov}(d\mathbf{u}_x, d\mathbf{u}_y) = \text{inv}\left(\begin{bmatrix} \sum I_x^2 & \sum(I_x I_y) \\ \sum I_x I_y & \sum I_y^2 \end{bmatrix}\right).$$

It is well-known that larger image gradients lead to more precise motion estimation. Clearly the image noise due to warping error is not only a function of flow error but also of image gradients. In particular, relatively large motion errors due to small gradients are balanced by the small gradients as shown in Eq. (8). In other words, even if the motion is not very accurate, the warped image is still very close to the warped image based on true motion. In summary, in the case of small noise, optical flow can be used for the purpose of super-resolution.

3.2 Computing Consistent and Accurate Flows

Though we showed that it is image warping that directly influences the super-resolution process, flow is especially critical for reconstruction of high-frequency components.

Computing Consistent Flow. Consistent flow [19] between a pair of frames guarantees that the pair of flow fields, from frame 1 to frame 2 and from 2 to 1, will be consistent. In many applications, one-sided traditional flow algorithms are independently applied in the two directions, and points where the two flows are inconsistent are rejected. However, for reconstruction based super-resolution, consistent flow is essential since the maximum-likelihood estimator typically minimizes error between an iteratively reconstructed super-resolved image and the original low resolution images. Depending on the specific iterative technique used for the reconstruction, pixels are mapped both ways between the low and the high-resolution coordinate systems.

Traditional flow estimation algorithms ([15], for instance) compute a flow field between and image pair, I_1 and I_2, using *brightness constancy*:

$$I_1(\mathbf{p}_1) = I_2(\mathbf{p}_2), \tag{9}$$

where $\mathbf{p}_1$ and $\mathbf{p}_2$ are the coordinates of frame 1 and 2 respectively. At each iteration, a linearized approximation to the above equation if employed to solve for increments in the flow field.

$$I_t(\mathbf{p}_2) \approx \nabla I_2(\mathbf{p}_2)^T J_{12}^T \mathbf{u}_2[\mathbf{p}_2], \tag{10}$$

where J_{12} is the Jacobian partial derivative matrix of $\mathbf{p}_1$ w.r.t $\mathbf{p}_2$. Equation (10) is the basic equation of iterative multi-grid algorithms that computes the flow field from I_1 to I_2. The following approximation is employed for the Jacobian:

$$J_{12}\nabla I_2(\mathbf{p}_2) \simeq \frac{1}{2}(\nabla I_2(\mathbf{p}_2) + \nabla I_1(\mathbf{p}_2)) \tag{11}$$

The above technique can be used to compute the pair of flow fields from I_2 to I_1 and vice-versa. However, such a computation does not guarantee the following *consistency* constraint:

$$\begin{aligned}\mathbf{p_2} &= \mathbf{p_1} + \mathbf{u_1}[\mathbf{p_1}]\\ \mathbf{u_2}[\mathbf{p_2}] &= -\mathbf{u_1}[\mathbf{p_1}]\end{aligned} \quad (12)$$

To enforce the two-way flow consistency, we propose computing just one flow field, the consistent flow satisfying Eq (12) between any frame pair. Using the consistency constraint and the brightness constraint (Eq. 9), we can derive the *consistent* brightness constraint equation

$$I(\mathbf{p}) = I_1(\mathbf{p} - \frac{1}{2}\mathbf{u}[\mathbf{p}]) = I_2(\mathbf{p} + \frac{1}{2}\mathbf{u}[\mathbf{p}]), \quad (13)$$

where $I(\mathbf{p})$ is the virtual middle frame between the two frames. Using Taylor series expansion, we obtain the following differential form:

$$\begin{aligned}I_t(\mathbf{p}) &\stackrel{\text{def}}{=} I_1(\mathbf{p}) - I_2(\mathbf{p})\\ &\approx \tfrac{1}{2}(\nabla I_1(\mathbf{p}) + \nabla I_2(\mathbf{p}))^T \mathbf{u}[\mathbf{p}].\end{aligned} \quad (14)$$

All the coordinates are in the coordinate system of I. An iterative version of this new method can be readily derived. The advantages of computing consistent flow are: 1) only one consistent flow needs to be estimated for an image pair, and 2) the estimated flow by definition guarantees backward-forward consistency and hence may be more accurate.

Computing Bundled Flow Fields. We can generalize the notion of flow consistency over many frames by computing a consistent bundle of flow fields. Suppose consistent flow is to be computed between three frames, I_1 and I_3 to frame I_2 with the flow fields designated as $\mathbf{u_1}$ and $\mathbf{u_3}$, respectively. Frame I_2 is chosen as the reference frame I. Traditional two-frame methods to compute the two flows $\mathbf{u_1}[\mathbf{p}]$ and $\mathbf{u_3}[\mathbf{p}]$ are based on two independent constraints: $I_1(\mathbf{p_1}) - I(\mathbf{p})$ and $I_3(\mathbf{p_3}) = I(\mathbf{p})$. Again, consistency between $\mathbf{u_1}$ and $\mathbf{u_3}$ is not guaranteed if the two are computed independently. A straightforward way to enforce the consistency among flows is to add the following constraint: $I_3(\mathbf{p_3}) = I_1(\mathbf{p_3})$.

The iterative version of these constraints can be expressed in the common coordinate system of $\mathbf{p}$ as:

$$\begin{aligned}I'_{t1} &= I'_1 - I \approx \tfrac{1}{2}(\nabla I + \nabla I'_1))^T \delta \mathbf{u_1}\\ I'_{t3} &= I'_3 - I \approx \tfrac{1}{2}(\nabla I + \nabla I'_3))^T \delta \mathbf{u_3}\\ I'_{t13} &= I'_1 - I'_3 \approx \tfrac{1}{2}[(\nabla I'_1)^T \delta \mathbf{u_1} - (\nabla I'_3)^T \delta \mathbf{u_3}]\end{aligned} \quad (15)$$

where I'_i are the warped version of I_i using motion from the previous iteration, $\delta \mathbf{u_1}[\mathbf{p}]$ and $\delta \mathbf{u_3}[\mathbf{p}]$ are the incremental flows computed at each iteration. The bundled flow can be solved for by formulating the normal equations within a window centered at each pixel by assuming a constant flow model inside the window. For brevity, we omit the normal equations since these can be derived easily from Eq. 15.

Accurate and Consistent Flow Fields. Note that the error minimized above does not take into consideration the consistency between each pair of frames. This is not possible for pairs of frames other than the reference frame since to enforce pairwise consistency we need to use virtual coordinate systems for each pair of frames. To handle this issue, we propose the following algorithm:

- First compute consistent pairwise flow $\mathbf{u}_{i,i+1}$.
- Then cascade the consistent flows to obtain the initial flow estimates $\mathbf{u}_j$ from frame j to the reference frame.
- Bundle adjust the initial flow estimates.

3.3 Flow-Based Super-Resolution

We have analyzed the performance of super-resolution using a popular reconstruction based super-resolution algorithm [1]. However, any of the other algorithms [2-11] would also show a similar behavior since the error measures minimized in all of them are similar. Although in [1] only parametric motion models were employed, we use general flow as the alignment model.

Let us denote $I_h^{(n)}$ as the recovered high-resolution image and $g_k^{(n)}$ as the simulated low-resolution image of the k-th frame, at the n-th iteration. The iterative update of high-resolution image is expressed in [1] as:

$$I_h^{(n+1)} = I_h^{(n)} + \frac{1}{K} \sum_{k=1}^{K} \{[(g_k - g_k^{(n)}) \uparrow s]^{F_k} \cdot p\} \qquad (16)$$

where K is the number of low-resolution images, p is a back-projection kernel, $\uparrow s$ denotes a up-sampling operator by a factor s, $[\cdot]^{F_k}$ denotes a forward-warping process. The simulated image $g_k^{(n)}$ is generated as follows:

$$g_k^{(n)} = [I_h^{(n)}]^{B_k} \cdot h\} \downarrow s \qquad (17)$$

where $[\cdot]^{B_k}$ denotes a backward-warping process and h is a blurring kernel.

One important quantity embedded in the above formulation is the projection error that measures the quality of the super-resolution

$$E_p = \frac{1}{K} \sum_{k=1}^{K} (g_k - g_k^{(n)}) \qquad (18)$$

In Section 4, we will investigate how flow algorithms can affect this important quality.

Estimating motion and performing super-resolution is a chicken-egg problem. To resolve this issue, the following incremental strategy can be used:

Iterative motion estimation and super-resolution.

1. Compute motion from original low-resolution images.

2. Interpolate low-resolution motion and perform super-resolution.
3. Use the super-resolved images to refine the motion at the high-resolution. (This step and the next are optional.)
4. Perform super-resolution using the refined motion and repeat steps 3 & 4 if needed.

Reject Warping Outliers. In order to cover all aspects of motion error, a reconstruction algorithm needs to account for warping errors in spite of accurate and consistent motion estimation procedures. Recall that the error analysis is based on small errors in flow computation. But this may not always be true for general scene or video content. For example, in the case of large object occlusions or scene changes in the video, the alignment is inherently wrong and super-resolution is not possible. In such cases, we need to detect anomalies in flow based on warping. We compute the cross-correlation between a target frame and the warped frame, and if the correlation score at a point is below a certain threshold, the corresponding warped pixels are ignored in the super-resolution process. The correlation scores can also be used as weights with a maximum-likelihood super-resolution estimator.

4 Experiments

We present experimental results with three types of datasets:

- Synthetic data that has synthetic motion and sub-sampled images. This data is generated from one high-resolution image by creating multiple images with synthetic motion.
- Semi-synthetic data that has synthetically sub-sampled images but real motion. This is generated from a real sequence of high-resolution images.
- Real sub-sampled image sequence.

The three different types of data allow us to systematically evaluate flow computation, the relation among flow error, warping error and super-resolution error, and the super-resolution results. We emphasize that for the last two sequences, rigid 3D motion (parallax) and non-rigid motions are present, therefore global motion estimates cannot be utilized.

For the back-projection algorithm, we choose the forward and backward filters as suggested by the authors in [1]. In our experiment, we use the interpolated reference image as the initial high-resolution image.

4.1 Purely Synthetic Data

We select a single high-resolution image from a real video sequence that consists of a rich scene with man-made rigid objects, text, and natural textures. Three synthetic motions are used to create three more frames: $[-0.5, -0.5]$, $[0.5, 1]$, and $[1, 0.5]$. In the following experiments, statistics are computed from all the frames.

For example, the flow error statistics are based on all flows from the reference image to the other images. Note that although a parametric model is chosen for the synthesized motions, for the experiments a non-parametric optical field is computed to assess the various aspects of flow accuracy.

Comparison of Flow Estimation. We compare three different methods for flow computation: 1) Least-squares based flow [15] (LSQ flow), 2) consistent flow (CONS flow), and 3) bundled flow with CONS flow as the initial input (CB flow).

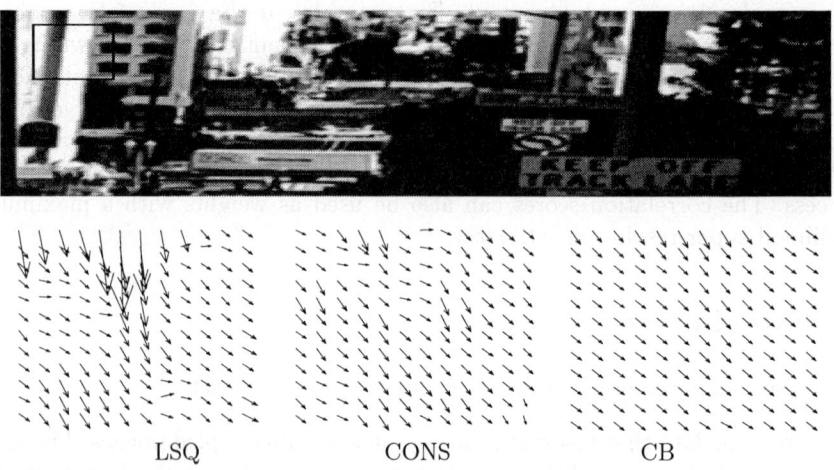

Fig. 1. Top row: the reference image and the selected region of interest (ROI). Bottom row: a close-up look at the computed flows in the selected ROI.

Fig. 1 shows the three flow fields for a region-of-interest (ROI) highlighted in one frame at the top. The qualitative nature of the flow and the relative errors are clear from the pictures. In addition, we compute quantitative errors in the flow in two different ways. If we define the *error flow* as the difference vector between the perfect flow and the computed flow, then the histograms of the two directional components, and the histograms of flow magnitude and angle can be used. To represent the error flow using just one measurement, we define the signed magnitude which is the product of its magnitude and the tangent of its direction. A similar quantity has been used to represent the probability distribution of the flow error in [16].

Figure 2 plots the two histograms, one for x-direction flow and the other for the signed magnitude of flow, for the three different methods. Furthermore, we also compute a measure of flow inconsistency, called *reprojection error flow*, as the difference between the forward and backward flows at corresponding points. That is, $\mathbf{e}12(\mathbf{p}) = \mathbf{p} - \mathbf{u}21(\mathbf{p} + \mathbf{u}12(\mathbf{p}))$, where $\mathbf{e}12, \mathbf{u}12, \mathbf{u}21$ are the reprojection error flow and the flow fields for frames 1-2 and 2-1, respectively. Table 1

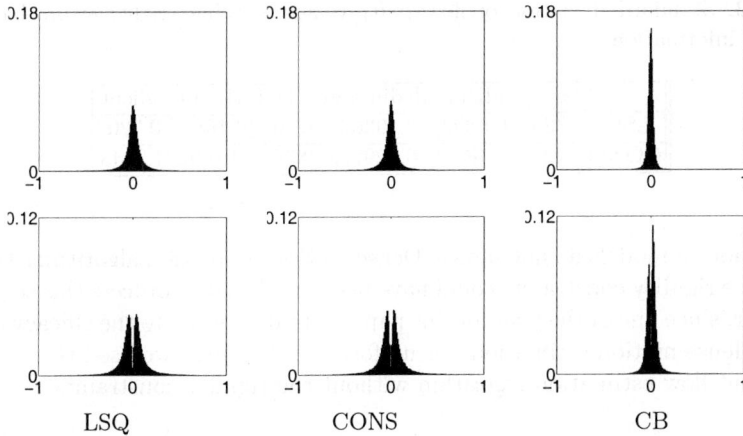

Fig. 2. Comparison of flows computed from synthetic low-resolution images. The top row plots the histogram of flow error in x-direction while the bottom row plots the histogram of the signed magnitude of error flows.

compares the peaks and standard deviations of the histograms of reprojection error flow for the three methods.

Table 1. Histogram peak (left) and standard deviation (right) of error flows corresponding to Fig. 2

	LSQ	CONS	CB
x-dir	.0748/.1685	.0795/.1163	.1601/.0417
signed mag	.0464/.8272	.0493/.1580	.1130/.0769
reproj. signed mag	.0308/.7093	none	small

Gradient-based Flow Error vs. Warping Error. We have computed the statistics for flow error and corresponding errors in image warping based on the gradient of the images. First, regardless of gradient information, if flow error is small, e.g., less than half pixel, then the warping error at the same location has a well-behaved Gaussian-shape distribution. Second, when gradient information is considered, relatively large flow error due to small gradients does not cause large warping error as pointed out in Section 3. This behavior is shown in Table 2 for the three methods using data from regions of three different gradient types..

4.2 Semi-synthetic Data

The second set of results are on a 9-frame video sequence captured with a DV (digital video) camcorder inside an office. There is parallax in the sequence so

Table 2. Standard deviation of flow (left) versus warping (right) errors based on gradient information.

	Low gradient	Medium gradient	High gradient
LSQ	0.3235/0.5802	0.1930/1.9736	0.1686/0.7202
CONS	0.1254/0.4836	0.1292/2.0864	0.1602/1.3643

global motion models do not suffice. Dense motion estimation algorithms that incorporate rigidity constraints could have been employed to process this sequence. However, since one of the goals of this paper is to demonstrate the efficacy of consistent dense motion estimation, for uniformity of results, we used the proposed consistent flow estimation algorithm without the rigidity constraints.

Super-resolution Error. We have experimented with the super-resolution algorithm with the three flows computed earlier plus the true flow. In Fig. 3, we plot the projection error (Eq. 18) as a function of the number of iterations for an ROI highlighted in the original frame on the top left in Fig. 4. For comparison purposes, the reconstructed images are also shown in Fig. 3. Note that errors in non-consistent flow tend to increase the reconstruction error as is evident both in the plot as well as the reconstructed image. The error becomes larger with more iterations. However, consistent flow does not suffer from this problem.

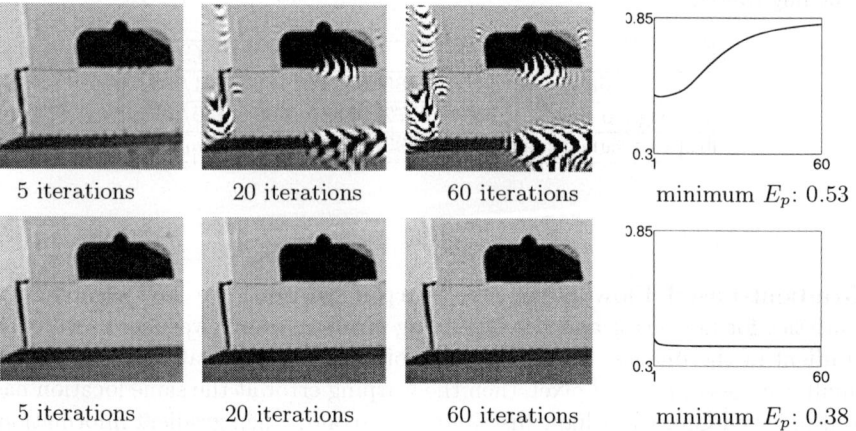

| 5 iterations | 20 iterations | 60 iterations | minimum E_p: 0.53 |
| 5 iterations | 20 iterations | 60 iterations | minimum E_p: 0.38 |

Fig. 3. Comparison of reconstruction results. An ROI is selected (as shown in the top frame in in Fig. 4) and its super-resolved image is zoomed up for display. The figures are arranged in a way that rows from one to two correspond to LSQ flow, and CONS flow, respectively. The first column plots the reconstructed image at iteration 5 while images in the second column are results at iteration 60. The last column plots projection error curves of LSQ and CONS flow for 60 iterations.

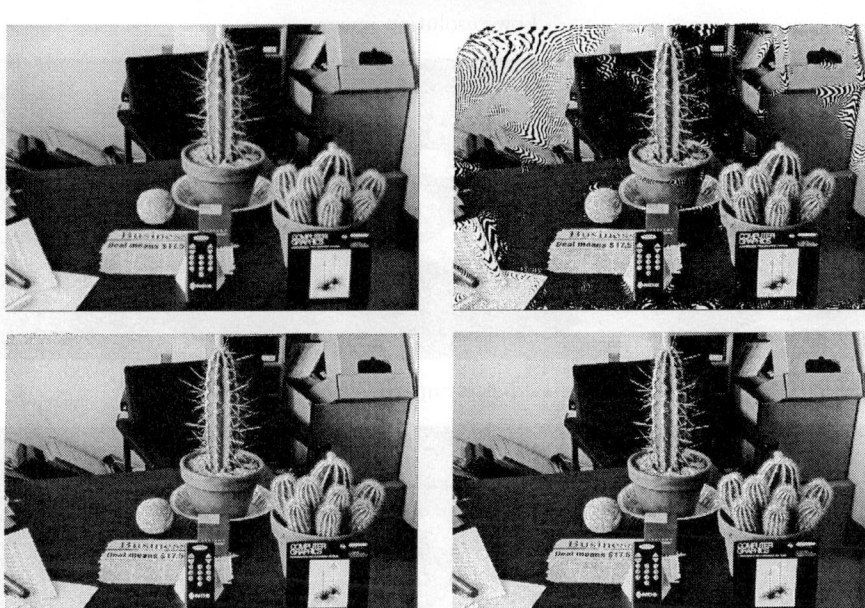

Fig. 4. Reconstruction results using one reference images and eight other images. The top row shows a low-resolution reference image with an ROI marked. Figures plotted in the second row are bicubic interpolation result and LSQ flow based super-resolved image. Finally, figures in the last row are CONS flow based super-resolved image and the true high-resolution image.

4.3 Real Video Sequences

The final results are with one sequence for which there is no ground truth. So the result is for visual quality assessment only. Again, we emphasize that no 2D/3D global motion model is valid for this sequence since the bee and the flower are swaying in the wind while the camera is moving. Fig. 5 shows one original frame and two super-resolved frames, one with LSQ flow and another with CONS flow. The superior quality in terms of sharpness and detail for the latter is evident.

5 Conclusions

We have studied the feasibility of reconstruction-based super-resolution with respect to errors in image alignment. An analysis of errors in optical flow indicates

Low-resolution image

LSQ flow based super-resolved image

CONS flow based super-resolved image

Fig. 5. Comparison of super-resolved images from high-quality DV.

that optical flow based super-resolution may be feasible in the small noise case since warping errors are well-behaved. However, even in the small noise case, flow accuracy is important. We introduced the concept of flow consistency and showed both quantitatively and qualitatively that flow consistency is critical for super-resolution. In the context of flow consistency, we presented algorithms that enforce consistency and demonstrated their efficacy. We plan to test these ideas with other reconstruction based super-resolution algorithms. We are also developing fully consistent bundled flow fields.

References

[1] Irani, M. and Peleg, S. 1993. Motion Analysis for Image Enhancement: Resolution, Occlusion, and Transparency. *Journal of Visual Comm. and Image Repre.*, Vol. 4, pp. 324-335.

[2] Elad, M. and Feuer, A. 1997. Restoration of a single superresolution image form several blurred, noisy and undersampled measured images. *IEEE Trans. on Image Processing*, pp. 1646–1658.

[3] Patti, A., Sezan, M., and Tekalp, M. 1997. Superresolution video reconstruction with arbitrary sampling lattices and nonzero aperture time. *IEEE Trans. on Image Processing*, pp. 1064–1078.

[4] Bascle, B., Blake, A., and Zisserman, A. 1996. Motion deblurring and super-resolution from an image sequence. In *Proc. European Conf. Comp. Vision*, pp 573–581.

[5] Schultz, R.R. and Stevenson, R.L. 1996. Extraction of high resolution frames from video sequences. *IEEE Trans. on Image Processing*, pp. 996–1011.

[6] Hardie, R., Barrard, K., and Armstrong E. 1997. Joint MAP Registration and High-resolution Image Estimation Using a Sequence of Undersampled Images. *IEEE Trans. on Image Processing*, pp. 1621-1633.
Multi-resolution

[7] Marziliano, P. and Vetterlli, M. 1999. Reconstruction of Irregularly Sampled Discrete-Time Bandlimited Signals. *IEEE Trans. on Signal Processing*, pp. 3462-3471.

[8] Shekarforoush, H. and Chellappa, R. 1999. Data-driven multi-channel super-resolution with application to video sequences. *Journal of the Optical Society of America A*, pp. 481–492.

[9] Tsai, R.Y. and Huang, T.S. 1984. Multi-frame Image Restoration and Registration.*Advances in Computer Vision and Image Processing*, JAI Press Inc.

[10] Baker, S. and Kanade, T. 1999. Super-Resolution Optical Flow. CMU-RI-TR-9936.

[11] Baker, S. and Kanade, T. 2000. Limits on Super-Resolution and How to Break Them. In *Proc. Conf. Comp. Vision and Patt. Recog.*

[12] Freeman, W. and Pasztor, E. 1999. Learning low-level vision. In *Proc. Int. Conf. Comp. Vision.*

[13] Bonet, J.S.D. 1997. sampling procedure for analysis and synthesis of texture images. In *Proceedings of SIGGRAPH*, pp. 361-368.

[14] B. D. Lucas and T. Kanade. 1981. An iterative image registration technique with an application to stereo vision. In *Proc. 7th Int. Joint Conf. on Art. Intell.*.

[15] Bergen, J., Anandan, P., Hanna, K., and Hingorani, R. 1992. Hierarchical Model-Based Motion Estimation. In *Proc. European Conf. Comp. Vision*, pp. 237-252.

[16] Simoncelli, E.P. and Adelson, E.H. 1990. Computing Optical Flow Distribution Using Spatio-Temporal Filters. MIT Media Lab Technical Report 165.

[17] Sha, N. R. and Zakhor, A. 1999. Resolution Enhancement of Color Video Sequences. In *IEEE Trans. on IP*, Vol. 8, No. 6, June, 1999, pp. 879–885.

[18] Oppenheim, A. V. and Schafer, R. W. Discrete-Time Signal Processing. Prentice Hall, Englewood Cliffs, NJ, USA, 1989.

[19] Birchfield, S. Derivation of Kanade-Lucas-Tomasi Tracking Equation. Unpublished, May 1996. *http://vision.stanford.edu/ birch/klt/*.

New View Generation with a Bi-centric Camera

Daphna Weinshall[1,2], Mi-Suen Lee[2], Tomas Brodsky[2], Miroslav Trajkovic[2], and Doron Feldman[1]

[1] School of Computer Science and Engineering, The Hebrew University of Jerusalem
91904 Jerusalem, Israel, daphna@ca.huji.ac.il
[2] Philips Research, 345 Scarborough Road, Briarcliff Manor, NY 10510, USA
mi-suen.lee@philips.com

Abstract. We propose a novel method for new view generation from a rectified sequence of images. Our new images correspond to a new camera model, which we call a bi-centric camera; in this model the centers of horizontal and vertical projections lie in different locations on the camera's optical axis. This model reduces to the regular pinhole camera when the two projection centers coincide, and the pushbroom camera when one projection center lies at infinity. We first analyze the properties of this camera model. We then show how to generate new bi-centric views from vertical cuts in the epipolar volume of a rectified sequence. Every vertical cut generates a new bi-centric view, where the specific parameters of the cut determine the location of the projection centers. We discuss and demonstrate applications, including the generation of images where the virtual camera lies behind occluding surfaces (e.g., behind the back wall of a room), and in unreachable positions (e.g., in front of a glass window). Our final application is the generation of movies taken by a simulated forward moving camera, using as input a movie taken by a sideways moving camera.

1 Introduction

Existing approaches to the problem of new view generation from images can be divided along the line of 3-D realism as follows:

- The goal of the first class of techniques is the generation of high quality and veridical new images. One class of techniques involves image generation by interpolation from dense samples [4,8]. The basic idea is to initially build a lookup table using many images of the given scene taken from many different viewpoints. New views are then generated by resampling this (huge) lookup table. Another class of techniques achieves view interpolation and extrapolation via image transfer, using the epipolar geometry and structures such as the trifocal tensor [1]. See additional references in [7].
- The goal of the second class of techniques is the generation of new images for such purposes as compression and visualization. To this end the realistic quality of the image is sacrificed, emphasizing instead the generation of a "visually compelling" image. This class includes mosaicking techniques, which

paste images together based on image similarity in overlapping areas [11]. Other techniques achieve view interpolation and extrapolation by learning the mapping between a set of stored images and various types of new images. Once again, see [7] for references.

Both classes of techniques can be very useful when used within the domain in which they are designed to operate. But these domains exclude many interesting cases. Ray sampling techniques require a lot of carefully collected data and huge memory. View transfer and learning techniques require image correspondence and often use or compute geometric constraints. Finally, mosaicking techniques generate images which do not typically deliver veridical sense of the three dimensional environment, and cannot be used reliably for purposes such as 3-D planning and reasoning.

Our approach to new view generation combines mosaicking and ray sampling methods, enjoying (we believe) the advantages of both. The new image is generated similarly to a "regular" panorama, by taking overlapping image strips from successive images. But, as in ray sampling methods, strips corresponding to different rays are sampled from each image in a systematic way. Like mosaicking, our method is an image based approach, which uses minimal assumptions and constraints about the input stream. But like ray-sampling, it is designed to generate geometrically veridical views that can be generated by a known camera model. Our new images are designed to give a geometrically consistent sense of the three-dimensional environment.

In Section 2, we present the mathematical properties of the projection model which describes the new views generated by our approach. It is not a true perspective camera model and therefore our new images cannot (even in principle) be taken by an ideal pinhole camera. Therefore the examples which we give should be used to judge whether the new images really give a compelling sense of three-dimensions.

In Section 3 we describe how to generate new bi-centric views. Specifically, we describe how to generate views taken from arbitrary new camera positions by simply taking different vertical cuts in the epipolar volume of the original sequence, and pasting the columns together. This simple setup requires that the input stream be generated by a camera translating along a line in 3-D, without changing its orientation or internal calibration (see discussion in Section 3).

In Section 4 we demonstrate a number of applications of our method: Starting from a rectified sequence taken by a camera moving sideways, we can generate images taken from virtual locations behind or in front of the moving camera. This allows us to generate large field of view images taken (virtually) from impossible locations, such as behind walls. Take, for example, an indoors scene; typically it is not possible to photograph a whole room even from the position at the back wall of the room, because the required field of view can be close to 180°. What we propose to do instead is: (i) first take a sequence of images by moving along the back wall of the room; (ii) then generate a bi-centric image taken from a virtual position which is *far behind* the back wall of the room. Our examples below show that the effect can be quite striking.

We can use the same principle in order to generate a simulated sequence where the simulated camera moves towards a scene, using as input a sequence generated by a camera moving sideways. This allows us to generate forward moving movies under conditions that do not normally make the generation of such movies possible; for example, when there are occluding surfaces in the scene (such as a wall behind the camera) or obstacles to motion (such as a glass window in front of the camera).

As our examples show, our simulated sequences are much more compelling than the alternative, which is the simulation of forward motion by zoom. When a camera zooms, all that happens is that the relative size of objects changes; the overall scene, however, remains the same - no occluded objects come to view. This is one reason why a zooming sequence does not give the viewer a sense of forward motion. Our simulated sequences, on the other hand, give the impression of real forward motion, with occluded objects appearing and disappearing in accordance with the 3-D geometry.

Other applications of our method include: (i) the representation of a sequence by a bi-centric panorama instead of the pushbroom panorama, which is typically used when the camera is translating; (ii) new view generation for stereo viewing or 3-D TV.

The idea of sampling columns from images has been explored before, most recently in [9,13,12]. While [12] only used the constant sampling function (as in the traditional pushbroom panorama), [9,13] indeed used a varying sampling function for the columns (where [9] dealt with a sequence obtained by a camera rotating off-axis on a circle, and [13] dealt with a sequence obtained by a translating camera as we do here). However, like the other ray-sampling methods described above, the proposed sampling methods in [9,13] relied on the precise measurement (or prior knowledge) of camera location and orientation along the way. In addition, the "vertical distortion" was considered an artifact that needed to be eliminated via the use of some domain knowledge or 3-D reconstruction; consequently no analysis of the distortion and its geometric meaning was offered.

2 The Bi-centric Camera Model

A camera model is, in general, a mapping from $\mathcal{R}^3$ to $\mathcal{R}^2$, describing which point in the real world ($\in \mathcal{R}^3$) is mapped to which point in the image ($\in \mathcal{R}^2$). In particular, a pinhole camera is such linear mapping when using homogenous (projective) coordinates to describe both world and image coordinate systems.

To describe the mapping of a projective camera, we use the following coordinate systems of the so-called "standard camera" [3] (see Fig. 1(a)). The world coordinates (X, Y, Z) of a point M in $\mathcal{R}^3$ are measured in the 3-D coordinate system whose origin is the focal center of the camera, X, Y denote the directions parallel to the horizontal and vertical image dimensions respectively, and Z denotes the direction of the optical axis of the camera (perpendicular to the image plane). The focal length of the camera, denoted by f, is the distance between the camera's focal center and the image plane in this coordinate system.

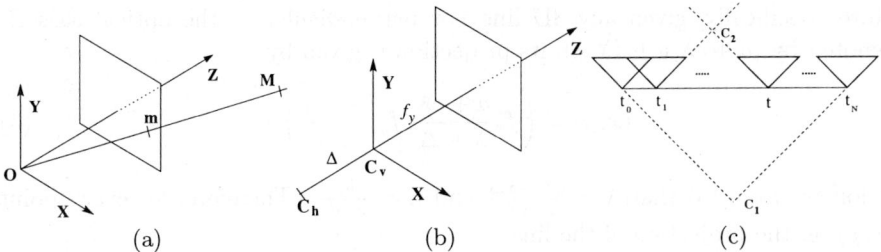

Fig. 1. (a) The standard camera. (b) Bi-centric camera. (c) A camera translating sideways; we show two virtual bicentric camera centers behind the scene (C_1) and in the scene (C_2).

Finally, the image coordinates (x, y) of a point m in $\mathcal{R}^2$ are measured in the coordinate system whose origin is the intersection of the optical axis with the image plane, and x, y denote the directions of the horizontal and vertical image axes respectively.

Using this notation, an ideal calibrated pinhole camera can be described by the following mapping:

$$M = (X, Y, Z) \implies m = (x, y) = (f\frac{X}{Z}, f\frac{Y}{Z}) \tag{1}$$

To describe the calibrated bi-centric camera, we use the same 3-D coordinate system, see Fig. 1(b). The center of vertical projection in all the images C_v is fixed at the origin, but the center of horizontal projections C_h is located at another point $(0, 0, -\Delta)$ on the optical axis. This dissociation is the reason why we call our camera bi-centric.

The focal length in the vertical dimension is denoted by f_y and the focal length in the horizontal direction is denoted $f_x = f_y + \Delta$. It follows that the bi-centric camera model used in our method corresponds to the following mapping from $\mathcal{R}^3$ to $\mathcal{R}^2$:

$$(X, Y, Z) \implies (x, y) = \left(f_x \frac{X}{Z + \Delta}, f_y \frac{Y}{Z}\right) \tag{2}$$

In general, an image created by a bi-centric camera cannot be generated by an ideal pinhole camera unless $\Delta = 0$. When $\Delta = \infty$, the bi-centric camera becomes a pushbroom camera, which corresponds to a vertical strip of sensors translating sideways [5]). In this case (2) reduces to

$$(X, Y, Z) \implies (x, y) = \left(X, f_y \frac{Y}{Z}\right)$$

One peculiarity of the bi-centric camera is the fact that straight lines are not mapped to straight lines (which is also the case for the pushbroom camera).

More specifically, given any 3D line not perpendicular to the optical axis Z, denoted by $(a + c\lambda, b + d\lambda, \lambda)$, its projection is given by

$$(x,y) = \left(f_x \frac{a+c\lambda}{\lambda + \Delta}, f_y \frac{b+d\lambda}{\lambda}\right) \quad (3)$$

It follows from (3) that $\lambda = \frac{af_x - x\Delta}{x - cf_x}$ and $\lambda = \frac{bf_y}{y - df_y}$. Therefore, for every point (x,y) on the projection of the line

$$\frac{-\Delta}{f_x f_y}xy + \frac{d\Delta - b}{f_x}x + \frac{a}{f_y}y + (bc - ad) = 0$$

Thus the line is projected to hyperbolic segment. The boundaries of the projected hyperbolic segment correspond to the visible end-points of the line $Z = f_y$ (considering all points in front of the image plane) and $Z = \infty$. The image coordinates at these boundaries can be shown to be:

$$\begin{aligned} Z = f_y : & \quad x = a + cf_y, y = b + df_y \\ Z = \infty : & \quad x = cf_x, y = df_y \end{aligned} \quad (4)$$

Another interesting property of the bi-centric camera is the geometry of the projection rays describing all the points which are projected to the same single point in the image. These rays determine the occlusion properties of this camera model: among all the points on the same projection ray, the one closest to the camera occludes the others. In an ideal pinhole camera, a projection ray is an optical ray – a 3-D line which passes through the focal center of the camera.

We find the projection rays of the bi-centric camera by solving directly from (2) for all 3-D points which are projected to an image point (x, y):

$$\left\{ \left(\frac{x}{f_x}(\lambda + \Delta), \frac{y}{f_y}\lambda, \lambda\right) \mid \lambda \in \mathcal{R} \right\}$$

This equation describes a ray (as in the models studied in [10,12]). For all points with $x = x_0$, these rays intersect at $\left(\frac{x_0 \Delta}{f_x}, 0, 0\right)$, whereas for all points with $y = y_0$, these rays intersect at $\left(0, \frac{-y_0 \Delta}{f_y}, -\Delta\right)$. Note also that, rather than having a single intersection as in the pinhole model, all camera rays intersect one horizontal line $(\lambda, 0, 0)$ $\forall \lambda$ and one vertical line $(0, \mu, -\Delta)$ $\forall \mu$.

A bi-centric image contains distortions reminiscent of lens distortions (but otherwise very different). Let us look at the difference between the image coordinates of a 3-D point projected through a bi-centric camera to (x, y), and the image coordinates of the same point projected through a pinhole camera to (x', y'). The pinhole camera is assumed to be identical to the bi-centric camera with $\Delta = 0$. From (2) it follows that:

$$x' = f_y \frac{X}{Z}, \quad x = f_x \frac{X}{Z + \Delta}, \quad y = y' = f_y \frac{Y}{Z}$$

and the bi-centric distortion is

$$\frac{x'}{x} = \frac{f_y \frac{X}{Z}}{f_x \frac{X}{Z+\Delta}} = \frac{f_y}{f_x}\left(1 + \frac{\Delta}{Z}\right) \tag{5}$$

It follows from (5) that the distortion of a bi-centric image depends on depth. There is no distortion near the image plane, for $Z = f_y$, because $x'/x = 1$. The distortion then increases as a function of $\frac{1}{Z}$ as the depth Z increases, for maximal distortion of $\frac{f_y}{f_x}$ for distant points.

It is interesting to compare bi-centric distortions to pushbroom distortions, where the depth-dependency of the distortion is maximal. Imagine a pushbroom camera recording a scene which contains the full moon at its center. The moon, being very far away, will be seen in the center of each image as the camera sweeps sideways; in the final pushbroom image, the image of the full moon will be a strip of light crossing the image horizontally from left to right. In the bi-centric image, on the other hand, the full moon will be projected to an ellipse with aspect ratio of f_x/f_y.

3 New View Generation and the Epipolar Volume

In this section we describe a method to generate new bi-centric views from a rectified sequence of images. We initially assume (Section 3.1) that the camera is internally calibrated, and that it translates with constant speed in a direction parallel to the horizontal axis of its image plane. The uncalibrated case is addressed in Section 3.2.

For a camera translating along a line in 3-D space, we can construct the so-called "epipolar volume", i.e., the box obtained by stacking the images one in front of the other. Our key result is that every planar cut of this volume, which is parallel to the Y axis of the box (or the vertical axis of the images), corresponds to a new view of the scene taken with a bi-centric camera.

3.1 An Internally Calibrated Camera

Assume that the input is a sequence of images, taken by an internally calibrated pinhole camera whose projection model is given in (1). Assume further that the camera is translating with constant speed sideways from left to right, in a direction parallel to the horizontal axis of its image plane. A schematic illustration of this setup is given in Fig. 1(c), showing a top-down view of the sequence of positions covered by the real camera's focal center, and their corresponding fields of view.

Suppose now that we generate a new image by taking successive vertical strips from successive images (as is often done in mosaicking algorithms). However, instead of taking the central strip from each image, we do something else: As the first strip in our new image, we take the left-most strip from the first image in the sequence. As the last strip in our new image, we take the right-most strip from the last image. In between, we incrementally sample successive columns

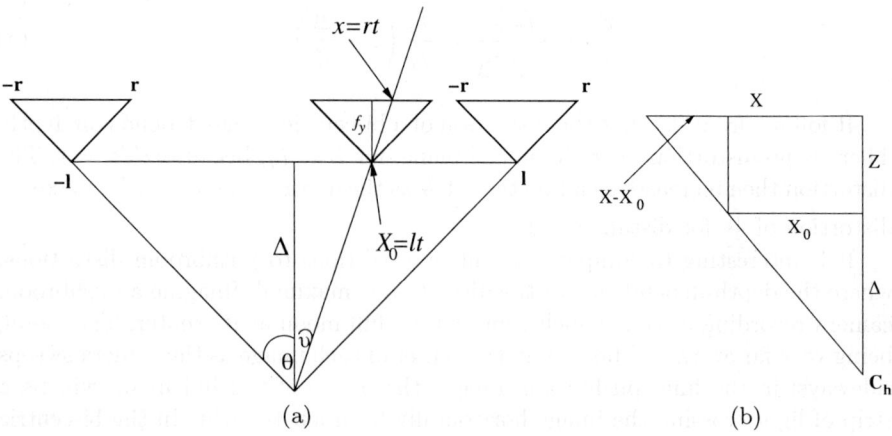

Fig. 2. (a) Bi-centric image formation; (b) bi-centric projection into the X-Z plane.

of the successive images and paste them side by side. The result is a bi-centric image, whose horizontal size is larger than its vertical size.

Fig. 2(a) illustrates how this image can be generated by a single virtual bi-centric camera. More specifically, suppose we have a sequence of images taken with a pinhole camera with focal length $f = f_y$ at different positions along a segment of the X axis. The projection model of the pinhole camera positioned at $(X_0, 0, 0)$ is given by $(x, y) = (f\frac{X-X_0}{Z}, f\frac{Y}{Z})$. We use $[-r, r]$ to denote the horizontal range of each pinhole image, and $X \in [-l, l]$ to denote the range of positions of the pinhole camera centers in R^3.

The horizontal range of the new image is $[-(r+l), (r+l)]$. For each $t \in [-1, 1]$, we define the $(l+r)t$ column of the new image to be the rt column of the pinhole camera positioned at $(lt, 0, 0)$ ($lt = X_0$ above). Now, for each column $x \in [-(r+l), (r+l)]$ in the new image, $t = \frac{x}{l+r}$ and therefore it follows from $f\frac{X-lt}{Z} = rt$ that

$$X = \frac{rt}{f}Z + lt = x\left(\frac{r}{l+r} \cdot \frac{Z}{f} + \frac{l}{l+r}\right) = \frac{x(Z+\Delta)}{f_x} \implies x = f_x\frac{X}{Z+\Delta}$$

where

$$f_x = f\frac{l+r}{r}, \quad f_y = f, \quad \Delta = f\frac{l}{r}$$

The above, together with the invariable property of the pinhole cameras $y = f_y\frac{Y}{Z}$, yield the same model as described by (2).

In order to generalize this scheme, we first need to define the epipolar volume (see Fig. 3). It is the volume obtained by stacking the images one in front of the other; its axes are the horizontal image axis X, the vertical image axis Y, and time T. A vertical planar cut in this volume is defined by a generating line in

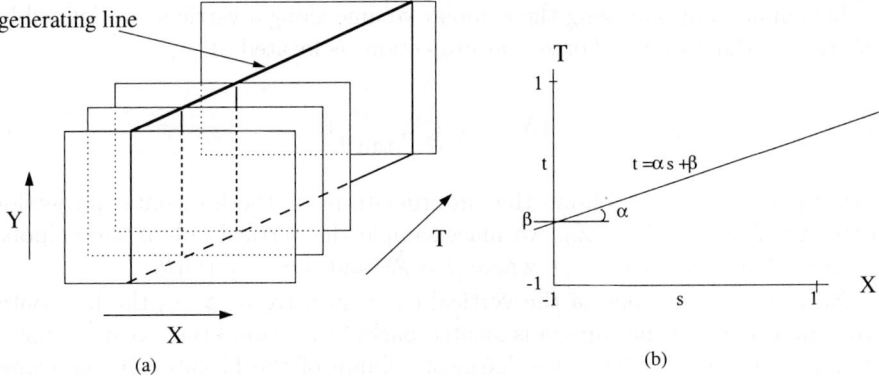

Fig. 3. The epipolar volume: (a) an oblique view and an example vertical cut, (b) top view.

the $X - T$ plane. Every such cut defines a collection of successive vertical image strips, which are combined to generate a new image - the *vertical cut image*. Assuming dense epipolar volume, we state the following result:

> **Result:** every *vertical cut image*, defined by a vertical cut in the epipolar volume, provides a bi-centric image.

In order to understand this result, consider the 2-D graph where one axis corresponds to the columns in each image, the second axis corresponds to all positions of a pinhole camera along the X axis (or equivalently, the $X - T$ plane of the epipolar volume). Let $s \in [-1, 1]$ denote the index of the column axis (X), and t denote the index of the motion axis (T), corresponding to all pinhole camera positions $(lt, 0, 0)$ for some $l \subset \mathcal{R}$. If the pinhole cameras have a field of view of 2θ, then $s = \frac{\tan \nu}{\tan \theta}$ for the bi-centric column at the location X_0 and angle ν from the optical axis (see Fig. 2(a)).

Let us consider now the line in s-t space given by $t = \alpha s + \beta$ (see Fig. 3(b)). For each s, the points projected by the camera located at $(lt, 0, 0)$ onto that camera's s column come in 3-D from the line (see Fig. 2(a)):

$$X = l(\alpha s + \beta) + \lambda s f_y \tan \theta, \quad Y = \lambda y, \quad Z = \lambda f_y \quad \forall \lambda$$

This 3-D line is projected onto point $(sf_x \tan \theta, y)$ in the vertical cut image; therefore

$$x = f_x \tan \theta s = f_x \tan \theta \frac{X - \beta l}{\alpha l + \lambda f_y \tan \theta} = f_x \tan \theta \frac{X - \beta l}{\alpha l + Z \tan \theta}$$

as well as $y = f_y \frac{Y}{Z}$. Setting $X_0 = \beta l$ and $\Delta = \alpha l / \tan \theta$, we obtain

$$x = f_x \frac{X - X_0}{Z + \Delta}$$

Finally, we set $f_x = f_y + \Delta$.

In summary, by sampling the epipolar volume along a vertical cut defined by $t = \alpha s + \beta$, the center of horizontal projections is located at

$$(X, Z) = (\beta l, \frac{-\alpha l}{\tan \theta}) \qquad (6)$$

Vice versa, from (6) it follows that in order to move the horizontal projection center to $X = X_0$, $Z = Z_0$, we must sample the vertical cut of the epipolar volume defined by $t = \alpha s + \beta$, where $\beta = \frac{X_0}{l}$ and $\alpha = -\frac{Z_0}{l} \tan \theta$.

Note that if the slope of the vertical cut is positive ($\alpha > 0$), the horizontal projection center of the camera is located backwards behind the moving camera. In this case (see Fig. 1(c)), the leftmost column of the bicentric image comes from the leftmost column of one of the input images. The rightmost column of the bicentric image comes from the rightmost column of another input image that occurs later in the sequence. On the other hand, if the slope is negative ($\alpha < 0$), the horizontal projection center of the camera is located forwards, *inside* the scene. In this case, the leftmost column of the bicentric image comes from the *rightmost* column of one of the input images. The rightmost column of the bicentric image comes from the *leftmost* column of a later input image. Consequently, to generate a consistent forward moving sequence, the inside-the-scene images have to be mirrored.

The construction above gives us a bi-centric image where the virtual image plane is located at $Z = f_y$. The analysis of the bi-centric depth-dependent distortion in Section 2 tells us the following: if we photograph a fronto-parallel square at depth Z, it will appear in the image as a rectangle with aspect ratio of $\frac{f_y}{f_x}\left(1 + \frac{\Delta}{Z}\right)$. Only squares on the image plane $Z = f_y$ will appear as squares. This is not an optimal choice for best "visual appeal". Thus we choose some fixed depth Z_0 by which we wish to normalize the image, and in the last step of the new view construction we shrink the image vertically by the factor $(1 + \frac{\Delta}{Z_0})$. As a result, planar objects at depth Z_0 appear in the image with veridical aspect ratio. When $\Delta > 0$, planar objects at depth $Z > Z_0$ appear horizontally elongated, while planar objects at depth $Z < Z_0$ appear vertically elongated (and vice versa, when $\Delta < 0$).

The rationale for this specific normalization is the following: The distortion on the *image plane* of points at depth Z_0 is $\frac{f_y}{f_x}\left(1 + \frac{\Delta}{Z_0}\right)$. Since we wish to preserve the *horizontal* angular field-of-view, we use the full range of columns (i.e., leftmost to rightmost), which effectively means that we have canceled a factor $\frac{f_y}{f_x}$ out of the distortion; thus the remaining $1 + \frac{\Delta}{Z_0}$ is the factor by which we must shrink the image vertically. Note that Δ is a value of our choice (e.g., by setting α in (6)), and Z_0 is the (physical) depth of the object we wish to normalize by. Thus the normalization procedure is fully automatic.

We note that before normalization, as we move the horizontal projection center, the image of a scene point moves horizontally on the image plane towards the line $x = 0$. Thus the optical flow is linear and horizontal, and the FOE is a vertical line (instead of a point). The final image scaling adds a vertical component to the optical flow, as a result of which the (combined) 2-D motion field is not linear.

3.2 The Uncalibrated Camera

Suppose that the camera is not internally calibrated, and that its internal calibration remains fixed throughout the sequence. Let **K** denote the 3 × 3 upper diagonal internal calibration matrix of the original camera. It can be shown that when we construct a new image from a vertical cut in the epipolar volume, the resulting image is still bi-centric, with the following effective internal calibration matrix:

$$\mathbf{K}_{bi-centric} = diag[\frac{f_x}{f_y}, 1, 1] \cdot \mathbf{K}$$

(Details of the proof are omitted. The notation $diag[\frac{f_x}{f_y}, 1, 1]$ denotes a 3 × 3 diagonal matrix whose diagonal elements are $\frac{f_x}{f_y}, 1, 1$ respectively.)

4 Results

We used a simulated 3-D scene and two real sequences to study bi-centric images and demonstrate the applications discussed above.

4.1 Simulations

The simulated scene includes a set of boxes, whose organization on the plane forms a grid, surrounded by a wall. A sequence was generated by the simulation of a pinhole camera moving sideways behind the boxes but inside the wall. Then virtual bicentric images were generated at different locations, including behind the wall. We compared virtual bicentric images (Fig. 4(a)) with the ideal perspective images taken from the location of the new horizontal projection center with and without occluding surfaces (Fig. 4(b),(c)). We also compared with panoramic images generated by traditional methods - pushbroom and panning panorama (Fig. 4(d),(e)).

4.2 Real Sequences

We took two real sequences using a camera with 48° field of view. We moved the camera on a straight track, with the image plane roughly parallel to the direction of motion, at approximately constant speed. In Fig. 5 we show three frames from each sequence. For the cafeteria scene, 208 frames were captured on a 4.4m track. For the laboratory scene, 360 frames were captured on a 2m track. The bicentric images generated by our method are shown in Fig. 6 (a) and (b). For comparison, we used the same camera to take an image with roughly the same field of view in the laboratory (Fig. 6(c)).

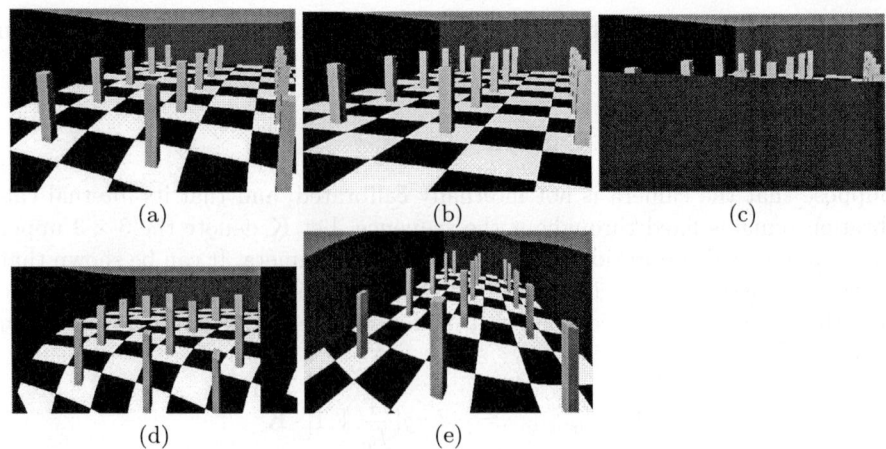

Fig. 4. Simulation results: a virtual bicentric image (a) is compared with the corresponding pinhole image as it would have looked without (b) and with (c) occluding surfaces. We also show two traditional panoramic images generated from roughly the same position as (a): (d) pushbroom, (e) cylindrical projection (panning, or self-rotating, camera).

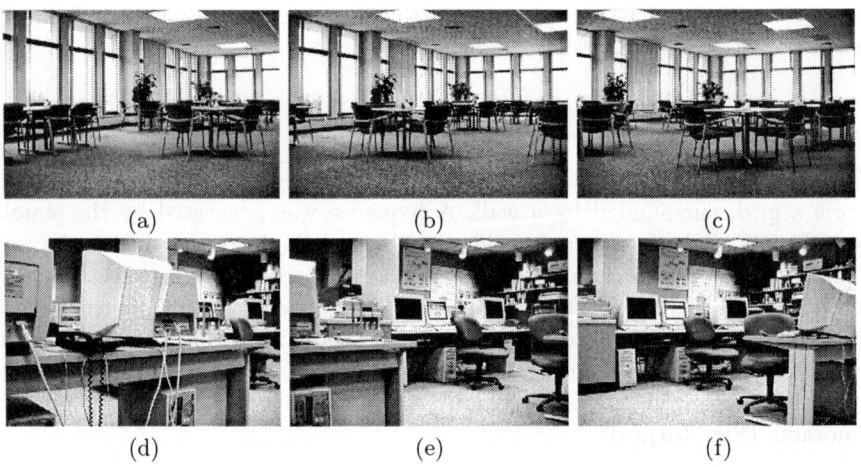

Fig. 5. A few frames (360x240) of the input sequences. In the cafeteria scene: (a) first frame; (b) middle frame; and (c) last frame. In the laboratory scene: (a) first frame; (b) middle frame; and (c) last frame.

We also generated a dolly (move in) and a tracking (move in and sideway) sequence for each scene, by picking subsets of consecutive frames in the input sequence to produce a series of bicentric images. The sequences start with the images shown in Fig. 6(a) and (b) respectively. Fig. 7 shows the middle and last

Fig. 6. Bicentric images generated from the sequences: (a) cafeteria scene; (b) laboratory scene. (c) Same scene in the laboratory captured by a projective camera at approx. 2m back from where the sequence was taken.

frames of the output sequences of the cafeteria scene. We scaled the height of the last frame so that the aspect ratio of the windows at the back maintained its veridical value. We interpolated the height for the rest of the frames. As another application, a stereo pair of the cafeteria scene is shown in Fig. 7(e).

Similarly, Fig. 8 shows the middle and last frames of the two output sequences of the laboratory scene. In this case, the height of the last frame is chosen to maintain the veridical aspect ratio of the column in the middle of the scene.

Lastly, for comparison, we generated panoramas using the pushbroom camera model. Figs. 9(a),(b) were generated by sampling the middle column of each frame in the input sequences. For the cafeteria scene, the panorama was scaled such that the aspect ratio of the table and chairs in the middle is veridical. For the laboratory scene, the scale was fixed such that the computer, the table and the monitor on the left side of the image have the correct aspect ratio.

5 Conclusions and Future Work

We presented a novel method for new view generation from rectified sequences of images. Our method borrows from mosaicking and ray sampling approaches, enjoying the advantages of both. As in regular mosaicking, a new image is created by overlapping image strips from consecutive input images. However, as in ray sampling methods, strips are sampled from each image in a consistent and systematic manner. Newly created images correspond to a new camera model

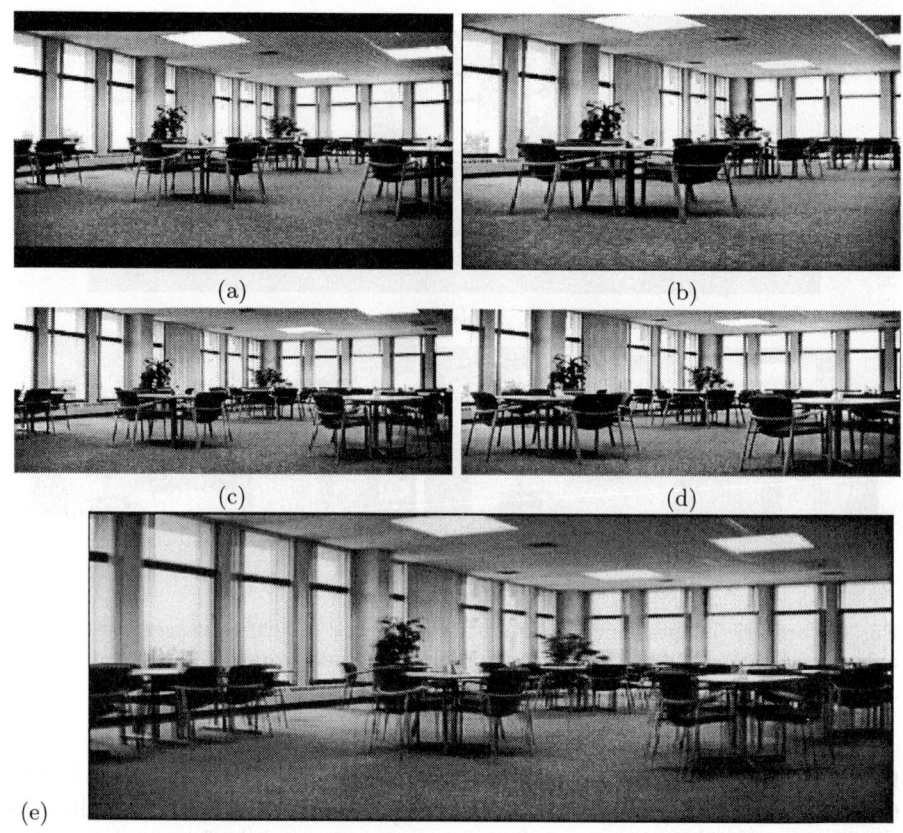

Fig. 7. Bicentric sequences of the cafeteria scene: (a) Middle frame of the dolly sequence (260 frames), generated from frames 70-137 of the input sequence; (b) Last frame of the dolly sequence. The virtual camera center is *in-the-scene*. This frame is generated from frames 77-130 of the input sequence, with leftmost column from the leftmost column of frame 130 and rightmost column from the rightmost column of frame 77. (c) Middle frame of the tracking sequence (208 frames), generated from frames 78-182; (d) Last frame of the tracking sequence, generated from frames 52-53. (e) A stereo pair - two bi-centric images obtained from two nearby positions; to view, use red-green stereo glasses and put the red lense on the left eye. The sequences can be obtained from http://www.cs.huji.ac.il/~daphna/bicentric-movies/ as: original sequence - cafe-original.mpg, dolly sequence - cafe-dolly.mpg, tracking sequence - cafe-tracking.mpg, stereo sequence - cafe-stereo.avi.

that we call a bi-centric camera; in this model the centers of horizontal and vertical projections lie in different positions on the camera optical axis. We have analyzed the properties of this model and demonstrated several applications, including the generation of panoramic images, the generation of images where the virtual camera lies in unreachable positions, and finally the generation of

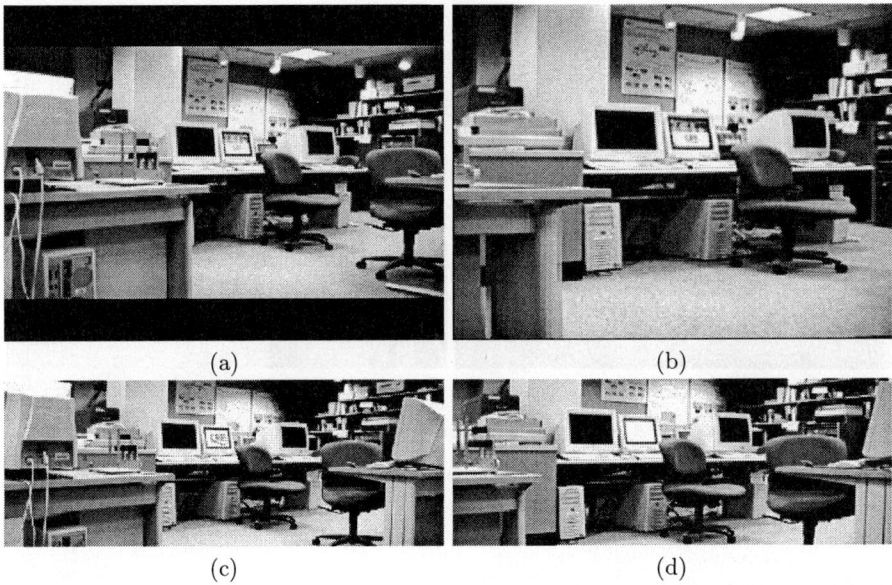

Fig. 8. Bicentric sequences of the laboratory scene: (a) Middle frame of the dolly sequence (300 frames), generated from frames 135-225 of the input sequence; (b) Last frame of the dolly sequence. The virtual camera center is *in-the-scene*. This frame was generated from frames 90-270 of the input sequence, with leftmost column from the leftmost column of frame 270 and rightmost column from the rightmost column of frame 90. (c) Middle frame of the tracking sequence (360 frames), generated from frames 117-297; (d) Last frame of the tracking sequence, generated from frames 53-54. Once again, the sequences can be obtained from http://www.cs.huji.ac.il/~daphna/bicentric-movies/ as: original sequence - lab-original.mpg, dolly sequence - lab-dolly.mpg, tracking sequence - lab-tracking.mpg.

movies taken by a simulated forward moving camera using as input a sequence obtained by a sideways moving camera.

While our present approach is constrained by the requirement that the input sequence is obtained by a camera which translates sideways in constant speed, our ultimate goal is to generate new views and new movies from an arbitrary sequence of images. One solution involves the registration of the original images with each other using the homography of the plane at infinity. This computation requires either internal calibration, or some domain knowledge such as parallel lines in the scene. Our current efforts focus on the elimination of jitter that might be added to the motion of the camera, and/or deviation from constant speed.

(a)   (b)

Fig. 9. (a) Pushbroom panorama of the cafeteria scene. (b) Pushbroom panorama of the laboratory scene.

References

1. S. Avidan, and A. Shashua. *Novel view synthesis in tensor space.* in *Proc. CVPR*, pp. 1034–1040, June 1997.
2. A. Criminisi, I. Reid, and A. Zisserman. Duality, rigidity and planar parallax. In *Proc. ECCV*, pp. 846–861, Springer-Verlag, June 1998.
3. O. Faugeras. *Three-Dimensional Computer Vision.* MIT Press, Cambridge, MA, 1993.
4. S. J. Gortler, R. Grzeszczuk, R. Szeliski, and M. F. Cohen. *The lumigraph.* In *Proc. SIGGRAPH'96*, pp. 43–54, Aug 1996.
5. R. I. Hartley and A. Zisserman. *Multiple View Geometry in Computer Vision.* Cambridge University Press, ISBN: 0521623049, 2000.
6. M. Irani, P. Anandan and D. Weinshall. From reference frames to reference planes: Multi-view parallax geometry and applications. In *Proc. ECCV*, pp. 829–845, 1998.
7. S. B. Kang. A survey of image-based rendering techniques. In *Videometric VI*, vol. 3641, pp. 2-16, Jan 1999.
8. M. Levoy, and P. Hanrahan. *Light field rendering.* In *Proc. SIGGRAPH'96*, pp. 31–42, Aug 1996
9. H. Shum and L. He. Rendering with concentric mosaics. In *SIGGRAPH'99*, pages 299–306, Los Angeles, California, August 1999. ACM.
10. Tomáš Pajdla. Stereo with oblique cameras. TR CTU–CMP–2001–32, K333 FEE Czech Technical University, Prague, Czech Republic, 2001.
11. S. Peleg and J. Herman. Panoramic mosaics by manifold projection. In *Proc. CVPR*, pp. 338–343, June 1997.
12. S. M. Seitz, *The Space of All Stereo Images.* In *Proc. ICCV*, 2001.
13. T. Takahashi, H. Kawasaki, K. Ikeuchi, and M. Sakauchi. Arbitrary view position and direction rendering for large-scale scenes. In *Proc. CVPR*, pp. 296–303, June 2000.

Recognizing and Tracking Human Action

Josephine Sullivan and Stefan Carlsson

Numerical Analysis and Computing Science, Royal Institute of Technology, (KTH), S-100 44
Stockholm, Sweden. {sullivan,stefanc}@nada.kth.se

Abstract. Human activity can be described as a sequence of 3D body postures. The traditional approach to recognition and 3D reconstruction of human activity has been to track motion in 3D, mainly using advanced geometric and dynamic models. In this paper we reverse this process. View based activity recognition serves as an input to a human body location tracker with the ultimate goal of 3D reanimation in mind. We demonstrate that specific human actions can be detected from single frame postures in a video sequence. By recognizing the image of a person's posture as corresponding to a particular key frame from a set of stored key frames, it is possible to map body locations from the key frames to actual frames. This is achieved using a shape matching algorithm based on qualitative similarity that computes point to point correspondence between shapes, together with information about appearance. As the mapping is from fixed key frames, our tracking does not suffer from the problem of having to reinitialise when it gets lost. It is effectively a closed loop. We present experimental results both for recognition and tracking for a sequence of a tennis player.

Keywords: Human motion, tracking, shape, correspondence

1 Introduction

Two of the most important applications of the analysis of human motion in image sequences are 3D reconstruction and action recognition. Using dynamic models of interrelated shape primitives is traditionally the dominant approach to these problems often resulting in very impressive demonstrations [4,8,15,9,11,16,17,18]. Successful 3D dynamic human modelling would simplify the task of inferring the underlying human activity. The main drawback of this approach, however, is that the tracking is not performed in a closed loop. Once the tracking fails, it has to be manually reinitialised. Automatic initialisation of a model based tracker requires the recognition of the 3D pose of the person being tracked. Recognizing the pose of a person is very often equivalent to recognizing the action taking place. If the main purpose of the 3D dynamic modelling is to recognize actions, this creates a paradox. Automating 3D model based tracking requires solving the problem for which the tracking was devised: action recognition. This applies, of course, only if we consider human pose and activity recognition as being equivalent. This remains to be proved. However, the problems of tracking, 3D modelling and recognition seem far more interrelated than has so far been considered. Introducing pose recognition into the tracking paradigm makes it into a closed loop system and one capable of automatic recovery from failure modes. However, if we have a system for 3D pose detection it could equally well be used permanently during the tracking, not just for error recovery.

The idea that recognition and stored prior information should precede tracking, or even totally replace it, has been expressed explicitly in recent works. Howe et. al [12] use manual initialisation and subsequently rely on prior learned 3D information, combined with image tracking, to capture the motion of body parts. Brand [3] uses shadows and silhouettes to recognize complete 3D motion sequences. Toyama and Blake [19] use the idea of key frame recognition. This totally replaces the goal of tracking specific body parts. In contrast to these, our aim is to show that recognition of specific key frames, similar to that in [19] can be used in order to aid the frame to frame tracking and to close the tracking loop. The idea is to store a set of key frames to represent a specific action. These key frames are matched to the frames of an actual image sequence using an algorithm for computing qualitative shape equivalence [5]. This algorithm produces point to point correspondence between the key frame and the actual frame. Using this correspondence field we can transfer any body location on the key frame to that of the actual frame. Point transfer using the shape matching can, of course, also be computed from frame to frame in the actual sequence. This, however, is still a standard open loop tracker. The use of the key frames for point transfer closes the tracking loop and allows for error recovery at any instant, provided there is a key frame similar enough to the actual frame to allow for matching.

The paper focuses on three distinct but interrelated topics. Initially the shape matching algorithm is described. It is an improved version of the algorithm in [5] using combinatorial geometric hashing. Its power is demonstrated by applying it to the problem of action recognition, in our case this equates to the detection of action-specific poses. In particular the beginning of forehand strokes are extracted from a long sequence of tennis footage. At this stage we now know that it is possible to locate image frames similar to specific key frames. Our tracking paradigm is then explained. It is based upon transferring body locations from appropriately matched key frames. The last part of the paper describes how to achieve robust point transferral in the presence of imperfect data.

2   Shape Correspondence by Combinatorial Geometric Hashing

If we subjectively consider two images to be similar as in figure 1 we are almost always able to map a certain point in one image to a specific point in the other. This ability to define a correspondence field between the two images can be taken as a starting point for defining equivalence between shapes. If the field represents a smooth deformation of one shape into the other we are likely to consider the shapes as similar or belonging to the same category. The smaller the deformation the larger the similarity. Computing a correspondence field between two shapes enables us to measure the similarity of the shapes without any prior segmentation. The process of computing correspondence relies on the ability to define invariants i.e properties common to the two shapes. Since correspondence is between points on the shapes, these invariants should be computed from local pointwise information. For well defined transformations such as rigid or linear, invariants can be computed by simple algebraic manipulations. For general smooth deformations however, invariants are associated with qualitative topological shape properties. In order to compute correspondence fields between shapes that are smooth deformations of each other we are faced with the problem of computing qualitative invariants from sets of points on the shapes.

A certain point on a shape has a location and in general also a tangent direction. A complex of points and lines is formed by sampled shape points and their associated tangent lines. Consider these complexes from two shapes when the points are in "perceptual correspondence". Note that a certain line in one complex intersects between two points in exactly the same way in the two shapes. The order of the points $a_1 \ldots a_4, b_1 \ldots b_4$ is preserved as they are traversed e.g clockwise and so is the order of the line directions.

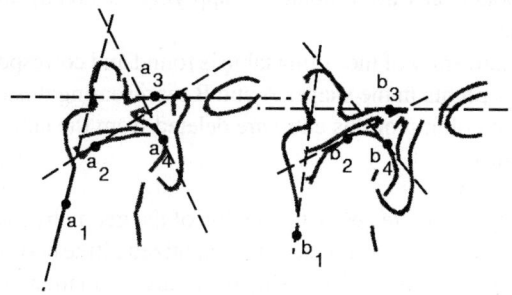

Fig. 1. Two point-line sets with the same topological type.

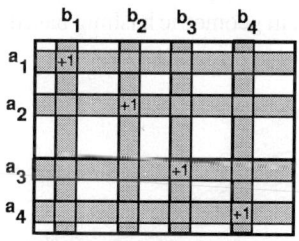

Fig. 2. A voting matrix with rows and columns corresponding to the points on the two shapes is updated whenever two 4-point-line complexes have the same topological type. The exact scenario is displayed for the example in figure 1.

The three components:

point order, line direction order, and relative intersection of the lines and the points in a complex

define the *topological type* of the point-line complex. By defining the leftmost point to be the first point, we get a canonical ordering of the points.

It should be noted that this definition of invariants actually defines the class of smooth transformations that relate equivalent shapes. This class will contain any linear transformation of shapes that preserves orientation of points and lines, i.e. any linear transformation associated with viewpoint changes and planar shapes.

Point to point correspondence between two shapes can now be computed in the following way:

- Points are sampled equidistantly on the shapes A and B and every four point combination $a_1 \ldots a_4, b_1 \ldots b_4$ is selected.

- Whenever two sets of 4-point combinations have the same topological type, the matching table is updated by one vote for the correspondences $a_1 \leftrightarrow b_1 \ldots a_4 \leftrightarrow b_4$, figure 2.

- Unique correspondences are computed by applying the greedy algorithm to the final matching table:
    1. The maximum entry of the voting table is found and correspondence is declared between the points in the shapes A and B representing this entry.
    2. The row and column of this entry are deleted from the table.
    3. Repeat from 1.

This is essentially a discrete geometry version of the geometric hashing algorithm of [13] where topological type index replaces the quantized affine coordinates of the fourth point in the basis of the first three. By basing the index on qualitative geometric properties the bins of geometric hashing are defined generically and we avoid the sometimes arbitrary choice of defining the bins in based on metric or affine coordinates.

Figure 3 shows an example correspondence field found after applying this algorithm. Computing the voting matrix, in geometric hashing based shape correspondence, can be

Fig. 3. The full set of correspondences computed between two frames.

formulated very efficiently as a matrix product [6]. The rows in these matrices actually correspond to the "shape context" vectors of [1] which have been recently applied to shape matching with considerable success.

3 Key Frame Based Action Recognition

The correspondence field that is computed from the shape matching algorithm contains all the information about the relations between image A and image B. If A and B are images with a well defined deformation between them, ideally this will be captured by the correspondence field. Let $p_1^a \ldots p_n^a$ and $p_1^b \ldots p_n^b$ be the coordinates of the corresponding points in image A and B respectively and $\mathbf{T}$ the class of transformations that, we know a priori, defines the relation between A and B. The decision that A and B are related by a member of this class of transformations can be based on the magnitude of the residual:

$$\min_{T \in \mathbf{T}} \sum_{i=1}^{n} ||p_i^b - T(p_i^a)||^2 \qquad (1)$$

It is important that the class of deformations is chosen to match the expected deformations expected. If it is chosen too large it may easily generate false positives by deforming images outside the class of interest. The class of transformations, $\mathbf{T}$, will obviously be problem dependent. In our case we want to identify a specific pose for a certain person at different time instants. The transformations should then reflect the projected image shape variation between the different instances. This transformation will obviously be quite complex, involving motions of several body parts. As a simple preliminary measure we tried various linear transformations: pure translation, similarity and affine transformations. Pure translation gave the best results in terms of discriminating image frames. Therefore the transformation used is simply:

$$T(p_i^a) = p_i^a + t$$

and the matching distance was computed as the residual:

$$\min_{t} \frac{1}{n} \sum_{i=1}^{n} ||p_i^b - p_i^a - t||^2 \qquad (2)$$

Evaluation of the complete algorithm of action recognition was made on a 30 sec sequence of tennis. The sequence contains forehand and backhand shots and mainly the player in a stand-by position.

The player was coarsely tracked automatically and a region of interest for each frame specified. In the upper half of this region Canny edge detection was applied. The edges were traced and subsampled to every fourth pixel. At each sample, the tangent direction was estimated. The number of edge points varied, in general, between $100 - 200$. No effort was made to delete the sometimes substantial number of background edges which occur in some frames. The upper half of the window is chosen as the upper body follows more consistent and distinctive patterns than the legs during different tennis strokes.

A specific frame (251 of the sequence) was selected as the key frame and the matching algorithm was applied to all frames in the sequence and a matching score was computed, see figure 4. There are clearly 9 local minima in the distance scores and each of these corresponds to the start of a forehand stroke as displayed.

4 Tracking by Point Transfer from Representative Key Frames

Motion capture requires body locations to be tracked over time, generally in multiple views in order to compute 3D representations of the body motion. In commercial and medical contexts this requires fitting visible markers to the person's body and recording with multiple calibrated cameras. Some attempts have been made to automate the tracking of body locations, notably rotational joints [16,12], but no general solution has so far been presented. The problem is, of course, very difficult. This is partly because the points of interest are skeletal and are embedded within the body and a surface protrusion is all that is seen. This surface projection is therefore view dependent. Nevertheless, we believe that a crude estimation of these point can be tracked automatically. If this is done in multiple views, the 3D reconstruction problem will be overconstrained, allowing for filtering of tracking errors to some degree.

Without specific body markers, the projected image point to be tracked, for example the knee, may not have very much special *local* information to allow its determination. However, if correspondence for edge elements of the projected body has been computed between the image frame to be tracked and some frame in which the body locations are known a priori, this can be used to compute the body locations in the actual frame. This transfer of body locations could, of course, be from the previous frame in which they have been previously determined. This would imply, though, a standard open loop tracker where errors are propagated. Consider instead that a set of key frames of body postures are defined. In each of these frames the body locations are determined, most probably manually, at an earlier stage. Then if any frame in the actual sequence matches to at least one key frame, body locations can be transferred from the matched key frames. Thus a closed tracking loop has been established and tracking errors do not propagate indefinitely. Figure 7 illustrates how the correspondence field in figure 3 can be used selectively around specific body locations in order to transfer interior points between the two frames.

Tennis, as well as sports in general, is very repetitive. It consists of a limited repertoire of actions and often seen from a limited number of camera angles. Sports events are therefore an ideal environment for exploiting the key frame based mapping. In order for this to be possible, every frame in a sequence has be sufficiently close to some key frame. The action recognition presented in the previous section is a promising indication that this should be possible. We have demonstrated that it is possible to find the forehand shots in a sequence. This can be seen even more clearly from figure 5. The figure displays the results of calculating the similarity measure between a specific forehand (503-514) and all other forehand frames. For the illustrated matrix the darker the shade the lower the distance score. The repetitive nature of the forehand shot is clearly seen in this matrix and it also indicates that finding a specific key frame for all frames in the sequence should be possible.

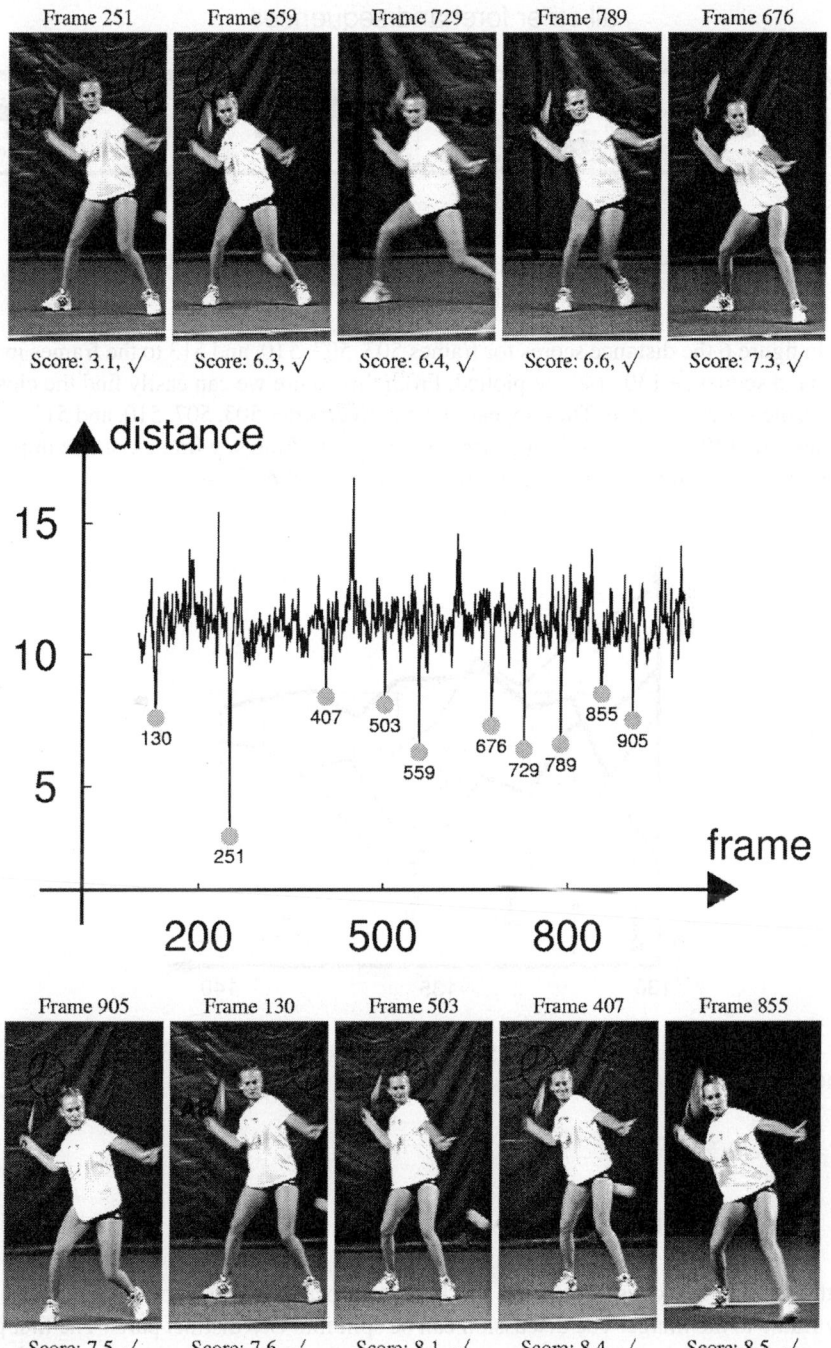

Fig. 4. Classified forehands for the sequence of the woman playing tennis. The displayed forehands correspond to the local minima of the distance scores.

all other forehand sequences

503
|
514

Fig. 5. Distance scores between forehand frames 503-514 and all other forehands.

In figure 6 the distance scores for frames 503, 507, 510, and 513 to the frames in the forehand sequence 130 -140 are plotted. From this figure we can easily find the closest key frame for each frame. They appear in the correct order 503, 507, 510, and 513 as the frames 130-140 are traversed. In general an ordering of the key frames can be imposed which would simplify the key frame selection even further.

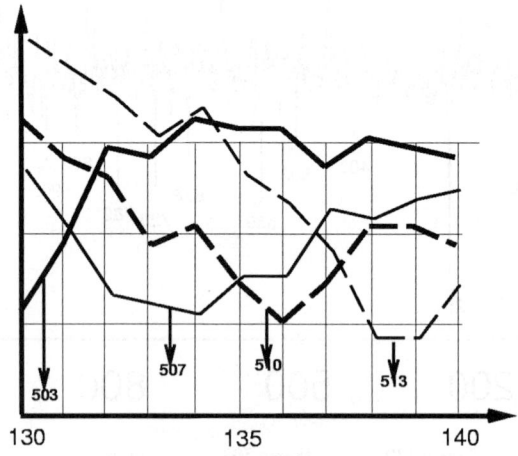

Fig. 6. Distance scores for frames 503, 507, 510, and 513 to all frames in forehand sequence 130 - 140.

5 Body Joint Localisation

In this section we focus on how the marked body locations can be transferred from the key frame to the image. The discussion can be split into two distinct parts. The first part describes how the body part locations are estimated just using the voting matrix V. In a completely constrained environment with the key frame being more or less exact replica of the image data this would probably be sufficient for successful localisation. However, as our data is not from such a world (though admittedly from a highly structured one) it is necessary to add another level of sophistication to the localisation. The other part is concerned with these issues. Priors are imposed upon the spatial arrangement of the points and also upon the anticipated colour of the intensity patches surrounding certain points. Crude tracking of the head and body regions is also implemented to give coarse prior estimates of their position. This latter information is used to refine the voting matrix V and to indirectly improve the estimates of the joint locations.

5.1 Point Transferral Using the Voting Matrix

Let $p_1^t, \ldots, p_n^t$ and $p_1^R, \ldots, p_n^R$ be the coordinates of the corresponding edge points in the test image, I_t, and the appropriately matched key frame image respectively. In the keyframe R the coordinates of the skeleton parts, P_k^R, are marked manually (see figure 10). For the upper-body keyframe these locations correspond to the left and right hand, elbow, and shoulders as well as the neck and the nose. These points are denoted by $\{P_k^R\}_{k=1}^K$. Let $P_k(t)$ be the location of the point corresponding to P_k^R in image I_t. It is assumed that a simple local translation, $\mathbf{v}_k(t)$, is sufficient to describe the transformation of the points from the key frame to the image:

$$P_k(t) = P_k^R + \mathbf{v}_k(t) \quad (3)$$

For each P_k^R a subset of the p_i^R's is chosen as support for this point from which $\mathbf{v}_k(t)$ is estimated, figure 7. This estimation is computed robustly to offset the influence of outliers.

Fig. 7. Examples of selective correspondences used for point transfer from key frame to actual frame.

Coarse Head and Body Tracking: Updating the Voting Matrix. The voting matrix V does not always give the correct correspondences. Thus if extra information can be obtained from other sources to adjust V that would be beneficial. An obvious candidate is to use the output of a conventional tracker.

Attempts to achieve automatic full body tracking on long sequences either using 3D fully articulate models or 2D appearance based ones have not meet with great success. However, tracking with less ambitious goals, for instance head and body localisation using colour information, have had very presentable results [7]. It was therefore decided to aid the matching process by tracking the head and body regions of the person. Each region is modelled as a quadrangle and a standard particle filter implemented for the tracking [2]. The likelihood function is based upon a sum-of-squares distance measure between a colour template and the image data. Examples of the localisation achieved are shown in figure 8.

Frame 130   Frame 133   Frame 136   Frame 139

Fig. 8. Output of the coarse head and body tracker when applied to the tennis sequence. This output can be used to guide the correspondences computed. It is relatively easy to successfully to achieve this level tracking for long sequences.

With the successful completion of this part of the tracking the new information is incorporated into the voting matrix V. This is done as follows:

Set $V(p_i^R, p_j^t) = 0$ if p_i^R and p_j^t are not close to the corresponding lines in corresponding matched quadrangles.

The above is not implemented for every point, but only for those points which are anticipated to have a consistent position with respect to the matched regions. For the upper-body example this corresponds to the points of the head and the shoulders and the torso. The points demarking the arms are omitted due to their varying relation to the body and head. The updated matrix can then be used to obtain estimates, $\{\mathbf{y}_k(t)\}$, of the interior points using the process previously described.

5.2 Incorporating Prior Constraints

The $\mathbf{y}_k(t)'s$ obtained will not in general be all inliers. This is mainly due to the fact that in the image data the edge information may be sparse in some areas. Numerous examples of this phenomenon can be seen in the pictures in figure 11, especially with regard to the feet and the right arm. (Note the time component will be dropped from the subsequent notation as we are dealing soley with matching to individual images.)

Spatial Constraints. A set of representative key frames has been chosen as being sufficient to represent the different topological shapes seen in a forehand stroke. Each key frame in the tracking process will be matched to an anticipated range of images. In these images the interior points should have a similar arrangement to the marked points in the key frame. This constraint can be mathematically stated using *Scaled Prismatic Models* of [14]:

$$P_{k+1} \sim f(P_{k+1}|P_k) = P_k + l_k(\cos(\theta_k)\sin(\theta_k))^T \qquad (4)$$

for $k = 1,\ldots, K-1$ and where $l_k \sim N(l_k^R, \sigma_k^2)$, $\theta_k \sim N(\theta_k^R, \delta_k^2)$. P_0 follows the distribution $p_0(P)$. Equation (4) corresponds to a state evolution equation. The estimates $\{y_k\}$ can be viewed as following the observation density:

$$\mathbf{y}_{k+1} \sim g(\mathbf{y}_{k+1}|P_{k+1}) = (1-\rho)N(P_{k+1}, \gamma^2 I_{2\times 2}) + \rho \text{Un}(A) \qquad (5)$$

where $0 \leq \rho \leq 1$ and $\text{Un}(A)$ is a uniform distribution over a region A. From the chain model described and the measurements it is desirable to obtain estimates of the body joint locations from the expected value of the smoothing distribution:

$$\hat{P}_{1:K} = E\{p(P_{1:K}|\mathbf{y}_{1:K})\} \qquad (6)$$

where $\mathbf{y}_{1:K} = (\mathbf{y}_1, \ldots, \mathbf{y}_K)$ and $P_{1:K} = (P_1, \ldots, P_K)$.

Finding the Smoothing Distribution. Given the non-Gaussian nature of the state evolution equation and the observations, a Monte Carlo algorithm is chosen to produce random samples from the smoothing density of equation (6). A procedure as described in [10] is used. It is assumed that a weighted set of particles $\{P_k^{(i)}, \pi_k^{(i)}\}_{i=1}^N$ for $k = 1,\ldots, K$ which are drawn approximately from $p(P_k|\mathbf{y}_{1:k})$, have been obtained by applying a particle-filtering technique. Smoothing is then performed by backward simulation as follows:

- Start with the final particle set $\{P_K^{(i)}, \pi_K^{(i)}\}$ and choose a particle $\tilde{P}_K = P_K^{(i)}$ with probability $\pi_K^{(i)}$.
- The positions of the nodes of the chain are now chosen in reverse order. New weights are calculated
  - $\pi_{k|k+1}^{(i)} \propto \pi_k^{(i)} f(\tilde{P}_{k+1}|P_k^{(i)})$

  and selections made
  - Choose $\tilde{P}_k = P_k^{(i)}$ with probability $\pi_{k|k+1}^{(i)}$.

  The above is repeated for $k = K-1, \ldots, 1$ to obtain $(\tilde{P}_1, \tilde{P}_2, \ldots, \tilde{P}_K)$ an approximate realisation from $p(P_{1:K}|\mathbf{y}_{1:K})$.

This procedure results in choosing the particles that are simultaneously consistent with the state evolution equation and the measurements. When applied to enforce the spatial chain constraints isolated outliers are spotted and corrected accordingly, as shown by figure 9.

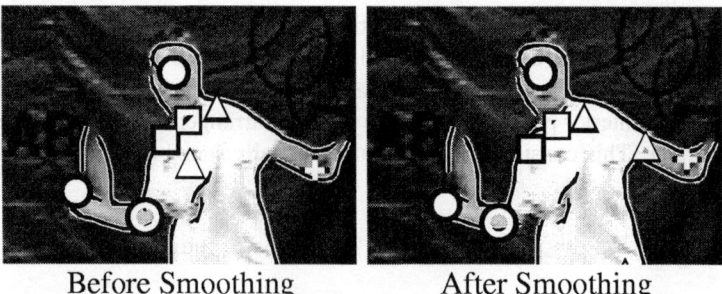

Before Smoothing   After Smoothing

Fig. 9. Applying the spatial constraints allows the rectification of the position of the right elbow.

Colour Constraints. In the keyframe each manually marked point P_k^R has an intensity patch associated with it. For example in figure 11 the left foot is surrounded by a predominantly white patch. This information can also be used to constrain the potential positions for the body joint locations and help to compensate for the cases when the edge data is insufficient and/or when the point matching partially fails. We exploit the information as follows.

An $L \times L$ template patch, $\mathbf{C}_k^R$, of RGB data centered at P_k^R is extracted from the key frame. For each particle $P_k^{(i)}$ a sum-of-squares distance score is made between the template and a patch from I_t centered at $P_k^{(i)}$ to obtain a measurement $z_k^{(i)}$. This measurement is turned into a probability:

$$p(z_k^{(i)}|P_k^{(i)}) = \exp{-\lambda_0 z_k^{(i)}} \tag{7}$$

The observation density equation (5) has to be updated to take account of this new measurement:

$$g'(\mathbf{y}_k, z_k^{(i)}|P_k^{(i)}) = g(\mathbf{y}_k|P_k^{(i)})p(z_k^{(i)}|P_k^{(i)}) \tag{8}$$

Particle filtering now results in each of the particle sets approximating $p(P_k|\mathbf{y}_{1:k}, z_{1:k})$ and the smoothing algorithm with samples drawn from the appropriately amended smoothing density.

Particle Filtering + Importance Function. A few words must be made with regard to the implementation of the particle filter and obtaining the initial particle sets. It is well known that the use of importance sampling greatly increases the efficiency of the filtering process. The first problem is to find an initial particle set $\{P_0^{(i)}, \pi_0^{(i)}\}$ that is an accurate representation of $p(P_0|\mathbf{y}_0, z_0)$ given that $p(P_0)$ is typically a broad uniform distribution. Particles are placed in the vicinity of $\mathbf{y}_0$. However, it is not guaranteed that $\mathbf{y}_0$ is an inlier, therefore the search must be wider. This is achieved initially by considering each $\mathbf{y}_k$ as an inlier and drawing samples from $p(\mathbf{y}_0|P_k = \mathbf{y}_k)$, which can be calculated from state evolution equation. Also in each keyframe the line joining P_k^R to P_{k-1}^R defines an intensity profile. In the image if each $\mathbf{y}_k$ is considered as an inlier then a search can easily be performed to find the $\mathbf{y}_{k-1}$ that allows the best replication of the corresponding keyframe intensity profile. More particles are placed in this area. The weights $\pi_0^{(i)}$ are updated appropriately to take into account the bias introduced. At each subsequent step the importance functions are normal distributions centred at $\mathbf{y}_k$ and the output of the profile intensity matching. ρ_1 of the particles are propagated using the state evolution equation while $(1 - \rho_1)$ are chosen using the importance functions where $0 \leq \rho_1 \leq 1$.

6 Results

The techniques described were implemented on a forehand stroke that had been segmented out from the tennis sequence using the methods in section 3. The frames 130–140 were used as the test data. Hand-drawn key frames were constructed by tracing out the silhouettes of the tennis player from the frames 503, 506, 509 and 512. The resulting key-frames for the upper-body are shown in figure 10. These key frames encompass the range of topological types seen in a forehand stroke. However, the frame rate of the data is only 25Hz and the motion of the arm can be quite rapid in the middle part of the stroke. Thus for a different forehand we are quite likely to see images that are inbetween the key frames as the camera is synchronised differently with the test stroke to the key frame stroke. However, the matching process combined with the colour information partially compensates for the differences between the key frame and the data. The upper and lower body are treated separately, with the matching and the point transferral being computed independently. The key frame with the lowest distance score to the image frame was used to implement the point transferral. This search was also guided by a simple Markov chain to reduce the computational aspect and also to prevent inappropriate key frames being chosen.

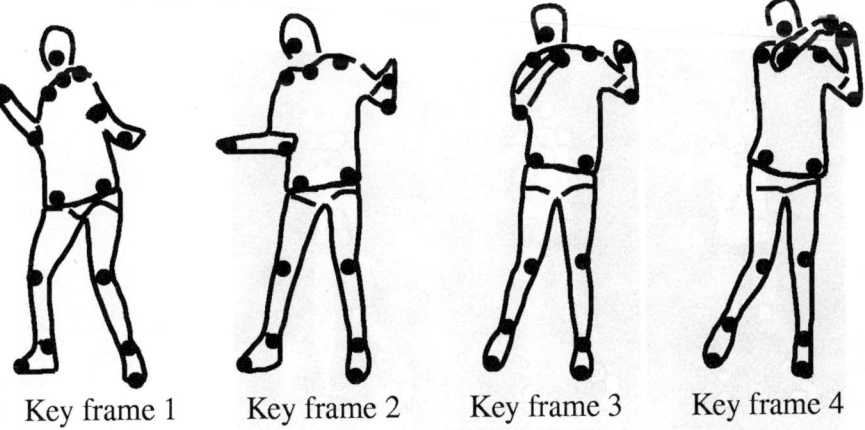

Key frame 1   Key frame 2   Key frame 3   Key frame 4

Fig. 10. Hand drawn key frames plus the manually marked interior points. These are the key frames used for matching to the forehand sequence.

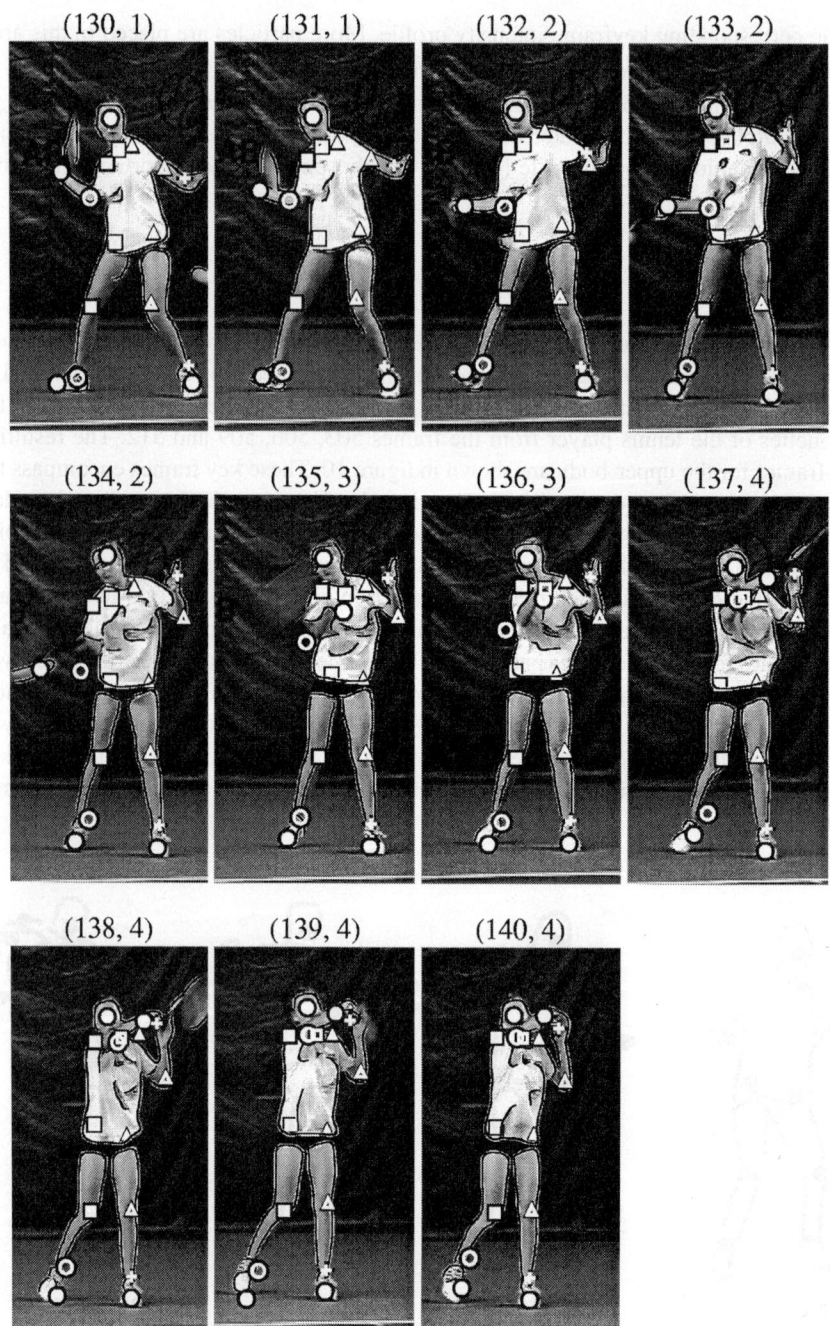

Fig. 11. Final estimates of the joint locations of the skeleton. Each point is displayed as a distinct shape. The edge data used in the matching process are also displayed. The numbers displayed correspond to the frame number of the sequence and to the matched key frame displayed in figure 10.

Finally a note must be made about about how the parameters of the state evolution equation and the observation were set. As of yet no coherent strategy has been developed to answer the questions how many key frames are needed and to which range of poses can a key frame be matched. Thus the parameters were set by hand upon the anticipated answer to the latter question and were set to allow a quite a great deal of variation. Ideally these should be learned from training data. However, this awaits the decision whether it is better to add a key frame to the database of key frames or to improve the matching process. Inspection of the results obtained in figure 11 show very promising results on a very challenging sequence.

7 Conclusions

This paper presents a shift in the traditional approach to the tracking process. It is motivated by the desire to create a closed loop system. This is achieved by being able to recognise specific poses which correspond to stored key frames in which body joint locations have been previously defined. The matching process based upon the concept of *topological type* is the machinery that allows this approach to work. To improve the robustness of the point transferral, the spatial relationship of the body points and colour information is exploited. Experimental evidence has been presented which displays the power of our approach to segment out specific actions of interest, ie a forehand stroke and then to localise the body points in these highlighted frames. Therefore the need for explicit initialisation of a complicated model has been by-passed. Errors obtained in one frame do not propagate to the next frame. Obviously a number of issues remain unanswered and should be subject to further research. How many key frames are needed for each stroke? Can generic key frames be defined that can be matched to different tennis players? Can the parameters for the smoothing process be learnt systematically? What range of actions can be successfully captured by this process? We have so far demonstrated that four key frames can be used to map most of the body locations in a sequence of a forehand stroke to their correct positions. The ultimate number of keyframes necessary to map correct body locations in a whole tennis game remains to be determined. The option of selecting keyframes as a collection of body parts will also be investigated. In this way multiple keyframes can be generated by combinations of a limited set of parts.

Acknowledgements. This work was supported by the European project VIBES IST-2000-26001 and the Swedish Research Council.

References

1. S. Belongie and J. Malik. Matching with shape contexts. In *IEEE Workshop on Content-based Access of Image and Video Libraries*, June 2000.
2. A. Blake and M. Isard. *Active Contours*. Springer, 1998.
3. M. Brand. Shadow puppetry. In *Proc. 7th Int. Conf. on Computer Vision*, pages 1237–1244, 1999.

4. C. Bregler and J. Malik. Tracking people with twists and exponential maps. In *Proc. Conf. Computer Vision and Pattern Recognition*, pages 8–15, 1998.
5. S. Carlsson. Order structure, correspondence and shape based categories. In *Shape Contour and Grouping in Computer Vision*, pages 58–71. Springer LNCS 1681, 1999.
6. S. Carlsson and J. Sullivan. Action recognition by shape matching to key frames. Workshop on Models versus Exemplars in Computer Vision at CVPR, 2001. Available at http://www.nada.kth.se/~stefanc.
7. D. Comaniciu, V. Ramesh, and P. Meer. Real-time tracking of non-rigid objects using mean shift. In *Proc. Conf. Computer Vision and Pattern Recognition*, volume 2, pages 142–149, Hilton Head Island, South Carolina, 2000.
8. J. Deutscher, A. Blake, and I. Reid. Motion capture by annealed particle filtering. *Proc. Conf. Computer Vision and Pattern Recognition*, 2000.
9. D.M. Gavrila. The visual analysis of human movement: A survey. *Computer Vision and Image Understanding*, 73(1):82–98, January 1999.
10. S.J. Godsill, A. Doucet, and M. West. Methodology for monte carlo smoothing with application to time-varying autoregressions. In *Proc. International Symposium on Frontiers of Time Series Modelling*, 2000.
11. D. Hogg. Model-based vision: a program to see a walking person. *J. Image and Vision Computing*, 1(1):5–20, 1983.
12. N. R. Howe, M. E. Leventon, and W. T. Freeman. Bayesian reconstruction of 3d human motion from single-camera video. In S. A. Solla T. K. Leen and K-R. Muller, editors, *Advances in Neural Information Processing Systems 12*, 2000.
13. Y. Lamdan, J. Schwartz, and H. Wolfson. Object recognition by affine invariant matching. In *Proc. Conf. Computer Vision and Pattern Recognition*, pages 335–344, 1988.
14. D.D. Morris and J.M. Rehg. Singularity analysis for articulated object tracking. In *Proc. Conf. Computer Vision and Pattern Recognition*, pages 289–296, 1998.
15. N. Paragios and R. Deriche. Geodesic active regions for motion estimation and tracking. *Proc. 7th Int. Conf. on Computer Vision*, 1999.
16. J. Rehg and T. Kanade. Model-based tracking of self-occluding articulated objects. *Proc. 5th Int. Conf. on Computer Vision*, 1995.
17. K. Rohr. Towards model-based recognition of human movements in image sequences. *Computer Vision, Graphics and Image Processing*, 59(1):94–115, 1994.
18. H. Sidenbladh, M. Black, and D.J. Fleet. Stochastic tracking of 3d human figures using 2d image motion. In *Poc of European Conference on Computer Vision*, pages 702–718, 2000.
19. K. Toyama and A. Blake. Probabilistic tracking in a metric space. In *Proc. 8th Int. Conf. on Computer Vision*, July 2001.

Towards Improved Observation Models for Visual Tracking: Selective Adaptation

Jaco Vermaak, Patrick Pérez, Michel Gangnet, and Andrew Blake

Microsoft Research Cambridge, Cambridge CB3 0FB, UK
http://www.research.microsoft.com/vision

Abstract. An important issue in tracking is how to incorporate an appropriate degree of adaptivity into the observation model. Without any adaptivity, tracking fails when object properties change, for example when illumination changes affect surface colour. Conversely, if an observation model adapts too readily then, during some transient failure of tracking, it is liable to adapt erroneously to some part of the background. The approach proposed here is to adapt selectively, allowing adaptation only during periods when two particular conditions are met: that the object should be both present and in motion. The proposed mechanism for adaptivity is tested here with a foreground colour and motion model. The experimental setting itself is novel in that it uses combined colour and motion observations from a fixed filter bank, with motion used also for initialisation via a Monte Carlo proposal distribution. Adaptation is performed using a stochastic EM algorithm, during periods that meet the conditions above. Tests verify the value of such adaptivity, in that immunity to distraction from clutter of similar colour to the object is considerably enhanced.

1 Introduction

Visual tracking of objects in video sequences is becoming an increasingly important technology in a wide range of computer vision applications, including video teleconferencing, security and surveillance, video segmentation and editing. Numerous visual tracking algorithms have been developed based on *e.g.* the Kalman Filter [2], and Extended Kalman Filter [6], the mean-shift technique [3], exemplars [12] and particle filters [7].

One important issue that remains to be resolved concerns the adaptation and individualisation of object observation models. Adaptation is important because of its contribution in distinguishing between different objects, and in making tracking more robust to appearance variations due to changing illumination and pose. The importance of adaptation for tracking has been acknowledged by the tracking community, and some recent progress in the application of adaptive luminance and colour models has been reported [9,13,14].

Whilst adaptation of observation models is necessary, over-eager adaptation is a hazard. This is because transitory failures of tracking are compounded if, while attending to a piece of clutter, the adaptation algorithm learns clutter characteristics and "forgets" the characteristics of the object. A solution to this problem, proposed here, is to allow adaption only *selectively* when two particular conditions are met. The first condition is that there is an object present, being tracked properly, as flagged by a binary indicator variable appended to the object state vector. The second condition is that the object should be moving, as a further protection against inadvertently adapting to a (stationary) background region. For this purpose, raw motion is observed via frame-difference signals in certain filter channels.

The setting for experiments is a somewhat complete tracking system. Information from the complementary modalities of motion and colour, are fused to enhance tracking accuracy and robustness. A novel aspect of the system is that observations are made entirely via a fixed bank of regularly spaced filters [8,11], some of which are colour sensitive while others are motion sensitive. When the object is moving strong localisation cues are provided by the motion measurements, whereas the colour measurements can undergo substantial fluctuations due to changes in the object pose and illumination. Conversely, when the object is stationary or near-stationary the motion information disappears, and colour information dominates to provides a reliable localisation cue. A Bayesian approach allows the balance between motion and colour to be captured automatically, using likelihood models for image measurements, both under the object hypothesis (foreground) and for the background.

The tracking engine itself is a particle filter [5,7], implementing Bayesian inference. The object of interest here is the face of a person in a video sequence, and its outline is modelled as an ellipse that is allowed to translate and scale subject to a Langevin dynamical model. Automatic object detection and particle filter initialisation are based on a segmentation of the motion measurements, and incorporated in a novel proposal distribution. Finally, adaptation of the object colour likelihood model is performed using a stochastic version of the EM algorithm during periods of motion.

The remainder of the paper is organised as follows. Section 2 formulates the tracking objectives in more detail and describes the object configuration and state-space, the measurement process, and the likelihood models for the motion and colour modalities. Section 3 outlines the particle filter tracking algorithm. The details of the particle proposal distribution and automatic initialisation strategy are presented in Section 4. Section 5 discusses the Monte Carlo EM algorithm to adapt the parameters of the object colour likelihood model. The performance of the proposed tracking algorithm is evaluated in Section 6. Finally, some conclusions are reached in Section 7.

2 Problem Formulation

The objective is to detect and track the face of a single person in a video sequence taken from a stationary camera. This section describes the necessary ingredients to achieve this within a particle filtering framework.

2.1 Object Description

For simplicity the face is modelled as an ellipse with a 1.25 aspect ratio, *i.e.* $(x/a)^2 + (y/b)^2 = 1$, with $b = 1.25a$. The object state is given by $\mathbf{x} = (x, y, s, r)$, where (x, y) is the location of the ellipse centre in the image, s is its scale, and r is a binary indicator signifying whether the object is present in the image ($r = 1$) or not ($r = 0$). The position and scale components are assumed to follow independent Langevin dynamical priors [1] when the object is present, whereas the priors for these components are undefined if the object is absent. The prior for the object indicator is taken to be a two state Markov process with initial state and state transition probabilities given by $P_0 = 0.5$ and $P_{01} = P_{10} = 10^{-3}$, respectively. More specifically, the prior model can be expressed as

$$p(\mathbf{x}_t|\mathbf{x}_{t-1}) = p(x_t|x_{t-1}, r_t, r_{t-1}) p(y_t|y_{t-1}, r_t, r_{t-1}) p(s_t|s_{t-1}, r_t, r_{t-1}) p(r_t|r_{t-1}),$$

where the first three factors are similarly defined, with the one for x given by

$$p(x_t|x_{t-1}, r_t, r_{t-1}) = \begin{cases} \text{undefined} & \text{if } r_t = 0 \\ p_L(x_t|x_{t-1}) & \text{if } r_t = 1 \text{ and } r_{t-1} = 1 \\ \mathcal{U}_{\mathcal{R}_x}(x_t) & \text{if } r_t = 1 \text{ and } r_{t-1} = 0, \end{cases}$$

where p_L denotes the Langevin dynamical model, $\mathcal{U}_\mathcal{R}$ denotes the uniform distribution over the set $\mathcal{R}$, and $\mathcal{R}_x$ is the valid range for the x location. In the above, the first case corresponds to objects being absent from the scene, whereas the second case corresponds to a valid object persisting in the scene. The third case corresponds to a new object entering the scene, in which case the prior for the state component is taken to be uniform over the valid range of the component.

2.2 Image Measurements

The raw image stream contains all the information necessary to detect and track objects. However, working with the raw images directly is difficult, and a certain amount of preprocessing is required to emphasise the salient features of the objects of interest. Two important modalities for visual tracking are motion and colour. These modalities complement each other in the sense that when the object is moving the colour information may become unreliable due to changes in the object pose and illumination, whereas strong localisation cues may be obtained from the motion information. Conversely, when the object is stationary or near-stationary the motion information disappears, whereas the colour information becomes more reliable. Here the hue and saturation parameterisation is used to capture the colour information to minimise the sensitivity to changes in illumination. The motion information is captured by computing the absolute value of the luminance frame-difference.

In the spirit of [8,11], the final image measurements are obtained by processing each of the channels (hue, saturation and frame-difference) on a regular filter grid. At each of the G gridpoints an isotropic Gaussian filter is applied to each channel independently, so that the measurement for the i-th gridpoint becomes $\mathbf{y}_i = (H_i, S_i, D_i)$, with H_i, S_i and $D_i = |\Delta I_i|$ the outputs of the filters on the hue, saturation and absolute frame-difference channels, respectively. The standard deviation for the Gaussian filters is set to a quarter of the gridpoint separation to ensure some degree of independence between the image measurements. The set of measurements over the entire image is denoted by $\mathbf{y} = (\mathbf{y}_1 \cdots \mathbf{y}_G)$.

2.3 Likelihood Models

Within a statistical framework a likelihood function facilitates the evaluation of the goodness of a hypothesis $\mathbf{x}$ in the light of a given set of measurements $\mathbf{y}$. Assuming all the gridpoints to be independent, the likelihood here is of the form

$$L(\mathbf{y}|\mathbf{x}) = \prod_{i=1}^{G} L_i(\mathbf{y}_i|\mathbf{x}) = \prod_{i \in F(\mathbf{x})} L^F(\mathbf{y}_i) \times \prod_{i \in B(\mathbf{x})} L_i^B(\mathbf{y}_i),$$

where $F(\mathbf{x})$ is the set of foreground gridpoints covered by the object parameterised by $\mathbf{x}$, and $B(\mathbf{x})$ is the set of remaining gridpoints in the background. Note that each gridpoint i is associated with a unique background likelihood model L_i^B, whereas there is a single likelihood model L^F for all the gridpoints in the foreground. The expression above can be divided by the product of all the background likelihoods, which is a constant for any valid hypothesis, yielding

$$L(\mathbf{y}|\mathbf{x}) \propto \prod_{i \in F(\mathbf{x})} L^F(\mathbf{y}_i) / L_i^B(\mathbf{y}_i).$$

Thus, the likelihood only needs to be evaluated over the gridpoints in the foreground, resulting in significant computational savings. At each gridpoint the channel measurements are assumed to be conditionally independent given the state, so that the foreground and background likelihoods can be further decomposed as

$$L^F(\mathbf{y}_i) = L^{FH}(H_i) L^{FS}(S_i) L^{FM}(D_i)$$
$$L_i^B(\mathbf{y}_i) = L_i^{BH}(H_i) L_i^{BS}(S_i) L^{BM}(D_i).$$

Note that each gridpoint is associated with unique background likelihood models for the colour components, whereas the background motion likelihood model is shared by all the gridpoints. For both the foreground and background colour likelihoods a histogram model with B bins is adopted. For a given scalar colour measurement c this model is defined as $L(c) = \gamma_{[c]}$, where $[c]$ is the index of the bin corresponding to the measurement, and $\sum_{i=1}^{B} \gamma_i = 1$. The background colour models are trained by collecting measurements at the gridpoints over a training sequence without any objects. The foreground colour models are initialised to skin-colour distributions by training on a set of labelled face images. To prevent numerical problems associated with empty bins each of the colour models is supplied with a uniform component for which the mixture weight is typically set to 10^{-3}.

As is shown by the empirical evidence in Figure 1, the background frame-difference are gamma distributed, *i.e.*

$$L^{BM}(D_i) \propto D_i^{a_\Delta - 1} \exp(-b_\Delta D_i), \tag{1}$$

with typical values for the parameters given by $a_\Delta = 2.62$ and $b_\Delta = 326.90$. This distribution accounts for small camera motions due to vibration and electronic noise in the image acquisition process.

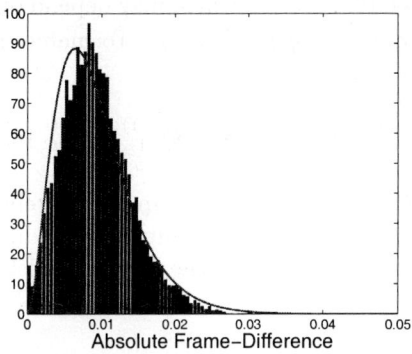

Fig. 1. Distribution of background frame-difference measurements. The absolute frame-difference measurements are gamma distributed if there is no motion in the scene.

Foreground frame-difference measurements depend on the magnitude of the motion, and the number and orientation of the foreground edges relative to the motion. Constructing a likelihood model to capture all these effects would be difficult. However, if the object is indeed moving, the foreground frame-difference measurements are generally substantially larger than the mean of the gamma background distribution, given by $\mu_\Delta = a_\Delta/b_\Delta$. For this reason a simple two component histogram model is adopted for the foreground frame-difference measurements, *i.e.*

$$L^{FM}(D_i) = \begin{cases} \beta & \text{if } 0 \leq D_i < n\mu_\Delta \\ m\beta & \text{if } n\mu_\Delta \leq D_i \leq D_{\max}, \end{cases} \tag{2}$$

where $D_{\max}$ is the maximum value for the absolute frame-difference measurements, and $\beta = (n(1-m)\mu_\Delta + mD_{\max})^{-1}$ is computed such that L^{FM} is a proper distribution. Typical values for the constants in the expressions above are $n = 3$ and $m = 10$. If the object is indeed moving the foreground frame-difference likelihood will typically be much larger than the background frame-difference likelihood, providing a strong localisation cue. However, if the object is present but stationary, the background frame-difference likelihood will dominate, in which case object localisation cues are provided by the colour likelihood.

3 Particle Filter Tracking

For non-linear multi-modal models, as the one introduced here, the particle filter [5] provides a Monte Carlo solution to the recursive filtering equation $p(\mathbf{x}_t|\mathbf{y}_{1:t}) \propto L(\mathbf{y}_t|\mathbf{x}_t) \int p(\mathbf{x}_t|\mathbf{x}_{t-1}) p(\mathbf{x}_{t-1}|\mathbf{y}_{1:t-1}) d\mathbf{x}_{t-1}$ necessary for tracking. Starting with a weighted particle set $\{(\mathbf{x}_{t-1}^{(i)}, \pi_{t-1}^{(i)})\}_{i=1}^N$ approximately distributed according to $p(\mathbf{x}_{t-1}|\mathbf{y}_{1:t-1})$, the particle filter proceeds by predicting new samples from a suitably chosen proposal distribution which may depend on the old state and the new measurements, i.e. $\mathbf{x}_t^{(i)} \sim q(\mathbf{x}_t|\mathbf{x}_{t-1}^{(i)}, \mathbf{y}_t)$. To maintain a consistent sample the new particle weights are set to

$$\pi_t^{(i)} \propto \pi_{t-1}^{(i)} L(\mathbf{y}_t|\mathbf{x}_t^{(i)}) p(\mathbf{x}_t^{(i)}|\mathbf{x}_{t-1}^{(i-1)}) / q(\mathbf{x}_t^{(i)}|\mathbf{x}_{t-1}^{(i)}, \mathbf{y}_t). \qquad (3)$$

The new particle set $\{(\mathbf{x}_t^{(i)}, \pi_t^{(i)})\}_{i=1}^N$ is then approximately distributed according to $p(\mathbf{x}_t|\mathbf{y}_{1:t})$. The particles are then resampled according to their weights to avoid degeneracy. Section 4 describes the proposal distribution used here in more detail.

4 Particle Proposal

The performance of the particle filter hinges on the quality of the proposal distribution. In [5] the optimal choice for the proposal distribution has been shown to be $p(\mathbf{x}_t|\mathbf{x}_{t-1}, \mathbf{y}_t) \propto L(\mathbf{y}_t|\mathbf{x}_t) p(\mathbf{x}_t|\mathbf{x}_{t-1})$. However, direct simulation from this distribution is intractable, calling for the design of a proposal distribution that best approximates it. Such a proposal should facilitate computationally efficient simulation and evaluation, and incorporate information about the measurements to guide the generation of new particles.

In terms of the behaviour of the object the particle filter exhibits three distinct operational phases, and the proposal must be designed to deal with each efficiently. The first phase is when an object first enters the scene. The proposal should be able to detect the object and spawn new particles in the region of the object. The second phase immediately follows the first and persists for as long as the object is in the scene. The proposal should allow the algorithm to successfully track the object, whether it is stationary or moving either slowly or rapidly. The third phase corresponds to the object leaving the scene. The proposal should detect this event and kill off the particles associated with the object. These ideas can be formalised by defining a proposal of the form

$$q(\mathbf{x}_t|\mathbf{x}_{t-1}, \mathbf{y}_t, \overline{P}_{1,t-1}) = q(r_t|r_{t-1}, \overline{P}_{1,t-1}) q(\mathbf{z}_t|\mathbf{z}_{t-1}, r_t, r_{t-1}, \mathbf{y}_t), \qquad (4)$$

with

$$\overline{P}_{1,t} = \sum_{i=1}^{N} \pi_t^{(i)} r_t^{(i)} \qquad (5)$$

$$q(r_t = 1 | r_{t-1} = 0, \overline{P}_{t-1}) = q_{10} = \begin{cases} P_{birth} & \text{if } \overline{P}_{1,t-1} = 0 \\ 0 & \text{otherwise} \end{cases}$$

$$q(r_t = 0 | r_{t-1} = 1) = q_{01} = P_{death}$$

$$q(\mathbf{z}_t | \mathbf{z}_{t-1}, r_t, r_{t-1}, \mathbf{y}_t) = \begin{cases} \text{undefined} & \text{if } r_t = 0 \\ p_L(\mathbf{z}_t | \mathbf{z}_{t-1}) & \text{if } r_t = 1 \text{ and } r_{t-1} = 1 \\ \mathcal{N}\left(\mathbf{z}_t; \widehat{\boldsymbol{\mu}}_t, \widehat{\boldsymbol{\Sigma}}_t\right) & \text{if } r_t = 1 \text{ and } r_{t-1} = 0, \end{cases}$$

where $\mathbf{z} = (x, y, s)$ denotes the continuous components of the state-space, and $\mathcal{N}(\cdot; \boldsymbol{\mu}, \boldsymbol{\Sigma})$ is the Gaussian distribution with mean $\boldsymbol{\mu}$ and covariance $\boldsymbol{\Sigma}$. Note that the proposal above also depends on the quantity $\overline{P}_{1,t-1}$, which is computed from the empirical particle distribution at the previous time step. Recent theoretical results [4] show that dependence on the empirical particle distribution in the proposal still leads to a particle filter that converges to the correct distribution.

From the proposal above it is evident that the birth of a new object is only allowed if there is not already an object alive in the scene, i.e. $\overline{P}_{1,t-1} = 0$. On the other hand, particles that are associated with an object that is alive in the scene are subjected to a fixed death probability. It is up to the reweighting and resampling stages to determine whether the decision to kill a particle should be enforced. Typical values for the birth and death probabilities are $P_{birth} = P_{death} = 0.1$. Note that these values are substantially larger than those for the corresponding parameters in the dynamical model. This is to ensure that a large enough proportion of the particles undergoes a birth/death process, enabling the instantaneous detection of objects entering/leaving the scene. If an object particle is dead ($r_t = 0$), the proposal for the object location and scale is undefined. If it is alive and persisting, the proposal for its location and scale is set to the object dynamics for these components. This is sufficient to maintain track under the assumptions that the particles are already locked on to the object, and the chosen dynamical model is broad enough to capture any expected object motion. For a new object entering the scene values for the object location and scale are simulated from a Gaussian birth proposal. The parameters of this proposal are computed using the motion measurements, as described below.

Object Detection

When an object enters the scene it is moving, and the motion measurements can be used to determine a rectangular region within which the object is likely to lie. This section proposes an efficient algorithm based on searching the horizontal and vertical projections of the frame-difference measurements to locate such a region. The size and location of this region can then be used to set the parameters of the birth proposal.

The image processing filters are arranged on a regular grid. Let G_x and G_y denote the number of filters in each row and column, respectively, with $G = G_x G_y$, and $\mathbf{y}_{i,j}$ the vector of measurements at the i-th row and j-th column of the grid. Since objects (faces) are assumed to be horizontally separated in most video sequences of interest, the object region boundaries in the x direction can be efficiently obtained by searching over the column projections of the frame-difference measurements. The object boundaries in the y direction can then be found by searching over the row projections of the frame-difference measurements within the region boundaries in the x direction. This two-step procedure is graphically illustrated in Figure 2.

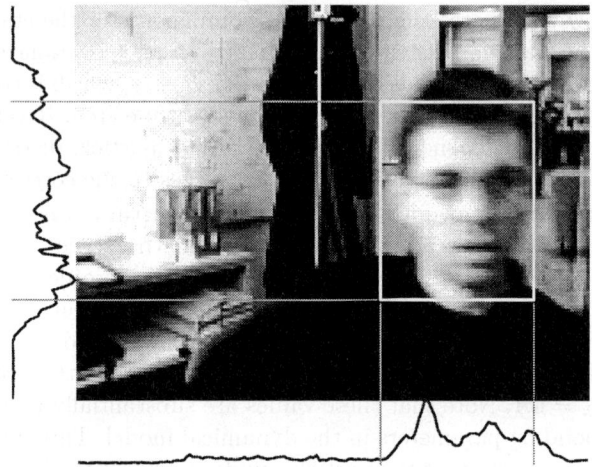

Fig. 2. Motion-based object detection. The object x region is located first by searching over the column projections of the frame-difference measurements (shown below the image). The object y region is then located by searching over the row projections of the frame-difference measurements within the object x region (shown to the left of the image). The size of the y region is constrained to yield within $\pm 10\%$ a 1.25 aspect ratio rectangular region.

The object search proceeds similarly in both directions, and only the first case is described in detail below. Let $\overline{\mathbf{D}}^x = (\overline{D}_1^x \cdots \overline{D}_{G_x}^x)$, with $\overline{D}_i^x = 1/G_y \sum_{j=1}^{G_y} D_{i,j}$, denote the vector of column projections of the frame-difference measurements, and denote by (d_x, W_x) the midpoint and halfwidth of the hypothesised object x region. Assuming the components of $\overline{\mathbf{D}}^x$ to be independent and following an argument similar to that in Section 2.3, the likelihood for the hypothesised object x region can be written as[1]

---

[1] The foreground and background likelihood models used here are identical to those defined in (2) and (1), respectively. Even though the statistics for the frame-difference projections (sums) are expected to differ from those for the single frame-difference measurements, the models were found to predict the projections equally well for the summation ranges in the application considered here.

$$L(\overline{\mathbf{D}}^x | d_x, W_x) \propto \prod_{i \in \mathcal{I}_x} L^{FM}(\overline{D}_i^x)/L^{BM}(\overline{D}_i^x),$$

with $\mathcal{I}_x = \{1 \cdots G_x\} \cap [d_x - W_x, d_x + W_x]$. An estimate of the object x region can then be obtained by maximising this likelihood, *i.e.*

$$(\widehat{d}_x, \widehat{W}_x) = \underset{(d_x, W_x)}{\arg \max} L(\overline{\mathbf{D}}^x | d_x, W_x),$$

under the constraint that $L(\overline{\mathbf{D}}^x | \widehat{d}_x, \widehat{W}_x) > 1$. This maximisation is performed by a computationally efficient coarse-to-fine hierarchical search over (d_x, W_x). An estimate of the object y region $(\widehat{d}_y, \widehat{W}_y)$ can be found in a similar way by maximising the likelihood over the vector of row projections within the object x boundaries. The size of the y region is constrained to yield within $\pm 10\%$ a 1.25 aspect ratio rectangular region.

Once the object region is determined the parameters of the birth proposal are set to (omitting the time subscript for brevity)

$$\widehat{\boldsymbol{\mu}} = (\widehat{d}_x, \widehat{d}_y, 0.5(\widehat{W}_x/a + \widehat{W}_y/b)), \quad \widehat{\boldsymbol{\Sigma}} = \text{diag}(0.1(\widehat{W}_x, \widehat{W}_y, 1))^2.$$

Thus, the location and scale parameters are proposed independently. The proposal is centred on the object region, with its uncertainty proportional to the size of the region. The chosen values were found to give good performance in practice.

5 Colour Model Adaptation

Recall from Section 2.3 that the parameters of the foreground colour likelihood are initialised using a set of labelled face images. As such the model may be too broad to facilitate accurate localisation for a specific individual. Furthermore, it may be particularly sensitive to changes in the object pose and illumination. Thus, there is a large potential benefit to be gained by devising a strategy to individualise the colour model to a particular object and to adapt to colour changes due to changes in object pose and illumination.

The largest variations in the object appearance occur when it is moving. In this case the colour likelihood becomes less reliable, but strong localisation cues are provided by the complementary frame-difference likelihood. These cues anchor the particles tightly around the moving object. The colour information within the particle extents can then be used to update the colour likelihood parameters. The degree to which each particle contributes to this adaptation should be proportional to the strength of its frame-difference likelihood. Within a probabilistic setting this can be achieved by a stochastic version of the EM algorithm [10]. It should be emphasised that adaptation is only allowed if an object is present in the scene and moving. An object is said to be present if $\overline{P}_1$ in (5) is bigger than some threshold T_{obj}, which is typically set to $T_{obj} = 0.9$. Object motion is detected by monitoring when the average output of the frame-difference filters covered by the particles encoding the object configuration, denoted by $\widetilde{D}$, exceeds some threshold T_Δ, which is typically set to $T_\Delta = 3\mu_\Delta$, where μ_Δ is the mean of the background frame-difference likelihood. The remainder of this section presents the details of the adaptation algorithm.

Denoting by $\boldsymbol{\theta} = (\boldsymbol{\gamma}^{FH}, \boldsymbol{\gamma}^{FS})$, with $\boldsymbol{\gamma}^{FH} = (\gamma_1^{FH} \cdots \gamma_B^{FH})$ and $\boldsymbol{\gamma}^{FS} = (\gamma_1^{FS} \cdots \gamma_B^{FS})$, the parameters of the histograms for the foreground colour likelihood, the objective at time t is to find the MAP parameter estimate, i.e. $\widehat{\boldsymbol{\theta}}_t = \arg\max_{\boldsymbol{\theta}_t} p(\boldsymbol{\theta}_t | \mathbf{y}_{1:t}, \widehat{\boldsymbol{\theta}}_{1:t-1})$. This estimation can be performed within the EM [10] framework by defining a Q-function of the form

$$Q(\boldsymbol{\theta}_t, \widehat{\boldsymbol{\theta}}_t) = \mathbb{E}\left[\log p(\boldsymbol{\theta}_t | \mathbf{y}_{1:t}, \mathbf{x}_{1:t}, \widehat{\boldsymbol{\theta}}_{1:t-1})\right]$$
$$\propto \mathbb{E}\left[\log p(\mathbf{y}_{1:t} | \mathbf{x}_{1:t}, \widehat{\boldsymbol{\theta}}_{1:t-1}, \boldsymbol{\theta}_t) + \log p(\mathbf{x}_{1:t} | \widehat{\boldsymbol{\theta}}_{1:t-1}, \boldsymbol{\theta}_t) + \log p(\boldsymbol{\theta}_t | \widehat{\boldsymbol{\theta}}_{1:t-1})\right],$$

where $\widehat{\boldsymbol{\theta}}_t$ is now a preliminary MAP estimate of the parameters, and the expectation is relative to the full filtering distribution $p(\mathbf{x}_{1:t} | \mathbf{y}_{1:t}, \widehat{\boldsymbol{\theta}}_{1:t})$. By eliminating terms independent of $\boldsymbol{\theta}_t$, this expression reduces to

$$Q(\boldsymbol{\theta}_t, \widehat{\boldsymbol{\theta}}_t) \propto \mathbb{E}\left[\log L(\mathbf{y}_t | \mathbf{x}_t, \boldsymbol{\theta}_t)\right] + \log p(\boldsymbol{\theta}_t | \widehat{\boldsymbol{\theta}}_{t-1}),$$

where the expectation is now relative to the marginal filtering distribution $p(\mathbf{x}_t | \mathbf{y}_{1:t}, \widehat{\boldsymbol{\theta}}_{1:t})$. This distribution is not known analytically, but using the particle set $\{(\mathbf{x}_t^{(i)}, \pi_t^{(i)})\}_{i=1}^N$ prior to resampling, a Monte Carlo approximation of the Q-function can be obtained as

$$\widehat{Q}_N(\boldsymbol{\theta}_t, \widehat{\boldsymbol{\theta}}_t) \propto \sum_{i=1}^N \overline{\pi}_t^{(i)} \log L(\mathbf{y}_t | \mathbf{x}_t^{(i)}, \boldsymbol{\theta}_t) \delta_1(r_t^{(i)}) + \log p(\boldsymbol{\theta}_t | \widehat{\boldsymbol{\theta}}_{t-1}),$$

where $\delta_x(\cdot)$ denotes the Kronecker delta function with mass at x, and $\overline{\pi}_t^{(i)} = \pi_t^{(i)} / \sum_{j=1}^N \pi_t^{(j)} \delta_1(r_t^{(j)})$. Note that the Monte Carlo approximation has been restricted to particles for which the object is alive in the scene, and the weights have been renormalised to sum to one over these particles. The M-step of the EM algorithm then updates the preliminary MAP parameter estimate by maximising this approximate Q-function, i.e.

$$\widehat{\boldsymbol{\theta}}_t \leftarrow \arg\max_{\boldsymbol{\theta}_t} \widehat{Q}_N(\boldsymbol{\theta}_t, \widehat{\boldsymbol{\theta}}_t). \tag{6}$$

Pure Monte Carlo EM, as described above, requires a redraw of the particles before proceeding with the next EM iteration. However, if the particle proposal is independent of the unknown parameters (as is the case here), a redraw is not strictly necessary, and the particle weights can simply be updated according to (3), using the new value of the parameters in the likelihood term. If the proposal distribution were to depend on the parameters, then after a few steps of the EM algorithm the particle approximation may deviate too much from the posterior with the current parameter estimate, so that the Monte Carlo approximation of the Q-function would be poor. In this case a particle redraw is required after every EM iteration. The algorithm is initialised with the final parameter estimate at the previous time step.

To complete the model it remains to specify a prior distribution on the model parameters $p(\boldsymbol{\theta}_t|\boldsymbol{\theta}_{t-1})$. It is desirable to choose a prior that facilitates a closed-form solution for the M-step in (6), and allows a large degree of flexibility in its specific form. For these reasons conjugate Dirichlet priors are adopted for the parameters. For both the hue and saturation models these distributions are specified by (omitting the time subscript for brevity)

$$\mathcal{D}i\left(\gamma_1\cdots\gamma_B;\alpha_1\cdots\alpha_B\right) \propto \prod_{i=1}^{B}\gamma_i^{(\alpha_i-1)},$$

where $\boldsymbol{\alpha} = (\alpha_1\cdots\alpha_B)$ are the parameters of the Dirichlet distribution, with $\alpha_i > 0$, $i = 1\cdots B$. The mean and variance of this distribution are given by $\mathbb{E}[\gamma_i] = \alpha_i/\alpha$ and $\mathbb{V}[\gamma_i] = \alpha_i(\alpha - \alpha_i)/(\alpha^2 + \alpha^3)$, respectively, with $\alpha = \sum_{i=1}^{B}\alpha_i$. The uniform prior is obtained if $\alpha_i = 1$, $i = 1\cdots B$. To maintain temporal coherence the prior can be centred on the previous parameter estimate, with the variance set to reflect the confidence in this estimate. This can be achieved by setting $p(\boldsymbol{\gamma}_t|\boldsymbol{\gamma}_{t-1}) = \mathcal{D}i\left(\boldsymbol{\gamma}_t; C\boldsymbol{\gamma}_{t-1}\right)$, with $C > 0$. The prior mean and variance then become $\mathbb{E}[\gamma_{i,t}] = \gamma_{i,t-1}$ and $\mathbb{V}[\gamma_{i,t}] = \gamma_{i,t-1}(1-\gamma_{i,t-1})/(1+C)$, respectively. Thus, as $C \to \infty$ the prior variance goes to zero.

With the Dirichlet priors and the form of the likelihood in Section 2.3, the M-step leads to update rules for the parameters of the hue and saturation models of the form

$$\gamma_i = \frac{\bar{n}_i + \alpha_i - 1}{\sum_{j=1}^{B}(\bar{n}_j + \alpha_j) - B}, \tag{7}$$

where $\bar{n}_i = \sum_{j=1}^{N}\pi^{(j)}n_i^{(j)}\delta_1(r_t^{(j)})$ is the weighted average bin counts for the i-th bin, with the i-th bin count for the j-th particle formally defined as $n_i^{(j)} = |\{k \in F(\mathbf{x}^{(j)}) : [c_k] = i\}|$, where $[c_k]$ denotes the histogram bin corresponding to a hue/saturation measurement at gridpoint k, and $|\cdot|$ denotes the set size operator. Note from (7) that in the case of a uniform prior the new parameters simply become the normalised weighted average bin counts.

The adaptation method described above is not the only one available. One alternative strategy would be to include the colour model parameters in the particle state-space. However, the corresponding increase in the state-space dimensionality increases the complexity of the estimation problem to a degree where many orders of magnitude more particles may be required to achieve the same performance as the Monte Carlo EM scheme. Furthermore, the colour model parameters are essentially auxiliary variables, and their posterior distribution is not of particular interest for tracking.

To conclude this section a summary of the complete tracking and adaptation algorithm is given below.

Algorithm 1: Monte Carlo EM Particle Filter

With $\{(\mathbf{x}_{t-1}^{(i)}, \pi_{t-1}^{(i)})\}_{i=1}^N$ and $\widehat{\boldsymbol{\theta}}_{t-1}$ the particle set and parameter estimate at the previous time step, proceed as follows at time t:

- Particle prediction: simulate $\widetilde{\mathbf{x}}_t^{(i)} \sim q(\mathbf{x}_t | \mathbf{x}_{t-1}^{(i)}, \mathbf{y}_t, \overline{P}_{1,t-1})$, $i = 1 \cdots N$ (see (4)).
- Parameter adaptation:
  If $\overline{P}_{1,t-1} > T_{obj}$ and $\widetilde{D} > T_\Delta$:
  - Initialisation: set $\boldsymbol{\theta}^{(0)} = \widehat{\boldsymbol{\theta}}_{t-1}$, $\boldsymbol{\alpha}^{FH} = C\widehat{\boldsymbol{\gamma}}_{t-1}^{FH}$, $\boldsymbol{\alpha}^{FS} = C\widehat{\boldsymbol{\gamma}}_{t-1}^{FS}$.
  - MCEM loop: for $j = 1 \cdots L$:
    - Weight update: $\kappa_j^{(i)} \propto \pi_{t-1}^{(i)} \frac{L(\mathbf{y}_t | \widetilde{\mathbf{x}}_t^{(i)}, \boldsymbol{\theta}^{(j-1)}) p(\widetilde{\mathbf{x}}_t^{(i)} | \mathbf{x}_{t-1}^{(i-1)})}{q(\widetilde{\mathbf{x}}_t^{(i)} | \mathbf{x}_{t-1}^{(i)}, \mathbf{y}_t, \overline{P}_{1,t-1})}$, $i = 1 \cdots N$.
    - Weight renormalisation: $\overline{\kappa}_j^{(i)} = \kappa_j^{(i)} / \sum_{k=1}^N \kappa_j^{(k)} \delta_1(r_t^{(k)})$, $i = 1 \cdots N$.
    - Parameter update (see (7)):
    $$\boldsymbol{\theta}^{(j)} = \arg\max_{\boldsymbol{\theta}} \sum_{i=1}^N \overline{\kappa}_j^{(i)} \log L(\mathbf{y}_t | \widetilde{\mathbf{x}}_t^{(i)}, \boldsymbol{\theta}) \delta_1(r_t^{(i)}) + \log p(\boldsymbol{\theta} | \widehat{\boldsymbol{\theta}}_{t-1}).$$
  - Termination: set $\widehat{\boldsymbol{\theta}}_t = \boldsymbol{\theta}^{(L)}$.
  Else:
  - Set $\widehat{\boldsymbol{\theta}}_t = \widehat{\boldsymbol{\theta}}_{t-1}$ and $\kappa_L^{(i)} \propto \pi_{t-1}^{(i)} \frac{L(\mathbf{y}_t | \widetilde{\mathbf{x}}_t^{(i)}, \widehat{\boldsymbol{\theta}}_t) p(\widetilde{\mathbf{x}}_t^{(i)} | \mathbf{x}_{t-1}^{(i-1)})}{q(\widetilde{\mathbf{x}}_t^{(i)} | \mathbf{x}_{t-1}^{(i)}, \mathbf{y}_t, \overline{P}_{1,t-1})}$, $i = 1 \cdots N$.
- Particle reweighting: set $\widetilde{\pi}_t^{(i)} = \kappa_L^{(i)}$, $i = 1 \cdots N$.
- Resampling: set $\mathbf{x}_t^{(i)} = \widetilde{\mathbf{x}}_t^{j(i)}$, $\pi_t^{(i)} = 1$, $j(i) \sim \{\widetilde{\pi}_t^{(k)}\}_{k=1}^N$, $i = 1 \cdots N$.

∎

6 Results

This section evaluates the performance of the proposed tracking and adaptation algorithm. For illustrative purposes the initial discussion will focus on the video sequence summarised in Figure 3[2]. The setting is a standard office environment with several objects in the background that can potentially confuse a generic skin-colour model. The first 50 frames are empty, and these were used to calibrate the background models. A person then enters the scene from the right and moves around, resulting in changes in pose. In the final part of the sequence the person is stationary. The size of the video frames is 160×120 and the video rate during acquisition was 30fps.

The algorithm was tested on this sequence with the adaptation first disabled, and subsequently enabled. In both cases $N = 100$ particles were used, with all the particles initialised to have no object alive in the scene. The free parameters

---
[2] Videos for all the results described in this section are available as AVI files at http://research.microsoft.com/users/jacov/msr_work.htm.

of the system were set according to the strategies described elsewhere in the text, but the algorithm proved to be robust over sensible ranges for these parameters. The adaptation algorithm was initialised with the colour model at the previous time step, and the prior was set to be centred on the initial values, with the variance constant fixed to $C = 100$. In all cases the adaptation algorithm was found to converge rapidly, and hence only a single EM iteration was performed at each time step. For the given image size and a 22×17 filter grid a non-optimised C++ implementation of the algorithm ran at 15fps on a 736MHz Pentium III with 512MB of RAM. With some care in the implementation real-time performance can easily be achieved.

The tracking results are summarised in Figure 3. In both cases the object is successfully detected and tracked during the period of motion when the frame-difference likelihood dominates. In the adaptive case the colour model is able to individualise to the specific object and adapt to changes in pose and illumination. When the object is stationary and the motion cues disappear, the generic skin-colour model is easily confused by skin-coloured objects in the background (the carpet in this case), and track is lost. In the adaptive case, however, the individualised colour model allows the algorithm to maintain lock on the object. Further results confirming that adaptivity allows successful tracking under adverse conditions are summarised in Figure 4.

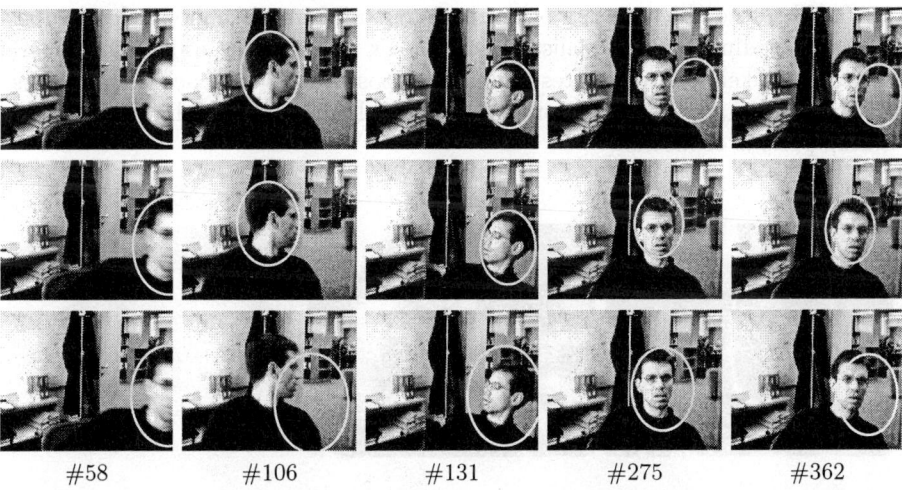

#58 #106 #131 #275 #362

Fig. 3. Tracking results with adaptation disabled (top), enabled (middle and bottom) and the frame-difference likelihood disabled (bottom). The object is successfully detected (#58) and tracked during periods of motion (#106, #131) if the frame-difference likelihood is enabled (top, middle). With the object stationary (#275, #362) track is lost in the non-adaptive case (top) due to the skin-coloured carpet in the background, whereas the individualised model maintains lock (middle). With the frame-difference likelihood disabled (bottom) lock is soon lost and the colour model drifts to the background.

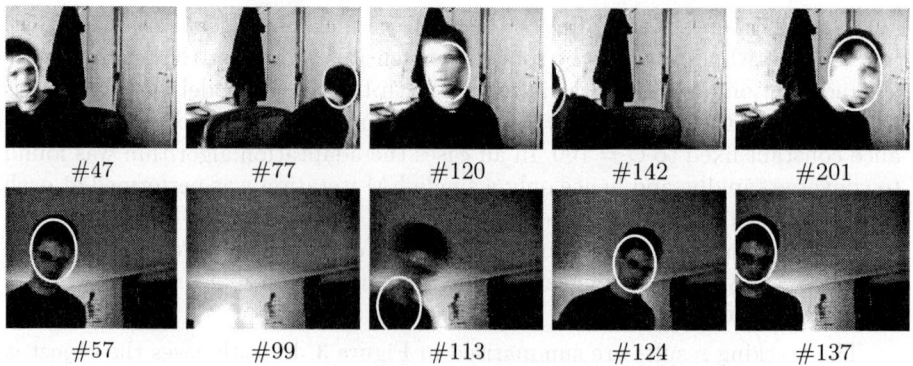

Fig. 4. Adaptivity allows tracking under adverse conditions. In the top sequence the head of the person is successfully detected and tracked despite substantial variations in pose and illumination, and the person momentarily leaving the scene. The first frame in the bottom sequence shows the face successfully tracked and the colour model adapted to the conditions. The person then leaves the scene and the particles are killed. Upon re-entering the tracker is wrongly initialised on the jumper, but the individualised colour model allows lock to be re-established after only a few frames, and the subsequent tracking proceeds successfully.

These results are further exemplified by the log-likelihood ratio maps in Figure 5. When the object is in motion the frame-difference likelihood clearly dominates, providing strong localisation cues. For a stationary object the generic skin-colour likelihood generates strong false positives in the background. These false positives are better suppressed if the colour model is allowed to adapt during periods of motion.

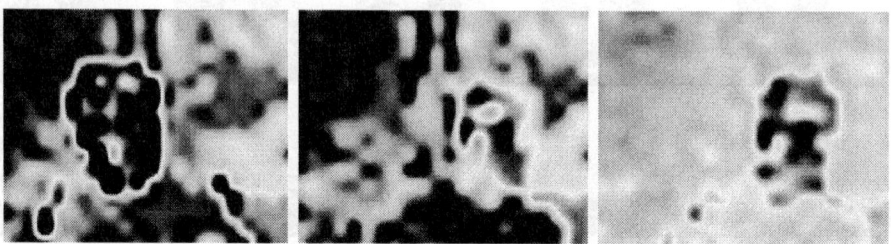

Fig. 5. Log-likelihood ratio maps. When the object is in motion the frame-difference likelihood dominates (left). With the object stationary the generic skin-colour model generates strong false positives in the background (middle). The false positives are better suppressed and the foreground model is stronger in the adaptive case (right).

The need for an anchor likelihood is easily demonstrated by disabling the frame-difference likelihood, and allowing adaptation at every time step, albeit with a stronger prior. In this case the colour model invariably drifts and becomes fixated on some part of the background, as is illustrated in the bottom of Figure 3.

7 Conclusions

This paper demonstrated how the fusion of motion and colour measurements, automatic initialisation and colour model adaptation can increase the accuracy and robustness of a particle filter tracker. The adaptation algorithm, based on a stochastic version of the EM algorithm, allows the individualisation of the colour model to a specific object, and accommodates changes in the object pose and illumination. It relies heavily on the frame-difference likelihood to anchor the particles and prevent drift to the background.

In the extension to multiple objects the adaptation strategy is of crucial importance to establish and maintain object identity. The adaptation strategy can also be applied to the background colour models when it is certain that the corresponding filters are not occluded by a foreground object. Furthermore, update rules based on the same principles can also be derived for the parameters of the Gaussian mixture colour models used in [8]. All these issues are topics of ongoing and future research.

References

1. K.J. Astrom. *Introduction to Stochastic Control Theory*. Academic Press, 1970.
2. A. Blake, R. Curwen, and A. Zisserman. A framework for spatio-temporal control in the tracking of visual contours. *Int. J. Computer Vision*, 11(2):127–145, October 1993.
3. D. Comaniciu, V. Ramesh, and P. Meer. Real-time tracking of non-rigid objects using mean shift. In *Proc. Conf. Comp. Vision Pattern Rec.*, pages II: 142–149, 2000.
4. A Doucet and D Crisan. A survey of convergence results on particle filtering for practitioners. *IEEE Trans. Signal Processing*, 2001. To Appear.
5. A. Doucet, J. F. G. de Freitas, and N. J. Gordon, editors. *Sequential Monte Carlo Methods in Practice*. Springer-Verlag, New York, 2001.
6. C. Harris. Tracking with rigid models. In A. Blake and A.L. Yuille, editors, *Active Vision*, pages 59–74. MIT, 1992.
7. M. Isard and A. Blake. CONDENSATION - conditional density propagation for visual tracking. *Int. J. Computer Vision*, 28(1):5–28, 1998.
8. M. Isard and J. MacCormick. BraMBLe: A Bayesian multiple-blob tracker. In *Proc. Int. Conf. Computer Vision*, pages II: 34–41, 2001.
9. H.T. Nguyen, M. Worring, and R. van den Boomgaard. Occlusion robust adaptive template tracking. In *ICCV*, pages I: 678–683, 2001.
10. C. P. Robert and G. Casella. *Monte Carlo Statistical Methods*. Springer-Verlag, New York, 1999.

11. J. Sullivan, A. Blake, M. Isard, and J. MacCormick. Bayesian object localisation in images. *IJCV*, 44(2):111–135, September 2001.
12. K. Toyama and A. Blake. Probabilistic tracking in a metric space. In *Proc. Int. Conf. Computer Vision*, pages II: 50–57, 2001.
13. Y. Wu and T. Huang. Color tracking by transductive learning. In *CVPR*, pages I: 133–138, 2000.
14. Y. Wu and T.S. Huang. A co-inference approach to robust visual tracking. In *Proc. Int. Conf. Computer Vision*, pages II: 26–33, 2001.

Color-Based Probabilistic Tracking

P. Pérez[1], C. Hue[2], J. Vermaak[1], and M. Gangnet[1]

[1] Microsoft Research, 7 JJ Thomson Av., Cambridge CB3 0FB, UK
{pperez, jacov, mgangnet}@microsoft.com
[2] Irisa, Campus de Beaulieu, F35042 Rennes Cedex, France
chue@irisa.fr

Abstract. Color-based trackers recently proposed in [3,4,5] have been proved robust and versatile for a modest computational cost. They are especially appealing for tracking tasks where the spatial structure of the tracked objects exhibits such a dramatic variability that trackers based on a space-dependent appearance reference would break down very fast. Trackers in [3,4,5] rely on the deterministic search of a window whose color content matches a reference histogram color model.

Relying on the same principle of color histogram distance, but within a probabilistic framework, we introduce a new Monte Carlo tracking technique. The use of a particle filter allows us to better handle color clutter in the background, as well as complete occlusion of the tracked entities over a few frames.

This probabilistic approach is very flexible and can be extended in a number of useful ways. In particular, we introduce the following ingredients: multi-part color modeling to capture a rough spatial layout ignored by global histograms, incorporation of a background color model when relevant, and extension to multiple objects.

1 Introduction

Tracking objects, and more generally features, through the frames of an image sequence is an omnipresent elementary task in online and offline image-based applications including visual servoing, surveillance, gestural human-machine interface and smart environments, video editing and compression, augmented reality and visual effects, motion capture, medical and meteorological imaging, etc.

The combination of tools used to accomplish a given tracking task depends on whether one tries to track (I) objects of a given nature, e.g., cars, people, faces, (II) objects of a given nature with a specific attribute, e.g., moving cars, walking people, talking heads, face of a given person, (III) objects of *a priori* unknown nature but of a specific interest, e.g., moving objects, objects of semantic interest manually picked in the first frame.

In each case part of the input video frame is searched against a reference model describing the appearance of the object. This reference can be based on image patches, thus describing how the tracked region should look like pixel-wise, on contours, thus describing the overall shape, and/or on global descriptors such as color models.

For problems of type (I) and (II), the instantiation of this reference model is exogenous. The reference is either chosen in an *ad-hoc* way, e.g., an ellipse outline for faces [1,18], or extracted from a set of examples like gray level appearance templates in [2] or outlines in [8,10,12].

In contrast, in problems of type (III) the instantiation of the reference has to arise from the sequence under consideration, thus being endogenous. In that case the reference can be extracted from the first frame and kept frozen, as color models in [3,4,5] and gray-level templates in [9], or adapted on the fly, using the tracking results from the previous frames, as gray-level templates in [14,15,17], deformable outlines in [16], and color models in [18,21,20].

This paper falls in the category of trackers using global color reference models and endogenous initialization. Such trackers have recently been proved robust and versatile for a modest computational cost [3,4,5]. They have in particular been proved to be very useful for tracking tasks where the objects of interest can be of any kind, and exhibit in addition drastic changes of spatial structure through the sequence, due to pose changes, partial occlusions, etc. This type of tracking problem arises for instance in the context of video analysis and manipulation. For such applications, most trackers based on a space-dependent appearance reference would break down very fast. In contrast, using a global, though sufficiently discriminant, model of the color distribution within the region of interest is an appealing way to address such complex tracking tasks.

The techniques introduced independently by Bradski ("CamShift" in [3]) and by Comaniciu *et al.* ("MeanShift" in [5]), and modified later by Chen *et al.* [4], are based on the following principle: the current frame is searched for a region, a fixed-shape variable-size window, whose color content best matches a reference color model. The search is deterministic. Starting from the final location in the previous frame, it proceeds iteratively at each frame so as to minimize a distance measure to the reference color histogram. Excellent tracking results on complex scenes are demonstrated in the three studies. This deterministic search might however run into problems when parts of the background nearby exhibit similar colors or when the tracked object is completely occluded for a while.

Improved handling of such situations is one of the benefits of the new color-based probabilistic tracking we propose. Relying on the same principle of comparing the color content of candidate regions to a reference color histogram, we embed it within a sequential Monte Carlo framework. This requires the building of a color likelihood based on color histogram distances, the coupling of this data model with a dynamical state space model, and the sequential approximation of the resulting posterior distribution with a particle filter. These different steps are described in Sect. 2. The use of a sample-based filtering technique permits in particular the momentary tracking of multiple posterior modes. This is the key to escape from background distraction and to recover after partial or complete occlusions, as demonstrated in Sect. 3.1.

This probabilistic approach is also very versatile in that is does not impose many constraints on the type of ingredients that can be incorporated in the state space, the dynamics, and the data likelihood definitions. Hence our color-based tracking can be extended in a number of useful ways:

- Extension to multi-part color modeling as a way of incorporating a gross spatial layout ignored by global histogramming in Sect. 3.2;
- Incorporation of a background color model when relevant in Sect. 3.3;
- Extension to multiple objects in Sect. 3.4.

The treatment of the two last items within a particle filtering approach bears connections with the "BraMBLe" tracker introduced in [11]. We discuss these connections in detail in Sect. 4.

2 Probabilistic Tracking

2.1 Sequential Monte Carlo Tracking

Sequential Monte Carlo techniques for filtering time series [6] and their use in the specific context of visual tracking [10] have been described at length in the literature.

The starting point is a standard state space model, where a Markovian prior on the hidden states is coupled with a conditionally independent observation process. Denoting by x_t and y_t respectively the hidden state and the data at time t, and fixing the order of the dynamics to one, the sequence of filtering distributions $p(x_t|y_{0:t})$ to be tracked obeys the recursion

$$p(x_{t+1}|y_{0:t+1}) \propto p(y_{t+1}|x_{t+1}) \int_{x_t} p(x_{t+1}|x_t)p(x_t|y_{0:t})dx_t, \quad (1)$$

with the notation $x_{0:t} \doteq (x_0,\ldots,x_t)$ and similarly for y. In the case of linear Gaussian state space models, (1) can be handled analytically yielding the Kalman filter.

Unfortunately, in visual tracking problems the likelihood is non-linear, and often multi-modal, with respect to the hidden state. The reason being that the hidden variables indicate which part of the data set to look at. As a result the Kalman filter and its approximations are usually not suitable.

The recursion can however be used within a sequential Monte Carlo framework where the posterior $p(x_t|y_{0:t})$ is approximated by a finite set $\{x_t^m\}_{m=1\cdots M}$ of M samples, the particles. The generation of samples from $p(x_{t+1}|y_{0:t+1})$ is then obtained as follows. All the particles are moved independently by sampling from an appropriate proposal transition kernel $f(x_{t+1}; x_t, y_{t+1})$. If the x_t^m's are fair samples from the filtering distribution at time t, the new particles, denoted by $\tilde{x}_{t+1}^m$, associated with the importance weights

$$\pi_{t+1}^m \propto \frac{p(y_{t+1}|\tilde{x}_{t+1}^m)p(\tilde{x}_{t+1}^m|x_t^m)}{f(\tilde{x}_{t+1}^m; x_t^m, y_{t+1})} \text{ with } \sum_{m=1}^{M} \pi_{t+1}^m = 1, \quad (2)$$

approximate the new filtering distribution well. Resampling these particle according to their weights provides a set $\{x_{t+1}^m\}_{m=1\cdots M}$ of fair samples from the filtering distribution $p(x_{t+1}|y_{0:t+1})$.

It can be shown (see [6]) that the optimal proposal density is proportional to $p(y_{t+1}|\tilde{x}_{t+1})p(\tilde{x}_{t+1}|x_t)$, but its normalization $\int_{\tilde{x}_{t+1}} p(y_{t+1}|\tilde{x}_{t+1})p(\tilde{x}_{t+1}|x_t)$ cannot be computed analytically in our case. The chosen proposal density must then be sufficiently close to the optimal one such that the weights do not become all extremely small in the re-weighting process, resulting in a degeneracy of the sample approximation. The default choice (bootstrap filter) consists in taking $f(x_{t+1}; x_t, y_{t+1}) = p(x_{t+1}|x_t)$. In this case the weights become the data-likelihood associated with each hypothesized state $\tilde{x}_{t+1}^m$.

Based on the discrete approximation of $p(x_t|y_{0:t})$, different estimates of the "best" state at time t can be devised. We use, in a standard way, the Monte Carlo approximation of the expectation $\hat{x}_t \doteq \frac{1}{M}\sum_{m=1}^M x_t^m \approx \mathbb{E}(x_t|y_{0:t})$ as the tracker output at time t.

After the different ingredients of the model are defined in the next section, the complete procedure will be summarized in Proc. 1.

2.2 State Space and Dynamics

We aim to track a region of interest in the image plane. The shape of this region is fixed *a priori* through the definition of a 0-centered window W. It can be an ellipse or a rectangular box as in [3,4,5]. In our case, there is no restriction on the class of shapes that can be used. More complex hand-drawn or learned regions can be used if relevant. In any case, tracking then amounts to estimating in each frame the parameters of the transformation to be applied to W. Affinity or similitude transforms are classically considered. Given the global nature of the color information on which the proposed tracking relies, the choice of a simple similitude seems appropriate. Moreover, when the aspect ratio of the chosen region is close to one, the color information gathered over transformed regions will be rather insensitive to the rotation component of the similitude. As in [3,5] we thus only consider here the location $d \doteq (x,y)$ in the image coordinate system and the scale s as the hidden variables to be estimated.

A second-order auto-regressive dynamics is chosen on these parameters. In accordance with the first-order formalism used in the previous subsection, we define the state at time t as $x_t = (d_t, d_{t-1}, s_t, s_{t-1})$. The dynamics then reads

$$x_{t+1} = Ax_t + Bx_{t-1} + Cv_t, \quad v_t \sim \mathcal{N}(0, \Sigma). \qquad (3)$$

Matrices A, B, C and Σ defining this dynamics could be learned from a set of representative sequences where correct tracks have been obtained in some way. For the time being we use an ad-hoc model composed of three independent constant velocity dynamics on x_t, y_t and s_t with respective standard deviations 1 pixel/frame, 1 pixel/frame, and 0.1 frame^{-1}.

2.3 Color Model

Color models are obtained by histogramming techniques in the Hue-Saturation-Value (HSV) color space [7] in order to decouple chromatic information from shading effects. Color information is however only reliable when both the saturation and the value are not too small. Hence, we populate an HS histogram with $N_h N_s$ bins using only the pixels with saturation and value larger than two thresholds set to 0.1 and 0.2 respectively in our experiments. The remaining "color-free" pixels can however retain a crucial information when tracked regions are mainly black and white. We thus found useful to populate N_v additional value-only bins with them. The resulting complete histogram is thus composed of $N = N_h N_s + N_v$ bins. We shall denote $b_t(\boldsymbol{u}) \in \{1, \ldots, N\}$ the bin index associated with the color vector $\boldsymbol{y}_t(\boldsymbol{u})$ at pixel location $\boldsymbol{u}$ in frame t.

Given an occurrence of the state vector $\boldsymbol{x}_t$, the candidate region in which color information will be gathered is defined as $R(\boldsymbol{x}_t) \doteq \boldsymbol{d}_t + s_t W$. Within this region a kernel density estimate $\boldsymbol{q}_t(\boldsymbol{x}) = \{q_t(n; \boldsymbol{x})\}_{n=1\cdots N}$ of the color distribution at time t is given by [5]

$$q_t(n; \boldsymbol{x}) = K \sum_{\boldsymbol{u} \in R(\boldsymbol{x})} w(|\boldsymbol{u} - \boldsymbol{d}|) \delta[b_t(\boldsymbol{d}) - n] \qquad (4)$$

where δ is the Kronecker delta function, K is a normalization constant ensuring $\sum_{n=1}^{N} q_t(n; \boldsymbol{x}) = 1$, w is a weighting function, and locations $\boldsymbol{u}$ lie on the pixel grid, possibly sub-sampled for efficiency reasons. This model associates a probability to each of the N color bins. In [3,4,5] the weight function is a smooth kernel such that the gradient computations required by the iterative optimization process can be performed. This is not required by our approach where competing hypotheses associated with the particles simply have to be evaluated. Hence we set $w \equiv 1$, which amounts to standard bin counting.

At time t, the color model $\boldsymbol{q}_t(\boldsymbol{x})$ associated with a hypothesized state $\boldsymbol{x}$ will be compared to the reference color model $\boldsymbol{q}^\star = \{q^\star(n)\}_{n=1\cdots N}$, with $\sum_{n=1}^{N} q^\star(n) = 1$. In our experiments, the reference distribution is gathered at an initial time t_0 at a location/scale $\boldsymbol{x}_{t_0}^\star$ (Fig. 1), which is either manually selected, as in [3,4,5], or automatically provided by a detection module (as in Sect. 3.5). In either case:

$$\boldsymbol{q}^\star = \boldsymbol{q}_{t_0}(\boldsymbol{x}_{t_0}^\star). \qquad (5)$$

The data likelihood must favor candidate color histograms close to the reference histogram, we therefore need to choose a distance D on the HSV color distributions. Such a distance is used in the deterministic techniques [3,4,5] as the criterion to be minimized at each time step. In [5], D is derived from the Bhattacharyya similarity coefficient, and defined as

$$D[\boldsymbol{q}^\star, \boldsymbol{q}_t(\boldsymbol{x})] = \left[1 - \sum_{n=1}^{N} \sqrt{q^\star(n) q_t(n; \boldsymbol{x})}\right]^{\frac{1}{2}} \qquad (6)$$

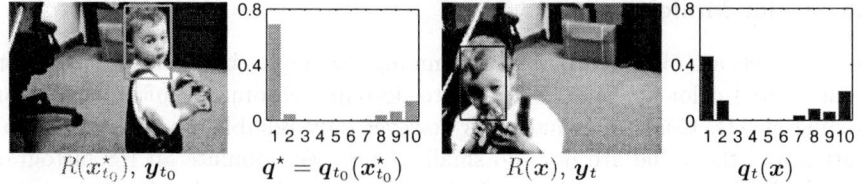

Fig. 1. Color histograms used for tracking. A reference color histogram $q^\star$ is gathered at time t_0 within a region picked either manually, or automatically if only a given class of objects is searched and a corresponding detector can be devised. At time t and for a hypothesized state x, the candidate color histogram $q_t(x)$ is gathered within the region $R(x)$.

with the argument that, contrary to the Kullback-Leibler divergence, this distance between probability distributions is a proper one, is bounded within $[0,1]$, and empty bins are not a source of concern.

We use the same distance. Gathering statistics on a number of window sequences obtained from successful tracking runs (obtained by a contour-based tracker on sequences with no background clutter), we observed a consistent exponential behavior for the squared distance D^2. Letting $p(y_t|x_t) \propto p(D^2[q^\star, q_t(x)])$,[1] we thus choose:

$$p(y_t|x_t) \propto \exp -\lambda D^2[q^\star, q_t(x_t)]. \qquad (7)$$

Lacking a way to estimate satisfactorily the parameter λ, we fixed it to the same value $\lambda = 20$ in all the experiments reported in the paper. This value is in good agreement with the range of values estimated on the labeled sequences mentioned above. As for the bin numbers, we used the default setting $N_h = N_s = N_v = 10$ in all experiments.

3 Results and Extensions

3.1 Base Tracker

The probabilistic color-based tracker introduced in the previous section is summarized in Procedure 1.

As the deterministic color-based trackers in [3,4,5] it allows robust tracking of objects undergoing complex changes of shape and appearance (Fig. 2). Due to its Monte Carlo nature, however it better handles the confusion caused by similar color spots in the background (Fig. 3) and by complete occlusions (Fig. 4).

---

[1] In fact, the likelihood can only obey this relation if the mapping $\{b_t(u), u \in R(x)\} \mapsto q_t(x) \mapsto D^2[q^\star, q_t(x)]$ from quantized sub-images to $\mathbb{R}^+$ is such that the size of the pre-image of any distance value is independent from this value. It is easy to exhibit counter-examples to show that this does not hold.

Procedure 1 Particle filter iteration for single object color-based tracking

Input: $q^* = \{q^*(n)\}_{n=1\cdots N}$ reference color histogram

- Current particle set: $\{x_t^m\}_{m=1\cdots M}$
- *Prediction*: for $m = 1 \cdots M$, draw $\tilde{x}_{t+1}^m$ from second-order AR dynamics.
- *Computation of candidate histograms*: for $m = 1 \cdots M$, compute $q_{t+1}(\tilde{x}_{t+1}^m)$ according to (4).
- *Weighting*: for $m = 1 \cdots M$ compute

$$\pi_{i+1}^m = K \exp \sum_{n=1}^{N} \lambda \sqrt{q^*(n) q_{t+1}(n; \tilde{x}_{t+1}^m)}$$

with K such that $\sum_{k=1}^{M} \pi_{i+1}^k = 1$
- *Selection*: for $m = 1 \cdots M$, sample index $a(m)$ from discrete probability $\{\pi_{i+1}^k\}_k$ over $\{1 \cdots M\}$, and set $x_{t+1}^m = \tilde{x}_{t+1}^{a(m)}$.

#1   #40   #64   #71   #77

Fig. 2. Color-based tracking. Using a global color reference model picked in the initial frame, a region of interest (player 75 here) can be tracked robustly, despite large motions, important motion blur, dramatic shape changes, and partial occlusions. These results, similar to those obtained by MeanShift in [5], were obtained with our Monte Carlo tracker. Note that the *football* sequence we used was in addition subsampled by a factor of two in time, which makes the displacement and appearance changes from one frame to another even more extreme.

As for the computational cost, a non-optimized implementation tracks regions of average size 25×25 pixels at a rate of 50fps with $M = 100$ particles on a 747Mhz Pentium III. The bottle-neck is the building of the M histograms at each time-step.

Beside the nice behavior demonstrated above, our approach can be extended in a number of useful ways. We introduce and demonstrate four extensions to the basic model in the remainder of this section. They respectively deal with the breaking up of tracked regions into several color patches, the introduction of a background model in the case of a still camera, the coupling with a skin detector for face tracking, and the extension to multi-object tracking.

3.2 Multi-part Color Model

If the tracked region contains different patches of distinct colors, e.g., the face and clothes of a person, the histogram-based modeling will capture them. However,

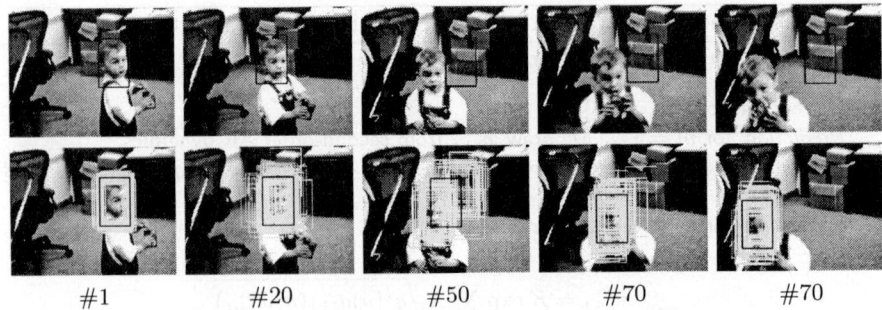

Fig. 3. Probabilistic color-based tracking under distraction. (Top) Deterministic color-based tracking can get stuck on local minima of the color-based metric, such as the boxes in the background. (Bottom) In contrast, by propagating a sample-based approximation of the filtering distribution, our Monte Carlo approach can be more robust to distraction. It can indeed track momentarily multiple modes (e.g., in frame 50) and then escape from distraction from the background.

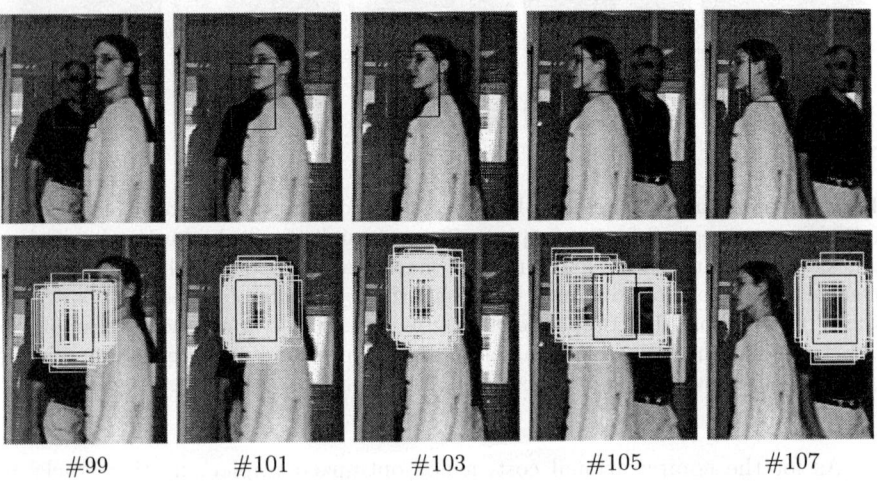

Fig. 4. Probabilistic color-based tracking through occlusions. (Top) Complete occlusion of the tracked region during a few frames (two in this case) can make deterministic color-based tracking break down. (Bottom) The ability of particle filtering to momentarily track multiple modes of the posterior (e.g., in frame 105) allows us to keep track of the region of interest even after the complete occlusion behind a region of similar color.

all information about the relative spatial arrangement of these different patches within the window will be lost. Keeping track of this coarse spatial layout might be beneficial to improve the tracker performance. Such a goal is easily achieved within our model by splitting the tracked region into sub-regions with individual reference color models. Formally, we consider the partition $R(\boldsymbol{x}) = \cup_{j=1}^{J} R_j(\boldsymbol{x})$ associated with the set $\{\boldsymbol{q}_j^\star\}_{j=1...J}$ of reference color histograms. These regions are rigidly linked in that the state space is kept unchanged with a unique location and scale vector per hypothesized object.

Assuming conditional independence of the image data within the different sub-regions defined by the state x_t, the likelihood becomes:

$$p(y_t| x_t) \propto \exp -\lambda \sum_{j=1}^{J} D^2[q_j^*, q_{j,t}(x_t)] \tag{8}$$

where the histogram $q_{j,t}(x_t)$ is collected in region $R_j(x_t)$ of image y_t.

By capturing the coarse spatial layout of colors, this multi-part extension to our probabilistic color-based tracker is more accurate (better positioning on the tracked object, better capturing of the scale) thus avoiding the drift, and possible subsequent loss, experienced sometimes by the single-part version. This is illustrated in Fig. 5.

Fig. 5. Multi-part color model improves tracking. (Top) Because a single histogram does not capture any information on the spatial arrangement of colors, a noticeable drift can occur in some cases. Here, the tracker shifted from the head and jumper of the baby, to the jumper and the legs, confusing two regions with similar global color contents but different spatial layouts. (Bottom) The splitting of the region of interest into two parts with individual color models improved drastically the tracking in this shaky video, with large and chaotic motions, distracting colors in the background (the sand, the face of the mother very close in frame 209), and important scale changes at the end.

3.3 Background Modeling

In particular situations such as surveillance, desktop interaction, or smart rooms, where the camera is fixed and views of the background can be acquired off-line, the robustness of tracking can be dramatically enhanced by incorporating background knowledge in the model. We assume here that a background reference image $\tilde{y}$ is available. The incorporation of the background information in the deterministic approach could be done by trying to minimize

$D^2[q^\star, q_t(x)] - D^2[q^\bullet(x), q_t(x)]$ where $q^\bullet(x)$ is the counterpart of $q_t(x)$ computed in the reference background image $\tilde{y}$ (Fig. 6).

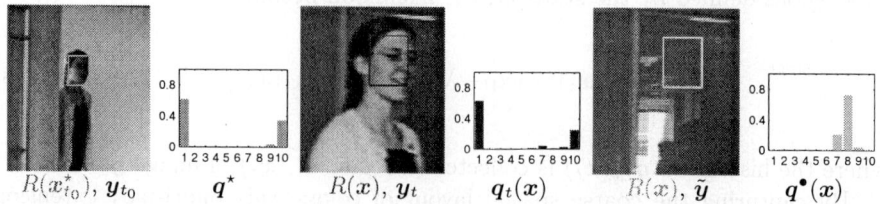

Fig. 6. Color histograms for tracking with background model. The color histogram $q_t(x)$ associated with the hypothesized region $R(x)$ at time t is not only compared to the reference $q^\star$ but also to the color histogram $q^\bullet(x)$ collected within the same region in the reference background image $\tilde{y}$.

As in Section 3.2, statistics of the difference of the squared Bhattacharyya distance, which lies in $[-1, 1]$, are gathered on a set of cropped training sequences, and exhibits a shifted exponential distribution. We thus choose the new likelihood as:

$$p(y_t | x_t) \propto \exp -\lambda \left(D^2[q^\star, q_t(x)] - D^2[q^\bullet(x), q_t(x)] \right) \quad (9)$$

where the shift is absorbed in the normalization factor. The merit of this complementary information will be illustrated in the challenging case of multiple face tracking with automatic initialization (Section 3.5).

3.4 Multiple Objects

We now extend the model to the simultaneous tracking of multiple objects. To this end, the likelihood is defined conditioned on the number of objects K_t present in the scene at time t. If $K_t = k$, then the state $x_t = (x_{1,t} \cdots x_{k,t})$ is a concatenation of k single-object states. Each object $x_{i,t}$ is associated with a reference color model $q_i^\star$. If the k corresponding regions $R(x_{i,t})$, $i = 1 \cdots k$, do not overlap, the data-likelihood is simply the product of single object likelihoods. As soon as at least two objects overlap, one has to be careful not to explain the same piece of image data several times [13]. In the overlapping case, we form the likelihood by marginalizing out all the possible relative depth orderings for each non-empty region intersection. For instance, for two overlapping objects indexed i and j the data likelihood reads:

$$p(y_t | x_{i,t}, x_{j,t}) = 0.5[p_{ij}(y | x_{i,t}, x_{j,t}) + p_{ji}(y | x_{i,t}, x_{j,t})] \quad (10)$$

where $p_{ij}(y_t | x_{i,t}, x_{j,t})$ is the data likelihood under the hypothesis that object i occludes object j. In the absence of background subtraction, and for single-part objects, it is defined as

$$p_{ij}(y | x_{i,t}, x_{j,t}) \propto \exp -\lambda \left(D^2[q_i^\star, q_t(x_{i,t})] + D^2[q_j^\star, q_t(x_{j,t} | x_{i,t})] \right) \quad (11)$$

where the histogram $q_t(x_{j,t}|x_{i,t})$ is obtained on the subregion $R(x_{j,t}) \setminus R(x_{i,t})$.

Note that the two possible relative depth orderings of the two objects are assumed equally likely. We could also enforce a temporal continuity constraint that prevents the depth ordering from changing during the time that objects cross. This would require, however, the capturing of the global depth ordering of the whole set of objects maintained in the state space. Note that when tracking is performed within the 3D space, as in [11], the depth ordering is directly accessible.

Figure 7 shows an example where two persons are tracked from a manual initialization. The ability to track an unknown and varying number of objects without manual initialization must rely on a prior knowledge of the background and/or a rough appearance model of the objects of interest. We already presented in Section 3.3 a simple way to incorporate background knowledge in our approach. To achieve a full fledged multiple object tracker, we address below the issue of appearance-based automatic initialization in the case of face tracking.

#99 #101 #103 #105 #107

Fig. 7. Multiple object tracking through occlusion. The combination of the state space dynamics along with the definition of one color-model per tracked entity and the averaging of the color-likelihood over possible depth orderings, permits to track objects that cross each other, without identity swapping or loss of track, even if the two color models are similar. This sequence is the same as in Fig. 4

3.5 Automatic Initialization on Skin

A number of tracking applications focus on people. Many trackers specialized for this use rely, at least partially, on skin color models (e.g., [1,18]). Such a specialization is easily incorporated within our system. A normalized HSV histogram $\tilde{q}$ with $N = N_h N_s + N_v$ bins is learned from hand-labeled face images, 20 frontal identity photographs with various illumination conditions, in our experiments. At each instant pixels are labeled as skin/non-skin by thresholding their likelihood under this skin color model. At time t, when a cluster of skin-labeled pixels falls within the specified size range for the objects of interest, and is not too close to an existing cloud of particles, if any, a new object is originated from this cluster. The large regions of false alarms produced by, e.g., wooden doors and desks, can be eliminated in the case of still camera, by passing detected pixels through a second motion-based sieve obtained by thresholding the frame-difference (Fig. 8). The good performance of the multiple face tracker with automatic initialization and reference background is illustrated in Fig. 9.

Fig. 8. Simple color-based face detection. A color histogram model learnt offline is used to assign each pixel with a probability to be in a skin region. (Middle) The thresholding of this probability, at level 0.3 in this example, already provides a good localization of skin patches, but a large number of false alarms in the background as well. (Right) Combining this skin detection with a very crude motion detection (thresholding the absolute frame difference, at level 10 here) permits the extraction of correct skin patches among which faces can be detected based on the aspect ratio of the region.

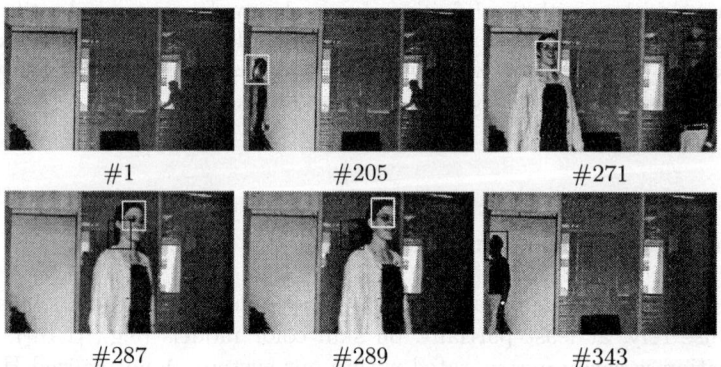

Fig. 9. Automatic multiple face tracking in still scenes. Combining the multi-object color-based tracker with a color modeling of the background in image 1 and the detection of moving skin patches, faces of moving persons can be detected as they enter the scene, and tracked without confusion even when they cross each other for a few frames.

4 Discussion

Embedding the color-based deterministic trackers introduced in [3,5] within a probabilistic framework we further improve their robustness and versatility. We achieve in particular the robust tracking of fast moving and changing regions within color distractions (Figs. 3 and 5), as well as the simultaneous tracking of multiple objects under temporary occlusions (Figs. 4 and 9).

In the case where a background model is used for multiple object tracking, our Monte Carlo tracker bears connections with the "Bramble" tracker introduced in [11]. In Bramble, an individual Gaussian mixture model capturing both colors and color gradients is associated with each point (on a subsampled grid) of the background. A generic Gaussian mixture model captures the same type of information for the foreground (e.g., the persons). The ratio of the two likelihoods over the grid-points within an hypothesized region (projection of a 3D generalized cylinder in the image plane) provides the weights for the particles.

As for the definition of hypothesis likelihood in terms of foreground and background models, an interesting connection can be worked out, as detailed in the Appendix. One nice aspect of the data likelihood in Bramble is that it explains the whole scene irrespective of the number of hypothesized objects. This enables the inclusion of the number of objects as part of the state space, since two particles maintaining different numbers of objects at the same instant can be legitimately compared using the weights based on this likelihood. Using birth and death processes, the handling of the varying object numbers can then be done consistently within the Bayesian framework. In practice, however, our experience of this type of approach is that after resampling, most of the particles share the same number of objects.

Another important difference related to the color modeling is that the instantiation of the foreground reference model in our approach makes it specific to the tracked object. As demonstrated in Sects. 3.5-6, this prevents swapping objects at crossings, a problem encountered by Bramble.

As for background modeling, the fact that it is related to individual spatial locations in Bramble, whereas it is built on the fly within the hypothesized region in our case, might make our use of the reference background more robust to slight camera motions. The experimental assessment of this could be part of the continuing exploration of our probabilistic tracking framework.

Other research perspectives concern the learning of the data likelihood, the automatic split of tracked regions into multiple color patches, the optimal combination of the color-based likelihood with more classic contour-based likelihoods with the following questions: how to assess adaptively which modality is the best to rely on at a given instant, and how to make the color and/or contour reference evolve in time for improved tracking robustness [19].

Acknowledgments. The authors thank Andrew Blake for his comments and encouragements.

References

1. S.T. Birchfield. Elliptical head tracking using intensity gradients and color histograms. In *Proc. Conf. Comp. Vision Pattern Rec.*, pages 232–237, Santa Barbara, CA, June 1998.
2. M. Black and A. Jepson. Eigentracking: Robust matching and tracking of articulated objects using a view-based representation. *Int. J. Computer Vision*, 26(1):63–84, 1998.
3. G.R. Bradski. Computer vision face tracking as a component of a perceptual user interface. In *Workshop on Applications of Computer Vision*, pages 214–219, Princeton, NJ, Oct. 1998.
4. H.T. Chen and T.L. Liu. Trust-region methods for real-time tracking. In *Proc. Int. Conf. Computer Vision*, pages II: 717–722, Vancouver, Canada, July 2001.
5. D. Comaniciu, V. Ramesh, and P. Meer. Real-time tracking of non-rigid objects using mean shift. In *Proc. Conf. Comp. Vision Pattern Rec.*, pages II:142–149, Hilton Head, SC, June 2000.
6. A. Doucet, S. Godsill, and C. Andrieu. On sequential Monte Carlo sampling methods for Bayesian filtering. *Statistics and Computing*, 10(3):197–208, 2000.
7. J. Foley, A Van Dam, S. Feiner, and J. Hughes. *Computer Graphics: Principles and Practice*. Addison-Wesley, 1990.
8. D. Gavrila. Pedestrian detection from a moving vehicle. In *Proc. Europ. Conf. Computer Vision*, Dublin, Ireland, June 2000.
9. G.D. Hager and P.N. Belhumeur. Efficient region tracking with parametric models of geometry and illumination. *IEEE Trans. Pattern Anal. Machine Intell.*, 20(10):1025–1039, 1998.
10. M. Isard and A. Blake. Condensation–conditional density propagation for visual tracking. *Int. J. Computer Vision*, 29(1):5–28, 1998.
11. M. Isard and J. MacCormick. BraMBLe: a Bayesian multiple-blob tracker. In *Proc. Int. Conf. Computer Vision*, pages II: 34–41, Vancouver, Canada, July 2001.
12. C. Kervrann and F. Heitz. A hierarchical Markov modeling approach for the segmentation and tracking of deformable shape. *Graph. Mod. Image Proc.*, 60(3):173–195, 1998.
13. J. MacCormick and A. Blake. A probabilistic exclusion principle for tracking multiple objects. In *Proc. Int. Conf. Computer Vision*, pages 572–578, 1999.
14. H.T. Nguyen, M. Worring, and R. van den Boomgaard. Occlusion robust adaptive template tracking. In *Proc. Int. Conf. Computer Vision*, pages I: 678–683, Vancouver, Canada, July 2001.
15. N.P. Papanikolopoulos, P.K. Khosla, and T. Kanade. Visual tracking of a moving target by a camera mounted on a robot: A combination of control and vision. *IEEE Trans. Robotics and Automation*, 9:14–35, 1993.
16. N. Peterfreund. The velocity snake: Deformable contour for tracking in spatio-velocity space. *Computer Vision and Image Understanding*, 73(3):346–356, 1999.
17. A. Rahimi, L.P. Morency, and T. Darrell. Reducing drift in parametric motion tracking. In *Proc. Int. Conf. Computer Vision*, pages I: 315–322, Vancouver, Canada, July 2001.
18. M. Spengler and B. Schiele. Towards robust multi-cue integration for visual tracking. In *Int. Workshop on Computer Vision Systems*, Vancouver, Canada, July 2001.
19. J. Vermaak, P. Pérez, M. Gangnet, and A. Blake. Towards improved observation models for visual tracking: selective adaptation. In *Proc. Europ. Conf. Computer Vision*, Copenhagen, Denmark, May 2002.

20. Y. Wu and T. Huang. Color tracking by transductive learning. In *Proc. Conf. Comp. Vision Pattern Rec.*, pages I:133–138, Hilton Head, SC, June 2000.
21. Y. Wu and T.S. Huang. A co-inference approach to robust visual tracking. In *Proc. Int. Conf. Computer Vision*, pages II: 26–33, Vancouver, Canada, July 2001.

Appendix: A Connection with Bramble [11]

If our histogram-based likelihood was defined using an exponential distribution on the Kullback-Leibler divergence (instead of the squared Bhattacharyya distance), but with arguments swapped as compared to the choice in [4], then the likelihood can be re-interpreted in terms of individual grid-point contributions. Indeed

$$KL[q_t(x)\|q^\star] = \sum_{n=1}^{N} q_t(n; x) \log \frac{q_t(n; x)}{q^\star(n)} = \mathbb{E}_{q_t(x)} \left[\log \frac{q_t(x)}{q^\star} \right]. \quad (12)$$

If the window is large enough, the expectation on the right-hand-side can be approximated by the average log-ratio over the window, since the $b_t(u)$ for $u \in R(x)$ can be seen as samples from $q_t(x)$:

$$\mathbb{E}_{q_t(x)} \left[\log \frac{q_t(x)}{q^\star} \right] \approx \frac{1}{|R(x)|} \sum_{u \in R(x)} \log \frac{q_t[b_t(u); x]}{q^\star[b_t(u)]}. \quad (13)$$

Using this approximation, we obtain:

$$\exp -\lambda KL[q_t(x)\|q^\star] \approx \prod_{u \in R(x)} \left(\frac{q^\star[b_t(u)]}{q_t[b_t(u); x]} \right)^{\frac{\lambda}{|R(x)|}} \quad (14)$$

In the case where background subtraction is incorporated, as described in Sect. 3.3, the likelihood ratio is then approximated by:

$$\exp -\lambda(KL[q_t(x)\|q^\star] - KL[q_t(x)\|q^\bullet(x)]) \approx \prod_{u \in R(x)} \left(\frac{q^\star[b_t(u)]}{q^\bullet[b_t(u); x]} \right)^{\frac{\lambda}{|R(x)|}}. \quad (15)$$

This is, as in [11] (apart from the raising to power $\frac{\lambda}{|R(x)|}$) the product over the grid points in the candidate region of the ratio of point-wise data likelihoods, under the foreground model and under the location-dependent background model respectively.

Dense Motion Analysis in Fluid Imagery

T. Corpetti, É. Mémin, and P. Pérez

[1] IRISA/Université de Rennes I, Campus Universitaire de Beaulieu 35042 Rennes Cedex, France
{tcorpett,memin}@irisa.fr
[2] Microsoft Research Center, 7 J J Thomson Avenue, Cambridge CB3 0FB, UK
pperez@microsoft.com

Abstract. Analyzing fluid motion is essential in number of domains and can rarely be handled using generic computer vision techniques. In this particular application context, we address two distinct problems. First we describe a dedicated dense motion estimator. The approach relies on constraints issuing from fluid motion properties and allows us to recover dense motion fields of good quality. Secondly, we address the problem of analyzing such velocity fields. We present a kind of motion-based segmentation relying on an analytic representation of the motion field that permits to extract important quantities such as singularities, stream-functions or velocity potentials. The proposed method has the advantage to be robust, simple, and fast.

1 Introduction

Since several years, the analysis of video sequences showing the evolution of fluid phenomenon gave rise to a great attention from the computer vision community [4,11,15,23,24]. The applications concern domains such as experimental visualization in fluid mechanics, environmental sciences (oceanography, meteorology, ...), or medical imagery.

In all these application domains, it is of primary interest to measure the instantaneous velocity of fluid particles. In oceanography one is interested to track sea streams and to observe the drift of some passive entities [9]. In meteorology, both operational and experimental, the task under consideration is the reconstruction of wind fields from the displacements of clouds as observed in various satellite images [19]. In medical imaging the issue is to visualize and analyze blood flow inside the heart, or inside blood vessels [21]. The images involved in each domain have their own characteristics and are provided by very different sensors. The huge amount of data of different kinds available, the range of applicative domains involved, and the technical difficulties in the processing of all these peculiar image sequences explain the interest of researchers of the image analysis community.

Extracting dense velocity fields from fluid images can rarely be done with the standard computer vision tools, which are originally designed for quasi-rigid motions with stable salient features. These generic approaches are based on a brightness constancy assumption and a spatial smoothness of the motion field. In contrast, fluid images usually exhibit high spatial and temporal distortions of luminance patterns. The design of alternate approaches dedicated to fluid motion thus constitutes a widely open domain of research. The first part of this paper is a contribution in that direction.

Once given a reliable description of the fluid motion, an other problem of interest consists in the extraction and the characterization of the *critical* – or *singular* – points of the flow. These points are the centers of kinematical events such as *swirl*, *vortices*, or *sinks/sources*. The knowledge of all these points is precious to understand and predict the flows of interest, but it also provides compact and hierarchical representations of the flow [11]. We propose, in the second part of this paper, a method to obtain such characteristics from a dense velocity field. This method is based on an analytic representation of the motion field, using the Rankine model.

This paper is organized as follows. In Section 2, we describe the dedicated technique to estimate a dense motion field for fluid phenomenon. The aim of Section 3 is first to present some properties of $2D$ motion fields, and then to show how quantities such as singularities, stream-function or velocity potential can be extracted analytically. Then, Section 4 presents a method to extract singular points and their associated parameters from dense motion fields. In section 5, we finally present some experimental results on meteorological sequences.

2 Fluid Optical Flow Estimator

Optical flow estimation aims at recovering the apparent displacement field between two consecutive frames in an image sequence. Let w denote the unknown displacement field defined over the continuous plane domain $s \in \Omega$ and $f(s,t)$ the luminance function at point s assumed to be continuous in space and time. The most accurate optical flow estimators used in computer vision are issued from Horn and Schunck method [13]. They are defined as the minimizer of an energy function $H = H_1 + H_2$ composed of two terms. The first one assumes the constancy of the luminance of a point along its trajectory ($\frac{df}{dt} = 0$). This so-called optical flow constraint (OFC) is captured by letting:

$$H_1(w, f) = \int_\Omega \rho[\nabla f(s) \cdot w(s) + \frac{\partial f(s)}{\partial t}]ds. \qquad (1)$$

The penalty function ρ is usually the L_2 norm but it may be changed to a robust function attenuating the effect of data that deviate significantly from the OFC-based data-model [5,17]. The second term H_2 of the energy function is usually a standard first-order spatial smoothness term:

$$H_2(w) = \alpha \int_\Omega \rho(\|\nabla w\|)ds, \qquad (2)$$

where $\alpha > 0$ is a parameter controlling the balance between the smoothness and the global adequacy to the brightness constancy assumption. Function ρ may be the quadratic penalty if the searched solution is smooth everywhere or a robust norm function if one wants to handle implicitly the spatial discontinuities of the field [5,14,16].

The standard dense estimator defined as the minimizer of H is generic. It is only based on the assumption of luminance conservation and of first-order spatial smoothness of the motion. Our aim is to devise a similar estimator that captures some specificities of image sequences with fluid motion.

2.1 Continuity Equation

As mentioned above, local deviations from the data-model as those occurring in small occlusion areas, can be handled with a robust cost function. In fluid imagery, the problem is much more complex. Image sequences representing fluid phenomena exhibit areas where the luminance function undergoes high temporal variations along the motion. These areas are often the center of tridimensional motions that cause the appearance or the disappearance of fluid matter within the bidimensional visualization plane. These regions are associated to divergent motions which influence greatly the shape of the velocity field in large surrounding areas. An accurate estimation of the 2D apparent motion in such regions is therefore of the highest importance and is hardly possible with the optical-flow constraint.

Instead of sticking to the intensity conservation assumption, we propose here to rely on the fluid law of mass conservation, also known as *continuity equation*:

$$\frac{\partial \chi}{\partial t} + \text{div}(\chi \mathbf{v}) = 0, \qquad (3)$$

where χ denotes the density of the fluid, $\mathbf{v}$ its 3D velocity and $\text{div}\mathbf{v} = \frac{\partial u}{\partial x} + \frac{\partial v}{\partial y} + \frac{\partial w}{\partial z}$ stands for the divergence of the vector field $\mathbf{v} = (u, v, w)$. Simple manipulations yield the alternative rewriting:

$$\frac{d\chi}{dt} + \chi \text{div}\mathbf{v} = 0. \qquad (4)$$

When the divergence of the 3D apparent flow vanishes, this equation is of the same form as the 2D optical flow constraint on luminance. The continuity equation originally introduced in [20] as a data model for motion estimation of intensity time varying images has been since incorporated in several works. It has been considered in the context of fluid imagery either for satellite meteorological images [4,7,24] or for experimental fluid mechanics [23]. It has also been introduced in medical imaging domain to recover 3D deformation fields of the heart [21] or to analyze blood flow [1]. In all these cases, this model has been proved appealing an alternative to standard luminance constancy assumption.

The use of continuity equation for image sequences analysis relies on two hypotheses. First, the luminance function is assumed to be directly related to a passive quantity transported by the fluid. Secondly, the continuity equation which holds in 3D, is assumed to hold as well for the bidimensional motion field captured by the image sequence. This latter assumption has been theoretically established in the case of transmittance imaging by Fitzpatrick [10] and extended by Wildes et al in [23]. The first assumption is difficult to validate, especially in meteorological images due to the complexity and the heterogeneity of the underlying physical processes. Nevertheless, as shown by several works, the use of the continuity equation in the case of meteorological data is appealing [4,24]. As the brightness consistancy is obviously not verified in that type of images, the equation of continuity provides us with an interesting alternative data-model. Instead of expressing a point-wise conservation of the luminance along the motion, this alternative model assumes the conservation of the total luminance of any moving elements of the image. This constraint reads:

$$\frac{df}{dt} + f \text{div} \boldsymbol{w} = 0. \qquad (5)$$

However, as OFC-based data models, a data-model based on the continuity equation is highly sensitive to the presence of noise and is very likely not to hold everywhere. Also, due to its differential nature, the continuity equation is not valid in case of large displacements. In fact, this equation concerns *velocity* and not *displacement* [18]. Unlike the brightness constancy expressed as $f(\boldsymbol{s}+\boldsymbol{d}(\boldsymbol{s}), t+\Delta t) - f(\boldsymbol{s},t) = 0$, which is explicitly based on displacement, the continuity equation (5), as it stands, cannot serve as the basis of an incremental data-model embedded in hierarchical estimation schemes. To cope with this problem, let us assume that the velocities are constant between the instants t and $t + \Delta t$. In that case, equation (5) constitutes a simple first-order differential equation which can be integrated from time t to time $t+\Delta t$ along trajectories [7]. Setting $\Delta t = 1$ for notational convenience, and incorporating the integral constraint thus obtained in a robust penalty function yields a new data-term:

$$H_1(\boldsymbol{w}) = \int_\Omega \rho \Big\{ f(\boldsymbol{s}+\boldsymbol{w}(\boldsymbol{s}), t+1) \exp(\text{div} \boldsymbol{w}(\boldsymbol{s})) - f(\boldsymbol{s},t) \Big\} d\boldsymbol{s}. \qquad (6)$$

We now turn to the definition of the smoothness prior to be used in conjunction with this new data energy term.

2.2 Adapted Div-Curl Regularization

By using Euler-Lagrange conditions of optimality, it is readily demonstrated that the standard first-order regularization functional $\alpha \int_\Omega \|\nabla \boldsymbol{w}(\boldsymbol{s})\|^2 d\boldsymbol{s}$ is equivalent from the minimization point of view, to the so-called *div-curl* regularization functional [22]:

$$\alpha \int_\Omega ([\text{div} \boldsymbol{w}(\boldsymbol{s})]^2 + [\text{curl} \boldsymbol{w}(\boldsymbol{s})]^2) d\boldsymbol{s}, \qquad (7)$$

where $\text{div} \boldsymbol{w} = \frac{\partial u}{\partial x} + \frac{\partial v}{\partial y}$ and $\text{curl} \boldsymbol{w} = \frac{\partial v}{\partial x} - \frac{\partial u}{\partial y}$ are respectively the divergence and the vorticity of the vector field $\boldsymbol{w} = (u,v)$.

A first-order regularization therefore penalizes the amplitude of both the divergence and the vorticity of the vector field. For fluid motion estimation, this does not seem appropriate since the apparent velocity field usually exhibits "concentrations" of vorticity and/or divergence. In addition, an under-estimation of the divergence would be all the more problematic in our case, because the data model includes an explicit use of this quantity. For these reasons, it would seem more appropriate to rely on second-order div-curl regularization [12,22]:

$$\int_\Omega \left(\|\nabla \mathrm{div} \boldsymbol{w}(s)\|^2 + \|\nabla \mathrm{curl} \boldsymbol{w}(s)\|^2\right) ds. \tag{8}$$

This regularization is nevertheless more difficult to implement. As a matter of fact, associated Euler-Lagrange equation is composed with two fourth-order coupled PDE's, which are tricky to solve numerically. We propose to simplify the problem by introducing auxiliary functions, and defining the alternative functional:

$$H_2(\boldsymbol{w}, \xi, \zeta) = \alpha \int_\Omega |\mathrm{div}\boldsymbol{w} - \xi|^2 + \lambda \rho(\|\nabla \xi\|) + \alpha \int_\Omega |\mathrm{curl}\boldsymbol{w} - \zeta|^2 + \lambda \rho(\|\nabla \zeta\|). \tag{9}$$

The new auxiliary scalar functions ξ and ζ can be respectively seen as estimates of the divergence and the curl of the unknown motion field, and λ is a positive parameter. The first part of each integral encourages the displacement to comply with the current divergence and vorticity estimates ξ and ζ, through a quadratic goodness-of-fit enforcement. The second part equips the divergence and the vorticity estimates with a robust first-order regularization favoring piecewise smooth configurations. Getting rid of the auxiliary scalar fields ξ and ζ in (9) (by setting $\xi = \mathrm{div}\boldsymbol{w}$ and $\zeta = \mathrm{curl}\boldsymbol{w}$) would amount to the original *second-order* div-curl regularization (8), if ρ is the quadratic penalty function.

From a computational point of view, regularizing functional (9) only implies the numerical resolution of first-order PDE's. It is shown in the appendix that, at least for the L_2 norm, the regularization we propose is a smoothed version of the original second order div-curl regularization.

2.3 Minimization Issue

We now turn to the minimization issue of the whole energy function $H = H_1 + H_2$. Two main sets of variables have to be estimated. The first one is the motion field $\boldsymbol{w}$, and the second one consists in the two scalar fields ξ and ζ. The estimation is conducted alternatively by minimizing $H_1 + H_2$ with respect to $\boldsymbol{w}$, ξ and ζ respectively. For the motion field, considering the div and curl estimates ξ and ζ as being fixed, the robust minimization with respect to $\boldsymbol{w}$ is solved with an iteratively reweighted least squares technique. This optimization is embedded in an efficient multi-parametric adaptive multigrid framework. In turn, $\boldsymbol{w}$ being fixed, the minimization of H with respect to ξ and ζ is in fact equivalent to the minimization of H_2 and is again conducted using an iteratively reweighted least squares technique. More details of the minimization issues can be seen in [7].

Dense displacements fields obtained by minimizing the proposed energy functional, with its data-term based on the integrated continuity equation and its compound div-curl regularization, will be presented in section 5. Before we address in the two next sections the issue of analyzing resulting motion fields in terms of potential functions and singularities.

3 Planar Vector Fields

In this section, we present known analytic results on planar vector fields. We shall rely on them to develop an original method to extract singularities, streamfunctions and velocity-potentials, and parametric descriptions from the motion fields extracted with the method presented in previous section.

A planar vector field w is a $\mathbb{R}^2$-valued map defined on a bounded set Ω of $\mathbb{R}^2$. We note $w(s) \triangleq (u(s), v(s))$ and we assume that each component of the vector field is twice continuous and differentiable: u and $v \in C^2(\Omega, \mathbb{R})$.

A vector field whose divergence is null everywhere is called *solenoidal*, and a vector field whose curl vanishes identically is called *irrotational*. A classical result, coming from the application of Green theorem shows that for irrotational fields there exists a scalar function ϕ, called the *velocity potential*, such that $w = \nabla \phi$. Similarly, for solenoidal fields there exists a scalar function ψ called the *stream function* such that $w^\perp = \nabla \psi$, with $w^\perp = (-v, u)^T$ is the orthogonal field of w. The equipotential curves, $\{\psi(x, y) = c\}$, are the streamlines of the flow. For a flow both irrotational and solenoidal, it is interesting to note that level curves of ϕ and ψ form an orthogonal network.

Irrotational and solenoidal fields play an important role in vector field analysis. As a matter of fact these two types of field can be combined to represent uniquely any arbitrary continuous vector field which vanishes at infinity. This is the Helmholtz representation of vector fields: $w = w_{so} + w_{ir}$ (with $w_{ir} = \nabla \phi$ and $w_{so}^\perp = \nabla \psi$), where ϕ and ψ are respectively the velocity potential of the irrotational component, and the stream function of the solenoidal part. When the null border condition at infinity can not be imposed, the representation is extended by the introduction of a third *laminar* component. A laminar field is a vector field that is both irrotational and solenoidal. The extended Helmholtz representation is then: $w = w_{lam} + w_{so} + w_{ir}$. In our applications, the laminar component accounts for a global transportation flow and for the effect of sources/sinks or vortices outside of the image plane. In the following we assume that this very smooth component is known. In practice, a sensible estimate of the laminar component can be obtained with standard motion estimation techniques under strong regularization. From now we will always refer to motion fields vanishing at infinity, and consequently to the original Helmholtz representation.

3.1 Irrotational and Solenoidal Field Separation

Taking the divergence of $\boldsymbol{w}_{ir}$ and $\boldsymbol{w}_{so}^\perp$ leads to $\nabla^2 \phi = \text{div}(\boldsymbol{w})$ and $\nabla^2 \psi = \text{curl}(\boldsymbol{w})$. Both potential functions are therefore the solution of Poisson equations. Assuming that the curl and divergence vanish at infinity, one has to face a well known Dirichlet problem whose solution may be obtained through convolution with 2D Green kernel. This direct solving is numerically tricky to implement since Green kernel lies on infinite support. Instead of that, using a spectral Fourier representation of the flow $\hat{\boldsymbol{w}} = (\mathcal{F}[u], \mathcal{F}[v])$ (such that $\mathcal{F}[f] = \hat{f}(\boldsymbol{k}) = \frac{1}{2\pi} \iint f(\boldsymbol{s}) e^{-i<\boldsymbol{k},\boldsymbol{s}>} dx dy$, with $\boldsymbol{k} = (\alpha, \beta)$ and $\boldsymbol{s} = (x, y)$) we have:

$$\begin{aligned}\mathcal{F}[\text{curl}(\boldsymbol{w}_{ir})] &= <\boldsymbol{k}^\perp, \hat{\boldsymbol{w}}_{ir}(\boldsymbol{k})>= 0, \\ \mathcal{F}[\text{div}(\boldsymbol{w}_{so})] &= <\boldsymbol{k}, \hat{\boldsymbol{w}}_{so}(\boldsymbol{k})>= 0,\end{aligned} \quad (10)$$

where $<\cdot,\cdot>$ is the scalar product. Therefore, assuming the vector field $\boldsymbol{w}$ is known, the irrotational and the solenoidal components can be respectively obtained through:

$$\hat{\boldsymbol{w}}_{ir}(\boldsymbol{k}) = <\boldsymbol{k}, \hat{\boldsymbol{w}}(\boldsymbol{k})> \frac{\boldsymbol{k}}{\|\boldsymbol{k}\|^2}, \text{ and } \hat{\boldsymbol{w}}_{so}(\boldsymbol{k}) = <\boldsymbol{k}^\perp, \hat{\boldsymbol{w}}(\boldsymbol{k})> \frac{\boldsymbol{k}^\perp}{\|\boldsymbol{k}\|^2}, \quad (11)$$

and the inverse Fourier transform.

3.2 Potential Functions Estimation

As we saw in the previous section, the knowledge of functions ϕ and ψ might be very useful as it allows a complete description of the velocity field. In turn, if the velocity field and its irrotational and solenoidal components are known, they can be easily estimated (as $\boldsymbol{w}_{ir} = \nabla \phi$ and $\boldsymbol{w}_{so}^\perp = \nabla \psi$). Noting that, if g is a C^2 function, $g(x,y) = g(0,0) + \int_\gamma \nabla g(x,y) \cdot d\gamma$, where γ is any path from $(0,0)$ to (x,y). Averaging this relation over the two paths joining $(0,0)$ to (x,y) along the sides of a rectangle, we get, taking $\phi(0,0) = \psi(0,0) = 0$:

$$\begin{cases} \phi(x,y) = \frac{1}{2}\left(\int_0^x u_{ir}(t,y)dt + \int_0^y v_{ir}(x,t)dt + \int_0^x u_{ir}(t,0)dt + \int_0^y v_{ir}(0,t)dt\right), \text{ and} \\ \psi(x,y) = \frac{1}{2}\left(\int_0^y u_{so}(x,t)dt - \int_0^x v_{so}(t,y)dt + \int_0^y u_{so}(0,t)dt - \int_0^x v_{so}(t,0)dt\right). \end{cases} \quad (12)$$

All terms of relation (12) may be numerically computed. They consist in integrations along the rows and the columns of the image.

3.3 Extrema of the Potential Function

It can be observed that characteristic points of the irrotational flow component (*i.e.*, points $\boldsymbol{s}$ for which $\boldsymbol{w}_{ir}(\boldsymbol{s}) = \nabla \phi(\boldsymbol{s}) = 0$) corresponds to local extrema of the velocity potential ϕ. Of course the same relation links extrema of the stream function and characteristic points of the solenoidal component. In addition, around a singular point s, the velocity distribution of a fluid flow can be accurately approximated (and characterized) by a so-called *linear phase portrait* [2]. Within some neighborhood around s, one can fit a parametric velocity model of the form $\boldsymbol{w} = A\boldsymbol{s}$ where A is a 2×2 matrix. The qualitative characterization of the motion field in the neighborhood of this singular point s relies on the structure of matrix A. Six typical motion configurations can be identified from its canonical Jordan form [2,11]. A second-order approximation of the velocity potential and the stream function around a singular point, $\boldsymbol{w}_{ir} = \nabla\phi(\boldsymbol{s}+\boldsymbol{\epsilon}) = H_\phi(\boldsymbol{s})\boldsymbol{\epsilon} + o(\boldsymbol{\epsilon})$ and $\boldsymbol{w}_{so}^\perp = \nabla\psi(\boldsymbol{s}+\boldsymbol{\epsilon}) = H_\psi(\boldsymbol{s})\boldsymbol{\epsilon} + o(\boldsymbol{\epsilon})$, provides phase portraits $A_\phi = \begin{bmatrix} \frac{\partial^2\phi}{\partial x^2} & \frac{\partial^2\phi}{\partial x\partial y} \\ \frac{\partial^2\phi}{\partial x\partial y} & \frac{\partial^2\phi}{\partial y^2} \end{bmatrix}$

and $A_\psi = \begin{bmatrix} \frac{\partial^2\psi}{\partial x\partial y} & \frac{\partial^2\psi}{\partial y^2} \\ -\frac{\partial^2\psi}{\partial x^2} & -\frac{\partial^2\phi}{\partial x\partial y} \end{bmatrix}$. Matrix A_ϕ is symmetric (it has real eigenvalues) and positive definite or negative definite around local extrema (the eigenvalues have all the same sign). The corresponding singular point is therefore a *node* or a *star node* (cf. [2]) which depicts well the behavior of sources or sinks. Concerning the solenoidal field, trace of A_ψ is null: the local extremum then corresponds to the singular point at the center of a rotating motion. This is the characterization of a vortex.

3.4 Rankine Model of Flows

One of the simplest models of velocity field for fluid flows at singularities is provided by the Rankine model of vortex [6]. It consists in approximating the velocity field as a vector field of constant curl inside a disk and null curl beyond this circular domain. The complex function $f(z) = u(x,y) + iv(x,y)$ associated to this velocity field reads:

$$f_i(z) \triangleq \begin{cases} g_i(z) = -\dfrac{i\beta_i(z-z_i)}{|z-z_i|^2} & \text{if} \quad |z-z_i| \geq r_i \\ h_i(z) = -\dfrac{i\beta_i(z-z_i)}{r_i^2} & \text{if} \quad |z-z_i| < r_i, \end{cases} \quad (13)$$

where r_i is the singularity radius, $z_i \triangleq x_i + iy_i$ denotes the complex vortex location, and β_i its strength. Based on a similar model, the velocity field associated to a source/sink in the plane can modeled as:

$$f_j(z) \triangleq \begin{cases} g_j(z) = \dfrac{\alpha_j(z-z_j)}{|z-z_j|^2} & \text{if} \quad |z-z_j| \geq r_j \\ h_j(z) = \dfrac{\alpha_j(z-z_j)}{r_j^2} & \text{if} \quad |z-z_j| < r_j \end{cases} \quad (14)$$

where α_j denotes the sink/source's strength. If $\alpha_j > 0$, this constitutes a source model, whereas if $\alpha_j < 0$ we are in presence of a sink. It is easy to verify that *i*) function f_i in (13) defines a solenoidal field, and function f_j in (14) defines an irrotational field; $ii)$ functions g_i is such that $\text{curl} g_i = \text{div} g_j = 0$ and function h_i is such that $\text{curl} h_i = \frac{2\beta_i}{r_i^2}, \text{div} h_j = \frac{2\alpha_j}{r_j^2}$.

These two types of fields can be composed to model a fluid flow with P vortices and N sources/sinks within $f(z) = \sum_{i=1}^{P} f_i(z) + \sum_{j=1}^{N} f_j(z)$.

4 Motion-Based Segmentation Based on Rankine Model Around Singularities

A global description of the flow based on the Rankine model allows to define a main characteristics of the flow in terms of interacting singularities and influence circular domains. Let us show how all the ingredients of such a motion-based segmentation may be identify from a dense motion field.

4.1 Localisation of Singular Points

Given a motion field w obtained by means of the technique introduced in section 2, the spectral technique described in section 3.1 enables to recover the associated stream-function ϕ and velocity potential ψ. We saw also that the knowledge of both potential functions gives a practical way to identify all the vortices and sinks/sources of the flow by extracting their respective extrema. In practice, these extrema are obtained through a simple morphological processing of the potential functions. Both are derived from dense motion field Helmholtz components $w_{ir} = \nabla \phi$ and $w_{so}^{\perp} = \nabla \psi$, using (12). Note that the laminar part of the motion field is assumed to be well approximated by the smooth motion field estimate obtained at the coarsest level of our multigrid setting.

4.2 Extraction of Rankine Parameters

Assuming that all singularities of the flow are known, a complete parametric representation of the flow as a superposition of individual rotational and divergent Rankine models can be sought. To this end, we need to estimate the strength and the circular linearity domain associated to each singular point.

Assuming that the solenoidal and irrotational components of the flow differ from the two corresponding components of the compound Rankine model by a white Gaussian noise of variance σ^2, we get:

$$f_{so}(z) = \sum_{i=1}^{P} \left(f_i(z) + a(z) + ib(z) \right) \quad \text{and} \quad f_{ir}(z) = \sum_{j=1}^{N} \left(f_j(z) + a(z) + ib(z) \right)$$

with $a(z)$ and $b(z) \sim \mathcal{N}(0, \sigma^2)$. Function $f_{so} \triangleq u_{so} + iv_{so}$ (resp. $f_{ir} \triangleq u_{ir} + iv_{ir}$) is the complex representation of w_{so} (resp. of w_{ir}), and P and N denote respectively the number of vortices and sources/sinks of the flow.

A maximum likelihood estimation of the Rankine model parameters leads to maximize with respect to the unknown parameters vector $\Theta \triangleq (r_i, \beta_i)_{i=1}^{P} \times (r_j, \alpha_j)_{j=1}^{N}$ the following log-likelihood defined on the whole image domain Ω:

$$\mathcal{L}(\Theta) = \underbrace{\iint_{\Omega} |f_{ir}(z) - \sum_{i} f_i(z)|^2 dz}_{\mathcal{L}_{so}} + \underbrace{\iint_{\Omega} |f_{so}(z) - \sum_{j} f_j(z)|^2 dz}_{\mathcal{L}_{ir}}. \quad (15)$$

With the assumption that two circular linearity domains of the same nature do not intersect each other, the two parts of this expression can be expressed as:

$$\mathcal{L}_{so}(\Theta) = \sum_{i=1}^{P} \iint_{\mathcal{D}_i} |f_{so}(z) - h_i(r_i, z) - \sum_{k \neq i} g_k(z)|^2 dz + \iint_{\overline{\mathcal{D}}} |f_{so}(z) - \sum_{i=1}^{P} g_p(z)|^2 dz, \quad (16)$$

and similarly for $\mathcal{L}_{ir}$, where $\mathcal{D}_i$ denotes the disk associated to the ith vortex singularity and $\overline{\mathcal{D}}_i \triangleq \Omega - \bigcup_{i=1}^{P} \mathcal{D}_i$. It is important to remark that the non-overlapping assumption only apply to domains associated to singularities of the same type. Likelihood (16) is still valid for a vortex and a source combined in a swirl.

Expanding expression (16) in the solenoidal case (the same computations may be carried out in the irrotational case) one gets:

$$\mathcal{L}_{so}(\Theta) = \sum_{i} \iint_{\mathcal{D}_i} \left\| w_{so}(s) + \frac{(s - s_i)^{\perp}}{r_i^2} \beta_i + \sum_{k \neq i} \frac{(s - s_k)^{\perp}}{\|s - s_k\|^2} \beta_k \right\|^2 ds$$

$$+ \iint_{\overline{\mathcal{D}}} \left\| w_{so}(s) + \sum_{k} \frac{(s - s_k)^{\perp}}{\|s - s_k\|^2} \beta_k \right\|^2 ds. \quad (17)$$

A maximizer of this likelihood is given by solving $\nabla \mathcal{L}_{so} = 0$, where $\nabla = (\frac{\partial}{\partial r_1}, ..., \frac{\partial}{\partial r_N}, \frac{\partial}{\partial \beta_1}, ..., \frac{\partial}{\partial \beta_N})^T$. The cancellation of the partial derivative w.r.t. the r_i's leads to (remarking with some efforts that $\frac{\partial}{\partial R}\left(\iint_{\mathcal{D}} f + \iint_{\overline{\mathcal{D}}} g\right) = \iint_{\mathcal{D}} \frac{\partial f(R)}{\partial R} + \iint_{\overline{\mathcal{D}}} \frac{\partial g(R)}{\partial R}$):

$$\frac{\pi}{2} r_i^2 = -\frac{1}{\beta_i} \iint_{\mathcal{D}_i} [(w_{so}(s) + \sum_{k \neq i} \frac{(s - s_k)^{\perp}}{\|s - s_k\|^2} \beta_k) \cdot (s - s_i)^{\perp}] ds. \quad (18)$$

Concerning the β_i's we get:

$$\beta_i = \frac{B+C}{A}, \text{with}$$

$$A = \iint_{\Omega-\mathcal{D}_i} \frac{1}{\|s-s_i\|^2} ds, B = \iint_{\overline{\mathcal{D}}} \left[w_{so}(s) + \sum_{k \neq i} \frac{(s-s_k)^\perp}{\|s-s_k\|^2} \beta_k \right] \cdot \frac{(s-s_i)^\perp}{\|s-s_i\|^2} ds,$$

$$C = \sum_{k \neq i} \iint_{\mathcal{D}_k} \left[w_{so}(s) + \frac{(s-s_k)^\perp}{r_k^2} \beta_k + \sum_{p \notin \{k,i\}} \frac{(s-s_p)^\perp}{\|s-s_p\|^2} \beta_p \right] \cdot \frac{(s-s_i)^\perp}{\|s-s_i\|^2}. \quad (19)$$

Equations 18 and 19 are solved alternatively. For fixed radius, 19 defines a linear system of equations w.r.t. the β_i's. In turn, the strength parameters β_i's being fixed, the independent non-linear equations (18) are solved with a kind of fixed point method: the integral is computed using the previous estimate of radius r_i (the initial radius is fixed to a small value (3 pixels in practice). The resolution of both systems is iterated until convergence (see [8] for details explanations). Let us note that an additional constraint which guaranty non-overlapping domains must be included to ensure an admissible solution.

4.3 Elimination of Noisy Singularities

In order to keep only the most significant singularities to describe the motion field, we consider the Bhattacharyya distance between two multidimensional Gaussian laws [3]:

$$d_B[\mathcal{N}_1(\boldsymbol{\mu_1}, \Sigma_1), \mathcal{N}_2(\boldsymbol{\mu_2}, \Sigma_2)] = \frac{1}{4}(\boldsymbol{\mu})^T(\Sigma_1 + \Sigma_2)^{-1}(\boldsymbol{\mu}) + \frac{1}{2}\ln(\frac{\det(\Sigma_2 + \Sigma_1)}{2\sqrt{\det(\Sigma_1 \Sigma_2)}}), \quad (20)$$

with $\boldsymbol{\mu} = \boldsymbol{\mu_2} - \boldsymbol{\mu_1}$. For each component (i.e., the irrotational one or the solenoidal one) we compute this distance for the two Gaussian distributions corresponding to the error between the considered Rankine model and the dense motion field for two consecutive numbers of singularities. For example for the solenoidal component we compute: $d_B[\mathcal{N}_1(\boldsymbol{\mu}^n, \Sigma^n), \mathcal{N}_2(\boldsymbol{\mu}^{n+1}, \Sigma^{n+1})]$ where, $\boldsymbol{\mu}^k$ and Σ^k are the mean and the variance of the difference field $(\boldsymbol{w}_{so} - \boldsymbol{w}^k_{\Theta_{so}})$. Parametric field $\boldsymbol{w}^k_{\Theta_{so}}$ correspond to a maximum likelihood estimate of Rankine model with k vortices. Starting with no singularities, we increase the number of singularities by considering the largest local maxima of its corresponding squared potential function. When the Bhattacharyya distance between two consecutive models is small enough (i.e., when the introduction of a new singularity does not bring additional information) the process is stopped.

5 Experimental Results

In this section we present some experimental results. Presented examples correspond to the motion between two consecutive images of the infra-red channel of

Meteosat, shot the 21st of January 1998 (Figs. 1a-b), and between two consecutive images of the water-vapor channel of Meteosat, shot the 4th of August 1995 (Figs. 1c-d). Both examples images exhibit a large through of low pressure. In addition, the two first images exhibit a set of moving cloud structures (top-right part of the image) and the two others an exploding convective cell. Corresponding estimated vector fields with their laminar component removed are visible in Figs. 2a and 2g. These motion fields seem visually plausible: both the main structures of the motion (counter-clockwise spiral of depressions, downward motion of cold clouds for the infrared image, the convective cell for the water vapor image) are captured.

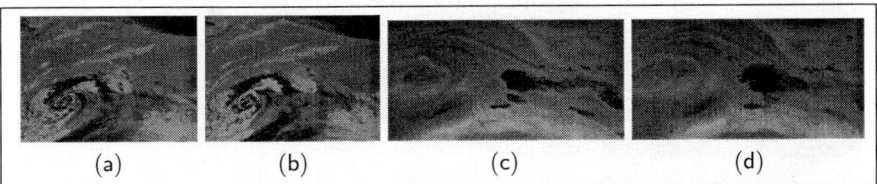

Fig. 1. Two consecutive images of each sequence treated: (a,b) Infrared images; (c,d) Water vapor images

The solenoidal and the irrotational components of these velocity fields are shown in the second column of Fig. 2. In the third column, we present for the first example the squared potential functions from which we extract the singularities by localizing their extrema. For the second example, we present the stream lines and the level curves of the velocity potential. The estimated singularity domains are superimposed to their corresponding motion fields. The parametric fields associated to estimated compound Rankine models are shown in Figs. 2d and 2j.

This method captures the main visible structures of the flow (seven vortices and four sources, for the first example, four vortices and one source for the second example). The associated parametric motion fields constitute fair "summaries" of the structure of the flows.

5.1 Comparison with Winding Number Technique

A popular method to extract singular points is based on the use of Poincaré indices also called winding numbers. The winding number of a closed curve in a vector field amounts to the number of turns, $\frac{1}{2\pi} \int d(\tan^{-1} u/v)$, that the field undergoes along the curve. Its value is +1 if the considered Jordan curve surrounds a vortex/sink/source. In practice, due to the image discretization, a small blob (whose size depends on the size of used curve) of +1 index pixels is obtained in the neighborhood of a singular point.

This method as the advantage to be fast. Nevertheless, it remains based on a local criterion which is not robust to noise. Furthermore, only blobs containing a

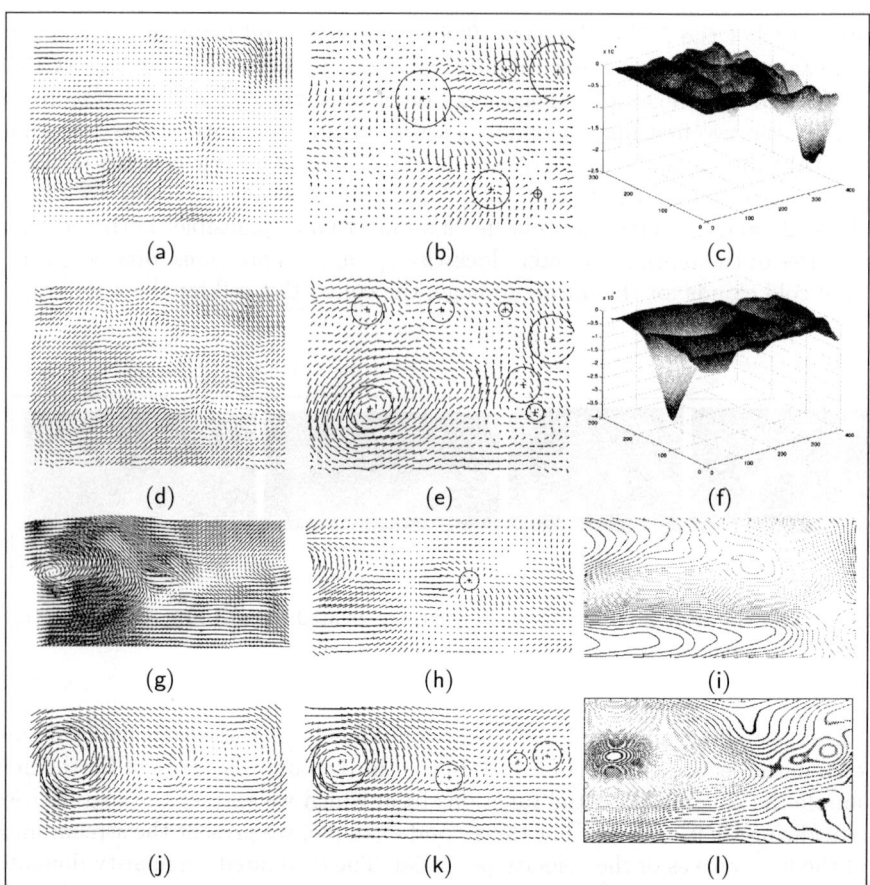

Fig. 2. (a-f) results for the IR images presented in Fig. 1a and (g-l) results for the WV images presented in Fig. 1b – (a,g): dense motion fields obtained with the proposed technique; (d,j): corresponding parametric Rankine flows; (b,h): estimated sources/sinks superimposed to the irrotational part of the flow; (e,k): estimated vortices superimposed to the solenoidal part of the flow; (c,f): squared velocity potential and squared stream function; (i,l): stream lines ($\psi = constant$) and level curves of the velocity potential ($\phi = constant$).

potential singular point may be detected with such technique. The exact location of the singularity has then to be extracted from such blobs with other adhoc techniques.

In order to illustrate the difference between such an approach and the one we propose, we present in Fig. 3, the different blobs detected via winding indices, from to dense motion fields estimated with the dedicated approach. Figure 3a corresponds to the singularities detected for the infrared sequence, whereas Fig. 3b corresponds to the ones obtained for the water-vapor example.

We can note that the correct singular points are also detected at least within the few pixel location accuracy associated to each blob. Nevertheless, the results are cluttered by a large number of false positives due to the sensitivity of the technique. These spurious points have then to be removed with some post-processing treatments.

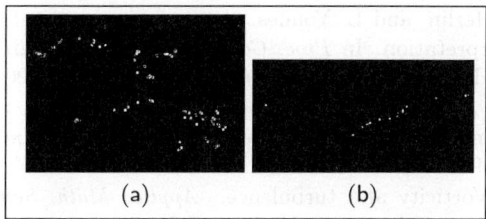

Fig. 3. Blobs of singularities estimated with winding number technique; (a) blobs corresponding to the infrared example and (b) blobs corresponding to the water vapor example .

6 Conclusion

In this paper, we have presented a complete method to analyze fluid flows from image sequences. We first presented a dedicated technique to estimate dense motion fields. This method modifies generic energy-based robust techniques through a new data term based on the continuity equation, and an original smoothness prior which preserves high concentrations of divergence and curl. We then have proposed an original technique to detect singular points and their associated domain of linearity from a dense motion field. This technique is based on the numerical decomposition of the motion field in terms of its irrotational and solenoidal components. From these components, we extract by integration the associated stream function and the velocity potential, whose local extrema provide the location of vortices and sinks/sources. The strength and linearity domain associated to each of these detected singular points are then obtained from a maximum likelihood estimation of a parametric Rankine model.

The whole approach has been demonstrated on two real meteorological examples. In [7], we shows that the fluid motion estimator provide better results than generic motion estimators based on brightness constancy assumption and a first-order smoothness. The singularities extraction method described here allows to extract the main structures of a motion field. Compared to an usual winding number technique, our approach is more robust to various sources of noise. As a by product, our approach provides a simple way to extract streamlines, velocity potential, solenoidal or irrotational components, which are central to many studies of fluids. As a final remark let us outline that the method described here requires no tuning of parameters.

References

1. A. Amini. A scalar function formulation for optical flow. In *Proc. Europ. Conf. Computer Vision*, pages 125–131, 1994.
2. V.I. Arnold. Ordinary differential equations. MIT Press, 1990.
3. M. Basseville. Distance measure for signal processing and pattern recognition. *Signal Processing*, (18):349–369, 1989.
4. D. Béréziat, I. Herlin, and L. Younes. A generalized optical flow constraint and its physical interpretation. In *Proc. Conf. Comp. Vision Pattern Rec.*, volume 2, pages 487–492, Hilton Head Island, South Carolina, USA, 2000.
5. M. Black and P. Anandan. The robust estimation of multiple motions: Parametric and piecewise-smooth flow fields. *Computer Vision and Image Understanding*, 63(1):75–104, 1996.
6. A. J. Chorin. Vorticity and turbulence. *Applied Math. Sciences* 103, Springer Verlag.
7. T. Corpetti, E. Mémin, and P. Pérez. Dense estimation of fluide flows. *IEEE Trans on Pattern Analysis and Machine Intelligence*, 24(3), March 2002.
8. T. Corpetti, E. Mémin, and P. Pérez. Extraction of singular points from dense motion fields: an analytic approach. *Journal of Math. Imag. and Vision*, 2002. Accepted under minor revisions.
9. S. Das Peddada and R. McDevitt. Least average residual algorithm (LARA) for tracking the motion of artic sea ice. *IEEE trans. on Geosciences and Remote sensing*, 34(4):915–926, 1996.
10. J.M. Fitzpatrick. The existence of geometrical density-image transformations corresponding to object motion. *Comput. Vision, Graphics, Image Proc.*, 44(2):155–174, 1988.
11. R.M. Ford, R. Strickland, and B. Thomas. Image models for 2-d flow visualization and compression. *Graph. Mod. Image Proc.*, 56(1):75–93, 1994.
12. S. Gupta and J. Prince. Stochastic models for div-curl optical flow methods. *Signal Proc. Letters*, 3(2):32–34, 1996.
13. B. Horn and B. Schunck. Determining optical flow. *Artificial Intelligence*, 17:185–203, 1981.
14. P. Kornprobst, R. Deriche, and G. Aubert. Image sequence analysis via partial differential equations. *Journal of Mathematical Imaging and Vision*, 11(1):5–26, September 1999.
15. R. Larsen, K. Conradsen, and B.K. Ersboll. Estimation of dense image flow fields in fluids. *IEEE trans. on Geoscience and Remote sensing*, 36(1):256–264, 1998.
16. E. Mémin and P. Pérez. Dense estimation and object-based segmentation of the optical flow with robust techniques. *IEEE Trans. Image Processing*, 7(5):703–719, 1998.
17. E. Mémin and P. Pérez. Hierarchical estimation and segmentation of dense motion fields. *Int. J. Computer Vision*, 46(2):129–155, February 2002.
18. A. Nomura, H. Miike, and K. Koga. Field theory approach for determining optical flow. *Pattern Recognition Letters*, 12(3):183–190, 1991.
19. A. Ottenbacher, M. Tomasini, K. Holmund, and J. Schmetz. Low-level cloud motion winds from Meteosat high-resolution visible imagery. *Weather and Forecasting*, 12(1):175–184, 1997.
20. B.G. Schunk. The motion constraint equation for optical flow. In *Proc. Int. Conf. Pattern Recognition*, pages 20–22, Montreal, 1984.

21. S.M. Song and R.M. Leahy. Computation of 3D velocity fields from 3D cine and CT images of human heart. *IEEE trans. on medical imaging*, 10(3):295–306, 1991.
22. D. Suter. Motion estimation and vector splines. In *Proc. Conf. Comp. Vision Pattern Rec.*, pages 939–942, Seattle, USA, June 1994.
23. R. Wildes, M. Amabile, A.M. Lanzillotto, and T.S. Leu. Physically based fluid flow recovery from image sequences. In *Proc. Conf. Comp. Vision Pattern Rec.*, pages 969–975, 1997.
24. L. Zhou, C. Kambhamettu, and D. Goldgof. Fluid structure and motion analysis from multi-spectrum 2D cloud images sequences. In *Proc. Conf. Comp. Vision Pattern Rec.*, volume 2, pages 744–751, Hilton Head Island, South Carolina, USA, 2000.

Appendix

In this appendix, we demonstrate (for the L_2 norm) that the regularization we propose in (9) corresponds to a smoothed form of the initial second-order regularization (8). To show that, let us consider only the div part of both functionals (the same deviations can be obtained for the curl part). Because of the Parseval theorem, the Fourier transform of the first term of (8) verifies:

$$\mathcal{F}\left(\int_\Omega \|\boldsymbol{\nabla}\mathrm{div}\boldsymbol{w}\|^2 ds\right) = \int |\mathcal{F}(\boldsymbol{\nabla}\mathrm{div}\boldsymbol{w})|^2 d\boldsymbol{k} = \int \|\boldsymbol{k}\|^2 |\boldsymbol{k}\cdot\hat{\boldsymbol{w}}(\boldsymbol{k})|^2 d\boldsymbol{k} \qquad (21)$$

Similarly, the Fourier transform of the corresponding term in (9) verifies (with $\mu = \frac{1}{\lambda}$):

$$\mathcal{F}\left(\int_\Omega \mu^2(\mathrm{div}\boldsymbol{w} - \xi)^2 + \|\boldsymbol{\nabla}\xi\|^2 ds\right) = \int \left(\mu^2 |\boldsymbol{k}\cdot\hat{\boldsymbol{w}}(\boldsymbol{k}) - \hat{\xi}|^2 + \|\boldsymbol{k}\|^2 |\hat{\xi}|^2\right) d\boldsymbol{k}. \qquad (22)$$

For a fixed $\boldsymbol{w}$, a minimizer of (22) is given by the resolution of the Euler-Lagrange equation ($\mu^2(\mathrm{div}\boldsymbol{w} - \xi) + \Delta\xi = 0$). In the Fourier domain, the minimizer is:

$$\hat{\xi}_{opt} = \frac{\mu^2 |\boldsymbol{k}\cdot\hat{\boldsymbol{w}}(\boldsymbol{k})|}{\|\boldsymbol{k}\|^2 + \mu^2}. \qquad (23)$$

Introducing $\hat{\xi}_{opt}$ in (22), after few manipulations leads to:

$$\mathcal{F}\left(\int_\Omega \mu^2(\mathrm{div}\boldsymbol{w} - \xi_{opt})^2 + \|\boldsymbol{\nabla}\xi_{opt}\|^2 ds\right) = \int \frac{\mu^2 \|\boldsymbol{k}\|^2}{\|\boldsymbol{k}\|^2 + \mu^2} |\boldsymbol{k}\cdot\hat{\boldsymbol{w}}(\boldsymbol{k})|^2 d\boldsymbol{k}$$
$$= \int \hat{g}(\boldsymbol{k}) |\mathcal{F}(\|\boldsymbol{\nabla}\mathrm{div}\boldsymbol{w}\|)|^2 d\boldsymbol{k} \qquad (24)$$

with $\hat{g}(\boldsymbol{k}) = \frac{\mu^2}{\mu^2 + \|\boldsymbol{k}\|^2}$. With $\mu = \frac{1}{\lambda}$ (in that case, the regularization is the same than (9)), one get $\hat{g}(\boldsymbol{k}) = \frac{1}{1+\lambda^2\|\boldsymbol{k}\|^2}$. For low frequencies, $\hat{g}(\boldsymbol{k}) \to 1$ and the regularization functions are the same. For high frequencies, $\hat{g}$ is a smoothing function. Nevertheless, as we assume that $\boldsymbol{w}$ is C^2, we have $\lim_{\|\boldsymbol{k}\|\to+\infty} \hat{\boldsymbol{w}}\cdot\|\boldsymbol{k}\|^2 = 0$ (i.e. $\hat{\boldsymbol{w}}$ tends to zero faster than $\frac{1}{\|\boldsymbol{k}\|^2}$ when $\boldsymbol{k}$ tends to $+\infty$).

A Layered Motion Representation with Occlusion and Compact Spatial Support

Allan D. Jepson [1]   David J. Fleet [2]   Michael J. Black [3]

[1] Department of Computer Science, University of Toronto, Toronto, Canada
[2] Palo Alto Research Center, 3333 Coyote Hill Rd., Palo Alto, CA 94304, USA
[3] Department of Computer Science, Brown University, Providence, USA

Abstract. We describe a 2.5D layered representation for visual motion analysis. The representation provides a global interpretation of image motion in terms of several spatially localized foreground regions along with a background region. Each of these regions comprises a parametric shape model and a parametric motion model. The representation also contains depth ordering so visibility and occlusion are rightly included in the estimation of the model parameters. Finally, because the number of objects, their positions, shapes and sizes, and their relative depths are all unknown, initial models are drawn from a proposal distribution, and then compared using a penalized likelihood criterion. This allows us to automatically initialize new models, and to compare different depth orderings.

1 Introduction

One goal of visual motion analysis is to compute representations of image motion that allow one to infer the structure and identity of moving objects. For intermediate-level visual analysis one particularly promising type of representation is based on the concept of layered image descriptions [4, 12, 26, 28]. Layered models provide a natural way to estimate motion when there are sevaral regions having different velocities. They have been shown to be effective for separating foreground objects from backgrounds. One weakness of existing layered representations is that they assign pixels to layers independently of pixels at neighboring locations. In doing so their underlying generative model does not manifest the constraint that most physical objects are spatially coherent and have boundaries, nor does it represent relative depths and occlusion.

In this paper we develop a new, 2.5D layered image representation. We are motivated by a desire to find effective descriptions of images in terms of a relatively small number of simple moving parts. The representation is based on a composition of layered regions called polybones, each of which has compact spatial support and a probabilistic representation for its borders. This representation of opaque spatial regions and soft boundaries, along with a partial depth ordering among the polybones, gives one an explicit representation of visibility and occlusion. As such, the resulting layered model corresponds to an underlying generative model that captures more of the salient properties of natural scenes than existing layered models.

Along with this 2.5D representation we also describe a method for parsing image motion to find global image descriptions in terms of an arbitrary number of layered, moving polybones (e.g., see Figure 1 (right)). Since the number of objects, their positions, motions, shapes, sizes, and relative depths are all unknown, a complete search of the model space is infeasible. Instead we employ a stochastic search strategy in which new parses are drawn from a proposal distribution. The parameters of the individual polybones within each such proposal are refined using the EM-algorithm. Alternative parses are then compared using a penalized-likelihood model-selection criterion. This allows us to automatically explore alternative parses, and to select the most plausible ones.

2 Previous Work

Many current approaches to motion analysis over long image sequences are formulated as model-based tracking problems. In most cases we exploit prior knowledge about the objects of interest. For example, one often uses knowledge of the number of objects, their shapes, appearances, and dynamics, and perhaps an initial guess about object position. With 3D models one can take the effects of directional illumination into account, to anticipate shadows for instance [14]. Successful 3D people trackers typically assume detailed kinematic models of shape and motion, and initialization is still often done manually [2, 3, 7, 21]. Recent success with curve-based tracking of human shapes relies on a user defined model of the desired curve [11, 17]. For complex objects under variable illuminants, one could attempt to learn models of object appearance from a training set of images prior to tracking [1, 8]. Whether one tracks blobs to detect activities like football plays [9], or specific classes of objects such as blood cells, satellites or hockey pucks, it is common to constrain the problem with a suitable model of object appearance and dynamics, along with a relatively simple form of data association [16, 19].

To circumvent the need for such specific prior knowledge, one could rely on bottom-up, motion-based approaches to segmenting moving objects from their backgrounds, prior to tracking and identification [10, 18]. Layered image representations provide one such approach [12, 20, 25, 28]. With probabilistic mixture models and the EM (Expectation-Maximization) algorithm [6], efficient methods have been developed for determining the motion and the segmentation simultaneously. In particular, these methods give one the ability to softly assign pixels to layers, and to robustly estimate the motion parameters of each layer. One weakness in most of these methods, however, is that the assignment of pixels to layers is done independently at each pixel, without an explicit constraint on spatial coherence (although see [23, 27]). Such representations, while powerful, lack the expressiveness that would be useful in layered models, namely, the ability to explicitly represent coherence, opacity, region boundaries, and occlusion.

Our goal here is to develop a compositional representation for image motion with a somewhat greater degree of generic expressiveness than existing layered models. Broadly speaking, we seek a representation that satisfies three criteria: 1) it captures the salient structure of the time-varying image in an expressive manner; 2) it allows us to generate and elaborate specific parses of the image motion within the representation in a computationally efficient way; and 3) it allows us to compare different parses in order to select the most plausible ones.

Towards this end, like previous work in [23, 24], we assume a relatively simple parametric model for the spatial support of each layer. However, unlike the Gaussian model in [23], where the spatial support decays exponentially from the center of the object, we use a *polybone* in which support is unity over the interior of the object, and then smoothly

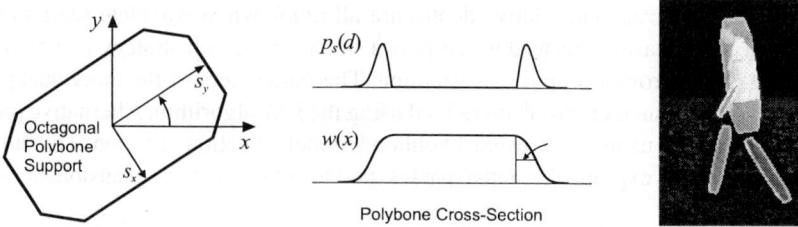

Fig. 1. (left) The spatial support of each polybone used in the experiments is a simple transform of a canonical octagonal shape. The allowed transforms include translation, rotation and independent scaling along two object-centered axes. (middle) These plots depict boundary position density $p_s(d)$ and the occupancy probability $w(x)$. The occupancy probability is unity inside the polygon with a Gaussian-shaped soft shoulder. (right) An example parse with polybones from an image sequence.

decays to zero only in the vicinity of the spatial boundary. This representation embodies our uncertainty about exact boundary position, it allows us to separate changes in object size and shape from our uncertainty about the boundary location, and it allows us to differentiate the associated likelihood function with respect to object shape and position. Most importantly, it allows us to explicitly express properties like visibility, occupancy, opacity and occlusion in a straightforward way.

One of the central issues in this research is whether or not the extraction and selection of a layered polybone description for image motion is computationally feasible. The space of possible descriptions is large owing to the unknown number of polybones, the unknown depth relations between the different polybones, and the dimension of the continuous parameter space for each polybone. We therefore require effective methods to search this space for plausible models.

3 Layered Polybones

A layered polybone model consists of a background layer and K depth-ordered foreground layers. Formally, a model **M** at time t can be written as

$$\mathbf{M} = (K(t), \mathbf{b}_0(t), ..., \mathbf{b}_K(t)), \tag{1}$$

where $\mathbf{b}_k \equiv (\mathbf{a}_k, \mathbf{m}_k)$ is the vector of shape and pose parameters, $\mathbf{a}_k$, together with the motion parameters, $\mathbf{m}_k$, for the kth polybone. By convention, the partial depth ordering of the layers is given by the order of the polybone indices. The background corresponds to $k = 0$, and the foremost polybone corresponds to $k = K$.

In the interests of a simple shape description, the interior of each polybone is defined by a closed convex polygon. These interior regions are assumed to be opaque, so anything behind a polybone interior is occluded. Given the simplicity of the polybone shape, we do not expect them to fit any particular region accurately. We therefore give each polybone a soft border to quantify our uncertainty in the true boundary location. More precisely, we define the probability density of the true boundary location, p_s, as a function of the distance, $d(\mathbf{x}; \mathbf{b}_k)$, from a location $\mathbf{x}$ to the polygon specified by $\mathbf{b}_k$ (see Fig. 1(middle)). Given p_s, the probability that $\mathbf{x}$ lies inside of the true boundary is then expressed as $w(\mathbf{x}; \mathbf{b}_k) = p_s(d > d(\mathbf{x}; \mathbf{b}_k))$, the cummulative probability that the distance d, in the direction $\mathbf{x}$, is greater than $d(\mathbf{x}; \mathbf{b}_k)$. This occupancy probability, $w(\mathbf{x}; \mathbf{b}_k)$, serves as our definition of spatial support from which we can formulate *visbility* and *occlusion*. As depicted in Fig. 1(middle), we model p_s so that the occupancy probability, $w(\mathbf{x}; \mathbf{b}_k)$, is unity in the interior of the polygon, and decays outside the polygon with the shape of a half-Gaussian function of the distance from the polygon. For convenience, the standard deviation of the half-Gaussian, $\sigma_{s,k}$, is taken to be a constant. In practice we truncate the polybone shoulders to zero after a distance of $2.5\sigma_s$.

With these definitions, the visibility of the jth polybone at a pixel $\mathbf{x}$ depends on the probabilities that closer layers do not occupy $\mathbf{x}$; i.e., the visibility probability is

$$v_k(\mathbf{x}) = \prod_{j=k+1}^{K} (1 - w(\mathbf{x}; \mathbf{b}_j)) = (1 - w(\mathbf{x}; \mathbf{b}_{k+1})) \, v_{k+1}(\mathbf{x}) , \qquad (2)$$

where all pixels in the foremost layer are defined to be visible, so $v_K(\mathbf{x}) = 1$. It may be interesting to note that transparency could also be modeled by replacing $(1 - w(\mathbf{x}; \mathbf{b}_j))$ in (2) by $(1 - \mu_j w(\mathbf{x}; \mathbf{b}_j))$, where $\mu_j \in [0, 1]$ denotes the opacity of the jth polybone (cf. [5, 22]). Previous layered models correspond to the special case of this in which $\mu_j = 0$ and each polybone covers the entire image, so $w(\mathbf{x}; \mathbf{b}_k) \equiv 1$.

In our current implementation and the examples below we restrict the polybone shape to be a simple transformation of a canonical octagonal boundary (see Fig. 1(left)), and we let $\sigma_s = 4$ pixels. The shape and pose of the interior polygon is parameterized with respect to its local coordinate frame, with its scale in the horizontal and vertical directions $\mathbf{s} = (s_x, s_y)$, its orientation θ, and the image position of the polygon origin, $\mathbf{c} = (c_x, c_y)$ (see Fig. 1(left)). Together with the boundary uncertainty parameter, σ_s, these parameters define the shape and pose of a polybone:

$$\mathbf{a}_k = (\mathbf{s}_k, \theta_k, \mathbf{c}_k, \sigma_{s,k}) . \qquad (3)$$

This simple description for shape and pose was selected, in part, to simplify the exposition in this paper and to facilitate the parameter estimation. It would be straightforward to include more complex polygonal or spline based shape descriptions in the representation (although local extrema in the optimization may be more of a problem).

Finally, in addition to shape and pose, the polybone parameters also specify the motion within the layer. In particular, the motion parameters associated with the kth polybone, denoted by $\mathbf{m}_k$, specify a parametric image warp, $\mathbf{w}(\mathbf{x}; \mathbf{m}_k(t))$, from pixels at time $t + 1$ to pixels at time t. In the current implementation we use similarity deformations, where $\mathbf{m}_k$ specifies translation, rotation and uniform scaling between frames.

4 Model Likelihood

The likelihood of a layered polybone model $\mathbf{M}_t$ depends on how well it accounts for the motion between frames t and $t + 1$. As is common in optical flow estimation, our motion likelihood function follows from a simple data conservation assumption. That is, let $d(\mathbf{x}, t)$ denote image data at pixel $\mathbf{x}$ and frame t. The warp parameters for the kth polybone specify that points $(\mathbf{x}, t)$ map to points in the next frame given by $(\mathbf{x}', t + 1) = (\mathbf{w}(\mathbf{x}; \mathbf{m}_k(t)), t + 1)$. The similarity of the image data at these two points is typically measured in terms of a probability distribution for the difference

$$\delta d_k(\mathbf{x}, t) = d(\mathbf{w}(\mathbf{x}; \mathbf{m}_k(t)), t + 1) - d(\mathbf{x}, t) . \qquad (4)$$

The distribution for the deviation δd is often taken to be a Gaussian density, say $p_1(\delta d)$, having mean 0 and standard deviation σ_m. To accommodate data outliers, a linear mixture of a Gaussian density and a broad outlier distribution, $p_0(\delta d)$, can be used. Such mixture models have been found to improve the robustness of motion estimation in the face of outliers and unmodelled surfaces [12, 13]. Using a mixture model, we then define the likelihood (i.e., the observation density) of a single data observation, $\delta d_k(\mathbf{x}, t)$, given the warp, $\mathbf{w}(\mathbf{x}; \mathbf{m}_k(t))$, to be

$$p_k(\delta d_k(\mathbf{x}, t)) = (1 - \pi_{0,k}) p_1(\delta d_k(\mathbf{x}, t)) + \pi_{0,k} p_0(\delta d_k(\mathbf{x}, t)), \quad (5)$$

where $\pi_{0,k} \in [0, 1]$ is the outlier mixing proportion. The additional parameters required to specify the mixture model, namely σ_m and π_0, are also included in the motion parameter vector $\mathbf{m}_k(t)$ for each polybone. Note that, as with the shape and pose parameterizations, we chose simple forms for the parametric motion model and the data likelihood. This was done to simplify the exposition and to facilitate parameter estimation.

The likelihood for the kth polybone at a pixel $\mathbf{x}$ can be combined with the likelihoods for other polybones in the model $\mathbf{M}_t$ by incorporating each polybone's visibility, $v_k(\mathbf{x})$, and occupancy probability, $w(\mathbf{x}, \mathbf{b}_k(t))$. It is straightforward to show that the likelihood of the entire layered polybone model at a single location $\mathbf{x}$ and frame t is given by

$$p(\{\delta d_k(\mathbf{x}, t)\}_{k=0}^{K} \mid \mathbf{M}_t) = \sum_{k=0}^{K} v_k(\mathbf{x}) w(\mathbf{x}; \mathbf{b}_k) p_k(\delta d_k(\mathbf{x}, t)). \quad (6)$$

Finally, given independent noise at different pixels, the log likelihood of the layered polybone model $\mathbf{M}_t$ over the entire image is

$$\log p(\mathbf{D}_t \mid \mathbf{M}_t) = \sum_{\mathbf{x}} \log p(\{\delta d_k(\mathbf{x}, t)\}_{k=0}^{K} \mid \mathbf{M}_t). \quad (7)$$

Note that the use of $\mathbf{D}_t$ here involves some abuse of notation, since the image data at both frames t and $t+1$ are required to compute the deviations $\delta d_k(\mathbf{x}, t)$; moreover, the model itself is required to determine corresponding points.

5 Penalized Likelihood

We now derive the objective function that is used to optimize the polybone parameters and to compare alternative models. The objective function is motivated by the standard Bayesian filtering equations for the posterior probability of the model $\mathbf{M}_t$, given all the data up to time t (denoted by $\mathcal{D}_t$). In particular, ignoring constant terms, the log posterior is given by

$$\mathcal{U}(\mathbf{M}_t) = \log p(\mathbf{D}_t \mid \mathbf{M}_t) + \log p(\mathbf{M}_t \mid \mathcal{D}_{t-1}). \quad (8)$$

The last term above is the log of the conditional distribution over models $\mathbf{M}_t$ given all the previous data, which is typically expressed as

$$\mathbf{p}(\mathbf{M}_t \mid \mathcal{D}_{t-1}) = \int_{\tilde{\mathbf{M}}_{t-1}} p(\mathbf{M}_t \mid \tilde{\mathbf{M}}_{t-1}) p(\tilde{\mathbf{M}}_{t-1} \mid \mathcal{D}_{t-1}), \quad (9)$$

given suitable independence and Markov assumptions. Given the complexity of the space of models we are considering, a detailed approximation of this integral is beyond the scope of this paper. Instead, we use the general form of (8) and (9) to motivate a simpler penalized likelihood formulation for the objective function, namely

$$\mathcal{O}(\mathbf{M}_t) = \log p(\mathbf{D}_t \mid \mathbf{M}_t) + q(\mathbf{M}_t, \mathbf{M}_{t-1}) \, . \tag{10}$$

The last term in (10), called the penalty term, is meant to provide a rough approximation for the log of the conditional probability distribution in (9).

The penalty term serves two purposes. First, when the data is absent, ambiguous, or noisy, the log likelihood term can be expected to be insensitive to particular variations in the model $\mathbf{M}_t$. In these situations the penalty term provides a bias towards particular parameter values. In our current implementation we include two terms in $q(\mathbf{M}_t, \mathbf{M}_{t-1})$ that bias the models to smaller polybones and to smooth shape changes:

$$q_1(\mathbf{M}_t) = \sum_{k=1}^{K} \log[L_1(s_{x,k,t} - 1) L_1(s_{y,k,t} - 1)] \tag{11}$$

$$q_2(\mathbf{M}_t, \mathbf{M}_{t-1}) = \sum_{k} \log N(\mathbf{a}_{k,t} - \tilde{\mathbf{a}}_{k',t}; \Sigma_a) \tag{12}$$

Here q_1 provides the bias towards small polybones, with $L_1(s)$ equal to the one-sided Laplace density $\lambda_s e^{-\lambda_s s}$. The second term, q_2, provides a bias for smooth shape changes with a mean zero normal density evaluated at the temporal difference in shape parameters. Here, k' is the index of the polybone in $\mathbf{M}_{t-1}$ that corresponds to the kth polybone in $\mathbf{M}_t$; if such a k' exists, then $\tilde{\mathbf{a}}_{k',t}$ denotes the pose of this polybone at time $t-1$ warped by the motion defined by $\mathbf{m}_{k',t-1}$. The sum in (12) is over all polybones in $\mathbf{M}_t$ that have corresponding polybones in $\mathbf{M}_{t-1}$.

The second purpose of the penalty function is to control model complexity. Without a penalty term the maximum of the log likelihood in (10) will be monotonically increasing in the number of polybones. However, beyond a certain point, the extra polybones primarily fit noise in the data set, and the corresponding increase in the log likelihood is marginal. The penalty term in (10) is used to ensure that the increase in the log likelihood obtained with a new polybone is sufficiently large to justify the new polybone. To derive this third term of $q(\mathbf{M}_t, \mathbf{M}_{t-1})$ we assume that each polybone parameter can be resolved to some accuracy, and that the likelihood does not vary significantly when parameters are varied within such resolution limits. As with conventional Bayesian model selection, the penalty function is given by the log volume of the resolvable set of models. In our current implementation, the third term in the penalty function is given by

$$q_3(\mathbf{M}_t) = \sum_{k=1}^{K} \log \left(\left[\frac{4\sigma_s^2}{n_x n_y} \right]^2 \frac{4\sigma_s}{\pi r} \frac{1}{10} \frac{2\sigma_{v,k}}{10} \frac{\log(2)}{\log(20)} \right) , \tag{13}$$

where the different factors in (13) correspond to the following resolutions: We assume the location and size parameters of any given polybone are resolved to $\pm \sigma_s$ over the image of size $n_x \times n_y$; the angle θ is resolved to $\frac{4\sigma_s}{r}$ where r is the radius of the polybone; the inlier mixing proportion used in the motion model is resolved to ± 0.05 out of the range $[0, 1]$; the inlier motion model has flow estimates that are resolved to within $\pm \sigma_{v,k}$ over a possible range of $[-5, 5]$; and $\sigma_{v,k}$ is estimated from the inlier motion constraints to within a factor of 2 (i.e. $\pm\sqrt{2}\sigma_{v,k}$), with a uniform prior for $\sigma_{v,k}$ having minimum and maximum values of 0.1 and 2.0 pixels/frame.

6 Parameter Estimation

Suppose $\mathbf{M}_t^0$ is an initial guess for the parameters (1) of the layered model. In order to find local extrema of (10) we use a form of gradient ascent. The gradient of the penalty term is easy to compute, while that of the log likelihood is simpler to compute if we exploit the layered structure of the model. We do this by rewriting $p(D(\mathbf{x}) \mid \mathbf{M})$ in a form that isolates the parameters of each individual polybone.

To simplify the likelihood expression, first note from (2) and (6) that the contribution to $p(D(\mathbf{x}) \mid \mathbf{M})$ from only those polybones that are closer to the camera than the kth bone can be expressed as

$$n_k(\mathbf{x}) = \sum_{j=k+1}^{K} v_j(\mathbf{x})\, w(\mathbf{x}; \mathbf{b}_j)\, p(D(\mathbf{x})|\mathbf{b}_j)$$
$$= v_{k+1}(\mathbf{x})\, w(\mathbf{x}; \mathbf{b}_{k+1})\, p(D(\mathbf{x}) \mid \mathbf{b}_{k+1}) + n_{k+1}(\mathbf{x}). \quad (14)$$

We refer to $n_k(\mathbf{x})$ as the *near term* for the kth polybone. Equations (14) and (2) provide recurrence relations, decreasing in k, for computing the near terms and visibilities $v_k(\mathbf{x})$, starting with $n_K(\mathbf{x}) = 0$ and $v_K(\mathbf{x}) = 1$.

Similarly, we collect the polybones that are further from the camera than the kth polybone into the 'far term',

$$f_k(\mathbf{x}) = \sum_{j=0}^{k-1} w(x; \mathbf{b}_j) \left[\prod_{l=j+1}^{k-1} (1 - w(\mathbf{x}; \mathbf{b}_l))\right] p(D(\mathbf{x})|\mathbf{b}_j)$$
$$= w(\mathbf{x}; \mathbf{b}_{k-1})\, p(D(\mathbf{x}) \mid \mathbf{b}_{k-1}) + (1 - w(\mathbf{x}; \mathbf{b}_{k-1}))\, f_{k-1}(\mathbf{x}). \quad (15)$$

Here we use the convention that $\sum_{j=n}^{m} q_j = 0$ and $\prod_{j=n}^{m} q_j = 1$ whenever $n > m$. Notice that (15) gives a recurrence relation for f_k, increasing in k, and starting with $f_0(\mathbf{x}) = 0$.

It now follows that, for each $k \in \{0, \ldots, K\}$, the data likelihood satisfies

$$p(D(\mathbf{x}) \mid \mathbf{M}) = n_k(\mathbf{x}) + v_k(\mathbf{x})\, w(\mathbf{x}; \mathbf{b}_k)\, p(D(\mathbf{x}) \mid \mathbf{b}_k)$$
$$+ v_k(\mathbf{x})(1 - w(\mathbf{x}; \mathbf{b}_k))\, f_k(\mathbf{x}). \quad (16)$$

Moreover, it also follows that $n_k(\mathbf{x})$, $v_k(\mathbf{x})$, and $f_k(\mathbf{x})$ do not depend on the parameters for the kth polybone, $\mathbf{b}_k$. That is, the dependence on $\mathbf{b}_k$ has been isolated in the two terms $w(\mathbf{x}; \mathbf{b}_k)$ and $p(D(\mathbf{x}) \mid \mathbf{b}_k)$ in (16). This greatly simplifies the derivation and the computation of the gradient of the likelihood with respect to $\mathbf{b}_k$.

The gradient of $\mathcal{O}(\mathbf{M})$ is provided by the gradient of $\log p(\mathbf{D}|\mathbf{M})$, which is evaluated as described above, along with the gradient of the penalty term, $q(\mathbf{M}, \mathbf{M}_{t-1})$. In order to optimize $\mathcal{O}(\mathbf{M})$ we have found several variations beyond pure gradient ascent to be effective. In particular, for a given model **M** we use a front-to-back iteration through the recurrence relations in (2) and (14). In doing so we compute the visibilities $v_k(\mathbf{x})$ and the near polybone likelihoods $n_k(\mathbf{x})$ (from the nearest polybone at $k = K$ to the furthest at $k = 0$), without changing the model parameters. Then, from the furthest polybone to the nearest, we update the kth polybone's parameters, namely $\mathbf{b}_k$, while holding the other polybones fixed. Once $\mathbf{b}_k$ has been updated, we use the recurrence relation in (15) to compute the corresponding far term $f_{k+1}(\mathbf{x})$. We then proceed with updating the parameters $\mathbf{b}_{k+1}$ for the next nearest polybone. Together, this process of updating all the polybones is referred to as one back-to-front sweep.

Several sub-steps are used to update each $\mathbf{b}_k$ during a back-to-front sweep. First we update the internal (motion) parameters of the kth polybone. This has the same structure as the EM-algorithm in fitting motion mixture models [12], except that here the near and far terms contribute to the data ownership computation. The M-step of this EM-algorithm yields a linear solution for the motion parameter update. This is solved directly (without using gradient ascent). The mixing coefficients and the variance of the inlier process are also updated using the EM-algorithm. Once these internal parameters have been updated, the pose parameters are updated using a line search along the gradient direction in the pose variables.[4] Finally given the new pose, the internal parameters are re-estimated, completing the update for $\mathbf{b}_k$.

One final refinement involves the gradient ascent in the pose parameters, where we use a line-search along the fixed gradient direction. Since the initial guesses for the pose parameters are often far from the global optimum (see Section 7), we have found it useful to constrain the initial ascent to help avoid some local maxima. In particular, we found that unconstrained hill-climbing from a small initial guess often resulted in a long skinny polybone stuck at a local maximum. To avoid this behaviour we initially constrain the scaling parameters s_x and s_y to be equal, and just update the mean position (c_x, c_y), angle θ, and this uniform scale. Once we have detected a local maximum in these reduced parameters, we allow the individual scales s_x and s_y to evolve to different values. This behaviour is evident in the foreground polybone depicted in Fig. 2.

7 Model Search

While this hill-climbing process is capable of refining rough initial guesses, the number of local maxima of the objective function is expected to be extremely large. Local maxima occur for different polybone placements, sizes, orientations, and depth orderings. Unlike tracking problems where one may know the number of objects, one cannot enumerate and compare all possible model configurations (cf. [19]). As a consequence, the method by which we search the space of polybone models is critical.

Here we use a search strategy that is roughly based on the cascade search developed in [15]. The general idea is that it is useful to keep suboptimal models which have small numbers of polybones in a list of known intermediate states. The search spaces for simpler models are expected to have fewer local maxima, and therefore be easier to search. More complex polybone models are then proposed by elaborating these simpler ones.

---

[4] Before this line-search, the angle parameter θ_k is first rescaled by the radius of the kth polybone to provide a more uniform curvature in the objective function.

Fig. 2. Growth of a single foreground polybone in the first 6 frames (shown in lexicographic order) of a short sequence. The background polybone that is occluded by the foreground layer covers the entire image but is not shown. For the first three frames the two scale parameters, s_x and s_y, are constrained to be equal, afterwhich they are allow to vary independently (see text).

This elaboration process is iterated, generating increasingly more complex models. Revisions in the simpler models may therefore cause distant parts of the search space for more complex models to be explored. This process creates, in a sense, a 'garden web' of paths from simpler models to progressively more complex ones. Our hypothesis is that optimal model(s) can often be found on this web.

In this paper, the suboptimal intermediate states that we retain in our search are the best models we have found so far having particular numbers of polybones. We denote the collection of layered polybone models at frame t by

$$\mathcal{M}(t) = (\mathcal{M}_0(t), \mathcal{M}_1(t), \ldots, \mathcal{M}_{\bar{K}}(t)) , \qquad (17)$$

where $\mathcal{M}_N(t)$ is a list of the best models found at frame t having exactly N foreground polybones and one background polybone, and $\bar{K}$ is a constant specifying the maximum number of foreground polybones to use. The sub-list $\mathcal{M}_N(t)$ is sorted in decreasing order of the objective function $\mathcal{O}(\mathbf{M})$, and is pruned to have at most L models (in the experiments, we used $L = 1$).

To describe the general form of the search strategy, assume that we begin with a partitioned list $\mathcal{M}(t-1)$ of models for frame $t-1$ and an empty list $\mathcal{M}(t)$ for a new frame t. We then use *temporal proposals* to generate seed models (denoted by $\mathbf{S}_t$) for frame t. These temporal proposals arise from the assumed model dynamics suggested by $p(\mathbf{M}_t \mid \mathbf{M}_{t-1})$, for each model $\mathbf{M}_{t-1} \in \mathcal{M}(t-1)$. These seed models are used as initial guesses for the hill-climbing procedure described in Sec. 6. The models found by the hill-climbing are then inserted into $\mathcal{M}(t)$, and if necessary, the sub-lists $\mathcal{M}_N(t)$ are pruned to keep only the best L models with N foreground polybones.

In addition to the temporal proposals there are *revision proposals*, which help explore the space of models. These are similar to temporal proposals, except that they operate on models $\mathbf{M}_t$ at the current time rather than at the previous time. That is, given a model $\mathbf{M}_t \in \mathcal{M}(t)$, a revision proposal generates a seed model $\mathbf{S}_t$ that provides an initial guess for hill-climbing. The resulting model $\tilde{M}_t$ is then inserted back into the partitioned list $\mathcal{M}(t)$. Broadly speaking, useful revisions include *birth and death proposals*, which change the number of polybones, and *depth ordering proposals* which switch the depth orderings among the polybone layers.

Finally, in order to limit the number of complex polybone models considered, we find the optimal model $\mathbf{M}_t^* \in \mathcal{M}(t)$ (i.e. with the maximum value of the objective function $\mathcal{O}(\mathbf{M})$) and then prune all the models with more polybones than $\mathbf{M}_t^*$. The temporal proposals for the next frame are obtained from only those models that remain in $\mathcal{M}(t)$.

Initially, given the first frame at time t_0, each sub-list in $\mathcal{M}(t_0)$ is taken to be empty. Then, given the second frame, one seed model S_{t_0} is proposed that consists of a background polybone with an initial guess for its motion parameters. The background polybone is always taken to cover the entire image. Here we consider simple background motions, and the initial guess of zero motion is sufficient. A parameterized flow model is then fit using the EM-algorithm described in Sec. 6.[5] This produces the initial model $\mathbf{M}_{t_0}$ that is inserted into $\mathcal{M}(t_0)$. Revision proposals are then used to further elaborate $\mathcal{M}_0(t_0)$, afterwhich the models for subsequent frames are obtained as described above.

Our current implementation uses two kinds of proposals, namely *temporal proposals* and *birth proposals*. Given a model $\mathbf{M}_{t-1} \in \mathcal{M}_N(t-1)$, the temporal proposal provides an initial guess, $\mathbf{S}_t$, for the parameters of the corresponding model in the next frame. Here $\mathbf{S}_t$ is generated from $\mathbf{M}_{t-1}$ by warping each polybone (other than the background model) in $\mathbf{M}_{t-1}$ according to the motion parameters for that polybone. The initial guess for the motion in each polybone is obtained from a constant velocity prediction. Notice that temporal proposals do not change the number of polybones in the model, nor their relative depths. Rather they use a simple dynamical model to predict where each polybone will be found in the subsequent frame.

In order to change the number of polybones or find models with different depth relations, we currently rely solely on birth proposals. For a given $\mathbf{M}_t \in \mathcal{M}_N(t)$, the birth proposal computes a sparsely sampled outlier map that represents the probability that the data at each location $\mathbf{x}$ is owned by the outlier process, given all the visible polybones within $\mathbf{M}_t$ at that location. This map is then blurred and downsampled to reduce the influence of isolated outliers. The center location for the new polybone is selected by randomly sampling from this downsampled outlier map. Given this selected location, the initial size of the new polybone is taken to be fixed (we used 16×16), the initial angle is randomly selected from a uniform distribution, the initial motion is taken to be zero, and the relative depth of the new polybone is randomly selected from the range 1 to $N+1$ (i.e. it is inserted in front of the background bone, but otherwise at a random

---

[5] The camera was stationary in all sequences except that in Fig. 2, so only the standard deviation of the motion constraints and the outlier mixing coefficient needed to be fit for the background in these cases. For the Pepsi sequence a translational flow was fit in the background polybone.

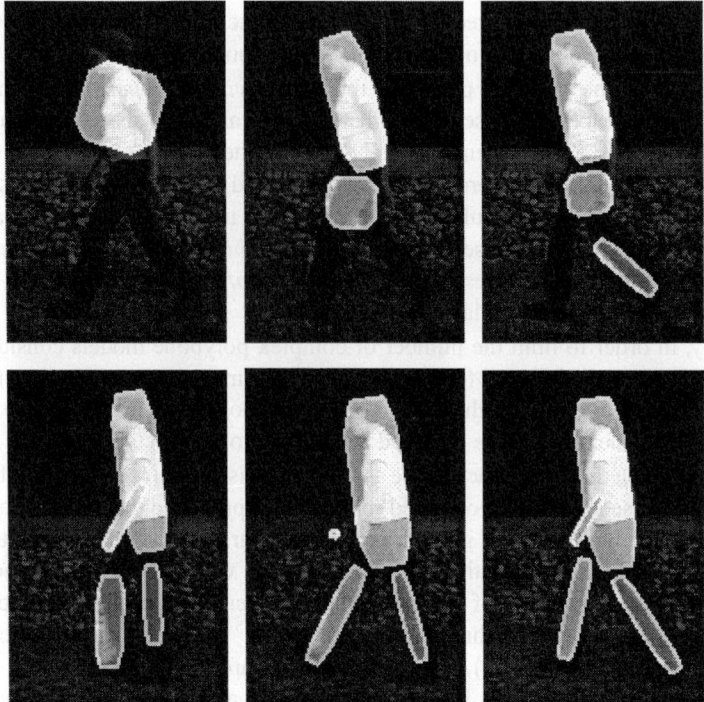

Fig. 3. The development of the optimal known model. The top row shows results for the first three frames. The bottom row shows results for frames 11, 15, and 19.

position in the depth ordering). Thus, the birth proposal produces a seed model S_t that has exactly one more polybone.

8 Examples

The results of the entire process are shown in Fig. 2. Here we limited the maximum number of foreground polybones to one in order to demonstrate the sampling and growth of a single polybone. The image sequence is formed by horizontal camera motion, so that the can is moving horizontally to the left faster than the background. Given the first two frames, the background motion was fit. An initial guess for a foreground polybone was generated by the birth process which, in this case, was sampled from the background motion outliers. The hill-climbing procedure then generated the polybone model shown in Fig. 2 (top-left). This polybone grows in subsequent frames to cover the can. The top of the can has been slightly underestimated since the horizontal structure is consistent with both the foreground and background motions, and the penalty function introduces a bias towards smaller polybones. Conversely, the bottom of the can was overestimated because the motion of the can and the table are consistent in this region. In particular, the end of the table is moving more like the foreground polybone than the background one, and therefore the foreground polybone has been extended to account for this data as well.

A more complex example is shown in Fig. 3, where we allow at most four foreground polybones. Notice that in the first few frames a new polybone is proposed to account for previously unexplained motion data. By the 10th frame the polybones efficiently cover the moving figure. Notice that the polybone covering the arm is correctly interpreted to be in front of the torso when it is moving differently from the torso (see Fig. 3 bottom left and right). Also, at the end of the arm swing (see Fig. 3 bottom middle) the arm is moving with approximately the same speed as the torso. Therefore the polybone covering the torso can also explain the motion of the arm in this region. The size prior causes the polybone on the arm to shrink around only the unexplained region of the hand.

A similar example of the search process is depicted in Fig. 4. In this case the subject walks towards the camera, producing slow image velocities. This makes motion segmentation more difficult than in Fig. 3. To alleviate this we processed every second frame. The top row in Fig. 4 shows the initial proposal generated by the algorithm, and development of a model with two foreground polybones. The two component model persisted until about frame 40 when the subject began to raise their right arm. A third foreground polybone, and then a fourth, are proposed to model the arm motion (frames 40-50). At the end of the sequence the subject is almost stationary and the model dissolves into the background model. This disappearance of polybones demonstrates the preferance for simpler models, as quantified by $q_3(\mathbf{M}_t)$ in (13).

The results on a common test sequence are shown in Fig. 5.[6] The same configuration is used as for the previous examples except, due to the slow motion of the people (especially when they are most distant and heading roughly towards the camera), we processed every fourth frame of the sequence. Shortly after the car appears in the field of view, the system has selected four polybones to cover the car (three can be seen in Fig. 5 (top-left) and the fourth covers a tiny region on the roof). But by frame 822 (five times steps later) the system has found a presumably better model using just two polybones to cover the car. These two polybones persist until the car is almost out of view, at which point a single polybone is deemed optimal. The reason for the persistence of two polybones instead of just one is that the simple spatial form of a single polybone does not provide a sufficiently accurate model of the shape of the car, and also that the similarity motion model does not accurately capture the deformation over the whole region. An important area for future work is to provide a means to elaborate the motion and shape models in this type of situation.

Fig. 5 (middle and bottom) shows that three pedestrians are also detected in this sequence, indicating the flexibility of the representation. Composite images formed from three successive PETS subsequences are shown in Fig. 5(bottom). All of the extracted foreground polybones for the most plausible model have been displayed in one of these three images (recall that only every fourth frame was processed). These composite images show that the car is consistently extracted in the most plausbile model. The leftmost person is initially only sporadically identified (see Fig. 5 bottom-left), but is then consistently located in subsequent frames when the image motion for that person is larger. The other two people are consistently detected (see Fig. 5 bottom middle and right).

---

[6] This sequence is available from the First IEEE International Workshop on Performance Evaluation of Tracking and Surveillance, March, 2000. We selected frames 750 to 1290 from the sequence as the most interesting.

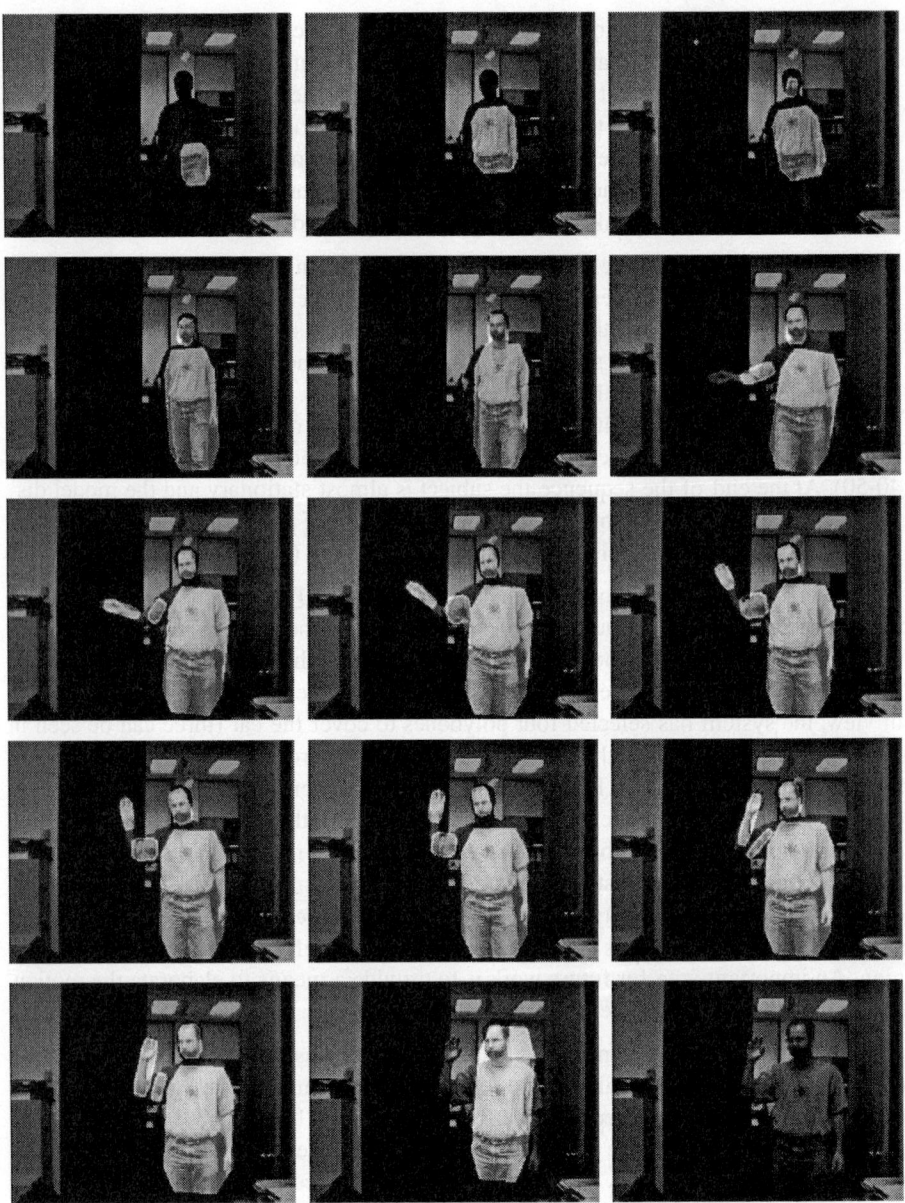

Fig. 4. The optimal known models for frames (top) 0, 2, 4, (second row) 10, 20, 40, (third) 42, 44, 46, (fourth) 48, 50, 60 and (bottom) 70, 80, 90 of the sequence.

9 Conclusions

We have introduced a compositional model for image motion that explicitly represents the spatial extent and relative depths of multiple moving image regions. Each region comprises a parametric shape model and a parametric motion model. The relative depth

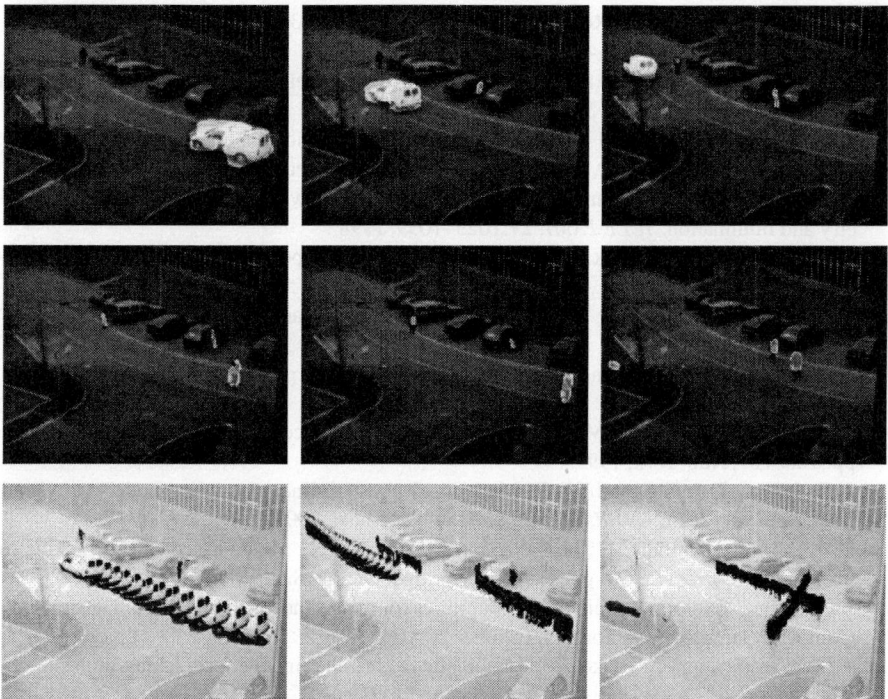

Fig. 5. The optimal models found for the PETS2000 sequence, (top) frames 802, 842, and 882, (middle) 1002, 1042, 1202. The the car, three pedestrians, and bushes blowing in the wind (middle-right) are detected. (bottom) Composite images formed from all the polybones of the optimal models in every fourth frame, for frames (bottom-left) 750 to 850, (bottom-middle) 850 to 1070, and (bottom-right) 1070 to 1290. Note that the car and the pedestrians are consistently detected.

ordering of the regions allows visibility and occlusion relationships to be properly included in the model, and then used during the estimation of the model parameters.

This modelling framework was selected to satisfy two constraints. First, it must be sufficiently expressive to be able to provide at least a preliminary description of the dominant image structure present in typical video sequences. Secondly, a tractable means of automatically estimating the model from image data is essential. We believe that our reported results demonstrate that both of these constraints are satisfied by our polybone models together with the local search technique.

References

1. M. J. Black and A. D. Jepson. EigenTracking: Robust matching and tracking of articulated objects using a view-based representation. *IJCV*, 26:63–84, 1998.
2. C. Bregler and J. Malik. Tracking people with twists and exponential maps. *Proc. IEEE CVPR*, pp. 8–15, Santa Barbara, 1998.
3. T. Cham and J.M. Rehg. A multiple hypothesis approach to figure tracking. *Proc. IEEE CVPR*, vol. II, pp. 239–245, Fort Collins, 1998.
4. T. Darrell and A. Pentland. Cooperative robust estimation using layers of support. *IEEE PAMI*, 17:474–487, 1995.

5. J.S. de Bonet and P. Viola. Roxels: Responsibility weighted 3d volume reconstruction. *Proc. IEEE ICCV*, vol. I, pp. 418–425, Corfu, 1999.
6. A.P. Dempster, N.M. Laird, and D.B. Rubin. Maximum likelihood from incomplete data via the EM algorithm. *J. Royal Stat. Soc. B*, 39:1–38, 1977.
7. J. Deutscher, A. Blake, and I. Reid. Articulated body motion capture by annealed particle filtering. *Proc. IEEE CVPR*, vol. II, pp. 126–133, Hilton Head, 2000.
8. G. D. Hager and P. N. Belhumeur. Efficient region tracking with parametric models of geometry and llumination. *IEEE PAMI*, 27:1025–1039, 1998.
9. S.S. Intille and A.F. Bobick. Recognizing planned, multi-person action. *CVIU*, 81:1077–3142, 2001.
10. M. Irani, B. Rousso, and S. Peleg. Computing occluding and transparent motions. *IJCV*, 12:5–16, 1994.
11. M. Isard and A. Blake. Condensation - conditional density propagation for visual tracking. *IJCV*, 29:2–28, 1998.
12. A. Jepson and M. J. Black. Mixture models for optical flow computation. *Proc. IEEE CVPR*, pp. 760–761, New York, 1993.
13. A.D. Jepson, D.J. Fleet and T.F. El-Maraghi. Robust on-line appearance models for visual tracking. *Proc. IEEE CVPR*, Vol. 1, pp. 415–422, Kauai, 2001.
14. D. Koller, K. Daniilidis, T. Thorhallson, and H.-H. Nagel. Model-based object tracking in traffic scenes. *Proc. ECCV*, pp. 437–452. Springer-Verlag, Santa Marguerita, 1992.
15. J. Listgarten. Exploring qualitative probabilities for image understanding. MSc. Thesis, Dept. Computer Science, Univ. Toronto, October 2000.
16. J. MacCormick and A. Blake. A probabilistic exclusion principle for tracking multiple objects. *Proc IEEE ICCV*, vol. I, pp. 572–578, Corfu, 1999.
17. J. MacCormick and M. Isard. Partitioned sampling, articulated objects, and interface-quality hand tracking. *Proc. ECCV*, vol. II, pp. 3–19, Dublin, 2000.
18. F.G. Meyer and P. Bouthemy. Region-based tracking using affine motion models in long image sequences. *CVGIP: Image Understanding*, 60:119–140, 1994.
19. C. Rasmussen and G.D. Hager. Probabilistic data association methods for tracking complex visual objects. *IEEE PAMI*, 23:560–576, 2001.
20. H. S. Sawhney and S. Ayer. Compact representations of videos through dominant and multiple motion estimation. *IEEE PAMI*, 18:814–831, 1996.
21. H. Sidenbladh, M.J. Black, and D.J. Fleet. Stochastic tracking of 3d human figures using 2d image motion. *Proc. ECCV*, vol. II, pp. 702–718. Springer-Verlag, Dublin 2000.
22. R. Szeliski and P. Golland. Stereo matching with transparency and matting. *IJCV*, 32:45–61, 1999.
23. H. Tao, H.S. Sawhney, and R. Kumar. Dynamic layer representation with applications to tracking. *Proc. IEEE CVPR*, vol. 2, pp. 134–141, Hilton Head, 2000.
24. P.H.S. Torr, A.R. Dick, and R. Cipolla. Layer extraction with a Bayesian model of shapes. *Proc. ECCV*, vol. II, pp. 273–289, Dublin, 2000.
25. N. Vasconcelos and A. Lippman. Empirical Bayesian motion segmentation. *IEEE PAMI*, 23:217–221, 2001.
26. J. Y. A. Wang and E. H. Adelson. Representing moving images with layers. *IEEE Trans. Im. Proc.*, 3:625–638, 1994.
27. Y. Weiss. Smoothness in layers: Motion segmentation using nonparametric mixture estimation. *Proc. IEEE CVPR*, pp. 520–526, Puerto Rico, 1997.
28. Y. Weiss and E. H. Adelson. A unified mixture framework for motion segmentation: Incorporating spatial coherence and estimating the number of models. *Proc. IEEE CVPR*, pp. 321–326, San Francisco, 1996.

Incremental Singular Value Decomposition of Uncertain Data with Missing Values

Matthew Brand

Mitsubishi Electric Research Labs, 201 Broadway, Cambridge 02139 MA, USA

Abstract. We introduce an incremental singular value decomposition (SVD) of incomplete data. The SVD is developed as data arrives, and can handle arbitrary missing/untrusted values, correlated uncertainty across rows or columns of the measurement matrix, and user priors. Since incomplete data does not uniquely specify an SVD, the procedure selects one having minimal rank. For a dense $p \times q$ matrix of low rank r, the incremental method has time complexity $O(pqr)$ and space complexity $O((p+q)r)$—better than highly optimized batch algorithms such as MATLAB's svd(). In cases of missing data, it produces factorings of lower rank and residual than batch SVD algorithms applied to standard missing-data imputations. We show applications in computer vision and audio feature extraction. In computer vision, we use the incremental SVD to develop an efficient and unusually robust subspace-estimating flow-based tracker, and to handle occlusions/missing points in structure-from-motion factorizations.

1 Introduction

Many natural phenomena can be faithfully modeled with multilinear functions, or closely approximated as such. Examples include the combination of lighting and pose [20] and shape and motion [12,3] in image formation, mixing of sources in acoustic recordings [6], and word associations in collections of documents [1,23]. Multilinearity means that a matrix of such a phenomenon's measured effects can be factored into low-rank matrices of (presumed) causes. The celebrated singular value decomposition (SVD) [8] provides a bilinear factoring of a data matrix $\mathbf{M}$,

$$\mathbf{U}_{p \times r} \operatorname{diag}(\mathbf{s}_{r \times 1}) \mathbf{V}_{r \times q}^\top \stackrel{\text{SVD}_r}{\longleftarrow} \mathbf{M}_{p \times q}, \quad r \leq \min(p, q) \tag{1}$$

where $\mathbf{U}$ and $\mathbf{V}$ are unitary orthogonal matrices whose columns give a linear basis for $\mathbf{M}$'s columns and rows, respectively. For low-rank phenomena, $r_{\text{true}} \ll \min(p, q)$, implying a parsimonious explanation of the data. Since r_{true} is often unknown, it is common to wastefully compute a large $r_{\text{approx}} \gg r_{\text{true}}$ SVD and estimate an appropriate smaller value $r_{\text{empirical}}$ from the distribution of singular values in $\mathbf{s}$. All but $r_{\text{empirical}}$ of the smallest singular values in $\mathbf{s}$ are then zeroed to give a "thin" truncated SVD that closely approximates the data. This forms the basis of a broad range of algorithms for data analysis, dimensionality reduction, compression, noise-suppression, and extrapolation.

The SVD is usually computed by a batch $O(pq^2 + p^2q + q^3)$ time algorithm [8], meaning that all the data must be processed at once, and SVDs of very large datasets are essentially unfeasible. Lanczos methods yield thin SVDs in $O(pqr^2)$ time [8], but r_{true}

A. Heyden et al. (Eds.): ECCV 2002, LNCS 2350, pp. 707–720, 2002.
© Springer-Verlag Berlin Heidelberg 2002

should be known in advance since Lanczos methods are known to be inaccurate for the smaller singular values [1]. A more pressing problem is that the SVD requires *complete* data, whereas in many experimental settings some parts of the measurement matrix may be missing, contaminated, or otherwise untrusted. Consequently, a single missing value forces the modeler to discard an entire row or column of the data matrix prior to the SVD. The missing value may be imputed from neighboring values, but such imputations typically mislead the SVD away from the most parsimonious (low-rank) decompositions.

We consider how an SVD may be updated by adding rows and/or columns of data, which may be missing values and/or contaminated with correlated (colored) noise. The size of the data matrix need not be known: The SVD is developed as the data comes in and handles missing values in a manner that minimizes rank. The resulting algorithms have better time and space complexity than full-data batch SVD methods and can produce more informative results (more parsimonious factorings of incomplete data). In the case of dense low-rank matrices, the time complexity is linear in the size and the rank of the data—$O(pqr)$—while the space complexity is sublinear—$O((p+q)r)$.

2 Related Work

SVD updating has a literature spread over three decades [5,4,1,10,7,23] and is generally based on Lanczos methods, symmetric eigenvalue perturbations, or identities similar to equation 2 below. Zha and Simon [23] use such an identity but their update is approximate and requires a dense SVD. Chandrasekaran et alia [7] begin similarly but their update is limited to single vectors and is vulnerable to loss of orthogonality. Levy and Lindenman [14] exploit the relationship between the QR-decomposition and the SVD to incrementally compute the left singular vectors in $O(pqr^2)$ time; if p, q, and r are known in advance and $p \gg q \gg r$, then the expected complexity falls to $O(pqr)$. However, this is also vulnerable to loss of orthogonality and results have only been reported for matrices having a few hundred columns.

None of this literature contemplates missing or uncertain values, except insofar as they can be treated as zeros (e.g., [1]), which is arguably incorrect. In batch-SVD contexts, missing values are usually handled via subspace imputation, using an expectation-maximization-like procedure: Perform an SVD of all complete columns, regress incomplete columns against the SVD to estimate missing values, then re-factor and re-impute the completed data until a fixpoint is reached (e.g., [21]). This is extremely slow (quartic time) and only works if very few values are missing. It has the further demerit that the imputation does not minimize effective rank. Other heuristics simply fill missing values with row- or column-means [19].

In the special case where a matrix $\mathbf{M}$ is nearly dense, its normalized scatter matrix $\Sigma_{m,n} \doteq \langle \mathbf{M}_{i,m} \mathbf{M}_{i,n} \rangle_i$ may be fully dense due to fill-in. In that case Σ's eigenvectors are $\mathbf{M}$'s right singular vectors [13]. However, this method does not lead to the left singular vectors, and it often doesn't work at all because Σ is frequently incomplete as well, with undefined eigenvectors.

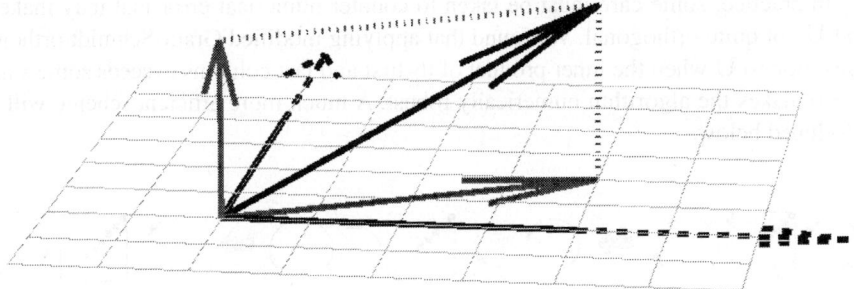

Fig. 1. A vector is decomposed into components within and orthogonal to an SVD-derived subspace. The parallel component causes the singular values and vectors to be rotated (see figure 2), while the orthogonal component increases the rank of the SVD.

3 Updating an SVD

We begin with an existing rank-r SVD as in equation 1. We have a matrix $\mathbf{C}_{p \times c}$ whose columns contain additional multivariate measurements. Let $\mathbf{L} \doteq \mathbf{U}\backslash\mathbf{C} = \mathbf{U}^\top \mathbf{C}$ be the projection of $\mathbf{C}$ onto the orthogonal basis $\mathbf{U}$, also known as its "eigen-coding." Let $\mathbf{H} \doteq (\mathbf{I} - \mathbf{U}\mathbf{U}^\top)\mathbf{C} = \mathbf{C} - \mathbf{U}\mathbf{L}$ to be the component of $\mathbf{C}$ orthogonal to the subspace spanned by $\mathbf{U}$. ($\mathbf{I}$ is the identity matrix.) Finally, let $\mathbf{J}$ be an orthogonal basis of $\mathbf{H}$ and let $\mathbf{K} \doteq \mathbf{J}\backslash\mathbf{H} = \mathbf{J}^\top \mathbf{H}$ be the projection of $\mathbf{C}$ onto the subspace orthogonal to $\mathbf{U}$. For example, $\mathbf{JK} \stackrel{QR}{\Longleftarrow} \mathbf{H}$ could be a QR-decomposition of $\mathbf{H}$. Consider the following identity:

$$[\mathbf{U}\ \mathbf{J}] \begin{bmatrix} \mathrm{diag}(\mathbf{s}) & \mathbf{L} \\ \mathbf{0} & \mathbf{K} \end{bmatrix} \begin{bmatrix} \mathbf{V} & \mathbf{0} \\ \mathbf{0} & \mathbf{I} \end{bmatrix}^\top = [\mathbf{U}\ (\mathbf{I}-\mathbf{U}\mathbf{U}^\top)\mathbf{C}/\mathbf{K}] \begin{bmatrix} \mathrm{diag}(\mathbf{s}) & \mathbf{U}^\top \mathbf{C} \\ \mathbf{0} & \mathbf{K} \end{bmatrix} \begin{bmatrix} \mathbf{V} & \mathbf{0} \\ \mathbf{0} & \mathbf{I} \end{bmatrix}^\top$$

$$= [\mathbf{U}\,\mathrm{diag}(\mathbf{s})\mathbf{V}^\top\ \mathbf{C}] \ =\ [\mathbf{M}\ \mathbf{C}] \qquad (2)$$

Like an SVD, the left and right matrices in the product are unitary and orthogonal. The middle matrix, which we denote $\mathbf{Q}$, is diagonal with a c-column border. To update the SVD we must diagonalize $\mathbf{Q}$. Let

$$\mathbf{U}'\,\mathrm{diag}(\mathbf{s}')\mathbf{V}'^\top \stackrel{SVD}{\Longleftarrow} \mathbf{Q} \qquad (3)$$

$$\mathbf{U}'' \leftarrow [\mathbf{U}\ \mathbf{J}]\,\mathbf{U}'; \quad \mathbf{s}'' \leftarrow \mathbf{s}'; \quad \mathbf{V}'' \leftarrow \begin{bmatrix} \mathbf{V} & \mathbf{0} \\ \mathbf{0} & \mathbf{I} \end{bmatrix} \mathbf{V}' \qquad (4)$$

Then the updated SVD is

$$\mathbf{U}''\,\mathrm{diag}(\mathbf{s}'')\mathbf{V}''^\top = [\mathbf{U}\,\mathrm{diag}(\mathbf{s})\mathbf{V}^\top\ \mathbf{C}] = [\mathbf{M}\ \mathbf{C}].$$

The whole update procedure takes $O((p+q)r^2 + pc^2)$ time[1], spent mostly in the subspace rotations of equation 4. To add rows one simply swaps $\mathbf{U}$ for $\mathbf{V}$ and $\mathbf{U}''$ for $\mathbf{V}''$.

---
[1] An SVD of an $r \times r$ matrix would ordinarily take $O(r^3)$ time but since $\mathbf{Q}$ is a c-bordered diagonal matrix, it can be rotated into bidiagonal form in $O(cr^2)$ time [22], and thence diagonalized

In practice, some care must be taken to counter numerical error that may make **J** and **U** not quite orthogonal. We found that applying modified Gram-Schmidt orthogonalization to **U** when the inner product of its first and last columns exceeds some small $\epsilon \approx 0$ makes the algorithm numerically robust. A much more efficient scheme will be developed below.

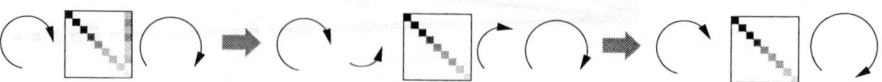

Fig. 2. Visualization of the SVD update in equation 2. The quasi-diagonal **Q** matrix at left is diagonalized and the subspaces are counter-rotated to preserve equality.

3.1 Automatic Truncation

Define $v \doteq \sqrt{\det(\mathbf{K}^\top \mathbf{K})}$, which is the volume of **C** that is orthogonal to **U**. If $v < \epsilon$ for some small ϵ near the limits of machine precision, then **J** must have zero norm, since there is no orthogonal component (else **J** is contaminated by numerical or measurement noise). In this case the noise should be suppressed by setting $\mathbf{K} \leftarrow 0$ prior to the SVD in equation 3. Since the resulting SVD will have r rather than $r+1$ singular values, equation 4 can be replaced with the truncated forms

$$\mathbf{U}'' \leftarrow \mathbf{U}\mathbf{U}'_{1:r,1:r}; \qquad \mathbf{s}'' \leftarrow \mathbf{s}'_{1:r}; \qquad \mathbf{V}'' \leftarrow \mathbf{V}'_{:,1:r}.$$

This automatically sizes the SVD is to the effective rank of the data matrix.

To explicitly suppress measurement noise, one truncates the completed update to suppress singular values below a noise threshold, derived from the user's knowledge of noise levels in the measurements.

The update procedure enables online SVDs and SVDs of datasets whose size defeats non-incremental SVD algorithms. The update can be used to add individual vectors, batches of vectors, or to merge SVDs from partitions of the data. We will now concentrate on the vector update and leverage it into linear-time and missing-value SVD algorithms.

4 Fast Incremental SVD of Low-Rank Matrices

A useful special case is when $\mathbf{c} = \mathbf{C}$ is a single column vector, for which scalar $k = \mathbf{K} = \|\mathbf{c} - \mathbf{U}\mathbf{U}^\top \mathbf{c}\|$ and vector $\mathbf{j} = \mathbf{J} = (\mathbf{c} - \mathbf{U}\mathbf{U}^\top \mathbf{c})/k$ can be computed very quickly[2]. To compute a full SVD by adding rows and/or columns, we take the first measurement

---

in an $O(r^2)$ time bidiagonal SVD [9]. If $c = 1$, the eigenvalues $\mathbf{s}'^2$ and eigenvectors $\mathbf{U}'$ of arrowhead matrix $\mathbf{Q}^\top \mathbf{Q}$ can be computed in $O(r^2)$ time [17]; the remaining singular vectors can also be recovered in $O(r^2)$.

[2] In practice, some care should be taken to order operations in computing k to get the most accurate result from floating point machines. We use $k \leftarrow \mathbf{c}^\top \mathbf{c} - 2\mathbf{L}^\top \mathbf{L} + (\mathbf{U}\mathbf{L})^\top (\mathbf{U}\mathbf{L})$.

$m \in M$ and set $s \leftarrow \|m\|$, $U \leftarrow m/\|m\|$, $V \leftarrow 1$. Then we iterate the update procedure above with truncation. The total procedure takes $O(pqr^2)$ time, which is essentially linear in the number of elements in M. This can be substantially faster than the $O(pq^2)$ time of a batch SVD when the rank $r \ll q$. The advantage over the Lanczos methods is that we now have an online algorithm whose in-memory storage requirements are reduced from $O(pq)$—the size of the data—to $O(r(p+q+r))$—the size of the results.

4.1 Preserving Orthogonality and Reducing Complexity

Because U and V are tall thin matrices, repeatedly rotating their column spaces makes loss of orthogonality through numerical error an issue. Instead of updating large matrices, we may keep U, V, U', V' separate and only update the small matrices U', V', with U and V growing strictly by appends.

In this fastest incarnation of SVD updating, we build an extended SVD,

$$\mathbf{U}_{p\times r}\mathbf{U}'_{r\times r}\operatorname{diag}(\mathbf{s}_{r\times 1})\mathbf{V}'^{\top}_{r\times r}\mathbf{V}^{\top}_{q\times r} \stackrel{\text{SVD}_r}{\longleftarrow} \mathbf{M},$$

with orthogonal U, U', UU' and VV'. The large outer matrices are built by appending columns to U and rows to V, while rotations of the subspace are handled by transforms of the much smaller U', V' matrices. This makes the update much faster and more robust to numerical error: Let Q and j be defined as above, and let A, B diagonalize Q as $A \operatorname{diag}(s) B^\top \stackrel{\text{SVD}}{\longleftarrow} Q$. The left-hand side is updated $U' \leftarrow U'A$ when the rank does not increase, otherwise $U' \leftarrow \begin{bmatrix}U' & 0\\ 0 & 1\end{bmatrix}A$ and $U \leftarrow [U, j]$. Due to its small size, U' loses orthogonality very slowly. Numerical error can be contained by occasionally re-orthogonalizing U' via modified Gram-Schmidt when the inner product of its oldest (first) column with its newest (last) column is more than some small ϵ away from zero.

The right side is somewhat more complicated because we are adding rows to V but must guarantee that VV' is orthogonal. To do so, we will also have to calculate and update the pseudo-inverse V'^+. Let r be the rank of the SVD prior to the update. When the rank increases, the right-hand side update is simply

$$\mathbf{V} \leftarrow \begin{bmatrix}\mathbf{V}' & 0\\ 0 & 1\end{bmatrix}, \quad \text{then } \mathbf{V}' \leftarrow \begin{bmatrix}\mathbf{V}' & 0\\ 0 & 1\end{bmatrix}\mathbf{B}, \quad \text{then } \mathbf{V}'^+ \leftarrow \mathbf{B}^\top\begin{bmatrix}\mathbf{V}'^+ & 0\\ 0 & 1\end{bmatrix}.$$

When the rank does not increase, we split $\mathbf{B} \to \begin{bmatrix}\mathbf{W}\\ \mathbf{w}\end{bmatrix}$ where matrix $\mathbf{W} \doteq \mathbf{B}_{(1:r,1:r)}$ is a linear transform that will be applied to V', and row-vector $\mathbf{w} \doteq \mathbf{B}_{(r+1,1:r)}$ is the eigen-space encoding of the new data vector. The update is

$$\mathbf{V}' =\leftarrow \mathbf{V}'\mathbf{W}, \quad \text{then } \mathbf{V}'^+ \leftarrow \mathbf{W}^+\mathbf{V}'^+, \quad \text{then } \mathbf{V} \leftarrow \begin{bmatrix}\mathbf{V}\\ \mathbf{V}'^+\mathbf{w}\end{bmatrix}.$$

It can be verified algebraically that $\mathbf{V}_{new}\mathbf{V}'_{new}$ is identical to the first r columns of $\begin{bmatrix}\mathbf{V}_{old}\mathbf{V}'_{old} & 0\\ 0 & 1\end{bmatrix}\mathbf{B}$.

Remarkably, W^+ can be computed in $O(r^2)$ time using the identity $\mathbf{W}^+ = (\mathbf{I} + \mathbf{w}^\top\mathbf{w}/(1 - \mathbf{w}\mathbf{w}^\top))\mathbf{W}^\top$ (when $\begin{bmatrix}\mathbf{W}\\ \mathbf{w}\end{bmatrix}^\top\begin{bmatrix}\mathbf{W}\\ \mathbf{w}\end{bmatrix} = \mathbf{I}$; see appendix 1 for the proof). This can be restructured to eliminate the $O(r^3)$ matrix-matrix product in favor of an $O(r^2)$ vector-vector outer product:

$$\mathbf{W}^+ = \mathbf{W}^\top + (\mathbf{w}^\top/(1 - \mathbf{w}\mathbf{w}^\top)))(\mathbf{w}\mathbf{W}^\top).$$

This eliminates the costliest steps of the update—rotation and re-orthogonalization of $\mathbf{U}, \mathbf{V}$—and requires that we only keep $\mathbf{U}'$ orthogonal. The time complexity falls to $O(pr^2)$ for the r rank-increasing updates and $O(pr+r^3)$ for the $q-r$ non rank-increasing updates, with an overall complexity of $O(pqr + qr^3) = O(pqr)$, assuming that the rank is small relative to the dimensionality of the samples, specifically $r = O(\sqrt{p})$. For a high-dimensional low-rank matrices, we effectively have a *linear-time* SVD algorithm.

4.2 Subspace Tracking

For nonstationary data streams, the best we can do is track an evolving subspace $\mathbf{U}$. In the incremental SVD, this is neatly and inexpensively accomplished between updates by decaying the singular values $\mathbf{s} \leftarrow \gamma \mathbf{s}$; $0 < \gamma < 1$. All updates of $\mathbf{V}$ are simply dropped.

5 Missing Data

Consider adding a vector $\mathbf{c}$ with missing values. In our implementation, these are indicated by setting entries in $\mathbf{c}$ to the IEEE754 floating point value *NaN* (not-a-number). Partition $\mathbf{c}$ into $\mathbf{c}_\bullet$ and $\mathbf{c}_\circ$, vectors of the known and unknown values in $\mathbf{c}$, respectively, and let $\mathbf{U}_\bullet, \mathbf{U}_\circ$ be the corresponding rows of $\mathbf{U}$. Imputation of the missing values via the normal equation

$$\hat{\mathbf{c}}_\circ \leftarrow \mathbf{U}_\circ \operatorname{diag}(\mathbf{s})(\operatorname{diag}(\mathbf{s})\mathbf{U}_\bullet^\top \mathbf{U}_\bullet \operatorname{diag}(\mathbf{s}))^+(\operatorname{diag}(\mathbf{s})\mathbf{U}_\bullet^\top \mathbf{c}_\bullet) = \mathbf{U}_\circ \operatorname{diag}(\mathbf{s})(\mathbf{U}_\bullet \operatorname{diag}(\mathbf{s}))^+ \mathbf{c}_\bullet, \quad (5)$$

yields the completed vector $\hat{\mathbf{c}}$ that lies the fewest standard deviations from the origin, with respect to the density of data seen thus far ($\mathbf{X}^+$ denotes pseudo-inverse). Substituting equation 5 into the $\mathbf{Q}$ matrix yields

$$\mathbf{Q} = \begin{bmatrix} \operatorname{diag}(\mathbf{s}) & \mathbf{U}^\top \hat{\mathbf{c}} \\ 0 & k \end{bmatrix} = \begin{bmatrix} \operatorname{diag}(\mathbf{s}) & \operatorname{diag}(\mathbf{s})(\mathbf{U}_\bullet \operatorname{diag}(\mathbf{s}))^+ \mathbf{c}_\bullet \\ 0 & \|\mathbf{c}_\bullet - \mathbf{U}_\bullet \operatorname{diag}(\mathbf{s})(\mathbf{U}_\bullet \operatorname{diag}(\mathbf{s}))^+ \mathbf{c}_\bullet)\| \end{bmatrix}, \quad (6)$$

where $\mathbf{U}^\top \hat{\mathbf{c}}$ is the projection of the vector onto the left singular vectors and k is the distance of the vector to that subspace. As one might expect, with missing data it is rare that $k > 0$. In the worst case, imputation raises the per-update complexity to $O(pr^3)$, but we find in practice that the per-update run time stays closer to $O(pr^2)$, because with missing data the pseudo-inverse problem tends to be small and thus dominated by the problem of rediagonalizing $\mathbf{Q}$.

5.1 Minimizing Rank Growth

The importance of the imputation in equation 5 is that it minimizes k. We show here that this in turn controls the effective rank of the updated SVD:

Theorem 1. *Minimizing k maximizes concentration of variance in the top singular values.*

Proof. Denoting the pre-update singular values as $s_i \in \mathbf{s}$, elements of the $\mathbf{Q}$ matrix as $Q_{i,j} \in \mathbf{Q}$, and the post-update singular values of $\mathbf{Q}$ as σ_i, we compute the determinant of the new singular value matrix:

$$k \prod_i^r s_i^2 = \prod_i^{r+1} Q_{i,i}^2 = \det(\mathbf{Q}^\top \mathbf{Q}) = \prod_i^{r+1} \sigma_i^2 = \exp 2 \sum_i^{r+1} \log \sigma_i. \quad (7)$$

The second equality follows from the special sparsity structure of $\mathbf{Q}$. This shows that minimizing k is equivalent to minimizing the log-volume ($\sum_i \log \sigma_i$) of the post-update singular value matrix, which is half the log-volume of the completed data's scatter matrix. Since the amount of total variance in the singular value matrix is lower-bounded by the variance in the known data values, by the log-sum inequality, the only way to minimize the log-volume is to concentrate the variance in a few dominant singular values[3]. Consequently equation 5 minimizes growth of the effective rank in the updated SVD. QED.

In a related forthcoming paper, we show how these methods can be extended to rapidly factor very large matrices (e.g. 5000 × 5000) in which more that 95% of the elements are missing. In such cases the minimal rank growth property plays a very important role in guaranteeing a parsimonious model of the data. We show that this translates into considerable improvements over the state-of-the-art in genetic classification and econometric prediction tasks.

6 Uncertainty, Priors, and Posteriors

In experimental settings the columns of $\mathbf{M}$ are uncertain in the sense that they are samples from a distribution. When the distribution is gaussian and its covariance Σ is known (often the case in vision), the eigen-basis $\Omega \Lambda \Omega^\top \stackrel{\text{eig}}{\Longleftarrow} \Sigma$ enables a directionally weighted least-squares solution for the SVD that maximizes the likelihood $p(\mathbf{M}|\mathbf{U},\mathbf{S},\mathbf{V}) \propto e^{-\operatorname{trace}(\mathbf{R}^\top \Sigma^{-1} \mathbf{R})}$ with respect to reconstruction residual $\mathbf{R} \doteq \mathbf{U}\operatorname{diag}(\mathbf{s})\mathbf{V}^\top - \mathbf{M}$. Let $\mathbf{R}' \doteq \Lambda^{-1/2} \Omega^\top \mathbf{R}$. Then $\operatorname{trace}(\mathbf{R}'^\top \mathbf{R}') = \operatorname{trace}(\mathbf{R}^\top \Sigma^{-1} \mathbf{R})$, which is to say that the left-handed *certainty warp* $\Lambda^{-1/2} \Omega^\top$ rotates and scales $\mathbf{M}$ to make its uncertainty or noise model gaussian i.i.d. Therefore the problem can be solved as

$$\mathbf{U}'\operatorname{diag}(\mathbf{s}')\mathbf{V}'^\top \stackrel{\text{SVD}}{\Longleftarrow} \Lambda^{-1/2} \Omega^\top \mathbf{M} \quad (8)$$

$$\mathbf{U}\operatorname{diag}(\mathbf{s})\mathbf{V}''^\top \stackrel{\text{SVD}}{\Longleftarrow} \Omega \Lambda^{1/2} \mathbf{U}' \operatorname{diag}(\mathbf{s}'); \qquad \mathbf{V} \leftarrow \mathbf{V}' \mathbf{V}''. \quad (9)$$

Equation 8 is an SVD in the i.i.d. certainty-warped space. The product in equation 9 unwarps[4] the results and its $O(pr^2)$ SVD restores orthogonality to the unwarped results $\mathbf{U}\operatorname{diag}(\mathbf{s})\mathbf{V}^\top$.

---

[3] Other imputation schemes minimize the entire rightmost column in $\mathbf{Q}$ (containing both the projection and the distance) thereby minimizing the trace norm $\operatorname{trace}(\mathbf{Q}^\top \mathbf{Q}) = \sum_i^{r+1} \sigma_i^2$, which actually encourages the spread of variance over many singular values.

[4] Irani & Anandan [12] developed certainty warps for SVD but do not consider unwarping and leave the result "determined up to an unknown affine transformation."

A gaussian subspace prior $p_\mathbf{U}(\mathbf{U}, \mathbf{S}, \mathbf{V}) \propto e^{-\text{trace}((\mathbf{U}-\mu_\mathbf{U})^\top \Sigma_\mathbf{U}^{-1}(\mathbf{U}-\mu_\mathbf{U}))}$ can be accommodated as another least-squares constraint simply by appending its own certainty-warped mean to the certainty-warped data columns, provided that all are rotated back into the same coordinate frame. equations 8–9 then become

$$\mathbf{U}' \operatorname{diag}(\mathbf{s}') \mathbf{V}'^\top \stackrel{\text{SVD}}{\Leftarrow} [\Omega \Lambda^{-1/2} \Omega^\top \mathbf{M}, \ \Omega_\mathbf{U} \Lambda_\mathbf{U}^{-1/2} \Omega_\mathbf{U}^\top \mu_\mathbf{U}] \tag{10}$$

$$\mathbf{V}'' \mathbf{F} \stackrel{\text{QR}}{\Leftarrow} \mathbf{V}'_{1:p,:}; \quad \mathbf{U} \operatorname{diag}(\mathbf{s}) \mathbf{V}''' \stackrel{\text{SVD}}{\Leftarrow} \Omega \Lambda^{1/2} \Omega^\top \mathbf{U}' \operatorname{diag}(\mathbf{s}') \mathbf{F}^\top; \quad \mathbf{V} \leftarrow \mathbf{V}'' \mathbf{V}''' \tag{11}$$

equation 10 calculates an SVD of data and prior, both warped into i.i.d. space. equation 11 drops the added column from $\mathbf{V}'^\top$ and reorthogonalizes in an $O(pq)$ QR downdate, then unwarps $\mathbf{U}'$ and reorthogonalizes in $O(pr^2)$ time to yield the maximum *a posteriori* (MAP) estimate.

In an incremental setting, each data vector must be warped according to $\mathbf{c}' \leftarrow \Lambda^{-1/2} \Omega^\top \mathbf{c}$ (or $\mathbf{c}' \leftarrow \Omega \Lambda^{-1/2} \Omega^\top \mathbf{c}$ if there is a prior) before it is incorporated into the SVD. After the last update, the final SVD is unwarped using equation 9 or equation 11. When the new vector $\mathbf{c}$ is both incomplete and uncertain, it cannot be warped until the missing elements are imputed. First we must *unwarp* the basis $\mathbf{U}$ to perform the imputation,

$$\hat{\mathbf{c}}_\circ \leftarrow (\Omega \Lambda^{1/2} \mathbf{U})_\circ (\Omega \Lambda^{1/2} \mathbf{U})_\bullet \backslash \mathbf{c}_\bullet), \tag{12}$$

then warp the completed $\hat{\mathbf{c}}$ and incorporate it into the SVD. Unless the covariance is diagonal, certainty warps require column-wise updating with at least some complete columns.

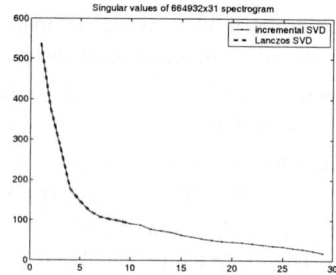

Fig. 3. Singular values from a very large SVD of dense audio data agree with the available Lanczos estimates.

7 Example Applications

7.1 Eigen-Coding

To test the numerical stability of our algorithm, we factored and eigen-coded a 664932×31 matrix containing a 31-band constant-Q spectrogram of roughly 2 hours of audio for a music classification study [6]. We also used matlab's built-in Lanczos thin SVD to get

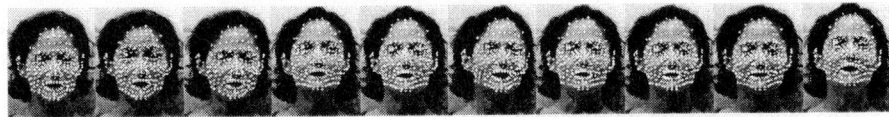

Fig. 4. Every 300th frame from a 3000-frame sequence tracked via rank-constrained optical flow with incremental SVD. Dots are superimposed on the video by the tracker.

the first 10 singular values (Lanczos estimates of small singular values are unreliable). These agreed with our results to 10 digits; the angle between the computed subspaces was a negligible 2×10^{-8} (see figure 3).

7.2 Subspace Optical Flow

The use of rank-constraints to regularize rigid-motion optical flow at many points in many frames was first introduced by Irani [11], and the general method has been extended to a variety of projective and motion models. Let $\mathbf{P}_{2F \times N}$ be the image projections of N points on a 3D surface viewed in F frames, arranged with horizontal and vertical projections on alternating rows. The main insight is that there is an upper rank-bound $r \geq \text{rank}(\mathbf{P})$, where r can be determined from inspection of the combined motion/projection model. Algebraically, it follows that $dr \geq \text{rank}(\mathbf{P}^{(d)})$ [11,3], where the vector-transpose operator $[]^{(d)}$ partitions a matrix into d-element vertical groups and transposes the groups [15]. This connects to optical flow through the premise that intensity variations through time time are locally linear in surface motion, consequently rank constraints apply directly to measured intensity gradients $\mathbf{Y} = \mathbf{X} \frac{d}{dt} \mathbf{P}^{(2)}$, which should have rank $2r$. In this context, it is useful to compute temporal intensity variations $\mathbf{Y}_{2F \times N}$ and spatial intensity variations $\mathbf{X}_{2F \times 2F}$ in the Kanade-Lucas-Tomasi normal-flow framework, because $\mathbf{X}$ may be understood as both the *precision matrix* of the flow estimate [2] and the *covariance matrix* of the uncertainty in $\mathbf{Y}$ [3]. It follows immediately that the certainty-warp methods in section 6 give the *optimal* rank-reduction of $\mathbf{Y}$ with regard to the information in $\mathbf{X}$.

Irani's subspace optical flow algorithm sweeps a W-frame temporal window over an image sequence: In each window of frames, $\mathbf{Y}, \mathbf{X}$ are measured at estimated correspondences from a reference frame. $\mathbf{Y}$ is rank-reduced to rank $2r$, then divided by $\mathbf{X}$ to estimate the flow, which is in turn rank-reduced to rank r and used to refine the correspondences. This iterates to convergence, and the window advances one frame. Many large SVDs must be computed per frame. We found that *most of this computation can be eliminated in favor of incremental* SVDs: a rank-$2r$ SVD of gradients $\mathbf{Y}$ and a rank-r SVD of correspondences $\mathbf{P}$. In fact, all that is needed are the right subspaces (singular vectors) and singular values of these two SVDs. When new measurements $\mathbf{Y}$ are made, they are incorporated into the rank-$2r$ gradient SVD, rank-reduced w.r.t. the updated subspace, divided by $\mathbf{X}$ to obtain flow, and cumulatively summed to obtain correspondences $\mathbf{P}^{(2)}$. These are then vector-transposed to $\mathbf{P}$ and similarly incorporated into the smaller rank-r SVD and rank-reduced w.r.t. its subspace.[5] When the flow has converged within a temporal window, the SVDs are permanently updated with the trusted correspondences, and the window advances.

The most important advantage of this method is that as the window advances, the SVDs accumulate information about how the points have moved and thereby "learn" a good basis for the surface being tracked. The tracker gets better and better, converging faster and faster until the SVDs need not be updated at all while processing a window; new measurements can be rank-reduced merely by projection onto the subspaces and then "unprojection" back to measurement space. The SVDs may be updated at window advances, but once the scene has exhibited most of its range of motions all updates become unnecessary. To automatically switch from SVD-based rank-reduction to projection-based rank-reduction, we monitor the angle between each newly updated subspace and an old subspace. When the subspace angle falls below a small threshold ϵ we may safely assume that the updates are not introducing new information about the range of motions exhibited by the scene.

Figure 4 shows some frames from a 3000-image sequence tracked in this manner using nonrigid-motion rank constraints derived by [3]. Please view the accompanying video, which shows every 6th frame with synthetic tracking dots superimposed on the original images. The rank was $r = 15$ and the temporal window size was $W = 31$ frames. The Irani tracker, modified to use the same rank constraints, "falls off" the surface after the first 290 frames, but survives another 220 frames if also modified to use certainty warps as per section 6. The Irani tracker required 5 iterations per window; the incremental SVD tracker performed well with 2 iterations per window and ceased SVD updates entirely roughly 900 frames into the sequence. We also note that once the subspaces are up to full rank (r and $2r$), the incremental subspace flow algorithm works quite well with temporal window sizes as small as one frame.

It is also worth noting that if occlusions are detected (e.g., see below), the imputative update can be used to continue tracking the unoccluded points while estimating the motion of the occluded points.

7.3 Structure from Motion with Occlusions

The problem of occluded points in (rigid) structure-from-motion factorizations have traditionally been handled through iterative methods [18,16]. Here we use the incremental imputative SVD to solve the same problem in a nonrigid context in a single pass through the data—and lower time complexity.

The subspace tracker was used to track points on a face in 150 frames of video. A recently developed SVD-based nonrigid factorization was used to factor the 2D motions into 3D rotations, translations, 3D shape and a linear basis set of 3D shape deformations, and per-frame deformation weights [3]. The K-mode forward model is

$$\mathbf{P}_{2F \times N} = \mathbf{M}_{2F \times 3K} \mathbf{S}_{3K \times N} \oplus \mathbf{T}_{2F \times 1} = [\searrow_f \mathbf{R}_f](\mathbf{S}^{(3)} \mathbf{C}_{K \times F})^{(3)} \oplus \mathbf{T}$$

---

[5] Some of the efficiency is lost because the updated subspaces must be discarded until the algorithm convergest to trusted correspondences and handling the uncertainty in $\mathbf{Y}$ obliges us to make an extra SVD, but we end up doing many small $O(Nr^2)$ or $O(NWr)$ SVDs rather than many large $O(NW^2)$ SVDs per frame.

Fig. 5. Video frames with profile views synthesized from a structure-from-motion analysis of the 70×80 pixel facial region. The profiles are mirror images except for differences in recovered 3D structure. The profiles on the left have poor structure between the mouth and nose because occlusion artifacts in the tracking were correlated with head nods. The profiles on the right have better shape from the tip of the nose to the top of the mouth because incomplete SVD was used to handle occlusions in the 3D reconstruction.

where Shape basis tensor, deformation Coefficients, Rotations, and Translations can be determined from F frames of N Points viewed in weak perspective. (Each $\mathbf{R}_f$ is the top two rows of a rotation matrix.) Both $\mathbf{P}$ and its precision matrix (inverse covariance matrix) $\mathbf{X}_{DF \times DF}$ are calculated from optical flow as described above.

The recovered shape was somewhat flawed because occlusions of the nostrils by the nose contaminated the tracking. The rank constraints cause the tracker to keep the nostril points below the nose tip point, even when they are occluded. This exaggerates the apparent motion of the nostrils and leading to overestimated depth estimates of the upper lip and underside of the nose. These occlusions can be detected in 2D by Delaunay-triangulating the points in a reference frame and watching for edge-crossings in the Delaunay mesh as the points move in time. The 3D factorization gives depth estimates that indicate which points are occluders and which are occluded. We estimated occlusions and near-occlusions and the corresponding entries in the matrix of tracking data were obliterated (set to *NaN*). The incomplete data was re-factored using incremental SVD with certainty warps, resulting in an improved 3D linear shape basis with a properly shaped nose and a better fit to the video (see figure 5).

8 Summary

We have examined the problem of finding good low-rank subspace models of datasets that may be extremely large, partly or mostly incomplete, contaminated with colored noise, and possibly even nonstationary. By combining an update rule with careful management of numerical noise, rank-minimizing imputations, and uncertainty transforms for MAP inference (with respect to measurement noise and user priors), we developed fast, accurate, and parsimonious online SVD methods, with better time/space complexity than widely used batch algorithms. This leads to fast online algorithms for vision tasks such as recovery of eigen-spaces, semi-dense optical flow on nonrigid surfaces with occusions, and automatic handling of occlusions in structure-from-motion.

Acknowledgments. Thanks to M. Casey for suggesting the audio problem and providing data.

References

1. Michael W. Berry. Large scale singular value computations. *International Journal of Supercomputer Applications*, 6:13–49, 1992.
2. Stan Birchfeld. Derivation of Kanade-Lucas-Tomasi tracking equation. Web-published manuscript at http://robotics.stanford.edu/~birch/klt/, 1996.
3. Matthew Brand. 3D morphable models from video. In *Proc. CVPR01*, 2001.
4. J. R. Bunch and C. P. Nielsen. Updating the singular value decomposition. *Numer. Math.*, 31:111–129, 1978.
5. P. Businger. Updating a singular value decomposition. *BIT*, 10:376–385, 1970.
6. Michael A. Casey. MPEG-7 sound-recognition tools. *IEEE Transactions on Circuits and Systems for Video Technology*, 11(6), June 2001.

7. S. Chandrasekaran, B. S. Manjunath, Y. F. Wang, J. Winkeler, and H. Zhang. An eigenspace update algorithm for image analysis. *Graphical models and image processing: GMIP*, 59(5):321–332, 1997.
8. Gene Golub and Arthur van Loan. *Matrix Computations*. Johns Hopkins U. Press, 1996.
9. Benedikt Großer and Bruno Lang. An $O(n^2)$ algorithm for the bidiagonal SVD. Technical Report BUGHW-SC 2000/4, University of Wuppertal Department of Mathematics, 2000.
10. M. Gu and S. C. Eisenstat. A stable and fast algorithm for updating the singular value decomposition. Tech. Report YALEU/DCS/RR-966, Department of Computer Science, Yale University, New Haven, CT, 1993.
11. Michal Irani. Multi-frame optical flow estimation using subspace constraints. In *Proc. ICCV*, 1999.
12. Michal Irani and P. Anandan. Factorization with uncertainty. In *Proc. European Conf. Computer Vision*, 2000.
13. J.E. Jackson. *A user's guide to principal components*. Wiley, 1991.
14. A. Levy and M. Lindenbaum. Sequential karhunenloeve basis extraction and its application to images. Technical Report CIS9809, Technion, 1998.
15. Jan R. Magnus and Heinz Neudecker. *Matrix differential calculus with applications in statistics and econometrics*. Wiley, 1999.
16. D.D. Morris and T. Kanade. A unified factorization algorithm for points, line segments and planes with uncertainty models. In *Proc. Sixth ICCV*, pages 696–702, Bombay, 1998.
17. D.P. O'Leary and G.W. Stewart. Computing the eigenvalues and eigenvectors of arrowhead matrices. Technical Report CS-TR-2203/UMIACS-TR-89-22, University of Maryland Department of Computer Science, February 1989.
18. Conrad Poelman and Takeo Kanade. A paraperspective factorization method for shape and motion recovery. Technical Report CMU-CS-93-219, Computer Science Department, Carnegie Mellon University, Pittsburgh, PA, December 1993.
19. B. M. Sarwar, G. Karypis, J. A. Konstan, and J. Riedl. Application of dimensionality reduction in recommender system—a case study. In *ACM WebKDD 2000 Web Mining for E-Commerce Workshop*. ACM Press, 2000.
20. J. B. Tenenbaum and W. T. Freeman. Separating style and content with bilinear models. *Neural Computation*, 12:1247 – 1283, 2000.
21. Olga Troyanskaya, Michael Cantor, Gavin Sherlock, Pat Brown, Trevor Hastie, Robert Tibshirani, David Botstein, and Russ B. Altman. Missing value estimation methods for DNA microarrays. *BioInformatics*, 17:1–6, 2001.
22. S. van Huffel and H. Park. Efficient reduction algorithms for bordered band matrices. *Numerical Linear Algebra with Applications*, 2(2), 1995.
23. Hongyuan Zha and Horst D. Simon. On updating problems in latent semantic indexing. *SIAM Journal on Scientific Computing*, 21(2):782–791, 1999.

A Pseudo-Inverse of a Submatrix of an Orthogonal Matrix

Lemma 1. *Let* $\mathbf{B} = \begin{bmatrix}\mathbf{W}\\\mathbf{Y}\end{bmatrix}$ *have orthogonal columns, such that* $\mathbf{B}^\top\mathbf{B} = \mathbf{W}^\top\mathbf{W} + \mathbf{Y}^\top\mathbf{Y} = \mathbf{I}$. *Then*

$$\mathbf{W}^+ = \mathbf{W}^\top + \mathbf{Y}^\top(\mathbf{I} - \mathbf{Y}\mathbf{Y}^\top)^+\mathbf{Y}\mathbf{W}^\top$$

and furthermore if $\mathbf{y} = \mathbf{Y}$ *is a row vector, then*

$$\mathbf{W}^+ = \mathbf{W}^\top + \frac{\mathbf{y}\mathbf{y}^\top}{1 - \mathbf{y}^\top\mathbf{y}}\mathbf{W}^\top$$

Proof. Define $\mathbf{Z} = \mathbf{Y}^\top \mathbf{Y}$.

$$\begin{aligned}
\mathbf{W}^+ &= \mathbf{W}^+ \mathbf{W}^{-\top} \mathbf{W}^\top \\
&= (\mathbf{W}^\top \mathbf{W})^+ \mathbf{W}^\top \\
&= (\mathbf{I} + (\mathbf{W}^\top \mathbf{W})^+ - \mathbf{I}) \mathbf{W}^\top \\
&= \mathbf{W}^\top + (\mathbf{I} - \mathbf{W}^\top \mathbf{W} - \mathbf{I} + \mathbf{W}^\top \mathbf{W} + (\mathbf{W}^\top \mathbf{W})^+ - \mathbf{I}) \mathbf{W}^\top \\
&= \mathbf{W}^\top + (\mathbf{Z} + ((\mathbf{W}^\top \mathbf{W})^+ - \mathbf{I})(\mathbf{I} - \mathbf{W}^\top \mathbf{W})) \mathbf{W}^\top \\
&= \mathbf{W}^\top + (\mathbf{Z} + (\mathbf{I} - \mathbf{W}^\top \mathbf{W})(\mathbf{W}^\top \mathbf{W})^+ (\mathbf{I} - \mathbf{W}^\top \mathbf{W})) \mathbf{W}^\top \\
&= \mathbf{W}^\top + (\mathbf{Z} + \mathbf{Z}(\mathbf{W}^\top \mathbf{W})^+ \mathbf{Z}) \mathbf{W}^\top \\
&= \mathbf{W}^\top + (\mathbf{Z} + \mathbf{Z}(\mathbf{I} - \mathbf{Z})^+ \mathbf{Z}) \mathbf{W}^\top \\
&= \mathbf{W}^\top + \mathbf{Z}(\mathbf{I} - \mathbf{Z})^+ \mathbf{W}^\top \\
&= \mathbf{W}^\top + \mathbf{Y}^\top (\mathbf{I} - \mathbf{Y}\mathbf{Y}^\top)^+ \mathbf{Y} \mathbf{W}^\top,
\end{aligned}$$

where the last equality holds from the Matrix Inversion Lemma. The special case of row vector $\mathbf{y} = \mathbf{Y}$ simplifies the pseudo-inverse to a scalar inverse, giving the second form of the this lemma.

Symmetrical Dense Optical Flow Estimation with Occlusions Detection

Luis Alvarez[1], Rachid Deriche[2], Théo Papadopoulo[2], and Javier Sánchez[1]

[1] Universidad de Las Palmas, Spain
{lalvarez,jsanchez}@dis.ulpgc.es
[2] INRIA Sophia-Antipolis, France
{der,papadop}@sophia.inria.fr

Abstract. Traditional techniques of dense optical flow estimation don't generally yield symmetrical solutions: the results will differ if they are applied between images I_1 and I_2 or between images I_2 and I_1. In this work, we present a method to recover a dense optical flow field map from two images, while explicitly taking into account the symmetry across the images as well as possible occlusions and discontinuities in the flow field. The idea is to consider both displacements vectors from I_1 to I_2 and I_2 to I_1 and to minimise an energy functional that explicitly encodes all those properties. This variational problem is then solved using the gradient flow defined by the Euler–Lagrange equations associated to the energy. In order to reduce the risk to be trapped within some irrelevant minimum, a focusing strategy based on a multi-resolution technique is used to converge toward the solution. Promising experimental results on both synthetic and real images are presented to illustrate the capabilities of this symmetrical variational approach to recover accurate optical flow.

1 Introduction and Motivation

A large number of methods have been proposed in the computer vision community to address the important problem of motion analysis from image sequences. In this paper, we are interested in computing the 2D optical flow field which is a specific type of motion defined as the velocity field obtained from the temporal changes of the intensity values of the image sequence. 2D optical flow estimation has been extensively addressed in the literature, and the most common methods are correlation, gradient, spatiotemporal filtering, Fourier phase and energy based approaches. We refer the interested reader to [6,17] for an excellent analysis and evaluation of important optical flow methods. Many of these approaches use the classical constraint equation that relates the gradient of brightness to the components u and v of the local flow to estimate the optical flow. Because this problem is ill-posed, additional constraints are usually required. The most used one is to add a quadratic constraint on the gradient magnitude of the flow to impose some form of smoothness on the flow field as done originally by Horn and Schunk [16]. Other formulations have been proposed using different smoothness constraints, but despite their interest, they clearly lacked robustness to the presence of occlusions and discontinuities. In order to estimate the optical flow more accurately, one have to explicitly take into account the problem of occlusions and discontinuities. See the following works, mostly based on variational approaches [20,19,10,24,15,14,22,13,5,18,11,3,31]. Due to the fact that the functional to be minimised is generally not convex, some focusing strategy embedding the method in a multi-resolution scheme or a linear scale-space have been successfully applied to reduce the risk to get trapped in some irrelevant minima [20,4,3].

The method presented here is inspired from this kind of variational framework that has also proven recently to be very useful in many other image processing and computer vision tasks [25,30,8,1]. We start explicitely with the method described in [4] and modify it using ideas similar to those developed in [9] to obtain an algorithm that will give the same solution if applied between images A and B or between images B and A. Contrarily to [9], we deal with discontinuities of the flow field and explicitly take into account the possibility of occlusions.

The article is organised as follows: in section 2, we will introduce some notations and basic concepts on which the approach will be based, section 3 describes the method which is demonstrated on some examples in section 4.

2 Notations and Previous Work

In this paper, images are represented as functions that map some coordinate space $\mathcal{D}$ to an intensity space $\mathcal{I}$. We consider that two images, I_1 and I_2, of the same scene are given:

$$I_1 : \mathcal{D}_1 \longmapsto \mathcal{I} \quad \text{and} \quad I_2 : \mathcal{D}_2 \longmapsto \mathcal{I} \ .$$

Note that it is assumed here that the two images share the same range $\mathcal{I}$. This assumption can be made without loss of generality as it is always possible to preprocess the images in order to normalize them. Preprocessing also allows us to limit ourselves on SSD-like (Sum of Squared Differences) criteria to compare the values of I_1 and I_2. The basic problem addressed by this paper is establishing dense correspondences between those two images. To do so, two unknown functions, h_1 and h_2, are introduced:

$$h_1 : \Omega_1 \subset \mathcal{D}_1 \longmapsto \Omega_2 \quad \text{and} \quad h_2 : \Omega_2 \subset \mathcal{D}_2 \longmapsto \Omega_1 \ .$$

For each point $\mathbf{m}_1 = (x_1, y_1)$ of Ω_1 (resp. $\mathbf{m}_2 = (x_2, y_2)$ of Ω_2), the function h_1 (resp. h_2) give its corresponding point $h_1(\mathbf{m}_1) = [u_1(x_1, y_1), v_1(x_1, y_1)]^T$ in Ω_2 (resp. the point $h_2(\mathbf{m}_2) = [u_2(x_2, y_2), v_2(x_2, y_2)]^T$ in Ω_1). Note that we have been careful to define these functions on subsets of $\mathcal{D}_1$ and $\mathcal{D}_2$ so that we can take account of occlusions in both images which are defined by the sets $\mathcal{D}_1 \setminus \Omega_1$ and $\mathcal{D}_2 \setminus \Omega_2$ respectively. Consequently, a good matching should satisfy the following two properties:

$$h_2 \circ h_1 = Id_{\Omega_1} \quad \text{and} \quad h_1 \circ h_2 = Id_{\Omega_2} \ , \tag{1}$$

where Id_{Ω_i} denotes the identity over the domain Ω_i. These equations mean that there is a one-to-one correspondence between the sets Ω_1 and Ω_2 (ie that the matched points are corresponding to each other) or equivalently that $h_1 = h_2^{-1}$ and $h_2 = h_1^{-1}$.

2.1 Dense Optical Flow

Given the previous notations, optical flow computation procedures have been defined as variational scheme that minimise an energy functional of the form:

$$E_1(h_1) = E_1^M(h_1) + \alpha E_1^R(h_1) , \qquad (2)$$

where α is a weighting factor and $E_1^M(h_1)$ and $E_1^R(h_1)$ represents the matching and regularisation costs, respectively. The matching term can be written as:

$$E_1^M(h_1) = \frac{1}{max\,\|\nabla I_1\|^2} \int_{\Omega_1} (I_1(\mathbf{m}_1) - I_2(h_1(\mathbf{m}_1)))^2 \, d\mathbf{m}_1$$

As announced previously, $E_1^M(h_1)$ corresponds to a SSD-like criterion, which is allowed by our assumptions. The factor in front of the integral is used to normalize the relative strength of the terms $E_1^M(h_1)$ and $E_1^R(h_1)$. Various different proposals have been made for the regularisation term. To prevent the flow map to be smoothed by the algorithm across images boundaries, we have chosen to use Nagel-Enkelmann operator [20], first because its efficiency has been demonstrated numerous times in the context of optical flow estimations [3,6,12,19,21,20,26,27] and because of its simplicity since the underlying second order differential operator is linear.

$$E_1^R(h_1) = \int_{\Omega_1} \Phi\left(D(\|\nabla I_1\|), \nabla h_1\right) d\mathbf{m}_1 ,$$

with:

$$\Phi\left(D(\nabla I_i), \nabla h_i\right) = trace\left(\nabla(h_i)^t D(\nabla I_i) \nabla(h_i)\right) ,$$

where $\nabla(h_i)$ denotes the Jacobian matrix of the function $h_i(\mathbf{m}_i)$. Since $h_i(\mathbf{m}_i) = [u_i(\mathbf{m}_i), v_i(\mathbf{m}_i)]^T$, the previous formula can also be written as:

$$\Phi\left(D(\nabla I_i), \nabla h_i\right) = \nabla u_1^t D(\nabla I_1) \nabla u_1 + \nabla u_2^t D(\nabla I_1) \nabla u_2$$

$D(\nabla I_1)$ is a regularised projection matrix in the direction perpendicular to ∇I_1

$$D(\nabla I_1) = \frac{1}{\|\nabla I_1\|^2 + 2\nu^2} \left\{ \begin{bmatrix} \frac{\partial I_1}{\partial y_1} \\ -\frac{\partial I_1}{\partial x_1} \end{bmatrix} \begin{bmatrix} \frac{\partial I_1}{\partial y_1} \\ -\frac{\partial I_1}{\partial x_1} \end{bmatrix}^t + \nu^2 Id \right\} . \qquad (3)$$

In this formulation, Id denotes the identity matrix and ν is a parameter used to control the desired level of isotropy.

It is interesting to note that the matrix $D(\nabla I_1)$ plays the role of a diffusion tensor. Its eigenvectors are $v_1 := \nabla I_1$ and $v_2 := \nabla I_1^\perp$, and the corresponding eigenvalues are given by

$$\lambda_1(\|\nabla I_1\|) = \frac{\nu^2}{\|\nabla I_1\|^2 + 2\nu^2}, \tag{4}$$

$$\lambda_2(\|\nabla I_1\|) = \frac{\|\nabla I_1\|^2 + \nu^2}{\|\nabla I_1\|^2 + 2\nu^2}. \tag{5}$$

In the interior of objects we have $\|\nabla I_1\| \to 0$, and therefore $\lambda_1 \to 1/2$ and $\lambda_2 \to 1/2$. At ideal edges where $\|\nabla I_1\| \to \infty$, we obtain $\lambda_1 \to 0$ and $\lambda_2 \to 1$. Thus, we have isotropic behaviour within regions, and at image boundaries the process smoothes anisotropically along the edge. This behaviour is very similar to edge-enhancing anisotropic diffusion filtering [29,28], and it is also close in spirit to the modified mean-curvature motion considered in [2,1].

At this point, two remarks can be made:

- Since Ω_1 is usually unknown, the domain $\mathcal{D}_1$ is used instead in the previous integrals.
- The criterion depicted above is clearly non-symmetrical in the images I_1 and I_2 so that the minimisation of $E_1(h_1)$ and that of the similarly defined $E_2(h_2)$ will not yield functions h_1 and h_2 that satisfy the constraints (1). In other words, the two procedures will not give the same matching which is unfortunate.

In the following section, we will discuss a method to reintroduce the symmetry across the two images while allowing simultaneously the detection of occlusions. Section 4 describes results obtained with this method.

3 Symmetric Optical Flow

Let us first assume that the function h_2 is known. The first step is to extend the energy depicted in equation (2) by adding a term $E_1^S(h_1)$ to impose the first of the two constraints (1):

$$E_1'(h_1, h_2) = E_1^M(h_1) + \alpha E_1^R(h_1) + \beta E_1^S(h_1, h_2), \tag{6}$$

where β is another weighting factor. $E_1^S(h_1)$ can be written as:

$$E_1^S(h_1, h_2) = \int_{\Omega_1} \Psi\left(\|h_2(h_1(\mathbf{m}_1)) - Id_{\Omega_1}(\mathbf{m}_1)\|^2\right) d\mathbf{m}_1,$$

where Ψ is a function that will be used to provide some robustness in the method. This function will be detailed in section 3.3. For the time being, we can assume that $\Psi(s) = s$. A large value of $\|h_2(h_1(\mathbf{m}_1)) - Id_{\Omega_1}(\mathbf{m}_1)\|$ means a lack of symmetry in the matching (h_2 being given). Assuming that h_2 is correct, when the solution for h_1 is reached, the most probable reasons for such a situation is an occlusion problem or an error in the estimated matching. Notice that taking only the first of the two constraints (1) just imposes that h_1 is injective and that h_2 is mapping from $h_1(\Omega_1)$ onto Ω_1.

It is possible to define $E_2'(h_1, h_2)$ in a similar fashion, with the roles of $h_i, i = 1..2$ and the $\Omega_i, i = 1..2$ reversed. A completely symmetric criterion is then obtained easily by:

$$E'(h_1, h_2) = E_1'(h_1, h_2) + E_2'(h_1, h_2).$$

3.1 A Multi-resolution Scheme Approach to Escape from Local Minima

In general, the Euler–Lagrange equation associated to the energy E' will have multiple solutions. As a consequence, the asymptotic state of the parabolic equation that will be used to minimize E', will depend on the initial data (h_1^0, h_2^0). Typically, we may expect the algorithm to converge toward a local minimum of the energy functional that is located in the vicinity of that initial data. To reduce the risk of being trapped into irrelevant local minima, we embed our method into a multi-resolution framework. At the coarsest-scale the problem is much smoother, so that many irrelevant local minima disappear. Using the coarse-scale solution as initialisation for finer scales helps in getting close to the most relevant global minimum. A detailed analysis of the usefulness of such a focusing strategy in the context of a related optic flow problem can be found for instance in [4].

3.2 Minimising the Energy

The previous energy function is minimised as the asymptotic solution of a gradient flow based on the Euler–Lagrange partial differential equation corresponding to the energy E'. In order to look for the minimum of this energy, we proceed in an iterative way as follows: first we begin with an initial approximation (h_1^0, h_2^0) and then obtain (h_1^{n+1}, h_2^{n+1}) from (h_1^n, h_2^n) as an iteration of a gradient descent method applied to the energy:

$$E'(h_1^{n+1}, h_2^{n+1}) = E_1'(h_1^{n+1}, h_2^n) + E_2'(h_1^n, h_2^{n+1})$$

The initial approximation is obtained by a classical correlation at the coarsest level of resolution. For the gradient descent, applying Euler-Lagrange, and using the notation $I^h = I \circ h$ for compactness, we obtain:

$$\frac{\partial E'}{\partial h_1} = -\left(I_1 - I_2^{h_1}\right)(\nabla I_2)^{h_1} - \alpha div\left(D(\|\nabla I_1\|)\nabla h_1\right) + \beta \Psi'\left(\|h_2 \circ h_1 - Id_{\Omega_1}\|^2\right)(\nabla h_2)^{h_1} \cdot (h_2 \circ h_1 - Id_{\Omega_1})$$

$$\frac{\partial E'}{\partial h_2} = -\left(I_2 - I_1^{h_2}\right)(\nabla I_1)^{h_2} - \alpha div\left(D(\|\nabla I_1\|)\nabla h_2\right) +$$
$$\beta \Psi'\left(\|h_1 \circ h_2 - Id_{\Omega_2}\|^2\right)(\nabla h_1)^{h_2} \cdot (h_1 \circ h_2 - Id_{\Omega_2})$$

Using coordinates, the updates for the evolution of the PDE are:

$$\begin{pmatrix} \frac{\partial u_1}{\partial t} \\ \frac{\partial v_1}{\partial t} \end{pmatrix} = -\frac{\partial E'}{\partial h_1} \qquad \begin{pmatrix} \frac{\partial u_2}{\partial t} \\ \frac{\partial v_2}{\partial t} \end{pmatrix} = -\frac{\partial E'}{\partial h_2}$$

Given a time step dt, these equations give the updates du_1, dv_1, du_2, dv_2 that must be applied to (h_1^n, h_2^n) to obtain (h_1^{n+1}, h_2^{n+1}).

3.3 Choosing the Function Ψ

As said above, $\Psi(.)$ can be chosen to improve the robustness of the algorithm. We have tested two possibilities:

$$\Psi_1(s) = s, \qquad \Psi_2(s) = \frac{s}{\gamma}e^{1-\frac{s}{\gamma}},$$

where γ is a threshold for which we consider there is a good matching. Note that the function Ψ_1 corresponds to standard least-squares (remember that the function Ψ is applied to the square of the error values), whereas Ψ_2 is similar in essence to least-trimmed-squares which can be used to deal with outliers. Indeed, with least-trimmed-squares, only the smallest residuals are summed up into the criterion. This is what achieves the function Ψ_2 (see figure 1): when the error is too large, the function Ψ_2 cancels its contribution to the criterion whereas for small errors it has a linear behaviour. These two constraints along with the fact that a variationnal approach is used so that the function chosen must be differentiable, imposes the general shape of the Ψ function. Ψ_2 is such a function (other choices obeying to the same constraints can be made).

In preliminary experiments, we have noticed that the locations where the flows obtained as the solutions of E_1 and E_2 are the least symmetrical with each other can be associated with the occlusions of the two images. We will use this property to recover those locations. To do so, the domain of integration will be extended to the whole images (ie $\mathcal{D}_1$ and $\mathcal{D}_2$ respectively), but the symmetry errors will be weighted by the Ψ_2 function. This weighting ensures that the large errors in symmetry will not affect the criterion. As a consequence the sub-domain Ω_1 can be found as the domain where the un-weighted errors are too large. A better choice of the function Ψ is under consideration [7].

4 Experimental Results

We now show results on both synthetic and real images. In both cases, the theoretical flow is available, and a comparison of the obtained and the expected

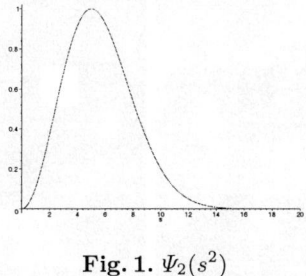

Fig. 1. $\Psi_2(s^2)$

results will be made. For both the experiments, the algorithm has been run for 200 iterations with a time step $dt = 10$. In [4], the non-symmetric method is compared with the other (the ones used in [6]) classical dense optical flow methods that give a density of matches of 100%. Typically, the non-symmetric method yields better results than the classical ones. Consequently, in this section, the comparison is limited to the non-symmetric and symmetric methods which have been depicted in the previous sections. This is the most relevant option.

4.1 Synthetic Images

We have first tried our algorithm with the set of synthetic images depicted in figure 2. Occlusion with these images is important so that they were processed with the robust version, ie $\Psi = \Psi_2$. Figure 3 show the theoretical result that should be obtained.

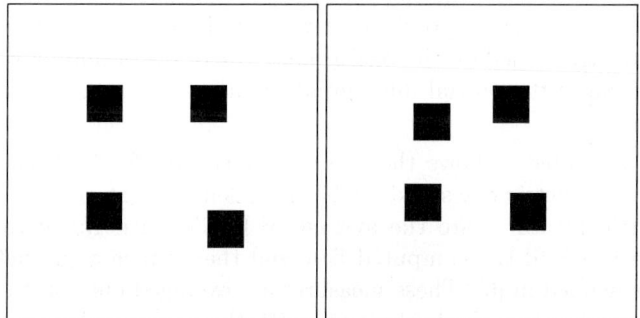

Fig. 2. The initial input images

Figure 4 shows the results obtained with our algorithm. A pyramid of three levels of resolution have been used with $\alpha = 1$, $\beta = 0.5$, $\gamma = 5$ and $\nu = 0.1$. Notice how the smoothness constraint, managed to give reasonnable results (of course there are multiple solutions, but the algorithm choose one of minimal cost with respect to the smoothness constraint) in homogeneous regions while being able to respect the discontinuities. Figure 5 shows the computed occlusion

728   L. Alvarez et al.

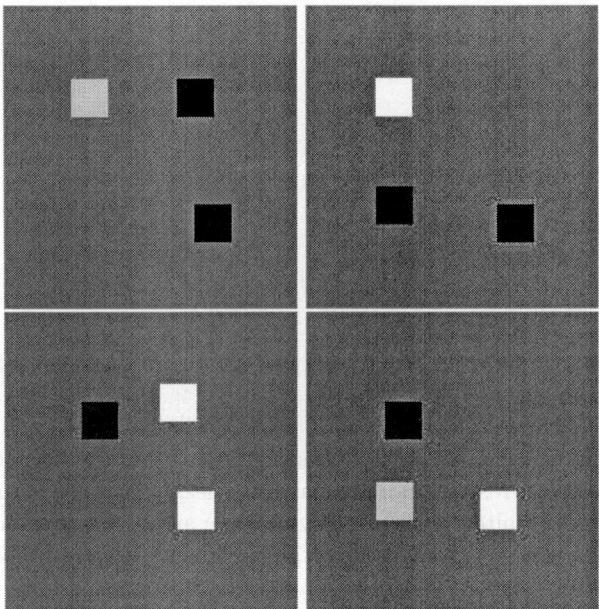

Fig. 3. The true optic flow. On the left (resp. right), the u (resp. v) component of the true flow. On the top (resp bottom) is the true function h_1 (resp. h_2).

images. These were obtained by selecting the image points where the symmetry conditions are violated by more than a fixed threshold ($\gamma = 5$). As it can be seen, these locations correspond fairly well to the occlusions. However, these have been slightly eroded on the background side of the occluding region, as the smoothing term of the partial differential equation has been in action at those locations.

In addition, table 1 shows the two error measures for both the symmetric and the non-symmetric cases and for both the left-to-right and the right-to-left flows. The two measures are the average of Euclidean norm of the difference between the true and the computed flow and the average angle between those two flows as defined in [6]. These measures are averaged only on the squares as the flow is undefined on the background with these images. It can be seen that errors are roughly divided by two with symmetrisation.

Finally, figure 6 shows the residual symmetry errors $\|h1 \circ h2 - Id\|$ and $\|h2 \circ h1 - Id\|$ over the images. Except in the occluded regions, these errors are very close to zero (black) everywhere, which shows that the algorithm indeed obtained a symmetric matching. The maximum symmetry error (outside of the occluded regions) is of about 1.0 for both $\|h1 \circ h2 - Id\|$ and $\|h2 \circ h1 - Id\|$ with the symmetrical method and of about 25.5 with the non-symmetric one (since the background is textureless there is no way the non-symmetric method can give symmetrical flows).

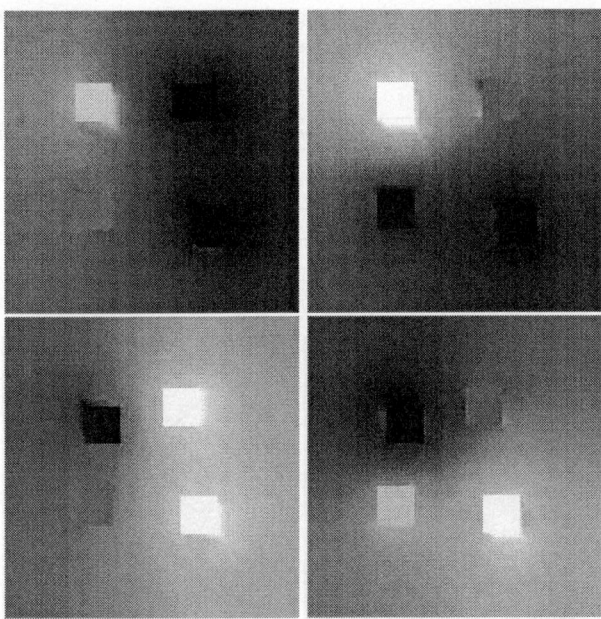

Fig. 4. The computed optic flow. On the left (resp. right), the u (resp. v) component of flow. On the top (resp. bottom) is shown h_1 (resp. h_2).

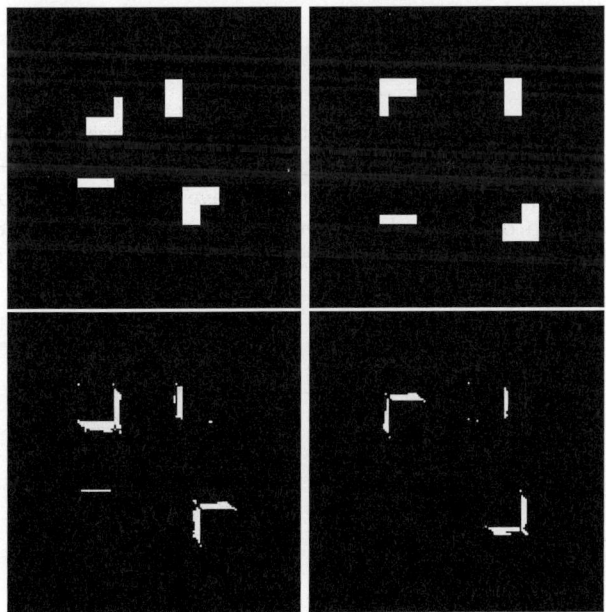

Fig. 5. The computed occlusions. On the left (resp. right), the occlusion mask computed for the first (resp. second) image. On the top (resp bottom) is the true (resp. the computed) occlusions.

Table 1. The mean errors in norm and angle between the computed and the true flow in the non-symmetric and the symmetric cases. LR (resp. RL) means left to right (resp. right to left) flow.

		Euclidean norm Error	Angular Error
Non symmetrical	LR	0.16	0.50
	RL	0.18	0.58
Symmetrical	LR	0.081	0.18
	RL	0.084	0.19

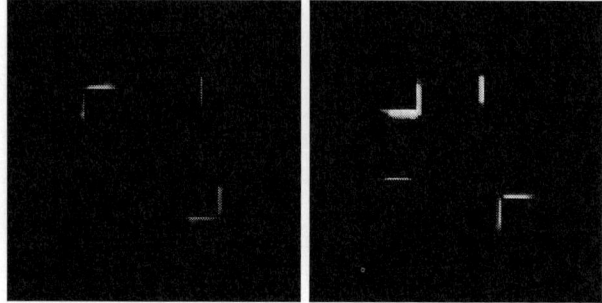

Fig. 6. The symmetry errors $\|h1 \circ h2 - Id\|$ (left) and $\|h2 \circ h1 - Id\|$ (right).

4.2 Real Images

The algorithm depicted above has also been run on various pairs of real images. One particularly useful pair is that provided in the paper [23] as it provides the ground truth optical flow. These images have been kindly provided by the KOGS/IAKS group of Karlsruhe University. Figures 7 and 8 show the input images and the two components of the true flow. As there is very little occlusion with these images, they were processed with the variant $\Psi = \Psi_1$.

Fig. 7. The initial input images

Figure 9 give the results obtained with this set of data both with (on the bottom) and without (on the top) the symmetrisation constraints. Three levels of resolution have been used with $\alpha = 0.3$, $\beta = 0.1$ and $\nu = 0.3$. As it can be seen, the symmetrisation constraints had several effects:

- The flow estimated on the floor is smoother.
- The computed flow on the column situated at the middle of the image is more homogeneous.
- The large error at the places marked with the letters A and C has disappeared at the cost of a much smaller one at the bottom right.
- The vertical component of the flow in the background is much more consistent with the ground truth solution (see the location marked with the letter B). In this very low-textured zone, the addition of the symmetry constraint resulted in a much better solution than the one obtained with just the regularisation constraint.

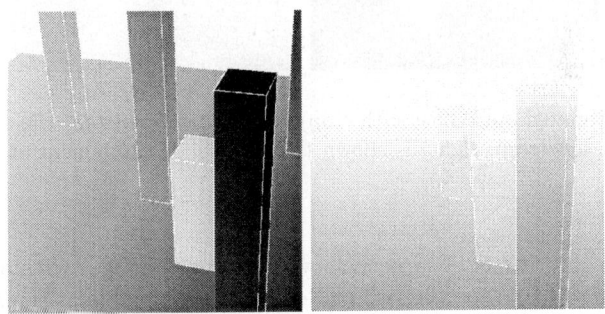

Fig. 8. The true optical flow. On the left (resp. right), the u (resp. v) component of the true flow.

In addition, figure 10 shows the two error measures: the Euclidean norm of the difference between the true and the computed flow, and the angle between those two flows as defined in [6]. Table 2 summarises the means of these two errors. Here again, errors are roughly divided by two with the symmetric method.

Table 2. The mean errors in norm and angle between the computed and the true flow.

	Euclidean norm Error	Angular Error
Non symmetrical	0.37	9.4
Symmetrical	0.17	5.2

Finally, figure 11 shows the the residual symmetry errors $\|h1 \circ h2 - Id\|$ and $\|h2 \circ h1 - Id\|$ over the images. Here again, these errors are very close to zero

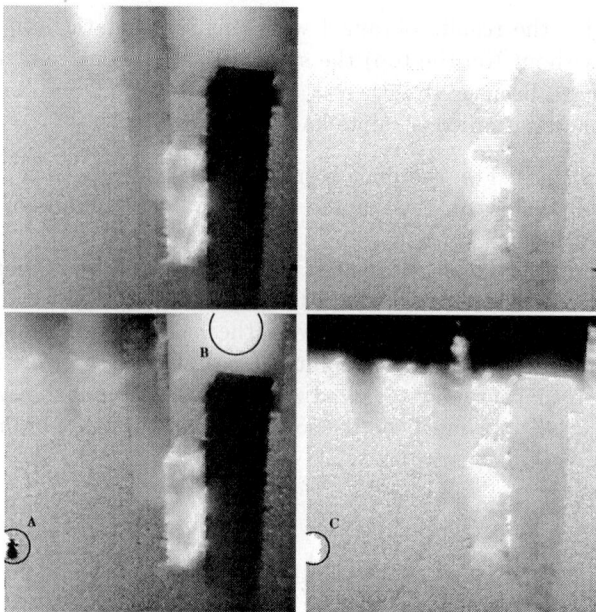

Fig. 9. The estimated optic flow with (top) and without (bottom) the symmetry constraint. On the left (resp. right) is shown the u (resp. v) component of the computed optical flow.

everywhere so that it has been necessary to show the images with a gamma correction of 2, in order to see the residual errors. Small problems remain along the edges of the marbled floor where the texture contours have affected the symmetry constraint. The maximal symmetry errors are of about 0.8 for $\|h1 \circ h2 - Id\|$ and 1.4 for $\|h2 \circ h1 - Id\|$ with the symmetric method and respectively of 1.5 and 1.9 with the non-symmetric one.

5 Conclusion

In this paper, we have presented a PDE based optical flow estimation that preserve the discontinuity of the flow field along the image contours in such a way that it is symmetrical with respect to both images. This is done by computing simultaneously the flow from image 1 to image 2 and from image 2 to image 1, while adding explicit terms in the PDE that constrain those two flows to be compatible. The places where this compatibility cannot be achieved correspond to occlusions, so that the process allows for the detection of sufficently large occlusions. The experimental results on synthetic and real images demonstrate the validity of the approach and the importance of the symmetry term, not only for the accuracy of the results but also as a tool to recover occluded regions.

It is important to note that the ideas developed can be generalized to many similar situations. For example, they can be very easily extended to deal with

Fig. 10. The errors on the optical flow with (top) and without (bottom) the symmetry constraint. On the left (resp. right) is shown the angular (resp. Euclidian) error of the computed optical flow.

Fig. 11. The symmetry errors $\|h1 \circ h2 - Id\|$ (left) and $\|h2 \circ h1 - Id\|$ (right). These images are displayed with a gamma correction of 4, otherwise they would have appeared totally black.

stereo images (ie when the matching is constrained to safisfy some given epipolar geometry). This is an ongoing research. More details will be given in a forthcoming research report.

Acknowledgments. This work was partially supported by the spanish research project TIC 2000-0585 (MCYT) and by the European IST project COGVISYS 3E010361.

References

1. L. Alvarez, R. Deriche, J. Weickert, and J. Sànchez. Dense disparity map estimation respecting image discontinuities: A PDE and scale-space based approach. In *IAPR International Workshop on Machine Vision Applications*, Tokyo, Japan, Nov. 2000. The University of Tokyo. A revised version has been accepted for publication in 2002 in *Journal of Visual Communication and Image Representation*.
2. L. Alvarez, P. Lions, and J. Morel. Image selective smoothing and edge detection by nonlinear diffusion (II). *SIAM Journal of Numerical Analysis*, 29:845–866, 1992.
3. L. Alvarez, J. Weickert, and J. Sànchez. A scale-space approach to nonlocal optical flow calculations. In M. Nielsen, P. Johansen, O. Olsen, and J. Weickert, editors, *Scale-Space Theories in Computer Vision*, volume 1682 of *Lecture Notes in Computer Science*, pages 235–246. Springer–Verlag, 1999.
4. L. Alvarez, J. Weickert, and J. Sànchez. Reliable estimation of dense optical flow fields with large displacements. *The International Journal of Computer Vision*, 39(1):41–56, Aug. 2000.
5. G. Aubert, R. Deriche, and P. Kornprobst. Computing optical flow via variational techniques. *SIAM Journal of Applied Mathematics*, 60(1):156–182, 1999.
6. J. Barron, D. Fleet, and S. Beauchemin. Performance of optical flow techniques. *The International Journal of Computer Vision*, 12(1):43–77, 1994.
7. M. Black and P. Rangarajan. On the unification of line processes, outlier rejection, and robust statistics with applications in early vision. *The International Journal of Computer Vision*, 19(1):57–91, 1996.
8. V. Caselles, J. Morel, G. Sapiro, and A. Tannenbaum. Introduction to the special issue on partial differential equations and geometry-driven diffusion in image processing and analysis. *IEEE Transactions on Image Processing*, 7(3):269–273, 1998.
9. G. E. Christensen. Consistent linear-elastic transformations for image matching. In A. K. et al, editor, *Proceedings of IPMI*, volume 1613 of *LNCS*, pages 224–237, Berlin, Heildelberg, 1999. Springer-Verlag.
10. I. Cohen. Nonlinear variational method for optical flow computation. In *Scandinavian Conference on Image Analysis*, volume 1, pages 523–530, 1993.
11. R. Deriche, P. Kornprobst, and G. Aubert. Optical flow estimation while preserving its discontinuities: A variational approach. In *Proceedings of the 2nd Asian Conference on Computer Vision*, volume 2, pages 71–80, Singapore, Dec. 1995.
12. W. Enkelmann. Investigation of multigrid algorithms for the estimation of optical flow fields in image sequences. *Computer Vision, Graphics, and Image Processing*, 43:150–177, 1988.
13. S. Ghosal and P. Vaněk. A fast scalable algorithm for discontinuous optical flow estimation. *IEEE Transactions on Pattern Analysis and Machine Intelligence*, 18(2):181–194, Feb. 1996.

14. F. Guichard and L. Rudin. Accurate estimation of discontinuous optical flow by minimizing divergence related functionals. In *Proceedings of the International Conference on Image Processing*, volume I, pages 497–500, 1996.
15. F. Heitz and P. Bouthemy. Multimodal estimation of discontinuous optical flow using markov random fields. *IEEE Transactions on Pattern Analysis and Machine Intelligence*, 15(12):1217–1232, Dec. 1993.
16. B. Horn and B. Schunk. Determining optical flow. *Artificial Intelligence*, 17:185–203, 1981.
17. B. McCane, K. Novins, D. Crannitch, and B. Galvin. On benchmarking optical flow. *Computer Vision and Image Understanding*, 84(1):126–143, 2002.
18. E. Memin and P. Perez. Multiresolution Markov random field and multigrid algorithm for discontinuity preserving estimation of the optical flow. In *Proceedings of the International Society for Optical Engineering*, San Diego, USA, July 1995.
19. H. Nagel. Constraints for the estimation of displacement vector fields from image sequences. In *International Joint Conference on Artificial Intelligence*, pages 156–160, 1983.
20. H. Nagel and W. Enkelmann. An investigation of smoothness constraint for the estimation of displacement vector fiels from images sequences. *IEEE Transactions on Pattern Analysis and Machine Intelligence*, 8:565–593, 1986.
21. H.-H. Nagel. On the estimation of optical flow: relations between different approaches and some new results. *Artificial Intelligence Journal*, 33:299–324, 1987.
22. P. Nési. Variational approach to optical flow estimation managing discontinuities. *Image and Vision Computing*, 11(7):419–439, Sept. 1993.
23. M. Otte and H. Nagel. Optical flow estimation: Advances and comparisons. In J.-O. Eklundh, editor, *Proceedings of the 3rd European Conference on Computer Vision*, volume 800 of *Lecture Notes in Computer Science*, pages 51–70. Springer–Verlag, 1994.
24. M. Proesmans, L. Van Gool, E. Pauwels, and A. Oosterlinck. Determination of Optical Flow and its Discontinuities using Non-Linear Diffusion. In *Proceedings of the 3rd ECCV, II*, number 801 in Lecture Notes in Computer Science, pages 295–304. Springer–Verlag, 1994.
25. G. Sapiro. *Geometric Partial Differential Equations and Image Analysis*. Cambridge University Press, 2001.
26. C. Schnörr. Determining optical flow for irregular domains by minimizing quadratic functionals of a certain class. *The International Journal of Computer Vision*, 6(1):25–38, 1991.
27. M. Snyder. On the mathematical fundations of smoothness constraints for the determination of optical flow and for surface reconstruction. *IEEE Transactions on Pattern Analysis and Machine Intelligence*, 13(11), Nov. 1995.
28. J. Weickert. *Anisotropic Diffusion in Image Processing*. PhD thesis, University of Kaiserslautern, Germany, Laboratory of Technomathematics, Jan. 1996.
29. J. Weickert. Theoretical foundations of anisotropic diffusion in image processing. *Computing Supplement*, 11:221–236, 1996.
30. J. Weickert. *Anisotropic Diffusion in Image Processing*. Teubner-Verlag, Stuttgart, 1998.
31. J. Weickert and C. Schnörr. A theoretical framework for convex regularizers in PDE-based computation of image motion. *The International Journal of Computer Vision*, 45(3):245–264, Dec. 2001.

Audio-Video Sensor Fusion with Probabilistic Graphical Models

Matthew J. Beal[1,2], Hagai Attias[1], and Nebojsa Jojic[1]

[1] Microsoft Research, 1 Microsoft Way,
Redmond, WA 98052, USA
{hagaia,jojic}@microsoft.com

[2] Gatsby Computational Neuroscience Unit, University College London,
17 Queen Square, London WC1N 3AR, UK
m.beal@gatsby.ucl.ac.uk

Abstract. We present a new approach to modeling and processing multimedia data. This approach is based on graphical models that combine audio and video variables. We demonstrate it by developing a new algorithm for tracking a moving object in a cluttered, noisy scene using two microphones and a camera. Our model uses unobserved variables to describe the data in terms of the process that generates them. It is therefore able to capture and exploit the statistical structure of the audio and video data separately, as well as their mutual dependencies. Model parameters are learned from data via an EM algorithm, and automatic calibration is performed as part of this procedure. Tracking is done by Bayesian inference of the object location from data. We demonstrate successful performance on multimedia clips captured in real world scenarios using off-the-shelf equipment.

1 Introduction

In most systems that handle digital media, audio and video data are treated separately. Such systems usually have subsystems that are specialized for the different modalities and are optimized for each modality separately. Combining the two modalities is performed at a higher level. This process generally requires scenario-dependent treatment, including precise and often manual calibration.

For example, consider a system that tracks moving objects. Such a system may use video data, captured by a camera, to track the spatial location of the object based on its continually shifting image. If the object emits sound, such a system may use audio data, captured by a microphone pair (or array), to track the object location using the time delay of arrival of the audio signals at the different microphones. In principle, however, a tracker that exploits both modalities may achieve better performance than one which exploits either one or the other. The reason is that each modality may compensate for weaknesses of the other one. Thus, whereas a tracker using only video data may mistake the background for the object or lose the object altogether due to occlusion, a tracker using also audio data could continue focusing on the object by following

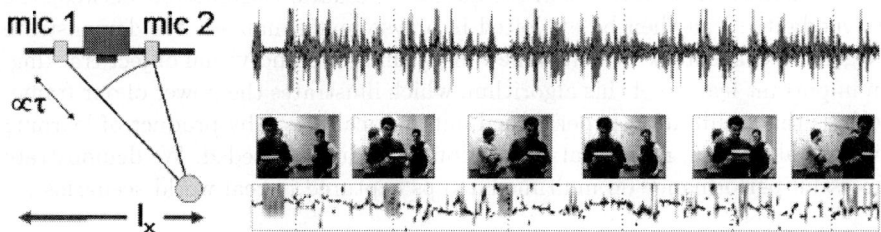

Fig. 1. (Top) audio waveform. (Middle) selected frames from associated video sequence (120×160 pixels^2). (Bottom) posterior probability over time delay τ (vertical axis, $\tau \in \{-15,\ldots,15\}$) for each frame of the sequence; darker areas represent higher probability, and each frame has been separately normalized. The horizontal direction represents time along the sequence.

its sound pattern. Conversely, video data could help where an audio tracker alone may lose the object as it stops emitting sound or is masked by background noise. More generally, audio and video signals originating from the same source tend to be correlated — thus to achieve optimal performance a system must exploit not just the statistics of each modality alone, but also the correlations among the two modalities.

The setup and example data in Fig. 1 illustrate this point. The figure shows an audio-visual capture system (left), an audio waveform captured by one of the microphones (top right), and a few frames captured by the camera (middle right). The frames contain a person moving in front of a cluttered background that includes other people. The audio waveform contains the subject's speech but also some background noise, including other people's speech. The audio and video signals are correlated on various levels. The lip movement of the speaker is correlated with the amplitude of part of the audio signal (see, e.g., [4]). Also, the time delay between the signals arriving at the microphones is correlated with the position of the person in the image (see, e.g., [9],[10]). It is the latter type of correlations that we aim for in this paper.

However, in order to use these correlations, a careful calibration procedure much be performed to establish a correspondence between the spatial shift in the image and the relative time delay between the microphone signals. Such a procedure needs to be repeated for each new setup configuration. This is a serious shortcoming of current audio-visual trackers.

The origin of this difficulty is that relevant features in the problem are not directly observable. The audio signal propagating from the speaker is usually corrupted by reverberation and multipath effects and by background noise, making it difficult to identify the time delay. The video stream is cluttered by objects other than the speaker, often causing a tracker to lose the speaker. Furthermore, audio-visual correlations usually exist only intermittently. This paper presents a new framework for fusing audio and video data. In this framework, which is based on probabilistic generative modeling, we construct a model describing the joint statistical characteristics of the audio-video data. Correlations between the two modalities can then be exploited in a systematic manner. We demonstrate the general concept by deriving a new algorithm for audio-visual object tracking. An important feature of this algorithm, which illustrates the power of our framework, is that calibration is performed automatically as a by-product of learning with the algorithm; no special calibration procedure is needed. We demonstrate successful performance on multimedia clips captured in real world scenarios.

2 Probabilistic Generative Modeling

Our framework uses probabilistic generative models (also termed graphical models) to describe the observed data. The models are termed generative, since they describe the observed data in terms of the process that generated them, using additional variables that are not observable. The models are termed probabilistic, because rather than describing signals, they describe probability distributions over signals. These two properties combine to create flexible and powerful models. The models are also termed graphical since they have a useful graphical representation, as we shall see below.

The observed audio signals are generated by the speaker's original signal, which arrives at microphone 2 with a time delay relative to microphone 1. The speaker's signal and the time delay are unobserved variables in our model. Similarly, the video signal is generated by the speaker's original image, which is shifted as the speaker's spatial location changes. Thus, the speaker's image and location are also unobserved variables in our model. The presence of unobserved (hidden) variables is typical of probabilistic generative models and constitutes one source of their power and flexibility.

The delay between the signals captured by the microphones is reflective of the object's position, as can be seen in Fig. 1 where we show the delay estimated by signal decorrelation (bottom right). Whereas an estimate of the delay can in principle be used to estimate of the object position, in practice the computation of the delay is typically not very accurate in situations with low signal strength, and is quite sensitive to background noise and reverberation. The object position can also be estimated by analyzing the video data, in which case problems can be caused by the background clutter and change in object's appearance. In this paper, we combine both estimators in a principled manner using a single probabilistic model.

Probabilistic generative models have several important advantages which make them ideal for our purpose. First, since they explicitly model the actual sources of variability in the problem, such as object appearance and background noise, the resulting algorithm turns out to be quite robust. Second, using a probabilistic framework leads to a solution by an estimation algorithm which is Bayes-optimal. Third, parameter estimation and object tracking are both performed efficiently using the expectation-maximization (EM) algorithm.

Within the probabilistic modeling framework, the problem of calibration becomes the problem of estimating the parametric dependence of the time delay on the object position. It turns out that these parameters are estimated automatically as part of our EM algorithm, and no special treatment is required. Hence, we assume no prior calibration of the system, and no manual initialization in the first frame (e.g., defining the template or the contours of the object to be tracked). This is in contrast with previous research in this area, which typically requires specific and calibrated configurations, as in [10],[3]. We note in particular the method of [9] which, while using a probabilistic approach, still requires contour initialization in video and the knowledge of the microphone baseline, camera focal length, as well as the various thresholds used in visual feature extraction.

Throughout this paper, the only information our model is allowed to use before or during the tracking is the raw data itself. The EM algorithm described below learns from the data the object's appearance parameters, the microphone attenuations, the mapping from the object position in the video frames to the time delay between the audio waveforms, and the sensor noise parameters for all sensors.

3 A Probabilistic Generative Model for Audio-Video Data

We now turn to the technical description of our model. We begin with a model for the audio data, represented by the sound pressure waveform at each microphone for each frame. Next, we describe a model for the video data, represented by a vector of pixel intensities for each frame. We then fuse the two model by linking the time delay between the audio signals to the spatial location of the object's image.

3.1 Audio Model

We model the audio signals x_1, x_2 received at microphones 1, 2 as follows. First, each signal is chopped into equal length segments termed *frames*. The frame length is determined by the frame rate of the video. Hence, 30 video frames per second translates into 1/30 second long audio frames. Each audio frame is a vector with entries x_{1n}, x_{2n} corresponding to the signal values at time point n.

x_1, x_2 are described in terms of an original audio signal a. We assume that a is attenuated by a factor λ_i on its way to microphone $i = 1, 2$, and that it is received at microphone 2 with a delay of τ time points relative to microphone 1,

$$x_{1n} = \lambda_1 a_n ,$$
$$x_{2n} = \lambda_2 a_{n-\tau} . \qquad (1)$$

We further assume that a is contaminated by additive sensor noise with precision matrices ν_1, ν_2. To account for the variability of that signal, it is described by a mixture model. Denoting the component label by r, each component has mean zero, a precision matrix η_r, and a prior probability π_r. Viewing it in the frequency

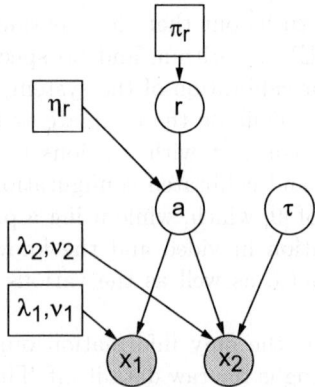

Fig. 2. Graphical model for the audio data.

domain, the precision matrix corresponds to the inverse of the *spectral template* for each component. Hence, we have

$$p(r) = \pi_r ,$$
$$p(a \mid r) = \mathcal{N}(a \mid 0, \eta_r) ,$$
$$p(x_1 \mid a) = \mathcal{N}(x_1 \mid \lambda_1 a, \nu_1) ,$$
$$p(x_2 \mid a, \tau) = \mathcal{N}(x_2 \mid \lambda_2 L_\tau a, \nu_2) , \qquad (2)$$

where L_τ denotes the temporal shift operator, i.e., $(L_\tau a)_n = a_{n-\tau}$. The prior probability for a delay τ is assumed flat, $p(\tau) = const$. A similar model was used in [2] to perform noise removal from speech signals. In that paper, the joint $p(a,r)$ served as a speech model with a relatively large number of components, which was pre-trained on a large clean speech dataset. Here, $p(a,r)$ has only a few components and its parameters are learned from audio-video data as part of the full model.

A note about notation. $\mathcal{N}(x \mid \mu, \nu)$ denotes a Gaussian distribution over the random vector x with mean μ and precision matrix (defined as the inverse covariance matrix) ν,

$$\mathcal{N}(x \mid \mu, \nu) \propto \exp\left[-\frac{1}{2}(x-\mu)^T \nu (x-\mu)\right] . \qquad (3)$$

Fig. 2 displays a graphical representation of the audio model. As usual with graphical models (see, e.g., [8]), a graph consists of nodes and edges. A shaded circle node corresponds to an observed variable, an open circle node corresponds to an unobserved variable, and a square node corresponds to a model parameter. An edge (directed arrow) corresponds to a probabilistic conditional dependence of the node at the arrow's head on the node at its tail.

A probabilistic graphical model has a generative interpretation: according to the model in Fig. 2, the process of generating the observed microphone signals

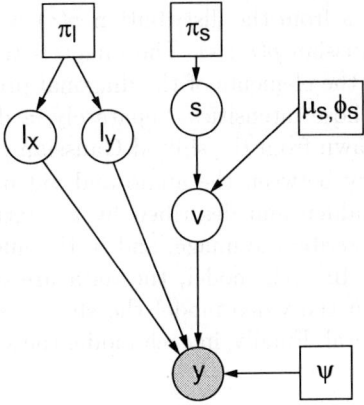

Fig. 3. Graphical model for the video data.

starts with picking a spectral component r with probability $p(r)$, followed by drawing a signal a from the Gaussian $p(a \mid r)$. Separately, a time delay τ is also picked. The signals x_1, x_2 are then drawn from the undelayed Gaussian $p(x_1 \mid a)$ and the delayed Gaussian $p(x_2 \mid a, \tau)$, respectively.

3.2 Video Model

In analogy with the audio frames, we model the video frames as follows. Denote the observed frame by y, which is a vector with entries y_n corresponding to the intensity of pixel n. This vector is described in terms of an original image v that has been shifted by $l = (l_x, l_y)$ pixels in the x and y directions, respectively,

$$y_n = v_{n-l} , \qquad (4)$$

and has been further contaminated by additive noise with precision matrix ψ. To account for the variability in the original image, v is modeled by a mixture model. Denoting its component label by s, each component is a Gaussian with mean μ_s and precision matrix ϕ_s, and has a prior probability π_s. The means serve as image templates. Hence, we have

$$\begin{aligned} p(s) &= \pi_s , \\ p(v \mid s) &= \mathcal{N}(v \mid \mu_s, \phi_s) , \\ p(y \mid v, l) &= \mathcal{N}(y \mid G_l v, \psi) , \end{aligned} \qquad (5)$$

where G_l denotes the shift operator, i.e. $(G_l v)_n = v_{n-l}$. The prior probability for a shift l is assumed flat, $p(l) = const$. This model was used in [5] for video based object tracking and stabilization.

Fig. 3 displays a graphical representation of the video model. Like the audio model, our video model has a generative interpretation. According to the model in Fig. 3, the process of generating the observed image starts with picking an appearance component s from the distribution $p(s) = \pi_s$, followed by drawing a image v from the Gaussian $p(v \mid s)$. The image is represented as a vector of pixel intensities, where the elements of the diagonal precision matrix define the level of confidence in those intensities. Separately, a discrete shift l is picked. The image y is then drawn from the shifted Gaussian $p(y \mid v, l)$.

Notice the symmetry between the audio and video models. In each model, the original signal is hidden and described by a mixture model. In the video model the templates describe the image, and in the audio model the templates describe the spectrum. In each model, the data are obtained by shifting the original signal, where in the video model the shift is spatial and in the audio model the shift is temporal. Finally, in each model the shifted signal is corrupted by additive noise.

3.3 Fusing Audio and Video

Our task now is to fuse the audio and video models into a single probabilistic graphical model. One road to fusion exploits the fact that the relative time delay τ between the microphone signals is directly related to the object position l. This is the road we take in this paper. In particular, as the distance of the object from the sensor setup becomes much larger than the distance between the microphones, which is the case in our experiments, τ becomes linear in l. We therefore use a linear mapping to approximate this dependence, and model the approximation error by a zero mean Gaussian with precision ν_τ,

$$p(\tau \mid l) = \mathcal{N}(\tau \mid \alpha l_x + \alpha' l_y + \beta, \nu_\tau) . \qquad (6)$$

Note that in our setup (see Fig. 1), the mapping involves only the horizontal position, as the vertical movement has a significantly smaller affect on the signal delay due to the horizontal alignment of the microphones (i.e., $\alpha' \approx 0$). The link formed by Eq. (6) fuses the two models into a single one, whose graphical representation is displayed in Fig. 4.

4 Parameter Estimation and Object Tracking

Here we outline the derivation of an EM algorithm for the graphical model in Fig. 4. As usual with hidden variable models, this is an iterative algorithm. The E-step of each iteration updates the posterior distribution over the hidden variables conditioned on the data. The M-step updates parameter estimates.

We start with the joint distribution over all model variables, the observed ones x_1, x_2, y and the hidden ones a, τ, r, v, l, s. As Fig. 4 shows, this distribution factorizes as

$$\begin{aligned} p(x_1, x_2, y, a, \tau, r, v, l, s \mid \theta) &= p(x_1 \mid a)\, p(x_2 \mid a, \tau)\, p(a \mid r) \\ &\quad \cdot p(r)\, p(y \mid v, l)\, p(v \mid s)\, p(s)\, p(\tau \mid l)\, p(l) . \end{aligned} \qquad (7)$$

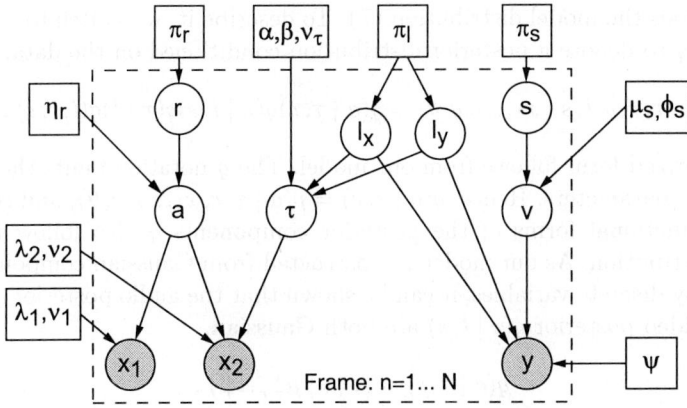

Fig. 4. Graphical model for the joint audio-video data. The dotted rectangle denotes i.i.d. frames and has the following meaning: everything it encompasses, i.e., all model variables, has value that is frame dependent; everything it leaves out, i.e., the model parameters, is frame independent.

This is the product of the joint distributions defined by the audio and video models and their link. The model parameters are

$$\theta = \{\lambda_1, \nu_1, \lambda_2, \nu_2, \eta_r, \pi_r, \psi, \mu_s, \phi_s, \pi_s, \alpha, \alpha', \beta, \nu_\tau\} \ . \tag{8}$$

Ultimately, we are interested in tracking the object based on the data, i.e., obtaining a position estimate $\hat{l}$ at each frame. In the framework of probabilistic modeling, one computes more than just a single value of l. Rather, the full posterior distribution over l given the data, $p(l \mid x_1, x_2, y)$, for each frame, is computed. This distribution provides the most likely position value via

$$\hat{l} = \arg\max_l p(l \mid x_1, x_2, y) \ , \tag{9}$$

as well as a measure of how confident the model is of that value. It can also handle situations where the position is ambiguous by exhibiting more than one mode. An example is when the speaker is occluded by either of two objects. However, in our experiments the position posterior is always unimodal.

4.1 E-step

Generally, the posterior over the hiddens is computed from the model distribution by Bayes' rule,

$$p(a, \tau, r, v, l, s \mid x_1, x_2, y, \theta) = \frac{p(x_1, x_2, y, a, \tau, r, v, l, s \mid \theta)}{p(x_1, x_2, y \mid \theta)} \ , \tag{10}$$

where $p(x_1, x_2, y \mid \theta)$ is obtained from the model distribution by marginalizing over the hiddens. In our model, it can be shown that the posterior has a factorized form, as does the model distribution (7). To describe it, we switch to a notation that uses q to denote a posterior distribution conditioned on the data. Hence,

$$p(a, \tau, r, v, l, s \mid x_1, x_2, y, \theta) = q(a \mid \tau, r) q(v \mid l, s) q(\tau \mid l) q(l, r, s) \,. \quad (11)$$

This factorized form follows from our model. The q notation omits the data, as well as the parameters. Hence, $q(a \mid \tau, r) = p(a \mid \tau, r, x_1, x_2, y, \theta)$, and so on.

The functional forms of the posterior components q also follow from the model distribution. As our model is constructed from Gaussian components tied together by discrete variables, it can be shown that the audio posterior $q(a \mid \tau, r)$ and the video posterior $q(v \mid l, s)$ are both Gaussian,

$$\begin{aligned} q(a \mid \tau, r) &= \mathcal{N}(a \mid \mu^a_{\tau,r}, \nu^a_r) \,, \\ q(v \mid l, s) &= \mathcal{N}(v \mid \mu^v_{l,s}, \nu^v_s) \,. \end{aligned} \quad (12)$$

The means $\mu^a_{\tau,r}$, $\mu^v_{l,s}$ and precisions ν^a_r, ν^v_s are straightforward to compute; note that the precisions do not depend on the shift variables τ, l. One particularly simple way to obtain them is to consider (11) and observe that its logarithm satisfies

$$\log p(a, \tau, r, v, l, s \mid x_1, x_2, y, \theta) = \log p(x_1, x_2, y, a, \tau, r, v, l, s \mid \theta) + const. \quad (13)$$

where the constant is independent of the hiddens. Due to the nature of our model, this logarithm is quadratic in a and v. To find the mean of the posterior over v, set the gradient of the log probability w.r.t. v to zero. The precision is then given by the negative Hessian, and we have

$$\begin{aligned} \mu^v_{l,s} &= (\nu^v_s)^{-1} (\phi_s \mu_s + G_l^T \psi y) \,, \\ \nu^v_s &= \phi_s + \psi \,. \end{aligned} \quad (14)$$

Equations for the mean and precision of the posterior over a are obtained in a similar fashion.

Another component of the posterior is the conditional probability table $q(\tau \mid l) = p(\tau \mid l, x_1, x_2, y, \theta)$, which turns out to be

$$q(\tau \mid l) \propto p(\tau \mid l) \exp(\lambda_1 \lambda_2 \nu_1 \nu_2 (\nu^a_r)^{-1} c_\tau) \,, \quad (15)$$

where

$$c_\tau = \sum_n x_{1n} x_{2, n+\tau} \quad (16)$$

is the cross-correlation between the microphone signals x_1 and x_2. Finally, the last component of the posterior is the probability table $q(l, r, s)$, whose form is omitted.

The calculation of $q(\tau \mid l)$ involves a minor but somewhat subtle point. Since throughout the paper we work in discrete time, the the delay τ in our model is generally regarded as a discrete variable. In particular, $q(\tau \mid l)$ is a discrete probability table. However, for reasons of mathematical convenience, the model distribution $p(\tau \mid l)$ (6) treats τ as continuous. Hence, the posterior $q(\tau \mid l)$ computed by our algorithm is, strictly speaking, an approximation, as the true posterior in this model must also treat τ as continuous. It turns out that this approximation is of the variational type (for a review of variational approximations see, e.g., [8]). To derive it rigorously one proceeds as follows. First, write down the form of the approximate posterior as a sum of delta functions,

$$q(\tau \mid l) = \sum_n q_n(l) \delta(\tau - \tau_n) , \qquad (17)$$

where the τ_n are spaced one time point apart. The coefficients q_n are nonnegative and sum up to one, and their dependence on l is initially unspecified. Next, compute the $q_n(l)$ by minimizing the Kullback-Leibler (KL) distance between the approximate posterior and the true posterior. This produces the optimal approximate posterior out of all possible posteriors which satisfy the restriction (17). In this paper we write $q(\tau \mid l)$ rather than $q_n(l)$ to keep notation simple.

4.2 M-step

The M-step performs updates of the model parameters θ (8). The update rules are derived, as usual, by considering the objective function

$$\mathcal{F}(\theta) = \langle \log p(x_1, x_2, y, a, \tau, r, v, l, s \mid \theta) \rangle , \qquad (18)$$

known as the averaged complete data likelihood. We use the notation $\langle \cdot \rangle$ to denote averaging w.r.t. the posterior (11) over all hidden variables that do not appear on the left hand side and, in addition, averaging over all frames. Hence, $\mathcal{F}$ is essentially the log-probability of our model for each frame, where values for the hidden variables are filled in by the posterior distribution for that frame, followed by summing over frames. Each parameter update rule is obtained by setting the derivative of $\mathcal{F}$ w.r.t. that parameter to zero.

For the video model parameters μ_s, ϕ_s, π_s we have

$$\mu_s = \frac{\langle \sum_l q(l,s) \mu_{ls}^v \rangle}{\langle q(s) \rangle} ,$$

$$\phi_s^{-1} = \frac{\langle \sum_l q(l,s)(\mu_{ls}^v - \mu_s)^2 + q(s)(\nu_{ls}^v)^{-1} \rangle}{\langle q(s) \rangle} ,$$

$$\pi_s = \langle q(s) \rangle , \qquad (19)$$

where the q's are computed by appropriate marginalizations over $q(l, r, s)$ from the E-step. Notice that here, the notation $\langle \cdot \rangle$ implies only average over frames. Update rules for the audio model parameters η_r, π_r are obtained in a similar fashion.

For the audio-video link parameters α, β we have, assuming for simplicity $\alpha' = 0$,

$$\alpha = \frac{\langle l_x \tau \rangle - \langle \tau \rangle \langle l_x \rangle}{\langle l_x^2 \rangle - \langle l_x \rangle^2}$$
$$\beta = \langle \tau \rangle - \alpha \langle l_x \rangle$$
$$\nu_\tau^{-1} = \langle \tau^2 \rangle + \alpha^2 \langle l_x^2 \rangle + \beta^2 + 2\alpha\beta \langle l_x \rangle - 2\alpha \langle \tau l_x \rangle - 2\beta \langle \tau \rangle \;, \qquad (20)$$

where in addition to averaging over frames, $\langle \cdot \rangle$ here implies averaging for each frame w.r.t. $q(\tau, l)$ for that frame, which is obtained by marginalizing $q(\tau \mid l)q(l, r, s)$ over r, s.

A note about complexity. According to Eq. (19), computing the mean $(\mu_s)_n$ for each pixel n requires summing over all possible spatial shifts l. Since the number of possible shifts equals the number of pixels, this seems to imply that the complexity of our algorithm is quadratic in the number of pixels N. If that were the case, a standard $N = 120 \times 160$ pixel array would render the computation practically intractable. However, as pointed out in [6], a more careful examination of Eq. (19), in combination with Eq. (14), shows that it can be written in the form of an inverse FFT. Consequently, the actual complexity is not $\mathcal{O}(N^2)$ but rather $\mathcal{O}(N \log N)$. This result, which extends to the corresponding quantities in the audio model, significantly increases the efficiency of the EM algorithm.

4.3 Tracking

Tracking is performed as part of the E-step using (9), where $p(l \mid x_1, x_2, y)$ is computed from $q(\tau, l)$ above by marginalization. For each frame the mode of this posterior distribution of l represents the most likely translation for the object template, and the width of the distribution the degree of uncertainty in this inference.

5 Results

We tested the tracking algorithm on several audio-video sequences captured by the setup in Fig. 1 consisting of low-cost, off the shelf equipment. The video capture rate was 15 frames per second, and the audio was digitized at a sampling rate of 16kHz. This means that each frame contained one 160×120 image frame and two 1066 samples long audio frames. No model parameters were set by hand, and no initialization was required; the only input to the algorithm was the raw data. The algorithm was consistently able to estimate the time delay of arrival and the object position while learning all the model parameters, including the calibration (audio-video link) parameters. The processing speed of our Matlab implementation was about 50 frames per second per iteration of EM. Convergence was generally achieved within just 10 iterations.

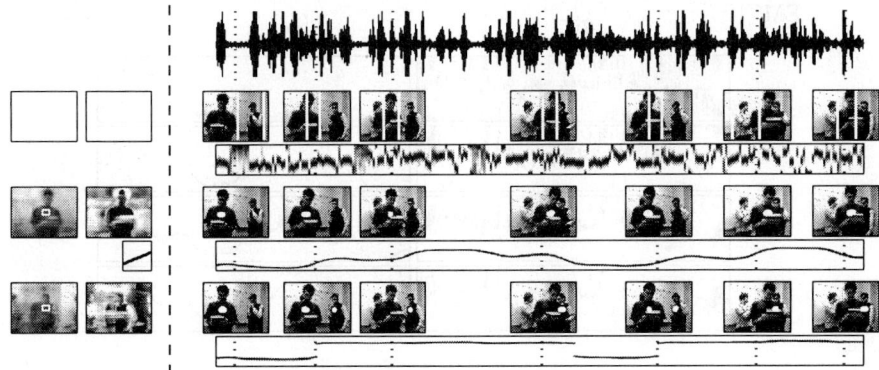

Fig. 5. Tracking results for the audio only (first row), audio-video (second row), and video only (third row) models. Each row consists of the inference for l_x (bottom), and selected frames from the video sequence (top), positioned in time according to the vertical dotted lines. Note that while the subject moves horizontally, the bottom row of each plot depicts l_x inference on its *vertical* axis for clarity. The area enclosed by the white dots, or *between* the white lines in the case of the audio only model (first row), represents the region(s) occupying the overwhelming majority of the probability mass for the inferred object location.

We present the results on two sequences that had substantial background audio noise and visual distractions. In Fig. 5, we compare the results of tracking using the audio only model (Fig. 2), full audio-video model (Fig. 4), and the video only model (Fig. 3) on the multimodal data containing a moving and talking person with a strong distraction consisting of another two people chatting and moving in the background (see Fig. 1). For tracking using the audio only model, a link between τ and l was added (whose parameters were computed separately) to allow computing the posterior $q(l)$. The left two columns in Fig. 5 show the learned image template and the variance map. (For the audio model, these images are left blank.) Note that the model observing only the video (third main row) failed to focus on the foreground object and learned a blurred template instead. The inferred position stayed largely flat and occasionally switched as the model was never able to decide what to focus on. This is indicated in the figure both by the white dot in the appropriate position in the frames and in the position plot (see figure caption). The model observing only the audio data (first main row) provided a very noisy estimate of l_x. As indicated by the white vertical lines, no estimate of l_y could be obtained, due to the horizontal alignment of the microphones.

The full audio-visual model (second main row) learned the template for the foreground model and the variance map that captures the variability in the person's appearance due to the non-translational head motion and movements of the book. The learned linear mapping between the position and delay variables is shown just below the template variance map. The tracker stays on the object

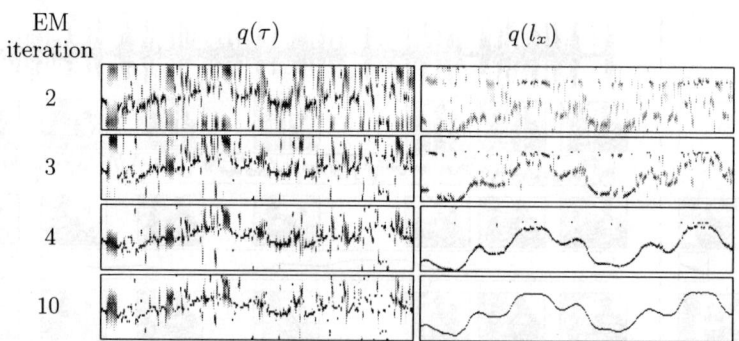

Fig. 6. Learning the combined model with EM iterations. (Left) uncertainty in τ represented by the posterior distribution $q(\tau)$, with darker areas representing more certainty ($\tau \in \{-15,\ldots,15\}$). Right uncertainty in horizontal position represented by the posterior distribution $q(l_x)$, similar shading. The four rows correspond to the inference after 2 (top), 3, 4 and 10 (bottom) iterations, by which point the algorithm has converged. In particular note how the final uncertainty in τ is a considerable improvement over that obtained by the correlation based result shown in Fig. 1.

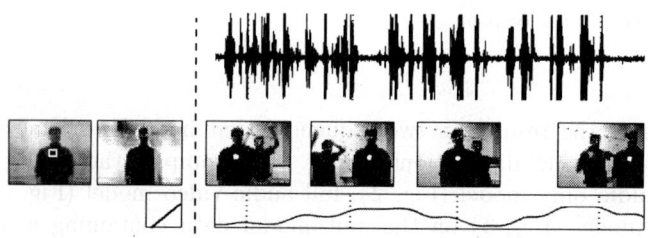

Fig. 7. Tracking results on a data set with significant visual noise.

even during the silent periods, regardless of the high background audio noise, and as can be seen form the position plot, the tracker had inferred a smooth trajectory with high certainty, without need for temporal filtering.

In Fig. 6 we illustrate the parameter estimation process by showing the progressive improvement in the audio-visual tracking through several EM iterations. Upon random initialization, both the time delay and location estimates are very noisy. These estimates consistently improve as the iterations proceed, and even though the audio part never becomes fully confident in its delay estimate, mostly due to reverberation effects, it still helps the video part achieve near certainty by the tenth iteration. In Fig. 7, we show another example of tracking using the full audio-video model on the data with strong visual distractions. One might note the step-like trends in the position plots in both cases, which really does follow the stepping patterns in the walk of the subjects.

6 Conclusions and Future Work

In this paper we have presented a new approach to building models for joint audio and video data. This approach has produced a new algorithm for object tracking, which is based on a graphical model that combines audio and video variables in a systematic fashion. The model parameters are learned from a multimedia sequence using an EM algorithm. The object trajectory is then inferred from the data via Bayes' rule. Unlike other methods which require precise calibration to coordinate the audio and video, our algorithm performs calibration automatically as part of EM.

Beyond self calibration, our tracker differs from the state of the art in two other important aspects. First, the tracking paradigm does not assume incremental change in object location, which makes the algorithm robust to sudden movements. At the same time, the estimated trajectories are smooth as the model has ample opportunity to explain noise and distractions using data features other than the position itself. This illustrates the power of modeling the mechanism that generates the data.

Second, the paradigm can be extended in several ways. Multi-object situations may be handled by replicating our single object model. Such cases typically involve occlusion, which may be approached using models such as the one proposed in [7]. Multi-object situations also pose the problem of interfering sound from multiple sources. This aspect of the problem may be handled by source separation algorithms of the type developed in [1]. Such models may be incorporated into the present framework and facilitate handling richer multimedia scenarios.

References

[1] H. Attias and C.E. Schreiner (1998), Blind source separation and deconvolution: the dynamic component analysis algorithm. Neural Computation 10, 1373-1424.
[2] H. Attias et al (2001), A new method for speech denoising and robust speech recognition using probabilistic models for clean speech and for noise. Proc. Eurospeech 2001.
[3] M. S. Brandstein (1999). Time-delay estimation of reverberant speech exploiting harmonic structure. Journal of the Accoustic Society of America 105(5), 2914-2919.
[4] C. Bregler and Y. Konig (1994). Eigenlips for robust speech recognition. Proc. ICASSP.
[5] B. Frey and N. Jojic (1999). Estimating mixture models of images and inferring spatial transformations using the EM algorithm. Proc. of IEEE Conf. on Computer Vision and Pattern Recognition.
[6] B. Frey and N. Jojic (2001). Fast, large-scale transformation-invariant clustering. Proc. of Neural Information Processing Systems, December 2001, Vancouver, BC, Canada.
[7] N. Jojic and B. Frey (2001). Learning flexible sprites in video layers. Proc. of IEEE Conf. on Computer Vision and Pattern Recognition, Maui, HI.

[8] Jordan, M.I. (Ed.) (1998). *Learning in Graphical Models*. MIT Press, Cambridge, MA.
[9] J. Vermaak, M. Gagnet, A. Blake and P. Pérez (2001). Sequential Monte-Carlo fusion of sound and vision for speaker tracking. Proc. IEEE Intl. Conf. on Computer Vision.
[10] H. Wang and P. Chu (1997). Voice source localization for automatic camera pointing system in videoconferencing. Proc. ICASSP, 187-190.

Visual Motion

Increasing Space-Time Resolution in Video

Eli Shechtman, Yaron Caspi, and Michal Irani

Dept. of Computer Science and Applied Math
The Weizmann Institute of Science
76100 Rehovot, Israel
{elishe,caspi,irani}@wisdom.weizmann.ac.il

Abstract. We propose a method for constructing a video sequence of high space-time resolution by combining information from multiple low-resolution video sequences of the same dynamic scene. Super-resolution is performed simultaneously in time and in space. By "temporal super-resolution" we mean recovering rapid dynamic events that occur faster than regular frame-rate. Such dynamic events are not visible (or else observed incorrectly) in any of the input sequences, even if these are played in "slow-motion".

The spatial and temporal dimensions are very different in nature, yet are inter-related. This leads to interesting visual tradeoffs in time and space, and to new video applications. These include: (i) treatment of *spatial* artifacts (e.g., motion-blur) by increasing the *temporal* resolution, and (ii) combination of input sequences of different space-time resolutions (e.g., NTSC, PAL, and even high quality still images) to generate a high quality video sequence.

Keywords. Super-resolution, space-time analysis.

1 Introduction

A video camera has limited spatial and temporal resolution. The spatial resolution is determined by the spatial density of the detectors in the camera and by their induced blur. These factors limit the minimal size of spatial features or objects that can be visually detected in an image. The temporal resolution is determined by the frame-rate and by the exposure-time of the camera. These limit the maximal speed of dynamic events that can be observed in a video sequence.

Methods have been proposed for increasing the spatial resolution of images by combining information from multiple low-resolution images obtained at sub-pixel displacements (e.g. [1,2,5,6,9,10,11,12,14]. See [3] for a comprehensive review). These, however, usually assume static scenes and do not address the limited temporal resolution observed in dynamic scenes. In this paper we extend the notion of super-resolution to the *space-time* domain. We propose a unified framework for increasing the resolution both in time and in space by combining information from multiple *video sequences* of dynamic scenes obtained at (sub-pixel) spatial and (sub-frame) temporal misalignments. As will be shown, this enables new visual capabilities of dynamic events, gives rise to visual tradeoffs between time

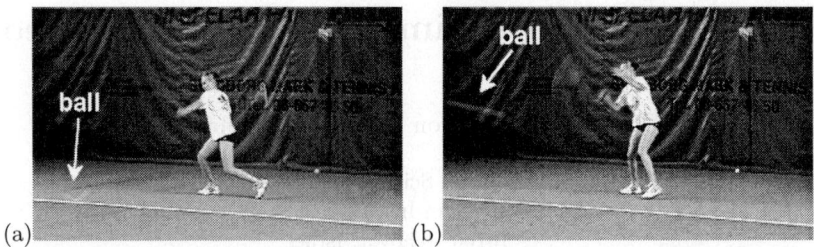

Fig. 1. Motion blur. *Distorted shape due to motion blur of very fast moving objects (the tennis ball and the racket) in a real tennis video. The perceived distortion of the ball is marked by a white arrow. Note, the "V"-like shape of the ball in (a), and the elongated shape of the ball in (b). The racket has almost "disappeared".*

and space, and leads to new video applications. These are substantial in the presence of very fast dynamic events.

Rapid dynamic events that occur faster than the frame-rate of video cameras are not visible (or else captured incorrectly) in the recorded video sequences. This problem is often evident in sports videos (e.g., tennis, baseball, hockey), where it is impossible to see the full motion or the behavior of the fast moving ball/puck. There are two typical visual effects in video sequences which are caused by very fast motion. One effect (motion blur) is caused by the exposure-time of the camera, and the other effect (motion aliasing) is due to the temporal sub-sampling introduced by the frame-rate of the camera:

(i) *Motion Blur:* The camera integrates the light coming from the scene during the exposure time in order to generate each frame. As a result, fast moving objects produce a noted blur along their trajectory, often resulting in distorted or unrecognizable object shapes. The faster the object moves, the stronger this effect is, especially if the trajectory of the moving object is not linear. This effect is notable in the distorted shapes of the tennis ball shown in Fig. 1. Note also that the tennis racket also "disappears" in Fig. 1.b. Methods for treating motion blur in the context of image-based super-resolution were proposed in [2, 12]. These methods however, require prior segmentation of moving objects and the estimation of their motions. Such motion analysis may be impossible in the presence of severe shape distortions of the type shown in Fig. 1. We will show that by increasing the *temporal resolution* using information from multiple video sequences, *spatial artifacts* such as motion blur can be handled without the need to separate static and dynamic scene components or estimate their motions.

(ii) *Motion-Based (Temporal) Aliasing:* A more severe problem in video sequences of fast dynamic events is false visual illusions caused by aliasing in time. Motion aliasing occurs when the trajectory generated by a fast moving object is characterized by frequencies which are higher than the frame-rate of the camera (i.e., the temporal sampling rate). When that happens, the high temporal frequencies are "folded" into the low temporal frequencies. The observable result is a distorted or even false trajectory of the moving object. This effect is illus-

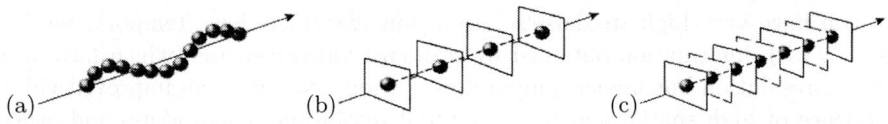

Fig. 2. Motion aliasing. *(a) shows a ball moving in a sinusoidal trajectory. (b) displays an image sequence of the ball captured at low frame-rate. The perceived motion is along a straight line. This false perception is referred to in the paper as "motion aliasing". (c) Illustrates that even using an ideal temporal interpolation will not produces the correct motion. The filled-in frames are indicated by the blue dashed line.*

trated in Fig. 2, where a ball moves fast in sinusoidal trajectory of high frequency (Fig. 2.a). Because the frame-rate is much lower (below Nyquist frequency of the trajectory), the *observed* trajectory of the ball is a straight line (Fig. 2.b). Playing that video sequence in "slow-motion" will not correct this false visual effect (Fig. 2.c). Another example of motion-based aliasing is the well-known visual illusion called the "wagon wheel effect": When a wheel is spinning very fast, beyond a certain speed it will appear to be rotating in the "wrong" direction.

Neither the motion-based aliasing nor the motion blur can be treated by playing such video sequences in "slow-motion", even when sophisticated temporal interpolations are used to increase the frame-rate (as in format conversion or "re-timing" methods [8,13]). This is because the information contained in a single video sequence is insufficient to recover the missing information of very fast dynamic events (due to excessive blur and subsampling). Multiple video sequences, on the other hand, provide additional samples of the dynamic space-time scene. While none of the individual sequences provides enough visual information, combining the information from all the sequences allows to generate a video sequence of high space-time resolution (Sec. 2), which displays the correct dynamic events. Thus, for example, a reconstructed high-resolution sequence will display the correct motion of the wagon wheel despite it appearing incorrectly in *all* of the input sequences (Sec. 4).

The spatial and temporal dimensions are very different in nature, yet are inter-related. This introduces visual tradeoffs between space and times, which are unique to spatio-temporal super-resolution, and are not applicable in traditional spatial (i.e., image-based) super-resolution. For example, output sequences of different space-time resolutions can be generated for the same input sequences. A large increase in the temporal resolution usually comes at the expense of a large increase in the spatial resolution, and vice versa.

Furthermore, input sequences of different space-time resolutions can be meaningfully combined in our framework. In traditional image-based super-resolution there is no incentive to combine input images of different spatial resolutions, since a high-resolution image will subsume the information contained in a low-resolution image. This, however, is not the case here. Different types of cameras of different space-time resolutions may provide *complementary* information. Thus, for example, we can combine information obtained by high-quality still cameras (which have very high spatial-resolution, but extremely low "temporal resolution"), with information obtained by standard video cameras (which have low spatial-resolution but higher temporal resolution), to obtain an improved video sequence of high spatial and high temporal resolution. These issues and other space-time visual tradeoffs are discussed in Sec. 4.

2 Space-Time Super-Resolution

Let S be a dynamic space-time scene. Let $\{S_i^l\}_{i=1}^n$ be n video sequences of that dynamic scene recorded by n different video cameras. The recorded sequences have limited spatial and temporal resolution. Their limited resolutions are due to the space-time imaging process, which can be thought of as a process of blurring followed by sampling in time and in space.

The blurring effect results of the fact that the color at each pixel in each frame (referred to as a "space-time point" and marked by the small boxes in Fig. 3.a) is an integral (a weighted average) of the colors in a space-time *region* in the dynamic scene S (marked by the large pink (bright) and blue (dark) boxes in Fig. 3.a). The temporal extent of this region is determined by the exposure-time of the video camera, and the spatial extent of this region is determined by the spatial point-spread-function (PSF) of the camera (determined by the properties of the lens and the detectors [4]).

The sampling process also has a spatial and a temporal components. The spatial sampling results from the fact that the camera has a discrete and finite number of detectors (the output of each is a single pixel value), and the temporal sampling results from the fact that the camera has a finite frame-rate resulting in discrete frames (typically 25 $frames/sec$ in PAL cameras and 30 $frames/sec$ in NTSC cameras).

The above space-time imaging process inhibits high spatial and high temporal frequencies of the dynamic scene, resulting in video sequences of low space-time resolutions. Our objective is to use the information from all these sequences to construct a new sequence S^h of high space-time resolution. Such a sequence will have smaller blurring effects and finer sampling in space and in time, and will thus capture higher space-time frequencies of the dynamic scene S. In particular, it will capture fine spatial features in the scene and rapid dynamic events which cannot be captured by the low-resolution sequences.

The recoverable high-resolution information in S^h is limited by its spatial and temporal sampling rate (or discretization) of the space-time volume. These rates can be different in space and in time. Thus, for example, we can recover a sequence S^h of very high spatial resolution but low temporal resolution (e.g., see Fig. 3.b), a sequence of very high temporal resolution but low spatial resolution (e.g., see Fig. 3.c), or a bit of both. These tradeoffs in space-time resolutions and their visual effects will be discussed in more detail later in Sec. 4.2.

We next model the geometrical relations (Sec. 2.1) and photometric relations (Sec. 2.2) between the unknown high-resolution sequence S^h and the input low-resolution sequences $\{S_i^l\}_{i=1}^n$.

2.1 The Space-Time Coordinate Transformations

In general a space-time dynamic scene is captured by a 4D representation (x, y, z, t). For simplicity, in this paper we deal with dynamic scenes which can be modeled by a 3D space-time volume (x, y, t) (see in Fig. 3.a). This assumption is valid if one of the following conditions holds: (i) the scene is planar and the dynamic events occur within this plane, or (ii) the scene is a general dynamic 3D scene, but the distances between the recording video cameras are small relative to their distance from the scene. (When the camera centers are very close to each other, there is no relative 3D parallax.) Under those conditions the dynamic scene can be modeled by a 3D space-time representation.

W.l.o.g., let S_1^l be a "reference" sequence whose axes are aligned with those of the continuous space-time volume S (the unknown dynamic scene we wish to reconstruct). S^h is a discretization of S with a higher sampling rate than that of S_1^l. Thus, we can model the transformation T_1 from the space-time coordinate system of S_1^l to the space-time coordinate system of S^h by a scaling transformation (the scaling can be different in time and in space). Let $T_{i \to 1}$ denote the space-time coordinate transformation from the reference sequence S_1^l to the i-th low resolution sequence S_i^l (see below). Then the space-time coordinate transfor-

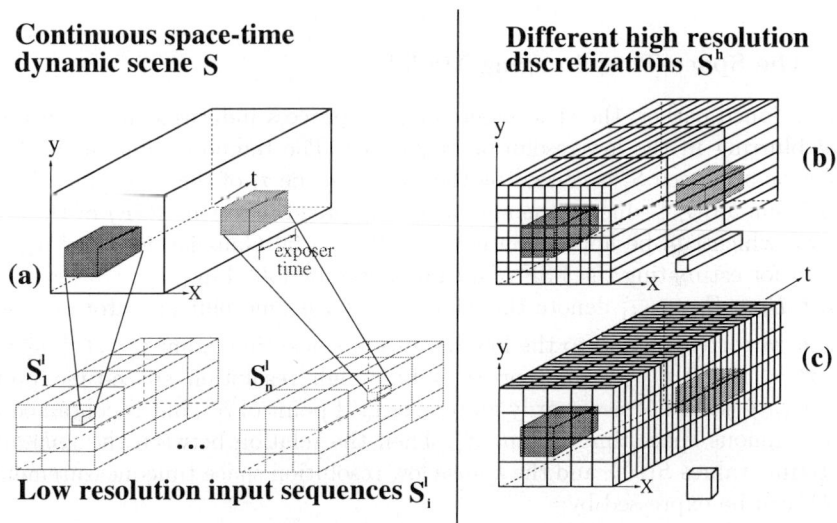

Fig. 3. The space-time imaging process. *(a) illustrates the space-time continuous scene and two of the low resolution sequences. The large pink (bright) and blue (dark) boxes are the support regions of the space-time blur corresponding to the low resolution space-time measurements marked by the respective small boxes. (b,c) show two different possible discretizations of the space-time volume resulting in two different high resolution output sequences. (b) has a low frame-rate and high spatial resolution, (c) has a high frame-rate but low spatial resolution.*

mation of each low-resolution sequence S_i^l is related to that of the high-resolution sequence S^h by $T_i = T_1 \cdot T_{i \to 1}$.

The space-time coordinate transformation between two input sequences ($T_{i\to 1}$) results from the different setting of the different cameras. A *temporal misalignment* between two sequences occurs when there is a time-shift (offset) between them (e.g., if the cameras were not activated simultaneously), or when they differ in their frame rates (e.g., PAL and NTSC). Such temporal misalignments can be modeled by a 1-D affine transformation in time, and is typically at sub-frame time units. The *spatial misalignment* between the two sequences results from the fact that the two cameras have different external and internal calibration parameters. In our current implementation, as mentioned above, because the camera centers are assumed to be very close or else the scene is planar, the spatial transformation can thus be modeled by an inter-camera homography. We computed these space-time coordinate transformations, using the method of [7], which provides high sub-pixel and high sub-frame accuracy.

Note that while the space-time coordinate transformations *between the sequences* ($\{T_i\}_{i=1}^n$) are very simple (a spatial homography and a temporal affine transformation), the motions occurring over time *within* the dynamic scene can be very complex. Our space-time super-resolution algorithm does *not* require knowledge of these motions, only the knowledge of $\{T_i\}_{i=1}^n$. It can thus handle very complex dynamic scenes.

2.2 The Space-Time Imaging Model

As mentioned earlier, the space-time imaging process induces spatial and temporal blurring in the low-resolution sequences. The temporal blur in the low-resolution sequence S_i^l is caused by the exposer-time τ_i of the i-th camera. The spatial blur in S_i^l is due to the spatial point-spread-function (PSF) of the i-th camera, which can be approximated by a 2D spatial Gaussian with std σ_i. (A method for estimating the PSF of a camera can be found in [11].)

Let $B_i = B_{(\sigma_i, \tau_i, p_i^l)}$ denote the combined space-time blur operator of the i-th camera corresponding to the low resolution space-time point $p_i^l = (x_i^l, y_i^l, t_i^l)$. Let $p^h = (x^h, y^h, t^h)$ be the corresponding high resolution space-time point $p^h = T_i(p_i^l)$ (p^h is not necessarily an integer grid point of S^h, but is contained in the continuous space-time volume S). Then the relation between the *unknown* space-time values $S(p^h)$, and the *known* low resolution space-time measurements $S_i^l(p_i^l)$, can be expressed by:

$$S_i^l(p_i^l) = (S * B_i^h)(p^h) = \int_x \int_y \int_t \atop p = (x,y,t) \in Support(B_i^h) S(p) B_i^h(p - p^h) dp \qquad (1)$$

where $B_i^h = T_i(B_{(\sigma_i, \tau_i, p_i^l)})$ is a point-dependent space-time blur kernel represented in the high resolution coordinate system. Its support is illustrated by the large pink (bright) and blue (dark) boxes in Fig. 3.a. To obtain a linear equation in the terms of the *discrete unknown* values of S^h we used a discrete approximation of Eq. (1). In our implementation we used a non-isotropic approximation in the temporal dimension, and an isotropic approximation in the spatial dimension (see [6] for a discussion of the different discretization techniques in the context of image-based super-resolution). Eq. (1) thus provides a linear equation that relates the unknown values in the high resolution sequence S^h to the *known* low resolution measurements $S_i^l(p_i^l)$.

When video cameras of different photometric responses are used to produce the input sequences, then a preprocessing step is necessary that histogram-equalizes all the low resolution sequences. This step is required to guarantee consistency of the relation in Eq. (1) with respect to all low resolution sequences.

2.3 The Reconstruction Step

Eq. (1) provides a single equation in the high resolution unknowns for each low resolution space-time measurement. This leads to the following huge system of linear equations in the unknown high resolution elements of S^h:

$$A\vec{h} = \vec{l} \qquad (2)$$

where $\vec{h}$ is a vector containing all the unknown high resolution color values (in YIQ) of S^h, $\vec{l}$ is a vector containing all the space-time measurements from all the low resolution sequences, and the matrix A contains the relative contributions of each high resolution space-time point to each low resolution space-time point, as defined by Eq. (1).

When the number of low resolution space-time measurements in $\vec{l}$ is greater than or equal to the number of space-time points in the high-resolution sequence S^h (i.e., in $\vec{h}$), then there are more equations than unknowns, and Eq. (2) can be solved using LSQ methods. This, however, implies that a large increase in the spatial resolution (which requires very fine spatial sampling in S^h) will come at the expense of a significant increase in the temporal resolution (which also requires fine temporal sampling in S^h), and vice versa. This is because for a given set of input low-resolution sequences, the size of $\vec{l}$ is fixed, thus dictating the number of unknowns in S^h. However, the number high resolution space-time points (unknowns) can be distributed differently between space and time, resulting in different space-time resolutions (see 4.2).

Directional space-time regularization. When there is an insufficient number of cameras relative to the required improvement in resolution (either in the entire space-time volume, or only in portions of it), then the above set of equations (2) becomes ill-posed. To constrain the solution and provide additional numerical stability (as in image-based super-resolution [9,5]), a space-time regularization term can be added to impose smoothness on the solution S^h in space-time regions which have insufficient information. We introduce a *directional* (or steerable [14]) space-time regularization term which applies smoothness only in directions where the derivatives are low, and does *not* smooth across space-time "edges". In other words, we seek $\vec{h}$ which minimize the following error term:

$$min(||A\vec{h} - \vec{l}||^2 + ||W_x L_x \vec{h}||^2 + ||W_y L_y \vec{h}||^2 + ||W_t L_t \vec{h}||^2) \qquad (3)$$

Where L_j ($j = x, y, t$) is matrix capturing the second-order derivative operator in the direction j, and W_j is a diagonal weight matrix which captures the degree of desired regularization at each space-time point in the direction j. The weights in W_j prevent smoothing across space-time "edges". These weights are determined by the location, orientation and magnitude of space-time edges, and are approximated using space-time derivatives in the low resolution sequences.

Solving the equations. The optimization problem of Eq. (3) has very large dimensionality. For example, even for a simple case of four low resolution input sequences, each one-second long (25 frames) and of size 128×128 pixels, we get: $128^2 \times 25 \times 4 \approx 1.6 \times 10^6$ equations from the low resolution measurements alone (without regularization). Assuming a similar number of high resolution unknowns poses a severe computational problem. However, matrix A is sparse and local (i.e., all the non zero entries are located in a few diagonals), the system of equations can be solved using "box relaxation" [15].

3 Examples: Temporal Super-Resolution

Empirical Evaluation. To examine the capabilities of temporal super-resolution in the presence of strong motion aliasing and strong motion blur, we first simulated a sports-like scene with a very fast moving object. We recorded a single video sequence of a basketball bouncing on the ground. To simulate high speed of the ball relative to frame-rate and relative to the exposure-time (similar to those shown in Fig. 1), we temporally blurred the sequence using a large (9-frame) blur kernel, followed by a large subsampling in time by factor of 30. This process results in a low temporal-resolution sequences of a very fast dynamic event having an "exposure-time" of about $\frac{1}{3}$ of its frame-time. We generated 18 such low resolution sequences by starting the temporal sub-sampling at arbitrary starting frames. Thus, the input low-resolution sequences are related by *non-uniform* sub-frame temporal offsets. Because the original sequence contained 250 frames, each generated low-resolution sequence contains only 7 frames. Three of the 18 sequences are presented in Fig 4.a-c. To visually display the event captured in each of these sequences, we super-imposed all 7 frames in each sequence. Each ball in the super-imposed image represents the location of the ball at a different frame. None of the 18 low resolution sequences captures the correct trajectory of the ball. Due to the severe motion aliasing, the perceived ball trajectory is roughly a smooth curve, while the true trajectory was more like a cycloid (the ball jumped 5 times on the floor). Furthermore, the shape of the ball is completely distorted in all input image frames, due to the strong motion blur.

We applied the super-resolution algorithm of Sec. 2 on these 18 low-resolution input sequences, and constructed a high-resolution sequence whose frame-rate is 30 times higher than that of the input sequences. (In this case we requested an increase only in the temporal sampling rate). The reconstructed high-resolution sequence is shown in Fig. 4.d. This is a super-imposed display of some of the

Fig. 4. Temporal super-resolution. *We simulated 18 low-resolution video recordings of a rapidly bouncing ball inducing strong motion blur and motion aliasing (see text). (a)-(c) Display the dynamic event captured by three representative low-resolution sequences. These displays were produced by super-position of all 7 frames in each low-resolution sequences. All 18 input sequences contain severe motion aliasing (evident from the falsely perceived curved trajectory of the ball) and strong motion blur (evident from the distorted shapes of the ball). (d) The reconstructed dynamic event as captured by the generated high-resolution sequence. The true trajectory of the ball is recovered, as well as its correct shape. (e) A close-up image of the distorted ball in one of the low resolution frames. (f) A close-up image of the ball at the exact corresponding frame in time in the high-resolution output sequence. For color sequences see: www.wisdom.weizmann.ac.il/~vision/SuperRes.html*

reconstructed frames (every 8'th frame). The true trajectory of the bouncing ball has been recovered. Furthermore, Figs. 4(e)-(f) show that this process has significantly reduced effects of motion blur and the true shape of moving ball has been automatically recovered, although no single low resolution frame contains the true shape of the ball. Note that no estimation of the ball motion was needed to obtain these results. This effect is explained in more details in Sec. 4.1.

The above results obtained by temporal super-resolution cannot be obtained by playing any low-resolution sequence in "slow-motion" due to the strong motion aliasing. Such results cannot be obtained either by interleaving frames from the 18 input sequences, due to the non-uniform time shifts between the sequences and due to the severe motion-blur observed in the individual image frames.

A Real Example – The "Wagon-Wheel Effect". We used four independent PAL video cameras to record a scene of a fan rotating clock-wise very fast. The fan rotated faster and faster, until at some stage it exceeded the maximal velocity that can be captured by video frame-rate. As expected, at that moment all four input sequences display the classical "wagon wheel effect" where the fan appears to be falsely rotating backwards (counter clock-wise). We computed the spatial and temporal misalignments between the sequences at sub-pixel and sub-frame accuracy using [7] (the recovered temporal misalignments are displayed in Fig. 5.a-d using a time-bar). We used the super-resolution method of Sec. 2 to increase the temporal resolution by a factor of 3 while maintaining the same spatial resolution. The resulting high-resolution sequence displays the true forward (clock-wise) motion of the fan, as if recorded by a high-speed camera (in this case, $75 frames/sec$). Example of a few successive frames from each low resolution input sequence are shown in Fig.5.a-d for the portion where the fan appears to be rotating counter clock-wise. A few successive frames from the reconstructed high temporal-resolution sequence corresponding to the same time are shown in Fig.5.e, showing the correctly recovered (clock-wise) motion. It is difficult to perceive these strong dynamic effects via a static figure (Fig. 5). We therefore urge the reader to view the video clips in www.wisdom.weizmann.ac.il/~vision/SuperRes.html where these effects are very vivid . Furthermore, playing the input sequences in "slow-motion" (using any type of temporal interpolation) will *not* reduce the perceived false motion effects.

4 Space-Time Visual Tradeoffs

The spatial and temporal dimensions are very different in nature, yet are interrelated. This introduces visual tradeoffs between space and time, which are unique to spatio-temporal super-resolution, and are not applicable to traditional spatial (i.e., image-based) super-resolution.

4.1 Temporal Treatment of Spatial Artifacts

When an object moves fast relative to the exposure time of the camera, it induces observable motion-blur (e.g., see Fig. 1). The perceived distortion is spatial, however the cause is temporal. We next show that by increasing the *temporal* resolution we can handle the *spatial* artifacts caused by motion blur.

Motion blur is caused by the extended temporal blur due to the exposure-time. To decrease effects of motion blur we need to decrease the temporal blur, i.e., recover high temporal frequencies. This requires increasing the frame-rate beyond that of the low resolution input sequences. In fact, to decrease the effect of motion blur, the output temporal sampling rate must be increased so that the distance between the new high resolution temporal samples is *smaller* than the original exposure time of the low resolution input sequences.

This indeed was the case in the experiment of Fig. 4. Since the simulated exposure time in the low resolution sequences was 1/3 of frame-time, an increase in temporal sampling rate by a factor > 3 can reduce the motion blur. The larger

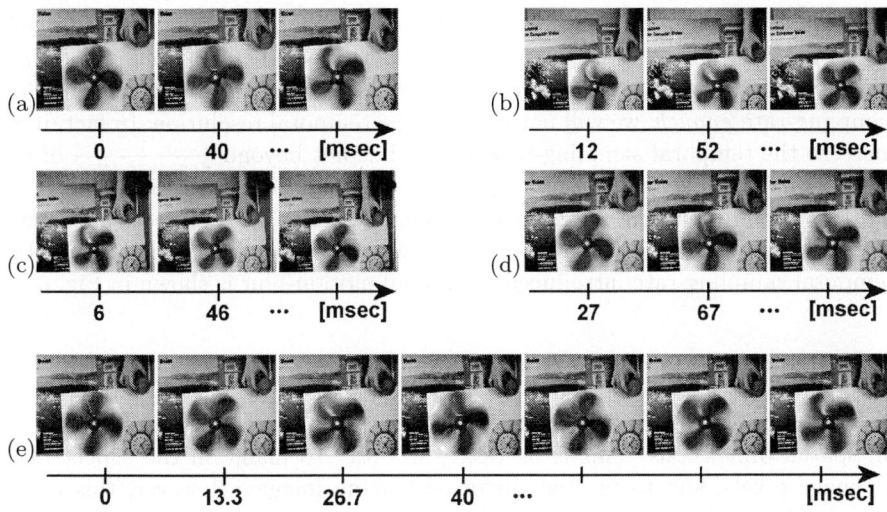

Fig. 5. Temporal super-resolution (the "wagon wheel effect"). *(a)-(d) display 3 successive frames from four PAL video recordings of a fan rotating clock-wise. Because the fan is rotating very fast (almost 90° between successive frames), the motion aliasing generates a false perception of the fan rotating slowly in the opposite direction (counter clock-wise) in all four input sequences. The temporal misalignments between the input sequences were computed at sub-frame temporal accuracy, and are indicated by their time bars. The spatial misalignments between the sequences (e.g., due to differences in zoom and orientation) were modeled by a homography, and computed at sub-pixel accuracy. (e) shows the reconstructed video sequence in which the temporal resolution was increased by a factor of 3. The new frame rate ($75 \frac{frames}{sec}$) is also indicated by a time bars. The correct clock-wise motion of the fan is recovered. For color sequences see:* www.wisdom.weizmann.ac.il/~vision/SuperRes.html

the increase the more effective the motion deblurring would be. This increase is limited, of course, by the number of input cameras.

A method for treating motion blur in the context of *image-based* super-resolution was proposed by [2,12]. However, these methods require a prior segmentation of moving objects and the estimation of their motions. These methods will have difficulties handling complex motions or motion aliasing. The distorted shape of the object due to strong blur (e.g., Fig. 1) will pose severe problems in motion estimation. Furthermore, in the presence of motion aliasing, the direction of the estimated motion will not align with the direction of the induced blur. For example, the motion blur in Fig. 4.a-c. is along the true trajectory and not along the perceived one. In contrast, our approach does not require separation of static and dynamic scene components, nor their motion estimation, thus can handle very complex scene dynamics. However, we require multiple cameras.

Temporal frequencies in video sequences have very different characteristics than spatial frequencies, due to the different characteristics of the temporal and the spatial blur. The typical support of the spatial blur (PSF) is of a few pixels ($\sigma > 1$ *pixel*), whereas the exposure time is usually smaller than a single frame-time ($\tau <$ frame-time). Therefore, if we do not increase the output temporal sampling-rate *enough*, we will not improve the temporal resolution. In fact, if we increase the temporal sampling-rate a little but not beyond $\frac{1}{exposure\ time}$ of the low resolution sequences, we may even introduce *additional* motion blur.

This dictates the number of input cameras needed for an effective decrease in the motion-blur. An example of a case where an insufficient increase in the temporal sampling-rate introduced additional motion-blur is shown in Fig. 6.c3.

4.2 Producing Different Space-Time Outputs

In standard spatial super-resolution the increase in sampling rate is equal in all spatial dimensions. This is necessary in order to maintain the aspect ratio of image pixels, and to prevent distorted-looking images. However, this is not the case in space-time super-resolution. As explained in Sec. 2, the increase in sampling rate in the spatial and temporal dimensions need not be the same. Moreover, increasing the sampling rate in the spatial dimension comes at the expense of increase in the temporal frame rate, and vice-versa. This is because the number of unknowns in the high-resolution space-time volume depends on the space-time sampling rate, whereas the number of equations provided by the low resolution measurements remains fixed.

For example, assume that 8 video cameras are used to record a dynamic scene. One can increase the spatial sampling rate alone by a factor of $\sqrt{8}$ in x and y, or increase the temporal frame-rate alone by a factor of 8, or do a bit of both: increase the sampling rate by a factor of 2 in all three dimensions. Such an example is shown in Fig. 6. Fig. 6.a1 displays one of 8 low resolution input sequences. (Here we used only 4 video cameras, but split them into 8 sequences of even and odd fields). Figs. 6.a2 and 6.a3 display two possible outputs. In Fig. 6.a2 the increase is by a factor of 8 in the temporal axis with no increase in the spatial axes, and in Fig. 6.a3 the increase is by a factor of 2 in all axes x,y,t. Rows (b) and (c) illustrate the corresponding visual tradeoffs. The "×1×1×8" option (column 2) decreases the motion blur of the moving object (the toothpaste in (c.2)), while the "×2×2×2" option (column 3) improves the spatial resolution of the static background (b.3), but increases the motion blur of the moving object (c.3). The latter is because the increase in frame rate was only by factor 2 and did not exceed $\frac{1}{exposure\ time}$ of the video camera (see Sec. 4.1). In order to create a significant improvement in all dimensions, more than 4 video cameras are needed.

4.3 Combining Different Space-Time Inputs

So far we assumed that all input sequences were of similar spatial and temporal resolutions. The space-time super-resolution algorithm of Sec. 2 is not restricted to this case, and can handle input sequences of varying space-time resolutions.

Increasing Space-Time Resolution in Video 765

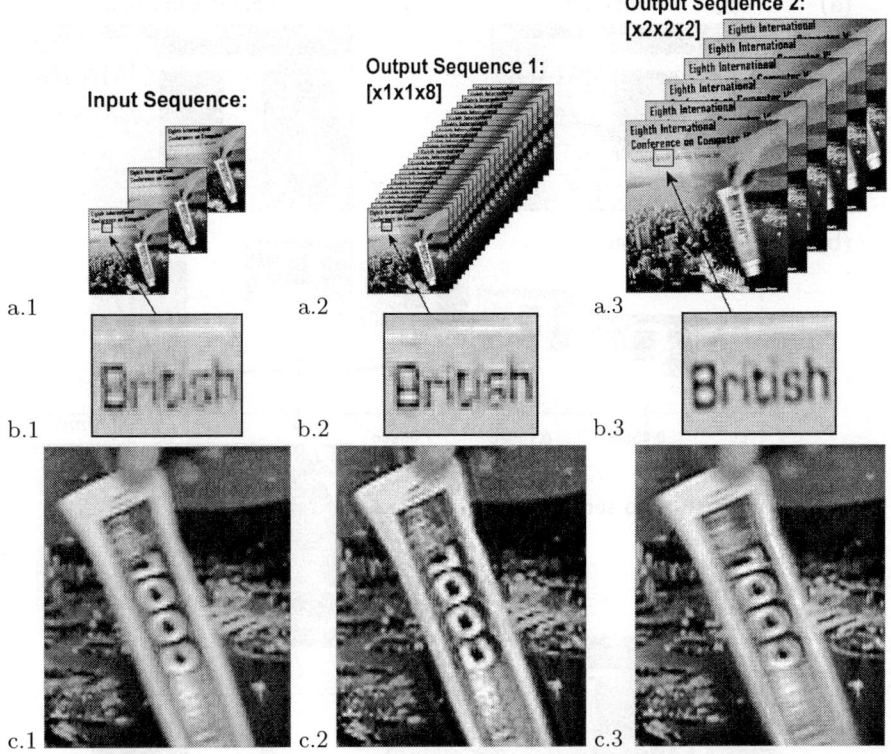

Fig. 6. Tradeoffs between spatial and temporal resolution. *This figure compares the visual tradeoffs resulting from applying space-time super-resolution with different discretization of the space-time volume. (a.1) displays one of eight low-resolution input sequences of a toothpaste in motion against a static background. (b.1) shows a close-up image of a static portion of the scene (the writing on the poster), and (c.1) shows a dynamic portion of the scene (the toothpaste). Column 2 (a.2, b.2, c.2) displays the resulting spatial and temporal effects of applying super-resolution by a factor of 8 in time only. Motion blur of the toothpaste is decreased. Column 3 (a.3, b.3, c.3) displays the resulting spatial and temporal effects of applying super-resolution by a factor of 2 in all three dimensions x, y, t. The spatial resolution of the static portions is increased (see "British" and the yellow line above it in b.3), but the motion blur is also increased (c.3). See text for an explanation of these visual tradeoffs. For color sequences see: www.wisdom.weizmann.ac.il/~vision/SuperRes.html*

Such a case is meaningless in image-based super-resolution, because a high resolution input image would always contain the information of a low resolution image. In space-time super-resolution however, this is not the case. One camera may have high spatial but low temporal resolution, and the other vice-versa. Thus, for example, it is meaningful to combine information from NTSC and PAL video cameras. NTSC has higher temporal resolution than PAL ($30 f/sec$

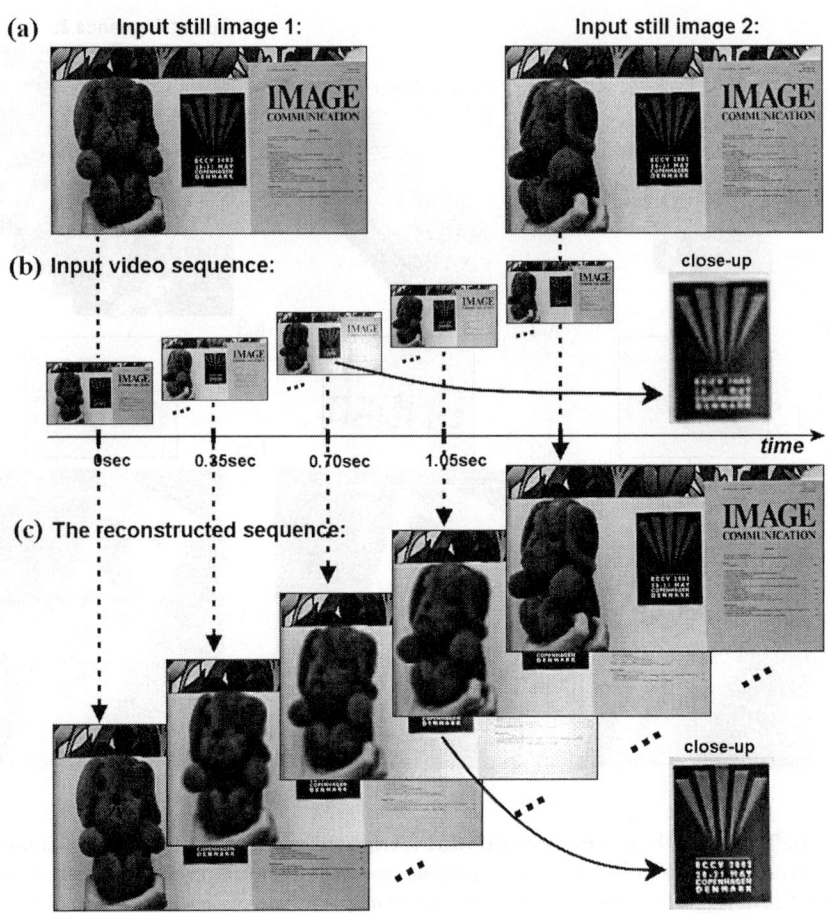

Fig. 7. Combining Still and Video. *A dynamic scene of a rotating toy-dog and varying illumination was captured by: (a) A still camera with spatial resolution of* 1120×840 *pixels, and (b) A video camera with* 384×288 *pixels at 50 f/sec. The video sequence was 1.4sec long (70 frames), and the still images were taken 1.4sec apart (together with the first and last frames). The algorithm of Sec. 2 is used to generate the high resolution sequence (c). The output sequence has the spatial dimensions of the still images and the frame-rate of the video* $(1120 \times 840 \times 50)$*. It captures the temporal changes correctly (the rotating toy and the varying illumination), as well the high spatial resolution of the still images (the sharp text). Due to lack of space we show only a portion of the images, but the proportions between video and still are maintained. For color sequences see:* www.wisdom.weizmann.ac.il/∼vision/SuperRes.html

vs. $25 f/sec$), but lower spatial resolution (640×480 pixels vs. 768×576 pixels). An extreme case of this idea is to combine information from *still* and *video* cameras. Such an example is shown in Fig. 7. Two high quality still images of high spatial resolutions (1120×840 pixels) but extremely low "temporal resolution" (the time gap between the two still images was 1.4 sec), were combined with an interlaced (PAL) video sequence using the algorithm of Sec 2. The video sequence has 3 times lower spatial resolution (we used fields of size 384×288 pixels), but a high temporal resolution ($50f/sec$). The goal is to construct a new sequence of high spatial and high temporal resolutions (i.e., 1120×840 pixels at 50 $images/sec$).

The output sequence shown in Fig. 7.c contains the high spatial resolution from the still images (the sharp text) and the high temporal resolution from the video sequence (the rotation of the toy dog and the brightening and dimming of illumination).

In the example of Fig. 7 we used only one input sequence and two still images, thus did not exceed the temporal resolution of the video or the spatial resolution of the stills. However, when multiple video cameras and multiple still images are used, the number of input measurements will exceed the number of output high resolution unknowns. In such cases the output sequence will exceed the spatial resolution of the still images and temporal resolution of the video sequences.

In Fig. 7 the number of unknowns was significantly larger than the number of low resolution measurements (the input video and the two still images). Yet, the reconstructed output was of high quality. The reason for this is the following: In video sequences the data is significantly more redundant than in images, due to the additional time axis. This redundancy provides more flexibility in applying *physically meaningful* directional regularization. In regions that have high spatial resolution but small (or no) motion (such as in the sharp text in Fig. 7), strong *temporal* regularization can be applied without decreasing the space-time resolution. Similarly, in regions with very fast dynamic changes but low spatial resolution (such as in the rotating toy in Fig. 7), strong *spatial* regularization can be employed without degradation in space-time resolution. More generally, because a video sequence has much more data redundancy than an image has, the use of *directional space-time regularization* in video-based super-resolution is physically more meaningful and gives rise to recovery of higher space-time resolution than that obtainable by image-based super-resolution with image-based regularization.

Acknowledgments. The authors wish to thank Merav Galun & Achi Brandt for their helpful suggestions regarding solutions of large scale systems of equations. Special thanks to Ronen Basri & Lihi Zelnik for their useful comments on the paper.

References

1. S. Baker and T. Kanade. Limits on super-resolution and how to break them. In *CVPR*, Hilton Head Island, South Carolina, June 2000.
2. B. Bascle, A. Blake, and A.Zisserman. Motion deblurring and super-resolution from an image sequence. In *ECCV*, pages 312–320, 1996.

3. S. Borman and R. Stevenson. Spatial resolution enhancement of low-resolution image sequences - a comprehensive review with directions for future research. Technical report, Laboratory for Image and Signal Analysis (LISA), University of Notre Dame, Notre Dame, July 1998.
4. M. Born and E. Wolf. *Principles of Optics*. Permagon Press, 1965.
5. D. Capel and A. Zisserman. Automated mosaicing with super-resolution zoom. In *CVPR*, pages 885–891, June 1998.
6. D. Capel and A. Zisserman. Super-resolution enhancement of text image sequences. In *ICPR*, pages 600–605, 2000.
7. Y. Caspi and M. Irani. A step towards sequence-to-sequence alignment. In *CVPR*, pages 682–689, Hilton Head Island, South Carolina, June 2000.
8. G. de Haan. Progress in motion estimation for consumer video format conversion. *IEEE Transactions on Consumer Electronics*, 46(3):449–459, August 2000.
9. M. Elad. Super-resolution reconstruction of images. Ph.D. Thesis, Technion Israel Institute of Technology, December 1996.
10. T.S. Huang and R.Y. Tsai. Multi-frame image restoration and registration. In *Advances in Computer Vision and Image Processing*, volume 1, pages 317–339. JAI Press Inc., 1984.
11. M. Irani and S. Peleg. Improving resolution by image registration. *CVGIP:GM*, 53:231–239, May 1991.
12. A. J. Patti, M. I. Sezan, and A. M. Tekalp. Superresolution video reconstruction with arbitrary sampling lattices and nonzero aperture time. In *IEEE Trans. on Image Processing*, volume 6, pages 1064–1076, August 1997.
13. REALVIZ^{TM}. Retimer. *www.realviz.com/products/rt*, 2002.
14. J. Shin, J. Paik, J. R. Price, and M.A. Abidi. Adaptive regularized image interpolation using data fusion and steerable constraints. In *SPIE Visual Communications and Image Processing*, volume 4310, January 2001.
15. U. Trottenber, C. Oosterlee, and A. Schüller. *Multigrid*. Academic Press, 2000.

Hyperdynamics Importance Sampling

Cristian Sminchisescu and Bill Triggs

INRIA Rhône-Alpes, 655 avenue de l'Europe, 38330 Montbonnot, France.
{Cristian.Sminchisescu,Bill.Triggs}@inrialpes.fr
http://www.inrialpes.fr/movi/people/{Sminchisescu,Triggs}

Abstract. Sequential random sampling ('Markov Chain Monte-Carlo') is a popular strategy for many vision problems involving multimodal distributions over high-dimensional parameter spaces. It applies both to *importance sampling* (where one wants to sample points according to their 'importance' for some calculation, but otherwise fairly) and to *global optimization* (where one wants to find good minima, or at least good starting points for local minimization, regardless of fairness). Unfortunately, most sequential samplers are very prone to becoming 'trapped' for long periods in unrepresentative local minima, which leads to biased or highly variable estimates. We present a general strategy for reducing MCMC trapping that generalizes Voter's 'hyperdynamic sampling' from computational chemistry. The local gradient and curvature of the input distribution are used to construct an adaptive importance sampler that focuses samples on low cost negative curvature regions likely to contain 'transition states' — codimension-1 saddle points representing 'mountain passes' connecting adjacent cost basins. This substantially accelerates inter-basin transition rates while still preserving correct relative transition probabilities. Experimental tests on the difficult problem of 3D articulated human pose estimation from monocular images show significantly enhanced minimum exploration.

Keywords. Hyperdynamics, Markov-chain Monte Carlo, importance sampling, global optimization, human tracking.

1 Introduction

Many vision problems can be formulated either as global minimizations of highly nonconvex cost functions with many minima, or as statistical inferences based on fair sampling or expectation-value integrals over highly multi-modal distributions. Importance sampling is a promising approach for such applications, particularly when combined with sequential ('Markov Chain Monte-Carlo'), layered or annealed samplers [8, 4, 5], optionally punctuated with bursts of local optimization [10, 3, 25]. Sampling methods are flexible, but they tend to be computationally expensive for a given level of accuracy. In particular, when used on multi-modal cost surfaces, current sequential samplers are very prone to becoming trapped for long periods in cost basins containing unrepresentative local minima. This 'trapping' or 'poor mixing' leads to biased or highly variable estimates whose character is at best quasi-local rather than global. Trapping times are typically exponential in a (large) scale parameter, so 'buying a faster computer' helps little. Current samplers are myopic mainly because they consider only the size of the integrand being evaluated or the lowness of the cost being optimized when judging 'importance'. *For efficient global estimates, it is also critically 'important' to include an effective strategy for reducing trapping, e.g. by explicitly devoting some fraction of the samples to moving between cost basins.*

This paper describes a method for reducing trapping by 'boosting' the dynamics of the sequential sampler. Our approach is based on Voter's 'hyperdynamics' [29, 30], which was originally developed in computational chemistry to accelerate the estimation of transition rates between different atomic arrangements in atom-level simulations of molecules and solids. There, the dynamics is basically a thermally-driven random walk of a point in the configuration space of the combined atomic coordinates, subject to an effective energy potential that models the combined inter-atomic interactions. The configuration-space potential is often highly multimodal, corresponding to different large-scale configurations of the molecule being simulated. Trapping is a significant problem, especially as the fine-scale dynamics must use quite short time-steps to ensure accurate physical modelling. Mixing times of 10^6–10^9 or more steps are common. In our target applications in vision the sampler need not satisfy such strict physical constraints, but trapping remains a key problem.

Hyperdynamics reduces trapping by boosting the number of samples that fall near 'transition states' — low lying saddle points that the system would typically pass through if it were moving thermally between adjacent energy basins. It does this by modifying the cost function, adding a term based on the gradient and curvature of the original potential that raises the cost near the cores of the local potential basins to reduce trapping there, while leaving the cost intact in regions where the original potential has the negative curvature eigenvalue and low gradient characteristic of transition neighborhoods. Hyperdynamics can be viewed as a generalized form of MCMC importance sampling whose importance measure considers the gradient and curvature as well as the values of the original cost function. The key point is not the specific form adopted for the potential, but rather the refined notion of 'importance': deliberately adding samples to speed mixing and hence reduce global bias ('finite sample effects'), even though the added samples are not directly 'important' for the calculation being performed.

Another general approach to multi-modal optimization is *annealing* — initially sampling with a reduced sensitivity to the underlying cost ('higher temperature'), then progressively increasing the sensitivity to focus samples on lower cost regions. Annealing has been used many times in vision and elsewhere[1], *e.g.* [18, 5], but although it works well in many applications, it has important limitations as a general method for reducing trapping. The main problem is that it samples indiscriminately within a certain energy band, regardless of whether the points sampled are likely to lead out of the basin towards another minimum, or whether they simply lead further up an ever-increasing potential wall. In many applications, and especially in high-dimensional or ill-conditioned ones, the cost surface has relatively narrow 'corridors' connecting adjacent basins, and it is important to steer the samples towards these using local information about how the cost appears to be changing. Hyperdynamics is a first attempt at doing this. In fact, these methods are complementary: it may be possible to speed up hyperdynamics by annealing its modified potential, but we will not investigate this here.

---

[1] Raising the temperature is often unacceptable in chemistry applications of hyperdynamics, as it may significantly change the problem. *E.g.*, the solid being simulated might melt...

1.1 What Is a Good Multiple-Mode Sampling Function?

'The curse of dimensionality' causes many difficulties in high-dimensional search. In stochastic methods, long sampling runs are often needed to hit the distribution's 'typical set' — the areas where most of the probability mass is concentrated. In sequential samplers this is due to the inherently local nature of the sampling process, which tends to become 'trapped' in individual modes, moving between them only very infrequently. More generally, choosing an importance sampling distribution is a compromise between tractable sampleability and efficient focusing of the sampling resources towards 'good places to look'.

There are at least three issues in the design of a good multi-modal sampler: (*i*) *Approximation accuracy*: in high dimensions, when the original distribution is complex and highly multi-modal (as is the case in vision), finding a good approximating function can be very difficult, thus limiting the applicability of the method. It is therefore appealing to look for ways of using a modified version of the original distribution, as for instance in annealing methods [18, 5]. (*ii*)*Trapping*: even when the approximation is locally accurate (*e.g.* by sampling the original distribution, thus avoiding any sample-weighting artifacts), most sampling procedures tend to get caught in the mode(s) closest to the starting point of sampling. Very long runs are needed to sample infrequent inter-mode transition events that lie far out in the tails of the modal distributions, but that can make a huge difference to the overall results. (*iii*)*Biased transition rates*: annealing changes not only the absolute inter-mode transition rates (thus reducing trapping), but also their relative sizes [27]. So there is no guarantee that the modes are visited with the correct relative probabilities implied by the dynamics on the original cost surface. This may seem irrelevant if the aim is simply to discover 'all good modes' or 'the best mode', but the levels of annealing needed to make difficult transitions frequent can very significantly increase the number of modes and the state space volume that are available to be visited, and thus cause the vast bulk of the samples to be wasted in fruitless regions[2]. This is especially important in applications like tracking, where only the neighboring modes that are separated from the current one by the lowest energy barriers need to be recovered.

To summarize, for complex high dimensional problems, finding good, sampleable approximating distributions is hard, so it is useful to look at sequential samplers based on distributions derived from the original one. There is a trade-off between sampling for local computational accuracy, which requires samples in 'important' regions, usually mode cores, and sampling for good mixing, which requires not only more frequent samples in the tails of the distribution, but also that these should be focused on regions likely to lead to inter-modal transitions. Defining such regions is delicate in practice, but it is clear that steering samples towards regions with low gradient and negative curvatures should increase the likelihood of finding transition states (saddle points with one negative curvature direction) relative to purely cost-based methods such as annealing.

---

[2] There is an analogy with the chemist's melting solid, liquids being regions of state space with huge numbers of small interconnected minima and saddles, while solids have fewer, or at least more clearly defined, minima. Also remember that state space volume increases very rapidly with sampling radius in high dimensions, so dense, distant sampling is simply infeasible.

1.2 Related Work

Now we briefly summarize some relevant work on high-dimensional search, especially in the domain of human modelling and estimation. Cham & Rehg [3] perform 2D tracking with scaled prismatic models. Their method combines a least squares intensity-based cost function, particle filtering with dynamical noise style sampling, and local optimization of a mixture of Gaussians state probability representation. Deutscher *et al* [5] track 3D body motion using a multi-camera silhouette-and-edge based likelihood function and annealed sampling within a temporal particle filtering framework. Their sampling procedure resembles one used by Neal [18], but Neal also includes an additional importance sampling correction designed to improve mixing. Sidenbladh *et al* [22] use an intensity based cost function and particle filtering with importance sampling based on a learned dynamical model to track a 3D model of a walking person in an image sequence. Choo & Fleet [4] combine particle filtering and hybrid Monte Carlo sampling to estimate 3D human motion, using a cost function based on joint re-projection error given input from motion capture data. Sminchisescu & Triggs [25] recover articulated 3D motion from monocular image sequences using an edge and intensity based cost function, with a combination of robust constraint-consistent local optimization and 'oversized' covariance scaled sampling to focus samples on probable low-cost regions.

Hyperdynamics uses stochastic dynamics with cost gradient based sampling as in [8, 17, 4], but 'boosts' the dynamics with a novel importance sampler constructed from the original probability surface using local gradient and curvature information. All of the annealing methods try to increase transition rates by sampling a modified distribution, but only the one given here specifically focuses samples on regions likely to contain transition states. There are also deterministic local-optimization-based methods designed to find transition states. See our companion paper [26] for references.

2 Sampling and Transition State Theory

2.1 Importance Sampling

Importance sampling works as follows. Suppose that we are interested in quantities depending on the distribution of some quantity $\mathbf{x}$, whose probability density is proportional to $f(\mathbf{x})$. Suppose that it is feasible to evaluate $f(\mathbf{x})$ pointwise, but that we are not able to sample directly from the distribution it defines, but only from an approximating distribution with density $f_b(\mathbf{x})$. We will base our estimates on a sample of N independent points, $\mathbf{x}_1, ..., \mathbf{x}_N$ drawn from $f_b(\mathbf{x})$. The expectation value of some quantity $V(\mathbf{x})$ with respect to $f(\mathbf{x})$ can then be estimated as $\bar{V} = \sum_{i=1}^{N} w_i V(\mathbf{x}_i) / \sum_{i=1}^{N} w_i$, where the **importance weighting** of $\mathbf{x}_i$ is $w_i = f(\mathbf{x}_i)/f_b(\mathbf{x}_i)$ (this assumes that $f_b(\mathbf{x}) \neq 0$ whenever $f(\mathbf{x}) \neq 0$). It can be proved that the importance sampled estimator converges to the mean value of V as N increases, but it is difficult to assess how reliable the estimate $\bar{V}$ is in practice. Two issues affect this accuracy: the variability of the importance weights due to deviations between $f(\mathbf{x})$ and $f_b(\mathbf{x})$, and statistical fluctuations caused by the improbability of sampling infrequent events in the tails of the distribution, especially if these are critical for estimating $\bar{V}$.

2.2 Stochastic Dynamics

Various methods are available for speeding up sampling. Here we use a stochastic dynamics method on the potential surface defined by our cost function (the negative log-likelihood of the state probability given the observations, $f(\mathbf{x}) = -\log p(\mathbf{x}|\cdot)$). Canonical samples from $f(\mathbf{x})$ can be obtained by simulating the phase space dynamics defined by the Hamiltonian function:

$$H(\mathbf{x}, \mathbf{p}) = f(\mathbf{x}) + K(\mathbf{p})$$

where $K(\mathbf{p}) = \mathbf{p}^\top \mathbf{p}/2$ is the kinetic energy, and $\mathbf{p}$ is the momentum variable. Averages of variables V over the canonical ensemble can be computed by using classical 2N-dimensional phase-space integrals:

$$\langle V \rangle = \frac{\iint V(\mathbf{x}, \mathbf{p}) e^{-\alpha f(\mathbf{x})} e^{-\alpha K(\mathbf{p})} \mathbf{dxdp}}{\iint e^{-\alpha f(\mathbf{x})} e^{-\alpha K(\mathbf{p})} \mathbf{dxdp}}$$

where $\alpha = 1/T$ is the temperature constant. Dynamics (and hence sampling) is done by locally integrating the Hamilton equations:

$$\frac{\mathbf{dx}}{dt} = \mathbf{p} \quad \text{and} \quad \frac{\mathbf{dp}}{dt} = -\frac{df(\mathbf{x})}{\mathbf{dx}}$$

using a Langevin Monte Carlo type integration/rejection scheme that is guaranteed to perform sampling from the canonical distribution over phase-space:

$$\mathbf{x}_{i+1} = \mathbf{x}_i - \frac{\Delta t_{sd}^2}{2} \frac{df(\mathbf{x})}{\mathbf{dx}} + \Delta t_{sd} \mathbf{n}_i \quad (1)$$

where $\mathbf{n}_i$ is a vector of independently chosen Gaussian variables with zero mean and unit variance, and Δt_{sd} is the stochastic dynamics integration step. Compared to so called 'hybrid' methods, the Langevin method can be used with a larger step size and this is advantageous for our problem, where the step calculations are relatively expensive (see [17] and its references for a more complete discussion of the relative advantages of hybrid and Langevin Monte Carlo methods)[3]. For physical dynamics t represents the physical time, while for statistical calculations it simply represents the number of steps performed since the start of the simulation. The simulation time is used in §3 below to estimate the acceleration of infrequent events produced by the proposed biased potential.

2.3 Transition State Theory

Continuing the statistical mechanics analogy begun in the previous section, the behavior of the physical system can be characterized by long periods of 'vibration' within one

---

[3] Note that the momenta are only represented implicitly in the Langevin formulation: there is no need to update their values after each leapfrog step as they are immediately replaced by new ones drawn from the canonical distribution at the start of each iteration. If approximate cost Hessian information is also available, the gradient in (1) can be projected onto the Hessian eigen-basis and its components weighted by the local eigen-curvatures to give an effective 'Newton-like' step. We use such steps near saddle points, where the hyperdynamic bias potential is essentially zero, to avoid the inefficiencies of random walk behavior there.

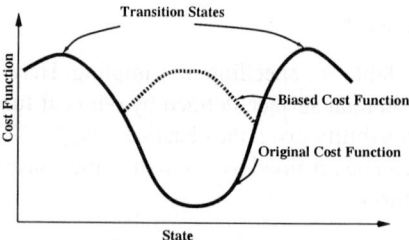

Fig. 1. The original cost function and the bias added for hyperdynamics.

'state' (energy basin), followed by infrequent transitions to other states via saddle points. In the 'transition state theory' (TST) approximation, the transition rates between states are computed using the sample flux through the *dividing surface* separating them. For a given state S, this is the $N - 1$ dimensional surface separating the state S from its neighbors. The rate of escape from state S is:

$$k_{S\to}^{tst} = \langle |\nu_S| \, \delta_S(\mathbf{x}) \rangle_S$$

where $\delta_s(\mathbf{x})$ is a Dirac delta function positioned on the dividing surface of S and ν_s is the velocity normal to this surface. Crossings of the dividing surface correspond to true state change events, and we assume that the system loses all memory of this transition before the next event.

3 Accelerating Transition State Sampling

In the above formalism, the TST rate can be evaluated as follows:

$$k_{S\to}^{tst} = \frac{\iint |\nu_S| \, \delta_S(\mathbf{x}) \, e^{-\alpha f(\mathbf{x})} \, e^{-\alpha K(\mathbf{p})} \, \mathbf{dx} \, \mathbf{dp}}{\iint e^{-\alpha f(\mathbf{x})} \, e^{-\alpha K(\mathbf{p})} \, \mathbf{dx} \, \mathbf{dp}}$$

Now consider adding a positive bias or boost cost $f_b(\mathbf{x})$ (with a corresponding 'biased' state S_b) to the original cost $f(\mathbf{x})$, with the further property that $f_b(\mathbf{x}) = 0$ whenever $\delta_S(\mathbf{x}) \neq 0$, i.e. the potential is unchanged in the transition state regions. The TST rate becomes:

$$k_{S\to}^{tst} = \frac{\iint |\nu_S| \, \delta_S(\mathbf{x}) \, e^{-\alpha[f(\mathbf{x})+f_b(x)]} \, e^{\alpha f_b(\mathbf{x})} \, e^{-\alpha K(\mathbf{p})} \, \mathbf{dx} \, \mathbf{dp}}{\iint e^{-\alpha f(\mathbf{x})} \, e^{-\alpha K(\mathbf{p})} \, \mathbf{dx} \, \mathbf{dp}} \qquad (2)$$

$$= \frac{\langle |\nu_S| \, \delta_S(\mathbf{x}) \, e^{\alpha f_b(\mathbf{x})} \rangle_{S_b}}{\langle e^{\alpha f_b(\mathbf{x})} \rangle_{S_b}} = \frac{\langle |\nu_S| \, \delta_S(\mathbf{x}) \rangle_{S_b}}{\langle e^{\alpha f_b(\mathbf{x})} \rangle_{S_b}} \qquad (3)$$

The boost term increases every escape rate from state S as the cost well is made shallower, but it leaves the *ratios* of escape rates from S, S_b to other states S_1, S_2 invariant:

$$\frac{k_{S\to S_1}^{tst}}{k_{S\to S_2}^{tst}} = \frac{k_{S_b\to S_1}^{tst}}{k_{S_b\to S_2}^{tst}}$$

This holds because all escape rates from S all have the partition function of S as denominator, and replacing this with the partition function of S_b leaves their ratios unchanged.

Concretely, suppose that during N_t steps of classical dynamics simulation on the biased cost surface, we encounter N_e escape attempts over the dividing surface. For the computation, let us also assume that the simulation is artificially confined to the basin of state S by reflecting boundaries. (This does not happen in real simulations: it is used here only to estimate the 'biased boost time'). The TST escape rate from state S can be estimated simply as the ratio of the number of escape attempts to the total trajectory length: $k_S^{tst} = N_e/(N_t \Delta t_{sd})$. Consequently, the mean escape time (inverse transition rate) from state S can be estimated from (2) as:

$$\tau_{esc}^S = \frac{1}{k_{S\to}^{tst}} = \frac{\langle e^{\alpha f_b(\mathbf{x})} \rangle_{S_b}}{\langle |\nu_S| \delta_S(\mathbf{x}) \rangle_{S_b}} = \frac{\frac{1}{N_t} \sum_{i=1}^{N_t} e^{\alpha f_b(\mathbf{x}_i)}}{N_e/(N_t \Delta t_{sd})} = \frac{1}{N_e} \sum_{i=1}^{N_t} \Delta t_{sd} \, e^{\alpha f_b(\mathbf{x}_i)}$$

The effective simulation time boost achieved in step i thus becomes simply:

$$\Delta t_{b_i} = \Delta t_{sd} e^{\alpha f_b(\mathbf{x}_i)} \qquad (4)$$

The dynamical evolution of the system from state to state is still correct, but it works in a distorted time scale that depends exponentially on the bias potential. As the system passes through regions with high f_b, its equivalent time Δt_b increases rapidly as it would originally have tended to linger in these regions (or more precisely to return to them often on the average) owing to their low original cost. Conversely, in zones with small f_b the equivalent time progress at the standard stochastic dynamics rate. Of course, in reality the simulation's integration time step and hence its sampling coarseness are the same as they were in the unboosted simulation. The boosting time (4) just gives an intuition for how much time an unaccelerated sampler would probably have wasted making 'uninteresting' samples near the cost minimum. But that is largely the point: the wastage factors are astronomical in practice — unboosted samplers can not escape from local minima.

4 The Biased Cost

The main requirements on the bias potential are that it should be zero on all dividing surfaces, that it should not introduce new sub-wells with escape times comparable to the main escape time from the original cost well, and that its definition should not require prior knowledge of the cost wells or saddle points (if we knew these we could avoid trapping much more efficiently by including explicit well-jumping samples). For sampling, the most 'important' regions of the cost surface are minima, where the Hessian matrix $\mathbf{H}$ has strictly positive eigenvalues, and transition states, where it has exactly one negative eigenvalue $e_1 < 0$. The gradient vector vanishes in both cases. The rigorous definition of the TST boundary is necessarily global[4], but locally near a transition state the boundary contains the state itself and adjacent points where the Hessian has a negative eigenvalue and vanishing gradient component along the corresponding eigenvector:

$$g_{p1} = \mathbf{V}_1^T \mathbf{g} = 0 \quad \text{and} \quad e_1 < 0 \qquad (5)$$

---

[4] The basin of state S can be defined as the set of configurations from which gradient descent minimization leads to the minimum S. This basin is surrounded by an $(n-1)$-D hypersurface, outside of which local descent leads to states other than S.

where **g** is the gradient vector and $\mathbf{V}_1$ is the first Hessian eigenvector. Voter [29, 30] therefore advocates the following bias cost for hyperdynamics:

$$f_b = \frac{h_b}{2}\left[1 + \frac{e_1}{\sqrt{e_1^2 + g_{p1}^2/d^2}}\right] \qquad (6)$$

where h_b is a constant controlling the strength of the bias and d is a length scale (*e.g.* an estimate of the typical nearest-neighbour distance between minima, if this is available). Note that Voter's f_b has all of the properties required in §3. In particular, it is zero on the dividing surface, as can be seen from (5) and (6).

Increasing h_b increases the bias and hence the nominal boosting. In principle it is even permissible to raise the cost of a minimum above the level of its surrounding transition states. However, there is a risk that doing so will entirely block the sampling pathways through and around the minimum, thus causing the system to become trapped in a newly created well at one end of the old one. Hence, it is usually safer to select a more moderate boosting.

One difficulty with Voter's potential (6) is that direct differentiation of it for gradient-based dynamics requires third order derivatives of $f(\mathbf{x})$. However an inexpensive numerical estimation method based on first order derivatives was proposed in [30]. For completeness we summarize this in the appendix. These calculations are more complex than those needed for standard gradient based stochastic simulation, but we will see that the bias provides a degree of acceleration that often pays-off in practice.

5 Human Domain Modelling

This section briefly describes the humanoid visual tracking models used in our hyperdynamic boosting experiments. For more details see [24, 25].

Representation: Our body models contain kinematic 'skeletons' of articulated joints controlled by angular joint parameters, covered by 'flesh' built from superquadric ellipsoids with additional global deformations [1]. A typical model has about 30-35 joint parameters $\mathbf{x}_a$; 8 internal proportion parameters $\mathbf{x}_i$ encoding the positions of the hip, clavicle and skull tip joints; and 9 deformable shape parameters for each body part, gathered into a vector $\mathbf{x}_d$. The complete model is thus encoded as a single large parameter vector $\mathbf{x} = (\mathbf{x}_a, \mathbf{x}_d, \mathbf{x}_i)$. During tracking or static pose estimation we usually estimate only joint parameters.

The model is used as follows. Superquadric surfaces are discretized into meshes parameterized by angular coordinates in a 2D topological domain. Mesh nodes $\mathbf{u}_i$ are transformed into 3D points $\mathbf{p}_i(\mathbf{x})$, then into predicted image points $\mathbf{r}_i(\mathbf{x})$ using composite nonlinear transformations $\mathbf{r}_i(\mathbf{x}) = P(\mathbf{p}_i(\mathbf{x})) = P(A(\mathbf{x}_a, \mathbf{x}_i, D(\mathbf{x}_d, \mathbf{u}_i)))$, where D represents a sequence of parametric deformations that construct the corresponding part in its own reference frame, A represents a chain of rigid transformations that map it through the kinematic chain to its 3D position, and P represents perspective image projection. During model estimation, prediction-to-image matching cost metrics are evaluated between each predicted model feature $\mathbf{r}_i$ and nearby associated image features $\bar{\mathbf{r}}_i$, and the results are summed over all features to produce the image contribution to the overall parameter space cost function. The cost is thus a robust function of the prediction errors $\Delta \mathbf{r}_i(\mathbf{x}) = \bar{\mathbf{r}}_i - \mathbf{r}_i(\mathbf{x})$. The cost gradient $\mathbf{g}_i(\mathbf{x})$ and Hessian $\mathbf{H}_i(\mathbf{x})$ are also computed and assembled over all observations.

Estimation: We aim for a probabilistic interpretation and optimal estimates of the model parameters by maximizing the total probability according to Bayes rule:

$$p(\mathbf{x}|\bar{\mathbf{r}}) \propto p(\bar{\mathbf{r}}|\mathbf{x})\,p(\mathbf{x}) = \exp\left(-\int e(\bar{\mathbf{r}}_i|\mathbf{x})\,di\right) p(\mathbf{x}) \quad (7)$$

where $e(\bar{\mathbf{r}}_i|\mathbf{x})$ is the cost density associated with observation i, the integral is over all observations, and $p(\mathbf{x})$ is the prior on the model parameters. Discretizing the continuous problem, our MAP approach minimizes the negative log-likelihood for the total posterior probability:

$$f(\mathbf{x}) = -\log p(\bar{\mathbf{r}}|\mathbf{x}) - \log p(\mathbf{x}) = f_l(\mathbf{x}) + f_p(\mathbf{x}) \quad (8)$$

Observation Likelihood: In the below experiments we actually only used a very simple Gaussian likelihood based on given model-to-image joint correspondences. The negative log-likelihood for the observations is just the sum of squared model joint reprojection errors. Our full tracking system uses this cost function only for initialization, but it still provides an interesting (and difficult to handle) degree of multimodality owing to the kinematic complexity of the human model and the large number of parameters that are unobservable in a singular monocular image. In practice we find that globalizing the search is at least as important for initialization as for tracking, and this cost function is significantly cheaper to evaluate than our full image based one, allowing more extensive sampling experiments.

Priors and Constraints: Both hard and soft priors are accommodated in our framework. They include anthropometric priors on model proportions, parameter stabilizers for hard to estimate but useful modelling parameters, terms for collision avoidance between body parts, and joint angle limits. During estimation, the values, gradients and Hessians of the priors are evaluated and added to the contributions from the observations.

6 Experiments and Results

In this section we illustrate the hyperdynamics method on a toy problem involving a two-dimensional multi-modal cost surface, and on the problem of initial pose estimation for an articulated 3D human model based on given joint-to-image correspondences. In both cases we compare the method with standard stochastic dynamics on the original cost surface. The parameters of the two methods (temperature, integration step, number of simulation steps, *etc.*) are identical, except that hyperdynamics requires values for the two additional parameters h_b and d that control the properties of the bias potential (6).

6.1 The Müller Cost Surface

Müller's Potential (fig. 2, left) is a simple 2D analytic cost function with three local minima M_1, M_2, M_3, and two saddle points S_1, S_2, which is often used in the chemistry literature to illustrate transition state search methods[5]. The inter-minimum distance is

---

[5] It has the form $V(x,y) = \sum_{i=1}^{4} A_i\, e^{a_i(x-x_i)^2 + b_i(x-x_i)(y-y_i) + c_i(y-y_i)^2}$ where $\mathbf{A} = (-200, -100, -170, 15)$, $\mathbf{a} = (-1, -1, -6.5, 0.7)$, $\mathbf{b} = (0, 0, 11, 0.6)$, $\mathbf{c} = (-10, -10, -6.5, 0.7)$, $\mathbf{x} = (1, 0, -0.5, -1)$, $\mathbf{y} = (0, 0.5, 1.5, 1)$.

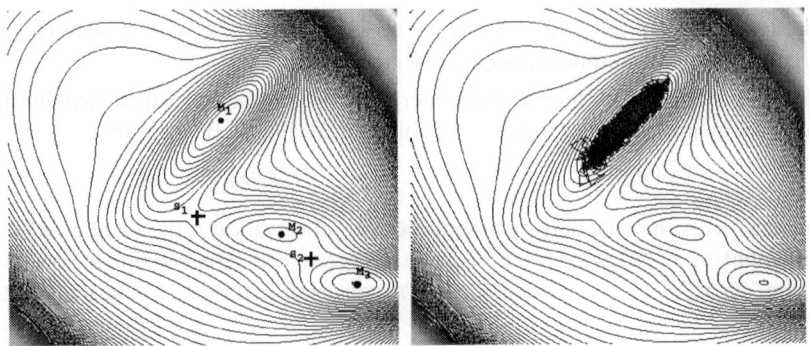

Fig. 2. The Müller Potential (left) and a standard stochastic dynamics gradient sampling simulation (right) that gets trapped in the basin of the starting minimum.

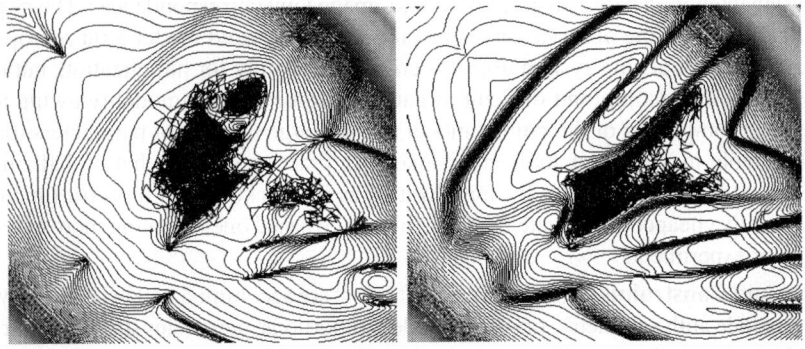

Fig. 3. Hyperdynamic sampling with $h_b = 150, d = 0.1$ and $h_b = 200, d = 0.5$.

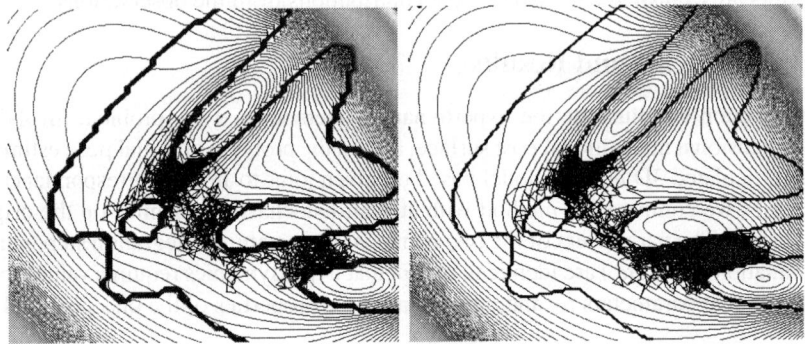

Fig. 4. Hyperdynamic sampling with $h_b = 300, d = 10$ and $h_b = 400, d = 100$.

of order 1 length unit, and the transition states are around 100–150 energy units above the lowest minimum.

Fig. 2(right) shows the result of standard stochastic dynamic sampling on the original cost surface. Despite 6000 simulation steps at a reasonable step size $\Delta t_{sd} = 0.01$, only

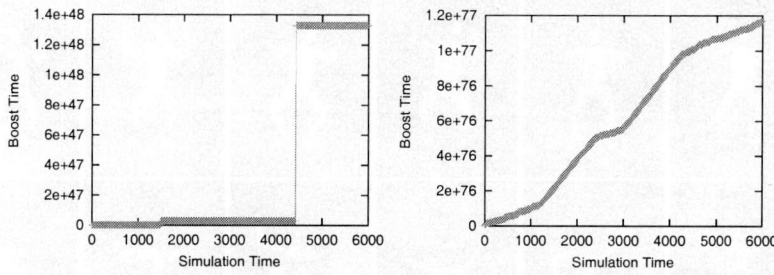

Fig. 5. Effective boost times for mild (left) and more aggressive (right) bias potentials.

the basin of the starting minimum is sampled extensively, and no successful escape has yet taken place. Fig. 3 shows two hyperdynamics runs with parameters set for moderate boosting. Note the reduced emphasis on sampling in the core of the minimum — in fact the minimum is replaced by a set of higher energy ones — and the fact that the runs escape the initial basin. In the right hand plot there is a clear focusing of samples in the region corresponding to the saddle point linking the two adjacent minima M_1 and M_2. Finally, fig. 4 shows results for more aggressive bias potentials that cause the basins of all three minima to be visited, with strong focusing of samples on the inter-minimum transition regions. The bias here turns the lowest positive curvature region of the initial minimum into a local maximum.

The plots also show that the Voter potential is somewhat 'untidy', with complicated local steps and ridges. Near the hypersurfaces where the first Hessian eigenvalue e_1 passes down through zero, the bias jumps from h_b to 0 with an abruptness that increases as the length scale d increases (sic) or the gradient projection g_{p1} decreases, owing to the $e_1 / \sqrt{e_1^2 + g_{p1}^2 / d^2}$ term in (6). A small d makes these $e_1 = 0$ transitions smoother, but increases the suddenness of ridges in the potential that occur on hypersurfaces where g_{1p} passes through zero.

Fig. 5 plots the simulation boosting time for two bias potentials. The left plot has a milder potential that simply encourages exploration of saddle points, while the right plot has a more aggressive one that is able to explore and jump between individual modes more rapidly. (Note the very large and very different sizes of the boosting time scales in these plots).

6.2 Monocular 3D Pose Estimation

Now we explore the potential of the hyperdynamics method for monocular 3D human pose estimation under model to image joint correspondences. This problem is well adapted to illustrating the algorithm, as its cost surface is highly multimodal. Of the 32 kinematic model d.o.f., about 10 are subject to 'reflective' kinematic ambiguities (forwards vs. backwards slant in depth), which potentially creates around $2^{10} = 1024$ local minima in the cost surface [13], although some of these are not physically feasible and are automatically pruned during the simulation (see below). Indeed, we find that it is very difficult to ensure initialization to the 'correct' pose with this kind of data.

The simulation enforces joint limit constraints using reflective boundary conditions, *i.e.* by reversing the sign of the particle's normal momentum when it hits a joint limit.

Fig. 6. Human poses sampled using hyperdynamics on a cost surface based on given model-to-image joint correspondences, seen from the camera viewpoint and from above. Hyperdynamics finds a variety of different poses including well separated reflective ambiguities (which, as expected, all look similar from the camera viewpoint). In contrast, standard stochastic dynamics (on the same underlying cost surface with identical parameters) essentially remains trapped in the original starting mode even after 8000 simulation steps (fig. 8).

We found that this gives an improved sampling acceptance rate compared to simply projecting the proposed configuration back into the constraint surface, as the latter leads to cascades of rejected moves until the momentum direction gradually swings around.

We ran the simulation for 8000 steps with $\Delta t_{sd} = 0.01$, both on the original cost surface (fig. 8) and on the boosted one (fig. 6). It is easy to see that the original sampler gets trapped in the starting mode, and wastes all of its samples exploring it repeatedly. Conversely, the boosted hyperdynamics method escapes from the starting mode relatively quickly, and subsequently explores many of the minima resulting from the depth reflection ambiguities.

Fig. 7 plots the estimated boosting times for two different bias potentials, $h_b = 200, d = 2$, and $h_b = 400, d = 20$. The computed mean state variance of the original estimator was 4.10^{-6}, compared to 7.10^{-6} for the boosted one.

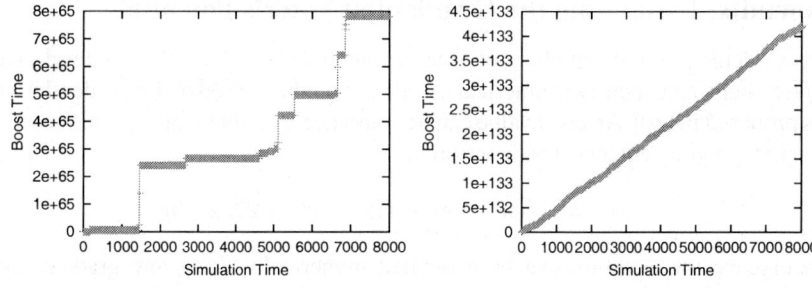

Fig. 7. Boosting times for human pose experiments, with mild (left) and strong (right) bias.

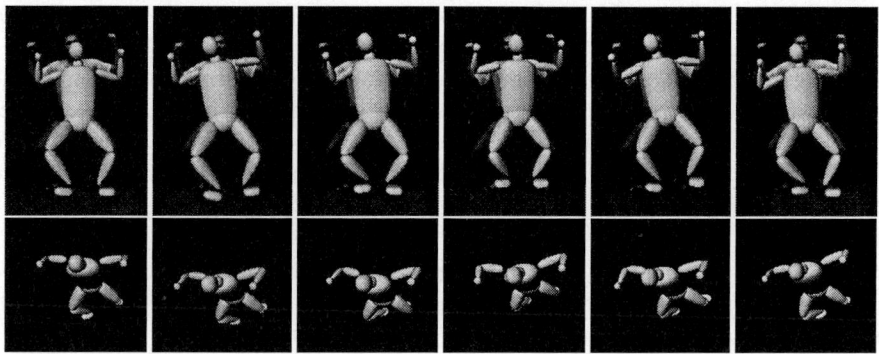

Fig. 8. Stochastic dynamics on the original cost surface leads to "trapping" in the starting mode.

7 Conclusions and Future Work

We underlined the fact that for global investigation of strongly multimodal high dimensional cost functions, importance samplers need to devote some of their samples to reducing trapping in local minima, rather than focusing only on performing their target computation. With this in mind, we presented an MCMC sampler designed to accelerate the exploration of different minima, based on the 'hyperdynamics' method from computational chemistry. It uses local cost gradients and curvatures to construct a modified cost function that focuses samples towards regions with low gradient and at least one negative curvature, which are likely to contain the transition states (low cost saddle points with one negative curvature direction) of the original cost. Our experimental results demonstrate that the method significantly improves inter-minimum exploration behaviour in the problem of monocular articulated 3D human pose estimation.

Our future work will focus on deriving alternative, computationally more efficient biased sampling distributions.

Acknowledgements. This work was supported by an EIFFEL doctoral grant and European Union FET-Open project VIBES. We would like to thank Alexandru Telea for implementation discussions.

Appendix: Estimating the Gradient of Voter's Potential

Direct calculation of the gradient of Voter's potential (6) requires third order derivatives of $f(\mathbf{x})$, but an inexpensive numerical estimation method based on first order derivatives was proposed in [30]. An eigenvalue can be computed by numerical approximation along it's corresponding eigenvector direction $\mathbf{s}$:

$$e(\mathbf{s}) = [f(\mathbf{x} + \eta\mathbf{s}) + f(\mathbf{x} - \eta\mathbf{s}) - 2f(\mathbf{x})]/\eta^2 \qquad (9)$$

The eigenvector direction can be estimated numerically using any gradient descent method, based on a random initialization s or on the one from the previous dynamics step, using:

$$\frac{de}{d\mathbf{s}} = [\mathbf{g}(\mathbf{x} + \eta\mathbf{s}) - \mathbf{g}(\mathbf{x} - \eta\mathbf{s})]/\eta \qquad (10)$$

The lowest eigenvector obtained from the minimization (10) is then used to compute the corresponding eigenvalue via (9). The procedure can be repeated for higher eigenvalue-eigenvector pairs by maintaining orthogonality with previous directions. The derivative of the projected gradient g_{1p} can then be obtained by applying the minimization to the matrices $\mathbf{H} + \lambda \mathbf{g} \mathbf{g}^\top$ and $\mathbf{H} - \lambda \mathbf{g} \mathbf{g}^\top$. One thus minimizes:

$$\frac{de_i}{d\mathbf{x}} = \left\{[\mathbf{g}(\mathbf{x} + \eta\mathbf{s}) + \mathbf{g}(\mathbf{x} - \eta\mathbf{s}) - 2\mathbf{g}(\mathbf{x})]/\eta^2\right\}_{\mathbf{s}=\mathbf{s}_i}$$

where:

$$e_{\pm\lambda} = e(\mathbf{s}) \pm \lambda\left[\frac{f(\mathbf{x} + \eta\mathbf{s}) - f(\mathbf{x} - \eta\mathbf{s})}{2\eta}\right]^2$$

A good approximation to g_{p1} can be obtained from [30]:

$$g_{p1} = \frac{1}{2\lambda}(e_{+\lambda} - e_{-\lambda}), \quad \text{and} \quad \frac{dg_{p1}}{d\mathbf{x}} = \frac{1}{2\lambda}\left(\frac{de_{+\lambda}}{d\mathbf{x}} - \frac{de_{-\lambda}}{d\mathbf{x}}\right)$$

References

[1] A. Barr. Global and Local Deformations of Solid Primitives. *Computer Graphics*, 18:21–30, 1984.
[2] M. Black and A. Rangarajan. On the Unification of Line Processes, Outlier Rejection, and Robust Statistics with Applications in Early Vision. *IJCV*, 19(1):57–92, July 1996.
[3] T. Cham and J. Rehg. A Multiple Hypothesis Approach to Figure Tracking. In *CVPR*, volume 2, pages 239–245, 1999.
[4] K. Choo and D. Fleet. People Tracking Using Hybrid Monte Carlo Filtering. In *ICCV*, 2001.
[5] J. Deutscher, A. Blake, and I. Reid. Articulated Body Motion Capture by Annealed Particle Filtering. In *CVPR*, 2000.
[6] J. Deutscher, B. North, B. Bascle, and A. Blake. Tracking through Singularities and Discontinuities by Random Sampling. In *ICCV*, pages 1144–1149, 1999.
[7] S. Duane, A. D. Kennedy, B. J. Pendleton, and D. Roweth. Hybrid Monte Carlo. *Physics Letters B*, 195(2):216–222, 1987.

[8] D. Forsyth, J. Haddon, and S. Ioffe. The Joy of Sampling. *IJCV*, 41:109–134, 2001.
[9] D. Gavrila and L. Davis. 3-D Model Based Tracking of Humans in Action: A Multiview Approach. In *CVPR*, pages 73–80, 1996.
[10] T. Heap and D. Hogg. Wormholes in Shape Space: Tracking Through Discontinuities Changes in Shape. In *ICCV*, pages 334–349, 1998.
[11] N. Howe, M. Leventon, and W. Freeman. Bayesian Reconstruction of 3D Human Motion from Single-Camera Video. *ANIPS*, 1999.
[12] O. King and D. Forsyth. How does CONDENSATION Behave with a Finite Number of Samples? In *ECCV*, pages 695–709, 2000.
[13] H. J. Lee and Z. Chen. Determination of 3D Human Body Postures from a Single View. *CVGIP*, 30:148–168, 1985.
[14] J. MacCormick and M. Isard. Partitioned Sampling, Articulated Objects, and Interface-Quality Hand Tracker. In *ECCV*, volume 2, pages 3–19, 2000.
[15] N. Metropolis, A. W. Rosenbluth, M. N. Rosenbluth, A. H. Teller, and E. Teller. Equation of State Calculations by Fast Computing Machines. *J. Chem. Phys.*, 21(6):1087–1092, 1953.
[16] D. Morris and J. Rehg. Singularity Analysis for Articulated Object Tracking. In *CVPR*, pages 289–296, 1998.
[17] R. Neal. Probabilistic Inference Using Markov Chain Monte Carlo. Technical Report CRG-TR-93-1, University of Toronto, 1993.
[18] R. M. Neal. Annealed Importance Sampling. *Statistics and Computing*, 11:125–139, 2001.
[19] R. Plankers and P. Fua. Articulated Soft Objects for Video-Based Body Modeling. In *ICCV*, pages 394–401, 2001.
[20] R. Rosales and S. Sclaroff. Inferring Body Pose without Tracking Body Parts. In *CVPR*, pages 721–727, 2000.
[21] E. M. Sevick, A. T. Bell, and D. N. Theodorou. A Chain of States Method for Investigating Infrequent Event Processes Occuring in Multistate, Multidimensional Systems. *J. Chem. Phys.*, 98(4), 1993.
[22] H. Sidenbladh, M. Black, and D. Fleet. Stochastic Tracking of 3D Human Figures Using 2D Image Motion. In *ECCV*, 2000.
[23] C. Sminchisescu. Consistency and Coupling in Human Model Likelihoods In *CFGR*, 2002.
[24] C. Sminchisescu and B. Triggs. A Robust Multiple Hypothesis Approach to Monocular Human Motion Tracking. Technical Report RR-4208, INRIA, 2001.
[25] C. Sminchisescu and B. Triggs. Covariance-Scaled Sampling for Monocular 3D Body Tracking. In *CVPR*, 2001.
[26] C. Sminchisescu and B. Triggs. Building Roadmaps of Local Minima of Visual Models. In *ECCV*, 2002.
[27] M. R. Sorensen and A. F. Voter. Temperature-Accelerated Dynamics for Simulation of Infrequent Events. *J. Chem. Phys.*, 112(21):9599–9606, 2000.
[28] G. H. Vineyard. Frequency factors and Isotope Effects in Solid State Rate Processes. *J. Phys. Chem. Solids*, 3:121–127, 1957.
[29] A. F. Voter. A Method for Accelerating the Molecular Dynamics Simulation of Infrequent Events. *J. Chem. Phys.*, 106(11):4665–4677, 1997.
[30] A. F. Voter. Hyperdynamics: Accelerated Molecular Dynamics of Infrequent Events. *Physical Review Letters*, 78(20):3908–3911, 1997.

Implicit Probabilistic Models of Human Motion for Synthesis and Tracking

Hedvig Sidenbladh[*,1], Michael J. Black[2], and Leonid Sigal[2]

[1] Computational Vision and Active Perception Laboratory (CVAP)
Dept. of Numerical Analysis and Comp. Sci. KTH, SE-100 44 Stockholm, Sweden
hedvig@nada.kth.se http://www.nada.kth.se/~hedvig/
[2] Department of Computer Science, Brown University, Box 1910
Providence, RI 02912, USA.
black@cs.brown.edu http://www.cs.brown.edu/~black/

Abstract. This paper addresses the problem of probabilistically modeling 3D human motion for synthesis and tracking. Given the high dimensional nature of human motion, learning an explicit probabilistic model from available training data is currently impractical. Instead we exploit methods from texture synthesis that treat images as representing an *implicit empirical distribution*. These methods replace the problem of *representing* the probability of a texture pattern with that of *searching* the training data for similar instances of that pattern. We extend this idea to temporal data representing 3D human motion with a large database of example motions. To make the method useful in practice, we must address the problem of efficient search in a large training set; efficiency is particularly important for tracking. Towards that end, we learn a low dimensional linear model of human motion that is used to structure the example motion database into a binary tree. An approximate probabilistic tree search method exploits the coefficients of this low-dimensional representation and runs in sub-linear time. This probabilistic tree search returns a particular *sample* human motion with probability approximating the true distribution of human motions in the database. This sampling method is suitable for use with particle filtering techniques and is applied to articulated 3D tracking of humans within a Bayesian framework. Successful tracking results are presented, along with examples of synthesizing human motion using the model.

1 Introduction

Probabilistic models of human motion provide a representation that can be used both for synthesizing novel animations and for constraining the search in Bayesian tracking algorithms [37]. While the learning of such models from training sets of 3D human motions (e.g. joint angles over time) is an active area of research, the problem is made difficult by the dimensionality of the human

---

[*] Address at the time of publication: Dept. of Data and Information Fusion, Swedish Defense Research Institute (FOI), SE-172 90 Stockholm, Sweden. hedvig@foi.se.

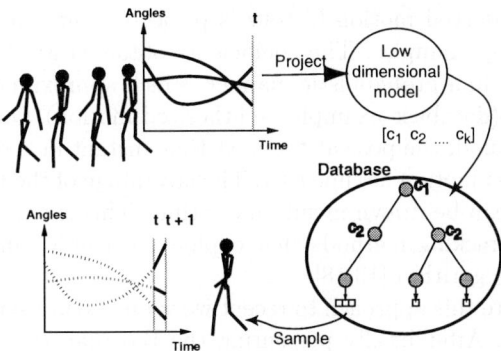

Fig. 1. Implicit probabilistic model of human motion (see text).

body, the variability in human motion, correlations among joint angles, and the correlations in motion over time. While recent work has seen some success at learning probabilistic models in small training sets or in supervised situations where the activities are known and clearly delimited, the general problem remains unsolved. Rather than attempt to learn a general probabilistic model in the high dimensional space of human motions we exploit recent work on texture synthesis that treats an image as an *implicit probability distribution*. As with human motion, there has been some limited success at learning probabilistic models of the spatial statistics of images that allows texture synthesis [30,32,44]. Recent synthesis methods, however, replace the problem of learning with that of search [7,8,9,14,16,40]. One incrementally constructs new textured regions by searching in the training images for example textures that have a similar neighborhood structure. The observation is that the important high order statistics are implicitly represented in the data and it is easier to *match* regions with similar statistics than it is to model them.

Here we extend these approaches to the problem of human motion modeling. The key idea with our motion model is to replace the problem of probabilistic *learning* with efficient probabilistic *search*. The idea is summarized in Figure 1. Given a large set of example human motions, over a time window of length d, we first construct a low dimensional model of the motion, by taking the time series of joint angles of length d and reducing the dimensionality using principal component analysis (PCA). Each length d subsequence in the set is then projected onto the resulting low-dimensional representation to give a vector of coefficients at each time instant. The database is then structured into a binary tree using these coefficients with the top node in the tree corresponding to the coefficient that captures the dimension of largest variance in the database. Lower levels in the tree capture the finer motion structure. Each of the leaf nodes contains an index into the motion database. This index gives the location of a time series corresponding to the body pose parameters (3D position and orientation of the body and the relative angles of all the joints).

Given a synthesized or observed motion from time $t-d$ to t, the goal is to predict (with the correct probability) the pose of the body at time $t+1$. The synthesized or observed motion history is projected onto the subspace learned from the database examples. The coefficients obtained are then used to index into the database in a probabilistic manner, which approximates sampling from the distribution p(database example | synthesized motion). Once a example from the database is found, the pose at the next time instant in the database is taken to be the predicted motion at time $t+1$. The advantage of the tree representation is that a sample can be drawn in sub-linear time. This is particularly important for synthesis or tracking methods that exploit stochastic sampling such as the CONDENSATION algorithm [13,18].

Below we relate this approach to recent work on texture synthesis and human motion modeling. After briefly presenting the Bayesian tracking framework in which the model is employed, we describe the database and the probabilistic tree search algorithm. We illustrate the implicit probabilistic model by using it to synthesize realistic motion sequences and by using it to provide a prior probability distribution over human motions for tracking. While our focus here is on developing a rigorous probabilistic model for Bayesian tracking, we expect the method to be useful for computer graphics applications and we will suggest extensions to make it more practical for human motion synthesis.

2 Related Work

There have been many approaches for modeling human motion. For narrow classes of motion such as walking, specific analytic functions of the joint angles have been proposed [17,34]. For more general human motion, dynamical systems have been developed for tracking [41,29] or animation (c.f. [5]). These systems can be computationally expensive and they may lack a clear probabilistic interpretation. Instead of explicitly modeling the physics of the human body, one can *learn* statistical properties of human motion from 3D motion capture data. This approach has been used both for synthesis and tracking.[1] The learned statistical properties may be captured by wavelets [33], PCA [22,37,42,43], polynomial basis functions of motion trajectories [12], or Hidden Markov Models (HMM) [3,4,26]. Full probabilistic models, however, remain difficult to learn given the dimensionality of the models and the limited availability of training data.

In contrast to traditional statistical learning methods, we make the most of available 3D motion capture data by keeping *all* of it. The challenge for probabilistic tracking is then to search it efficiently and to do so in a way that captures the underlying, implicit, probabilistic structure.

In formulating this implicit motion model, we exploit recent work in texture synthesis. This work can be roughly viewed on a continuum from approaches that attempt to learn statistical models of texture [15,30,32,44] to those that

---

[1] It is worth noting that the goals of synthesis and tracking are somewhat different. In synthesis, a good deal of effort is expended to make sure that transitions are "smooth", visually pleasing, and physically meaningful. For tracking, what we need is a representative set of plausible motions. Image data will tell us which of these are reasonable.

essentially treat an input texture as an implicit probabilistic model and use search to find matches between similar textures [7,8,9,14,16,40].

The non-parametric texture models most similar to the approach here generate new textures from an example texture in roughly the following way. Given a randomly selected starting block of texture in the image, propagate out from it generating new texture blocks. For each new block in the image, examine any neighboring blocks that have already been generated and search the example image (or images) for similar textures. Find the k best such matches and then randomly choose the corresponding new texture patch from among them. The methods [8,9,14,16,40] all vary in how the blocks are represented, how similarity is determined, and how the search is performed.

The approach described here is a natural extension of this texture synthesis idea to sequences of joint angles. Previous extensions to time have focused on synthesis and prove unsuitable for Bayesian tracking [1,35,40]. For cyclic articulated motion, Pullen and Bregler [33] use a frequency decomposition of joint angles with a learned, non-parametric, kernel density estimate of the conditional statistics across frequency bands [7,15]. Sampling from this model produces synthetic repetitive motions with natural variation. More closely related to the work described here is the work on video textures [35] which uses a pixel-based match metric to construct a matrix of probabilities that captures the similarities between frames in a video sequence and that can be used to transition between frames to construct an infinitely looping video sequence with apparently natural variation. In contrast to our approach, the method uses relatively short sequences of a single type of motion and, hence, all possible transitions can be pre-computed (and even optimized for display). Molina and Hilton [26] use a similar approach for modeling human motion. Since this type of motion is more diverse and has structure over longer time intervals, it is not possible to learn transition probabilities between all possible poses. Instead, a large set of example poses are grouped using vector quantization, and transition probabilities between the different groups are learned using an HMM formulation. A pose in the group found at each time step is selected based on constraints of smoothness over time. Our approach differs in that we do not *learn* transition probabilities between states. Instead, at each time step of the synthesis, we *search* among a large set of previously observed motions to find a plausible motion that fits with the synthesized motion history. We have thus replaced the problem of learning with that of searching a large database.

The most recent motion texture models for image sequences assume stationary statistics and use simple autoregressive models to capture temporal image change [10,39]. It is not clear whether these methods will scale to the problem of representing general human motion where the assumption of stationarity is violated.

For general motions an example-based model such as ours will only be practical if efficient search methods can be employed. Moreover, if it is to be used for Bayesian tracking, it must have a sound probabilistic interpretation. There are two issues to be addressed: defining a match metric and a search procedure

[21,40]. Exhaustive search in a large dataset is prohibitive and an algorithm with sub-linear time complexity is required. Thus, the metric must be defined so as to allow a hierarchical search in the dataset. Matching can be be performed using wavelet coefficients [1,21] and various pyramid representations [7, 15,40]. Here we use a database-specific basis set learned using PCA. This provides an approximate representation of the data and has the property that the basis functions provide a decomposition of the data ordered by the variance accounted for. Various search approaches have been proposed and include kd-trees [2,14], approximate nearest neighbor search (ANN) with PCA coefficients [16, 24,27], dynamic space partitioning [28] and tree-structured vector quantization [16,40]. Our approach extends these ideas to provide a probabilistic tree search using PCA coefficients.

It is worth noting that Chenney and Forsyth [6] have shown that samples such as those generated by our probabilistic tree search can be used to generate motions satisfying various external constraints.

3 Probabilistic Tracking Framework

The motion model described in this paper is employed in a probabilistic tracking framework. Given a model of a human, parameterized at time $t-1$ by the m parameters[2] $\boldsymbol{\phi}_{t-1} = [\phi_{1,t-1}, \ldots, \phi_{m,t-1}]^T$, the tracking of the model parameters over time can be formulated using Bayes' rule as

$$p(\boldsymbol{\phi}_t \mid \mathbf{I}_t) = \kappa\, p(I_t \mid \boldsymbol{\phi}_t) \int p(\boldsymbol{\phi}_t \mid \boldsymbol{\phi}_{t-1})\, p(\boldsymbol{\phi}_{t-1} \mid \mathbf{I}_{t-1})\, d\boldsymbol{\phi}_{t-1} \qquad (1)$$

where I_t is the image at time t, $\mathbf{I}_t$ the image sequence up to t, and κ a normalizing constant independent of $\boldsymbol{\phi}_t$. At each time step, the *posterior* distribution $p(\boldsymbol{\phi}_t \mid \mathbf{I}_t)$ is estimated. This distribution is represented by a set of samples or particles, which are propagated in time using a particle filter [13,18]. Each particle i represents a certain pose $\boldsymbol{\phi}_t^i$ of the human model, i.e. a certain location in the parameter space.

The distribution $p(I_t \mid \boldsymbol{\phi}_t)$ is the *likelihood* of observing the image I_t, conditioned on model configuration $\boldsymbol{\phi}_t$. In the particle representation, each model configuration $\boldsymbol{\phi}_t^i$ is projected into the image I_t and assigned a likelihood according to an image-model similarity measure. For details on the likelihood model and the tracking framework, the reader is referred to [36,37].

The motion model presented here, is used to formulate the *temporal prior* $p(\boldsymbol{\phi}_t \mid \boldsymbol{\phi}_{t-1})$. This conditional distribution is used to propagate the particles in time so that the correct part of the parameter space is covered at each time instant. Due to the particle representation, it is sufficient to design a motion model that allows *drawing samples* $\boldsymbol{\phi}_t^s$ from the distribution $p(\boldsymbol{\phi}_t \mid \boldsymbol{\phi}_{t-1})$. Details are described in the following section.

---

[2] The model is a 3D articulated assembly of truncated cones, with 50 parameters comprising the position and velocity of the torso, the joint angles between the cones (limbs), and the angular velocities [36]. However, the framework applies to any parameterized model.

4 Implicit Probabilistic Motion Model

The motion database consists of multiple sequences of body pose parameters recorded with a 3D motion capture system; sequences include two male and two female actors walking, running, dancing, skipping and lifting. Let $\psi_i = [\psi_{1,i}, \ldots, \psi_{m,i}]^T$ be a recorded vector of m pose parameters of the human model, stored at index location i in the database. More specifically, the pose parameters are the global position and orientation of the model, as well as joint angles, and the velocities of all these parameters. Let $\Psi_i = [\psi_i^T, \ldots, \psi_{i-d}^T]^T$ be the dm-dimensional vector containing the sequence of the d vectors of parameters up to and including the angles at location i. Similarly, let $\phi_t = [\phi_{1,t}, \ldots, \phi_{m,t}]^T$ represent the m pose parameters in a synthesized (or in a tracking framework, estimated) pose at time t, and let $\Phi_t = [\phi_t^T, \ldots, \phi_{t-d}^T]^T$ be the synthesized (or estimated) sequence between time $t-d$ and t. In all experiments here we take $d = 10$ [22] which corresponds to 1/3 sec.

In the standard formulation of the probabilistic motion model, the temporal prior $p(\phi_t \mid \phi_{t-1})$ satisfies a first-order Markov assumption. Here, instead of drawing samples ϕ_t^s from the the Markov prior, we augment the state space to store the history, Φ_{t-1}, over the previous d time instants and draw samples from a distribution $p(\phi_t \mid \Phi_{t-1})$ [3]. In the example based formulation, to draw samples ϕ_t^s from $p(\phi_t \mid \Phi_{t-1})$ we rewrite it as

$$p(\phi_t \mid \Phi_{t-1}) = p(\phi_t \mid \Psi_{i-1}) \, p(\Psi_{i-1} \mid \Phi_{t-1}),$$

where

$$p(\phi_t \mid \Psi_{i-1}) = \begin{cases} 1 & \text{if } \phi_t = \psi_i, \\ 0 & \text{otherwise.} \end{cases}$$

Thus, sampling from the prior $p(\phi_t \mid \Phi_{t-1})$ corresponds to drawing samples Ψ_{i-1}^s from $p(\Psi_{i-1} \mid \Phi_{t-1})$, and selecting $\phi_t^s = \psi_i^s$, where ψ_i^s is the pose directly following the stored motion Ψ_{i-1}^s. The key idea is that sampling from $p(\Psi_{i-1} \mid \Phi_{t-1})$ is approximated by an efficient probabilistic search of the database of motions as described below.

First, the variance of each pose parameter in the database is computed and stored in an $m \times m$ diagonal covariance matrix Γ. Let Γ_d be the $dm \times dm$ covariance matrix created by storing d copies of Γ along the diagonal.

We define a generative model that states that the stored human motion data looks like the synthesized data plus Gaussian noise

$$\Psi_i = \Phi_t + \eta(\Gamma_d) \tag{2}$$

where $\eta(\Gamma_d)$ is an dm-dimensional vector of Gaussian noise. Then the probability that any length d segment, Ψ_i, in the database matches a synthesized sequence Φ_t is given by

$$p(\Psi_i \mid \Phi_t) = \kappa \, e^{-\frac{1}{2}(\Psi_i - \Phi_t)^T \Gamma_d^{-1}(\Psi_i - \Phi_t)} \tag{3}$$

---

[3] The violation of the Markov assumption in (1) can be dealt with by treating $p(\phi_t \mid \Phi_{t-1})$ as a proposal distribution and appropriately re-weighting samples in our particle filtering framework [19].

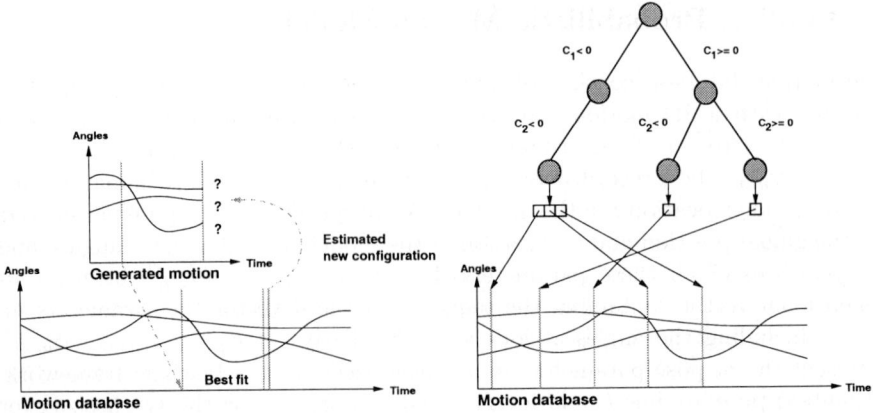

Fig. 2. Indexing into the database (see text).

(a) The history of generated motion is compared with examples of motion, and the next time step is selected from an example whose history fits well with the generated history.

(b) Binary search tree structure. Each leaf contains a list of pointers to motion examples in the database with coefficients corresponding to the search path to that leaf.

where $\kappa = (2\pi)^{-\frac{dm}{2}}(\det(\Gamma_d))^{-\frac{1}{2}}$. For simplicity, we assume a diagonal covariance matrix.

As illustrated in Figure 2a a naive approach to synthesis would compute $p(\Psi_i \mid \Phi_t)$ for every subsequence Ψ_i in the database. Then, $i = \arg\max_i p(\Psi_i \mid \Phi_t)$ would be chosen and the index $i+1$ would provide the new pose parameters, ψ_{i+1}. However, this search strategy would have a time complexity of $\mathcal{O}(n)$ where n is the number of entries into the database, and would not scale to the large databases needed for tracking of human motion in general. A search strategy performing in sub-linear time has to be developed, which means that the database has to be structured to avoid comparison with all database elements.

This search exploits a low-dimensional model of the data. Let $\bar{\Psi} = (\sum_{i=1}^{n} \Psi_i)/n$ be a length dm vector representing the mean of all subsequences in the database of motions. Let $\hat{A} = [\hat{\Psi}_1, \cdots, \hat{\Psi}_n]$ be the $dm \times n$ matrix of all subsequences where the mean motion has been subtracted; that is, $\hat{\Psi}_i = \Psi_i - \bar{\Psi}$.

Performing singular value decomposition (SVD), we write $\hat{A}$ as $\hat{A} = U\Sigma V^T$ where the $dm \times n$ matrix U contains the principal components of $\hat{A}$ and Σ is a diagonal matrix in which the diagonal entries represent the standard deviation σ_l accounted for by each of the principal components $l = 1, \ldots, n$.

We select the first b principal components where $b = \lfloor \log_2(n) \rfloor$. Given our training set of $n \approx 50000$ time points, $b = 16$ and accounts for 89% of the variance in the training data; that is, $\sum_{l=1}^{b} \sigma_l^2 / \sum_{l=1}^{n} \sigma_l^2 \geq 0.89$. Let $\tilde{U}$ be the b first columns of U, and $\tilde{\Sigma}$ the matrix with the b first singular values σ_l, $l = 1, \ldots, b$ along the diagonal. Using this sub-space representation, we can approximate any subsequence, Ψ_i, in the database as

$$\Psi_i \approx \tilde{\Psi}_i = \bar{\Psi} + \tilde{U}(\tilde{U}^T \hat{\Psi}_i) = \bar{\Psi} + \tilde{U}\mathbf{c}_i \ . \tag{4}$$

where the vector of coefficients $\tilde{U}^T\hat{\Psi}_i = \mathbf{c}_i$ provides a "descriptor" for the motion parameters Ψ_i. Analogously, the generated motion Φ_t can be approximated as

$$\Phi_t \approx \tilde{\Phi}_t = \bar{\Psi} + \tilde{U}\mathbf{c}_t \qquad (5)$$

where $\mathbf{c}_t = \tilde{U}^T\hat{\Phi}_t$, and $\hat{\Phi}_t = \Phi_t - \bar{\Psi}$.

4.1 Tree Representation

There are many ways to represent data such as ours for nearest neighbor search; e.g. given a probe motion (set of coefficients) find the k nearest neighbors. Our goals are somewhat different. For our tracking task, we seek a representation that can be searched such that each search result corresponds to a sample from some underlying distribution. These samples will only approximate the true distribution and the formulation trades off accuracy for efficiency. The method proposed here exploits the structure of our problem and may not be applicable to other search problems with a different probabilistic structure.

The motion examples in the database are sorted into a binary tree of depth b according to their coefficients $\mathbf{c}_i = [c_{i,1}, ..., c_{i,b}]^T$ (Figure 2b). The top node of the tree corresponds to the coefficient $c_{i,1}$. The database is split based on the sign of $c_{i,1}$ for each motion example i. Similarly, at the next level, the data is divided again at each node based on the sign of $c_{i,2}$. For each node (at depth l), the left subtree contains motion examples with eigencoefficient $c_{i,l} < 0$, while the right subtree contains samples with eigencoefficient $c_{i,l} \geq 0$. The process continues to the leaves of the tree at the depth b. Each leaf of the tree contains a list of pointers to the actual motion sequences in the database.

This process does not guarantee a balanced tree and, thus, some parents will have one child instead of two, and some leaves will contain more than one sample (see Figure 2b). In practice, the PCA representation results in a tree that is approximately balanced. Leaf nodes in our experiments contain between zero and several hundred samples. A balanced tree could be obtained by computing the median of the coefficients at each node and dividing based on that value [2].

4.2 Probabilistic Search

The tree described above can be searched in a probabilistic fashion so that searching the tree roughly approximates sampling from the distribution $p(\Psi_i \mid \Phi_t)$ (Equation (3)). The approach exploits the generative model above and uses the coefficients $c_{i,l}$ at each level l to randomly select the left or right subtree.

Observation 1 *If $\tilde{U}$ are the b axes with largest variation in the space of motion examples Ψ_i, $\bar{\Psi}$ the center of this space, $\mathbf{c}_i = \tilde{U}^T(\Psi_i - \bar{\Psi}) = \tilde{U}^T\hat{\Psi}_i$ the projection of Ψ_i into the sub-space spanned by $\tilde{U}$, and $\mathbf{c}_t = \tilde{U}^T(\Phi_t - \bar{\Psi}) = \tilde{U}^T\hat{\Phi}_t$ the projection of a generated motion Φ_t, then*

$$p(\Psi_i \mid \Phi_t) \approx p(\mathbf{c}_i \mid \mathbf{c}_t).$$

Explanation: $p(\Psi_i \mid \Phi_t)$ in Equation (3) can be written as

$$p(\Psi_i \mid \Phi_t) = \kappa\, e^{-\frac{1}{2}((\Psi_i-\bar{\Psi})-(\Phi_t-\bar{\Psi}))^T \Gamma_d^{-1}((\Psi_i-\bar{\Psi})-(\Phi_t-\bar{\Psi}))} =$$
$$= \kappa\, e^{-\frac{1}{2}(\hat{\Psi}_i-\hat{\Phi}_t)^T \Gamma_d^{-1}(\hat{\Psi}_i-\hat{\Phi}_t)} = \kappa\, e^{-\frac{1}{2}(\hat{\Psi}_i^T \Gamma_d^{-1}\hat{\Psi}_i - \hat{\Phi}_t^T \Gamma_d^{-1}\hat{\Phi}_t)}. \qquad (6)$$

This can be characterized by the *Mahalanobis* distances [25] of the two motions from the learned feature space:

$$d(\Psi_i) = \hat{\Psi}_i^T \Gamma_d^{-1} \hat{\Psi}_i, \quad d(\Phi_t) = \hat{\Phi}_t^T \Gamma_d^{-1} \hat{\Phi}_t.$$

Using the learned basis $\tilde{U}$ and the diagonal matrix of singular values $\tilde{\Sigma}$ of size $b \times b$, containing the b first diagonal elements from Σ, the Mahalanobis distance can be approximated by projecting it onto the subspace spanned by $\tilde{U}$ [25]:

$$d(\Psi_i) = \hat{\Psi}_i^T \Gamma_d^{-1} \hat{\Psi}_i \approx \hat{\Psi}_i^T \tilde{U} \tilde{\Sigma}^{-2} \tilde{U}^T \hat{\Psi}_i = (\tilde{U}^T \hat{\Psi}_i)^T \tilde{\Sigma}^{-2} \tilde{U}^T \hat{\Psi}_i = \mathbf{c}_i^T \tilde{\Sigma}^{-2} \mathbf{c}_i.$$

Similarly, $d(\Phi_t) \approx \mathbf{c}_t^T \tilde{\Sigma}^{-2} \mathbf{c}_t$. Inserting these approximations into (6) gives

$$p(\Psi_i \mid \Phi_t) \approx p(\mathbf{c}_i \mid \mathbf{c}_t) = \kappa\, e^{-\frac{1}{2}(\mathbf{c}_i^T \tilde{\Sigma}^{-2} \mathbf{c}_i - \mathbf{c}_t^T \tilde{\Sigma}^{-2} \mathbf{c}_t)} = \kappa\, e^{-\frac{1}{2}(\mathbf{c}_i - \mathbf{c}_t)^T \tilde{\Sigma}^{-2}(\mathbf{c}_i - \mathbf{c}_t)}. \quad \square$$

Thus, the samples in the database can be compared to a generated motion using only the eigencoefficients $\mathbf{c}$. The error in the approximation can be estimated from the residual eigenvalues σ_l, $l = b+1, \ldots, dm$, i.e. the eigenvalues of the dimensions in U that are not included in $\tilde{U}$ [25].

Search Algorithm. Given a "probe" motion, Φ_t, project it onto the basis set to compute the coefficients $\mathbf{c}_t$. Starting at the top of the tree with coefficient $c_{t,1}$ and proceeding down the tree for each level l, decide which branch to chose (left or right) based the probabilities

$$p_{\text{right subtree}} = p(c_{i,l} \geq 0 \mid c_{t,l}) = \frac{1}{\sqrt{2\pi\beta\sigma_l}} \int_{z=-\infty}^{c_{t,l}} e^{-\frac{z^2}{2\beta\sigma_l^2}} dz, \qquad (7)$$

$$p_{\text{left subtree}} = 1 - p_{\text{right subtree}}, \qquad (8)$$

where β is a "temperature" parameter described below.

Assuming the Gaussian model from Observation 1, a branch at level l is selected with the probability that the coefficient value $c_{t,l}$ falls on that side of the tree. Since this choice is probabilistic, "sampling" from the tree many times will result in different paths through the tree to the leaf nodes. Note that for simplicity, σ_l is derived from the entire data set rather than being conditioned on the choices above.

When a leaf is reached using this probabilistic search, one of the examples in the leaf, Ψ_i^s, is selected. This can be done by computing $p(\mathbf{c}_i \mid \mathbf{c}_t)$ for each i in the leaf and then using a Monte Carlo sampling technique to chose a particular i. As suggested by Observation 1, this approximates sampling from the leaf using $p(\Psi_i \mid \Phi_t)$ (Equation (3)). Alternatively, one can sample uniformly from the leaf node; this works well in practice and is more efficient.

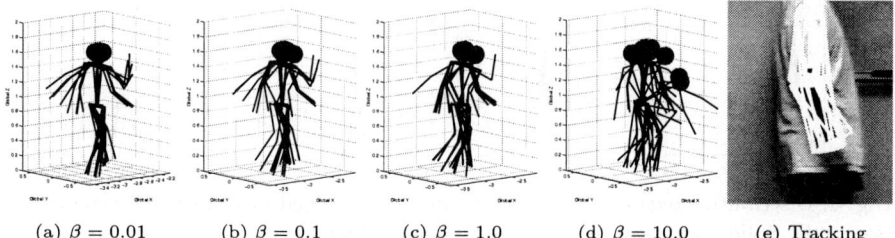

(a) $\beta = 0.01$ (b) $\beta = 0.1$ (c) $\beta = 1.0$ (d) $\beta = 10.0$ (e) Tracking

Fig. 3. Sampling from the database. The temperature parameter β affects the randomness in the sampling. In each figure, 10 pose candidates ϕ_{t+1} were sampled from the database using a generated motion Φ_t (a) Very low temperature. (b) Low temperature. (c) Neutral temperature. (d) High temperature. (e) Samples from an example of arm tracking (see also Section 6).

The new state, sampled from the example database, is defined as $\phi^s_{t+1} = \psi^s_{i+1} + \eta$ where ψ^s_{i+1} is the pose directly following Ψ^s_i in time, and η is a small Gaussian noise term with empirically determined variance. This noise is added in both synthesis and tracking to generate samples that differ slightly from the training data. ϕ^s_{t+1} is concatenated to the $d-1$ most recent entries in Φ^s_t to create Φ^s_{t+1} which is the motion history of particle s at time $t+1$.

The temperature parameter β controls the amount of randomness in the probabilistic tree search. Figure 3 illustrates the effect of β with samples drawn from the database using Equation (7). A generating motion example Φ_t was first selected from the database. Then, a probabilistic tree search was performed 10 times. For each of the 10 found database examples Ψ_i, the pose ψ_{i+1} directly following the motion example was selected and plotted. Thus, the variance within the 10 found poses reflects the accuracy with which the examples were found. A low temperature (e.g. 3a) results in samples that are similar to Φ_t. Alternatively, a very high temperature (e.g. 3d) will lead to an almost uniform sampling of the search tree, which means that the distribution over possible body poses will roughly approximate the *prior* probability distribution, $p(\Psi_i)$, over all motions. In a tracking application, the temperature parameter controls how strongly the motion prior guides the tracking. Furthermore, a lower temperature is typically needed if the model will be used for synthesis, since it is not guided by image measurements.

The total search cost for a single sample involves a logarithmic time tree search followed by a search that is linear in the number of elements in the leaf node. The relationship between the size of the leaf nodes, the depth of the tree, and the size of the database requires further study. The overall cost, however is significantly better than linear in the size of the database. This efficiency is particularly important if the samples are to be used for particle filtering where predicting each particle involves sampling the tree with a different probe.

Observation 2 *The "true" distribution $p(\Psi_i \mid \Phi_t)$ or $p(\mathbf{c}_i \mid \mathbf{c}_t)$ is unknown. The probabilistic tree search provides an approximate model and samples from the tree search are more "realistic" than those from the Gaussian model in (3).*

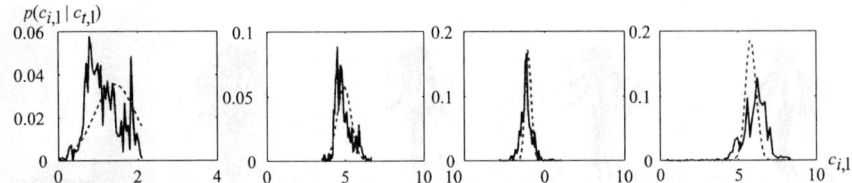

Fig. 4. Distribution over coefficients c_3, c_7, c_{11}, c_{15} obtained by probabilistic tree search (see text). Solid: empirical distribution from sampling. Dashed: Gaussian model.

Intuition: In the general case, there is no guarantee that the probabilistic tree search will approximate sampling from $p(\Psi_i | \Phi_t)$. For example, if the coefficients c_l for each basis direction l were actually normally distributed and statistically independent, then the tree search could provide a poor approximation to sampling the true distribution.

Given the nature of human motion however, PCA does not result in bases that make the coefficients statistically independent and, hence, these dependencies are represented in the branching structure of the tree. Intuitively, similar motions have similar sets of coefficients and these motions end up being grouped in the leaf nodes.

This can be seen in Figure 4 which plots the empirical distribution over a few coefficients using 1000 samples, Ψ_i, drawn for a single probe, Φ_t (with $\beta = 1$). For comparison, the figure also plots the distribution over each coefficient assuming independent Gaussian noise. This example illustrates the general agreement between the independent Gaussian model and samples drawn with the tree. By adopting our model however, we can also capture the non-Gaussian nature of the human motion data present in the database.

Further work needs to be done to formalize the tree search procedure, understand the nature of the approximation, and characterize the problems to which it is applicable.

5 Visualizing the Model (Synthesis)

Although our primary application for this motion model is as a prior to guide probabilistic tracking, the probabilistic model can also be used for synthesis. The goal of the visualization is to generate a new synthetic motion incrementally, by indexing into the database at each time step, using the generated motion at the previous d time steps. Note that the synthesis does not have a goal function. The type of motion can be controlled up to a certain point by the choice of start motion. However, due to the probabilistic tree search there is a certain randomness in the synthesis.

In Figure 5, a 2 second long running motion is visualized.[4] Note that the database contains several types of activities, not just running. The regularity with which the feet are planted (Figure 5) indicates that the periodicity is well

---

[4] A movie of the generated motion in Figure 5, along with other synthesis examples, can be found at http://www.nada.kth.se/~hedvig/mpegs/movies.html.

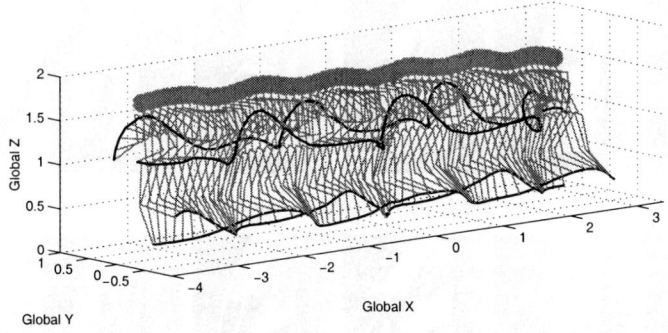

Fig. 5. Generated running motion, 2 s at 30 Hz. The pose every frame is shown in gray. Trajectories for hands and wrists are plotted in black.

preserved in the synthesized running sequence, even though the phase of the running cycle is not explicitly modeled.

To generate more varied and non-cyclic motion, a larger database of examples is needed to find smooth transitions between many different types of motion (β can be used to control the probability of changing motions). Finally, it is important to note that the motion model has no notion of gravity, friction, and position of the feet relative to the floor. To be able to generate plausible-looking motions for longer periods, constraints need to be introduced on the position and rotation of the human model so that it fulfills basic kinematic and dynamic requirements [6,11]. Furthermore, in general it is desired to be able to edit the generated motion iteratively, and to introduce goals in the motion generation [26]. Therefore, the motion model is, in its present state, more suited for tracking than for motion synthesis. However, the example based scheme introduces fine realistic details that are often lost in a learned motion model.

6 Tracking Results

The example-based motion model is now evaluated in terms of its performance as a temporal prior for *monocular* 3D tracking, as described in Section 3. We compared it to a very general temporal model of constant (angular) velocity in the parameters, where all parameters are considered independent [36]. The generality of the constant velocity model allows tracking of any type of motion, but introduces problems in high-dimensional spaces. Using particle filtering methods as we do here is problematic given that the number of required particles is $N \propto 1/\alpha^d$ where $\alpha \ll 1$ depends on the generality of the motion model, and d is the number of parameters [23]. The use of a strong prior model such as the one developed here is one way of coping with the dimensionality problem. See [38] for recent work on human motion tracking that places particles more effectively thus allowing more general motion priors.

As an initial illustration, a version of the database is built using only the joint angles and angular velocities of the right arm. The model has 8 DOF; 3 Euler angles in the shoulder, one angle in the elbow, and their angular velocities.

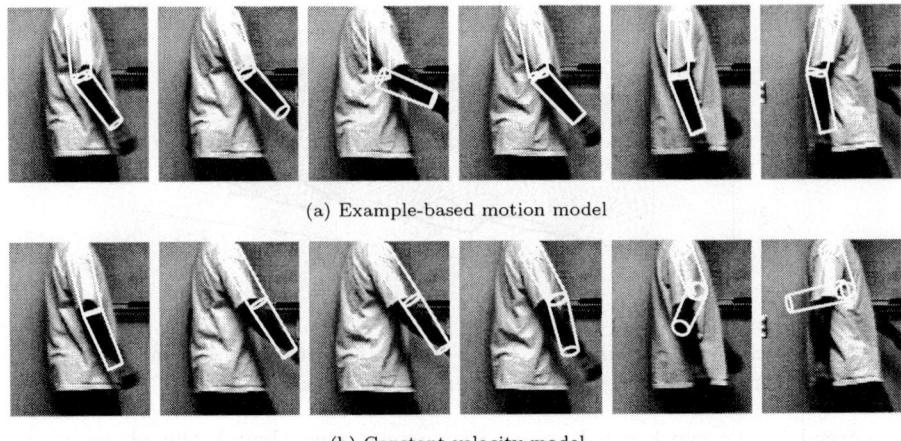

Fig. 6. Tracking an arm using 300 samples. Frames 5, 10, 15, 20, 25 and 30, with the expected value of the posterior distribution overlaid, are shown. (a) The example based model enables tracking with a small number of samples. (b) The same number of samples is insufficient using the constant velocity model.

The sequence used for tracking is stabilized so that the shoulder has the same position in all images and the configuration of the arm at frame 0 is manually set. To initialize the example-based temporal model, a linear search is performed in the database, and N arm motion samples, whose last time step correspond well with the manually set joint angles, are chosen using Monte Carlo sampling.

In Figure 6a, the arm is tracked with the example-based motion model as the temporal prior. $N = 300$ samples are used for particle filtering. In frame 15, the elbow of the model arm is more bent than the real elbow in the sequence. The reason for this is that the real arm position is not present in the database – none of the example subjects moved their arm to this position. This may be an artifact of the marker placement during motion capture. However, in frame 20, the arm is again correctly estimated. A typical set of particles is illustrated in Figure 3e. The variation in the set of sampled poses can be controlled by the temperature parameter β, as discussed in Section 4.

For comparison, the arm is also tracked using the constant velocity prior. The number of particles, N (and the likelihood model) are the same as in the previous tracking case, i.e. much lower than the number of particles used in similar experiments [36]. Since the constant velocity model is not able to predict the arm motion as well as the example-based model, the arm model loses track after a few frames, due to the small number of particles. However, if the number of particles is raised to $N = 3000$, the constant velocity prior is sufficient.

If the number of parameters d is larger, the constant velocity model is too general (i.e. α is too low). Given that $N = 3000$ is sufficient to track an 8-dimensional arm model using this motion model, the relation $N \propto 1/\alpha^d$ gives an estimate of the number of particles needed to track a 50-dimensional model such as human. Using this estimate, $N \approx 10^{16}$.

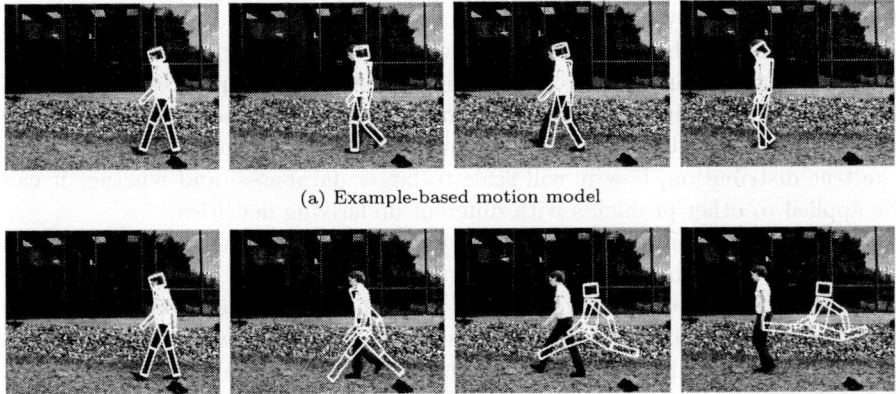

Fig. 7. Tracking a walking human using 300 samples. Frames 5, 10, 15, 20, 25 and 30, with the expected value of the posterior distribution overlaid, are shown. (a) Even though the dimensionality is higher than in Figure 6 the example based model enables tracking with the same number of samples. (b) This number of samples is, again, insufficient using the constant velocity model.

The result of tracking a full 3D body using the example-based model is shown in Figure 7a. $N = 300$ particles were used for tracking. Since the database of motions is quite small ($n \approx 50000$), and the examples are taken from the motion of professional dancers (a quite biased selection in terms of motion pattern), the deviations in pose between the model and the human in the sequence is at times large. Apart from the pose deviations, the example-based motion model enables successful tracking of the person in this 30 frame sequence. This is in contrast to the smooth motion model for which $N = 300$ particles is far from sufficient (Figure 7b). Note that the example-based motion model is more versatile than learned models of walking [17,34,37] in that it can be used for all kinds of motion (present in the database), as well as transitions between activities. Furthermore, some generalization to novel motions is made possible by the addition of Gaussian noise to the samples.

7 Conclusions

Learning a concise probabilistic model of 3D human motion is a challenging task (though recent work [4] suggests that it is possible). Here we make the simple observation that a database of motion capture data can, itself, serve as an implicit probabilistic model in a way that is directly analogous to recent work on texture synthesis. Unlike work on texture synthesis, our goal is human tracking and, hence, we must model general human motion rather than narrow "textural" motions. This results in a large database of heterogeneous motions. Consequently, practical algorithms for either synthesis or tracking necessitate an efficient algorithm for searching the database. We have proposed a method for structuring the database as a binary tree based on the coefficients of a low-dimensional approximation to the data. Furthermore, we described a probabilistic search method that uses the binary tree to stochastically generate sample motions from the database that match a synthesized input motion. The algorithm has sub-linear complexity and is suitable for synthesizing novel motion sequences and for generating predictions in a Bayesian tracking framework. Further work needs to be done however to understand how well this heuristic search method approximates the true distribution, how it will scale to larger databases, and whether it can be applied to other problems with different underlying densities.

One advantage of this method over traditional learning methods is that it uses all the data and hence captures subtle variations that may be lost using other methods. It is also extremely simple to implement. The disadvantage however is that the representation does not readily generalize to new motions. To allow more variation in the generated motion, and to lower the number of needed example motion sequences, the method described here could be used to learn separate motion models for different parts of the body (as was illustrated with the arm tracking example in Section 6 and Figure 6). The natural tree structure of the body can be exploited in sampling the motions of the joints. More research is needed to model the correlations between these limbs and to perform Bayesian inference using such a model.

While our tracking results are preliminary, they suggest that an implicit motion model may prove effective for tracking high dimensional human motion. To reduce the problems with extrapolation from the database, the example-based motion priors could be combined with more general priors using mixture models. In a particle framework, this would correspond to propagating a certain portion of the particles with a general temporal prior, and another portion with the example-based temporal prior.

The model also shows promise as a method for generating varied synthesized motion with natural detail. However, to exploit the example-based method for synthesis, further work must be done. The most obvious extension is to perform some simple blending or smoothing of the synthesized poses [35,31], and to introduce a predictive mechanism to avoid "dead ends" [35]. The issue of retargetting the synthesized motions to new actors remains open [11,20,31] as does the application of these techniques to facial motions or other time series data. Finally, realistic synthesis will require the addition of constraints such as contact between feet and the ground plane and, more generally, controllability/editability for animation [11]. The formulation of such constraints within our sampling framework seems plausible (cf. [6]) but remains an area for future research.

Acknowledgments. We thank Michael Gleicher for providing the 3D motion capture database and Yaser Yacoob for the walking image sequence used for the arm tracking experiment. We also thank Nancy Pollard, Fernando De la Torre, and Thomas Hofmann helpful discussions on motion synthesis, and Jan-Olof Eklundh for his support and encouragement.

HS was sponsored by the Foundation for Strategic Research under the "Center for Autonomous Systems" contract. MJB was supported by the DARPA HumanID Project (ONR contract N000140110886) and by a gift from the Xerox Foundation.

References

1. J. Bar-Joseph, R. El-Yaniv, D. Lischinski, and M. Werman. Texture mixing and texture movie synthesis using statistical learning. *IEEE Trans. Visualization and Computer Graphics*, 7(2):1120–135, 2001.
2. J. S. Beis and D. G. Lowe. Shape indexing using nearest-neighbour search in high-dimensional spaces. *CVPR*, pp. 1000–1006, 1997.
3. M. Brand. Shadow puppetry. *ICCV*, vol. 2, pp. 1237–1244, 1999.
4. M. Brand and A. Hertzmann. Style machines. *SIGGRAPH*, pp. 183–192, 2000.
5. A. Bruderlin and T. W. Calvert. Intelligence without representation. *Computer Graphics*, 23:233–242, 1989.
6. S. Chenney and D. A. Forsyth. Sampling plausible solutions to multi-body constraint problems. *SIGGRAPH*, pp. 219–228, 2000.
7. J. de Bonet. Multiresolution sampling procedure for analysis and synthesis of texture images. *SIGGRAPH*, pp. 361–368, 1997.
8. A. A. Efros and W. T. Freeman. Image quilting for texture synthesis and transfer. *SIGGRAPH*, pp. 341–346, 2001.
9. A. A. Efros and T. K. Leung. Texture synthesis by non-parametric sampling. *ICCV*, vol. 2, pp. 1033–1038, 1999.
10. A. Fitzgibbon. Stochastic rigidity: Image registration for nowhere-static scenes. *ICCV*, vol. 1, pp. 662–669, 2001
11. M. Gleicher. Retargeting motion to new characters. *SIGGRAPH*, pp. 33–42, 1998.
12. L. Goncalves, E. Di Bernardo, and P. Perona. Reach out and touch space (motion learning). *IEEE International Conference on Automatic Face and Gesture Recognition*, pp. 234–238, 1998.
13. N. Gordon. A novel approach to nonlinear/non-gaussian Bayesian state estimation. *IEE Proceedings on Radar, Sonar and Navigation*, 140(2):107–113, 1993.
14. P. Harrison. A non-hierarchical procedure for re-synthesis of complex textures. *WSCC*, 2001.
15. D. J. Heeger and J. R. Bergen. Pyramid-based texture analysis/synthesis. *SIGGRAPH*, pp. 229–238, 1995.
16. A. Hertzmann, C. E. Jacobs, N. Oliver, B. Curless, and D. H. Salisin. Image analogies. *SIGGRAPH*, pp. 327–240 2001.
17. D. C. Hogg. Model-based vision: A program to see a walking person. *IVC*, 1(1):5–20, 1983.
18. M. Isard and A. Blake. CONDENSATION – conditional density propagation for visual tracking. *IJCV*, 29(1):5–28, 1998.
19. M. Isard and A. Blake. ICONDENSATION: Unifying low-level and high-level tracking in a stochastic framework. *ECCV*, vol. 1, pp. 893–908, 1998.
20. J. K. Hodgins and N. S. Pollard. Adapting simulated behaviors for new characters. *SIGGRAPH*, pp. 153–162, 1997.
21. C. E. Jacobs, A. Finkelstein, and D. H. Salesin. Fast multiresolution image querying. *SIGGRAPH*, pp. 277–286, 1995.
22. M. E. Leventon and W. T. Freeman. Bayesian estimation of 3-d human motion from an image sequence. MERL Tech. Rep. TR–98–06, Cambridge, MA, 1998.
23. J. MacCormick and M. Isard. Partitioned sampling, articulated objects, and interface quality hand tracking. *ECCV*, vol. 2, pp. 3–19, 2000.
24. J. McNames. A fast nearest-neighbor algorithm based on a principal axis search tree. *PAMI*, 23(9):964–976, 2001.

25. B. Moghaddam and A. Pentland. Probabilistic visual learning for object representation. *PAMI*, 19(7):696–710, 1997.
26. L. Molina and A. Hilton. Realistic synthesis of novel human movements from a database of motion capture examples. *IEEE Workshop on Human Motion*, pp. 137–142, 2000.
27. H. Murase and S. Nayar. Visual learning and recognition of 3-D objects from appearance. *IJCV*, 14:5–24, 1995.
28. S. A. Nene and S. Nayar. A simple algorithm for nearest neighbor search in high dimensions. *PAMI*, 19:989–1003, 1997.
29. V. Pavolvić, J. Rehg, T-J. Cham, and K. Murphy. A dynamic Bayesian network approach to figure tracking using learned dynamic models. *ICCV*, vol. 1, pp. 94–101, 1999.
30. K. Popat and R. W. Picard. Cluster-based probability model and its applications to image and texture processing. *IEEE Trans. Image Proc.*, 6(2):268–284, 1997.
31. Z. Popovic and A. Witkin. Physically Based Motion Transformation. *SIGGRAPH*, pp. 11–20, 1999.
32. J. Portilla and E. P. Simoncelli. A parametric texture model based on joint statistics of compex wavelet coefficients. *IJCV*, 40(1):49–71, 2000.
33. K. Pullen and C. Bregler. Animating by multi-level sampling. *IEEE Computer Animation*, pp. 36–42, 2000.
34. K. Rohr. Towards model-based recognition of human movements in image sequences. *CVGIP - Image Understanding*, 59(1):94–115, 1994.
35. A. Schödl, R. Szeliski, D. H. Salesin, and I. Essa. Video textures. *SIGGRAPH*, pp. 489–498, 2000.
36. H. Sidenbladh and M. J. Black. Learning image statistics for Bayesian tracking. *ICCV*, vol. 2, pp. 709–716, 2001.
37. H. Sidenbladh, M. J. Black, and D. J. Fleet. Stochastic tracking of 3D human figures using 2D image motion. *ECCV*, vol. 2, pp. 702–718, 2000.
38. C. Sminchisescu and B. Triggs. Covariance scaled sampling for monocular 3D body tracking. *CVPR*, vol. 1 pp. 447–454, 2001.
39. S. Soatto, G. Doretto, Y. Wu. Dynamic Textures. *ICCV*, pp. 439–446, 2001.
40. L-Y. Wei and M. Levoy. Fast texture synthesis using tree-structured vector quantization. *SIGGRAPH*, pp. 479–488, 2000.
41. C. R. Wren and A. P. Pentland. Dynaman: Recursive modeling of human motion. *IVC*, to appear.
42. Y. Yacoob and M. J. Black. Parameterized modeling and recognition of activities in temporal surfaces. *CVIU*, 73(2):232–247, 1999.
43. Y. Yacoob and L. Davis. Learned models for estimation of rigid and articulated human motion from stationary or moving camera. *IJCV*, 36(1):5–30, 2000.
44. S. C. Zhu, Y. N. Wu, and D. Mumford. Minimax entropy principle and its application to texture modeling. *Neural Computation*, 9:1627–1660, 1997.

Space-Time Tracking

Lorenzo Torresani and Christoph Bregler

Computer Science Department,
Stanford University,
Stanford, CA 94305, USA
{ltorresa, bregler}@cs.stanford.edu

Abstract. We propose a new tracking technique that is able to capture non-rigid motion by exploiting a space-time rank constraint. Most tracking methods use a prior model in order to deal with challenging local features. The model usually has to be trained on carefully hand-labeled example data before the tracking algorithm can be used. Our new model-free tracking technique can overcome such limitations. This can be achieved in redefining the problem. Instead of first training a model and then tracking the model parameters, we are able to derive trajectory constraints first, and then estimate the model. This reduces the search space significantly and allows for a better feature disambiguation that would not be possible with traditional trackers. We demonstrate that sampling in the trajectory space, instead of in the space of shape configurations, allows us to track challenging footage without use of prior models.

1 Introduction

Most of the tracking techniques that are able to capture non-rigid motion use a prior model. For instance, some human face-trackers use a pre-trained PCA model or parameterized 3D model, and fit the model to 2D image features. Combining these models with advanced sampling techniques (like particle filters or multiple hypothesis approaches) result in algorithms capable of overcoming many local ambiguities. There are many cases where a prior-model is not available. In fact, often the main reason for performing tracking is to estimate data that can be used to build a model. In this case, model-free feature trackers have to be used. Unfortunately many non-rigid domains, such as human motion, contain challenging features that make tracking without a model virtually impossible. Examples of such features are points with degenerate or 1D texture (points along lips and eye contours, cloth and shoe textures). We propose an innovative model-free tracking solution that can overcome such limitations. This can be achieved in redefining the tracking problem.

1. **Traditional Tracking**: *Given* $\mathbf{M} \to$ *Estimate* α:
   Standard model-based approaches assume a known (pre-trained) parameterized model $\mathbf{M}(\alpha)$. The model $\mathbf{M}$ stays constant over the entire time sequence (for example $\mathbf{M}$ might coincide with a set of basis-shapes). The parameters

α change from time frame to time frame (for example the interpolation coefficients between the basis shapes). Traditional tracking solves by estimating frame by frame the parameters $\alpha(1)..\alpha(F)$ that would fit $\mathbf{M}(\alpha)$ to the data.

2. **Reverse-Order Tracking**: *Estimate $\alpha \to$ Estimate $\mathbf{M}$*:
   Our new technique first estimates the $\alpha(1)..\alpha(F)$ without knowing the model. Given the α parameters, it then estimates the model $\mathbf{M}$.

To reverse the order of computations we have to overcome two major hurdles: 1) How can the parameters α be estimated in a model-free fashion? 2) How can a model $\mathbf{M}$ be derived from the parameters α? We will also demonstrate why the reverse order tracking is advantageous over the traditional order.

Based on the assumption that the non-rigid motion can be factorized into a rigid motion and a blend-shape (non-rigid) motion component, we can establish a global low-rank constraint on the measurement-matrix (of the entire image sequence). This low-rank constraint allows us to estimate model-free all deformation parameters α over the entire image sequence. It is inspired by recent work by Irani [8] for the rigid case, and by extensions to non-rigid motion [17].

Since our tracking is based on direct image measurements, we have to minimize over a nonlinear error surface. In traditional tracking the search space grows with the number of time frames and the degrees of freedom of the model, and is therefore prone to many local minima (even with the use of nonlinear sampling techniques). With this new setup, and by fixing α over the entire sequence, we can show that the model estimation becomes a search in a very low-dimensional space. Sampling techniques in this small search space allow us to estimate models with high accuracy and overcome many local ambiguities that would exist in the traditional tracking framework.

We demonstrate this new technique on video recordings of a human face and of shoe deformations. Both domains have challenging (degenerate) features, and we show that the new algorithm can track densely all locations without any problem.

Section 3 describes the general rank constraint, and section 4 details how to exploit it for the two-step tracking. In section 5 we summarize our experiments and we conclude by discussing the results in section 6.

2 Previous Work

Many non-rigid tracking solutions have been proposed previously. As mentioned earlier, most methods use an a-priori model. Examples are [11,3,5,14,1,2,10]. Most of these approaches estimate non-rigid 2D motion, but some of them also recover 3D pose and deformations based on a 3D model.

What is most closely related to our approach, and in part inspired this solution, is work by Irani and Anandan [8,9] as well as methods for non-rigid decompositions [4,17], although these are either in the framework of rigid scenes, based on preexisting point tracks or related to Lucas-Kanade tracking.

3 Low-Rank Constraint for Non-rigid Motion

Our tracking algorithm relies on the assumption that the non-rigid 3D object motion can be approximated by a 3D rigid motion component (rotation and translation) and 3D non-rigid basis shape interpolations.

In this section we describe how we can justify a rank bound on the tracking matrix W without the prior knowledge of a specific object model. This gives an important insight on the roles of two matrices Q and M resulting from the decomposition of the tracking matrix. Section 4 shows how this decomposition is used in the tracking process.

3.1 Matrix Decomposition

The tracking matrix W describes the dense optical flow of P pixel or the tracks of P feature points over a sequence of F video frames:

$$W = \begin{bmatrix} \mathbf{U}^{F \times P} \\ \mathbf{V}^{F \times P} \end{bmatrix} \quad (1)$$

Each row of $\mathbf{U}$ holds all x-displacements of all P locations for a specific time frame, and each row of $\mathbf{V}$ holds all y-displacements for a specific time frame. It has been shown that if $\mathbf{U}$ and $\mathbf{V}$ describe a 3D rigid motion, the rank of $[\frac{\mathbf{U}}{\mathbf{V}}]$ has an upper bound, which depends on the assumed camera model [16,8]. This rank constraint derives from the fact that $[\frac{\mathbf{U}}{\mathbf{V}}]$ can be factored into two matrices: $Q \times M$. $Q^{2F \times r}$ describes the relative pose between camera and object for each time frame, and $M^{r \times P}$ describes the 3D structure of the scene which is invariant to camera and object motion.

In previous works we have shown that a similar rank constraint holds also for the motion of deforming objects [4,17]. Assuming the non-rigid 3D deformations can be approximated by a set of K modes of variation, the 3D shape of a specific object configuration can be expressed as a linear combination of K basis-shapes $(S_1, S_2, ... S_K)$. Each basis-shape S_i is a $3 \times P$ matrix describing the 3D positions of P points for a specific "key" shape configuration of the object [1]. A deformation can be computed by linearly interpolating between basis-shapes: $S = \sum_k l_k S_k$.

Assuming weak-perspective projection, at a specific time frame t the P points of a non-rigid shape S are projected onto 2D image points $(u_{t,i}, v_{t,i})$:

$$\begin{bmatrix} u_{t,1} & \cdots & u_{t,P} \\ v_{t,1} & \cdots & v_{t,P} \end{bmatrix} = R_t \cdot \left(\sum_{i=1}^{K} l_{t,i} \cdot S_i \right) + T_t \quad (2)$$

where R_t contains the first two rows of the full 3D camera rotation matrix, and T_t is the camera translation. The weak perspective scaling (f/Z_{avg}) of the

---
[1] We want to emphasize that no prior knowledge of the basis-shapes of the object will be assumed by the method: the K unknown key-shapes will instead be implicitly estimated by the tracking algorithm.

projection is implicitly coded in $l_{t,1},...l_{t,K}$. As in [16], we can eliminate T_t by subtracting the mean of all 2D points, and henceforth can assume that S is centered at the origin.

We can rewrite the linear combination in (2) as a matrix multiplication:

$$\begin{bmatrix} u_{t,1} & ... & u_{t,P} \\ v_{t,1} & ... & v_{t,P} \end{bmatrix} = \begin{bmatrix} l_{t,1}R_t & ... & l_{t,K}R_t \end{bmatrix} \cdot \begin{bmatrix} S_1 \\ S_2 \\ ... \\ S_K \end{bmatrix} \quad (3)$$

We stack all point tracks from time frame 1 to F into one large tracking $2F \times P$ matrix W. Using (3) we can write:

$$W = \underbrace{\begin{bmatrix} l_{1,1}R_1 & ... & l_{1,K}R_1 \\ l_{2,1}R_2 & ... & l_{2,K}R_2 \\ & ... & \\ l_{F,1}R_F & ... & l_{F,K}R_F \end{bmatrix}}_{Q} \cdot \underbrace{\begin{bmatrix} S_1 \\ S_2 \\ ... \\ S_K \end{bmatrix}}_{M} \quad (4)$$

Since Q is a $2F \times 3K$ matrix and M is a $3K \times P$ matrix, in the noise free case W has at most rank $r \leq 3K$.

Beyond the important derivation of the rank constraint, the analysis above allows us to conclude that it is possible to separate the components of non-rigid motion, represented in Q in form of rotation matrices and deformation coefficients, from the structure (basis-shape model) of the object stored in M.

In the following sections we will show how we can take advantage of this decomposition to derive a solution to the tracking problem.

4 Tracking Algorithm

Section 3 described how W can be decomposed into a matrix Q and M. We do not have the tracking matrix W yet, this is the goal of our tracking algorithm. As outlined in section 1, we achieve this in reversing the traditional tracking order: first estimating the motion parameters Q, and then estimating the model M that fits the data.

4.1 Non-rigid Motion Estimation

The motion parameters are the interpolation coefficients $l_{t,k}$ and the rotation matrices R_t that are coded in the $Q^{2F \times r}$ matrix of equation (4).

It is possible to estimate Q without the full availability of W. It is based on the following observation (inspired by [8]): if the rank of $W^{2F \times P}$ is r, a subset of r point tracks (non-degenerate columns in W) will span the remaining tracks of W.

We reorder W into a set of m known "reliable" tracks W_{rel}, and a set of n unknown "unreliable" tracks W_{unrel} ($n = P - m$):

$$W^{2F \times P} = [W_{rel}^{2F \times m} | W_{unrel}^{2F \times n}] = Q^{2F \times r} \cdot [M_{rel}^{r \times m} | M_{unrel}^{r \times n}] \quad (5)$$

Usually r is significantly smaller than P and it is easy to find at least $m > r$ reliable tracks [17] that can be computed for the entire image sequence. Assuming W_{rel} is of rank r, we can estimate a matrix $\hat{Q}^{2F \times r}$ with following factorization:

$$W_{rel}^{2F \times m} = \hat{Q}^{2F \times r} \cdot \hat{M}_{rel}^{r \times m} \quad (6)$$

The factorization is not uniquely defined. Any invertible matrix $G^{r \times r}$ defines another valid solution: $\hat{Q}_2 = \hat{Q} \cdot G$ and $\hat{M}_{rel2} = G^{-1} \hat{M}_{rel}$. Since W_{rel} has rank r, the original matrix Q for the full W matrix (in equation (4) and (5)) is also related to $\hat{Q}$ with an invertible matrix G: $Q = \hat{Q} \cdot G$. In [4,17] several methods are described for how to calculate G (specifically for non-rigid reconstruction). In the context of our tracking problem here, we do not have to know G, since it does not change W. We only need to know that $\hat{Q}$ and Q are related by some (unknown) invertible G. The model M that we obtain in section 4.2 is then just multiplied by G^{-1} to get a correct 3D model (using results from [17]).

We calculate $\hat{Q}$ and $\hat{M}_{rel}$ in the standard way with SVD:

$$svd(W_{rel}) = U \cdot S \cdot V^T = \underbrace{U \cdot C}_{\hat{Q}} \cdot \underbrace{C \cdot V^T}_{\hat{M}_{rel}} \quad (7)$$

where C is the upper $r \times r$ sub-block of $\sqrt{S}$.

This factorization gives us (up to unknown G) the motion parameters $\hat{Q}$ and the 3D shape coordinates of the reliable points $\hat{M}_{rel}$.

4.2 Non-rigid Shapes Estimation

The task we have left is that of estimating the shape elements in the $r \times n$ matrix M_{unrel}.

The corresponding image features for point i has degenerate texture, and no reliable feature extraction and tracking schema for those points is assumed to work. Even probabilistic point tracks (as assumed in [9]) with uncertainty measures are not available. Nonlinear probabilistic trackers (e.g. particle filter-based) fail since the density for each feature location has too much spread or is a-priori uniformly distributed. Obviously in those cases, a known basis-shape model would help dramatically and would constrain the possible feature locations in a reliable way, but we do not have such a model M_{unrel} yet.

Let us consider a single column m_i of M_{unrel} which represents the spatial (unknown) positions of point i for the K main deformations of the object. It turns out that if we multiply $\hat{Q}$ with m_i, we obtain an r-dimensional family of image trajectories $w_i = \hat{Q} \cdot m_i$. Now we have a very strong parameterized model for the unreliable point, but along the time axis instead of the space axis: the low-dimensional variability is expressed as temporal variations of the trajectory curve of a single point across time. In a sense we have a very accurate high resolution "dynamical model" of the point, without having the "kinematic constraints" in place yet. The probability of each possible trajectory in this constrained (r-dimensional) subspace can be computed much more reliably from the image data. As local texture might be ambiguous in a single frame, it is unique across the entire sequence of F frames, if constrained in the trajectory subspace. For instance, the famous aperture problem of 1D texture vanishes in this framework, as noted by [8] already.

Sampling in trajectory space. Since we only use the image sequence itself as features, the probability density for our trajectory family is nonlinear. Also any possible initialization heuristic for the trajectory of the unknown point track i might be far of. We therefore adopt a stochastic estimation technique based on factored sampling [7] to find the most likely values for m_i.

Factored sampling is a Monte Carlo technique for estimation of conditional probability densities. Let us assume we are trying to estimate the function $p(\mathbf{X}|\mathbf{Z})$ where $\mathbf{X}$ and $\mathbf{Z}$ are continuous random variables statistically related by some unknown dependency. When $p(\mathbf{X}|\mathbf{Z})$ cannot be sampled directly but the function $p(\mathbf{Z}|\mathbf{X}=x)$ can be computed for any x, factored sampling proposes the following recipe. Let $x_1, ..., x_N$ be N samples drawn from the prior $p(\mathbf{X})$ and let us generate a third random variable $\mathbf{Y}$ by choosing samples $y = x_s$ at random with probabilities

$$p_s = \frac{p(\mathbf{Z}|\mathbf{X}=x_s)}{\sum_{k=1}^{N} p(\mathbf{Z}|\mathbf{X}=x_k)} \quad (8)$$

It has been shown that the probability distribution of $\mathbf{Y}$ tends to $p(\mathbf{X}|\mathbf{Z})$ as $N \to \infty$ [7]. An approximation of the mean of the posterior can be computed as

$$E[\mathbf{X}|\mathbf{Z}] = \sum_{s=1}^{N} x_s p_s \quad (9)$$

In our case $p(\mathbf{X}|\mathbf{Z}) = p(\mathbf{m_i}|\mathbf{Z})$ where $\mathbf{Z}$ are measurements derived from the image sequence. We evaluate each hypothesis (sample) $m_i^{(s)}$ for $\mathbf{m_i}$ by computing for each frame f the sum of squared differences between a small window around the point i in the reference frame and the corresponding window in frame f translated according to $m_i^{(s)}$:

$$p(\mathbf{Z}|\mathbf{m_i} = m_i^{(s)}) \propto exp\{-\sum_{f=1}^{F} \sum_{(x,y) \in ROI_i} \frac{(I_0(x,y) - I_f(x + u_f^{(i,s)}, y + v_f^{(i,s)}))^2}{2\sigma^2}\} \quad (10)$$

where $u_f^{(i,s)} = q_u^{(f)} \cdot m_i^{(s)}$, $v_f^{(i,s)} = q_v^{(f)} \cdot m_i^{(s)}$, and $q_u^{(f)}, q_v^{(f)}$ are the f-th rows of Q_u and Q_v, with $\hat{Q} = [\frac{\mathbf{Q_u}}{\mathbf{Q_v}}]$.

Alternatively, the outputs of a set of steerable filters tuned to a range of orientations and scales could be used to compare image patches [6,13].

At the end of this density estimation process, each column m_i of M_{unrel} is computed as the expected value of the posterior using equation (9).

Note again how each hypothesis is tested against all the frames of the sequence. This large amount of measurements per sample is the key reason of the robustness of this approach.

The speed of convergence to the posterior density depends on how well the samples $m_i^{(s)}$ are chosen with respect to the unknown distribution $p(\mathbf{m_i}|\mathbf{Z})$. Also, evaluating the likelihood is computationally expensive. Ideally we would like to draw the $m_i^{(s)}$ from areas where the likelihood $p(\mathbf{Z}|\mathbf{m_i})$ is very large instead of wasting computational resources on samples with negligible p_s, that are clearly of little contribution for a first approximation of the unknown density. This is the intuitive idea underlying the theory of importance sampling [15].

Suppose we are given an auxiliary function $g_i(x)$ describing the areas of the random variable space that are believed to better characterize the posterior. Now we can use the importance function $g_i(x)$ to draw the samples $m_i^{(s)}$ and thus achieve faster convergence. We simply need to introduce a correction term in equation (8) to reflect our use of a different sampling distribution:

$$p_s = \frac{p(\mathbf{Z}|\mathbf{X}=x_s)p(x_s)/g(x_s)}{\sum_{k=1}^{N} p(\mathbf{Z}|\mathbf{X}=x_k)p(x_k)/g(x_k)} \quad (11)$$

In this case we define the importance function $g_i(x)$ by assuming the object has smooth surface[2]: we compute μ_{M_i}, for $i = 1, ..., n$, by interpolation from the shapes of the reliable points. $g_i(x)$ is then defined as a Gaussian around μ_{M_i}:

$$g_i(x) = \frac{1}{(2\pi)^{r/2}|\Sigma_i|^{1/2}} exp\{-\frac{1}{2}(x - \mu_{M_i})^T \Sigma_i^{-1}(x - \mu_{M_i})\} \quad (12)$$

We apply this technique for each of the n unreliable m_i separately.

Again, it is important to emphasize the fact that by sampling in the space of deformations as opposed to estimating the inter-frame relationships, we fully exploit the information in the sequence by evaluating each sample on ALL of the images. Whereas for conventional approaches the number of frames represents the number of sub-problems to solve, with this technique images are only measurements. The longer the sequence the more data we have available to constrain the solution.

5 Experiments

The method presented in this article has been tested on two separate video recordings of human motion with different types of deformations. The first sequence was originally employed in [17] to evaluate the algorithm of tracking and

---

[2] The smoothness assumption is clearly violated at depth discontinuities, but this hypothesis is not critical for the convergence of the method. It is used here only to speed up the process of density estimation.

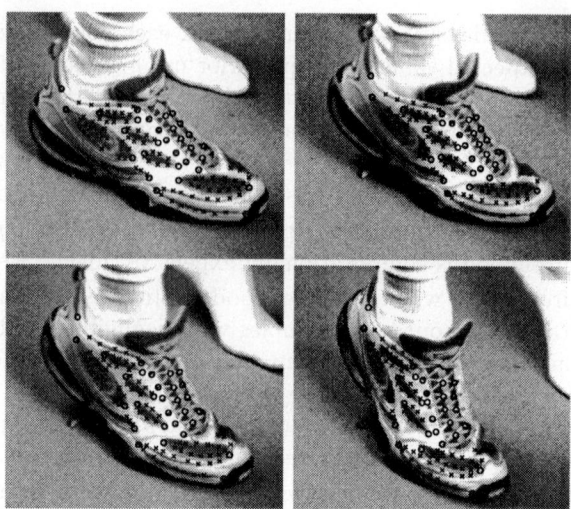

Fig. 1. Example tracks of the shoe sequence. The blue circles are the reliable points utilized to derive Q. The red crosses are edge features: their optical flow is determined by estimating the model M.

non-rigid 3D reconstruction described in that article. Here we show the improved tracking performance that is achievable with this new approach. The video consists of a 500 frames-long sequence of a shoe undergoing very large rotations and non-rigid deformations. While the reliable points are features with 2D texture tracked using the technique of Lucas-Kanade [12], the other 80 points are edges or degenerate features whose optical flow cannot be recovered using local operators. In order to prevent drifting along edges and 1D texture the solution

Fig. 2. Samples distribution. The shape samples are reprojected onto the images according to the occurring non-rigid motion. This is reflected in the sample distributions in the two frames: the principal motion is eyebrow deformation in the first image and head rotation in the second.

in [17], based on an integration of the rank constraint and the Lucas-Kanade linearization, had to be augmented with a regularization term enforcing smooth flow among neighboring features. We have tried to run the tracking solution presented in this article on the shoe sequence making sure that parameters ($r = 9$) and feature points were the same as those used in the original experiment. Although we are now not using any spatial smoothness heuristic, we found the results derived with the new technique even more accurate than those presented in the previous work. Figure 1 shows some examples of the non-rigid motion characterizing the sequence, together with the tracks recovered by our new solution based on sampling trajectories with rank constraints.

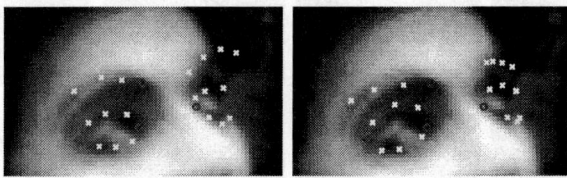

Fig. 3. Eyebrow detail. The left figure shows the initialization of the tracking with shapes extrapolated from the reliable points. The final optical flow recovered by trajectory sampling is shown on the right.

The second group of experiments was carried out on equally challenging data. We extracted 400 frames of digital footage from a Charlie Chaplin film originally recorded in 1918. The old technology used for the recording as well the non-uniform light of the outdoor scene make the sequence very difficult for a tracking task. We focused on a segment of the movie containing a close up of the actor with the goal of capturing his famous facial expressions. The rigid head motion is very large and causes considerable changes in the features appearance. The non-rigid deformations are similarly extreme and mostly due to eyebrow, lips and jaw motion. We restricted the tracking to important facial features such as eyebrows, eyes and the moustache: most of these points are edges and they are virtually impossible to track with conventional model-free techniques without incurring in features drifting. We could find only 9 features that could be tracked over the entire sequence with the technique of Lucas-Kanade employing affine transformations for the local windows centered at these points. The locations of these reliable points are marked with pink circles in figure 2. These points proved to be anyway sufficient for capturing the main modes of deformations of the face. All the results on this footage reported in the article were obtained with $r = 4$ or $r = 5$. The tracks of these points were used to estimate Q and to consequently recover the main elements of non-rigid motion. Figure 2 shows the reprojections onto the image of the shape samples for different non-reliable features in example frames. It is very apparent how the search for the best feature match takes place along the direction of the occurring non-rigid motion encoded in the Q matrix. The samples in the left frame are spread vertically because

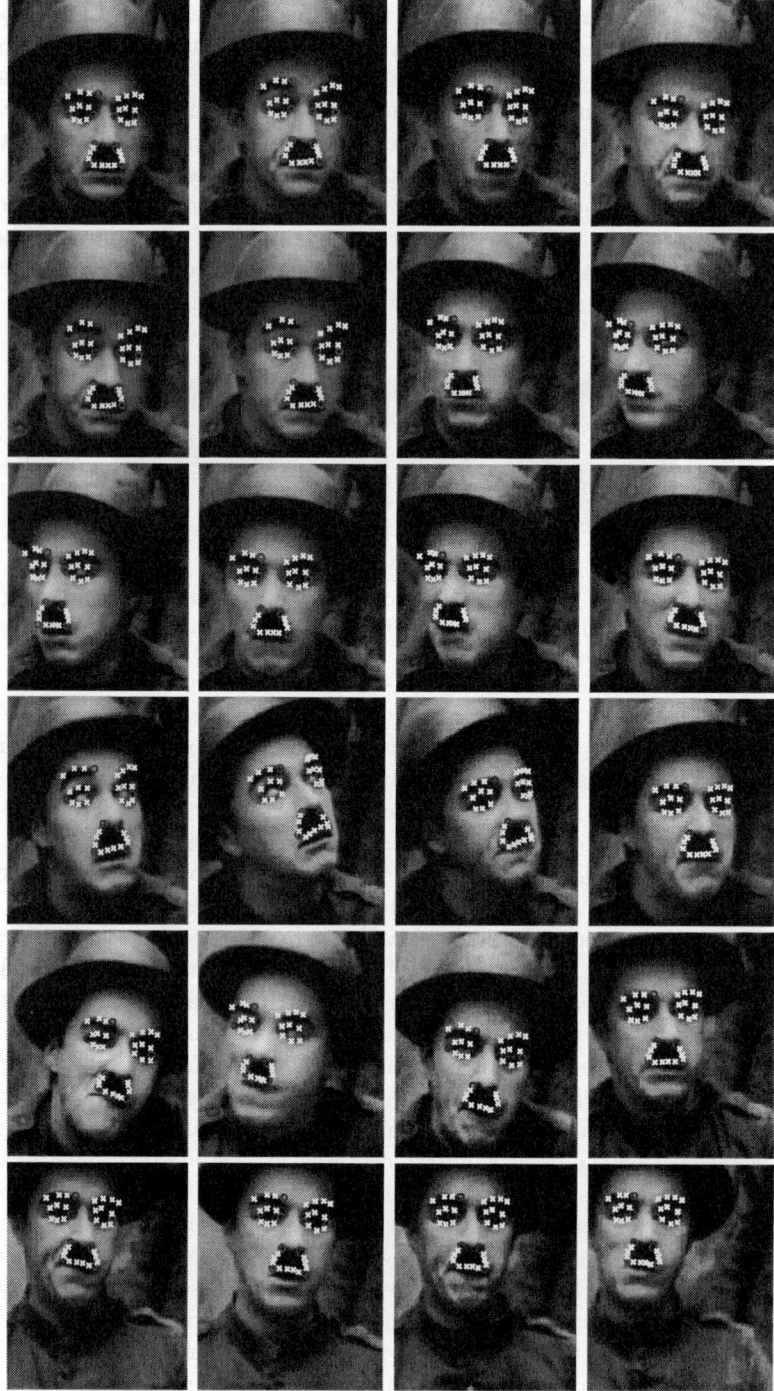

Fig. 4. Tracking of degenerate features on the Chaplin footage. The pink circles are reliable points.

of the large deformation along that direction picked up by the reliable point located on the left eyebrow. Similarly the sample distributions in the right image match the occurring head rotation. This experimentally validates the motion-shape decomposition expressed by equation (4) and shows the reduced size of the search space.

The shape initialization extrapolated from the reliable points provides only a very rough initial approximation, especially in frames where the non-rigid component of the motion is large. The optical flow resulting from the initialization that is shown on the left of figure 3 misses completely to capture deformation and correct 3D position of the right eyebrow. This initialization is not critical for the convergence of the algorithm as exemplified in the right image.

Using our unconventional approach we could track reliably and accurately all of the 29 degenerate features throughout the whole sequence of 400 frames, a task extremely difficult to achieve without the use of prior models. Example frames taken from the footage together with their estimated tracks are shown in figure 4. See http://movement.stanford.edu/nonrig for mpeg or quicktime video showing the results of tracking on the entire sequence.

The tracking algorithm described in this article was implemented in interpreted Matlab code and tested on a PC Pentium 3 with a 900MHz CPU and 512M RAM. The number of samples per feature point was chosen to be 500 for all the experiments presented. With this setup the average time to estimate the trajectory of one feature in a video of 400 frames is 2-3 seconds.

6 Discussion

We have presented a new algorithm that is able to track non-rigid object motion and disambiguate challenging local features without the use of a prior model. The key idea of the algorithm is the exploitation of a low-rank constraint that allows us to perform a sampling-based search over trajectory subspaces instead of over the space of shape configurations. From this result we derive a robust solution for tracking without models.

We demonstrated the algorithm on tracking of film footage of Charlie Chaplin's facial expressions, and of sport-shoe deformations. In both cases, model-free point trackers are able to track only a few corner features. With the use of this new technique we were able to track challenging points suffering from the aperture problem and other degenerate features.

Acknowledgements. We would like to thank Hrishikesh Deshpande for providing advice and help with the experiments. This research was funded in part by the National Science Foundation and the Stanford BIO-X program.

References

1. M.J. Black and Y. Yacoob. Tracking and recognizing rigid and non-rigid facial motions using local parametric models of image motion. In *ICCV*, 1995.

2. M.J. Black, Y.Yacoob, A.D.Jepson, and D.J.Fleet. Learning parameterized models of image motion. In *CVPR*, 1997.
3. A. Blake, M. Isard, and D. Reynard. Learning to track the visual motion of contours. In *J. of Artificial Intelligence*, 1995.
4. C. Bregler, A. Hertzmann, and H. Biermann. Recovering Non-Rigid 3D Shape from Image Streams. In *CVPR*, 2000.
5. D. DeCarlo and D. Metaxas. Deformable model-based shape and motion analysis from images using motion residual error. In *ICCV*, 1998.
6. W. Freeman and E Adelson. The design and use of steerable filters. *IEEE Trans. Pattern Anal. Mach. Intell.*, 1991.
7. U. Grenander, Y. Chow, and D.M. Keenan. *HANDS. A Pattern Theoretical Study of Biological Shapes*. Springer Verlag. New York, 1991.
8. M. Irani. Multi-frame optical flow estimation using subspace constraints. In *ICCV*, 1999.
9. M. Irani and P. Anandan. Factorization with uncertainty. In *ECCV*, 2000.
10. M. Isard and A. Blake. Contour tracking by stochastic propagation of conditional density. In *ECCV*, 1996.
11. A. Lanitis, Taylor C.J., Cootes T.F., and Ahmed T. Automatic interpretation of human faces and hand gestures using flexible models. In *International Workshop on Automatic Face- and Gesture-Recognition*, 1995.
12. B.D. Lucas and T. Kanade. An iterative image registration technique with an application to stereo vision. *Proc. 7th Int. Joint Conf. on Artif. Intell.*, 1981.
13. P. Perona. Deformable kernels for early vision. *IEEE Trans. Pattern Anal. Mach. Intell.*, 1995.
14. F. Pighin, D. H. Salesin, and R. Szeliski. Resynthesizing facial animation through 3d model-based tracking. In *ICCV*, 1999.
15. B.D. Ripley. *Stochastic Simulation*. Wiley. New York, 1987.
16. C. Tomasi and T. Kanade. Shape and motion from image streams under orthography: a factorization method. *Int. J. of Computer Vision*, 9(2):137–154, 1992.
17. L. Torresani, D.B. Yang, E.J. Alexander, and C. Bregler. Tracking and Modeling Non-Rigid Objects with Rank Constraints. In *CVPR*, 2001.

Author Index

Adams, N.J.   IV-82
Agarwal, S.   IV-113
Ahuja, N.   IV-685
Alvarez, L.   I-721
Anandan, P.   II-883
Aner, A.   IV-388
Ansar, A.   IV-282
Araujo, H.   IV-237
Attias, H.   I-736
Aubert, G.   III-365
Auf der Maur, D.   III-180
August, J.   III-604
Avidan, S.   III-747

Bajaj, C.   III-517
Barla, A.   IV-20
Barlaud, M.   III-365
Barnard, K.   IV-97
Barreto, J.P.   IV-237
Bartoli, A.   II-340
Bazin, P.-L.   II-262
Beal, M.J.   I-736
Belhumeur, P.N.   III-869
Bell, J.W.   IV-358
Belongie, S.   III-21, III-531
Bhat, K.S.   I-551
Bhotika, R.   III-112
Bischof, H.   IV-761
Black, M.J.   I-476, I-692, I-784, IV-653
Blake, A.   I-645, IV-67
Blanz, V.   IV-3
Bø, K.   III-133
Borenstein, E.   II-109
Botello, S.   IV-560
Boult, T.   IV-590
Boyer, E.   IV-221
Brand, M.   I-707
Bregler, C.   I-801
Bretzner, L.   III-759
Breuel, T.M.   III-837
Brodsky, T.   I-614
Buehler, C.   III-885
Buhmann, J.M.   III-577

Caenen, G.   III-180
Calderon, F.   IV-560
Carcassoni, M.   I-266
Carlsson, S.   I-68, I-629, II-309
Carneiro, G.   I-282, I-297
Caspi, Y.   I-753
Castellani, U.   II-805
Chang, J.T.   II-31
Chantler, M.   III-289
Charbonnier, P.   I-492
Chaumette, F.   IV-312
Chazelle, B.   II-642
Cheeseman, P.   II-247
Chefd'hotel, C.   I-251
Chellappa, R.   II-277, III-681
Chen, H.   I-236
Chen, Y.   IV-546
Chung, F.   III-531
Cipolla, R.   II-155, II-852
Clerc, M.   II-495
Cobzas, D.   II-415
Cohen, L.D.   III-807, IV-531
Cohen, M.F.   III-885
Collins, R.   II-657
Comaniciu, D.   I-173, III-561
Cootes, T.F.   III-3, IV-621
Cornelis, K.   II-186
Corpetti, T.   I-676
Costeira, J.   II-232
Coughlan, J.M.   III-453
Cremers, D.   II-93
Criminisi, A.   I-508
Crouzil, A.   IV-252
Cufí, X.   III-408

Daniilidis, K.   II-140, IV-282
Darrell, T.   III-592, III-851
David, P.   III-698
Davies, R.H.   III-3
Davis, L.S.   I-18
DeCarlo, D.   IV-327
Del Bue, A.   III-561
DeMenthon, D.   III-698
Deriche, R.   I-251, I-721
Deschamps, T.   III-807
Deutscher, J.   IV-175

Dick, A.R.   II-852
Dickinson, S.   III-759
Dobkin, D.   II-642
Donato, G.   III-21
Doorn, A.J. van   I-158
Dornaika, F.   IV-606
Drbohlav, O.   II-46
Drew, M.S.   IV-823
Duci, A.   III-48
Duraiswami, R.   III-698
Duygulu, P.   IV-97
Dyer, C.   IV-131

Eklundh, J.-O.   III-469
Elder, J.   IV-606
Ernst, F.   II-217
Everingham, M.   IV-34

Fablet, R.   I-476
Faugeras, O.   I-251, II-790
Favaro, P.   II-18, II-735
Feldman, D.   I-614
Felsberg, M.   I-369
Ferrari, V.   III-180
Ferreira, S.J.   III-453
Ferrie, F.P.   IV-267
Finkelstein, A.   II-642
Finlayson, G.D.   IV-823
Fisher, J.W.   III-592, III-851
Fisher, R.B.   IV-146
Fitzgibbon, A.   III-304, III-487
Flandin, G.   IV-312
Fleet, D.J.   I-692, III-112
Florack, L.   I-143, I-190
Forsyth, D.A.   III-225, IV-97
Fossum, R.   II-201
Fowlkes, C.   III-531
Freitas, J.F.G. de   IV-97
Freixenet, J.   III-408
Frey, B.J.   IV-715
Fua, P.   II-325, II-704, III-163
Fukui, K.   III-195
Funkhouser, T.   II-642
Fusiello, A.   II-805

Gangnet, M.   I-645, I-661
Gao, X.   IV-590
Gee, J.   III-621
Georgescu, B.   II-294
Gérard, O.   III-807

Geusebroek, J.-M.   I-99
Geyer, C.   II-140
Giannopoulos, P.   III-715
Giblin, P.   II-718
Gilboa, G.   I-399
Goldberger, J.   IV-461
Goldenberg, R.   I-461
Gomes, J.   II-3
Gong, S.   IV-670
Gool, L. Van   II-170, II-186, II-572, II-837, III-180, IV-448
Gortler, S.J.   III-885
Graham, J.   IV-517
Granger, S.   IV-418
Greenspan, H.   IV-461
Greff, M.   III-807
Grenander, U.   I-37
Grossberg, M.D.   I-220, IV-189
Guo, C.-e.   III-240, IV-793
Gurdjos, P.   IV-252

Hadjidemetriou, E.   I-220
Han, F.   III-502
Hancock, E.R.   I-266, II-63, II-626, III-822
Hartley, R.I.   II-433, II-447
Harville, M.   III-543
Hassner, T.   II-883
Hayman, E.   III-469
Hebert, M.   III-651, III-776
Heidrich, W.   II-672
Hermes, L.   III-577
Hertz, T.   IV-776
Hillenbrand, U.   III-791
Hirzinger, G.   III-791
Hordley, S.D.   IV-823
Huang, K.   II-201
Hue, C.   I-661
Huggins, P.S.   I-384

Ieng, S.-S.   I-492
Ilic, S.   II-704
Irani, M.   I-753, II-883
Isard, M.   IV-175

Jagersand, M.   II-415
Javed, O.   IV-343
Jehan-Besson, S.   III-365
Jelinek, D.   II-463
Jepson, A.D.   I-282, I-692
Jiang, G.   I-537

Jin, H.   II-18
Jönsson, C.   III-759
Jojic, N.   I-736, IV-715

Kahl, F.   II-447
Kam, A.H.   IV-297
Kamberov, G.   II-598
Kamberova, G.   II-598
Kambhamettu, C.   II-556, IV-206
Kaminski, J.Y.   II-823
Kanatani, K.   III-335
Kang, S.B.   I-508, III-210
Kaucic, R.   II-433
Kazhdan, M.   II-642
Kender, J.R.   IV-388, IV-403
Khosla, P.K.   I-551
Kim, J.   III-321
Kimia, B.B.   II-718, III-731
Kimmel, R.   I-461
Klein, P.N.   III-731
Koenderink, J.J.   I-158, IV-808
Kohlberger, T.   II-93
Kolmogorov, V.   III-65, III-82
Košecká, J.   IV-476
Kozera, R.   II-613
Kriegman, D.J.   III-651, III-869
Krüger, V.   IV-732
Kuehnel, F.O.   II-247
Kuijper, A.   I-143, I-190
Kutulakos, K.N.   III-112

Lachaud, J.-O.   III-438
Lafferty, J.   III-776
Lasenby, J.   I-524
Lazebnik, S.   III-651
Leclerc, Y.   III-163
Lee, A.B.   I-328
Lee, M.-S.   I-614
Lee, S.W.   II-587
Leonardis, A.   IV-761
Levin, A.   II-399, III-635
Lhuillier, M.   II-125
Li, S.Z.   IV-67
Li, Y.   III-210
Lin, S.   III-210
Lindeberg, T.   I-52, III-759
Liu, C.   II-687
Liu, T.   IV-403
Liu, X.   I-37
Liu, Y.   II-657

Lo, B.P.L.   III-381
Loy, G.   I-358
Lu, W.   IV-297
Luong, Q.-T.   III-163

Ma, Y.   II-201
MacCormick, J.   IV-175
Maciel, J.   II-232
Mahamud, S.   III-776
Maki, A.   III-195
Malik, J.   I-312, III-531, III-666
Malis, E.   IV-433
Malladi, R.   I-343
Malsburg, C. von der   IV-747
Maluf, D.A.   II-247
Manning, R.   IV-131
Markham, R.   IV-502
Marroquin, J.L.   I-113, IV-560
Martinec, D.   II-355
Martí, J.   III-408
Mathiassen, J.R.   III-133
Maybank, S.   IV-373
Mayer, A.   IV-461
McGunnigle, G.   III-289
McMillan, L.   III-885
Medioni, G.   III-423
Meer, P.   I-236, II-294
Mémin, É.   I-676
Mikolajczyk, K.   I-128
Mindru, F.   IV-448
Mirmehdi, M.   IV-502
Mitran, M.   IV-267
Mittal, A.   I-18
Mitter, S.   III-48
Mojsilovic, A.   II-3
Moons, T.   IV-448
Mori, G.   III-666
Morris, R.D.   II-247
Muller, H.   IV-34
Muñoz, X.   III-408
Murino, V.   II-805
Murray, D.W.   I-82

Nakashima, A.   III-195
Narasimhan, S.G.   III-148, IV-636
Nayar, S.K.   I-220, I-508, III-148, IV-189, IV-636
Ng, J.   IV-670
Ng, T.K.   I-205

Nicolescu, M.   III-423
Noakes, L.   II-613

Odone, F.   IV-20
Oliensis, J.   II-383
Osareh, A.   IV-502
Overveld, K. van   II-217

Pajdla, T.   II-355
Pal, C.   IV-715
Papadopoulo, T.   I-721
Paragios, N.   II-78, II-775
Pavel, M.   IV-776
Payrissat, R.   IV-252
Pece, A.E.C.   I-3
Pedersen, K.S.   I-328
Pennec, X.   IV-418
Pérez, P.   I-645, I-661, I-676
Perona, P.   II-759
Petrou, M.   III-289
Plaenkers, R.   II-325
Pollefeys, M.   II-186, II-837
Ponce, J.   III-651
Pont, S.C.   IV-808
Popović, J.   I-551
Prados, E.   II-790
Prince, J.L.   IV-575

Qian, G.   II-277
Quan, L.   I-537, II-125

Raba, D.   III-408
Ragheb, H.   II-626
Ramesh, V.   I-173, II-775, III-561, IV-590
Ravve, I.   I-343
Ren, X.   I-312
Richard, F.   IV-531
Ringer, M.   I-524
Rivera, M.   I-113, III-621
Rivlin, E.   I-461
Robertson, D.P   II-155
Robles-Kelly, A.   II-63
Rogers, M.   IV-517
Romdhani, S.   IV-3
Ronchetti, L.   II-805
Ronfard, R.   IV-700
Rosin, P.L.   II-746
Roth, D.   IV-113, IV-685
Rother, C.   II-309
Rousson, M.   II-78, II-775

Rouy, E.   II-790
Rudzsky, M.   I-461

Samaras, D.   III-272
Samet, H.   III-698
Sánchez, J.   I-721
Šára, R.   II-46, III-900
Savarese, S.   II-759
Sawhney, H.S.   I-599
Schaffalitzky, F.   I-414
Scharstein, D.   II-525
Schiele, B.   IV-49
Schmid, C.   I-128, III-651, IV-700
Schmidt, M.   III-289
Schnörr, C.   II-93
Schwartz, S.   I-173
Schweitzer, H.   IV-358, IV-491
Sebastian, T.B.   III-731
Seitz, S.M.   I-551
Sénégas, J.   III-97
Sethi, A.   III-651
Shah, M.   IV-343
Shakhnarovich, G.   III-851
Sharp, G.C.   II-587
Shashua, A.   II-399, III-635
Shechtman, E.   I-753
Shental, N.   IV-776
Shokoufandeh, A.   III-759
Shum, H.-Y.   II-510, II-687, III-210, IV-67
Sidenbladh, H.   I-784
Siebel, N.T.   IV-373
Sigal, L.   I-784
Skavhaug, A.   III-133
Skočaj, D.   IV-761
Smelyansky, V.N.   II-247
Smeulders, A.W.M.   I-99
Sminchisescu, C.   I-566, I-769
Soatto, S.   II-735, III-32, III-48
Sochen, N.A.   I-399
Sommer, G.   I-369
Speyer, G.   I-432
Srivastava, A.   I-37
Strecha, C.   II-170
Sturm, P.   II-867, IV-221
Sullivan, J.   I-629
Sun, J.   II-510
Sung, K.K.   I-205
Swaminathan, R.   I-508
Szeliski, R.   I-508, II-525

Tam, R. II-672
Tarel, J.-P. I-492
Taton, B. III-438
Taylor, C.J. II-463, III-3, IV-621
Teicher, M. II-823
Tell, D. I-68
Terzopoulos, D. I-447
Thacker, N. IV-621
Thomas, B. IV-34, IV-502
Tohka, J. III-350
Tong, X. III-210
Tordoff, B. I-82
Torr, P.H.S. II-852
Torre, F. De la IV-653
Torresani, L. I-801
Torsello, A. III-822
Trajkovic, M. I-614
Triggs, B. I-566, I-769, IV-700
Tschumperlé, D. I-251
Tsin, Y. II-657
Tsui, H.-t. I-537
Tu, Z. III-393, III-502
Twining, C.J. III-3

Ullman, S. II-109

Varma, M. III-255
Vasconcelos, N. I-297
Vasilescu, M.A.O. I-447
Veltkamp, R.C. III-715
Vemuri, B.C. IV-546, IV-560
Verbiest, F. II-837
Vermaak, J. I-645, I-661
Verri, A. IV-20
Vetter, T. IV-3
Vézien, J.-M. II-262
Vidal, R. II-383
Vogel, J. IV-49

Wang, B. I-205
Wang, C. III-148
Wang, S.-C. I-583
Wang, Y. I-583, III-272, IV-793
Wang, Z. IV-546
Waterton, J.C. III-3
Wehe, D.K. II-587
Weijer, J. van de I-99
Weinshall, D. I-614, IV-776

Werman, M. I-432
Werner, T. II-541
Wexler, Y. III-487
Wieghardt, J. IV-747
Wilczkowiak, M. IV-221
Wilinski, P. II-217
Williams, C.K.I. IV-82
Wolf, L. II-370
Worrall, A.D. I-3
Wu, F. IV-358
Wu, Y.N. III-240, IV-793
Würtz, R.P. IV-747
Wyngaerd, J. Vanden II-572

Yang, G.-Z. III-381
Yang, M.-H. IV-685
Yang, R. II-479
Yau, W.-Y. IV-297
Yezzi, A.J. III-32, III-48, IV-575
Yu, Y. II-31
Yu, Z. III-517

Zabih, R. III-65, III-82, III-321
Zalesny, A. III-180
Zeevi, Y.Y. I-399
Zelinsky, A. I-358
Zhang, C. II-687
Zhang, H. IV-67
Zhang, W. IV-476
Zhang, Y. II-556
Zhang, Z. II-479, IV-67, IV-161
Zhao, W.Y. I-599
Zheng, N.-N. II-510
Zhou, S. III-681, IV-732
Zhou, W. IV-206
Zhu, L. IV-67
Zhu, S.-C. I-583, III-240, III-393, III-502, IV-793
Zhu, Y. I-173
Zhu, Y. I-583
Zickler, T. III-869
Zisserman, A. I-414, I-537, II-541, III-255, III-304, III-487
Zöller, T. III-577
Zomet, A. II-370
Zucker, S.W. I-384
Žunić, J. II-746

Lecture Notes in Computer Science

For information about Vols. 1–2266
please contact your bookseller or Springer-Verlag

Vol. 2267: M. Cerioli, G. Reggio (Eds.), Recent Trends in Algebraic Development Techniques. Proceedings, 2001. X, 345 pages. 2001.

Vol. 2268: E.F. Deprettere, J. Teich, S. Vassiliadis (Eds.), Embedded Processor Design Challenges. VIII, 327 pages. 2002.

Vol. 2269: S. Diehl (Ed.), Software Visualization. Proceedings, 2001. VIII, 405 pages. 2002.

Vol. 2270: M. Pflanz, On-line Error Detection and Fast Recover Techniques for Dependable Embedded Processors. XII, 126 pages. 2002.

Vol. 2271: B. Preneel (Ed.), Topics in Cryptology – CT-RSA 2002. Proceedings, 2002. X, 311 pages. 2002.

Vol. 2272: D. Bert, J.P. Bowen, M.C. Henson, K. Robinson (Eds.), ZB 2002: Formal Specification and Development in Z and B. Proceedings, 2002. XII, 535 pages. 2002.

Vol. 2273: A.R. Coden, E.W. Brown, S. Srinivasan (Eds.), Information Retrieval Techniques for Speech Applications. XI, 109 pages. 2002.

Vol. 2274: D. Naccache, P. Paillier (Eds.), Public Key Cryptography. Proceedings, 2002. XI, 385 pages. 2002.

Vol. 2275: N.R. Pal, M. Sugeno (Eds.), Advances in Soft Computing – AFSS 2002. Proceedings, 2002. XVI, 536 pages. 2002. (Subseries LNAI).

Vol. 2276: A. Gelbukh (Ed.), Computational Linguistics and Intelligent Text Processing. Proceedings, 2002. XIII, 444 pages. 2002.

Vol. 2277: P. Callaghan, Z. Luo, J. McKinna, R. Pollack (Eds.), Types for Proofs and Programs. Proceedings, 2000. VIII, 243 pages. 2002.

Vol. 2278: J.A. Foster, E. Lutton, J. Miller, C. Ryan, A.G.B. Tettamanzi (Eds.), Genetic Programming. Proceedings, 2002. XI, 337 pages. 2002.

Vol. 2279: S. Cagnoni, J. Gottlieb, E. Hart, M. Middendorf, G.R. Raidl (Eds.), Applications of Evolutionary Computing. Proceedings, 2002. XIII, 344 pages. 2002.

Vol. 2280: J.P. Katoen, P. Stevens (Eds.), Tools and Algorithms for the Construction and Analysis of Systems. Proceedings, 2002. XIII, 482 pages. 2002.

Vol. 2281: S. Arikawa, A. Shinohara (Eds.), Progress in Discovery Science. XIV, 684 pages. 2002. (Subseries LNAI).

Vol. 2282: D. Ursino, Extraction and Exploitation of Intensional Knowledge from Heterogeneous Information Sources. XXVI, 289 pages. 2002.

Vol. 2283: T. Nipkow, L.C. Paulson, M. Wenzel, Isabelle/HOL. XIII, 218 pages. 2002.

Vol. 2284: T. Eiter, K.-D. Schewe (Eds.), Foundations of Information and Knowledge Systems. Proceedings, 2002. X, 289 pages. 2002.

Vol. 2285: H. Alt, A. Ferreira (Eds.), STACS 2002. Proceedings, 2002. XIV, 660 pages. 2002.

Vol. 2286: S. Rajsbaum (Ed.), LATIN 2002: Theoretical Informatics. Proceedings, 2002. XIII, 630 pages. 2002.

Vol. 2287: C.S. Jensen, K.G. Jeffery, J. Pokorny, Saltenis, E. Bertino, K. Böhm, M. Jarke (Eds.), Advances in Database Technology – EDBT 2002. Proceedings, 2002. XVI, 776 pages. 2002.

Vol. 2288: K. Kim (Ed.), Information Security and Cryptology – ICISC 2001. Proceedings, 2001. XIII, 457 pages. 2002.

Vol. 2289: C.J. Tomlin, M.R. Greenstreet (Eds.), Hybrid Systems: Computation and Control. Proceedings, 2002. XIII, 480 pages. 2002.

Vol. 2290: F. van der Linden (Ed.), Software Product-Family Engineering. Proceedings, 2001. X, 417 pages. 2002.

Vol. 2291: F. Crestani, M. Girolami, C.J. van Rijsbergen (Eds.), Advances in Information Retrieval. Proceedings, 2002. XIII, 363 pages. 2002.

Vol. 2292: G.B. Khosrovshahi, A. Shokoufandeh, A. Shokrollahi (Eds.), Theoretical Aspects of Computer Science. IX, 221 pages. 2002.

Vol. 2293: J. Renz, Qualitative Spatial Reasoning with Topological Information. XVI, 207 pages. 2002. (Subseries LNAI).

Vol. 2294: A. Cortesi (Ed.), Verification, Model Checking, and Abstract Interpretation. Proceedings, 2002. VIII, 331 pages. 2002.

Vol. 2295: W. Kuich, G. Rozenberg, A. Salomaa (Eds.), Developments in Language Theory. Proceedings, 2001. IX, 389 pages. 2002.

Vol. 2296: B. Dunin-Kęplicz, E. Nawarecki (Eds.), From Theory to Practice in Multi-Agent Systems. Proceedings, 2001. IX, 341 pages. 2002. (Subseries LNAI).

Vol. 2297: R. Backhouse, R. Crole, J. Gibbons (Eds.), Algebraic and Coalgebraic Methods in the Mathematics of Program Construction. Proceedings, 2000. XIV, 387 pages. 2002.

Vol. 2298: I. Wachsmuth, T. Sowa (Eds.), Gesture and Language in Human-Computer Interaction. Proceedings, 2001. XI, 323 pages. 2002. (Subseries LNAI).

Vol. 2299: H. Schmeck, T. Ungerer, L. Wolf (Eds.), Trends in Network and Pervasive Computing – ARCS 2002. Proceedings, 2002. XIV, 287 pages. 2002.

Vol. 2300: W. Brauer, H. Ehrig, J. Karhumäki, A. Salomaa (Eds.), Formal and Natural Computing. XXXVI, 431 pages. 2002.

Vol. 2301: A. Braquelaire, J.-O. Lachaud, A. Vialard (Eds.), Discrete Geometry for Computer Imagery. Proceedings, 2002. XI, 439 pages. 2002.

Vol. 2302: C. Schulte, Programming Constraint Services. XII, 176 pages. 2002. (Subseries LNAI).

Vol. 2303: M. Nielsen, U. Engberg (Eds.), Foundations of Software Science and Computation Structures. Proceedings, 2002. XIII, 435 pages. 2002.

Vol. 2304: R.N. Horspool (Ed.), Compiler Construction. Proceedings, 2002. XI, 343 pages. 2002.

Vol. 2305: D. Le Métayer (Ed.), Programming Languages and Systems. Proceedings, 2002. XII, 331 pages. 2002.

Vol. 2306: R.-D. Kutsche, H. Weber (Eds.), Fundamental Approaches to Software Engineering. Proceedings, 2002. XIII, 341 pages. 2002.

Vol. 2307: C. Zhang, S. Zhang, Association Rule Mining. XII, 238 pages. 2002. (Subseries LNAI).

Vol. 2308: I.P. Vlahavas, C.D. Spyropoulos (Eds.), Methods and Applications of Artificial Intelligence. Proceedings, 2002. XIV, 514 pages. 2002. (Subseries LNAI).

Vol. 2309: A. Armando (Ed.), Frontiers of Combining Systems. Proceedings, 2002. VIII, 255 pages. 2002. (Subseries LNAI).

Vol. 2310: P. Collet, C. Fonlupt, J.-K. Hao, E. Lutton, M. Schoenauer (Eds.), Artificial Evolution. Proceedings, 2001. XI, 375 pages. 2002.

Vol. 2311: D. Bustard, W. Liu, R. Sterritt (Eds.), SoftWare 2002: Computing in an Imperfect World. Proceedings, 2002. XI, 359 pages. 2002.

Vol. 2312: T. Arts, M. Mohnen (Eds.), Implementation of Functional Languages. Proceedings, 2001. VII, 187 pages. 2002.

Vol. 2313: C.A. Coello Coello, A. de Albornoz, L.E. Sucar, O.Cairó Battistutti (Eds.), MICAI 2002: Advances in Artificial Intelligence. Proceedings, 2002. XIII, 548 pages. 2002. (Subseries LNAI).

Vol. 2314: S.-K. Chang, Z. Chen, S.-Y. Lee (Eds.), Recent Advances in Visual Information Systems. Proceedings, 2002. XI, 323 pages. 2002.

Vol. 2315: F. Arhab, C. Talcott (Eds.), Coordination Models and Languages. Proceedings, 2002. XI, 406 pages. 2002.

Vol. 2316: J. Domingo-Ferrer (Ed.), Inference Control in Statistical Databases. VIII, 231 pages. 2002.

Vol. 2317: M. Hegarty, B. Meyer, N. Hari Narayanan (Eds.), Diagrammatic Representation and Inference. Proceedings, 2002. XIV, 362 pages. 2002. (Subseries LNAI).

Vol. 2318: D. Bošnački, S. Leue (Eds.), Model Checking Software. Proceedings, 2002. X, 259 pages. 2002.

Vol. 2319: C. Gacek (Ed.), Software Reuse: Methods, Techniques, and Tools. Proceedings, 2002. XI, 353 pages. 2002.

Vol.2320: T. Sander (Ed.), Security and Privacy in Digital Rights Management. Proceedings, 2001. X, 245 pages. 2002.

Vol. 2322: V. Mařík, O. Štěpánková, H. Krautwurmová, M. Luck (Eds.), Multi-Agent Systems and Applications II. Proceedings, 2001. XII, 377 pages. 2002. (Subseries LNAI).

Vol. 2323: À. Frohner (Ed.), Object-Oriented Technology. Proceedings, 2001. IX, 225 pages. 2002.

Vol. 2324: T. Field, P.G. Harrison, J. Bradley, U. Harder (Eds.), Computer Performance Evaluation. Proceedings, 2002. XI, 349 pages. 2002.

Vol 2326: D. Grigoras, A. Nicolau, B. Toursel, B. Folliot (Eds.), Advanced Environments, Tools, and Applications for Cluster Computing. Proceedings, 2001. XIII, 321 pages. 2002.

Vol. 2327: H.P. Zima, K. Joe, M. Sato, Y. Seo, M. Shimasaki (Eds.), High Performance Computing. Proceedings, 2002. XV, 564 pages. 2002.

Vol. 2329: P.M.A. Sloot, C.J.K. Tan, J.J. Dongarra, A.G. Hoekstra (Eds.), Computational Science – ICCS 2002. Proceedings, Part I. XLI, 1095 pages. 2002.

Vol. 2330: P.M.A. Sloot, C.J.K. Tan, J.J. Dongarra, A.G. Hoekstra (Eds.), Computational Science – ICCS 2002. Proceedings, Part II. XLI, 1115 pages. 2002.

Vol. 2331: P.M.A. Sloot, C.J.K. Tan, J.J. Dongarra, A.G. Hoekstra (Eds.), Computational Science – ICCS 2002. Proceedings, Part III. XLI, 1227 pages. 2002.

Vol. 2332: L. Knudsen (Ed.), Advances in Cryptology – EUROCRYPT 2002. Proceedings, 2002. XII, 547 pages. 2002.

Vol. 2334: G. Carle, M. Zitterbart (Eds.), Protocols for High Speed Networks. Proceedings, 2002. X, 267 pages. 2002.

Vol. 2335: M. Butler, L. Petre, K. Sere (Eds.), Integrated Formal Methods. Proceedings, 2002. X, 401 pages. 2002.

Vol. 2336: M.-S. Chen, P.S. Yu, B. Liu (Eds.), Advances in Knowledge Discovery and Data Mining. Proceedings, 2002. XIII, 568 pages. 2002. (Subseries LNAI).

Vol. 2337: W.J. Cook, A.S. Schulz (Eds.), Integer Programming and Combinatorial Optimization. Proceedings, 2002. XI, 487 pages. 2002.

Vol. 2338: R. Cohen, B. Spencer (Eds.), Advances in Artificial Intelligence. Proceedings, 2002. X, 197 pages. 2002. (Subseries LNAI).

Vol. 2345: E. Gregori, M. Conti, A.T. Campbell, G. Omidyar, M. Zukerman (Eds.), NETWORKING 2002. Proceedings, 2002. XXVI, 1256 pages. 2002.

Vol. 2347: P. De Bra, P. Brusilovsky, R. Conejo (Eds.), Adaptive Hypermedia and Adaptive Web-Based Systems. Proceedings, 2002. XV, 615 pages. 2002.

Vol. 2350: A. Heyden, G. Sparr, M. Nielsen, P. Johansen (Eds.), Computer Vision – ECCV 2002. Proceedings, Part I. XXVIII, 817 pages. 2002.

Vol. 2351: A. Heyden, G. Sparr, M. Nielsen, P. Johansen (Eds.), Computer Vision – ECCV 2002. Proceedings, Part II. XXVIII, 903 pages. 2002.

Vol. 2352: A. Heyden, G. Sparr, M. Nielsen, P. Johansen (Eds.), Computer Vision – ECCV 2002. Proceedings, Part III. XXVIII, 919 pages. 2002.

Vol. 2353: A. Heyden, G. Sparr, M. Nielsen, P. Johansen (Eds.), Computer Vision – ECCV 2002. Proceedings, Part IV. XXVIII, 841 pages. 2002.

Vol. 2359: M. Tistarelli, J. Bigun, A.K. Jain (Eds.), Biometric Authentication. Proceedings, 2002. XII, 373 pages. 2002.